D1283034

Greek Waters Pilot

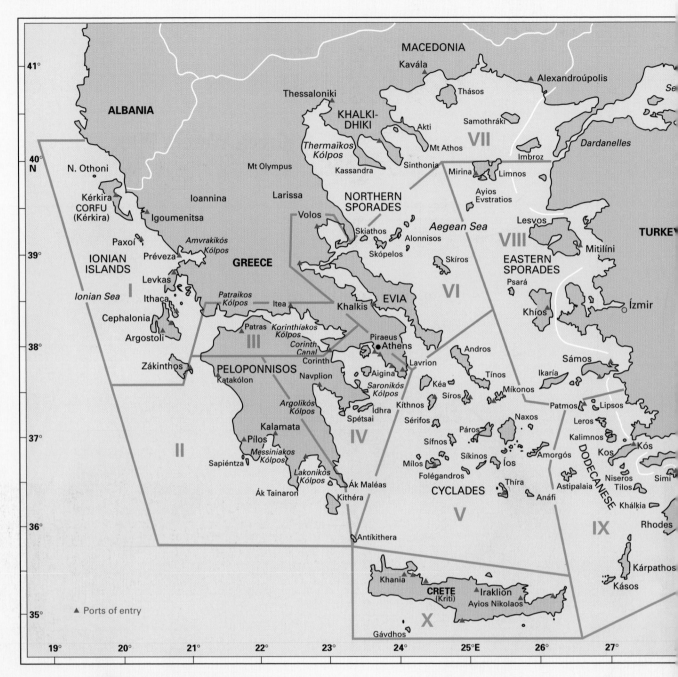

Map legend: ▲ Ports of entry

Contents

ISTANBUL

Imray

Greek Waters Pilot

A yachtsman's guide to the coasts and islands of Greece

ROD HEIKELL

29°

Imray Laurie Norie & Wilson Ltd

Rod Heikell

Rod Heikell has spent more than twenty-five years cruising the coasts and islands of the Mediterranean.

In the 1970s he took time off from academic life and sailed *Roulette*, a 1950s JOG plywood hard chine sloop all of 20ft LOA and 6ft beam, from England to Greece. He fell in love with the life and stayed in the Mediterranean. For a number of years he worked in the yacht charter business, delivered yachts and was a freelance photographer.

In 1979 he bought *Fiddlers Green*, a 28ft Cobra 850, and sailed it down to the Mediterranean in the winter months. Three years later he acquired *Tetra (Tetranora)*, a 31ft Cheverton New Campaigner built in 1962. In Tetra he travelled extensively around the Mediterranean researching his pilots and sailed her to Southeast Asia and back. In 1987 he sailed down the Danube and on to the Aegean in a 19ft Mirror Offshore, *Rozinante*. His latest yacht, *seven tenths*, a Cheoy Lee Pedrick 36, is his fifth and is now in the Mediterranean from the Caribbean.

Rod Heikell is the acknowledged expert on sailing in the Mediterranean. His pilots have become the model for others and are often referred to as 'the bible'! Since the publication of his first book, *Greek Waters Pilot*, in 1982 and now in its ninth edition, he has written over a dozen others on related matters and also edits the Imray-Tetra chart series.

He is currently working on several new books including one on cruising strategies and at the same time updating his back list of pilots. He prefers gunk-holing to long passages, and sails with Lu his partner, an eclectic mixture of music, a lot of books and the BBC World Service for company.

Danny Da Costa Studio

Imray Mediterranean Almanac (editor)
Mediterranean Cruising Handbook
Mediterranean Sailing
Mediterranean France & Corsica Pilot
Italian Waters Pilot
Greek Waters Pilot
Ionian
West Aegean
Turkish Waters & Cyprus Pilot
East Aegean
The Turquoise Coast of Turkey
The Danube – A river guide
Indian Ocean Cruising Guide
Yacht Charter Handbook
The RYA book of Mediterranean Cruising

Author's note

Photocopies and downloaded information from my books circulate around the Mediterranean. For those of you sitting and reading a photocopy or information downloaded off internet sites, I suggest you reflect on the fact that you forfeit your own moral basis for objecting to any theft from yourself or your boat. You have after all stolen something from me and my publishers, both in a moral and legal sense, so when you have something stolen, think about how it feels.

RJH

Published by
Imray Laurie Norie & Wilson Ltd
Wych House The Broadway St Ives Cambridgeshire PE27 5BT
England
☎ +44(0)1480 462114 *Fax* +44(0)1480 496109
Email ilnw@imray.com
2004

1st edition 1982
Revised reprint 1983
2nd edition 1985
3rd edition 1987
4th edition 1990
5th edition 1992
6th edition 1994
7th edition 1998
8th edition 2001
9th edition 2004

A catalogue record for this book is available from the British Library.

ISBN 0 85288 701 9

CAUTION
Every effort has been made to ensure the accuracy of this book. It contains selected information and thus is not definitive and does not include all known information on the subject in hand; this is particularly relevant to the plans, which should not be used for navigation. The author believes that his selection is a useful aid to prudent navigation, but the safety of a vessel depends ultimately on the judgement of the navigator, who should assess all information, published or unpublished.

PLANS
The plans in this guide are not to be used for navigation. They are designed to support the text and should at all times be used with navigational charts.

CORRECTIONAL SUPPLEMENTS
This pilot book will be amended at intervals by the issue of correctional supplements. These are published on the internet at our web site www.imray.com and may be downloaded free of charge. Printed copies are also available on request from the publishers at the above address.

This work has been corrected to February 2004.

Printed in Italy by Eurolitho, SpA, Milan.

Preface

For this edition *seven tenths* and her crew criss-crossed Greece for two full seasons. There has been a lot of building going on around the islands and mainland coast. New harbours have been built. Old harbours have been improved and breakwaters built or extended. New concrete quays have been built where once there was rock or a sandy foreshore. Most of the marinas built by the Tourist Board are now privatised and new marinas have been built – some in pretty unlikely spots. Lu and I have been kept busy measuring, sounding and photographing harbours and anchorages. New plans have been drawn and old plans modified. Inevitably there has to be a cut-off point and even as I read the last set of page proofs there are emails coming in noting changes going on. Remember to check the Imray website (www.imray.com) for updates.

Greece has become more affluent since it joined the EU and it shows around the coast. Many Greeks have built second homes or small hotels. The latter are usually empty as Greece now has a surfeit of hotel rooms. Small runabouts and RIBS owned by Athenians or rich locals clutter some of the new harbours and I have a bit of a beef about this. I'm not unhappy about them being there, but I wish they weren't parked in the deep-water berths taking up all the room in a small harbour where a visiting yacht might get in. Local taverna owners I know are just as miffed that they miss out on passing waterborne trade. Perhaps some small harbours could have a few deepwater berths earmarked for visitors and everyone would be happy.

By the time this edition is out the 2004 Olympics will be about to start and Greece will be winding up for the big event. Some are predicting disaster, but I think everything will come together in that wonderful haphazard way that things happen here and that these games will be remembered as the friendly games. Everyone is hoping that the visitors coming to the games will take some time out and travel around the islands and the rest of the mainland. I'm sure there will be more people sailing around Greek waters in 2004 and that would be a relief for those here who have seen a decline in visiting yachts over the last few years. Certainly fewer yachts have been around with the introduction of the tedious paperwork involved with the Transit Log and Cruising Permit. Let's hope the European Court sorts this bureaucratic nightmare out and Greece becomes as easy to cruise as the rest of the EU countries. In the meantime the relative absence of yachts in some areas means it's a bit like cruising around Greece ten or fifteen years ago, except you can get a latte and a ciabatta ashore along with your moussaka and chips.

At times other yachtsmen will say to me that it must have been wonderful cruising around Greece 25 years ago. Well, yes it was. And it is today. Things change, but there is still that wonderful light, the turquoise water merging into inky black, the mountains fading into rosy outlines at dusk, the lights ashore of some taverna overlooking the water and the smell of fish grilling over charcoal. It is still there and it is wonderful.

Acknowledgements

My thanks to all of you who have contributed information for this edition. Lu as always has helped me sail *seven tenths*, sounded harbours and measured quays, climbed mountains to take photos and generally put up with the somewhat cramped quarters on board to read and edit the proofs. The book benefits from all her care and attention, and so do I. The following people and organisations provided information and help: the Cruising Association Med. Section as always provided valuable information; Conrad Jenkin put together information from the RCC; Dick & Janice Taverne; David & Pat Teale of SY R*etreat from Battle II*; Jim Baerselman of SY *Rapaz*; Michael & Christine Ratcliffe of SY *Sea Topaz*; Nigel Patten of SY *Magellan*; Steve Goulden of SY S*mall Consolation*; Ove Hansen of SY *Vildgas*; Mike Johnston of SY *Arran Comrades*; Anton Stanwix of SY *Anatina*; Steve Miller of SY *Ithaca*; Marc Labaume; Matthew Hunter of SY *Outlandish*; Jeremy Shaw of SY *Zingano*; Rene Ortmans of SY *Fare Nui*; Jim Parish of SY *Red of Hull*; Bill Atkinson; W. Schreiber; M. Hontebeyrie; M. Hirtz; M. Hourcade; Buck Creel; Manos Ioannidis; Peter Sailer; Tomasz Cwizewicz; Marc L.Verhoeven; Bernd Gruneberg; Th.A.C. Spoor; John Hollamby SY *Bali Hai*; Dick Casteldine; Mrs C. Collins; Mr P Braddock; Mr B Sommerlad; Roland Harris; Pekka Roine of SY *Carmencita*; Bill and Hilary Keatinge; Boguslaw Syrek. Also thanks to Robyn, Joe and all at CYS, Richard and Andreas at Greek Sails and Nikos Koutsodontis of K & G Med Marinas. At Imrays Willie Wilson put together the book, not to mention coping with the corrections on two sets of page proofs couriered to Greece and then here in Antigua, and nursed everyone at Imrays through the text and plan corrections. My thanks to everyone at Imrays for their toil and care over the book.

Rod Heikell
Antigua 2004

v

KEY TO SYMBOLS USED ON PLANS

 depths in METRES

 shallow water with a depth of 1m or less

 rocks with less than 2 metres depth over them

 rock just below or on the surface

a shoal or reef with the least depth shown

wreck partially above water

wreck

dangerous wreck with depth over it

eddies

rock ballasting on a mole or breakwater

above-water rocks

cliffs

anchorage

prohibited anchorage

harbour with yacht berths

yacht harbour/marina

church

mosque

windmill

chimney

castle

airport

ruins

houses

port police

port of entry

customs

waypoint

travel-hoist

shower

water

electricity

fuel

post office

tourist information

pine

trees other than pine

visitors berths

fish farm

yacht berth

local boats (usually shallow or reserved)

beacon

port hand buoy

starboard hand buoy

mooring buoy

Characteristics

light

lighthouse

F	fixed

Fl.	flash

Fl(2)	group flash

Oc.	occulting

R	red

G	green

W	white

M	miles

s	sand

m	mud

w	weed

r	rock

KEY TO QUICK REFERENCE GUIDES

Shelter
A Excellent
B Good with prevailing winds
C Reasonable shelter but uncomfortable and sometimes dangerous
O In calm weather only

Mooring
A Stern-to or bows-to
B Alongside
C Anchored off

Fuel
A On the quay
B In the town
O None or limited

Water
A On the quay
B In the town
O None or limited

Provisioning
A Excellent
B Most supplies can be obtained
C Meagre supplies
O None

Eating out
A Excellent
B Average
C Poor
O None
(Note These ratings are nothing to do with the quality of food served in restaurants, but relate only to the number of restaurants.)

Plan
• Harbour plan illustrates text

Charges
Charges are for the daily high season rate for a 12-metre yacht, with approximate exchange rates.

1 No Charge
2 Low Cost   Under €25 (c. £15)
3 Medium Cost   €25–40 (c. £16–25)
4 High Cost   €41–55 (c. £26–35)
5 Very High Cost Over €55 (£35+)

USEFUL CONVERSIONS

1 inch = 2.54 centimetres (roughly 4in = 10cm)
1 centimetre = 0.394 inches

1 foot = 0.305 metres (roughly 10ft = 3 metres)
1 metre = 3.281 feet

1 pound = 0.454 kilograms (roughly 10lbs = 4.5kg)
1 kilogram = 2.205 pounds

1 mile = 1.609 kilometres (roughly 10 miles = 16 km)
1 kilometre = 0.621 miles

1 nautical mile = 1.1515 miles
1 mile = 0.8684 nautical miles

1 acre = 0.405 hectares (roughly 10 acres = 4 hectares)
1 hectare = 2.471 acres

1 gallon = 4.546 litres (roughly 1 gallon = 4.5 litres)
1 litre = 0.220 gallons

Temperature scale
$t°F$ to $t°C$: $5/9(t°F–32) = t°C$
$t°C$ to $t°F$: $9/5(t°C+32) = t°F$

So 70°F = 21.1°C   20°C = 68°F
   80°F = 26.7°C   30°C = 86°F

Introduction

What to expect

Greece has more coastline than any other Mediterranean country, over 7000 miles once you unravel all the coastlines of all those islands and the mainland coast. Importantly, this coast is much indented with bays and gulfs so there is an abundance of natural harbours and anchorages around the islands and mainland coast. There are relatively few marinas in Greece although more are being built, though many of these are not fully functional. What you will find are a multitude of harbours where yachts can berth, ranging from commercial ports to small fishing harbours where a yacht can squeeze in alongside the local *caïques*. Throughout Greece anchorages lie an easy day's sail away (or usually less) and you don't need to visit a harbour until you choose to do so.

For many people their first introduction to sailing in Greece is on a charter yacht.

Chartering a yacht in Greece

Yacht charters in Greece fall into three main categories:

Flotilla

This involves a group of boats, usually ten or so, sailing in company around a more or less planned route. The flotilla lead boat stays with the flotilla, with a skipper, hostess and engineer on board to help and guide the flotilla. In this way people with only a little experience can skipper their own boat, but remain confident that help is at hand should anything go wrong.

Bareboat

Bareboat charter has grown enormously in recent years and now accounts for the majority of charter boats in Greece. Basically you charter the yacht and sail independently within a given area. They are typically a return-to-base charter, although some companies will arrange a one-way charter from one base to another. Bareboats are far from bare and should carry everything you might need bar provisions. In fact, most companies will provision for you as well. When booking your bareboat it is worth checking the inventory for anchors, nav equipment, charts and such. You should also enquire about the back-up team, should you need repairs whilst on charter.

Skippered

Some people with little experience opt for a skippered charter. It gives the freedom of your own boat, without the responsibility. Experience levels of the skippers vary enormously and it is worth enquiring when you book.

For more information see *Yacht Charter Handbook* published by Imray.

Berthing Mediterranean-style

For the most part berthing is stern or bows-to in the Mediterranean. In some harbours yachts berth alongside, mostly commercial or fishing harbours little frequented by yachts, where an anchor line would obstruct passage in the harbour, or where a current makes going stern or bows-to difficult. There are advantages to going stern or bows-to:

1. A yacht can leave comparatively easily from a berth. When alongside there may be three or four yachts outside making it a difficult process to leave.
2. *Privacy* When alongside there will always be people walking over the decks if you are on the inside of any boats. When bows-to there is increased privacy from the gaze of onlookers on the quay.
3. *Safety* If there is a surge in a harbour a yacht will not be squashed and scratched on the quay and yachts on the inside will not have unfair loads put on their hulls and mooring lines from boats on the outside. When stern or bows-to it is possible to ease off on the lines ashore and pull yourself off the quay a short distance if there is a surge in a harbour.
4. *Vermin* Going stern or bows-to makes it less likely that cockroaches and rats, and other animals, can get on board.

It takes some skill to go stern-to, especially if there is a strong crosswind and a narrow gap to fit into between other yachts. Always have plenty of fenders out and when close to the quay warp the yacht into place rather than using the engine. For yachts up to 10–13m long it is easier to go bows-to as a yacht can more easily be manoeuvred into a berth when going forward. If ballasting extends a short distance underwater (as it often does) then damage to the rudder is avoided by going bows-to. Moreover there is a gain in privacy as people on the quay cannot see into the cockpit or into the cabin.

1.Stern-to
2. Bows-to

Berthing Mediterranean-style

Berthing bows-to may be necessary in some places where ballasting extends underwater from the quay

There are increasing numbers of laid moorings in Greece and these will nearly always be a line tailed from the mooring to the quay or a small buoy. However, fishermen often have laid moorings with a line tailed to the quay and this will almost always be a floating line which can easily get caught around the rudder and propeller of a yacht berthing amongst or near to fishing boat berths.

For more information see *The RYA Book of Mediterranean Cruising* or *Mediterranean Cruising Handbook* for more detail.

Berthing lines
It is useful to have two stout lines made up for the stern lines when mooring stern or bows-to. A short loop of chain on the end of the line which can be

Going stern-to can be a bit of a tricky business until you get used to it. Just have everything ready and take it easy

dropped over a bollard (or unfastened with a carbine clip or shackle to go through a mooring loop) will reduce chafe on the line. Care is needed not to brain bystanders or anyone helping you to berth when throwing the lines ashore. The line should be fairly heavy as the surges which can develop in some harbours with gale force winds can be greater than those encountered in many other cruising grounds.

Yacht facilities

Water
The English quarrel about the respective merits of different beers, the French about wines, and the Greeks about water. Water is important above all else in Greece and to abuse it is to insult it. In many of the islands and some mainland areas water is in short supply. Towards the end of the summer is the most critical period and at this time some places which normally have water will turn off public supply points.

In most harbours a local is appointed as the 'water-man' who controls the water and charges for it. The charges for water are normally fixed by the local council, but usually vary according to what the 'water-man' thinks he can get. Ask beforehand and if the charge seems excessive, haggle a bit. In some harbours a local entrepreneur will truck water in and in this case there is no fixed charge and the cost will inevitably be higher because of the costs of operating a tanker service. A length of hosepipe (about 25m) with a selection of connectors is useful for refilling the water tanks.

The water is nearly always safe to drink except where a sign states otherwise or in a few places I have mentioned. To any water of doubtful quality add the requisite number of proprietary water-purifying tablets (such as *Puritabs*) or a little bleach solution (around 3%) or potassium permanganate.

It is now possible to buy bottled water all over Greece, though I don't encourage it. It is an affectation encouraged by the bottling companies that does not reflect upon the quality of most of the tap water available. Enough thoroughly obnoxious plastic mineral water bottles already litter the seas and shores of Greece and as far as I am concerned the practice of drinking bottled mineral water should be actively discouraged.

The recent mild and dry winters in Europe have meant that summer water supplies in the Mediterranean have been steadily eroded. For several summers water has been in short supply in Athens and water rationing was imposed. Though many optimistically pin their hopes on a mini-climatic aberration that will right itself in a few years, evidence for the 'greenhouse effect' continues to accumulate and if this is so then water poverty in the Mediterranean will become a fact of life.

Already I see yachtsmen, both local and foreign, surreptitiously washing their boats down when there is a ban on this activity, and they have only themselves to blame if they are denied water altogether. In recent years small communities have denied yachtsmen water because the precious stuff is in short supply and yachtsmen have abused it. It is an insult to wash your boat down when the supplies in a small village may not last the summer and just because you are paying for it, don't assume you can abuse it. I can see the day when water-makers become a common piece of equipment on board cruising yachts.

Fuel

Where fuel is shown in the pilotage notes as being close to or on the quay I am referring in most cases to diesel fuel. In some cases petrol will also be available, but often you will have to go to a petrol station in the town to obtain it. There are a number of dedicated fuel quays for yachts in Greece, but in most places fuel is delivered by mini-tanker, usually a pick-up with a tank on the back and a petrol powered delivery pump. In many places the telephone number for the fuel truck is on a notice-board at the yacht quay. If not, enquire locally and someone will usually give you a phone number or will ring up the fuel supplier for you.

Duty-free fuel is no longer available to EU registered yachts. Theoretically non-EU registered yachts can obtain duty-free fuel, although in practice it is difficult to find anyone prepared to do so. If you are going to the trouble of trying to get duty-free fuel it is only worth doing so for large amounts. Briefly it works like this:

1. Get a form from the bank showing you have changed foreign currency to Euros.
2. Get a pink slip from customs.
3. Locate the supplier and customs will annotate the pink slip.

Electricity

In all marinas and some other harbours it is possible to plug into mains electricity on the pontoon or quay. Most marinas include electricity in the berthing charge so it is worthwhile being equipped to take advantage of it. Unfortunately this will mean a variety of connectors to plug into whatever socket a marina is using and it is really a matter of adapting what you have in the best way possible. Most connections are 220V 50Hz, but some marinas also have 380V. In some of the municipal harbours where electricity and water 'boxes' have been installed the connections can be potentially dangerous and the supply is prone to surges. Turn off any sensitive equipment on board or it may be damaged by the irregular nature of the supply.

When you are away from fully equipped marinas then you will have to rely on generating the stuff yourself. Around the gulfs and in any of the anchorages and in some harbours you must be pretty well self sufficient for electricity on board and that means totting up your consumption and fitting batteries with sufficient capacity and the means to charge them. Most yachts opt for solar panels or wind generators to top up the charging from the engine alternator. In addition it is worthwhile fitting a 'smart' regulator to the alternator in place of the standard regulators supplied by the manufacturer. It may also be possible to fit two alternators to an engine depending on the relative size of the engine to the boat.

If at all possible don't rely on running a generator to top up batteries and run equipment. There is nothing more irritating than to be near a boat with its generator running in what would be an otherwise tranquil anchorage. If you really need to pollute the air with engine and exhaust noise and pollute the water with exhaust emissions please go to a noisy harbour, preferably one that is already suffering from a diesel slick, and stay there to run your generator.

Gas

In most of the larger towns Camping Gaz can be obtained, but it may be difficult to find in the islands where stocks of full canisters can run down and may not be replenished for weeks. If a yacht is fitted with Calor Gas type bottles an adaptor can be bought in Greece to take Greek gas bottles. As elsewhere the common practice is to change the old empty bottle for a full new one.

If staying for an extended period and if a lot of gas is used for hot water, heating and cooking, then it is worth changing over to Greek gas which is comparatively cheap. There are gas filling stations at Gouvía, Kalamata, Piraeus, Kalimnos, Rhodes and Iraklion.

Yacht spares

Much yacht equipment is now available in Greece or can be ordered now that Greece is part of the EU. On the whole the cost of equipment, including major items like marine engines, is cheaper than in many other EU countries. At worst it will be only marginally more expensive and it is hardly worth going to the trouble of bringing most items in.

Any equipment shipped or mailed to Greece is subject to Greek VAT.

Locally produced goods can often be used instead of imported goods – especially paint, adhesives, sealants, bronze and stainless steel gear like cleats and fairleads, batteries and cordage.

Small engineering works are good at making boat bits and pieces for more ancient bits of equipment for which spares are not readily available.

Antifouling

A yacht bottom fouls more quickly in the warm waters of the Mediterranean than it would in more northerly waters. Consequently a more potent antifouling must be used. Eroding antifoulings such as International Micron, Blake's SeaTech, and Hempel's Mille work well as long as your boat is moving and not sitting still at anchor or berthed for long periods, when the build-up of weed and coral worm overcomes the antifouling's ability to erode itself and rubbing down just takes the antifouling off. Hard scrubbable antifoulings like Blake's tin-free Tiger, International Cruiser, and Veneziani Rafaello 3 work well and although they tend to foul more quickly than eroding antifoulings, they can be satisfactorily rubbed down without removing all the antifouling. Brands like Yotun and an Israeli paint called Tammarin that a friend of mine swears by can also be found.

Local antifouling of the soft type (TransOcean is popular and works well) is widely available, cheap, and effective. You cannot of course rub it down through the season, but generally for an eight-month sailing season and four months on the hard I find it copes well, with fouling just beginning in the eighth month. If you haul every winter then in terms of cost effectiveness the local soft antifouling is difficult to beat – working out at around one third the cost or less of more sophisticated antifoulings.

Fast ferries

The advent of new fast ferries running between Greece and Italy and in some places through the Aegean islands has brought with it the problem of massive ferry wash. At speed these ferries push a massive wall of water that crashes into what were otherwise protected anchorages and harbours causing damage to yachts and other small craft. When the ferries first began running they caused a lot of damage and there were hundreds of claims against the ferry companies involved. This has caused the ferries to slow down in coastal waters, but some of them still push a lot of water even at slower speeds.

The main problem area is in the northern Ionian, particularly around Corfu, Cephalonia and Ithaca. In a few places in the Aegean such as Ios and Siros there can also be a problem. The only solution is to anchor off with a long line ashore rather than go on jetties exposed to the wash but otherwise sheltered from the wind, and in harbour, to pull yourself well off the quay.

If you do experience damage from one of these ferries document the time, damage, etc. and make a claim. If possible take photographs and if you get no satisfaction, get in touch with the Greek Tourist

Hauling and boatyards

The following list gives the current location of yards with travel-hoists in Greece. There are also a number of yards which have hydraulic trailers or slipways using the old fashioned sledge on wooden runners or a modern variant on the slipway method. Yachts are also hauled by crane in a number of places, but I only include yards here which are well organised and not places where yachts are craned onto any old bit of hardstanding that is around. It is important to remember that whether hauling by travel-hoist, slipway or crane, there may be constraints on draught, beam and LOA that limit the size of yacht that can be hauled even though the dead weight of the boat is within the tonnage limit.

Gouvía 75-ton travel-hoist
Préveza Three yards. 50-ton travel-hoists and 50-ton hydraulic trailer. Also sledge and runners in the N bay.
Levkas Sledge and runners.
Levkas Marina 60-ton travel-hoist.
Nidri/Vlikho Sledge and runners.
Katakólon Crane and trailer.
Kalamata 50-ton travel-hoist to be installed. 30-ton crane.
Patras Yachts craned ashore.
Isthmia Yachts craned ashore.
Salamís Sledge and runners.
Ambelákia 100-ton travel-hoist.
Pérama Slipways to 1000-tons. 250-ton travel-hoist.
Kalamáki Marina Yachts craned ashore.
Aigina 60-ton travel-hoist and sledge and runners.
Póros 20-ton crane.
Porto Kheli 40-ton crane.
Koiládhia 100-ton travel-hoist.
Síros 65-ton hydraulic lift. Sledge and slipway.
Olympic Boatyard 50/200-ton travel-hoists.
Angistri (S Gulf of Evia) To 55ft on hydraulic trailer.
Volos Yachts craned ashore.
Pafkakia Hydraulic trailer
Vathoudhi Sledge and runners.
Aretsou (Thessaloníki) Yachts craned ashore.
Porto Carras 50-ton travel-hoist to be installed.
Khíos Marina Travel-hoist planned.
Pithagorion Marina (Samos) Travel-hoist planned.
Lakkí (Léros) 50-ton travel-hoist.
Partheni (Léros) 70-ton travel-hoist
Kós Marina 100-ton travel-hoist.
Rhodes 60-ton travel-hoist. 200-ton travel-hoist planned.
Iraklion Yachts craned out. Also sledge and runners.
Áy Nikólaos (Crete) 40-ton crane. Travel-hoist to be installed.

There are plans to install more travel-hoists around parts of Greece, but it is best to adopt a 'wait and see' policy in case the hoist fails to materialise. There are also a lot of smaller yards that haul a few yachts using either a sledge and runners or a crane with strops.

Wintering afloat

Greece has a good climate for wintering afloat, although it can be colder than you think. It snows in Athens sometimes. Just as certain yards are popular with cruising yachts, so too are certain harbours and marinas popular for wintering afloat.

The following places have been used:

Gouvia (Corfu)	Póros
Préveza	Porto Kheli
Levkas & Nidri	Lakki (Léros)
Kalamata Marina	Kos
Trizonia	Rhodes
Zea Marina	Ayios Nikólaos (Crete)
Aigina	Khania

Board. Eventually the ferry operators will get the message that speeding in coastal waters is not only environmentally damaging, but it is also going to cost them.

Macho man

In recent years there has been an increase in small craft based in Greece and, sad to say, many of these are driven by souls with the money to acquire a boat but none of the wit to learn seamanship and care for others using the sea. Most of these newly acquired craft are motorboats and while some are skippered in a sensible and seamanlike way, others are driven by macho man and all the baggage he carries with him. While I am quite happy for these sad souls to crash around where they affect no one else, not surprisingly they seem to frequent those places where others are quietly enjoying themselves. Dangerous situations have developed with craft entering and leaving harbour at high speed, creating large amounts of wash that damage craft berthed in the harbour as well as posing a danger to any craft manoeuvring within the harbour. Dangerous situations have also arisen with boats navigating around an anchorage at speed where people are swimming or pottering around in dinghies. Often RIBs or waterbikes navigate carelessly and at speed in bays where people are swimming and it should be made plain to anyone doing so that not only is their sport antisocial in such situations, but it is also dangerous should they hit anyone swimming in the water.

Rubbish

The steady increase in man-made disposables found in the oceans and seas of the world is saddening. Around the seas of Greece the amount of rubbish, particularly plastic, has steadily increased. Locals are partly to blame for this – in many Greek villages you will see garbage thrown into the sea – but shore-based tourists and sadly some yachtsmen are also to blame. No one on a yacht has any excuse for polluting somebody else's waters and anybody who does so should not be there. In most harbours there are containers for garbage and it is here and not in the sea that it belongs.

New harbours

Around Greece a number of new harbours have been built with EU money to promote tourism in the area. Other harbours have been improved and extended. Sadly many of these new berths are occupied by small boats, often owned by Athenians or others from the large cities, which unnecessarily take up deep water berths with what are effectively dinghies or small motorboats. This means that there are generally few or no berths for visitors so yachts must move on to other places. A lot of the locals I have spoken to are upset by this as their tavernas or minimarkets are missing out on custom from yachts, but there is often little they can do about it. Perhaps someone in the appropriate tourism department might want to do something about it before the locals themselves take it into their own hands.

Formalities

Entry formalities

All yachts entering Greece should fly the Greek courtesy ensign and should proceed to a port of entry. Yachts entering from outside the EU should also fly a Q flag. All yachts must visit Customs and Immigration, and purchase a Cruising Permit and Transit Log. Passports and yacht registration papers will usually be requested. Proof of VAT status, insurance cover, radio licences and certificates of competence may also be requested. Marinas and boatyards at a port of entry will usually assist with the paperwork.

VAT

Greece as part of the European Union (EU) comes under EU legislation regarding the implementation of the Single Market Agreement.

EU Registered Yachts

Since 1 January 1993 all yachts registered in EU countries are required to have proof that VAT has been paid or that the yacht is exempt from payment. The only exemption is for yachts built before 1 January 1985 which were in an EU country before 1 January 1993. All yachts built after 1 January 1985, and older craft imported into the EU after 1 January 1993, are liable for VAT payment.

If liable, VAT may be paid in any EU country.

Non-EU Registered Yachts

From 1 July 2002 yachts registered in countries outside the EU are allowed 18 months Temporary Importation into the EU in any 24-month period without incurring VAT liability.

If a yacht is hauled out and placed under customs bond in an EU country, it is probable that this time will not count against the 18-month limit. Thus a non-EU yacht can remain within the EU for up to 2 years, as long as it is hauled out and under customs bond for a period of 6 months. Yacht owners who are not EU nationals must also leave the EU for this 6-month period. It is essential that these terms be agreed with the relevant customs officials before assuming this interpretation of the ruling.

Alternatively you can leave the EU and haul the yacht in a non-EU country such as Malta or Croatia and then return to the EU for another 18-month period, as long as the yacht has been out of the EU for 6 months.

Obviously any non-EU nationals' visa obligations must be observed over and above the VAT regulations.

Note

1. VAT can be paid in the EU country in which a boat is based or in the EU country of registration. In practice boats have moved from one country to another to pay VAT, usually to take advantage of a lower VAT rate or valuation by customs.
2. Evidence of VAT payment or exemption from VAT must be obtained unless you want to be

Ports of entry

Adhamas (Milos)	(Cyclades)
Ayios Nikólaos	(Crete)
Alexandroupolis	(Northern Greece)
Argostoli (Cephalonia)	(Ionian)
Corinth	(Gulf of Corinth)
Dhafni (Khalkidhiki)	(Northern Greece)
Ermoúpolis (Síros)	(Cyclades)
Gaios (Paxoí)	(Ionian)
Glifada	(Attic Coast)
Igoumenitsa	(Ionian)
Iraklion	(Crete)
Itéa	(Gulf of Corinth)
Kalamata	(Peloponnisos)
Kali Limenes	(Crete)
Katakólon	(Peloponnisos)
Kavala	(Northern Greece)
Kérkira (Corfu)	(Ionian)
Khalkis	(Evia Channel)
Khania	(Crete)
Khíos	(Eastern Sporades)
Kós	(Dodecanese)
Lavrion	(Saronic Gulf)
Levkas	(Ionian)
Mikonos	(Cyclades)
Mirina (Limnos)	(Eastern Sporades)
Mitilíni (Lésvos)	(Eastern Sporades)
Navplion	(Argolic Gulf)
Patmos	(Dodecanese)
Patras	(Gulf of Patras)
Pílos	(Western Peloponnisos)
Pithagorion (Sámos)	(Eastern Sporades)
Preveza	(Ionian)
Rethimno	(Crete)
Rhodes	(Dodecanese)
Sami(Cephalonia)	(Ionian)
Sími	(Dodecanese)
Sitia	(Crete)
Soudha	(Crete)
Stilidhos	(Evia Channel)
Thessaloniki	(Northern Greece)
Thira	(Cyclades)
Vathi (Ithaca)	(Ionian)
Vathi (Samos)	(Eastern Sporades)
Volos	(Northern Greece)
Vouliagméni Marina	(Saronic Gulf)
Yithion	(Peloponnisos)
Zákinthos	(Ionian)
Zéa Marina	(Saronic Gulf)

Cruising Permit Charges

(Private Pleasure Yacht Permission For Stay and Maritime Traffic)

These are issued by the Port Authority and cost €6 per metre LOA and are payable each time a yacht enters Greek waters, valid for 6 months. EU yachts may renew on an unlimited basis. Non-EU yachts may renew for a further 6 months. This is likely to fall in line with the VAT Temporary Importation rules. (See also Note 1 below).

Transit Log
(Private Pleasure Maritime Traffic Document)

All yachts cruising in Greek Waters must also have a valid Transit Log. These are purchased on entry along with the Cruising Permit and are valid for fifty ports of call. A Transit Log must be presented to port police on entering and leaving each port where it will be stamped. It costs €30.

Other charges
Compulsory Customs processing fee	€15
Solidarity Tax for Sailors Social Security	€15
Total charges for a 12m EU yacht	€132

Special Reciprocal Charge €15 (per metre LOA). Levied to non-EU yachts. Valid for three months and levied at the end of the period.

NOTES
1. Yachts with an annual contract with a marina, boatyard or other service company may apply for a three year Cruising Permit for a small additional charge. It would appear that his permit remains valid even if the yacht leaves Greece for up to 30 days in a year.
2. This Cruising Tax appears to contravene EU regulations for free travel within the EU and it is possible that the law will be repealed or reformed to conform to EU regulations. It also contravenes EU legislation on equal treatment for all member states as Greek-flagged yachts are exempt from this law.

   The European Commission has taken Greece to the European Court of Justice on grounds that this is an illegal import duty under the EU Treaty of Paris after Greece formally refused to remove the tax.
3. These charges are intended as a guide only. There seems to be some interpretation and re-interpretation by individual Port Authorities, so implementation of the regulations varies throughout Greece.

STOP-PRESS - CRUISING TAX RESCINDED
Just as this book was going to press the Greek government responded to the findings of the EU court and passed Law L3182/2003 which effectively ended the cruising tax. EU yachts will now only have to buy a Transit Log (cost €30) on entering Greece. Any further changes to the law will be posted as a supplement on the Imray website.

---

liable for VAT payment. In the UK customs introduced a simple method of paying VAT or acquiring proof of exemption with the SAD (Single Administrative Document) form. In Greece customs have been slow to implement the rule on VAT.

3. Very little notice has been taken of the requirement to pay VAT on yachts built after 1985 and yachts subsequently brought into Greece. Until recently there was no paperwork in place to obtain a certificate to show exemption from VAT and it was extremely rare for the authorities to ask for any relevant paperwork. There have been a few cases of customs requesting a certificate from foreign flag yachts but all in all the VAT situation remains fairly

fluid. If you are contemplating paying VAT the rates are:

18% on new craft.
18% on non-Greek-flagged second-hand craft.
3·6% on Greek-flagged second-hand craft.

Insurance

A comprehensive insurance policy for the eastern Mediterranean is not excessively expensive, although substantial increases in premiums (up to 30%) have been noticeable over the last year or so. Shop around various companies or brokers to get the best deal. Most policies do not cover east of 34°E, but since all Greek waters are inside this limit there is no problem here.

In 1999 new insurance requirements for all yachts

(regardless of flag) in Greek waters were introduced. Details of the requirements, mostly to do with third party liability, are outlined below, but most reputable insurance policies will already provide the amounts required by the new Greek law. What you may not have is a certificate stating the amounts for which you are covered; this must now be carried on board the yacht. A Greek translation of all Third Party Liability policy details must also be carried. Contact your insurance company and they will be able to provide the necessary documentation. It may also be worth checking that you are covered for liability for pollution.

Greek insurance requirements
All yachts must have:
1. Insurance for liability for death or injury for those on board and any third party for a minimum of €295,000 (approx. £190,000).
2. Insurance for liability for damage of at least €145,000 (approx. £93,500).
3. Liability for pollution resulting from an incident of €60,000 (approx. £40,000).

Small Craft Licences

At the time of publication there was no clear EU directive on small craft licences and it appeared to be up to individual countries to determine agreement on what licence or certificate corresponded with what.

The RYA *International Certificate of Competence* (ICC) is generally accepted as a minimum requirement. Check the RYA website for details: www.rya.org.uk

Yacht Registration Documents

Full Part 1 or SSR papers or their equivalent are required.

Radio Licences

All yachts fitted with a VHF radio or SSB radio should carry the appropriate licence. The new DSC radios require a new Short Range Certificate (SRC) user licence; the set is registered and an MMSI (Maritime Mobile Service Identity) number unique to that radio is issued.

Recreational Craft Directive

On 15 June 1998 the Recreational Craft Directive came into existence. There is still a lot of wrangling about the exact interpretation of the directive, but a brief summary is outlined below.

- The RCD applies to all recreational craft in the EU between 2·5 and 24 metres LOA.
- Any craft built after 15 June 1998 must have a CE mark and rating.
- Craft built before 15 June 1998 are exempt, as long as they were in the EU before this date.
- If they were imported into the EU after 15 June 1998 they should apply retrospectively. (This is the main point of contention.)
- Home built craft are exempt if not sold for five years. Historical replicas are also exempt.

It appears that the original brief, to have certain common standards of construction for the EU market so that trade within the EU could be

facilitated by one kitemark, has been extended to exclude a large number of craft from being sold on in the EU market.

In practice most Mediterranean countries are ignoring the daft requirements of the RCD for the simple reason that it is just not enforceable.

Immigration

As it is part of the EU, any EU nationals may enter Greece freely with no visa requirements. Everyone on board a yacht must carry a valid passport. It is likely that all passports will be checked when Cruising Permits and Transit logs are issued. An official identity card for EU residents may also be accepted. Normally when entering Greece non-EU passport holders are allowed to stay three months without a visa (two months for some passport holders including those from the USA) and after that period is up, an extension for a further three months' stay must be applied for. However, when you enter on a yacht you can stay indefinitely provided you remain with the yacht. A problem arises if you enter on a yacht and depart by some other means. It is worthwhile obtaining a photocopy of the transit log to present to immigration when departing other than by yacht.

EU Expansion

United Kingdom, Ireland, Denmark, Sweden, Finland, the Netherlands, Belgium, Luxembourg, Germany, Austria, Portugal, Spain, France, Italy, and Greece comprise the EU in 2003.

Planned expansion of the EU from May 2004 will include, amongst others, Malta, Slovenia and Cyprus. Any countries that join the EU will be covered by the rulings outlined above. This in turn will limit the options for non-EU yachts in the Mediterranean leaving the EU under the temporary importation rules, not to mention the further complication of RCD regulations.

Port formalities

Port police

The port police offices are generally on or near the waterfront. They can be easily recognised by the crossed anchors next to the sign saying port police (*Limenario*) and the very large Greek flag flying from the building. The port police handle most of your papers and now work closely with the Greek coastguard. In practice the coastguard and the traditional port police now handle paperwork and in more remote places you will often find there is only a coastguard station

An interesting point is that the port police can keep yachts in harbour if the weather forecast predicts winds of over Force 6. (Often they will not bother.) Should they make such a ruling skippers of yachts can sign a form which states in effect that they have been warned and any misfortune due to bad weather is entirely their own fault.

In my dealings with the port police I have invariably found them to be courteous and helpful, although business may be conducted with that typical Greek disdain for time that the Anglo-Saxons find so infuriating. Occasionally the yachtsman will come across an official who is rude and difficult, but this does not characterise officialdom only in Greece – it can be encountered everywhere.

Harbour dues

Harbour dues are levied in Greek harbours where there are port police or someone else appointed to collect the dues. The charge is administered by the *Limeniko Tameio* (harbour financial committee) and not the *Limenario* (port police) although in practice it is usually collected by the port police.

For a 12-metre yacht the charge amounts to around €5. This is not an unreasonable charge for sheltering within a harbour and those who complain that there are no facilities for the money they pay should try heading for shores where there is a marina and somewhat higher berthing charges, though no doubt they will moan about that as well.

These are the charges made when the port police (or *Limeniko Tameio* collector) bothers to charge you. In the last season in Greece I was charged in around 30% of the harbours I visited. The collection of the charge is neither dedicated nor consistent, but I strongly suggest that you are polite and civil towards those port policemen forced to make out the receipts for your boat. They did not devise the charges and already have more than enough other paperwork they wish they did not have to do.

Other laws for yachtsmen

There are a number of laws which, while not specifically maritime law, nonetheless are of special relevance to the yachtsman.

Antiquities This concerns the acquisition and export of antiquities. Greece loses valuable and irreplaceable antiquities every year and some of these are smuggled out of the country on yachts. Any antiquities found in Greece must be surrendered to the state. Any yacht with antiquities on board is liable to be impounded and confiscated and I know of several instances when this has occurred. This law also applies to antiquities and works of art which have been sold to you so it would pay to find out if an article can be exported before you exchange any money.

Diving regulations This law forbids the use of compressed air tanks for underwater fishing. You may use a spear gun with a snorkel and mask but not with compressed air tanks. Scuba gear may be used for pleasure or filming except in areas where there may be antiquities on the seabed. These prohibited areas are so extensive that the National Tourist Board of Greece finds it easier to list those areas where compressed air tanks can be used for pleasure and filming. These are:

Kassandra promontory (Khalkidhiki peninsula)

All along a 500-metre belt of sea stretching out from the eastern shore of the promontory from the village of Polihrono to Ák Glarokavos.

Sinthonia promontory (Khalkidhiki peninsula)

All along a similar belt of the eastern shore of the promontory from Ák Armenistís to Ák Dhrépanon.

Athos promontory (Khalkidhiki peninsula)

a. Along a 500-metre belt from the shore in Órmos Provlaka from Pirgos Oranoupolis to Xerxes Canal.

b. Along the northern shore of Nisís Ammouliani from Ák Trigona to Ák Kókkino, within a 300-metre belt running parallel with the shore.

Míkonos

Within a 500-metre belt around the island's shores, save for the stretch from Ák Ayios Yeóryios to Ák Alogomandra.

Kérkira (Corfu)

a. Within a 500-metre belt around the island's shores from Ák Rodha to Ák Dhrastis.

b. Within a similar belt of sea from Palaiokastrita to Ák Arkoudila, with the exception of the waters surrounding Nisídhes Langoudhia.

c. Within a similar 500-metre belt of sea from Ák Koundhouri to Ák Agni, with the exception of the waters surrounding the islands of Vidho and Lazaretto.

Paxoí

Within a 500-metre belt of sea round the island's shores except for the area of Voutsi.

Levkas

a. Within the usual 500-metre belt along the island's western shores from Yiropetra to Ák Dhoukaton.

b. Within a similar 500-metre belt along the island's eastern shore from the point on the beach in line with the village of Katouna as far as the eastern entrance to Órmos Rouda, but not within the bay itself nor around the island of Madhouri.

c. Within a 500-metre belt of sea all round the island of Meganísi.

Cephalonia

a. Within a 500-metre belt along the island's shores, except for Dhíavlos Ithaca from the level of Fiskárdho to Órmos Andísami and Órmos Samí to Áy Eufimia.

b. Also excluded are the stretches of coast from Ák Kapri to Ák Mounda, the waters round the Variani islets and the coast from Ák Ortholithia to Ák Atheras.

Zákinthos

All around the island's shore, along a 500-metre belt.

Obviously it would pay to check with the local port police since any of these areas can be designated 'out of bounds' if the Archaeological Service suspect there are antiquities on the seabed.

Divers caught diving in prohibited areas face large

fines, confiscation of their equipment and in some cases confiscation of the dive vessel if it is thought that the diving activities have been carried out to retrieve antiquities from the sea bottom.

In most areas you go to there will be a commercial operation that organises diving courses and holidays. It makes sense to talk to the operators in an area to find out exactly what restrictions there are and what local conditions are like. There have been a number of accidents over the years where divers have got into trouble with currents which, although not always strong, can be tricky in tight situations.

Chartering your yacht

It seems to be a commonplace dream among impoverished yachtsmen arriving in Greece that they will quickly replenish their coffers by chartering – until they learn of the regulations governing charter. Up until 2003 if your yacht was to be chartered in Greek waters then it had to be registered in Greece. The amount of paperwork was prodigious and the charter agreement might be checked at any port.

In 2003 the laws on cabotage and Law 438 changed so that Greece now falls in line with the other EU countries. This theoretically means that any EU-flagged boat can charter in Greece as long as it complies with Greek safety regulations for charter boats.

For more detailed information on the whys and wherefores of chartering I suggest you get in touch with the National Tourist Board of Greece. On a more practical level you would do better to talk to someone in the charter game in Greece. A number of companies will put your boat under the Greek flag and charter it, paying you a percentage of the returns as well as allowing you the use of your boat in the off-season and for a limited period (usually two weeks) in the season. Just be sure you choose a reputable company or your beautiful new yacht may be a wreck by the end of a season of bareboat charter.

General information

Tourist offices
In the cities and larger towns there are tourist offices which can often provide useful maps and pamphlets relevant to the local area.

Banks and ATMs
Major credit cards (Visa, MasterCard and American Express) and travellers' cheques are accepted in the cities, larger towns and popular tourist spots. Many places have ATMs (Automatic Teller Machines – or 'hole in the wall machines' to you and me), which work well with the major credit cards and a PIN number. In general there are few places of any size where you cannot change money either at an ATM, in a bank, post office, or at a tourist agent who will usually have a sideline changing money. Banks are open from 0800–1300 Monday–Friday.

Getting money sent to Greece from outside the country is a tedious and prolonged affair – expect it to take literally weeks longer than you anticipate.

Public holidays
January 1 New Year's Day
January 6 Epiphany
March 25 Independence Day
May 1 Labour Day
August 15 Assumption Day
October 16 St Dimitrius' Day (Salonika)
October 28 *Ochi* ('no') Day
December 25 Christmas Day
December 26 St Stephen's Day
Moveable
First day of Lent
Good Friday
Easter Monday
Ascension

Health and medicines
All cities and large towns have a hospital and for the most part treatment is good. Smaller towns and tourist areas will often have a health centre which can attend to more minor injuries and assess whether the patient should be taken to a hospital for further treatment.

In most cases treatment for EU nationals is free of charge with Form E111. In some cases you may have to pay part of the cost of treatment. It is worthwhile taking out comprehensive medical insurance which includes the costs of repatriation if necessary.

Dental treatment is good in the cities and large towns, with well equipped practices and dentists who have often trained abroad.

Specially-prescribed drugs should be bought in sufficient quantities in England before departure. Most drugs and medical requisites are freely available over the counter in Greece (including contraceptive pills, wide-spectrum antibiotics, antibiotic powder etc.) although they may be under unfamiliar brand names

Drugs
There are very strict penalties for the importation of drugs (hashish, cocaine, etc.) in Greece and severe sentences are handed out for possession of even small amounts of 'soft' drugs such as marijuana. Your yacht can be confiscated if drugs are found on board so play it safe and avoid them and anyone associated with them. A momentary 'high' is hardly worth the loss of your yacht and a stiff jail sentence.

Security
By and large Greece is an honest country, but in the cities and larger resorts crime is on the increase. Take all sensible precautions. In general the harbours around Athens have a bad reputation for theft.

Security around the Albanian border appears more settled in recent months, although caution is still advised. Refer to the notes in the relevant chapters.

More worrying is the increase in the people-smuggling trade. A number of yachts have been implicated in high profile illegal immigration cases, particularly around the Eastern Sporades and Dodecanese. In 2002 I was moored next to an impounded yacht which had been chartered from a reputable company, but was allegedly used to smuggle people into the EU. When stopped by the coastguard patrol there were fifty people on this 42' yacht. The wider issues of immigration aside, it is a very real problem for the Greek Authorities. Increased security around Greece's enormous sea border is now the norm. NATO warships and Greek Coastguard high-speed RIBs patrol these borders and regularly contact commercial sea traffic. Yachts are rarely contacted but a listening watch on VHF Ch 16 is recommended.

Laundry

In most places there will be someone who takes in laundry or a laundry will often be associated with a dry-cleaner. There are few self-service launderettes in Greece. Prices vary considerably, and are usually comparatively high, so ascertain the cost first.

Mail

The postal system is reliable and efficient for letters, but packages take a long time to be distributed. A private address is preferable to *Poste Restante*. Most marinas and boatyards will hold mail for you.

Telecommunications

Telephone

Most of Greece is served by a good telecommunications network, much of which has been upgraded in recent years.

Over the last few years Greek telephone codes have change more times than could have been dreamt of by business card printers. The main changes are:

Area codes begin with a 2 and end in a 0
i.e. an area code of 0645 is now 26450
This also applies to international calls to Greece.
i.e. 0030 645 is now 0030 26450

All mobile numbers now begin with a 6
i.e. 0974 becomes 6974

All towns and most villages have an overseas telephone exchange (OTE) where international calls can be made. Even the smallest village will have a metered telephone in a hotel, shop, taverna, or commonly in a *periptero* (the kiosks that sell everything from cigarettes to sweets), though charges will be slightly more (in hotels considerably more) than in the OTE.

Telephone cards are now widely available in Greece and can be purchased from grocery and other shops, even from the *periptero* that have metered telephones.

IDD is now possible from all phones except for a few ancient exchanges on the smallest islands. Now new equipment has been installed the communication services in Greece are considerably improved and direct dialling to other countries is normally fairly quick, although delays occur at peak periods when a lot of business calls are made.

Fax

Many travel agents and stationery shops operate a fax service, although charges vary enormously.

Mobile phones

Digital cellular phones with GSM (Global System for Mobile Communications) capacity can be used in Greece. Your own service provider will need to have an agreement with the main service providers in Greece (Panafon, Telestet, and OTEnet). In practice the system is seamless and your phone will register with a provider in Greece when you turn it on. Most phones will automatically register, although at times it is worth manually changing provider where your phone 'sticks' on one provider even though the signal is weaker than a rival's signal.

Most UK service providers have their 'preferred partners' and using these can mean lower call charges. Check with your service provider for details of their 'roaming rates'. As well as high charges for calls you make, you will also be charged for receiving calls. Receiving international calls incurs the cost of your service provider's signal to and from Greece at international rates; the caller pays only the cost of a point-to-point call in the UK. You may also be charged for receiving local calls.

If you are going to spend some time in Greece it is worth getting a Greek chip for your phone with a Greek number. You can then ask people to phone you on the Greek number rather than your home country mobile where the call is costing YOU a lot of money. I use my UK mobile number for collecting email and making short calls out.

Email

There are a number of ways of sending and receiving email while cruising. The following is a brief round-up of ways and means of doing so:

1. Using a laptop computer, a GSM phone and dedicated connection cord you can connect at 9600 baud wherever you can get a signal. 9600 baud is not a very fast speed these days but it is sufficient for text-based email. Transmission charges vary not only with your local provider in Greece, but also with your provider in the UK or wherever your phone is registered.

   Improved transmission speeds are claimed for many new phones, but it is worth remembering that these speeds are reliant on the capability of the local network. In practice most networks are a long way from supporting the speeds quoted by the phone manufacturers.

2. Internet cafés. Many quite small places have an internet café these days and if you have an internet email provider then it takes little time to download and send mail using a floppy disk. If you do not have a laptop to compile mail on and download it from the desktop in the café then most internet cafés will let you print out the mail for a small fee. Costs are low and of course connection rates are high at typically 56K. I use

this method of connecting when emailing or receiving large files or when I feel like a coffee with my mail.

3. Acoustic couplers. This sort of connection (whereby you use an acoustic coupler onto the mouthpiece of a public phone) used to be popular but connection rates are slow and errors can creep in. It is unusual to get connection rates much over 2400 baud.

4. HF Radio. There are a number of companies who will transmit data via HF radio including Sail Mail, Pinoak, GlobeEmail and the Ham Radio Network. Data rates are slow, typically less than 2400 baud, and costs for the service are relatively expensive for the commercial concerns (the Ham network is a co-operative group and you must be a licensed ham operator to use it). In addition you must make a substantial investment in a HF modem and the appropriate software. For the Mediterranean the system is probably too expensive in investment and running costs but does have the advantage of operating in many parts of the world.

5. Magellan GSC 100. This is a combined GPS and email device. The email is sent and received via the ORBCOMM satellite network. Because of the cost of the service it is really only suitable for short messages, and besides the small keypad interface would make it tedious to send long messages. Like the HF radio services it does offer near global coverage.

6. Using a satellite system such as INMARSAT you can send and receive email just about anywhere in the world. INMARSAT transmissions vary depending on the system used. INMARSAT B (replacing INMARSAT A) offers fast enough speeds for video conferencing, but is also the most expensive and biggest of the range. The costs of the systems are expensive and transmission charges are expensive, typically $2–6 a minute.

7. Other satellite phone services. A number of new satellite phone services are beginning operation using either high (GEO), medium (MEO) or low (LEO) earth orbiting satellites.
Iridium The failed Iridium system formerly run by Motorola has been bought by a consortium and is now operational. Data transmission rates are 9600 baud. Coverage is worldwide using LEO satellites.
Globalstar Coverage over most land areas and the Mediterranean using LEO satellites, but patchy or non-existent (as yet) for offshore waters. Data transmission at 9600 baud.
Thuraya Using one GEO satellite, covers mid-Atlantic to India except for low latitudes. Another GEO satellite planned. Data transmission and the phone incorporates a GPS receiver.
Emsat Uses one GEO satellite, giving coverage of northern Europe and the Mediterranean.

8. Plugging into a conventional socket. If you can find somewhere to plug into a conventional telephone socket ashore with (usually) a meter on the time used, then this is a quick and easy way to send and receive email using your own laptop.

Internet

As well as web-based email services, the internet provides many services for the cruising yachtsman. The options for connecting to the internet are the same as for email, only transmission rates really need to be at least 14400 baud. The cost of using a mobile phone and laptop is prohibitive until transmission rates improve. Internet cafés are the cheapest way of accessing the web and they can be found in most towns, and even in some villages on the smaller islands. Many marinas have an online computer for public use. Transmission rates are good and generally match those of other parts of Europe. Obtaining weather forecasts is probably the most obvious application, but I also use the internet to keep track of bank accounts and bills at home.

Provisioning

In all but the smallest villages you will have few problems obtaining the basic provisions. In the larger towns and popular tourist resorts there is now a wide range of imported goods available and even in small villages you will find the ubiquitous fare that some tourists feel they cannot do without. Why some people should feel an overwhelming need for Heinz baked beans or spaghetti hoops in Greece is beyond me, but they are there.

Fresh fruit and vegetables are seasonal, although now Greece is an EU member there is a better selection over a longer period.

In the 2002 change over from Drachma to Euro, price hikes of up to 30% on some goods were not uncommon. Price differences are considerable in places, and although it is reasonable to expect small variations, depending on location, it is wise to shop around.

Shopping hours are 0800–1300 and 1630–2000, although shopkeepers will stay open through the siesta period or later at night if there are enough customers to warrant it. Shops often close on Monday afternoon and sometimes on Wednesday afternoon as well.

Fish is expensive. Large fish such as red snapper and grouper are very expensive and the prices of prawns and lobsters are considerable – certainly comparable to or higher than in Italy and France. Fish from fish farms is a lot cheaper than the wild variety and farmed shellfish, predominantly mussels, are also available

Fruit and vegetables are reasonably priced and usually fresh. Outdoor native tomatoes, the knobbly ones, taste better than any of the ubiquitous greenhouse tomatoes now distributed throughout the EU. In the smaller centres fruit and vegetables are seasonal. All fresh produce should be washed.

Bread Bakers are a growth industry in Greece and even small villages often have a good bakers with all sorts of bread from white through all shades of brown. They will also often have mini-pizzas, cheese or spinach pies, bacon and egg pies, stuffed croissant, in fact whatever the baker reckons he can sell.

Coffee and tea Most popular brands of instant coffee are commonly available although it costs more than in some of the other European countries. Good filter coffee is also widely available and is not too expensive. Some of the specialist coffee shops and larger supermarkets do freshly ground coffee. Local teabags make an insipid cup of tea and if you want something akin to English tea then you will have to pay for imported tea bags. I usually take a couple of boxes of Earl Grey with me. Some of the loose tea packed locally is cheap and good.

Wines, beers and spirits Bottled wines are numerous and vary from excellent to terrible. Local wine can often be bought cheaply from the barrel, but taste it first. The ubiquitous retsina is an acquired taste. Wine is on the whole cheap. Local beer is quite palatable and cheap. Local spirits, ouzo (akin to Pernod) and brandy (sweetish) are excellent value, especially when bought in bulk.

Food and wine

Compiled by Bridgit Marsh

Greece is not a country for the gourmet. Eating out is as much a part of life in Greece as in other Mediterranean countries, but the food is not the sophisticated fare found in Italy or France or the carefully prepared food of the Levant. Not that the Greeks don't eat well – they do. The food is invariably fresh, simply cooked, and appetizing, but the choice will often be limited, the food sometimes served cold or lukewarm, and the garnishing meagre. In the larger towns and cities a wider choice will be found on the menu than in the smaller islands and villages.

In some areas, especially the more touristy areas, you get the 'kidnap and hustle' tavernas. Waiters stand outside the taverna and actively and often physically attempt to hustle you inside. Some of these will proffer enticements like a free drink or free entertainment. Generally these tavernas have to resort to hustling because their food is mediocre and the prices high. Those offering a freebie of some sort will make sure it is recovered by charging more for other items. My advice is you pass them by and resist being kidnapped until you have inspected the other tavernas nearby. You can always go back if you decide the taverna-with-hustle was worth visiting anyway.

One of the things which will be most noticeable is the seasonality of the food. Although most fruits and vegetables are available in Greece they may only be available during the ripening season. Apricots for instance ripen in early June and will only be in the shops for two to three weeks. This can be quite surprising to the visitor who is used to being able to buy fruit over an extended season. The seasonality of ingredients leads to a variation in the dishes served in the tavernas. This of course applies with special significance to the small village tavernas where only those foods in season will be served, whereas places with access to better markets will be able to serve such things as *moussaka* (normally only served when aubergines are in season) most of the year round.

Now that increasing numbers of tourists arrive in the summer the bigger tourist areas have to import considerable amounts of foodstuffs for the bulging taverna tables. Often your *kalamari* will come frozen from Californian waters, your lamb will come frozen from New Zealand, your *feta* was probably manufactured in Denmark, and even the aubergines in your *moussaka* may have come from Spain. Only in the smaller, more out-of-the-way places will you get locally grown produce tossed into the salad or grilled over the charcoal.

A taverna generally prepares its dishes for the day in the morning and these will be cooked in time for the midday meal when they will be served hot. These oven dishes will stand on a hot plate or by the oven for the rest of the day and by evening will be lukewarm at best. You will find that it is better in Greece to eat the baked dishes such as *moussaka*, stuffed vegetables, or *pastitsio*, at midday and in the evening order something grilled or fried which will be served hot. In recent years the introduction of the convenient microwave has meant food can now be warmed quickly for the evening meal, but this is really stale midday food reheated and not that appetizing.

When you first go into a taverna do not be confused by the menu. It will probably (if there is one, that is) have printed on it a large variety of food and drink. Some of the items will have prices beside them. These are the ones available that day and the menu should be dated at the top. The service charge is always included in the bill, and extra tipping is at your own discretion.

Greece is not a gourmet destination but the location of the tavernas is as good as you get

Butcher with good home-made sausages in Ermoúpolis on Síros

A word of advice: do not order your food all at once or your main course, side orders and starters will arrive at the table at the same time. Eating is done slowly and leisurely in Greece and it is quite alright to occupy a table all night.

The menu

You can start with appetizers. Common appetizers are: *tzatziki* (yoghurt flavoured with grated cucumber and garlic); *taramasalata* (cod roe ground into a paste); aubergine salad; *merithes*, small fried fishes (eaten whole, head and all); *kalamaris* (fried baby squid); peas or green beans in a tomato sauce; and invariably a Greek salad consisting of some or all of the following – tomatoes, onions, green peppers, olives, cucumber, *feta* (sheep's milk cheese) dressed in oil and oregano.

This can be followed with soup or a vegetable dish: fish, tripe or bean soups are common; vegetables are often stuffed and you will find tomatoes, green peppers and aubergines stuffed with a rice and cheese mixture as well as *dolmades* (stuffed vine leaves often cooked in a tomato sauce mixture). Garlic is a favourite seasoning and is used frequently and liberally. Lemon is probably the second most popular seasoning and you will find it by the side of most of your dishes and in the cooking of everything from egg and lemon soup to the flavouring of rice pudding.

The main course will probably be a choice of the following: grilled chops (beef, pork or lamb); grilled fish depending on what the local fishermen have caught; *souvlaki* (pieces of pork or beef on a skewer grilled over charcoal); kebabs which are a bigger version of *souvlaki*, usually with pieces of tomato and onion between the meat; lamb baked in a pastry case; a beef stew (*stifado*) or beef cooked in a garlic sauce (*sofrito*); *moussaka* (Greek shepherd's pie); *pastitsio* (lamb or beef with pasta); barbecued chicken, lamb or beef; spaghetti with a variety of sauces ranging from terrible to passable; meatballs;

Sign language. Fish and chicken and chips on the menu

and probably a variety of leftover baked dishes from the midday meal.

In the larger towns choice will be good and there may be specialities depending on the skill and whims of the cook, but in the smaller islands and villages you must get used to a more limited choice. Chips are served with everything and they are usually home-made and not the instant packaged 'French fries'.

It is usual to finish a meal with fresh fruit, but occasionally some form of sweet may be offered such as *crème caramel* or ice cream. Cakes, pastries and sweets are more often eaten in a 'cake shop'. Here you will find *baklava* (pastry filled with walnuts and steeped in honey); *loukamathes* (fritters coated in honey); *kadaifi* (nuts and honey in shredded pastry); and the best yoghurt in the world which can be eaten plain or mixed with honey and fruit.

Wines

Wine has been made and drunk in Greece for centuries and in ancient times was carried to most parts of the known world. It is thought the wine was stored in amphoras and pine resin poured on top to seal them – from this ancient practice it is believed we get the retsina wines which are artificially produced today.

You either like or hate retsina. Do not be put off by the bottled varieties which are much inferior to retsina from the barrel. Retsina is made locally all over Greece and often a café or taverna will be famous not only for its food or company, but also for its retsina.

Locally produced wines, resinated and unresinated, are available in bulk in some places and are served in tavernas by the litre or half litre. They vary a great deal, can be quite palatable, and if awful at least have the merit of being cheap. Do not try to carry them for any distance as they do not usually travel or keep.

At The Real Greek restaurant in London the owner has put together a fine list of bottled wines that are reproduced here and would be hard to better. The cooking is good too, with the normally robust Greek cuisine refined and fused into one of the best Greek menus in London (book ahead for a table).

Beer is also brewed in Greece and the common Heninger, Mythos, and Amstel beers are cheap and palatable.

Besides wine and beer there are several other drinks deserving a mention. Firstly, ouzo which qualifies as the national tipple of Greece. It is similar to French *pastis* and may be drunk with or without water. Greek cognac or brandy is another popular drink and makes a refreshing long drink mixed with

Coca-Cola and ice. Metaxa and Botrys are two of the better known brands. Ouzo and brandy can be bought in bulk from the barrel and are very cheap and not at all inferior when purchased like this. Take along a bottle to a *cava* or wine shop (or in the smaller villages the local grocer or café) and you will be able to get a litre or more of either ouzo or brandy for very little.

Miscellaneous

There are a few sundry items not often found on the menu but nonetheless an important part of Greek life. First, in the *galaktopolia* or dairies, you will find fresh yoghurt made from cow's or sheep's milk. The dairy will also probably stock the variety made in Athens and strained so that you believe you are eating not yoghurt, but tasty whipped cream. These shops also have *feta* (a soft cheese made from sheep's milk), local honey and eggs.

In some of the cafés you will see a long homemade sausage cooking on the spit. Made from lamb's offal and cooked with garlic and herbs, it is called *kokoretsi* and is delicious. Technically it is illegal under EU law to make and sell *kokoretsi* as it includes offal not prepared and cooked in the required EU manner, but like some other EU laws, it is disregarded by many.

At every bus station or ferry terminal you will find a kiosk where pork or beef *souvlaki* are soused in lemon juice and herbs and cooked on the spot as a snack. You may also find the Greek hamburger which is pitta bread (unleavened) filled with a *souvlaki*, tomato, onion and a dollop of yoghurt. The kiosk will probably also have cheese pies (*tiropitta*) or spinach pies (*spinakopitta*).

Kali oretsi – bon appetit!

Marine life

The marine life in the Mediterranean is at first disappointing to the yachtsman used to life around the English coast. It is not as prolific or as diverse as you might imagine; there are fewer seabirds, good eating fish are scarce and difficult to catch and in places the sea bottom can be quite bereft of interest compared with, say, the Red Sea or the west coast of France.

There are a number of reasons for the relative paucity of marine life. The first is the non-tidal nature of the sea which means there is not the inter-tidal zone in which a varied and rich amount of life can live and contribute to the whole marine ecosystem and nor are there the bottom currents to stir up the waters of the eastern Mediterranean basin and provide the nutrients that plankton need to feed on. Add to that the fact that the Mediterranean has been fished for longer and more intensively than any other region and you do not have the ideal conditions for marine life to flourish. Historically this is nothing new. The Mediterranean is the watery equivalent of marginal land like the prairies or steppes and has never been rich in sea life. The Romans used to complain about poor fish stocks

---

THE REAL GREEK WINE LIST

All-rounders
Whites Cambas White, Kretikos White, Asprolithi, Ilioni, Semeli White, Viognier.
Reds Cambas Red, Kretikos Red, Nemea, Porfyros.
Crustacea and fish
Whites Spiropoulos Mantinea, Roditis Alepo, Tselepos Mantinea, Adoli Ghis, Robola of Kefallonia, Thalassitis White, Athiri-Assyrtiko, Tselopos Barrique, Traminer (Averoff), Sauvignon Blanc (Hazimichalis).
Poultry and pork
Whites Strofilia White, Notios White, Megas Oenos, Chateau Julia Chardonnay (Lazardis).
Reds Athanassiadi, Notios Red, Ampellochora, Katogi Averoff, Domaine Mercouri, Satirikon (Oenotekhniki).
Red meat and game
Whites Amethystos (Lazaridis), Minoiko, Antonopoulos Chardonnay.
Reds Naoussa, Strofilia Red, Ramnista, Naousa Grand Reserve, Amethystos, Kava Red, Megas Oenos, Cabernet New Oak (Antonopoulos).

and bad catches and you can hardly say that their fishing methods and craft were raping the sea. Oddly enough the fabled clarity of the Mediterranean, all that transparent blue and turquoise water, comes from the relative absence of plankton.

In Greece fishing methods like the use of dynamite which began after the First World War have decimated the local ecosystems. Despite the fact that the practice carries heavy penalties and some considerable risk, it still goes on in isolated areas. In many coastal villages you will see a man without a hand or an arm, lost when he miscalculated on the fuse.

Although the marine life is initially disappointing, the yachtsman is in a unique position to discover and explore the life in the eastern Mediterranean. Dolphins, whales, turtles, flying fish, tuna, swordfish and sunfish will be seen in many places and, with a mask and a snorkel, the warm waters invite exploration.

Marine mammals

Whales and dolphins (cetaceans)

Dolphins, sadly, are becoming less common in Greek waters than they were even a few years ago. You will still see dolphins and occasionally a school of dolphins will come up to a yacht and play around it. At night the phosphorescence created by dolphins around a yacht is something marvellous to behold. The numbers of dolphins have decreased for several reasons. Food stocks, normally mackerel and tuna, have decreased. Drift netting, common in Italy and unfortunately recently resumed there, catches dolphins as well as swordfish and tuna. Estimates of the numbers killed in this manner vary, but are thought to be in the thousands rather than hundreds. Lastly, pollution in the form of heavy metals, PCBs and other carcinogenic compounds, and spills of toxic chemicals, has caused a form of 'flu' similar to that which killed many seals around British coasts. I can only suggest you support any of those groups fighting for the continued survival of this magnificent mammal which has never harmed humans and, anecdotal trivia aside, is known actively to have aided humans in distress in the water. Renew your subscription to Greenpeace, Friends of the Earth, or the Environmental Investigation Agency.

In antiquity the dolphin was mentioned and often depicted in mosaics. Aristotle and Pliny mentioned it as a friend of man and Herodotus tells of the poet Arion of Lésvos who was thrown overboard by mutinous sailors and rescued by a music-loving dolphin. The modern Greek fisherman is not so fond of the dolphin as his ancestors were, believing it to rob him of fish and there are stories (though I cannot vouch for any of them) that the friendly animals have been killed by fishermen.

Cetaceans are divided into toothed and non-toothed whales. In the eastern Mediterranean most of the cetaceans seen belong to the toothed whales,

Edible fish

Although Greece is fished out to some extent, there are still sufficient good eating fish remaining. If you despair of catching any then treat yourself in a taverna. The fish is mostly grilled and arrives without a sauce or other trimmings. Particularly good for eating are the following:

Tuna (*Tonnos*) Frequents northern waters in the summer and travels south to the Mediterranean in winter. The white flesh is a little oily but delicious

Swordfish (*Xsifia*) As above and just as delicious. In years past the swordfish was not considered a good fish to eat and local lore reckoned if you ate swordfish you went mad. Times have changed and now Greeks consider it one of the best eating fish

Grouper (*Sfiritha*) Prefers sandy or rocky bottoms and you may be lucky enough to get one in the less populated areas. Pleasant white flesh

Red mullet (*Barbouni*) Tasty white flesh but full of small bones

Bream (*Fagri, Sinagritha*) Tasty and not too bony

Whitebait (*Merithes*) Often served as a starter, the little fish are cooked and eaten whole

Octopus (*Octopothi*) Sometimes a bit tough but always tasty. Pickled octopus is delicious

Squid (*Kalamari*) Normally deep-fried. Delicious.

Prawns (*Garides*) Often expensive and not always fresh. Buy them off a fishing boat and cook them yourself for the best results

Crayfish (*Astakós*) Just as delicious as lobster. Normally boiled or grilled

which are fish-eaters and so possess teeth to grip their prey. To this class belong the porpoise, dolphin, pilot whale and killer whale. The common dolphin (*Delphinus delphis*) will often be seen. Less common are the larger bottle-nosed dolphin (*Tursiops truncatus*) and the common porpoise (*Phocoena phocoena*). The pilot whale (*Globicephala melaena*) is fairly common and grows up to 8·5m long. The bottle-nosed whale (*Hyperoodon ampullatus*), Risso's dolphin (*Grampus griseus*) and the killer whale (*Orcinus orca*) have been reported in the eastern Mediterranean.

Monk seals

The Mediterranean monk seal, *Monachus monachus*, is numbered amongst the twelve most endangered animals in the world and is the rarest species of seal left. It is specific to the warm waters of the Mediterranean, although small numbers are found on the Atlantic coast of Morocco. There are estimated to be only 500 to 800 of these animals left, with approximately half the population in Greece.

One of the big problems is the encroachment of tourism into the habitat occupied by the seals. Illegal spear-fishing using subaqua equipment is eroding the food supply – visitors have been cited as the chief culprits and there have been several convictions, but the blame does not lie solely here. Small powerboats and inflatables with powerful outboards exploit quiet places and the coastal caves where these retiring animals live. Those on the water and the land can help by keeping away from coastal caves and rocky coastlines and at all times should avoid making too much noise – the seals are easily frightened. Any illegal fishing whether by subaqua divers or dynamiting should be reported to the port police or any other authority.

Dangerous marine animals

In the Mediterranean there are no more dangerous marine animals than you would encounter off the English coast, but the warm sea temperatures mean that you are in the water more often and therefore more likely to encounter these animals.

Sharks Probably the greatest fear of a swimmer, yet in all probability the least to be feared. Films such as *Jaws* and *Blue Water, White Death* have produced a phobia amongst swimmers that is out of all proportion to the menace. After many years of sailing around the eastern Mediterranean I have positively identified a shark in the water on only three occasions. Fishermen occasionally bring in sharks from the deep water – usually the mackerel shark or sand shark. I have not been able to establish one fatality from a shark attack in Greece and so far as I know the total recorded number of fatalities for the Mediterranean is six.

Moray eels Of the family *Muraenidae*, these eels are quite common in the eastern Mediterranean and are often caught by fishermen. They inhabit holes and crevices in rocks and can bite and tear if molested. Usually they will retire and are not aggressive unless wounded or sorely provoked.

Octopus Are very shy and do not attack. They have much more to fear from man than man from them.

Stingrays The European stingray (*Dasytatis pastinaca*) is common in the Mediterranean. It inhabits shallow waters, partially burying itself in the sand. If it is trodden on accidentally it will lash out with its tail and bury a spine in the offending foot. Venom is injected which produces severe local pain, sweating, vomiting and rapid heart beat, but rarely death. Soak the foot in very hot water and seek medical help.

Weeverfish Members of the family *Trachinidae*. The two most common are the great weever (*Trachinus draco*) and lesser weever (*Trachinus vipera*). The dorsal and opercular fins contain venom spines. When disturbed or annoyed the weever will erect its dorsal fin and attack. The venom injected produces instant pain which spreads to other parts of the body and is very painful. The victim may lose consciousness and death sometimes occurs. There are no known antidotes. Bathe the wound in hot water and seek medical help as soon as possible.

Note When walking in the water where stingrays or weevers are thought to be, wear sand-shoes and shuffle the feet along the bottom. Do not handle dead weevers or stingrays.

Jellyfish Of all the animals described, the ones you are most likely to encounter are jellyfish. At certain times of the year and in certain places there will be considerable numbers of jellyfish in the water. All jellyfish sting, for this is the way they immobilize their prey, but some species have more powerful stings than others and consequently deserve greater respect.

Aurelia aurita The common jellyfish. It is a transparent dome-shaped body with four purple-violet crescents grouped around the centre. Transparent or light violet mouth arms hang below. Up to 25cm in diameter. A light contact with the stings is something like a nettle, but prolonged contact can hurt.

Pelagia noctiluca A mushroom-shaped jellyfish up to 10cm in diameter. It is easily identified, being light brown-yellow in colour and covered in 'warts'. It has long trailing tentacles and can inflict severe and painful stings.

Cyanea lamarckii A blue-violet saucer-shaped jellyfish up to 30cm across. It can be identified by the frilly mass of mouth arms underneath. It has long tentacles which can inflict severe and painful stings. There is a brown variety (*Cyanea capillata*) which can grow up to 50cm in diameter.

Charybdea marsupialis Mediterranean sea-wasp. A transparent, yellow-red box-shaped 'umbrella' up to 6cm high. Rarely seen but can inflict severe and painful stings.

Physalia physalis Portuguese man-o'-war. Has a large conspicuous float (pneumatophore) above water growing to 30cm long and 10cm wide. Below it stream very long tentacles. Rarely seen but can inflict dangerous stings.

Chryassaora hysoscella Compass jellyfish. Common browny-biscuit coloured 'umbrella' up to 30 cm in diameter with brown patches and radiating 'stripes' from the centre. Frilly lobes and tentacles. Can inflict stings although these are usually not severe.

Velella velella By-the-wind-sailor. Flattened oval disc with a gas-filled central float. Silvery float with blue and purple disc and tentacles underneath. In places you can see quite a few of these and they can inflict a severe and painful sting. I've always quite liked their evolutionary stance of having a curved float so that they sail on a beam reach rather than being blown downwind with all the other jellyfish.

Rhizostoma pulmo Dome-shaped blue-white jellyfish up to 90cm in diameter. Its mouth arms are fused in a grey-green 'cauliflower' mass below the body. It has no long tentacles and is not known as a vicious stinger.

There are no known antidotes to jellyfish stings, but there are a number of ways of obtaining relief. Diluted ammonium hydroxide, sodium bicarbonate, olive oil, sugar and ethyl alcohol have been used. A tip which I have not tried but which sounds promising is to use a meat tenderizer, which apparently breaks down the protein base of the venom. Gloves should be worn when hauling up an anchor in jellyfish-infested water as the tentacles, especially those of *Pelagia*, can stick to the anchor chain.

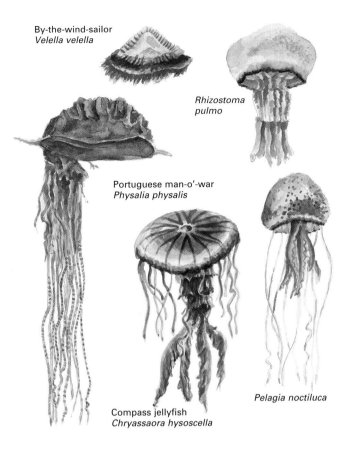

By-the-wind-sailor
Velella velella

Rhizostoma pulmo

Portuguese man-o'-war
Physalia physalis

Compass jellyfish
Chryassaora hysoscella

Pelagia noctiluca

Bristleworms In some locations numbers of bristleworms, probably of the family *Nereidae*, will be found. They are black and may grow up to 25cm long. The *setae* can produce a mild irritation similar to a stinging nettle if touched.

Sea urchins In some places on rocky coasts large colonies of sea urchins (*Paracentrotus lividus* and *Arbacia lixula*) will be found. While they do not have a venom apparatus, the spines penetrate and break off when the urchin is trodden on and are very painful. Care must be taken not to get an infection.

Marine reserves

All over the Mediterranean Marine Reserves are being established to protect marine flora and fauna from pollution, over-fishing or general disturbance. It is likely that more Marine Reserves will be established in Greece, but at the time of writing, only Kolpos Lagana, Zakinthos has restrictions on fishing and navigation.

Greek fishing methods

When a fishing boat is sighted a good look-out must be kept for floats and lines in the water. Some of the fishing methods could be dangerous to a yacht if it is not understood what is going on. The following methods are used:

1. Trawling either singly or in pairs.
2. Purse seine netting, in Greek *grigia*, in which a large *caïque*, a smaller net-*caïque* and two to four small *caïques* or light-floats are used. The smaller

caïques and/or light floats are set adrift with powerful gas or arc lamps to attract fish to the surface. The large *caïque* and its helper then lay the net in a semicircle around the fish and haul them in. Large catches of mackerel and sardines are made. The gas lamps are conspicuous from a long distance off.

3. Netting off the land. A long rope is run out to a net and then to a *caïque* which circles to enclose any fish. Particularly dangerous to a yacht as the rope is generally just under the water between the *caïque* and the shore.
4. A set net in a bay or near the shore. Usually weighted to be below the surface although sometimes a surface net is laid.
5. *Lampera*. A gas lamp on a *caïque* is used to attract fish which are speared or hooked. Often used for octopus. The *lampera* method can be confusing at night as the light bobbing up and down on the swell can easily be mistaken for a navigation light and, human beings being what they, the longer you look at it, the more convinced will you become that it is the Fl.2s you have been searching for.
6. Long-lining from a *caïque*: the lines are attached to a float which is allowed to drift.

Fish farms

With Greece's entry into the EU grants were made available for all sorts of enterprises. One of these was for the establishment of fish farms and in recent years they have proliferated everywhere. Unfortunately for the yachtsman the requirements for a fish farm are much the same as those for a good anchorage – shelter from strong winds and reasonable depths to anchor the farm in. Consequently a number of coves and bays formerly frequented only by yachtsmen and fishing boats have now sprouted fish farms which may obstruct much of the cove or bay.

In most places the operators of the fish farm are content to allow yachts to use the anchorage if there is room, but in some places the operators have expressed disapproval and actively chased yachts out of anchorages. The legality of this is somewhat dubious since it is impossible to own anything below the high-water mark. Even the late Onassis and Niarchos did not own that section of the beach or the sea bed below the high-water mark on their private islands (much to their consternation), so unless legislation has been passed exempting fish farms, it may be illegal. Certainly town councils in the vicinity of some fish farms have had them removed and others have denied operators permission to set up.

I appreciate that fish farms are a possible solution to the natural poverty in fish in the eastern Mediterranean, but such a programme needs to be carefully administered and the operators properly trained. I am sceptical of the ability of many of the operators to safely handle the restricted chemicals necessary to eliminate disease amongst the intensively farmed fish. I suggest that you enquire where the fish in a restaurant has come from before ordering it, especially if it has a muddy taste.

Note Fish farms must be moved at regular intervals because of the build-up of detritus under the farm. Consequently the location of fish farms on the plans may vary from that shown and should be interpreted as a general guide to the vicinity of a fish farm, not a precise position.

Pollution

Being a closed sea it was inevitable that as the population around the shores grew, so pollution in the Mediterranean increased. The less densely-populated eastern Mediterranean is comparatively less polluted than the western half, but around the heavily-populated Saronic Gulf and Thessaloniki Gulf there is some pollution. Around Athens it has been estimated there is more than 50% of Greece's industry and the air and water quality suffers badly because of this. Down by the Ionian Islands there is also some hydrocarbon pollution from the numerous oil-tankers cleaning out their tanks after leaving the Adriatic.

For a long time nothing was being done about the increasing pollution in the Mediterranean, but in 1975 the United Nations Environment Programme decided to get together the culturally and politically diverse countries around the Mediterranean and work out a programme to clean up the sea. In 1980 all the countries (except Albania) agreed to a ten billion dollar plan to go ahead. Some progress has been made since then, but much remains to be done and it may be that the political will to do something has weakened and that it is up to environmental pressure groups to force the pace of the clean-up programme.

Part of the antipollution plan will probably affect yachtsmen in the future. No thinking yachtsman should ever dump garbage in the sea – especially plastic. In harbour, regulations already exist by which a yachtsman can be fined up to €500 Euros for pumping out a toilet or dumping waste oil overboard, although these regulations are not rigidly enforced. All charter boats must now be fitted with holding tanks and these should be used when in harbour and pumped out only when well out to sea. It is likely that in the future antipollution measures affecting the yachtsman will be introduced and this is only right. The yachtsman may curse the extra cost, but must acknowledge the necessity of such regulations when so much of the Mediterranean, and for that matter the other seas and oceans of the world, is threatened by pollution of one sort or another.

Amended Port Authority extract on pollution

The protection of the environment and particularly of the marine environment is a basic obligation of all concerned due to the known consequences to public health and to the economy of this country.

Rubbish, including all non-biodegradable products, when put into the sea, may pose a serious threat to marine life and degrade the aesthetic view of the beaches in the areas affected. In order to reduce pollution by garbage generated on board vessels a new international law came into effect on 31.12.88.

These regulations, MARPOL 73/78 Convention annex Y, are applied to all vessels concerning the dumping of rubbish overboard. The provisions govern the following:

Plastics Any disposal is prohibited
Floating Disposal is prohibited in a distance of less than 25M offshore
Paper, rags, glass, metal Disposal is prohibited in a distance of less than 12M offshore
Food waste not ground As above
Food waste ground and in solution Disposal is prohibited in a distance of less than 3M offshore.

Following the above-mentioned legal requirement please make sure that on-board handling of rubbish is carried out in the proper manner. The port authority is sensitive to the protection of the marine environment and in cases where discharges of rubbish at sea are substantiated severe penalties will be imposed.

Note MARPOL requirements can be applied to pleasure craft and some yachts have been fined substantial amounts for indiscriminate disposal of rubbish around the coast.

History

Sailing in Greece

When you think of Greece you think of the sea and the islands. The bowl of the Aegean Sea is dotted with islands, hundreds of islands with comparatively small distances between them, so that navigation is a matter of looking for the next island and heading in that direction. In this way it is possible to island-hop from one side of the Aegean to the other. Add to this seascape a regular summer wind blowing steadily from a northerly direction and you have the ideal climate for the evolution of sailing craft and associated skills. For this reason the development of sailing craft occurred relatively early on in this part of the world and until the introduction of petrol and diesel motors, sail was the principal method of moving people and goods.

In this setting it would be surprising if the indigenous folklore and mythology were not concerned with the sea and ships. Homer wrote the first great epic of sailors and shipwrecks in the *Odyssey*. The saga of Jason and the Argonauts in pursuit of the Golden Fleece added another classic to bedtime reading. In this atmosphere of sailing craft and adventure it is surprising that there are so few records of sailing for pleasure. Pausanias records that in Ermioni during the festival of Dionysus 'they hold a musical contest in his honour and offer prizes for a diving competition and boat race.' There is some difficulty with the translation of the word for boat race and it may mean a swimming race, so even this brief mention of boating for pleasure is suspect.

Not until the Roman occupation of Greece do we find a concrete reference to sailing for pleasure in the poems of Catullus. Catullus is little known today, but in his time he instigated something of a revolution in poetic style. A contemporary of Cicero, he moved in high government circles and is believed to have entertained Caesar several times. In addition to his literary credits, Catullus had a small sailing boat constructed for his own pleasure, and in this craft he achieved some notable passages. After visiting his brother in the Troad he sailed across the Aegean and up the Adriatic to the river Po. He sailed up the Po as far as he could and then hauled the boat out and transported it overland to Lake Garda. Catullus retired to a villa on the shores of Lake Garda, spending his last years writing poetry and sailing with friends around the lake.

Not until the 19th and 20th centuries do we know that pleasure craft again sailed around the Greek islands, although during the interim there must have been such craft around. In the late 19th and early 20th centuries gentlemen on their yachts cruised around the Mediterranean, often combining their sailing with shooting expeditions or amateur archaeology. In those days a yacht meant a small ship by today's standards. Some of them still survive – marvellous creations of the boatbuilder's art which would cost a small fortune to duplicate today and must cost the same to maintain. Some are available for charter, but not by the impecunious.

Until thirty years ago Greece was relatively unknown to the cruising yachtsman. A few yachts cruised around the islands simply for the fun of it and a few took charter parties around the islands. To read an account of sailing in Greek waters written then is much like reading an account today of sailing in the Pacific – it all seemed a long way away and somehow exotic. Today, the improved design of small yachts has made the long passages possible and it is now commonplace to see yachtsmen in all manner and size of craft sailing in Greece.

General

Most people, like myself, arrive in Greece without the benefit of a classical education. We may have heard of Homer, Herodotus, Thucydides, Plato, Aristotle, Pausanias, Livy, Pliny and Catullus and we may even have read some of their works, but we do not know them in the way that schoolboys of old did. The glories of Greece, the might of Rome, the splendour of Byzantium, the atrocities of the Saracens and Turks, the romantic passions of Byron and other Philhellenes we may know of only superficially. In Greece my outstanding difficulty was to put the places inhabited by the ancients, the monuments, castles and forts, into some sort of historical order. The following brief history will sort

---

The voyage of the Heroes

In 1984 author Tim Severin set out from Volos (ancient Iolcos) to trace the path sailed by Jason and the Argonauts in their search for the Golden Fleece. The craft sailed by Tim Severin and his crew was a twenty-oared scouting galley, a replica of the sort of craft that would have been around in Homeric times. The galley crossed the northern Aegean in May and passed through the Dardanelles to arrive in Istanbul in June. From here it passed through the Bosphorus to the Black Sea and voyaged along its north coast to the mouth of the Rhion in Soviet Georgia, the Land of the Golden Fleece.

In 1985 the same craft investigated the wanderings of Odysseus in the Mediterranean on his way home from the Trojan War. This is the first time a practical experiment to trace the routes of these two early voyages has been carried out and Severin came to some unorthodox conclusions about the voyage of Odysseus. Formerly it was assumed Odysseus was blown around the Mediterranean to such diverse places as Libya, Tunisia, Gibraltar, Malta and Italy, but according to Severin Odysseus took the prudent and logical route home to Ithaca, and all of the places mentioned in Homer's *Odyssey* can be identified in Greece. For instance the one-eyed Cyclops historians assumed to have lived in Sicily can be identified with tales of triamates in Crete. It is a startling hypothesis that anyone sailing in Greek waters will find fascinating. I leave it up to you to determine which holds up best: Severin's hypothesis or the more conventional interpretation of the voyage of Odysseus.

The vessel for the voyage of the heroes, a replica of a Homeric scouting galley, was built in Spétsai according to ancient techniques using mortice and tenon joints to join the planks of Sámos pine. The galley is 16m (54ft) LOA, 2·85m (9ft 4ins) beam, and 0·30m (1ft) draught. It carries a square sail of approximately 300sq ft and is steered with twin steering oars over the stern. The crew was a polyglot bunch that at one time or other contained Greeks, Turks, Russians, a Bulgarian, a Syrian, an Australian, Americans and Norwegians as well as English and Irish members.

---

out some of that chaos, but for more detail and for scholarly wrangling over precise dates and alternative explanations the reader must turn elsewhere.

Pre-Cycladic times

Little is known of early Neolithic life in the Aegean. A number of Aegean islands were inhabited, and people must somehow have travelled between them to get there in the first place. Mílos was of considerable importance because of the obsidian (volcanic glass) found there which was used to make knives, razors, spears and so on.

Cycladic civilisation

By about 4000BC Neolithic colonists were living on Crete and the Cyclades. It flourished mostly as a farming and fishing community, and artwork in stone, clay, obsidian and later metal has been discovered. The civilisation produced a distinctive form of geometric sculpture which has been found on the Greek mainland and in Asia Minor as well as in graves in the Cyclades. Some of the statuettes are of harp players and the civilisation has been nicknamed 'harpist' after these. From widespread distribution of the geometric statuettes it is believed that sailing craft regularly plied across the Aegean and even as far as France and Spain.

Minoan civilisation (2000BC–1450BC)

Around 2000BC new peoples bringing with them the advances of the Bronze Age filtered into the Aegean from the Balkans and Turkey. They brought not only the art of working in bronze, but also the Mesopotamian pottery wheel and the eastern Mother Goddess. The Minoan empire based on Crete and Thíra expanded and flourished until it was the dominant civilisation in the eastern Mediterranean.

It was a remarkably advanced and peaceful culture. Knossos on Crete was not a fort but a palace which was both beautiful and functional; the Minoan art form worked into frescoes, pottery, and jewellery was both intricate and graceful and compares with any modern pottery and jewellery; and the Minoan fleet traded all round the Mediterranean and established order and peace under the aegis of the Mother Goddess. The civilisation ended abruptly, probably with the cataclysmic eruption of Thíra round 1450BC – one of the biggest eruptions known to have occurred on the Earth. The tidal waves, earthquakes and ash destroyed the Minoan civilisation overnight.

Mycenaeans, Dorians and Phoenicians (1500BC–1100BC)

With the demise of the Minoans, the Mycenaeans based at Mycenae on the Peloponnisos became the power to be reckoned with in the Aegean. These are the Achaeans of Homeric fame and were dominant from 1300BC–1100BC. The Mycenaeans were supplanted by the Dorians who invaded from the north and brought with them the Iron Age. For some two centuries between 1100BC and 900BC Greece lay in the grip of an era which is known now as the Greek 'Dark Age'. In this period writing and painting disappeared. The Dorians settled around the eastern Sporades and Dodecanese, while the Phoenicians from the southern shores of the Mediterranean took control of the sea-routes. By 800BC a distinct language was emerging from the chaos of the 'Dark Age'.

Greek civilisation (800BC–27BC)

What we know as the Classical and Hellenic periods began about 800BC and lasted until the Romans arrived. This era saw the birth of the city-state (polis) and for this period there was never a united Greece, more a collection of city-states – some of which were more powerful and existed in alliance with others. Colonies were established all around the Mediterranean and Black Sea.

Homer, Sappho, Alcaeus, and Archilochus belong to the early Greek period. Around 500BC the first threat to the Greeks came from the east when the Persians invaded and captured Naxos. Nine years later they were back and the famous battles of Marathon and Salamís were fought. The latter destroyed the Persian fleet and removed the Persian threat. Athens, the most powerful city-state, formed the Delian league based around the island of Delos to which all other city-states contributed and so Athens, through the league, controlled Greece.

The lonely hermitage on Cape Malea

At various times some of the city-states fell out with Athens, but not until the Peloponnesian War (431–404BC) was Athens really threatened. Sparta was the eventual winner, though its influence was not as great as Athens' had been. The islands on the eastern seaboard, Rhodes, Kós, Khíos and Lésvos, became powers unto themselves. In 330BC, Philip II of Macedon conquered most of Greece and later his remarkable son, Alexander the Great, completed the job. Greece continued to prosper, but the country was gradually coming under Roman domination.

The Romans (27BC–AD330)

By 27BC Greece was part of the Roman Empire. For nearly four centuries Rome controlled Greece, but for the most part had little cultural influence on it. Greek remained the official language and most cities were allowed to remain autonomous. Little by little Christianity filtered into Greece and merged with the ancient rituals and beliefs. The greatest change came with the conversion of the Emperor Constantine to Christianity and the beginning of the Byzantine period.

Byzantium (330–1204)

The foundation of Constantinople and the rise of Christianity marks the rise of the first Christian Empire. In 6AD numerous tribes from the north, the Slavs, Avars, Huns and Bulgars, raided Greece, although the forces of Byzantium afforded protection to many cities. Nonetheless many islands were depopulated and towns contracted in size. Later the Saracens were active in the Aegean and some islands were to become completely deserted. The Saracens completely occupied Crete for some time (810–961). The Emperor Nicephorus regained control of some of the islands, but the power of the Byzantine Empire was waning. The churches, particularly the mosaics and frescoes within, are the most enduring monument of Byzantium.

The Franks and Venetians (1204–1550)

In 1204 the Fourth Crusade sacked Constantinople and the Byzantine Empire was divided up between

Venice and numerous other Italian adventurers. In the eastern Sporades the Gattelusis and Giustianinis, on Naxos Marco Sanudo, and in the Peloponnisos Villehardouin, were the most notable duchies established. On Rhodes, the Knights of St John established a castle stronghold which they lost to the Turks in 1522. During this period the Venetians established castles and forts at the principal ports along the Aegean trade routes. Many of these strongholds were held well into the Turkish occupation of Greece.

The Turkish occupation (1460–1830)

In 1453 the Turks took Constantinople and ended the rule of Byzantium. By the end of the 16th century most of Greece was under Turkish rule. The Turkish occupation was partly one of oppression and neglect, although the horrors of Turkish rule have often been exaggerated. In the 17th century the Venetians regained some possessions in the west and English adventurers travelled around Greece collecting the antiquities which can now be seen in British museums. Few remains of the Turkish occupation are to be seen today as after the War of Independence most of the minarets and mosques were torn down, except in Crete and the Eastern Sporades.

The War of Independence (1822–1830)

In 1822 the Turks massacred 25,000 people on Khíos and so aroused Greek passions that many parts of Greece revolted against their Turkish masters. Hydra and Spétsai greatly aided the war effort by committing their fleets to the cause, and the war was won when the combined English, Russian and French fleets bottled up the Turkish fleet in Navarino and destroyed it.

The twentieth century

The newly born republic got off to a shaky start and after a series of assassinations the West put a Bavarian prince on the throne. He was unpopular and was replaced by George I from Denmark who proved to be acceptable. Greece gradually acquired more territory, Thessaly and the Epirus in 1881 and the northern Aegean islands after the Balkan Wars in 1913. The Greeks fought on the allied side in the First World War and with the defeat of the Turks on the Axis side embarked on a disastrous campaign to acquire territory in Asia Minor. When the Greeks were finally driven out the Turkish population remaining in Greece was exchanged for Greeks in Turkey.

Greece fought with the Allies in the Second World War and obtained the Dodecanese at the end of the war. Greece had attempted to remain neutral at the onset of the war, but when Mussolini proposed a coalition with the then Prime Minister of Greece, Metaxa, he declined it with a curt telegram which simply read *Ochi* (No). British, New Zealand and Australian troops fought in Greece, but the Germans overwhelmed them and occupied it until 1944.

After the war a bloody civil war split the country until 1947, when a series of conservative governments ruled until the notorious junta of the Colonels in 1967 which ushered in seven years of autocratic and repressive rule. Democracy returned in 1974 with Karamanlis. The first socialist government, PASOK, under Papandreou, was elected in 1981. In 1986 Greece joined the European Union.

The twenty-first century

In January 2002 the Euro was finally introduced, linking Greece to the other 10 countries that adopted the new currency. 2003 saw the presidency of the European Commission move to Greece for the first time. In 2004 the Olympic Games returns to its spiritual home for the first time since the first modern Olympics were held here in 1896.

On many of the islands the main settlement, the *chora*, was built on the highest part of the island so that you could see the pirates coming and at least have some time to get out of the way with your daughters and valuables. This is Skála on Astipálaia

Technical information

Navigation

A yacht will require no more navigation equipment than would be used around other areas and in all probability will use less in practice.

In a lot of places navigation is using the Mk1 eyeball and you can often see the next island or coast along a mainland coast to where you are going. All the usual instruments; a speedo/log, wind strength and direction and a depth-sounder come in handy. A GPS repeater is useful for checking things in the cockpit or you can mount a handheld GPS in a convenient place near the helm.

Most boats will have a VHF. SSB radio has only limited usefulness in the Med compared to other more remote parts of the world where radio nets are more common. Navtex works well in the Med with good coverage in most places. Radar is also a lot more common than it used to be.

When using GPS and dedicated chart plotters or chart plotters running on a laptop read the comments below carefully. Without doubt GPS is a wonderful aid to navigation as a stand-alone unit or incorporated into a chart plotter, but is does have limitations and some care is needed. Read on.

Electronic navigation aids

The new breed of electronic navigation equipment has revolutionised position finding, but some care is needed if you are using it in Greece.

GPS (Global Positioning System) The first GPS satellites were launched over 25 years ago. Since then GPS has become the cheapest form of position finding around, with a handheld set now costing less than a decent hand-bearing compass. Selective availability (SA) – the function where the military would reduce the accuracy of civilian positioning signals – has been turned off for several years now.

Modern GPS receivers are all multi-channel and can receive from three to twelve signals at any one time and decode them to determine a position. The speed at which a GPS receiver can do a cold start and produce a position is now around 30 seconds. The ease with which we retrieve data has been simplified by software that enables us to scroll through pages and pick out how we want to view the data. From the stream of position data we get speed over the ground, course heading in true and magnetic, distance off course from a waypoint, and a graphic display of our course.

DGPS There are currently no DGPS stations in Greece and in any case now that selective availability has been turned off there is little point in using DGPS add-ons.

SDGPS (Satellite Differential GPS) Works by a network of ground reference stations receiving GPS signals and then correcting them for known errors: GPS satellite orbit, clock errors, and transmission errors. A GPS correction signal is then transmitted to geostationary satellites on the same frequency as GPS signals. An accuracy of 2–3 metres is claimed.

WAAS (Wide Area Augmentation System) is the US SDGPS system. In Europe EGNOSS is the WAAS equivalent, which should be operational in 2004.

GPS Accuracy

You can currently expect an accuracy of around ±20 metres with a standard receiver. Repeated accuracy testing tends to give a figure higher than this though, and in some tests over a 24 hour period errors have been greater than ±200 metres (with SA turned off). SDGPS gives errors of only ±2–3 metres but is presently only available in the US with WAAS equipped receivers. In 2004–2005 SDGPS will use EGNOSS satellites in Europe to give a similar accuracy. When Galileo (see below) is up and running some time around 2008–2009 it will also give an accuracy of around 5 metres.

The very accuracy of GPS can be misleading and seeing a position to two or three decimal points can induce a false sense of confidence in the user. The problem is simply that we do not have charts accurate enough to make full use of such precise positions. Read over the caution carefully at the end of this section.

Although satellites are turned off for maintenance every now and again and in places coverage by the satellites is not enough to give an accurate position, in my experience these gaps in coverage have never exceeded an hour. Nonetheless it is worthwhile thinking carefully before linking the GPS to the autopilot so that the autopilot is steering a true course relative to currents, tide, etc.; or you may end up like the yacht in the Caribbean which hit a reef because the inattentive owner missed the error warning on his GPS. Without coverage the GPS kept a course using the last data that had arrived from the satellite and without any new data to correct for currents and other errors steered straight towards a reef.

Note Recent research in the US has revealed problems with corruption of GPS signals by some marine television antennas. A small number of marine TV aerials emit spurious radiation which interferes with the L1 GPS frequency at 1575·42MHz. It is only a problem with land-based broadcast TV – satellite TV antennas operate on different frequencies and are not a problem.

Gallileo The EU alternative to GPS has been approved for start-up costs and operational uses. When the satellites necessary are launched and the system is operational (around 2008) it is envisaged users will pay a licensing fee to some authority. Since GPS is free this is likely to be a contentious issue.

Chart plotters A number of yachts are fitting dedicated chart plotters which, when interfaced to an electronic position-finding system, show a yacht's position on a chart. Dedicated chart plotters are a useful adjunct to the navigation table or cockpit and I use one on *seven tenths*. Despite the usefulness of a plotter it does not replace the usefulness of a chart in the cockpit for me. With that old-fashioned paper chart I can put it anywhere, hold it up while looking at a feature or danger to navigation and quickly pan from one side of the chart to the other. You can get irritated with the *please wait, chart loading* message on chart plotters as you either zoom in or out or pan from one part to another. If the chart plotter is located at the chart table then you must constantly run up and down to check the map against the view above and this can make it difficult to mentally fit the 3D real view to the 2D chart view. A chart in the cockpit lets you constantly scan from one to the other and fit the chart to the real world. In addition the problems outlined below are exacerbated on electronic charts where an electronically derived 'real' position is displayed on a cartographically inaccurate chart.

Laptop computers Many yachts now have laptop computers on board. There are a number of software packages which reproduce charts and if GPS, radar and the boat instruments are interfaced this can be a useful navigation tool. One of the problems with most systems is that the laptop is not fitted into the navigation area and so is difficult to use when conditions are rough. Most people don't want to risk their laptop slithering all over the place when things get a bit bumpy. If you are contemplating a laptop-based navigation system incorporating charts and instrumentation, then some thought needs to go into securing the laptop on the navigation table or as a modular unit with the screen on a bulkhead and the keyboard secured on the chart table. There are also a number of remote waterproof screens available which can be installed in the cockpit to reproduce the charts, GPS position and other data where it is easy to see when sailing. The following points should be kept in mind when looking at plotting software.

1. You will need to choose between raster and vector charts. Basically, raster charts are scanned originals. Vector charts are redrawn digitally from the original. In practice the best choice is to go for vector charts. They occupy less space on the hard disk, load more quickly and, importantly, can be read when you zoom in or out. Raster charts are scanned at one resolution so when you zoom in or out you lose definition and get a fuzzy pixellated image. That is intensely irritating and the only answer is to buy a large folio of charts, although that means the laptop grinding away to load a chart on a smaller or larger scale. Raster charts also take longer to reload, which is annoying when you are trying to get from one side of the chart to the other on a 15 inch laptop screen.

2. Don't go for a chart plotter that has all the bells and whistles. Even a basic plotter has more than enough for practical navigation and the more you squeeze onto a toolbar the more confusing it gets when conditions are a bit bumpy at sea. Even a basic plotter will insert waypoints, construct routes, let you keep an automatic log off the GPS input and an annotated log as well. Just as most of us never use half of the functions on a word processor, so you will never need to use a lot of the functions on some chart plotters.

3. Ease of use and large icons are important when it's blowing half a gale and the boat is bucketing to windward. You don't want to have to work out how to construct a route when the rest of the crew are sick and you are not feeling too bright yourself. And get a mouse for your laptop instead of using the touchpad or that little joystick stuck in the middle of the keys, or every time the boat hits a wave the mouse pointer will shoot across the screen as you twiddle with the touchpad or the miniature joystick.

Handheld computers (PDA's) are also just starting to gain the processing power necessary to run plotting software. They may become a smaller alternative to a laptop with all the pros and cons, (mostly cons), that that brings.

Radar Now radar is more compact and more economical with your amps, it can be used as a useful navigation tool. Its great value is in reproducing a map of what is there, rather than a latitude and longitude that you then plot on an (inaccurate) chart. Some are combined with a chart plotter.

A caution

Most of the charts for Greece were surveyed in the 19th century using celestial fixes and basic triangulation techniques. Subsequent observations have shown considerable errors, in some cases up to 1 minute of longitude. While you may know your latitude and longitude to within 20 metres, the chart you are plotting it on may contain errors of up to 1 mile, though normally less. The practice of including the datum point for a chart and an offset to be used with electronic position-finding equipment only confuses a very complicated picture because the old charts have varying inaccuracies over the area they cover. For instance, one cape may be in position and another half a mile out of position. For the most part errors have been corrected, but there are still discrepancies and you should not be lulled into a false confidence because everything appears to be turning up in the right place. The next time it may not happen and the situation may be more critical.

The solution to the problem lies in the hands of the relevant hydrographic authorities who could use satellite-derived photographs to resurvey the areas and produce new charts – however this seems unlikely to happen in the near future and so we are left with what amounts to basically 19th-century charts patched up here and there as best the hydrographic departments are able. The problem is further complicated because the old 19th-century 'fathoms' charts are being metricated and so look like new surveys – even when the attribution is to a recent Greek survey, this will be for only a part, often a small part, of the chart, while the basis for the chart will still have been the original Admiralty 19th-century survey.

It hardly needs to be stated that you should exercise great caution in the vicinity of land or hazards to navigation – eyeball navigation rules OK.

Climate and weather

I will make only some general comments here as there is a detailed description of the weather patterns for a particular area at the beginning of each chapter.

Wind strength
All wind strengths are described as a force on the Beaufort Scale (see below under *Weather Forecasts*).

Winds
In the summer months the winds in the Ionian and Aegean are predominantly from the north. In the Aegean the constancy of the northerly winds in the summer has been noted from ancient times when they were called the *etesians* from *etos* (annual). Today they are commonly called by the Turkish name – the *meltemi*. This wind begins blowing in June and early July, reaches full strength in July and August, and dies off at the end of September and early October. In the northern Aegean the *meltemi* blows from the NE, in the middle Aegean from the north, and in the southern Aegean from the NW–WNW: in effect the wind describes an arc from the NE through to NW from the northern Aegean to the southern Aegean. In strength it varies from Force 4 to Force 7–8. The *meltemi* blows less strongly in the north and south than it does in the central Aegean.

The *meltemi* is a consequence of a pressure gradient between a low-pressure area over Pakistan (the Asian monsoon low) which extends its influence as far as the eastern Mediterranean, and the high-pressure area over the Azores which affects the western Mediterranean. The pressure gradient between these two stable pressure areas produces the constant northerlies in the summer.

Where the *meltemi* is not found or when it is not blowing a sea breeze predominates, though the direction is much affected by the local topography. For the most part the sea breeze is from the SW/S/SE.

In the spring and autumn the *sirocco* may blow strongly from the S. Sometimes it may blow up to gale force and exceptionally to more. In May 2001 a *sirocco* blew through the Aegean reaching Force 10 at Paros and blowing several yachts ashore. A *sirocco* will often kick in with little advance warning from weather forecasts.

In the winter the pressure gradients over the eastern Mediterranean are not pronounced at all and the winds are not from any constant direction. An almost equal proportion of northerly and southerly winds can be expected. Gales in the winter result from small depressions moving in an easterly direction, either southeastward towards Cyprus or northeastward to the Black Sea. Although these depressions are usually of small dimensions they can give rise to violent winds. In the winter of 1979–80 one such storm was recorded at Force 10–11 and in Corfu a yacht was blown off its cradle in an exposed yard. The depressions can develop rapidly and are often difficult to track as they move rapidly and then stop before moving off rapidly again. Depressions often linger in the Ionian Sea and the southern Aegean.

Katabatic winds
Katabatic winds will sometimes blow at night off steep mountain slopes. These winds can sometimes blow at Force 5–6 although usually less. They seldom last longer than 2–3 hours.

Fog
Fog is very rare. It has been reported in the winter and spring, with the highest incidence recorded in January at the entrance to the Dardanelles (3·8 per cent) and in Saronikos Kólpos (2·6 per cent). In all my years of sailing around Greek waters in every month of the year, I have encountered fog only rarely.

Radiation fog
In some areas, especially the northern Ionian and northern Greece, there can be radiation fog in the early morning when conditions are right. This fog will usually be coastal and rarely reaches more than a mile to seaward. The fog has normally burned off by early morning, but in exceptional circumstances may linger to midday.

Visibility
In the summer, dust particles suspended in the air may reduce visibility to as little as 2 miles, but rarely to less.

Thunderstorms
These occur most frequently in the spring and autumn and are often accompanied by a squall. They are usually of short duration and are over in one to three hours. The distribution of thunderstorms is reported to vary over the mainland and the islands: thunderstorms are more frequent over the mainland in the spring and autumn and over the islands in the winter.

Waterspouts
Waterspouts have been reported in some areas in the winter and the spring. Reliable reports of waterspouts have come mostly from the northern Ionian and Saronic. Areas known to be affected are the entrance to Patraikos Kólpos, the channel between Cephalonia and Zákinthos, the northern and eastern side of Corfu and the area around Ídhra and Spetsai. There are certainly other areas prone to waterspouts, but there is a dearth of reliable reports. One story I recently heard was of a yacht knocked down and partially flooded in the sea area between Ídhra and the mainland. It would have been interesting to know if the water was fresh, as waterspouts typically release large amounts of fresh water at the base of the column.

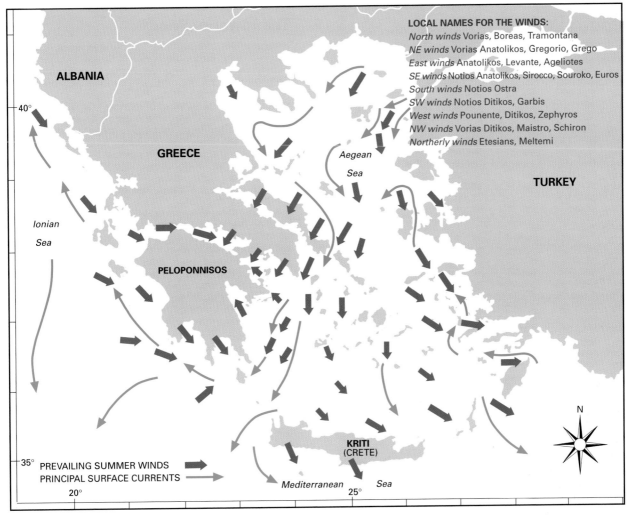

LOCAL NAMES FOR THE WINDS:
North winds Vorias, Boreas, Tramontana
NE winds Vorias Anatolikos, Gregorio, Grego
East winds Anatolikos, Levante, Ageliotes
SE winds Notios Anatolikos, Sirocco, Souroko, Euros
South winds Notios Ostra
SW winds Notios Ditikos, Garbis
West winds Pounente, Ditikos, Zephyros
NW winds Vorias Ditikos, Maistro, Schiron
Northerly winds Etesians, Meltemi

PREVAILING SUMMER WINDS ▶
PRINCIPAL SURFACE CURRENTS →

WINDS AND CURRENTS

Humidity

The relative humidity is low in the eastern Mediterranean. At 1400 local time the average value in winter is 50–75% and in summer 35–55%.

Sea temperature

The monthly average values vary considerably. In the winter (February) it is 10°C in the north and 16°C in the south. In the summer (August) it is 23°C in the north and 25°C in the south.

Cloud

In the summer cloud is rare. Over the land typical fairweather cauliflower cumulus will form as the day progresses, but unless any weather systems are around there is seldom any other cloud. In the winter there is more cloud in the northerly regions and the Ionian than in the more southerly regions.

Swell

Although there is never the large swell encountered in the Atlantic, at times winds from the west and south can build up a large swell. The seas in the Mediterranean with any winds are much shorter, steeper and more powerful than seas around, for instance, the English Channel. Going to windward in a Force 5–6 is a very wet and uncomfortable process.

Currents

In the eastern Mediterranean there is roughly an anticlockwise current: this flows towards the north up the coast of Asia Minor and then turns to flow towards the west and southwest in the north and middle Aegean before turning to flow towards the northwest in the Ionian close to the Greek coast. The many islands and channels in Greek waters means that this flow can be diverted, so that in places the current flows in a completely opposite direction to the direction of the general flow. Wherever possible I mention particular currents with the description of a specific channel or sea area.

Sea levels

In most of the eastern Mediterranean the sea level is more influenced by the wind than the tide. The barometric pressure also influences the sea level. With a high barometric pressure and an offshore wind the sea level is lowered, and conversely with a low barometric pressure and an onshore wind the sea level is raised.

Tides

The spring rise of tides varies from 10 centimetres to 0·8m (2·5ft). The greatest spring rise is in Pagasitikós Kólpos (Gulf of Volos) and Evvoïkós Kólpos (Evia Gulf). Tidal streams are weak in

WIND DIRECTION AND FREQUENCY

Note For 0800 and 1400 the two most common directions are given with the relevant frequencies.

At Corfu

	frequency 0800		frequency 1400		Calms
Jan	E-SE/30%	N-NE/17%	E-SE/38%	N-NE/16%	27%
Feb	E-SE/26%	var	E-SE/38%	NW/13%	21%
Mar	SE/19%	var	E-SE/40%	NW/11%	15%
Apr	SE/12%	var	E-SE/37%	NW/15%	17%
May	SE/10%	var	E-SE/29%	NW/13%	17%
Jun	NW/12%	var	NW/29%	SE/20%	15%
Jul	NW/14%	var	NW/32%	NE/21%	10%
Aug	NW/12%	var	NW/36%	NW/16%	14%
Sep	SE/13%	var	SE/25%	NW/23%	15%
Oct	SE/18%	var	SE/26%	NW/14%	26%
Nov	SE/25%	var	SE/32%	var	26%
Dec	SE/25%	var	SE/33%	var	23%

At Athens

	frequency 0800		frequency 1400		Calms
Jan	NE/29%	N/16%	N-NE/37%	S-SW/35%	9%
Feb	NE/24%	N/20%	N-NE/40%	S-SW/38%	8%
Mar	NE/20%	N/14%	S-SW/43%	N-NE/27%	5%
Apr	N-NE/18%	S-SW/18%	S/35%	SW/26%	5%
May	S-SW/27%	N-NE/17%	S-SW/58%	NE/17%	5%
Jun	S-NE/29%	S-SW/12%	S-SW/51%	NE/23%	2%
Jul	N-NE/33%	SW/7%	N-NE/43%	S-SW/39%	1%
Aug	N-NE/35%	SW/6%	N-NE/36%	S-SW/32%	3%
Sep	N-NE/36%	var	N-NE/42%	S-SW/37%	5%
Oct	N-NE/28%	var	S-SW/51%	N-NE/27%	3%
Nov	N-NE/39%	var	N-NE/34%	S-SW/28%	20%
Dec	N-NE/34%	var	S-SW/37%	N-NE/36%	11%

At Rhodes

	frequency 0800		frequency 1400		Calms
Jan	N-NW/32%	SE/24%	N-NW/37%	S-SE/32%	6%
Feb	N-NW/37%	S-SE/24%	N-NW/38%	SE/19%	4%
Mar	W-NW/39%	SE/15%	W-NW/44%	S-SE/29%	6%
Apr	W-NW/50%	SE/14%	W-NW/53%	SE/16%	4%
May	W-NW/65%	SE/10%	W-NW/67%	SE/13%	6%
Jun	W-NW/81%	SW/10%	W-NW/81%	SW/12%	2%
Jul	W-NW/73%	SW/14%	W-NW/71%	SW/23%	3%
Aug	W-NW/84%	SW/12%	W-NW/83%	SW/12%	1%
Sep	W-NW/75%	var	W-NW/78%	var	3%
Oct	W-NW/58%	var	W-NW/55%	SE/16%	7%
Nov	W-NW/36%	SE/14%	W-NW/45%	SE/20%	9%
Dec	S-SE/40%	W-NW/25%	S-SE/50%	W-NW/28%	9%

TEMPERATURE AND PRECIPITATION (AT ATHENS)

	Av max °C	Av min °C	Highest recorded	Relative humidity	Days 0·1mm rain	Sea temp °C
Jan	13	6	21	62%	16	13
Feb	14	7	23	57%	11	12
Mar	16	8	28	54%	11	13
Apr	20	11	32	48%	9	14
May	25	16	36	47%	8	15
Jun	30	20	42	39%	4	18
Jul	33	23	42	34%	2	22
Aug	33	23	43	34%	3	24-25
Sep	29	19	38	42%	4	24
Oct	24	15	37	52%	8	23
Nov	19	12	28	56%	12	20
Dec	15	8	22	63%	15	16

Greece except in the narrow channel between Evia and the Greek mainland where at springs it may reach 7 knots at Khalkís.

For those interested there are a number of software programmes that include data for some Greek ports. These programmes all use standard port offsets and the reliability for Greek waters is dubious to say the least. If you want to see what is available there is a free software package called *WXTide32* which has port offsets for Greece. I suggest doing a general search on the internet as it is can be downloaded from a number of sources.

The Tower of Winds

If you wander around Pláka, the old quarter of Athens, you will come across the Tower of Winds standing just outside the site of the Roman market place. Built in the first century BC by the Macedonian astronomer, Andronikos of Kyrrhos, the octagonal tower is remarkable for a number of reasons. On each of the eight marble sides there is a relief of a winged figure representing the wind that blows from that direction. Originally the tower was capped by a revolving bronze Triton holding a wand which pointed to the prevailing wind. It was also a clock-tower. Beneath the figures of the winds are eight sundials. Within the tower a water clock registered the hours, fed by a reservoir on the south side of the roof.

But what is most remarkable is that each of the eight sides of the tower faces the cardinal and half-cardinal points of the compass, although the compass in its most rudimentary form was not introduced from the east until over a thousand years later. Moreover, the figures depicting the wind fly around the tower in an anticlockwise direction, which is the direction in which any cyclonic system entering the Mediterranean also revolves, with the winds of a depression following the same pattern and sequence as that shown on the tower.

The figures

North: *Boreas*, the violent and cold north wind, represented by a bearded old man wrapped in a thick mantle with the folds being plucked by the wind.

Northeast: *Kaikias*, a cold bitter wind represented by a man holding a vessel from which olives are being scattered, representing the valuable olive crop being destroyed by this wind.

East: *Apeliotes*, a handsome young man, carries flowers and fruit, depicting the mild and kindly nature of the wind.

Southeast: *Euros*, represented by an old man with his right arm muffled in his mantle, heralds the stormy southeast wind.

South: *Notios*, a sour-looking figure, empties an urn, implying rain and sultry weather.

Southwest: *Lips*, represented by a figure pushing the prow of a ship, signifies the wind that is unfavourable for ships leaving Athens.

West: *Zephyros*, the mild west wind, is represented by a handsome youth showering a lapful of flowers into the air.

Northwest: *Skiron*, represented by a bearded man with a vessel in his hands, is interpreted in various ways. Either he is carrying a vase denoting occasional rain showers, or a charcoal vessel with which he dries up rivers.

Routes

The constancy of the summer wind from the north makes the planning of routes quite straightforward. In the spring a yacht should keep to the north and plan to go south and east with the summer northerlies. It can then return to the north and west in the autumn.

At the beginning of each chapter there is a brief section on routes for that area and routes to and from other areas. Because Greece has so many islands and a much indented coastline, there are really any number of routes to and from one place to another. Whatever the weather, there are so many places to shelter within short distances of one another that you can make up your own itinerary, covering as much or as little ground as you want.

At the beginning of each chapter there is also a list of useful waypoints to facilitate route planning. See the section on waypoints under *About the plans and pilotage*.

Buoyage

IALA Maritime Buoyage System 'A' was introduced in 1983–84. This is the normal European system where green buoys/beacons are left to starboard and port buoys/beacons are left to port WHEN ENTERING A HARBOUR. (I include this for our American cousins who use IALA System 'B'.) Around large and medium-sized ports which handle commercial traffic and in waters used for navigation by commercial traffic the system is in place and well maintained. In small harbours and areas not frequented by commercial traffic IALA 'A' buoyage is not always used and maintenance of the buoyage system is not always consistent.

Lights

The coast and islands are surprisingly well lit given the extent of coastline which must be covered. Many of the lights have been converted to solar power with automatic photo-sensitive switches to turn them on when light levels drop below a pre-determined level. In a few places lights are not always maintained as well as they should be although NAVTEX will usually carry a notice advising that a particular light is not working.

Weather forecasts

Because of the high and large landmasses close to all sea areas in Greece it is extremely difficult to predict what local winds and wind strength will be. The Greek Meteorological Service does its best, but nonetheless cannot give really accurate forecasts for many areas. Warnings of approaching depressions will be given, but again the erratic progress of these makes forecasting difficult.

VHF frequencies

A forecast for all Greek waters in Greek and English is given at 0600, 1000, 1600, 2200 UTC. For local time add 2 hours in the winter and 3 hours in the summer. The forecast covers all Greek waters for Z+12 hours. Gale warnings are given at the beginning of the broadcast.

A *sécurité* warning on Ch 16 gives all the VHF channels for the different shore stations and you will need to choose whichever shore station is closest to you. In practice the advice notice on shore stations is often mumbled and at such a speed that it can be difficult to hear, but is worth listening to in case VHF frequencies for the different shore stations are changed.

At the beginning of each chapter the relevant VHF channels and times for the weather forecasts are annotated onto the introduction map for that chapter.

The Ch 86 continuous weather forecast broadcast for the Saronic is stated still to be in operation, but I was not able to pick it up in 2003.

A weather forecast from Italy is transmitted continuously on VHF Ch 68. It can be picked up in

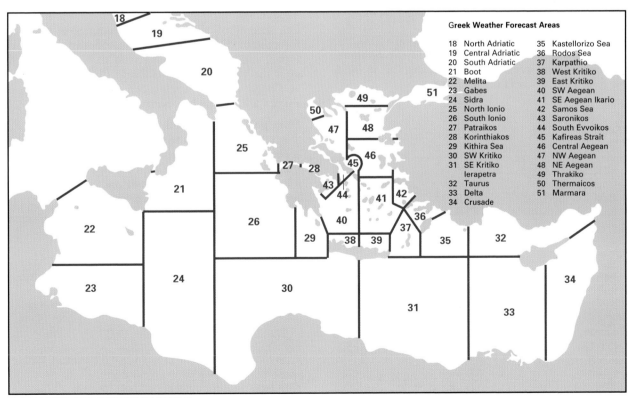

Greek Weather Forecast Areas

18 North Adriatic	35 Kastellorizo Sea
19 Central Adriatic	36 Rodos Sea
20 South Adriatic	37 Karpathio
21 Boot	38 West Kritiko
22 Melita	39 East Kritiko
23 Gabes	40 SW Aegean
24 Sidra	41 SE Aegean Ikario
25 North Ionio	42 Samos Sea
26 South Ionio	43 Saronikos
27 Patraikos	44 South Evvoikos
28 Korinthiakos	45 Kafireas Strait
29 Kithira Sea	46 Central Aegean
30 SW Kritiko	47 NW Aegean
31 SE Kritiko	48 NE Aegean
Ierapetra	49 Thrakiko
32 Taurus	50 Thermaicos
33 Delta	51 Marmara
34 Crusade	

GREEK WEATHER FORECAST AREAS

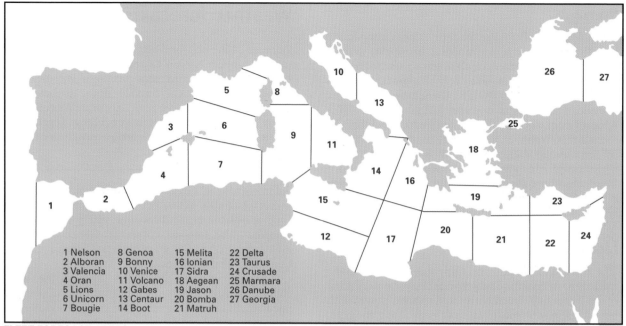

FLEET FORECAST AREAS

1 Nelson	8 Genoa	15 Melita	22 Delta
2 Alboran	9 Bonny	16 Ionian	23 Taurus
3 Valencia	10 Venice	17 Sidra	24 Crusade
4 Oran	11 Volcano	18 Aegean	25 Marmara
5 Lions	12 Gabes	19 Jason	26 Danube
6 Unicorn	13 Centaur	20 Bomba	27 Georgia
7 Bougie	14 Boot	21 Matruh	

the Ionian and in fact all the way across to Minorca in the Balearics. It is transmitted using a synthesised voice similar to some US forecasts and gives a forecast for the whole of the Mediterranean, first in Italian and then in English. The format is identical to that for Italian forecasts (see *Italian Waters Pilot*).

HF Radio
A forecast in Greek and English is broadcast on the following frequencies for SSB radios. (Receivers only will need a BFO switch.)

Kerkira	2830kHz	0633, 0903, 1533, 2133 UT
Limnos	2730kHz	0633, 0903, 1533, 2133 UT
Iraklion	2799kHz	0633, 0903, 1533, 2133 UT
Rhodes	2624kHz	0633, 0903, 1533, 2133 UT

Broadcast Radio
Weather forecasts are transmitted on the National Programme in Greek only. The forecasts are at 0430 (1 hour later when DST is in force).

	kHz	*MHz*
Athens	729	91·6
Corfu	1008	99·3

Iraklion	954	97·5
Kavala	1602	96·3
Rhodes	1494	92·7
Khania	1512	104·0
Patras	1485	92·5
Volos	1485	100·7
Zakinthos	927	95·2

Around Athens ERA radio 91·6FM is reported to have a forecast in English at 0630–0700 local time. For the eastern Mediterranean a marine weather forecast is given by the Austrian short wave service (in German only) on 6150MHz/49m at 0945 and 1400 local time (from 1 May to 1 October only).

Television
On several of the television channels a weather forecast in Greek with satellite photos and wind forces and directions shown on the map is given after the news around 2100 local time. Many cafés and bars will have a television somewhere and you should ask for *o kairos parakalo*.

Port police and marinas
The port police get a weather forecast faxed to them several times a day. Depending on the inclination of the port police it may be worthwhile asking them for a forecast. Most of the few marinas in Greece post a forecast, often taken off the internet.

VHF Shore station list	
Corfu (Kérkira)	Ch 02
Cephalonia	Ch 27
Petalidhi (Kalamata)	Ch 83
Kithera	Ch 85
Saronic	Ch 25
Salamis	Ch 23
Siros	Ch 04
Parnis (Khalkhi)	Ch 25
Pilio (Volos)	Ch 60
Sfendarni (Thessaloniki)	Ch 23
Thasos	Ch 85
Limnos	Ch 82
Lesvos	Ch 01
Khíos	Ch 85
Rodhos	Ch 63
Knossos (Kriti)	Ch 83

SMS text message forecast
Poseidon provide a website weather forecast and can now send a basic forecast by text message to your mobile phone. Text: W GPS (co-ordinates of position for forecast) and send to 4264.

e.g. W GPS 38 50 20 43 requests a forecast for the area around Levkas.

The message gives wind strength and direction for 24 hours in three 6 hour intervals.

e.g. 24/9 15 4B (NW) indicates Force 4 NW wind at 1500 hrs UTC on 24 September

The service costs around 25 cents per message.

Navtex

Navtex is part of GMDSS and sets automatically receive MSI (Maritime Safety Information). See the section on *Rescue Services* at the end of the Introduction. The data for Navtex stations in Greece is shown in the table.

There has been some discussion in the past over message errors and non-recording of messages. In 2003 I experienced no problems with any of the stations listed below and received messages at the times given.

The mounting of the aerial for Navtex reception is often mentioned as critical. My aerial is mounted on the pushpit clear of other aerials and I have had no problems. Others who have experienced problems have connected the aerial to a shroud for better reception. I've also met one boat where the aerial is inside the aft cabin where it gets a clear signal.

In areas where there is high ground surrounding the harbour or anchorage some problems can be experienced getting a clear signal, though less than might be expected. I use a Navtex Pro Plus with the Navtex active aerial. The set is earthed, though I'm uncertain of how good the earth connection really is.

Navtex has three message priorities:

Vital For immediate broadcast
Important For broadcast at the next available period
Routine For broadcast at the next scheduled transmission period

The following subject indication characters are used:

A Navigational warnings
B Meteorological warnings
C Ice reports
D Search and rescue information
E Meteorological forecasts
F Pilot service messages
G Decca messages
H Loran messages
I Omega messages
J Satnav messages
K Other electronic navaid messages
L Navigational warnings
Z No messages on hand

Weatherfax (WX)

Weatherfax services are usually accessed using an HF receiver and appropriate computer and software or a dedicated weatherfax receiver.

For weatherfax station frequencies, transmission times and data please consult:

Imray *Mediterranean Almanac*
Admiralty *ALRS Small Craft* NP289

or the following websites:
HF-Fax Listing of stations, frequencies and data
www.hffax.de
Frank Singleton Links and explanations
www.franksingleton.clara.net
NOAA Worldwide stations. PDF download
www.nws.noaa.gov/om/marine/radiofax.htm

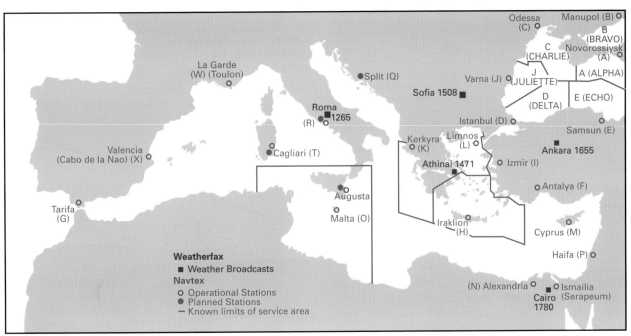

NAVTEX AND WEATHERFAX SERVICES

NAVTEX (N4) transmitters

	Transmitter identification character	Freq kHz	Times (Weather bulletins in bold type)	Language used	Range NM	Status of implementation character
Kérkira	K	518	0140, **0540**, **0940**, 1340, **1740**, **2140**	English	280	Operational
Limnos	L	518	0150, **0550**, **0950**, 1350, **1750**, **2150**	English	280	Operational
Iraklion	H	518	0110, **0510**, **0910**, 1310, **1710**, **2110**	English	280	Operational

Weather on the Internet

There are a number of services on the Internet which provide up-to-date surface forecasts, text forecasts and satellite pictures. Details of ways to access the internet from a boat are in the section on *Telecommunications*. See also *GRIB weather files* below.

Internet sites

Poseidon weather for Greece
www.poseidon.ncmr.gr/weather_forecast.html
Up to 72 hour surface wind forecasts for Greece. The best source of weather for Greek waters and adjacent Turkish waters.

University of Athens
weather.noaa.gov/weather/GR-cc.html
Weather observations at Greek airports.

DWD Mediterranean Forecast
www.dwd.de/forecasts/seemm.htm
3-day text forecasts for a number of Mediterranean areas including the eastern Mediterranean. In German only but easily read in table form.

Mediterranean Sea Weather Page
www.sto-p.com/atol/
Bracknell surface analysis map, surface analysis maps from NEMOC and wind charts from the University of Athens.

Jcomm by Meteo-France
weather.gmdss.org/III.htm
A text only forecast identical to the NAVTEX forecast.

Weather Online
www.weatheronline.co.uk/sail.htm
Current satellite and radar imagery and text forecasts

Mediterranean sailing
www.medsail.nildram.co.uk
Rod Heikell's site for sailing in the Mediterranean, with a weather page and links to those sites he considers most useful in terms of content and download time. Includes forecasts for Greece.

Yahoo!
The weather data available from Yahoo! includes satellite maps and aviation forecasts.

GRIB weather files

GRIB files are highly compressed weather files which cut download speeds compared to earlier compression formats. They can contain all sorts of data though commonly they have information on wind speed and pressure. The files can be downloaded off the internet or received by email and their small size makes them particularly suitable for receiving using slow modems such as SSB. You will need a GRIB viewer and for some forecasts you will have to pay a subscription fee to the provider.

- A number of software plotting systems have a GRIB viewer including later versions of Raytech Navigator (this is the software I use), Max-Sea, and Nobeltec. In the future other software plotting systems are likely to include a GRIB viewer.
- There are a number of free GRIB viewers available including Airmail's Weather Fax Companion at www.siriuscyber.net/wxfax/ and I'm sure there are others out there.
- GRIB files are generated by various agencies, including NOAA, which many of the other sources rely on for their raw data. You can download free GRIB files from various sources, but typically you will have to pay for some email services and for longer range data. Raytech, for example, allow free internet downloads (usually 3-day forecasts), but you must subscribe to the email service (up to 7-day forecasts). Have a look at the list below for sourcing GRIB data.
- It is important to know that GRIB files are entirely computer generated and have no human at the helm interpreting the data.
- GRIB files are compressed in different ways and you may need some software to decompress the files depending on the viewer you are using. Compression can be .zip (use Winzip) .grb or .bz2 and there may be others. Shareware or relatively cheap software can be downloaded to decompress the file formats.
- These weather files are all fairly broad stroke and do not provide the sort of detailed information found in more dedicated websites for a country or sea area. They provide an overall picture for a large sea area rather than detailed data for planning your sailing within a country.

For more information and GRIB data sources look at Airmail www.siriuscyber.net/wxfax/
Unzipping software
EF Commander www.bhs.com or
WinRar 3.0 www.rarlab.com .
Raytech Navigator (all-in-one GRIB viewer and receiver) www.raymarine.com
Xaxero (I use their weatherfax software, the GRIB viewer is a later addition) www.xaxero.com/gribplot
Maxsea (via Setsail which has a good site for the basics) www.setsail.com/maxsea
Sailmail www.sailmail.com
Marinenet www.marinenet.net
Navcenter www.navcenter.com

Note It seems as if weatherfax transmissions are gradually being phased out as more and more large ships use INMARSAT or internet weather maps. (I should stress this is my opinion and not the official line.)

Local weather lore

The following is a collection of local weather lore gathered at various times in various places. I vouch for none of it, but it may come in useful when planning passages or deciding where you are going.

1. A warning sign of the *meltemi* is a long white cigar-shaped cloud over an island (particularly in the Cyclades). The cloud will normally form before the wind arrives and will remain in place when the wind is blowing. In the Ionian, low dense cloud hugging the summit of the islands warns of a strong *maistro*.

2. In the summer, dry decks in the early morning forecast wind while dewy decks mean there will be little or no wind.

3. The formation of the stages of the new moon forecast whether there will be strong winds or not in the month. If the phases of the new moon form vertically or sideways (the moon 'can't hold water') then there will not be strong winds. If the phases of the moon form horizontally or from the bottom up (the moon 'can hold water') then strong winds will blow in the month.

4. In the eastern Aegean and Crete the Coptic calendar (reproduced in *Turkish Waters and Cyprus Pilot* and *Mediterranean Cruising Handbook*) showing the dates of gales and their direction and duration could prove useful.

BEAUFORT SCALE OF WIND STRENGTH

Sea State	Beaufort No.	Description	Velocity in knots	Velocity in km/h	Term	Code	Wave height in metres
Like a mirror	0	Calm, glassy	<1	<1	Calm	0	0
Ripples	1	Light airs Rippled	1–3	1–5	Calm	1	0–0.1
Small wavelets	2	Light breeze Wavelets	4–6	6–11	Smooth	2	0.1–0.5
Large wavelets	3	Gentle breeze	7–10	12–19	Slight	3	0.5–1.25
Small waves, breaking	4	Moderate breeze	11–16	20–28	Moderate	4	1.25–2.5
Moderate waves, foam	5	Fresh breeze	17–21	29–38	Rough	5	2.5–4
Large waves, foam and spray	6	Strong breeze	22–27	39–49			
Sea heads up, foam in streaks	7	Near gale	28–33	50–61	Very rough	6	4–6
Higher long waves, foam in streaks	8	Gale	34–40	62–74			
High waves, dense foam, spray impairs visibility	9	Strong gale	41–47	75–88	High	7	6–9
Very high tumbling waves, surface white with foam, visibility affected	10	Storm	48–55	89–102	Very high	8	9–14
Exceptionally high waves, sea covered in foam, visibility affected	11	Violent storm	56–62	103–117	Phenomenal	9	Over 14
Air filled with spray and foam, visibility severely impaired	12	Hurricane	>63	>118			

Coastal radio stations

Piraeus (SXE2) (Hellenic Coastguard)
Note This station does not accept public correspondence; accepting distress, safety and urgent traffic, port operations and pollution reports. Meteorological bulletins available on request.
RT (MF) Transmits on 1698, 1904, 2182kHz. Receives on 2182kHz
VHF Transmits and receives on Ch 07, 18, 19, 20, 21

Aspropyrgos Attikis (SXE) (JRCC)
Note This station does not accept public correspondence; accepting distress, safety and urgent traffic, port operations and pollution reports. Meteorological bulletins available on request.
RT (MF) Transmits on 1698, 1734, 2182kHz. Receives on 2123, 2078, 2182kHz

The call sign to Greek coastal radio stations on VHF and on 2182kHz is OLYMPIA RADIO. The best policy to elicit a reply is to use a callsign rather than the yacht's name.

All port police stations have a VHF and listen out on Channels 8, 12, 16 and 19. The following stations are the major OLYMPIA RADIO installations:

Olympia Radio (SVO)
Call *Olympia Radio*

Kerkyra	02, 03, 16, 64	Gerania	02, 16, 64
Kefallinía	16, 26, 27, 28	Pérama	25, 86
Patra	16, 85	Andros	16, 24
Petalidi	16, 23, 83, 84	Syros	03, 04, 16
Kythira	16, 85, 86	Chios	16, 85
Moystakos	04, 16	Mytilíni	01, 02, 16
Knossos	16, 83, 84	Parnis	16, 25, 26, 84
Faistos	16, 26, 27	Lichada	01, 16
Sitía	16, 85, 86	Pilio	03, 16, 60
Kárpathos	03, 16	Sfendami	16, 23, 24
Rodos	01, 16, 63	Tsoukalas	16, 26, 27
Astypalea	16, 23	Limnos	16, 82, 83
Pátmos	16, 24	Thásos	16, 25, 85
Thíra	16, 61, 62	Pyrgas	16, 86
Mílos	16, 85	Skyros	16, 86
Póros	16, 26, 27, 28	Broychas	16, 28

All stations H24

Safety and rescue services

Piraeus Coastguard JRCC
MMSI 237 673 000

VHF Ch 16	DSC VHF
MF 2182kHz	DSC MF 2187.5kHz
	DSC HF

☎ 210 411 2500 *Fax* 210 411 5798

The SAR co-ordinating centre for all rescues is in Piraeus.

There are also five local SAR stations

Patras	Ionian	☎ 2610 327136
		Fax 2610 327136
Mitilini	Central Aegean	☎ 22510 40827
		Fax 22510 47888
Thessaloniki	North Aegean	☎ 2310 531504
		Fax 2310 531506
Rhodes	SE Aegean	☎ 22410 22220
		Fax 22410 29294
Khania	SW Aegean	☎ 28210 98888
		Fax 28210 28387

All Greek Port Authorities operate an SAR unit with Coastguard officers. Coast radio and Olympia radio monitor DSC, VHF, MF and HF frequencies including 2182kHz and VHF Ch 16.

A number of harbours operate patrol boats which, while not strictly lifeboats, are often heavy-weather craft. A number of lifeboats and large RIBS are also operated around the coast. For major operations the navy and air force will be called up and rescue helicopters, aircraft and large offshore vessels can be called out. At the beginning of each chapter the relevant coastguard stations are shown on the introductory map with all radio frequencies including DSC capability if applicable.

For salvage operations a tug can be called out from large harbours or in some cases large trawlers undertake salvage.

GMDSS (Global Maritime Distress and Safety System)

GMDSS consists of several integrated systems which are now required on all ships with the exception of the following:

Ships other than passenger vessels of less than 300 gross-tonnage.
Passenger ships carrying less than 6 passengers.
Ships of war.
Ships not propelled by engines.
Pleasure yachts not engaged in charter.
Fishing vessels.

The integrated system is composed of the following components:

DSC Digital Selective Calling VHF, MF and HF will utilise DSC for ship-to-ship, ship-to-shore, shore-to-ship and will also generate a pre-formatted distress signal giving a location position if connected to GPS or any other position-finding receiver.

MSI Marine Safety Information NAVTEX is the main method of transmitting Navigation and Met Warnings, Met Forecasts and other urgent safety related messages. Sat Coms and HF Radio are also used for long range warnings.

Safety Of Life At Sea Regulations (SOLAS)

From 1 July 2002 skippers of craft under 150 tons are required to conform to the following SOLAS V regulations. The regulations will almost certainly be applied in piecemeal fashion in the Mediterranean countries. What follows is very much a précis of the regs and at the time of writing clarification is ongoing.

R19 A radar reflector (3 & 9 GHz) must be exhibited.
R29 A table of life-saving signals must be available to the skipper/helmsman at all times.
R31 Skippers must report to the coastguard on dangers to navigation including (R32) wrecks, winds of Force 10 or more and floating objects dangerous to navigation.
R33 Vessels must respond to distress signals from another vessel.
R34 Passage planning is now mandatory. If a vessel involved in an incident can be shown not to have engaged in detailed passage planning the skipper can be prosecuted. This is a very messy regulation and may involve having corrected charts and up-to-date pilotage instructions on board and keeping a ship's log.
R35 Distress signals must not be misused.

EPIRB Emergency Position Indicating Radio Beacon Uses COSPAS-SARSAT international satellites to pick up the 406MHz signal.

SART Search and Rescue Transponders Portable radar transponders.

SAT COMs INMARSAT is currently the main provider of maritime satellite communication systems.

Of all these it is really DSC which most affects pleasure yachts. All GMDSS equipment had to be fitted to ships by 1 February 1999. Ships are no longer required to keep a listening watch on 2182MHz and will not have to keep a listening watch on VHF Ch 16 after 1 February 2005. It is uncertain yet whether shore stations will likewise stop listening on VHF Ch 16. Ch 70 is now banned for voice transmission and is the DSC distress frequency.

DSC stations have been introduced in Greece and details are given on the area maps for specific chapters.

About the plans and pilotage notes

Nomenclature

The spelling of Greek names presents many problems, not the least of which is the difficulty of transforming demotic Greek accurately into English. For instance, the island of Evia (my spelling) may be Euboea, Evvoia, or Evoia. Even if you get the modern Greek nearly right you may find the place is normally talked of in the diminutive, so Levkas, for example, becomes Levkadha. To add to the confusion an alternative name from the Venetian, Turkish, French, Italian or English occupation may be the name by which a place is commonly called. For example, Thíra is commonly called by its Italian name of Santorini.

In this edition I have adopted the convention, in common with all hydrographic departments, of calling a place by the Greek name transliterated into the Latin alphabet. One interesting point here is that if the rules for transliteration are followed inflexibly, the result can at times be nonsense. Consequently I have modified the rules where I think the end result is truer to the name in Greek. For several places I have used the name commonly used and familiar to English-speaking readers, so Crete is not called Kriti, Corfu is not called Kérkira and Piraeus is not Pireefs. After the familiar name I have added the alternative names and any confusing variations so readers can sort through the different names themselves.

Abbreviations

In the pilotage notes for a harbour or anchorage all compass directions are abbreviated to the first or first and second letters in capitals as is common practice: e.g. N is north, SE is southeast, etc.

Harbour plans

The harbour plans and charts are designed to illustrate the accompanying notes which are set out in a standard format.

Some smaller places and many anchorages will have just a simple description with an abbreviated form of the above or just a straight description.

It is stressed that many of these plans are based on the author's sketches and therefore should only be used in conjunction with the official charts. They are not to be used for navigation.

Photographs

Most of the photographs were taken by the author. Many were taken under difficult conditions – when navigating short-handed or single-handed or under poor light conditions – and consequently the quality is not all that might be desired. Because of the sheer number of anchorages and harbours in Greece it is not possible to include shots of all the harbours and anchorages mentioned. Some areas are also out of bounds for military reasons.

Bearings

All bearings are in 360° notation and are true.

Magnetic variation

The magnetic variation in Greece is very small and for the normally quite short voyages made, the variation can be ignored. It varies from half a degree to two degrees, but is mostly just over one degree east.

Soundings

All soundings are in metres and are based on mean low-water springs. In the case of my own soundings there will sometimes be up to half a metre more water than the depth shown when the sea bottom is uneven, but in most cases there is the depth shown.

For those used to working in fathoms and feet the use of metres may prove difficult at first and there is the danger of reading the depths in metres as the depths in fathoms. For all practical purposes one metre can be read as approximately three feet and two metres is approximately equal to one fathom. Therefore as an instant check on the depths in fathoms without reference to the conversion tables in the appendix, it is possible simply to divide the depth in metres by two and that will be approximately equal to the depth in fathoms: e.g. 3 metres = 1½ fathoms (whereas accurately 3 metres = 1 fathom 3·8ft).

Waypoints

Waypoints are given for all harbours and anchorages. The origins of the waypoints vary and in a large number of cases the datum source of the waypoint is not known. Where I have taken waypoints for a harbour or anchorage it has a note after it reading WGS84. All these waypoints are to World Geodetic Survey 1984 datum which it is intended will be the datum source used throughout the world. Most GPS receivers automatically default to WGS84.

It is important to note that plotting a waypoint onto a chart will not necessarily put it in the position shown. There are a number of reasons for this:

1. The chart may have been drawn using another datum source. Many of the Imray-Tetra charts use European Datum 1950 (Europe 50). There are many other datum sources that have been used to draw charts.
2. All charts, including those using WGS84, have errors of various types. Most were drawn in the 19th century and have been fudged to conform to WGS84 (the term 'fuzzy logic' could aptly be used).
3. Even when a harbour plan is drawn there is still a significant human element at work and mistakes easily creep in.

The upshot of all this is that it is important to eyeball your way into an anchorage or harbour and not just sit back and assume that all those digits on the GPS display will look after you. In the case of waypoints I have taken and which are appended WGS84, the waypoint is indeed in the place shown. Other waypoints may be derived from the light position, from reports in my files, or from other sources.

In this edition I have also included useful waypoints which are listed at the beginning of the relevant chapter and included on the location maps. As above, any that are appended WGS84 are from my own observations, using the radar for distance off and a compass bearing for the direction. Given that some radar distance off readouts can be a bit of a guestimate, these should be used with every caution. In most cases I have endeavoured to keep a reasonable distance off so that an error of, say, 50 metres, should be unimportant when the waypoint is 0·5M from the land. There are other occasions when I have shaved a cape or islet and the distance off is considerably less.

All waypoints are given in the notation:

degrees   minutes   decimal place of a minute

It is important not to confuse the decimal place of a minute with the older 60 second notation.

Quick reference guide

At the beginning of each chapter there is a summary of the important information: Ports of Entry, Prohibited Areas, and Major Lights. Following this there is a list of all the harbours and anchorages described in the chapter with a classification of the shelter offered, mooring, and whether fuel, water, provisions and tavernas are available. Compressing information about a harbour or anchorage into such a framework is difficult and not a little clumsy, but the list can be useful for route planning and as an instant memory aid to a harbour.

I. The Northern Ionian
Corfu (Kérkira) to Zákinthos

From the heel of Italy most yachts cross the Otranto Strait to Corfu only 70 miles away. Corfu is the first of the Heptanesoi, the seven islands of the Ionian. Proceeding south from Corfu you come to the islands of Paxoí and Andípaxoi, Levkas, Ithaca, Cephalonia and Zákinthos, and the island of Kíthera (now administered separately). Along the eastern shores of the Ionian are Albania, mainland Greece and the Peloponnisos. Some yachts cross direct from Sicily or Malta to Preveza on the mainland, Levkas, Argostoli on Cephalonia or to Zákinthos.

The Ionian derives its name from the goddess Io. Io was a priestess of Hera and for a short time a mistress to Zeus. Inevitably there was conflict when Hera discovered Zeus was deceiving her and, fearing what Hera in her wrath might do, he changed Io into a white cow. Not to be outdone, Hera sent a gadfly to torment the unfortunate Io, who plunged into the sea to rid herself of the stinging pest – hence the Ionian Sea.

Historically the importance of the Ionian was as a stepping-stone route from the Aegean to Italy and Sicily. Corfu has always been identified as the Homeric island home of the Phaeacians, those mythical ancient sailors who ferried Odysseus home to Ithaca. On a more substantive level Corfu was the ancient Corcyra, a colony of Corinth and the stepping-stone to another important Corinthian colony – Siracusa in Sicily.

The seven islands were not united as a historical group until the 14th century when the islands appealed to Venice for protection from their tyrannical Norman and Genoese overlords. Venice seized the chance to consolidate her trade route from Venice around the Peloponnisos to the Aegean and thus the seven islands became one political unit. It was this long occupation by the Venetians that gave the Ionian its Italianate qualities. Many of the old gnarled olive trees seen today were planted during the Venetian occupation so the local population could pay its taxes in olive oil. Later the French and English added their own flavour to the islands until, in 1864, the seven islands reverted to Greece.

To those of you who visualize a Greece of sun-baked rock dotted with dazzling whitewashed houses, the Ionian comes as a gentle surprise. This is not the Greece of the popular travel brochure but a shaded green country, sheltering red-tiled Latin houses – an eccentric collection of Italian and French architecture and English tastes (in Corfu the locals play cricket and you can buy currant buns and ginger beer) welded together into a whole that is indubitably Greek. Evergreen cypress, pine, elm, green fields, flowers even in the height of summer, and everywhere the dull dark sheen of the olive, characterise the lower land, while higher up the slopes are covered in pine and the tenacious Mediterranean maquis. If the wind is in the right direction you can smell the pungent herby aroma a mile out to sea.

The green luxuriance of the islands is in direct contrast to the high eroded mountains of Albania and mainland Greece that form the eastern boundary to the Ionian. Here there is a barren backdrop to the islands that gives a taste of the topography to come. In between there are protected waters where the wind seldom blows too strongly, and a multitude of little anchorages accessible only by yacht. From the inland sea bordered by Levkas, Ithaca and Cephalonia you leave the rolling, almost English, landscape of Zákinthos to confront the rocky slopes of the Peloponnisos.

Weather patterns in the North Ionian

Winds are consistent in the summer. From June to the end of September the normal wind in the northern Ionian is from the NW to WNW. Generally it arrives around noon, blows between Force 2 and 5 and dies at sunset. In the morning there may be a light E or SE wind, but it rarely reaches Force 1–2. After October until April/May winds can be from the N or S, though gales tend to be more from the S–SE.

In July and August a wind known as the *maistro* may blow from the N–NW with a little more strength than the normal NW wind. Care needs to be taken at this time of gusts off the lee side of high islands, especially in the inland sea, where there can be strong gusts off Levkas, Ithaca, Cephalonia and Zákinthos. Usually when the wind is going to be strong, dense white cigar-shaped clouds hug the tops of the mountains on the islands. In the evening there may be a katabatic wind off the high mainland mountains for several hours. It generally blows from a NE direction and can get up to Force 5–6.

In summer the climate in the northern Ionian is sunny with little rain. The temperature can reach 32°C plus in July and August. In the spring and autumn there are often thunderstorms and associated squalls but these seldom last for very long. In the winter Corfu has one of the highest rainfalls in Greece. As you proceed further south and east the rainfall decreases dramatically. So too does the prolific greenery that goes with a high winter rainfall.

Routes

The geography determines that routes are generally northerly or southerly ones. The prevailing NW winds in the summer mean that going S is pretty much a matter of plotting which harbours and anchorages on the islands and mainland you want to visit and then coasting down to them. You may encounter a few problems coming into bays or entrances which face the prevailing wind such as Palaiokastrita, the northern entrance to the Levkas Canal or the approaches to Argostoli, but generally you will have few problems getting to where you are going.

In places the prevailing NW wind tends to curve around the top and bottom of the high islands and sometimes it is accelerated when it is channelled or where it gusts down valleys. Areas where the wind tends to blow around the land are on the northern side of Corfu where it blows from the WNW and then is channelled down the North Corfu Channel, around the southern end of Corfu and Paxos, around the southern end of Levkas where it blows from the WNW and then the W closer to the Meganísi Channel, down the Ithaca Channel between Cephalonia and Ithaca, around the southern end of Cephalonia, and around the northern and southern sides of Zákinthos. Gusts will be experienced on the lee sides of some islands, especially Paxos and Antipaxos, the E and S sides of Levkas, the E side of Ithaca especially in Kólpos Aetou, around Kólpos Argostoliou, and on the E side of Zákinthos.

Going N in the summer is usually a matter of bashing up against the prevailing NW wind. If you want to make up ground then the NW wind will not normally get up until around midday, so if you leave early in the morning you can generally motor to destinations in the N. The trip from Levkas going N can often be a bit of a bash and many yachts choose to leave Levkas early and motor at least part of the way to Paxos or Parga.

In the winter there are more southerlies and route planning becomes more of a lottery. Really the only thing you can do here is get a forecast and make your plans from there. Remember that many of the harbours which are safe in the prevailing summer northerlies can be less comfortable and even untenable in strong southerlies.

From the Ionian you can reach the Aegean by one of two routes: around the capes of the Peloponnisos following the old trade route, or through the Gulf of Patras and the Gulf of Corinth to the Corinth Canal that severs mainland Greece from the Peloponnisos.

Data

PORTS OF ENTRY
Kérkira (Corfu)
Igoumenítsa
Préveza
Gaios (Paxos)
Levkas
Vathi (Ithaca)
Argostoli
Sami
Zákinthos

PROHIBITED AREAS
The NE coast of Corfu and mainland coast 1M offshore from the Albanian border to Nisís Prasoúdhi. Limín Vathi immediately N of Préveza.

Theoretically permission must be obtained from the navy before entering the prohibited areas around Corfu and the adjacent mainland coast, but in practice this is not normally necessary and no problems have arisen from not obtaining formal permission. Likewise Vathi near Préveza is used by yachts without permission. However it should be remembered that these areas are still classified as prohibited areas on the latest Greek charts.

Note
In the past there have been a number of incidents of piracy off the Albanian coast, the nearby Greek mainland coast and in Corfu. Albania now appears more settled and recent reports are that there is less anarchy ashore. When approaching the North Corfu Channel keep as close as practicable to the Greek coast. At present there is a strong Greek naval presence and this should ensure the safety of craft in the area. However it would pay to keep an eye on developments and act accordingly.

One thing that is for sure is that predicting the political path of a newly emerging country such as Albania is next to impossible. After the demise of communism in Albania it was thought the country would soon open up to yachts and tourism to help out the ailing economy. How wrong we were.

MAJOR LIGHTS
Nisís Othoní NE Point (Ákra Kastrí)
Fl.10s21M
Nisís Othoní SW Point Fl(2)6s6M
Nisís Erikoússa Ákra Potamópoulo
Fl(3)15s6M

Kérkira (Corfu)
Ákra Aikateríni Fl.10s6M
Ákra Sidhero (Citadel/Corfu town)
Fl(2)6s13M
Ákra Levkímmis Fl.6s7M
Vrákhoi Lagoúdhia Fl(3)14s7M
Nisís Prasoúdhi (Igoumenítsa)
Fl(2)9s8M
Nisís Sívota Fl(3)20s12M

Nísos Paxoí
Lákka Fl(3)24s20M
Nisís Panayía Fl.WR.5s10/8M
Nísos Andípaxoi Fl.WR.6s12/9M

Ákra Mítikas (Préveza)
Fl.WR.3s7/5M

Nísos Levkas
Fort Santa Maura (Levkas Canal N Entrance)
Fl(2)WR.12s8/5M
Nisídha Sésoula Fl.4·5s8M
Ákra Dhoukaton Fl.10s24M

Nísos Kefallinia (Cephalonia)
Ákra Yero-Gómbos LFl(2)15s24M
Nisís Vardhiánoi Fl.WR.7·5s6/4M
Nisís Kalóyeros Fl.4s8M
Nisís Pondikos Fl.3s8M
Ákra Kateliós Fl(2)WR.15s11/8M
Ákra Kapri Fl(3)WR.9s6/4M
Ákra Fiskárdho Fl.3s7M

Ithaca (Ithaki)
Ákra Áy Nikoláou Fl(3)15s7M
Ákra Áy Ioánnis Fl.10s10M
Ákra Pisaitós Fl.5s6M
Ákra Oxiá Fl(2)15s17M

Zákinthos (Zante)
Ákra Skinári Fl.5s20M
Nisidhia Áy Nikólaos Fl.2s7M
Ákra Krionéri Fl(2)16s6M
Ákra Kerí Fl.10s17M

For more detail on the Ionian as covered in Chapters I and II see *Ionian* from the publishers

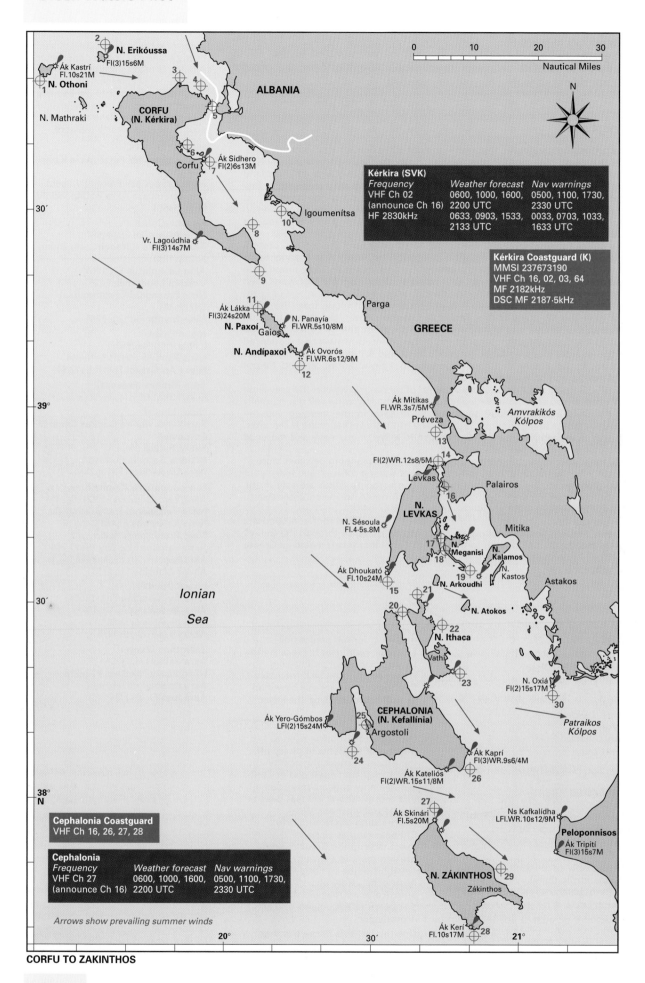

Scale: 0 10 20 30 Nautical Miles

N. Erikóussa
Fl(3)15s6M

Ák Kastrí
Fl.10s21M
N. Othoni

N. Mathraki

ALBANIA

CORFU
(N. Kérkira)

Corfu
Ák Sidhero
Fl(2)6s13M

Igoumenítsa

Kérkira (SVK)

Frequency	Weather forecast	Nav warnings
VHF Ch 02	0600, 1000, 1600,	0500, 1100, 1730,
(announce Ch 16)	2200 UTC	2330 UTC
HF 2830kHz	0633, 0903, 1533,	0033, 0703, 1033,
	2133 UTC	1633 UTC

Kérkira Coastguard (K)
MMSI 237673190
VHF Ch 16, 02, 03, 64
MF 2182kHz
DSC MF 2187·5kHz

Vr. Lagoúdhia
Fl(3)14s7M

Parga

GREECE

Ák Lákka
Fl(3)24s20M
N. Paxoí
Gaios
N. Panayía
Fl.WR.5s10/8M

N. Andípaxoi
Ák Ovorós
Fl.WR.6s12/9M

Ák Mitíkas
Fl.WR.3s7/5M
Préveza

Amvrakikós
Kólpos

Fl(2)WR.12s8/5M
Levkas
Palairos

N. Sésoula
Fl.4·5s.8M

N.
LEVKAS

Mitika

N.
Meganisi
N.
Kalamos

Ák Dhoukató
Fl.10s24M

N. Arkoudhi
N. Kastos

Astakos

Ionian

Sea

N. Atokos

N. Ithaca

Vathi

N. Oxiá
Fl(2)15s17M

Patraikos
Kólpos

CEPHALONIA
(N. Kefallínia)

Ák Yero-Gómbos
LFl(2)15s24M
Argostoli

Ák Kaprí
Fl(3)WR.9s6/4M

Ák Kateliós
Fl(2)WR.15s11/8M

Ns Kafkalídha
LFl.WR.10s12/9M
Peloponnisos

Ák Skinári
Fl.5s20M

Ák Tripití
Fl(3)15s7M

Cephalonia Coastguard
VHF Ch 16, 26, 27, 28

Cephalonia

Frequency	Weather forecast	Nav warnings
VHF Ch 27	0600, 1000, 1600,	0500, 1100, 1730,
(announce Ch 16)	2200 UTC	2330 UTC

N. ZÁKINTHOS
Zákinthos

Arrows show prevailing summer winds

Ák Kerí
Fl.10s17M

20° 30' 21°

USEFUL WAYPOINTS

⊕1 0·5M S of Othoní SW point light
39°49'·7N 19°23'·2E

⊕2 0·5M N Erikoússa Ák Skotini
39°54'·5N 19°34'·8E

⊕3 0·35M N of Ák Aikateríni (Corfu N)
39°49'·70N 19°51'·05E WGS84

⊕4 Mid-channel between Nisís Peristeraí and Ák Psaromíta
39°47'·29N 19°57'·19E WGS84

⊕5 0·25M E of Ifalos Sérpa (Corfu N Channel)
39°46'·24N 19°57'·86E WGS84

⊕6 0·5M E of Ák Kommeno (Gouvia)
39°39'·82N 19°52'·45E WGS84

⊕7 0·5M E of Ák Sidhero (Corfu E side)
39°37'·36N 19°56'·61E WGS84

⊕8 1M E of Ák Levkímmis light
39°27'·6N 20°05'·7E

⊕9 1M S of Asprokavos (Corfu S end)
39°20'·7N 20°06'·8E

⊕10 Igoumenitsa Channel (Outer buoys)
39°30'·10N 20°12'·06E WGS84

⊕11 0·5M N of Lákki entrance
39°15'·0N 20°08'·0E

⊕12 1M S of Nds Dhaskalia (S end Andipaxoi)
39°06'·8N 20°15'·0E

⊕13 Entrance to Préveza channel (outer buoys)
38°55'·90N 20°43'·66E WGS84

⊕14 N entrance to Levkas Canal
38°50'·79N 20°43'·27E WGS84

⊕15 0·5M S of Ák Dhoukato (Levkas SW end)
38°33'·17N 20°32'·46E WGS84

⊕16 S end of Levkas Canal
38°47'·54N 20°43'·58E WGS84

⊕17 N end Meganísi Channel
38°40'·10N 20°43'·72E WGS84

⊕18 S end Meganísi Channel
38°37'·88N 20°43'·88E WGS84

⊕19 1M SE of Ák Kefáli (Meganísi S end)
38°34'·8N 20°49'·8E

⊕20 N end Ithaca Channel
38°28'·47N 20°35'·73E WGS84

⊕21 0·25M N of Ák Marmara (Ithaca N end)
38°30'·47N 20°38'·93E WGS84

⊕22 0·25M E of Ák Áy Illias (Ithaca NE end)
38°26'·07N 20°42'·91E WGS84

⊕23 0·25M E of Ák Áy Íoannis (Ithaca SE end)
38°19'·20N 20°46'·36E WGS84

⊕24 1M S of N. Vardhiánoi light (Cephalonia SW end)
38°06'·9N 20°25'·6E

⊕25 0·5M W of Ák Áy Theodhoroi (Kólpos Argostoliou)
38°11'·5N 20°27'·5E

⊕26 2·25M E of Ák Mounda (Cephalonia SE end)
38°03'·20N 20°49'·97E WGS84

⊕27 1M N of Ák Skinari light (Zákinthos N end)
37°56'·9N 20°42'·2E

⊕28 1M S of Ák Marathia (Zákinthos SW end)
37°37'·9N 20°50'·0E

⊕29 0·5M E of Ák Krioneri light (Zakinthos E side)
37°48'·26N 20°54'·89E WGS84

⊕30 0·5M S of Ák Oxiá
38°16'·60N 21°05'·95E WGS84

Nisoi Othoní and Erikoússa

When crossing from Italy to Corfu there are two islands, Othoní and Erikoússa, lying off the N end of Corfu island, which have useful anchorages often used by yachts to break the passage between Italy and Corfu.

Nisís Othoní
(Othonoí Fano)

BA206

Imray-Tetra G11

Nisís Othoní is a bold precipitous island (500m high with a sheer cliff face on the western side), but with the normal summer haze it will often not be seen until two or three miles off. There are two anchorages, Fiki on the N and Ammou on the S. Ammou is the bay normally used in the summer with the prevailing N–WNW winds.

ÓRMOS AMMOU

Approach

From the N the lighthouse on the NE corner will be seen. From the W head for the SW tip of the island – the light tower on the SW cannot be seen until closer in. The houses of the hamlet will not be seen until you open the bay.

Dangers Care needs to be taken in the approaches of Ifalos Aspri Pétra (1·8m), a reef lying directly in the S approach. Care also needs to be taken of underwater rocks lying off the coast on the E side of the entrance. The approach should be made from a SW direction with a lookout forward conning you in.

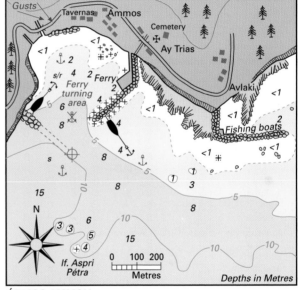

ÓRMOS AMMOU
⊕39°50'·2N 19°24'·2E

Mooring

Anchor in 2–10m where convenient without blocking the immediate approaches to the small harbour. The ferry charges in here at speed and needs all the space at the entrance to manoeuvre. The bottom is sand and weed, mostly good holding, although there are some anchor-snagging rocks closer in. It is possible to go bows-to part of the quay when the ferry is not due, though care must be taken as the bottom comes up quickly off parts of the quay. Alternatively anchor and take a long line to the outside of the breakwater.

Shelter With the normal NW wind there are mild gusts out of the bay and some swell works its way

Quick reference guide

	Shelter	Mooring	Fuel	Water	Provisioning	Tavernas	Plan
Corfu and outlying islands							
Nisís Othoní							
Órmos Fiki (N Bay)	C	C	O	O	O	O	
Órmos Ammou (S Bay)	B	C	O	O	C	C	•
Erikoússa (S Bay)	B	AC	O	O	C	C	•
Plakes	B	AB	O	B	C	C	
Nísos Kérkira (Corfu I)							
¹Kassiopi	B	A	B	B	B	A	•
¹Ayios Stefanos	B	C	O	O	C	B	•
¹Kouloura	C	C	O	O	O	C	•
Kalami	C	C	O	O	O	C	•
Agni	C	C	O	O	O	C	•
Gouvía Marina	A	A	A	A	A	A	•
Limín Kérkira (Corfu)	A	AB	A	A	A	A	•
Mandraki	B	A	B	A	A	A	
Naok YC	B	A	O	A	A	A	
Benitses	O	C	O	O	C	B	
Petriti	B	AC	O	A	C	B	•
Kavos (Levkimmi)	C	AB	O	B	O	O	•
Áy Stefanos (Avliotes)	B	AC	O	B	C	C	•
Áy Yeoryiou	C	C	O	O	O	C	
Palaíokastrita	B	AC	B	B	B	A	•
Nísos Paxoí							
Lákka	B	AC	B	B	C	B	•
Longos	C	C	O	O	C	C	
Gaios	A	A	B	B	B	B	•
Mongonisi	A	AC	O	O	O	C	•
Mainland coast adjacent to Corfu							
¹Pagania	A	C	O	O	O	O	•
¹Sayiadha	B	A	O	A	B	B	•
Ormiskos Valtou (Igoumenítsa Creek)	A	C	O	O	O	O	•
Igoumenítsa	C	AB	B	B	B	B	•
Platarias	B	A	B	A	B	B	•
Nisís Sívota and Moúrtos	B	AC	B	B	B	B	•
Parga	B	AC	B	B	B	A	•
Áy Ioannou	C	C	O	O	O	O	•
Ó. Fanari	C	C	O	B	C	B	
Ligia	B	A	O	O	C	C	•
Préveza	B	AB	B	A	A	B	•
Amvrakikós Kólpos (Gulf of Amvrakia)							
Vónitsa	B	A	B	B	B	C	•
Loutráki	C	C	O	O	C	C	
Amfilokhia	C	BC	B	B	B	C	
Menidhion	B	AC	O	O	C	C	•
Koronisía	B	AB	O	O	C	C	
Nísos Levkas and adjacent islands							
Levkas							
Levkas Town	A	AB	A	A	A	A	•
Levkas Marina	A	A	A	A	B	B	•
Ligia	C	AC	O	B	C	B	
Nikiana	B	A	B	A	C	B	•
Nidri	B	A	B	A	B	A	•

	Shelter	Mooring	Fuel	Water	Provisioning	Tavernas	Plan
Tranquil Bay	A	C	O	O	O	O	•
Órmos Vlikho	A	AC	B	B	C	C	•
Sívota	A	AC	O	A	C	B	•
Vasilikí	B	A	B	A	B	B	•
Nísos Meganísi							
Spartakhori	B	AC	B	B	C	C	•
Port Vathi	A	AC	O	O	C	C	•
Abelike and Kapali	B	C	O	O	O	O	•
Port Atheni	B	AC	O	B	C	C	•
Nísos Ithaca (Itháki)							
Frikes	B	A	O	B	C	C	•
Kióni	B	AC	O	O	C	C	•
Port Vathi	A	AC	B	B	B	B	•
Pera Pigadhi	B	AC	O	O	O	O	•
Áy Andréou	C	C	O	O	O	O	
Ó. Pis'Aitou	O	C	O	O	C	C	
Port Polis	C	C	O	O	C	C	
Nísos Kefallinia (Cephalonia)							
Argostoli	A	AB	B	A	A	B	•
Argostoli Marina	A	A	B	B	B	B	•
Maistratos Harbour	A	A	B	A	A	B	•
Lixouri	B	A	B	A	B	C	•
Áy Kiriakis	C	A	O	O	O	C	
Assos	C	AC	O	B	C	B	•
Fiskárdho	A	AC	B	A	B	A	•
Áy Eufimia	B	AC	B	A	C	B	•
Sami	C	AB	B	A	B	C	•
Póros	B	AC	B	A	B	B	•
Mainland coast adjacent to the inland sea							
Palairos (Zaverda)	B	A	B	A	B	B	•
Vounaki	B	A	A	A	C	C	•
Mitika	B	AC	B	B	C	C	•
Nísos Kálamos							
Port Kalamos	B	A	O	B	C	C	•
Port Leone	B	C	O	O	O	O	•
Episkopi	B	AB	O	O	C	C	
Nísos Kastos							
Port Kastos	B	A	O	O	C	C	•
Mainland coast							
Nisís Atoko	C	C	O	O	O	O	•
Astakós	B	A	B	A	B	C	•
Marathia	C	C	O	O	O	O	
Port Pandelimon	AB	C	O	O	O	O	
Nisís Petalas	B	C	O	O	O	O	
Nisís Oxiá	C	C	O	O	O	O	
Nísos Zákinthos (Zante)							
Áy Nikólaos	B	A	B	B	C	C	•
Port Zákinthos	A	A	B	A	A	A	•
Porto Roma	O	C	O	O	O	C	
Lagana	C	AC	O	O	C	B	•
Órmos Kerí	C	C	O	O	O	C	•
Port Vroma	C	C	O	O	O	O	

1. See 'Prohibited Areas'

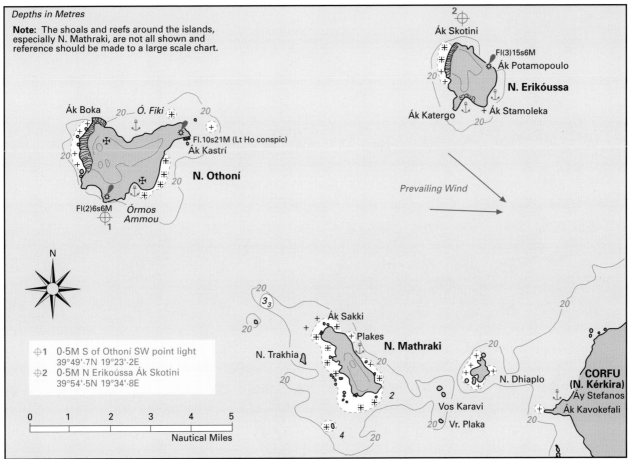

Depths in Metres

Note: The shoals and reefs around the islands, especially N. Mathraki, are not all shown and reference should be made to a large scale chart.

Ák Skotini

Fl(3)15s6M
Ák Potamopoulo
N. Erikoússa
Ák Katergo
Ák Stamoleka

Prevailing Wind

Ák Boka 20 Ó. Fiki 20
Fl.10s21M (Lt Ho conspic)
Ák Kastrí
N. Othoní
Fl(2)6s6M
Órmos Ammou
1

N

Ák Sakki
Plakes
N. Mathraki
N. Trakhia
N. Dhiaplo
CORFU (N. Kérkira)
Áy Stefanos
Ák Kavokefali
Vos Karavi
Vr. Plaka

⊕1 0·5M S of Othoní SW point light
39°49'·7N 19°23'·2E
⊕2 0·5M N Erikoússa Ák Skotini
39°54'·5N 19°34'·8E

0   1   2   3   4   5
Nautical Miles

NISOI OTHONI, ERIKOUSSA AND MATHRAKI

around into here, but it is secure enough in settled conditions. The new stubby breakwater on the W side of the bay provides some additional shelter from the ground swell that can work its way in. Open S.

Facilities
Ashore there are several tavernas which often have fresh fish. Limited provisions can be obtained. Telephone in the local shop.

Note Yachts should not attempt to enter the small fishing harbour to the E (Avlaki) as the entrance is rock-bound and depths in the harbour are variable.

ÓRMOS FIKI
The bay on the N side of the island offers a good anchorage in the event of winds from the S and SE. Care must be taken of the numerous above and below-water rocks in the vicinity of the bay. When anchoring try to find a patch of sand for plough-type anchors although a fisherman can be hooked on the rocky bottom – attach a trip line. A reef extends out a little way from the middle of the bay so caution is necessary close to the shore. I have used this anchorage to ride out a gale from the SE and the shelter from that quarter is excellent.

Erikoússa
(Merlera, Mérikha)

The island lying about 7 miles due E of Othoní. It is a lower island than Othoní and like Othoní difficult to spot until 1½–2 miles off with the normal summer heat haze. The only village is on the shores of the large sandy bay on the S side which affords good shelter from the prevailing NW winds.

PORT ERIKOÚSSA
BA 206
Imray-Tetra G11

Approach
The port is on the western side of the large bay on the S side of Erikoússa. The approach is free from dangers except for the reefs running out about 100m from Ák Katergo and Ák Stamoleka on either side of the bay.

By night There are no lights, but the lights of the village and the arc lights around the electricity generating plant to the E of the village can be identified.

Mooring
Anchor off in the bay or go stern or bows-to on the W quay of the small harbour. When the tripper boats are not in you can go alongside the end of the jetty off the village. In the bay anchor in 3-6 metres on a sandy bottom, good holding. In the harbour the

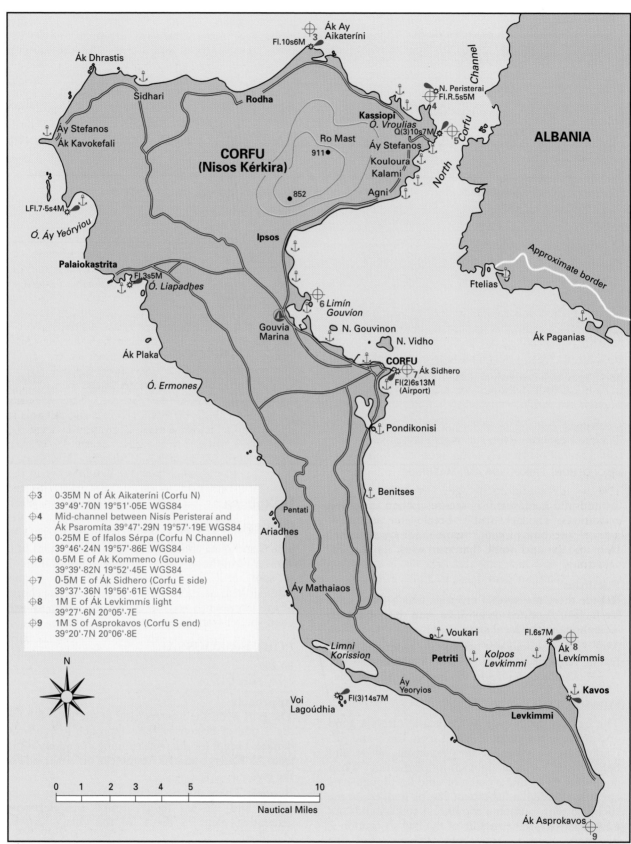

Ák Ay Aikateríni
Fl.10s6M ⊕3

N. Peristerai ⚓
Fl.R.5s5M ⊕4

Ák Dhrastis

Sidhari

Rodha

Kassiopi
Ó. Vroulias
Q(3)10s7M ⊕5

North Corfu Channel

ALBANIA

Áy Stefanos
Ák Kavokefali

CORFU
(Nisos Kérkira)

Ro Mast
911●

Áy Stefanos
Kouloura
Kalami

Agni

LFl.7.5s4M ⊕

Ó. Áy Yeóryiou

852●

Ipsos

Approximate border

Ftelias

Palaiokastrita
Fl.3s5M ⊕
Ó. Liapadhes

Ó Limín
Gouvíon
⊕6

Ák Paganias

Ák Plaka

Gouvia
Marina

N. Gouvinon

N. Vidho

Ó. Ermones

CORFU
⊕7 Ák Sidhero
Fl(2)6s13M
(Airport)

Pondikonisi

Benitses

Pentati

Ariadhes

⊕3 0·35M N of Ák Aikateríni (Corfu N)
    39°49'·70N 19°51'·05E WGS84
⊕4 Mid-channel between Nisís Peristeraí and
    Ák Psaromíta 39°47'·29N 19°57'·19E WGS84
⊕5 0·25M E of Ifalos Sérpa (Corfu N Channel)
    39°46'·24N 19°57'·86E WGS84
⊕6 0·5M E of Ak Kommeno (Gouvia)
    39°39'·82N 19°52'·45E WGS84
⊕7 0·5M E of Ák Sidhero (Corfu E side)
    39°37'·36N 19°56'·61E WGS84
⊕8 1M E of Ák Levkimmís light
    39°27'·6N 20°05'·7E
⊕9 1M S of Asprokavos (Corfu S end)
    39°20'·7N 20°06'·8E

N

Áy Mathaiaos

Voukari

Fl.6s7M ⊕
Ák 8
Levkímmis

Limni
Korission

Petriti

Kolpos
Levkimmi

Kavos

Áy
Yeoryios

Voi
Lagoúdhia
Fl(3)14s7M

Levkimmi

0 1 2 3 4 5   10
Nautical Miles

Ák Asprokavos ⊕
9

NÍSOS KERKIRA (CORFU)

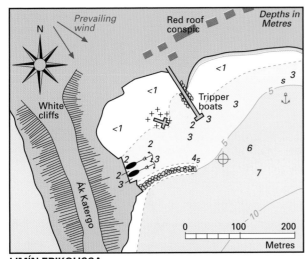

LIMÍN ERIKOUSSA
⊕39°52'·6N 19°34'·8E

bottom is mud and rubble, generally good holding.

Shelter Good shelter at anchor from the prevailing NW winds although there are gusts into the bay. Reasonable shelter in the harbour although you are side-on to the gusts. Some shelter from southerlies in the harbour although strong SE winds could make it untenable.

Facilities
Tavernas ashore, several of which have good fresh fish. Limited provisions. Ferry service to Corfu.

General
The bay is a useful anchorage, well sheltered from the prevailing summer northerlies, when en route between Greece and Italy. The sandy beach attracts tripper boats from Corfu, but they all disappear by 1600 and the anchorage is then a peaceful one. The only thing that disturbs the night air is the noise from the electricity generating plant on the shore.

NOTE
On the E side of the island there are some delightful coves and bights that a yacht can explore in calm weather or with light NW winds.

NISÍS MATHRAKI
This island off the NW tip of Corfu is surrounded by above and below-water rocks. When navigating in the vicinity of the island every care is needed, especially when the prevailing NW wind is blowing and it can be difficult to pick out the rocks and reefs. If you are heading here it is generally best to do so in the morning before the breeze picks up. On the E side of the island there is the small harbour of Plakes.

PLAKES 39°46'·9N 19°31'·3E
The harbour lies on the E side somewhat more towards the NW end. Make the approach from a northerly direction as shoals extend out from the shore to the SE of the harbour. Two rough stone breakwaters extend out from the shore enclosing the old mole that protects the fishing boat basin. There are 5m depths in the entrance and 2–2·5m depths

on the outside of the mole protecting the inner basin. Go stern or bows-to the mole leaving the space on the end free for the ferry. There is room for perhaps half a dozen yachts here provided no fishing boats are using the outside of the mole. The harbour is very small so you need to have everything ready before you enter. Good shelter and open only NE.

There are several tavernas nearby and basic provisions can be found. Wonderful sandy beaches nearby.

Nísos Kérkira
(Corfu Island)

Most people know little of the Ionian but there are few who have not heard of Corfu. The references to Corfu from Homer to the present day praise the island as a lush green paradise spinning a soothing spell over all who visit it. In an age of package holidays the Corfu magic is continuously battered by jets winging in with yet more holidaymakers – and far, far more go to Corfu than to the rest of the Ionian – so it is surprising to find there are still charming and beautiful places on the island.

Corfu lies like a plump sickle off the west coast of Albania and mainland Greece. The channel between the northern end of Corfu and Albania is just one mile across – from Corfu you can see the military outpost at Butrino quite clearly. In contrast to the bare mountains of Albania, Corfu is a luxuriant green island from Mt Pandokrator in the north sloping down to the coastal plains in the south. In the centre are broken slopes cut by green valleys and grassy fields. Seeing cows grazing on the slopes of the hinterland it is sometimes difficult to believe you are in Greece.

North coast of Corfu

NOTE Care is needed when approaching the NE corner of Corfu because of the unsettled political situation in Albania. See the note at the beginning of this chapter.

ÁK AIKATERÍNI
39°49'·07N 19°50'·59E WGS84

At the NW end of Almiros beach in Ormos Ay Yeoryios is a tiny fishing harbour west of Ak Ay Aikaterini. Depths are mostly <1m and in any case it is too small for all but the smallest yachts.

ÓRMOS IMEROLIA
Fishing boat quay 39°47'·44N 19°54'·56E WGS84

The bay on the W side of Ák Kassiopi. With light NW–W winds it is possible to anchor on mud, sand and weed, not everywhere good holding.

In the SW corner of the bay a concrete apron has been built out to provide a quay for local fishing boats. There may be space to go alongside here, but you may need to move if you take a fishing boat berth.

Tavernas open in the summer.

41

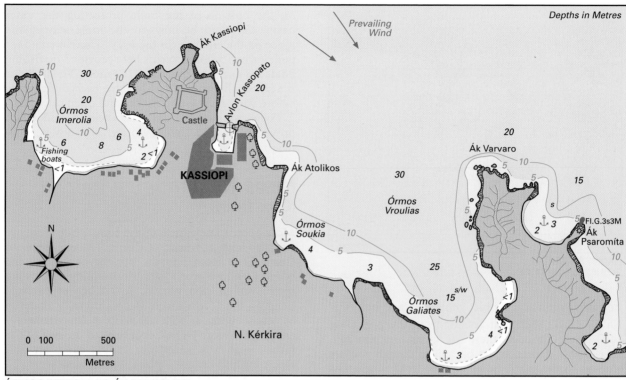

ÓRMOS IMEROLA TO ÁK PSAROMITA
⊕39°47′·48N 19°55′·40E WGS84

KASSIOPI (Avlon Kassapeto)

BA 206

Approach

From the W the castle on the headland and a number of houses around Órmos Imerolia will be seen. From the E the buildings of Kassiopi are readily identified. The small harbour itself will not be seen until you are right into the bay.

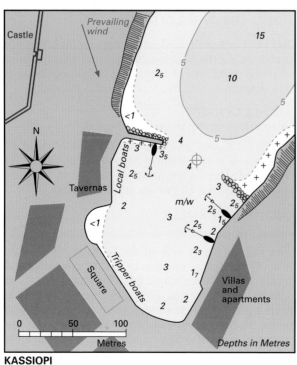

KASSIOPI
⊕39°47′·48N 19°55′·40E WGS84

Mooring

Yachts should go stern-to the quay on the E side under the stubby breakwater. Depths here are irregular so some care is needed. The bottom is mud and weed, adequate holding once the anchor is in.

Shelter Adequate shelter from the prevailing NW-W breeze although some swell penetrates. If the wind goes around to the N or NE it can get very uncomfortable and may become untenable in here.

Facilities

Water from private sources. A fuel station in the town. Good shopping for provisions and numerous tavernas and restaurants of all types. Bank. ATM. PO. Hire cars and motorbikes.

Kassiopi looking SW into the harbour   *Lu Michell*

Nisís Peristeraí and lighthouse at the northern end of North Corfu Channel looking ESE

General

Kassiopi is a thriving tourist spot with numerous small hotels and self-catering apartments around the original village. In July and August it is crowded with holidaymakers, but outside high season it retains some of the charm of what was a small fishing village.

ÓRMOS VROULIAS

The large bay immediately E of Kassiopi. In settled weather there are several attractive anchorages on the W side and at the head of the bay. The bottom is mostly sand and weed. On the E side of Ák Varvaro there are two small coves affording reasonable shelter on either side of Ák Psaromíta.

East coast of Corfu

NORTHERN CORFU CHANNEL (VORION STENÓN KÉRKIRAS)

BA 206

Imray-Tetra G11

From the N pass between Nisís Peristeraí and Corfu and proceed with caution into the channel until the platform E cardinal beacon on Ifalos Sérpa is sighted. Leave the beacon well to starboard – it is not on the extremity of the reef. When you pass through the channel outside Ifalos Sérpa you are less than a mile from the Albanian coast. At night the light on Nisís Peristeraí Fl.R.5s5M is easily seen from the distance stated and once into the channel the light Q(3)10s7M on the beacon on Ifalos Sérpa will be seen.

Note See caution on Albania at the beginning of this chapter.

AYIOS STEFANOS[1]

A small inlet immediately S of Ifalos Sérpa in the North Corfu Channel. Although just below a military post no objection is normally made to anchoring here.

Proceed into the middle of the bay and anchor in 3–6m depths. The bottom is mud and thick weed which can be difficult to get through. Excellent

Corfu history

One of the spin-offs of tourism is the proliferation of guides describing the history, places-to-see and things-to-do in Corfu and so rather than attempt to condense the whole history of the island from such guides I have prepared instead a brief synoptic history. This little history also describes, somewhat more loosely, the chain of events and invasions determining the character of the other islands in the Ionian.

c.1200BC It is surmised that Homer's Skheria, the island home of the Phaeacians, was Corfu. Palaíokastrita is thought to be the site of the castle of King Alkinoos. The Phaeacians ferried Odysseus home to Ithaca, in so doing arousing the wrath of Poseidon who turned their ship to stone. The island of Gravia off Palaíokastrita is said to be this petrified ship although some say it is the island of Pondokonisi (Mouse Island) near Kanoni.

c.734 to 434BC Corfu is colonised by the Corinthians. Corfu, itching for independence from the mother city, called on the Athenians to aid it against the Corinthians who naturally enough asked the opposing Spartans to give them a hand in quelling Corfu. Thus Corfu was indirectly the cause of the disastrous Peloponnesian War that effectively obliterated Athens and classical Greece.

229BC Corfu colonised by Rome.

722AD Corfu passed to the eastern Byzantine Empire.

1080 to 1386 After a collection of Norman and Sicilian rulers, Corfu invites the Venetians to restore order. Corfu remained under Venetian rule until 1797.

1460 The body of St Spiridon is brought to the island and becomes the patron saint of Corfu. Every year there are four processions on which the body of St Spiridon is brought out: Palm Sunday, Easter Saturday, the 11th of August, to commemorate the defeat of the Turks in 1716, and the first Sunday in November to commemorate the end of a plague. Every second male in Corfu seems to be called Spiros after the patron saint.

1431, 1537, 1716 Major assaults by the Turks on Corfu.

1797 Corfu taken over by the French. The French laid out a regular street plan for Corfu and began the construction of the arcaded buildings on the esplanade in Corfu town.

1814 Corfu occupied by the British who began many public works as well as introducing ginger beer, fruit cake and cricket.

1864 Corfu ceded to Greece. Today Corfu reflects many of these influences in its own special Corfiot architecture and culture. The eerie Medusa in the museum, the Venetian forts and galley port, the French architecture raising a second Rue de Rivoli far from Paris, cricket and cake on Sundays, Byzantine churches. . .yet undeniably Greek, as Lawrence Durrell will tell you:

`A glance at the synoptic history of the place will do nothing to decrease the sense of being out of one's depth, submerged by too much data. But as time goes on, as sunny Greek mornings succeed each other, you will find everything sinking to the bottom of your mind's harbour, there to take up shapes and dispositions which are purely Greek and have no frame or reference to history anywhere else.'

Lawrence Durrell *The Greek Islands*

shelter from the NW wind. On the S side of the bay there is a rough stone mole, but this is usually occupied by local boats. Some tavernas have short jetties off the beach where yachts can go bows-to, although you are rightly obliged to use the taverna.

Some provisions can be obtained and there are numerous tavernas around the shore. Although a

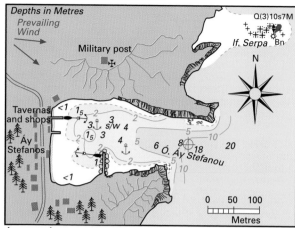

ÓRMOS ÁY STEFANOU
⊕39°45′·90N 19°57′·09E WGS84

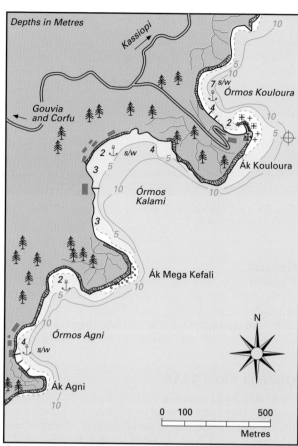

ÓRMOS KOULOURA, KALAMI AND AGNI
⊕39°44′·60N 19°56′·50E WGS84

Áy Stefanos looking SE

number of holiday villas have been built here, the bay retains a calm and beauty well worth the stop for the night.

KOULOURA[1]

A small bay S of Áy Stefanos. There is a miniature harbour surrounded by shoal water at the SE end of the bay. A yacht drawing one metre or less can enter with care from the N. Excellent shelter inside. Alternatively anchor in 5–10m depths immediately W of the small harbour and take a long line ashore or anchor in the W of the bay in 8–15m. There are two stub jetties off the taverna. The bottom is covered in thick weed. Good shelter from the prevailing NW wind.

Ashore above the small harbour is a taverna which though frequently crowded for lunch is less hectic at night.

KALAMI[1]

Immediately S of Kouloura is Órmos Kalami. Open to the S and E, it offers good shelter from the prevailing NW wind. Anchor in 4–6m depths in the NW of the bay. There is also a jetty off the taverna on the W side of the bay that can be used. Some provisions and tavernas ashore.

AGNI

The bay immediately S of Kalami. Anchor at the N end or at the S end. There are several jetties off the tavernas at the S end of the bay that can be used. Good shelter from the NW wind although it gusts into the bay. Tavernas ashore.

Recently the slopes have been carved up for hotel and villa complexes, a sort of pastoral extension to greater Corfu. Down on the water you are in the best place, away from the coast road and its incessant traffic.

NOTE

Care is needed if you are using any of the jetties from Kouloura to Agni as a considerable wash is created by the fast ferries steaming in and out of the North Corfu Channel. Several yachts have been damaged by the wash when moored overnight so it may be wise to anchor off (with a long line ashore) rather than going stern-to a jetty.

1. These harbours lie within an officially prohibited area though the prohibition is disregarded in practice.

IPSOS 39°41'·72N 19°50'·38E WGS84

Ipsos is part of the ribbon development of holiday complexes that have sprung up around the coast to the north of Gouvia in an attempt to accommodate some of the tourist overflow from Corfu town.

The small harbour lies towards the south end of the beach and is used mainly by small fishing boats and trip boats. To the north of the harbour is a boarding platform for watersports and trip boats that extends out for some distance from the beach.

There are 2–3m depths in the entrance and 2–2·5m depths a few metres off the E breakwater. The quay running around the head of the harbour is shallow with depths mostly less than 1m and in any case is taken up with local boats. Anchor and take a

long line to the rough stone breakwater. You will need to use your dinghy to get ashore. Adequate shelter from the prevailing NW–W wind but open N–NE.

Tavernas and bars ashore. Good shopping for provisions. Ipsos is a pretty noisy resort area and if you are looking for peace and quiet then head elsewhere.

ÓRMOS GOUVÍON (Gouvía)

BA 2406

Imray-Tetra G11

The large enclosed bay NW of Corfu town with Gouvía Marina at the S end.

Approach

Conspicuous Nisís Gouvíon in the S approach and Ákra Kommeno and Vrakhos Foustanopidhima on the N are readily identified. Two large hotels on the N side of the entrance are conspicuous. Once up to the entrance to the bay the red and green buoys marking the channel into the bay are readily seen. Entering the bay keep to the N side of the entrance to avoid the extensive shallows on the S.

By night There are no major lights to guide you in, but the conical buoys marking the channel are lit Fl.G and Fl.R, range probably about one mile. The lights on the channel buoys cannot always be relied upon. The end of the marina pier is lit 2F.R(vert)3M.

VHF Ch 16, 69 (24/24). Call sign *Gouvía Marina.*

Dangers The southern half of the entrance is obstructed by a shallow mud bank. The aforementioned buoys show the channel into the bay clear of the shoal water.

Mooring

Yachts should head for the marina where they will be directed to a berth. Normally you will be met at the entrance to the marina by an inflatable and guided into your berth.

Data 960 berths to be expanded to 1200 berths. Visitors' berths. Max LOA 80m. Depths 2–6m.

Berths Berth where directed in the marina where you will be assisted by marina staff on the quay. There are laid moorings tailed to the quay.

Shelter The shelter in the marina is now much improved with the construction of new piers and is generally good. However some berths are still uncomfortable with the prevailing wind, especially those on the far west quay, and in strong N–NE winds berths here can get uncomfortable.

Authorities Harbourmaster and marina staff. Entry procedures may be completed here. Charge band 2/3.

South Anchorage Can no longer be used as the new pontoons installed by the marina cover most of this area. It is prohibited to anchor in the North Bay.

Facilities

Services Water and electricity (220 and 380V) at all berths. Telephone connections. Shower and toilet

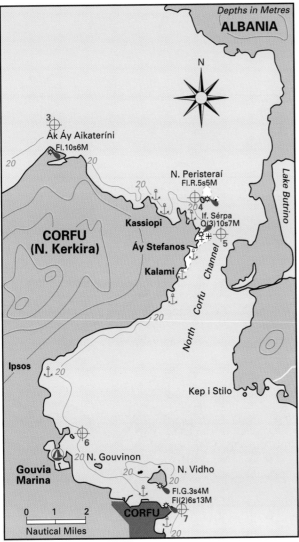

CORFU: NORTH CHANNEL

⊕3   0·35M N of Ák Aikateríni (Corfu N)
      39°49'·70N 19°51'·05E WGS84
⊕4   Mid-channel between Nisís Peristerai and Ák Psaromíta
      39°47'·29N 19°57'·19E WGS84
⊕5   0·25M E of Ifalos Serpa (Corfu N Channel)
      39°46'·24N 19°57'·86E WGS84
⊕6   0·5M E of Ák Kommeno (Gouvia)
      39°39'·82N 19°52'·45E WGS84
⊕7   0·5M E of Ák Sidhero (Corfu E side)
      39°37'·36N 19°56'·61E WGS84

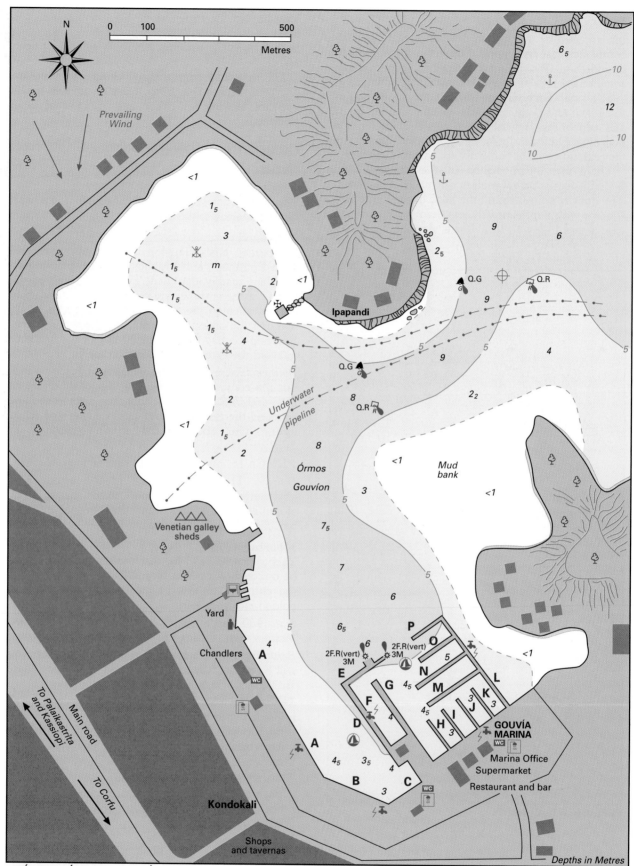

N

0   100   500
Metres

Prevailing
Wind

<1

1₅

3

m

1₅

1₅

2

<1

1₅

<1

5

4

2

1₅

2

6₅

10

12

10

10

Q.G

Q.R

Ipapandi

9

Q.G

9

5

4

8

Q.R

2₂

<1

Mud
bank

<1

Órmos

Gouvíon

8

3

<1

5

7₅

5

7

6

5

5

Venetian galley
sheds

Yard

Chandlers

A 4

A

WC

To Palaikastríta
and Kassiópi

Main road

To Corfu

Kondokali

Shops
and tavernas

6₅

6

2F.R(vert)
3M

2F.R(vert)
3M

E

G

F

D

A

4₅

3₅

B

4

3

C

WC

P

O

N

M

5

4₅

4₅

H

I

J

K

3

3

3

3

L

GOUVÍA
MARINA

WC

Marina Office
Supermarket
Restaurant and bar

Depths in Metres

LIMÍN GOUVÍON AND GOUVÍA MARINA
⊕39°39′·53N 19°51′·35E WGS84

Gouvía Marina looking SE   *K & G Marinas*

blocks. Laundry. 24 hour security.

Fuel At the N end of the W quay. Depths are reported to be 3m.

Repairs 65-ton travel-hoist. Most yacht repairs can be arranged here including mechanical and engineering repairs, sail repairs, electrical and electronic repairs, GRP and wood repairs. The best policy is to get in touch with the base manager who will organise the necessary repairs. Chandlers in the marina and in Kondokali (Force 5 Chandlers).

Nautilus Yacht Chandlers, Marina Gouvía, 49100 Corfu, GR. ☎ 26610 90343 *Fax* 26610 99277.

Provisions There is a supermarket within the marina and supermarkets in Kondokali.

Eating out Restaurant at the marina. Others in Kondokali.

Other PO and ATM in Kondokali. Camping Gaz in chandlers. Buses to Corfu town from Kondokali. Taxis. Corfu International airport.

K & G Med. Marinas Management
Marina Gouvia, PO Box 60, 49083 Tzavros, Corfu
☎ 26610 91900 *Fax* 22610 91829
Email gouvia@medmarinas.com
www.medmarinas.com

General

Kondokali was once a small fishing village, but that was long ago before hotels and self-catering apartments were built around the coast. Now it plays host to predominantly English tourists who can find all things English here – English newspapers, English breakfasts, an English pint, English Sunday lunches – but few things Greek.

The marina is owned and run by K & G Med. Marinas Management, the group that also runs Levkas, Kalamata and Zea Marinas. The marina is the base for a large number of charter craft and also a popular spot for yachties to spend the winter. It is around 15 minutes from Corfu airport. To get into Corfu either take a bus (every half hour on the main road) or get a taxi.

NEARBY BOATYARDS

Between Gouvía and Corfu there are several yards which haul yachts. Yachts up to 20–30 tons can be hauled out here on a cradle and slipway. Associated with the yards are various companies who can carry out most yacht repairs including GRP repairs, woodwork, engineering and mechanical work, electrical work, sail repairs and canvas work.

LIMÍN KÉRKIRA (Corfu Harbour)

BA 2406
Imray-Tetra G11

Approach

Conspicuous From the N Nisís Vidho obscures part of the town. Nisís Vidho and the rock (Vrak Navsika) nearby are conspicuous from the distance. As you near the harbour the buildings of the town will be seen. From the S the Venetian citadel on Ák Sidhero and the lighthouse atop it are clearly visible from some distance off. A red belfry in the town and the two radio masts to the W of the town are also conspicuous.

By night Use the light on Ák Sidhero Fl(2)6s13M and closer in the lights of the harbour. The old harbour is lit at the E end Fl.R.2s.4M and on the W end Q.R.9m3M. The detached breakwater is lit: Q.G.3M and Fl.R.2s4M. The end of the commercial breakwater is lit Fl.G.2s7M. The red lights atop the radio masts in the town are clearly visible and the citadel is often spotlit in the summer.

Notes

1. It is safe to pass between Nisís Vidho and Vrak Navsika.
2. The harbour is used by considerable numbers of ferries from Italy and smaller landing-craft-type ferries from Igoumenítsa. A yacht should give way to these ferries at all times and a good lookout should be kept for them in the approaches to the harbour.

Mooring

If you need to clear in go on the customs quay. After obtaining your papers moor in the old harbour to the E of the customs quay. If there is a strong NW wind you can sometimes moor in the old harbour and obtain your papers from there as the customs quay can be dangerous with the prevailing NW wind. In the summer it is best to arrive early in the morning aiming to be off the customs quay before the NW wind arrives about noon. In the old harbour the most comfortable place is alongside the outer breakwater where the NW wind will hold you off. The old harbour is full of tripper boats and it can be difficult to find a berth. Often you will have to go

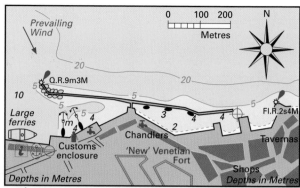

LIMÍN KERKIRA (PALAIO LIMANI)
⊕39°37'·66N 19°55'·15E WGS84

two or three out from the mole and move when the tripper boats are ready to go.

Shelter Good shelter in the old harbour where only southerly gales set up a surge. As mentioned the quay off the customs area is open to the prevailing NW wind which blows straight down onto it.

Authorities Customs, immigration, and port police in the customs enclosure. A transit log can be obtained here and as all the relevant authorities are grouped close together this is a comparatively easy process. Entry procedures may also be completed at Gouvia Marina.

Note There is talk of turning the old harbour into a marina although no plans are available yet and work had not started at the time of publication.

Facilities

Water On the customs quay and a tap behind the toilet block in the old harbour.
Fuel On the customs quay.
Repairs Chandlers nearby on the waterfront.
Provisions Good shopping for all provisions. There

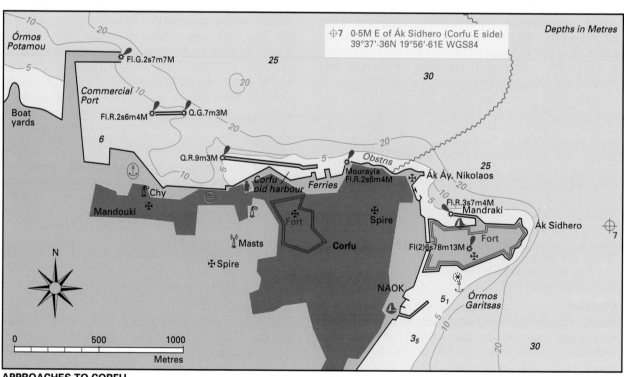

APPROACHES TO CORFU

Ák Sidhero on Corfu looking SW into Órmos Garítsas. Corfu old harbour is just out of the picture right

Peter Kleinoth/MareTeam

are several small mini-markets on the waterfront, but you are better off going into town where there is a better choice. Ice can be ordered.

Eating out A wide choice of tavernas. Those clustered around the square SE of the harbour are as good as any or wander around and find your own favourite. Numerous bars dotted about everywhere.

Other PO (open 24 hours and will change foreign banknotes). OTE. Banks and exchange offices. ATMs. Greek gas and Camping Gaz. Hospital. Hire cars, motorbikes, bicycles. Bus service to most parts of the island. Ferry service to Brindisi, Patras and Igoumenítsa. International flights and regular internal flights to Athens.

General

Corfu town is one of those special places that grows on you the longer you stay. Unfortunately Corfu old harbour is smelly and crowded in the summer which adversely affects your views on the town. Gouvía is too far away unless you have your own land-based transport. The myriad tourists choking the narrow alleys can also put you off. Nonetheless persevere until Corfu charms you. There are many things to do and see in and around Corfu, but as much as anything it is just wandering around that gives pleasure and despite the increase in 'tourist alleys' selling nondescript knick-knacks, there is still much of the old town remaining intact and alive.

MANDRÁKI

The harbour in Mandráki on the N side of Ák Sidhero belongs to two yacht clubs: POIATH, the Hellenic Offshore Racing Club, and IOK, the Corfu Sailing Club. You may be able to find a berth in here if there is room. The best bet is to go by land to contact the *marinero* in charge or alternatively try

approaching the entrance and see if you are directed to a berth.

An L-shaped mole protects the harbour and the masts of the yachts inside are easily identified. The mole head is lit Fl.R.3s4M. There are 3–4m depths in the entrance and mostly 1·5–3m depths inside off the outer mole. Off the quay and on the E side depths are less. Laid moorings tailed to the quay or buoys. Good shelter inside. A charge is made.

The harbour is in an enviable situation under the steep walls of the fort on Ák Sidhero and it is a short walk into the middle of town.

ÓRMOS GARÍTSAS

A yacht can anchor off on the S side of Ák Sidhero in Órmos Garítsas where there is good shelter from the prevailing NW wind. Anchor in 5–12m on mud, good holding.

NAOK YACHT CLUB

⊕ 39°37'·32N 19°55'·65E

The yacht harbour on the W side of Órmos Garítsas belongs to NAOK, the Nautical Club of Corfu. There are a limited number of berths for visiting yachts in the summer.

There are 3–4m depths in the entrance and 3m depths on the outer end of the mole decreasing further into the harbour. Off the W quay and piers there are a number of shallow patches. Go stern or bows-to the mole where directed or where convenient. Yachts can also go stern-to the outside of the mole. Good shelter from the prevailing NW winds. In strong southerlies the harbour is reported to be untenable.

Showers and toilets at the clubhouse. Charge band 2. It is a short walk up to the esplanade and the centre of town.

BENITSES (Benitsai)

39°32'·92N 19°54'·75E WGS84

An exposed anchorage 5 miles S of Corfu town. A large white hotel complex is conspicuous N of Benitses. Anchor in 3–10m. The anchorage is only really tenable in calm weather as the prevailing wind funnelled between Corfu and the mainland coast blows down from the N and pushes a swell in. There is a small harbour, but it is always full of local and tripper boats.

Ashore Benitses is a booming resort full of tavernas and bars for the tourists in the hotels and apartments around the original village.

VOUKARI (Boukari)

⊕ 39°27'·57N 19°58'·68E WGS84

A small village approximately 1·5M W of Ak Voukari. You can anchor off here in calm weather. There is a very small and shallow harbour not suitable for most yachts. Tavernas ashore.

PETRITI
Approach
Seven miles SE of Benitses and just around Ák Voukari is the bay and little fishing port of Petriti. From the N the hamlet will not be seen but an eroded escarpment just S of Ák Voukari is conspicuous. Once the bay is opened the harbour mole and houses will be seen. From the E the houses of the hamlet are easily identified.

Dangers In the approach from the E care must be taken of the shoal water extending off the low-lying Ák Levkímmis.

Mooring
If there is room in the harbour go stern or bows-to the W quay or on the end of the mole. The harbour is often crowded with fishing boats and it may be difficult to find a berth. Alternatively anchor in the bay in 2–4m on mud, sand, and weed.

Shelter Good shelter from prevailing NW wind although some swell creeps around into the anchorage.

Facilities
Water on the quay. Most provisions can be found. Tavernas around the harbour.

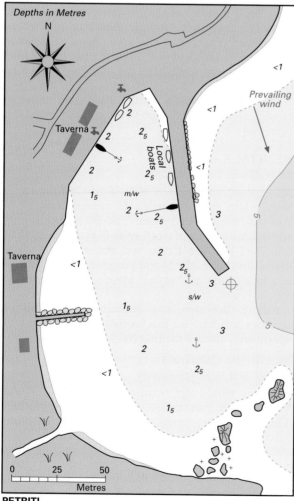

PETRITI
⊕39°27'·20N 20°00'·19E WGS84

General
Petriti gets few visitors by land and is one of those sleepy hollows you quickly develop an affection for. It is a green place, watered by a stream, with a good sandy beach and clear water.

AK LEVKIMMIS

⊕8 1M E of Ak Levkimmis light 39°27'·6N 20°05'·7E

The low-lying cape E of Petriti. It is difficult to pick out from the distance though the light structure near the end will eventually be seen. Shoal water extends for up to half a mile E and nearly a mile N of the cape and you should keep a healthy distance off.

SKALA POTAMOU
(Levkimmi Canal entrance)
39°26'·11N 20°05'·16E WGS84

1·5M south of Ak Levkimmi is the mouth of the canal which leads a mile or so inland to Levkimmi town. A training wall extends out from the beach on the south side, with a light structure on the extremity. The canal is liable to silt and depths are uneven, reported to be just 1–1·5m. In calm weather yachts can anchor off the beach in 4–10m, but with the prevailing northerlies this anchorage is not tenable except in the morning calm. Taverna on the beach at Skala Potamou, more choice in Levkimmi town. Levkimmi is the administrative centre for the south of Corfu and is the second largest town. More amazingly, it is seemingly immune from the onslaught of tourism which happily has missed this sleepy gem of a town.

KAVOS (Levkimmi)
A square-shaped harbour constructed for the ferries from the mainland. The entrance is lit Fl.R/Fl.G. The ferries berth on the west quay, smaller trip boats use the southwest corner. The harbour has been dredged to 4–5m and yachts can go alongside the quay on the N side or stern-to on the S side. Good shelter in the N corner although the prevailing northerlies blow into the entrance and can set up a surge and strong northerlies may make the harbour untenable. Some yachts use the harbour as a refuge when beating northwards to Corfu town. The new main road to the north runs out of the port and bypasses Levkimmi town centre, 1½km away. The port itself is pretty isolated, with just a café in the ferry ticket office providing drinks and snacks. Although the port is known as Kavos, it shouldn't be confused with the package tour resort of the same name further to the south.

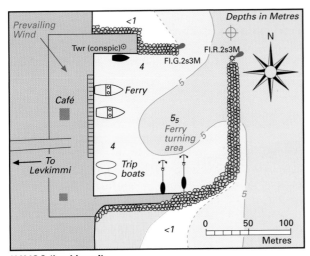

KAVOS (Levkimmi)
⊕39°24'·96N 20°06'·09E WGS84

West coast of Corfu

ÁY STEFANOS (Avliotes)

39°45'·24N 19°38'·00E WGS84

A small harbour on the N side of Ák Kavokefali.

Approach

Should be made from the N. The breakwater will not be seen until close to the harbour. Care is needed at the entrance which silts and it would be wise to reconnoitre in the dinghy to see if depths are adequate. With the normal NW–W prevailing winds in the summer this can be difficult so if possible try to get here in the morning before the prevailing wind gets up.

Note In 2003 depths in the entrance were around 2·5m in approximately the middle of the entrance channel.

Mooring

Most of the quay space is occupied by local craft. Anchor and take a long line to the breakwater or go bows-to on the S quay. The bottom is sand and good holding. Good all-round shelter.

Facilities

Tavernas and bars open on the beach to the N in the summer. The village of Avliotes is a little further on and here you can find provisions and tavernas.

AYIOS YEÓRYIOU (Agios Georgis)

Ák Arilla light 39°42'·7N 19°39'·3E

A wide sandy bay just N of Palaíokastrita. Anchor in 4–5 metre depths in the N corner of the bay or off Ayios Yeóryiou if it is calm. If the prevailing NW–W wind is blowing with any strength a swell works its way around into the bay. Open S.

Tavernas and bars around the long sandy beach open in the summer.

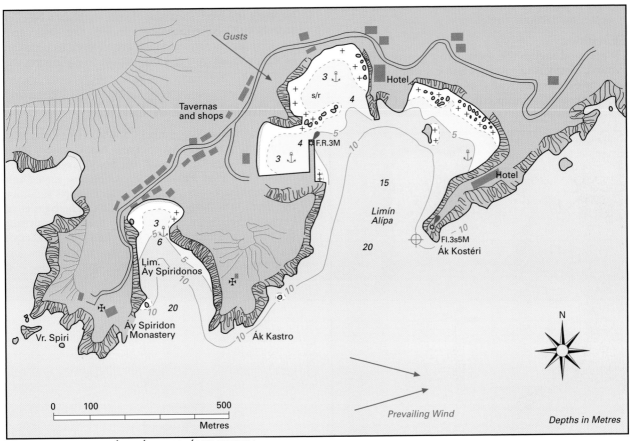

APPROACHES TO LIMÍN ALÍPA (PALAÍOKASTRITA)
⊕39°40'·24N 19°42'·75E

PALAÍOKASTRITA (Limín Alípa)

BA 2402

Imray-Tetra G11

Approach

Difficult by day and night.

Conspicuous The village of Lakones on the hill above Palaiokastrita is conspicuous from the distance. Nearer the coast the monastery and the large hotels around the bay are the best marks. You will not see the harbour mole until you are right into the bay.

By night Use the light on Ák Kostéri Fl.3s5M and the light at the end of the mole F.R.3M. A night entrance is not recommended.

Dangers

1. Entering the harbour proper stay close to the head of the mole to avoid the rocky shoal on the N side which is easily visible (rocks awash) by day but not by night.
2. With the prevailing NW wind a heavy swell is pushed onto the coast which rebounds off causing a wicked cross sea.

Mooring

Go stern or bows-to the mole. The harbour is full of local boats but there is normally space somewhere. Alternatively anchor in the N bay, taking care of the rocks near the entrance to the harbour. The bottom is sand, good holding.

Shelter Good shelter from the prevailing NW winds. The harbour is dangerous with strong southerlies when a surge develops and waves break over the mole. If strong southerlies are likely a yacht should vacate the harbour straight away.

Facilities

Water and fuel in the town. Most provisions can be found. Numerous tavernas and bars although prices can be expensive because of the captive customers in the large hotels around the bay. Bus to Corfu.

Palaíokastrita harbour looking SW. Note the rocks off the N side of the entrance (in the foreground)

General

In a watercolour by Edward Lear, Palaíokastrita is depicted as it was before the hotels – a beautiful bay guarded by the monastery of Áy Spiridonos and a few fishermen's houses. Today the giant hotels surrounding the bay considerably mar the landscape, yet the seascape and the view from the monastery are still superb. Now no more hotels are to be built – the authorities consider there are enough here – though service buildings still keep popping up every summer. By the harbour a NATO storehouse is concealed under the hill and theoretically no photographs are allowed to be taken of this, though you can buy a postcard showing the prohibited view!

Southwest Coast of Corfu

Much of the coast south of Paleokastrita running right down to Ak Asprokavos has devoted itself entirely to land-based tourism. Some larger resorts, notably the Pink Palace at Ay Giordios, have built miniature harbours to shelter water-sports facilities but there is nothing of use to yachts. The hamlet of Pentati is relatively untouched by the mass tourism, but the tiny fishing harbour is packed with local craft and in any case is shallow in the approaches and inside the harbour, mostly <1m.

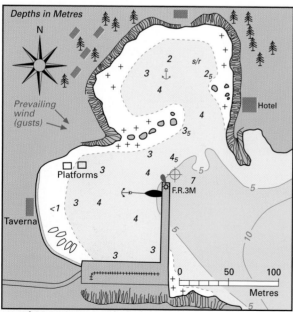

PALAÍOKASTRITA (LIMÍN ALÍPA)
⊕39°40'·4N 19°42'·6E

Nisoi Paxoí and Andípaxoi
(Paxos and Anti-Paxos Islands)

Seven miles south of Corfu lies Paxoí and its diminutive Andípaxoi. Five miles long and two miles wide, Paxoí until recently produced little else except olive oil for which it is famous. Harrods apparently sells only olive oil from Paxoí. Now tourists from Corfu regularly visit the island and in recent years a large number of villas have been built. The island is also popular with flotilla companies and in the summer the harbours and anchorages are full of yachts.

It was off Paxoí that a significant historical event occurred – little remembered now, but of momentous importance in ancient times. The Egyptian pilot Thamus was bound for Italy when he was becalmed off Paxoí. A voice came over the water commanding him to announce that the great god Pan was dead. Twice he disobeyed until the third command, whereupon he obeyed. Immediately a great wail of lamentation arose from the sea. It is a strange story, recorded for us by Plutarch in the *Moralia*, and yet when Pausanias visited Greece a century later he found Pan was still actively worshipped.

Andípaxoi, immediately south of Paxoí, is only sparsely populated. It has some attractive anchorages but none safe except in settled weather. The few inhabitants cultivate their vines and olives and are dependent on Paxoí for their needs and entertainment.

ÓRMOS LÁKKA

BA 2402

Imray-Tetra G11

A virtually landlocked bay on the N end of Paxoí.

Approach
Conspicuous The exact location of the bay is difficult to determine from the distance. From the W the lighthouse is conspicuous. From the N and E the light structures at the entrance will be seen when you are closer in.

By night Use the main light Fl(3)24s20M and closer in the lights at the entrance: Fl.G.2s3M/Fl.R.2s3M.

Mooring
Anchor off in the bay where convenient or anchor in the NW corner with a long line ashore. There is some room on the quay for small yachts to go bows-to, but care is needed as the depths are uneven. The bottom is sand and weed, good holding.

Shelter Good shelter from the prevailing winds although if there is more N than W in the wind it can get uncomfortable in here. Uncomfortable and untenable in places with strong NE winds. With NE winds tuck into the E side as far as possible.

Note At times it can get a bit smelly from sewage at the SE end of the bay.

Facilities
Water Sometimes available on the quay.
Provisions Most provisions can be obtained.
Eating out Tavernas and bars.
Other PO. OTE. Ferry to Parga.

General
The anchorage is picturesque under olive-clad slopes with the huddle of houses of the hamlet at the head of the bay. The anchorage is popular in the summer and this is a lively place rather than a quiet hide-away.

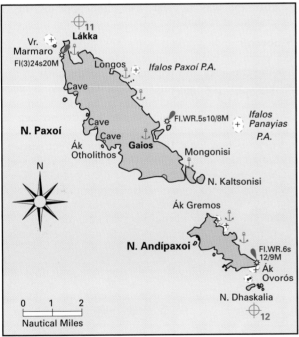

NISOI PAXOÍ AND ANDÍPAXOI

⊕11 0·5M N of Lákka entrance
39°15'·2N 20°08'·0E
⊕12 1M S of Nds Dhaskalia (S end (Andíipaxoi)
39°06'·8N 20°15'·0E

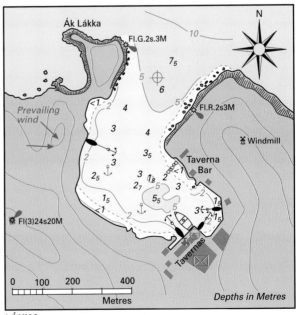

LÁKKA
⊕39°14'·65N 20°07'·75E WGS84

Lákka on the N end of Paxos   *Nigel Patten*

LONGOS (Logos)

39°13'·61N 20°09'·75E WGS84
BA 2402

A small harbour on the E coast of Nísos Paxoí between Lákka and Gaios. The harbour is very small and yachts are restricted from berthing inside, where all the space is reserved for local and tripper boats.

Either go stern-to the outside of the mole with a long line to it or anchor and take a long line to the N side of the bay. With the prevailing wind a swell works its way around making these berths uncomfortable. The new breakwater N of the harbour does not yet provide useful berthing space.

Ashore most provisions can be obtained and there are numerous tavernas and bars around the waterfront. It is a pity there is not a comfortable berth to be had at Longos as the small fishing village is an attractive place, with whitewashed houses huddled around the miniature harbour under olive-clad slopes.

IFALOS PAXOÍ

100m N of Ifalos Paxoí
39°13'·72N 20°10'·27E WGS84

Approximately half a mile E of Longos there is a reef, Ifalos Paxoí, which is difficult to see even in calm weather. It is possible to pass between the reef and the island, though care is needed and it is prudent to have someone up front keeping an eye out for it. Some believe the charted position is in error and it is closer to Nísos Paxoí than shown.

IFALOS PANAYIAS

A reef lying approximately 2½ miles E of Port Gaios. The reef and shoal water around it is difficult to see with the wind whipping up a chop on the water so it should be given a prudent berth. The reef lies just S of the direct route from Gaios to Parga so care is needed. Some believe it should be closer to the mainland than its charted position, though I think it looks about right.

PORT GAIOS (Port Gayo, Limín Paxon, Limín Paxoí)

BA 2402
Imray-Tetra G11

Approach

Conspicuous From the N the entrance to the harbour is difficult to see. From the distance the houses and tall chimney at Longos can be seen and as you close the port the lighthouse enclosed by a whitewashed wall on Nisís Panayía marks the entrance to the N channel. From the S the lighthouse on Nísos Andípaxoi is conspicuous and closer to Gaios a number of large white villas S of the town and the lighthouse and wall on Nisís Panayía are visible before the buildings of Port Gaios itself.

By night Use the light on Andípaxoi Fl.WR.6s12/9M (red sector over If Panayías) and on Nisís Panayía Fl.WR.5s10/8M. The N entrance is lit: Fl.R.3s3M/Fl.G.3s3M and the bend in the channel Fl.R.2s3M. The N end of the quay is lit F.G.3M. The S entrance is lit: Fl.G.2s3M/F.R.2M, though the lights should not always be relied on.

Dangers
1. Care needs to be taken of Ifalos Panayías in the approach from the E.
2. Ferries and tripper boats are constantly churning in and out of the harbour. In the N entrance care must be taken of the blind bend in the channel where you cannot see what is coming the other way.
3. In the S entrance there are barely 2m depths in the middle and no room to manoeuvre so wait until the way is clear. On either side of the S channel it is shallow.

Mooring

Go stern or bows-to either side of the town quay leaving the ferry and tripper boat berths clear in the middle. In the summer the town quay is very crowded and the alternative is to berth on the quayed section in the N channel. The bottom is

Gaios on Paxos looking NE with Nisís Panayía at the top of the photo   *Peter Kleinoth/MareTeam*

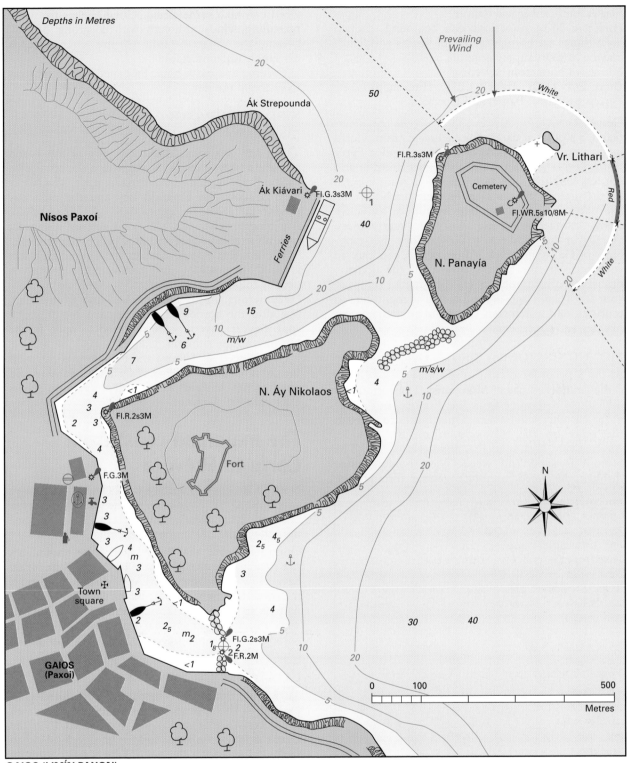

GAIOS (LIMÍN PAXON)
⊕₁ 39°12·22N 20°11'·47E WGS84
⊕₂ 39°11·80N 20°11'·32E WGS84

mud and generally good holding. Large yachts can anchor under the causeway between Nisís Áy Nikólaos and Nisís Panayía although the holding has been reported to be suspect here.

Shelter Good shelter from the prevailing summer winds. Strong southerlies cause a surge on the town quay and a yacht may have to move to a berth in the N channel.

Note Crossed anchors are a fact of life with all the boats using Gaios and there is not a lot you can do about it except remain cool and use some muscle power in the morning when you leave.

Authorities Port police and customs.

Facilities

Water Water can be delivered by mini-tanker. With so much tourist infrastructure water is scarce on the island.

Fuel A mini-tanker will deliver.

Provisions Most provisions can be found, though most things are brought in on the ferries and hence may be in short supply at times.

Eating out Numerous tavernas.

Other PO. OTE. Bank. ATM. Hire motorbikes. Ferries to Patras, Parga, and Corfu.

General

Gaios is a popular choice for excursions from Corfu making it a very crowded place in the summer. Ferry boats, flotilla yachts and private yachts churn in and out, choking the little harbour. If you want a berth in the height of summer be here early in the afternoon. For all this, Gaios is still an attractive town. Sitting in the cockpit of your yacht you are literally in the middle of town watching the hurly-burly of Gaios life go by. Alternatively, you can sip your ouzo in the square amidst all the activity, probably with a number of cats begging for scraps at your feet (Gaios appears to possess as many cats as tourists), and watch your yacht and any others who may try and squeeze in.

MONGONISI (Órmos Spuzzo, Ozias)

At the S tip of Paxoí, just over a mile SE of Gaios, is the landlocked bay of Mongonisi. The entrance is difficult to determine from the distance, but closer in the entrance will be seen. Once inside go bows-to the quay on the NE side or on the S side. Alternatively anchor in the middle in 3–5m. The bottom is sand and weed, good holding once through the weed, although getting through the

MONGONISI (ÓRMOS SPUZZO)
⊕39°11'N 20°12·5E

weed can take some doing. Good shelter from the prevailing winds although with a strong N–NW breeze the western side of the anchorage is extremely uncomfortable.

Taverna and bar ashore. Fast speedboat ferry runs to Gaios in the day.

NÍSOS ANDÍPAXOI

(Anti-Paxos)

There are two bays on the NE side of the island popular as day anchorages. Approach the coast with care as there are numerous fringing reefs. The N bay here is known as Emerald Bay and the next bay down is Órmos Agrapidhia. Anchor where convenient. When the NW wind gets up it can get uncomfortable in here and may become untenable.

There is a miniature harbour at Agrapidhia but it is really too small for most yachts and in any case is usually full of local boats.

Numerous tripper boats run to and from Paxoí, but after the hordes have departed it is a peaceful spot. Several tavernas are reported to open in the NE bays in the summer.

Care is needed of above and below-water rocks off the coast of Andípaxoi especially at the southern end and yachts should keep well out from Nisís Dhaskalia off the southern tip.

The mainland coast from Corfu to Préveza

Note At the time of writing yachts should take extra care around the bays close to the Albanian border because of the unsettled political situation there. See the note at the beginning of this chapter.

Opposite Corfu the Albanian-Epirote mountains rise to an impressive 1300m. The craggy peaks often have snow on them even in April. Proceeding south the mountain range curves inland and the coastline flattens to salt marsh around Préveza and Levkas. The much-indented coastline has some good harbours and anchorages, some of them much removed from the island tourism.

FTELIAS 39°41'·4N 20°00'·5E

Tucked up under the Albanian border is the bay of Ftelias. In the approaches a high rugged island on the Albanian side and a low rocky island on the Greek side will be seen. Leave the Greek island to starboard and enter the bay. There is a fish farm on the N side. Good depths in the entrance decreasing to 10m off the fish farm and 3m around the dogleg. Anchor where convenient on mud. No facilities.

PAGANIA

Approach

From the S it is difficult to see the entrance. From the distance the road cut into the hill appears to disappear where Pagania headland obscures it. Once into the entrance to the bay the farm buildings will be seen.

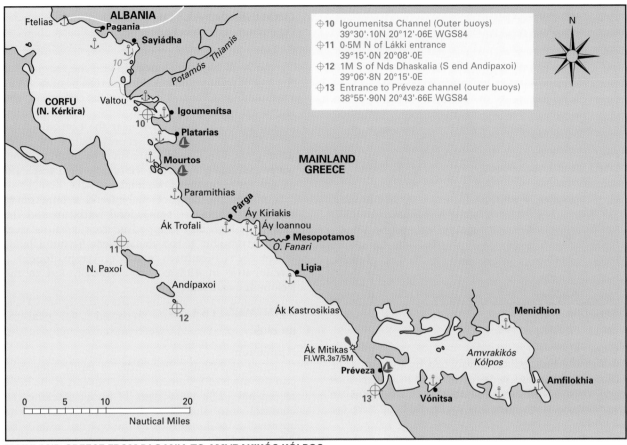

MAINLAND GREECE FROM PAGANIA TO AMVRAKIKÓS KÓLPOS

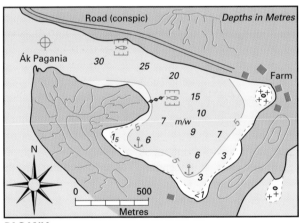

PAGANIA
⊕ 39°39′·8N 20°06′·0E

Note A fish farm extends out from the W side of the bay. It is easily seen by day. There are also other fish farms in the bay.

Mooring
Anchor in the SW or SE corner. The bottom is mud and weed, good holding. Good all-round shelter.

Facilities
You may get a few eggs from the farm, but otherwise none.

General
An idyllic spot little visited by yachts or anyone at all for that matter. The only inhabitants are the farmer and his family on the NE side of the bay. Occasionally a Greek patrol boat will turn up and may order yachts here to leave.

SAYIÁDHA

Approach
The buildings of the hamlet can be identified from the distance and closer in the harbour will be seen.

Mooring
Only shallow-draught yachts drawing less than 1·5m should attempt to enter. The new entrance on the SE side is narrow and bordered by rocks. It was probably opened by the simple Greek method of dynamiting a gap in the old wall. It is best to go alongside the outer mole as the holding is poor. Care must be taken of a shallow patch near the middle of the harbour. Shelter in the harbour is much improved with the new entrance. A yacht can also go alongside the quay just outside the entrance where there is reasonable shelter from the prevailing wind.

Anchorage You can anchor off under the rough mole to the N of the harbour in calm weather or light NW winds. If the wind gets up this is not a safe place to be.

Facilities
Port police. Water near the quay. A grocery shop, baker, and several tavernas.

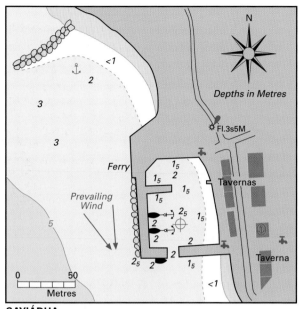

SAYIÁDHA
⊕39°37'·52N 20°10'·83E WGS84

General

A friendly little village untouched by tourism. The hinterland here is intensively farmed in wheat, corn and cotton and Sayiádha mostly functions as an agricultural town – the few yachts that call here are a bonus.

Note Pagania and Sayiádha fall within the restricted area where theoretically permission should be obtained for a visit. In practice this is not normally necessary.

ORMISKOS VALTOU
(Igoumenítsa Creek)

BA 2406

To the N of Nisídha Prasoúdhi and the entrance to the bay of Igoumenítsa is the deserted bay known as Igoumenítsa Creek. Care must be taken of the shoals off the river mouth (Potamós Thiamis) when entering. In the third cove near the bottom of the inlet there is excellent all-round shelter in 3–8m depths, mud and weed. Care must be taken of shoal water extending out from the shore. Fish traps cut off the very bottom of the inlet.

Just over the neck of the inlet is a long sandy beach and there are some good walks around the area. The high land trapped in the silt of the river delta is thought to be the ancient Sívota Islands where the Corinthians and Corcyreans fought a naval battle in 433BC that eventually led to the Peloponnesian War.

IGOUMENÍTSA

BA 2406

Approach

Conspicuous Nisídha Prasoúdhi is easily identified and the town of Igoumenítsa can be seen at the head of the bay. The three pairs of buoys marking the channel into the bay stand out clearly. The approaches and entrance to the bay can usually be determined by the constant coming and going of car ferries to Corfu.

By night Use the light on Nisídha Prasoúdhi Fl(2)9s8M and the light on the S side of the

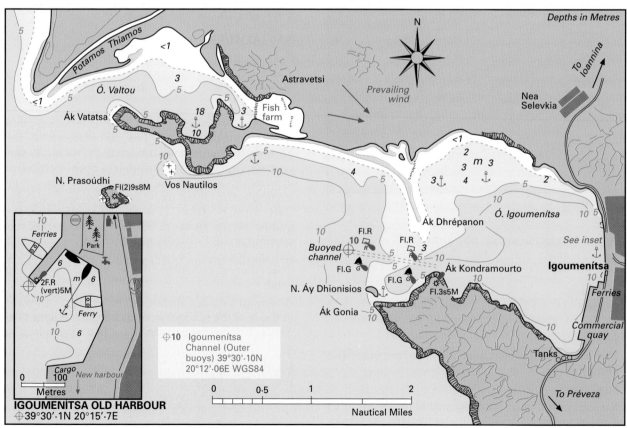

IGOUMENÍTSA OLD HARBOUR
⊕39°30'·1N 20°15'·7E

⊕10 Igoumenítsa Channel (Outer buoys) 39°30'·10N 20°12'·06E WGS84

ÓRMOS VALTOU AND ÓRMOS IGOUMENÍTSA

Órmos Igoumenítsa looking WNW towards the entrance with Ák Dhrépanon on the right side of the photo

entrance (Ák Kondramoúrto) Fl.3s5M. The buoys marking the channel are lit Q.G/Q.R and a 2F.R(vert)5M is exhibited on the pier head at Igoumenítsa.

VHF Ch 14 (harbourmaster)

Note

1. The massive harbour works to create a new commercial harbour beginning at the southern extremity of the old harbour and extending for virtually the length of the E side of the bay have been completed. As yet the ferries continue to use their usual berths, and it may be that the new quay is purely for cargo ships.
2. A VTS (Vessel Traffic Service) is in operation. Listen out on VHF Ch 14 for instructions although the VTS is really for ships using the port. Yachts are sometimes advised to enter the harbour to the N or S of the buoyed channel where depths are adequate at least a boat's length outside the buoys.

Mooring

Go stern or bows-to or alongside the quay. The bottom is mud – good holding.

Shelter Reasonable shelter although with strong NW winds it can be uncomfortable here and it may be better to anchor at the N end of the bay. There is a small fishing harbour N of the main pier but it is usually crowded and the depths are uneven (1–2m).

Anchorage Yachts can anchor at the N end of the bay where there is good shelter from the prevailing wind. There is also reported to be a good lee under Nisís Áy Dhionisios in attractive surroundings.

Authorities A Port of Entry. Port police, customs and immigration.

Facilities

Water On the quay.

Fuel Near the quay.

Provisions Good shopping for provisions.

Eating out Numerous tavernas and a number of fast-food places.

Other PO. OTE. Banks. ATMs. Greek gas and Camping Gaz. Infrequent buses to Préveza and Athens. Car ferry to Corfu. Ferries to Patras and Italy (Brindisi, Ancona and Bari).

General

Igoumenítsa is a rather unattractive convenience ferry-terminal town, although the large bay is attractive. In 1979 an earthquake destroyed some of the buildings and 200 people lived in tents for some 6 months after the event. The development of the new commercial quay is intended as the maritime feeder for the pan-Ionia motorway linking Igoumenítsa and Patras over the new Rhio-Andirhio suspension bridge. Completion of the bridge is expected at the end of 2004 and the motorway should be complete by 2005.

PLATARIAS

Approach

A small harbour in the NE corner of Órmos Plataria. The approach is straightforward.

Mooring

Go stern or bows-to or alongside on the new breakwater extension.

Shelter Good shelter from the prevailing NW wind although it tends to funnel into the bay and kick up a bit of a chop.

Facilities

Water on the quay though you may have to find the 'waterman' to unlock it. Petrol station up on the main coast road which can deliver fuel by mini-tanker. Most provisions can be found. Tavernas and bars on the waterfront.

General

Platarias is now a popular detour for yachts heading up and down the coast from Corfu to Párga. The improved harbour and the small resort make it a wonderful place, with a good sandy beach and shallow water for swimming and just enough in the way of tourists for there to be some good tavernas and cafés.

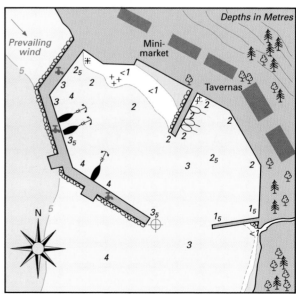

PLATARIAS

⊕ 39°27'·12N 20°16'·51E WGS84

MOÚRTOS AND ADJACENT ISLANDS

Just S of Órmos Platarias lie the Sívota islands with the village of Moúrtos on the mainland nearby. There are three islands: Nisís Sívota (Sybota), Nisís Áy Nikólaos, and Nisís Mavros Notos.

Approach

Conspicuous From the N the lighthouse on Nisís Sívota and a large three-storeyed house on the mainland are conspicuous. As you close Moúrtos village the houses on the hill above can be easily identified. From the S the islands are more difficult to identify, but the lighthouse on Nisís Sívota will be seen.

By night There is only the light on Nisís Sívota Fl(3)20s12M and a light on the pierhead at Moúrtos Fl.R.3M. A night approach is not recommended for the first time.

Dangers
1. Do not attempt to pass between Nisís Sívota and Nisís Áy Nikólaos as the channel is obstructed by the reef running across the S end.
2. The passage between the mainland and the islands has only 2m depths at one point (see plan). The deepest part of the bar is approximately one third off Nisís Áy Nikólaos.

3. In the approach from the S keep to the eastern side of the passage to avoid the reef jutting out from Nisís Sívota. Waves break on some of the rocks of the reef.

Mooring

There are a number of possibilities:
1. ***Moúrtos*** Go stern-to the SE quay making sure your anchor is well dug in. There are mostly 2-metre depths along the quay except for the NE end where it shallows. The prevailing wind blows straight down onto the quay making it uncomfortable and at times untenable. There is often damage sustained to boats here both from the wind and swell and also from ferry wash pushing boats onto the quay. A large harbour has been built enclosing the N side of the bay. As yet yachts are discouraged from berthing here, and little is known of completion plans. When open and finished it is likely to have laid moorings and services. The shelter in here is excellent.
2. ***Monastery Bay*** The cove NW of Moúrtos quay. Anchor and take a line to the shore or the jetty. Shelter here is better than it looks.

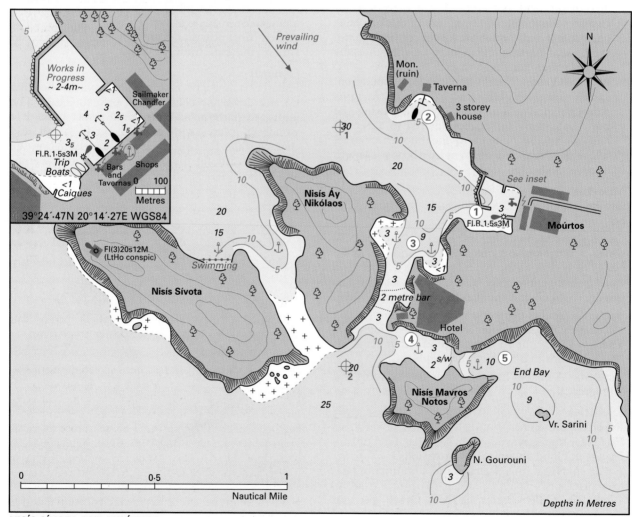

NISÍS SÍVOTA AND MOÚRTOS
⊕₁ 39°24′·66N 20°13′·82E WGS84
⊕₂ 39°23′·88N 20°13′·72E WGS84

3. ***Middle Bay*** In the cove on the SE just inside the N entrance to the channel. Anchor in 3–7m and take a long line ashore if possible. The bottom is mud and thick weed, good holding once through the weed. This is the best place to be with good shelter and a short dinghy trip to Moúrtos. The cove opposite on the NW side is mostly too shallow and has underwater rocks fringing it. In any case space is limited by permanently moored yachts.

4. ***Sand Bar Bay*** At the S end of the channel there is a cove sheltered by Nisís Mavros Notos. Much of the cove is taken up with moorings for sailing dinghies from the hotel on the slopes above. There are now signs around the bay prohibiting anchoring, although the legality of these is in doubt as anything up to the high water mark is owned by the state and cannot be bought or sold. Booms have been reported, laid across the bay restricting access. In any case the channel between Nisís Áy Nikólaos and the mainland south of the bar is the primary water-skiing area, so don't expect peace and tranquility here.

5. ***End Bay (or Fourth Bay)*** On the E side of Nisís Mavros Notos a yacht can find reasonable shelter from the prevailing winds. Anchor in 4–10m on sand and weed. If there are a lot of yachts in here the best thing to do is take a long line ashore to the N or S side rather than swinging to anchor. Care needed of dinghy moorings laid near the beach. Water-sports centre ashore.

Notes
1. Depths in the channel between Nisís Áy Nikólaos and the mainland decrease abruptly to a 2m bar before increasing quickly again.
2. There can be a S-going current in the channel with the prevailing wind.

The N entrance and anchorage in the channel at Nisís Sívota looking across to Nísos Áy Nikólaos   *Nigel Patten*

Facilities
(Moúrtos)
Services Water and electricity points on the quay.
Fuel In the village about 600m away. It may be possible to get a mini-tanker down to the quay.
Provisions Most provisions can be found on the waterfront. There are also grocery shops 600m away in the village.
Eating out Good tavernas on the waterfront and up in the village.
Other PO. OTE. Bank. ATM. Sailmaker. Chandlery. Bus to Igoumenítsa.

General
Moúrtos village is a pleasant place in a wooded setting with friendly locals. The anchorages around Mourtos have always been a popular spot for yachties to hole up, but now there is a lot more competition from shore-based holidays. It remains an enchanting spot and Mourtos town quay has all been redeveloped in a sympathetic and convivial way that does not spoil the ambience of the place. The same cannot be said of Sand Bar Bay or the strangely out-of-place water-slide feature in Monastery Bay.

Although called the Sívota Islands, these are not thought to be the ancient Sybota Islands off which the Corinthians and Corcyraeans fought their battle in 433 BC. The ancient Sybota Islands are probably the low hills around the creek immediately N of Igoumenítsa.

PÁRGA

BA 2402

Approach
Conspicuous From the W the fort at Kastelli in the hills NW of Párga is conspicuous and closer in the belfry on Ák Áy Spiridhonos will be seen. From the S the belfry, fort and the buildings of Parga village are conspicuous. The small white chapel on Nisídha Áy Nikólaos also stands out well.

By night The light on the fort at Párga Fl(2)6s6M will be seen from the S but is obscured in the approach from the W. The small harbour in Órmos Valtou is not lit.

Dangers Care needs to be taken of the reef Voi Spiridhonia lying approximately 100m off Ák Áy Spiridhonos. In calm weather it is easily spotted, but with any whitecaps it can be difficult to pick out.

Mooring
Most yachts head for the small harbour on the W side of Órmos Valtou. Go stern or bows-to. In general it is better to go bows-to as rock ballasting projects out from the quay in places. Alternatively anchor S of the mole and take a line ashore or to the old mole. Difficult holding so ensure your anchor is well in. The new breakwater S of the old mole provides some shelter if you are tucked right under it with a line ashore – it is likely it will be extended some time in the future to provide additional berths for yachts. Although the wharf at Párga village appears to be adequately protected a swell rolls

around into here with the afternoon breeze and in southerlies it is untenable. In any case it is normally occupied by local ferries and tripper boats.

Shelter In the harbour at Órmos Valtou is good.

Anchorage In the height of summer yachts tend to anchor off on the W side of Ormos Valtou. Try not to anchor off the section of beach further E used by the water-ski and paragliding boats. It is sometimes possible to anchor in the cove under Nisís Panayia. The best policy is to arrive in the early evening when the swimmers have gone home. Anchor fore and aft as there is little room to swing here.

Note Of late there have been numerous reports of theft from yachts here. Make sure you lock up well and put any loose items away.

Facilities

Water At the root of the mole in Valtou.
Provisions At the eastern end of the beach or in Párga itself.
Eating out Numerous tavernas and bars along the beach and in Párga.
Other Water taxis run between Órmos Valtou and Párga town in summer. PO. Bank. ATM. Taxis. Hire cars and motor bikes. Ferry to Paxos.

General

Párga has developed into a major resort with the consequence that development spreads all the way around Órmos Valtou and only stops just before the harbour. There are more tavernas and bars than you can shake a stick at and in the day the beach is packed to overflowing. On a yacht you are at least lucky to be just beyond all this in the little harbour.

The castle on the promontory between the two bays is of Norman origin (c.1337). Well defended to seaward and landward by the monolithic rock on

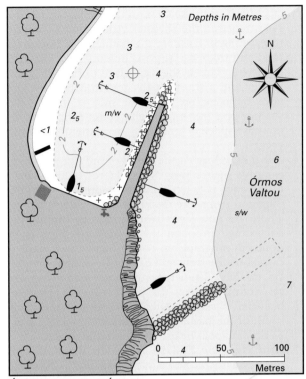

ÓRMOS VALTOU (PÁRGA)
⊕39°16′·9N 20°23·3E

which it sits, this castle has always been difficult to capture. The Venetians considered it 'the eye and ear of Corfu' and consequently the Parganiotes enjoyed special trade privileges with Venice. The notorious Ali Pasha attempted to capture the castle many times, finally succeeding in a roundabout way with the help of the English. In 1814, when the French held Párga, British agents managed to persuade the Parganiotes to overthrow the garrison

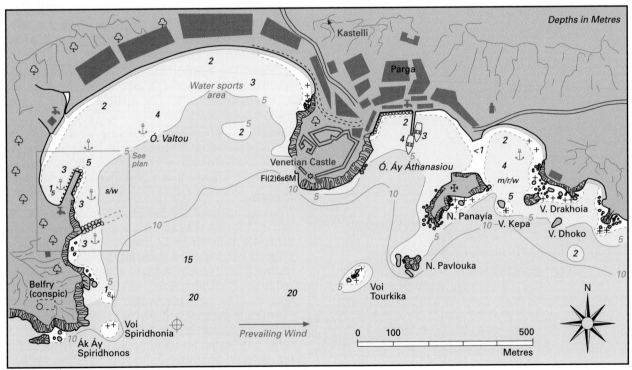

ÓRMOS PÁRGA
⊕39°16′·75N 20°23′·55E

and hand it over to the English. After holding Párga for two years the English then sold it to Ali Pasha to strengthen their claim with the Turks to the Ionian Islands. The inhabitants were evacuated to the islands, only returning generations later. Párga only became Greek in 1913.

ÓRMOS ÁY KIRIAKIS
39°16'·6M 20°26'·5E

A large bay a mile E of Nisídha Áy Nikolao (Kiriakis). A yacht can find reasonable protection from the prevailing wind in the NW corner. Anchor in 3–10m on sand and weed, good holding. Hotel and villas ashore and several taverna/bars open in the summer.

ÓRMOS ÁYIOU IOANNOU

Three miles east of Párga is Áy Ioannou, affording good shelter from the NW wind, although some swell does work its way around into the bay. Anchor in the NW corner of the bay in 4–10m on mud, rock and weed, bad holding in places. The cove in the NW corner is now obstructed by a mussel farm. On the W side of the bay a freshwater spring wells up from the bottom into the sea and the murky slow whirlpool of fresh water is easily spotted.

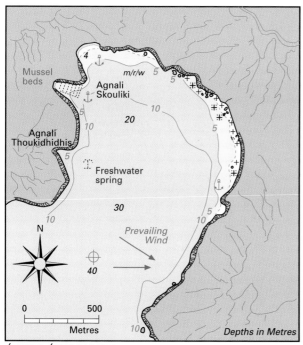

ÓRMOS ÁY IOANNOU
⊕39°16'·2N 20°28'·2E

ÓRMOS FANÁRI 39°14'·18N 20°28'·58E WGS84

Two miles south of Ioannou there is the bay of Fanári. Depths in the bay gradually shelve to the shore with 8–9m depths in the entrance decreasing to 2m around 150–200 metres off the beach at the head of the bay. Anchor under the N side of the bay outside the buoyed swimming area on mud and sand. If the prevailing NW–W wind is blowing strongly the bay is not really comfortable and may be untenable as a swell is pushed straight into it.

At the entrance on the S side is the Akheron River and it is possible to navigate up the river. Yachts usually berth upriver from the village on a wooden catwalk along the left bank of the river. The river is periodically dredged but often silts to less than 1·5m, so it would pay to reconnoitre in a dinghy first. Tavernas serving good fresh fish near the quay on the river.

TWO ROCK BAY

A cove lying approximately 2 miles S of Fanári which offers surprisingly good shelter from the NW wind. Several large rocks just in the entrance identify it. A small yacht can squeeze in – depths are not great – and anchor in 1·5–2m over a sandy bottom. There are reported to be greater depths on the S side and a yacht can anchor here in 3m.

LIGIA

A small fishing harbour lying 6M SE of Two Rock Bay. Care is needed of a reef approximately 1M NW of the harbour which is some distance off the coast. The harbour entrance is rockbound and extreme care is needed in the final approach. If any swell is running the entrance can be difficult and it is best approached in calm conditions with someone up front to con the way in. The approach is from the SE between a rocky ledge on either side. If there is space among the fishing boats go bows-to on the N quay or anchor and take a line ashore to the rough stone breakwater. Good shelter from the prevailing winds. Southerlies may send a swell in.

Taverna near the harbour and others in the village about 20 minutes' walk away. Limited provisions.

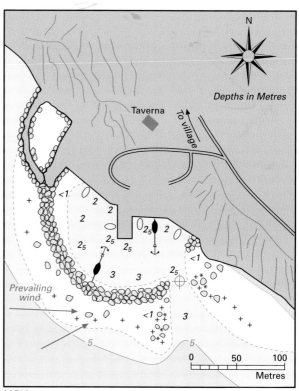

LIGIA
⊕39°09'·07N 20°34'·01E WGS84

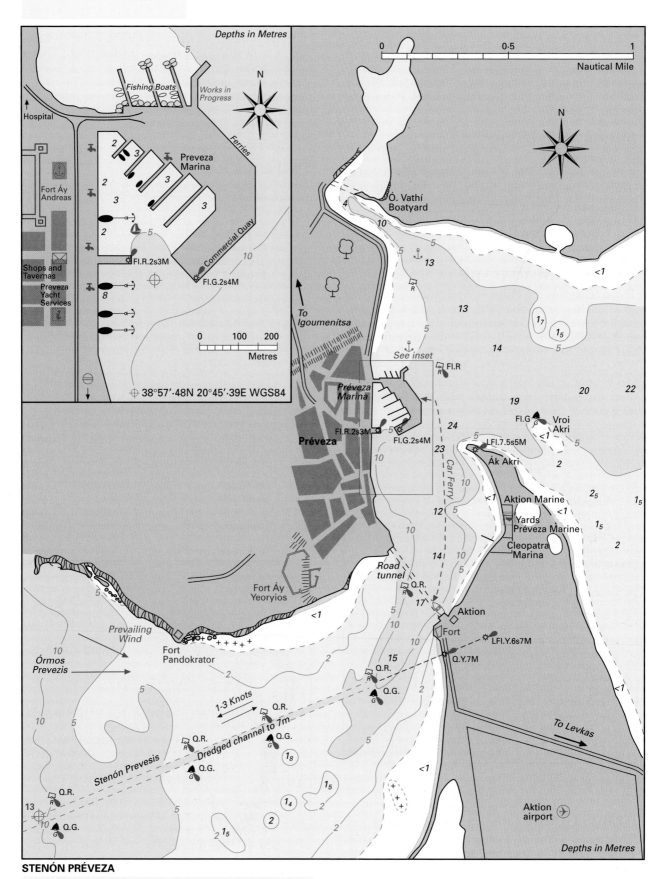

Depths in Metres

Fishing Boats

Works in Progress

Hospital

N

2

3

3

Preveza Marina

2

3

3

Fort Áy Andreas

3

3

2

Ferries

5

Commercial Quay

10

Shops and Tavernas

Preveza Yacht Services

8

Fl.R.2s3M

Fl.G.2s4M

0   100   200
Metres

⊕ 38°57'·48N 20°45'·39E WGS84

Depths in Metres

0   0·5   1
Nautical Mile

N

Ó. Vathí Boatyard

4

10

5

13

5

To Igoumenítsa

R

13

5

See inset

Fl.R

R

Préveza Marina

1₇

1₅

5

14

20   22

19

Fl.G Vroi Akri

24

Ák Akri

LFl.7.5s5M

Fl.R.2s3M

5

Fl.G.2s4M

23

Car Ferry

10

12

Aktion Marine

Yards
Préveza Marine

2₅

1₅

1₅

2

Cleopatra Marina

Préveza

10

Fort Áy Yeoryios

Road tunnel

Q.R.
R

17

14

10

5

Aktion

Fort

LFl.Y.6s7M

Q.Y.7M

<1

10

Prevailing Wind

Fort Pandokrator

Q.R.
R

5

15

Q.R.
R

10

Órmos Prevezis

10

5

2

2

Q.G.
G

2

5

<1

To Levkas

1-3 Knots

Q.R.
R

Q.G.
G

Dredged channel to 7m

Q.R.
R

Q.G.
G

1₈

5

1₅

Stenón Prevesis

Q.G.
G

1₄

2

13

Q.R.
R

<1

Aktion airport

10

Q.G.
G

2

1₅

STENÓN PRÉVEZA

⊕**13** Entrance to Preveza channel (outer buoys)
38°55'·90N 20°43'·66E WGS84

PRÉVEZA

BA 2405

Approach

Conspicuous From the N and S, a low thickly-wooded hill and Fort Áy Yeóryios on the N side of the channel are conspicuous. Aktion Airport is on the S side of the channel and planes will often be seen landing or taking off in the summer. The buoys marking the narrow channel are difficult to see from the distance. Closer in the buoys will be seen and the navigable channel is obvious.

By night Use the light on Ák Mítikas: Fl.WR.3s7/5M, the red sector covers 078°-135°. There are leading lights into the channel on 066°: Q.Y.7M and LFl.Y.6s7M. The buoys marking the channel are lit Q.G/Q.R. Ák Akrí is lit LFl.7·5s5M and the entrance harbour is lit Fl.G.2s4M/Fl.R.2s3M.

Dangers
1. A current will often be running in the buoyed channel – sometimes as much as 3 knots. The prevailing wind from the NW blowing down over the shallowing water and against the current kicks up a confused swell – uncomfortable rather than dangerous in the summer.
2. The channel is claimed to be dredged to 7m but is only 5–6m in places. Outside the channel the depths can also vary from those shown on the chart due to silting.

Mooring

Go alongside or stern or bows-to in the 'marina' or stern-to along the town quay.

Shelter Good shelter in the marina although strong SE winds cause a surge. Good shelter from the prevailing winds on the town quay but with southerlies it can be uncomfortable and may become untenable in a southerly gale.

Note Progress on the 'marina' stalled after the jetties were completed. Service boxes are installed but not connected. Moorings are yet to be laid. There is no official management and a number of charter operators and private yachts occupy much of the quay space. Works continue on the N side of the commercial quay, and care is needed of submerged concrete blocks in the area.

Authorities A port of entry. Port police, customs and immigration. Marina staff when the marina is up and running. A charge will be made.

Anchorage Órmos Vathi to the N of the harbour provides good shelter from the prevailing NW winds. Depths come up gradually as you head towards the causeway at the neck of the lagoon. Anchor where convenient on mud, good holding. The boatyard in Órmos Vathi hauls yachts.

Facilities

Services Water and electricity points are being installed. A shower and toilet block is to be constructed.

Fuel Can be delivered by mini-tanker.

Repairs **Preveza Yacht Services** can arrange repairs, spares, gardiennage, laundry and offers email services.
☎ 26820 60940 *Email* pys@pre.forthnet.gr

On Aktion to the N of the ferry pier and road tunnel are three yards, from S to N:

Cleopatra Marina Not a marina but a boatyard. 50-ton travel-hoist. 350-yacht capacity ashore. Cleopatra Marina has plans to build a mini-marina outside the yard. The small basin will have approximately 80 berths and all services. Work is yet to begin on the project.
Cleopatra Marina, PO Box 25, 48100 Préveza, Greece
☎ 26820 23015 *Fax* 26820 21414
Email clmarina@otenet.gr

Préveza Marine 50-ton travel-hoist. Large hardstanding area.
Préveza Marine, PO Box 26, 48100 Préveza, Greece
☎ 26820 24305 *Fax* 26820 29805
Email prevmar@otenet.gr

Aktion Marine Hauling by hydraulic trailer. Large hardstanding area.
Aktion Marine, Aktion, PO Box 42, Préveza, Greece
☎ 26820 61305 *Fax* 26820 61306
Email aktiomar@hol.gr; VHF Ch 09.

All of these yards can carry out most yacht repairs or arrange to have work carried out. I have had various recommendations for stainless steel work, paint jobs and mechanical repairs, but as any of these are dependant on the skills of the local contractor or the staff employed, it is best to enquire locally in case the person who once carried out excellent work has been replaced by someone who is not up to scratch. Overall the three yards attract a fair range of skills and between the yards there are good facilities for the care and repair of yachts. There are some restrictions on outside contractors in some of the yards so check before hauling if you want someone else to do work on the boat. The yards all have water, electricity, showers and toilets, workshops and other facilities.

Chandlers at the Aktion yards and hardware shops in Préveza.

Provisions Good shopping for all provisions. Ice can be ordered.

Eating out Numerous tavernas on the waterfront and in the back streets.

Other PO. OTE. Banks. ATMs. Greek gas and Camping Gaz. Buses to Igoumenítsa (limited), Levkas, and Athens. European charter flights from Aktion Airport in the summer and internal flights.

Note Since the road tunnel was completed the ferries run much less frequently, leaving the yards at Aktion a little isolated. There has been talk of the yards providing a 'ferry' service, otherwise a sturdy dinghy and outboard should be adequate for small shopping trips.

General

In the last few years Préveza has cast aside its ugly duckling status and turned into a swan, if not yet a graceful one. The waterfront has been pedestrianised and now has numerous trendy bars and cafés along it. The back streets still have the charm they always had when Préveza was a provincial market town and most people find the place grows on them.

About 3 miles N of the town are the ruins of Nikopolis built by Octavian to commemorate his victory over Anthony in the Battle of Actium. This battle fought in the approaches to Préveza effectively determined the course of the Roman Empire. The ruins are well worth a visit: a large theatre, a villa and the city walls are well preserved and a small museum houses an interesting collection of artifacts.

Amvrakikós Kólpos
(Gulf of Amvrakia)

The Gulf of Amvrakia offers some good sailing and interesting anchorages. There are also a multitude of ancient sites dotted around the edge of the gulf: Nikopolis, erected by Octavian after his defeat of Anthony; the Venetian castle at Vónitsa built on a Byzantine original; the remains of Limnaea near Karvasarás; ancient Arta and its famous bridge up the Arakthos river.

When entering the gulf from Préveza clear the harbour taking care of the works around the commercial quay. Vroi Akri and the shallows to the E are marked by two green buoys (Fl.G). Once into the gulf there are reasonable depths except around the N coast where it has silted in places and shallows may extend further than shown on the chart. Care is also needed of the reef and foul ground around N. Kefalos and close to the coast on the S side.

VÓNITSA
Approach
Once into Órmos Vónitsa the buildings of the town and the castle will be seen. The cove on the W side will not be seen until you are in the entrance. The detached breakwater off Vónitsa is easily identified.

Mooring
Go stern or bows-to on the town quay. In most places it pays to go bows-to as ballasting extends out underwater and there are bits of rock and rubble that could damage the rudder when going stern-to. Mooring bollards and rings are scarce and a jury-rigged mooring rope along the quay may be necessary.

Note Work is in progress extending the town quay westwards in front of the fort. The blocks are in place but the quay is unfinished, although much of it is already occupied with local craft.

Shelter Now the outer breakwater has been extended there is good protection from the prevailing wind on the town quay.

Anchorage Anchor in Órmos Áy Markou, the cove on the W side of the bay. It is quite deep in here, mostly 8–15m up to the edges, so take a long line ashore. Care is needed in case there is debris on the bottom from the mussel farm that used to be along the N side. It may be better to anchor off the shoal patch in 5m on the S side of the entrance. Good all-round shelter in here.

It is also possible to anchor off on the E side of Nisís Koukouvitsa. The islet, (joined to the mainland by a causeway), provides a good lee from the prevailing wind.

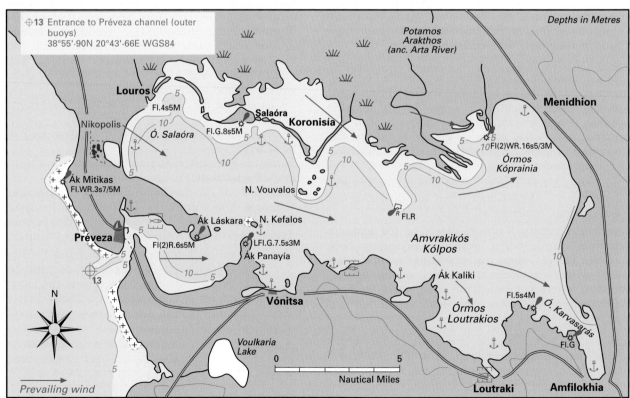

AMVRAKIKÓS KÓLPOS (Gulf of Amvrakia)

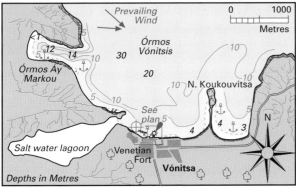

VÓNITSA AND APPROACHES
⊕38°55'·39N 20°53'·14E WGS84

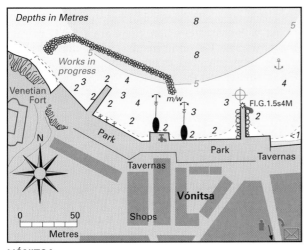

VÓNITSA
⊕38°55'·27N 20°53'·31E WGS84

Facilities

Water on the quay. Fuel in the town. Most provisions can be obtained and there are numerous tavernas. PO. OTE. Bank. The bus to Athens and Levkas stops here.

General

Above the town is a large Venetian fort (built on the site of a Byzantine fort) which offers excellent views out over the Gulf. According to Alexander Paradissis, Robert Guiscard died here of an epidemic along with 10,000 of his Norman troops . . . however, he is also supposed to have died in Fiskárdho on Cephalonia.

ÓRMOS PALAIOMILOU

38°54'·0N 21°01'·3E

A bay on the W side of Órmos Loutrakios. There is sometimes a fish farm in here although it was recently reported abandoned. Good shelter from the NW wind.

LOUTRAKI

38°52'·5N 21°04'·5E

The anchorage under the small village of the same name. Like Palaiomilou this is now obstructed by a fish farm, but you may find somewhere to squeeze in. Limited provisions and taverna in the village.

Nikopolis

After the assassination of Julius Caesar in 44BC a civil war was intermittently waged until 31BC when Octavian's victory over Anthony decided the fate of the known world. Anthony had assembled his soldiers and ships at Actium intending to invade Italy. Octavian based his fleet at Mítikas to forestall Anthony and all through the summer the opposing fleets waited for the other to move. Eventually Anthony decided to initiate an action by moving his fleet to the mouth of the estuary. Octavian waited for the afternoon NW wind and when it arrived his swifter and more manoeuvrable galleys attacked the rival fleet. The rout of Anthony's fleet was completed when Cleopatra fled taking her Egyptian ships (Anthony followed leaving his men and ships to be scattered by Octavian).

To commemorate the victory Octavian built Nikopolis (Victory City) on the site from which he commanded his victory. It soon grew to be the capital for the area and to populate it many of the inhabitants of the surrounding countryside were resettled here. The present walls encompass a city about one fifth of the area of the original city which boasted theatres, temples, baths and three harbours – one at Mítikas and two on the Gulf of Amvrakia. Here the Apostle Paul stayed a winter and wrote his Epistle to Titus. Towards the end of 4AD the city was destroyed by Alaric the Goth and though rebuilt on a smaller scale, it was soon abandoned in the face of the Slavic invasion from the North.

AMFILOKHIA (Karvasarás)

38°52'·1N 21°09'·8E

A small harbour in Órmos Amfilokhia in the SE corner of the gulf. It is possible to go alongside the quay with an anchor out to hold you off. However with a strong afternoon wind a considerable chop is pushed onto the quay and it is better to anchor off. It is very deep in here and you will have to anchor in 12–15m. The harbour is invariably uncomfortable with the prevailing wind and may become untenable.

Fuel and water in the town. Good shopping and tavernas.

Near the town are the remains of the ancient Arcanian city of Limnaea. According to H. M. Denham, in the 19th century a small volcano erupted in this bay (1847 and 1885) killing most of the fish in the gulf.

MENIDHION (Kópraina)

In the NE corner of the gulf in Órmos Kópraina is the small harbour of Menidhion. There is normally room for small to medium-sized yachts to go bows-to squeezed onto the end of the mole. Alternatively anchor off on a mud bottom – good holding. Shelter is adequate under the mole but it can become bumpy when anchored off here. If it gets untenable head for Ák Kóprainis where you can anchor under the lee of the cape and obtain good shelter from westerlies.

Several tavernas ashore, and limited provisions can be obtained in the village. A taxi can be hired here to visit Arta (18km). Little remains of ancient Arta (Ambracia), but its medieval bridge (with a

Menidhion harbour looking E

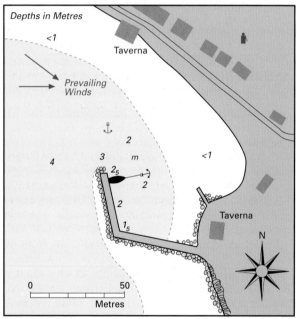

MENIDHION
⊕39°02′·5N 21°07′·1E

delightful little museum nearby) and an eccentric Byzantine church are well worth the visit.

Note
At one time it was possible to ascend the Arakhitkos River near Menidhion to Arta upriver, but the construction of a hydroelectric dam on the river now so restricts the flow of water in the summer that this is virtually impossible and moreover dangerous. Water is sometimes run off from the dam and levels increase very quickly.

VOUVALOS AND ADJACENT ISLANDS
38°59′·0N 20°55′·0E
Good shelter from the prevailing wind can be found under these islets. The islets are connected by a gravel bar and a yacht should anchor off the E side of the group. Some yachts have reported anchoring off the E side of Vouvalos although care is needed of depths. Poor holding reported. Reasonable shelter from the prevailing wind. At one time there used to be lots of mussels around the islets.

KORONISIA 39°00′·9N 20°54′·8E
A small fishing harbour between Ák Salaóra and Nisídhes Vouvalos. The entrance to the harbour has silted but small yachts can enter with care. Make the approach on a NE course and keep close to the end of the W breakwater where there are 1·5m depths in the entrance. Reconnoitre first if in doubt. Once inside there are 2m depths along the SW mole. Good shelter inside.
Tavernas ashore.

Nísos Levkas, Nísos Meganísi, and adjacent islands

Levkas is an island only because of the canal which separates it from the mainland. The present canal was built just after the turn of the century by the Greek government, although earlier canals were dug by the Corinthians around the 7th century BC and by Augustus during the Roman occupation. What appears to be an old canal cut can be seen running through the salt marsh just to the E of the present canal. The line of ruined stone on the W is the remains of an old Turkish/Venetian bridge.

The main town of Levkas is sited on a bend of the canal and in common with many other towns on this earthquake belt was rebuilt after the 1953 earthquake. Unlike Vathi on Ithaca or Zákinthos, it was not rebuilt to a style and consequently the town is a riotous jumble of corrugated iron and brick houses leaning over narrow streets. It has its own charm despite the chaotic housing and hand-me-down appearance and is in fact a major cultural centre for the area. Every August the town council sponsors music, dance and theatre from all over the world. The local band practices for weeks before to perfect its cacophonous contributions, storekeepers decorate their shops, the police bedeck the street with flags and banners and Levkas fairly bustles with locals and visitors out to enjoy themselves.

The flat salt marsh and sand spits at the northern end of the island are in marked contrast to the steep-to limestone mountain range forming the rest of the island. Most of the population is around the S and E sides of the island, which are attractively wooded in places. The large fort at the N entrance to the canal, called Santa Maura after a small chapel within its walls, was built in the Middle Ages (c.1300). Later it was used by the Turks and the Venetians. It is worth a visit to wander around the

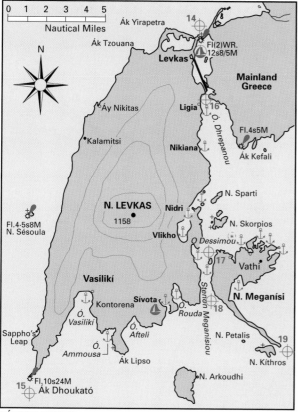

NÍSOS LEVKAS

⊕**14** N Entrance to Levkas Canal 38°50'·79N 20°43'·27E WGS84
⊕**15** 0·5M S of Ák Dhoukató (Levkas SW end)
  38°33'·17N 20°32'·46E WGS84
⊕**16** S end of Levkas Canal 38°47'·54N 20°43'·58E WGS84
⊕**17** N end Meganísi Channel 38°40'·10N 20°43'·72E WGS84
⊕**18** S end Meganísi Channel 38°37'·88N 20°43'·88E WGS84

Much of the factual basis of this book is derived from excavations by the German archaeologist Dorpfeldt who discovered Neolithic remains near Evgiros on the S of Levkas. Dorpfeldt also put forward the controversial theory that Levkas fulfills all the requirements for the Ithaca of Homer and indeed he uncovered Mycenaean remains near Sívota and Vasilikí. Dorpfeldt contended that during the Middle Ages the inhabitants of Levkas were driven from their homeland to the more remote Ithaca of today and so transferred their name and cultural identity to that island. However, archaeological opinion still favours the present Ithaca as the original home of Odysseus.

LEVKAS CANAL

BA 2405

Imray-Tetra G12, G121

Levkas canal, cut through the salt marsh between the island proper and the mainland, effectively severs it from the mainland and provides a passage for boats down the E coast of the island.

The canal is kept dredged to a minimum depth of 6m although some of it is deeper than this. The southern end of the canal is buoyed but the rest of the canal is marked by poles with red or green triangles on top. Some of the poles are missing, but normally it is fairly easy to distinguish the shallow brown water marking the edge of the dredged channel from the murky green water of the canal itself.

Approach from the N

The first approach to the northern end of the canal can be hair-raising. With the prevailing NW wind pushing you down onto a lee shore with just the canal entrance to get you out of it, most people are on tenterhooks the first time around. You should have everything prepared, all sails down and stowed, the engine ticking over and someone up front to keep an eye on any traffic coming out of the canal.

Approaching the island in the afternoon haze it is not easy to identify where the entrance to the canal is. At times the haze can obscure even the high mountains of the island and you may be only 3 or 4 miles off before you see it. Closer in the wine co-op factory and warehouse on the W side of the canal and Ayios Mavros (Santa Maura) fort on the E side will be seen against the flat sandbanks of Yera spit to the W and Pláka spit to the E. From the NW two windmills stand out on Yera spit and behind the buildings of Levkas town will be seen.

On rounding the protecting mole, two rusty 44-gallon drums (sometimes painted red) are the buoys marking the underwater rocks and shallows on the SE side of the canal entrance, though they cannot always be relied on to be in place. A sand bar extends a short distance from the western entrance-point to the canal. Although it is periodically dredged, care must be taken as it silts up and extends rapidly in the summer with the prevailing northerlies.

large complex, especially the small galley port adjacent to the E wall. At the S end of the canal is a fort built by the Venetians to guard the approaches to Órmos Dhrepanou.

On the SW corner of the island is a precipitous white cliff called Leukatas from which Levkas takes its name. This is the cliff presumed to be Sappho's Leap from which Sappho of Lésvos, the famous lyric poetess of the 6th century BC, is supposed to have flung herself. After Sappho there are records of criminals being flung from the cliffs; if they succeeded in reaching the sea unharmed, they were recovered and pardoned. There is no anchorage here although the small port of Vasilikí is nearby.

The E coast of Levkas is fringed by a number of small green islands including Skorpios, the private parkland island of the late Aristotle Onassis, and Meganísi, looking like a giant tadpole on the chart and indented on its N coast with half a dozen sheltered anchorages. This area is the setting for Hammond Innes' novel *Levkas Man* which supposes that these islands are the remains of a land bridge over which primitive man crossed from Africa to Europe.

Levkas canal N end and Levkas town looking N
Peter Kleinoth/MareTeam

Just beyond this is the floating bridge with a section that can be raised. When the section of the floating bridge is raised it leaves a 9m wide gap on the W side of the canal. For larger craft the floating bridge swivels to lie parallel to the E bank. When the bridge is going to open a siren sounds and theoretically the signal on the bridge is lowered. If that doesn't work the operator will make it plain that you are to go with much waving of the hands.

Contrary to conventional IMO regulations, traffic heading *southwards* has right of way according to a special regulation. In practice, though, northbound traffic is usually waved through first to clear traffic in the canal. Keep an eye on the operator and play it by ear. There may be a current in the canal at times, occasionally up to 1½ knots, which makes manoeuvring difficult. Levkas town is a short distance down the canal.

Note The bridge uses VHF Ch 12. Between 2100 and 0600 you will need to call up to get the bridge to open. During daylight hours the bridge opens on the hour.

Approach from the S

Fort Áy Yeoryiou is conspicuous on a summit above the E side of the entrance to the canal. Closer in you will see Nisís Voliós, an islet at the entrance with a light structure on it, and the first set of buoys marking the channel. The channel is then shown by pairs of buoys and beacons and in the salt marsh by poles with red and green triangles atop. The direction of buoyage is from Órmos Dhrepanou.

A yacht should not attempt to cut outside the buoys marking the channel: there is a reef on the E and the remains of an old breakwater on the W.

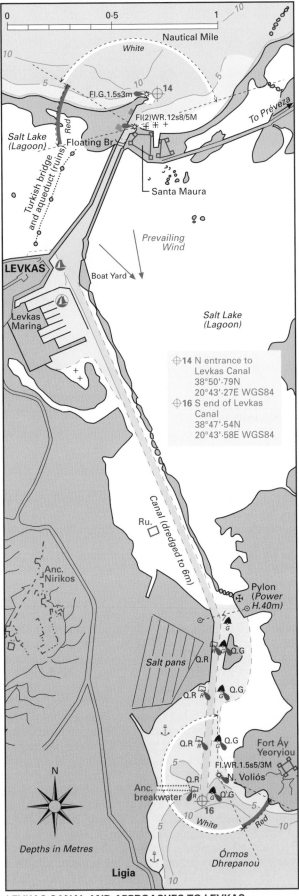

LEVKAS CANAL AND APPROACHES TO LEVKAS

The floating bridge at the N end of the Levkas Canal. For small yachts the end section of the bridge lifts up vertically and for larger yachts the whole bridge swivels out of the way, as here

By night From the N use the light on Ayios Mavros (Santa Maura) fort Fl(2)WR.12s8/5M, (red sector covers 075°-120°) and the light on the end of the short mole sheltering the entrance to the canal Fl.G.1·5s3M. Care is needed as a hotel on the waterfront in Levkas has a quick flashing red and blue neon sign which is easily mistaken for the entrance lights. In the summer the Kastro near the beach has bright spotlights at night and along with the lights of Levkas town this makes spotting the entrance lights difficult. In the summer Fort Áy Yeoryiou at the S end of the canal is spotlit and shows up well.

From the S use Ák Kefáli Fl.4s5M, Nisís Voliós Fl.WR.1·5s5/3M, (red sector covers 293°-335°), and the lights of the buoys and beacons marking the channel Q.G/Q.R.

LEVKAS TOWN

Levkas town lies a short distance down the canal at the point where the canal turns to run SE. The buildings of the town are easily seen and the location of the harbour is hard to mistake.

Mooring

Go stern or bows-to the town quay on the NE or S side. Care needs to be taken on the S side as the ballasting runs out underwater in places and a yacht should really go bows-to rather than stern-to. The bottom is sticky mud, good holding, although in places a bit soft, so your anchor pulls through it. If the harbour is very crowded a yacht can go stern or bows-to the W side of the canal just above the road bridge.

Shelter Good all-round shelter. The berths on the S side have the advantage that you are blown off the quay by the prevailing NW–W wind, but care is needed of the underwater ballasting and the wind also blows all the dust from the town across your boat. Berths on the NE quay have the prevailing wind blowing beam-on which is not normally a problem unless it is very strong or your anchor drags. Berths above the road bridge also have the prevailing wind blowing you off the quay. Southerlies set up a considerable surge for a landlocked harbour and care is needed.

Authorities A port of entry. Customs, port police and immigration.

Facilities

Services Water on the quay.

Fuel On the quay at the E corner.

Repairs A boatyard nearby. Most mechanical repairs can be carried out. Light engineering work. GRP and wood repairs. Electrical and minor electronic repairs. Some sail repairs. Chandlers. See Contract Yacht Services or Levkas Marine Centre below.

Provisions Good shopping for all provisions. Several supermarkets near the quay and other shops in the town. A good town for restocking the larder. Ice from the supermarket behind Contract Yacht Services.

Eating out Numerous tavernas on the waterfront and in the town.

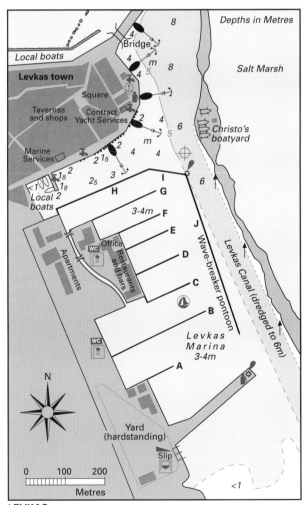

LEVKAS
⊕38°49′·98N 20°42′·78E WGS84

Other PO. OTE. Banks. ATMs. Greek gas and Camping Gaz. Hire cars and motorbikes. Occasional buses around Levkas Island. International and internal flights from Aktion.

Contract Yacht Services Contract Yacht Services will winter your yacht and get it ready for the summer. All work can be carried out: mechanic, electrical and engineering work, wood and GRP work, rigging, sail repairs and life raft servicing including certification. Chandlers and fast order system for spares and equipment from the UK.

Contact Joe Charlton, Petrou Filippa 3a, 31100 Levkas
☎ 26450 24446 *Fax* 26450 24490
Email cys@acn.gr
www.c-y-s.com

Yacht Assist Operated by Contract Yacht Services. Operates a mobile workshop and high speed RIB to attend to yacht breakdowns in the area between Corfu and Cephalonia.
☎ 26450 24446 *Fax* 26450 24490 VHF Ch 08.

Levkas Marine Centre Situated down the quay from Contract Yacht Services. Carries out mechanical and engineering work. Chandlers. Gardiennage. Life raft certification.

Levkas Marine Centre, Golemi 18-20, 31100 Levkas.
☎ 26450 25036 *Fax* 26450 25550
Mobile ☎ 693 231595

Chandlers and hardware shops in town.

General

Levkas town, as I indicated in the introduction to the island, is an odd sort of place that you either like or regard as a convenient stop en route to the north or south. I first came here in 1977 and so I have a long and ongoing association with the place that does not let me regard it objectively. For me it is a real working town that has benefited from a little tourism, but still remains mostly a business hub for the island that does not close down for the winter when the tourists have left. It will be interesting to see how it evolves when Levkas Marina is fully up and running and whether this substantially changes the nature of the place. I hope not.

Áyios Mavros (Santa Maura) fort at the N end of the canal is not the only fort on Levkas, merely the most obvious. S of present-day Levkas, the remains of ancient Levkas, or Nirikos as it was called in Mycenaean times, can just be discerned. Huge walls surrounded a town that was larger than present-day Levkas.

LEVKAS MARINA

The marina lies immediately S of Levkas town quay, with the entrance at the S end of the marina. The pontoon to enclose the N side of the marina will be installed in the near future.

Approach

VHF Ch 69.

Mooring

Data 434 berths. Visitors' berths. Max LOA 40m. Depths 2·5–4m.

Berth Berth where directed. Laid moorings tailed to the quay and pontoons.
Shelter Some berths may be uncomfortable with the chop kicked up across the harbour by the prevailing NW wind in the summer. Some berths may be affected by southerlies.
Authorities Harbourmaster and marina staff. Charge band 3.

K & G Med. Marinas Management, Lefkas Marina, 31100 Lefkas, Greece
☎ 26450 26645/6 *Fax* 26450 26642
Email lefkas@medmarinas.com
www.medmarinas.com

Facilities

Services Water and electricity (220 and 380V). Shower and toilet blocks.
Fuel Fuel quay on the S mole.
Repairs 60-ton travel-hoist. Hardstanding area. Workshops.
Provisions A minimarket in the marina. More in Levkas town.
Eating out Café/bars and restaurants in the marina.

General

Levkas Marina, open since July 2002, is part of the K & G Med. Marinas Group, who also run Gouvia, Kalamata and Zea marinas. It is a maturing development with restaurants and bars dotted around the waterfront and some shops and boutiques, but don't forget to stroll around Levkas town as well.

Note

After the recent earthquake in August 2003 (variously recorded as somewhere between 6·2 and 7·2) there has been some subsidence in the marina and around the town quay. None of it is critical but care is needed when walking around of tilted concrete slabs and sunken infill.

LIGIA

38°47'.34N 20°43'.32E WGS84

On Levkas near the southern entrance to the canal is Ligia, a small fishing harbour. Behind the mole there are 2–5m depths, but it is normally cluttered with the resident fishing boats. Go alongside or stern-to the end of the mole if there is room. Local fishing boats will soon let you know if you occupy their berth. The quay around from the mole is mostly too shallow although there are a few spots a small yacht can go bows-to if there is room amongst the local boats. Most yachts anchor off just N of the entrance in 3–7m on mud and thick weed. Make sure you get through the weed as the afternoon breeze gusts down into here and the anchor needs to be well in.

Water on the quay. Ashore limited provisions are available and there are several tavernas. The local fishing boats supply the tavernas with good fresh fish and they have some of the best fish on the island.

NIKIANA

A small harbour lying approximately 1½ miles S of Ligia. There are 2–4m depths along the outer half of

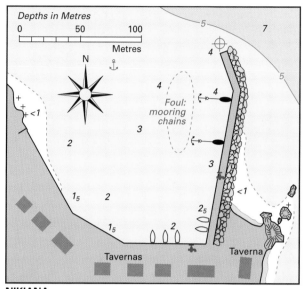

NIKIANA
⊕38°45'·6N 20°43'·25E

The baroque-style Vallaoritis villa on Nisís Madhouri

the breakwater. Go stern or bows-to the mole. Care is needed of old mooring chains fouling the bottom about 30 metres off the quay on the outer end of the mole. A number of charter boats are kept here and between the yachts and the local boats it can be difficult to find a berth. The bottom is mud, sand and weed, good holding once through the weed. Generally good shelter although it sometimes blows into here from the NNE–NE in the late afternoon making it uncomfortable.

Tavernas and some provisions ashore.

PERIYIALI

38°43'·1N 20°43'·4E

A long straight quay in the northern approaches to Nidri, partially obscured by Nisís Sparti. The quay is reasonably well sheltered from the prevailing NW wind, but should it blow overnight off the mountains on the mainland, which is not uncommon, it will blow straight onto the quay here, making it untenable. Go stern or bows-to where convenient. Ashore the main road runs adjacent to the quay and it can be quite noisy here.

NOTE

In the approaches to Nidri and Órmos Vlikho are three islands: Sparti, Kheloni and Madhouri. Off Nisís Sparti there is a 2m patch where care is needed. Between Nisís Kheloni and Levkas there are also some shallow patches off the islet and the coast of Levkas – care needed.

NIDRI

BA 2402
Imray-Tetra G121

Approach

Straightforward and there are no dangers by day. The town is obscured in the approach from the N, but the islands of Sparti, Kheloni and Madhouri make location easy and the town of Nidri will be seen in the closer approaches. From the S the town will not be seen until you are around the headland

opposite Nisís Madhouri. A night approach is not recommended for a first time entry.

Note Nidri is a watersports and yacht charter base and there are invariably yachts, motorboats, sailing dinghies, sailboards, water-bikes, tripper boats and ferries to watch out for.

Mooring

Go stern or bows-to the quay at Nidri. The quay is invariably crowded and you may have to anchor off to the S of the quay in the summer. The bottom is mud and weed, generally good holding.

To the S of the town quay there are two T-piers. The first belongs to a charter company and a berth may be available if yachts are not on turn-around. The second T-pier may also have berths available. Enquire first.

Shelter The prevailing wind tends to blow down onto the quay making it uncomfortable though not usually untenable. The wake from tripper boats and local ferries is also bothersome and berths on the quay are certainly not comfortable.

Authorities Port police.

Facilities

Water On the quay.
Fuel On the road to Vlikho. A mini-tanker can deliver to the quay.
Repairs A boatyard used to hauling yachts just S of the town and others nearby in Vlikho Bay. Hauling here is on a sledge and runners in the old-fashioned way. Mechanical repairs can be carried out. Stainless fabrication to a good standard by Steel Marine ☎ 26450 92243. Sail repairs by Sioux Sails opposite Nidri (look for the sign on the E side of the narrows going into Vlikho). Several well-stocked chandlers in Nidri.
Sioux Sails ☎/*Fax* 0030 26450 95525
Email s_sails@otenet.gr
www.siouxsails.net
Provisions Good shopping for all provisions. Ice from the fishmongers in the High Street.
Eating out Tavernas and restaurants stretch from

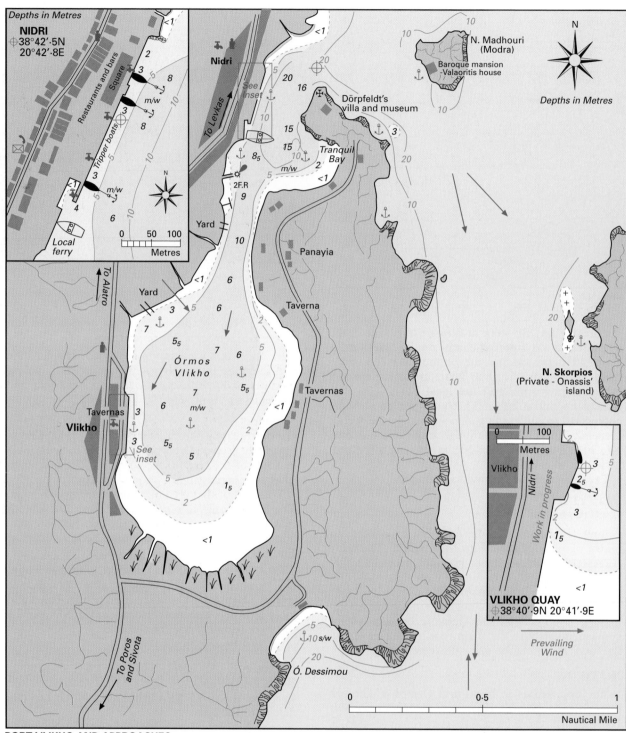

Depths in Metres
NIDRI
⊕ 38°42′·5N
20°42′·8E

Restaurants and bars
Square
Tripper boats
Local ferry
Yard

2
3
8
m/w
3
8
3
<1
4
6
5
N
0   50   100
Metres

To Alatro

To Levkas

Nidri

See inset

<1
20
16
15
15
10
2
m/w
<1

8 5
2F.R
9
Yard

10

<1
6
Yard
3   5
7   5 5
7
Órmos Vlikho
7
m/w
6
5 5
5 5
5
5
2
1 5
<1

To Poros and Sivota

Tavernas
Vlikho
3
See inset

Panayia

Taverna

Tavernas
<1

Ó. Dessimou
5
10 s/w
20

N. Madhouri (Modra)
Baroque mansion -Valaoritis house

Dörpfeldt's villa and museum

Tranquil Bay

10
10
10
20
3
10

N
Depths in Metres

N. Skorpios
(Private - Onassis' island)
20

VLIKHO QUAY
⊕ 38°40′·9N 20°41′·9E
0   100
Metres
Vlikho
Nidri
Work in progress
3
2 5
3
2
1 5
<1
5

Prevailing Wind

0   0·5   1
Nautical Mile

PORT VLIKHO AND APPROACHES
⊕ 38°42′·38N 20°42′·87E WGS84

one end of the town to the other.

Other PO. OTE. ATMs. Bank. Greek gas and Camping Gaz. Hire cars and motorbikes. Occasional bus to Levkas. Ferries to Meganísi.

General

Nidri is a busy little centre in the summer, something of a crossroads for private and flotilla yachts going N or S. Add a large watersports centre and a lot of land-based accommodation and you come up with one of the busiest resorts on Levkas.

The busy square by the harbour has a superb view out over the bay and across to the islands and the mountains of the mainland opposite.

The Baroque villa on Nisís Madhouri in the approaches to Nidri belongs to the Vallaoritis family, descendants of Aristoteles Vallaoritis (1824–79), Greece's national poet and composer of the national anthem.

Nidri and Órmos Vlikho on Levkas looking SSW

Peter Kleinoth/MareTeam

TRANQUIL BAY

Opposite Nidri town there is the large bay called (some time ago when the name was accurate) Tranquil Bay. It provides good all-round shelter in attractive surroundings. Anchor in 8–12m on soft mud and weed, good holding once your anchor is dug in. Yachts often anchor and take a long line ashore to the N side of the bay. Care needs to be taken of a shallow muddy shelf extending around the S and E side of the bay – it can be difficult to see at times. On the edge of the mudbank is the wreck of a small coaster which yachts sometimes tie onto after putting an anchor out.

The slopes around the bay are heavily wooded, mostly with olives and cypress, and there is little habitation to intrude on the peace and quiet, only the numerous other yachts that use it. A number of yachts have wintered afloat here. It is a longish row over to Nidri town for supplies or a cold beer (an outboard helps) but water can be obtained from a tap near the chapel at the entrance to the bay.

Dorpfeldt, the archaeologist who challenged the orthodox theories about the homeland of Odysseus, claiming Levkas to be the original Ithaca of Homer, is something of a folk hero in Nidri. On the N side of the bay an obelisk has been erected to his memory; just above is his beautiful villa, now administered by the Director of Antiquities in Athens. In Levkas town museum some of his finds are exhibited.

ÓRMOS VLIKHO

From Nidri and Tranquil Bay, Órmos Vlikho extends S through a bottleneck opening and opens up into an oval landlocked bay. There is good all-round shelter here and you can anchor in a number of places. The bottom is everywhere mud and weed, good holding once through the weed.

1. On the NE side of the bay. Anchor in 5–6m. Good shelter from the prevailing wind which tends to gust down from the N. Good tavernas nearby on the E side.
2. On the NW side off the boatyard. Anchor in 5–6m taking care of a shallow ledge off the NW corner. Good shelter.
3. Off Vlikho village. Anchor in 5–6m on mud and weed. Good holding. The wind tends to gust into here but the holding is good and there is no fetch for any chop to build up.
4. On the quay at Vlikho. Where the quay projects there are 1·5–2·5m depths and you can go stern-

75

to here if you can find room. There are a number of yachts which seem to berth permanently alongside taking up most of the quay space. It can be quite uncomfortable on the quay as the prevailing wind tends to push a chop onto the quay. Make sure your anchor is well dug in.

Facilities

Water On the quay, although it has been reported to be non-potable.

Fuel Fuel station on the road to Nidri or a mini-tanker can deliver if you are on the quay.

Repairs Several yards nearby. Electrics and electronics repair shop on the road to Nidri. Second-hand chandlers. Also see details for Nidri.

Provisions Minimarket. Better shopping in Nidri.

Eating out Several tavernas dotted around.

General

After Nidri, Vlikho is a quiet relaxed spot where the tourists seem either to pass by or dally for only a short time. There is talk of improving the facilities at Vlikho, but as yet little has happened and it remains a sleepy hollow compared to the booming resort at Nidri.

ÓRMOS DESSIMOU

A large bay across the isthmus from Órmos Vlikho and opposite the NW point of Meganísi. It is very deep for anchoring – anchor in the N corner in 10–15m. Good shelter from the prevailing wind. Camping ground and taverna ashore.

ÓRMOS ROUDA

38°38'·2N 20°42'·0E

A large bay on the SE corner of Levkas. A swimming area is cordoned off with small buoys at the head of the bay and you need to anchor outside this area in 12 to 15 metres. The prevailing wind gusts out of the bay but a swell may still work its way in. A number of tavernas ashore.

In the NE corner is Mikró Yialis and a short quay. The quay has mostly 1·5–2m depths off it and if there is room you could go stern-to. Most of the quay is the preserve of the local fishing boats so if you do berth here, enquire whether or not you are occupying someone's place.

ÓRMOS SÍVOTA

Approach

Entrance is easy in all weather. The entrance is difficult to make out from the distance, but closer in a number of houses on the slopes on the W side of the entrance will be seen. The houses of the hamlet cannot be seen until you are around the dogleg of the bay.

Note With the prevailing wind there will sometimes be strong gusts off the high land in the vicinity of the bay.

Mooring

Anchor where convenient in 3–10m although when there are large numbers of yachts using the bay you will be forced to anchor further out in 10–20m. The

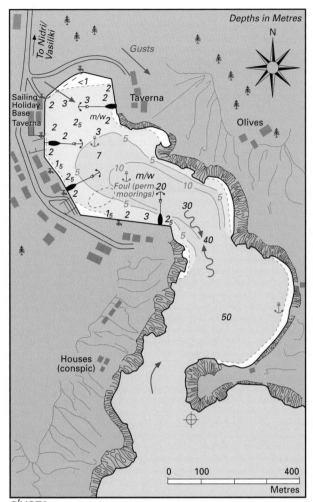

SÍVOTA
⊕38°36'·87N 20°41'·52E WGS84

bottom is mud and thick weed, good holding once through the weed though this can take some doing.

The quay along the W and S side has mostly 2–3m depths. If there is room go stern or bows-to, though it is often crowded with charter boats.

Sívota looking SE from the slopes behind

Sívota quay looking SE   *Peter Sewell*

Shelter Good all-round shelter. With the prevailing wind there are gusts into the bay so make sure your anchor is well in. Yachts are wintered afloat here.

Dangers In the SW corner of the bay there are some heavy chains on the bottom which were used as permanent moorings.

Facilities
Water Metered water on the quay.
Provisions Most provisions can be obtained.
Eating out Tavernas around the bay. Make your own choice. Also a number of bars for post dinner drinks.
Other Metered telephone. Taxis.

General
The enclosed bay with olive trees around the steep slopes is a picturesque place, though several new clusters of self-catering apartments threaten the character of the bay. The local community is largely engaged in accommodating the large numbers of yachts visiting the bay – on which the tavernas and bars largely depend for their income.

ÓRMOS VASILIKÍ (Vasilikas)

BA 2402
Imray-Tetra G121

Approach
Conspicuous The white lighthouse on Ák Dhoukaton is easily identified and once you are into the large bay the houses of Pondi at the W end of the beach will be seen. From the E the houses of Vasilikí village will not be seen until you are right into the bay.

By night Care is needed in a night approach. Use the light on Ák Dhoukaton Fl.10s24M and the light on the end of the harbour mole F.G.3M.

Dangers With the prevailing wind there are strong gusts out of the bay.

Mooring
Go stern or bows-to where convenient. The bottom is mud, good holding.

Shelter Good shelter although the prevailing wind tends to blow into the harbour. This is usually bothersome rather than troublesome, although some correspondents reckon it can be more dire than that when the wind is really gusting.

Anchorage A yacht can anchor in the bay in calm weather or light NW winds. Anchor off Pondi in 2–5m on sand.

Note The harbour is prone to silting and since my first surveys depths have already decreased substantially in the harbour.

Facilities
Water On the quay. A natural spring favours this corner of Levkas and keeps the extensive plains watered. Immediately S of the town an outdoor washing house contains four tubs through which cold spring water constantly runs.
Fuel On the outskirts of the village. You may be able to get fuel delivered to the quay.
Provisions Most provisions can be found.
Eating out Tavernas in the village.
Other PO. Metered telephone. Exchange office. Ferry to Fiskárdho.

General
Until the arrival of watersports centres here, Vasilikí was a sleepy little agricultural and fishing village. Now it deals with the summer flock of tourists in its own homespun way without neglecting the fertile agricultural plain behind the beach. For sailboard buffs the regular strong downdraughts into the bay make Vasilikí one of the top ten spots in the world for the sport – so I am told.

This is the nearest secure anchorage to the white cliffs of Sappho's leap close to Ák Dhoukaton. Here also is the site of a temple dedicated to Apollo where in antiquity panhellenic games were held to

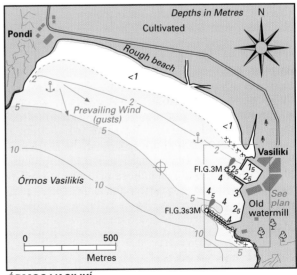

ÓRMOS VASILIKÍ
⊕38°37'·7N 20°36'·15E

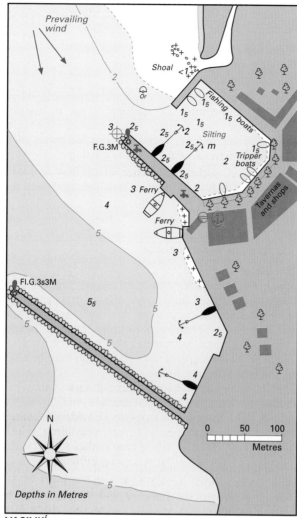

VASILIKÍ
⊕38°37'·7N 20°36'·4E

celebrate the god. Today only a few fragments and shards mark the site.

Nisís Skorpios and Skorpidhi
(Scorpio Island)

Close E of Órmos Vlikho are the twin islands of Skorpios and Skorpidhi. These are the private islands of the Onassis family, originally bought by the late Aristotle Onassis. Sailing between Skorpidhi and Skorpios you used to see *Christina*, the late Onassis' motor yacht (read ship), moored to two large buoys. The whole of Skorpios has been planted as a park and requires a considerable full-time staff to maintain it. On the SW corner there is a farm to supply fresh milk and meat, on the E side are the generating plant, warehouses and employees' houses. Unfortunately for those who buy islands to gain privacy, the very scale of the acquisition seems to attract sightseers and from Nidri a number of *caïques* run day trips around Skorpios.

You can sail around the islands, you can even anchor off the coast, but you cannot land above the high water mark. Anchor on the N or S sides where convenient. The best shelter is in the coves on the S

side. There is a cove on the SW with a small beach house that Jackie Onassis favoured. Further E is a sandy isthmus and a yacht can anchor on either side of it. The best spot is on the E side of the isthmus off a sandy beach. Anchor in 6–12m on a mud and weed bottom.

Nísos Meganísi

Imray-Tetra G121

This Rorschach blob of an island lies immediately E of Levkas. The strait between Meganísi and Levkas, Stenón Meganisiou, is one of the loveliest channels in the Ionian, with the high precipitous slopes of Levkas on one side and the lower more gentle slopes of Meganísi fringed by a beach on the other. Winds in the channel are fickle and often you will have wind from a southerly direction at the S end and a northerly wind at the N end.

The N side of Meganísi is much indented with several natural harbours and numerous enclosed bays. Most of the bays are fringed by olive and cypress with clear blue water – a combination that makes them popular with yachts though there is always somewhere to anchor in high season and a little more solitude outside of July and August.

On the SW coast of Meganísi, on the 'tail' of the island, are a number of caves. The most famous of these, 'Papa Nicolis', is quite large and rumoured by the locals to be the hiding place of a Greek submarine during the Second World War.

NÍSOS MEGANÍSI

⊕17 N end Meganísi Channel
　　38°40'·10N 20°43'·72E WGS84
⊕18 S end Meganísi Channel
　　38°37'·88N 20°43'·88E WGS84
⊕19 1M SE of Ák Kefáli (Meganísi S end)
　　38°34'·8N 20°49'·8E

Further south of this cave are a number of small but deep caves which lead 60 to 70 feet in. There is some good fishing to be had around this part of the island.

For some unknown reason Meganisi seems to be home to more wasps than anywhere else in the Ionian. It takes them seconds to locate a yacht with lunch on the go, and at times you can be inundated with these persistent, though usually benign, insects.

IFALOS HIEROMITI

Between Nisís Skorpios and Nísos Meganísi there is a shoal patch and reef. The reef is scheduled to be marked with a light structure (light characteristic unknown) which will make it a good deal easier to identify. Until the structure is installed some sort of pole is occasionally fixed to the reef. In calm weather the shoal and reef are easily seen, but with the chop from the prevailing wind it can be difficult to see. On a calm day it is possible to anchor off on one of the shoal patches and dive on the reef. If you see any yachts approaching, curious about what you are doing, please stand on the reef to give an indication that there is something there which could stop them abruptly.

SPARTAKHORI (Port Spiglia)

Approach
The village of Spartakhori perched on top of a hill on the W side of the bay is easily seen from the N and W. Once you are into the bay the small harbour will be seen.

Mooring
Go stern or bows-to the quay or short pier where possible. Most berths have laid moorings tailed to the quay to pick up. You can also go stern or bows-to the quay at the head of the bay off taverna Spilia

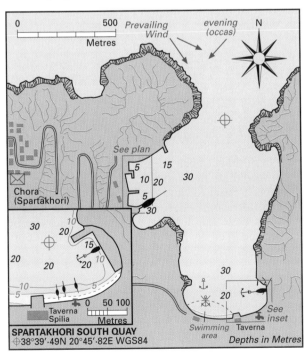

SPARTAKHORI SOUTH QUAY
⊕38°39'·49N 20°45'·82E WGS84

SPARTAKHORI (SPIGLIA)
⊕38°40'·10N 20°45'·82E WGS84

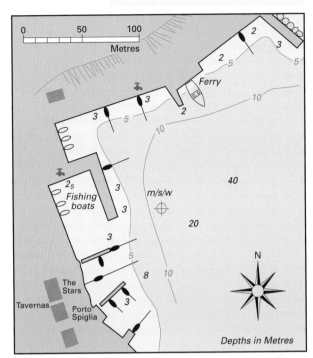

SPARTAKHORI
⊕38°39'·75N 20°45'·6E

which also has laid moorings. A new quay has recently been built around the SE corner with a stubby breakwater built out to provide additional shelter. Good shelter with the prevailing winds although the evening NE breeze makes some berths on the W side of the harbour uncomfortable.

Anchorage Anchor off the beach at the head of the bay. It is deep here and you will be anchoring in considerable depths as the buoyed swimming area means you must anchor a fair way out.

Facilities
Minimarket at the harbour and limited water from the tavernas. Fuel by mini-tanker. Tavernas by the harbour, at the head of the bay, and in the village.

General
The village is reached by a winding cypress-lined road and is worth the hot walk to reach it. From a bend in the road before you get to the village you have a view over the whole of the N part of the inland sea. Even if you eat at the bottom, it is well worth the steep climb up to the village for both the stupendous view and the enchanting village itself.

PORT VATHI

Approach
The entrance to the bay is difficult to determine and you cannot see the houses of the hamlet until you are well into the bay itself.

Mooring
Anchor in the bay or go stern or bows-to in the harbour. Good shelter from the prevailing winds. A NE wind can blow in the evening making things a bit rolly, although it generally dies down after a few hours.

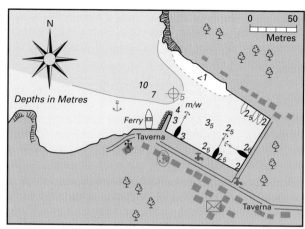

VATHI
⊕38°39′·8N 20°47′·0E

VATHI MARINA

On the W side of the bay at Vathi a small yacht harbour has been planned. It is not known when, or even if, work will begin.

ÓRMOS KAPALI AND ABELIKE

Two large indented bays between Vathi and Atheni. There are no dangers apart from a few reefs, easily seen, extending a short distance off the rocky coast. From the plan it is apparent there are numerous places in which a yacht can anchor.

There are considerable depths in both bays, mostly 10–15m until close to the coast. Anchor where convenient and take a long line ashore – there is little room in the bays to swing to an anchor. The bottom is mud and weed, good holding once through the weed.

The coves in the two bays can get crowded in the summer, but these are peaceful places for all that. There are no facilities and nor should there be. It is about a 10-minute walk from Kapali over the saddle to Vathi.

Note

1. In Abelike part of the bay is now buoyed off for swimmers. A road has been cut around the coast from Vathi and it is likely more land-based tourists will use the bays in the future.
2. In some of the bays laid moorings have been put down, but the legality of these is dubious so play it by ear.
3. There have been reports here of bold rats attracted to the rubbish left by yachts on the shore. Since I and a lot of other skippers expended some energy keeping the place clean in years gone by, I'd suggest that anyone visiting here do likewise. It is not a place to dump or bury rubbish.

Port Spiglia looking W with the *chora* of Spartakhori on top of the hill *Lu Michell*

Facilities

Water close to the quay, although it is often turned off in the summer. Limited provisions and several tavernas.

General

The small village is the nominal capital of the island, though the dusty little place hardly acknowledges it. It is a charming place, seemingly half asleep in summer. Good walks inland through the olive groves.

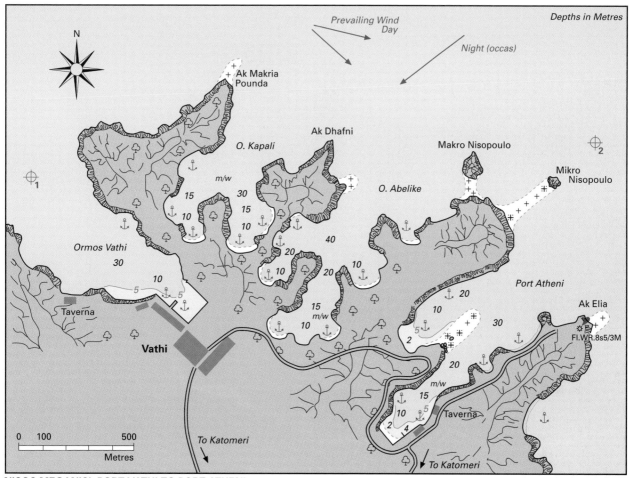

Depths in Metres

Prevailing Wind Day

Night (occas)

Ak Makria Pounda

O. Kapali

Ak Dhafni

Makro Nisopoulo

Mikro Nisopoulo

O. Abelike

m/w

15 30

15

10 10

40

Ormos Vathi

30

20

10 20 10

10 20

Port Atheni

Ak Elia

Fl.WR.8s5/3M

Taverna

Vathi

10

5 5

Taverna

15 *m/w*

10

20

10

30

20

m/w

15

10 5

2 4

Taverna

To Katomeri

To Katomeri

0 100 500

Metres

NISOS MEGANISI: PORT VATHI TO PORT ATHENI
⊕₁ 38°40′·60N 20°48′·70E WGS84
⊕₂ 38°40′·26N 20°46′·60E WGS84

PORT ATHENI

Approach

From the N and W the two islets of Megálo Nisopoulo and Mikró Nisopoulo are easily identified. From the E the light structure on the E side of the entrance will be seen. Pass to seaward of the two islets as a reef connects them to Meganísi.

Note There is a reef running out into the middle of the bay. Most of it is just underwater and numbers of yachts run up on it in the summer. Care needed!

Mooring

There are several places to anchor.

1. Most boats anchor on the NW side of the bay with a long line ashore. Most of the bay is quite deep, 10–20m except at the head of the bay. The bottom is sand and weed, good holding.
2. On the E side of the bay.
3. At the head of the bay clear of the concrete quay. It is quite deep until the very end. The bottom is mud, sand, and thick weed, good holding once through the weed.
4. Bows-to the rough quay off the *Niagas* taverna. It shallows up to the quay so go bows-to rather than stern-to.
5. Bows-to the concrete quay further into the bay. A quay now runs right around the head of the bay. The south end is crowded with local boats, but in

any case is mostly shallow, with less than 1m depths off the quay. Depths of 2–4m can be found along the outer end of the quay.

Shelter There is generally good shelter although a NE wind sometimes blows at night. It usually dies down after several hours.

Port Atheni on Meganisi

Meganísi looking SE to Port Vathi and across to Órmos Kapali,
Abelike and Port Atheni   *Peter Kleinoth/MareTeam*

Facilities

Niagas taverna on the E side. Some provisions and
tavernas at Katomeri. Fuel in Katomeri. It may be
possible to arrange delivery by mini-tanker.

General

It is about 15 minutes' picturesque walk through the
olive groves to the small village of Katomeri, though
remember to take a torch if returning at night –
there are no streetlights here.

ÓRMOS EPANO ELIA

The bay tucked under the E side of Ák Elia. Anchor
off the beach. The afternoon wind will often not
reach here until later and sometimes not at all. A
useful lunch stop and in settled weather a possible
overnight anchorage.

ÓRMOS KATO ELIA

The more indented bay further S. Anchor in 6–10m.
A few local fishing boats use the bay. You can walk
up to Katomeri from here.

Nísos Ithaca
(Ithắki)

According to Homer this is the island home of
Odysseus. Archaeologists can dispute whether or
not this is so, but Homer still provides the best
description of the island:

'In Ithaca there are not wide courses, nor meadowlands
at all. It is a pasture land of goats, and more pleasant in
my sight than one which pastureth horses...,

Homer *Odyssey*

The island consists of two peninsulas connected
by a narrow isthmus which is the backbone to
Kólpos Aetou (Gulf of Molo). The steep-to
mountains are bare and rocky, although in a few of
the valleys there is a swathe of green fed by some
small subterranean spring.

In common with many of the Ionian Islands,
Ithaca has a strong seafaring tradition and many of
the young make their living in the merchant navy.
Many more have emigrated to Australia or South
Africa, although a substantial number do return and
it is not unusual to be greeted by an Australian
'G'day sport!' around the island.

The important port on the island is Port Vathi, although there are a number of other harbours and anchorages. At Port Polis, a bay below the town of Stavrós, the local school teacher looks after a small museum housing a collection of items from excavations on the supposed site of Odysseus' palace. Although the site of the palace has not been conclusively proved, a number of tripods and masks indicating later hero worship of Odysseus have been unearthed. Certainly the fact that Ithaca is on a major fault line may mean that the Homeric palace was completely buried by an earthquake, or perhaps the subject of Homer's epic lived in a comparatively modest dwelling.

ITHACA CHANNEL (Stenón Ithakis)

Caution With the prevailing afternoon W–NW breeze there are strong gusts off the high land into the Ithaca Channel and off the E side of Ithaca. In July and August when the *maistro* is blowing these gusts can be quite severe. The most notorious spots are the S end of the Ithaca Channel, Órmos Frikou, and Kólpos Aetou (Gulf of Molo).

FRIKES

Imray-Tetra G121

Approach

A small harbour tucked into the W corner of Órmos Frikou on the NE of Ithaca. The buildings of the hamlet will not be seen until closer in, when two windmills on a bluff by the hamlet are conspicuous. Care must be taken of above and below-water rocks around the islets under Ák Áy Nikoláou.

By night The end of the mole is lit Fl.R.2s3M. The floating pontoon is lit with weak white lights along its length.

Note With the prevailing wind there are strong gusts out of Órmos Frikou and care is needed.

Mooring

Go stern or bows-to wherever there is room. In the summer many yachts go alongside because of the strong gusts into the harbour and you may well find that you will have to go alongside another yacht if the harbour is crowded. It is intended to install laid moorings at some time. Larger yachts can go stern-to the outside of the mole with a long line to it, keeping clear of the ferry berth.

Shelter The prevailing wind gusts down into here but once tied up it is a safe harbour. Strong NE winds could cause a problem. Southerlies cause a surge. Wash from fast ferries now rebounds inside the harbour and can damage yachts.

Authorities Port police. Charge band 2.

Note The recently installed pontoon has an alarming undulation with a southerly swell. It is likely that a good southerly blow will damage it in its present exposed position.

Facilities

Services Water and electricity on the quay and pontoon.

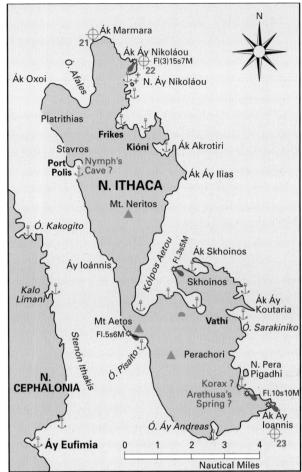

NÍSOS ITHACA

⊕21 0·25M N of Ák Marmara (Ithaca N end)
     38°30'·47N 20°38'·93E WGS84
⊕22 0·25M E of Ák Áy Illias (Ithaca NE end)
     38°26'·07N 20°42'·91E WGS84
⊕23 0·25M E of Ák Áy Íoannis (Ithaca SE end)
     38°19'·20N 20°46'·36E WGS84

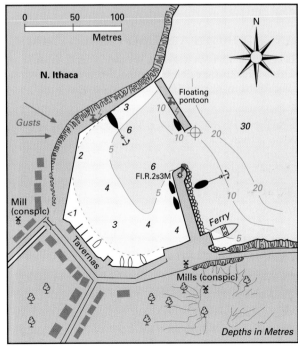

FRIKES
⊕38°27'·60N 20°39'·91E WGS84

Ithaca and Odysseus

Despite the paucity of archaeological evidence for Ithaca as the island home of Odysseus and despite Dorpfeldt's claim that Levkas is the real Ithaca, the Ithaca of today remains the favoured archaeological choice. Consequently the places on the island mentioned in Homer have nearly all been identified on Ithaca.

Port Polis is the harbour of ancient Polis which stood on the ridge above. Just N on the summit of a hill called Pelikata are the ruins of a Bronze Age settlement which is generally accepted to be the palace of Odysseus. Some of the walls and a section of paved road are all that remain. On the N side of Port Polis there existed a cave, the Cave of the Nymphs, where archaeologists have found Mycenaean pottery and bronze relics including a number of tripods and terra cotta masks indicating later hero worship of Odysseus.

Port Frikes can be identified with the Reithron of the *Odyssey*.

Órmos Pera Pigadhi lies at the bottom of Arethusa's spring. The spring still flows today and above it is the raven's rock (*Korax*) of the *Odyssey*, still called by the same name today. Above here lies the plateau of Marathia and it is probably here that Odysseus met Eumaneus the swine herd.

On Mt Aetos, on the narrow peninsula joining the two halves of the island, are the scanty remains of what may have been a shrine or temple.

All of this is largely speculation, and indeed Dorpfeldt was able to single out equally convincing sites on Levkas.

Provisions Most provisions can be found.
Eating out Tavernas around the waterfront.
Other Ferries to Fiskardho and Vasiliki in the summer.

General

The village is a picture postcard place, set at the bottom of a wooded ravine with a stream running down to the sea keeping everything green through the summer. A couple of windmills sit above the village on a rocky crag. Inevitably this once isolated village has begun to attract tourists, but it is still a gem and well worth a visit.

ANCHORAGES AROUND ÓRMOS FRIKOU

In general the anchorages on the N and W side of Órmos Frikou are the best with the prevailing wind. The bottom is mostly mud, shingle and weed, not everywhere good holding.

Port Áy Nikólaos The bay under Ák Áy Nikoláou. Good protection though there are gusts.

Khondri Pounda Reasonable shelter though some swell may work its way into here.

Limenia A two-headed bay under Ák Khondri Pounda. There is a watersports centre in the W cove. Reasonable shelter.

Damouri Immediately E of Frikes. Poor shelter.

Mavrounas Calm weather anchorage.

Vathi Limani Calm weather anchorage. Ruined monastery ashore.

PORT KIÓNI

BA 2402

Approach

Straightforward, and there are no dangers from N or S. The three ruined windmills on the S point of the bay and the cluster of houses on the saddle of the hill are easily distinguished.

By night The end of the short mole in the bay is lit F.G.3M.

Note With the prevailing NW wind there are strong gusts down into the bay.

Mooring

Go stern or bows-to the quay. As the bottom shelves steeply you must drop your anchor in quite deep water, so have plenty of scope ready. Alternatively anchor off, though again, because it is so deep, you will be anchoring in 10+m. Because of limited swinging room it is probably better to anchor and take a long line ashore to the SW side of the bay or to the head of the bay. The bottom is hard mud and weed, uncertain holding in places.

Shelter With the prevailing wind there are strong gusts down into the bay, so ensure that your anchor is well in and holding. In southerlies a surge builds up and the harbour can become untenable. In strong southerlies it is better to head for Vathi.

Note In calm weather or light W winds a yacht can anchor off the cemetery in the SE, though again depths are considerable for anchoring.

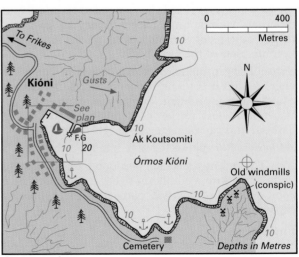

ÓRMOS KIÓNI
⊕38°26'·84N 20°42'·17E WGS84

Frikes looking W into the harbour

Kióni looking WNW into the bay   *Nigel Patten*

Kióni harbour looking NE from just inside the stub mole

Facilities

There is no water supply other than cisterns. Some provisions (baker, grocer) can be found. Tavernas on the waterfront.

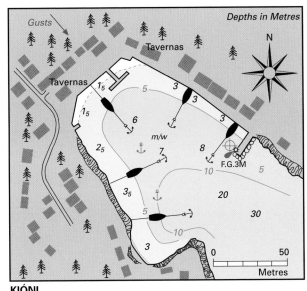

KIÓNI
⊕38°27'·0N 20°41'·5E

General

Kióni is an attractive huddle of whitewashed houses around the slopes at the head of the bay. If the place seems to have more houses than people, this is because a large part of the population has emigrated to Australia and the USA and many of the houses are still owned by these expatriates. In twenty years the school roll has fallen from some 600 to 20. A *caïque* runs from here to Port Vathi in the season. Pleasant walks over the saddle to a number of small coves.

ANCHORAGES AROUND KÓLPOS AETOU

Imray-Tetra G12

Órmos Aetou In calm weather you can anchor in the SW corner of the gulf. Anchor in 5–10m on the W. Care is needed of the reef about half way along the bay.

Órmos Dexia The bay under Nísos Katzurbo. In calm weather anchor in 5–12m.

Órmos Skhoinos The large bay under Ák Skhoinos. Anchor in 8–12m in the NE or SW corner. Tenable in light W winds.

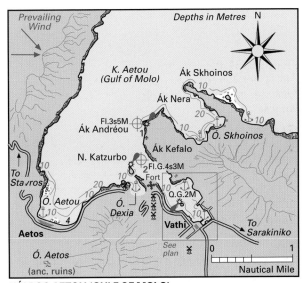

KÓLPOS AETOU (GULF OF MOLO)
⊕1 38°23'·14N 20°42'·01E WGS84
⊕2 38°22'·66N 20°42'·06E WGS84

VATHI (Ithaca)

BA 2402
Imray-Tetra G12

Approach

Conspicuous From the N and S a belfry and the earthworks scar of the road on Mt Korini are conspicuous. Once into Kólpos Aetou (Gulf of Molo) the light structure and the chapel on Ák Áy Andréou are easily distinguished. The light structure on Nisís Katzurbo, the small island at the bottleneck entrance to Port Vathi, will also be seen.

By night Use the lights on Ák Áy Andréou Fl.3s5M and on Nisís Katzurbo Fl.G.4s3M. Once into Port Vathi use the light on the small islet in the harbour Q.G.2M.

Dangers With the prevailing wind there are severe gusts down into Kólpos Aetou.

Mooring

Go stern or bows-to the quay on the W under the ferry berths. Alternatively go stern-to the outside of the mole sheltering the basin. Yachts also go stern or bows-to the protruding bit of quay at the head of the bay. The quay in the NE corner of the bay has been widened, making it possible for yachts to go stern or bows-to, keeping clear of fishing boat berths. The depths increase quickly off the quay and you will be dropping the anchor in depths of 10–15m so have plenty of scope ready. The bottom is everywhere mud and thick weed, not the best holding until you get your anchor through the weed.

Shelter The prevailing wind tends to blow into the bay with some force so make sure your anchor is well in and holding. Once the breeze dies at dusk you will have no further worries. No sea enters with the wind and as long as care is taken in anchoring there is good all-round protection.

Authorities Port police and customs.

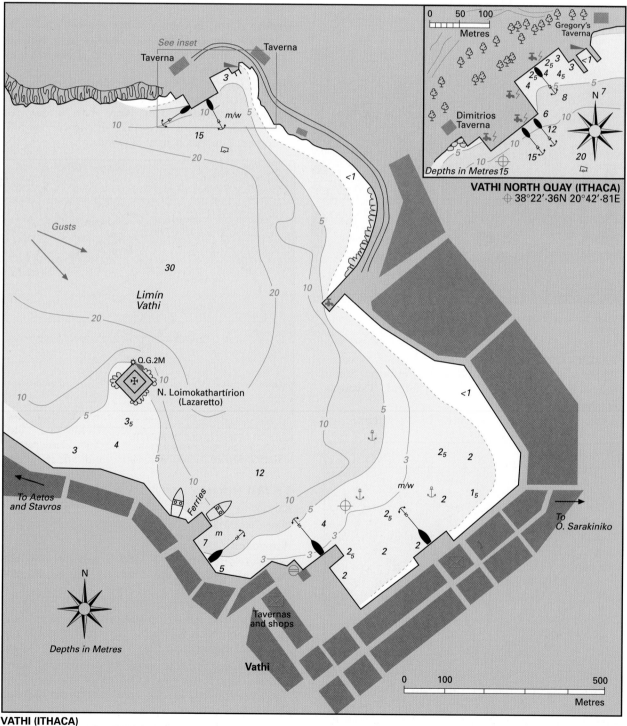

VATHI NORTH QUAY (ITHACA)
⊕ 38°22'·36N 20°42'·81E

VATHI (ITHACA)
⊕ 38°21'·95N 20°43'·14E WGS84

Vathi on Ithaca looking NW out to Kólpos Aetou
Peter Kleinoth/MareTeam

Anchorage Anchor off at the head of the bay in 2–5m. The anchorage is exposed to the gusts blowing in, but as long as your anchor is in and holding it is safe enough here.

Facilities
Services Water can be delivered by mini-tanker to the town quay. Water and electricity boxes on the north quay.
Fuel Can be delivered by mini-tanker to the town quay and the north quay.
Repairs Limited mechanical repairs only.
Provisions Good shopping for all provisions. Ice available.
Eating out Numerous tavernas in the town. There are also two tavernas in the N bay.
Other PO. OTE. Bank. ATM. Motorbike and car hire. Ferries to Patras, Corfu and Italy.

General
Vathi suffered severe damage in the 1953 earthquake, but although most of the town around the harbour is new, it is not an unattractive place. The port hums and bustles with *caïques* coming and going and when the Patras–Brindisi ferry arrives most of the town turns out to watch. Vathi is the best place to leave a yacht and hire a car or motorbike to explore the island – Stavrós, the likely site of Odysseus' palace, is about a one hour drive.

In late August there is an Ithaca theatre festival at Vathi.

ÓRMOS SARAKINIKO
38°21'·9N 20°44'·4E

A bay on the E coast of Ithaca immediately below Ák Sarakiniko (Ák Áy Koutaria). Anchor in 3–10m off the beach on sand, rock and weed. Reasonable protection from the prevailing wind which gusts down from the W. The bay is a delightful spot and in settled weather can be used as an overnight anchorage. Just over the saddle of the ridge is Vathi town, about an hour's walk.

PERA PIGADHI
Imray-Tetra G121

On the SE side of Ithaca the small islet of Pera Pigadhi lies close to the coast. It is difficult to distinguish until you are close to. South of the islet on Ithaca is Órmos Pera Pigadhi.

Anchor in Órmos Pera Pigadhi or just S of the islet. There is room for a few yachts to go alongside the small quay on the islet. There are 4m least depths through the channel between the islet and Ithaca, though the water is so clear it is difficult to believe you are not going to touch bottom. Outside the channel depths drop off quickly and you will

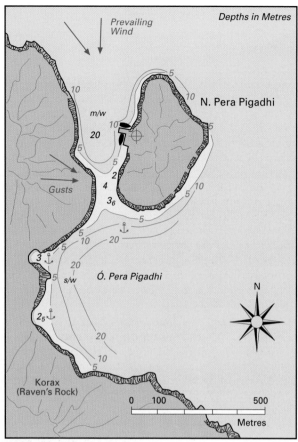

PERA PIGADHI
⊕38°20'·15N 20°44'·80E

usually be anchoring in 10–20m in the bay or S of the islet. The bottom is sand and weed, good holding.

The afternoon breeze does not get here until mid-afternoon, when, unless you are tucked right into Órmos Pera Pigadhi or securely on the quay, it may become untenable. There have been a number of reports of very big and bold rats on the island that have no hesitation in invading a yacht moored overnight on the quay.

The steep-to slope above Órmos Pera Pigadhi is called Koraka, corresponding to the *Korax* in the *Odyssey*.

ÁYIOS ANDREAS

38°18'·2N 20°43'·5E

An impressive deserted anchorage on the S of Ithaca. Anchor in 8–15m at the head of the bay or in the cove on the W with a long line ashore. Some swell enters with the prevailing wind pushing down the Ithaca channel, uncomfortable rather than untenable. Open to the S.

ORMOS PIS'AITOU

⊕ 38°21'·0N 20°41'·1E

A bight on the waist of the W coast of Ithaca opposite Kolpos Aetou. The anchorage is suitable only in calm weather as the prevailing NW wind sends a considerable swell in. Anchor in 5–15m on mud and weed. There is a miniature harbour and a ferry quay, but there is little room for yachts.

PORT POLIS

38°26'·4N 20°38'·5E

A large bay on the NW side of Ithaca. Anchor off the beach or go stern-to on the end of the small mole. The bottom shelves steeply, so you will have to anchor in 10–20m. With the afternoon breeze gusting down the channel between Cephalonia and Ithaca it can be uncomfortable in here, but usually not untenable. Southerlies blow straight into the anchorage and a yacht should go to Fiskárdho in the event of S winds.

Cephalonia
(Nísos Kefallínía)

Across the narrow sea strait from Ithaca lies Cephalonia, the largest in area of the Ionian Islands. Like Ithaca, Cephalonia is rugged and steep-to. Starting at the N end of the island a jagged mountain spine runs S to the highest mountain of the Ionian Islands, Mount Nero, standing over 1,600m (5200ft) above sea level. Most of the slopes are bare rock, but in the valleys, particularly on the E side of the island, beautiful pine forests run down to the sea. Much of this forest is composed of a local

CEPHALONIA (NÍSOS KEFALLÍNÍA)

⊕20 N end Ithaca Channel
38°28'·47N 20°35'·73E WGS84
⊕23 0·25M E of Ák Áy Íoannis (Ithaca SE end)
38°19'·20N 20°46'·36E WGS84
⊕24 1M S of N.Vardhiánoi light (Cephalonia SW end)
38°06'·9N 20°25'·6E
⊕25 0·5M W of Ák Áy Theodhoroi (Kólpos Argostoliou)
38°11'·5N 20°27'·5E
⊕26 2·25M E of Ák Mounda (Cephalonia SE end)
38°03'·20N 20°49'·97E WGS84

fir tree, *Abies cephalonica*, a tall slim pine which, despite its name, grows elsewhere in Greece.

In ancient times Cephalonia formed part of the kingdom of Odysseus, and here at least archaeologists have been able to find evidence of the ancient sites mentioned in Homer. There were four important towns: Pale, Krane, Same, and Pronoi. Same or Sami (similarly Pale-Pali and Krane-Krani) was the most important town built on the heights immediately N of the small ferry port of the same name. Extensive ruins of all four towns remain, those at Krani being particularly well preserved relics of Mycenaean occupation. The tombs here are said to be the best examples of Mycenaean tombs in Greece.

Like many of the Ionian Islands, Cephalonia has close links with Italy, and a wartime story is often told which illustrates just how strong this association can be. The Italians invaded the islands in the early days of the Second World War but failed to gain real control. In 1943 the Germans landed in Cephalonia, but the occupying Italian force, some 9,000 troops of the Alpine Division, not only refused to co-operate but actually fought against them for seven days. Of the Italian force only 3,000 survived, and these were brutally lined up and shot, it is said on Hitler's personal orders. Only 34 survived and, so the story goes, one of the survivors swam to Ithaca where he was sheltered by the local Greeks until he escaped. Until recently he was captain on one of the Patras–Brindisi ferries and every time he passed Ithaca gave a long toot on the ship's horn to salute his Greek friends.

Captain Corelli's Mandolin, the novel by Louis de Bernières, picks up on this theme and is well worth reading for a fictional account that incorporates this awful bit of Second World War history. Recently it has been made into a film, though interestingly the governor of Cephalonia censored some of the material on the role of the communists in the war, and the film is neutered by this censorship.

Cephalonia produces some good wines, though not from its Italian connection but from local initiative, the French and, surprisingly, an Englishman. Although not cheap by Greek standards (in fact nearly double the price of the ubiquitous Demestica), the Robola whites and reds are excellent and for those who like a rosé, the Manzavino is also good.

The earthquake belt that blights the other Ionian Islands likewise touches Cephalonia. Edward Lear, when he was touring the Ionian Islands, recorded 43 small tremors in 1863 alone. The major earthquake of 1953 effectively demolished every town on Cephalonia except Fiskárdho, because, it is said, it sits on a bed of soft clay. One inhabitant of Argostoli who experienced the '53 quake described to me how the ground undulated like a three-foot swell on the sea. In some of the rebuilding of Cephalonia there is a sameness about the reinforced concrete architecture that contrasts poorly with the gentle nineteenth-century grace of Fiskárdho.

ARGOSTOLI (Argostolion)

BA 2402

Imray-Tetra G12

Approach

Conspicuous From the W the large lighthouse on Ák Yero-Gómbos is conspicuous. From the E Nisís Thionisi and a white hotel on Ák Pelagia are easily identified. Closing the low-lying Nisís Vardhiánoi it is safe to pass between it and Cephalonia, but a more prudent course is to stand off leaving the island to port and then proceed up the Gulf of Argostoli. Once you are in the Gulf of Argostoli, the town of Lixouri and a Doric-style lighthouse on Ák Áy Theodhoroi are conspicuous. Rounding the green wooded slopes of Ák Áy Theodhoroi keep to the middle of the inlet that forms the harbour of Argostoli. Leave the concrete beacon to starboard – although there are three metre depths between the beacon and the docks, there are also shoal patches close to the docks.

By night Use the light on Ák Yero-Gómbos LFl(2)15s24M and closer in the light on Nisís Vardhiánoi Fl.WR.7·5s6/4M (red sector covers 080°-107°). (The range of the light on Nisís Vardhiánoi appears to be less than stated.) Once into the gulf use the light on Ák Áy Theodhoroi Fl.3s5M and the light on the beacon Fl.G.3s3M.

The marina entrance is lit Fl.R/Fl.G.

Dangers Care is needed of the reef running SE from Ák Pelagia and of the reef running W from Ák Áy Nikólaos.

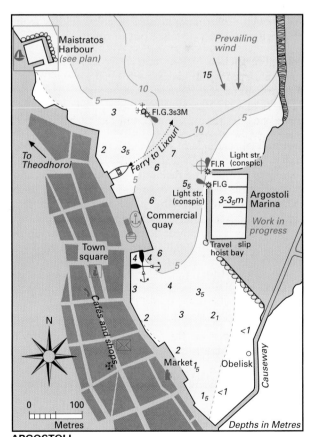

ARGOSTOLI
⊕38°10'·90N 20°29'·76E WGS84

Note With a fresh afternoon breeze blowing down into the approaches to Argostoli (regularly Force 5–6 in the summer) it can be hair-raising entering this dead-end inlet for the first time.

Mooring
Berth stern or bows-to the S of the ferry quay or on the N end of the W quay. If clearing into Greece go on the S side of the ferry quay within the customs enclosure. The bottom is mud, good holding.

Shelter The ferry quay provides a good lee from the prevailing wind whistling down into the inlet.

Authorities A port of entry. Port police, customs and immigration.

Note See entries which follow for Argostoli Marina and Maistratos harbour.

Facilities
Water On the quay.

Fuel Can be delivered by mini-tanker. The nearest fuel station is near the market to the S of the yacht quay.

Repairs Mechanical and engineering work can be carried out. Electrical work. According to reports good emergency repairs have been carried out here. Good hardware shops but limited chandlery available. A small boatyard at Maistratos Harbour can haul yachts but there is limited hard-standing.

Provisions Good shopping in the town for provisions. Ice can be delivered.

Eating out Numerous tavernas in the town.

Other PO. OTE. Banks. ATMs. Greek gas and Camping Gaz. Hire cars, motorbikes and bicycles. Buses to most parts of Cephalonia. Regular car ferry to Lixouri. International and internal flights from the airport a short distance out of town.

General
In previous editions I have described Argostoli as looking 'like a frontier town – a Greek setting for a spaghetti western'. In recent years the town has metamorphosed into something which can almost be called chic. The pedestrianised main street has become all caffè latte and baguette, with outdoor cafés in between fashionable boutiques and jewellery shops. The residents take their coffee and conversation in a relaxed atmosphere and the hum of conversation lends the place an Italianate feel which of course is not out of place.

On Ák Áy Theodhoroi there is a reconstruction of the mill built by an Englishman, Stevens, in the 19th century. It is powered by the sea pouring into subterranean channels – a team of Austrian scientists, by putting a dye in the water, showed that it eventually reappears at Melissani near Sami. The flow of water is now much reduced after the 1953 earthquake. Also on the headland is the Doric-style lighthouse, which is conspicuous from seawards.

ARGOSTOLI MARINA
38°10'·90N 20°29'·76E WGS84

Note At the time of writing a large sign prohibits any boats from entering and, given that the local

Argostoli Marina looking across to the town quay

boat owners have not moved in, I think we can assume the authorities mean it.

Approach
The marina is on the E side of the arm running S to Argostoli docks. The light structures on the entrance are conspicuous.

By night The marina entrance is lit Fl.R/Fl.G.

Mooring
Data c.250 berths. Max LOA c.30m. Depths 3–3·5m.

Berths Will be stern or bows-to with laid moorings. The marina has been dredged to 3–3·5m.

Shelter All-round shelter.

Facilities
Yet to be installed. Planned are water and electricity, toilet and shower block, fuel quay, and there is a travel-hoist bay with large hardstanding area nearby.

General
The structure of the marina is complete but as yet no facilities have been installed. It may be that the marina will be sold to a private operator or that the NTOG will hand the marina over to the local council.

MAISTRATOS HARBOUR
Approach
This small harbour with a mix of fishing boats and yachts lies approximately 1000m N of the commercial docks. The breakwater and boats inside are easily identified when heading down into the inlet towards Argostoli.

By night The entrance is lit Q.Y(occas).

Mooring
There is little room for visiting yachts. The best policy is to head for Argostoli and then walk up and enquire about a berth here. Yachts berth stern or bows-to on the NE and SE quay. The rest of the berths are occupied by fishing boats.

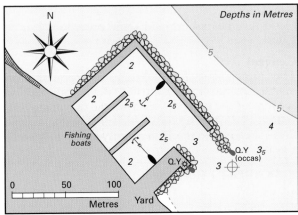

MAISTRATOS HARBOUR
⊕38°11′·4N 20°29′·1E

Shelter Good all-round shelter.

Facilities

Water on the quay. Provisions and tavernas nearby. Argostoli town is a short walk away.

Close to the entrance is a yard which can haul yachts. Yachts are craned out but the hardstanding area is relatively small. Mechanical and engineering repairs.

LIXOURI

BA 2402
Imray-Tetra G12

Approach

Directly across the Gulf from Argostoli is Lixouri. The buildings of the town and the harbour moles are easily identified. The entrance is lit: Fl.R.1·5s3M/Fl.G.1·5s3M.

Mooring

Berth stern or bows-to the N or W mole. The bottom is soft mud, poor holding until the anchor digs in. The prevailing NW wind sets up a surge in the harbour which can be uncomfortable.

Port police and customs.

Facilities

Fuel and water near the quay. Shower on the S mole. PO. OTE. Bank. Good shopping and tavernas in the town. Regular car ferry to Argostoli.

General

Between the surge with the prevailing wind and the constant smell of sewers, few yachts visit the sister town to Argostoli. That said, the town itself is a likeable place, mostly busy with agricultural concerns and its own little cottage industries.

ÁY KIRIAKIS

38°18′·6N 20°28′·6E

A small harbour in Órmos Kiriakis is suitable only for small yachts in calm weather. The harbour is very small and partially rock-bound. There are 2–3m depths in the entrance and 1–3m depths inside. Berth under the outer breakwater with a long line to it. Depths inside the harbour are irregular with shallows extending from the middle of the E

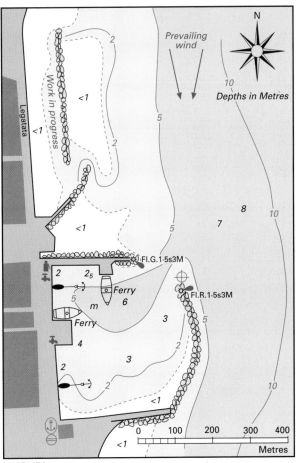

LIXOURI
⊕38°12′·1N 20°26′·6E

breakwater and around the shore for approximately 20–30m out.

The little harbour is a gem, with just local fishing boats and a couple of simple tavernas ashore.

PORT ASSOS

Approach

A natural harbour on the W coast 6 miles S of Ák Dafnoudhi (Vlioti). A large Venetian fort on the headland forming the W side of the harbour is not as conspicuous as it might appear on the plan, but can usually be made out from the distance. Closer in the houses of the village and the mole will be seen.

Mooring

Go stern or bows-to the mole with a long line ashore, or anchor off. The short mole and the quayed area have mostly 1·5–2m depths, but the ballasting extends a considerable distance underwater, making it difficult to get close in. It is quite deep in the bay, some 7–10m mostly, coming up quickly to the quay. The bottom is mud, shingle, and weed, not everywhere good holding. With the normal NW winds a swell rolls into the harbour – uncomfortable and untenable with strong NW winds. There is no nearby shelter as the swell is just as bad on the S side of the headland in nearby Órmos Mirto.

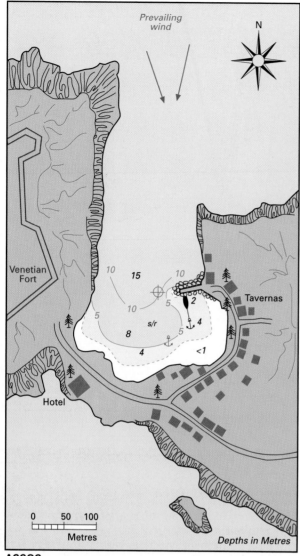

ASSOS
⊕38°22′·8N 20°32′·2E

Assos

Facilities

Good tavernas ashore and some provisions can be found.

General

The picturesque little harbour is popular with tourists in the summer but few yachts call here on account of the poor shelter from the prevailing NW winds. The Venetian fort, which enclosed a sizeable town, was built in the 16th century and is well worth a visit.

FISKÁRDHO (Phiscardo)

BA 2402

Imray-Tetra G121

Approach

Conspicuous It can be difficult to work out just where the bay is, though the general location at the N end of the Ithaca Strait is obvious. From the NE a number of new buildings in the bay immediately N of Fiskárdho are conspicuous. Closer in the twin ruined towers, the large stone lighthouse and the smaller Venetian lighthouse on the N side of Órmos Fiskárdho will be seen, although from the NE they can be difficult to pick out when the sun is low in the sky. The new villas and the hotel on the S side of the bay will also be seen. From the S the houses in the bay are easily discerned once you are past Nisís Dhaskalio which has a small chapel on it.

By night Use the light on Ák Fiskárdho (Fl.3s7M).

Mooring

Go stern or bows-to on the S or W quay or on the new pontoon on the W side. Care is needed on the S quay where the ballasting protrudes underwater in places. Do not berth in the SW corner where local *caïques* moor. In the summer the harbour gets crowded and you may have to anchor with a long line ashore to the N side. The bottom is sand, rocks and weed, reasonable holding.

Shelter Excellent shelter from all directions, although strong prolonged southerlies cause a surge, troublesome rather than dangerous.

Authorities Port police.

Facilities

Services Water and electricity on the pontoon. You may also be able to get water on the quay from a taverna or bar

Fuel Can be delivered by mini-tanker.

Provisions Good shopping for all provisions. Ice available.

Eating out Good tavernas and bars.

Other PO. OTE. Bank. ATM. Hire cars and motorbikes. Ferry to Frikes and Vasilikí.

General

Fiskárdho is a popular spot for yachts, and in the season the quay is stacked two or three deep. The safe port and picturesque 19th-century houses set amid green pine groves remain pretty much original and a historical preservation order will hopefully keep them that way. This was the only place on Cephalonia that escaped damage in the 1953 earthquake that devastated much of the Ionian.

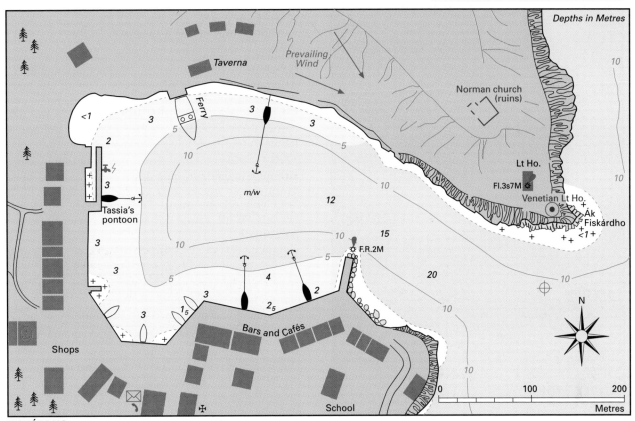

FISKÁRDHO
⊕38°27'·53N 20°34'·94E WGS84

The village is named after Robert Guiscard (thus Guiscardo/Phiscardo/Fiscardho), a Norman adventurer who briefly ruled these parts and who is said to have died of fever here in 1085. Unfortunately for local folk history, it is also recorded that he died in Vónitsa in the Gulf of Amvrakia – also of fever. The ruined Norman towers in the N of the bay are believed to be part of a church built in his memory.

Modern lighthouse and Venetian lighthouse (looking NE) on the N side of the entrance to Órmos Fiskárdho

THE EAST COAST BETWEEN FISKÁRDHO AND AYIOS EUFIMIA

On this green wooded stretch of coastline there are a number of small bays suitable for an overnight stay. Palaiokaravo, Órmos Kakogito and Kalo Limení are all sheltered from the NW wind, although there may be gusts off the high hills above and some swell may roll into some of them. The bays are deserted except for Kalo Limení, where there are a few houses ashore. Exercise some caution when anchoring as the bottom is loose shingle in places.

Fiskárdho on Cephalonia looking S   *Peter Kleinoth/MareTeam*
(The new pontoon is not shown)

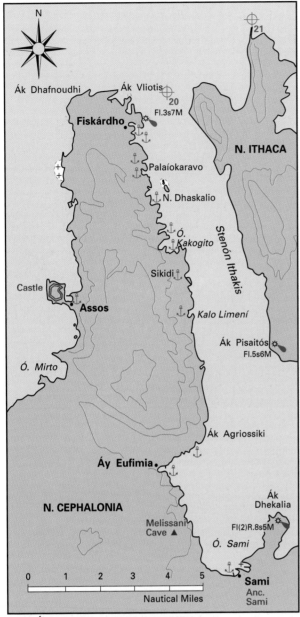

STENÓN ITHAKIS (ITHACA CHANNEL)

⊕**20** N end Ithaca Channel
38°28'·47N 20°35'·73E WGS84
⊕**21** 0·25M N of Ák Áy Marmara (Ithaca N end)
38°30'·47N 20°38'·93E WGS84

ÁY EUFIMIA (Sta Eufemia, Pilaros Cove)

Imray-Tetra G121

Approach

Conspicuous From the N you will not see the town and the mole until you round Ák Agriossiki. From the E the town is conspicuous from the S end of Ithaca and as you close the port you will see the mole.

By night Use the light on Ák Dhekalia Fl(2)R.8s5M and closer in the light on the end of the mole Q.G.3M.

Note The channel between Cephalonia and Ithaca has a reputation for being very windy. The wind tends to blow either up or down the channel (usually down from the N) and you will also get gusts down the valleys and out of Áy Eufimia.

Mooring

Go stern or bows-to on the N quay where shown. Alternatively anchor off keeping clear of the area where yachts berth. The bottom is sand, rocks and weed, not everywhere the best holding. In the SW corner there are sandy patches where the holding is better.

Shelter Good shelter from the prevailing wind, although it tends to gust down the valley and blow beam on, so ensure that your anchor is well in to hold you off the quay. The wind dies off in the evening. With strong SE winds a swell enters the harbour.

Facilities

Services Water and electricity on the N quay.
Fuel Can be delivered by mini-tanker. The fuel station is on the S side of the bay.
Provisions Most provisions can be found.
Eating out Numerous tavernas. The one around the

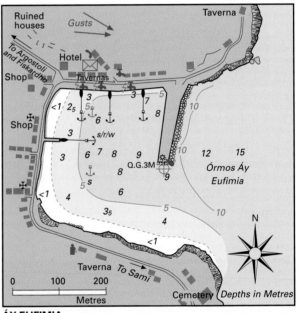

ÁY EUFIMIA
⊕38°18'·2N 20°36'·1E

Áy Eufimia looking NNW from the S entrance point

coast from the root of the mole is worth a visit.
Other PO. OTE. Bank. ATM. Ferry to Vathi and
Astakós.

General

This used to be the main port for the east of
Cephalonia, but after the 1953 earthquake it was
abandoned and Sami became the major port for the
area. It is a better port than Sami for visiting Lake
Melissani and the Cave of Drogarati.

Lake Melissani is an underground cave and lake
which is fed by seawater entering at Ák Áy
Theodoroi near Argostoli and then travelling
underground across the island to the lake and the
sea on the east coast. A boatman will row you
around and although it is crowded in the summer it
is still worth a visit, as much for the subterranean
cool as for the limpid waters of the lake.

SAMI

BA 2402

Approach

Conspicuous From the N the double-storeyed
buildings lining the quay are easily visible under the
green wooded slopes. From the S the harbour will
not be seen until you are around Ák Dhekalia.
Closer in the outer mole is easily identified.

By night Use the light on Ák Dhekalia Fl(2)R.8s5M
and the light on the mole head Fl.R.2s4M.

Mooring

Go stern or bows-to or alongside the new pier inside
the basin. The bottom is mud and good holding.

Shelter Reasonable shelter from the prevailing
N–NW wind although a surge can develop as the sea
is pushed through the arches let into the new pier.

Authorities Port police and customs.

Facilities

Water On the quay at the root of the mole, though it
can be difficult to find the man to turn it on.
Fuel Near the quay.

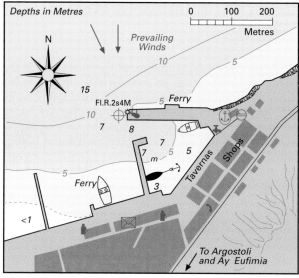

SAMI
⊕38°15′·3N 20°38′·8E

Provisions Good shopping for provisions near the
quay.
Eating out Numerous tavernas and bars.
Other PO. OTE. Bank. ATM. Hire cars and
motorbikes. Ferry to Patras.

General

Sami was completely rebuilt after the 1953
earthquake as the ferry terminal for Cephalonia.
The green wooded slopes above Sami are attractive,
but the town itself is mostly new, though now
mellowing with the patina of a few years' ageing. It
is an alternative to Áy Eufimia for visiting the semi-
underground Lake Melissani and the Cave of
Drogarati. The ruins of ancient Sami (Aegiala) are
close to the SE of present-day Sami but there is little
to see. Parts of the town and adjacent coast were
used during the filming of *Captain Corelli's
Mandolin.*

PÓROS (Pronos Bay)

Approach

A small harbour tucked under Ák Pronos.

Conspicuous From the N the buildings of the village
will be seen and closer in the breakwater is easily
identified. From the S the village and harbour will
not be seen until you round Ák Pronos.

By night Use the light on Ák Kapri Fl(3)WR.9s6/4M
and on the end of the mole Q.G.3M.

Dangers With the prevailing wind there can be
strong gusts off the coast.

Mooring

Go stern or bows-to the new quay in the SW corner.
The bottom is mud and weed, mostly good holding.

Shelter Uncomfortable but tenable with the
prevailing wind which blows down from the N.
When the wind dies down at night things become
more comfortable although at times it may blow
through the night making it difficult to get any sleep.

Authorities Port police.

Note Yachts should keep well clear of the ferry berth.
The ferry normally comes in and drops an anchor
and then takes a line to one of the mooring buoys in
the harbour.

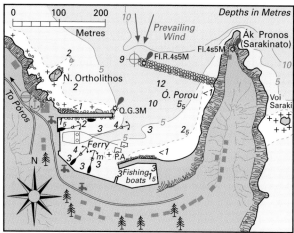

PÓROS
⊕38°09′·0N 20°46′·9E

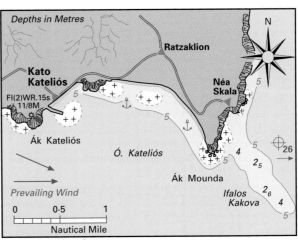

ORMOS KATELIÓS

⊕26 2·25M E of Ak Mounda (Cephalonia SE end)
38°03'·20N 20°49'·97E WGS84

Póros looking down onto the harbour from Ák Pronos

Facilities

Water On the SW quay.
Fuel On the road to the village. A mini-tanker can deliver to the quay.
Provisions Minimarket nearby. Other shops in the village.
Eating out Tavernas nearby and others in the village and around the road running out to Ák Pronos.
Other PO. Bank. Greek gas. Buses to Argostoli. Ferry to Killini.

General

The village is set in a spectacular position on a strip of flat land between a precipitous gorge and the sea. It has a modest tourist trade, though most people arriving here on the ferry from Killini hardly stop and are on the bus to Argostoli before you even notice they have arrived. Recently a number of villas and houses have been built around Ák Pronos and the village is expanding as a resort, though still in a low-key sort of way.

IFALOS KAKOVA

The old BA 203 recommends the following to avoid the Kakova Shoal off the SE tip of Cephalonia: for N–S traffic Ák Kapri kept open of the W end of Nisís Atoko; for E–W traffic Áy Yeoryios castle in line with Ák Koroni clears the shoal. While the marks for E–W traffic are easily located the mark of Nisís Atoko for N–S traffic is difficult to locate with the summer heat haze. Although quite large *caïques* cut across the shoal, it is wise to give it a good offing.

KATO KATELIÓS

38°04'·0N 20°45'·0E

In the NW corner of the large bay under Ák Mounda a yacht can find some shelter from the prevailing wind which blows from the W around the bottom of Cephalonia. A detached rough stone breakwater shelters fishing boats here, but a reef obstructs the entrance and a yacht is not advised to

try to enter. Depths within the harbour are uneven and mostly less than 1m. Anchor off the beach on the N taking care of the off-lying reefs.

PESSADES

38°06'·2N 20°34'·5E

A miniature ferry harbour connecting with Áy Nikólaos on Zákinthos. The tiny harbour and the ferry apron are tucked up in Órmos Lourtha under Ák Sosti. Yachts go stern-to the outside breakwater with a long line ashore. Work is in progress extending the ferry quay at the root of the breakwater.

NOTE

Between Ák Liakas and the entrance to Kólpos Argostoliou there are a number of reefs and shoal water lying up to a mile off the coast. Keep well off when sailing along this stretch coast.

The mainland coast and adjacent islands to Oxiá Island

Following the east boundary of the inland sea is the steep-to coast of mainland Greece. The eroded brown mountains rise straight out of the sea to some 1550m in places, providing an impressive backdrop to the islands dotting the sea. The two principal islands near the coast and the only inhabited islands are Kálamos and Kastos. Kálamos lies like a great stranded whale in the sea with skinny Kastos alongside. Further S the Dragonera and Echinades (meaning 'sea urchin') islands lie scattered off the marshlands at the foot of the mountains. These numerous small islands are all uninhabited, although sheep and goats are grazed on the larger islands. The southern part of this area is little visited by yachts although it contains a number of safe anchorages and ports, possibly because it is off the

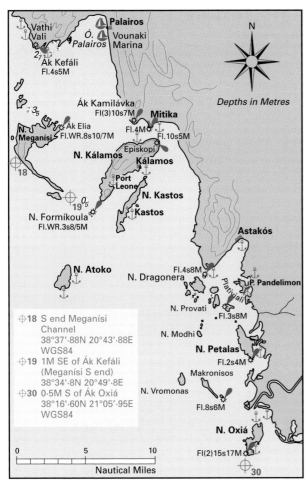

THE MAINLAND COAST AND ADJACENT ISLANDS
(Meganísi to Nisís Oxiá)

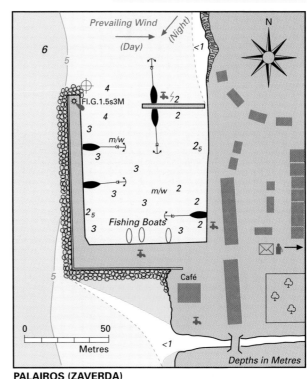

PALAIROS (ZAVERDA)
⊕38°46'·94N 20°52'·64E WGS84

yacht 'motorway' to the Gulf of Patras and the Aegean and the few towns in the area are poor in tavernas. For those yachtsmen who like remote anchorages and spectacular, if desolate, scenery, this area makes a good cruising ground.

VATHI-VALI

Ák Kefáli light 38°45'·4N 20°45'·9E

A small inlet on the mainland coast just S of the Levkas canal around the headland of Ák Kefáli. A fish farm now obstructs most of this inlet though it is still possible to squeeze in. Good shelter except from the S.

PALAIROS (Zaverda)

Approach

The buildings of the village straggling down the hillside to the harbour are easily identified. Closer in the harbour mole will be seen. The mole head is lit: Fl.G.1·5s3M.

Mooring

Go stern or bows-to the quay or pontoon where convenient. The harbour is used by a charter company and it can get crowded in the summer. The bottom is mud and weed, reasonable holding.

Shelter Good shelter from the prevailing wind. At night a katabatic breeze may blow in from the NE, but dies down after 2–3 hours.

Facilities

Services Water on the quay. Water and electricity boxes on the pontoon.
Fuel A mini-tanker can deliver to the harbour.
Provisions Good shopping for provisions in the town.
Eating out Numerous tavernas near the harbour and in town.
Other PO. OTE. Bank. Irregular bus service to Vónitsa and Mitika.

General

A largely agricultural village that now adds to its income from the charter company based here. The village is attractive in a proper working way, serving the needs of the surrounding farmers, and the inhabitants are a friendly lot. Above the village the slopes of the Arkarnanika rise abruptly to 1,590m (5,167ft) with barren stony slopes bereft of trees and even maquis.

VOUNAKI MARINA

Approach

Situated just S of Palairos. The harbour is easily identified from the hotel complex behind and the harbour breakwaters show up well closer in. The approach should be from the W as the dinghy mooring area directly N of the harbour is shallow.

By night The shelter breakwater is lit Fl.G.3s7m3M.

VHF Ch 10.

Mooring

Data 60 berths. Depths 2–6m.

Berth stern or bows-to where directed or convenient. There are laid moorings with lines tailed to the quay.

97

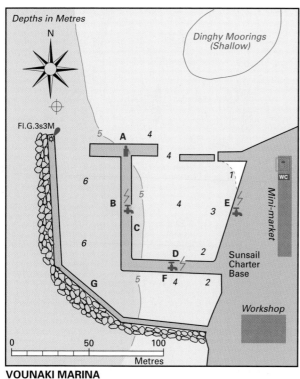

VOUNAKI MARINA
⊕38°46'·16N 20°52'·62E WGS84

Note Work has been completed on the new extension to the breakwater. The W side of the harbour has been dredged and the quay on this side has been widened and extended.

Shelter Good shelter although strong westerlies might cause some bother. The breakwater extension has improved shelter inside.

Authorities Dockmaster. Charge band 2.

Sunsail Vounaki Marina, Palairos, A.K. 30012, Greece. VHF Ch 10. ☎/Fax 26430 41944.

Facilities

Services Water and electricity at or near every berth. Showers and WC.

Fuel Fuel dock in the harbour.

Repairs 15-ton crane. Mechanical and engineering repairs. GRP workshop. Sail loft. Chandlers.

Provisions Minimarket. Better shopping in Palairos 15 minutes' walk away.

Eating out Taverna. Others in Palairos.

Other Laundry service. Gas available. Telephone and Fax. Car hire. Air tickets.

General

Vounaki is a major Sunsail charter base in the area but cruising yachtsmen can use the harbour and its resources. The hotel is exclusively for Sunsail clients but the other facilities are available to visiting yachties.

MITIKA

There is a quay on the W side of Ák Mitika in Órmos Mitika, but this is only tenable in the morning calm before the afternoon breeze gets up. On the S side of Ák Mitika a new fishing harbour has been built.

MITIKA HARBOUR

Approach

Straightforward. There are no lights for a night entry.

Mooring

Note Work is in progress improving the existing harbour on the east side of Ak Mitika, and completing a new harbour immediately south of this. There are depths of 2–3m inside both basins, although I suspect that the primary use for the harbours is for small local craft rather than yachts. The harbours are both quite small so manoeuvring space inside is very limited. Go stern or bows-to wherever there is room, taking care of floating mooring lines. Good shelter.

Shelter Good shelter from the prevailing NW–W wind.

Anchorage You can anchor off to the E of the harbour, but the prevailing wind pushes swell through the channel between Mitika and Kalamos and the anchorage is not really comfortable.

Facilities

Water Tap on the NE quay.

Fuel Some way out of town.

Provisions Good shopping for provisions.

Eating out Numerous tavernas on the waterfront on the W, some with good fresh fish.

Other PO. Bank. *Caïque* ferry to Kalamos and Kastos.

General

Mitika is a very Greek workaday place with little in the way of tourism and the better for it. It can get a bit dusty in the summer, but once you are safely tucked into a berth then you can wander around to the western side for a drink and dinner overlooking the sea, in a setting which is just charming.

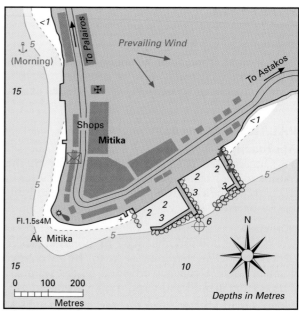

MITIKA
⊕38°40'·05N 20°56'·91E WGS84

Nísos Kálamos

PORT KÁLAMOS

Approach

Straightforward. From the N the houses of Kálamos village on the hill will be seen. From the S a number of old windmills, including one on a rocky outcrop before the harbour, will be seen.

By night The end of the mole is lit Fl.R.3s3M.

Note Care is needed in the afternoon when the prevailing wind gusts up the channel between Kálamos and Kastos.

Mooring

Go stern or bows-to the mole. In places it is best to go bows-to as there are patches of underwater ballasting extending out from the quay. There are some laid moorings tailed to the quay and if one is available then use one of these. At the head of the harbour and around the quay there are insufficient depths. The bottom is mud, sand and weed, mostly good holding.

Shelter Good shelter from the prevailing wind. although at night a NE katabatic may blow into the harbour for a while. A strong SE wind can make the harbour uncomfortable and even dangerous if it is a prolonged blow.

Note Most works on the mole extension are complete, but work continues on the W side of the harbour and care is needed in the vicinity.

Facilities

Minimarket and bakery in the village. Several tavernas. PO.

General

At Kálamos town and on the NE of the island there are cool green pine glades running down to the sea. The islanders make a living from fishing and a little agriculture and, one suspects, remittances from abroad. Sadly, the village is dying as the young move away to more lucrative jobs on the mainland and the local population is skewed to the elderly.

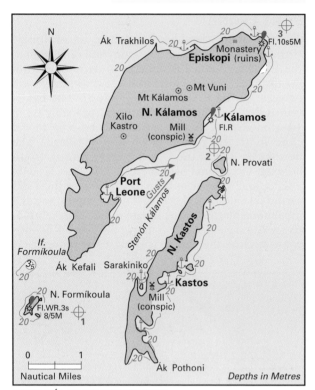

NISOI KÁLAMOS AND KASTOS
⊕1 38°34'·00N 20°52'·03E WGS84
⊕2 38°37'·01N 20°56'·26E WGS84
⊕3 38°39'·28N 20°57'·78E WGS84

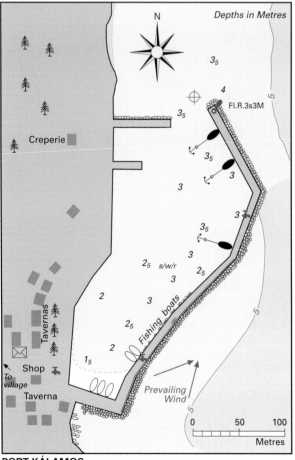

PORT KÁLAMOS
⊕38°37'·41N 20°55'·94E WGS84

Port Kalamos   *Nigel Patten*

PORT LEONE

To the S of the island lies Port Leone, an anchorage sheltered from the prevailing winds and only open to the E. The entrance is difficult to determine from the distance, though closer in two old windmills will be seen on the E side of the entrance. The bay is very deep to anchor in and you will probably be in 10–15m depths. A few yachts will be able to get close in to the ruined piers off the village. The bottom is sand, mud and weed, mostly good holding. Occasional bar ashore.

The small village has been deserted since the 1953 earthquake destroyed the local water supply and the inhabitants decided to emigrate rather than rebuild. Every Sunday three or four people from Kálamos come to clean the church and say a few prayers.

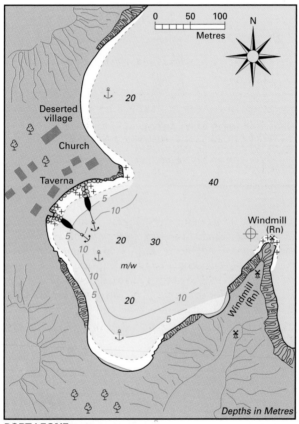

PORT LEONE
⊕38°35′·96N 20°53′·36E WGS84

EPISKOPI

⊕ 38°38′·92N 20°55′·57E WGS84

A small harbour on the N side of Kálamos. A few small yachts can get in here though care is needed as there is little room to maneouvre and the depths decrease from 2m on the outer mole to 1·5m in the middle and less towards the beach. Small taverna on the beach.

Nísos Kastos

PORT KASTOS

Approach

From the N the flat island of Prasonisi and the houses of Kastos identify where the harbour is. From the S a mill on the headland sheltering Port Kastos will be seen, but you will not see the village until you round the headland.

By night The end of the mole is lit Fl.R.4s8m5M.

Mooring

Stern or bows-to the outer end of the small mole, or anchor off with a long line to the W side of the harbour. The bottom is mud and weed, good holding once through the weed.

Shelter Behind the mole is good, and anchored off you are safe enough, though the prevailing wind sends in a residual swell that sets yachts rolling. At night a NE katabatic wind may blow but the harbour is usually tenable.

Facilities

Several tavernas and a few provisions if you are lucky. Most provisions arrive from Mitika by *caïque*.

General

In previous editions I have written that the population was evacuated in 1976 because of a suspected typhoid outbreak (that's what I was told in 1977 by a local!), though the locals now contest this. The islanders are gradually returning, although the population in the winter is still only 80 or so. The village and its setting are beautiful, all prickly pear and olives that supports a surprising assortment of livestock including cows, sheep and the ubiquitous goats. Good snorkelling in the waters around the island.

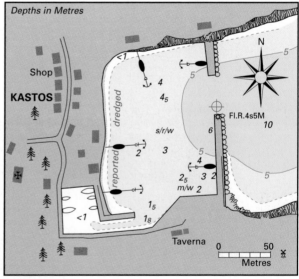

PORT KASTOS
⊕38°34′·12N 20°54′·73E WGS84

ANCHORAGES AROUND NÍSOS KASTOS

Port Sarakiniko 38°34'·0N 20°54'·2E The indented bay on the W side of the island. In calm weather you can anchor in the bay in 5–10m. When the prevailing NW–W wind is blowing a swell is sent into here. At the head of the bay is a short mole (25m long) with 2–3m depths behind it shallowing to less than a metre off the rough quay. If there is space a small yacht may be able to go bows-to or take a long line ashore.

Prasonisi anchorage The rocky islet NE of Kastos harbour. In the channel between the islet and Kastos there are least depths of 4m in the fairway at the N end of the channel and least depths of 7m at the S end in the fairway. In calm weather you can anchor in the bay opposite the islet.

SE Bay On the E side of Kastos and S of the harbour there is an indented bay which affords some shelter from the prevailing wind. It is quite deep in here for anchoring and the best policy is to take a long line ashore in the N arm.

Nisís Atoko

Around 6 miles E of Frikes on Ithaca lies Nisís Atoko, a dome-shaped island easily identified from the distance.

There are two anchorages on the island. In calm weather or light NW winds Cliff Bay on the S side can be used, although it is very deep (10–15m at either end) to anchor in.

On the SE side One House Bay affords better shelter and more suitable depths for anchoring and consequently is more popular. Anchor in 5–12m on sand, good holding. Shelter from the prevailing NW wind is good and it is possible to stay overnight in settled weather. Clear turquoise water and a solitary house ashore. Sweet water from a well ashore.

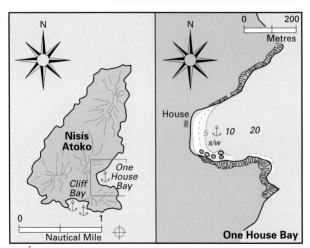

NISÍS ATOKO
⊕38°28'·4N 20°49'·1E

One House Bay on Nisís Atoko   *Nigel Patten*

The mainland coast

ASTAKÓS (Astokos, Dragonmestre)

Approach

Conspicuous Once you are into Órmos Astakou the buildings of the small town will be seen, and closer in the harbour breakwater is easily identified. Close E of the breakwater is the newly constructed fishing harbour.

By night The end of the breakwater is lit: Fl.R.4s3M.

Mooring

Go stern or bows-to the N quay, leaving the ferry berth clear. Yachts may have to move off part of the quay when the hydrofoil arrives so if there is a space on the mole it may be worthwhile going there. Care is needed as rock ballasting extends out underwater in places along the mole. The bottom is mud, good holding.

Shelter Good shelter from the prevailing winds. Open to southerlies.

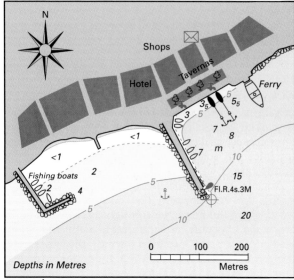

ASTAKÓS
⊕38°31'·91N 21°04'·94E WGS84

Facilities

Water On the quay.

Fuel About 1km out of town.

Repairs Caïques are hauled in a yard across the bay. Limited mechanical repairs. Chandlers.

Provisions Good shopping for provisions in the town.

Eating out Several tavernas on the waterfront and in the town.

Other PO. OTE. Banks. Ferry to Ithaca and Póros on Cephalonia.

General

Astakós has a little tourist trade, mostly from Greeks on holiday here, but is principally a fishing and agricultural town. Astakós means 'lobster' but despite this promise the restaurants in the town never seem to have the delectable crustacean. Do the locals keep them for themselves or are there really no lobsters in the town called 'Lobster'?

ANCHORAGES NEAR ASTAKÓS

Port Marathia A deserted inlet SW of Astakós tucked in behind Ák Tourkovigla. Good shelter from the prevailing wind. Anchor near the head of the bay on mud. The new coast road running across the N of the bay and a camping ground erode the calm and beauty of the place.

Boulder Bay A bight just before Astakós that can be recognised by the prominent boulder/rock near the shore. Anchor off the beach where convenient. Gusts with the prevailing WNW wind.

ANCHORAGES AROUND THE DRAGONERA AND ECHINADES ISLANDS

Note Many of the bays around the islands are wholly or partially obstructed by fish farms. Some are mentioned or marked on the plans, but exact positions will change as they are regularly moved to fresh areas.

Nisís Dragonera On the SE tip of the island there is a miniature inlet that a small yacht can use. On the N side are two coves suitable in calm weather before the prevailing wind gets up.

Nisís Karlonisi Small yachts can tuck themselves into the narrow channel between Karlonisi and Provati. Care is needed of the reef running out from the W side.

PORT PANDELIMON

A double-headed inlet now partially obstructed by fish farms. The perimeter of the two fish farms here is marked by small plastic buoys. At times the fish farm caretakers have objected to yachts anchoring in the inlet, although in recent years this seems not to be the case.

Anchor in the E or the S creek with the latter giving the best shelter. The bottom is mud and weed, good holding once through the weed. The E creek can become uncomfortable with the chop pushed in by the prevailing wind, though rarely dangerous. In the S creek it is a good idea to take a long line ashore. No facilities unless you can get a fish or two from the fish farm.

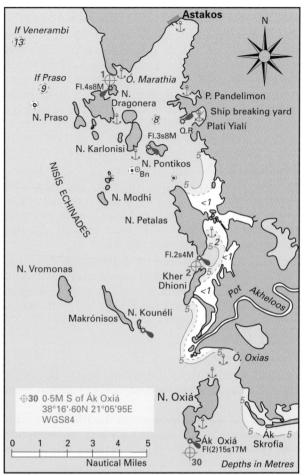

NISÍS DRAGONERA AND ECHINADES AND ADJACENT COAST
⊕1 38°29′·83N 20°01′·90E WGS84
⊕2 38°23′·49N 21°06′·00E WGS84

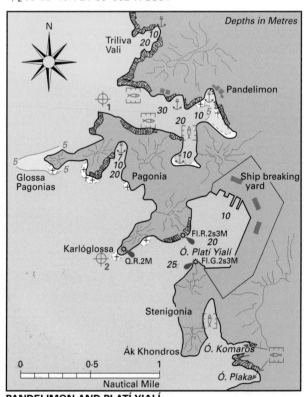

PANDELIMON AND PLATÍ YIALÍ
⊕1 38°29′·52N 21°04′·81E WGS84
⊕2 38°28′·38N 21°04′·81E WGS84

Note The fish farms are often moved because of the debris (uneaten food and excrement) that builds up under them over time. Consequently do not rely on the buoyed off areas for the fish farms being in the exact position shown.

PLATÍ YIALÍ (Plateali)

The large bay lying immediately S of Pandelimon. For some time massive engineering work has been carried out to create huge concrete aprons and quays and the infrastructure ashore for a ship-breaking yard. Despite the massive amount of money that has been spent it seems that there may be some uncertainty over its future.

A patrol boat now operates here, preventing yachts from berthing or even approaching the installations too closely.

KOMAROS

A small inlet S of Platí Yialí, now effectively obstructed by a fish farm.

Nisís Petalas

150m S Ák Aspro 38°23'·49N 21°06'·00E WGS84

The large island lying close off the coast 2½ miles S of Platí Yialí. A yacht can find good shelter from the prevailing winds tucked in behind the island. Anchor behind the SE corner of the island in 2–3m. The bottom shelves gently towards the marshland at the N end. Shelter here is much better than it looks and the holding is good in glutinous mud.

Above the anchorage a cave is conspicuous. On one late autumn evening I spied a huge bird sitting by the cave and from a pinion feather retrieved from the cave the breeding pair of vultures here were estimated to have a wing-span of around eight feet. They are shy birds and it is unlikely you will see them through the summer, when they retire to even more remote areas.

POTAMOS AKHELOOS (River Achelos)

This river, the longest in Greece, empties into the sea about 3 miles S of Nisís Petalas. The exact mouth of the river is difficult to identify and shoal water from the silt brought down extends at least a mile offshore. The shoal water appears to extend further than charted and care is needed to keep a safe distance off.

Note The fast ferries passing W and S of the shoal water cause heavy breaking waves with their wash in this area. One 80ft yacht suffered damage from wash here.

Nisís Oxiá

⊕30 0·5M S of Ák Oxia 38°16'·60N 21°05'·95E WGS84

The high island with a jagged ridge running down the spine at the entrance to the Gulf of Patras. Once seen its spiny outline is unmistakable. The lighthouse on the S end Fl(2)15s17M is conspicuous from the W and E. There are only two indifferent anchorages, both very deep.

1. **North Bay** There is now a fish farm in North Bay, leaving no room to anchor.
2. **East Bay** A bay on the E side affording some shelter from the prevailing westerlies. Anchor in 15–20m with a long line ashore. Spectacular surroundings and utter isolation except for a few fishing boats.
3. ***Órmos Oxias*** Some shelter from the prevailing wind can be obtained under the spit of land formed by the river delta of the Akheloos. Anchor in 4–6m on mud, sand and weed.

Nísos Zákinthos
(Zante Island)

Zákinthos, the ancient name now officially readopted, is the southernmost of the Heptanesoi. (Kíthera and Andíkithera, although originally part of the Heptanesoi, are now administered separately.) Like a bowl holding something precious, the mountains of Zákinthos enclose the fertile central plain except where it overflows onto

NÍSOS ZÁKINTHOS

⊕27 1M N of Ák Skinari light (Zákinthos N end)
37°56'·9N 20°42'·2E
⊕28 1M S of Ák Marathia (Zákinthos SW end)
37°37'·9N 20°50'·0E
⊕29 0·5M E of Ák Krionéri light (Zakinthos E side)
37°48'·26N 20°54'·89E WGS84

the sands of Lagana Beach. The Venetians called Zákinthos 'the flower of the Levant' and looking down on the plain planted with vines, mostly of the dwarf variety for currants, figs, olives, orange and lemon groves, it is easy to see why.

The first time I saw Zákinthos was in the autumn. After the baked islands of the Cyclades, the green slopes dotted with grazing cows were reminiscent of England. Yet despite English rule before Greece became independent, and English commercial interests in the currant trade, there is little apart from the green fields to remind you of England – Zákinthos is an Italianate island. Until the 1953 earthquake destroyed much of the Venetian architecture it must have appeared to be almost a cameo left behind by Venice.

'Only in Italy itself could one find this sort of baroque style, fruit of the seventeenth and eighteenth-century mind. Then in 1953 came the definitive earthquake which engulfed the whole of the Venetian past and left the shattered town to struggle to its knees once more. This it has done, in a manner of speaking; but it is like a beautiful woman whose face has been splashed with vitriol. Here and there, an arch, a pendent, a shattered remains of arcade, is all that is left of her renowned beauty.'

Lawrence Durrell *The Greek Islands*

Lawrence Durrell goes on to slate the modern town, which I personally do not find so distasteful – but then I never saw the old Venetian town.

Zákinthos town overlooks a sheltered bay that has harboured naval fleets since ancient times. Anybody who wanted to move south needed Zákinthos to control the strait into the Gulf of Patras and the route south around the Peloponnisos. First the Athenians, then Philip of Macedon, the Romans, Vandals, Normans, Turks, Venetians, French, Russians and finally the British held the island. While under British rule the island was a constant source of irritation to the Turks, since Greeks could easily escape to it and seek protection under the neutral Ionian flag – only to venture out again to fight the Turks on the mainland.

Twenty-five miles to the south of Zákinthos lie the remote Strophades Islands (Nisídhes Strofadhes). Administered from Zákinthos, the largest island was once a prosperous monastery until the Turks sacked it.

ÓRMOS ÁY NIKÓLAOS

A bay on the northern tip of Zákinthos partially sheltered by the islet of Áy Nikólaos in the entrance to the bay. Entry can be made on either side of the islet, though care is needed of the reef and shoal water extending from either side of the N entrance. Blocks have been laid on the reef out from the islet to improve shelter inside the bay, although some blocks are now under the surface. The end of the blocks is marked with a small stick beacon. A light is exhibited on the SE side of the islet Fl.2s7M.

A large concrete apron has been built around the southern side of the bay, where yachts can berth stern or bows-to on the northwest end. The southern end is used by the larger trip boats and the ferry to Cephalonia. The south side of the southern quay and the quayed area in the north of the bay are full of fishing boats. The depths drop off quickly in the bay so make sure you have plenty of scope. With any swell entering the bay all the trip boat and ferry wash rebounds off the quays, making berths uncomfortable. There can be severe gusts into the bay with the afternoon breeze, so make sure your anchor is well in.

Tavernas and provisions ashore. One enterprising family with a restaurant, a minimarket, the petrol station and several trip boats can arrange water, fuel by mini-tanker and fresh bread. Ferry to Pessades on Cephalonia in the summer. Local *caïques* run excursions from here to caves near the northern tip of the island which are said to rival the Blue Grotto on Capri.

ALYKANAS (Alikes)
37°50'·68N 20°46'·83E WGS84

A small harbour at the S end of Órmos Alikon. A rough stone breakwater encloses a U-shaped basin with the mouth of the U located on the beach side.

There is no quay to tie up to so you will have to anchor and take a long line to the breakwater. The space inside is largely taken up by local boats so really the best option is to anchor off the beach outside the buoyed swimming area.

Tavernas ashore.

KAVOS
37°50'·41N 20°49'·18E WGS84

A small fishing harbour about 2M ESE of Órmos Alikon. The miniature harbour is only really suitable for very small yachts drawing less than 1·5m. Berth where convenient taking care of uneven depths inside the harbour. Excellent shelter if you can get in amongst the local boats.

ÁY NIKÓLAOS
⊕37°54'·33N 20°42'·57E WGS84

PORT ZÁKINTHOS (Zante, Zakynthos)

BA 2404

Imray-Tetra G12

Approach

Conspicuous From the N the hills dominated by Mt Skopio (520m) to the E of the central plain look like a separate island from the distance. As you near Ák Krionéri the hotels on the beach to the N of the cape and a tower on the hills immediately above are conspicuous. The buildings of Zákinthos are obscured until you round the cape when the N mole will be easily identified. From the S the buildings of Zákinthos stand out well against the eroded cliffs behind.

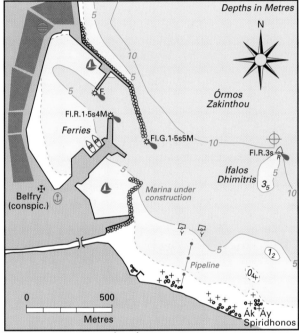

APPROACHES TO LIMÍN ZÁKINTHOU
⊕37°46'·84N 20°54'·91E WGS84

Zákinthos looking SE   *Peter Kleinoth/MareTeam*

Zákinthos yacht quay looking towards the town

By night From the N use the lights on Ák Skinári Fl.5s20M, Áy Nikólaos Fl.2s7M and on Ák Krionéri Fl(2)16s6M and Ák Krionéri Fl(2)16s6M. From the S use the lights on Ák Kerí Fl.10s17M. A constant red aerobeacon just W of the town is visible for about 5 miles and two alternate flashing red aerobeacons are also visible for about 3 miles to the W of the town. The entrance to the harbour is lit: Fl.G.1·5s5M/Fl.R.1·5s4M, though in the approach from the S the lights at the entrance are difficult to make out against the lights of the town until you are near the harbour.

Dangers

1. Care is needed of Ifalos Dhimitris, a reef and shoal water lying approximately 900m ESE of the harbour entrance. There are reported least depths of 3·5m. It is marked by a red conical buoy.
2. Closer to the coast there is a group of unlit mooring buoys off the end of an oil pipeline.
3. A good lookout should be kept for ferries, which are constantly coming and going from the harbour.

Mooring

Berth stern or bows-to on the NE or NW quays. The NE quay is the base for many of the large trip boats which use the top half of the quay. There is usually space to go south of them, clear of the ferry berth marked on the plan. The town quay on the NW side has been dredged and there is plenty of room to go stern or bows-to on the northern half of the quay. Further south has not been dredged and it is too shallow for most yachts. The bottom is mud and good holding.

Shelter Good shelter from the prevailing NW wind. With strong southerlies a surge builds up in the harbour and it may make berths on the NW quay untenable.

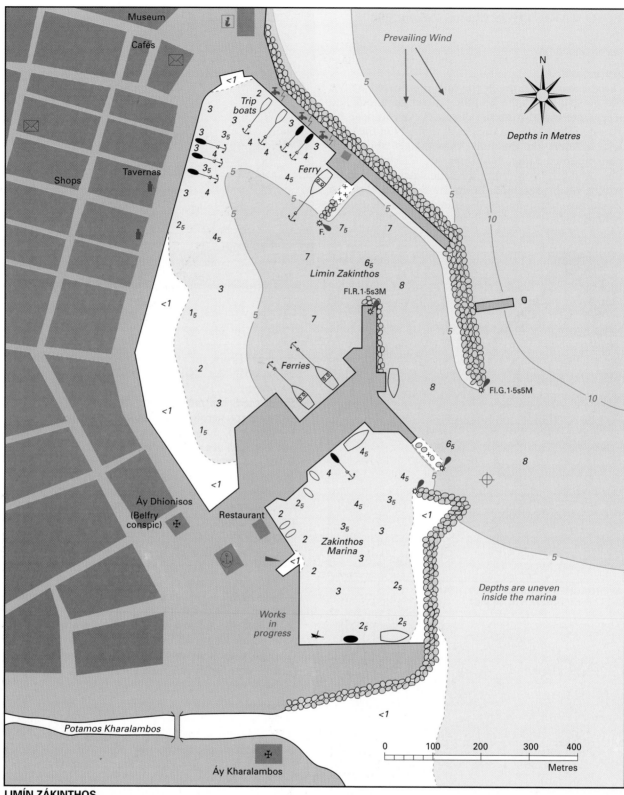

LIMÍN ZÁKINTHOS
⊕ 37°46'·69N 20°54'·36E WGS84

Note Any craft entering at speed (such as the coastguard boat) creates a significant wash so ensure your anchor is well in and you are pulled far enough off the quay to prevent damage.

Authorities A port of entry. Port police, customs and immigration.

Facilities

Services Water and electricity on the NE quay.

Fuel A mini-tanker can deliver. Also petrol stations around the waterfront.

Repairs Caïques are hauled out at the root of the S mole. Some mechanical repairs. Hardware shops. Chandlers.

Provisions Good shopping for all provisions in the town.

Eating out Tavernas in the town. Komi's fish restaurant at the waterside in the marina and others nearby.

Other PO. OTE. Banks. ATMs. Greek gas and Camping Gaz. Hire cars and motorbikes. Ferries to Killini. International and internal flights.

General

Until its total destruction in the 1953 earthquake the town consisted largely of Venetian buildings. In the rebuilding of the town a Venetian aura has been retained – spacious boulevards, arcaded shops, central square and imposing public buildings, yet somehow the town cannot be described as anything approaching an aesthetic reconstruction of the pre-'53 town. There is just too much slab-sided reinforced concrete and too little sympathetic detail. A museum in the town houses some of the relics, particularly some fine icons, recovered after the earthquake. Zákinthos is the logical spot to leave a yacht and explore the interior of the island – I suggest you head for the W side where there is some spectacular scenery, small villages, and fewer tourists.

ZÁKINTHOS MARINA

The marina has been 'under construction' for many years now, but finally the infrastructure at least appears to be reaching completion. The quays are in place, although mooring rings and bollards are scarce. Light structures guard the almost finished breakwaters, but rusting hulks hog much of the quay

space. Although this rush of activity has provided local boats with new berths, a viable yacht marina still seems to be some way off.

PORTO ROMA

A fair-weather anchorage on the SE tip of the island on the E coast. Porto Roma is sheltered from the prevailing NW–W wind, but a swell tends to roll into here. Taverna on the beach and several others a short walk away.

Kólpos Lagana

ÓRMOS YÉRAKAS

The bay lying immediately N of Ák Yérakas. Entry should be made on approximately 040° towards the beach. The rocks which extend on either side of the entrance are easily identified by day. Anchor where convenient. Good protection from the prevailing NW wind although it will sometimes blow around the bottom of Zákinthos and into the anchorage. Yérakas lies within Zone A of the regulations below.

Tavernas ashore. The beach is a turtle breeding ground and nobody is allowed on the beach after sunset.

LAGANA BEACH

In settled weather a yacht can anchor off Lagana Beach when the restrictions allow. The sandy bottom shelves gently to the shore. The anchorage is entirely open to southerlies when a heavy swell sets into the bay. The beach has been much developed

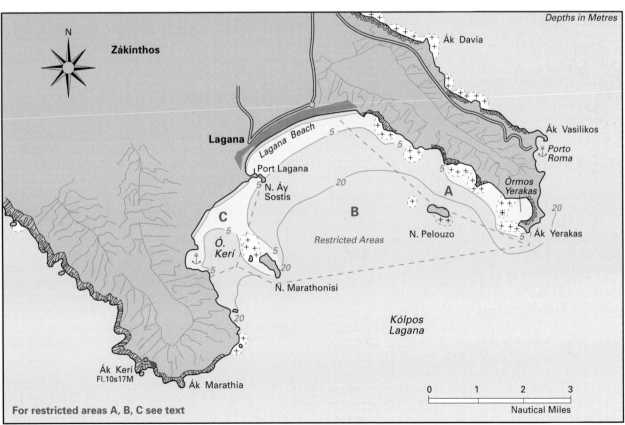

KÓLPOS LAGANA

Boating restrictions in Kólpos Lagana

Reproduced below is the advice note from the Greek authorities restricting navigation and mooring in Kólpos Lagana. I have reproduced the advice note and zones rather than my interpretation of it so there can be no doubt regarding the wording and advice given.

Bay of Laganas

The Bay of Laganas on Zakythnos is the most important nesting area for the loggerhead sea turtle (*Caretta caretta*) in the Mediterranean. Apart from specific legislation (Presidential Decree of 5/7/90, Government Gazette 347/D) that has been enacted to protect the nesting beaches and a broader surrounding area, the Coast Guard of Zakythnos has issued two Local Port Regulations (Ref. Num. 19/91 and 20/94 Government Gazettes 585/B/91 & 591/B/94). According to these, the Bay is divided into three zones, in which the following laws are effective from 1 May through to 31 October each year.

Maritime Zone A It is forbidden for any boat or vessel to enter or moor within this zone. Fishing with any kind of fishing gear is prohibited.

Maritime Zone B It is forbidden for any boat or vessel to travel at a speed greater than 6 knots, and to moor or anchor within this zone.

Maritime Zone C It is forbidden for any boat or vessel to travel at a speed greater than 6 knots within this zone.

What this effectively means is that Yérakas, Órmos Lagana and Lithakia cannot be used in the summer and early autumn. Yachts should observe the restrictions diligently as there have been a number of fines (around £200) for infringements of the regulations.

Now the sea area is effectively policed it is to be hoped that the beach development will be managed as well so the turtles get a chance to breed safely without interference from the lager louts who tend to inhabit parts of this resort area. Kólpos Lagana may be better policed now, but sadly the same may not be said for the beaches. By day almost every square metre of the main turtle egg-laying beaches are covered with sunbathing bodies, and by night lights and noise from the hotels pollute the bay. There seems to be a greater demand in selling cuddly toy turtles than providing protection for real ones.

I have left the plan and notes on the anchorages in this restricted area intact in this edition in case any yachts want to go there out of the restricted times but even then yachts should exercise caution and it may be prudent to enquire with the authorities at Limín Zákinthos on the legality of navigating and anchoring in these zones outside the time limits given.

Vroma looking W   *Nigel Patten*

The harbour lies within Zone B of the regulations above, but is still used by local boats during the prohibited summer season.

ÓRMOS KERÍ (Kierí)

37°40'·95N 20°50'·19E WGS84

An anchorage on the E side of Ák Marathia and to the W of Nisís Marathonisi. Anchor in 2–4m depths off the rough stone mole. The ballasting on the mole extends a considerable distance underwater making it difficult to moor close to it. Care needed of permanent moorings close in. Excellent shelter from the NW–W wind, but open to the S and E.

The famous pitch wells recorded by Herodotus still exist close inland.

ÓRMOS VROMA

37°49'·2N 20°38'·3E

A deep inlet close to the NW corner of Zákinthos. It affords reasonable shelter from the prevailing NW–W wind although there may be gusts down into it. It is dangerous in southerlies when a swell rolls in. Anchor and take a long line ashore as there can be katabatic gusts at night off the high land. The bay is spectacular, although the new road takes away some of the solitude of the place. Tripper boats run here and a simple taverna opens in the summer.

In the bay to the N of Vroma is the much photographed 'Wreck Bay' that appears in just about every book on Greece. Numerous tripper boats zip in and out of the picturesque bay bringing tourists with yet more cameras and film.

for tourism recently and there are numerous tavernas and hotels along it.

The beach is a breeding area for turtles and they are now protected in the breeding season. The area lies within Zone B of the boating restrictions in Kólpos Lagana.

PORT LAGANA (Ay Sostis)

37°42'·97N 20°51'·88E WGS84

The fishing port for the village of Lithakia. The harbour sits under the small islet of Nisís Áy Sostis at the W end of Lagana beach. There are 1·5–3m depths in the harbour but beware of large ropes stretched between the moles just under the water. The harbour is usually packed with fishing boats and local craft. Open to the SE. Taverna and, worse, a disco on the beach.

II. The Southern Ionian

Katakólon to Kíthera

The images retained of the northern Ionian are seldom anything but fond memories of rolling green islands and fine sailing days. By contrast the southern Ionian is more rugged and fierce: the shores are for the most part bordered by high mountains, often still snow-capped in spring, under which there is a thin coastal plain washed down over time by the winter torrents. These mountains run irregularly from the centre of the Peloponnisos into the sea in all directions although the two principal mountain ranges, the Taiyetos and the Parnon, run south ending in Cape Matapan (Ák Tainaron) and Cape Malea (Ák Maléas) respectively.

Like the mountains, the peoples of this country have been rugged and tough. It was known in ancient times as the Island of Pelops (hence Peloponnese or Peloponnisos) after Pelops, son of Tantalus. His bizarre history included being sliced up and stewed for the gods by his father (Zeus later brought him back to life) and outwitting King Oenomaus for the hand of his daughter Hippodamia in a chariot race by removing the pins from the wheels of his competitor's chariot. On a more substantive basis we know that around 2000 BC the Peloponnese was invaded by the first Greek-speaking peoples, a warrior race from whom the hero legends of Perseus and Pericles were probably derived. Later came the Mycenaeans (the Homeric Achaeans) and later still (around 850 BC), the warrior race supreme, the Spartans, emerged as a power.

Ancient Sparta occupied a spectacular site sandwiched between the Taiyetos and Parnon mountains – in a gorge in the Taiyetos the weak and deformed children considered unfit to belong to this militaristic race were left to die. Nothing much remains of ancient Sparta, but the word 'spartan' has passed into our vocabulary to describe what was a way of life.

With the decline of Sparta the peoples occupying the Mani peninsula formed themselves into the Free Laconian League and their descendants acquired the name Maniotes. The Maniotes have been the most fierce race to people the Peloponnisos – the Spartans notwithstanding. They lived in clans, and feuds within and between clans were common. Families built towers to shelter from reprisals and these strange structures still exist on the Mani peninsula. While the rest of the Peloponnisos was subjugated by a succession of invaders, the Mani remained independent – both Rome and Turkey failed to defeat these fierce warriors.

Along the coastline the forts and castles at strategic points – Pílos, Methóni, Koroni, Kíthera – tell of the importance of the Peloponnisos as part of the trade route between the Aegean and Europe. Until the Corinth canal was cut most of the trade between east and west passed around this lonely stretch of coast. Whoever controlled this route controlled the flow of spices (especially pepper), silk, precious metals and stones, pearls, opium, perfumes – all the exotic wealth of the Indian Ocean – to Europe. The Venetians and, to a lesser extent, the Turks have left the lasting monuments, but often their forts incorporate masonry from more ancient colonists. Even today a lot of the shipping traffic in the eastern Mediterranean travels down this coast rather than through the Corinth Canal.

The forbidding physical geography of the Peloponnisos is perhaps the reason why comparatively few yachts cruise down this coast. Certainly the twin capes at the bottom of the Peloponnisos, Matapan and Malea, have acquired a reputation as minor Cape Horns. Yet the weather is really no worse than that of many other areas of the Aegean and there are sufficient harbours and anchorages to provide refuge in the event of bad weather. Moreover you are off the tourist track and the impecunious will also save the Corinth Canal dues.

Weather patterns in the South Ionian

In the northern half of the south Ionian, from Katakólon to Methóni, the weather pattern in the summer is very nearly identical to that of the northern Ionian: a NW wind gets up about noon and dies down in the evening. Sometimes it may be more from the W than NW and a little fresher than the Force 3–5 of the northern Ionian.

In the southern half of the south Ionian the wind is more from the W and SW and may last longer into the evening than in the northern Ionian. The wind tends to blow up into Messiniakos Kólpos and Lakonikós Kólpos although it can also gust off the W side of the gulfs. It is rare to get a land breeze in the morning. Around Ák Maléas and Kíthera, and sometimes in Lakonikós Kólpos, there is a NE wind which may blow all day although it rarely exceeds Force 4 – more often Force 2–3. The exception to

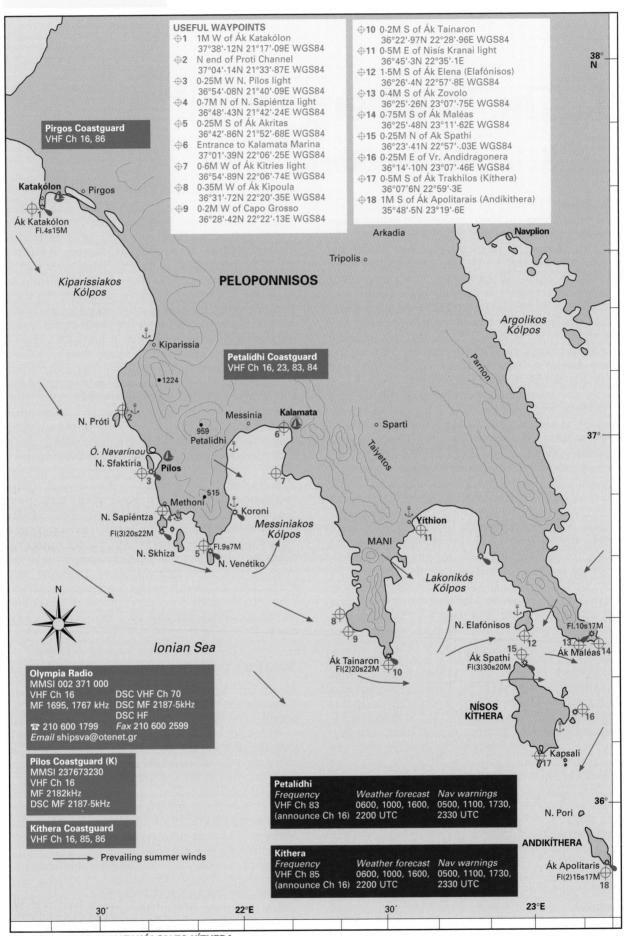

USEFUL WAYPOINTS

⊕1 1M W of Ák Katakólon
37°38'·12N 21°17'·09E WGS84

⊕2 N end of Proti Channel
37°04'·14N 21°33'·87E WGS84

⊕3 0·25M W N. Pílos light
36°54'·08N 21°40'·09E WGS84

⊕4 0·7M N of N. Sapiéntza light
36°48'·43N 21°42'·24E WGS84

⊕5 0·25M S of Ák Akritas
36°42'·86N 21°52'·68E WGS84

⊕6 Entrance to Kalamata Marina
37°01'·39N 22°06'·25E WGS84

⊕7 0·6M W of Ák Kitries light
36°54'·89N 22°06'·74E WGS84

⊕8 0·35M W of Ák Kipoula
36°31'·72N 22°20'·35E WGS84

⊕9 0·2M W of Capo Grosso
36°28'·42N 22°22'·13E WGS84

⊕10 0·2M S of Ák Tainaron
36°22'·97N 22°28'·96E WGS84

⊕11 0·5M E of Nisís Kranai light
36°45'·3N 22°35'·1E

⊕12 1·5M S of Ák Elena (Elafónisos)
36°26'·4N 22°57'·8E WGS84

⊕13 0·4M S of Ák Zovolo
36°25'·26N 23°07'·75E WGS84

⊕14 0·75M S of Ák Maléas
36°25'·48N 23°11'·62E WGS84

⊕15 0·25M N of Ak Spathi
36°23'·41N 22°57'·.03E WGS84

⊕16 0·25M E of Vr. Andidragonera
36°14'·10N 23°07'·46E WGS84

⊕17 0·5M S of Ák Trakhilos (Kíthera)
36°07'6N 22°59'·3E

⊕18 1M S of Ák Apolitarais (Andíkithera)
35°48'·5N 23°19'·6E

Pirgos Coastguard
VHF Ch 16, 86

Katakólon ○ Pirgos

Ák Katakólon
Fl.4s15M

Kiparissiakos Kólpos

PELOPONNISOS

Arkadia

Navplion

Tripolis ○

○ Kiparissia

Petalídhi Coastguard
VHF Ch 16, 23, 83, 84

•1224

Argolikos Kólpos

Parnon

N. Próti

Messinia ○ **Kalamata**

○ Sparti

959
Petalídhi

37°

Ó. Navarínou
N. Sfaktiria

Pílos

Taíyetos

515
Methoni

○ Koroni

N. Sapiéntza
Fl(3)20s22M

Messiniakos Kólpos

Yíthion

MANI

N. Skhiza   Fl.9s7M

N. Venétiko

Lakonikós Kólpos

N. Elafónisos

Fl.10s17M

N

Ák Tainaron
Fl(2)20s22M

Ák Spathi
Fl(3)30s20M

15   12   13
Ák Maléas 14

Ionian Sea

8

9

Olympia Radio
MMSI 002 371 000
VHF Ch 16   DSC VHF Ch 70
MF 1695, 1767 kHz   DSC MF 2187·5kHz
                    DSC HF
☎ 210 600 1799   Fax 210 600 2599
Email shipsva@otenet.gr

NÍSOS KÍTHERA

16

Pilos Coastguard (K)
MMSI 237673230
VHF Ch 16
MF 2182kHz
DSC MF 2187·5kHz

Kapsali
17

Petalídhi

Frequency	Weather forecast	Nav warnings
VHF Ch 83	0600, 1000, 1600,	0500, 1100, 1730,
(announce Ch 16)	2200 UTC	2330 UTC

36°

N. Pori ○

Kíthera Coastguard
VHF Ch 16, 85, 86

ANDIKÍTHERA

→ Prevailing summer winds

Kíthera

Frequency	Weather forecast	Nav warnings
VHF Ch 85	0600, 1000, 1600,	0500, 1100, 1730,
(announce Ch 16)	2200 UTC	2330 UTC

Ák Apolitaris
Fl(2)15s17M
18

38°
N

30'   22°E   30'   23°E

SOUTHERN IONIAN: KATAKÓLON TO KÍTHERA

Routes

Routes around the Peloponnese are pretty much a matter of following the coast around from Katakólon to Cape Malea. The prevailing NW–W winds will give you a sleigh ride from the Ionian to the Aegean whereas coming from the Aegean generally means a slog against the wind. For boats needing to get a move on there is a fairly well defined route either way that takes in Katakólon, Pilos or Methoni, Koroni, Porto Kayio, Sarakiniko on Elafonisos and on around Cape Malea. Reverse the route when on passage from the Aegean to the Ionian.

As in the northern Ionian, the prevailing NW–W wind will often not get up until late morning. If you are heading from the Aegean to the northern Ionian then you can make up some miles under engine if you leave early in the morning. When heading S and E it pays to leave a little later in the morning so you get a good downwind sail.

Anyone heading up into the gulfs will get a mixture of weather. Generally the prevailing wind will curve around and blow from the S–SW up into the gulfs. At times the NW wind will gust down through the valleys on the W side of the gulfs and at times these gusts can be severe. At the head of the gulfs there can be a pronounced land and sea breeze effect. The land breeze generally blows from the N–NE and the sea breeze from the S–SW. This means you need to choose anchorages carefully as although the land breeze rarely gets above F4, it can be enough to make it uncomfortable in anchorages exposed to a fetch from that direction.

The biggest problem most people encounter is getting around Cape Malea and into the Aegean. From the E you will usually have a NE wind to help you get around. From the W it is not unusual to sit in Sarakiniko on Elafonisos or at Neapolis waiting for a strong NE wind to die. Yachts have been known to wait a week and I suggest you read my notes for getting around in the section on Cape Malea at the end of the chapter. The advice is not infallible, but I have often found it to work, as have others.

In the winter there are more southerlies and route planning becomes more of a lottery. Really the only thing you can do here is get a forecast and make your plans from there. Remember that many of the harbours which are safe in the prevailing summer northerlies can be less comfortable and even untenable in strong southerlies.

Data

PORTS OF ENTRY
Katakólon
Pílos
Kalamata
Yithion

PROHIBITED ANCHORAGES
Nisís Skhiza is used for target practice by the air force. Vessels should not navigate in the immediate vicinity and anchoring and landing are prohibited.

MAJOR LIGHTS
Ák Katakólon Fl.4s15M
Nisís Stamfáni Fl(2)15s17M
Nisís Próti Fl.1·5s6M
Nisís Pílos Fl(2)10s9M
Ák Karsí (Nisís Sapiéntza) Fl.3s5M
Nisís Sapiéntza (SW Summit) Fl(3)20s22M
Nisís Venétiko Fl.9s7M
Ák Kitries Fl(2)12s7M
Ák Tainaron (Cape Matapan) Fl(2)20s22M
Nisís Kranai (Yíthion) Fl(3)18s9M
Ák Xílis Fl.3s5M
Órmos Vatíka Fl.3s7M
Ák Zóvolo Fl.7s12M
Ák Maléas Fl.10s17M

this is when the *meltemi* is in full swing and you can get strong NE winds from Elafonisos to Cape Malea. (See the weather note in this section). After October and until March–April the winds are predominantly from the SE although there may be strong winds from the N associated with nearby depressions.

There are two problem areas as regards the weather in the south Ionian. The first is to do with the very high mountain ranges down which there can be severe gusts on the lee side. Gusts off the mountains are particularly severe on either side of Ák Maléas and Ák Tainaron (the gusts are coming off the Taiyetos and Parnon mountains) and off Kíthera. At night there may be a katabatic wind which can be quite strong and arrive without warning.

The second problem in this area is that of the six generalised depression tracks over Greece; three of these tracks converge in the strait between Ák Maléas and Crete. Consequently the weather can deteriorate rapidly around the bottom of the Peloponnisos, especially in spring and autumn. It should be borne in mind when seeking shelter in the summer that strong southerlies will often veer to strong northerlies. This is not quite so true in the spring and autumn when a strong southerly may be prolonged and followed by only a weak northerly.

In the summer there may be thunderstorms around the coast with associated squalls but these seldom last for very long. The temperatures in the summer are marginally warmer than those in the northern Ionian except on Kíthera where the climate is more like that on Crete.

You can find more detail on the coast from Katakolon to Methoni in Ionian published by Imray.

For more detail on the Ionian as covered in Chapters I and II see *Ionian* from the publishers

Quick reference guide

Katakólon to Órmos Navarínou	Shelter	Mooring	Fuel	Water	Provisioning	Tavernas	Plan
Katakólon	A	A	B	A	B	B	•
Kiparissia	C	BC	B	A	B	B	•
N. Strofadhes	C	C	O	O	O	O	•
Agrilos	C	B	B	B	C	C	
Nisís Próti	C	C	O	O	O	O	•
Marathoupolis	C	A	B	B	C	C	•
Vromoneri	B	C	O	B	O	C	
Voidhokoilia	C	C	O	O	O	C	
Pílos	C	AB	B	A	B	A	•
Pílos Yacht Harbour	A	AB	B	B	B	A	•
Órmos Navarínou	B	C	O	O	O	C	•
Messiniakos Kólpos (Gulf of Messinia)							
Methóni	B	AC	O	B	B	B	•
Port Longos	B	C	O	O	O	O	•
Finakounda	B	AC	O	A	C	B	•
Maratho	C	C	O	O	O	O	
Koroni	B	C	B	B	B	B	•
Petalídhion	B	A	B	B	B	B	•
Kalamata Marina	A	A	A	A	A	A	•
Kitries	C	AC	O	O	O	C	•
Kardamila	C	C	O	O	B	B	•

	Shelter	Mooring	Fuel	Water	Provisioning	Tavernas	Plan
Limení	C	C	O	O	C	C	•
Diros	O	C	O	O	O	C	•
Mezapo	C	C	O	O	C	C	•
Yerolimena	O	C	O	O	C	C	•
Lakonikós Kólpos (Gulf of Lakonika)							
Porto Káyio	B	AC	O	O	C	C	•
Kotronas	C	AC	O	O	B	B	•
Órmos Skoutari	C	C	O	O	O	O	•
Yíthion	B	AB	B	A	A	A	•
Elaia	B	AC	B	B	B	C	•
Plítra	B	A	O	B	O	C	•
Nísos Elafónisos	C	C	O	O	O	C	•
Elafónisos village	B	AC	O	B	B	C	•
Neapolis	C	AC	B	B	B	B	•
Palaiokastro	B	AC	O	O	O	C	•
Kíthera and Andíkithera							
Pelagia	C	AB	B	A	B	C	•
Dhiakofti	B	AB	B	A	C	C	•
Ó. Áy Nikólaos	C	C	O	O	C	O	•
Avelomona	B	AC	O	O	C	C	•
Órmos Kapsáli	C	ABC	B	A	B	B	•
Órmos Potamóu	O	C	O	O	C	C	•

Katakólon to Órmos Navarínou

Approaching Kiparissiakos Kólpos (Gulf of Arcadia) from the north the coastline is low and featureless. The land beyond the wide sweep of the bay is largely salt marsh until the low hills behind. Towards the southern end of the gulf the hills rise abruptly to the mountains behind Kiparissia.

Immediately south of the gulf is the large protected bay of Navarinon – a large natural harbour approximately three and a half miles by two miles. In settled weather a yacht can anchor off the northern end of the bay either near the Sikia channel (not navigable) or further east on the low sandy mainland shore. From here the scene of the Sphakteria incident can be explored and easily visualized in the craggy deserted landscape. The incident described by Thucydides occurred when a group of Athenians under Demosthenes besieged a force of 400 Spartans of which 120 eventually surrendered, thus destroying the myth that Spartans always fought to the death. Later the bay was the scene of the Battle of Navarinon which effectively decided the Greek War of Independence. (See the section on Órmos Navarínou).

KATAKÓLON (Limín Katakólou)

BA 2404
Imray-Tetra G16

Approach

Conspicuous From the N and S the lighthouse on Ák Katakólon is conspicuous. The low-lying cape

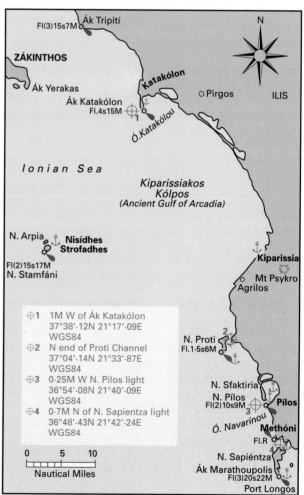

KATAKÓLON TO METHONI

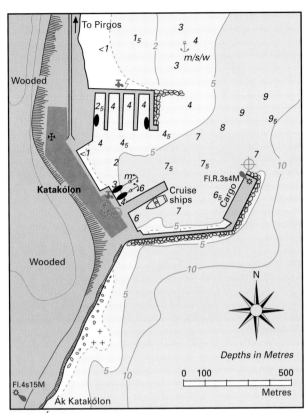

KATAKÓLON
⊕37°38'·81N 21°19'·66E WGS84

Katakólon town quay looking NE towards the new 'marina'
Lu Michell

looking like an aeroplane wing in cross section can be identified a long way off. From the N the harbour breakwater and village will not be seen until around Ák Katakólon, but from the S the breakwater is easily identified.

By night Use the light on Ák Katakólon Fl.4s15M and the light on the end of the breakwater Fl.R.3s4M.

Dangers Care is needed off the E side of Ák Katakólon not to shave the reef and shoal water here – keep at least 700m off the coast.

Mooring

The main structure of the new yacht basin is complete, but there are no facilities yet. Go alongside the west or east end of the basin where convenient. It is likely that laid moorings will be installed eventually.

On the town quay berth stern or bows-to on the N side of the central pier. Alternatively anchor NE

of the harbour. The bottom is mud and clay, excellent holding.

Shelter Good shelter from the prevailing winds.

Authorities A port of entry: port police, customs and immigration.

Facilities

Water On the town quay. Reported to be of poor quality. Water and electricity boxes in the 'marina'.
Fuel In the town. A mini-tanker delivers to the quay.
Repairs **Ionian Yacht Services** run by Yannis Kalofonos can haul yachts up to 16 tons. Larger yachts can be hauled by arrangement. He uses a crane and puts yachts onto a specially designed trailer to trundle them to the boatyard. The only disadvantage is that your mast must come down. Mechanical and engineering work can be carried out. Some GRP and general repairs. Gardiennage ☎ 26210 31353 www.pyrgosnet.gr/ionian.yacht
Provisions Most provisions can be found in the village.
Eating out Numerous tavernas and an inordinate number of pizzerias for the size of the place.
Other PO. ATM. Bus to Pirgos. Taxis. Hire motorbikes and cars.

Ák Katakólon looking W

OLYMPIA

Although it seems a bit of a trek from Katakólon, the site at Olympia is well worth the effort. The actual site is a rambling muddle of a place with a jumble of ruins overgrown by olive and maquis. The site itself, situated in a wooded valley with the twin rivers of Alfios and Kladhios running through it, is magnificent and even the coach park and tacky souvenir stalls cannot detract from it. It is difficult to imagine that this site hosted the ancient Panhellenic games for over a thousand years and that many of the Greek heroes we read about proved their worth on track and field here.

One of the wonderful things about these ancient games was that a sacred truce, the *Ekeheiria*, was observed for the duration of the games and warring states would put aside their differences to partake in the events, presumably resuming hostilities after the games. It evokes those wonderful moments in the First World War when the British and Germans laid down their arms and played a game of football at Christmas. At the first games the prize for winning was purely symbolic, a palm leaf and an olive branch, but later some professionalism crept in and winners could expect monetary rewards as well as kudos from their home state. Under the Romans large monetary prizes were awarded at the games at Olympia.

The modern Olympic games were revived by Baron Pierre de Coubertin in 1896 and when he died his heart was brought here to be buried at Olympia. There is a small Museum of the Olympic Games in Olympia town and an excellent Archaeological Museum at the site.

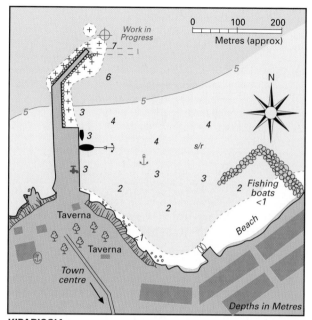

KIPARISSIA
⊕37°15′.51N 21°39′.76E WGS84

General

Katakólon was built in 1875 for the then thriving currant trade. Now it is used by small cargo ships and by cruise ships as a base for the visit to Olympia about 25 miles away. This is the best place to leave a yacht if you wish to visit Olympia – usually you will be accosted by a taxi driver as soon as you arrive. Alternatively hire a motorbike or car or take the bus to Pirgos and another bus on to Olympia.

KIPARISSIA (Órmos Kiparissias)

BA 189
Imray-Tetra G16

Approach

From the N the town of Kiparissia is conspicuous under the steep-to Mt Psikro (1350m). From the W the Disney-esque castle situated on the seafront near Agrilos is conspicuous.

By night There are no lights.

Dangers If the prevailing NW wind blows strongly there can be a confused swell in the approaches.

Mooring

Go stern or bows-to the quayed section of the breakwater or anchor off. The bottom is hard sand with some rocks, good holding once the anchor is in though this can take some doing.

Shelter from the N and W is just adequate and with the regular NW–W wind there is an uncomfortable surge in the harbour. With strong winds from the N the nearest shelter is in Órmos Navarínou or Methóni. With strong winds from the N or W the harbour is untenable – locals report that in the winter of 1990 a northerly gale sank every boat in the harbour.

Note 1. At the time of writing it is reported that the breakwater is being extended in an easterly direction which should improve the shelter here dramatically.

Note 2. The small fishing harbour in the SE corner is normally full of local fishing boats. You may be able to find a berth here although the locals will often wave you away. There are 2–3m depths in the entrance and 1–2m depths in the outer part of the harbour. Better shelter from the NW–W winds than under the outer breakwater.

Facilities

Services Water on the quay. Showers on the beach.
Fuel In the town about 500m away. A mini-tanker may be able to deliver to the quay.
Provisions Good shopping in the town.
Eating out Tavernas on the waterfront and in the town.
Other PO. OTE. Bank. ATM. Greek gas and Camping Gaz. Buses to Pílos and Patras.

General

Once an important harbour for nearby Messene, today only a few fishermen keep their boats here because of the poor shelter. This is a pity for yachtsmen because the town and the surrounding countryside are wonderful – as you sail along the coast you realise you are going to miss it all unless you take a chance here. It is worth wandering up to the Byzantine-Frankish castle and the old town below it. The castle and both the old and the new town sit on the lower slopes of Mt Psikro, a conical peak of the Egaleo mountain range rimming the Bay of Kiparissia. The houses of the old town are crumbling now, but this was once a prosperous place of rich merchants. Get up here early in the morning and you can get back before the maistro picks up and makes life uncomfortable in the harbour.

Nisídhes Strofadhes

Nisís Stamfáni light 37°14'·9N 21°00'·2E

These lonely islands lie approximately 32 miles due W of Kiparissia and 26 miles due S of Ák Yérakas on Zákinthos. A light is exhibited on Nisís Stamfáni: Fl(2)15s17M. On Nisís Arpia, the N island, a church is conspicuous at the N end. On Nisís Stamfáni the lighthouse and the monastery are conspicuous.

The islands once supported a prosperous monastery, but today there is just one monk who with the aid of a tractor looks after a flock of sheep, poultry, a vineyard, and a vegetable garden! At one time the island was plagued by rabbits, but a recent visitor reported there were no rabbits, but a lot of spent cartridges lying around!

Recent visitors report that the last monk here may have left this lonely monastery.

Órmos Tavernas A bay on the S side of Nisís Arpia. The approach to the bay should be made from the E only – the W side of the channel between Arpia and Stamfáni is obstructed by above and below-water rocks. Anchor in 4–10m. on a sand and rock bottom, good holding once the anchor is in. Good shelter from the prevailing NW wind. Water from a number of wells ashore.

Órmos Limani On the W side of Nisís Arpia there is a crescent bay with a tiny rockbound harbour at the N end. The approaches to this bay from either the S or NW are littered with above and below-water rocks. The passage into the bay from the NW can be made on a SE heading, but you should reconnoitre first by dinghy before attempting the approach. Anchor in the N end of

Órmos Tavernas on the S side of Nisís Arpia. The monastery on Stamfáni is conspicuous behind   *Nigel Patten*

The monastery on Nisís Stamfáni   *Nigel Patten*

the bay where there is only poor shelter from the prevailing NW wind.

Órmos Panayia In calm weather you can anchor off the monastery on the N side of Nisís Stamfani. Anchor in 5–6m on sand and rock. When the NW wind gets up it is advisable to leave here and return to the bay on the S side of Arpia. The monastery of Áy Panayia (13th century) ashore is an impressive fortified structure more like a fort than a monastery – not surprising given the certainty of pirate attacks in days past. Recently the monastery building has been beefed up with steel bands to hold the walls in place – no doubt after earthquake damage in the last few years.

Órmos Prasa A bay on the S side of Nisís Stamfáni. Not recommended as an anchorage as the coast is one long, low sea cliff and the sea bed is littered with large boulders.

Note In unsettled weather a yacht should not remain at Nisídhes Strofadhes. The waters around the island with gales from any direction have been likened to a giant washing machine swirling around

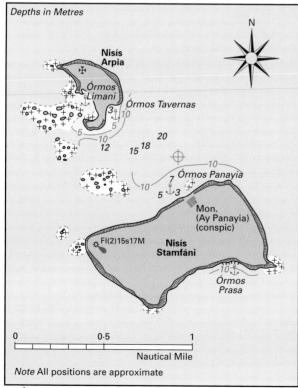

NISÍDHES STROFADHES
⊕37°15'·4N 21°00'·7E

– a potent image that should have you moving as soon as bad weather brews up.

AGRILOS 37°12'·74N 21°35'·68E WGS84

A small harbour approximately 5 miles SW of Kiparissia. The harbour is easily identified by the Kastro Paramython, a disneyesque castle on the coast. The harbour is very small and mostly 1–1·5m or less, so only small yachts (max. 8m LOA) will be able to get in here, much less find a berth amongst the fishing boats. Adequate shelter from the NW–W winds although a bit of a surge can build up.

Nearby the bizarre castle on the coast was built by Haris Fournakis (Harry Fournier), a local boy made good who returned from America to build this and other follies. The Kastro Paramython (Castle of the Fairytales) has battlements, towers and a thirty-five foot statue of Poseidon's horse and another of Athena. The castle is open in the summer (0900–1400/1700–2000) if you want to visit, or just coast in close for a look.

ÁY KIRIAKI 37°07'·11N 21°34'·52E WGS84

A very small harbour off the village of Áy Kiriaki. The entrance is rockbound and depths inside the harbour are mostly less than 1 metre and unsuitable for yachts.

NISÍS PRÓTI AND CHANNEL (Stenón Protis)

On the E coast of Nisís Próti there is a small bay which fishing boats sometimes use to shelter from NW winds. Care is needed of permanent moorings with floating lines on the surface. Depths are considerable and it is not a good anchorage. Above the anchorage there is a monastery which has been undergoing some recent renovation.

Local fishing boats also anchor on the SW side of Marathoupolis village where there is a surprisingly good lee from NW winds although some swell still penetrates.

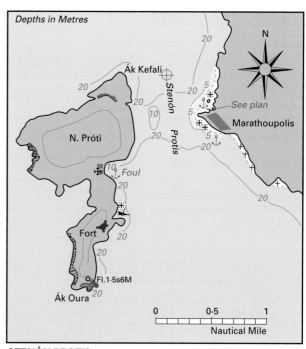

STENÓN PROTIS
⊕37°04'·14N 21°33'·87E WGS84

MARATHOUPOLIS

Approach

A small *caïque* harbour on the NE corner of Próti Channel to the N of Ák Marathoupolis. Suitable for small yachts perhaps up to 10m. The entrance is difficult with rock-bound shallows on either side of the channel. By day enter from the N keeping an eye open for the shallows.

Conspicuous A church with two blue cupolas is conspicuous.

By night There are no lights and entry at night would be dangerous.

Dangers With moderate NW winds there is a considerable swell at the entrance and care is needed. With strong NW–W winds a heavy sea builds up in the approaches and entry is not advised.

Note The new extension to the W breakwater was destroyed recently in a Force 11 winter gale. Care needed in the immediate approaches and the entrance.

Marathoupolis village on the E side of the Próti Channel looking NE. The small *caïque* harbour is 'around the top' of the headland

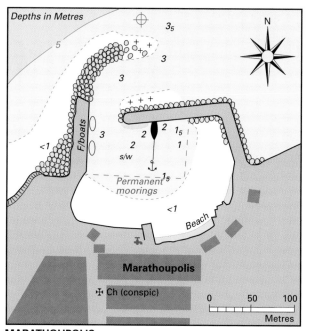

MARATHOUPOLIS
⊕37°03'·69N 21°34'·42E WGS84

Mooring

There are 2m depths off the extremity of the mole running E–W on the N side of the harbour. Go bows-to tucked just inside the mole or alongside on the W mole, keeping clear of fishing boat berths. The E side of the harbour is taken up with permanent moorings. The harbour is very crowded with fishing boats and you may have difficulty finding a berth here.

Shelter Reasonable shelter from moderate N–NW winds. Good shelter from S winds.

Facilities

Water in the village. Fuel about 1km away. Taverna and limited provisions in the village.

General

The village cannot be described as an attractive place, but it is convivial and the situation on the edge of the channel looking across to Nisís Próti is wonderful.

VROMONERI

37°01'·01N 21°37'·21E WGS84

A miniature cove with a diameter of around 100 metres. In calm weather a small yacht could investigate.

ÓRMOS VOIDHOKOILIA

36°56'·97N 21°39'·64E WGS84

The oval bay located just N of the N end of Nísos Sfaktiria. In calm weather or light NW winds it is an attractive spot to stop over. With any wind from the NW–W a swell is pushed into the bay and it is not a good place to be, making it effectively a calm weather anchorage only. Anchor in 2–3m at the N end of the bay on sand.

Above the anchorage to the S is the rocky crag with Palaiokastro on top. The castle is basically Frankish and Venetian although it is built on the site of an ancient Acropolis. On the way up you pass a cave dubbed the Cave of Nestor which may or may not be the cave mentioned in the *Odyssey* where Nestor and Neleus kept their cows and where Hermes hid Apollo's sacred cattle.

PÍLOS (Pylos, Navarino, Neokastro)

BA 2404

Imray-Tetra G16

Approach

Conspicuous Nisís Sfaktiria (ancient Sphakteria) and Nisís Pílos are easily identified. Nisís Pílos has a huge natural arch through it and the lighthouse and a white memorial on it are conspicuous. On entering Órmos Navarínou the large Venetian fort with a conspicuous church on the S side of the entrance is easily identified. Once in Órmos Navarínou the small town of Pílos will be seen.

By night Use the light on Nisís Pílos Fl(2)10s9M, the light on Ák Neókastron off the Venetian fort Fl.G.3s6M and the light on the extremity of the pier F.G.3M. The entrance to the new marina is lit: Fl.G.3s3M/Fl.R.3s3M though the lights appear to be unreliable.

VHF Ch 12 for Pílos port police.

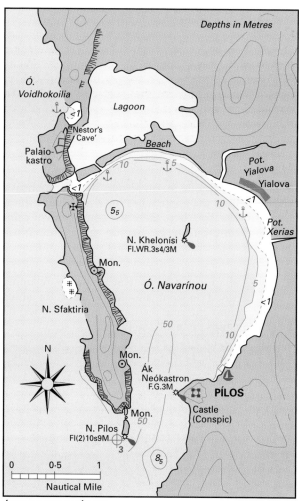

ÓRMOS NAVARÍNOU

⊕3   0·25M W N. Pílos light 36°54'·08N 21°40'·09E WGS84

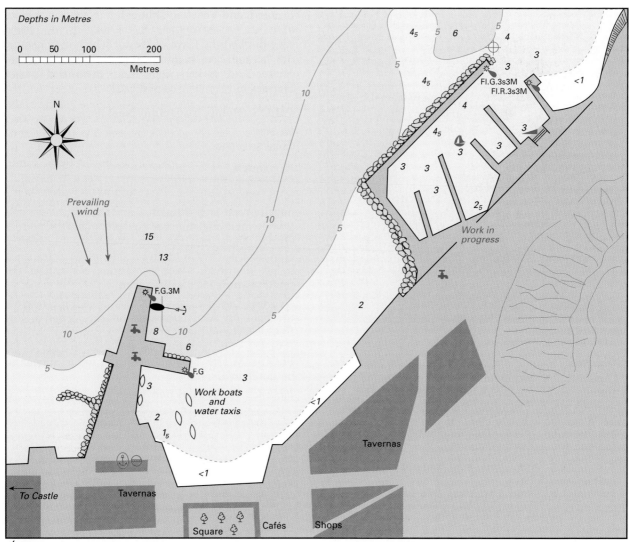

PÍLOS
⊕ 36°55´·16N 21°42´·02E WGS84

Dangers With moderate to strong W winds a heavy sea piles up in the approaches to Órmos Navarínou. Once inside the bay there is comparative calm although there can be strong gusts off Nisís Sfakteria.

Note

1. Large ships use Órmos Navarínou to resupply and a good lookout should be kept for ships leaving and entering the bay. There will often be several ships at anchor in the bay.

2. When approaching the marina entrance you are literally heading straight for the cliffs before you turn hard to starboard to enter the marina. If the prevailing NW wind is blowing there is a bit of slop at the entrance but not really anything to worry about.

Mooring

Data c.180 berths. Visitors' berths. Max LOA c.20m. Depths 2·5–3·5m.

Nísos Pílos looking E into Órmos Navarínou

General

Pílos was largely built by the French in the 19th century after the Battle of Navarinon and it shows with elegant buildings arranged around a large square. The shaded square has a memorial to the three admirals who commanded the fleet which destroyed Turkish sea power – Admirals Codrington, de Rigny and von Heyden. In the evening the locals wander around the square and everyone chooses the café of choice and relaxes as the sun goes down – you could almost be in some provincial French town.

The fort to the W of the harbour, so prominent from seawards, was originally built by the Venetians and added to by the Turks. It has an impressive mosque, now a church, inside the walls. The castle is open from 0930 hours.

Pílos is the place to organise a visit to Ano Englianos and ancient Pílos, the Mycenaean city believed be King Nestor's. You really need a car or motorbike to get there – around 30 minutes' drive. The palace seems to have been abandoned after a fire around 1200BC and later covered over, so it is one of the best preserved sites of a Mycenean palace.

Pilos Marina looking out over the pier at Pilos town to the entrance to Ormos Navarinou

Berths At present yachts berth alongside the outer wall and piers of the marina. Laid moorings are to be installed and berthing will then be stern or bows-to.

Yachts can go stern or bows-to under the end of the town pier if there is room, though it is uncomfortable here both from the prevailing wind and wash from the workboats.

Shelter Good all-round shelter although N–NW winds push a swell onto the cliffs at the entrance which rebounds into the marina and makes some berths near the entrance uncomfortable.

Authorities A port of entry: port police, customs and immigration. The authorities are housed in a building at the root of the town pier. Charge band 2. Charging for the use of the marina seems to be fairly haphazard at the time of publication although it is likely charges will be applied in the future.

Note The future of the marina is uncertain at the moment. A number of private companies have looked at the marina and decided against buying it, but in the future it is more than likely a private company will acquire it and finish the development.

Facilities

Services Water tap at the root of the marina breakwater. Service boxes for water and electricity are being installed. Toilets completed but not serviced. A shower block is planned.

Fuel In the town. A mini-tanker will deliver to the marina.

Repairs 20-ton crane at the marina. Limited mechanical repairs.

Provisions Good shopping for all provisions.

Eating out A number of good tavernas to the E of the square on the road leading up the hill. Others around the square and waterfront.

Other PO. OTE. ATM. Banks. Greek gas and Camping Gaz. Hire motorbikes and cars. Buses to Methóni, Kalamata, and Kiparissia.

The Battle of Navarinon

At the very time when the Greek forces were at their lowest ebb during the War of Independence, the fortuitous naval engagement in the Bay of Navarinon changed the whole order of things and effectively won the war. On 6 July 1827, the Treaty of London between Great Britain, France and Russia provided that Greece should be autonomous but under the control of the Turks. This piece of legal chicanery was implemented so that the three powers might remain friendly to both Greece and Turkey and allowed for their fleets to guarantee the treaty. The senior admiral, Codrington, was given wide powers of discretion in the policing of the treaty.

Presented with the terms of the treaty, the Greeks agreed (they had little option) while the Turks did not. Codrington decided to enter the Bay of Navarinon where the Turko-Egyptian fleet was assembled, even though his fleet was outnumbered and outgunned (the allied fleet numbered 26 ships and 1270 guns; the Turko-Egyptian fleet numbered 89 warships and 2450 guns) and despite the fact that his country was not at war with the opposing fleet. The Turko-Egyptian fleet was anchored in a three quarter circle facing the entrance, in theory a trap in which ships sailing in would be caught by fire from all sides before they could sail out again. Codrington led his fleet in, the bands playing on the deck and the gun ports half open, and anchored in the middle of the trap. An Egyptian ship fired a shot and the battle began. 'The bloody and destructive battle was continued with unabated fury for four hours; and the scene of wreck and devastation which presented itself at its termination was such as has been seldom before witnessed', Codrington wrote in his dispatch.

It was an unremitting battle fought at anchor which Codrington won, proving that European gun crews were more efficient in the heat of battle than their eastern counterparts. Codrington was not censured over this action although the English government expressed regret over it. France mopped up any remaining opposition in the Peloponnisos and in the end Greece was free.

ÓRMOS NAVARÍNOU – N END

A yacht can anchor at the N end of Órmos Navarínou where convenient. The bottom comes up quickly to the sandy beach so you will have to anchor in 8–12m. The bottom is sand and mud, good holding once the anchor has dug in, though this can take a bit of doing for some reason. Good shelter from the prevailing wind which blows in from between NW and N. At night after the wind has died down it can be a bit uncomfortable here with the residual swell creeping in through the entrance and up into the bay.

There are a couple of snack bars that open in the summer, but little else. If you anchor in the NW corner you can walk across to Nísos Sfaktiria. A shallow bar shuts off the northern entrance to the bay and it is possible to wade across to the island.

The energetic may like to hike up to the summit of Ák Korifasion to Palaiokastro and down the other side to Voidhokoilia. Take some water and stout shoes.

Methóni Roadstead and Messiniakos Kólpos

Five miles south of Órmos Navarínou, the once important port of Methóni is tucked behind a small headland dominated by a large fort. Following the coast east for some 12 miles, the wide gulf of Messiniakos Kólpos (Gulf of Messina, Gulf of Kalamata) opens up between Nisís Venétiko and Ák Tainaron (Cape Matapan). Bordered on the west by comparatively tame mountains, the country is for the most part green and wooded down to sandy beaches. The harbours of Koroni and Petalídhion offer reasonable shelter in the summer months. At the head of the gulf lies the low marshland of the Makaria plain with the large port of Kalamata at its eastern end.

Towering above Kalamata is the Taiyetos (2307m/7500ft high) running south to the Mani peninsula ending in Ák Tainaron. Tainaron, a.k.a Matapan, was the ancient Tenaron, the entrance to the underworld, and for all that exists around the cape it might as well be the end of the world for yachtsman and ancient alike. Tainaron is very nearly the most southerly cape of mainland Europe and only Cape Tarifa at the entrance to the Gibraltar Strait is further south by 14 miles.

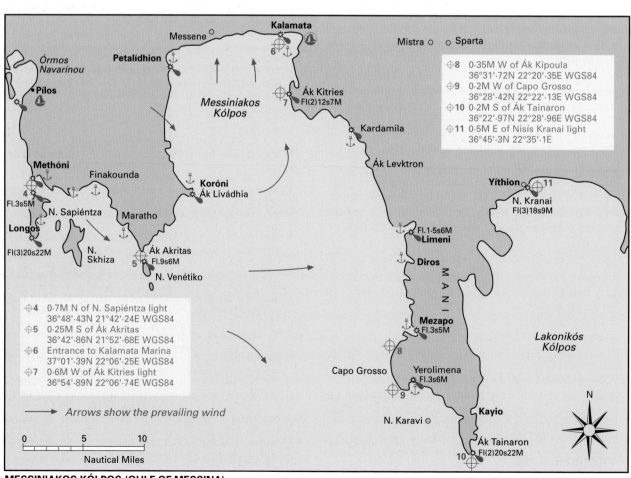

MESSINIAKOS KÓLPOS (GULF OF MESSINA)

METHÓNI (Modon)

BA 1683

Imray-Tetra G15

Approach

Conspicuous From the N and S the Venetian fort and the Turkish tower on the extremity of Ák Soukouli are conspicuous. The silhouette of the Turkish tower is unmistakable once seen. From the W and S the lighthouse on the S end of Nisís Sapiéntza stands out clearly. Once in Methóni Roadstead the small harbour is easily identified.

By night Use the light on S end of Nisís Sapiéntza Fl(3)20s22M, the light on Ák Karsí at the N end of Sapiéntza Fl.3s5M, and the light on the end of the breakwater Fl.R.3s3M.

Dangers

1. With westerlies a confused swell piles up between Ák Soukouli and Ák Karsí, but a short distance into the roadstead things quieten down.
2. Care should be taken of the reef around Nisís Kouloura – there is usually broken water around it.
3. A yacht should keep well clear of Nisís Skhiza which is used by the air force for target practice.

Mooring

Anchor off under the breakwater. The bottom is mud or sand and weed. The weed is quite thick in places so make sure your anchor is well in.

Shelter Good shelter from all but strong SE winds.

The conspicuous Turkish tower at Methóni, looking SW from the harbour. (It looks pretty much the same from all angles)

Facilities

Water At the root of the breakwater or on the beach.

Fuel In the town about 500m from the beach.

Repairs Limited mechanical repairs.

Provisions Good shopping in the village.

Eating out Tavernas on the beach and in the town.

Other PO. OTE. Bank. Greek gas and Camping Gaz. Bus to Pílos.

General

The harbour, bounded by the large fort and the sandy beach, is one of my favourite places on the W Peloponnisos. Methóni was mentioned by Homer as being 'rich in vines' and later under the Venetians it was famous for its wine and pork. Today the hinterland is still intensively cultivated and you will see the greenhouses flashing in the sun as you near the harbour.

The Venetian fort guarded the shipping route around the Peloponnisos and Methóni, along with Koroni, was called 'the eye of the Republic'. Later

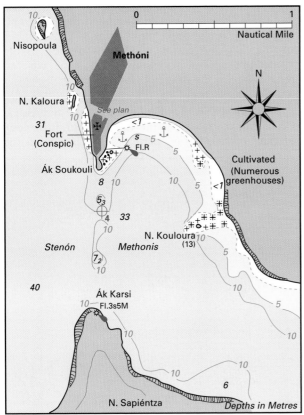

STENÓN METHONIS

⊕4   0·7M N of N. Sapiéntza light 36°48'·43N 21°42'·24E WGS84

Methóni harbour and anchorage looking E from the castle

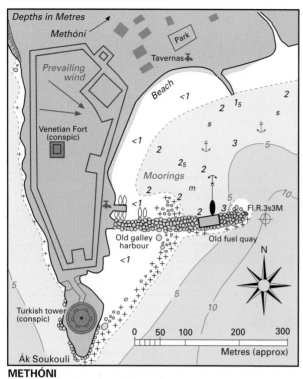

METHÓNI
⊕36°48'·83N 21°42'·58E WGS84

reported to be bad in places so make sure your anchor is well dug in. Good shelter, although strong easterlies send a swell in and there can be gusts off the land with the prevailing wind.

The lighthouse can be reached by a track from the bay and is now surrounded by an impressive bank of solar cells. Greece was comparatively late in modernising its lights and as a consequence was able to bypass other outmoded 'modern' methods and convert its remote lights (which used to be mostly powered by bottled gas) to solar power.

NISÍS SKHIZA

The island is a prohibited area. The air force use it for bombing practice and unless you happen to get a thrill out of F111s approaching at masthead height on a bombing run, it is wise to keep well clear of the whole island. And yes, they do use live bombs and rockets.

Despite the frequent use of the island for target practice, local fishermen can often be seen pottering around the W coast and they sometimes use the cove on the SW end of the island. I have not investigated it (that live ammunition has deterred me somewhat) and would not recommend it.

ÁK KOLIVRI 36°46'·77N 21°45'·61 WGS84

With westerlies there is a lee under Ák Kolivri. Local fishing boats sometimes anchor here to sort the catch and in settled weather it might be a useful overnight stop. Open S and E.

FINAKOUNDA

Note At the time of publication it was reported that the end of the breakwater had been damaged and there was underwater rubble and shoal water surrounding the entrance. Care is needed in the immediate approaches and it would be wise to reconnoitre in the dinghy before entering.

The small harbour in Órmos Finakounda lies approximately 5 miles E of Ák Karsí on Sapiéntza. Once into the large bay the village around the edge of the beach is easily identified. A church on the

the Turks captured it and Cervantes was a prisoner here – the tale in *Don Quixote* of the captive may relate his experiences as a Turkish prisoner. The entrance is in the NE wall and the fort is open from 1000–1600.

PORT LONGOS

On the SE end of Nisís Sapiéntza there is the deserted bay of Port Longos. The lighthouse is conspicuous from some distance off. A fish farm now occupies the E side of the bay, but there is still room for 3 or 4 yachts to anchor. Anchor under the saddle between the hills or in the S of the bay in 5–6m on a sandy bottom. The holding has been

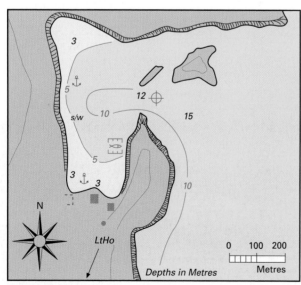

PORT LONGOS
⊕36°45'·4N 21°42'·4E

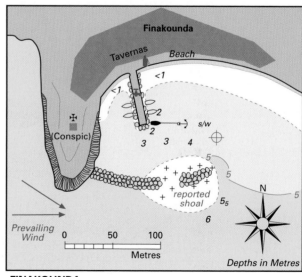

FINAKOUNDA
⊕36°48'·3N 21°49'·3E

headland sheltering the harbour is conspicuous. The rough stone breakwater will be seen closer in. There are no lights. With the prevailing wind funnelled W there is often a considerable swell rolling across the entrance to the harbour.

Berth bows-to the end of the pier or anchor off under the shelter of the breakwater. Good shelter from the prevailing W winds but open to the S.

Fuel in the village near the new pier. Water on the pier. Ashore provisions are available and there are numerous tavernas. The once tranquil fishing village has been somewhat shattered by the arrival of a watersports centre and has become something of a backpackers' resort, but retains a likeable character. The setting is wonderful, with the village huddled around the beach under a low rocky bluff and a fertile hinterland.

PORT MARATHO

36°46'·4N 21°50'·0E

A small inlet 3½ miles NW of Ák Akritas. The inlet is difficult to identify from the distance, but the beach around its head will be seen between the rocky sides to the cove. Care is needed of a group of rocks awash off the N side of the entrance. Anchor in 2–4m on mud and sand, good holding. Reasonable shelter from westerlies and from the N–E winds which sometimes blow out of Messiniakos Kólpos.

KORONI (Coron)

BA 1683

Imray-Tetra G15

Approach

Conspicuous The fort atop the headland is conspicuous from the N and S. From the N the buildings of Koroni village under the castle are conspicuous. From the S the buildings of the town on the crown of the hill and around the bay to the S are conspicuous. From the S the harbour will not be seen until around Ák Livádhia.

By night Use the light on Ák Livádhia Fl.1·5s5M and the light on the end of the harbour breakwater Fl.R.1·5s3M.

Mooring

Anchor in 2–5m depths on the W side of the bay – the depths come up slowly so you can usually potter in until satisfied and then anchor. The bottom is

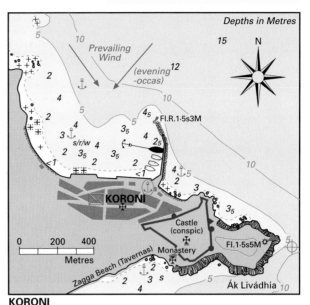

KORONI
⊕36°47'·62N 21°58'·40E WGS84

mostly mud, sand and weed, not everywhere good holding so make sure your anchor is well in. Very large boulders litter the bottom in places and care should be taken not to snag one of these. Although there are 2m depths at the extremity of the concrete walkway on the mole where a yacht can moor bows-to, this is not advised as the prevailing wind normally blows onto here and the bottom is littered with permanent moorings.

Shelter Good shelter from the prevailing wind which normally blows across the headland from the S or off the hills from the NW–W. At night a NE wind may blow which can be uncomfortable but rarely dangerous. Make sure your anchor is well in and if in doubt don't leave the boat unattended.

Alternative anchorages

1. In calm weather or light westerlies a yacht can anchor off on the E side of the harbour breakwater. This is an idyllic place under the bastions of the castle.
2. A yacht can anchor off on the S side of the headland ending in Ák Livádhia. Zanga beach stretching around the coast from here is wonderful and popular with the locals in the summer.

Koroni approach looking E

Koroni castle looking from the harbour. The Venetians called it 'the eye of the Republic'

Facilities
Water Not easily available. Can be delivered by tanker.
Fuel 1½km out of the village.
Provisions Good shopping in the village.
Eating out Good tavernas around the waterfront. Good *ouzeries*.
Other PO. OTE. Bank. Greek gas and Camping Gaz. Regular bus service to Kalamata.

General
Built on the steep slopes under and partly inside the Venetian fort, Koroni is an attractive town with some fine old houses. The town acquired the name Korone (corrupted to Coron) via migrants from ancient Korone, now Petalídhion. The Venetians rightly perceived that the headland was the ideal site for a fort to defend their trade route around the Peloponnisos. Much of it is still largely intact and incorporates bits of ancient masonry from nearby Asine. The fort, entered through the massive gateway at the eastern end of the village (follow the road up from the harbour mole), is a wonderfully tranquil place, much overgrown and now mostly occupied by a monastery. This fort was the second 'eye of the Republic' after Methóni.

The harbour front, though a bit smelly in places from the sewage emptying into it, is alive at night with the locals promenading and a few tourists relaxing in the tavernas – there are several good *ouzeries* specialising in charcoal-grilled octopus.

KORONI TO PETALÍDHION
The coast between Koroni and Petalídhion is pleasantly wooded and there are a number of attractive bays with sandy beaches where a yacht can anchor in calm weather. In Homeric times this was part of ancient Messene and later was conquered by the Spartans. Many of the Messenians fled to Sicily around about this time. Their descendants captured Zancle, renaming it Messana, hence modern Messina and the Messina Strait.

PETALÍDHION (Petalidi)
An attractive sheltered bay in the NW corner of the gulf. A church, a two-storeyed building, and the light structure are conspicuous.

Mooring
A new harbour has been constructed to the W of the old mole. Depths 1·5–3·5m. If there is room berth stern or bows–to on the N side. Bows–to is better as depths come up to 1·5m in places close to the quay. Good shelter from the prevailing winds.
Anchorage Anchor off to the N of the harbour in 3-5 metres. The bottom is sand and weed, generally good holding. Shelter in the anchorage is good in settled weather and only strong NE winds would make it untenable.

Facilities
Water On the beach or in town.
Fuel On the outskirts of town. You may be able to get a mini-tanker down to the quay or go to the fuel quay at Kalamata Marina a short distance away.
Provisions Good shopping for most provisions in town.
Eating out Good local tavernas on the waterfront.
Other PO. Bank. Bus to Kalamata. Taxis.

General
Petaídhion is a somewhat ramshackle town although the old villas around the shore hint at an affluent past. Although little is recorded of the place it was probably a trading port for the flat coastal plain at the head of the gulf until the commercial harbour at

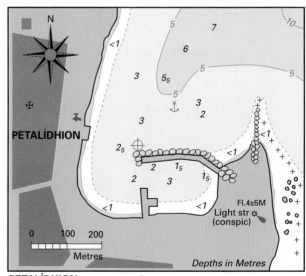

PETALÍDHION
⊕36°57′·50N 21°55′·95E WGS84

Kalamata was built. It seems to have sat here pretty much unmolested over time. On the hills to the SW are a few remains of ancient Aereia, later renamed as Korone. This was the original Korone until the inhabitants moved further down the coast to present-day Koroni. It is a laid-back place with a little local tourism in the summer that is well worth the detour into this NW corner of the gulf.

WEATHER NOTE

In the late summer there are frequently black clouds over the plain behind Kalamata and over the Taiyetos and the Mani. More often than not these come to nothing even though they look threatening, but on occasion there will be some rain and an associated squall. The locals in Kalamata say their summer begins in May and ends in the middle of August.

The weather over the land sometimes affects the weather further out over Messiniakos Kólpos and there may be squalls in the gulf. Normally the prevailing wind blows from the W into the bottom of the gulf and then curves to blow from the SW and finally from the S at Kalamata.

KALAMATA (Kalami, Kalamón)

BA 2404
Imray-Tetra G15

Approach

Straightforward by day and night.

Conspicuous The cluster of buildings of the small city is conspicuous. The exact location of the harbour is difficult to see from the distance but closer in a large flour mill at the W end of the harbour and the harbour breakwater will be seen. Yachts should head for the marina and not the commercial harbour.

The lighthouse on Ák Kitries looking NE

By night Use the light on Ák Kitries Fl(2)12s7M and the lights at the entrance to the marina Fl.G.3s3M/Fl.R.3s3M. The lights at the marina entrance are difficult to make out against the loom of the lights behind. The entrance to the commercial harbour is lit Fl.G.1·5s3M/Fl.R.1·5s3M.

VHF Ch 69 for marina office. Call sign *Kalamata Marina*.

Dangers With the prevailing onshore breeze blowing there is some confused swell in the narrow entrance – more difficult with a fresh breeze than dangerous.

Mooring

Data 255 berths. Visitors' berths. Max LOA 30m. Depths 2-3·5m.

Berth Where directed. Marina staff will assist you to berth. There are laid moorings tailed to the quay. The rope tail is substantial and smaller yachts may need to tie a smaller diameter line to it.

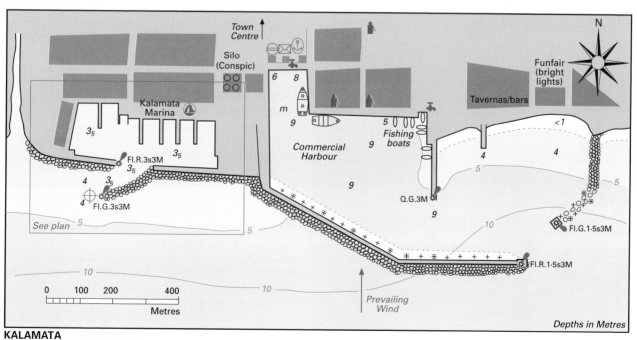

KALAMATA
⊕37°01'·39N 22°06'·25E WGS84

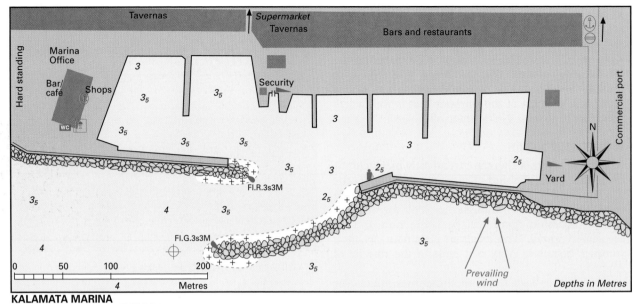

KALAMATA MARINA
⊕37°01′·39N 22°06′·25E WGS84

Shelter Good all round shelter. The prevailing onshore breeze causes a little surge at some berths near the entrance which can be mildly uncomfortable.

Authorities Harbourmaster and marina staff. Port police office in the marina. Charge band 2.

Kalamata Marina, 24100, Greece
☎ 27210 21054/21037 *Fax* 27210 26079
Email kalamatamarina@yahoo.com
www.kalamatamarina.tsx.org
www.medmarinas.com

Facilities

Services Water and electricity at every berth. Shower and toilet block. Laundry operated by tokens.
Fuel Fuel quay near the entrance. Care needed of the rock ballasting near the W end of the fuel quay.
Repairs 30-ton crane. 50-ton travel-hoist to be installed soon. Hardstanding area for c.130 boats. Most mechanical and engineering work. The marina will carry out gardiennage and maintenance on the boat according to what is needed. Chandlers. Hardware shops in town.
Provisions Good supermarket a block away heading N from the entrance. Other good supermarkets with all sorts of hard-to-get items nearby.
Eating out A bar and café in the marina. Tavernas close by and others along the waterfront. Some good tavernas in the hills to the E.
Other PO. OTE. Banks. ATMs. Greek gas and Camping Gaz (from the service station E of the basin). Hire cars and motorbikes. Buses to Athens and most destinations around the Peloponnisos. Internal flights and some European flights.

Note A regular bus service operates past the harbour into the centre of town – Bus No.1.

General

Kalamata was once the principal port of the Peloponnisos, but now its commercial traffic is much diminished. The harbour and town are more undistinguished than unattractive. The recent earthquake in 1968 caused much damage and consequently parts of the town have an abandoned appearance while the rest is undergoing reconstruction.

Despite this, Kalamata is a place I like, a real Greek place supported by the agricultural hinterland, especially the production of fat black olives famous throughout the world as 'Kalamata olives'. Kalamata Marina is such a friendly well-run marina that it adds to the charm of the place and makes it a pleasure to visit here.

There are all sorts of surprises in the town. From the basin if you walk straight up from the W corner you will come to a park you can walk through nearly into the middle of town. The park incorporates the old railway station and on the tracks around it are numerous restored locomotives and carriages from all ages – a must for railway buffs and a pleasant walk into town for the mildly curious.

Kalamata Marina looking ESE   *Nikitas Kiriakoulis*

Kalamata was the capital for the Franks when they controlled the area and the redoubtable Guillaume de Villehardouin (1218–1287) was born and died here – above the town are the remains of the castle he built, though most of what remains are later modifications and additions from the Venetians. Modern Kalamata was built by the French in the 19th century, though many of the old buildings from this period have decayed. Kalamata is the nearest safe harbour to Messene and the safest harbour for visiting Mistra, although Yíthion is also suitable.

ÓRMOS KITRIES

⊕7 0·5M W of Ák Kitries 36°31'·7N 22°07'·1E

On the N side of Ák Kitries lies the large bay of Kitrou. The bay provides good shelter from the prevailing southerlies and reasonable shelter from northerlies which do not normally blow home.

Anchor off the harbour where possible. Shelter is not the best here although there is some shelter from the breeze blowing up into the gulf and it is usually calm at night. Occasionally a NE wind will blow off the mountains and if it blows strongly you may have to move up to the head of the gulf or to Kalamata Marina. The bottom is sand and weed, good holding once through the weed.

In the SE corner there is a short mole providing shelter for local boats. Small yachts may be able to find a berth on the end of the mole where there are 1·5–2m depths.

Tavernas ashore. The slopes around the bay are terraced and planted in olive and citrus with villas dotted around the beach and lower slopes. It is an entrancing spot and in settled weather can be used as an overnight anchorage.

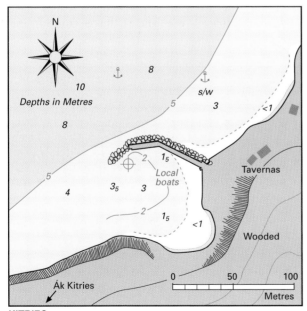

KITRIES
⊕36°55'·7N 22°08'·5E

KARDAMILA

An open anchorage lying about 5 miles SSE of Ák Kitries. There is a small harbour off the village but there are barely 2m depths in the entrance and 1–1·5m depths inside. Anchor off the mole under the islet in 4–8m or in the bay to the S. There is nearly always some swell in here making it uncomfortable, and in unsettled weather it would be untenable.

Numerous tavernas in the village and good shopping for provisions ashore. Fuel available in the village.

The village is an attractive place, all creepers and tiled roofs, though somewhat overrun with visitors with a professorial gait, in search of inspiration from the village's literary inhabitant Patrick Leigh Fermor (though I suspect he escapes from the summer visitors). For wonderful writing on Greece and all sorts of esoteric information difficult to locate elsewhere, Leigh Fermor's two books on Greece, *Mani* and *Roumeli*, should go on everybody's list of books to read.

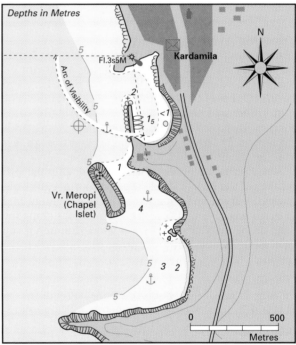

KARDAMILA
⊕36°53'N 22°13'·7E

ÁK LEVKTRON

Care is needed of extensive reefs and shallows extending up to 1M SW from the cape. There is a miniature fishing harbour at Áy Nikólaos to the S of Ák Levktron, not suitable for yachts, but it is lit Fl.3s5M.

PORT LIMENÍ (Órmos Limeniou)
Approach

This large bay lies 18 miles SE of Ák Kitries. The bay is difficult to identify from the distance, but once up to the entrance the ravine splitting the land at the head of it stands out well and closer in the houses around the bay will be seen. The neo-

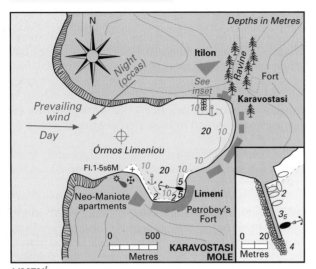

LIMENÍ
⊕36°41′·15N 22°22′·3E

Maniote village above Limení and the church by the light structure on the S entrance point are conspicuous.

By night The S side of the entrance is lit Fl.1·5s6M but a night entrance should be made with caution.

Mooring
Anchor on the E side of Limení cove on the S side of the bay and take a long line ashore or anchor off on the W side of the cove. It is quite deep here and you will have to drop anchor in 10–12m. The bottom is sand and weed with a scattering of rocks over it. In settled weather the prevailing wind tends to blow only lightly in the summer and though it is a little uncomfortable, it is quite tenable.

An alternative anchorage is tucked into the NE corner of the bay. A short stone breakwater runs out from the shore and you may be lucky enough to find a berth on the end. There are 3–4m depths along the end of the quay. Shelter here is good although it can get a bit bumpy if it gusts from the NE down the ravine.

Facilities
Water from local sources ashore. Provisions at Limení. Several tavernas at Limení and Karavostasi.

General
The large bay lies approximately halfway down the W side of the Mani peninsula, ideally placed to break the voyage between Kalamata and Porto Káyio. The fact that the bay is open to westerlies puts most people off, but for those willing to chance it, and in the summer you will have no problems most of the time, this is a wonderful place in a magnificent setting. The small hamlet at Limení has a little tourism in the summer, but nothing overwhelming. The tavernas serve simple but good fare with views out over the cove and the bay.

There are two architectural anomalies in the bay. The first is the Maniote village on the hillside above Limení, which is not a Maniote village but a hotel and apartment complex built in neo-Maniote style – only the large windows and the large building at the rear give it away. The second is what appears to be

a reproduction of a Scottish Presbyterian church in the village, which is in fact a fortress built in the 19th century by Petros Mavromichalis, a clan leader from Areopolis, on the hilltop above.

DIROS (Dyros)
A bay about 3 miles S of Limení. The entrance is difficult to make out from the distance. A tall tower in Pirgos village N of the bay is conspicuous, but then there are a lot of towers along this stretch of coast. The shelter from the prevailing winds is poor, but in the morning calm a yacht can put in here to visit the Caves of Diros. Anchor in the NE corner or in the SE corner where a few local boats are kept on moorings. The caves and the reception buildings are housed on the SE side of the bay.

The caves are spectacular – one of those sights that stays with you a long time and which few adjectives adequately describe. The viewing of the caves is strictly controlled and it is best to go early before the coaches and cars of other sightseers arrive. The ticket booth is a short distance up the road from the caves. A guide punts and pushes a flat-bottomed boat around the subterranean passages which literally drip with stalactites – unfortunately in recent years the guides have taken to racing through the caves as quickly as possible and a protest is in order if you receive such treatment. The interconnected passages are lit for the convenience of tourists and although the tour is an extensive one, you emerge with the feeling that there are many more passages trailing off into an inky blackness than you have seen from the boat.

The apocryphal story of the discovery of the caves relates that a shepherd, chasing one of his sheep, fell through a hole into one of the caves and thus the cave complex was discovered. In fact evidence of prehistoric occupation has been discovered here and it is likely the caves have been known for a long time. Perhaps this is the real entrance to the underworld rather than Cape Matapan.

Although I am not a speleologist, caves have always fascinated me and I have toured and

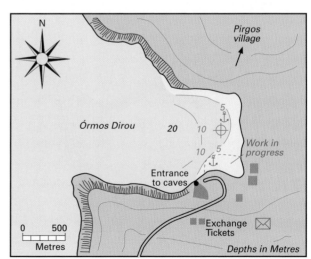

DIROS
⊕36°38′·8N 22°22′·5E

explored a good number. The Caves of Diros rank with the best of them. Between Limení and Diros and indeed further S of Diros there are a great many caves in the cliffs and it would appear that this whole area is riddled with them. If it is too rough to anchor at Diros, go to Yíthion or Kalamata and take a bus from there.

At Diros there is a small PO and money exchange booth, a bar, café, and taverna.

Note There are works in progress in the SE corner of the bay, but no information is available as yet on what the construction is for. I'd plump for a new entrance to the caves.

MEZAPO (Órmos Mezapou)

A large bay some 10 miles S of Limení. The vast mountainous bulk of Capo Grosso just S is difficult to miss. On the thin peninsula partially sheltering the bay (Tigani = frying pan, because of its shape) the remains of a fort will be seen when closer in. Once at the entrance to the bay the village of Mezapos will be seen.

Anchor off the small harbour and take a long line ashore. Very small yachts may find a space in the harbour, though care is needed as the bottom is uneven. The bay affords some shelter from the prevailing winds but at night a strong katabatic wind may blow in from the N–NE making it uncomfortable and possibly untenable. Tavernas ashore and limited provisions are available.

The small fishing harbour under vertical cliffs is a spectacular spot. Mezapo for a long time had a reputation as a local pirating and smuggling village and it continues to give that impression. Tim Severin on his voyage to retrace the route of Odysseus identified the place with the harbour of the Laestrygones, the cannibal giants who threw stones down on Odysseus and his men, killing many of them and sinking all but the galley of Odysseus.

Ák Taínaron (Matapan) and lighthouse looking W

Formerly Bonifacio on Corsica was identified with the harbour of the Laestrygones. Make up your own mind on the matter.

CAPO GROSSO

Immediately SW of Mezapo lies the vast bulk of Capo Grosso, a huge precipitous mass of rock that is unmistakable once seen – if any large cape should be called 'gross' it is this one. The cliffs rise sheer from the sea to 250m (800ft) and more, split by ravines and peppered with caves. Some of the caves have been walled up and it is said these contained the wealth of the Mezapo pirate families, but you would need to be a rock climber to get to them.

On the S side of Grosso just before Yerolimena there is a huge natural cave in the cliffs, easily identified from seawards, and this cave would be a

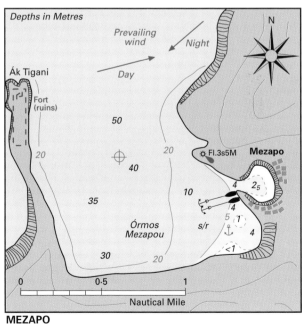

MEZAPO
⊕36°32′·9N 22°22′·6E

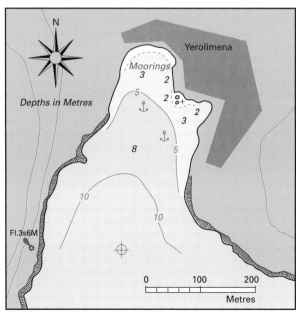

YEROLIMENA
⊕36°28′·8N 22°24′·0E

natural choice for the ancients' entrance to Hades, rather than the traditional site situated at Tainaron (Matapan) further south.

YEROLIMENA

36°28'·9N 22°24'·04E

A bay tucked in S of Capo Grosso. There is a small quay for fishing boats where two or three small yachts could berth with care. The bay is open W and S and invariably has some swell rolling into it. In calm weather anchor off in 4–6m on sand and rock, poor holding in places. If there is a hint of strong winds from almost any direction then you should leave and seek shelter elsewhere. In strong southerlies head for Porto Káyio or Kalamata.

Provisions and tavernas ashore.

At one time this was the principal ferry port for the Mani.

Lakonikós Kólpos
(Gulf of Lakonika, Gulf of Kolokythia)

Around Ák Tainaron (Cape Matapan) lies the steep-sided and heavily indented Lakonikós Kólpos. Bordered on the west by the Taiyetos and on the east by the Parnon, it is a forbidding place, although the weather at the head of the gulf is often more settled than around the southern end. On the eastern side Nísos Elafónisos must be rounded before Ák Maléas is encountered.

Now, as in ancient times, the channel between Ák Maléas and the island of Kíthera is an important channel for ships leaving and entering the Aegean. The chances are you will encounter a fair number of large ships in this channel and a sharp lookout must be kept.

Ák Maléas is a mountainous headland some 780m high. It has a formidable reputation and mariners leaving Greece coined the saying: 'Round Malea, forget your native country'. It was the *Formidatum Maleae caput* of the Roman poet Statius and the cape where Odysseus was blown south to the land of the Lotus Eaters.

'I might have made it safely home, that time, but as I came round Malea the current took me out to sea, and from the north a fresh gale drove me on, past Kythera.'

Odyssey

Today, even with the aid of weather forecasts, it pays to treat the cape with respect.

PORTO ASOMATO AND ÓRMOS VATHI

Porto Asomato 36°24'·4N 22°29'·4E
Órmos Vathi 36°23'·8N 22°29'·4E

These two inlets on the E side of Ák Tainaron are suitable overnight anchorages in calm weather. Both are subject to severe gusts with W–SW winds and are open to the SE whence a heavy swell rolls in. Only one mile N is the better shelter of Porto Káyio.

It was off here on 29 March 1941 that the British fleet from Alexandria surprised the Italian fleet and sank five Italian ships. Despite this success the Axis powers soon pushed down through Greece and two months later Crete fell and British troops were hurriedly evacuated to Alexandria.

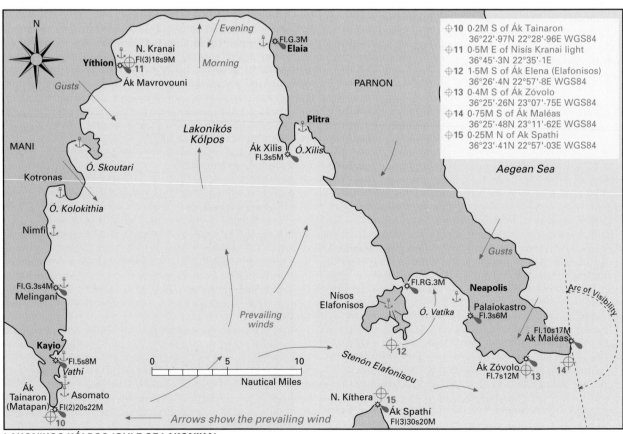

LAKONIKOS KÓLPOS (GULF OF LAKONIKA)

PORTO KÁYIO (Kaio)

BA 1092

Approach

Conspicuous The Maniote towers of the two small villages on the hilltops and the ruined monastery on the NW side are conspicuous. Closer in a small church on the S entrance point and the light structure will be seen. The houses of the hamlet will not be seen until into the bay.

By night Use the light on Ák Tainaron Fl(2)20s22M and the light at the entrance Fl.5s8M.

Dangers With strong westerlies there can be strong gusts out of the bay and off the high land in the approaches.

Mooring

With the normal W–SW wind anchor in 4–10m in the S cove of the bay. The gusts off the hills are not violent or frequent here. The holding in the S cove is not always to be relied upon. The bottom is hard sand with weed and some rocks. It is also possible to anchor and take a long line ashore to the quay in the SE corner where you are nicely tucked into the coast with good shelter from E–NE winds. The quay has only 1m or less depths off it so it is not possible to berth here. Strong NE winds may blow in unsettled weather and in that case the N cove is the best place to be. Here the bottom comes up very quickly from 30m to the shore so there is really only space for 2 or 3 yachts to anchor in reasonable depths. The bottom here is sand and weed, good holding.

Shelter Good shelter from the prevailing W–SW winds. Good shelter in the N cove from NE winds.

Pórto Káyio in Lakonikós Kólpos looking WNW into the anchorage *Peter Kleinoth/MareTeam*

Facilities

Water from local sources. Several tavernas in the summer. Fruit and vegetables from a small truck that calls at the bay.

General

The bay was called Psamathous in ancient times and Porto Quaglio by the Venetians, from which the present name probably comes – 'Quaglio' means quail and apparently great numbers of quail were caught here and salted for export. The bay was used by the Venetians, the Turks, and by various Maniote pirates of whom the most famous was Katsonis – a monument to the freedom fighter-cum-pirate stands near the quay in the SE corner.

In 1980 there were only a few families including the fishermen living in the small hamlet in the S of the bay. Since then the summer arrival of yachts on passage around the Peloponnisos and numbers of camper-vans has rejuvenated the hamlet.

ÓRMOS MELINGÁNI

36°30'·5N 22°29'·5E

Five miles N of Porto Káyio is the bay of Melingáni offering indifferent shelter. It is easily identified by a few houses at its head and the white light structure Fl.G.3s4M on the N side of the bay.

PORTO NIMFI (Nymphi)

Four miles N of Melingáni is a narrow inlet open to the E. The village is situated on the hill above the inlet. Subject to squalls with W winds.

KOTRONAS

A small village at the head of Órmos Kolokithias under Ák Kolokithia. There are often severe gusts out of the bay, but when the gusts are not severe it is possible to anchor in the bay for a lunch stop or overnight if the weather remains calm. Open S and if southerlies blow you should vacate the bay. Anchor in 5–8m off the village and mole. The bottom is sand and gravel, not everywhere good

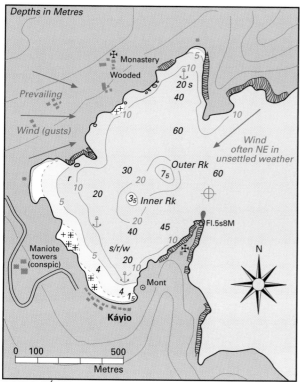

Depths in Metres

Monastery
Wooded
5
10
20 s
40
Prevailing
10
60
10
Wind (gusts)
Wind often NE in unsettled weather
30
Outer Rk
7₅
60
20
10
20
(3₅) Inner Rk
5
r
20
10
40
45
Fl.5s8M
Maniote towers (conspic)
s/r/w
20
10
4
5
Mont
4
1₅
N
Káyio

0   100   500
Metres

PORTO KÁYIO
⊕36°25'·98N 22°29'·48E WGS84

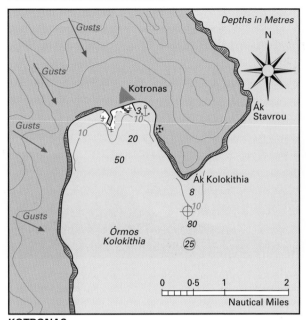

KOTRONAS
⊕36°36'·5N 22°30'·5E

holding. It may be possible to find a spot on the end of the pier to go alongside. There are 2–3m depths on the outer half of the mole.

Some provisions and tavernas ashore in the village. The fishing village tucked under the steep slopes is an attractive spot that has inevitably developed into a small resort. On the headland to the W are the remains of a prehistoric settlement.

ÓRMOS SKOUTARI (Scutari Bay)

The large bay between Ák Stavri and Ák Pagania. There are several anchorages around the large bay which can be used in settled weather.

Skoutari Anchor off the beach below the village or in the rocky cove by a prominent cave in the N. Generally you can anchor in 3–5m on a sand and weed bottom, adequate holding once the anchor is in. There can often be severe gusts down off the high land onto these anchorages and if staying for

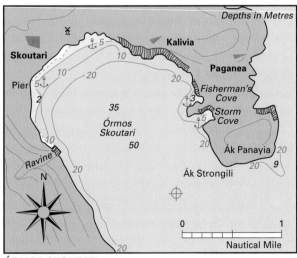

ÓRMOS SKOUTARI
⊕36°38'·6N 22°31'·9E

a while it would be prudent to lay a second anchor.

Fisherman's Cove A cove with a beach at the head on the E side of Órmos Scoutari. Anchor in 3–6m on a sandy bottom. Depending on the severity of the gusts off the land, this is an attractive anchorage open W–NW.

Storm Cove A cove immediately S of Fisherman's Cove. Anchor in 4–5m on sand. It may be useful to anchor and take a long line ashore to the N side depending on the wind and sea. Reasonable shelter tucked into here.

Weather note

The severity of gusts off the land in the vicinity of Skoutari varies greatly. Sometimes there may be next to no wind at all and another time there can be severe gusts. The latter usually arrive in the afternoon and continue until dusk. If on passage between Yíthion and Melingáni exercise some caution or leave early in the morning. The two last mentioned coves afford good shelter from the NE winds which sometimes blow in the gulf.

YÍTHION (Githion, Gytheoin)

BA 1683
Imray-Tetra G15

Approach

Conspicuous From the SE, especially if you are approaching at dusk, it is difficult to pick out just where Yíthion town is. By day the village of Mavrovouni atop Ák Mavrovouni and the tall white

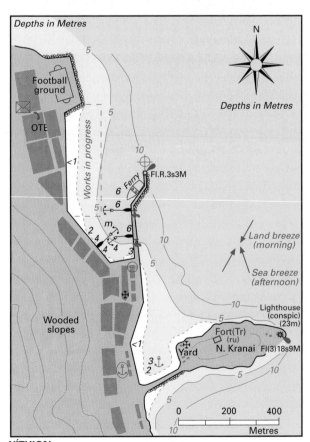

YÍTHION
⊕36°45'·6N 22°34·2E

Yíthion in the NW corner of Lakonikós Kólpos looking WNW
across Nisís Kranai in the foreground

Peter Kleinoth/MareTeam

Yíthion from above the town *Nigel Patten*

octagonal lighthouse on Nisís Kranai are
conspicuous. From the S the buildings of Yíthion
town are not visible until you round Ák
Mavrovouni.

By night Use the light on Nisís Kranai Fl(3)18s9M
and the light on the extremity of the mole
Fl.R.3s3M.

Dangers Care needs to be taken of gusts off the high
land in the approaches.

Mooring

Go stern or bows-to or alongside the mole as
directed. Good depths and good holding in mud.

Shelter Good from the prevailing winds. With strong

winds from the NW (not common in my
experience) there may be strong gusts off the
Taiyetos mountains – in this case the best place is
bows-to the W quay where you will be held off the
quay by the wind. Strong NE winds are reported to
cause a surge.

Authorities Port police and customs.

Note There are plans to build a mole out from the
coast to the E to improve the shelter in the harbour.

Facilities

Water On the quay.
Fuel Some distance out of town. A mini-tanker can
deliver.
Repairs Limited mechanical repairs.
Provisions Good shopping for all provisions close by.
Eating out Good tavernas nearby including good fish
restaurants.
Other PO. OTE. Banks. ATM. Greek gas and
Camping Gaz. Buses to Sparta and Athens. Ferry to
Piraeus and Kíthera.

General

Yíthion is seldom visited by yachts, yet it is an
excellent base for exploring Lakonikós Kólpos and a
pleasant low-key place in itself. Yíthion has a long
pedigree: claimed to have been founded by Heracles
and Apollo, it has seen Mycenaean and Phoenician
colonists and was the chief port of Sparta. With the
decline of Sparta, Yíthion became the most
important town of the Free Laconian League and
later of the Maniotes. Before all this Kranai was the
island mentioned by Homer in the *Iliad* where Paris
and Helen spent their first night after eloping
together.

'...when I snatched thee first
From lovely Lacedaemon's vale, put out to sea in hollow
ships,
And on Kranai lay with thee upon a couch of love'

Homer *Iliad* Book 3

The result was of course the siege of Troy and the
battle of the heroes, not to mention the birth of
Greek literature.

Yíthion makes a good base for exploring the
medieval town of Mistra – a remarkable fortified
town of narrow streets crowned by a large castle. It
is the completeness and size of the town in a
forbidding setting that visually impresses one,
although here some of the finest Byzantine
architecture is preserved. Mistra can be visited by
taxi or bus from Yíthion.

ELAIA (Elea)

Across the gulf directly E of Yíthion the large village
of Elaia is conspicuous.

There is a short mole off the village, but this is
often crowded with local boats. Anchor off the
beach in 2–4m on sand and weed. There are some
patches with rock under the sand where it is difficult
to get the anchor to hold. If there is room go stern
or bows-to the end of the mole. Good shelter from
all but strong NW–W winds.

Some provisions and tavernas ashore. Additional
facilities in Yithion or Molaous.

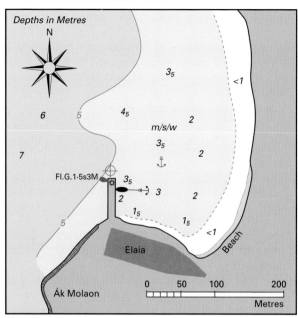

ELAIA
⊕36°45'·2N 22°48'·0E

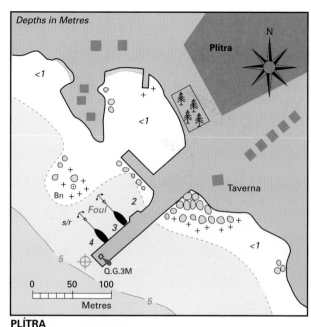

PLÍTRA
⊕36°41'·2N 22°50'·3E

ÓRMOS XÍLIS AND PLÍTRA (Xyli Bay, Plythra)

Approach

Conspicuous From the W and S the steep-to craggy Ák Xílis is conspicuous. Nearing Plítra the buildings of the small village and the mole are easily identified.

By night Use the light on Ák Xílis Fl.3s5M and the light on the end of the mole Q.G.3M.

Dangers Caution is called for to avoid the above and below-water rocks lying approximately 30m N of the extremity of the mole. The rocks are marked by an iron pipe beacon. A night entry is possible, but care

must be taken of the rocks N of the mole as the beacon is not lit.

Mooring

Go stern or bows-to the outer end of the mole if there is room. The harbour is very small and often crowded with local yachts. The bottom is largely rock and there are numerous permanent moorings on the bottom. Care is needed and it may be wise to use a trip-line on the anchor.

Shelter Good protection from all but strong southerlies although the fishermen say they leave their boats here all year round. With the normal SW wind a limited swell of no consequence creeps around the end of the mole making it a bit uncomfortable.

Anchorage Depending on the weather you can anchor off the beach at the head of Órmos Xíli. Anchor in 3–5m on sand and rock, once you find a good sandy patch that the anchor will dig into. Taverna ashore.

Facilities

Water from local sources only. In the summer there are several tavernas around the shore. The nearest village for supplies is 4km away.

General

Plítra is an unprepossessing village but manages to attract a few tourists to its sandy beaches in the summer. It is a pleasant sleepy little place that grows on you. On the seaward side of the mole are the remains of the ancient town of Plithra, now mostly submerged. You can snorkel over the remains that are scattered around the sea-bed in shallow water.

Note

Some yachts use Arkhangelos in the SE corner of Órmos Xíli. It is open N–NW but may be tenable with the prevailing wind which tends to curve and blow from the W–SW into Órmos Xili. The bottom

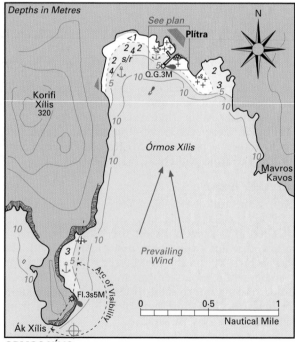

ORMOS XÍLIS
⊕36°39'·15N 22°49'·0E

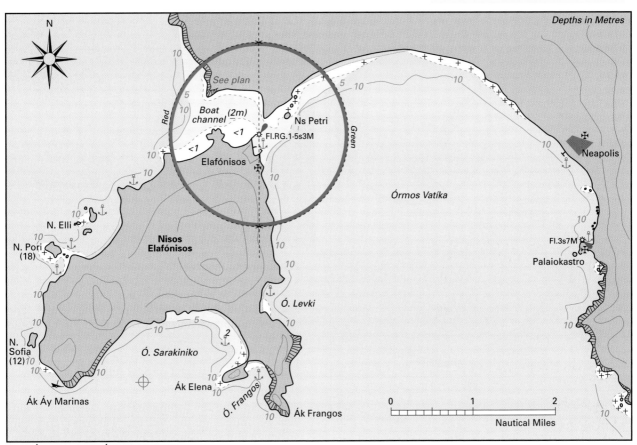

ELAFÓNISOS AND ÓRMOS VATIKA
⊕36°27'·9N 22°56'·8E

here is reported to be mostly rock so unless you find a sandy patch and the weather is relatively calm, it is better to move elsewhere.

Nísos Elafónisos and channel

Nísos Elafónisos is the island on the N side of the channel between Nísos Kíthera and the Peloponnisos. It is separated from the Peloponnisos by a shallow boat channel that those with iron nerve can negotiate if they so desire. Elafónisos means 'deer island' although nobody, myself included, has ever seen any here. In antiquity there was a trading post here and the island was known as Onugnathos, 'ass's jaw', which with a little imagination the island can be seen to resemble.

There are a number of anchorages around the island and a small harbour at the village of Elafónisos on the NE corner.

Anchorages around Elafónisos
1. **W coast** There are several anchorages in and around Nisís Pori and Nisís Elli. Anchor where convenient on sand. Good shelter from the S–SE and from E–NE.
2. **Órmos Sarakiniko** The large bay on the S of the island. Anchor off the beach on the E side on sand, good holding. In the summer there will often be a NE–E wind blowing over Elafónisos and around Ák Malea. Good shelter here from

NE–E and in fact you will often be in company with others waiting to get around Malea. A beach taverna/bar in the summer.
3. **Ormiskos Frangos** The bay immediately E of Sarakiniko. Anchor off the beach on sand. Good shelter and suitable as an overnight anchorage in settled weather.
4. **Órmos Levki** The bay on the E side of the island. It affords limited shelter from the prevailing wind. The bottom is sand and rock with good holding reported at the S end of the bay, although bad holding has been reported in

Órmos Sarakiniko and Órmos Frangos abut one another on the S end of Elafónisos
Nigel Patten

135

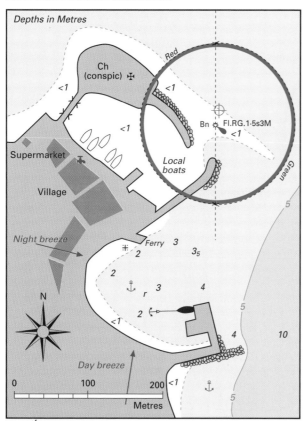

ELAFÓNISOS VILLAGE
⊕36°30′·8N 22°59′·0E

Elafónisos *caïque* harbour

other parts of the bay.

The attractions of all these anchorages are wonderful sandy beaches and translucent water in deserted surroundings, although camper vans somehow seem to have penetrated to Sarakiniko and Frangos in the summer.

WEATHER NOTE
The normal summer breeze is from the W curving up to blow from the S in Órmos Vatíka. At night a NE wind may blow and may continue to do so through the day. In unsettled weather care is needed as there can be violent winds around this area.

ELAFÓNISOS VILLAGE
Approach
Conspicuous From the S the church sitting out in the channel is conspicuous. The houses of the village will also be seen, but the rough stone mole of the harbour will not be seen until closer in.

By night Use the light on the E side of Órmos Vatíka Fl.3s7M and the light on the beacon (Vrakhos Stavrós: Fl.RG.1·5s3M). The harbour entrance is not lit.

Mooring
Anchor in the bay or go stern or bows-to the mole at the S entrance. The bottom is rock covered by a minuscule amount of sand, bad holding. Snorkel over your anchor to make sure it has snagged on something and preferably use a fisherman anchor.

Shelter Good shelter from the prevailing winds. The harbour is open E and in strong southerlies I would expect a surge in here.

Note The fishermen's harbour N of the ferry harbour is shallow and packed full of local boats.

Facilities
Water tap near the fishing harbour. Most provisions can be found in the village. Tavernas and bars around the waterfront. OTE. Ferry to the mainland opposite. Ferry to Kíthera.

General
The village is a ramshackle sort of place, but convivial. Greek tourists come here and camp on the mainland opposite off the magnificent beach fronted by the turquoise waters of the boat channel. At night the entertainment for the locals and tourists can reach fairly high decibel levels.

ELAFÓNISOS BOAT PASSAGE
Separating Elafónisos from the Peloponnisos is the shallow boat channel which can be seen as the expanse of turquoise water N of Elafónisos village. Passage through the channel is possible for yachts drawing less than 2m in calm weather, but with any swell a yacht should go S of the island. It is essential to have someone up front conning you through and a careful eye should be kept on the depth sounder.

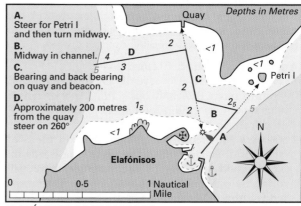

ELAFÓNISOS BOAT PASSAGE

Even so the passage requires an iron nerve and a calm day. Every feature on the bottom can be clearly identified and the depths are such that you are never out of 2–2·5m for nearly a mile.

NEAPOLIS

The large town on the E side of Órmos Vatíka is visible from some distance off. A large church is prominent behind the town. Shelter off here is rarely comfortable and depends on what has been happening with the weather outside Órmos Vatika. If there has been a lot of wind from almost any direction then it will not be that comfortable in here. With southerlies of any sort it will be uncomfortable and can be untenable. With the E–NE wind that often blows in the summer it is tenable but a swell is pushed around into Órmos Vatika.

Anchor to the S of the ferry pier in 4–8m on mud and weed, generally good holding. The ferry pier is quite high to go alongside or stern or bows-to, but in calm weather it is possible. The S side is used by the ferry to Kíthera.

Water and fuel in the town. Good shopping for provisions and numerous tavernas. PO. OTE. Banks. Ferry to Kíthera and Piraeus.

Neapolis is an interesting place which has a little local tourism, but otherwise functions as the main town for the area. It is not the most attractive place with a lot of 'pour-and-fill' buildings, but it is a proper working town serving this outpost of the Peloponnese. The Bay of Vatika takes its name from ancient Voiai (the Voiatic Gulf), the remains of which are said to be underwater somewhere S of Neapolis.

Nearby to the NW the tiny fishing harbour of Neapolis is too small and shallow for a yacht. The entrance is rock-bound with around 1·7m depths in the entrance and less inside. A rock with less than 2m over it is reported to lie in the immediate approaches. Not recommended for yachts, though very small motorboats drawing less than a metre might find some shelter inside. Extreme care needed here.

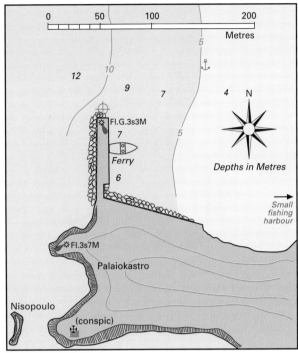

PALAIOKASTRO
⊕36°29'·4N 23°03'·8E

PALAIOKASTRO

About 1½M S of Neapolis, a new quay has been built under the headland on which stands a conspicuous church. The headland (Ák Vatíka or Palaiokastro) is lit Fl.3s7M and the end of the mole is lit Fl.G.3s3M.

A ferry that serves Kithera during the summer uses the quay. The ferry runs several times during the day, and stays overnight here. There may be some quay space left that can be used, alternatively anchor off in 3–10m tucked as far under the headland as you can. Good shelter from southerlies and from the E–NE winds which often blow. On the quay there is also good protection from westerlies.

The name Palaiokastro (old castle) indicates there has been ancient occupation here although little is recorded.

ÁK MALÉAS

Ák Maléas has a bit of a fearsome reputation and at times it lives up to it. At other times you can motor around it in a flat calm. Coming from the W most yachts will hole up in Órmos Sarakiniko or nearby if there are strong adverse winds in order to wait for the wind to die down. Often in the summer a whole gaggle of yachts can build up here waiting for the right time to leave. The problem is that the winds around Elafónisos are not always a good indication of the wind around Maléas and I have left here (watched curiously by all the other yachts) with two reefs down and a pocket handkerchief for a jib, only to end up motoring around Maléas and up to Monemvasía. I have also left here and returned to Elafónisos after being battered by 40-knot gusts near the cape. There is no accurate method of judging what the wind is doing around the cape in

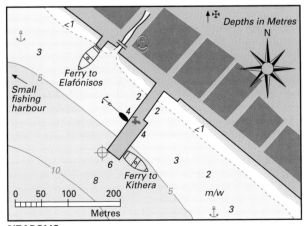

NEAPOLIS
⊕36°29'·6N 23°03'·9E

The lighthouse on Ák Maléas

Ak Spathi lighthouse looking W   *Lu Michell*

the summer and you can only use your nose to sniff things out as best you can.

In spring and autumn any depressions in the vicinity of Maléas will bring strong winds and confused seas. It is quite simply a windy place to be when depressions are nearby and if in doubt hole up somewhere secure. While this is not much consolation, I can assure you, having hurtled around here in a winter gale when en route from the Saronic to the Ionian, that once bitten you treat this place with respect. And don't forget to wave to the monks in the hermitage who watch over ships large and small rounding this lonely place.

Nísoi Kíthera and Andíkithera
(Kythera, Cerigo and Anti-Kíthera, Cerigotto, Lious)

Kíthera and Andíkithera form an island bridge between the Peloponnisos and Crete. As a convenient lee or port of refuge, the islands have played an important part as stepping-stones on the ancient trade routes around the Peloponnisos to the Aegean and east along Crete. Near Avelomona, a small village on the south of Kíthera, a Minoan trading post (c.2000–1450 BC) has been excavated. Later the Phoenicians (the island was reputed to be rich in murex from which the Phoenicians extracted their famous purple dye), Mycenaeans, Romans and Venetians used the island.

Kíthera has another claim to classical fame and it is that Aphrodite was born here, though other islands, notably Cyprus, also lay claim to the goddess. Her worship was probably introduced to this lonely rocky island by the Phoenicians and when she was later adopted by the Greeks, her birthplace was assumed to be Kíthera. This seems as good a place as any to let Lawrence Durrell describe this most human of goddesses:

'Under her title Urania, she stood for pure and ideal love; as Genetrix or Nymphia, she was the protector of lawful marriage and favoured all serious unions; as Pandemos or Porne she was the patron of all prostitutes and favoured all lust and venal love. Everything to do with passion, from the noblest to the most degraded, came within her scope. It is her completeness, compounded of many attributes, which wins our hearts. Her loving had a comprehensiveness that accepted every human foible, good or bad.

Nor was she averse to using her powers mischievously – as when she took it into her head to light a short fuse under the chair of Zeus in Olympus, which gave him one of the worst attacks of skirt-fever ever to win a place in the Olympian version of 'The Guinness Book of Records'. Was there nothing sacred, he asked her, all lit up like a Christmas tree? Yes, she must have answered, everything is sacred, without distinction, even laughter. Especially laughter.'

Lawrence Durrell *The Greek Islands*

When the Union of the Seven Islands was declared, Kíthera and Andíkithera were declared to be part of the Heptanisoi, despite the distance separating them from the other Ionian islands. After the War of Independence the islands gradually came under the administration of Athens. Today a few tourists who enjoy quiet places visit Kíthera, but on the whole the island remains a comparatively untouched spot.

Eighteen miles south of Kíthera lies its diminutive Andíkithera (Anti-Kíthera) – a pitted rocky island rising sheer from the sea and inhabited by around fifty hardy souls. Few yachts call here as the only harbour is unsafe in all except calm weather. Early this century a wreck of the 1st century BC was discovered near the island and a number of valuable bronze and marble statues recovered. These are now displayed in the National Museum in Athens.

PLATIA AMMOS

36°22'·0N 22°57'·7E

A small bay approximately 2 miles SE of Ák Spathi. A short mole provides some shelter from NE winds, although even a moderate NE breeze makes it uncomfortable in here and if it blows strongly from the NE it is untenable. With westerlies there are strong gusts into the bay.

PELAGIA
Approach

The old ferry port lies approximately 4 miles SE of Ák Spathi. The mole for the ferry is easily located.

By night The end of the mole is lit Fl.R.1·5s3M.

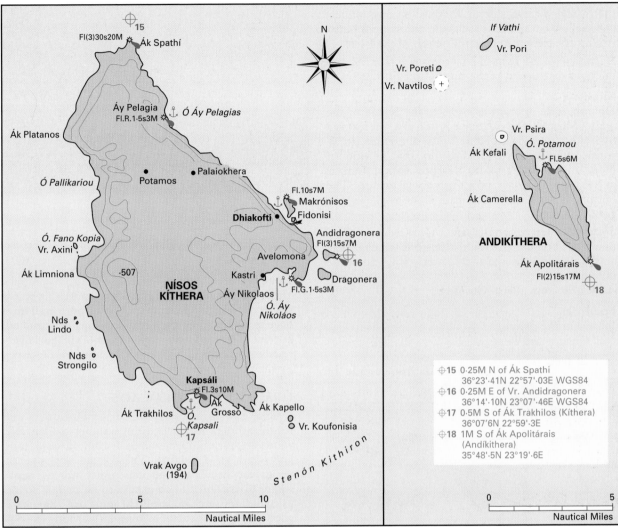

KÍTHERA AND ANDIKÍTHERA

Dangers When close, care is needed of the shoal water off the coast in the vicinity of the mole.

Mooring

If there is room go alongside or stern or bows-to the mole. Alternatively anchor off on either side of the mole. The bottom is sand and weed, good holding.

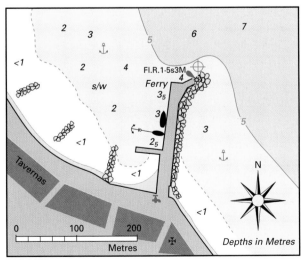

PELAGIA
⊕36°19'·59N 22°59'·21E WGS84

Shelter The harbour is useful only in calm weather or light offshore winds. With westerlies there are strong gusts into the harbour and it is completely open to NE winds. With any wind from the NE you should vacate the harbour and go elsewhere.

Authorities Port police.

Facilities

Water At the root of the mole.
Provisions Minimarket near the mole.
Eating out Tavernas around the waterfront.

General

The harbour and village have become a bit of a ghost town now that the new ferry port at Dhiakofti has opened, although there is still a modest tourist trade here, and during the summer a ferry runs to Palaiokastro.

DHIAKOFTI

The main ferry port for Kíthera, situated on the W side of Makrónisos.

Approach

Makrónisos joined by a causeway is easily recognised from the N and closer in the breakwater sheltering the ferry quay will be seen. The wreck of the *Nordland* cargo ship on Fidonisi is conspicuous, especially from the S. It looks like the skipper had a run up to attempt to perch it on top of the islet.

By night Use the light of Makrónisos Fl.10s7M and the light on the end of the breakwater Fl.R.3s3M.

Mooring

Go alongside or stern or bows-to the S side of the quay. Most of the W quay is for the ferries and hydrofoils running to Kíthera. An alternative in W winds would be to anchor on the E side of Makrónisos tucked under Vrakhoi Mikró. Care is needed as Mikro is only just above water. The bottom is sand and weed with some rock, mostly good holding.

Shelter Shelter is better than it looks when tucked under the breakwater. With strong NE winds it may get bumpy in here and with easterly gales could be untenable.

Authorities Port police. Customs.

Facilities

Water On the quay.
Fuel Outside the village.
Provisions Minimarket.
Eating out Tavernas on the waterfront, some of which have good fresh fish.

Dhiakofti looking SE into the harbour from the entrance
Lu Michell

Other Exchange. Ferries and hydrofoil to Neapolis and Yíthion.

General

Until the construction of the ferry port this was a sleepy little fishing hamlet. A few more buildings have gone up since the ferry port was constructed, but in a sympathetic way and the village largely remains a peaceful little spot. The only real activity is when the ferry arrives.

ÓRMOS ÁYIOS NIKOLAOS

A large bay immediately SE of the Dragonera and Andidragonera islets. In calm weather or light NE winds anchor off the beach in 4–10m on sand, mud and weed, good holding. The bottom slopes gently up to the beach so you can pretty much choose where to anchor though it pays to be in 4–5 metres to avoid the ground swell heaping up. Shelter is good in settled weather from NE around to SW although some swell does creep around into the bay – more uncomfortable than dangerous. Southerlies send in a swell. Beach bar at the NE end of the bay.

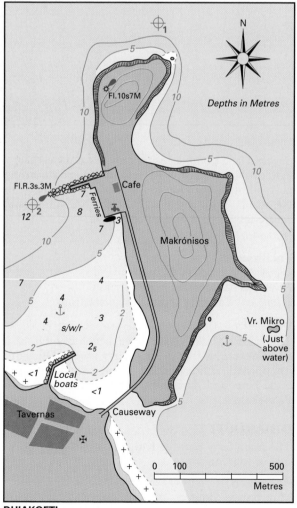

DHIAKOFTI
⊕₁36°16'·62N 23°04'·71E WGS84
⊕₂36°16'·20N 23°04'·55E WGS84

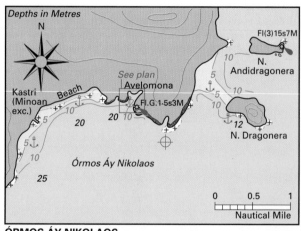

ÓRMOS ÁY NIKOLAOS
⊕36°13'·04N 23°05'·40E WGS84

AVELOMONA

Approach

The twin-headed inlet lies in the NE corner of Órmos Áy Nikolaos.

By night Use the light on Andidragonera Fl(3)15s7M and the light on the E side of the entrance to Avelomona Fl.G.1·5s3M.

Note The two coves are very small and you should have everything ready before entering.

Mooring

Go stern or bows-to where possible on the stubby mole or on the quay just inside the mole. Alternatively anchor and take a long line ashore to the NE side. If you cannot get into the cove then it is possible to anchor with a long line ashore or fore and aft in the W cove. The bottom is sand and weed, good holding.

Note 1. There are some permanent moorings on the bottom which can foul an anchor so care is needed where you drop the anchor. It may be useful to rig a trip-line.

Note 2. The small harbour is easily crowded and you should reckon on not finding a berth here. Use the W cove or anchor in Ay Nikolaos if you cannot get in.

Shelter Reasonable shelter from NE and W winds although there is often a surge in here if NE winds are fresh. Open S.

Facilities

Some provisions available and several tavernas ashore.

General

The little hamlet tucked into the corner of Áy Nikolaos is a sweet little place that has experienced something of a renaissance in recent years and has now been smartened up. Numbers of smart new villas have been built here, but there are still enough rough old fishermen and locals to make it real. There is evidence that the harbour has been used since antiquity and around the bay at Kastrí a Minoan settlement has been excavated which was occupied from c.2000–1450 BC. The Venetians also used it and built the small fort on the W headland of Avelomona.

ÓRMOS KAPSÁLI (Kíthera)

Approach

Conspicuous From the distance Vrak Avgo (Ovo Island) which means Egg Island – it is roughly egg-shaped – is conspicuous. From the S and E a windmill on Ák Grosso and the fort above the *chora* are conspicuous. From the W the fort can be seen as you near Ák Trakhilos. Once into the large bay, two large white villas to the W of the harbour and the

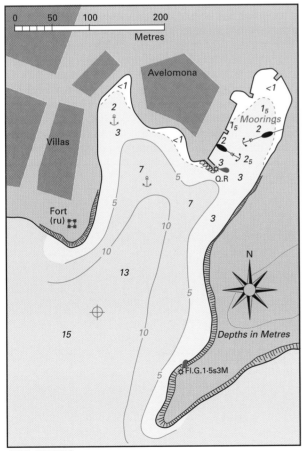

AVELOMONA
⊕36°13'·46N 23°04'·89E WGS84

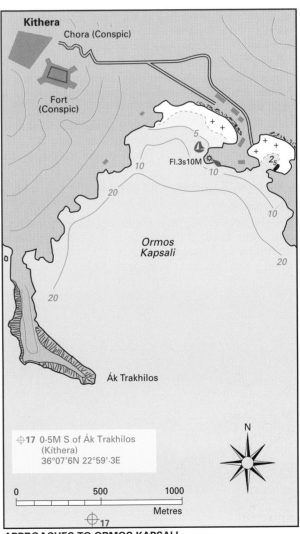

APPROACHES TO ORMOS KAPSALI

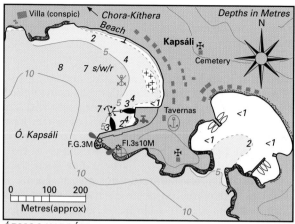

ÓRMOS KAPSÁLI
⊕36°08′·6N 23°00′·0E

lighthouse on the bluff above the harbour are conspicuous.

By night Use the light on the bluff (Fl.3s10M) and the light on the end of the quay (F.G.3M).

Dangers With strong westerlies there are gusts off the high land and a considerable swell around the coast.

Mooring

Only the W bay is deep enough for a yacht. The E bay is shallow and rock-bound. Moor stern-to or alongside the outer half of the quay if there is not a swell. The bottom is sand, rock and weed, reasonable holding once the anchor is in.

Shelter Whatever the wind direction I have invariably encountered a swell in the harbour, making it uncomfortable. With strong S winds the harbour is untenable.

Note It is reported that it is now prohibited to anchor in the harbour without permission from the port police. A yacht can be fined for contravening this regulation.

Authorities Port police and customs.

Facilities

Water From a café on the quay, by hose.
Provisions Limited provisions at the harbour, better shopping in the *chora*.
Eating out Tavernas on the waterfront.

Órmos Kapsáli looking SW onto the quay

Other PO and OTE in the *chora*.

General

Órmos Kapsáli is picturesque as are the walled *chora* and fort, a steep climb above. The walled *chora* is the capital of Kíthera, although nowadays Potamós is the commercial centre. The fort, on what looks like an impregnable rocky bluff, was first built by the Venetians in 1316 to protect their new trade route around the Peloponnisos. Despite the poor shelter in the harbour it is well worth a visit to this picturesque place – most of the time in the summer it is tenable, if sometimes uncomfortable.

ÓRMOS POTAMOU (Andíkithera)

At the northern end of Andíkithera the natural harbour of Órmos Potamou is a narrow inlet running southwards and open to the N. Anchor in 6–12m at the S end of the inlet. At the head of the bay there are above and below-water rocks. The bottom is sand and rock. There is invariably a swell in the bay and with even moderate N winds the harbour is untenable. With SW–W winds there are gusts into the harbour.

Meagre supplies can be obtained ashore. Taverna in the hamlet.

Andikithera was the site of a remarkable discovery by Greek sponge divers sheltering here in bad weather. In October 1900 they dived on a wreck 180ft down and recovered a number of artefacts. Among them was an encrusted bronze item which when cleaned up proved to be a type of astrolabe. The wreck has been dated to around 100BC and the astrolabe has an inscription on it dating it to 200BC. The mystery of it all is that this astrolabe is a sophisticated device comprising 40 interlocking cogs and nine adjustable scales. It is surmised that it related the cycles of the sun and a 19-year cycle of the moon and probably some planets as well. The intricacy of the device and its construction (some of the layers inside are just 2mm thick) may earn it the label of the first proto-computer known to man.

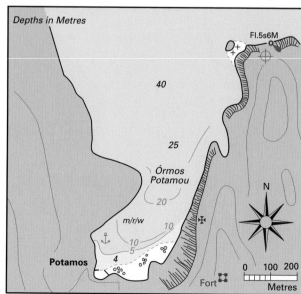

ÓRMOS POTAMOU
⊕35°53′·5N 23°17′·7N (Fl.5s6M)

III. The Gulf of Patras and the Gulf of Corinth
(Patraikos Kólpos and Korinthiakós Kólpos)

Approaching the Gulf of Patras from the west, the coast is low-lying although backed by high land. Much of this coast is shallow salt marsh and shoal water extends some distance offshore, particularly on the north side of the gulf. Approaching the narrow western entrance to the Gulf of Corinth, the coast rises abruptly to high mountains. The sides of the Gulf of Corinth are flanked by two high mountain ranges scarred by winter torrents and split by deep gorges. On the south coast Mt Killini (Zyria) rises to 2,377m (7,800ft) and on the north coast Mt Parnassos reaches 2,454m (8051ft). Well into late spring these mountains are capped with snow.

The Gulf of Corinth is 60 miles long from the Straits of Ríon and Andírrion (once known as the 'little Dardanelles') to the Corinth Canal. Surrounded by high mountains, the gulf is much like a large lake and indeed the scenery resembles that of an Alpine lake. The narrow alluvial plain on the south coast is extensively cultivated with vineyards and citrus and fringed by attractive beaches. On the north coast the mountains are for a large part bare of vegetation although in places, particularly Návpaktos and Itéa, there are patches of green contrasting with the barren mountains behind.

The history of the gulfs has largely revolved around the fortunes of Corinth. Using the Corinth Canal saves a distance of approximately 150 miles between the Ionian Sea and Athens. In antiquity, vessels were transported across the isthmus on rollers on a road called the *diolkos* and Corinth controlled this passage between the Ionian and the Aegean. From the Archaic period right up to the end of Roman rule the city flourished and grew fat on its income from the *diolkos*. In 522 and 551 AD earthquakes destroyed the city and it never regained its former prosperity.

The city and control of the gulf passed through successive invaders: the Normans sacked it in 1147; Villhardouin captured it in 1212; the Turks took it in 1458; the Knights of Malta in 1612; the Venetians in 1687; and, in 1715, the Turks acquired it yet again until it finally became a part of Greece at the beginning of the War of Independence. Today Corinth has little to exercise the perceptions, but its former feats and glories have passed into our language and culture.

At the entrance to the Gulf of Patras two maritime incidents took place – one of historical note and the other just a footnote to history.

Proceeding down the channel between Oxiá Island and Ak Scrofa the coast becomes low-lying for some 25 miles before the town of Mesolóngion appears hovering over the salt marsh. In and around the channel off Oxiá the Battle of Lepanto took place. The Turks prepared their fleet in Návpaktos, then known as Lepanto, and engaged the combined Christian fleet under Don John of Austria in this desolate spot. The Christian fleet with galleys from Venice, Genoa, the Papal States, Spain, Sicily and Naples defeated the Turks, sinking and capturing some 250 galleys and freeing 15,000 galley slaves. This was the last major sea battle fought with galleys rowed by slaves and effectively demolished Turkish control of the sea. It is recorded that Cervantes, the author of *Don Quixote*, lost the use of his left hand here. The late Peter Throckmorton attempted to locate some of the galleys lost in this action but uncovered nothing from the thick silt that covers the bottom.

It was also here under the lee of Scrofa that a small ship Byron was on put in to evade a Turkish brig-of-war on New Year's Eve in 1823. En route to Mesolóngion from Cephalonia, his Ionian skipper elected to anchor until the Turks passed. Apparently feeling unsafe they later went further north to Astakós, then called Dragomestre. Eventually three ships from Mesolóngion found Byron's ship and escorted it safely into the marshy fortress. Although Byron liked the sea and ships he knew very little about them and his companions were even more ignorant of matters nautical. David Howarth records this amusing episode on the trip to Mesolóngion in his *The Greek Adventure*:

'The passengers in this boat were a land-lubberly lot, except perhaps Tita the gondolier, and the crew seems not to have been much better. Fletcher the valet had caught a cold and had to lie down on the only mattress on board, Dr Bruno was prone to wring his hands and weep at any threat of disaster, and Loukas could not swim. Byron himself liked boats, but had never learned much about them. And as they returned through the Oxiá channel, the boat missed stays and ran aground in a squall. Two thirds

Quick reference guide

	Shelter	Mooring	Fuel	Water	Provisioning	Tavernas	Plan
Gulf of Patras							
Killini	B	AB	B	A	C	C	•
Kato Achaia	A	A	O	O	C	C	•
Missalonghi	A	ABC	B	A	B	B	•
Krionéri	O	C	O	O	O	C	
Patras	B	A	B	A	A	A	•
Patras Yacht Harbour	A	A	B	A	A	B	•
Gulf of Corinth N side							
Návpaktos	B	A	A	A	A	A	•
Khiliadhou	B	AB	O	B	C	C	•
Monastiraki	C	C	O	B	C	C	
Nisís Trizónia	A	ABC	O	B	C	C	•
Kallithea	B	C	O	O	C	C	•
Eratini	C	C	B	B	B	C	•
Panormos	C	C	O	O	C	C	•
Vidhavis	C	C	O	O	O	C	•
Anemokambi	B	O	O	O	O	C	•
Galaxidhi	A	A	B	A	B	A	•
Itéa	A	A	B	B	B	B	•
Andíkiron	B	ABC	B	A	C	B	•
Áy Saranda	B	C	O	B	C	C	•
Kólpos Domvrainis	B	C	O	O	O	O	
Porto Germeno	A	AB	O	B	O	C	•
Kato Alepochori	A	A	B	B	C	C	•
Nisídhes Alkonidhes	C	C	O	O	O	O	•
Agriliou	O	C	O	O	O	O	
Loutráki	O	C	B	B	B	B	
Gulf of Corinth S side							
Aiyíon	C	AC	B	B	B	A	•
Xilokastro	A	A	O	A	C	C	•
Kiato	B	A	B	A	A	B	•
Vrakhati	B	A	O	O	C	C	•
Corinth	A	AB	B	A	A	B	•
Posidhonía	C	AC	O	O	O	C	•
Isthmia	B	B	O	O	O	C	•

of the crew climbed out on the bowsprit and jumped ashore, Byron told Loukas he would save him, and Dr Bruno stripped to his flannel waistcoat and running about like a rat (it was Byron's description) shouted 'Save him indeed! By God, save me rather – I'll be the first if I can.' Thereupon, after striking twice, the boat blew off again. The crew was removed from the rocks by one of the escort ships, and that evening, without any more alarms, Byron reached the entrance of Missalonghi.'

Byron accomplished little in Mesolóngion. The guerrilla chiefs assembled around him for the money he had brought. The collection of Philhellenes gathered in Mesolóngion for the most part grumbled and argued amongst themselves and with the Greeks. Byron was appointed a 'commander' but could do little to organise the ill-assorted groups around him. It was more his death of fever on 19 April 1824 that inspired the world and focussed

Data

PORTS OF ENTRY
Patras
Itéa
Corinth

PROHIBITED AREAS
The small harbour on the E side of Órmos Andíkiron and the area immediately surrounding it.

MAJOR LIGHTS
Ák Oxiá Fl(2)15s17M
Nisís Kavikalidha (Cape Killini) LFl.WR.10s12/9M
Ák Páppas LFl(2)20s10M
Ák Áy Sóstis Fl.WR.5s17/14M
Ríon Fl.6s6M
Andírrion Fl(2)10s10M
Ák Mórnos Fl(3)15s7M
Ák Dhrépanon Fl.10s22M
Nisís Trizónia Fl.4s4M
Ák Psaromíta Fl(2)15s21M
Ák Andromákhi Fl(3)15s10M
Nisís Apsifía (Galaxidhi) Fl.7s5M
Ák Mákri-Nikólaos Fl.4·5s5M
Ák Likoporiá Fl(2)16s10M
Ák Kefálí Fl.3s4M

Routes

Given the confines of the two gulfs, yachts will pretty much be heading east or west most of the time.

When heading E into the Gulf of Patras the prevailing wind in the summer is the NW breeze which is funnelled into a W wind and blows right through the Gulf of Patras and into the Gulf of Corinth from a westerly direction. The funnelling effect can substantially increase the strength of the wind, especially where it is squeezed by the land at the Strait of Ríon and Andírrion and for some distance into the narrow W part of the Gulf of Corinth. For yachts headed E this is no real problem as once into the gulfs the seas are relatively slight and you are on a downwind run to Corinth.

When heading W from Corinth you will be plugging into the wind most of the time. As the prevailing summer wind tends to gradually extend into the gulfs from the Ionian, if a yacht leaves early in the morning it will generally be able to motor some of the way in the morning calm. If you are beating into the wind when headed W then it pays to stay on the N side of the gulfs where you will often pick up a bit of a lift with the wind getting a bit of northerly in it. You will also have less sea under the N side of the gulfs.

When heading out of the Gulf of Patras into the Ionian, care is needed not to get too close to the shoal water on the N side of the gulf. Keep an eye on the depthsounder and on your position. Once up to Oxiá it is better to continue out past the S end of the island for a bit before putting a tack in as the wind tends to follow the contours of the inside channel between Oxiá and the coast.

At times in the summer you will have N–NE winds at the E end of the Gulf of Corinth and there can be fierce gusts off the high land on the N side. In this case stick close in to the N coast before turning down to Corinth. If you arrive off the Corinth Canal with strong westerlies it is often better to stay overnight in Corinth harbour and venture out in the morning calm to transit the canal.

For weather for the Gulf of Patras listen to **Cephalonia**		For weather for the Gulf of Corinth listen to **Perama**		**Patras Coastguard (O)**
Frequency	Weather forecast Nav warnings	Frequency	Weather forecast Nav warnings	MMSI 237673140
VHF Ch 27	0600, 1000, 1600, 0500, 1100, 1730,	VHF Ch 86	0600, 1000, 1600, 0500, 1100, 1730,	VHF Ch 16, 85
(announce Ch 16)	2200 UTC 2330 UTC	(announce Ch 16)	2200 UTC 2330 UTC	MF 2182kHz
				DSC MF 2187·5kHz

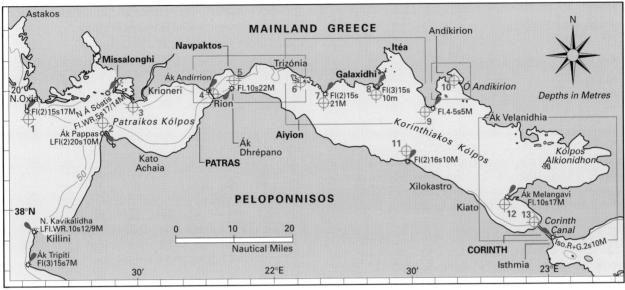

GULF OF PATRAS AND GULF OF CORINTH

USEFUL WAYPOINTS

⊕1 0·5M S of Ák Oxiá
   38°16'·60N 21°05'·95E WGS84
⊕2 2M N of Ák Páppas light
   38°14'·9N 21°22'·4E
⊕3 0·2M S of lightbuoy off Ák Evinos
   38°16'·86N 21°29'·16E WGS84
⊕4 Mid-channel of Ríon – Andírrion Strait
   38°19'·25N 21°46'·45E
⊕5 Mid-channel: Ák Mórnos – Ák Dhrépano
   38°21'·22N 21°52'·19E WGS84
⊕6 SE end of Nísos Trizónia
   38°21'·49N 22°05'·47E WGS84
⊕7 0·5M S of Ák Psaromíta light
   38°18'·9N 22°11'·1E
⊕8 0·5M S of Ák Andromákhi light
   38°19'·5N 22°22'·7E
⊕9 1M S of Ák Mákri Nikólaos light
   38°16'·0N 22°33'·1E
⊕10 0·5M E of Ák Kefáli (Andíkiron)
   38°21'·6N 22°39'·4E
⊕11 1M N of Ák Likoporia light
   38°09'·2N 22°29'·5E
⊕12 1M S of Ák Melangávi light
   38°00'·8N 22°51'·0E
⊕13 0·5M W of Corinth Canal entrance (Posidhonia)
   37°57'·29N 22°56'·88E WGS84

attention on the Greek struggle than his presence – as he lay dying he is reported to have said: 'I do not lament for to terminate my wearisome existence I came to Greece. My wealth, my abilities, I devoted to her cause. Well, there is my life to her.'

Many yachts pass through the Gulf of Patras and the Gulf of Corinth – most are using it simply as a short cut to the Aegean, saving 150 miles on the trip around the Peloponnisos. For the yachtsman who is not in a hurry to reach the Aegean, the two gulfs, in particular the Gulf of Corinth, are good cruising areas with a lot of attractive harbours and anchorages. In the Gulf of Corinth the south coast is relatively straight and offers few secure anchorages, but the north coast is much indented with many attractive and safe anchorages separated by short distances.

Weather patterns in the Gulf of Patras and the Gulf of Corinth

The prevailing winds in the summer are from the W. Across the low salt marsh on the N side of the Gulf of Patras the wind is from the NW to WNW. In the Gulf of Corinth the high mountains funnel the wind so it comes from the W. It normally blows from midday until well into the evening and may reach Force 5–6 in July and August. The wind may also blow from the NE at Corinth and sometimes blows right down to the Gulf of Patras. Again it is funnelled into an E wind in the two gulfs. In Krissaíos Kólpos (Gulf of Krissa) and Órmos Andíkiron (Antikyrra) there is frequently no wind even when it is blowing strongly in the middle of the gulf.

In the spring and autumn the winds vary between W and E – depending largely on the winds in the Ionian and the Aegean. In the Gulf of Patras there are frequently violent thunderstorms which may last for some time in the spring and autumn. Waterspouts are fairly frequent here in unsettled weather and, believe me, you don't want to see a big waterspout in action.

Although gusts off the high mountains could be expected, in my experience they have been little stronger than the winds in the middle of the two gulfs. The mountains appear to funnel the wind (W or E) for the length of the gulf rather than act as obstacles off which gusts might blow. Only at the

145

Corinth end is this not the case with NE winds, where gusts blow off the high land with some violence.

Gulf of Patras
(Patraikos Kólpos)

KILLINI (Kyllini, Glarenza)

BA 2404

Imray-Tetra G16

Approach

The harbour actually lies outside the Gulf of Patras 20 miles SW of Ák Pappas. Castel Tornese on a hill inland of Killini is conspicuous from some distance away. The lighthouse on Nisís Kavikalidha is also conspicuous. Closer in the buildings of Killini and the harbour mole will be seen against the low-lying coast.

By night Use the light on Nisís Kavikalidha LFl.WR.20s12/9M (red sector 059°-092°) and the light on the buoy at the entrance Fl.G.3s. Castel Tornese above Killini is floodlit in the summer and can be seen from a considerable distance, up to 20M depending on visibility.

Dangers A reef If Khelona runs out from the headland immediately NW of the harbour and it should be given a good offing as it can be difficult to see. Make the immediate approach to the harbour from the NE.

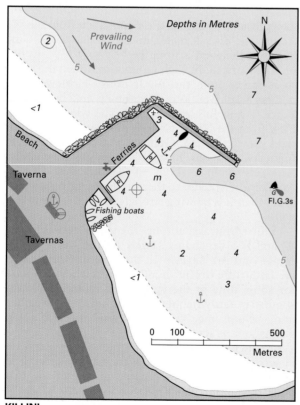

KILLINI

⊕37°56′·18N 21°08′·86E WGS84

Mooring

Berth stern or bows-to the quay under the outer breakwater. The bottom is mud, good holding.

Shelter Good shelter from the prevailing NW–W winds although a strong *maistro* sets up a bit of a surge in here and the coming and going of the ferries also creates some uncomfortable wash.

Authorities Port police and customs.

Anchorage Yachts can also anchor off the beach clear of the port area proper. The bottom shelves gently to the shore and is shallow for some distance off it. Anchor in 2–3 metres on mud. Good holding although there may be a bit of chop rolling around the end of the mole until the prevailing northwesterlies die down.

Facilities

Water On the quay.

Fuel In the village.

Provisions Most provisions can be obtained.

Eating out Tavernas along the waterfront.

Other PO. OTE. ATM. Bus and train to Patras. Ferry to Zákinthos and Cephalonia.

General

Known in Venetian times as Glarenza, the port was once an important link in the trade route around the Peloponnisos. It is difficult to think of this dusty little place, now the ferry terminal for Zákinthos and Cephalonia, being a thriving cosmopolitan place full of the sights and sounds of foreign sailors and merchants en route to or from the Orient. The port is not exactly a 'glam' spot to visit, but it can be a useful harbour en route to and from the southern Ionian.

The castle on the heights to the S was built in 1220 by Geoffrey Villehardouin and later passed to the Venetians who named it Castel Tornese. It was taken by the Turks during their occupation of the Peloponnisos and finally partially destroyed by Ibrahim Pasha in 1825. It is now being restored and is worth a visit – it commands superb views over the surrounding countryside and the approaches to the Gulf of Patras.

ÁK SKROFA

On the northern entrance to Patraikos Kólpos around Ák Skrofa extensive works have been in progress for some years. The purpose of the land reclamation here is not known but may be linked to the huge harbour works at Plátiyiali or may be a separate project altogether. The results are unlikely to be of use to yachts.

KATO ACHAIA

A small fishing harbour lying approximately 9M ESE of Ák Páppas. It is quite shallow and only yachts drawing less than 1·5m should attempt to enter it. The approach to the harbour should be made with caution and in calm weather as there is shoal water in the vicinity. Make the approach on a SSE course keeping an eye on the depthsounder and colour of the water. The end of the mole is lit

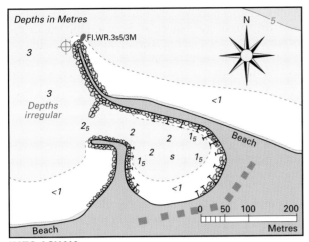

KATO ACHAIA
⊕38°09'·6N 21°32'·4E

Fl.WR.3s5/3M, but the light should not be relied on.

The entrance to the harbour is very narrow so have everything ready for berthing before entering. The harbour is usually quite full of fishing boats so berth stern or bows-to where possible. Catwalks have been built out from the rubble along the inside and if you cannot find one of these free you will have to take a long line to the shore. Good shelter.

Ashore there are a couple of tavernas which have good fresh fish.

MISSALONGHI (Mesolóngion)

Imray-Tetra chart G13

Approach

Conspicuous The white lighthouse on Nisís Áy Sóstis and the group of houses at the entrance to the canal will be seen first. The red and green buoys marking the entrance to the dredged channel are difficult to pick out from the distance and in bad visibility it can be quite a job finding them until close to. Once the buoys are located the canal is marked out by four pairs of beacons.

By night Use the light on Nisís Áy Sóstis Fl.WR.5s17/14M (red sector 293°-010°) and the lights on the outer buoys Fl.R.4·5s and Fl.G.4·5s. The channel beacons are lit (all Q.R and Q.G.3M). The lights on the buoys at the seaward end can be very difficult to locate and the lights of the beacons marking the channel are not easily seen against the lights of the town.

Note The canal is dredged to a least depth of 6m. In parts there are depths of 8m. At the entrance to the basin don't cut the corner but head for the middle of the basin to clear the shallows on the E.

Mooring

Stern or bows-to or alongside the N quay. Most yachts elect to go alongside. The bottom is mud, excellent holding.

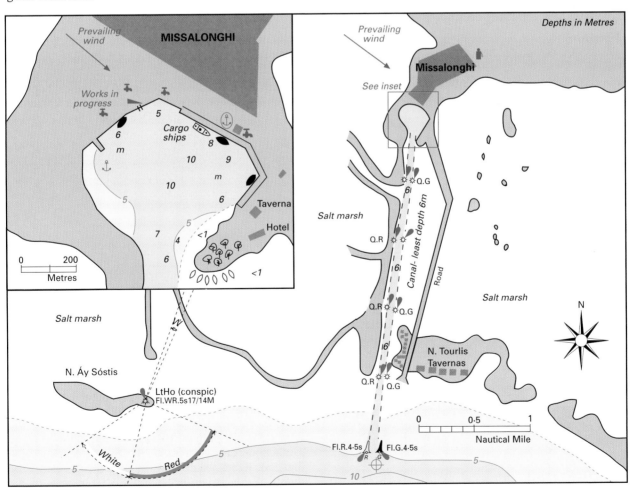

MISSALONGHI
⊕38°18'·17N 21°24'·84E WGS84

Stilt houses at the entrance to Missalonghi

Shelter Excellent shelter from all winds although the prevailing wind pushes a chop across the large basin into the NE corner.

Authorities Port police and customs.

Note The W end of the harbour now has a quay along it with a pier in the SW corner. There is talk of this becoming a marina, but at the time of publication no further works were in evidence. At present yachts can berth alongside where there is good shelter with the prevailing wind blowing you off the quay.

Anchorage Yachts can anchor in the SW corner where there is good shelter.

Facilities

Water On the quay. Showers in the hotel SE of basin.

Fuel In the town a considerable distance (30 minutes' walk) away. You may be able to arrange for a mini-tanker to come to the quay.

Repairs Some mechanical repairs. Hardware shops.

Provisions Good shopping for all provisions. Ice available.

Eating out Hardly a good taverna for a town of this size. Avoid any in the town that are labelled 'Self Service Caféteria'. The taverna at the harbour is as good as any. The cafés around the central square are pleasant enough.

Other PO. OTE. Bank. ATM. Bus to Athens.

General

Neither the harbour nor the town of Missalonghi has much charm, but the locals are friendly and somehow Missalonghi grows on you. When you eventually get through all the reinforced concrete and dust to the town square and sit down in a café for a beer or two, Missalonghi seems a little more charming and after a while you quite get to like the place.

The entrance to the canal has some interesting fishermen's houses (*pelades*) standing on stilts in the shallow water, looking like something out of SE Asia. The picture is reinforced by locals up to their knees in the salt marsh pushing rakes through the mud to collect shellfish, mostly the enormous golden-shelled fan mussel, or harpooning fish.

Many of the huts are now used as holiday homes and they have got bigger and more fancy than the original *pelades*. The surrounding salt marsh supports a variety of water birds.

Those visiting Missalonghi for its associations with Byron will be disappointed for there is little to see and little to remind us that Byron died here. There is a statue of the poet and a small museum houses a few relics from the War of Independence, but just as it had never been heard of before Byron died here, so it seems to have slipped back into an anonymity fostered by the featureless salt marsh all around it.

I have been taken to task by the Byron Society which points out that Missalonghi is a 'sacred town'. This title was bestowed on it in 1937 for its part in the Greek War of Independence; the title doesn't really do much for the architecturally challenged town, though efforts are being made to preserve some of the old centre of the place and it does have more going on than in times past. A new Byron museum is being built, though it is on the outskirts of the town and I'm not sure what they are going to put in it.

KRIONERI

38°20'·5N 21°36'·5E

Situated under the steep slopes of Mt Varasavon (922m) the open bay offers limited protection from the prevailing winds. There are 2–5m depths in the middle section of the short pier off the village where some shelter from E winds can be gained. The extremity and E side of the pier is shallow. Taverna on the waterfront.

Caution The shoal water off Ák Evinos between Missalonghi and Krionéri is marked at its extremity by a S cardinal lightbuoy Q(6)+LFl.15s.

⊕3 0·2M S of lightbuoy off Ák Evinos 38°16'·86N 21°29'·16E WGS84

PATRAS (Limín Patron, Pátrai)

BA 2404

Imray-Tetra G13

Approach

Conspicuous The buildings of the city are easily identified from some distance off. The dome of Áy Andreas church is conspicuous close to the S entrance to the harbour. A chimney is conspicuous just inland from the N entrance. The outer breakwater is quite low and it can be difficult to identify until closer in, but the cargo ships and ferries within the harbour show up well.

By night The S entrance is lit: Fl.G.3M on the inner breakwater/Fl.R on the buoy off the breakwater. The N entrance is lit: Fl.G.5s8M and F.R on the buoy off the yacht 'marina'. The elbow of the detached breakwater is lit Fl.G.1·5s3M. The harbour lights are difficult to distinguish against the lights of the city until 1–2 miles off. On calm nights there are numerous fishing boats with bright lamps

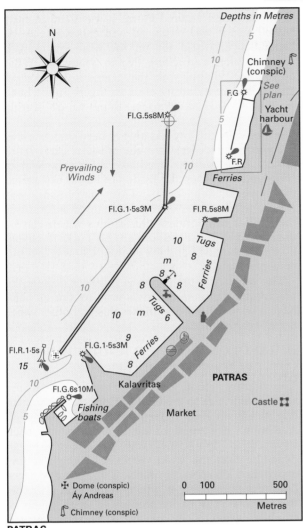

PATRAS
⊕38°15'·6N 21°44'·0E

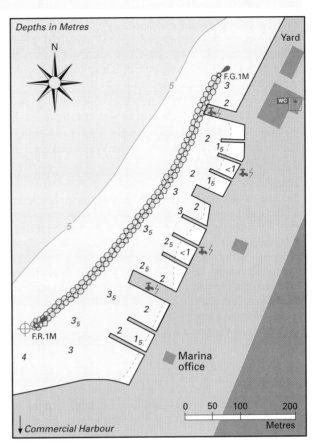

PATRAS YACHT HARBOUR
⊕38°15'·7N 21°44'·2E

moorings tailed to the quay or to a small buoy.

Shelter All round shelter.

Authorities Harbourmaster. Charge band 2/3.

Yacht harbour guardian Llanos Vasilli ☎ 2610 429130

Nautilus Yachting Can assist with berthing at the marina and provides other services including clearing yachts in and out of Greece (non-EU flags), fuel, water, provisioning and so on. A charge is made for services and it is mostly concerned with larger yachts.

VHF Ch 12
☎ 2610 622676/270019
Fax 2610 621400.

outside the harbour whose bright lights bobbing up and down in the swell give the appearance of navigation lights. The aero beacon Fl.R on Profitis (6½ miles SE of Ák Páppas) shows up well.

VHF Ch 16, 12 for port authorities. Ch 12 for Nautilus Yachting (call sign *Nautilus*).

Dangers
1. With the brisk prevailing breeze from the W there can be a confused sea off the breakwater, bothersome rather than dangerous.
2. Large ferries are constantly coming and going from the port and a good lookout must be kept in the approaches and the harbour itself.

Note Yachts should make for the yacht harbour at the N end of the commercial harbour. Large yachts should call up the harbour authorities in advance to arrange a berth in the commercial harbour.

Mooring
Patras Yacht Harbour
The entrance to the yacht harbour is difficult to identify until close to. Once into the entrance keep close to the breakwater as the harbour shallows towards the quay. Go stern or bows-to where directed or where convenient. Most berths have laid

S entrance to Patras commercial harbour

Patras commercial harbour

Go alongside or stern-to the central pier. It is often difficult to find a berth here as workboats and tugs occupy much of the quay space. Large yachts should arrange a berth in advance.

Shelter Adequate shelter although the coming and going of tugs, workboats and ferries creates a lot of wash in the harbour.

Authorities Port police. Customs. Immigration. A port of entry.

Facilities

Services Water and electricity in the yacht harbour. Toilets and showers in the yacht harbour.
Fuel A mini-tanker may deliver to the yacht harbour.
Repairs A yard near the yacht harbour can haul up to 20 tons. Most yacht work can be arranged but for specialist work you will need to go elsewhere. Hardware shops and chandlers near the marina.
Provisions Excellent shopping for all provisions in town. Supermarket about 500m going towards Patras from the yacht harbour.
Eating out Tavernas and restaurants of all types in town. Bars and cafés near the waterfront.
Other PO. OTE. Banks. ATMs. Greek gas and Camping Gaz. Hire cars and motorbikes. Regular buses to Athens, around a 2½ hour trip. Ferries to Ithaca, Cephalonia, Corfu and Italy.

General

Patras is the largest city in the Peloponnisos and the third largest in Greece. The city and the harbour are noisy and grubby but lively. You enter Patras thinking you will dislike it and slowly you end up quite liking it. The carnival (in late February and early March – traditionally ten days before Lent) is celebrated with as much gusto as Easter in Patras.

The first time I entered Patras it was 0100 in early March and it was rather an odd experience to be handed sweets and hit on the head by masked strangers after a gruelling slog to windward. What do you do? You buy your own plastic club and mask and walk around hitting other strangers on the head as this seemed the proper thing to do during carnival.

Historically the city has always been important as a commercial centre and the western gateway to Greece. The city was celebrated during the War of Independence when the Bishop of Patras first raised the Greek flag here. This patriotism was remembered all over Greece for many years and was the subject of countless illustrations which can be seen in many of the museums. The Turks retaliated by razing the town and the present city was laid out on a grid system.

The wine from the region is excellent despite the ubiquitous *Demestica*, and a visit to the Achaia-Klauss wine factory that makes this and other wines is well worth while.

DHIAVOLOS RÍON AND ANDÍRRION
(Strait of Rhion and Anti-Rhion)

This narrow strait, only one mile wide, is the western entrance to the Gulf of Corinth. A Venetian fort stands on Ríon (conspicuous) and another on Andírrion. A current of up to 2 knots has been reported to flow either way through this strait depending on the wind direction, though in my experience there is normally a W–going current despite the prevailing W winds. If the wind is against the current it is easily seen as a small patch of troubled water. Care needs to be taken of the numerous car ferries plying between Ríon and

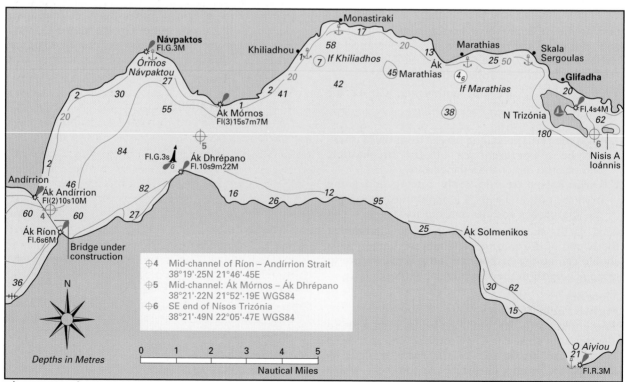

RÍON TO TRIZÓNIA

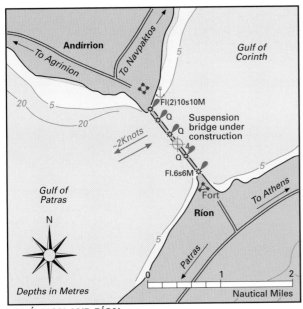

ANDÍRRION AND RÍON

⊕4   Mid-channel of Rion – Andírrion Strait 38°19'·25N 21°46'·45E

Andírrion, at least until the bridge is finished.

The strait is lit on either side: Rion Fl.6s6M and Andírrion Fl(2)10s10M.

In 1999 construction began on the Rion Andirrion suspension bridge across the strait. At the time of writing construction is in full swing with all four of the cable columns in place. The bridge will be a five span cable suspension structure with a total length of 2,290 metres. Air height for the bridge is not known at this stage, but will probably be in the vicinity of 80–100 metres under the main navigable span.

At present the cable columns are lit by quick flash lights atop the structures or the cranes and are visible for a considerable distance off. The navigable channel in either direction is buoyed and will change as work proceeds. When the bridge is complete it is likely the channels E or W will be buoyed and the navigable channel indicated on the bridge. Completion is scheduled for the end of 2004.

Communication with bridge coastguard VHF Ch 14. Yachts should call up *Rion traffic* 5 miles off and then again at 2 miles off to get permission to pass.

ANDÍRRION 38°19'·7N 21°46'·0E

Immediately E of the car ferry ramps there is a very small basin. The entrance is around 20m wide and the basin itself is approximately 100m by 30m wide. There are 2m depths in the entrance and 1·5m depths in the outer part of the basin. It is recommended you do not use the basin as a matter of course, but in an emergency it could be useful for very small yachts. At the time of writing it is in the middle of the construction site for the bridge project.

Gulf of Corinth
(Korinthiakós Kólpos)

The Gulf of Corinth extends from Rion and Andírrion to the Corinth Canal. It is considerably indented on the N side with numerous natural bays and gulfs in which a yacht can find shelter. There are also man-made harbours on both the N and S sides of the gulf. Many yachts charge through the gulf intent on getting to or from the Aegean, and miss out on the delights of the places around the coast. You can usefully spend a couple of weeks dawdling around the gulf should you decide to take it easy and there are a number of sites ashore (Delphi and Corinth spring to mind) which are well worth a visit.

Gulf of Corinth north side from Navpaktos to Corinth

NÁVPAKTOS (Lepanto)

Approach

Conspicuous From the distance the castle walls on the hill above the town and the buildings of the town are conspicuous. Closing the town, the castellated walls of the harbour will be seen.

By night The entrance is lit Fl.G.2s3M.

Note The medieval harbour is very small so a yacht should have everything ready for berthing before entering. A large yacht should not attempt to get in here as there simply isn't room.

Mooring

Go stern or bows-to on the S side of the harbour or off the fuel jetty or wherever there is room. Beware of floating lines from the local fishing boats. The bottom is soft mud, not always the best holding. The small harbour gets very crowded in July and August so you may not be able to find a berth – after all it doesn't take too many yachts to fill a harbour of this size. Crossed anchors are also something you can do little about given the difficulties of manoeuvring once inside and the lack of space.

Shelter Reasonable shelter from the prevailing wind although a prolonged westerly sets up a surge. Winds from the SW and SE funnelling into the bay cause a surge, though in the summer this is more uncomfortable than dangerous.

Anchorage If the harbour is impossibly full then you can anchor off the beach in settled weather. This is not the most comfortable place to be with the prevailing westerlies although they will usually die down at night. Large yachts (over c.16m) should anchor off anyway or they will simply block access to most parts of the miniature harbour. Off the beach the bottom is sand or mud, good holding.

Facilities

Water On the quay.

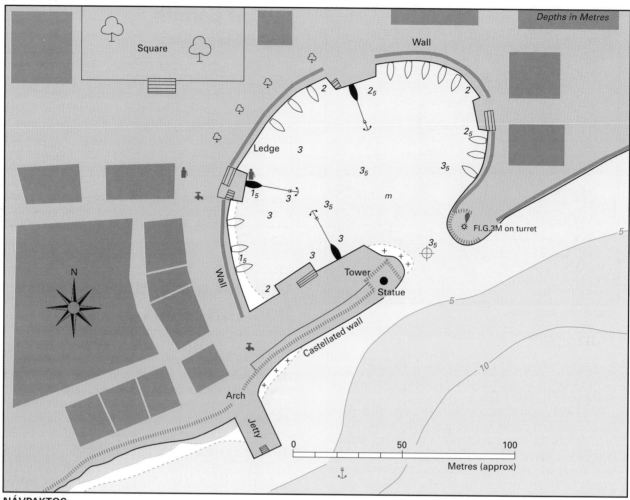

NÁVPAKTOS
⊕38°23´·55N 21°49´·72E WGS84

Fuel Close to the quay – a hose can be led down to the fuel quay.

Repairs Minor mechanical repairs. Hardware shops.

Provisions Good shopping for all provisions. Ice available.

Eating out Numerous tavernas around the harbour and in the town.

Other PO. OTE. ATM. Bank. Greek gas and Camping Gaz. Bus to Andírrion where you can get a ferry across to Ríon and catch the bus to Athens or Patras.

General

The minute medieval harbour bordered by old plane trees and under the shadow of the Venetian castle (now a park) is a captivating place. It is a pity the same cannot be said for the reinforced concrete sprawl on either side of the old town. Nor is the harbour a quiet place – traffic rumbles and buzzes around the road by the harbour, the locals are an animated lot and it all goes on in the square by the harbour. Around the harbour some of the old houses have been turned into convivial cafés and restaurants. Take a wander around the E side of the harbour.

It is well worth a walk up to the castle to escape the hubbub. Návpaktos is well-watered and in the summer heat it is strange to hear water bubbling away when not so far away it is scarce. The town was known in medieval times as Lepanto and it was here that the Turks refitted before the disastrous (for them) Battle of Lepanto. The medieval harbour is one of the best examples of its type in the Mediterranean and should not be missed.

Návpaktos looking NW from just outside the entrance to the harbour

Návpaktos harbour looking NE to the entrance and E side

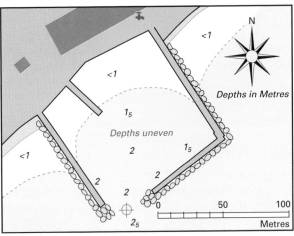

KHILIADHOU
⊕38°23'·4N 21°55'·0E

KHILIADHOU

A small harbour on the E side of the low land running out to Ák Mornos. The entrance is prone to silting so care is needed in the immediate approach. Go stern or bows-to or alongside in the outer part of the harbour where possible. Care is needed as depths are uneven in the harbour and only yachts drawing 1·5m or less should try to get in here. Good shelter from all but strong S–SE winds.

Water in the village square and several tavernas ashore.

MONASTIRAKI 38°24'·2N 21°56'·4E

With the prevailing westerlies you can anchor off the village here. Anchor in 5–8m on mud. Generally some swell tends to creep around into the bay and it is not the most comfortable place to stay for the night. The short pier and quay off the village has mostly less than 1m depths except near the end of the pier where there are 1–1·5m depths.

Water tap near the quay. Several tavernas.

MARATHIAS 38°23'·3N 22°00'·7E

Marathias village sits tucked under the W side of Ák Marathias approximately halfway between Monastiraki and Trizonia. Off the village there is a very small harbour in which a small yacht drawing 1·5m or less may be able to find a berth. There are 2m depths in the entrance decreasing to 1–<1m further in. Good shelter.

Tavernas ashore.

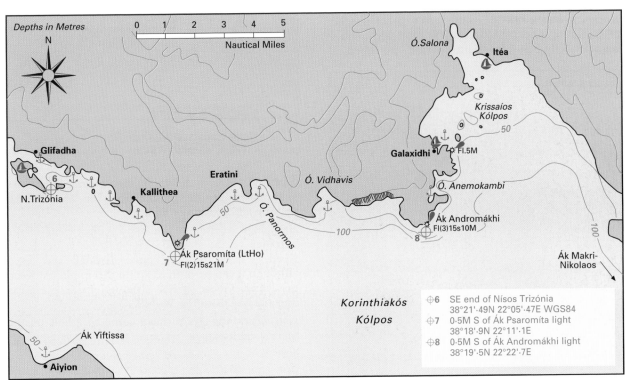

TRIZÓNIA TO KRISSAÍOS KÓLPOS

⊕6   SE end of Nísos Trizónia
38°21'·49N 22°05'·47E WGS84

⊕7   0·5M S of Ák Psaromíta light
38°18'·9N 22°11'·1E

⊕8   0·5M S of Ák Andromákhi light
38°19'·5N 22°22'·7E

GLIFADHA 38°22'·8N 22°04'·5E

A very small harbour on the mainland opposite Trizonia. The harbour is around 80m long by 40m wide. Entrance is at the SE end with around 2m depths in the entrance. A very small yacht may be able to go alongside the end of the outer mole where there are 1·5–2m depths.

Minimarket and taverna ashore.

Nisís Trizónia

Approach

From the distance the island is difficult to make out against the nearby hills of the mainland. From the W a villa on the saddle of Nisís Trizónia stands out well and several other villas on the S side will be seen. From the E an escarpment on Nisís Áy Ioánnis is conspicuous. Closer in the village on the mainland opposite the island will be seen, but the small hamlet on the island and the entrance to the bay are not visible until you are near the anchorage.

By night With care a night approach is possible. The N entrance is lit Fl.4s4M. The fish farm in the bay opposite the SE end of Trizónia is lit by bright arc lights. The marina is unlit.

Dangers If proceeding between Trizónia and the mainland coast care is needed of the reef running out from the island for around 300m off the N side of Trizónia. Keep closer to the mainland coast than to Trizónia.

Mooring

At present yachts go alongside in the marina. In the summer when it gets more crowded yachts should go stern or bows-to. Care is needed off the two jetties running out from the shore as it has been reported that there are large mooring chains running parallel to them ready to take mooring lines. If going alongside on the outside of the moles care is needed of ballasting and rubble near the mole although I found mostly 2·5–3·5m depths despite the rubble.

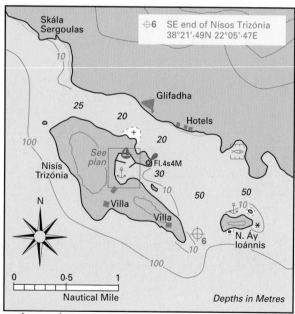

NISÍS TRIZÓNIA

Trizónia 'marina' looking E towards the entrance to the bay

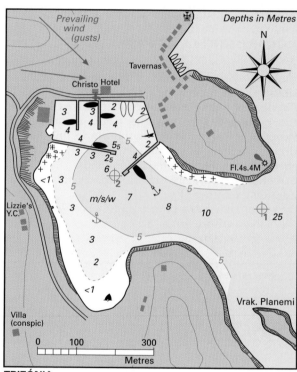

TRIZÓNIA
⊕1 38°22'·06N 22°04'·77E WGS84
⊕2 38°22'·10N 22°04'·57E WGS84

Shelter All round shelter in the marina. There are gusts down into the marina from the W–NW with the prevailing summer wind.

Anchorage Anchor in the bay keeping clear of the entrance to the marina. The bottom is mud and weed – good holding once through the weed although it can be difficult to do this in places. Keep persisting. Good shelter although there are gusts into the bay from the W–NW.

Note Work appears to have come to a halt on the marina, although in its present state it is perfectly usable.

Facilities

Services Water available from Christo on the N side of the marina near the hotel. You will have to be in a berth on the N side of the marina. Hotel Dryma behind the marina offers showers and laundry facilities, as does the YC (see below).

Fuel Some distance from Glifadha, the village on the mainland opposite.

Repairs Christo in the house near the hotel can carry out gardiennage including engine and boat maintenance, and he has acquired a good reputation. He also has the metered water hose.

Provisions Minimarket in the village. Navpaktos is the nearest place for all provisions.

Eating out Several tavernas in the village and a restaurant at the Hotel Dryma and at the YC.

Other Caïque ferry to the mainland opposite.

The Yacht Club Not really a yacht club as such but a convivial restaurant and bar. Also showers, laundry, book-swap library and they will hold mail. Reached by road from the 'marina' or take your dinghy across to a small wooden landing stage.

The Yacht Club, Trizónia Island, Gulf of Corinth, 33058 Doridos, Greece.
☎ 22660 71580.

General

The land around the bay is green and lush – mostly vines and olives. The small fishing hamlet has changed little over the years despite the number of yachts using the sheltered bay. A few more villas have now been built on the island, but as yet it is still an out-of-the-way spot that has now attracted a surprising number of yachts for the winter.

Even if you do not eat ashore it is well worth your while to go ashore for an ouzo or brandy and coffee – sitting around the little square overlooking the small harbour you'll easily lose an evening.

NISÍS ÁY IOÁNNIS

In calm weather you can anchor off this delightful islet in the eastern approaches to Trizónia. Anchor on the N side taking care of the rock off the N and E ends. With the prevailing westerlies it is usually too bumpy to stay here.

SKALA KALLITHEA (Áy Nikoláos)

Situated 4 miles SE of Nisís Trizónia. On the E side of the entrance is the small islet of Lagonisi and further into the bay there is another small islet with a chapel on it. Care is needed of the above water rock off Lagonisi. The bay hooks NW to give good shelter from W winds although E winds send in some swell. Open to the S. Anchor in 3–6m where convenient. The bottom is sand – good holding.

Some provisions ashore. Tavernas. Ferry to Aiyíon.

ÁK PSAROMITA

The lighthouse on the cape is easily spotted from some distance off. On the E side there is reasonable shelter from the prevailing westerlies. The best place to be is tucked up in the NW corner where there are 5–10m depths to anchor in.

Kallithea looking NW towards the town and islet

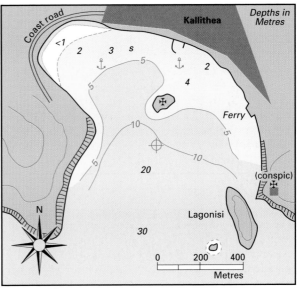

KALLITHEA
⊕38°20´·8N 22°09´·6E

On the beach nearby is a large hotel with a taverna.

ERATINI

A bay situated situated 3 miles NE of Ák Psaromíta. The large white hotel behind the beach to the W of Eratini is conspicuous and closer in a church in the village stands out well. The bay affords reasonable shelter from the prevailing winds though some swell rolls into it. It is not a secure spot in unsettled weather. Anchor in 5–10m off the village. A small pier has 3m depths at its extremity and a yacht can go bows-to if there is room.

On the E side of the bay a small *caïque* harbour has been built. There is usually room in here for a small to medium size yacht to go stern or bows-to or alongside. Good all-round shelter in the *caïque* harbour.

Most provisions can be found and tavernas open in the summer. PO. OTE.

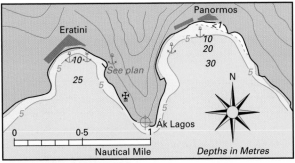

ERATINI AND PANORMOS
⊕38°21'·0N 22°14'·2E

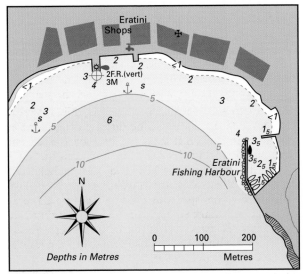

ERATINI
⊕38°21'·6N 22°13'·8E

Eratini *caique* harbour looking SW   *Lu Michell*

Ák Andromákhi looking E. The light structure is difficult to make out until close-to

ÓRMOS PANORMOS

The bay situated over the headland immediately E of Eratini. Anchor in 5–10m tucked up into the NW side. The bottom is sand and weed, good holding. Adequate shelter from the prevailing westerlies. E winds send in a swell. If anchoring in the NE corner care is needed of shoal water off the coast – easily seen in calm weather.

Tavernas open in the summer and limited provisions are available.

ÓRMOS VIDHAVIS (Áy Pandes)

Lying 2 miles to the E of Panormos on the E side of Ák Dounos. The islet of Xeronisi off the cape is easily identified and Vidhavis lies at the W end of the conspicuous escarpment dropping down into the sea along this stretch of coast. Vidhavis affords good shelter from W winds but E winds send in some swell. Open to the S. Anchor in 3–6m at the head of the bay. Good holding. A small harbour at the E end has just 2m depths at the end of the quay. Minimarket, telephone and tavernas ashore.

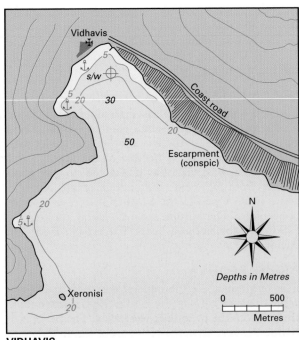

VIDHAVIS
⊕38°21'·2N 22°17'·9E

156

The bay is marred by the awful road scar right around it, but otherwise is an attractive place. In calm weather there is a pleasant anchorage in the bay just N of Xeronisi.

ÓRMOS ANEMOKAMBI (Andromákhi)

An almost landlocked bay lying just N of Ák Andromákhi. The light structure on the cape is difficult to see until close to. In the approaches Ifalos Trakhilou lying 0·4 miles E of Ák Trakhilou, the S entrance point of Anemokambi Bay, has 3m depths over it. It is easily seen in calm weather. In the bight before Anemokambi inlet and on the N side of the bay there are now fish farms. Large buoys mark the limits of the fish farms and by day entry to the bay is straightforward, but at night care is needed.

Anchor where convenient in 3–12m. The bottom is mud and weed, good holding. Good shelter. There is a hotel at the head of the inlet with a restaurant. The new road around the bay has brought the hotel and campers in the summer, but it is still an attractive place and worth a visit.

GALAXIDHI

Imray-Tetra G13

Approach

The approach to the harbour should be made between Nisís Apsifiá and Nisís Áy Yeóryios until past the stone beacon on the reef E of the entrance and then into the harbour as shown on the plan.

Conspicuous Once up to Ák Pounda, Nisís Apsifiá and Nisís Áy Yeóryios can be distinguished. Apsifiá has a single tree on it and a white shed next to the light structure. Áy Yeóryios has a church on the S end and another on the NW end. On the headland sheltering Galaxidhi the buildings of the naval college are conspicuous. The beacon (roughly rectangular) marking the reef off the entrance to Galaxidhi is easily identified. Once up to Áy Yeóryios the buildings of Galaxidhi (the cathedral is conspicuous) will be seen.

By night There is a light on Nisís Apsifiá Fl.7s5M and a light off the W side of the entrance to the harbour (Fl.RG.1·5s3M 080°-R-216°-G-347°). A night entry is not recommended.

Dangers
1. Care needs to be taken of the reefs fringing Nisís Apsifiá and Nisís Áy Yeóryios – see plan.

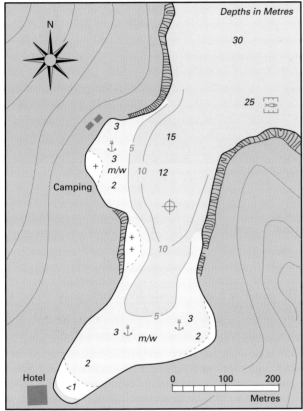

ÓRMOS ANEMOKAMBI
⊕38°21′·0N 22°22′·9E

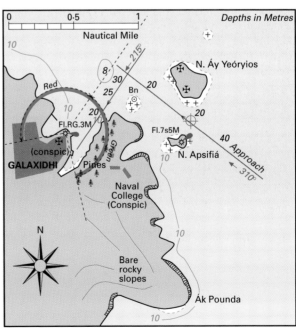

GALAXIDHI APPROACHES
⊕38°22′·80N 22°24′·28E WGS84

Órmos Anemokambi looking S

Nisís Áy Yeóryios with the church conspic looking NE

2. Care needs to be taken of the reef off the E side of the entrance marked by a stone beacon. Although local boats pass between this reef and the coast, this passage is not recommended even with local knowledge.

Mooring
Go stern or bows-to the quay on the W. It is better to go bows-to as ballasting extends some distance under the water. The bottom is mud and weed, mediocre holding.

Shelter Good all-round shelter. NE winds send some swell in – more uncomfortable than dangerous. It has been reported that there can be a tidal surge similar to the *marrobio* experienced in some harbours on the S of Sicily, but I have yet to encounter any reliable reports of its occurrence here.

Authorities Port police.

Facilities
Water On the quay. You need to find the 'waterman'.

Fuel Can be delivered by mini-tanker.

Repairs Limited mechanical repairs. Hardware shop.

Provisions Good shopping for most provisions.

Eating out Tavernas around the waterfront and others in the village. Pension Gannymede does an excellent luxury breakfast in the garden.

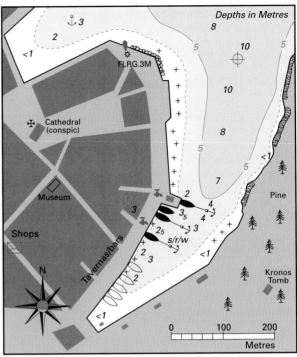

GALAXIDHI
⊕38°22′·69N 22°23′·36E WGS84

Other PO. OTE. ATM. Greek gas. Bus to Itéa and then on to Delphi. Hire cars. Taxi to Delphi.

General
From the distance the rocky islets and stony hills hide the tranquil narrow inlet of Galaxidhi harbour. Hemmed in by a pine-studded peninsula to the E and the town hunched on a rocky mound to the W, this harbour is one of the most pleasing in the Gulf of Corinth. In the 18th and early 19th centuries it was a prosperous port until the Turks occupied the area and captured the fleet. Near the harbour there is an interesting small museum displaying curios including some fine figureheads from its heyday as a thriving shipping town.

Today it lies as quietly as it has done for over a century and offers shelter only to yachts. It has a modest amount of tourism and some fairly sophisticated restaurants and gift shops (with

Approach to Galaxidhi harbour looking SW. The rectangular beacon marking the reef (left) and the cathedral in the town are easily identified

Galaxidhi looking from the E side of the inlet

sophisticated prices) will be found on the waterfront. This is a useful safe harbour near Delphi, which can be reached by the local bus, hire car or by taxi.

ÓRMOS SALONA (Krissa)

BA 2405

Imray-Tetra G13

Lying at the NW extremity of Krissaíos Kólpos, there are a number of sheltered coves bordering the bay, but the opencast mines on the coast hideously scar it and with any wind a haematite red stains the sea and the surrounding land. Recently fish farms have been built in some of the coves so there is really little point in heading up into the bay.

It was in this bay that Frank Abney Hastings proved the worth of a steam-powered ship in more ways than one. With a small escort he steamed into the bay and destroyed a much bigger Turkish fleet. Not only could he manoeuvre under power but his iron hull was less susceptible to damage. According to H M Denham he used hot shot (heated in the boilers) because he feared solid shot would simply go straight through an enemy ship without doing any real damage. It is somewhat ironic that the place where an iron ship was first used for combat in Greece is now a mass of mines extracting iron ore.

ITÉA

Imray-Tetra G13

Approach

Conspicuous The buildings of Itéa are easily identified. A large church on the waterfront and the silos of a flourmill near the W end of the marina are conspicuous.

By night The end of the pier is lit Fl.RG.3s4M (295°-G-355°-R-030°-G-111°).

Dangers In the approaches keep well clear of the islets of Molimenos and Stafidha which have reefs and shoal water around them.

Note Yachts should make for the marina. The entrance is difficult to see until close to, but it is obvious where it is.

Mooring

Note At the time of publication work is still in progress on parts of the marina, although the harbour works are basically complete.

At present yachts go alongside where convenient. In the future laid moorings will be installed and yachts will go stern or bows-to.

Shelter Good all-round shelter although a surge can build up with southerlies.

Authorities Port police. Customs.

Facilities

Services Water and electricity points to be installed. There are some water points near the marina where you may be able to get water.

Fuel In the town. Can be delivered by mini-tanker.

Repairs Basic mechanical and engineering repairs.

Provisions Good shopping for all provisions nearby. Ice available.

Eating out Numerous restaurants and bars along the waterfront. Some more ethnic haunts in the back-streets.

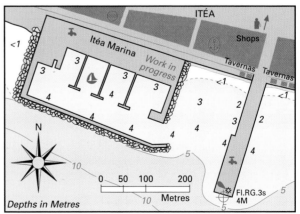

ITÉA
⊕38°25'·8N 22°25'·5E

Itéa Marina looking in through the entrance

Other PO. OTE. Banks. ATM. Bus to Athens which stops at Delphi.

General

Itéa is an odd little town. It survives on the dark red haemetite iron ore extracted just around the coast and also services the agricultural hinterland. The waterfront is a line of tavernas and bars and a thoroughly pleasant spot to stroll along if the wind is not blowing its usual cloud of gritty red dust over the town. Itéa is a dusty spot and everything gets covered by the greasy red dust, including any yachts in the marina.

Behind the waterfront the town is a pleasantly old-fashioned place as it gets few tourists except those stranded here en route to or from Delphi.

ITÉA FISHING HARBOUR

On the W side of the town there is a fishing harbour affording good all-round protection. However there are only 1–1·5m depths in the entrance and along the outer breakwater. Most of the harbour is very shallow. Small craft drawing less than 1m could get in here with care. Good all-round shelter inside.

DELPHI

Ancient Delphi is easily visited from Galaxidhi or Itéa and although acknowledged as one of the most spectacular and beautiful classical sites in Greece, it is for my taste, also spectacularly overcrowded in summer, when there are frequently twenty to thirty coaches lining the road. It is best visited in spring or autumn.

Delphi was regarded by the ancients as the centre of the world. Its spectacular site amidst ravines, rocky bluffs and sheer cliffs on the side of Mt Parnassos contributes for a large part to its air of mystery. It takes its name from Apollo Elphinos when the god was worshipped in the shape of a dolphin. As well as Apollo other gods were associated with Delphi, notably Dionysus and Athena. The Delphic oracle was famous throughout Greece - it is interesting to note that the interpretations were vague and often obscene, but had the reputation of being more truthful than elsewhere. Its fame diminished during Roman times.

The French school began excavating the site in 1892 and have continued to do much of the work. A museum houses most of the important finds.

ÓRMOS ANDÍKIRON (Antikyrra)

BA 2405

Imray-Tetra G13

This large bay to the E of Ák Mákri-Nikólaos has a number of anchorages around it that can be used by a yacht depending on wind and sea. The whole bay is surrounded by steep slopes and split by spectacular ravines. It is an impressive coast to sail around although the high mountains mean that there can be severe gusts at times.

Órmos Veresses Lies immediately NW of Ák Trakhilos. Affords good shelter with W winds. Untenable with NE–E winds. Anchor in 3–10m.

Órmos Isidhorou Lies on the S side of Kefalí, the high headland on the W side of Andíkiron proper. Good shelter from W and NE–E winds, although

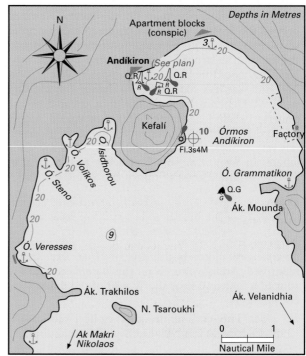

ÓRMOS ANDÍKIRON

⊕10 0·5M E of Ák Kefáli (Andíkiron)
38°21'·6N 22°39'·4E

Andíkiron looking NE onto the town quay

Órmos Grammatikon The bay in the SE of Andíkiron. The bay is designated as a military zone and although a yacht may anchor here, photographs of the area are forbidden.

ÓRMOS ÁY SARANDA (Saranti)

The large bay lying 6 miles E of Ák Velanidhia. The bay affords reasonable shelter from westerlies, but with easterlies a swell runs into the bay and unless you can get into the small harbour it can be uncomfortable. Depths are considerable right up to the head of the bay and you will usually have to anchor in 12–15m. It is difficult to tuck right up into the NW corner because of the local boats on permanent moorings here. If you can get in go stern or bows-to or alongside the end of the mole of the small harbour in the NW corner. Good shelter in here from W and E winds.

Some provisions available ashore and several tavernas.

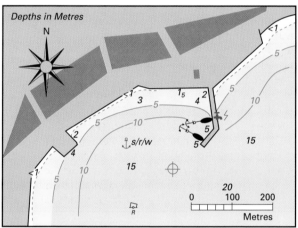

ANDÍKIRON
⊕38°22'·6N 22°37'·9E

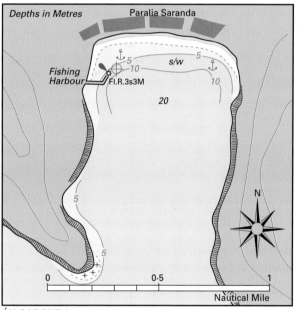

ÁY SARANDA
⊕38°14'·2N 22°53'·2E

westerlies may creep around Ák Pangalos and up into here. Anchor in 5–10m. Care needs to be taken of large concrete mooring blocks on the bottom off the beach by the café. Café ashore.

Immediately W of Isidhorou are two other bays worth exploring.

Andíkiron The large bay entered between Kefalí on the W and Ák Mounda on the E. The town of Andíkiron (Aspra Spitia) around the head of the bay and the factory 'suburb' on the NE (tower blocks conspicuous) is easily identified. On the SE side of the bay there is a military base and on the SW side two large red and white mooring buoys (lit: Q.R). Yachts can go stern or bows-to on the W side of the new pier. Care is needed of some underwater rubble, but on the outer end depths are deep enough so that you can easily get close to the pier. Good shelter behind the pier.

Alternatively anchor off although the depths drop off considerably so you will be anchoring in 10–15m.

Water and electricity points on the pier. Fuel in the town. Good shopping for provisions and tavernas and cafés on the waterfront. PO. Bank.

KÓLPOS DOMVRAINIS (Dobrena)

The much-indented gulf lying E of Ák Tambourlo. A number of small islands are peppered across the entrance. In the gulf the prevailing wind is often an E–NE wind which can gust down off the steep slopes around the gulf. There are a number of anchorages around the gulf.

Órmos Vathi Naoussa A deeply indented bay in the NW corner of the gulf. Harbour works are in progress at the head of the bay where a large commercial quay and approach roads have been built. This rather restricts its usefulness for yachts although you may still be able to anchor here, depending on future plans for the place.

Órmos Áy Ioannou A double-headed bay immediately E of Vathi. Anchor off the hamlet in the NW arm of the bay in 5–10m. The setting of the

161

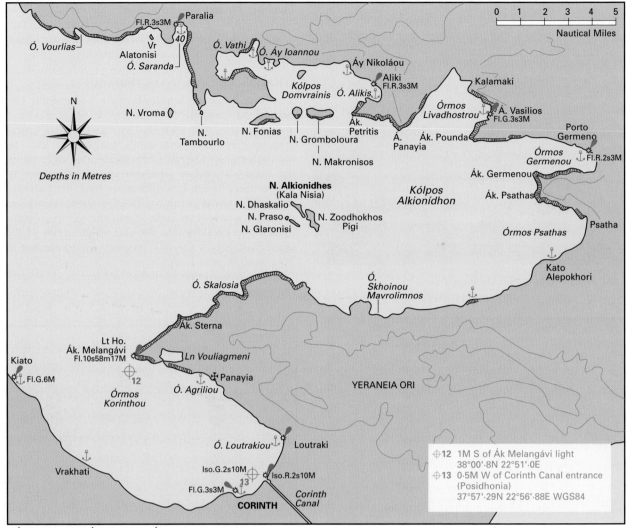

0 1 2 3 4 5
Nautical Miles

Ó. Vourlias

Paralia
Fl.R.3s3M
Vr
Alatonisi
Ó. Saranda
40

Ó. Vathi
Ó. Áy Ioannou
Áy Nikoláou
Aliki
Fl.R.3s3M

Kalamaki

Kólpos
Domvrainis
Ó. Alikis

Órmos
Livadhostrou
Á. Vasilios
Fl.G.3s3M

Porto
Germeno

N

N. Vroma

N.
Tambourlo

N. Fonias

N. Gromboloura

Ák.
Petritis

Á.
Panayia

Ák. Pounda

Órmos
Germenou
Fl.R.2s3M

Depths in Metres

N. Makronisos

Ák. Germenou

N. Alkionidhes
(Kala Nisia)

Kólpos
Alkionídhon

Ák. Psathas

N. Dhaskalio
N. Praso
N. Glaronisi

N. Zoodhokhos
Pigi

Órmos Psathas

Psatha

Ó.
Skhoinou
Mavrolímnos

Kato
Alepokhori

Ó. Skalosia

Ák. Sterna

Lt Ho.
Ák. Melangávi
Fl.10s58m17M

Ln Vouliagmeni

YERANEIA ORI

Kiato
Fl.G.6M

12

Panayia

Órmos
Korinthou

Ó. Agriliou

Ó. Loutrakiou

Loutraki

⊕12 1M S of Ák Melangávi light
       38°00'·8N 22°51'·0E
⊕13 0·5M W of Corinth Canal entrance
       (Posidhonia)
       37°57'·29N 22°56'·88E WGS84

Vrakhati

Iso.G.2s10M
Fl.G.3s3M

13

Iso.R.2s10M

Corinth
Canal

CORINTH

KÓLPOS ALKIONÍDHON AND ÓRMOS KORINTHOU

bay is spectacular under steep slopes. You can also anchor in the NE arm of the bay in 6–10m.

Áy Nikoláou An exposed anchorage off the beach in the NE corner. Suitable in calm weather.

Alikis 38°11'·9N 23°02'·8E

The bay on the E side of the gulf. A light is exhibited at the end of a stub mole: Fl.R.3s3M. Anchor off the village in 6–12m. The bottom drops off quickly. Good shelter from all sectors except the W. There can be gusts from the N–NE into the bay. The stub mole has just 2m depths at the end decreasing to 1m near the root.

Provisions and taverna ashore.

ÓRMOS LIVADHOSTROU

38°10'·9N 23°08'·5E

A large bay immediately E of Kólpos Domvrainis. On the E side Órmos Áy Vasilios affords shelter from E–NE winds. The bay is open W. Anchor in 6–12m depths in the SE corner off the village. Taverna ashore.

The stub mole off the village has 1·5–1m depths off it, but is full of local boats. The end of the mole is lit Fl.G.3s3M.

PORTO GERMENO

Approach

Órmos Germenoú is the large bay at the NE end of Kólpos Alkionidon. At the head of Órmos Germenoú is Porto Germeno.

By night The entrance is lit Fl.R.2s3M/Fl.G.2s3M.

Mooring

If there is room go alongside the end of the outer mole. There are good depths here up to the elbow, but further in it quickly becomes shallow and depths are irregular.

Shelter Good shelter under the outer mole.

Anchorage You can anchor off in 5–10m. The bottom is reported to be shingle and rock, poor holding.

Facilities

A water tap near the root of the mole. Tavernas open in the summer. Bus to Athens.

General

Porto Germeno is a local resort that attracts a fair number of Athenians in the summer. One reason to make the voyage up here is to look at the 4th-

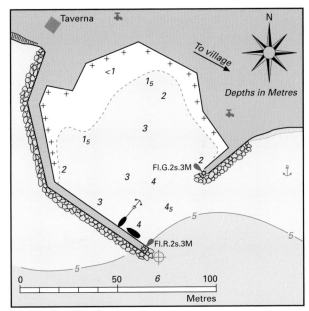

PORTO GERMENO
⊕38°09'·5N 23°13'·2E

MAVROLIMNOS 38°03'·7N 23°06'·4E

A large harbour on the S side of Kólpos Alkionidhon. Depths inside are unknown, although reported to be adequate for small to medium-sized yachts. Probably the best thing to do is send someone in with a dinghy to reconnoitre.

NISOI ALKONIDHES (Kala Nisia)

A group of three small islands lying to the S of Kólpos Domvrainis in Kólpos Alkionidhon. With W or E winds shelter can be found anchored between Dhaskalio and Zoodhokos. A bar with depths of 1m or less connects the southernmost tip of Dhaskalio to the middle of Zoodhokos. Anchor in the cove to the S of the bar off the monastery on Zoodhokos (sheltered from the E and NE) or on the N side of the bar between Dhaskalio and Zoodhokos (sheltered from the W). The bottom is sand – good holding.

Once the islands supported a prosperous monastery, the buildings of which still stand on these lonely islands.

century BC fort of Aegosthena above the mouth of a valley to the S. The ancient walls are impressive with two towers still standing. The site was not historically that important, which may account for why it has remained intact for so long. (Important sites tended to be rebuilt using state-of-the-art military architecture.) Inside are the remains of a medieval monastery.

ÓRMOS PSATHAS

The large bay in the SE corner of Kólpos Alkionidhon. Depths are considerable right up to the shore. On the S side of the bay is Kato Alepochori which has a small harbour off it.

Kato Alepochori The harbour is small and cramped so have everything ready before entering. Most of the quay is occupied by local boats and depths off the quayed areas are mostly 1m or less. You may be able to go stern or bows-to on the E quay. Alternatively anchor and take a long line ashore to the rough stone breakwater. Good shelter.

Ashore provisions can be found and there are several tavernas.

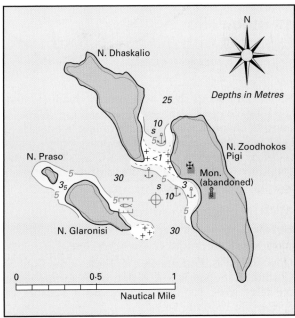

NISOI ALKONIDHES
⊕38°06'·7N 22°59'·4E

ÓRMOS AGRILIOU

38°00'·5N 22°55'·4E

A shallow bight lying 3 miles E of Ák Melangávi (the lighthouse on the cape is conspicuous from the distance), this open anchorage has been used by some yachts waiting to go through the canal. It offers some shelter from the NE but is open to all other directions.

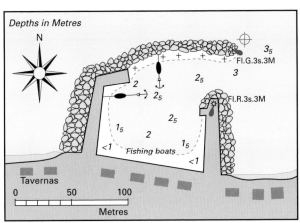

KATO ALEPOCHORI
⊕38°05'·4N 23°11'·2E

ÓRMOS LOUTRAKIOU

37°58'·8N 22°58'·4E

BA 2404

Imray-Tetra G13

The open bay lying N of the Corinth Canal. Used by some yachts while waiting to go through the Corinth Canal. Large hotels conspicuous from the distance line the edge of the bay. It offers shelter from the NE but is open to the W and S. Anchor where convenient in 3–6m. The bottom is sand and weed with some rocks – the holding is uncertain in places.

Gulf of Corinth south side from Ák Dhrepano to Corinth

The south side of the Gulf of Corinth is less indented than the north coast, with few natural harbours. Rivers flowing down off the Peloponnisos have created a fertile plain between the mountains and the coast. Shallow water extends some distance off the coast, particularly around the river mouths.

ÁK DHREPANO

⊕5 Mid-channel: Ak Mornos – Ak Dhrepano
38°21'·22N 21°52'·19E WGS84

At Ák Dhrepano there is a cement loading quay used by coasters. Entrance is from the W by a buoyed channel. With the prevailing westerlies a swell is pushed directly onto the quay.

Off Ák Dhrepano a lightbuoy (Fl.G.3s) marks the extremity of an old sunken pier and shoal water off the cape.

AIYÍON (Aigion, Vostitsa)

BA 2404

Imray-Tetra G13

Opposite Nisís Trizónia on the S side of the Gulf of Corinth, the open bay of Aiyíon is the terminus for the ferry from Kallithea. There are a number of options for mooring here.

1. In calm weather go stern-to or alongside the E end of the ferry quay. If it blows strongly from the W or E it is not secure here.
2. Anchor in the bay on the W side under the small fishing harbour. Depths here are less than elsewhere and you will be able to anchor in 4–6m on mud and weed. Exposed to E winds and only moderate shelter from W winds.
3. Small yachts may be able to get into the small fishing harbour on the W side. There are 1·5m depths in the entrance and 1–1·5m depths inside. Good shelter here.

Ashore there is good shopping for provisions and tavernas and cafés. Aiyíon is something of a provincial centre and generally has good facilities ashore.

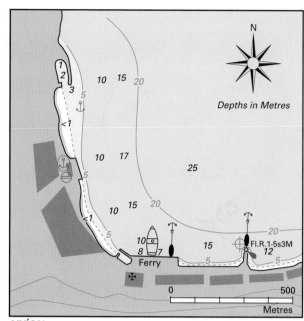

AIYÍON
⊕38°15'·3N 22°05'·0E

XILOKASTRO

A private yacht harbour situated at the E end of Xilokastro village. The harbour is small with a difficult narrow entrance. Depending on members' boats in here you may or may not find a berth. The inner part of the harbour is 1–<1m, so berth in the outer part of the harbour. Good shelter inside although strong E–NE winds may make some berths uncomfortable.

Water on the quay. Tavernas at the harbour. It is around a 5-minute walk into Xilokastro to the E.

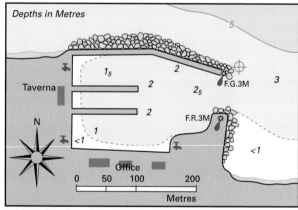

XILOKASTRO
⊕38°05'·0N 22°37'·5E

KIATO

Imray-Tetra G13

Approach

Conspicuous The town of Kiato can be seen from the distance and closer in the high retaining wall of the harbour mole is easily identified. A cathedral with a red tile cupola and belfry is conspicuous behind the harbour.

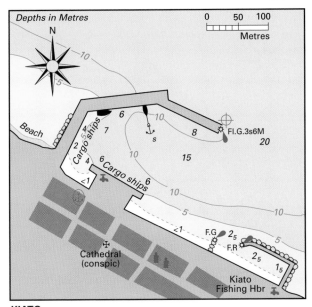

KIATO
⊕38°00′·9N 22°45′·3E

Eating out Tavernas near the waterfront.
Other PO. OTE. Bank. Greek gas and Camping Gaz. Hire cars. Bus to Athens.

General

Kiato is developing into a popular tourist resort based on the good bathing beaches nearby. The surrounding land is intensively cultivated with citrus and the vine.

VRAKHATI

A harbour lying approximately 7 miles W of Corinth on the S side of Órmos Korinthou. Off Vrakhati the mole extends out from the coast providing shelter from westerlies. The harbour is completely open to E–NE winds and you should not attempt to shelter here in these conditions. Go stern or bows-to or alongside the outer end of the mole. Care is needed as ballasting extends underwater from the quay in places. The inner part of the harbour is shallow.

Provisions in the village about 10 minutes' walk away. Taverna nearby.

By night The end of the breakwater is lit Fl.G.6M. A green neon light to the E of the harbour also has a good range!

Mooring

Go stern or bows-to or alongside the mole wherever there is sufficient room. The harbour is 15m deep near the extremity of the mole so if possible go alongside.

Shelter Good protection from W winds although some swell works its way around the end of the mole. Open to the E and dangerous with winds from that direction. With strong N winds it has been suggested yachts go under the high part of the sea wall rather than the low part near the root of the mole as sheets of spray come over the low part drenching any yacht berthed there.

Note Part of the quay is reported to have detached itself from the outer part of the end of the mole and to have subsided to sea level. Attention is needed on entry and yachts should berth elsewhere in the harbour.

Authorities Port police and customs.

Kiato fishing harbour The small fishing harbour immediately E of Kiato commercial harbour is usually full of local boats. The outer part of the harbour has 1·5–2·5m depths, but off the shore it is <1m. Small yachts may be able to find a berth in here although usually the locals or the port police will wave you away. If you manage to tie up, just feign incomprehension. Go stern or bows-to off the end of the outer mole taking care of depths off the quay. Good shelter from E–NE winds in here.

Facilities

Water Close to the quay.
Fuel In the town. A mini-tanker can be arranged to deliver to the harbour.
Provisions Good shopping for all provisions in the town.

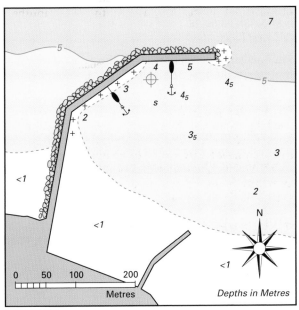

VRAKHATI
⊕37°58′·0N 22°48′·8E

CORINTH HARBOUR

BA 1600
Imray-Tetra G13

Approach

Conspicuous The harbour is difficult to locate from the distance. The high-rise buildings of Corinth city are easily identified and the harbour lies immediately NE of the cluster of buildings. The harbour mole will be seen closer in.

By night Use the light on Ák Melangávi Fl.10s17M and the lights at the entrance to the Corinth Canal Iso.R.2s10M/Iso.G.2s10M (although the range of the canal lights appears less). The harbour mole is lit on the extremity (Fl.G.3s3M) although it is difficult to pick up against the loom of the town lights. There

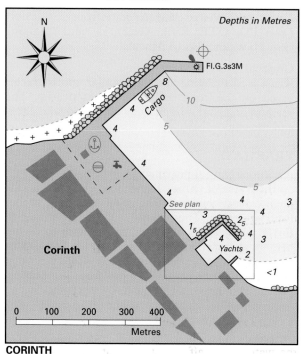

CORINTH
⊕37°56'·8N 22°56'·1E

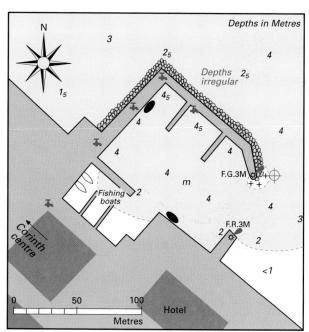

CORINTH YACHT HARBOUR
⊕37°56'·6N 22°56'·0E

are four large floodlights along the quay. The yacht harbour is lit F.R.3M and F.G.3M, though these should not be relied on.

Dangers
1. With strong NE winds there can be severe gusts down into this end of the Gulf of Corinth.
2. With strong westerlies a swell piles up at this end of the gulf although once behind the mole you are out of it.

Note Yachts up to 20m or so should head for the yacht harbour. Yachts over 20m may have to berth in the commercial harbour and should contact the port authorities on VHF Ch 12 or 16 to obtain permission.

Mooring
Berth alongside or stern or bows-to where possible. The harbour is now crowded with local boats and it may be difficult to find a berth here. If you cannot squeeze in somewhere then the only alternative is the commercial harbour. The bottom is mud, good holding. Very large yachts should berth alongside in the commercial port where possible.

Shelter Good all-round shelter in the new yacht harbour. The outer harbour is considered dangerous in strong NE winds.

Authorities Port police and customs.

Facilities
Water On the quay. You will need to find the water man.
Fuel In the town. A mini-tanker can be arranged to deliver fuel to the quay.

Corinth harbour looking S   *Claude Mauge*

Corinth yacht harbour looking NE towards the entrance

Repairs Mechanical and engineering repairs possible. Good hardware shops in the town.

Provisioning Good shopping for all provisions. Several large supermarkets in the town and a small fruit and vegetable market at the N end several streets in from the quay.

Eating out Tavernas in the town.

Other PO. OTE. Banks. ATMs. Greek gas and Camping Gaz. Hire cars and motorbikes. Bus to Patras and Athens.

General

Corinth is a bustling modern and thoroughly nondescript city – just the sort of place you would expect of a city that has been hastily erected after a series of earthquakes demolished previous cities here. It seems to be more of a crossroads for people going elsewhere than a centre for anything.

That said, it is also a pleasant enough place to wait for a transit through the canal and the yacht harbour is a safe place to leave the boat if you wish to visit ancient Corinth. Buses run on the hour not far from the yacht harbour and it is best to visit in the morning when the site is usually open 0900–1400.

Corinth Canal

(Dhiórix Korínthou)

BA 1600

Imray-Tetra G13

The canal is 3·2 miles long, 25m (81ft) wide, the maximum permitted draught is 7m (23ft) and the limestone from which it is cut rises to 76m (250ft) above sea level at the highest point. The canal is closed on Tuesdays to repair the crumbling limestone sides and for dredging.

A current of 1–3 knots is stated to flow either way in the canal depending on the wind direction. Certainly I have been through when strong westerlies have been blowing for several days and there was at least a 2 knot current. If you happen to get stuck behind a large ship in the canal further complications can ensue from the wash produced by its propellers which create a washing machine effect behind it.

There are two hydraulic bridges across the canal near either end. The bridges are lowered down into the water and traffic lights indicate when to go or stop. When you are clear to transit the canal the bridges will be ordered to lower from the canal offices. The following signals concerning entry into the canal are displayed on a signal mast at either end of the canal.

By day	*By night*	*Signal*
Blue flag	One white light	Entry permitted
Red flag	Two vertical white lights	Entry prohibited

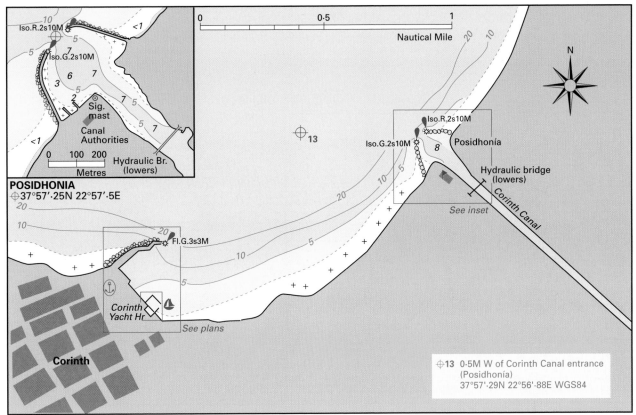

CORINTH CANAL - WEST ENTRANCE

Corinth Canal going E

The canal zone authorities use VHF Ch 11.

A yacht may have to wait up to three hours before entering the canal. Yachts normally go through at the end of the ship convoy heading in their direction. The paperwork and canal fees are done at Isthmia at the Aegean end of the canal. Moor alongside the quay on the S side of the canal. Large yachts may pay the pilot outside the canal – he will come alongside in a launch.

The ancients used to drag ships across the isthmus on a paved road (the *dhiolkos*), parts of which can still be seen on the N side. Octavian in pursuit of Antony after the Battle of Actium had his ships dragged across here. At various times the Greek and Roman rulers worked out schemes for a canal but Nero was the only one to start digging. Using 6,000 Jews, he didn't even get to the rock before insurrection in Gaul diverted his energies. The present canal was started by a French company and

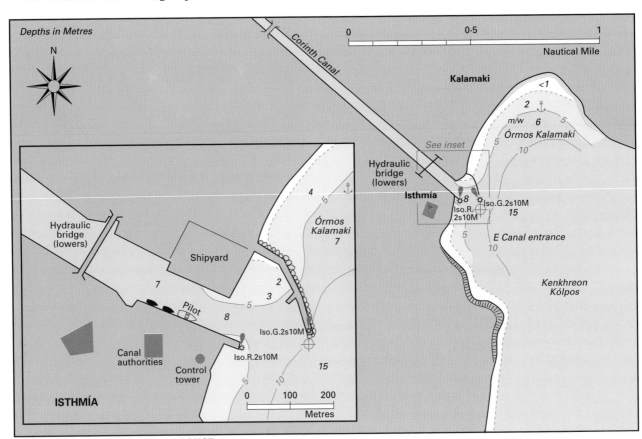

CORINTH CANAL - EASTERN ENTRANCE
⊕37°54′·9N 23°00′·6E

finished by the Greeks in 1893. It was enlarged after damage suffered in the Second World War. Three bridges, a railway bridge and two road bridges, cross it at the maximum height of the cut.

Caution Severe gusts blow off the surrounding high land at either end of the canal. They are particularly bad at the Aegean end with NE winds.

POSIDHONÍA
(Corinth Canal W end)

From the Gulf of Corinth the breakwaters protecting the W end of the canal are difficult to see. Closer in the canal office buildings for the W end and the signal mast will be seen. The entrance is lit Iso.R.2s10M/Iso.G.2s10M although the effective range seems much less.

When waiting to transit the canal the normal procedure is to potter around outside. This can be uncomfortable if westerlies are blowing strongly, but there are few alternatives. I have anchored inside the S breakwater, but the holding is bad here and the authorities frown on the practice. It is also possible to go alongside the very end of the N pier where there are just 2m depths at the end quickly becoming less.

Note When crossing between Posidhonía and Corinth Harbour, keep a reasonable distance off the shore as it is reported that shallows extend further

than shown on the chart. A sort of semi-circle route out from the shore is best.

ISTHMIA
(Corinth Canal E end)

In effect you head for the NW corner of Kenkhreon Kólpos. When closer in the tower of the canal office and the breakwater protecting the entrance will be seen. The entrance is lit Iso.G.2s10M/Iso.R.2s10M.

Small to medium yachts proceed into the entrance and tie up alongside the quay on the S side. This is fendered with large rubber bumper rails, but the quay itself is quite high and the black rubber bumper fenders are pretty unforgiving to topsides, so you should hang out every fender you have. Large yachts (25m plus) should call up the control tower and request the pilot boat to come out so the paperwork can be completed. You can also arrange an agent in Piraeus to do the necessary paperwork and pay on account.

Once tied up, go to the office in the tower and fill in the requisite paperwork and pay the canal fees. You then hang around until you can transit the canal. If a large ship is transiting either way pay attention to your warps as the water pushed by large ships in the confines of the canal significantly adds and then removes a large mass of water as the ship passes. This can snap mooring lines, with dire consequences. It may be better, if a large ship is going to pass, to go outside the canal entrance and hang around until it is time for you to enter the canal.

The small harbour on the N side under the breakwater does not have berths for transiting yachts. If you do decide to berth here for any reason care is needed of the ballasting which extends underwater for a short distance.

Ancient Corinth

Ancient Corinth sits on a plateau behind modern Corinth, and the ruins of this infamous city deserve a visit. The ancient city commanded the passage of trade between the mainland and the Peloponnisos and across the isthmus between the Ionian and the Aegean. Consequently it was an important and rich city. The Corinthians were fine seamen and possessed a large fleet with which they founded and protected colonies in Corfu and Syracuse. Some believe the first trireme was built here. They paid particular attention to the gods of the sea, Poseidon and Palaimon. The latter was the protector of harbours and myth has it that he was originally Melikertes who was transported to Corinth on a dolphin.

The hard-living Corinthians were evidently hard-working as well. Their pottery was esteemed throughout the Mediterranean and from the 5th century BC the Corinthian style of architecture embodied in the Corinthian column became one of the most popular styles – continuing on through Byzantium and to the present day. From the 4th to the 2nd centuries BC Corinth earned a reputation for itself of a fast-living city where (in an age of loose living) the inhabitants were notorious for their vices. From this hedonistic age we get the term Corinthian, used in the early 19th century to describe a hard-living sportsman devoted to pugilism, horse racing and yachting! The term survives today as the name of various yacht clubs and football teams.

IV. The Saronic and Eastern Peloponnisos

The Aegean Sea is entered from the west round Cape Malea or through the Corinth Canal, the southwestern and northwestern limits of the sea area covered in this chapter.

The Aegean takes its name from Aegeus, the father of Theseus, who flung himself into the sea when he believed his son to have been killed in Crete. Theseus had gone to Crete as part of the annual tribute of young Athenian men and women to the Minotaur, but with the help of Ariadne slew the monster and escaped. Ariadne was unceremoniously dumped on Naxos and perhaps the gods clouded his memory after this foul deed, because he forgot the prearranged signal to his father to tell him that all was well. If his ship carried a black sail then Aegeus would know his son had perished; a white sail would mean he was alive. Aegeus, seeing the black sail on the approaching ship, was overcome with grief and leapt to his death.

The Aegean geographically divides Europe from Asia, although the islands in the sea form a bridge between the two continents. Between the islands, without compass or sextant, the merchants of ancient times could cross the Aegean and be out of sight of land for only a few hours. Almost as important as the island bridge across the sea were the regular summer winds blowing from the north. These winds, now called by the Turkish name, the *meltemi*, were then called the *etesian* winds from the Greek *etos*, a year, because they blow regularly every year. Traders could sail across the Aegean with this wind and return in the spring or autumn when the northerlies are light and southerlies sometimes blow. The winter winds can be fierce and some ancient states forbade traders to cross the sea in the winter months.

The area covered in this chapter encompasses three significant historical centres. Mycenae at the head of the Argolic Gulf was the centre of the Mycenaean period, which succeeded the Minoans and provided the material for Homer's epics. Athens was of course the centre of Classical Greece, although it is all too easy to attribute too much to this ancient city and forget the contributions to art, oratory, science, and commerce from other city-states all over Greece. Lastly, the fleets of Ídhra (Hydra) and Spétsai were of key importance in determining the outcome of the War of Independence and both Navplion and Aigina were at different times the capitals of the newly liberated Greece.

Weather patterns in the Saronic and Eastern Peloponnisos

The normal summer wind differs radically depending on where you are in this area. Along the mainland coast from the Corinth Canal to Ák Sounion and the sea area between the mainland coast and Methana, the *meltemi* is the normal wind. It blows from the NNE to NE at about Force 4–6, although it may be stronger around Ák Sounion. Around the Methana peninsula and Póros it is usually less. The *meltemi* starts blowing in July and dies in October. If the *meltemi* does not blow, (and it is not as regular here as in the Cyclades or the Dodecanese), the wind in this sea area is generally from the south, usually getting up about midday, blowing Force 2–4, and dying off about sunset.

Moving south and west, in Kólpos Idhras (Gulf of Hydra) and Argolikós Kólpos (Argolic Gulf), the prevailing wind is from the SE. It gets up about midday, blows Force 3–5, occasionally more, and dies down at night. In Argolikós Kólpos this wind can be relied upon in the summer for 90% of the time. Down the eastern Peloponnisos the wind may be a *meltemi* from the NE or a southerly from the SE or SW. In the spring and autumn the wind is predominantly from the S over the whole area and is generally weak.

In general there are few weather problems in the area. When the *meltemi* is blowing there are strong gusts off the high land near the entrance to the Corinth Canal and around Ák Sounion. Along the eastern coast of the Peloponnisos there may be a katabatic wind at night. Ástrous is particularly notorious for this wind which arrives without warning and often reaches Force 6–7 where previously there was no wind. It usually lasts for 4–6 hours. In the spring and autumn there may be thunderstorms accompanied by a squall, but these last only one or two hours on average. In the winter the Saronic and Argolic Gulfs have a mild sunny climate, making them popular places for yachts to spend the winter.

This chapter is covered in more detail in *West Aegean* by the publishers

Routes

Routes in the area covered by this chapter can be divided into three categories.

In the Saronic Gulf the yachtsman will come upon the greatest concentration of yachts in Greece. Most of these are based at the marinas along the Attic coast from where a considerable number of charter companies operate. Many charter yachts follow the Saronic trail to Aigina, Póros, Ídhra and Spétsai and to nearby harbours and anchorages, so if you wish to avoid the crowds in the summer stay away from the charter yacht milk run and head for the eastern coast of the Peloponnisos where there are less crowded harbours and anchorages.

1. **From the Corinth Canal heading E along the Attic coast and down towards the Argolic Gulf and Cape Maléa**
   The prevailing wind in the Saronic Gulf is the *meltemi* blowing from the N–NE. To get to the marinas around Athens it is best to stick close to the Attic coast. Gusts can be fierce off the coast but the sea is generally fairly flat. Heading down towards Aigina and Póros you will be close or beam reaching and as you get towards Póros the wind usually moderates and may even turn to the S–SE.

   If you are heading towards the Cyclades from Athens then stick to the Attic coast until Sounion before departing for the islands. It can get very windy and bumpy around the Kea Channel and will get no better further E if the *meltemi* is at full strength. When I used to skipper charter boats from Athens it was not unusual for charterers who just had to visit the Cyclades to change their minds and enquire if there was somewhere a little less windy to go to. It was a relief to jibe over and head to Póros and the 'milk run'.

   From Póros to the Argolic Gulf the prevailing summer wind is the SE sea breeze and in general seas are slight to moderate. As the breeze does not get up until midday or so you can motor in the morning calm if you need to. Down the coast of the Peloponnisos the wind will often be variable or a light S–SE wind or, if the *meltemi* gets through, a fresh NE breeze.

2. **The reverse route from Cape Maléa to the Argolic Gulf and the Attic coast**
   See the notes on rounding Cape Maléa at the end of Chapter II. Often you will find that once around Cape Maléa the *meltemi* is light and often variable up the coast to Monemvásia. At times it does blow hard and if that is the case you have few options except to bash up against it. It is worth trying to leave early in the morning when the wind is often lighter although there is usually a residual swell from the central Aegean making things uncomfortable. As you get closer to the Argolic Gulf the wind will become fluky and then eventually turn to the SE sea breeze. It is worth threading your way up through Kólpos Idhras to Póros and Aigina as although the SE breeze can be brisk, the sea is usually moderate.

   To get from Póros and Aigina back to the marinas around Athens will entail either a wet and bruising beat against the *meltemi*, or if it is not blowing too hard, a more pleasant sail but still a beat to windward. At either end of the summer there is a higher frequency of southerly sea breezes and this makes the return to Athens an altogether more pleasant experience.

3. **Routes coming W from the Cyclades**
   This is probably the most debated of routes by charter skippers. When the *meltemi* is blowing strongly I think it is worth doing a bit more distance and heading for Ídhra or Póros from the Cyclades. Generally you will get a good close reach from the southern Cyclades or a beam reach from the middle Cyclades. Once up to Ídhra or Póros you can run up to Aigina and on back to Athens.

   Some charter skippers disagree and reckon you may as well beat back to Athens, though if you question them closely, what they mean is motorsail back to Athens. It really depends on how hard the *meltemi* is blowing as to whether it is worth beating back directly or taking the circular route via Ídhra, Póros and Aigina.

Data

PORTS OF ENTRY
Zéa Marina
Vouliagméni
Navplion

PROHIBITED AREAS
1. It is prohibited to navigate in Órmos Salamís in an area half a mile off the southern shore between a point one mile and a point two miles E of Ák Petritis.
2. It is prohibited to enter an area NE of Órmos Elevsinos, one mile E of Limín Elevsis.
3. It is prohibited to navigate between Salamís and the NE side of the mainland except in a narrow channel in the fairway. It is prohibited to navigate in this channel at night.
4. It is prohibited to anchor outside the channel mentioned above.
5. It is prohibited to navigate and anchor in the northern part of the bay immediately N of Póros town where there is a naval college.
6. Nisís Ipsilí is used for target practice by the Greek Navy.
7. Although not listed as such, Nisídhes Karavi (36°46'N 23°36'E), three barren islets lying off the eastern Peloponnisos, are also used for target practice by the Greek air force.

MAJOR LIGHTS
Corinth Canal (W side) Iso.R.2s10M
Corinth Canal (mole head) Iso.G.2s10M
Órmos Sofikoú (Korfos) Fl.4s5M
Ák Kalamáki Fl.2s6M

Mainland coast
Ák Sousáki Fl.G.10s12M
Ák Káras Fl.4s8M
Ák Kónkhi Fl.4s9M
Nisís Psittália Fl(2)15s25M
Ák Filatoúri Fl(2)14s5M
Póros Themistokléous LFl.G.6s9M
Piraeus Harbour LFl.R.6s9M
Zéa Marina (S mole) Fl(2)R.6s7M
Mounikhías (N mole) Iso.G.2s6M
Mounikhías (S mole) Iso.R.2s8M
Ellinikón (aero beacon) AlFl.WG.6s15M
Nisís Fléves Fl(3)10s8M
Vouliagméni (mole head) Fl(3)R.12s7M

Aigina
Ák Plakákia Fl(2)15s7M
Ák Toúrlos Fl.3·6s5M
Nisís Moní Fl(2)WRG.10s11·8M
Nisís Lagoúsa LFl.7·5s5M

Póros
Ák Dána (N entrance) Fl.WR.4s8/5M
Ák Stavrós S Point Fl.RG.3s4/4M

Ídhra
Ák Zoúrva Fl(3)20s17M
Nisís Dhokós (SE point) Fl(2)WR.12s6/4M
Nisís Áy Yeóryios (SE end) Fl(2)15s17M

Spétsai
Ák Fanári (Báltiza) Fl.WR.5s18/14M
Ák Mavrókavos Fl.WR.2s5/3M
Nisís Petrokáravo Fl(2)9s7M

Argolikós Kólpos
Ák Kórakas Fl.7s11M
Nisís Ipsilí (SW point) Fl.5s9M

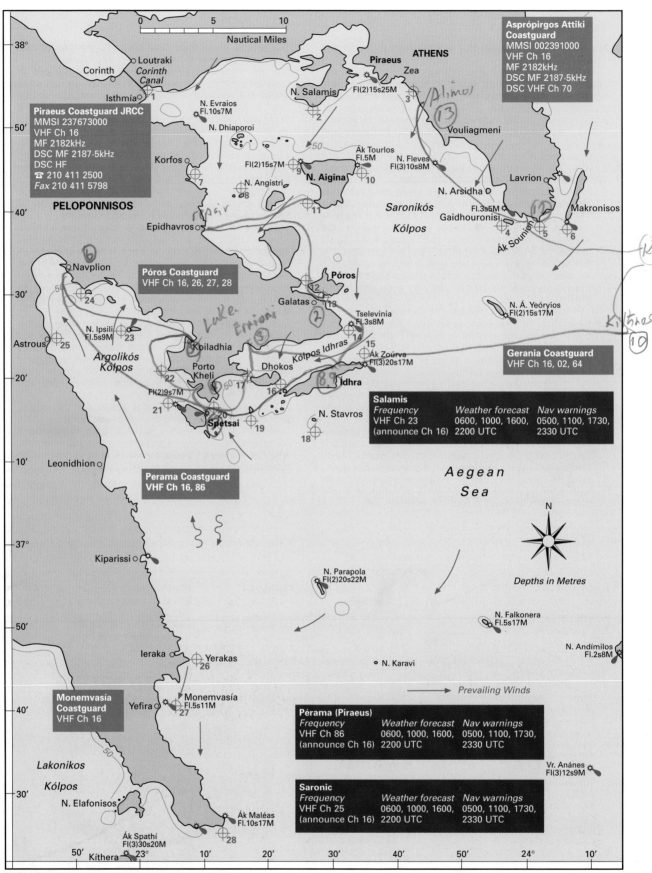

THE SARONIC AND EASTERN PELOPONNISOS

Limín Khäidhari (E point)
Fl(3)WR.15s5/3M
Ák Skála (Nisís Toló)
Fl(2)WR.10s6/4M
Ák Panayítsa Fl.1·5s5M
Ák Ástrous Fl.5s7M
Ák Sambateki LFl.7·5s6M

E Peloponnisos
Nisís Parapóla Fl(2)20s22M
Nisís Falkonéra (S end) Fl.5s17M
Nisís Monemvasía Fl.5s11M
Ák Maléas Fl.10s17M

USEFUL WAYPOINTS

⊕1 E entrance to Corinth Canal
37°54'·9N 23°00'·5E

⊕2 ½M S of Ák Kónkhi (Salamina
SW end)
37°52'·0N 23°27'·2E

⊕3 Marina Alimos
(Kalamáki/Athens)
37°54'·8N 23°42'·1E

⊕4 0·5M S of W end of
Gaidhouronisi
37°38'·45N 23°56'·04E WGS84

⊕5 0·25M S of temple on
Sounion
37°38'·63N 24°01'·31E WGS84

⊕6 0·15M S of S end of
Makronisos
37°38'·56N 24°06'·25E WGS84

⊕7 1M S of Ák Trelli (Órmos
Sofikou)
37°44'·49N 23°08'·93E WGS84

⊕8 0·25M N of N. Kira
37°42'·82N 23°16'·38E WGS84

⊕9 0·25M W of Ák Plakákia
(Aigina)
37°45'·70N 23°24'·77E WGS84

⊕10 0·75M E of Ák Toúrlos light
37°45'·73N 23°03'·91E WGS84

⊕11 S end Stenón Monis (Aigina)
37°41'·26N 23°26'·82E WGS84

⊕12 N Channel into Póros
37°31'·62N 23°25'·31E WGS84

⊕13 SE Channel into Póros
37°29'·61N 23°27'·74E WGS84

⊕14 S end of Tselevinia Channel
37°26'·05N 23°32'·15E WGS84

⊕15 0·5M N of Ák Zoúrva (Ídhra)
37°22'·56N 23°34'·74E WGS84

⊕16 0·5M S of Dhokós SE light
37°19'·30N 23°21'·48E WGS84

⊕17 Ák Mouzáki – N. Dhokós
Channel
37°20'·74N 23°16'·98E WGS84

⊕18 1·75M S of N. Stavrós
37°13'·33N 23°26'·61E WGS84

⊕19 0·5M S of N. Tríkeri
37°15'·05N 23°16'·46E WGS84

⊕20 0·5M S of Ák Aimilianós
37°16'·82N 23°12'·00E WGS84

⊕21 0·1M W of Petrokárovo light
37°17'·08N 23°04'·67E WGS84

⊕22 0·25M W of Ák Kórakas
37°21'·09N 23°03'·59E WGS84

⊕23 1M W of Nisís Ipsilí light
37°25'·9N 22°57'·1E

⊕24 1M W of Ák Megalí (Toló)
37°30'·6N 22°50'·3E

⊕25 0·5M E of Ák Ástrous
37°24'·86N 22°46'·87E WGS84

⊕26 0·25M E of Ák Yérakas
36°46'·17N 23°06'·90E WGS84

⊕27 0·25M E of Monemvásia
headland
36°41'·52N 23°03'·89E WGS84

⊕28 0·75M S of Ák Maléas
36°25'·48N 23°11'·62E WGS84

Athens and the mainland Attic coast

This section from the Corinth Canal to Ák Sounion is mostly mountainous barren terrain. Around Athens there is the large flat Attic Plain, much of which is covered by Athens and Piraeus and their outlying suburbs. There are a considerable number of industrial installations along the coast: the large petrochemical refinery near the canal (the gaseous by-products burning off are conspicuous at night); the shipyards and naval base near Pérama and on Salamínas; and numerous factories and mills between Pérama and Piraeus – in fact some 60% or more of Greek industry surrounds the capital. Between Piraeus and Glifadha the coast is lined by high-rise apartment blocks. A motorway and railway run parallel to the coast between Athens and the canal.

Athens is a comparatively modern city whose modern architecture compares badly with the ancient monuments in the centre. It has grown rapidly as the young from the islands and rural mainland have arrived here by the thousands looking for work. Consequently the outlying

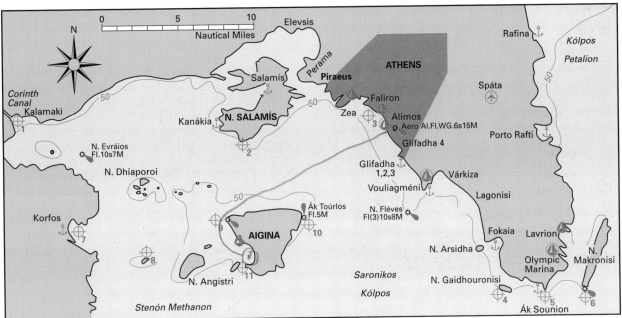

CORINTH TO SOUNION

Quick reference guide

Attic Coast	Shelter	Mooring	Fuel	Water	Provisioning	Tavernas	Plan
Órmos Kalamáki	C	C	O	O	C	C	
Salamís	B	AC	B	A	B	B	•
Ambelakia	A	AB	B	A	C	C	
Pakhi	B	AB	B	A	C	B	
Elefsina	A	AB	B	A	B	B	
Zéa Marina	A	AB	A	A	A	A	•
Mounikhías	A	A	B	A	A	A	•
Faliron	B	A	B	A	A	A	•
Kalamáki (Alimos)	A	A	A	A	A	A	•
Glifadha 4	A	A	B	A	B	A	•
Glifadha 1, 2, 3	A	A	A	A	B	A	•
Voula	B	AB	B	A	B	B	
Vouliagméni	A	A	A	A	C	B	•
Várkiza	B	A	B	A	B	B	•
Órmos Anavíssou	B	C	B	B	C	B	•
Sounion	C	C	O	O	O	B	•
Peloponnisos and off-lying islands to Póros							
Órmos Linari	C	C	O	O	O	O	
Frangolimani	C	C	O	O	O	O	
Órmos Dimani	C	C	O	O	O	O	
Korfos	A	AC	B	A	B	B	•
Órmos Selonda	B	C	O	O	O	O	
Néa Epidhavros	B	AC	O	B	C	C	•
Epidhavros	B	AC	B	A	B	B	•
Vathi (Methana)	A	AC	O	A	O	C	•
Áy Yeoryios	B	A	O	B	O	C	
Methana	A	A	B	A	A	B	•
Limín Aigina	A	A	B	A	A	A	•
Perdika	C	AC	B	B	B	B	•
Áy Marina	O	C	O	O	O	B	
Souvalas	C	A	O	O	C	C	
Angistri	C	A	O	B	C	C	•
Skála (Angistri)	C	C	O	B	C	C	

	Shelter	Mooring	Fuel	Water	Provisioning	Tavernas	Plan
Dhoroussa	B	C	O	O	O	C	
Póros	A	ABC	B	A	A	A	•
Kólpos Ídhras and Argolikós Kólpos							
Nisís Soupia	C	C	O	O	O	O	
Hydra Beach Hotel	A	AB	O	A	O	C	
Ermioni	A	AC	B	A	A	B	•
Órmos Kapari	C	C	O	O	O	C	
Limín Idhras	B	A	O	A	A	A	•
Mandráki (Ídhra)	C	C	O	O	O	C	•
Órmos Skindos (Dhokós)	B	C	O	O	O	C	•
Báltiza (Spétsai)	A	AC	A	A	A	A	•
Dápia (Spétsai)	C	A	B	B	A	A	•
Órmos Zoyioryia (Spétsai)	B	C	O	O	O	C	
Porto Kheli	A	AC	B	B	A	B	•
Nisís Korakonisia	C	C	O	O	O	O	
Iria	B	A	O	B	O	C	
Koiládhia	A	AC	B	B	B	C	•
Khäidhari	A	C	O	B	B	B	•
Toló	C	AC	B	B	A	A	•
Navplion	A	AB	B	A	A	A	•
Ástrous	A	A	B	A	B	B	•
Tíros	B	A	B	B	B	C	•
Leonídhion	C	A	O	A	C	B	•
Poúlithra	C	A	O	O	C	C	
Fokianas	C	C	O	O	O	O	
Peloponnisos							
Kiparíssi	B	AC	B	B	C	B	•
Ieraka	A	AC	O	O	C	B	•
Monemvasía	AB	AC	B	B	A	A	•
Palaio Monemvasía	B	C	O	O	O	O	•

suburbs have been built to house these migrants with little planning or thought and are particularly unattractive. The geographical situation of a flat coastal plain surrounded by mountains is similar to that of Los Angeles, so Athens has a smog problem that is often worse than that of the smog capital of the USA – at times you will see the green-grey cloud of the dreaded *nefos* hanging over the city as you approach from seawards. It is not surprising that many have voted Athens the worst capital city in Europe. The city's population is over three million, about one third of the total population of Greece.

Although the natives of a particular island or region will always run down the natives of another island or region ('they are liars/cheats/thieves/etc.'), between the natives of Athens and the rest of the population there is a very real enmity. There are effectively two races in Greece: those Greeks who live in Athens and the others. I well remember being introduced to an Athenian on Spétsai with the admonition that he was an Athenian, but a 'good person' despite that handicap.

Athens, partly because of its position and communications and partly because much of the wealth is concentrated here, is the Greek equivalent of the Hamble or the French Riviera. Along the coast there are six marinas. The marinas are all crowded and although many of the yachts are owned by Greeks, still a very small percentage of the overall population takes to the water purely for pleasure. Most of the bareboat charter companies and the skippered yachts for charter are based at Zéa or Kalamáki. A yacht entering the Aegean will inevitably home in on Athens and its string of marinas for the facilities and availability of spares and nautical items which will only be found there. Apart from that, there is little point in going there as the surrounding sea is dirty and polluted and the scenery quite unrepresentative of the rest of Greece. You will have seen Athens but not Greece.

In 2004 the Olympic Games returns to its spiritual home for the first time since the first modern Olympics were held here in 1896. It has brought with it regeneration of much of downtown Athens and the Olympic sailing events base in Ayios Kosmas is likely to become a yacht marina after the games, providing the berths so much in demand along this coast.

Spáta Airport

The new airport, properly called Eleftherios Venizelos International Airport, opened in 2001. For the marinas around Athens, the benefit from a massive reduction in noise pollution from passenger aircraft taking off and landing at the old airport at Ellinikon is difficult to describe unless you have sat in Kalamáki or Glifadha with aircraft a few hundred metres above you. Athens too will benefit, with less unburnt aircraft fuel being dropped over the city and adjacent coastline.

The new airport is situated at Spáta 27km NE of Athens. The road link goes to the Athens ring road and then you hit the massive traffic jam that constantly afflicts the city. From the airport there are taxis (around 25 Euros in 2003) and buses to downtown Athens. The rail connection from the airport to the Athens Metro is under construction and due to open before the Olympic Games in 2004. The airport is closer to Rafina and its ferry connections than it is to Athens and it may be worthwhile thinking of linking up via one of the ferry (and fast catamaran and hydrofoil services) connections from Rafina (currently to Evia, the Cyclades and a few routes to the Dodecanese and northern Greece), rather than going into Athens itself.

CORINTH CANAL See Chapter III Gulf of Patras and Corinth.

Caution For about 6 miles E of the Corinth Canal in Kólpos Kenkhreon (Gulf of Kenkhreo) there are strong gusts off the mountains on the N side of the gulf when the *meltemi* is blowing. The gusts become less fierce the further E and S you go.

NAVY PRACTICE AREA

The sea area between the Corinth Canal and Salamís is often used by the navy for exercises. Nisís Ipsilí in this area is used for target practice.

ÓRMOS KALAMÁKI

37°55'·2N 23°01'·0E

While waiting to proceed through the canal or after coming through from the Gulf of Corinth, a yacht can anchor in Órmos Kalamáki immediately N of the canal entrance. Anchor in 4–6m at the head of the bay. Good shelter from the *meltemi* although there are strong gusts off the high land above. The bottom is sand and weed – only mediocre holding. Tavernas ashore. Fishing boats are kept on moorings here all year round.

ÁK SOUSAKI BOATYARD

37°55'·0N 23°03'·5E

On the W side of Ák Sousaki approximately 2 miles E of Órmos Kalamáki there is a large boatyard. Anchor in the bay and go ashore to enquire at the boatyard. Boats are hauled from a concrete apron on the E point which has a reported depth of 4m. Hauling is by crane and the yacht is then stored ashore.

The yard is somewhat remote, but has become increasingly popular and there are now good facilities ashore. Most yacht repairs can be arranged. Taverna and café nearby.

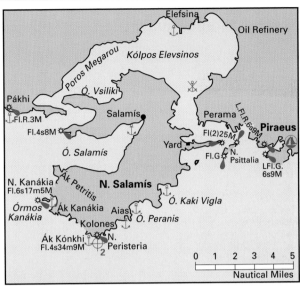

SALAMÍS TO PIRAEUS

⊕2 0·5M S of Ák Kónkhi (Salamís SW end)
37°52'·0N 23°27'·2E

Nísos Salamís
(Nísos Salamina)

An arid rocky island devoid of vegetation. It is much indented, but there are few anchorages available to yachts because of the extensive naval installations around the coast near which anchoring is prohibited. This is no great loss as the water is very polluted (a dirty oily brown colour with all sorts of objectionable flotsam) and the nearby coast is an industrial wasteland.

Prohibited Areas
1. In Órmos Salamís navigation is prohibited within half a mile of the shore between one and two miles E of Ák Petritis (the southern entrance of the bay).
2. Navigation is prohibited in an area around Elevsis in the Kólpos Elevsinos.
3. Except for a narrow channel in the fairway, navigation is prohibited between the NE side of Salamís and the mainland coast opposite. Navigation at night is prohibited. Large ships are not permitted to navigate (without special permission) in the area enclosed by Nisís Psittália, Salamís and the mainland (Órmos Keratsiniou). Anchorage is prohibited in the area.

SALAMÍS (Salamina)
Approach
Salamís village lies at the head of Órmos Salamís. The boatyard on the N side of the bay and the houses of the village are easily identified.

By night Use the light on Ák Káras Fl.4s8M and the light on the pier head at Salamís 2F.R(vert)3M.

Mooring
Go alongside or stern or bows-to in the inner basin if you can find a berth. The mole and the pier are usually crowded with fishing boats.

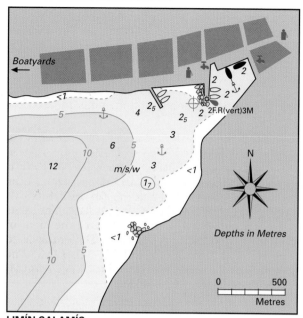

LIMÍN SALAMÍS
⊕37°57'·7N 23°29'·6E

Shelter Good shelter from the *meltemi*. Southerlies whip up a short chop across the large bay.

Anchorage Anchor in 3–5m in the bay clear of the approaches to the harbour. In the summer the anchorage is well protected although there can be gusts with the *meltemi*. The bottom is mud, sand and weed, good holding.

Facilities

Services Water on the quay in places. You may be able to get a connection for electricity.
Fuel Close to the mole.
Provisions Good shopping for provisions.
Eating out Tavernas.
Other PO. OTE. Bus to Paloukia and ferries to the mainland (Pérama and Piraeus).

General

The village has a run-down appearance, but the locals are friendly and it is a convivial enough place if you are hauled out at the boatyard. There are some good local tavernas nearby which often have fresh fish.

BOATYARDS

To the W of the village there are a number of yards which can haul out yachts up to 40 tons. Hauling is by cradle and sledge in the old-fashioned way. They can carry out general repairs including some engine repairs and welding and machining jobs. Anchor off the boatyard where there is reasonable shelter from all but strong SW winds.

ANCHORAGES AROUND SALAMÍS

Kanákia N. Kanákia light 37°54'·3N 23°23'·5E
The bay on the SW end of Salamís with the islet of Kanákia lying off it. Care is needed of the reef and shoal water off the N and SE side of Nisís Kanákia and off the shore of the bay. Anchor at the N or S end of the bay where convenient. Good shelter from N–NE winds in the N end of the bay. The bay is a

Battle of Salamís

Around 22 September 480 BC in the narrow winding channel between the NE side of Salamís and the mainland opposite (the same area where navigation is restricted), the Battle of Salamís was fought between the Greeks and the invading Persians under Xerxes. The Greek battle plan was worked out by Themistocles in considerable detail (as was discovered only recently with the recovery of the Troezein Stone in the Tríkeri Channel) and ranks as one of the great strategic victories in the history of naval warfare.

The Persians were based at Faliron and intended to take the Greeks in a pincer movement between their fleet and a land force marching along the coast. A conventional battle between the two forces would probably have meant a resounding defeat for the numerically inferior Greek force. Themistocles devised a trap. He leaked information to the Persians that the Greek force was going to withdraw and Xerxes immediately dispatched his ships to bottle the Greeks up in Salamís. Two hundred Egyptian ships blockaded the western entrance while the remainder of Xerxes' fleet was arrayed across the eastern entrance. Xerxes had a silver throne set up on the mainland to view the defeat of the Greeks.

The Greek fleet emerged and then retired, apparently in confusion, to a position behind a promontory where they again formed up in battle order. The enemy fleet advanced and were totally surprised to find the Greek fleet waiting for them. The more handy Greek triremes caused chaos in the narrow channel and the Persian fleet became hopelessly confused, so much so that it was recorded they accidentally sank some of their own ships. This battle effectively destroyed the Persian fleet and with it the Persian threat in the Aegean.

pleasant spot with pine down to the shore. Taverna opens in the summer.

Kolones 37°52'·6N 23°26'·5E
A very small harbour under the cliffs. The entrance is rockbound and you should reconnoitre first by dinghy. There are 3m depths in the entrance, but the inner part of the harbour has <1m depths.

Aias 37°53'·4N 23°28'·9E
This small bay affords good shelter from the *meltemi*. Anchor off the beach in 4–6m on sand. Care is needed of the reef running out from the shore in places. There is a short mole in the NE corner, but this is used by the local fishing boats. Tavernas ashore.

Órmos Peranis 37°53'·7N 23°29'·4E
The large bay immediately E of Aias. Anchor on the NW side or in the NE cove. Care is needed of the reefs on the W and N sides of the bay. Good shelter from the *meltemi*. Tavernas in the summer.

Kaki Vigla 37°54'·6N 23°30'·7E
The large bay under Ák Tourlos. Anchor in N of the bay. Mediocre shelter only. Tavernas ashore.

AMBELAKIA BOATYARD
37°57'·1N 23°32'·9E

At Ambelakia on the E side of Salamís there is a large boatyard in the SW corner of the bay with a quayed area and short pier where yachts can berth.

Data 25 berths. 40 places ashore. Excellent shelter.

Facilities WC and showers. Fuel on the quay. 100-ton travel-hoist.

All manner of repairs including steel and stainless steel fabrication, wood and GRP repairs, mechanical and general engineering repairs are undertaken and other work can be arranged in Piraeus.

Tasso Lathouras, Bekris & Co Ltd, 18902 Ambelakia, Salamís ☎ 210 467 1588/4120 *Fax* 210 467 5332

ATTIC COAST OPPOSITE SALAMIS

Before pottering up around Salamis read the notes on 'Prohibited Areas' at the beginning of the chapter. Around the Attic coast there are two fishing harbours where you may find a berth.

Pakhi 37°58'·4N 23°21'·7E

A small fishing harbour on the mainland coast N of Nisídhes Pakhi. The entrance is lit Fl.R.3s3M/ Fl.G.3s3M. There are 5m depths in the entrance and 1·5–7m depths inside. If there is space go alongside the outer end of the mole. Good shelter. Water on the quay. Tavernas ashore.

Elefsina 38°02'·2N 23°32'·2E

A small fishing harbour off Elefsina which is virtually a suburb of Athens. The entrance is lit Fl(2)G.12s3M. There are 5m depths in the entrance. Care is needed off the quayed areas which have <1m in places. Go stern or bows-to where possible. Good shelter. Water and electricity on the quay. Provisions ashore. Tavernas.

PERAMA

Perama is largely the industrial area on the E side of Piraeus. There are a number of shipyards here with associated facilities for engineering and mechanical work. One of these yards is equipped for work on yachts.

Halkitis Urania Boatyard Uses a 280-ton travel-hoist. Max capacity is as follows: Weight 280-tons/LOA 45 metres/Beam 9 metres/Draught 5·2 metres.

All facilities at the yard including water, 220/380V, compressed air, showers and toilets, communications, 24 hour security. All yacht repairs carried out or arranged.

Halkitis Urania Boatyards, 104-6 Dimokratis Av, 18863 Perama, Piraeus ☎ 210 441 0182/402 0256 *Fax* 210 402 0262.

PIRAEUS COMMERCIAL HARBOUR

This large harbour is for ferries, hydrofoils and commercial cargo ships only. A yacht should not attempt to enter or berth here.

ZÉA MARINA

BA 1596

Imray-Tetra G14

Approach

The roadstead between the coast of Salamís and Piraeus is crowded with ships (cargo and ferries) at anchor and under way. Care is needed when navigating through this maze, especially at night.

Conspicuous The multi-storey apartment blocks of Piraeus and the outlying suburbs of Athens are spread along the coast, making it difficult to identify exactly where Piraeus and Zéa Marina are. Two tall chimneys with red and white bands are conspicuous W of Piraeus and the stadium at Faliron to the E is easily identified. Between Piraeus and Zéa there is a rocky bluff covered in apartments. Closer in, Piraeus Commercial Harbour (there are always ferries coming and going) and the outer mole of Zéa can be identified.

By night The lights which stand out are: Ák Khónkhi light on the SE tip of Salamís Fl.4s9M; the light on Nisís Psittália Fl(2)15s25M; the lights at Piraeus Commercial Harbour LFl.R.6s9M; the light on the extremity of the outer mole of Zéa Fl(2)R.6s7M; and the light on Nisís Fléves Fl(3)10s8M. The lights are not always easy to pick up against the loom of the lights of Athens and Piraeus. The entrance to Zéa is lit: Fl(2)R.6s7M and Fl(2)G.6s4M. The channel into Paşalimani is lit: Fl.G.1·5s4M, Fl.G.1·5s4M and Fl.R.1·5s3M.

VHF Ch 09 for Zéa Marina and A1 Yachting.

Dangers

1. Care is needed of the large amount of shipping coming and going from Piraeus and the anchorage off it. Some of the new ferries and the hydrofoils approach at considerable speed (25–30 knots) so keep a good lookout aft. There are traffic separation zones for ships coming and going from the Aegean, but do not count on shipping sticking to the correct zone.

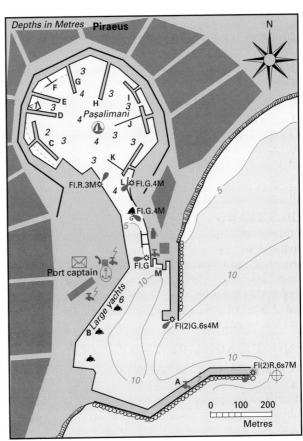

ZEA MARINA
⊕37°55'·93N 23°39'·22E WGS84

Zea Marina

K & G Marinas

2. With the *meltemi* there can be gusts in the approaches.

Mooring

Data 700 berths. Visitors berths. Max LOA c.100m. Depths 2-10m. A marina attendant will direct you to a berth, probably alongside the outer end of the outer mole if you are only staying for a short period. The inner harbour (Paşalimani) is generally full as most of the berths are permanently occupied by Athens-based yachts.

Shelter Paşalimani has excellent all-round shelter. The outer harbour can be uncomfortable in strong southerlies when a reflected swell causes a surge to develop.

Authorities A port of entry: port police, customs, and immigration. Port captain and marina staff. Charge band 3/4.

Enquiries Zéa Marina ☎ 210 428 4100
Fax 210 428 7533 *Email* zea@medmarinas.com www.medmarinas.com

Note The marina has recently been taken over by K&G Marina Management of which Kiriacoulis provide the management. There are plans to develop the infrastructure and it is likely that details will be different in the near future.

Facilities

Services Water and electricity (220v and 380v).
Fuel A tanker will deliver. A fuel quay is planned for the outer harbour where shown on the plan.
Repairs Mechanical repairs. All types of engineering work possible. Wood and GRP repairs. Most spares for marine engines and boat gear can be found or ordered. All repairs can be carried out including specialist marine diesel repairs, GRP work and electrical and electronic work. Sailmakers. Good chandlers near the marina. Most charts and relevant nautical publications can be obtained. Excellent hardware and tool shops.

A1 Yachting offer a range of services to yachts including arranging a berth in Zéa, spares and repairs, chandlers, provisioning, bunkering and related services. All repairs and gardiennage can be arranged.

A1 Yacht Trade Consortium SA (Sea Trade Marine), PO Box 80150, Akti Themostocleous 8, Zea Marina, Piraeus GR 185 36 ☎ 210 458 7100
Fax 210 452 3629 *Email* piraeus@a1yachting.com www.a1yachting.com

Provisions Excellent shopping for all provisions. Several markets nearby. Ice can be ordered.
Eating out All types of tavernas and restaurants nearby.
Other PO and OTE at the marina. Banks and ATMs nearby. Consular offices in Athens for all European and most overseas countries. Greek gas and Camping Gaz. Hire cars and motor bikes. Bus to Athens and from there to all over Greece. Underground to Athens. Ferries and hydrofoils from Piraeus to most destinations in the Aegean. Internal and international flights from Spata Airport around 45 minutes away.

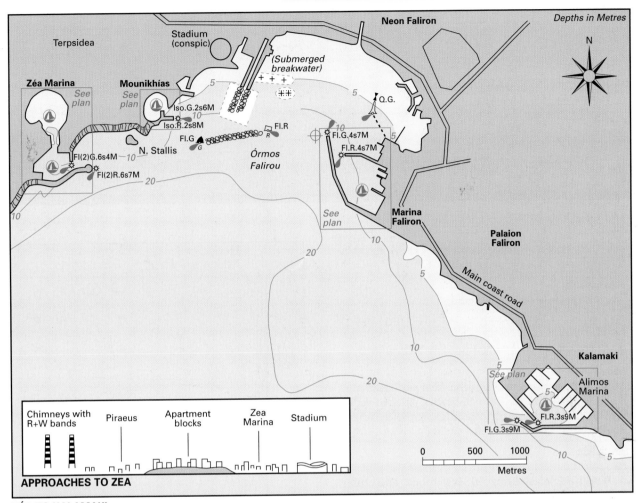

ZÉA TO KALAMAKI
⊕37°57´·1N 23°40´·8E

General

Zéa is a dirty, noisy, crowded harbour and if you don't have a headache after arriving from some comparatively peaceful island you will be one of the lucky few. Yet Piraeus city grows on you. It has many amenities not found elsewhere in Greece: movie theatres with the latest films from the West End; a choice of restaurants (Chinese, Indian, steak houses, French, Italian); bars and nightclubs; English magazines and newspapers; and shop windows crammed with all the consumer goods you don't need (especially on a boat), but like to look at.

Near the commercial harbour over the hill from Zéa the markets and a warren of alleys with tiny shops stocked with a miscellany of wares are intriguing places to wander around. In the outer harbour of Zéa the luxury yachts of the very rich line the quay outside the marina offices – the brass gleams, the brightwork is immaculate despite the blistering sun, and the flower arrangements on the saloon table would probably pay for a week's mooring of a small yacht. And when you have finished with Piraeus then a trip into Athens – at the very least to visit the Acropolis and the National Museum – must be made now that you are here.

MOUNIKHÍAS (Turkolimani, Mikrólimani)

Imray-Tetra G14

The almost circular harbour immediately east of Zéa. The harbour is administered by the Royal Hellenic Yacht Club and visiting yachts are not always welcome here. The best policy is to go to Zéa

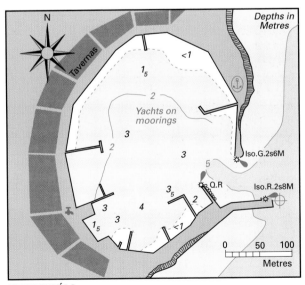

MOUNIKHÍAS
⊕37°56´·3N 23°39´·7E

179

Mounikhías looking ESE

and then check with the authorities at Mounikhías to see if there is a berth available.

Approach

The entrance is straightforward.

By night The entrance is lit Iso.G.2s6M/Iso.R.2s8M.

VHF Ch 09.

Mooring

Moor where directed by the marina attendant. There are laid moorings to all berths. A lot of yachts are kept on fore and aft moorings in the middle of the harbour. Good all-round shelter.

Facilities

Around the marina are numerous, mostly expensive, restaurants (specialising in sea food) and cafés. Provisions nearby. Yacht club.

FALIRON (Flísvos)

BA 1599

Imray-Tetra G14

Approach

The harbour on the E side of Órmos Falírou. The outer breakwater is easily identified.

By night The outer breakwater is lit on the extremity Fl.G.4s7M and the N breakwater is lit on the extremity Fl.R.4s7M.

VHF Ch 09.

Mooring

Data 195 berths. Limited visitors berths. Max LOA c. 120m. Depths 3–13m. Go stern or bows-to where directed or where convenient. Large yachts berth along the outer S mole. There are few berths for visiting yachts and most prefer to go to Zéa or Kalamáki.

Shelter The harbour is open to the N–NW and with strong N–NW winds it can get very choppy in the harbour.

Authorities Port police and harbourmaster.
☎ 210 982 9218 *Fax* 210 988 7354

Note The LAMDA group (which also operates Porto Carras) has recently taken over Faliron Marina. There are plans to develop the infrastructure and it is possible that details will be

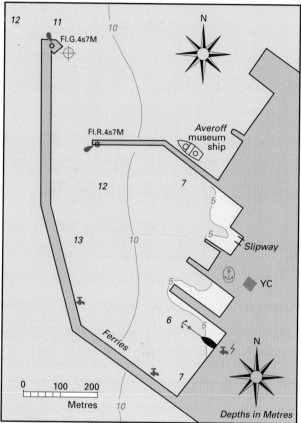

FALIRON
⊕37°56′·1N 23°40′·8E

different in the near future. No details were available at the time of publication.

Facilities

Services Water and electricity can be connected to most berths.
Fuel A tanker can deliver to the quay.
Provisions Good shopping for provisions in Faliron.
Eating out Tavernas in Faliron.

ALIMOS MARINA (Kalamáki)

Imray-Tetra G14

Approach

The marina lies about 1½ miles to the SE of Faliron.

Conspicuous It is difficult to make out exactly where

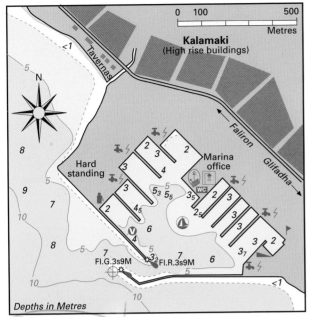

ALIMOS MARINA (KALAMAKI)
⊕37°54'·8N 23°42'·1E

the marina is along this built-up coast. Following the coast, the outer moles and masts of yachts moored within will soon be seen. Immediately W of the marina a green lawn in a cemetery with a conspicuous white cross can be identified. The entrance is not apparent until you are right up to the marina.

By night The entrance is lit: Fl.G.3s9M/Fl.R.3s9M. Despite the range of the lights they can be difficult to see against the bright flashing lights along the waterfront.

VHF Ch 09, 16.

Dangers Care must be taken of the reef running SW from Ák Áy Kósmas about 1 mile S of the Marina. A W cardinal (YBY) tower stands towards the end of the reef: light Q(9)15s5M.

Mooring

Data 900 berths. Visitors berths. Max LOA c.40m. Depths 2–4·5m. Go stern or bows-to under the W mole wherever you can. There are laid moorings tailed to a buoy or to the quay. The visitors' quay is theoretically along the inner W mole (berths A–E), but it is so congested here with permanent berth holders that it can be exasperating trying to find a berth. Asking at the office normally doesn't help at all.

Shelter Excellent all-round shelter.

Authorities Port police and customs. Port captain and marina staff. Charge band 3.

☎ 210 988 0002.

Note 1. The marina has little security and a number of yachtsmen have asked me to mention that a 'minder' is virtually mandatory. Lone females should be wary of wandering around at night.

Note 2. The marina has recently been taken over by a private consortium and it is likely there will be significant changes in the near future. No details were available at the time of publication.

Facilities

Services Water and electricity (220v) near every berth. Showers and toilets near the office.

Fuel On the quay just inside the entrance.

Repairs Most mechanical repairs. Light engineering work including stainless steel work can be arranged. Wood and GRP repairs. Electrical and electronic repairs. Sailmaker. Chandlers along the main coast road. Yachts can be craned onto the hard in the marina if there is room.

Provisions Good shopping for provisions nearby. Ice available.

Eating out Tavernas along the coast road and also on the beach side. There are some good local tavernas tucked up in the streets behind the main coast road.

Other PO, OTE, banks and ATMs in Faliron. Greek gas and Camping Gaz. Hire cars and motorbikes. Regular buses into Athens and Piraeus from outside the marina.

General

The surrounding suburbs are drab apartment blocks and the marina is not much better. One of the things which has blighted Kalamáki and its environs, the noise of large jet aircraft taking off from the nearby airport, has disappeared now the new airport at Spáta has opened. At night a disco within the marina blasts out enough decibels to shiver your GRP. If you get the impression I don't much like the place you are right and neither, for that matter, do most people who visit here. Hopefully the acquisition of the marina by a private consortium will sort out some of the problems that have given it such a bad reputation in the past.

AYIOS KOSMAS (OLYMPIC SAILING CENTRE)

37°53'·6N 23°42'·7E

Between Alimos and Glifadha a yacht harbour has been built at Ay Kosmas to stage the events for the 2004 Olympic Sailing Regatta. Following the Olympics Ayios Kosmas may provide much needed yacht berths along this coast.

GLIFADHA MARINA 4 (Glyphada)

Although called 'Marina 4', this is in fact the first of the Glifadha marinas to be encountered when bound down the coast from Athens.

Approach

The harbour lies approximately 3 miles SE of Kalamáki. Care must be taken of the reef running SW from Ák Áy Kósmas.

By night Áy Kosmás is lit Q(9)15s5M. The entrance is lit: F.G.3M/F.R.3M.

VHF Ch 09.

Mooring

Go stern or bows-to where directed. There are laid moorings tailed to the quay. The harbour is normally very crowded and you will be lucky to find a berth.

Shelter Good all-round shelter.

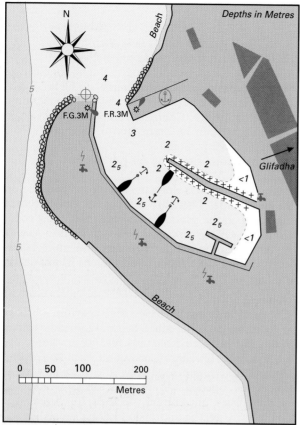

GLIFADHA MARINA 4
⊕37°52′·3N 23°44′·0E

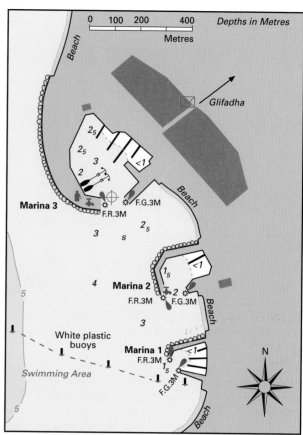

GLIFADHA MARINA 1,2,3
⊕37°51′·8N 23°44′·6E

Authorities Port police and a port captain. Charge band 2/3.
☎ 210 894 7290.

Facilities

Services Water and electricity at every berth.
Fuel A mini-tanker can deliver to the quay.
Repairs Most repairs can be arranged.
Provisions Good shopping for provisions nearby in Glifadha.
Eating out Tavernas and restaurants in Glifadha.
Other PO. OTE. Banks. ATMs. Hire cars and motorbikes.

General

If you can arrange a berth here this is one of the more agreeable marinas near Athens. You are far enough away from the main coast road for it to be comparatively peaceful and yet it is a short hop into the hurley-burley of downtown Athens.

GLIFADHA MARINA 1, 2, 3 (Glyphada)

Approach

Conspicuous The large hotels around Ormiskos Glifadha and a church with a blue cupola behind the harbour are conspicuous. Closer in, the masts of yachts in the marina and a hoarding on the extremity of the mole of Marina 3 are conspicuous.

By night The entrances to all three marinas are lit F.G.3M and F.R.3M which could conceivably lead to confusion. The loom of the lights behind makes identification of the lights difficult anyway.

Mooring

Go stern or bows-to where directed in Marina 3. There are laid moorings tailed to the quay. The marina is small, crowded, and you will be lucky to find a berth here.

Shelter Good shelter although strong southerlies send in an uncomfortable swell.

Authorities Port police and port captain. Marina charges are made.

Facilities

Services Water and electricity at or near every berth.
Fuel On the quay.
Repairs Some mechanical repairs. Chandlers.
Provisions Good shopping for provisions in the town.
Eating out Tavernas in Glifadha. Buses to Piraeus and Athens.

General

The marinas are essentially private with few places for visitors.

VOULA 37°50′·3N 23°45′·7E

A small harbour S of Glifadha. A mole running S from the coast and curving around to the E has 2–3m depths behind it. A small buoy marks the shallows beyond the channel into the entrance. The harbour is full of local yachts and it can be difficult to find a berth. Good shelter if you can get in here. Tavernas and shopping nearby.

VOULIAGMÉNI

Approach

Conspicuous A large white hotel on the hill above the marina is conspicuous. Once into Órmos Vouliagmenos the marina will be seen on the W side of the bay.

By night Use the light on Nisís Fléves (Fl(3)10s8M) and the lights at the entrance: outer entrance Fl.G.1·5s3M/Fl.R.1·5s3M and inner entrance Fl.G.1·5s3M/Fl(3)R.12s7M.

VHF Ch 09 (don't rely on getting a reply).

Dangers Care must be taken of Vrak Kasidhis, the reef lying approximately 350m S of the W entrance to Órmos Vouliagménos. There is an inside passage but the prudent course is to pass to seaward of the rock.

Mooring

Data c.75 berths. Limited visitors berths. Max LOA c.50m. Depths 2–4m. Berth stern or bows-to where directed. There are laid moorings tailed to the quay or a small buoy. The marina is usually fully booked although for a short stay there may be a vacant berth.

Shelter Good shelter although strong southerlies cause a reflected swell that makes it uncomfortable inside.

Authorities A port of entry: port police, customs, and immigration. Port captain and marina staff. Charge band 3/4.

☎ 210 896 0012/0415.

Facilities

Services Water and electricity (220v and 380v) at or near every berth. Shower and toilet block.
Fuel On the quay.
Repairs Most repairs can be arranged.
Provisions Most provisions can be obtained. Ice available.
Eating out Tavernas nearby.
Other Taxis available at the marina.

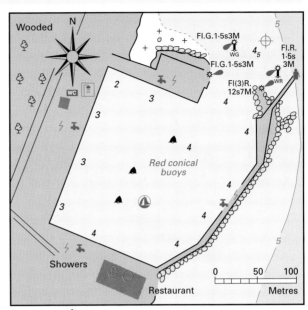

VOULIAGMÉNI
⊕37°48′·3N 23°46′·6E

General

Vouliagméni was the first marina to be built in Greece and the developers chose a wonderful site in the bay away from the hustle and bustle of Athens and Piraeus. The peninsula on the W side of the bay is an upmarket suburb with very expensive bits of real estate discreetly scattered around the wooded slopes. Likewise the marina is an upmarket place full of millions of dollars' worth of little ships.

VÁRKIZA (Varkilas)

Approach

A small harbour in the NW corner of the large bay immediately E of Órmos Vouliagmenos.

By night The entrance is lit: F.R.3M.

Mooring

Berth stern or bows-to the outer mole or inside the basin if there is room. The bottom is sand, rocks and

Vouliagméni looking S into the entrance

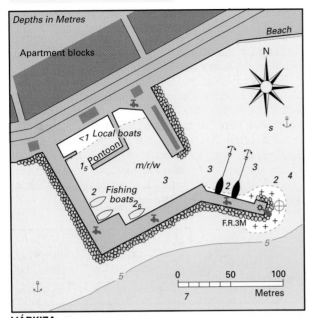

VÁRKIZA
⊕37°49'·1N 23°48'·3E

weed, poor holding.

Shelter Good shelter in the basin. Mediocre shelter from the *meltemi* on the mole.

Anchorage Depending on wind and sea it is possible to anchor off the beach or on the SW side of the breakwater of Varkiza. Anchored off the beach there is reasonable shelter from the *meltemi*.

Facilities

Water On the quay.
Fuel A mini-tanker can deliver to the quay.
Provisions Most provisions can be found nearby.
Eating out Tavernas nearby.

General

The small harbour is crowded with local boats, but a small yacht may find a berth here. Várkiza is an outer suburb of Athens, mostly bland apartment blocks and the wide coast road to whisk commuters in and out of Athens.

Várkiza looking E towards the entrance

LAGONISI 37°47'·0N 23°53'·2E

A small harbour at the S end of the beach. There are 3–4m depths off the end of the mole, but it is usually crowded with local boats. Anchor off the beach in 3–6m. Good shelter from the *meltemi*. Tavernas.

ÓRMOS ANAVÍSSOU

The large bay with Nisís Arsidha lying off the entrance. There are a number of anchorages around the bay.

1. ***Chapel cove*** The enclosed bay on the W side of Órmos Anavíssou. Much of the cove is taken up by boats on permanent moorings. Anchor clear of any permanent moorings where possible. Good shelter from the *meltemi*. A *cantina* opens in the summer.

2. In the NW corner where a number of boats are kept on permanent moorings. The holding is reported to be poor. Reasonable shelter from the *meltemi*.

   Note The holding in both these coves has been reported as suspect in places. The bottom is hard sand and rock, good holding once the anchor is in.

3. ***Palaia Fokaia*** The small harbour has 2–3m depths along the outer half of the mole, but it is usually full of local boats. The inner part of the harbour has <1m. Care is needed in the approach to the harbour as the depths are uneven and there are areas of underwater rocks protruding up to 2–2·5m in the vicinity of the harbour. The best policy is to anchor off the harbour in 3–6m. Care must be taken of patches of coral-like rock that can foul an anchor. Good shelter from the *meltemi* although there are gusts into the bay.

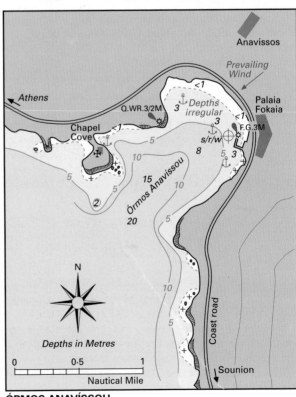

ÓRMOS ANAVÍSSOU
⊕37°43'·2N 23°56'·7E

Chapel Cove on the W side of Órmos Anavíssou. Some yachts are kept here on permanent moorings throughout the summer

Looking S across Palaia Fokaia harbour to the anchorage off the small harbour

Water and electricity on the mole. Fuel nearby. Good shopping for provisions and tavernas in the village.

A word of warning about the tavernas on the waterfront: in one of these I had one of the most expensive and least satisfactory meals in Greece. Touts outside will promise you everything gastronomic, but deliver awful food. Choose your own taverna with care.

NISÍS GAIDHOURONISI (Patróklou)

⊕4 0·5M S of W end of Gaidhouronisi
37°38'·45N 23°56'·04E WGS84

The humpbacked islet lying close off the coast S of Ák Katafiyí. It is lit on the NE side: LFl.10s6M. It is possible to pass inside the islet though care must be taken of the reef just under the water lying near the middle of the fairway at the eastern end.

There is a useful anchorage on the NE end if W–SW winds are blowing. There is a fish farm in here but still room for a number of yachts to anchor.

SOUNION

The bay under Ák Sounion is often used by yachts waiting for the *meltemi* to die before proceeding into Kólpos Petalíon or returning to Athens.

The temple on the cape is conspicuous from the distance. Anchor where convenient. The bottom is sand and weed – bad holding. In the N of the bay there is a 3·5m patch of sand off the chapel which is good holding. Make sure your anchor is well in and holding as the gusts into the bay have caused numerous yachts to drag anchors here. Good shelter from the *meltemi* although there are strong gusts into the bay. Tavernas on the shore.

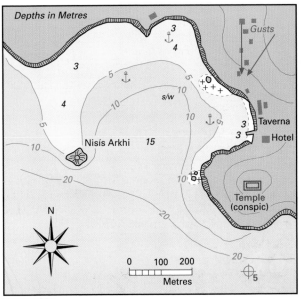

SOUNION

⊕5 0·25M S of temple on Sounion
37°38'·63N 24°01'·31E WGS84

The anchorage at Sounion looking W

The temple of Poseidon on the cape is easily reached after a short walk from the shore. It was built around 444 BC, probably to a design by Hephaisteion of Athens. Visit it in the morning as in the afternoon and evening it is overrun by day-

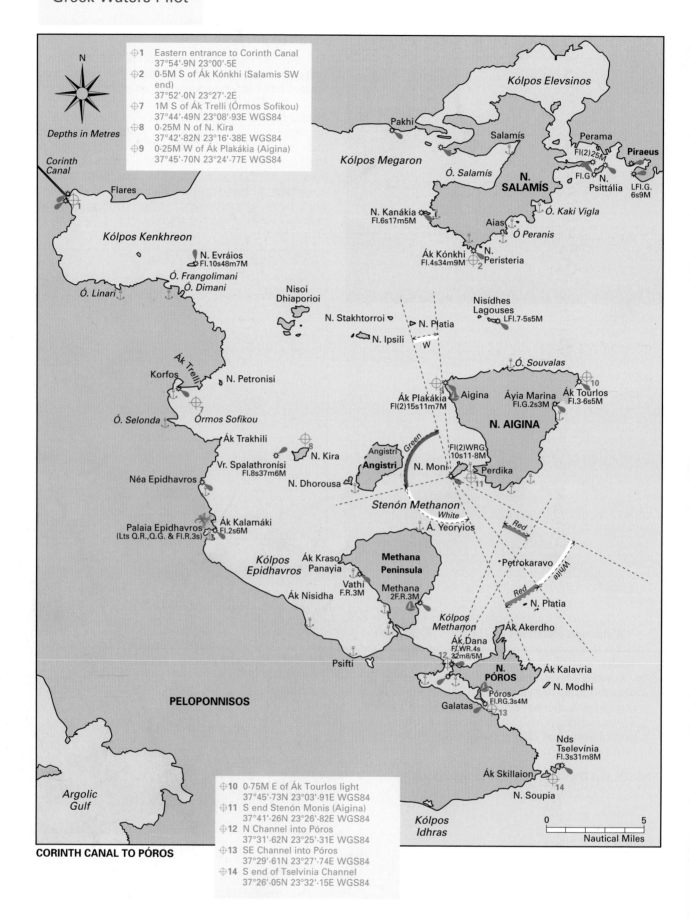

N

Depths in Metres

⊕1 Eastern entrance to Corinth Canal
37°54'·9N 23°00'·5E
⊕2 0·5M S of Ák Kónkhi (Salamis SW end)
37°52'·0N 23°27'·2E
⊕7 1M S of Ák Trelli (Órmos Sofikou)
37°44'·49N 23°08'·93E WGS84
⊕8 0·25M N of N. Kira
37°42'·82N 23°16'·38E WGS84
⊕9 0·25M W of Ák Plakákia (Aigina)
37°45'·70N 23°24'·77E WGS84

Corinth Canal

Flares

Kólpos Kenkhreon

Ó. Linari

N. Evráios
Fl.10s48m7M

Ó. Frangolimani
Ó. Dimani

Ák Trelli

Korfos

N. Petronisi

Ó. Selonda

Órmos Sofikou

Ák Trakhili

Vr. Spalathronísi
Fl.8s37m6M

N. Kira

Néa Epidhavros

N. Dhorousa

Palaia Epidhavros
(Lts Q.R.,Q.G. & Fl.R.3s)

Ák Kalamáki
Fl.2s6M

Kólpos
Epidhavros

Ák Kraso
Panayia

Vathí
F.R.3M

Methana
Peninsula

Methana
2F.R.3M

Ák Nisidha

Kólpos
Methanon

PELOPONNISOS

Psifti

Argolic
Gulf

Pakhi

Kólpos Megaron

Ó. Salamís

N. Kanákia
Fl.6s17m5M

Ák Kónkhi
Fl.4s34m9M

Kólpos Elevsinos

Salamís

Perama
Fl(2)25M

N.
SALAMÍS

Fl.G

Piraeus

N.
Psittália

LFl.G.
6s9M

Ó. Kaki Vigla

Aias

Ó Peranis

N.
Peristeria

Nisoi
Dhiaporioi

N. Stakhtorroi

N. Platia

N. Ipsili

W

Nisídhes
Lagouses
LFl.7·5s5M

Ó. Souvalas

Ák Plakákia
Fl(2)15s11m7M

Aigina

 Áyia Marina
Fl.G.2s3M

Ák Toúrlos
Fl.3·6s5M

N. AIGINA

Angistri

Angistri

Green

Fl(2)WRG
10s11·8M

Perdika

N. Moni

Stenón Methanon

White

Á. Yeóryios

Red

Petrokaravo

White

Red

N. Platia

Ák Akerdho

Ák Dana
Fl.WR.4s
32m8/5M

N.
PÓROS

Ák Kalavria

N. Modhi

Póros
Fl.RG.3s4M

Galatas

Nds
Tselevínia
Fl.3s31m8M

Ák Skillaion

N. Soupia

Kólpos
Idhras

⊕10 0·75M E of Ák Tourlos light
37°45'·73N 23°03'·91E WGS84
⊕11 S end Stenón Monis (Aigina)
37°41'·26N 23°26'·82E WGS84
⊕12 N Channel into Póros
37°31'·62N 23°25'·31E WGS84
⊕13 SE Channel into Póros
37°29'·61N 23°27'·74E WGS84
⊕14 S end of Tselvinia Channel
37°26'·05N 23°32'·15E WGS84

0   5

Nautical Miles

CORINTH CANAL TO PÓROS

The temple at Sounion

trippers from Athens. The young Byron is supposed to have carved his name on one of the columns and afterwards he penned a few lines on his visit:

'Sunium's marbled steep
Where nothing save the waves and I
May hear our mutual murmurs sweep.'

The Saronic Islands and the adjacent coast

The coast

This section covers the coast from the Corinth Canal down to Ák Skillaion and around the corner to Ák Mouzaki opposite the NW tip of Nísos Dhokós. It is mostly mountainous with a ridge running along the coast between 600 and 900m (2,000–3,000ft) high reaching the summit at Ortholithi (112m/3,625ft) opposite Methana peninsula. The upper slopes are rocky and devoid of vegetation, but the lower slopes along the coast are densely wooded in pine. Methana peninsula, properly Khersónisos Methanon (almost an island but for a narrow isthmus), is an extinct volcano.

ÓRMOS LINARI

37°50'·6N 23°04'·8E

Lies on the S shore of Kólpos Kenkhreon 5 miles SE of the canal. Poor shelter as a swell enters with strong northerlies. Open to the NW–W. No facilities.

FRANGOLIMANI

37°50'·7N 23°07'·0E

A bay 3½ miles E of Linari. It is steep-to until close to the shore. A beach around the SW side. You will have to drop your anchor in 15–20m and take a line ashore. The bottom is hard sand and weed – bad holding. A swell enters with strong northerlies and shelter is not as good as it looks. The slopes above are being developed for summer villas.

ÓRMOS DIMANI

A bay approximately 1M E of Frangolimani. Suitable in settled weather. From here on in the coast is littered with fish farms tucked into any and every cove until Korfos. It could be renamed Fish Farm Coast.

NISOI DHIAPORIOI

A group of uninhabited islands lying to the E of Ák Spiri. The channel between the two largest islands, Áy Thomas and Áy Ioánnis, does not have the depths shown on BA 1657. A reef joins the two islands with the deepest part (3–4m) nearest to Nisís Áy Ioánnis.

NISÍS ÍPSILI

Lies to the ESE of Nisoi Dhiaporioi and is used for target practice by the Greek Navy.

KORFOS (Limín Sofikoú)
Approach

A nearly landlocked bay 1½ miles W of Ák Trelli. The islet of Petronisi with fish farms around it is easily identified in the approaches. The houses of the village will not be seen until into the bay.

By night The E side of the entrance is lit: Fl.4s5M. With care a night entry is possible.

Dangers
1. Care must be taken of the reef running out from Ák Trelli for nearly 400m. With any chop on the water it can be difficult to see and because Ák Trelli is low-lying it is difficult to determine where the reef starts and finishes.
2. With W–NW winds there are fierce gusts off the land.

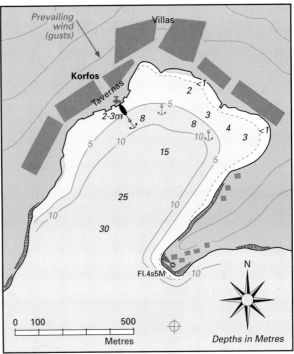

KORFOS
⊕37°45'·32N 23°07'·72E WGS84

Korfos looking NE into the bay

Mooring

Anchor in the bay in 5–10m or go stern or bows-to off the quayed area on the N side just off several tavernas here. Two of the tavernas each have a concrete quay with 2–3m metre depths off them. Some laid moorings tailed to the quay. Between the two concrete quays depths are shallow and even off the quays depths are variable. The bottom is mud and weed, poor holding in places, so make sure your anchor is well in.

Shelter Good all-round shelter although there are strong gusts with westerlies.

Facilities

Water On the quay.
Fuel A mini-tanker can deliver to the quay.
Provisions Good shopping for provisions in the village.
Eating out Good tavernas along the waterfront.
Other PO. OTE. Camping Gaz.

General

The bay is attractive enough, but the same cannot be said for the awful concrete villas that have been thrown up around the slopes. The best part of Korfos is the waterfront and the tavernas with views out over the bay.

ÓRMOS SELONDA
37°43'·8N 23°07'·8E

A deep inlet 2 miles S of Korfos. It is now largely obstructed by a fish farm, but it is possible to find a space to anchor in. It is mostly very deep for anchoring. Even with the fish farm here it is a spectacular spot at the foot of a deep ravine cutting through the cliffs. Open to the E–SE only.

NÉA EPIDHAVROS

Approach

A small harbour off the hamlet set at the foot of a flood plain. The approach is straightforward with good depths up to the entrance.

By night The entrance is lit Fl.G.3s.3M and Fl.R.3s3M.

Mooring

Go stern or bows-to the pontoon off the taverna in the NE of the harbour. The pontoon is a bit rickety and semi-sunk in places so care is needed. Alternatively go alongside the end of the stubby mole.

Shelter Good shelter from the prevailing NE wind although there can be a bit of a surge.

Anchorage In calm weather anchor off the beach in 2–4m on sand and weed, good holding.

Facilities

Water at the taverna. Limited provisions. If you berth on the pontoon then really you should eat in the taverna above which has wonderful views.

General

The hamlet on the small flood plain is a convivial place that has a little tourism to augment the income from the citrus groves extending back from the beach into the valley. The harbour here is like some secret place locked in by the cliffs and the steep-sided valley. The river that formed the flood plain now runs under the cliffs and empties into the N corner of the harbour.

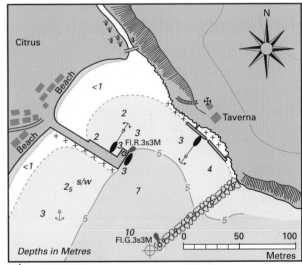

NÉA EPIDHAVROS
⊕37°40'·8N 23°09'·3E

EPIDHAVROS (Old (Palaia) Epidavros, Epidhavro, Epidauros)

Approach

Conspicuous The entrance to Órmos Palaia Epidhávrou is difficult to see from seaward. A road scar on the hill on the S side of the bay is conspicuous. Closer in, the light structure and a church on the N side of the bay will be seen. The village of Palaia Epidhavros at the head of the bay will not be seen until you are in the entrance. Once into the bay proceed between the two beacons marking the channel to the quay.

Epidhavros looking S into the bay

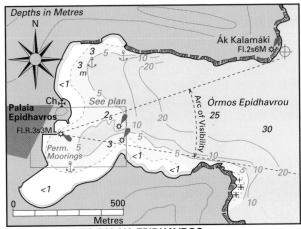

APPROACHES TO PALAIA EPIDHAVROS
⊕37°38′·5N 23°10′·2E

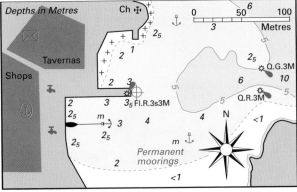

PALAIA EPIDHAVROS
⊕37°38′·3N 23°09′·5E

By night Use the light on the N side of the entrance Ák Kalamáki Fl.2s6M, on the two beacons Q.G.3M, Q.R.3M and on the pierhead Fl.R.3s3M.

Mooring
Go stern or bows-to the pier or the quay or anchor in the bay. The bottom is mud and weed, reasonable holding.

Shelter Good shelter. Although the bay is open E, winds from the E rarely blow in the summer with any force.

Authorities Port police.

Note The port police and local hoteliers do not like you anchoring too close to the beach. This is understandable as boats have loos and I for one don't like swimming in pumped out liquid goo.

Facilities
Water On the quay.
Fuel In the town.
Provisions Good shopping for most provisions.
Eating out Tavernas on the waterfront and in the town.
Other PO. OTE. Bank. ATM. Greek gas. Hire motorbikes. Taxis can be hired to go to Epidhavros theatre.

General
Set at the base of steep wooded slopes, Palaia Epidhavros is an attractive small village. However the real attraction is Epidhavros theatre about 30 minutes away by taxi – the easiest way of getting there.

The theatre is accepted as the best preserved of all Greek theatres and one of the finest pieces of classical architecture in existence. Some sensible restoration has been carried out, but the theatre is mostly original. The acoustics of the theatre are perfect: a piece of paper rustled on the stage or a coin dropped on the floor can be clearly heard from any one of the 14,000 seats. There is a festival of ancient Greek drama in the summer and seats and transport can be booked at Palaia Epidhavros.

The site was renowned in ancient times not for its theatre but as a sanctuary of the Askeplion: a religious centre for curing the sick and infirm. Extensive temples, hospitals, sanatoriums and the bath-houses covered a site comparable to Delphi. Little remains of the buildings today but the site on the pine-clad slopes has a certain feeling of quiet and calm about it. A museum on the site houses local finds.

Methana Peninsula

VATHÍ (Methana)
Approach
Vathi is a small fishing harbour on the W coast of the Methana peninsula. The rough stone breakwater and houses of the village will not be seen until close to in the approach from the N.

By night A F.R.3M is exhibited on the end of the breakwater.

Mooring
Go stern or bows-to the quay off the tavernas on the S side. Alternatively anchor and take a long line ashore to the rough stone breakwater. The bottom is mud and weed, mostly good holding, although a bit soft in places.

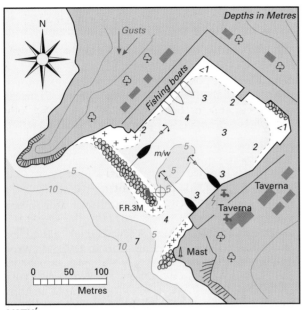

VATHÍ
⊕37°35′·7N 23°20′·3E

Shelter Good shelter, although strong N–NE winds gust into the harbour, more bothersome than troubling.

Facilities
Water and electricity on the quay. Several café/tavernas ashore. Infrequent bus to Methana town.

General
The hamlet is a delightful spot and well off the Saronic charter milk run. On the black basalt slopes a short distance N there is an old caldera, betraying the peninsula's recent volcanic origins.

Vathi looking SE from the NW side of the harbour

NEARBY ANCHORAGES
To the S of Vathi there are several deserted bays that can be used in calm weather. A yacht can also anchor off on the SW side of Kólpos Epidhávrou in calm weather.

ÁY YEORYIOS (Áy Georgis)
37°38′·38N 23°23′·72E WGS84

A small harbour on the NE corner of the Methana peninsula. A large church is conspicuous close behind the harbour and closer in the outer breakwater an old coaster that has been sunk and filled with ballast will be seen. There is room for a few yachts to go stern or bows-to behind the outer breakwater where there are 2–3m along the outer half of the quay. Further into the harbour it becomes progressively shallow. Care is needed off the quay as depths are uneven. Good shelter from the prevailing winds although with strong northerlies it can get bumpy in here.

Limited provisions and tavernas ashore.

METHANA
Approach
Conspicuous The town of Methana is easily identified from some distance off. The marina lies near the S end of the town and it is difficult to identify the entrance tucked under the wooded headland until close to.

By night Use the light on the headland Fl.G.3s3M and the lights at the narrow entrance Q.G.3M/Q.R.3M – care needed.

Dangers Care is needed negotiating the narrow entrance into the harbour.

Mooring
Go stern or bows-to the quay on the W or N. Depths off the quay are variable, between 1·5–2·5m, but if you touch bottom it is all mud. The bottom of

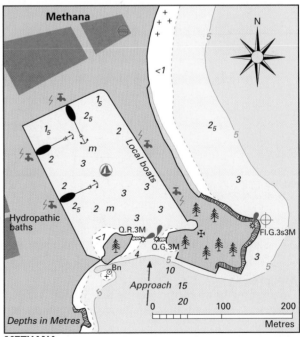

METHANA
⊕37°34′·6N 23°23′·5E

Fuel Near the quay. A mini-tanker can deliver to the quay.
Repairs Some mechanical repairs. Hardware shops.
Provisions Good shopping for provisions. Ice available.
Eating out Tavernas in the town.
Other PO. OTE. Greek gas and Camping Gaz. Ferries to Piraeus and to the islands in the Saronic Gulf.

General

The lasting impression of Methana is not visual but olfactory. The characteristic rotten-egg smell of the sulphuretted hydrogen bubbling up into the harbour is so pungent that the village above Methana is called Vromolimani or 'stinking shore'. The buildings on the west side of the harbour house sulphur baths to which people suffering from rheumatic diseases come. You can have a free bath in the harbour if you fancy it. Boats moored here are said not to have fouling problems as the sulphur in the water kills off weed and barnacles.

Methana looking NW   *Peter Kleinoth/MareTeam*

sticky black mud is excellent holding, but messy when you haul the anchor up again. Some yachts use rope rather than chain because of the corrosive action of the sulphurous water on chain.
Shelter Good all-round shelter. Yachts are wintered afloat here.
Authorities Port police and customs. Charge band 2.

Facilities

Services Water and electricity points around the quay.

Nísos Aigina

(Aiyina, Aegina, Egina)

Aigina is the roughly triangular island lying some 12 miles SW of Zéa Marina. The summit of Aigina, Oros (532m/1,745ft), is near the southern end of the island. The island is mostly rocky and barren, but there are a few wooded areas around the coast.

The position of Aigina guarding the northwestern approaches to the Aegean has meant that it was important from the very early days of trade. It was occupied by a Neolithic people who were in turn supplanted by a Bronze Age people around 2000

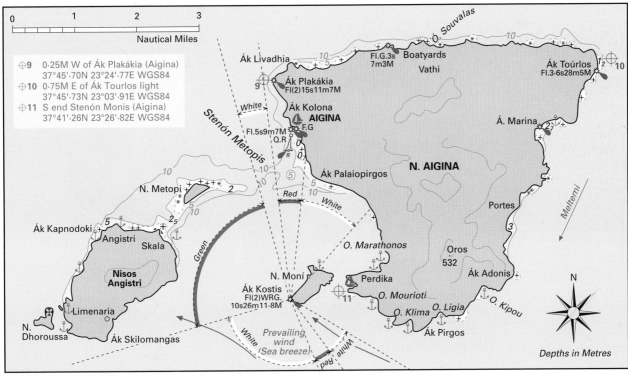

AIGINA AND ANGISTRI

     9   0·25M W of Ák Plakákia (Aigina)
        37°45'·70N 23°24'·77E WGS84
     10 0·75M E of Ák Tourlos light
        37°45'·73N 23°03'·91E WGS84
     11 S end Stenón Monis (Aigina)
        37°41'·26N 23°26'·82E WGS84

BC. The Mycenaeans occupied it about 1400 BC, but appear to have abandoned it after a couple of centuries. Later it was recolonized and the inhabitants began to build up their own merchant marine fleet. In the Battle of Salamís the fleet from Aigina was said by Herodotus to have distinguished itself above all others. The growth of the maritime fleet aroused the envy of the Athenians to the extent that Aristotle remarked that the island was 'the eyesore of Piraeus'.

At the beginning of the Peloponnesian War the island opted for the Spartan side (its relationship with Athens had never been a happy one), and was subsequently subdued by Athens. It never recovered and thereafter endured the usual succession of invaders: the Romans, Byzantines, the Saracens, Venetians and Turks. From 1826–28 the city was the capital of the newly liberated Greece and the first modern Greek coins were minted here and the new Greek national flag flown.

The island is very popular with tourists and Athenians alike. By hydrofoil from Zéa it is only 20 minutes away and is a popular excursion for the smog-bound Athenians. Tourists visiting Athens often come on a day trip here. Consequently the strip of water between Aigina and Athens is constantly churned up with ferries and hydrofoils hurrying back and forth, and at the weekends with Athens-based pleasure boats scurrying to get out or back to the capital.

AIGINA (Aegina, Egina)

Imray-Tetra G14
BA 1657

Approach

Conspicuous The town of Aigina is conspicuous from the distance. Closer in a Doric column on Ák Kolóna immediately NW of the town and a white chapel near the outer end of the W mole are conspicuous. A red conical buoy marks a rock with 3m over it off the marina and another red conical buoy marks a shoal patch with 2·4m least depths just W of the entrance.

By night Use the light on Ák Plakákia Fl(2)15s7M, Nisís Moní (Ák Kóstis Fl(2)WRG.10s11-8M; the white sector 296°-322° covers the safe passage across the shoal water between Aigina and Angistri), and the lights at the entrance: Fl.5s7M, Fl.R.3M and F.G.3M. The entrance to the marina is lit Fl.G.3s.

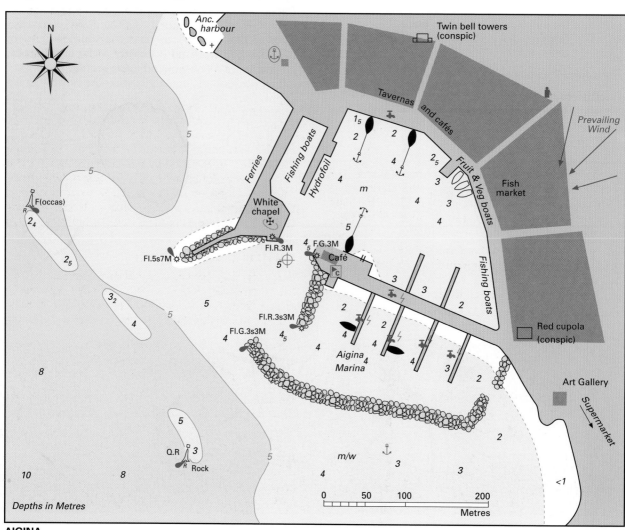

AIGINA
⊕37°44′·66N 23°25′·59E WGS84

Aigina looking NW with the new 'marina' in the foreground.
This picture does not show the later additions to the 'marina'
Peter Kleinoth/MareTeam

Dangers
1. Care should be taken when making an approach from the S as shoal water extends E from Nisís Metopi across to Aigina. There are least depths of 8–9m through the fairway of the channel.
2. Care is needed at the entrance to the harbour as numerous ferries and hydrofoils use it and they enter and leave at speed. A good lookout is needed.

Mooring
Go stern or bows-to the town quay or off the café on the S quay. If you want to berth in the marina then apply to the port police for a berth. The harbour gets very crowded with yachts in the summer months.

Shelter Good all-round shelter although strong southerlies send in an uncomfortable swell. The bottom is mud with some rocks – poor holding in places. Some yachts winter afloat here.

Authorities Port police and customs.

Aigina Marina The marina is now in use and yachts berth stern or bows-to the pontoons. There are laid moorings tailed to the quay at some berths. If you use your anchor then a trip line is advisable. At the time of writing many of the berths are occupied by local boats and yachts permanently based here. The marina is still not finished and the situation is in a state of flux. If you can find a berth here use it. Otherwise it is really better to be on the town quay if space is available. Shelter in the marina is generally good and only NW winds cause a swell to enter.

Facilities
Services Water and electricity points on the town quay and in the marina. The service points in the marina are not yet connected.
Fuel Some distance from the harbour. A mini-tanker can deliver to the quay.
Repairs Limited mechanical repairs. Chandlers. For hauling see section on Boatyards on the N side of Aigina.
Provisions Good shopping for provisions. Large supermarket on the coast road going S out of town (turn left at Miranda Hotel). Fruit and vegetables can be bought from *caïques* moored on the town quay. Ice available.
Eating out Good tavernas around the waterfront.
Other PO. OTE. Banks. ATM. Greek gas and Camping Gaz. Hire motorbikes and bicycles. Buses to the other villages on the island. Ferries to Piraeus and to the other islands in the Saronic Gulf.

General
The small town around the harbour is a pleasant homely sort of place despite the large numbers of tourists deposited here in the summer months. It has the distinction of being the first place in Greece where the Greek flag was raised at the end of the Greek War of Independence. This flag differed from the present-day one, being red and gold in colour. The single column on Ák Kolóna is all that remains of the Temple of Aphrodite that formerly stood on the cape.

ORMOS MARATHONOS
The large bay between Aigina and Perdika. In the SE corner there is a cove that provides reasonable shelter from the *meltemi* and SE winds. It has been called Profitis Ilias Cove by one cruiser and he says

Entrance to Aigina harbour looking NE

that it provides good shelter when Perdika is so full you can't get a berth. Anchor in the SE cove. Good holding and several tavernas ashore.

PERDIKA

Approach
The small bay on the SW end of Aigina. The small village on the N side of the bay is easily identified from seaward.

By night Use the light on Nisís Moní Fl(2)WRG.10s11-8M and the light on the end of the outer mole Fl.R.1·5s2M.

Mooring
It's always a bit of a squeeze trying to get into Perdika in the summer. Go stern or bows-to either side of the centre mole, the new pontoon immediately E or on either side of the outer mole where possible. Depths are variable around the centre mole and in general you are better off trying to go bows-to.

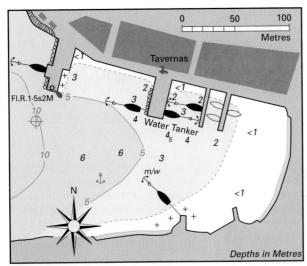

PERDIKA
⊕37°41'·43N 23°27'·06E WGS84

Perdika pier looking SW

Note Do not obstruct the end of the centre mole where the water tanker berths alongside.

Shelter Good shelter from the normal summer winds. The bay is open to the W and with fresh to strong NW–W winds the outer part of the harbour is very uncomfortable and may become untenable.

Anchorage There is room for a few yachts to anchor and take a long line to the stubby mole on the S side.

Facilities
Water on the quay. Fuel 500m out of the village, although he may deliver to the quay. Several mini-markets. Good tavernas on the waterfront, some of which specialise in seafood.

General
The bay is an attractive place, but fills up quickly in the summer with visiting yachts. Get here early and take some time off for a wander around the village and a beer on the seafront.

NISÍS MONÍ
In calm weather a yacht can anchor in the bay on the N side of the island. Anchor in 8–10m. A taverna opens in the summer. The S side of the island is bare weathered rock, but on the N side it is partially wooded.

SOUTH SIDE ANCHORAGES
⊕0·10M S of Ák Pirgos 37°40'·29N 23°28'·82E WGS84

In settled weather yachts can anchor off in the bays on the S side of Aigina. Órmos Mourioti and Órmos Klima afford the best shelter. Órmos Ligia and Órmos Kipou can be used in calm weather.

AYIA MARINA
Ayia Marina light (Fl.G.2s3M) 37°44'·7N 23°32'·4E

An open bay near the NE corner of the Nísos Aigina. A large hotel on the waterfront is conspicuous. In calm weather anchor near the NW corner of the bay in 4–6m. Sand and weed bottom. With the *meltemi* this anchorage is not really tenable. A small quay in the NW corner is reserved for *caïque* ferries bringing tourists to see the Temple of Aphaia. It would be prudent to leave someone on board the yacht while visiting the temple in case there is a sudden change in the weather.

The Temple of Aphaia (5–6 BC) on the NE corner of the island has been called the most perfectly developed classical temple in Greece. Cruise ships anchor in Ayia Marina to disembark passengers wishing to view it. In calm weather this is the nearest anchorage to the temple for a yacht – alternatively buses run from Aigina town to Ayia Marina.

ÁK TOÚRLOS
⊕10   0·75M E of Ák Toúrlos light
      37°45'·73N 23°03'·91E WGS84

The NE corner of Aigina. Care is needed of two patches of shoal water and rocks lying approximately 250 metres off the cape. Give it a wide berth when rounding it.

SOUVALAS

37°46'·4N 23°29'·3E

A small harbour situated midway along the N coast. A short mole (50m long) runs W from the E side of the coast and has 2m depths just inside. If there is room moor bows-to the mole although it is usually full with trip boats. Care must be taken as the depths inside are uneven and there is little room for manoeuvring. Care is also needed not to obstruct the ferry berth. Tavernas ashore.

BOATYARDS

On the N of Nísos Aigina to the W of Souvalas are two boatyards.

Asprakis Boatyard 60-ton travel-hoist. 2·5m depths. Limited yacht repairs. Few facilities. A bit out of the way but transport can be arranged.

☎ 22970 23925 *Fax* 22970 26112

Kanonis Boatyard 37°46'·3N 23°27'·6E

50/20-ton hydraulic trailers. 2m max depths.

☎/*Fax* 22970 24151.

METOPI SHOALS

Between Aigina and Angistri lies Nisís Metopi, a low flat islet, with shoal water extending from either side. Between Metopi and Angistri there is a passage with 2·5–3m least depths on a course of approximately N–S around the mid-channel point. This passage is not recommended and in general a yacht should not attempt to pass in between Metopi and Angistri where the depths are variable and there are numerous underwater rocks either side of the passage. Between Metopi and Aigina the channel has 8–9m depths approximately one third of the way across from Aigina.

Nísos Angistri

(Aykistri)

Angistri is the small island lying 4 miles to the west of Aigina and connected to it by the strip of shoal water. Angistri is hilly, with the summit on the eastern side (296m/965ft). It is covered in pine for the most part and supports a small population.

There are two harbours on Angistri, but only Angistri harbour on the NW is suitable for yachts, whereas Skala on the NE side is not.

ANGISTRI (Miloi, Megalohorio, Saint Georgis)

Approach

A small harbour on the NW corner of Angistri. Care must be taken when approaching the harbour from the E because of the reefs and shoal water between Angistri and Nisís Metopi.

By night The entrance is lit Fl.G/Fl.R.

Mooring

Go stern or bows-to the quay if there is room. More usually you will have to anchor and take a long line to the rough stone breakwater on the NE side. Care

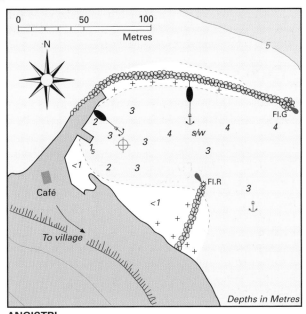

ANGISTRI
⊕37°42'·8N 23°20'·9E

is needed of large mooring chains fouling the bottom.

Shelter Local ferries spend the night on the quay, taking up most of the room available. Good shelter except for strong NE–E winds when it can get very uncomfortable.

Facilities

Tavernas and cafés at the harbour. Provisions available in Angistri village.

General

Tripper boats run across to here from Aigina in the summer, but the island retains a simplicity and charm of its own. Recently a number of villas have been built on the slopes around the harbour.

SKALA

37°42'·5N 23°22'·1E

This ferry harbour lies on the S side of the shoal water connecting Angistri to Metopi. The ferry pier is constantly in use and should not be approached. The small harbour to the NW of the ferry pier offers poor shelter from N–NE winds. There are 2–2·5m depths in the entrance and mostly 2m depths along the outer part of the rough stone breakwater. Anchor and take a long line to it. Care is needed of permanent mooring chains on the bottom.

NISÍS DHOROUSSA ANCHORAGES

N end of Dhoroussa Channel 37°41'·08N 23°19'·18E WGS84

Nisís Dhoroussa lies off the SW tip of Angistri. The narrow channel between the two islands is deep and clear of dangers. Opposite Nisís Dhoroussa there are a number of small bays offering good shelter from the normal summer winds (SE or NE) in attractive wooded surroundings. Anchor where convenient. A delightful little corner, with a taverna opening in the summer.

Petrokaravo ('rock ship') looking N with Nísos Aigina behind

Ák Nédha looking SE to Póros in the N Channel

PETROKARAVO

⊕ 0·25M E of the rocks 37°36'·82N 23°29'·07E WGS 84

The group of jagged rocks (the highest is 15m/49ft), lying 3½ miles S of the southern tip of Aigina. There are considerable depths close to the rocks. They are covered by one of the red sectors of the light on Nisís Moní (Fl(2)WRG.10s11-8M) and the red sector of the light on the W tip of Póros (Ák Dána Fl.WR.4s8/5M).

NISÍS PLATIA

The small island (7m/23ft high) approximately 1½ miles NE of the northern tip of Póros. It is surrounded by a reef and is unlit.

Nísos Póros

The Rorschach blob island of the Saronic. It lies close to the coast of the Peloponnisos, separated from it by a narrow and in places shallow channel. The island is extensively wooded (mostly pine but also olive and citrus groves) and is cultivated in places.

In ancient times the island was known as Kaularia and was the centre of the Kaularian league, a

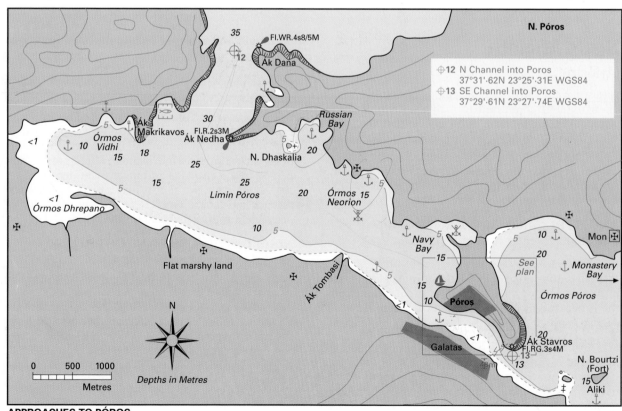

APPROACHES TO PÓROS

maritime confederacy of the 7th century BC amongst whose members were Athens, Aigina, Epidhavros, Troezein, Ermioni, Navplion, Praisiai and Póros. Its patron was Poseidon and a few remains of a temple to Poseidon (about 6 BC but built on an earlier site) can be found on a picturesque site on the east coast of the island.

In 1831 at the end of the Greek War of Independence the islanders opposed the first Greek government and formed a constitutional committee to replace it which had widespread support from the surrounding islands. The Greek ships *Hellas* and *Hydra* were blown up in the harbour by Admiral Miaoulis in defiance of the new government when it sent forces to crush the rebellion. A Greek naval establishment and naval cadet school are situated immediately north of Póros town, perhaps to ensure that there are no further insurrections on the island.

Póros town looking ESE towards the yacht quay on the N side of the peninsula

PÓROS

BA 1599
Imray-Tetra G14

Approach

Conspicuous From the N the narrow channel leading into the large landlocked bay is difficult to see from the distance. The numerous ferries plying this stretch of water will seem to disappear or appear from nowhere. Closer in the lighthouse on the E side of the entrance will be seen. Once in the large bay, the town of Póros will be clearly seen. A light blue clock-tower is conspicuous.

From the S the buildings on the low-lying isthmus can be seen, but it is difficult to see the entrance to the narrow channel. Keep close to the Póros side of the channel and keep a good lookout for the numerous ferries which come rocketing out of the narrow channel.

By night From the N use the two lights on the E side of the entrance: Ák Dána Fl.WR.4s8/5M and Ák Nédha Fl.R.2s2M.

From the S a night entrance is difficult because of the unlit islands in the approaches. The red sector of the light on the S point of Póros covers the islands: Ák Stavrós Fl.RG.3s4M: 284°-R-309°.

VHF Ch 16, 27, 28, 88 for coastguard.

Dangers
1. Care is needed of the shallows on the Peloponnisos side of the channel through Póros

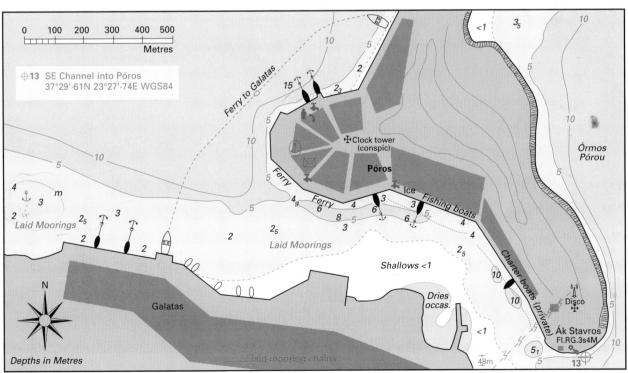

PÓROS

town. Stick close to the Póros side. Local *caïques* make a good living pulling inattentive yachtsmen off the sticky mud.

2. Care is needed of the ferries and hydrofoils entering and leaving at speed.

Mooring

Go stern or bows-to the quay on the N side of town or stern-to the quay on the S quay in the narrow channel. The wash from ferries, particularly the hydrofoil, can be uncomfortable and you must ensure your anchor is well in so that you are not violently pushed onto the quay. The holding off the N quay is patchy. The bottom in the channel is mud – excellent holding.

Note Mooring blocks and chains have been laid in the places shown on the plan. The mooring lines were long ago removed, allegedly by the local diver who thought he would lose out on charging for recovering fouled anchors. On the S quay the chains are around 20m off the quay at the W end and around 30m off at the E end. On the N quay there is only a short section of chain on the W side around 25m off. Recently it was reported the chains have been removed but I would still counsel caution until it can be confirmed.

Shelter Good all-round shelter although strong westerlies cause some slop on the N quay. There are strong gusts off the hills of the Peloponnisos with strong southerlies.

Authorities Port police and customs. A charge is sometimes made.

Note A current normally flows through the Póros Strait, usually from W to E though it can reverse and flow in the opposite direction. The current can be up to 1 knot although usually less. The only real problem with the current is when berthing on the town quay in the strait when it can push you about as you go stern-to at slow speed. Likewise when you leave you may have to be a bit snappy about it so you do not get pushed down onto your neighbours.

Facilities

Water On the quay. The water man usually does the rounds in the morning and evening. Showers available in several of the bars on the waterfront.

Fuel A mini-tanker delivers to the quay.

Repairs Some mechanical repairs. Hardware shops. Two chandlers.

Greek Sails A charter company which operates from the quay at the SE end of the channel, can arrange various repairs including engine, engineering and sail repairs.

Richard Kouvaras, Greek Sails, Punta Poros, Trizinias, 18020 Greece
☎ 22980 22332 *Fax* 22980 23147
Mobile ☎ 6944 683 678 *Email* grsails@x–treme.gr

Póros looking SE out to the SE entrance and Órmos Pórou

Peter Kleinoth/MareTeam

Poros Yachting Centre Provides gardiennage and can arrange haul–outs and repairs.

Antonios Vikos, Poros Yachting Centre
☎ 22980 24019 *Fax* 22980 24110
Mobile ☎ 6932 321001
Email avikos@b–online.gr

Provisions Good shopping for all provisions. Ice available.

Eating out Numerous tavernas on the waterfront and behind. Also tavernas at Galatas across the strait. Yorgiou at the Café Remetzo on the waterfront serves a good breakfast or a cool beer in the evening. *Other* PO. OTE. Banks. ATMs. Greek gas and Camping Gaz. Laundrette close to the N quay. Hire cars, motorbikes and bicycles. *Caïque* ferries across to Galatas. Ferries to Piraeus and the other islands in the Saronic Gulf.

General

The small volcanic peninsula on which Póros town is built was known in ancient times as Sphaeria. Póros means a 'strait' or 'ferry' and is a later name. The town built on the rocky slopes is attractive and the approach by sea one of the most beautiful in Greece. Póros is a popular tourist spot as well as being popular with day-trippers from Athens. In the season they pour into Póros, yet it somehow manages to stand up to it all and remains a likeable place.

If you are berthed on the S quay it can get smelly at the height of the season from the sewage emptying into the harbour. If the smell doesn't prevent you from sleeping, the latest in popular music will assail your eardrums from the numerous bars along the waterfront.

GALATAS

The town on the S side of the Poros channel, served by numerous ferries and water taxis to Poros.

Approach

Care needed of the shallows on the S side of the channel. Many yachts are on moorings off the town and are unlit at night. Approach from the NW where depths come up gradually towards the quay.

Mooring

There is usually room to berth stern or bows–to on the W end of the quay. Keep clear of the ferry quay and local berths. Care is needed of floating mooring lines for fishing boats dotted along the quay. Depths 2–3m. Alternatively anchor off to the W, clear of the moorings.

Facilities

Water on the quay. Supermarket nearby. Restaurants and tavernas. Ferries to Poros.

ANCHORAGES NEAR PÓROS

1. *Órmos Vidhi* Anchor in the bay or any of the coves on the N side. A fish farm obstructs one of the bays, but you can still get in. The water here is a bit murky. Taverna on the beach at the head of the bay.

2. *Ák Dána* Anchor in the cove tucked under the cape. Good shelter from the prevailing winds and clear water.

3. *Russian Bay* Nisís Dhaskalia under Ák Nédha is easily recognised by the conspicuous white chapel on it. Care is needed of the reef running out for approximately 50m from the E side of the islet. Anchor in the bay under the islet. The bottom is mud and weed, good holding once through the weed. Good shelter from the prevailing winds.

4. *Órmos Neorion* In the bay SE of Russian Bay where a number of charter yachts have permanent moorings there is good shelter.

5. *Aliki* A reef connects the small islets to the SE of Póros Channel to the mainland. Pass between the islets and Nisís Bourtzi. Good shelter. Sandy bottom. Taverna on the beach.

6. *Órmos Pórou* Is quite deep until a short distance off. Poor holding. Taverna on the beach.

7. *Monastery Bay* As for Órmos Pórou.

ALIKI BOATYARD

At Aliki Beach Póros Marine can haul yachts up to 17 tons. There is around 2m off the short quay where hauling takes place. Hauling is by crane and then yachts are shored up on the hard. Most yacht repairs can be arranged. Go around to Aliki Beach or contact Richard at Greek Sails in Póros.

Kolpos Idhras
(Gulf of Hydra)

NISIDHES TSELEVINIA

⊕14   S end of Tselevinia Channel
        37°26'·05N 23°32'·15E WGS84

These two islands, Spathí and Skilli, lie to the S of Póros just before you 'turn the corner' to head into Kólpos Idhras (the Hydra Gulf). The passage between the two islands is deep and clear of dangers in the fairway. However, great care is needed of the numerous ferries and hydrofoils which charge through the narrow channel at full speed (the ferries come through at 15–20 knots, the hydrofoil at around 30 knots).

The passage between Nisís Spathí and the Peloponnese is obstructed by a reef just below the surface. Off the SW tip of Spathí there is a small islet and behind it a secluded anchorage.

NISÍS SOUPIA

⊕ 0·2M S of N. Soupia 37°25'·00N 23°29'·60E WGS84

An islet lying close off the coast about 1½ miles W of Nisís Spathí. The islet looks like a crouching frog when viewed from the E. Anchor behind the islet where convenient. Depths shallow up on the NE side of the islet. Good shelter in settled weather. The bottom is covered in thick weed and is poor holding in parts. Mulberry trees around the shore and a villa development above.

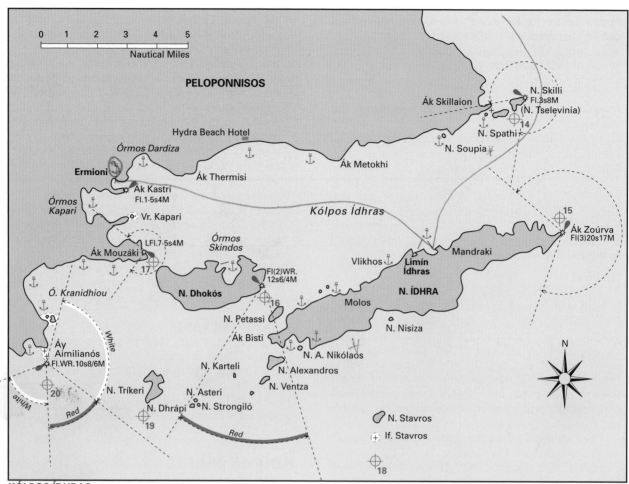

KÓLPOS ÍDHRAS

⊕**14** S end of Tselevinia Channel
37°26'·05N 23°32'·15E WGS84
⊕**15** 0·5M N of Ák Zoúrva (Ídhra)
37°22'·56N 23°34'·74E WGS84
⊕**16** 0·5M S of Dhokós SE light
37°19'·30N 23°21'·48E WGS84
⊕**17** Ák Mouzáki – N. Dhokós Channel
37°20'·74N 23°16'·98E WGS84
⊕**18** 1·75M S of N. Stavrós
37°13'·33N 23°26'·61E WGS84
⊕**19** 0·5M S of N. Tríkeri
37°15'·05N 23°16'·46E WGS84
⊕**20** 0·5M S of Ák Aimilianós
37°16'·82N 23°12'·00E WGS84

Nisís Soupia looking NE

HYDRA BEACH HOTEL

37°24'·8N 23°20'·4E

This large hotel complex lies approximately 8½ miles W of Nisís Spathí. It is easily identified from seaward. There is a small boat harbour attached to the complex, but it is usually crowded with *caïque* ferries and water taxis.

Small yachts may find a berth here, but the entrance is barely 20m wide and the basin itself is very small. There are 3·5m depths in the entrance and 2–3·5m depths on the W side of the basin. Bar and tavernas ashore, although the complex has a run-down feel to it.

ERMIONI (Hermioni, Kastrí)
Approach
Conspicuous The village of Ermioni saddling the headland is easily identified from seaward. The end of the headland is wooded (mostly conifers).

By night Use the light on Ák Kastrí Fl.1·5s4M and on the mole head F.R.2M. The breakwater head is lit Fl.G.2s3M.

Dangers Care needs to be taken of the remains of the ancient mole on the N side of the headland.

Mooring
Go stern or bows-to behind the outer mole if there is room. Larger yachts can anchor in the bay. The harbour can get crowded in the summer. The

bottom is mud and weed with some rocks – poor holding in patches.

Shelter Good all-round shelter behind the mole. One or two yachts have wintered afloat here. The stone breakwater running out from the shore on the W provides additional shelter from northerlies though not from northeasterlies which can blow fiercely off the hills.

Anchorage Yachts can anchor in the N part of the bay. Anchor in 2–4m and try to get as far N as you can without going aground, where there is better shelter from the swell pushed into the bay. If you go aground it is mostly mud. There is a fair amount of weed so make sure the anchor is well in.

Authorities Port police.

Ermioni South Quay

On the S side of the peninsula there is a protruding quayed area with 2–5m depths off it. The bottom drops off quickly to 10m and more. The rest of the quayed area is bordered by underwater rubble. The S quay is entirely open to southerlies and easterlies so does not provide all-round shelter. However, with offshore winds it is a delightful spot and comparatively peaceful in the summer compared with the other side of the headland.

Ermioni in Kólpos Idhras looking NE across Ák Kastrí with the harbour centre left   *Peter Kleinoth/MareTeam*

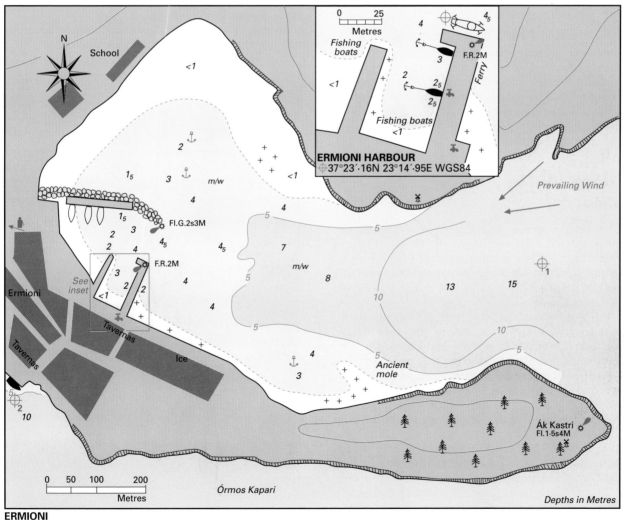

ERMIONI
⊕1 37°23´.24N 23°15´.68E WGS84
⊕2 37°22´.88N 23°14´.97E WGS84

Facilities

Water On the quay.

Fuel In the town. Delivered by mini-tanker.

Repairs Limited mechanical repairs. Hardware shop.

Provisions Good shopping for most provisions. Ice available.

Eating out Tavernas on the waterfront and on the S side of the headland.

Other PO. OTE. Bank. Greek gas and Camping Gaz. Car and motorbike hire. Hydrofoils to Piraeus and the islands in the Saronic Gulf.

General

The village has been relatively untouched by tourism although there are now several small hotels of what has been called the 'pour and fill' variety. Walk over the saddle of the town to the S side of the headland where things are peaceful and you can sit in a bar on the waterfront with wonderful views over the water.

In ancient times Ermioni was of some importance. The remains of an ancient mole and parts of a wall can be seen on the N side of Ák Kastrí. Pausanias records that a festival in honour of Poseidon was held here and depending on your interpretation of the ancient Greek, either swimming or boat races were held – it is possible Ermioni was the site of the first small boat regatta in recorded history.

ÓRMOS KAPARI

The large bay immediately S of Ermioni. In the SW corner there is good shelter from the normal summer winds. Anchor in 2–5m. The bottom is sand and weed – good holding. Care must be taken of Vrak Kapari, an islet and rocks lying to the E of the southern entrance point. Some of the rocks are only just above water and are difficult to see.

Nísos Ídhra

(Hydra)

The long narrow island lying parallel to the Peloponnisos coast and bordering the south side of Kólpos Ídhras. It is mountainous throughout, rising to the summit, Mt Eros (590m/1935ft), near the centre. It is everywhere arid and sterile and devoid of vegetation.

Ídhra appears not to have been of any importance in ancient times. It was during the centuries of Turkish rule that it prospered and built up a large mercantile marine fleet. It paid no taxes but supplied sailors for the Turkish fleet. In 1821 it was the first of the islands to pledge its sizeable fleet (some 150 ships) to the Greek cause. Admiral Miaoulis, admiral of the Greek fleet, was an Hydriot as were many of the other captains and sailors who distinguished themselves against the Turks. It has been said that but for the Hydriot fleet and sailors, the War of Independence would not have been won.

The Hydriot fleet never recovered from the war effort and Ídhra declined in importance to become a backwater of the Saronic until it was discovered by discerning travellers. It became a fashionable resort,

and in the early days of tourism the rich and famous holidayed in Ídhra, though now it is visited by larger numbers ferried in daily from Piraeus.

LIMÍN ÍDHRAS (Hydra, Ydra)

Approach

Conspicuous A white monastery on the hill above the harbour is conspicuous from some distance off. Closer in the small town of Ídhra built around the natural amphitheatre above the harbour will be seen.

By night Use the light on the E side Fl.R.1·5s3M and the lights at the entrance F.R.2M/F.G.2M.

Dangers Care is needed of the numerous craft, ferries and hydrofoils and pleasure craft, entering and leaving the narrow entrance, often at speed.

Mooring

Go stern or bows-to the town quay or the N mole. The latter has underwater ballasting projecting a short distance out in places so care is needed when berthing there. If possible go on the N mole in case N–NW winds blow. In the summer the harbour is very crowded and it is not unusual for yachts to be berthed three out from the quay. Crossed anchors are a fact of life here and there is little you can do about it. The bottom is mud and weed with some rocks – poor holding in places.

In settled weather very large yachts anchor outside the harbour with a long line to the mole.

Shelter With strong N–NW winds a dangerous surge develops and the only safe place is on the N mole.

Authorities Port police and customs.

Facilities

Water On the quay.

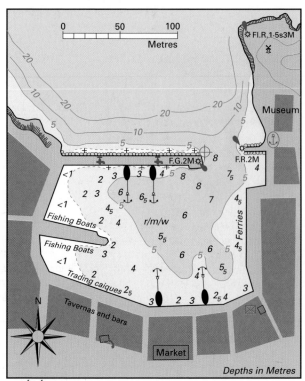

LIMÍN ÍDHRAS
⊕37°21′·1N 23°28′·0E

Ídhra (Hydra) harbour looking SE   *Peter Kleinoth/MareTeam*

Provisions Good shopping for most provisions. Ice from the market.
Eating out Tavernas on the waterfront and in the town. I suggest you go into the town away from the overpriced tavernas and bars on the waterfront.
Other PO. OTE. Bank. ATM. Greek gas and Camping Gaz. Ferries to Piraeus and the other islands in the Saronic Gulf.

General

Among the buildings of the town there are many large stately houses built in the time when Ídhra was a prosperous town and possessed a large mercantile fleet. In the 1950s and 60s Ídhra became a fashionable artists' colony attracting, amongst others, songwriter and performer Leonard Cohen, the champion of depressive and suicidal ballads. He still has a house here.

Later it became a popular tourist island, but it has not experienced the extensive development of Míkonos or Rhodes and remains architecturally very much of the 18th and 19th centuries. In the summer months there are about 10 ferries a day and perhaps one or two cruise ships anchored off or berthed in the tiny harbour.

MANDRAKI

A bay about ¾ mile E of Hydra. A hotel at the head of the bay is conspicuous. Good shelter from southerlies but open to northerlies. Anchor in

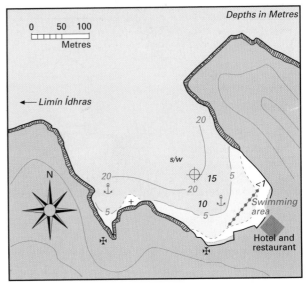

MANDRAKI
⊕37°21′·5N 23°28′·8E

5–10m. The bottom is sand, mud and weed – good holding. Tavernas ashore. Water taxi to Ídhra.

ANCHORAGES SW OF LIMÍN IDHRAS

Along the northern side and at the SW end of Ídhra there are several anchorages affording some shelter from the prevailing SE wind. At times there may be gusts off Ídhra though they vary in strength and duration.

1. **Vlíkhos** Anchor off the hamlet. Taverna ashore.
2. **Órmos Molos** A small bay opposite Nisís Kivolos. Taverna ashore.
3. **Petassi** Opposite the NE end of Nisís Petassi there are several small coves that can be used.
4. **Bisti** Under Ák Bisti there is a bay that can be used though it is quite deep.
5. **Áy Nikólaos** NE of Nisís Áy Nikólaos there is a large bay that can be used in calm weather. Marvellous surroundings and clear water make it very busy in the summer. When the prevailing wind gets up a swell is pushed in here.

NISÍS DHOKÓS

The bluff barren island off the SW end of Ídhra. Stenón Petassi, the channel between Ídhra and Dhokós, is deep and clear of dangers. The winds in this channel are variable and often die away altogether so it is best to motor through until they pick up again. One or two families live in Órmos Skindos on the north side of the island.

The island has a number of archaeological remains around the E side of Órmos Skindos and at times parts of it are closed off for archaeological digs. The remains here date from Mycenean and the early Hellenistic period. In the bay at the top there has been some excavation of an early Hellenistic trading ship.

Nisís Dhokós. Anchorage in the NW cove of Órmos Skindos

ÓRMOS SKINDOS

A large bay with a number of coves around the edges providing good shelter from the normal summer winds.

Órmos Skindos E side On the E side where possible. Anchor in 2–5m with a line ashore if necessary. Yachts also anchor SW of this anchorage. Reasonable shelter from the prevailing wind although at times it can be uncomfortable. The bay is popular as a lunch stop but is often deserted at night. Open W across the bay and NW.

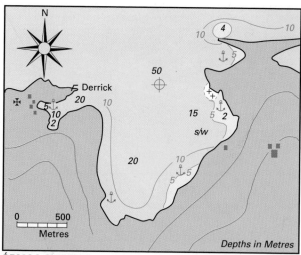

ÓRMOS SKINDOS
⊕37°20'·8N 23°20'·2E

Derrick Cove In the NW corner a small inlet with a number of houses around the shore provides good shelter. Anchor in 7–10m. Sand and weed bottom. The large buoy formerly in here has been moved but its substantial mooring chain is still on the bottom.

NISÍS TRIKERI

The islet midway between Ídhra and Spétsai. Fishing boats will often be seen around it. Between Tríkeri and Ídhra there is a chain of islets and islands: Asteri, Dhrápi, Strongiló, Dhisakki, Tagari, Karteli, Ventza and Alexandros. The red sector of the light on the E side of Báltiza Creek (Ák Fanári Fl.WR.5s18/14M red sector covers 254°-278°) covers these islands and rocks as well as Ifalos Tríkeri (least depth 5m) and Ifalos Aimilianos (least depth 7m) lying between Nisís Tríkeri and Spétsai.

Argolikós Kólpos

Argolikós Kólpos reaches back up to the north from the more southerly Saronic Islands of Spétsai and Ídhra. It is surrounded by high mountains except at the head of the gulf where there is the flat plain of Argos. The mountains on the western side of the gulf are the first of the Parnon range which continues right down the eastern side of the Peloponnisos to Ák Maléas. The mountains are rugged and barren and the shore inhospitable. Generally there are good depths close off the coast as the mountains drop sheer into the sea. The highest peaks are covered with snow in the winter and often well into the spring.

AIMILIANOS (Ak Aimilianos)

⊕20 0·5M S of Ák Aimilianós
37°16'·82N 23°12'·00E WGS84WGS84

A reef partly under the water on which the sea breaks extends about ¼ mile S of the cape. A white church on the cape is conspicuous. A small light structure marks the extremity of the reef

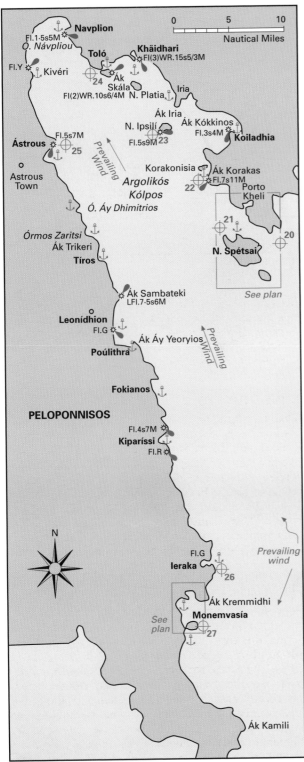

ARGOLIKOS KÓLPOS AND THE EASTERN PELOPONNISOS

⊕20 0·5M S of Ák Aimilianós
    37°16'·82N 23°12'·00E WGS84
⊕21 0·1M W of Petrokárovo light
    37°17'·08N 23°04'·67E WGS84
⊕22 0·25M W of Ák Kórakas
    37°21'·09N 23°03'·59E WGS84
⊕23 1M W of Nisís Ipsilí light
    37°25'·9N 22°57'·1E
⊕24 1M W of Ák Megalí (Toló)
    37°30'·6N 22°50'·3E
⊕25 0·5M E of Ák Ástrous
    37°24'·86N 22°46'·87E WGS84
⊕26 0·25M E of Ák Yérakas
    36°46'·17N 23°06'·90E WGS84
⊕27 0·25M E of Monemvásia headland
    36°41'·52N 23°03'·89E WGS84

(Fl.WR.10s8/6M red sector covers 314°-357° over Ifalos Milianós and Ifalos Tríkeri).

In the bay immediately W of Ák Milianós there are several attractive calm-weather anchorages.

Nísos Spétsai

The roughly oval island lying in the eastern approaches to Argolikós Kólpos. It has a gentler aspect than either Ídhra or Dhokós and the climate is described by the Admiralty *Pilot* as 'exceedingly healthy'. Much of the island is covered by pine trees planted in an inspired afforestation programme implemented in the early part of the last century. Unfortunately with the dawn of this century some of the forest has been destroyed by forest fires, many apparently caused deliberately. Most of the population lives in Spétsai town on the northern coast (conspicuous from the east).

Spétsai has the distinction of being the first island (with Ídhra) to revolt against the Turks and commit her merchant fleet to the Greek cause. The local heroine was Boubalina (many of the local boats are named after her) who commanded the Spétsai fleet – her most daring deed was the destruction of part of the Turkish fleet at Navplion with fire ships. The deed is commemorated by a regatta in September when a small *caïque* rigged out as an old trader is set on fire in the harbour accompanied by a noisy fireworks display and much merriment. Like Ídhra, the mercantile power of Spétsai declined after the War of Independence.

Spétsai town is more akin to the Italian Riviera than a Greek town although recent architectural additions have reduced the effect. Of late a number of large hotels have been built in the town to cater for the large numbers of tourists who descend on the island in the summer.

Just outside the town the buildings of the large public school, the Anarghyrios and Korghialenios School of Spétsai, was modelled on an English public school. John Fowles taught at the school for a time and his novel *The Magus* is set on the island – most of the places in the novel can be easily identified including the Villa Yasemia on the west coast where most of the action in the novel takes place. The school closed in 1984.

SPÉTSAI (BALTIZA CREEK) (Spetses, Balza, Palaio Limani)

BA 1683
Imray-Tetra G14

Approach

Conspicuous From the distance the houses of Spétsai town around the northern shores and on the gentle slopes are easily seen. Closer in, the lighthouse on Ák Fanári, the headland forming the E side of the harbour, and a number of whitewashed windmill towers (now converted to houses) are conspicuous.

By night Use the light on Ák Fanári Fl.WR.5s18/14M and the light on the extremity of the headland Q.R.3M.

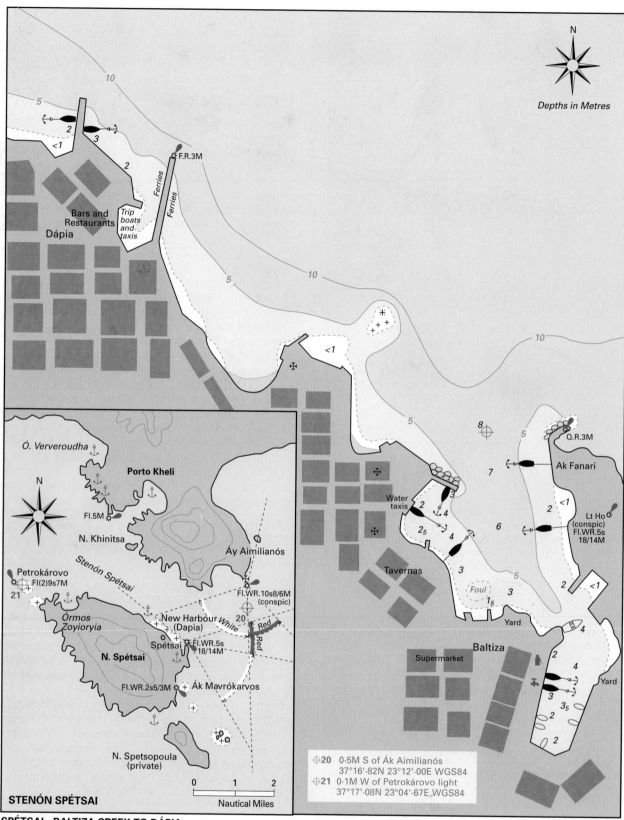

SPÉTSAI - BALTIZA CREEK TO DÁPIA
⊕ 37°15′·85N 23°09′·85E WGS84

Dangers

1. Care should be taken rounding the extremity of the headland where there are some above-water rocks and a short reef.
2. There is often a confused swell at the entrance with S winds.

Note A large unlit mooring buoy lies between Spetsai and Spetsopoula.

Mooring

Anchor in the bay with a long line ashore or stern or bows-to in the inner harbour if there is room. Báltiza Creek is a popular destination for yachts in the

Báltiza Creek on Spétsai looking NE out to the conspicuous lighthouse on the headland sheltering the E side of the creek
Peter Kleinoth/MareTeam

season and the inner harbour will usually be full to bursting and the outer harbour too crowded for you to swing at anchor. In the outer harbour the bottom is sand and weed (poor holding in patches) and in the SW corner there is a large permanent mooring chain fouling the bottom. In the inner harbour the bottom is mud – excellent holding.

Shelter With strong NW winds the outer harbour is uncomfortable and possibly dangerous for small yachts. Wash from the water–taxis in the outer harbour can be uncomfortable though not usually dangerous. The inner harbour has excellent all-round protection and a number of yachts are wintered afloat here.

Authorities Port police and customs in the new harbour. Charge band 2 in the inner harbour.

Facilities

Water On the quay. A € 10 charge for water in 2003.
Fuel On the quay.
Repairs Yachts can be hauled out in any one of the yards around the harbour, though you will need to book early to get a place. Some mechanical repairs. Old-fashioned wood repairs. Small chandlers. Hardware shops.
Provisions Good shopping for provisions near the harbour and in town. Ice available.
Eating out Good tavernas near the harbour and others in town.

Other PO. OTE. Banks. ATMs. Greek gas and Camping Gaz. Hire motorbikes and bicycles. Horse drawn gharries. Car ferry to Kósta across the Spétsai Strait and ferries and hydrofoils to Piraeus and the other islands in the Saronic Gulf.

General

Spétsai is an attractive town popular with tourists and Athenians alike. Spétsai restaurants often have an excellent dish peculiar to the island, fish *à la Spetsiosa*, a casserole of fish, tomatoes and green peppers covered in cheese – which is well worth sampling.

Spétsai old harbour and environs is a wonderful place to wander around. There are several yards building *caïques* and Spetsiot boats are said to be among the best in Greece. Tim Severin had his replica galley built here for his voyages tracing the routes of Jason and the Argonauts and Odysseus wandering home from the Trojan War.

Surrounding the harbour are many grand old houses built in the prosperous era of the 18th and 19th centuries when Spetsiot ships traded all over the eastern Mediterranean, and because no cars are allowed on the island (motorbikes unfortunately are), walking around the old quarter is a delight.

Nisís Petrokárovo off the NW tip of Spétsai looking SE

SPÉTSAI REEF

Between Baltiza Creek and Spétsai New Harbour (Dápia), a reef projects nearly 200m from the coast with 1m depths over it. Make sure when you are moving between the Dápia and Baltiza you do not cut the corner and come to grief on it.

SPÉTSAI NEW HARBOUR

Off the Dápia at Spétsai town there is a mole and a small boat harbour. The mole is reserved for ferries and the small boat harbour for local *caïque* ferries. A yacht will be turned away by the port police.

On the W side of the ferry mole and boat harbour there is a short mole and a quay. There are underwater rocks off the quay, but on the W side of the mole there are 2–5m depths. Go stern-to where convenient. There is usually an uncomfortable swell with the normal summer winds and it is untenable with northerlies.

ÓRMOS ZOYIORYIA

37°17'·0N 23°06'·4E

A large bay on the NW corner of Spétsai. Anchor in the bay in 5–8m. On the W side of the bay there is a small cove offering good shelter from all but NE–E winds. The bottom is sand with some rock – good holding. Sometimes at night a katabatic wind will blow out of Argolikós Kólpos from the NW making the bay uncomfortable and sometimes untenable. The cove on the W affords shelter from this wind.

The surroundings here are attractive with a wooded foreshore and clear water. A taverna on the shore.

NISÍS PETROKÁROVO

⊕21   0·1M W of Petrokárovo light
      37°17'·08N 23°04'·67E WGS84

The islet off the NW tip of Spétsai. It is lit: Fl(2)9s7M. Between the islet and Spétsai there is a reef which has a deep passage through it nearer to Spétsai than Petrokárovo. The reef is sometimes marked by 3 red buoys along its length although this cannot be relied upon. The prudent course is to go around the outside of Petrokáravo.

SPETSOPOULA

The small island lying off the SE tip of Spétsai. It is the private property of Stavrós Niarchos, (the ship owner whose fleet rivals that of the late Onassis), and landing is prohibited on it. There is a private harbour on the N end of the island where Niarchos' large yacht is sometimes moored. Care must be taken when navigating between Spétsai and Spetsopoula as there are a number of reefs in the general vicinity.

PORTO KHELI (Heli)

BA 1683
Imray-Tetra G14

Approach

Conspicuous A large white hotel on the SE side of the entrance and a number of large villas on the E side of the channel are conspicuous from the W. From the E Nisís Khinitsa is easily identified. Closer in the light structure on the W side and the beacon (white with a green band) marking the reef off the E side of the entrance will be seen.

By night Use the lights at the entrance: Fl.1·5s5M on the N side and Fl.G.3s3M on the beacon on the E side.

Porto Kheli anchorage and moorings on the NW side of the bay

The two beacons on the S side of the entrance to Porto Kheli
Lu Michell

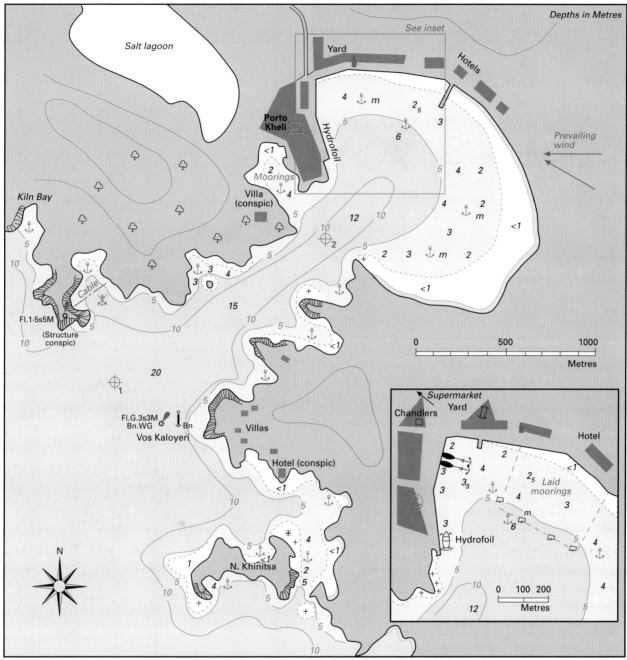

Depths in Metres

Salt lagoon

Yard

Hotels

Porto Kheli

Hydrofoil

Prevailing wind

Moorings

Villa (conspic)

Kiln Bay

Cable

Fl.1·5s5M

(Structure conspic)

Vos Kaloyeri

Fl.G.3s3M
Bn.WG
Bn

Villas

Hotel (conspic)

N. Khinitsa

N

0   500   1000
Metres

Supermarket

Chandlers   Yard

Hotel

Laid moorings

Hydrofoil

0   100   200
Metres

PORTO KHELI
⊕₁ 37°18′·67N 23°07′·85E WGS84
⊕₂ 37°19′·07N 23°08′·56E WGS84

Caution The channel between Nisís Khinitsa S of the entrance and the mainland has 2m depths in the fairway, but the bottom is uneven and extreme caution is needed when navigating through the channel. The prudent course is to keep to seaward of the island.

Mooring

Go stern or bows-to the quay or anchor off. The area in which you can anchor is marked by buoys around the outer limits. In fact much of this area is taken up by permanent moorings and yachts anchor outside the buoyed off area. The bottom is sticky mud – excellent holding.

Shelter Excellent all-round shelter. However, with the regular SE day breeze the berths on the quay can be uncomfortable with the slop that is kicked up across the bay. Numbers of yachts are wintered afloat here.

Authorities Port police and customs.

Anchorages On either side of the entrance channel into Porto Kheli there are numerous coves where a yacht can anchor depending on the wind direction (see plan). Shelter in the coves is generally good enough to overnight in most of them.

Facilities

Water Local water is brackish. Drinking water is delivered by tanker.

Fuel Near the quay. A mini-tanker delivers to the

Looking S down the quay at Porto Kheli   *Lu Michell*

quay.

Repairs Yachts are hauled at the boatyard here. Some mechanical repairs. Two chandlers. Frank's Yacht Station will look after yachts afloat (on moorings) or ashore. Wintering and repair work can be carried out. Most mechanical and light engineering work can be arranged. Life raft servicing. Yachts up to 20 tons can be craned out.

Frank's Yacht Station, Frank Wenzloff, Odos Costa 2, Porto Kheli, 21300 Greece

☎ 27540 52380 *Fax* 27540 51364

Provisions Good shopping for provisions. Ice available.

Eating out Tavernas around the waterfront and in the village. There seems to be a paucity of good tavernas, given the numbers of tourists here.

Other PO. OTE. Bank. ATM. Greek gas, Camping Gaz. Bus to Athens. Ferry (hydrofoil) to Piraeus and the islands in the Saronic Gulf.

General

The long quay was built in the 1960s when Porto Kheli was zoned as a NATO base. The plan was eventually shelved and the unfinished harbour and airstrip nearby, used today by small planes, are all that remain of the scheme. Over the years trees have been planted and roads laid so that what was a dust bowl is now more convivial.

Kheli or *heli* means eel in Greek, probably referring to the numbers of eels which once lived here, especially in the landlocked saltwater lagoon on the W side. The landlocked bay is not unattractive and is custom-made for water sports, so it is not surprising that a number of hotels have been built – in the summer the bay is busy with sailboards, dinghy sailors, paragliding, jet skis, water skiers, and a few swimmers taking their chances amongst the flotsam of skimming plastic and whirling propellers.

ÁK KÓRAKAS TO ÁK ÁY NIKÓLAOS

⊕22 0·25M W of Ák Kórakas
    37°21'·09N 23°03'·59E WGS84

NISÍS KORAKONISIA

⊕22 0·25M W of Ák Kórakas
    37°21'·09N 23°03'·59E WGS84

A small island lying immediately N of Ák Kórakas (light: Fl.7s11M). On the coast just N of the island there is a small bay sheltered from the normal summer wind. Anchor where convenient. The bottom is sand and rock – good holding. A few houses around the shore. You can also anchor in the cove on the E side of the island. Wonderful surroundings.

ÁK ÁY SPIRIDHION

Just N of this headland with a white church on it there is a bay affording reasonable shelter from the prevailing wind. Anchor in 4–5m off the beach. Taverna ashore in the summer.

In calm weather there are several other anchorages off sandy beaches in the vicinity.

KOILÁDHIA (Koilas, Kilas)

Approach

The large bay in the easternmost part of the gulf with the islet of Koiládhia in the entrance.

Conspicuous The white church on Ák Kókkinos is conspicuous and closer in the large church in the village will be seen. Nisís Koiládhia in the entrance is easily identified.

Koiládhia looking NW towards the village and conspicuous church

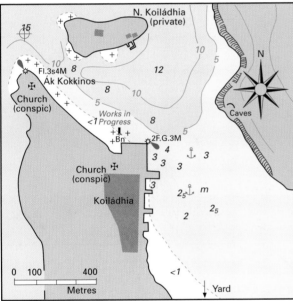

KOILÁDHIA
⊕37°25′·54N 23°06′·75E WGS84

By night A night entrance should be made with care. Use the light on Ák Kókkinos Fl.3s4M and the light on the pierhead 2F.G(vert)3M.

Dangers Care must be taken of the reefs bordering the channel off Ák Kókkinos and Nisís Koiládhia.

Mooring
Anchor off the village in 2–3m. The short pier off the village is usually crowded with fishing boats, but there may be spaces available. The bottom is mud – excellent holding.

Shelter Good all-round shelter in the bay. Boats are left on moorings here all year round.

Dangers
1. A submarine electricity cable runs across the entrance channel to the island. Anchoring is prohibited in the vicinity.
2. Works in progress on the N quay. It is likely that the quay will be extended out over the shallow water off the quay.

Note Nisís Koiládhia is privately owned by a ship owner and the small harbour on the SE side is private.

Facilities
Water On the quay.
Fuel Out of town. A mini-tanker can deliver to the quay.
Provisions Most provisions can be found. Ice available.
Repairs The boatyard round from Koiladhia still builds wooden *caïques* and can arrange to haul yachts. A 2m channel has been dredged to the boatyard and is marked with buoys. A 100-ton travel-hoist is reported to be in operation here. Take the dinghy across or walk around to check on details first.
Eating out Several tavernas on the waterfront which often have good fresh fish.
Other PO. OTE. Greek gas. Taxis.

General
Koiládhia is very much a proper working and fishing village with a large resident fleet. The look-alike reinforced concrete houses are not the image you may have of a Greek village, but the place grows on you and the locals are a friendly bunch.

In the Franchthi Caves, prominent on the E side of the anchorage, numerous prehistoric remains have been found, including a skeleton from the Mesolithic period, the oldest found in Greece.

NISÍS IPSILÍ AND NISÍS PLATIA

On the NE side of the gulf there are two islands. Nisís Ipsilí, the southern of the two, is a bold crescent-shaped island. Nisís Plátia to the N is of lower aspect.

There are no anchorages around Ipsilí as the depths are considerable right up to the edge. On Plátia there is an anchorage on the N side sheltered from the afternoon breeze blowing up the gulf, but fish farms now obstruct much of the anchorage.

OTHER ANCHORAGES

All around Ormos Vourlias, fish farms have sprung up to occupy every bight and bay that would otherwise be a good lunch stop anchorage.

On the E side of Ák Iria there is a solitary anchorage in a cove worth exploring. In settled weather a yacht can anchor off the long sandy beach by the hamlet of Kantia. The anchorage is exposed to the afternoon breeze so be prepared to move off when the wind gets up. Taverna ashore.

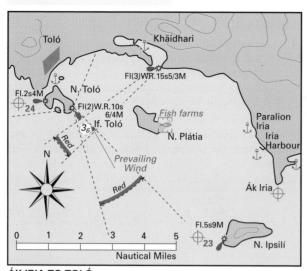

ÁK IRIA TO TOLÓ
⊕ 0·3M S of Ák Iria
37°27′·25N 23°00′·24E WGS84

⊕**23** 1M W of Nisís Ipsilí light 37°25′·9N 22°57′·1E
⊕**24** 1M W of Ák Megalí (Toló) 37°30′·6N 22°50′·3E

IRIA

37°28′·7N 22°59′·9E

A small harbour off the village of Iria. The harbour is very small and mostly occupied by local boats. There are just 2m depths in the entrance and 1–1·5m depths inside. With the normal SE sea breeze there is a swell at the entrance and it would be tricky trying to get in. Taverna ashore.

KHÄIDHARI (Dhrepano Vivari)

Approach

The entrance to the inlet is difficult to make out from the distance. When closer in the ruins of the fort on the W side and the light structure on the SE side will be seen. The entrance is deep and free of dangers.

By night The SE point is lit Fl(3)WR.15s5/3M. There are no other lights but with care a night entrance is possible.

Mooring

Go stern or bows-to the pier if there is room. There are 5m depths on the end and 1·5–3·5m depths on either side although care is needed as the depths are irregular in places. Alternatively anchor in 6–12m keeping clear of the permanent moorings in the W corner. The bottom is mud and weed, good holding.

Shelter Good all-round shelter.

Facilities

Water on the pier. Limited provisions in the village. Numerous tavernas on the waterfront.

General

Most people like Khäidhari and the entrance into the long inlet under the cliffs on either side makes it an impressive natural anchorage. The fort on the point is of Venetian origin signifying the harbours importance to Venetian trading ships.

Khäidhari looking E to the pier

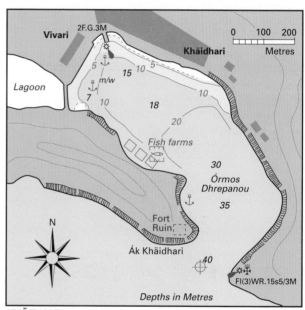

KHÄIDHARI
⊕37°31′·33N 22°55′·94E WGS84

TOLÓ (Tolon)

Approach

Conspicuous Nisís Plátia and Nisís Toló lying close off the coast are easily identified. A white chapel on a conical peak behind Toló village is conspicuous. The small harbour lies in Stenón Toló at the SW end of the village.

By night Use the light on the S end of Nisís Toló (Ák Skála Fl(2)WR.10s6/4M), on Ák Khäidhari (Fl(3)WR.15s5/3M) and on Ák Megalí (Fl.2s3M). The end of the mole is lit: 2F.R(vert)3M.

Dangers Ifalos Toló is a reef approximately ¾ of a mile SE of Ák Skála, the SE extremity of Nisís Toló. The reef has 3·5m least depth over it and is covered by the red sectors of the light on Ák Skála (315°–343°) and on Ák Khäidhari (046°–058°).

Mooring

Anchor off the village or go alongside or stern or bows-to the outside of the S mole. Much of the anchorage off the town is covered with permanent moorings. Inside the little harbour is usually crowded with fishing boats whose owners take exception to visiting yachts taking their spaces. The bottom is sand, good holding.

Shelter Off the village it can get bumpy with the afternoon breeze, but the holding on sand is good. Alongside the outside of the mole you are protected from the afternoon breeze, but completely exposed to westerlies.

Facilities

Water On the quay in the small harbour.
Fuel In the town. A mini-tanker can deliver to the quay.
Provisions Good shopping for provisions.
Eating out Numerous tavernas on the waterfront.
Other PO. OTE. Bank. ATM. Greek gas and Camping Gaz. Hire cars. Bus to Navplion. *Caïque* ferry to Astrous. Hydrofoil to Piraeus.

General

Toló was a small fishing village that has developed into a tourist resort on the strength of its sandy beach. Of late it has become very crowded with tourists on package holidays and little remains to remind you that fish, and not people, was once the principal industry here.

ÓRMOS KARATHONA

⊕ 37°32'·22N 22°48'·99E WGS84

The large bay between Toló and Navplion. A yacht can anchor at the southern end of the bay where there is some protection from the prevailing southerlies blowing up the gulf. The breakwater here provides additional shelter if you can get under it and take a long line to it. The passage between the islet and the breakwater has minimum depths of 5m in the fairway. In calm weather anchor in the N of the bay near the miniature fishing harbour. All around the bay the bottom slopes up gradually to the beach, and it is possible to anchor outside the buoyed swimming area in 6–8m. Tavernas ashore.

NAVPLION (Nauplion, Nauplia)

BA 1683

Approach

Conspicuous The large town will not be seen until around Akronavplia. A chapel on Ák Khondrós and a hotel on Akronavplia will be seen. The fortress of Palamidi will also be seen. Once close to the point the small fort on Nisís Bourtzi will be seen.

By night Use the light on Ák Panayítsa Fl.1·5s5M and the lights at the entrance (light buoy Q.R and Fl.G.3s3M).

VHF Ch 12, 16 for port authorities.

Mooring

Go alongside or stern or bows-to the quay in the large inner basin. The bottom is gooey mud which plough anchors will sometimes pull through.

Shelter Good shelter although strong NW winds cause an uncomfortable slop. If the swell becomes dangerous anchor off.

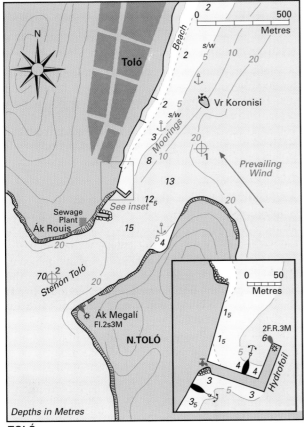

TOLÓ
⊕₁ 37°30'·97N 22°52'·02E WGS84
⊕₂ 37°30'·66N 22°51'·22E WGS84

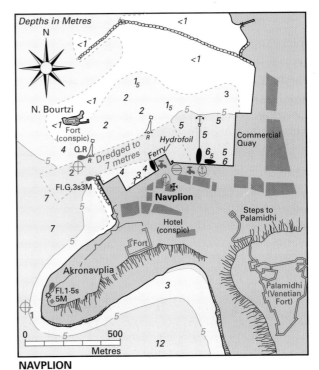

NAVPLION
⊕₁ 37°33'·76N 22°47'·34E WGS84
⊕₂ 37°34'·03N 22°47'·48E WGS84

213

Navplion looking W down from Palamidi. Yachts berth along the quay right of picture *Lu Michell*

Navplion quay looking NW to Nisís Bourtzi

Authorities A port of entry: port police, customs, and immigration.

Note Sewage empties into the harbour and with the summer heat it can get very smelly.

Facilities
Water On the quay when you can find the 'water man'.

Fuel In the town. A mini-tanker can deliver to the quay.

Repairs Some mechanical repairs. Good hardware shops.

Provisions Excellent shopping for provisions. Ice available.

Eating out Numerous tavernas in the town, including some quite sophisticated places in and around the old streets.

Other PO. OTE. Banks. ATM. Greek gas and Camping Gaz. Hire cars and motorbikes. Buses to Athens. Hydrofoil to Piraeus.

General
The large town of mostly 18th and 19th-century buildings, mainly two or three-storeyed and shuttered and balconied, is a gem. The stone houses seem to be engulfed in vegetation as they vie with each other to grow the biggest swathe of bougainvillea or clematis. The narrow cobbled streets wind in and out of modest mansions and less modest public buildings, many of them built in a golden sandstone that seems to absorb colour from the sun. Shops and tavernas are tucked away in streets everywhere. It is the sort of place you could willingly live in and has always been the most important city of the Argolid. At the beginning of the fledgling Greek Republic after the War of Independence, Navplion was briefly capital before Athens was chosen.

In the square the museum is the large building, originally built by the Venetians as a naval arsenal. It has a number of interesting exhibits including a suit of Mycenaean armour, a reminder that this whole area was the heartland of the Mycenaeans and in fact Navplion may have been a Mycenaean naval base at one time. Navplion is also thought to be the birthplace of Palamedes who is credited with the invention of lighthouses, the art of navigation, and the games of dice and knucklebones.

The Venetian citadel, Palamidi, is reached by a winding track of about 1000 steps. The hot climb is worthwhile, not only to view the most finely-preserved piece of Venetian military architecture in existence, but also for the view over the Argolic Gulf. Alas, the vast structure was out of date not long after it was completed. The citadel is open 0800–1845.

KIVERION 37°31'·4N 22°44'·0E
A bight on the coast opposite Navplion which is really only suitable before the afternoon breeze gets up. There is a short mole here with 1·5–3m depths off it, but it is usually occupied by fishing boats. If you can tuck behind it there is good shelter from the SE breeze. Alternatively in calm weather anchor off in 3–5m on mud and weed.

Good fish tavernas ashore.

ÁSTROUS (Astros, Paralion Astros)
Approach
Conspicuous The rocky headland, connected by a low isthmus (on which the village is built) to the Peloponnisos, looks like an island from the distance. Closer in, the castle and some houses on the headland and the lighthouse are conspicuous. From the N and E the village will not be seen until you are around the headland.

By night Use the light on Ák Ástrous Fl.5s7M and the lights at the entrance F.R.5M/F.G.5M.

Mooring
Go stern or bows-to either mole where convenient. The S mole usually has space free. Along the S mole the ballasting projects some distance underwater in places. The bottom is mud and weed – poor holding in places.

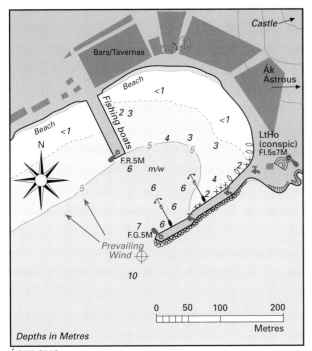

ÁSTROUS
⊕37°24´·76N 22°46´·01E WGS84

Shelter Good shelter from the prevailing southerlies. Care is needed at night as Ástrous is notorious for katabatic winds which blow strongly off the mountains from the NW–W in the evening – it is generally over in 3–4 hours.

Authorities Port police.

Facilities
Water On the quay.
Fuel On the outskirts of the village.
Provisions Most provisions can be obtained. Ice available.
Eating out Good tavernas on the waterfront and in the village.
Other PO. OTE. Irregular bus service to Ástrous town and Tripolis. Hydrofoil to Navplion and Piraeus.

Ástrous looking SW from the castle

Mycenae
(Mikinai)

This ancient city situated some nine miles from the head of Argolikós Kólpos was the centre of a great Helladic civilization between about 1650 and 1100 BC. Despite scholarly conjecture, it is widely accepted that the period dominated by Mycenae (and therefore called the Mycenaean period) fits in with the Achaeans of Homer's *Odyssey* and *Iliad*, although he probably telescoped events occurring over five centuries into a smaller timescale.

The site was occupied very early on, but not until 1700–1650 BC did it become important. Its position guards the approaches to the Argolic Gulf and the natural land route through the mountains to Corinth. The Mycenaeans were a militant race that quickly came to dominate Greece: their domain covered the whole of the Peloponnisos, the Aegean Islands, the Greek mainland and Crete.

Their cultural influence spread even further, to Asia Minor, Cyprus, Egypt and the Ionian Islands. The wealth of Mycenae was legendary and the dead were buried with lavish amounts of treasure, much of which was lost to grave robbers in later centuries. Particularly notable are the gold death masks, of which the mask of Agamemnon found by Heinrich Schliemann is the most famous. The Mycenaean period came to an abrupt end around 1000 BC and scholars are still at a loss to explain just what it was that stopped a great civilization in its tracks and put the clock back for four centuries in the Greek `Dark Ages'.

The site can be conveniently visited from Navplion (by taxi or bus) and there is enough for the layman to see to make it a worthwhile excursion. The site on a virtually treeless hill can be unbearably hot in the summer and it is recommended you go early in the morning and take a hat and water.

General
Ástrous is a bustling fishing village and tourist resort. The village is built around the slopes above the harbour with the new development along the long sandy beach around the bay. The harbour is one of my favourite places in the gulf and even with its tourism remains a likeable and very Greek village.

The medieval castle on the top of the hill is in reasonable condition and well worth the short walk up to it for the views over the gulf. Local folklore tells of a subterranean passage leading from the castle to the cave at sea level on the S side of the headland, but I haven't been able to find any trace of it. On the tip of the headland are the ruins of a large classical building.

The village around the harbour is properly called Paralion Ástrous and the main village of Ástrous is some 2½ miles inland. It is a down-to-earth agricultural town in the middle of a region which is noted for its orchards and particularly for its peaches. Also nearby is Moní Loukous, a large monastery approximately 2½ miles from the village, which is worth a visit.

ANCHORAGES BETWEEN ÁSTROUS AND TIROS

Along the steep-to coast between Ástrous and Leonídhion are several anchorages suitable as lunch stops in calm weather.

Áy Dhimitrios 37°20'·0N 22°48'·5E
   The bay under Ák Áy Dhimitrios. Tucked into the cove on the S you can overnight with care although any northerlies will mean you must leave.

Órmos Krionéri Anchor in the SW corner. Really only a lunch stop.

TIROS

Approach

A short mole on the S side of Órmos Tiros. From the S it will not be seen until you are around Ák Tiros which has 3 windmills running down the ridge.

By night The end of the mole is lit Fl.R.3s3M.

Mooring

If you can find a space behind the mole go stern or bows-to. Make sure you do not obstruct the hydrofoil quay although I have been told it now only runs in July and August. Care is needed of a patch of rock ballasting about one third up from the root of the mole. Care is also needed of permanent mooring lines everywhere.

Shelter Good shelter from the SE sea breeze.

Anchorage In calm weather anchor in the S part of the bay tucked under the mole as much as possible and take a long line ashore.

Facilities

Water On the mole.
Fuel Some way out of town.
Provisions Good shopping for provisions
Eating out Tavernas and cafés along the waterfront.
Other PO. Bank. Hire cars and motorbikes. Hydrofoil to Piraeus.

General

Tiros is a busy resort popular with the Germans and French. The long sandy beach is permanently occupied and the waterfront hums with the sounds of drinking and eating and having fun. In July and August it is a bit too busy for my taste, but in the spring and autumn it is well worth a visit.

LEONÍDHION (Leonideon, Pláka)

Approach

Conspicuous The harbour is difficult to locate from the distance. A mill converted to a house on the beach to the N of the harbour and a white church behind the harbour can be identified closer in. The hotel in the village will also be seen. Only a small part of the mole is visible as most of it is behind a continuation of the beach.

By night Use the light on Ák Sambateki LFl.7·5s6M and the light on the extremity of the mole Fl.G.1·5s3M.

Dangers With the normal southerly sea breeze there is a confused swell in the entrance.

Note The extension to the mole has been completed although care is needed in the approaches by night until the light is re-sited at the new head. The extremity of the works has been marked by a buoy Fl.G.2·4s.

Mooring

Go stern or bows-to the mole. The bottom is hard sand with some rocks – poor holding in patches. Care is needed of underwater ballast in places. The iron ladder roughly halfway along the mole marks the end of the underwater ballast off the quay.

Shelter Shelter is much improved with the extension to the mole although there is still a bit of a surge from the prevailing SE wind until it dies at night.

Authorities Port police.

Facilities

Water On the quay.
Provisions Some provisions.
Eating out Good tavernas on the waterfront.
Other Bank in Leonídhion town. Taxis. Hydrofoil to Piraeus.

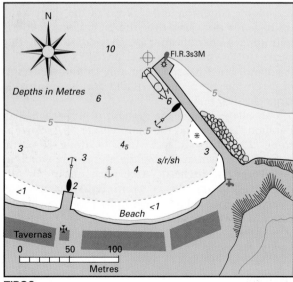

TIROS
⊕37°14'·8N 22°52'·1E

Leonídhion (Pláka) looking NE before the breakwater was extended

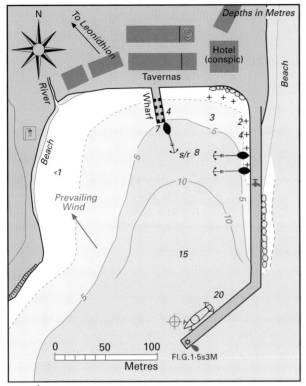

LEONÍDHION
⊕37°08´·7N 22°53´·6E

General

The small hamlet under the towering cliffs is a pleasant, mostly unspoilt spot. The fertile valley (citrus, olives, figs and market gardening) winds between the high mountains to Leonídhion town – a modest place untouched by tourism. About 30 minutes away by taxi is the small monastery of Elonas, on a spectacular cliffside site reminiscent of those at Meteori. It is well worth visiting. The surrounding Parnon range is rugged and steep-to with cliffs dropping sheer for 600–700m (2,000–2,300ft).

In the region around Leonídhion a dialect known as 'Tsakonika' used to be spoken by the older inhabitants and is considered to be a link between ancient (Doric) and modern (Demotic) Greek.

POÚLITHRA

Poúlithra light F.R.3M 37°07´·1N 22°54´·2E

A small fishing harbour 2 miles S of Leonídhion. A white church near the harbour is conspicuous. There is room for one or maybe two yachts amongst the fishing boats on the stubby mole. Go stern or bows-to the short mole. Care is needed of rock ballasting extending underwater from the quay so it is best to go bows-to here. Good shelter from the normal summer southerlies. With northerlies a swell works its way into the harbour. Tavernas ashore. The hamlet of Poúlithra is about 15 minutes' walk away and enjoys a modest tourist trade in the summer.

FOKIANAS (Phokianos)

37°04´·1N 22°59´·2E

A bay lying just S of Ák Turkoviglia. With the normal summer wind from the SE it is untenable, but it affords good shelter from the northerlies. A cove in the NE corner has reasonable shelter. Care is needed of large permanent moorings on the bottom which may foul an anchor. Permanent bottom nets have also been reported. A beach runs around the head of the bay under the steep slopes behind – wonderful wild surroundings.

KIPARÍSSI (Kyparissi)

Approach

This large bay lies about 5 miles S of Fokianas. On the N side of the entrance a conspicuous road scar runs around the coast and on the S side a pylon communications tower is conspicuous. The houses of the hamlet cannot be seen until you are in the entrance to the bay and it can be difficult to identify just where it is from the distance.

By night There are lights on either side of the entrance: N side (Ák Aspro Kórtia) Fl.4s7M and S side (Ák Nisáki) Fl.R.1·5s3M.

Mooring

There are several places a yacht can go, depending on wind and sea.

1. *Kiparíssi town pier* When southerlies are blowing the ferries and hydrofoil use the town pier. Care is needed of the reef running out from the shore approximately 50 metres NW of the pier. Go alongside the SW side of the pier. Alternatively you can anchor off the village in 3–8m keeping clear of the pier. Adequate shelter in calm weather or light southerlies. Untenable with strong NE winds.
2. *N ferry pier* If the N pier is not being used by the ferry go alongside. Alternatively anchor to the

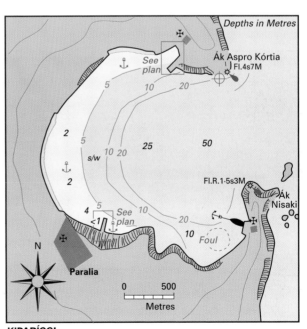

KIPARÍSSI
⊕36°59´·1N 23°00´·4E

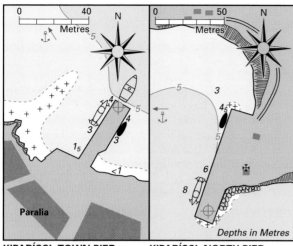

KIPARÍSSI: TOWN PIER
⊕36°58'·3N 22°59'·7E

KIPARÍSSI: NORTH PIER
⊕36°59'·0N 23°00'·0E

Kiparíssi. The anchorage off the village   *Nigel Patten*

W of the pier keeping clear of the approaches for the ferry. Reasonable shelter when it blows from the NE.

3. ***Chapel Cove*** In the SE corner of the bay there is a short quay close off the chapel here. Go stern or bows-to if there is room. It is very deep (15–20m) a short distance off so you will be dropping the anchor in fairly deep water. Good shelter from southerlies and adequate from NE winds.

Note The bottom is mostly sand and thick weed, not everywhere good holding.

Facilities
Provisions and tavernas in the village. PO. OTE. Hydrofoil and ferry to Piraeus and Monemvasía.

General
The small village is quite unspoilt and the bay, surrounded by mountains, a spectacular spot. Chapel Cove in the SE corner is my favourite spot in Kiparíssi with good shelter and just a few fishermen cleaning their nets under the chapel for company.

The short quay off the chapel on the SE side of Kiparíssi

IERAKA (Yérakas)
Approach
The narrow entrance between the high cliffs is difficult to locate even quite close in.

Conspicuous From the N a church on a knoll about one mile NW of Ák Vathi is conspicuous. The light structure will only be seen from a short distance off when approaching from the N.

By night The approach is difficult as the light at the entrance (Ák Kástro Fl.G.3s5M) is partially obscured by the surrounding hills.

Dangers With strong northerlies there is a confused reflected swell in the approaches and in the entrance.

Mooring
Go bows-to the quay keeping clear of the ferry and hydrofoil berths. Some care needs to be taken as the depths are uneven and underwater rocks litter the bottom off the quay. Some of the tavernas have depths marked on the quay, but these depths are usually a bit out from the quay so take care. Shallow-draught craft can go through the bottleneck and anchor at the entrance to the lagoon. The bottom is mud with some rocks and weed, reasonable holding.

Shelter Good all-round shelter, although a surge develops with strong northerlies – uncomfortable, but not normally dangerous. If you are on the quay the surge causes yachts to roll considerably, making things uncomfortable – go ashore for a meal!

Facilities
Tavernas and a café ashore. Some provisions from a little shop. Ferry to Piraeus in the summer.

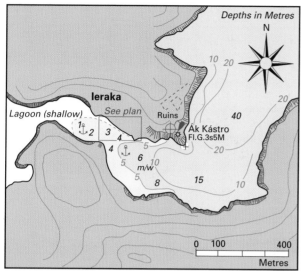

IERAKA
⊕36°47′·2N 23°05′·3E

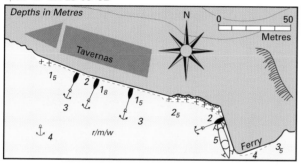

General

The small hamlet surrounded by the hostile mountains of the Parnon is hardly touched by outside influences. In the hot afternoon sun out of the cooling reach of the *meltemi* the whole hamlet snoozes until the cool of evening when things come to life again. On the summit of the entrance is an extensive ruined acropolis, probably of Mycenaean origin.

Ieraka looking W from Ák Kástro

MONEMVASÍA (Monemvassi)

BA 1683
Imray-Tetra G15

Approach

Conspicuous The humpbacked island of Monemvasía (likened to a little Gibraltar) connected to the Peloponnisos by a causeway is easily identified from the distance. Closer in the village of Yefira on the mainland will be seen.

From the S the old village of stone houses on the S side of Monemvásia tends to blend into the rocky background and is difficult to see until closer in. If heading for the marina it can be difficult to pick out the breakwater. Head for the last white house on the outskirts of Yefira.

By night Use the light on the end of Nisís Monemvasía Fl.5s11M and the light on the end of the mole Fl.R.2s3M. The end of the marina breakwater is not lit.

Dangers With the *meltemi* there are fierce gusts in the approaches to the bay.

Mooring

If there is space in the marina then go alongside the outer breakwater or alongside the end of the pontoons. The outer pontoon is partially sunk and reported unusable. Inner berths at the marina are occupied by local boats. If the marina is full, as it often is in the summer, then there may be space on the inside of the ferry mole on the N side of the causeway or anchor off on the S side of the causeway.

Note In the 'marina' the square concrete mooring blocks for the pontoons have been laid on the bottom and reduce depths by around 0·4–0·6m. They are easily seen.

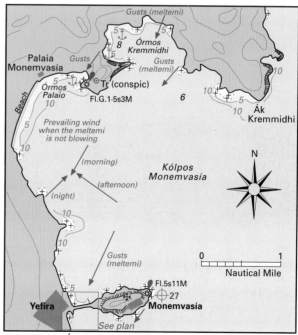

MONEMVASÍA APPROACHES

⊕27 0·25M E of Monemvásia headland
36°41′·52N 23°03′·89E WGS84

219

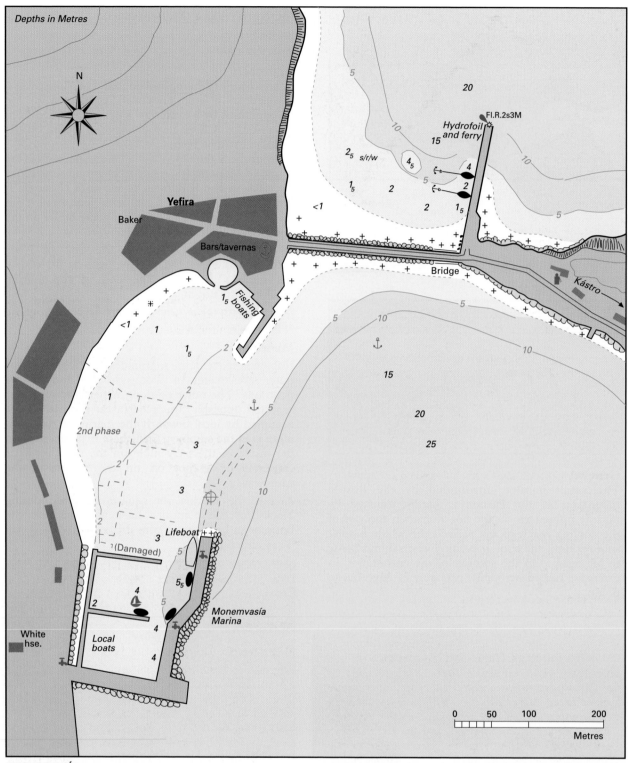

MONEMVASÍA
⊕36°41′·03N 23°02′·38E WGS84

Shelter Good shelter in the marina. Good shelter from southerlies under the ferry mole and adequate with the NE *meltemi*. The *meltemi* causes a surge behind the ferry mole and you will roll around, so make sure you have plenty of fenders out to avoid damage to the topsides from boats on either side. The anchorage on the S side of the causeway is adequate with light southerlies and provides reasonable protection from the *meltemi*, although some swell works its way around the headland and you will roll at anchor.

Authorities Port police and customs in Yefira.

Anchorage If anchoring under the causeway you will be in reasonably deep water, typically around 12–15m. Try to anchor as close towards the fishing harbour as possible. The bottom is sand, rocks and weed, poor holding in patches.

Monemvasía 'marina' looking ENE towards Monemvasía

Facilities
Water On the breakwater quay in the marina.
Fuel Near the root of the mole. A mini-tanker can deliver.
Repairs Minor mechanical repairs. Hardware shop.
Provisions Good shopping for all provisions. Ice available.
Eating out Good tavernas. In the old village on the island there are a number of excellent tavernas in a romantic setting between the steep slopes and the sea. Good *ouzeries* around the fishing harbour.
Other PO. OTE. Bank. ATM. Greek gas and Camping Gaz. Ferry (hydrofoil and regular ferry) to Piraeus.

General
Monemvasía Island was called Minoa in ancient times, suggesting a Cretan influence. Until the 20th century it was an important port, the last port of call before setting off around Cape Malea. The old fortified village is of Byzantine origin although the Venetians rebuilt much of it.

You should not miss an opportunity to visit the old village which is slowly coming to life again in a sympathetic way. The gift shops and restaurants do not detract from its character if you squint your eyes and don't dally too long. There are a number of interesting churches in the village, but to get to the best of them, Ayia Sofia, you will have to climb up the zig-zag path behind the village to the summit. The fortified path and tunnel into the fort with its iron gates still intact is as impressive as the fortifications at the top, and if you run out of breath on the way up it is a good excuse to sit down and enjoy the superb views down onto the roofs of the old village and out over the sea.

Ayia Sofia stands on the very edge of a sheer cliff on the N side with what the *Blue Guide* quaintly describes as a 'view of wild grandeur at sunset'. The church has interesting frescoes and its situation on the edge of the cliff affords a view of the wild hinterland of the Peloponnisos and the grand sweep of Kólpos Monemvasias.

In the past Monemvasía was called Malmsey or Malvoise by the French, hence the name of the famous red and white wines shipped (but not necessarily grown in the region) from the port in its heyday. The strong sweet red wine was known to travel well and hence was much in demand on the extended voyages in the age of sail – and from this we should learn the lesson that a small yacht is not the place for good wine, especially delicate whites and some of the more fragile reds, so drink up before any of that good wine you have on board goes off.

ANCHORAGES IN KÓLPOS MONEMVASÍA
Órmos Palaio Palaio light 36°43'·9N 23°02'·4E
In the NW corner of Kólpos Monemvasía this small bay offers good shelter from all but W–SW winds. Care must be taken of the reef off the southern entrance. The S entrance is lit: Fl.G.1·5s3M. Anchor in 6–8m on a sandy bottom. From about the 6m line into the head of the bay large permanent moorings foul the bottom. There are a few villas and fishermen's houses around the bay.

Órmos Kremmidhi Lies just around the cape from Órmos Palaio. Open to the S–SE. Anchor in 5–8m on a sandy bottom. The severe gusts into the bay with the *meltemi* mean you must be sure your anchor is in. If in doubt lay a second anchor.

Islands lying off the Peloponnisos
Between the Peloponnisos coast and Mílos and Sífnos there are several small and uninhabited islets.

Nisís Parapóla (Belopoula) light 36°55'·8N 23°17'·2E
An islet lying approximately 21 miles off the coast from a point midway between Kiparíssi and Ieraka. It is quite high at 227m (745ft) and easily seen by day. It is lit on the N: Fl(2)20s22M. It is reported that the bay on the SW side affords some shelter from NE winds.

Nisídhes Karavi 36°46'·2N 23°36'·4E
A group of three small islets that look like one from the distance. Although the maximum height is only 33m (110ft) they are easily identified by day. Care is needed to give the islets a wide berth as they are sometimes used by the Greek air force for target practice and I would suggest, having been one mile off while live rockets were used, that a yacht keep at least 3 and preferably more miles off the islets. (There is no mention in the relevant publications of the fact that it is a prohibited zone.)

Nisís Falkonéra 36°50'·4N 23°53'·4E
The high bold islet lying approximately midway between Parapóla and Mílos. It is easily identified by day and is lit on the S end Fl.5s17M. It is reported that a bay on the SW side affords shelter from N winds, but as with other islands in the vicinity, there are likely to be fierce gusts off the lee side.

V. The Cyclades
(Kikladhes Nisoi)

This is the central group of islands in the Aegean, so named because they more or less surround Delos, the ancient centre of trade and worship (*kukloi* = rings). I will not attempt to describe the islands here, but describe each separately when I come to them. To impose some order on the scattered islands they are broken down into three sections: northern, middle and southern Cyclades.

Northern Cyclades Kéa, Kíthnos, Síros, Andros, Tínos, Míkonos, Delos and Rinia.

Middle Cyclades Sérifos, Sífnos, Andíparos, Páros, Naxos, Dhenoussa, Iráklia, Skhinoússa, Koufonisia, Amorgós and Lévitha.

Southern Cyclades Mílos, Kímolos, Folégandros, Síkonos, Ios, Thíra and Anáfi.

Weather patterns in the Cyclades

The prevailing wind in the summer is the infamous *meltemi* blowing from the NE–N–NW. The *meltemi* begins to blow fitfully at first in June, blows strongest in July, August and September, and dies during October. In July and August the *meltemi* blows at Force 5–6 and may reach Force 7–8 on occasions. It may blow for 1–3 days or it may sometimes blow for 2 weeks at a time. There is no way of knowing just how long it will blow. It has a

Síros		
Frequency	Weather forecast	Nav warnings
VHF Ch 04	0600, 1000, 1600,	0500, 1100, 1730,
(announce Ch 16)	2200 UTC	2330 UTC

Saronic		
Frequency	Weather forecast	Nav warnings
VHF Ch 25	0600, 1000, 1600,	0500, 1100, 1730,
(announce Ch 16)	2200 UTC	2330 UTC

Pérama		
Frequency	Weather forecast	Nav warnings
VHF Ch 86	0600, 1000, 1600,	0500, 1100, 1730,
(announce Ch 16)	2200 UTC	2330 UTC

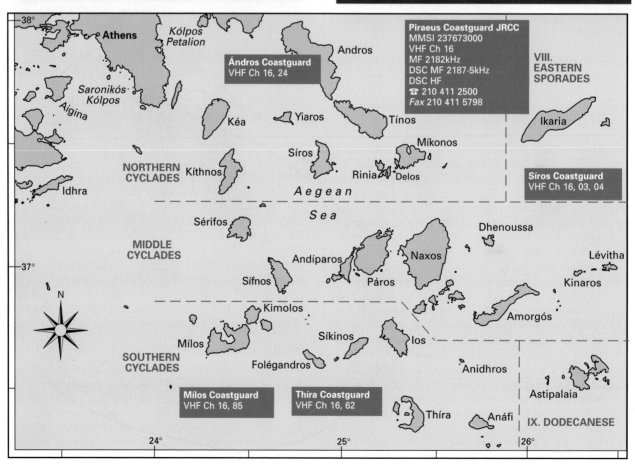

thermal component in that it loses some strength at night and increases again in the day.

In June and again in late September the wind strength is considerably less at about Force 4–5 and there may be wind from other directions. The direction of the *meltemi* varies down through the Cyclades. In the northern Cyclades it blows from the NE, curving to blow from the N in the middle Cyclades and curving again to blow from the NW–WNW in the southern Cyclades. In the SW islands of the Cyclades the wind is marginally less strong than in the northern and eastern islands.

In the spring and autumn the wind is predominantly from the N although there are also winds from the S. Gales are commonly from the N or the SE.

Note Care must be taken of violent gusts off the high land on the lee side of the islands when the *meltemi* is blowing. These gusts may be considerably stronger than the wind strength on the open sea – gusts of Force 7–8 may be experienced when the wind on the open sea is Force 5–6. At times small whirlwinds may accompany the gusts which strike with great force and very quickly. Places noted for these squalls are the Doro Channel between Evia and Andros, the south coasts of Andros and Tínos, Yiaros, the Kéa Channel, Míkinos, Naxos and the islands S of it, the S coast of Amorgós, Kímolos, Folégandros, and the S side of Ios.

In the summer months the Cyclades are hot and temperatures average 25°–26°C (79°F) and often reach 33°–35°C (95°F). In the summer there is very little if any rain and many of the islands run short of water towards the end of the season. Snow will only fall on the peaks of Andros and occasionally Tínos in the winter.

Routes

Route planning in the Cyclades is really a matter of going E or W. Anyone who has sailed there will know that getting back through the islands from the E against the *meltemi* is the problem. If you are going E the *meltemi* blowing down from the NE–N–NW will give you a sleigh ride to the Dodecanese or Crete. At times there will be too much wind even for a beam reach and you may have to bear off under headsail alone, but overall choosing the route to the E is more a matter of personal choice than of weather considerations.

How to get back to windward through the Cyclades is a much debated point. I favour going S in a great semicircle around the southern Cyclades where the wind is less strong and you can make to the N through the Saronic islands. From Kós or Kalimnos head for Astipálaia, Anáfi, Thíra, Íos, Folégandros, Kímolos and Mílos. At times the *meltemi* can be just as strong around Íos/Folégandros/Mílos as elsewhere, so you may need to keep going to the Peloponnisos! Others maintain that you should go N in the eastern Cyclades or the Dodecanese and then W through the northern Cyclades. One thing is clear – going E through the Cyclades is infinitely preferable to going W when the *meltemi* is blowing.

Data

PORTS OF ENTRY
Ermoúpolis (Síros)
Mikonos
Adhamas (Milos)
Thira

PROHIBITED AREAS
Nisídhes Karavi is sometimes used for target practice by the air force.

MAJOR LIGHTS
Northern Cyclades
Kéa
Áy Nikólaos Fl(2)10s15M
Ák Tamélos Fl(2)15s17M

Kíthnos
Ák Kéfalos Fl.4s9M
Ák Áy Dhimítrios Fl.10s12M
Ák Mérikha Fl.WR.5s5/3M

Síros
Nisís Gáïdharos Fl.6s12M
N Aspronisi Fl(2)12s7M
Nisís Náta Fl.3s6M
Ermoúpolis Fl.G.3s6M
Ák Trímeson Fl(2)14s12M

Ák Velostási Fl(3)12s6M

Andros
Ák Fássa Fl.10s25M
Ák Kastrí Fl.6s8M
Ák Kolóna Fl.3s5M
Órmos Kástrou Fl(2)15s6M
Ák Griá Fl.10s25M
Vrákhoi Kalóyeroi (Kaloyeri Reef) Fl(2)15s17M
Ák Áy Kosmás Fl.3s.7M

Tínos
Nisís Dhisvaton Fl.10s16M
Ák Livádha Fl.15s7M
Limín Tínou Fl.R.3s7M
N Planitís Fl(2)14s10M

Míkonos
Ák Armenistís Fl.10s22M
Nisídhes Prassonisía Fl.3s6M

Middle Cyclades
Sérifos
Ák Spathí Fl(3)30s19M
Ák Kíklops Fl(2)14s9M

Sífnos
Ák Fílippos Fl.5s9M
Ák Kokkála Fl(2)10s9M
Ák Maistros Fl.2s7M
Ák Stavrós Fl.1·5s5M

Páros
Vk Portes Fl(2)10s7M
Ák Áy Fokas Fl.4s6M
Ák Kratzi Fl(3)WG.15s12/10M
Ák Kórakas LFl.12s14M
Vk Mirmingas Fl.5s8M
Ns Strongilo Fl(2)14s5M

Naxos
Limín Náxou Fl.R.4s7M
Ák Stavrós Fl(2)16s13M
Vrákhoi Amarídhes Fl.WR.4s5/3M
Vrakhónisos Kopriá Fl(2)12s10M

Dhenoussa
Ák Kalota Fl.(3)15s10M

Iráklia
Nisís Mikró Avélos Fl(3)10s7M

Skhinoúsa
Mirsini Fl.4s6M

Amorgós
Ák Goniá Fl.8s11M
Órmos Katápola/Ák Áy Ilías Fl(2)10s12M
Áy Annas/Ák Langadhia Fl.5s8M
Nisídhes Liadhi (N) Fl(2)20s9M

Lévitha
Ák Spanó Fl.10s11M

Southern Cyclades
Mílos
Nisídhes Akrádhia Fl.10s10M
Ák Bombárdha Fl.5s12M
Andímilos Fl.2s8M
Nisís Paximádhi Fl(2)15s12M
Nisís Ananes Fl(3)12s9M

Políagos
Ák Máskoula Fl.5s19M

Folégandros
Ák Asprópounda Fl(3)30s17M

Síkinos
Órmos Skála Fl.5s8M

Íos
Ák Fanári Fl.5s9M

Thíra
Ák Akrotíri Fl.10s24M
Epanomeria Fl.4s7M
Nisídhes Khristianá Fl(3)9s10M

Quick reference guide

Northern Cyclades	Shelter	Mooring	Fuel	Water	Provisioning	Tavernas	Plan
Kéa							
Áy Nikólaou	B	AC	B	A	B	B	●
Órmos Pisa	C	C	O	O	O	O	
Órmos Kavia	B	C	O	B	C	C	●
Khalidhoniki	B	C	O	O	O	C	●
Órmos Polais	O	C	O	O	O	O	●
Kíthnos							
Órmos Kolóna	B	C	O	O	O	O	●
Órmos Fikiadha	B	C	O	O	O	O	●
Mérikha	B	AC	B	B	B	B	●
Loutra	A	ABC	B	A	C	B	●
Áy Stefanos	B	C	O	B	O	C	●
Kanala	O	C	O	O	O	O	
Síros							
Ermoúpolis	AB	A	B	A	A	A	●
Nisís Gáïdharos	B	C	O	O	O	O	●
Órmos Varis	B	C	O	O	C	C	●
Finikas	A	AC	B	A	B	B	●
Posidhonía	C	C	O	B	C	C	●
Órmos Galissas	C	C	O	B	C	C	●
Órmos Kini	C	C	O	B	C	C	●
Órmos Delfino	B	C	O	O	O	O	●
Órmos Aetou	C	C	O	O	O	O	●
Órmos Grammata	B	C	O	O	O	O	●
Andros							
Gavrion	B	AC	B	A	B	B	●
Órmos Petros	C	C	O	B	O	C	
Órmos Fournos	C	C	O	B	O	C	
Batsí	B	AC	B	A	B	B	●
Palaioupolis	O	C	O	O	O	C	
Órmos Plaka	C	C	O	O	O	O	
Kástro	B	AC	B	A	B	B	●
Korthion	C	AC	O	B	C	C	●
Tínos							
Tínos	A	A	B	A	A	B	●
East coast anchorages	C	C	O	O	O	C	
Órmos Panormou	C	C	O	B	C	C	●
Órmos Kolombithra	C	C	O	O	O	O	
Míkonos							
Míkonos Marina	A	AB	B	B	C	C	●
Órmos Ornos	B	C	O	O	O	C	●
Órmos Áy Annas	B	C	O	O	O	C	●
Panormos	C	C	O	O	O	C	
Rinia							
Delos Channel	B	C	O	O	O	O	●
Órmos Skhinou	C	C	O	O	O	O	●
South Bay	B	C	O	B	O	O	●
Órmos Miso	B	C	O	O	O	O	●
Órmos Kormou Ammos	C	C	O	O	O	O	
Middle Cyclades							
Sérifos							
Livádhi	A	AC	B	A	B	B	●
Órmos Koutala	B	C	O	B	C	C	●
Mega Livádhi	B	C	O	O	O	O	
Sífnos							
Áy Yeóryios	B	C	O	O	O	C	
Kamáres	B	AC	B	A	B	B	●
Órmos Vathí	B	AC	O	B	C	C	●
Órmos Fikiadha	C	C	O	O	O	O	●
Órmos Platí Yialos	C	C	O	O	C	C	●
Faros	B	C	O	B	C	C	●
Kástro	O	C	O	B	B	C	●
Andíparos							
Órmos Dhespotico	B	C	O	O	O	O	●

	Shelter	Mooring	Fuel	Water	Provisioning	Tavernas	Plan
Andíparos	C	C	O	O	B	C	●
Páros							
Paroikía	B	AC	B	B	A	A	●
Órmos Naoúsis	A	C	O	B	O	C	●
Náoussa	B	AC	B	A	B	B	●
Órmos Filizi	C	C	O	O	O	O	●
Órmos Marmara	C	C	O	O	O	O	
Piso Livádhi	B	AC	O	A	C	B	●
Órmos Faranga	C	C	O	O	O	O	●
Aliki	B	C	O	O	O	C	●
Naxos							
Naxos	B	ABC	B	A	A	A	●
Órmos Áy Prokopiou	C	C	O	O	O	C	●
Áy Annas	B	AC	O	A	C	B	●
Órmos Kouroupa	C	C	O	O	O	O	●
Órmos Kalando	C	C	O	O	O	O	
Órmos Panormou	C	C	O	O	O	O	
Órmos Moutsouna	O	C	O	O	O	C	
Apollonia	O	C	O	B	C	C	●
Dhenoussa							
Órmos Roússa	C	C	O	O	O	C	●
Órmos Dhendhro and Stavrós	B	C	O	O	C	C	●
Iráklia							
Áyios Yeóryios	C	C	O	O	C	C	●
Órmos Livadhi	C	C	O	O	O	C	
Órmos Pigadhi	C	C	O	O	O	O	
Skhinoúsa							
Órmos Mirsini	B	AC	O	O	C	C	●
Agrilos	C	C	O	O	O	O	●
Koufonisia							
Koufonisia	C	C	O	B	C	C	●
Parianós	B	AC	O	O	O	O	●
Dhrima and Andíkaros	C	C	O	O	O	O	●
Amorgós							
Katápola	B	AC	B	A	B	B	●
Órmos Kalotaritissa	B	AC	O	O	O	C	●
Órmos Akrotíri	C	C	O	O	O	C	
Kalotiri	C	C	O	O	O	C	●
Órmos Áy Annas	B	AC	O	B	C	C	●
Órmos Vilakardha	O	C	O	O	O	O	
Lévitha and Kinaros							
Órmos Lévitha	A	C	O	O	O	C	●
Órmos Vathi	B	C	O	O	O	O	
Órmos Pningo	B	C	O	O	O	O	
Southern Cyclades							
Mílos							
Adhamas	B	AC	B	A	A	A	●
Apollonia	B	AC	O	B	C	B	●
Voudhia	C	C	O	O	O	C	●
Kímolos							
Sikia	C	C	O	O	O	O	●
Psathi	C	AC	O	O	C	C	●
Sémina	C	C	O	O	O	O	
Pirgonisi	B	C	O	O	O	O	●
Prasonisi	O	C	O	O	O	O	
Políagos							
Nisís Manolonisi	C	C	O	O	O	O	●
Folégandros							
Karavostási	B	AC	O	O	C	B	●
Vathi	C	C	O	O	O	O	●
Síkinos							
Skála	B	C	O	B	C	C	●
Íos							
Íos	A	A	B	B	B	B	●
Órmos Koumbaras	C	C	O	O	O	C	

	Shelter	Mooring	Fuel	Water	Provisioning	Tavernas	Plan
Órmos Milopotamou	C	C	O	O	O	C	•
Órmos Manganari	B	C	O	O	O	C	•
Órmos Tris Klises	B	C	O	O	O	O	•
Thíra							
Áy Nikólaos (Thirasia)	C	C	O	O	C	C	
Finikia	C	C	O	O	C	C	
Skála Thíra	C	AB	O	B	A	A	•
Vlikadha	A	AB	B	B	C	C	•
Monolithos	C	A	O	B	O	O	•
Néa Kammeni							
(SE cove)	B	AB	O	O	O	O	•
Anáfi							
Skála	C	C	O	O	O	C	•

Northern Cyclades

Nísos Kéa
(Zéa, Tzia)

A craggy and mountainous island lying a little over 12 miles east of Ák Sounion in the approaches to the Kólpos Petalíon. A high mountain ridge runs down the east coast with the summit, Mt. Ayias Ilías (561m/1,840ft), near the east coast 4 miles south of the northern extremity of Kéa. Most of the inhabitants live in the *chora* (Kéa) or at Áy Nikólaos. The island is mostly barren although there are patches of cultivated and wooded ground near the coast.

In ancient times the island was considerably more important than it is now. It had four cities and produced the lyric poets Simonides and Bacchlides and the physician Erasistratos. A few ruins of the cities remain and there is a large lion with a face like a big pussy cat carved out of a rock face (about 6m/20ft long) to the east of the *chora*. The ancient Kéans were apparently noted for their modesty and temperance. Today the population is much diminished (about 2,000), as the young leave the island to find work in Athens.

USEFUL WAYPOINTS FOR N. CYCLADES
Note: waypoints follow the order of the islands in this chapter.
⊕1 1M N of Ák Perlevos (Kéa)
    37°42'·3N 24°21'·0E
⊕2 0·2M S of Ák Tamelos (Kéa)
    37°31'·14N 24°16'·50E WGS84
⊕3 0·25M N of Ák Kéfalos (Kíthnos)
    37°29'·21N 24°26'·01E WGS84
⊕4 1M S of Ák Áy Dhimítrios (Kíthnos)
    37°17'·1N 24°21'·9E
⊕5 0·5M N of Ák Trímeson (Síros)
    37°31'·4N 24°53'·0E
⊕6 0·2M S of Ák Velostási (Síros)
    37°21'·58N 24°52'·53E WGS84
⊕7 0·2M S of Ák Khondra (Síros)
    37°22'·75N 24°56'·60E WGS84
⊕8 Mid-channel Stenón Kafírevs (Andros/Evia)
    37°58'·4N 24°37'·7E
⊕9 Mid-channel Stenón Dhisvaton (Andros/Tínos)
    37°40'·6N 24°58'·0E
⊕10 Mid-channel Stenón Mikonou (Tínos/Míkonos)
    37°30'·9N 25°16'·4E
⊕11 0·75M N of Ák Via (Rinia)
    37°27'·12N 25°13'·58E WGS84
⊕12 0·25M off Delos E side (Prasonísia channel)
    37°23'·63N 25°17'·11E WGS84
⊕13 1M S of Nisís Khatapodhia light
    37°23'·7N 25°33'·8E

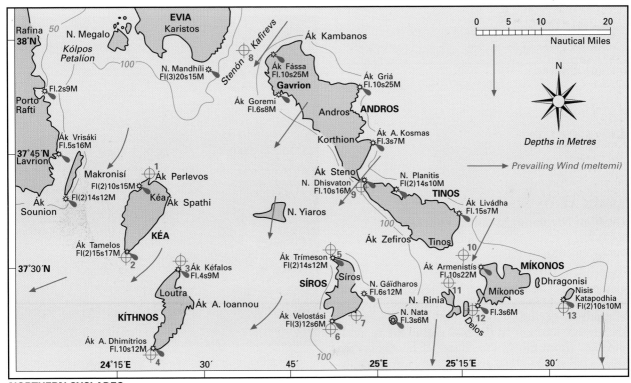

NORTHERN CYCLADES

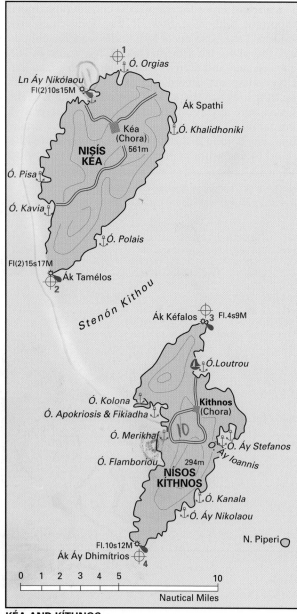

KÉA AND KÍTHNOS

⊕1 1M N of Ák Perlevos (Kéa)
   37°42'·3N 24°21'·0E
⊕2 0·2M S of Ák Tamelos (Kéa)
   37°31'·14N 24°16'·50E WGS84
⊕3 0·25M N of Ák Kéfalos (Kíthnos)
   37°29'·21N 24°26'·01E WGS84
⊕4 1M S of Ák Áy Dhimítrios (Kíthnos)
   37°17'·1N 24°21'·9E

LIMÍN ÁYIOS NIKÓLAOU

(Aghiou Nicolaou, Livádhi, Vourkari)
BA 1538
Imray-Tetra G31

Approach

Conspicuous The village or *chora* (Kéa) on the hill behind the harbour is visible from the N. The entrance is not easy to spot from the distance but the general location on the NW end of the island is obvious. From the W the cluster of houses on the slopes behind Vourkari will be seen. Closer in the chapel and light (on top) on the N side and a church

on the S side of the entrance are conspicuous.

By night Use the lights on either side of the entrance: N side Fl(2)10s15M/S side Fl.1·5s5M. The mole at Korissía is lit: Fl.G.3s3M.

Note With the *meltemi* there are strong gusts off the high land in the vicinity of the harbour.

Mooring

There are three possibilities:

1. ***Órmos Livádhi*** The S arm of the bay. Moor stern or bows-to the quay at Korissía keeping clear of the ferry berth behind the mole. Reasonable shelter from the *meltemi*. Alternatively anchor off in the bay in calm weather. The bottom is mud and weed, not everywhere good holding.

2. ***Vourkari*** The NE arm of the bay. Anchor in the bay or go stern or bows-to the quay in the space indicated on the plan. The bottom comes up quickly just before the quay and consequently it is best to go bows-to if possible. On either side of

The chapel-cum-lighthouse on the N side of the entrance to Limín Áy Nikólaou

Áyios Nikólaou on Kéa looking W with Voukari in the foreground and Órmos Livádhi top left

Peter Kleinoth/MareTeam

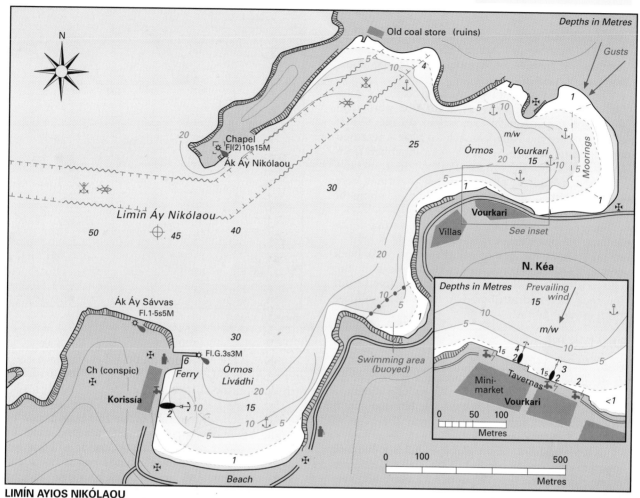

LIMÍN AYIOS NIKÓLAOU
⊕37°39′·89N 24°18′·67E WGS84

this space it is too shallow off the quay. The bottom drops off quickly here (over 10m depths 30m out from the quay) so make sure you have an adequate length of chain or line to let go. The bottom is mud and weed and not everywhere good holding. It is reported there is a cable fouling the bottom about 30m off the quay. As the *meltemi* blows straight on to the quay ensure your anchor is holding before tying up to the quay. If you are anchoring off there are laid moorings off the E side of the bay, but you can anchor amongst the moored boats with care. Alternatively anchor outside the area with laid moorings in 8–12m.

In the summer there are a lot of yachts using this bay.

3. **Coal Bunker Bay** Anchor off the old coal bunkering depot in the N arm of the bay clear of the underwater cables. Good shelter from N winds. The bottom is mud and weed, indifferent holding.

Authorities Port police at Korissía.

Facilities

Services Water and electricity points on the quay at Vourkari. Water on the quay at Korissía. Water is often in short supply in the summer and may be rationed.

Fuel Near the quay at Korissía. A mini-tanker can deliver to the quay (☎ 24100).
Provisions Some provisions available at Vourkari and Korissía.
Eating out Tavernas at Vourkari and Korissía.
Other Telephone. Irregular bus to the *chora*. Ferry to Lavrion.

The quay at Vourkari

General

Áyios Nikólaos is more often than not crowded in the summer with Athens-based yachts, the picturesque hamlet of Vourkari being the most popular.

The bay was once important as a coaling station for steamers plying between Black Sea ports and western Europe. Recent excavations on the N side of the bay by the American school have unearthed an important Bronze Age settlement inhabited from around 2000 BC to 1400 BC. Pottery, domestic and ornamental, and the classic Cycladic figurines have been unearthed amongst the buildings, many of which are now just under the sea.

The *chora* on the hill, a huddle of glaring white houses, is picturesque and well worth a visit – enquire about the bus to get there and walk back downhill. About 20 minutes' walk to the E of the village is the large lion (the 'pussy cat') carved from the rock face and attributed to an Ionian sculptor from around 600 BC.

ÓRMOS PISA (Pisses)

37°36'·1N 24°16'·6E

A small bay on the W coast about 1½ miles N of Ák Makropoundha. Open to the W and S. With the *meltemi* some swell creeps into the bay making it uncomfortable. Anchor in 4–8m near the head of the bay. Sandy bottom.

Tavernas ashore. The valley behind is a startling green in comparison to most of the island. There are a few ruins of ancient Piessa here, a comparatively minor ancient town of the island.

There is a cove immediately N of Órmos Pisa that looks good, but it is very deep even close in.

ÓRMOS KAVIA (Koundouros)

A small bay lying approximately one mile to the E of Ák Makropoundha. Care must be taken of a reef lying about ¼M SSW of Makropoundha. Waves break on it with a slight swell and it is relatively easy to spot. A number of windmills on the slopes around the bay are conspicuous as well as a large building on the N side of the entrance to the bay.

Anchor in 3–6m on sand and rock. The holding is mediocre so make sure the anchor is well in. Good shelter from the *meltemi*, although some swell creeps around into the bay making it uncomfortable. A

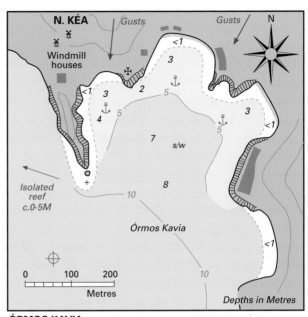

ÓRMOS KAVIA
⊕37°34'·44N 24°16'·13E WGS84

number of old mooring blocks and chains have been reported on the bottom so it may be wise to use a trip-line on the anchor.

The bay is being developed with new hotels and houses which, with the exception of a brown blob of a building, fit reasonably well into the landscape. In spite of reports to the contrary Manos still has his taverna in Ormos Kavia. Manos can arrange for provisions, gas, ice, water, fuel, showers, indeed anything it is possible to procure on Kéa. He speaks English, French, Arabic and a little German. Well worth a visit if only to sample his first-rate ouzo. Limited provisions and tavernas ashore.

ORGIAS (Otzias) 37°40'·5N 24°21'·3E

A small cove on the N side of Kéa suitable in calm weather only. Anchor in 5–6m near the head of the inlet. A line of small buoys marks the limit of the swimming area at the head of the cove. There are a few houses around the slopes and a taverna opens in the summer.

Órmos Kavia looking NNE from the entrance   *Lu Michell*

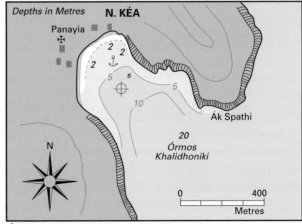

ÓRMOS KHALIDHONIKI (Spathi)
⊕37°38'·6N 24°24'·5E

Note A rock above water has been reported 0·4M E of the entrance to Orgias.

KHALIDHONIKI

A small cove on the NE corner of the island under Ák Spathí. Anchor near the head of the cove in 3–5m on a sandy bottom. Good shelter from the *meltemi* although some swell is pushed into the cove. Open S. A small hamlet ashore and a taverna at the head of the bay.

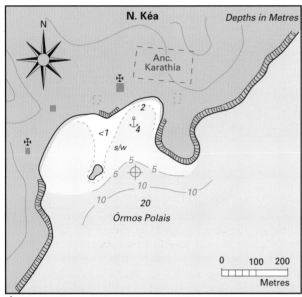

ÓRMOS POLAIS
⊕37°33′·4N 24°20′·05E

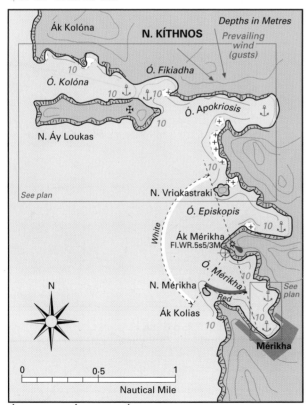

ÓRMOS KOLÓNA TO MÉRIKHA
⊕37°23′·65N 24°23′·5E

ÓRMOS POLAIS

An open bay on the SE coast of Kéa 3 miles NE of Ák Tamélos. In the middle of the bay there is a small islet joined by a reef to the shore. Anchor to the E of the islet and the reef in 3–4m. The bottom is sand and weed with some rock and not everywhere good holding. The *meltemi* tends to send some swell in here so use it in light northerlies or calm weather.

There are a few ancient ruins ashore including the remains of a temple belonging to ancient Karathia. Some of the ancient city walls and the theatre can also be found.

Nísos Kíthnos
(Kythnos, Thermia)

A barren rocky island lying a little over 6 miles SE of Kéa. The hump of the island is highest in the middle where the summit reaches 294m (965ft). Despite its modest height, the island is so folded and steep-to that it gives the impression of being more savage and higher from seawards than figures suggest. The population mostly lives in the *chora* (Kíthnos) on the hill above Órmos Apokriosis and in Mérikha. The island has some tourist trade in the summer, but on the whole is little touched by tourism.

KOLÓNA, APOKRIOSIS AND FIKIADHA
Approach
These bays are situated about one mile to the N of Mérikha where the huddle of houses around the harbour is conspicuous. Care should be taken of the underwater rocks on the S side of the entrance to Órmos Apokriosis and on the NE side of the entrance to Fikiadha.

By night There are no lights.

Dangers With the *meltemi* there are strong gusts into the approaches and the bays.

Mooring
Órmos Kolóna (Sand Bar Bay) Anchor in the NE corner in 3–6m on sand. In the summer the bay is popular so it is common practice to take a long line ashore to the N side. The bottom is sand and good holding. Good shelter from the *meltemi*. Open W.

Órmos Fikiadha Anchor in 3–5m on sand and weed, good holding once the anchor is through the weed. Good shelter from the *meltemi* although there are gusts into the bay. Open S for a limited sector.

Órmos Apokriosis Anchor in 5–10m on sand and weed. You can take a long line ashore to the N side for added security. Good shelter from the *meltemi*. Open SW–W.

Facilities
Taverna at Apokriosis and Fikiadha.

General
The bays provide good shelter in pleasant surroundings. Development has slowly been

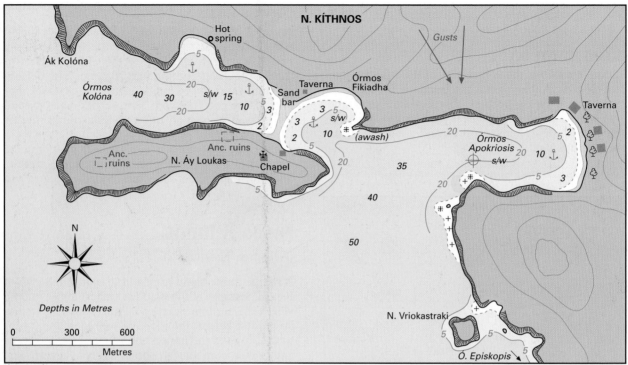

Ó. KOLÓNA, FIKIADHA AND APOKRIOSIS
⊕37°24'.9N 24°23'.5E

extending northwards from Merikha, but has not really affected these bays yet.

On Nisís Áy Louka, the islet connected to Kíthnos by the sand bar, are a few ancient remains including traces of walls, a temple and *agora*. On the N side of Órmos Kolona it is reported there is a hot spring.

EPISKOPIS

Lies in between Mérikha and Órmos Apokriosis. With the *meltemi* some swell enters the bay. In calm weather or with SE–E winds anchor in 3–10m where convenient. Open to the W. A taverna opens in the summer.

MÉRIKHA (Merikhas)

Approach

A small harbour on the W coast and the ferry port of Kíthnos. The buildings of the town are conspicuous from seaward.

By night Use the light on Ák Mérikha Fl.WR.5s5/3M: the red sector covers Vrak Mérikha on the S side of the entrance 340°-R-030°. The end of the ferry mole is lit Fl.R.3s3M.

Mooring

Go stern or bows-to the quay inside the ferry berth or anchor off. Make sure you let out plenty of scope and that the anchor is well in to cope with the ferry and the fast ferry which will often use the propellers to keep them off the quay and in so doing create a lot of wash.

Shelter Reasonable shelter from the *meltemi* although there are strong gusts into the bay that can be uncomfortable. Any wind with any W in it sends a swell into the harbour. Strong SW–W winds may make it untenable.

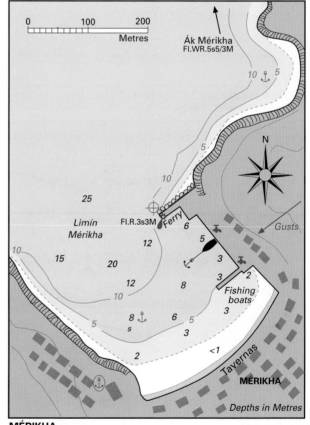

MÉRIKHA
⊕37°23'.45N 24°23'.75E WGS84

Mérikha on Kíthnos looking NW with Fikiadha and Apokriosis at the top of the photo — *Peter Kleinoth/MareTeam*

Authorities Port police and customs.

Facilities

Water On the quay, but you will need to track down the water man

Fuel Can be delivered by mini-tanker.

Provisions Some provisions can be found although supplies are much dependent on the ferry. Ice.

Eating out Tavernas on the waterfront.

Other PO. Greek gas. Bus to the *chora*. Ferry to Lavrion.

General

Mérikha is a comparative newcomer of a village, really built to service the ferry port. It is effectively the biggest place on Kíthnos (the *chora* has more houses but less in the way of services) and the tavernas on the beach are pleasant enough places to while away an evening while the *meltemi* screams down into the bay.

It is worth hiring a motorbike from here to look around the island, though care is needed on the roads which are both steep and in poor repair in many places.

LOUTRA (Loutron, Port Irene)

Approach

The entrance to the bay is difficult to pick out from the distance until close to. The light structure on the S side of the entrance is difficult to spot. Once up to the entrance some of the houses on the S side of Loutra will be seen.

By night Use the light on Ák Kéfalos Fl.4s9M and the light on the S side of the entrance Fl.1·5s5M.

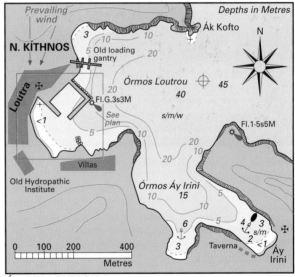

ÓRMOS LOUTROU
⊕37°26′·66N 24°25′·97E WGS84

The dogleg corner of the basin at Loutra is lit Fl.G.3s3M.

Caution With the *meltemi* there is a considerable amount of wind and sea pushing you into the bay. As the basin has limited manoeuvring space it is prudent to prepare the boat for berthing in the outer part of the bay.

Mooring

Loutra Go alongside either side of the outer arm of the basin or stern or bows-to the NE mole.

Yachts normally go alongside the outer quay because otherwise anchors would be criss-crossed inside the small basin. Excellent shelter inside the basin although there are gusts with the *meltemi*. In settled weather or when the basin is full yachts can go stern or bows-to the quay N of the basin. Care is needed of underwater ballasting in places.

Áy Irini Anchor and take a long line ashore to the NE side. There are a number of rings set into the rock for lines. The quay is too shallow to berth stern or bows-to. Reasonable shelter from the *meltemi* although some swell is pushed into here making it uncomfortable.

Facilities

Services Water and electricity points on the quay at Loutra. Showers in the taverna ashore.

Fuel May be able to get a mini-tanker down to the harbour.

Provisions Some provisions.

Loutra on Kíthnos looking NNW with Órmos Áy Irini bottom right and the yacht quay off the village middle left (taken before the new basin was built)   *Peter Kleinoth/MareTeam*

Loutra harbour looking NW

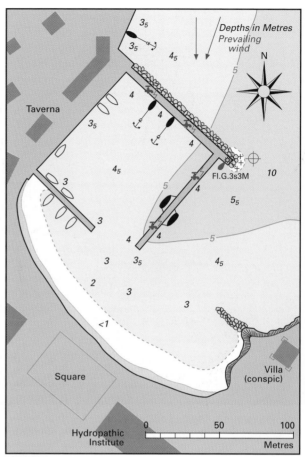

LOUTRA
⊕37°26′·6N 24°25′·7E

Eating out Several tavernas and cafés. Taverna at Áy Irini.

Other PO. Telephone.

General

The hot mineral springs have been esteemed throughout history except for the present age when spa resorts have become unfashionable. The ancient Greeks and Romans used them and King Otto, Greece's first king, built the institute now standing. The hot springs still run and you can take a bath at the institute although it is pretty run-down these days. Alternatively, hot springs bubble up at the S end of the beach and you can take your own spa bath there.

Near Ák Kéfalos (about two hours' walk) are the ruins of a medieval citadel and town, though few buildings remain intact.

ÁYIOS STEFANOS AND ÁYIOS ÍOANNIS

BA 1538

Two bays on the E coast of Kíthnos affording good shelter from the *meltemi*. There are gusts off the high land at the entrance. Care should be taken of the reef lying 100m SE of the headland separating the two bays.

Anchor near the head of either bay and take a line ashore to a tree or a rock. The bottom is sand and weed – bad holding in places. Good shelter from the *meltemi* despite the gusts once you are securely anchored.

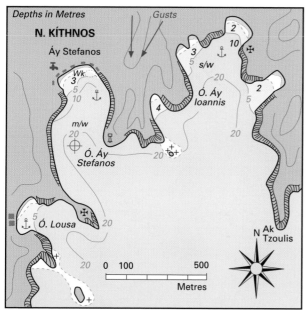

Ó. AYIOS STEFANOS AND Ó. AYIOS IOANNIS
⊕37°23′·6N 24°27′·6E

There is an uncharted wreck reported lying in the NE corner of Ormos Ayios Stefanos in 5–6m, with 1·5–2m over.

Limited water ashore. The taverna at Áy Stefanos offers showers, ice and water in the summer.

A number of modest villas and one palatial villa have been built here in these beautiful bays. The slopes behind drop precipitously down to the sea which is the clearest blue. It is an enchanting spot once you have got used to the wind whistling down into it and well worth a visit.

LEFKES

37°22′·4N 24°27′·0E

A tiny cove approximately 1M S of Órmos Lousa. It would probably not pay to be here with the *meltemi*, but in calm weather the cove at the foot of a ravine is a spectacular spot. Taverna ashore.

ÓRMOS KANALA AND ÓRMOS ÁY NIKOLAOS (Skillou)

Ó Kanala 37°20′·7N 24°26′·2E

Ó Áy Nikolaos 37°19′·8N 24°25′·3E

These lie respectively 4½ and 6¼ miles SW of Ák Áy Ioannis, the easternmost tip of Kíthnos. They offer indifferent shelter from the *meltemi*, but can be visited in calm weather. Both are open to the S and E. Care is needed of an isolated reef off the entrance to Órmos Kanala. No facilities.

Near Kanala is the monastery of the Panayía Kanala, the Virgin of the Canal, because reputedly the icon of the virgin in the monastery was discovered in a canal, though exactly where is uncertain. Her feast days are 15 August and 8 September when large numbers of pilgrims are said to come here.

Nísos Síros
(Syros, Syra)

A hilly, mostly barren island. The north is rugged and mostly uninhabited while the south has gentler slopes and is cultivated near the coast. Most of the population live in Ermoúpolis, the port and also the nominal capital of all the Cyclades.

Nothing much remains of ancient Síros which was sited where Ermoúpolis now stands. In the Middle Ages the inhabitants moved inland until the Venetians, ever mindful of the potential of the harbour and the strategic position of Síros along the Aegean trade route, occupied the island and restored its prosperity. In the 17th century the island came under the protection of the French and so escaped Turkish occupation. Síros took no part in the Greek War of Independence, but did take refugees from Psará and Khíos.

In the steam age Síros became the principal port in the Aegean and a major coal-bunkering station for ships on passage through the Cyclades. Its importance declined when oil replaced coal and ships could do longer passages without the need to refuel.

The twin villages on the two hills behind the harbour reflect the island's history. Old Síros

NÍSOS SÍROS

⊕5 0·5M N of Ák Trímeson (Síros)
    37°31′·4N 24°53′·0E
⊕6 0·2M S of Ák Velostási (Síros)
    37°21′·58N 24°52′·53E WGS84
⊕7 0·2M S of Ák Khondra (Síros)
    37°22′·75N 24°56′·60E WGS84

became the Venetian and Genoese Roman Catholic village and the descendants remain predominantly Roman Catholic. The Psariote and Khiot refugees established Ermoúpolis (Hermoupolis: named after Hermes, the god of traders) which is the Greek Orthodox quarter. Ermoúpolis has spilled over from its original site and now spreads around the waterfront. The port is still a mercantile centre and a major ferry port. The island is also famous for the production of *loukoumi* or Turkish Delight which here is excellent and not to be confused with some of the sickly-sweet imitations made elsewhere.

ERMOÚPOLIS (Limín Sirou)

BA 1538

Imray-Tetra G31

Approach

Conspicuous The twin villages on the hill above the harbour are easily seen from the distance. The most conspicuous object is the lighthouse on Nisís Gaïdharos which is easily identified from a considerable distance off. Closer in a large cathedral on the slopes behind the town and the breakwaters are conspicuous.

By night Use the light on Nisís Aspronisi Fl(2)12s7M and Nisís Gaïdharos Fl.6s12M. The entrance to the harbour is lit: Ák Kondoyiánnis Fl.3s5M; the N breakwater head Fl.G.3s6M and S breakwater Fl.R.3s6M and F.Y. Ifalos Karfomeni is marked by a light buoy Q.R though it is not to be relied upon.

Danger
1. Care is needed of Ifalos Karfomeni, a reef and shoal water on the SW side of the harbour. It is marked by a light buoy Q.R(occas).

   If a yacht keeps close to the end of the N breakwater where there are good depths, the bunkering station and reef are easily avoided.
2. Care is needed of the large ferries constantly churning in and out of the harbour.

Mooring

Go stern or bows-to the quay on the NE side of the harbour. Use the shorelines supplied and keep well pulled off the quay. No laid moorings but the

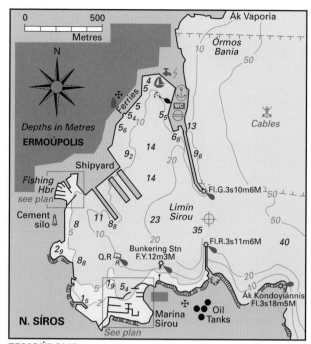

ERMOÚPOLIS
⊕37°26'·15N 24°56'·9E

bottom is mud – good holding.

Shelter Good shelter from the *meltemi* although there are gusts and a surge develops making it uncomfortable, as does the wash from ferries. With SE winds a swell rolls in making the harbour very uncomfortable and possibly dangerous for small yachts.

Note The harbour is very smelly in places from sewage emptying into it.

Authorities A port of entry: customs, port police and immigration authorities.

For Marina Sirou and the fishing harbour on the W side of the harbour see below.

Facilities

Services Water and electricity points on the quay.

Fuel Near the W quay. ☎ 22810 23784 or call on VHF Ch 8 for a mini-tanker.

Repairs There are several yards here which can haul yachts.

Approaches to Ermoúpolis looking NNW

Lefteris Akilas 65-ton hydraulic lift. 4m depths at slipway.

☎ 22810 23682 *Fax* 22810 23445.

Vangelis Tzortis Sledge and slipway. Used to hauling yachts.

☎ 22810 87086 *Fax* 22810 86000.

The commercial dry-dock is now open again and can take very large craft. Mechanical and engineering repairs. Chandlers near the yacht yards. Sail repairs can be carried out – go to the cheese shop at Chiou 28!

Provisions Good shopping for all provisions nearby. Near the W end of the town quay there is a market street leading up into town with all manner of butchers, fruit and veg shops, cheese shops and mini-markets. Sirou sausages are excellent.

Eating out Good tavernas around the waterfront and others in the town.

Other PO. OTE. Banks. ATMs. Greek gas and Camping Gaz. Hospital. Hire cars and motorbikes. Buses to the principal villages. Ferries to Piraeus, nearby Cyclades, Crete, and Sámos.

General

Ermoúpolis is still the capital of the Cyclades and although it may not have the commercial power it once did, it still bustles and buzzes with the self importance and assurance of a cultural and commercial hub. It is still the largest town and it feels like it.

The buildings around the harbour reflect the past power and glory. An 18th-century square paved with marble and shaded by trees and complete with bandstand. Impressive public buildings, including an opera house modelled on La Scala. Elegant 19th-century mansions with wrought iron balconies, and an extra-large Catholic cathedral. Ermoúpolis repays a wander around the back streets where neo-classical buildings and ship-owners mansions are impressive although crumbling here and there.

The quay is alive all day and night with a wide choice of bars and cafés to while away the time watching the ferries churn in and out of the harbour. In the back streets and around the west quay are some old-fashioned *ouzeries* and cafés while on the east quay and the east side of the old town are some traditional tavernas. It all comes as a bit of a shock after the quieter places, but the hustle and bustle is genuine and Ermoúpolis grows on you as something more essential and Greek than other tourist-orientated places.

MARINA SIROU

The basic structure of the marina is now complete, although it is not yet open to yachts. Construction work continues on shore.

Approach

Once into Limin Sirou the N mole of the marina will be seen when past the bunkering station.

By night The bunkering station is lit F.Y.12m3M. A buoy marking If. Karfomeni is lit Q.R. The marina entrance is not lit.

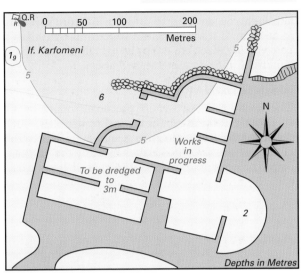

MARINA SIROU

Mooring

When the marina opens berth stern or bows-to where directed. Laid moorings to be installed. Manoeuvring inside the marina in larger yachts could be difficult with any wind.

Facilities

Water and electricity points to be installed. Shower and toilet block planned.

General

When complete Marina Sirou will offer all facilities, but it is sadly some distance away from the charms of Ermoúpolis on the other side of the harbour. Estimated completion date is 2004–2005.

ERMOÚPOLIS FISHING HARBOUR

The fishing harbour is complete and also full. Yachts can berth alongside the outer wall where shown and shelter here is good although there is some wash from craft entering and leaving Ermoúpolis. You are not too far away from town

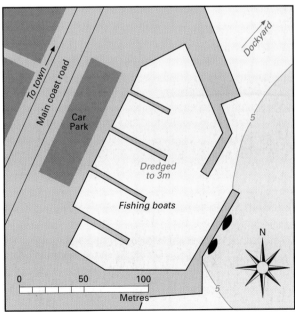

ERMOÚPOLIS FISHING HARBOUR

although you do need to dodge the traffic speeding in and out of town along the waterfront road. It is a convenient place to stop at if enquiring about hauling in the yards mentioned above.

NISÍS GAÏDHAROS

The island lying close off the coast opposite Ák Kondoyiánnis at the entrance to Ermoúpolis.

On the SE corner of the island there is a small cove that provides good shelter from the *meltemi*. Approximately halfway into the cove there is a bar with 2·5m depths over it. On the W side of the bar near the coast there is a sunken obstruction. Once over the bar anchor in 3m on a sand and weed bottom. No facilities.

Caution A reef (Tripita Reef) with 1·6m least depth over it lies one mile W of Nisís Aspronisi. N. Aspronisi is also fringed by reefs.

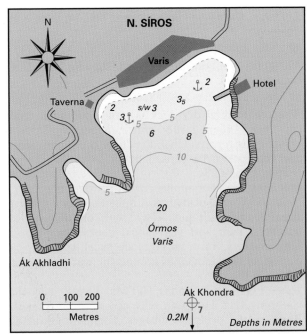

ÓRMOS VARIS

⊕7   0·2M S of Ák Khondra (Síros) 37°22'·75N 24°56'·60E WGS84

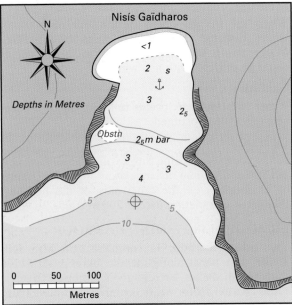

NISÍS GAÏDHAROS ANCHORAGE
⊕37°25'·6N 24°58'·7E

ÓRMOS VARIS

A deeply indented bay on the SE side of Síros immediately W of Ák Khondra. Anchor near the head of the bay in 2–4m or in the cove on the W side in 3–5m. The bottom is sand and good holding. Good shelter from the *meltemi* although there are gusts and a swell can be reflected into the anchorage.

Several tavernas around the waterfront and a hotel at the head of the bay. Fuel about 800m away on the road to Ermoúpolis.

FINIKAS (Foinikas, Foinikou)

BA 1538
A sheltered bay on the SW coast of Síros.

Approach

Conspicuous The villas around the slopes of Órmos Finikou will be seen and closer in the light structure on Psathonisi can be identified. Psathonisi is low-

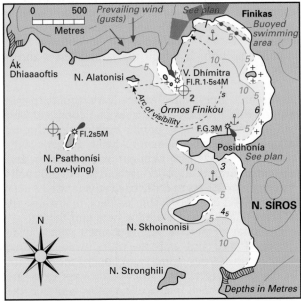

FINIKAS APPROACHES
⊕1 37°23'·23N 24°52'·17E WGS84
⊕2 37°23'·51N 24°52'·48E WGS84

lying and difficult to make out from the distance. The rough stone breakwater built out from the point to Vrak Dhimitra on the W side of Órmos Foinikou will also be seen.

By night Use the light on Psathonísi Fl.2s5M and the light on Vrak Dhímitra Fl.R.1·5s4M vis only over 198°–085°. The end of the mole at Posidhonía is lit F.G. The entrance to the harbour is lit Fl.G.4s5M/Fl.R.4s5M.

Dangers There are strong gusts into the bay with the *meltemi*. With southerlies a confused sea builds up in the approaches to the bay.

Finikas (Órmos Finikou) on Síros looking NNW across Ák Velostási into the bay of Órmos Finikou. The yacht pier and anchorage can just be discerned on the NW side of the bay
Peter Kleinoth/MareTeam

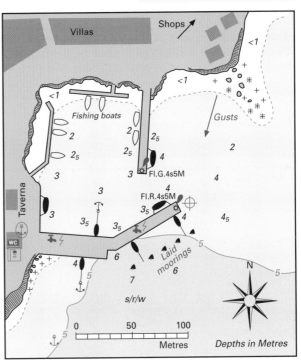

FINIKAS
⊕37°23'·83N 24°52'·62E WGS84

Finikas harbour looking NE

Mooring

Go stern or bows-to the S side of the outer mole at Finikas. There are laid moorings tailed to a small buoy that you need to pick up on the outer dogleg end of the mole. On the inner section you will need to use your own anchor although there are plans to lay moorings here as well. Yachts can also berth inside the basin if there is room. Go stern or bows-to the mole or alongside the inner mole.

Shelter With the *meltemi* blowing the best place to be is on the outside of the mole where the *meltemi* is blowing you off the quay. In unsettled weather and with southerlies berth in the basin. With strong southerlies the outside berths are untenable and you need to be inside the basin where there is a surge, but it is tenable.

Dangers There have been reports that the wash from high speed ferries affect the berths on the outside of the harbour. Keep pulled well off.

Authorities Harbour attendant. Charge band 2.

Anchorage With the *meltemi* you can anchor off in the bay. The beach area has a line of small buoys marking out the swimming area, but there is plenty of room left to anchor. The bottom is sand and weed with some rocks, good holding once the anchor is in.

Note The area S of the basin has a number of laid moorings. Care is needed when navigating in the area and also if you intend to anchor here.

Facilities

Services Water on the quay. You may be able to get electricity connected. A shower and toilet block although it is not always the most sanitary.

Fuel Can be delivered by mini-tanker (☎ 281858).

Repairs A number of yacht service companies can be called out for repairs. There is a notice board at the harbour with telephone numbers. Small chandlers around the waterfront.

Provisions Most provisions can be found.

Eating out Taverna at the harbour and others around the waterfront.

Other PO. Hire cars and motorbikes. Taxi and buses to Ermoúpolis.

General

The bay and the beach are most attractive so it is not surprising that a number of hotels and villas have been built around the bay. Nearly everyone who visits here likes the place and it is well worth stopping here with the bonus in the *meltemi* season of excellent shelter.

POSIDHONÍA

The military harbour in the SE corner of Órmos Finikou. Yachts are not permitted to berth inside the harbour which in any case is usually occupied by naval craft. Yachts can anchor off in the SE corner just clear of the prohibited area. The anchorage is not well sheltered from the *meltemi*, but is useful if it blows from the S. Taverna ashore.

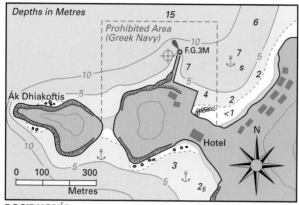

POSIDHONÍA
⊕37°23'·3N 24°52'·9E

ÓRMOS GALISSAS

A small bay lying immediately S of Ák Katakefalos. Anchor in 4–5m at the head of the bay. There are 3m depths about 50m off the beach. The bottom is sand and good holding. Reasonable shelter from the *meltemi* although some swell penetrates into the bay. On the S side of the bay a short mole has been built and several yachts can squeeze in behind it getting better shelter from the *meltemi*. Care is needed of underwater ballasting off the mole so take a long line to it.

Minimarket and tavernas ashore as well as a disco producing industrial sound levels.

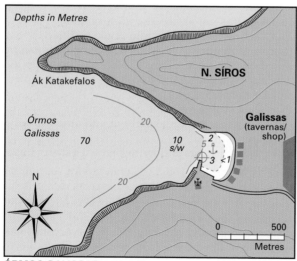

ÓRMOS GALISSAS
⊕37°26'·88N 24°53'·86E WGS84

ÓRMOS KINI

A small bay on the W coast of Síros immediately opposite Ermoúpolis on the E coast. Care must be taken of the reef lying just over half a mile off the coast WNW of the bay. Care must also be taken of a sand bar just under the water that extends from the S side of the bay to halfway across it. Anchor in 3–5m in the NE corner. There are numerous laid moorings here so care is needed not to foul your anchor. The mole on the N side of the bay has 2–3·5m depths off the quayed area, but is always full of tripper and local boats. Reasonable shelter from the *meltemi* although some swell is pushed into the bay. Open W.

Tavernas ashore and limited provisions can be obtained.

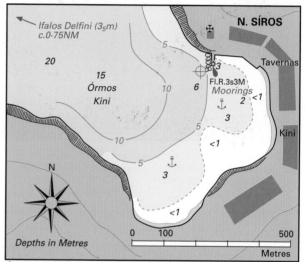

ÓRMOS KINI
⊕37°26'·52N 24°54'·68E WGS84

Órmos Kini looking W

ÓRMOS DELFINO

A small bay approximately one mile N of Kini. It can be recognised when close in by the small islet in the middle. Care is needed of Ifalos Delfini with a

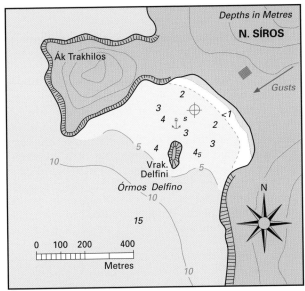

ÓRMOS DELFINO
⊕37°27'·5N 24°53'·8E

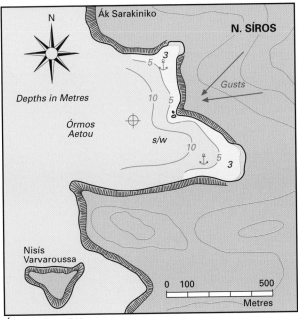

ÓRMOS AETOU
⊕37°28'·6N 24°53'·8E

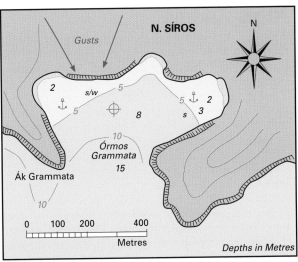

ÓRMOS GRAMMATA
⊕37°30'·0N 24°53'·3E

western side of the bay. Anchor on the W or E side of the bay in 4–5m. Although the bottom is sandy it does not appear to be good holding. With the *meltemi* there are severe gusts off the high land and it is prudent to take a long line ashore. No facilities.

Ák Grammata is covered with the names and dates of seafarers who have sheltered here over the centuries waiting for the infernal *meltemi* to die down, and no doubt many readers of this book will likewise add their names to the list.

NÍSOS YIAROS (Yioura)

The island nearly midway between Kéa and Tínos about 8 miles NW of Síros. It is a barren uninhabited lump of rock with no anchorages. When the *meltemi* is blowing there are strong gusts off the south coast and a yacht should keep a prudent distance off.

DORO STRAIT (Stenón Kafirevs/Kafireos)

⊕8 Mid-channel Stenón Kafirevs 37°58'·4N 24°37'·7E

This strait lies between the N end of Andros and the S end of Evia. The strait is 6 miles across at its narrowest part. A current runs through the strait in a SW direction at 2–4 knots but the Admiralty *Pilot* reports that a southerly current of 7 knots was recorded with a strong northerly gale. The *meltemi* is funnelled through the strait and accompanying it are steep confused seas.

With gales from the N small yachts should exercise considerable caution in the vicinity of the strait. I have seen large ships anchor in the roadstead off Karistos rather than proceed through the strait and during a Force 10 gale which lasted several days I counted over twenty ships anchored off waiting for the gale to abate. Even after the *meltemi* dies down a confused sea will remain for some time. In the event of strong northerly winds a yacht can shelter at Karistos on Evia or the bays to the E of it (see Chapter VI).

least depth of 3·5m over it lying just under one mile W of the anchorage. Anchor in 3–4m behind the islet. Reasonable shelter from the *meltemi* although there are gusts off the high land. Taverna opens in the summer.

ÓRMOS AETOU

A bay approximately 1M N of Delfino. The best anchorage is in the cove on the N side with a long line ashore. Anchor in 4–5m. Alternatively anchor at the head of the bay in 3–5m on sand. Adequate shelter from the *meltemi* although some swell rolls into the bay. Taverna opens in the summer.

ÓRMOS GRAMMATA (Megas Lakkos)

Lies at the N end of Órmos Megas on the NW of Síros. Ák Grammata, a bell-shaped light yellow rocky bluff conspicuous from seaward, forms the

Nísos Andros

The northernmost and second largest of the Cyclades. It is mountainous throughout with the summit in the middle of the island, Mt Kouvarion, rising to 1,134m (3,721ft), and another peak, Mt Petalon, about a mile to the NE, rising to 944m (3,097ft). These peaks are snowcapped in the winter and in early spring. It is well wooded and cultivated in places.

The island is named after Andreus, a general from Crete. During the Persian invasions Andros sided with the invaders, which cost it dearly after the Athenian sea victory off Salamís. During the Peloponnesian War it sided with Sparta – it must have had some longstanding grudge against Athens. The ancient capital was at Palaioupolis on the west coast, but few ruins remain. It passed in turn to the Romans and to Byzantium and eventually to the Venetians in 1207 who built many of the fortified towers and the distinctive dovecotes dotted around it. It was occupied by the Turks in 1556 and became Greek after the War of Independence.

Today Andros is popular with Greek holidaymakers, although a few foreign tourists are discovering it. The *chora* at Kástro is well worth a visit by land if you decide not to take on the *meltemi* and sail around to it in the summer. In recent years the island has become something of a 'weekend cottage' suburb of Athens and the new bland villas of the Athenians have appeared around the coast, giving the island a case of villa-pox. It is still enchanting in places though you need to try harder to get away from it all.

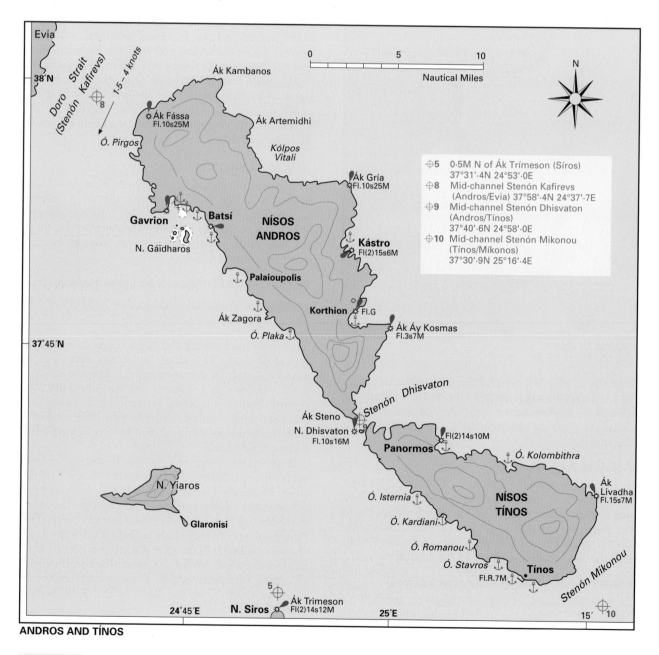

ANDROS AND TÍNOS

GAVRION

BA 1538

Imray-Tetra G31

Approach

Conspicuous The entrance to Órmos Gavrion is difficult to see from the distance. The group of islands to the S of the entrance (Platí, Gáïdharos, Akamatis, Prasso, and Megálo) are easily identified and closer in the light structure on the W entrance point and the buildings of the village will be seen. Once at the entrance to the bay things are straightforward.

By night Use the lights on either side of the entrance to the bay: Ák Kastrí Fl.6s8M and Ák Mármara Fl.RG.2s3M, (the red sector covers If Vouvi and the islands described above over 248°-005°). The breakwater is lit on the extremity Q.G.3M. The reefs and the unlit islands lying to the S of the entrance make a night approach from the S difficult and possibly dangerous. (See *Dangers* below.)

Dangers

1. Care must be taken of Ifalos Vouvi, a reef and shoal water approximately half a mile SE of the entrance.
2. Shoal water extends some distance off the islets in the approach from the S, especially Nisís Akamatis and Nisís Platí.
3. If coasting towards Gavrion from Batsí care is needed of Vrak Rosa, an above-water rock and reef approximately 200m ESE of Ák Marmara.

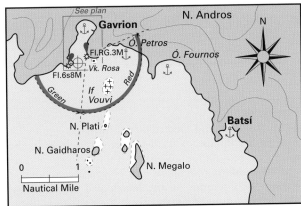

APPROACHES TO GAVRION AND BATSÍ
⊕37°52´·6N 24°43´·8E

Gavrion looking ENE   *Nigel Patten*

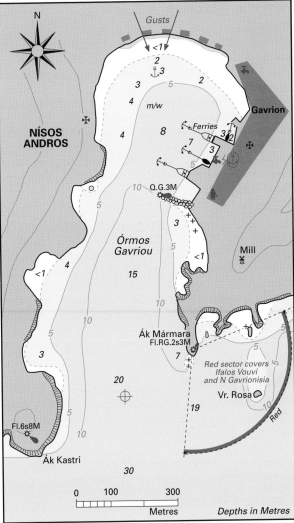

GAVRION
⊕37°52´·6N 24°43´·8E

4. With the *meltemi* there are strong gusts down into Gavrion. Although there is good shelter inside, the gusts can make manoeuvring difficult off the quay.

Note The ferries using Gavrion enter and leave at speed. A good lookout should be kept for them in the vicinity of the bay.

Mooring

Anchor at the head of the bay or go stern or bows-to or alongside the quay between the ferry piers. It is also possible to tuck into the E corner of the ferry pier, though one of the ferries often spends the night here and will take a line across to the quay, effectively blocking yachts in until it leaves. When anchoring tuck as far into the NW corner as you can to ensure you leave sufficient room for the large ferries to manoeuvre. The sight of one of these maritime juggernauts steaming towards you before dropping its anchor and going hard astern towards the ferry quay takes a bit of getting used to. The bottom is mud and weed, mostly good holding once through the weed.

Shelter Good shelter from the *meltemi* although there are strong gusts off the land.

241

Authorities Port police.

Facilities
Services Water on the quay. Electricity can be connected.
Fuel Near the quay. A mini-tanker can deliver to the quay.
Provisions Good shopping for most provisions. Ice near the quay.
Eating out Tavernas in the village and around the beach.
Other PO. OTE. Bank. ATM. Hire cars and motorbikes. Bus to Kástro and Batsí. Ferry to Rafina and Piraeus.

General
The natural harbour of Gavrion offers the best shelter on Andros. The village is a modest uninspired little place, but not unpleasant. It is the ferry port for Andros and the ferries come and go frequently in the summer, bringing Athenians getting away from the smog of Athens to the clear air of the islands and tourists getting away from more crowded islands. Gavrion is a safe enough place to leave your boat (put out a second anchor for security) and explore inland.

ÓRMOS PETROS

37°52'·9N 24°44'·5E

The large bay immediately E of Gavrion. Poor shelter from the *meltemi* as a swell inevitably rolls into here.

Anchor in 3–5m in the NW corner on sand and weed. Tavernas and bars on the beach.

ÓRMOS FOURNOS

37°52'·6N 24°45'·6E

The large bay after Petros on the E side of Ák Kourouni. Some shelter from the *meltemi* tucked into the NW corner although there is still some swell pushed into the bay. Anchor in 3–5m on sand and weed. Above the anchorage is a Hellenistic tower (Áy Petros). Tavernas and bars on the beach.

BATSÍ

Approach
A small harbour 2¾ miles SE of Gavrion. Batsí village is conspicuous from seaward.

By night Use the light on Ák Kolóna Fl.3s5M and the light on the extremity of the mole Fl.G.2s3M.

Dangers With the *meltemi* there are strong gusts down into the bay and approaches.

Mooring
Go stern or bows-to the quay near the root of the mole if there is room. The mole itself is reserved for the hydrofoil and fishing boats. There are 2–3m depths for most of the quay. Alternatively anchor off in the N or W of the bay.

Shelter Good shelter from the *meltemi*, although the gusts off the land from the E can make it uncomfortable. With strong southerlies a surge develops and the harbour may become untenable.

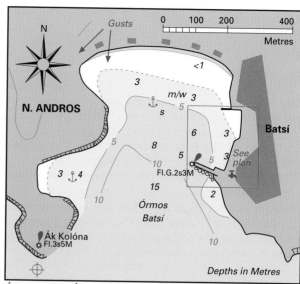

ÓRMOS BATSÍ
⊕37°51'·0N 24°46'·7E

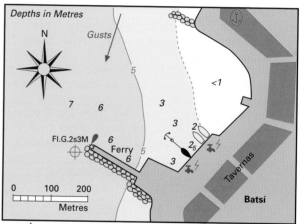

BATSÍ
⊕37°51'·4N 24°47'·1E

Facilities
Services Water and electricity on the quay.
Fuel In the village. A mini-tanker can deliver to the quay.
Provisions Most provisions can be found.
Eating out Tavernas on the beach and in the village and bars around the waterfront.
Other PO. OTE. Banks. ATM. Hire cars and motorbikes. Taxis. Bus to Gavrion and Kástro.

General
Batsí is a pleasant enough little place, if somewhat overwhelmed by tourists. The locals who aren't cashing in on the tourism with bars and boutiques seem mesmerized by the parade of foreigners through their village, who apparently come here to do little else than lie in the sun and drink in the bars.

ÓRMOS PALAIOUPOLIS

37°48'·9N 24°48'·2E

An open bay 5 miles SE of Gavrion. Anchor at the N end of the bay under Ák Thiakion where there is reasonable shelter from the *meltemi* although some swell penetrates. There have been reports that the holding is suspect. Clear water and delightful surroundings. In calm weather it is possible to anchor off the small fishing hamlet built near the ruins of ancient Palaioupolis.

There are few ruins remaining (part of an ancient breakwater can be seen on the sea bottom), but the site is enchanting and a good lunch stop in calm weather.

ÓRMOS PLAKA

37°46'·0N 24°52'·7E

A small bay under Ák Zagora. Anchor in 2–4m on a sandy bottom. The bay is subject to strong gusts off the high land with the *meltemi*.

Ashore on a plateau at Ák Zagora are the ruins of ancient Zagora, a fortified Geometric town excavated in the 1970s.

E COAST OF ANDROS

Along the E coast are a number of bays that can be used in calm weather or in light southerlies. When the *meltemi* is blowing a heavy sea is set onto this coast and it can be hard work getting along it.

KÁSTRO (Kástron, Port Andros)

BA 1538

Approach

The harbour faces directly into the *meltemi* and the approach is difficult. The reef running out from the headland can be identified by the seas breaking on it and the spume over it. Stick close to the N side where there are good depths off the end of the mole.

By night During the *meltemi* season a night approach is not recommended for first time visitors to the harbour. Use the light Nisís Tourlítis on the reef running out from Kástro Fl(2)15s6M and the light on the end of the mole Fl.G.2s3M.

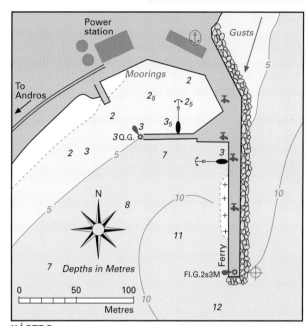

KÁSTRO
⊕37°50'·8N 24°56'·4E

Dangers The *meltemi* gusts down the coast into here pushing considerable seas onto the coast. Care needed in the approach to the harbour.

Mooring

Go stern or bows-to behind the mole. The bottom is rock and weed, poor holding, but there may be a laid mooring free behind the mole. Care must be taken of ballasting along the quay in places.

Shelter With the *meltemi* there is a surge in the harbour – more uncomfortable than dangerous in the inner basin.

Facilities

Water On the quay.

Fuel On the outskirts of the village. You may be able to get a mini-tanker to deliver.

Provisions Good shopping in the village.

Eating out A taverna and bar near the harbour and others around the waterfront and in the village.

Other PO. OTE. Banks. ATM. Irregular bus to Batsí and Gavrion.

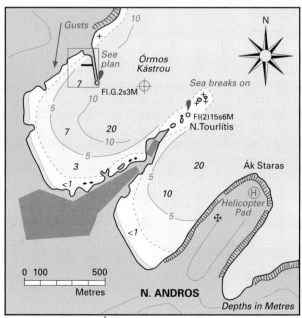

APPROACHES TO KÁSTRO
⊕37°50'·6N 24°56'·2E

Kástro looking NW into the inner basin   *Nigel Patten*

General

Kástro, or more properly Andros, is the capital of the island. It is a long hot walk around the bay to the village which straggles out along the rocky tongue forming the S side of the harbour, but it is well worth the effort to visit it. The town sits hunched over its rocky headland with the houses looking out over brown rock and the wind-tossed waters of the bay. On the end of the headland there is a small maritime museum and in the central square an archaeological museum and a museum of modern art.

Unfortunately a noisy power station has been built in the N corner of the port, which adds noise and visual pollution to this otherwise beautiful and savage coast.

KORTHION

Approach

The large bay and harbour lies approximately 6M S of Kástro. The houses of Korthion will be seen on the NW of the bay.

By night Use the light on Ák Áy Aikaterína Fl.2s3M and the light on the extremity of the mole F.R.3M.

Dangers As at Kástro the *meltemi* gusts down the coast and pushes a big sea into the bay.

Mooring

If there is room go stern or bows-to behind the mole. In calm weather you can anchor off, but with the *meltemi* the only place to be is under the mole.

Shelter Adequate if uncomfortable shelter from the *meltemi* under the mole. Southerlies are reported to make it untenable here.

Facilities

Water near the root of the mole. Limited provisions. Several tavernas and cafés.

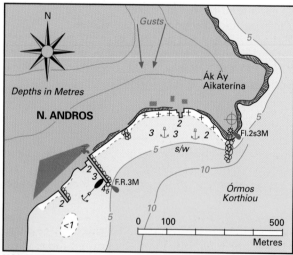

KORTHION
⊕37°46′·8N 24°57′·6E

STENÓN DHISVATON

⊕9 Mid-channel Stenón Dhisvaton (Andros/Tínos)
37°40′·6N 24°58′·0E

This strait separates the S end of Andros and the N end of Tínos. Two islands, Nisís Dhisvaton and Nisís Kaloyeri, lie off the NW tip of Tínos. The strait is a little over half a mile across at its narrowest part. A current setting towards the SW runs through the strait, but not with the strength of the current in the Doro Strait. With the *meltemi* there are strong gusts through the channel.

Nísos Tínos

A mountainous rugged island lying immediately south of Andros across a narrow strait. The summit, Korifi Tsiknias (713m/2,340ft), lies at the SE end of the island and Polemos Kambos in the centre of the island rises to 637m (2,090ft). The island is wooded and the slopes are extensively terraced and cultivated. There are a large number of villages (there are said to be 64) peppered around the island and many Venetian dovecotes and towers. The main port and capital is Tínos.

The ancient name of the island was Ophiousa, referring to the large number of snakes to be found here in ancient times. The name Tenos, corrupted to Tínos, may be derived from the Phoenician word, *tenok*, for snake. Poseidon was credited with ridding Tínos of snakes by sending storks to devour them. The Venetians occupied the island and held it for 500 years until the Turks took it in 1714.

The long Venetian occupation established Catholicism on Tínos and today Catholic convents, schools and churches are scattered around the island. In 1822 the discovery of the miracle-working icon of the Virgin ironically transformed this very Catholic island to a place of pilgrimage for those of the Orthodox faith.

TÍNOS

BA 1538

Approach

Conspicuous The large town of Tínos is clearly visible from the distance. Above the town the church of the *Panayía* is conspicuous. Closer in the harbour breakwater and the entrance are easily identified.

By night Use the lights on the extremities of the breakwaters Fl.R.3s7M/Fl.G.2s3M and the light on the inner mole Fl.R.2s3M.

Dangers
1. With the *meltemi* there are strong gusts off the high land in the vicinity of the harbour.
2. Care is needed of the reef and shoal water extending S from Ák Akrotíri, the cape in the S approaches to Tínos.

Mooring

Proceed into the inner harbour and go stern or bows-to the N quay between the cargo mole and the ferry quay or immediately E of the ferry quay. Care should be taken of the ledge protruding a short

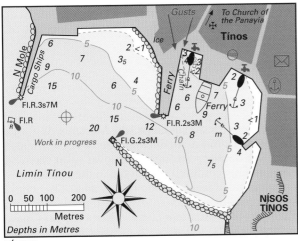

TÍNOS
⊕37°32′·25N 25°09′·4E

distance underwater from the quay. Care is also needed of a large ship's anchor chain fouling the bottom approximately where the pecked line is on the plan. In calm weather it is reported there is a usable quay in the SE corner although care is needed of underwater ballasting. The bottom is mud, good holding.

Note Do not anchor in the harbour as the ferries need the whole area to manoeuvre in when berthing.

Shelter Good all-round shelter although strong southerlies are said to cause a surge. Wash from the ferries can also be uncomfortable.

Authorities Port police and customs.

Facilities
Water On the quay (reputed to be the purest in Greece!).

Tínos harbour looking WNW across Ák Akrotíri in the foreground   *Peter Kleinoth/MareTeam*

Fuel In the town. A mini-tanker can deliver to the quay.
Repairs Some mechanical repairs and light engineering. Hardware shops.
Provisions Good shopping for all provisions close by. Ice available near the quay.
Eating out Tavernas nearby.
Other PO. OTE. Banks. ATM. Greek gas and Camping Gaz. Hire motorbikes. Buses to the principal villages. Ferries to Piraeus.

General
Despite a sizeable Catholic population, Tínos is a centre of the Orthodox faith and the Church of the Panayía (the Virgin Mary/Our Lady – also called Tiniotissa and Evangelistria) is the focus of this faith. The modern church is sited above the town and is devoted to the miracle-working icon of Our Lady of Good Tidings discovered in 1822. Twice a year, on 25 March and 15 August, thousands of sick and crippled pilgrims come to Tínos seeking a cure. This Greek Orthodox 'Lourdes' has apparently cured many, if the innumerable gold and silver votive offerings adorning the already ornate interior are anything to go by.

The church also contains a shrine commemorating the sinking of the Greek cruiser *Helle (Elli)*. On 15 August 1940 the cruiser was anchored outside the port attending the celebrations. An unknown submarine, probably Italian, torpedoed the ship, sinking her and killing many of the crew. Greece was not at war at this stage and the atrocity caused an uproar all over the country. Just below the church a museum contains some interesting finds including a sundial from the first century BC.

ANCHORAGES ON THE EAST COAST OF TÍNOS
Most of these anchorages afford limited or poor shelter from the *meltemi* as a swell tends to be pushed down the coast and curve into any bays. They can be used in calm weather or when the *meltemi* is not blowing strongly.

Órmos Isternia 37°36′·9N 25°02′·4E
The bay under Ák Isternia. Keep to seaward of the islet off the cape. Anchor in 6–10m off the hamlet. There is a quayed area off the hamlet with 3–4m depths off it, but you are better off at anchor because of the swell in here. The holding is reported to be mediocre only. Strong gusts with the *meltemi* and a swell curves around into the anchorage. Tavernas ashore.

Órmos Kardiani
The small bay 2½M SE of Ák Isternia. Tuck up into the N cove in the bay. Poor shelter from the *meltemi*.

Órmos Romanou 37°34′·2N 25°06′·5E
A bay affording some shelter from the *meltemi*. Anchor in 3–6m off the beach. A swell is pushed into the anchorage with a fresh to strong *meltemi*.

Órmos Stavrós 37°33′·0N 25°07′·9E
The large bay immediately NW of Tínos harbour. With the *meltemi* there are strong gusts into the bay.

Anchor in 5–10m at the NW end of the bay. Care is needed of the reef and shoal water extending off the beach. Tavernas on the beach.

Órmos Akrotíri The bay under Ák Akrotíri in the southern approach to Tinos harbour. Suitable in calm weather as a swell is pushed into it with the *meltemi*.

ÓRMOS PANORMOU

Approach
A bay on the NE side of Tínos providing some protection from the *meltemi*. Nisís Planitís, with a light structure (Fl(2)14s10M) on it and connected by a narrow isthmus to Tínos, forms the N side of the bay and is easily identified. A beacon on the N side of the bay marks a reef.

Mooring
The only place to be with the *meltemi* is in the cove (Áy Thalassa) on the N side of the bay. Anchor where possible in the cove. Care is needed as there are a number of permanent moorings here. In calm weather or with westerlies you can go on the quay at the head of the bay. The easternmost quay jutting out has 4–5m depths off it while the longer inner quay has 1·5–2m depths off it.

Facilities
Water on the quay. Some provisions. Tavernas around the waterfront.

General
Panormos used to be used for shipping marble from the hinterland and may still be used by small coasters at times. It has now become a modest tourist spot with much of the building of the 'pour-and-fill' variety.

ÓRMOS KOLOMBITHRA

37°38'·5N 25°08'·5E

A large bay approximately halfway along the N coast of Tinos. It is of no use when the *meltemi* is blowing, being completely open to that direction, but would provide useful shelter from southerlies and westerlies. The approach is straightforward leaving

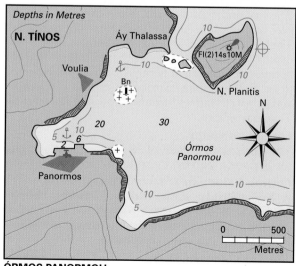

ÓRMOS PANORMOU
⊕37°39'·2N 25°04'·1E

the islet (Drakonissi) off the W entrance point to starboard. Anchor in either of the two coves at the head of the bay in 3–5m.

STENON MIKONOU

⊕10 Mid-channel Stenón Mikonou 37°30'·9N 25°16'·4E

The channel between Tinos and Míkonos. With the *meltemi* the wind is channelled through here and can blow substantially stronger than over open water. A considerable confused sea occurs in the channel and care is needed when sailing in this area. There have been a number of masts lost and more blown sails than in the Americas Cup when skippers have underestimated the strength of wind from the gusts down through this channel.

Nísos Míkonos
(Mykonos)

A rocky barren island which is mostly low-lying. Mt Áy Ilías rises to 364m (1,194ft) in the NW and Mt Anomeritis rises to 351m (1,152ft) in the SE. The population mostly lives in Port Míkonos or in Tourliani in the middle of the island. The town of Míkonos, the tourist Mecca of Greece, is the real attraction because, apart from fine sandy beaches, the island has scenically little else.

Note Between Naxos and Míkonos a strong southerly current has been reported after a prolonged *meltemi*.

MÍKONOS MARINA (Toúrlos)
Note
All boats must now berth in the marina and not in Míkonos old harbour. You will be turned away from the old harbour if you try to enter.

Approach
The harbour lies just over a mile N of the old harbour. From the W a large hotel looking a bit like the radiator grille of an American car is conspicuous. Normally the most conspicuous objects will be the cruise ships tied alongside the outside quay of the marina. Yachts should make for the E basin.

By night The W basin is lit at the entrance Fl.G.3s3M. The E basin is lit on the end of the mole Fl.R.3s3M. The central quay area is spotlit.

Dangers The *meltemi* gusts down into the bay making manoeuvring difficult although, unlike the old harbour, there is plenty of room here.

Mooring
Berth stern or bows-to or alongside on the S side of the basin. As work progresses pontoons and laid moorings will be installed.

Shelter Good all-round shelter although the *meltemi* gusts into the harbour.

Authorities Port police.

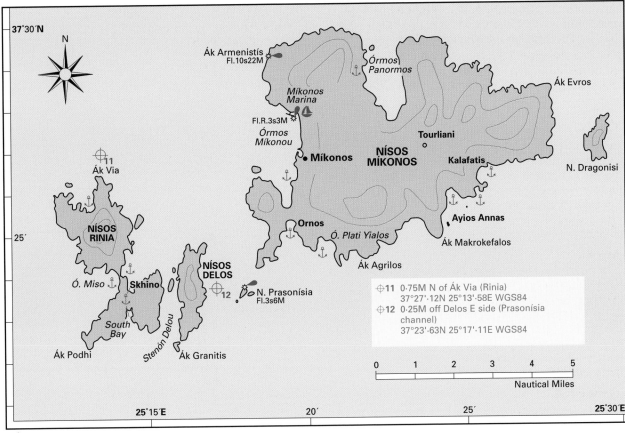

MÍKONOS, DELOS AND RINIA

| ⊕11 | 0·75M N of Ák Via (Rinia)
37°27'·12N 25°13'·58E WGS84 |
| ⊕12 | 0·25M off Delos E side (Prasonísia channel)
37°23'·63N 25°17'·11E WGS84 |

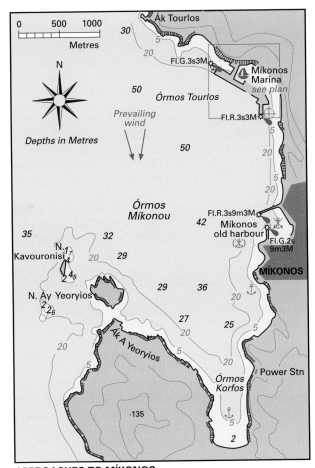

APPROACHES TO MÍKONOS
⊕37°27'·74N 25°19'·54E WGS84

Note At the moment no charge is made for using the harbour, but this will change when work is more advanced and services are installed.

Facilities

Services None at the time of writing. It is planned to install water and electricity points and a shower and toilet block. You may be able to get a water tanker to deliver.

Fuel Can be delivered by mini-tanker to the quay.

Repairs Limited mechanical repairs only. Limited chandlers in Míkonos town.

Provisions Good shopping for all provisions in Mikonos town.

Eating out Wide choice of tavernas and restaurants in Míkonos town.

Other PO. OTE. Banks. ATMs. Hospital. Greek Gas and Camping Gaz. Hire cars and motorbikes on the N side of the marina. Ferries to Piraeus, Siros, Paros and Rhodes. Internal and European flights.

General

Míkonos Marina The marina is a dusty deserted place at present, a sort of boon-docks miles away from the glitz of Míkonos town. That said, I think I speak for many, especially a lot of charter skippers pressured by clients to come here, when I say that the shelter in the marina is wonderful compared to the perils the old harbour used to present. At Míkonos old harbour you gritted your teeth as you came into it to berth between ferries, the howling *meltemi*, whistling port police and other boatowners

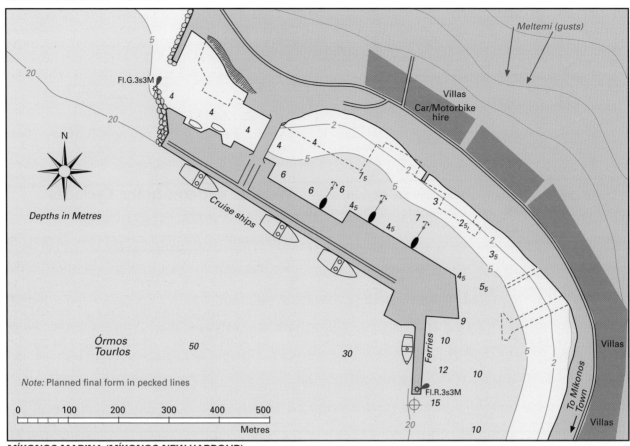

MÍKONOS MARINA (MÍKONOS NEW HARBOUR)
⊕37°27'·74N 25°19'·54E WGS84

swearing at you as anchors became crossed and topsides were gashed. It was a nightmare. The best thing to do at the marina is hire a motorbike or car from the agency on the N side and use that to zip in and out of town.

Míkonos town Míkonos has almost passed into the English language to describe a certain type of touristy island in the way that Benidorm describes the most down-market of resorts. To 'mikonos'

means to take the most wonderful place and completely change the values and worth of the community so that while physically little appears to have changed, the place is soulless and possesses little that was valuable in the old community. So it is that in the summer the locals rub shoulders with the yacht set, the jet set, backpackers, artists – real and pseudo, nudists and recently the gay set as well as plain ordinary holidaymakers. Míkonos is bright and breezy by day and by night the hum of the bars and throb of discos into the wee hours is all part of the scene.

The town is a dazzling white cluster of cubes stacked around a natural amphitheatre above the harbour. Míkonos epitomizes the Greek flair for choosing a superb site and tailoring a natural architecture to it. The houses, the churches (there are said to be 365 of them, a bit of an exaggeration), and the narrow winding alleys appear to be a naturally evolved form sculpted from the rocks of the island itself. There may be hordes of tourists from all over the world, and more photographs of Míkonos than of any other town in Greece, films and documentaries may have featured it, yet Míkonos retains that wonderful appearance and certain architectural something that so many flock to see. For the yachtsman the cosmopolitan flavour of Míkonos may be a refreshing contrast to the simpler pleasures of the other islands.

Míkonos Marina looking W

ÓRMOS MÍKONOU

In light southerlies or easterlies it is possible to anchor off Míkonos town. Anchor off in either of the two coves S of the old harbour. The bottom comes up fairly quickly in both bays so you will need to anchor in 7–10m.

In southerlies you can anchor in Órmos Korfos. Anchor in 4–6m on mud and weed.

ÓRMOS ORNOS

The bay on the S side of Míkonos immediately E of Ák Alogomandra. Anchor in 5–10m at the head of the bay. The bottom is sand and weed – poor holding in places. Good shelter from the *meltemi* although there are strong gusts into the bay. Open to the S.

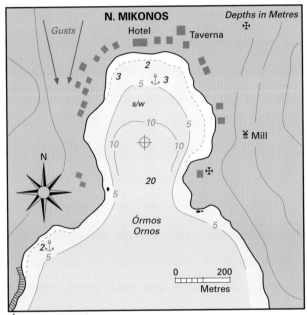

ÓRMOS ORNOS
⊕37°25'·3N 25°19'·5E

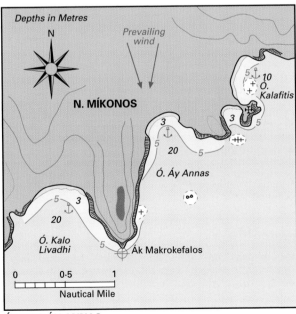

ÓRMOS ÁY ANNAS
⊕37°24'·8N 25°24'·0E

There is a hotel on the beach and several tavernas. Supermarket nearby. It is two miles to Míkinos town, buses every hour. Just to the E of Ornos there are a number of small bays sheltered from the *meltemi*. They have sandy beaches and tavernas nearby.

ÓRMOS KALO LIVADHI

An open bay on the W side of Ák Makrokefalis. Anchor off the beach in 3–6m. Reasonable shelter from the *meltemi*. A taverna opens in the summer. Inland there is at last some agriculture and cultivated fields.

ÓRMOS ÁYIOS ANNAS (Baraga)

Lies immediately E of Ák Makrokefalos. Anchor in 3–6m. The bottom is sand and weed. Good shelter from the *meltemi*. Open S. A taverna opens in the summer. Some of these beaches are unofficially 'no clothes' beaches and some are the preserve of men only, who may take exception to being invaded from the sea. Mikonos after all is an island where reputedly anything goes, and outside town you are on the fringe of 'anything goes'. Avert your eyes and have another drink.

ÓRMOS KALAFATIS

A bight offering reasonable protection from the *meltemi* although completely open to the S and E. It lies immediately E of Órmos Áy Annas and Ák Tarsanas. Care must be taken of a reef on the W side of the bight. Anchor off the N end of the beach in 3–4m off the hotel complex. Taverna and café ashore.

PANORMOS

37°30'·0N 25°17'·3E

The large bay on the N side of Míkonos. The *meltemi* blows straight down into the bay so most of it is a lee shore during the summer. On the W side of the bay at Áy Sostis there is a bight where you can get some shelter from the *meltemi*. Care is needed of Vrak. Moles, a group of rocks and a reef which should be left to starboard before turning up into Áy Sostis.

With southerlies the bay affords good shelter and you can anchor at Áy Sostis or at the head of the bay.

Tavernas at Áy Sostis and Ftelia at the head of the bay. The bay is popular with windsurfers who come here for the wind and sea pushed into the bay by the *meltemi*.

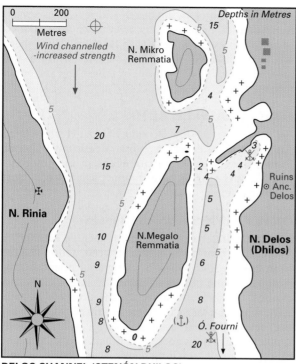

DELOS CHANNEL (STENÓN DHILOS)
(⚓) until 1500 hours
⊕37°24'·2N 25°15'·5E

Nísos Delos
(Dhilos, Mikró Delos)

A small low barren island with the extensive ruins of ancient Delos on the west coast. Every day in the summer tripper boats ferry sightseers over from Míkonos to see these ruins. It used to be prohibited for a yacht to berth or anchor at Delos. A large notice at the small harbour says simply 'No Yachts' and in Órmos Foúrnoi a notice prohibits landing and anchoring overnight. Recently it was reported that yachts could anchor off, but must depart before 1500 hours. Other yachts have reported staying overnight.

DELOS CHANNEL (Stenón Dhilos)

A yacht transiting the channel must exercise caution when the *meltemi* is blowing. The channel between Delos and Rinia and the Nisídhes Remmatia is fringed by reefs. When the *meltemi* is blowing it is funnelled into the channel and may blow at Force 7 or more on occasions. The combination of a narrow shallow channel fringed by reefs and strong winds and short seas can make navigation a tricky business – care is needed.

Ancient Delos

Delos was once the political and religious centre of the ancient world. Legend has it that Apollo was born here and Artemis on nearby Rinia. The Delos oracle was consulted before major decisions and its fame was second only to that of Delphi. How did Delos become the centre of the ancient world? The most succinct answer is provided by Ernle Bradford:

'Delos, the hub around which the Cyclades (Kukloi – rings) radiate, was formed by nature to be the focal point of a seaman's world. If one is tempted to ask why so small an island, without any natural resources, ever became what it did, then the answer can be given by any sailor. Delos is the last, and best, anchorage between Europe and Asia. To the east it is shielded by Mykonos, to the north by Tínos, and to the west by Rheneia. Looking at a chart, it is easy to see how the direct sea route between the Gulf of Nauplia (with Argos at its head) flows straight across the latitude of 37°10' north of Pátmos and Sámos. Exactly in the centre of this trading route lies Delos. At the same time, it is almost in the centre of the trading route between the Dardanelles and Crete. Religious centres may sometimes, as at Rome or Lourdes, attract trade and commerce. But more often one will find that where the trade is, there are also temples. Merchants, then as now, are eager to purchase security in both worlds.'

Ernle Bradford The Greek Islands

In those days the ancient harbour was larger and better protected than it is today. The breakwater was some 165m long and the harbour extended south for half a mile and was divided by moles into five basins. Yet despite Ernle Bradford's praise for the natural attributes of Delos, I cannot help thinking there are other better natural harbours nearby. Órmos Náoussa on Páros or Órmos Dhespotico, for instance, are better protected and more accessible than Delos. In any case, for whatever reasons, the ancients settled on Delos and transformed this rocky little island into the centre of the world.

In 700 BC the island was under the protection of Naxos and the centre of the Ionian League of islands. Athens soon entered the league and before long was commanding Delian affairs. It was purified in 543 BC by Peristratos and thereafter the island was not to be defiled by human birth or death. The dying and any women nearing childbirth were taken across to nearby Rinia. The island was subsequently purified on several other occasions, presumably because someone had a heart attack or some similar fairly instant demise and died before they could be whisked off to Rinia.

After the defeat of the Persians, the first great period of prosperity for Delos began. In Macedonian times it enjoyed privileges akin to those of a 'free port' and its wealth and power were immense. By 200 BC the first Romans came to Delos and although the Athenians remained, the power soon shifted to Rome. Around 80 BC it was sacked and although it was rebuilt, its power was on the wane. A wall was built around it, but by AD 3 the island was finished. In that year it was put up for sale, but there were no takers.

The remaining ruins and the site should not be missed. The site has been likened to Pompeii, not for any architectural similarity, but for the completeness of the picture of ancient life that can be gleaned from it. Many of the ruins have been vandalised by past invaders and collectors of antiquities and of course by the Greeks themselves who have carted off the conveniently-hewn stone to build their houses on Míkonos, but much remains: the five lean lions guarding the sacred lake; the temple of Apollo in the great square of Apollo; the theatre; the bright mosaics of dolphins, panthers, birds, fruit and flowers; and the remains of what was the busiest harbour in antiquity.

Nísos Rinia

(Rhenea, Megálo Delos)

The barren rocky island separated from Delos by the narrow Delos Strait. The island is nearly divided into two by a narrow isthmus. The northern half is the higher of the two (149m/490ft). There are several sizeable farms on the island and even a herd of cows as well as sheep and goats.

ÓRMOS SKHINOU

The bay has numerous above and below-water rocks fringing it and care is needed in the bay itself. There are two possible anchorages.

1. In the N. Care is needed of the rocks off the E side which are marked by a small pillar on one of them. Care is also needed of an underwater rock in the middle of the entrance which is sometimes marked by a small buoy. Anchor in 4–5m on sand, good holding. Good shelter from the *meltemi*.
2. In the S. Care is needed of the reef on the E side fringing the coast. Anchor in 3–5m. The anchorage is not sheltered from the *meltemi* but is protected from the S.

Rinia. South Bay looking S   *Nigel Patten*

CHAPEL BAY

To the N of Órmos Skhinou is an islet with a chapel on it. It is possible to anchor under the SW end of the islet in 6–8m on sand, good holding. Some shelter from moderate northerlies.

ÓRMOS KORMOU AMMOS

The bay on the N end of Rinia. It is open to the *meltemi*, but would be useful with southerlies. Anchor in 3–5m near the head of the bay.

ÓRMOS MISO

A large bay on the W side sheltered from the *meltemi*. Anchor in one of the two coves at the northern end where shown on a sandy bottom. No facilities.

SOUTH BAY

On the S side of Rinia, affords good shelter from the *meltemi*. Anchor near the head of the bay in 3–5m on a sandy bottom; good holding. No facilities. Water from a well in the field nearby.

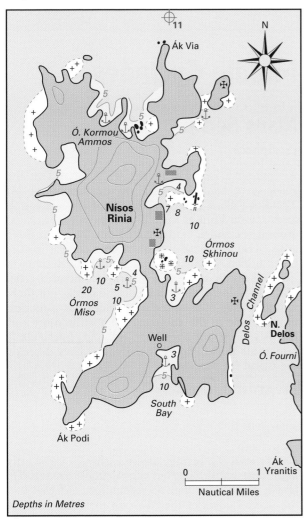

NÍSOS RINIA

⊕11 0·75M N of Ák Via (Rinia) 37°27'·12N 25°13'·58E WGS84

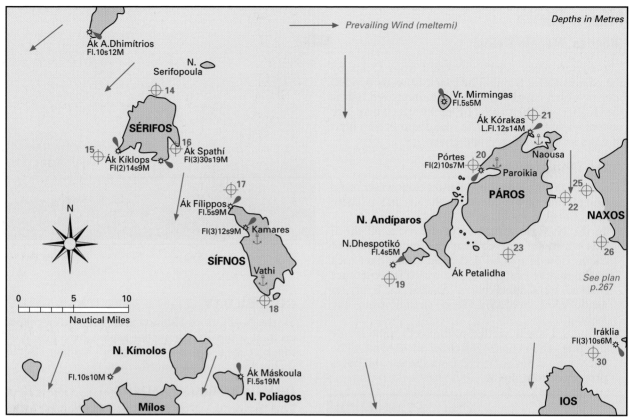

MIDDLE CYCLADES - WEST

Middle Cyclades

Nísos Sérifos

(Seriphos)

A dome-like island with the white houses of the *chora* on a conical hill SE of the summit of Mt Troullos (585m/1,919ft). The island appears barren from seaward but at Livádhi it is green and wooded around the shore, and inland from the *chora* there are several green valleys in startling contrast to the burnt brown mountain sides. There are a number of iron ore mines at Megálo Khorio on the west coast of the island and at Koutala on the south, but there is little active mining today. Livádhi has a modest tourist trade in the summer, but for the most part the island is populated by the old (particularly noticeable in the *chora*) as the young have deserted the island for Athens.

LIVÁDHI (Livadhiou)

BA 1538

Imray-Tetra G33

Approach

Conspicuous Coasting around the S coast the lighthouse on Ák Spathí is conspicuous. From the N and E Nisís Vous can be recognised and closer in the white houses of the *chora* on the hill above the harbour are easily seen. Once at the entrance to Órmos Livadhiou the approach is straightforward.

NÍSOS SÉRIFOS

Depths in Metres

N

100
⊕ **14**
Ák Volos

Ák Fournoi

Ó. Dhistomou

Ák Vouno

NÍSOS SÉRIFOS

Ó.Psili Ammou

Mega Livádhi

Serifos
See plan
Fl.R.3M

100

N. Vous

Ó. Mega Livádhi

15
⊕

Ák Amino

Ó.Koutala

Ó. Ambeli

Ó. Livadhiou

Ák Kíklops
Fl(2)14s67m9M

Ák Katano

16

Ák Spathí
Fl(3)30s67m19M

0 1 2 3 4 5
Nautical Miles

⊕**14** 0·5M N of Ák Volos (Sérifos)37°13'·14N 24°29'·49E WGS84
⊕**15** 1M W of Ák Kiklops (Sérifos)37°07'·4N 24°23'·7E
⊕**16** 0·2M W of Ák Amino (entrance to Ó. Livadhiou/Sérifos)
37°07'·66N 24°31'·68E WGS84

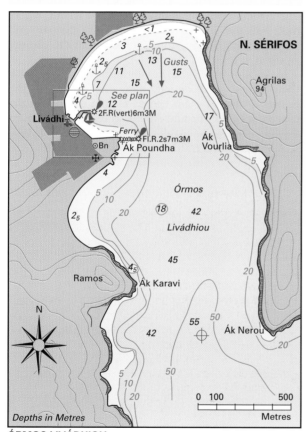

ÓRMOS LIVÁDHIOU
⊕37°07'·97N 24°31'·34E WGS84

By night From the S use the light on Ák Kíklops Fl(2)14s9M and Ák Spathí Fl(3)30s19M. The extremity of the breakwater is lit Fl.R.2s3M. The end of the yacht jetty is lit 2F.R(vert), but should not be relied on. From the N a night approach can be difficult, especially if visibility is not good. There are no useful lights and Nisís Vous is not lit – if coming from the Saronic the approach around the

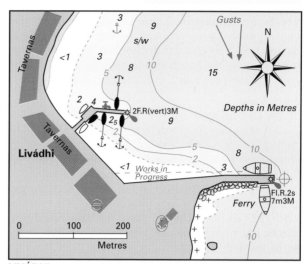

LIVÁDHI
⊕37°08'·49N 24°31'·19E WGS84

W and S side of the island is safer, if slightly longer.

Dangers With the *meltemi* there can be strong gusts off the lee side of the island and in the immediate approaches to Livádhi.

Mooring
Anchor in the bay or go stern or bows-to the jetty off the village on the SE side of the bay. In the summer when the *meltemi* is blowing the S side of the jetty is preferable. On the N side you will need a good anchor and all your chain as well as a bit of nerve when the *meltemi* gusts down into the bay. The bottom is sand and weed and not everywhere the best holding.

Note Works in progress widening the S quay.

Shelter Good shelter from the *meltemi* although there are gusts into the bay. With strong SE winds a swell works around into the bay although it is still tenable. In the summer the harbour is often crowded with yachts.

Authorities Port police.

Anchorage Anchor where convenient in the bay. The bottom is sand and weed and it can be difficult to

Livádhi looking down from the *chora*   *Lu Michell*

get the anchor dug in. There is really not much you can do except persevere and let out as much chain as possible. Some yachts anchor and take a long line ashore across the beach to a tree on the N side of the bay, but the port police will sometimes object.

Facilities
Water On the jetty.
Fuel A mini-tanker can deliver to the quay ☎ 22810 51512.
Provisions Most provisions can be obtained at Livádhi. Ice from a mini-market nearby.
Eating out Good tavernas in the village and around the beach.
Other PO and OTE at the *chora*. Exchange facilities. Greek gas. Bus to the *chora*. Hire motorbikes. Ferry to Mílos and Piraeus.

General
The nearly landlocked bay is fringed by tamarisk trees providing welcome shade from the sun, and the white houses of the *chora* on the hill above, like icing on a bun, are like a cliché of received ideas of the Cyclades. The view from the *chora* down onto the bay and over the sea and islands beyond is worth the trip, and the bus to the *chora* leaves from the root of the yacht mole. The *chora* remains much as it always was, but the settlement around the bay has acquired the usual trappings for the summer tourist trade including highly amplified disco music which, in this otherwise tranquil spot, pierces the night-time air with an unnatural cacophony.

ÓRMOS KOUTALA
An open bay on the S side of Sérifos offering good shelter from the *meltemi*. Anchor in either of the two coves at the head of the bay. In the NE cove anchor in 3–5m on a sandy bottom. In the NW cove care must be taken of a foul area where large mooring chains have been laid. Anchor where shown in 6–10m on a sandy bottom. Good shelter from the

meltemi although there are strong gusts into the bay.

On either side of the bay are the remains of iron ore mines and jetties and the concentration of ore is reported to cause local magnetic anomalies. Taverna. A number of villas have been built around the shores.

MEGA LIVÁDHI
37°08'·5N 24°25'·8E

An inlet NE of Ák Kíklops. It is reported to offer good shelter from the *meltemi*.

NISÍS SERIFOPOULA
A barren uninhabited island lying 4½ miles NE of Sérifos.

Nísos Sífnos
(Síphnos)

The high bold island lying 7 miles SE of Sérifos across the often windy Sífnos Channel. The island is hilly throughout, rising near the centre to Mt Áyios Ilías (694m/2,277ft). The west coast is barren and burnt rock, but on the east side of the island, where most of the population live, it is greener and cultivated in places. Most people live in the capital, Apollonia, on a hill inland.

In ancient times the inhabitants were vilified for their greed and deceit. On one occasion the Sifniotes offered a gilt egg at Delphi instead of the customary gold one and Apollo in revenge destroyed

NÍSOS SÍFNOS

⊕17 1·25M N of Ák Filippos (Sifnos) 37°03'·86N 24°38'·47E WGS84
⊕18 0·4M W of Ák Karavi (N. Kitriani/Sifnos) 36°53'·50N 24°42'·91E WGS84

ÓRMOS KOUTALA
⊕37°07'·8N 24°27'·3E

the gold mines which had formerly earned a great deal of revenue for the island. On the east coast the decaying medieval village of Kástro is a delightful place surrounded by a wall into which two and three-storey houses have been built. The village and former capital looks down onto Órmos Kástro and across to Andíparos and Páros.

Today the beaches on the SE coast of the island are popular and a number of small hotels have been built around the coast.

Note Vrakhos Tsoukala lies 0·5M NNW of Ák Filippos on the N tip of Sífnos. The rock extends only 1m above the surface but can be clearly seen in calm weather.

ÁYIOS YEÓRYIOS

A narrow inlet on the NW tip of the island. It provides good shelter from the *meltemi*, and indeed from all but W winds. There is a quay on the SW side where yachts can go stern or bows-to taking care of underwater rubble off the quay. There is also a quay on the NE side where there may be a space. A local tripper boat also uses the quay. There are 8–10m depths at the dogleg and 3–4m in the middle of the inlet with 2m depths until quite close to the edges. The head of the inlet is shallow.

Tavernas and a ceramics workshop ashore. At one time the last hand-formed giant amphora-like pots were made here.

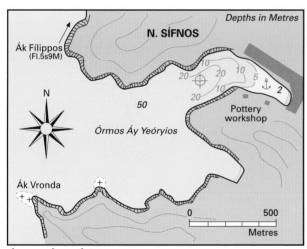

ÓRMOS ÁY YEÓRYIOS
⊕37°02'·2N 24°38'·8E

VOURLITHA

Lies between North Bay and Áyios Yeóryios. It has been recommended as an anchorage, but I find it a bleak desolate spot affording little shelter, certainly not as good as that offered by nearby anchorages.

NORTH BAY

Just N of Kamáres there is a small bay affording some shelter from the *meltemi*. Cliffs surround the bay except where two deep gullies descend into the bay. Anchor in 4–5m between the gullies. The bottom is sand and weed, not everywhere good holding. No facilities.

KAMÁRES

BA 1538

Approach

Conspicuous It is difficult to see where the entrance is to the bay – vessels appear to pop out of a slit in the cliffs. The light structure on the N side of the entrance is conspicuous. Once near the entrance the buildings of the town and the outer mole can be seen.

By night Use the light on Ák Kokkála Fl(2)10s9M. The breakwater is lit on its extremity: Fl.G.1·5s3M.

Dangers It is advisable to take down your sails before entering the bay as with the *meltemi* there are strong gusts from all directions at the entrance and inside the bay.

Mooring

Go alongside or stern or bows-to the inside of the mole. Ferries now berth on the outside of the mole. Alternatively anchor at the head of the bay. The bottom is hard sand and weed with some rocks – fair holding only.

Shelter Good shelter from the *meltemi* although there are gusts. With W winds a swell rolls into the bay.

Authorities Port police and customs.

Facilities

Water On the quay.

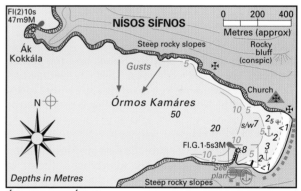

ÓRMOS KAMÁRES
⊕36°59'·50N 24°39'·21E WGS84

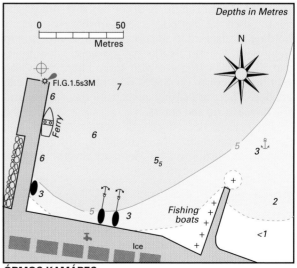

ÓRMOS KAMÁRES
⊕36°59'·42N 24°40'·47E WGS84

Sífnos. Kamáres looking WNW from the slopes behind the bay
Nigel Patten

Vathi on Sífnos looking SE   *Nigel Patten*

Fuel Can be delivered by mini-tanker to the quay.

Provisions Most provisions although supplies are much dependent on the ferries.

Eating out Good tavernas on the waterfront and around the beach.

Other Bank, ATM. Motorbike and car hire. A regular bus runs to Apollonia, the island capital, where there are a PO and OTE. Ferries to Mílos and Piraeus.

General

Kamáres is the ferry port for Sífnos and the setting between the high cliffs and hills is spectacular. During the summer it is a bustling little resort town, and a good base for a trip to Apollonia and Kástro.

ÓRMOS VATHI

A landlocked bay affording the best all-round shelter on Sífnos. The entrance is somewhat difficult to identify until you get there, when the cliffs on either side open up to an amphitheatre of a bay. There is a light structure on the S side of the entrance Fl.2s7M. Anchor in the N of the bay in 3–4m on the gently shelving bottom – sand and weed, patchy holding in places. Off the chapel there is a section of quay with 2–2·5m depths off it where a few boats can go stern or bows-to with care. There are a also number of coves on the S side where a yacht can anchor. There are strong gusts from the *meltemi* into the bay, but no sea enters.

Water near the church. Tavernas ashore. The surroundings here are wonderful, the water a translucent turquoise, and there are several tavernas on the beach for a run ashore.

FIKIADHA

A deserted inlet immediately S of Vathi which offers reasonable shelter from winds N through E to S. Open to the W only. Anchor in the inlet with a long line ashore or go bows-to the short pier below the chapel (1·5m depths at the extremity). The bottom

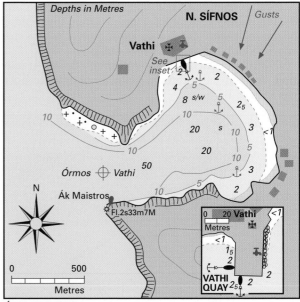

ÓRMOS VATHI
⊕36°55′·62N 24°41′·01E WGS84

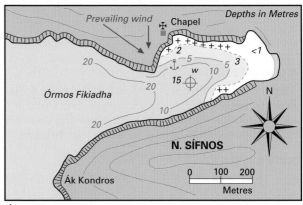

ÓRMOS FIKIADHA
⊕36°54′·4N 24°41′·6E

is sand and mud with some rock, not everywhere good holding. Apart from the chapel the inlet is quite deserted, magnificently so.

PLATÍ YIALOS

A U-shaped bay on the SE coast. Good shelter from the *meltemi* although there are strong gusts into the bay. Anchor off the NE corner in 5–7m. There are 2m depths approximately 80m off the beach. The bottom is sand and rock, not everywhere good holding. Tavernas and hotels on the beach.

Faros looking NE towards the head of the bay   *Nigel Patten*

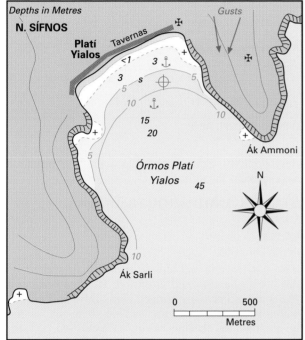

ÓRMOS PLATÍ YIALOS
⊕36°55'·6N 24°44'·0E

FAROS (Pharos)

BA 1538

An inlet near the SE tip of Sífnos providing good shelter from the *meltemi*. Open only to the S. The church on Ák Petalos, on the W side of the entrance, and the light structure on Ák Stavrós, on the E side of the entrance, are conspicuous. The best place to be is anchored off the bluff at the head of the bay with a long line ashore. There is a short quay with 2–3m depths on the E side of the bay where a few yachts may be able to go stern or bows-to. Often it is occupied by local and tripper boats. Alternatively anchor in one of the coves on the W and E side of the entrance. The bottom is sand and weed – good holding once through the weed. Good shelter from the *meltemi* although there are strong gusts into the bay.

Tavernas at the head of the bay and limited provisions. A number of villas and small hotels have been built around the adjacent coastline – mostly frequented by the young. The bay, hemmed in by high land, is a wonderful place with good swimming in the clear water and good snorkelling around the adjacent coast.

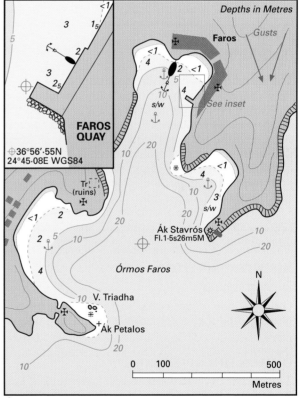

ÓRMOS FAROS
⊕36°56'·3N 24°45·2E

KÁSTRO

An open cove under the medieval village on the slopes above. The cove lying immediately N of Ák Miti is suitable only in calm weather, being entirely open to the prevailing summer northerlies. Anchor in 3–4m off the tiny beach and take a long line ashore. The bottom is sand and weed, mostly adequate holding.

There is a hamlet by the beach and a track leading up to the fascinating huddle of medieval houses

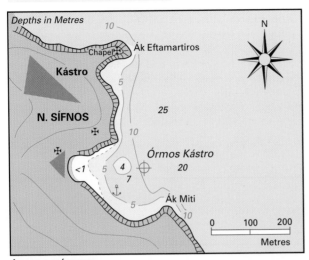

ÓRMOS KÁSTRO
⊕36°58'·3N 24°45'·1E

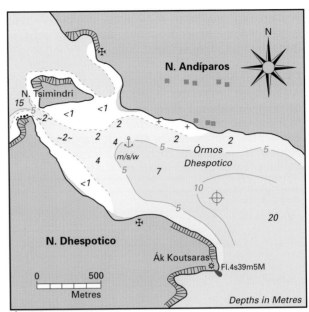

ÓRMOS DHESPOTICO
⊕36°58'·2N 25°02'·0E

perched on the steep slopes. If the weather does not permit a visit by yacht then take a bus or taxi from Kamáres to Apollonia and from there to Kástro.

Andíparos

(Anti-Páros)

The island of Andíparos lies close off the SW side of Páros, separated by a narrow shallow channel. It is low-lying (299m/981ft at the summit in the middle) and barren. The village of Andíparos lies on the east coast near the narrowest part of the channel. Near the south end of the channel there is a deep cave containing a small chapel and spectacular stalactites and stalagmites. Excursions from Andíparos village and Paroikia by tripper boat.

The two islands to the south of Andíparos, Nisís Dhespotico and Nisís Strongiló, are barren and uninhabited.

NISÍS DHESPOTICO

36°57'·4N 25°00'·6E

On the S side of this island there is a deserted bay offering good shelter from the *meltemi*. Open only to the S.

ÓRMOS DHESPOTICO

The large bay between Nisís Dhespotico and Andíparos. It is protected on the N and E by Andíparos and on the S and W by Nisís Dhespotico and the islet of Tsimindri in the NW. The channel on the N side of Nisís Tsimindri has less than one metre depths. The channel on the S side of Tsimindri has reported 2m depths in the fairway. It should be attempted in calm weather only with someone up front conning you through, and is not one for the faint-hearted.

Anchor in 2–4m where convenient on the N side. The bottom is sand and weed – good holding. In the 16th and 17th centuries the bay was a laying-up port for pirate galleys. The recent construction of a number of roads has opened up the area to development. Several tavernas on the Andíparos side open in the summer.

STENÓN ANDÍPAROU (Anti-Páros Channel)

BA 1539

Imray-Tetra G33

The narrow channel should only be attempted by day with due care and attention. Remmatonisi and the coast of Páros are fringed with above and below-water rocks and with the *meltemi* there are strong gusts down the channel raising a short disturbed sea. A deep-draught yacht should not attempt the channel and small to medium-sized yachts should do so with someone up front conning you through and one eye on the depth-sounder. A yacht

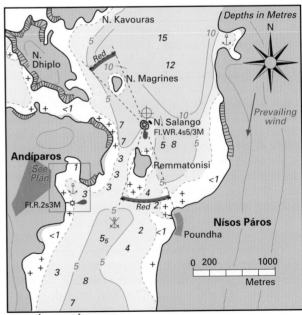

STENÓN ANDÍPAROU
(ANDÍPAROS CHANNEL – 14 FOOT PASSAGE)
⊕37°03'·1N 25°05'·8E (N. Salango light)

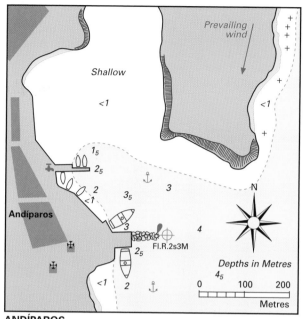

ANDÍPAROS
⊕37°02'·4N 25°05'·2E

attempting the passage for the first time should do so in calm weather if possible when the reefs fringing the passage are easily seen. With the *meltemi*, identifying the green of the safe passage and the brown of rocks in the underwater mosaic becomes more difficult.

The channel on the W side of Remmatonisi can also be used by shallow-draught yachts with due care and attention although there are less depths than on the E side.

Note Recent charts show the deeper passage to be on the W side of Remmatonisi, but in my experience the passage on the E side is better. Recently least depths of 3·8m were reported in the W Channel. If anyone out there wants to survey either passage again in calm weather, please let me know the results.

ANDÍPAROS

In the cove off the village on the W side of Andíparos channel a yacht can find some shelter from the *meltemi*. There is only a limited amount of space here. Try for a berth at the N pier. Spaces here are normally reserved for local boats and you should not occupy the ferry berth as ferries run frequently from Pountas on the other side of the channel. You can try anchoring off on the N side of the bay keeping clear of the piers although most of the bay is shallow. Anchor in 2–2·5m on sand and weed, good holding once the anchor is in. Reasonable shelter from the *meltemi* although gusts blow in from the channel.

Several tavernas on the waterfront and limited provisions can be found in the village.

Andiparos has been much developed in recent years and there are now numerous hotels and the accompanying bars and tavernas. Once you penetrate the concrete overcoat around the old village it reveals itself to be a wonderful fortified little town. The fortified wall that surrounds the village was built by Loredano in the mid-15th century to protect the population from pirate raids.

Around the southern end of the channel there are numerous enchanting coves to be explored in calm weather. The shallow water and sandy bottom produce those wonderful blues and greens so often reproduced on postcards.

POUNDHA

37°02'·3N 25°06'·0E

A small port on the Paros side of the channel for the ferries to Andiparos. There are 1·5–2m depths off the pier but there is really no room here for a yacht.

Páros

A large oval island which is essentially one mountain with two peaks: Mt Áyios Ilías (771m/2,530ft) to the NW and Mt Karamboli (747m/2,450ft) to the SE. The land slopes down evenly from the two peaks to the sea. The land is mostly barren and burnt rock with few trees. The port and capital is Paroikia on the NW coast.

The island was colonised early on by the Ionians from Asia Minor. In the 7th century BC the Parians sent a party to colonise Thásos. Archilochus, the lyric satirist credited with inventing Iambic verse, was born on Páros and accompanied the colonizing party to Thásos. Ernle Bradford relates some amusing details about the poet: he was thrown out of Sparta for his 'cowardice and licentious character' and when fighting the Thracians admitted on one occasion to throwing away his shield and running away. Unfortunately this likeable muse was killed whilst fighting the neighbouring Naxians. During the Persian invasions Páros sided with the Persians and with their defeat was consequently subdued and became subject to Athens. In the Middle Ages the island was colonised by the Venetians until falling to the Turks in 1537.

In ancient times Parian marble was famous. The marble was called *Lychnites* – won by lamplight – as it was mined underground in tunnels. Because the marble was difficult to mine, the mines were abandoned after classical times and were last used in 1844 when marble was required for Napoleon's tomb. The mines and tunnels can still be seen today. Parian wine was also famous in antiquity and today the red wine made on the island is passably palatable. Páros is a popular tourist island, Paroikiá fairly bulges at the seams in summer, and consequently facilities are well developed.

PAROIKIÁ

BA 1539

Approach

Conspicuous In the approaches to Paroikiá there are a number of islands and reefs encircling the bay. From the N these are: Pórtes, two in number and looking like a pair of bookends; Petrokáravo, an almost submerged rock difficult to identify in rough

259

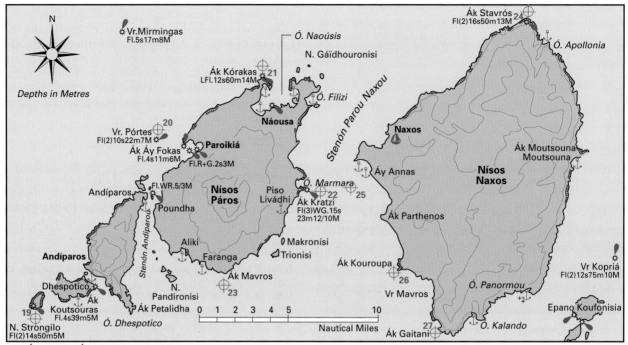

ANDÍPAROS, PÁROS AND NAXOS

⊕19 1·5M S of Ns. Strongiló light (Andíparos)
36°55'·21N 24°57'·04E WGS84

⊕20 0·5M N of Pórtes Rocks
37°06'·5N 25°06'·1E

⊕21 1M N of Ák Kórakas light (Páros)
37°10'·3N 25°13'·5E

⊕22 1M E of Ák Kratzi (Páros)
37°03'·0N 25°17'·7E

⊕23 1M S of Ák Mavros (Páros)
36°57'·6N 25°11'·0E

⊕24 0·6M N of Ák Stavrós (Naxos)
37°12'·85N 25°32'·38E WGS84

⊕25 0·5M E of Vr. Amaridhes (Stenón Parou-Náxou)
37°03'·0N 25°19'·6E

⊕26 0·35M W of Ák Kouroupa (Naxos)
36°58'·36N 25°22'·66E WGS84

⊕27 0·5M SW of Ák Gaitani (Naxos)
36°55'·24N 25°25'·18E WGS84

Ák Áy Fokas (light structure and church conspicuous), the N
entrance point to Órmos Paroikiás looking NW

seas; Vouves, low with a reef off the NE end and a
reef with 3m over it 0·2 miles to the SW; Nisídhes
Áy Spirídhonos, high and jagged (with a white
chapel on one) except for the easternmost islet
which is low; and Mavro Toúrlos off the N end of
Nisís Kavoúras, high and jagged. Further into the
bay, Kakí Skála and Peponas are low-lying. The
white houses of Paroikiá are easily seen once into the
bay. A white church with a blue cupola is
conspicuous on Ák Áy Fokas. The harbour off
Paroikiá is easily identified when close in.

By night Use the light on Pórtes Fl(2)10s7M and on
Ák Áy Fokas Fl.4s6M. Two pillar buoys Q.G/Q.R
mark the deep water channel into Limín Paroikiá.
Street lights illuminate the ferry quay.

Dangers
1. Care is needed of the reef and above-water rock
just N of Nisídhes Áy Spiridhonos and of the
shoal water just N of Vouves in the approaches to
Órmos Paroikiás.

2. Care must be taken of the reef and shoal water
extending out from Ák Áy Fokas. There are
depths of 3m or less some 300m S of the cape.

3. Care is needed of a reef running out from the
coast on the S side of the entrance to Órmos
Paroikiás.

4. There is an extensive shallow rock shelf on the E
side of Ák Krios. An old mole now underwater
runs out from the N side of the bay for 250m
between the more easterly of the two houses with
white arches (conspic.) in a roughly SE direction.
Depths over the submerged mole are less than
2m and in places only just 1m over.

5. The light structure on Ifalos Paroikiá has been
removed and the reef levelled. Two pillar buoys
now show the deep water channel into the
harbour.

Note On 26 September 2000 the ferry *Samina
Express* hit the Pórtes rocks in the approaches to
Paroikiá. The ship sank in 40 metres in the vicinity
of the rocks at 37°05'N 25°07'E. Over 80 people

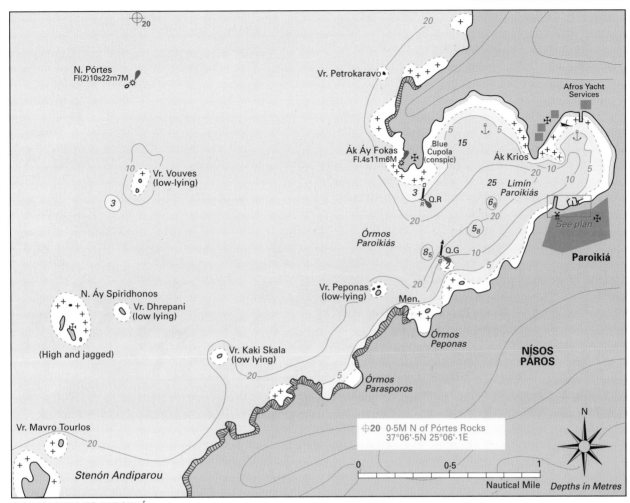

APPROACHES TO PAROIKIÁ

drowned in the worst maritime disaster in Greece for 35 years. Rob and Di Brown who have lived on Paros for 31 years make the following observations:

'It is a matter of observation that a sustained *meltemi* gale sets up a current that can exceed 2 knots going south around the Pórtes rocks and down the Antiparos channel. This was almost certainly the direct cause of the sinking of the *Samina*. (It is commonly believed on Paros that the ship was on a compass autopilot course, which would normally have carried it nearly 1/3 of a mile further north. My brother-in-law was swept close to the Pórtes himself three hours before the accident.) The rescue at night from the sea in a F8 gale in the no-go area itself of 400 of the 500 or so on board is little short of miraculous to those who know the area.

Except for a few fishermen, almost all local boats treat the sea between the Pórtes rocks and the Áy Spiridhones islets as a 'no-go' area. It is simply too easy to go wrong even in half-metre waves. The unmarked Vouves reef is awash in calm weather, and lost in white horses in any sea. The outliers from the Áy Spiridhones islets are underwater and run a long way north and also east towards Kaki Skala. There are two safe routes in and out of Paroikiá, used by the ferries: firstly passing N of Pórtes and keeping at least ¼ mile offshore and S of Áy Fokas headland; secondly passing about 300m N of Peponas and Kaki Skala (both easily visible by day), then keeping to the channel S of the Áy Spiridhones islets and N of the Mavros and Kókkinos Toúrlos pillars.'

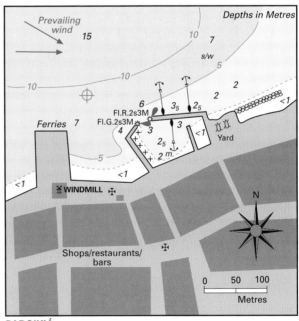

PAROIKIÁ
⊕37°05'·3N 25°09'·1E

Paroikiá on Páros looking NW across Órmos Paroikiás
Peter Kleinoth/MareTeam

Mooring

Berth stern or bows-to in the inner harbour or in calm weather off the outside of the mole. The bottom is mud and weed, mostly good holding.

Shelter Excellent shelter inside the harbour. If the inner harbour is crowded and the *meltemi* makes berthing on the outside of the moles impossible, it is best to anchor in one of the bays to the N of the harbour.

Note Works are in progress to the W of the ferry quay.

Authorities Port police and customs.

Anchorage A yacht can anchor in either of the two bays on the N side of Órmos Paroikiás. The bay in the NE affords the best shelter from the *meltemi* but you need to be careful of the rock shelf off the shore and the sunken mole running for 250 metres out from the shore mentioned in 'Dangers' above. Anchor in 4–6m on sand, mud and weed, good holding once through the weed. This anchorage is untenable in southerlies.

Facilities

Water On the quay once the 'water man' is located.
Fuel On the outskirts of town. A mini-tanker can deliver to the harbour.
Repairs Yacht service agency. Call *Afros Yacht Service* on VHF Ch 73 or ☎ 22840 23625. Mechanical repairs. Sailmaker. Chandlers. General hardware.

Provisions Good shopping for all provisions in the town. Ice available.
Eating out Good tavernas of all types. I favour some of the local tavernas in the streets behind the harbour, but there are all sorts of other tavernas in town.
Other PO. OTE. Banks. ATMs. Greek gas and Camping Gaz. Hire cars, motorbikes and bicycles. Buses to the other villages on the island. Ferries to Piraeus, Rhodes, Iraklion and nearby Cyclades islands.

General

Built on a gentle slope beside the sea with steep slopes behind, Paroikiá is typically Cycladic – houses, shops, churches are dazzling white cubes with bougainvillea and wisteria providing splashes of natural colour. The old quarter around the 13th-century *kástro* is an intriguing place full of narrow winding alleys and archways, stone houses and shops with wooden balconies.

Paroikiá possesses the finest church in the Aegean, the Katapoliani (Ekatontepiliani). The name is said to mean 'the church of the 100 doors', but more probably means simply 'below the town'. The church is in fact three churches under one roof and it is well worth a visit for the beautiful interior – a mixture of the original and some recent renovation in neo-Byzantine style. On 15 August pilgrims converge on the church although the celebrations cannot compete with the Tiniot festival. Near the church the archaeological museum houses some interesting finds including a slab of the Parian Chronicle recording Greek history from pre-Homeric times and some sculptures in Parian marble.

The harbour is busy in the summer with ferries constantly coming and going bringing throngs of holidaymakers to the main port. The town resounds to the babble of different languages, the entreaties of waiters wanting your custom, and the click of camera shutters, and no wonder – some of the streets ending literally at the sea on the W of the town rival those in Míkonos for wonderful Cycladic architecture.

NÁOUSA

BA 1539

Approach

This large much-indented bay lies on the N end of Páros between Ák Kórakas and the islet of Gaïdhouronísi.

Conspicuous The white lighthouse on Ák Kórakas is conspicuous and from the entrance to the bay the power station buildings on the S side of Órmos Langeri, the white houses of Náousa, and a large

Ák Kórakas and lighthouse on the W side of the entrance to Órmos Naoúsis looking SW

church with a red cupola behind the village, are conspicuous.

By night A night approach is not recommended. In good visibility use the light on Ák Korakas LFl.12s14M and the lights at the entrance to Náousa harbour Fl.R.1·5s3M/Fl.G.1·5s3M.

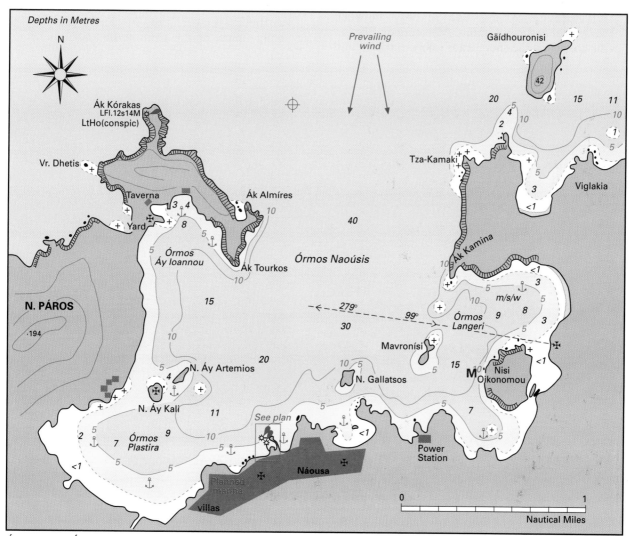

ÓRMOS NAOÚSIS ⊕37°09'·44N 25°14'·35E WGS84

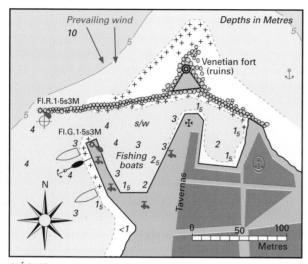

NÁOUSA
⊕37°07´·6N 25°14´·2E

Dangers Care is needed of the above and below water rocks fringing the islets and shores of the large bay.

Mooring
There are numerous anchorages around the bay.
1. **Órmos Langeri** Care is needed of the reef in the W entrance to the bay midway between Mavronísi and Ák Kamina. A bearing of 099° on the chapel on the shore leads safely into here and conversely, a back-bearing of 279° leads safely out. Anchor at the N end where convenient in 4–10m on mud, sand, and weed, good holding. Good shelter from the *meltemi* tucked into the N end. Yachts can also anchor at the S end of the bay in calm weather or southerlies. The S end is somewhat spoiled by the large power station there.
2. **Órmos Áy Ioannou** Care is needed of the reef running out from the chapel on the W. Anchor where convenient at the N end in 3–10m. The bottom is mud, sand and weed, good holding. Good shelter from the *meltemi*. A small chapel in the NW corner of the bay is conspicuous and nearby there is a small boatyard. This anchorage is idyllic: sun-baked rock eroded into wonderful shapes, clear turquoise water, a small white chapel perched on the rock near the water, even the boatyard with bright *caïques* hauled out fits into the scene, so consequently it is popular in the summer. Taverna ashore. A local tripper boat operates a service on the half hour to Náousa until 1800 in the summer.

Note The beaches around here are popular for nude swimming and sun-bathing. That so, it should always be remembered that in the vicinity of a church or chapel it is frowned upon. As the sign at the chapel here puts it: 'These grounds are holly – plese do not swim in the nude' *(sic)*.

Órmos Naoúsis looking NW across to Órmos Áy Ioannou and Ák Almires on the W side of the entrance. Náousa harbour is middle left
Peter Kleinoth/MareTeam

3. **Órmos Plastira** In calm weather anchor where convenient. With the *meltemi* some shelter can be found anchored in 3–4m under Nisís Áy Kali.

4. **Náousa** Most of the space in the harbour is taken up with local boats and tripper boats, although if you can find a berth inside then this is a good option. Yachts now go on the outside of the W mole leaving the striped area in the middle free for the ferry. There are mostly 1·5–3m depths off the quay although care is needed of underwater ballasting in places. Good holding and reasonable shelter from the *meltemi*.

In calm weather you can use the bay on the E side of the fort, although care is needed of a mooring chain lying approximately W–E in the bay. Yachts also anchor off just W of the harbour in 4–10m on sand and weed, good holding. The *meltemi* doesn't normally blow home here although at times when it is blowing strongly the anchorage off here is not the best and you are better off moving elsewhere in the bay.

Authorities Port police at Náousa.

Facilities
Water On the quay.
Fuel Can be delivered by mini-tanker to the harbour.
Repairs Minor repairs at Náousa. Yachts are hauled at the yard in Órmos Áy Ioannou using a cradle and slipway. It is a bit isolated but has the advantage that you can wander down to the water and have a swim.
Provisions Most provisions can be found at Náousa.
Eating out Good tavernas at Náousa.
Other PO. OTE. Bank. Greek gas. Hire motorbikes and bicycles. Bus to Paroikiá.

General
The bay is a much indented amoeboid shape of sun-baked rock enclosing clear blue and turquoise water. Much of the rock has been sculpted into weird and wonderful shapes that give the bay a desolate feel. Although popular in the summer, there is nearly always somewhere to tuck yourself into away from the others. Out of season it is positively lonely.

Náousa was a small fishing village that has grown into a large straggling tourist resort. The tavernas and bars clustered around the edge of the inner basin provide a pleasant spot to while away an evening. A windsurfing school operates from a hotel on the E side of the bay.

Note There are plans to build a marina immediately W of Náousa harbour utilising the bight in the coast here. At the time of writing work had not started and there was some uncertainty over when or if work would begin.

VIGLAKIA
This is the knobbly NE tip of Páros with a number of off-lying islets (Gaïdhouronisi, Tourlites, Ovriokastro and Fonisses). Local boats take a shortcut between the islands and Paros to get to the Parou-Naxou Channel and in calm weather with someone up front keeping an eye on things, navigating between the islands and Paros is

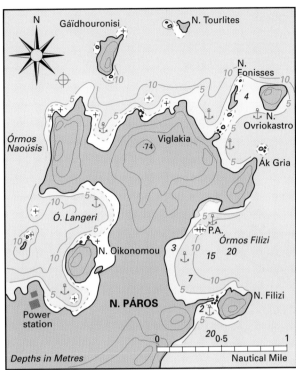

GAÏDHOURONISI TO NISÍS FILIZI
⊕37°09'·45N 25°15'·35E

straightforward. When the *meltemi* is blowing it is prudent to go around the outside of the islets. In calm weather there are a number of delightful anchorages, but with any hint of northerlies you should leave.

ÓRMOS FILIZI
37°08'·0N 25°17'·2E

The bay directly under Ák Gria. In calm weather or light westerlies it is an attractive anchorage. Care is needed of a wreck on the bottom on the N side of the bay. Anchor in 4–6m on sand and weed.

There is also a delightful anchorage tucked under Nisís Filizi which lies close off the S side of the bay.

ÓRMOS MARMARA
37°03'·4N 25°16'·1E

A large bay on the E coast. Although it looks as if there should be good shelter here, the *meltemi* blowing down the strait between Páros and Naxos sends a swell in. Anchor in the NW corner in light N winds or calm weather.

PISO LIVÁDHI (Marpissa, Tsipidho Bay)
Approach
A small harbour approximately 1½ miles SSW of Órmos Marmara.

Conspicuous A peak with a conspicuous white building on the summit immediately N of Piso Livádhi is easily identified. Closer in a cluster of villas and small hotels around the coast will be seen. The breakwater is easily identified once up to the bay.

By night There are no lights marking the reef and a night approach is not recommended (see *Dangers*

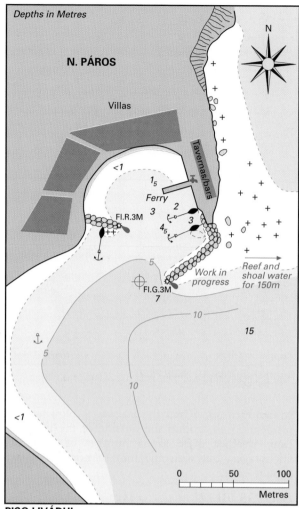

Depths in Metres

N. PÁROS

Villas

Tavernas/bars

Ferry

Fl.R.3M

Work in progress

Reef and shoal water for 150m

Fl.G.3M

0   50   100
Metres

PISO LIVÁDHI
⊕37°02'·0N 25°15'·5E

below).

Dangers A reef and shoal water extends E from the breakwater for about 250m. Keep well off and approach the bay from the SE.

Note Works are in progress inside the harbour repairing the breakwater and dredging parts of the basin. It is planned to extend the quayed area around the breakwater which will considerably increase the number of berths available. Care needed when entering the harbour.

Mooring

Go stern or bows-to the breakwater with a long line to it. Some care is needed of permanent moorings fouling the bottom and of a wreck on the bottom. With care you can also go bows-to the short W breakwater with a long line to it. Care is needed of underwater ballasting extending out in places. The bottom is sand and weed, good holding. When the ferry is not due in (it normally arrives in the morning and early evening, but does not stay for long) small yachts can go bows-to the short pier where there are 1·5–2m depths.

Shelter Reasonable shelter from the *meltemi* although with a prolonged blow there can be a surge in here. Open to the SE when it is uncomfortable and can become untenable.

Anchorage In calm weather a yacht can anchor in the S part of the bay.

Note Yachts should not anchor in the vicinity of the entrance where the ferry needs room to manoeuvre.

Facilities

Water At the root of the mole.
Provisions Some provisions available in the village.
Eating out Several tavernas around the waterfront with wonderful views over the harbour and the strait.
Other Ferry to Naxos and Amorgós.

General

The small village has a modest amount of tourism in the summer and is a convivial place much removed from the hustle and bustle of Paroikiá. The setting is wonderful under the slopes of Páros on the edge of Stenón Parou-Náxou. The anchorage in the S part of the bay makes a good lunch stop in calm weather.

FARANGA

A double-headed bay on the S side of Paros. Care is needed of the reef off the SW entrance point. Anchor in either of the two heads of the bay with the more easterly considered the best. In the E bay anchor off the beach in 4–7m on sand and weed. Reasonable shelter from the *meltemi* although some swell swings around from the Parou-Naxou Channel into the bay – uncomfortable rather than dangerous.

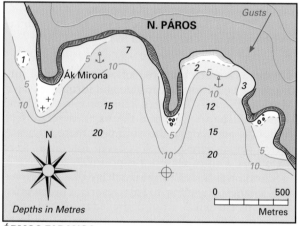

Gusts

N. PÁROS

Ák Mirona

N

Depths in Metres

0   500
Metres

ÓRMOS FARANGA
⊕36°58'·8N 25°09'·2E

ALIKI (Órmos Angaria)

A bay on the SW coast of Páros lying 2 miles NW of Ák Mavros. Anchor in 2–3m depths in the bay. Sandy bottom. On the E side of the bay a stubby breakwater shelters a quay and short pier. There are 1–2m depths off the quay and pier, but depths are irregular and there is some underwater rubble along the quay. You are better off at anchor in the bay. Good shelter from the *meltemi* although there are gusts. Open S.

A hotel and tavernas ashore.

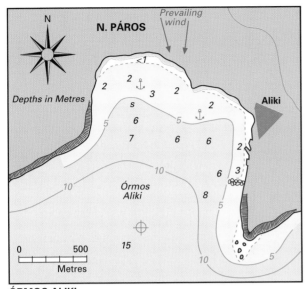

ÓRMOS ALIKI
⊕36°59'·7N 25°08'·0E

STENÓN PAROU-NAXOU (Páros-Naxos Strait)

This strait separating Páros and Naxos is fringed by rocks and reefs. There are also two reefs in the fairway: Ifalos Kalipso (Vrákhoi Tsamban), and Vrákhoi Amarídhes, which has a conspicuous light structure on it (Fl.WR.4s5/3M red sector covers 185°-015°) and a wreck at its S extremity, though the latter has now all but disappeared underwater. With the *meltemi* a current sets to the S at about ½–1½ knots, although with southerlies there is a N-going current. These currents also affect the group of islands to the S of Naxos, but are much modified by the channels between the islands and it is difficult to determine precise directions and rates.

Nísos Naxos

The largest and most fertile of the Cyclades. From seaward the west coast appears rocky and bare but inland the island is wooded and cultivated. The island is mountainous throughout with two high peaks: the summit Mt Zeus lies just to the south of the middle of the island and is 1,084m (3,308ft) high, and 6 miles to the north Mt Korna is 1,065m (3,250ft) high. In the interior valleys the slopes are

USEFUL WAYPOINTS FOR MIDDLE CYCLADES
⊕22 1M E of Ák Kratzi (Páros)
    37°03'·0N 25°17'·7E
⊕24 0·6M N of Ák Stavrós (Naxos)
    37°12'·85N 25°32'·38E WGS84
⊕25 0·5M E of Vr. Amaridhes (Stenón Parou-Náxou)
    37°03'·0N 25°19'·6E
⊕26 0·35M W of Ák Kouroupa (Naxos)
    36°58'·36N 25°22'·66E WGS84
⊕27 0·5M SW of Ák Gaitani (Naxos)
    36°55'·24N 25°25'·18E WGS84
⊕28 0·4M N of Ák Kalota (Dhenoussa)
    37°08'·63N 25°49'·78E WGS84
⊕29 0·5M E of Ák Megalí Poundha (Iráklia)
    36°52'·69N 25°28'·93E WGS84
⊕30 2M S of N. Mikros Avelos (Stenón Iou-Iráklia)
    36°47'·82N 25°23'·94E WGS84
⊕31 0·3M W of S end of N. Ofidhousa (Skhinoúsa)
    36°49'·87N 25°30'·96E WGS84
⊕32 0·5M S of S end of N. Dhrima
    36°49'·5N 25°40'·3E
⊕33 1M N of N. Gramvoúsa (N islet) light (Amorgós)
    36°50'·2N 25°44'·7E
⊕34 0·5M S of Ák Áy Ilias light (Amorgós/Katápola)
    36°49'·2N 25°50'·4E
⊕35 1M N of Ák Vlikadha (Amorgós)
    36°57'·3N 26°00'·2E
⊕36 1M S of Ák Goniá light (Amorgós)
    36°45'·2N 25°48'·0E
⊕37 1M S of Ák Spanó (Lévitha)
    36°58'9N 26°29'·8E

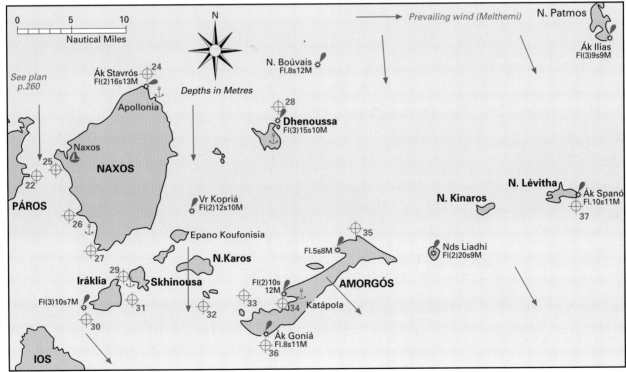

MIDDLE CYCLADES - EAST

terraced and olives, citrus orchards and cypresses grow. The lower plains are cultivated with figs, vines and market gardens.

Naxos is the island where Theseus abandoned Ariadne on his way back to Athens from Crete. It was with Ariadne's help that Theseus penetrated the labyrinth and slew Ariadne's half-brother the Minotaur. Ariadne, in love with Theseus and he apparently in love with her, sailed away from Crete and the first place they landed at was Naxos. Just why Theseus abandoned her has always puzzled classical scholars, but it at least provided the material for one of Catullus' best long poems:

'...Here are the never silent sands of Naxos
here Theseus vanishes towards the north,
a woman watches from the empty beach
unflagging grief in her heart
Ariadne doesn't yet believe, quite,
she is witnessing what her eyes see –
she's only just woken from a trap
(of sleep)
found herself alone on the island...'

Catullus transl. by Peter Whigham

Luckily Dionysus landed on the island and they fell in love at first sight. They appear to have been happy together and Ariadne bore the god many children. Dionysus, the god of the vine, appears to have been a gentler, less raucous god than his Roman namesake, Bacchus, and he blessed Naxos with great fertility and good wine. Today Naxian white wine is still quite palatable, though perhaps not good enough for Dionysus if he is around.

Naxos was sacked by the Persians in 490 BC and thereafter the island steadfastly aided the Athenians. In 1207 the Venetian adventurer Marco Sanudo occupied the island and it remained a Venetian duchy for 300 years. The succeeding dynasty of Sanudo, the Crispi, ruled over most the Cyclades until Naxos fell to the Turks in 1566. It became Greek in 1832.

If you decide to leave your yacht at Naxos town, the only really safe harbour on the island, then the magnificent interior is well worth visiting. The young Byron on visiting Naxos wanted to buy the island and return here to retire. In Apollonia a large unfinished marble statue some 10·5m high lies in the marble bed it was carved from. It was intended for Delos, but probably it was decided that the marble was of poor quality. There are also a number of Byzantine churches with good frescoes.

NAXOS

BA 1539
Imray-Tetra G33

Approach

Conspicuous Ák Moungri to the SW of the town has a conspicuous conical peak on it. Closer in the hump of white buildings of Naxos town and a marble arch on Nisís Apollonas (joined by a causeway to Naxos) will be seen. The breakwater and harbour are easily identified and there is usually a ferry or two in the harbour or coming or going to aid identification.

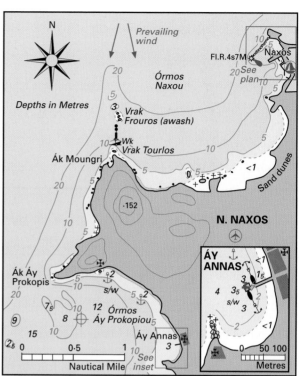

APPROACHES TO NAXOS AND ÓRMOS ÁY PROKOPIOU
⊕37°04'·4N 25°20'·2E

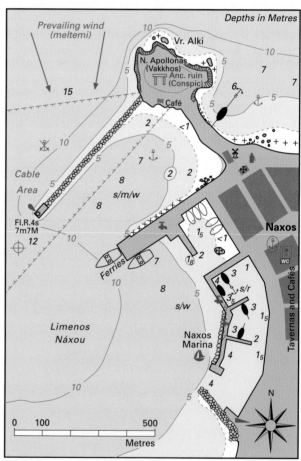

NAXOS
⊕37°06'·36N 25°21'·99E WGS84

Naxos harbour looking NE with Nisís Apollonas middle left. The photograph was taken before the marina was built

Peter Kleinoth/MareTeam

is reported still uncomfortable with ferry wash. With a strong *meltemi* a scend develops around the piers, particularly the outer pier, more uncomfortable than dangerous. In these conditions the quay wall becomes untenable.

Authorities Port police and customs. Charge band 2.

Anchorage
1. Anchor under the breakwater in the NE corner. There are convenient depths of 4–7m. Take care to avoid the 2m shoal shown on the plan. The bottom is sand, rock, and weed, good holding once the anchor bites properly. Care is needed of a number of permanent moorings in the anchorage. Good shelter from the *meltemi*. Southerlies send a swell in.
2. Anchor and take a long line ashore on the NE side of the isthmus joining Nisís Vakkhos to Naxos. The bottom is sand, rock, and weed, good holding once the anchor is in. Open to the *meltemi* but sheltered from southerlies.

Facilities
Services Water on the main ferry mole and near the café/bar on Apollonas. Water and electricity in the marina. Showers and WC near the marina.
Fuel Close to the root of the mole. A mini-tanker can deliver to the harbour.
Repairs Some mechanical repairs can be carried out. Hardware shops.
Provisions Good shopping for provisions in the town behind the 'marina'. Wine from the barrel. Ice available.
Eating out Good tavernas in the town.
Other PO. OTE. Banks. ATMs. Greek gas and Camping Gaz. Hire cars, motorbikes and bicycles. Buses to the main villages on the island. Ferries to Piraeus, Rhodes, Iraklion and nearby Cyclades islands.

General
The town, built on a low hummock by the water, is a typically whitewashed Cycladic place with a smattering of Venetian here and there. I have been reprimanded for calling it 'somewhat scruffy' in earlier editions, but it has been cleaned up since then. The warren of alleys, arches and tunnels around the Venetian castle on the summit of the hill is the most fascinating part of the town. It was the up-market end of town and many of the entrances sport coats of arms from the time when Naxos ruled over the surrounding islands.

The marble arch on Nisís Apollon Vakkhos (or Bacchus) is part of a temple begun about 530 BC and never finished. The archaeological museum in the town houses early Cycladic finds, Mycenaean pottery and gold jewellery and classical finds. The museum was once a schoolhouse where the writer Nikos Kazantzakis (best known for *Zorba the Greek*) taught for 12 years before returning to his native Crete.

By night The extremity of the breakwater is lit: Fl.R.4s7M.

Dangers
1. Care must be taken of Vrakhos Frouros, the reef lying approximately 1¼ miles WSW of the harbour and 0·3 miles N of Ák Moungri, the S extremity of Órmos Náxou. By day the reef, two rocks just above water surrounded by underwater rocks and shoal water, is easily identified in calm weather and there are no problems in passing between it and the cape. With any sea running the above-water rocks are more difficult to locate and it is prudent to go well outside them.

   In 2000 a small ferry hit the rocks and sank between Vrak. Frouros and the coast. The top of a mast on the superstructure is just above water and a buoy (conical Y with two balls vertical) has been laid just N of the wreck in the channel between Frouros and the coast. Navigation warnings give the position for the wreck as 37°06'N 25°21'E.
2. With the *meltemi* there are gusts and some swell at the entrance to the harbour.
3. A good lookout must be kept in the approaches to the harbour for the numerous ferries coming and going, often at considerable speed, until right up to the harbour.

Mooring

Naxos Marina
Note The marina has been privatised and the new management will take over in 2004. We can expect that facilities will be improved and additional infrastructure developed.

The basic structure is now completed and is open to yachts and fishing boats. Yachts go stern or bows–to the concrete piers. Laid moorings tailed to buoys, but sometimes left tangled up. The E quay has been widened and depths alongside are 1–1·5m.

Shelter Much improved with the mole extension, but

ÓRMOS ÁYIOS PROKOPIOU

Lies under the lee of Ák Prokopis about 3 miles S of Naxos. Anchor off in 4–6m. Sandy bottom. There is

Ák Katomeri looking SE

shelter from the *meltemi* but nearly always some swell in the bay.

Beach tavernas open in the summer.

ÁY ANNAS

A small resort at the southern end of Órmos Áy Prokopiou. Anchor off the resort in 4–6m on sand. Alternatively go stern or bows-to the outer end of the pier. Reasonable shelter from the *meltemi*.

Water and electricity on the pier. Limited provisions and tavernas ashore.

DANGERS IN PAROU-NÁXOU CHANNEL

1. Care must be taken of Ifalos Kalipso (Vrákhoi Tsamban) lying approximately 0·8 miles SW of Ák Prokopis.
2. Care must be taken of the reef lying 0·4 miles off Áy Nikólaos in the S of Órmos Prokopis.
3. Care must be taken of Vrákhoi Amarídhes.
4. From a position roughly parallel to Vrákhoi Amarídhes and extending down to Ák Parthenos, above and below-water rocks fringe the coast of Naxos up to just over a mile off.

ÓRMOS KOUROUPA (Áy Ioánnis)

An open bay under Ák Kouroupa. A large unfinished hotel complex on Ák Kouroupa is conspicuous from seaward. Anchor off in 4–6m. There is a short pier, but it is rock-bound. The bottom is sand with some rocks – good holding. The *meltemi* is funnelled down the Páros-Naxos Strait

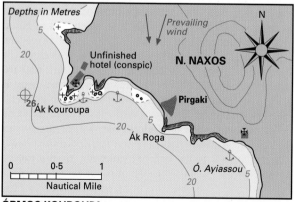

ÓRMOS KOUROUPA

⊕26 0·35M W of Ák Kouroupa (Naxos)
36°58'·36N 25°22'·66E WGS84

and pushes a swell around the cape, making it uncomfortable in here.

ÓRMOS KALANDO

A bay on the SE coast about 1½ miles NE of Ák Katomeri. Anchor near the head of the bay in 3–6m. Sandy bottom. Good shelter from the *meltemi* although there are gusts into the bay. No facilities.

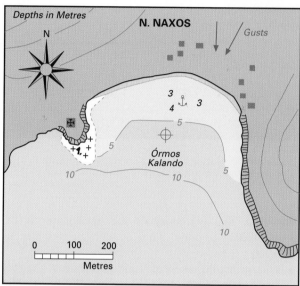

ÓRMOS KALANDO
⊕36°56'·2N 25°28'·4E

ÓRMOS PANORMOU

A bay under Ák Panormos on the SE tip of Naxos. Care is needed in the approaches of Ifalos Dhilos, an isolated reef lying off the coast. The approach is best made from the E towards Ák Panormos. Anchor in 3–5m at the head of the inlet. The bottom is sand and weed, good holding once dug in. There are severe gusts down into the bay with the *meltemi* and it is advisable to lay a second anchor.

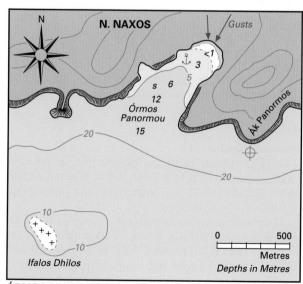

ÓRMOS PANORMOU
⊕36°57'·3N 25°32'·6E

ÓRMOS MOUTSOUNA

37°04'·7N 25°35'·25E

An anchorage under Ák Moutsouna on the E side of Naxos. A large ore loading pier is conspicuous in the bay. Indifferent shelter from the *meltemi*. Care is needed of a reef on the N side of the bay. Anchor S of the pier in 3–5m on sand and shingle, poor holding. Tavernas ashore on the beach.

APOLLONIA

A bight near the NE tip of Naxos. A short breakwater provides some protection from the *meltemi* although some swell is pushed around the end of it. Go stern or bows-to the outside of the short mole that protects the fishing harbour. Care is needed as depths are uneven off the mole. The small basin is shallow. Indifferent shelter from the *meltemi* and really only tenable in calm weather.

A small village ashore with several tavernas and a hotel. The unfinished statue of Apollo lies a short distance directly inland from the village.

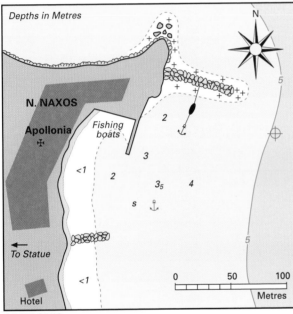

APOLLONIA
⊕37°11'·0N 25°33'·2E

Nísos Dhenoussa

(Dhonoussa)

A small high island (489m/1,064ft) lying nine miles off the east coast of Naxos. There are three anchorages: Órmos Roússa on the NE corner, Órmos Dhendro on the south, and in calm weather off the village of Stavrós.

The island has been settled since the Bronze Age period and was latterly used by the Romans as a prison island. Today it is still out on a limb off the tourist track, although sadly EU money has been used to score rude roads across the island and scar its natural if barren visage.

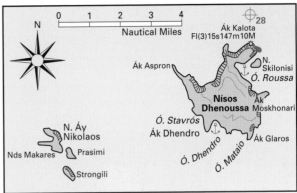

NÍSOS DHENOUSSA
⊕28 0·4M N of Ák Kalota (Dhenoussa)
37°08'·63N 25°49'·78E WGS84

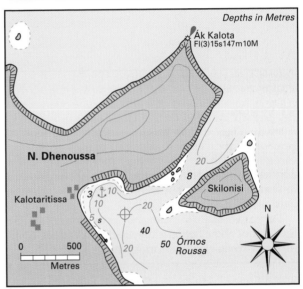

ÓRMOS ROUSSA
⊕37°07'·38N 25°49·52E WGS84

ÓRMOS ROUSSA

A bay on the E coast of Dhenoussa partially sheltered by Nisís Skilonisi (Trigono). Although there is a narrow channel between Skilonisi and Dhenoussa with good depths, the prudent course is to enter the bay from the SE. The cove in the NW corner (8–12m) affords the best shelter from the *meltemi*, but the holding on a rocky bottom is not the best. It may be better to anchor on the W side of the bay in 8–10m where the holding is better. The anchorage is safe enough when the *meltemi* is blowing but gets uncomfortable with the swell that rolls in.

Meagre provisions can sometimes be obtained from a 'shop' in a house near the shore. Simple taverna opens occasionally.

ÓRMOS DHENDRO (Khendro)

A bay on the S coast of Dhenoussa lying immediately E of Ák Dhendro. A chapel is conspicuous on the cape. Care must be taken of the reef lying off the cape. Anchor near the head of the bay in 5–6m. Further into the bay (in 3–4m) lies a wreck. Good shelter from the *meltemi* although there are gusts into the bay.

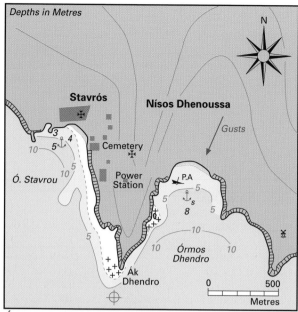

ÓRMOS DHENDRO AND STAVROU
⊕37°05'·2N 25°48'·0E

STAVRÓS

A small village on the western side of Ák Dhendro. Anchor off the village in 4–5m. If there is room you can go bows-to the quay where there are 1·5–2·5m depths in the middle. Shelter here is not as good as in Órmos Dhendro, but is useful in calm weather or light northerlies.

Tavernas ashore. Limited provisions can be found, but the islanders are much dependent upon the ferry from Naxos for most things.

Nísos Iráklia

A small barren island lying 3 miles SSE of Ák Katomeri. There is a small hamlet at Áyios Yeóryios.

Like the other islands, civilisation in the form of anonymous pour-and-fill concrete buildings has changed the face of the island in places, though it still remains a wild and mostly inaccessible island.

On the S side of the island is a cave which you will have to walk to from the *chora* Panayia – about an hour.

ÁYIOS YEÓRYIOS (Iráklia)

A deep inlet on the NE tip of Iráklia. The entrance is somewhat difficult to see from the N. The houses at the head of the bay can be seen from the entrance. Although open to the NE the *meltemi* does not always blow home although on other occasions it will do so. Anchor in 3–6m. There is just room for a few yachts to go bows-to inside the short mole. Care is needed of old mooring chains on the bottom so use a trip-line on the anchor. Good shelter from the

⊕26 0·35M W of Ák Kouroupa (Naxos)
36°58'·36N 25°22'·66E WGS84
⊕27 0·5M SW of Ák Gaitani (Naxos)
36°55'·24N 25°25'·18E WGS84
⊕29 0·5M E of Ák Megalí Poundha (Iráklia)
36°52'·69N 25°28'·93E WGS84
⊕30 2M S of N. Mikrós Avélos (Stenón Iou-Iráklia)
36°47'·82N 25°23'·94E WGS84
⊕31 0·3M W of S end of N. Ofidhousa (Skhinoúsa)
36°49'·87N 25°30'·96E WGS84
⊕32 0·5M S of S end of N. Dhrima
36°49'·5N 25°40'·3E

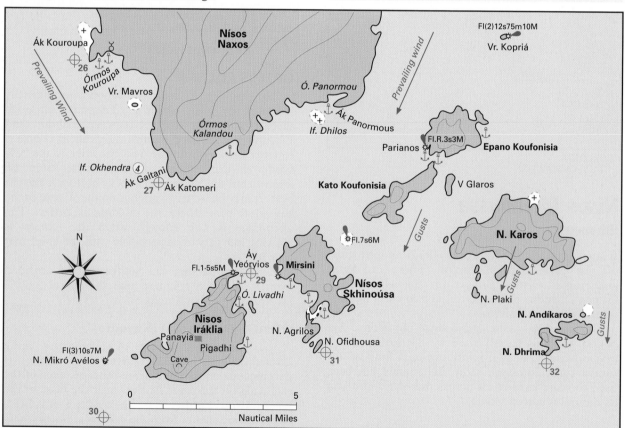

NAXOS AND ADJACENT ISLANDS

Áy Yeóryios on Iráklia looking NNE   *Nigel Patten*

PIGADHI (Pegadi)

36°50'·0N 25°28'·8E

A deep inlet near the SE tip of Iráklia. Open to the ENE and consequently a swell rolls in with the *meltemi*. In calm weather it is an attractive fjord to visit. Anchor in 6–10m near the head of the bay. The bottom is sand with some rocks – reasonable holding.

Nísos Skhinoúsa

MIRSINI (Myrseni)

Approach

A narrow inlet on the W side of Skhinoúsa, almost directly opposite Áyios Yeóryios on Iráklia. The entrance is difficult to locate until the small white chapel immediately due W of the entrance and the light structure are spotted. The entrance is lit Fl.4s6M, but a night approach needs care.

Mooring

Anchor in the bay in 5–8m. The bottom is sand and weed, not everywhere good holding. Small yachts can squeeze in bows-to just N of the ferry quay or go on the ferry quay when it is not in use. Good shelter from the *meltemi*, although there are gusts into the bay.

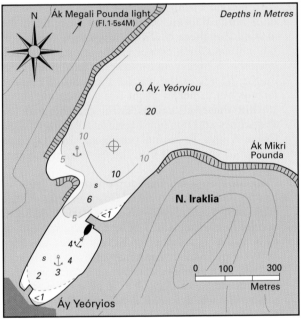

ÁYIOS YEÓRYIOS
⊕36°52'·3N 25°28'·6E

meltemi tucked in behind the mole. The bottom is sand with some rocks – good holding.

Tavernas ashore. The small hamlet in the rocky bay is most attractive despite the new houses that have been built around it.

ÓRMOS LIVÁDHI (Mourto)

Immediately S of Áy Yeoryios is Livádhi, not really tenable with the *meltemi*, but a suitable anchorage in calm weather. Anchor in 4–5m on sand with some rocks, good holding once dug in.

A taverna sometimes opens on the beach. Ashore on the hill is the village of Livádhi which was abandoned in 1940 and not re-inhabited after the war. The ruins of the houses built of and into Hellenistic and later Venetian ruins is a melancholy spot.

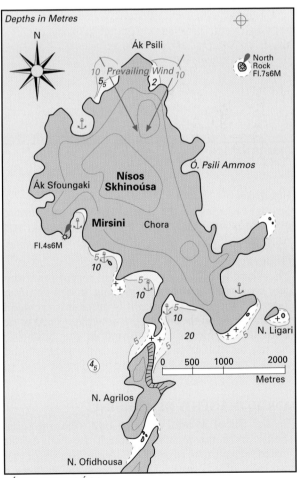

NÍSOS SKHINOÚSA
⊕ 0·3M N of light 36°53'·74N 25°32'·56E WGS84

Skhinoúsa. Mirsini looking ESE   *Nigel Patten*

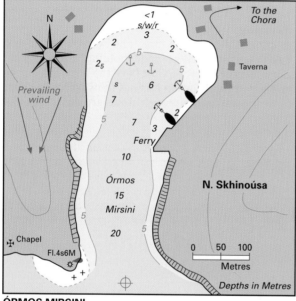

ÓRMOS MIRSINI
⊕36°51'·97N 25°30'·47E WGS84

Facilities
Several tavernas on the shore. Taverna and limited provisions in the *chora*. Ferry to Naxos and Amorgós.

General
The island has been 'discovered' in recent years and gets crowded with tourists arriving in the summer months. Out of high season it is much less crowded and the *chora* on the hill reverts to what it used to be with the old men sitting around in the cafeneion playing backgammon and the lads hanging around wandering what to do with no tourists around to ogle.

ANCHORAGES S OF MIRSINI
To the SE of Mirsini are two bays offering some shelter from the *meltemi* although they are better visited in calm weather. The southernmost of the two bays affords the best shelter from the *meltemi*.

NISÍS AGRILOS
The skinny islet running S from Skhinoúsa approximately a mile SSE of Mirsini. There is not a passage around the N end of the islet as stated in the Admiralty *Pilot*. The bay under the headland opposite the islet affords reasonable shelter from the *meltemi* in rugged but attractive surroundings.

Nísoi Koufonisia
Two islands about one mile NE of Skhinoúsa: Lower (Kato) Koufonisia is the southwestern island while Upper (Epano) Koufonisia lies to the NE.

There are three anchorages on Upper Koufonisia:

1. A bay on the NE tip of the island provides some shelter from the *meltemi* although a swell rolls in. Open to the E. Anchor in 3–5m. Sandy bottom. Deserted.

2. ***Koufonisia village***. Anchor in the bay in 3–5m on a sandy bottom. Reasonable shelter from the *meltemi* but there is always a residual swell with the *meltemi* which causes yachts at anchor to roll horribly. A breakwater and quay have been built on the W side of the bay for the ferry. When the ferry is not in here a yacht can go stern or bows-to, but the swell causes awful snatching at the shore lines and it is not a comfortable place to be. Open S and E. Some provisions and tavernas ashore. A quaint OTE in the bottom of a village house.

3. ***Parianós*** A small harbour on the SW side of Epano Koufonisia. A mole closes off part of the inlet with 5–6m depths in the entrance and 3m depths in the middle. The end of the mole is lit Fl.R.3s3M. A number of fishing boats are kept here on permanent moorings and the bottom is littered with permanent moorings. Anchor with a trip-line and you may also be able to pick up a mooring if one is free. It is possible to go bows-to the quay in a few places, but care is needed of

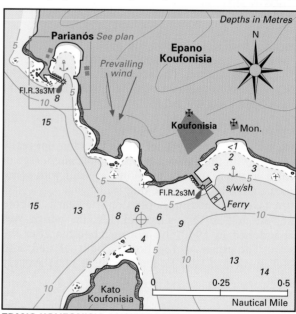

EPANO KOUFONISIA ANCHORAGES
⊕36°55'·8N 25°35'·9E

Parianós looking W   *Nigel Patten*

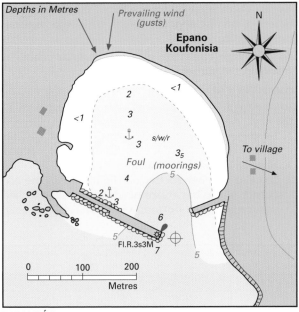

PARIANÓS
⊕36°56'·1N 25°35'·6E

Nísoi Karos (Keros) and Andíkaros

The southeasternmost of this group of islands off the south coast of Naxos. The SW tip of Amorgós lies 3 miles to the SE of Andíkaros. On the S side of Karos there is a tiny cove about halfway along (36°52'·7N 35°39'·3E), but there are severe gusts into here with the *meltemi*. Anchor in 4–5m near the head. The bottom is sand and rock and not everywhere good holding. The surroundings are bleak and inhospitable on this sun-baked barren island.

Andíkaros consists of two islands: Nisís Dhrima to the SW and Andíkaros to the NE. The narrow channel between them has 4m least depth. In calm weather a yacht can anchor at the SE end of the channel where there is reasonable shelter from the *meltemi* although there are severe gusts.

Note There is an above-water rock approximately ¼ mile N of the E end of Andíkaros. The rock sits on a shelf with least depths of 10m which extends approximately ½ mile N of the E end of Andíkaros. The above-water rock is normally easily spotted, but with the *meltemi* it can be difficult to see until close to. Sailing around here I spotted what I thought was a shallow area at the extremity of the shelf, but a Force 7 *meltemi* made investigation a little difficult.

Caution In the vicinity of Koufonisia, Karos and Andíkaros there can be severe gusts off the lee side of the islands with the *meltemi*. Care is needed with a strong *meltemi* when there can be extremely fierce gusts when on passage from Stenón Parou-Náxou to Amorgós.

rock ballasting along the quay and permanent moorings off it. Good shelter from the *meltemi* although there are gusts. The bay is a pleasant 20 minute stroll from the village. The fishing harbour has a bleak but beautiful aspect to it – and the water is clean enough to swim in.

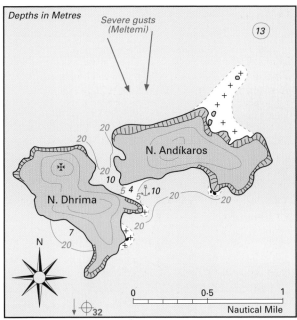

NISOI DHRIMA AND ANDÍKAROS
⊕**32** 0·5M S of S end of N. Dhrima 36°49'·5N 25°40'·3E

Nísos Amorgós

The easternmost of the Cyclades apart from the small islands of Kinaros and Levithia. It is mountainous throughout, dropping sheer into the sea in many places. Mt Krikelos is 821m (2,693ft) high at the NE end; Mt Áyios Ilías is 698m (2,290ft) high in the middle; and Mt Korax (Raven) is 607m (1,991ft) high at the SW end. The cliffs are spectacular, especially at the NE end and on the south coast where they drop straight down into the sea for 300m or so, giving you the impression that the island was simply sliced off here like a wedge of cheese. Most of the island is burnt barren rock though inland the valleys are cultivated in places.

In the past the islanders had a reputation as wreckers and pirates. The island was colonised in classical times but appears to have been of minor importance. The poet Simonedes settled here and became known as Simonedes of Amorgós. The island is off the main tourist route and mostly visited by backpackers. There is excellent fishing around the coast and a school of dolphins will often be seen in the vicinity of the island.

For film buffs the island is known as the setting for Luc Besson's film *Le Grand Bleu* (*The Big Blue*) and numerous locations around the coast were used during filming. In the rocky cove E of Órmos Kalotaritissa at the SW end of the island is the wrecked coaster *Olympia* which figures prominently in the film.

Note When the *meltemi* is blowing there are severe gusts off the S side of Amorgós and big seas on both the NW and SE sides.

KATÁPOLA (Vathi)

Approach

Conspicuous The *chora* and a line of windmills on the hill above the harbour are conspicuous from seaward. Houses straggle around the head of the bay with a monastery and church with a blue cupola conspicuous in the middle. Katápola lies in the SE corner of the bay.

By night Use the light on Ák Áyios Ilías: Fl(2)10s12M. Apart from this light there are no others, but with good visibility it is possible to make a night entrance.

Dangers With the *meltemi* there are strong gusts into the bay though these lift at Katápola.

Mooring

Go stern or bows-to the quay under the lee of the ferry quay. The bottom is mostly sand and weed with some rocks – good holding once the anchor bites.

Shelter The shelter under the lee of the ferry quay is better than it appears even with the *meltemi* funnelling in.

Note Sewage emptying into the harbour makes it smelly in the summer heat.

Authorities Port police.

Anchorage A yacht can anchor in several places in the bay.

1. In the cove immediately W of Katápola. Shelter in here is better than it looks as there is something of a lee from W–NW winds.
2. In calm weather anchor off the hamlet in the NE corner of the bay. Care needs to be taken of laid moorings on the bottom. Good tavernas ashore.

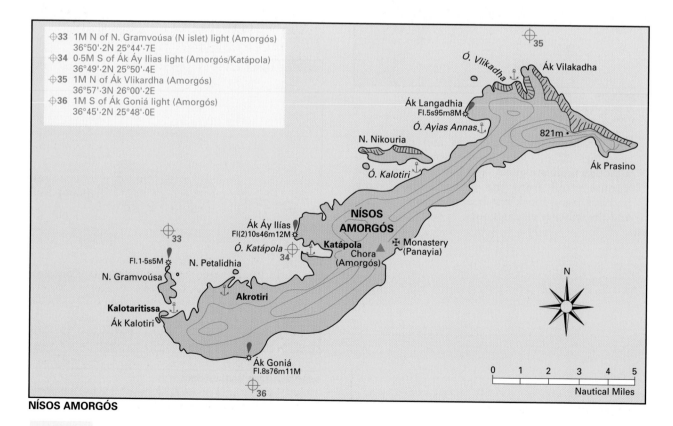

⊕33 1M N of N. Gramvoúsa (N islet) light (Amorgós)
36°50'·2N 25°44'·7E
⊕34 0·5M S of Ák Áy Ilias light (Amorgós/Katápola)
36°49'·2N 25°50'·4E
⊕35 1M N of Ák Vlikardha (Amorgós)
36°57'·3N 26°00'·2E
⊕36 1M S of Ák Goniá light (Amorgós)
36°45'·2N 25°48'·0E

NÍSOS AMORGÓS

Katápola on Amorgós looking N. Ák Áy Ilias is top left and the village and harbour middle right   *Peter Kleinoth/MareTeam*

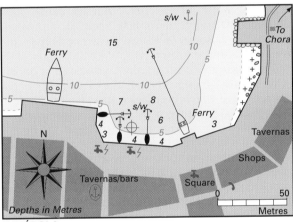

KATÁPOLA
⊕36°49'·62N 25°51'·80E WGS84

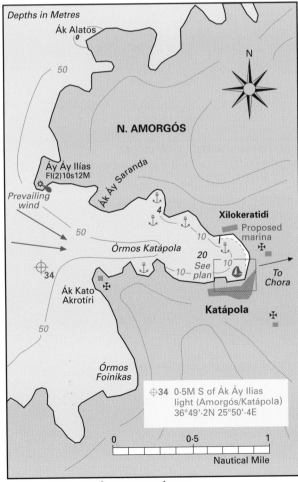

APPROACHES TO ÓRMOS KATÁPOLA

3. In the cove W of the NE hamlet. Shelter from the *meltemi* is not the best here.

Note There are plans to build a marina at Xilokeratidi opposite Katápola itself. At the time of writing no plans were available and work has yet to begin.

Facilities

Services Water and electricity on the quay.

Fuel Can be delivered by mini-tanker to the quay. Alternatively the nearest petrol station is a few kilometres away on the road to the *chora*.

Provisions Most provisions can be obtained.

Eating out Pleasant tavernas and bars on the waterfront. The Corner taverna has excellent Greek cuisine that I couldn't fault during an enforced stay with a Force 9 gale here.

Other PO. OTE. Bank. Greek gas. Hire motorbikes. Ferries to Naxos, Piraeus and Rhodes.

Nikouria Passage and Ormos Kalotiri looking N from Amorgós over N. Nikouria

General

Órmos Katápola is a magnificent deep bay with steep cliffs dropping sheer into the sea. The small village of Katápola is a pleasant relaxed spot and the harbour quite secure. Few tourists come here although recently there has been an influx of backpackers, some of whom have not helped the foreigner's image in Amorgós.

The *chora* above is typically Cycladic. It is on the way to the monastery of the Panayía of the Presentation which occupies a spectacular site on a cliff suspended between the sky and the sea below. The best way to get there is either to hire a motorbike or alternatively to get the local bus to the *chora* and then on to a stop nearby – the driver is used to dropping people off at the nearest stop to the monastery. It is then a hot steep climb (remember to take a bottle of water) to the monastery itself which, even in this secular age, manages to instill a feeling of reverence and monastic quiet into the most hardened of sceptics.

ÓRMOS KALOTARITISSA

An enclosed bay at the SW end of Amorgós lying under Nisís Gramvoúsa. Care is needed in the approaches of the reefs and low-lying islets in the approaches. Anchor in the bay in 3–5m or go stern-to the stubby quay on the N side. There are numerous moorings in the bay for the local fishing

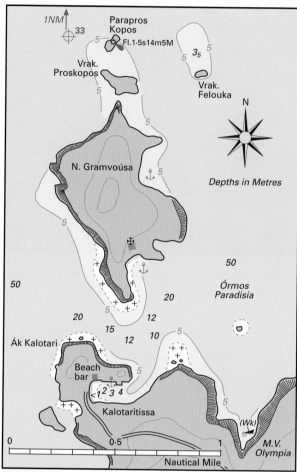

KALOTARITISSA AND APPROACHES

⊕33 1M N of N. Gramvoúsa (N islet) light (Amorgós)
36°50'·2N 25°44'·7E

Órmos Kalotaritissa looking N towards the bay and Nisís Gramvoúsa

boats. Reasonable shelter from the *meltemi* although a surge is generated with a prolonged blow from the N.

A beach taverna opens in the summer. In a rocky bight to the E of here is the wrecked coaster *Olympia* which was used during the filming of *The Big Blue*.

ÓRMOS AKROTÍRI

36°48'·8N 25°47'·4E

A long narrow inlet lying under Nisís Petalidhia. It is only useful during calm weather as the *meltemi* sends a swell in. Taverna opens in the summer. There is a pier in the bay with 2m depths at the extremity.

ÓRMOS KALOTÍRI

Lies on the SE side of Nisís Nikouria. Anchor on the NW side of the bay in 4–5m. Sandy bottom. Reasonable shelter from the *meltemi* although there are gusts into the bay which can be severe with a strong blow from the N.

Nisís Nikouria is connected to Amorgós by shoal water. The narrow passage, Stenón Kakoperator, has 5m depths close off Nisís Nikouria. Keep closer to the N side than the S side where a reef and shoal water extend out into the channel.

On the Amorgós side at Áy Pavlos several tavernas open in the summer.

Áy Annas looking NW

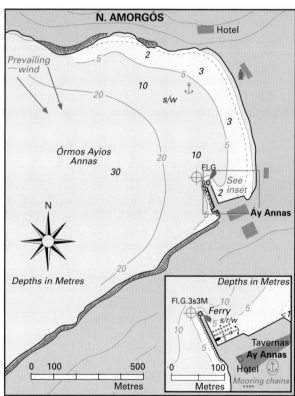

APPROACHES TO ÁYIOS ANNAS
⊕36°54'·15N 25°58'·51E WGS84

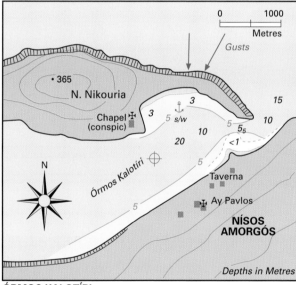

ÓRMOS KALOTÍRI
⊕36°52'·6N 25°55'·2E

ÓRMOS ÁYIOS ANNAS (Aghios Ioanna, Yialis, Aigiali)

Approach

The small harbour lies off the village of Yialis in the SE of Órmos Áy Annas. From the W the houses of the village are easily identified. From the E the houses will not be seen until into the bay, but the small islet N of Ák Langadhia is easily identified. Closer in the mole off the village is easily identified.

By night Use the light on Ák Langadhia Fl.5s8M and on the mole head Fl.G.3s3M.

Dangers With the *meltemi* there are strong gusts into the bay and big seas in the vicinity.

Mooring

Go stern or bows-to the mole or the quay clear of the ferry berth. The bottom is mostly rock and not good holding – make sure your anchor is well in. Care is needed of permanent moorings chains on the bottom in the approximate locations shown so it may be wise to use a trip-line on the anchor.

Shelter The bay is open to the W–NW and with the *meltemi* some swell rolls into the bay, but the harbour is tenable if not always comfortable. There are also strong gusts into the bay.

Anchorage In calm weather you can anchor in the bay in 3–6m on sand and weed. Some swell invariably rolls into the bay even when there is no wind and it can be very rolly at anchor.

Facilities
Water On the quay in front of the village.
Provisions Minimarket.
Eating out Tavernas on the waterfront.

General
The small bay has a modest tourist income, but is relatively untouched. The hinterland supports a few small villages, though how they survive is difficult to know in this barren baked landscape. For the visitor the steep-sided bay with small villages around the slopes is a wonderful spot well worth a visit despite the *meltemi*.

ÓRMOS VILAKARDHA
36°56'·2N 26°00'·0E

On the NE tip of Amorgós there is a magnificent fjord-like inlet which can be used in calm weather. With the *meltemi* a swell is pushed straight into it. Anchor near the head of the inlet where convenient – though depths are considerable. At the head of the inlet a ravine cuts through the high cliffs. Around Ák Vilakardha on the NE end of Amorgós are spectacular cliffs rising sheer to some 700m (2,275ft) in places.

Nísoi Kinaros and Lévitha

Kinaros is a barren jagged island 11 miles ENE of Amorgós. It is inhabited only occasionally by a solitary shepherd and his flock. Lévitha, lower in aspect than Kinaros, lies 5 miles to the east. The deep bay on the south coast affords good shelter and two families live at the head of the bay. A tale, probably anecdotal, relates that a member of one of the families here was suddenly taken ill while a large yacht belonging to a Greek minister was anchored off. He ordered up a helicopter to take the patient to hospital and, concerned by the lonely situation of the island, had a radio installed so that if help was needed again the inhabitants needed only to call for it and it would come – on his special authorisation.

Note A strong SE current is reported to flow in the vicinity of the islands and between the islands and Amorgós.

ÓRMOS LÉVITHA
A landlocked bay on the S coast. The entrance to the bay is located in the saddle between the higher ends of the island. There is a large conspicuous rock immediately W of the entrance.

The E arm of the bay offers good all-round shelter. Recently mooring buoys have been laid in the eastern arm and one of the locals makes a charge for using the moorings. Charge band 2.

Only a lighthouse keeper and a few fishermen inhabit the island. There is a small taverna in a farmhouse about 15 minutes' walk up the hill from the quay. Good fresh fish is served in pleasant

Lévitha. The anchorage in the creek on the E side of Órmos Lévitha *Nigel Patten*

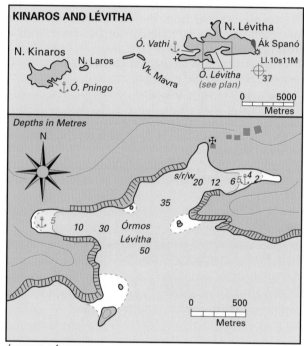

KINAROS AND LÉVITHA

N. Kinaros · N. Laros · Ó. Vathi · N. Lévitha · Ák Spanó · Ll.10s11M · Vk. Mavra · Ó. Lévitha (see plan) · 37 · Ó. Pningo

0 — 5000 Metres

Depths in Metres

s/r/w 20 12 6 4 2
35
10 30 Órmos Lévitha 50

0 — 500 Metres

ÓRMOS LÉVITHA

⊕37 1M S of Ák Spanó (Lévitha) 36°58'9N 26°29'·8E

surroundings. Remember to take a torch for the return trip.

You can also anchor in the W creek on Lévitha in 4–5m depths with a long line ashore.

ÓRMOS VATHI
36°59'·9N 26°25'·5E

On the W side of Lévitha there is a deep bay offering some shelter from the *meltemi* although some swell penetrates into here. Anchor in 4–5m near the head of the bay. The bottom is sand and rock, not everywhere good holding.

ORMISKOS PNINGO (Kinaros)
36°57'·96N 26°17'·85E WGS84

On the S side of Kinaros there is a long narrow inlet affording nearly all-round shelter. Anchor near the head of the inlet in 4–5m. The bottom is rock and not the best holding – it is prudent to get a line ashore if possible. Good shelter from the *meltemi*. Closed in by the inlet you feel closed off from the world in here. It is a lonely spot – wonderfully so.

Note Strong winds create a confused reflected swell off the sheer cliffs on the S coast of Kinaros.

Southern Cyclades
Nísos Mílos
(Melos)

The southwesternmost of the Cyclades, Mílos is an ancient volcano which, like Thíra, long ago erupted and scooped out the giant bay. The circular mountain ridge enclosing the bay is mostly barren and sterile. The summit at the SW end is Mt Profitis Ilías, rising to 751m (2,464ft). Alum, sulphur (hot sulphur springs still exist), barium and kaolin are mined and the open-cast mines around the slopes of the island are easily identified from seaward.

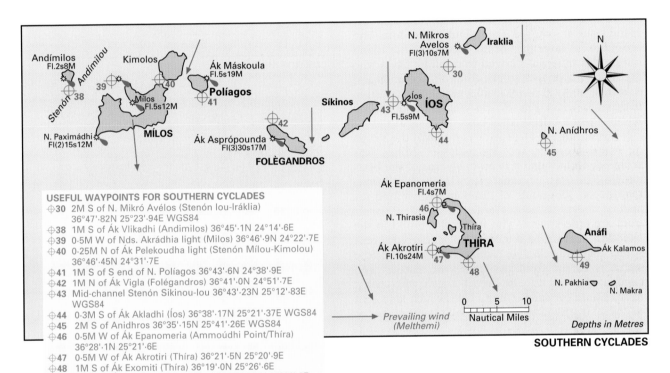

USEFUL WAYPOINTS FOR SOUTHERN CYCLADES
⊕30 2M S of N. Mikró Avélos (Stenón Iou-Iráklia) 36°47'·82N 25°23'·94E WGS84
⊕38 1M S of Ák Vlikadhi (Andímilos) 36°45'·1N 24°14'·6E
⊕39 0·5M W of Nds. Akrádhia light (Milos) 36°46'·9N 24°22'·7E
⊕40 0·25M N of Ák Pelekoudha light (Stenón Mílou-Kimolou) 36°46'·45N 24°31'·7E
⊕41 1M S of S end of N. Políagos 36°43'·6N 24°38'·9E
⊕42 1M N of Ák Vigla (Folégandros) 36°41'·0N 24°51'·7E
⊕43 Mid-channel Stenón Sikinou-Iou 36°43'·23N 25°12'·83E WGS84
⊕44 0·3M S of Ák Akladhi (Íos) 36°38'·17N 25°21'·37E WGS84
⊕45 2M S of Anidhros 36°35'·15N 25°41'·26E WGS84
⊕46 0·5M W of Ák Epanomeria (Ammoúdhi Point/Thíra) 36°28'·1N 25°21'·6E
⊕47 0·5M W of Ák Akrotiri (Thíra) 36°21'·5N 25°20'·9E
⊕48 1M S of Ák Exomiti (Thíra) 36°19'·0N 25°26'·6E
⊕49 1M S of Ák Petradhia (Skála Anáfi) 36°19'·7N 25°46'·2E

SOUTHERN CYCLADES

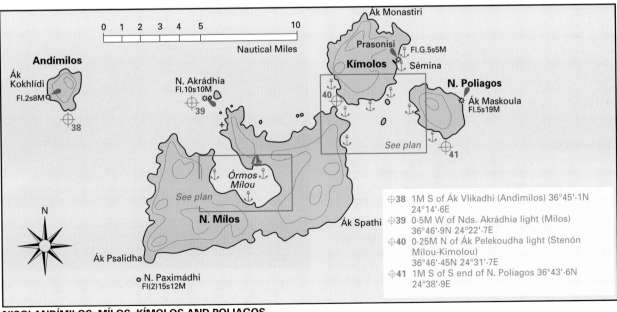

⊕38 1M S of Ák Vlikadhi (Andimilos) 36°45'·1N 24°14'·6E
⊕39 0·5M W of Nds. Akrádhia light (Milos) 36°46'·9N 24°22'·7E
⊕40 0·25M N of Ák Pelekoudha light (Stenón Mílou-Kimolou) 36°46'·45N 24°31'·7E
⊕41 1M S of S end of N. Políagos 36°43'·6N 24°38'·9E

NISOI ANDÍMILOS, MÍLOS, KÍMOLOS AND POLIAGOS

Mílos was the centre of a pre-Minoan Bronze Age civilization and finds on the island of the distinctive 'harpy' sculptures have added much to our knowledge of this early Cycladic civilization. No doubt these early settlers used the island as a stepping stone during their island by island colonization of the Aegean. Later it came under the Minoans and later still passed to the Mycenaeans.

Mílos opted for the Spartan side during the Peloponnesian War, thereby angering the Athenians to such an extent that they carried out the infamous massacre recorded by Thucydides. The Athenians besieged Mílos which, after some months, surrendered unconditionally, whereupon all able males were slaughtered and the women and children enslaved.

The Franks and later the Turks colonised the island, but it enjoyed considerable freedom and prospered. A large part of the income of the island during this time was derived from pirate fleets who used the remote anchorages around the islands and sold their booty at Mílos from where it was resold to merchants. In the First World War the large natural harbour was a British naval base.

It was during the Hellenistic period that the Venus de Milo, properly, the Aphrodite of Mílos, was sculpted, and though it is probably one of the best-known pieces of ancient Greek sculpture, reproduced thousands of times in history and art history books, its source and the island it comes from are little known. The statue was found in the late 19th century by a farmer collecting old Greek stones for fieldwalls. He removed the top half (the statue is carved from two pieces of marble) and negotiated to sell it to the French consul who took it to his house for safekeeping. The French ship sent to collect it arrived to find that the Sultan's governor had forcibly taken the statue and put it aboard a ship bound for Istanbul. Captain de Marcellus decided to retake the statue and landed an armed party which, after a brief skirmish, got it back and aboard the French ship. It is said that it was during this skirmish that the Venus de Milo lost her arms which were spirited away by a local. Despite reports of the arms being rediscovered at various times, the Venus still hasn't acquired them and probably shouldn't lest it change our accepted perception of the armless beauty art historians are so familiar with.

ADHAMAS (Port Mílos)

BA 1539

Approach

Conspicuous Approaching the entrance to Órmos Mílos the lighthouse on Nisídhes Akrádhia and the village of Mílos (the *chora*) on the peak on the E side of the entrance are conspicuous. Rounding Ák Bombárdha the village of Adhamas will be seen.

By night Use the light on Nisídhes Akrádhia Fl.10s10M and Ák Bombárdha Fl.5s12M. The jetties off the opencast mine on the E side of Órmos Mílou are lit: 2F.R.3M and F.R.3M.

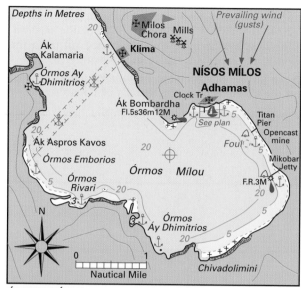

ÓRMOS MÍLOU
⊕36°42´·8N 24°26´·1E

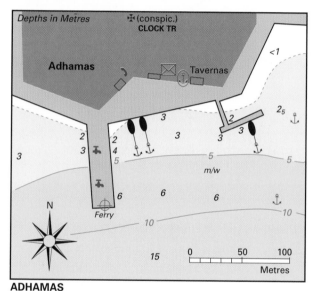

ADHAMAS
⊕36°43´·5N 24°26´·7E

Adhamas on Órmos Mílou looking NE. The town quay has been widened and the E pier extended *Peter Kleinoth/MareTeam*

Nisís Akrádhia and lighthouse in the approaches to Órmos
Mílou looking N

Dangers
1. With the *meltemi* there are heavy confused seas off
   the entrance to Órmos Mílou. Special care must
   be taken between Voi Kounidhi and Nisídhes
   Akrádhia where the waves rebound off the N side
   of Mílos and cause a heavy sea up to a mile off.
2. Care must be taken of rocks and reefs bordering
   the E side of the entrance to Órmos Mílou. Vos
   Monopodhro is a square rock easily identified.
   Off Ák Fourkovouni there are several detached
   above-water rocks eroded into fantastic wind-
   sculpted shapes.
3. At times the *meltemi* can gust down off the high
   land in the vicinity of Ák Bombárdha.

Mooring
Go stern or bows-to the town quay between the two
piers or the T-pier to the E. Alternatively anchor off
the village E of the short pier. The bottom is mud,
rocks and weed – poor holding in places.

Shelter Good shelter from the *meltemi* although there
is some residual swell. With strong S winds
Adhamas is dangerous from the long fetch across
the bay.

Authorities Port police and customs.

Facilities
Water On the ferry pier. Apply to the tourist office
nearby.
Fuel On the outskirts of town. A mini-tanker can
deliver.
Repairs Limited mechanical repairs. Hardware shop.
Provisions Good shopping for most provisions. Ice
available.
Eating out Tavernas at Adhamas. Others along the
waterfront.
Other PO. OTE. Bank. ATM. Greek gas and
Camping Gaz. Hire cars, motorbikes and bicycles.
Ferries to Piraeus, Thíra and Soúdha. Internal
flights to Athens.

General
The huge natural harbour is impressive to look at
but the yachtsman is liable to curse this very size for
the sea that can be raised inside in strong winds. I
have always found Adhamas an indifferent sort of
place – perhaps a few too many reinforced concrete
buildings to be classified as attractive and a few too
many tourists for the size of the place. Others
disagree and find it has its own charm.

The *chora* (Mílos) on the hill above is attractive
and the view over the bay superb. As at Thíra, the
eye sees the volcanic crater that is now the bay, but
the mind finds it difficult to compute the size of the
explosion that produced it.

OTHER ANCHORAGES IN ÓRMOS MÍLOU
1. *Titan and Mikobar piers* Anchor off under the
   piers where there is some shelter from the
   meltemi.
2. *Chivadolimini* An open bay to the E of Áy
   Dhimitrios. Anchor off the beach in calm weather
   or with southerlies. There are strong gusts off the
   slopes with southerlies.
3. *Órmos Áy Dhimitrios* A bay on the S side of
   Órmos Mílou approximately SSW of Ák
   Bombárdha. It looks to offer reasonable shelter
   from the *meltemi* and small yachts could creep in
   under the headland. Open to the E.
4. *Órmos Rivari* An enclosed bay on the SW side
   of Omos Mílou. Anchor in 3–4m. Poor shelter
   from the *meltemi* but good shelter from
   southerlies.
5. *Órmos Emborios* A large bay on the W side of
   Órmos Mílou. Anchor in the NW corner. Open
   to the NE–E and not really a good place to be in
   the *meltemi*.
6. *Klima* Suitable in light northerlies or calm
   weather only.

ÓRMOS PROVATAS
36°40'·0N 24°26'·7E

A large two-headed bay on the S side of Mílos W of
Ák Zefiros. In calm weather or light northerlies this
is a spectacular anchorage. Anchor in either of the
bays. Open S.

NÍSOS ANDÍMILOS (Anti-Mílos)

⊕**39** 0·5M W of Nds. Akrádhia light (Milos)
         36°46'·9N 24°22'·7E

A high steep-to island lying 5 miles WNW of Mílos.
It rises to 686m (2250ft). With the *meltemi* there are
severe gusts off the SW side of it, such that small
whirlwinds are created. Keep well off! On the W
side there is a light on Ák Kokhlídi: Fl.2s8M.

NÍSOS KIMOLOS
A low barren island lying immediately NE of Mílos
from which it is separated by a narrow channel. The
small population lives in the *chora* or at Psathi.
Formerly it was called Echinousa on account of the
sea urchins found here (Pliny) and Argentiera on
account of its silver mines. In the Middle Ages it was
an infamous pirate haunt.

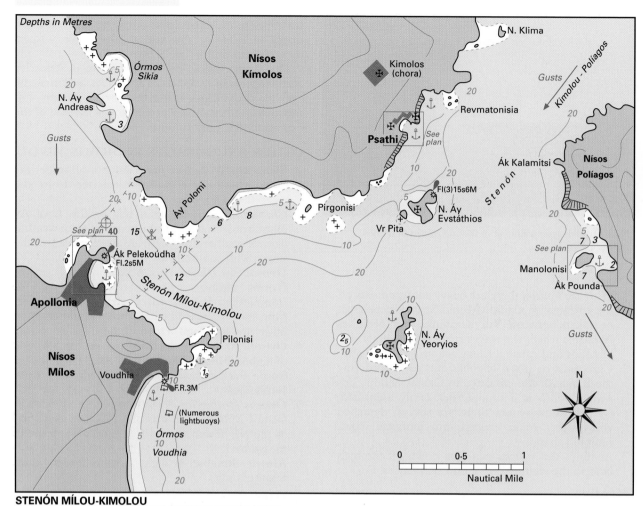

STENÓN MÍLOU-KIMOLOU

⊕40 0·25M N of Ák Pelekoudha light (Stenón Mílou-Kimolou)
36°46'·45N 24°31'·7E

STENÓN MÍLOU-KIMOLOU (Kímolos Channel)

BA 1539

Imray-Tetra G33

The area enclosed by Mílos, Kímolos and Políagos islands is an attractive mini-cruising area with a number of well-sheltered anchorages. In one or other of the anchorages shelter can be found from winds from any direction. Care must be taken of the reefs and shoals which fringe the islands and islets. In the plan these cannot be shown in great detail.

Caution With the *meltemi* there are severe gusts off the SW side of Nísos Políagos, down through Stenón Kimolou-Políagos (the channel between Kímolos and Políagos) and off the S side of Nísos Kímolos. Although there is not a big sea in the lee of the islands, the wind can be very strong indeed.

1. *Órmos Sikia* On the SW side of Kímolos. Open to the W–NW and unsuitable when the *meltemi* is blowing. With light northerlies and easterlies there is adequate protection in here. Anchor in 3–4m on the S side of the islet (Áy Andreas) in the middle of the bay. Care must be taken of the reef connecting Áy Andreas to Kímolos. A yacht can also anchor on the N of the islet in 3–5m.

2. *Apollonia* A bay on the S side of Stenón Mílou-Kimolou directly under Ák Pelekoúdha. Care is needed of the reefs running out from the N and S entrance points. Anchor in 2–4m on the E side of the bay off the beach or off the hamlet on the S side. A line of small buoys marks off a swimming area inside of which anchoring is not allowed. Alternatively in calm weather go stern or bows-to the pier which has 3m depths at the extremity. Good holding on a sandy bottom. The shelter from the *meltemi* is better than it might appear on the plan although there are still strong gusts into the bay. It is completely open to the E.

   Tavernas and a minimarket ashore.

3. *Órmos Voudhia* A bay lying about one mile SE of Apollonia. A 1·9m patch lies 0·2 miles S of Pilonisi (connected to Mílos by a causeway). Anchor in 5–8m in the N corner of the bay. You can also anchor under the bight further SW of the Pilonisi anchorage. There are a number of mooring buoys in the bay (Q.Y(occas)) for the ships that load here. Good shelter from the *meltemi*. There are open-cast mines ashore and a wharf and ore-carrier on the waterfront, so the bay is not really the most attractive place to bring up for the night.

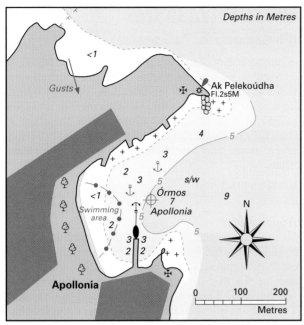

APOLLONIA
⊕36°45'·9N 24°31'·6E

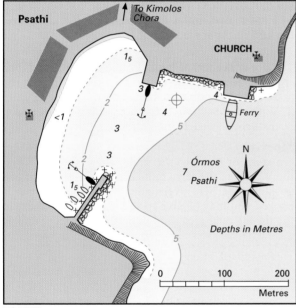

PSATHI
⊕37°47'·1N 24°35'·0E

Psathi on Kímolos looking SW   *Nigel Patten*

4. ***Pirgonisi anchorage*** A long sandy beach extends nearly right around the S side of Kímolos. A yacht can anchor anywhere off the beach and obtain excellent shelter from the *meltemi*. Care is needed of a rocky shelf running W–E approximately 1m underwater some way off the shore. At the E end of the beach a low rocky islet, Pirgonisi, is connected to the shore by a reef. A yacht can tuck under Pirgonisi off the beach in attractive surroundings. The bottom is sand and weed, good holding. A few villas have been built around the shoreline.

   Note An underwater rock (1·5m over) was reported approximately ¼M offshore in the middle of the bay. As no-one else has been able to locate it I suggest you disregard the report for now, though if anyone locates it please let me know.

5. ***Psathi*** A cathedral in the *chora* above and 4 windmills on a ridge are conspicuous. Closer in, the houses around Psathi Bay are conspicuous. A ferry uses the quay on the N side. Anchor in the bay in 2–3m on sand, weed and rock, not everywhere good holding so make sure your anchor is well in. Alternatively go stern or bows-to the stubby quay on the N side (W of the ferry quay) or bows-to the extremity of the S mole. Care is needed on the latter as rocks extend underwater from the quay. The bay is not well sheltered from the *meltemi* and should only really be used in calm weather. Open to the S–SE. Limited provisions and taverna/cafés ashore. *Caïque* ferry to Mílos.

6. ***Sémina Creek*** 36°48'·4N 24°35'·4E

   A fjord-like bay approximately 1¼ miles N of Psathi. The N side of the entrance is lit Fl.G.5s5M although the operation of the light is reported to be intermittent. There is a short mole which the fishing boats use. Anchor in the bay in 4–6m. Poor shelter from the *meltemi* which is funnelled straight down Stenón Kimolou-Políagos.

7. ***Prasonisi anchorage*** Under the NE tip of Kimolos (Ák Anatoli) is a small cove with an islet in the middle. Anchor in 3–4m on either side of the islet and take a line ashore. Care should be taken of the reef connecting the islet to Kímolos. Poor shelter from the *meltemi*.

NÍSOS POLÍAGOS (Poliagaios, Polino)

A barren island close SE of Kímolos.

MANOLONISI

On the W side of Políagos a yacht can anchor behind Manolonisi Island in 2–3m. Sandy bottom. Shelter from the *meltemi*. The islet is connected to Políagos by a sand bar with 1–1·5m depths over it. A delightful, utterly secluded spot.

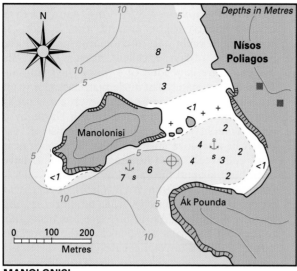

MANOLONISI
⊕36°46′N 24°36·5E

POLÍAGOS S SIDE

On the S side of Políagos there are several anchorages which can be used in calm weather. With the *meltemi* there are strong gusts off the land and a swell is pushed around into here making the anchorages uncomfortable.

Nísos Folégandros
(Pholegandhros, Polikandros)

A barren rocky island lying 14 miles east of Mílos. It is steep-to with some impressive cliffs on the south side. At the NW end the island is 311m (1,020ft) high and at the SE end Mt Elevtherios is 415m (1,361ft) high. The small *chora* sits on the edge of the cliff on the NE side and is a delightful oasis of green trees and shrubs in the otherwise barren island.

KARAVOSTÁSI
BA 1541

Approach
Conspicuous Nisídhes Adhelfia, the jagged islets lying E of Karavostási and SW of Nisís Kardhiotissa, are easily recognised. Closer in Dhio Adhelfia, the small islet in the middle of the entrance to Karavostási, will be seen. The white houses around the bay and a church on a low hill behind are also conspicuous.

By night A night approach is not recommended. Use the light on the N side of the entrance (Fl.WR.6s10/7M red sector covers 202°-248° and 322°-344° over Ifalos Poulioxeres) and the light on the end of the mole Q.G.3M.

Dangers
1. Care is needed of Ifalos Poulioxeresi to the NNE of the entrance and the reef running NE from the N entrance point to Karavostási.
2. With the *meltemi* there are strong gusts and a disturbed swell at the entrance to the bay.

Mooring
Go stern or bows-to the mole where shown. When the W side of the ferry mole is not in use a yacht can go alongside here overnight. When the harbour is packed you may be able to squeeze in somewhere in the fishing boat area though berths here are jealously

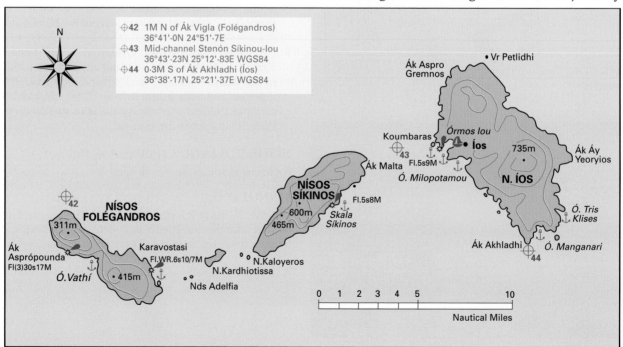

FOLÉGANDROS, SÍKINOS AND ÍOS

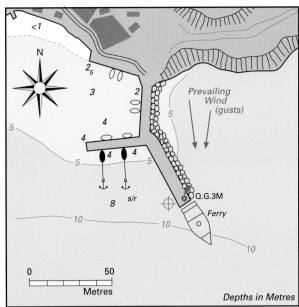

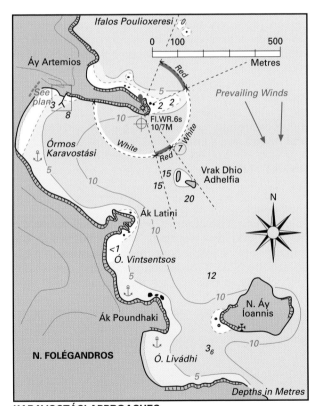

Karavostási on Folégandros looking NW. Nisís Áy Íoannis is
bottom right   *Peter Kleinoth/MareTeam*

KARAVOSTÁSI
⊕36°37'·0N 24°57'·2E

KARAVOSTÁSI APPROACHES

KARAVOSTÁSI
⊕36°36'·9N 24°57'E

guarded. The bottom is sand and rock – poor
holding in places.

Shelter Reasonable shelter from the *meltemi* although
a prolonged blow sets up a surge in the bay which
makes things uncomfortable though still tenable.
Open SE–E.

Anchorage In calm weather you can anchor off in
Órmos Karávostasi. It is uncomfortable and can be
untenable in here with the *meltemi*. Likewise in calm
weather Órmos Vintsentsos and Órmos Livádhi
have suitable depths for anchoring.

Facilities
Limited. Some provisions can be obtained although
supplies are much dependent on the ferry. Tavernas
and bars. Bus to the *chora*. Ferry to Íos and Mílos.

General
The bay with its jagged headland and small islets in
the approaches is attractive in a parched sun-baked
way. A few backpackers come here in the summer.
It is about an hour's walk (or much shorter bus ride)
to the *chora* sited on the edge of a cliff and
something of an oasis with trees and greenery
contrasting with the otherwise barren island. There
are a few tavernas and limited supplies here.

Karavostási literally means a 'ship-stop'. Before
the new ferry mole was built the ferry would anchor
in the bay and passengers and cargo were brought
ashore in small boats. Even a strong *meltemi* could
not stop the ferry and it literally roared into the bay,
unloading and loading again as quickly as possible,
before steaming off to some more secure port.

ÓRMOS VATHI
A large bay on the W side of Folégandros to the E of
Ák Aspropounda. With the *meltemi* there are very
strong gusts into the bay and a swell works its way
in. In calm weather anchor off in 4–5m. The bottom
is sand and weed, poor holding in places.

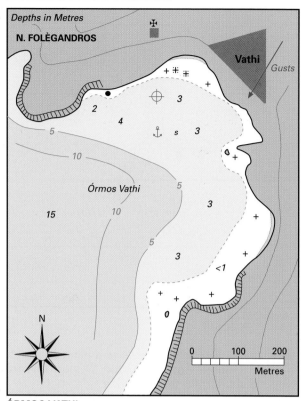

ÓRMOS VATHI
⊕36°37′·6N 24°53′·3E

Nísos Síkinos

A barren dry island to the E of Folégandros. It was once called the wine island because of the excellence of its wine, but I cannot attest to this fact today. The small *chora* lies inland under a ruined fortified monastery.

ÓRMOS SKÁLA

The only harbour on Síkinos, situated 3 miles SW of Ák Malta. The buildings around the bay are

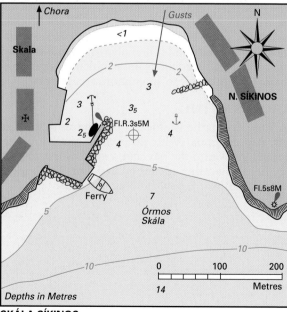

SKÁLA SÍKINOS
⊕36°40′·6N 25°08′·8E

conspicuous from the S, but not from the E. There is a light on the E side of the bay Fl.5s8M and the short mole is lit Fl.R.3s5M.

The mole and quayed area on the W side of the bay have been extended and there is room under the stubby mole to go alongside with an anchor out to hold the yacht off the quay. Local boats use the quayed area N of the stub mole. Alternatively anchor off in 3–5m. Good shelter from the *meltemi* although there are strong gusts. Open to the S.

Some provisions available and tavernas ashore. The small village around the bay is most attractive and popular with Greek tourists.

Nísos Íos

Lies to the east of Síkinos across a narrow (3½ miles) strait. The island is mountainous and barren but in the words of the Admiralty *Pilot* '. . . it has a softer and more genial aspect than either Folégandros or Síkinos.' Mt Pirgos in the middle of the island rises to 790m (2,410ft).

Íos is claimed to be the burial place of Homer. On a voyage from Sámos to Athens the old blind bard died. His body was thrown overboard and washed up on Íos where the sea buried him on the beach. His body is now said to be buried on the northern slopes of Mt Pirgos. An apocryphal story, but then you never know.

Today the island is extremely popular with young sun-lovers. Nude bathing is tolerated here (although it is still technically illegal in Greece) and the beaches around the island are packed with lobster-red bodies and some natural brown ones as well.

PORT ÍOS

BA 1541

Approach

Conspicuous The *chora* of Íos on the hill above the harbour and two windmills on the hill below the village are conspicuous from seaward. Nisís Dhiakofto NW of the entrance to Órmos Íou stands out clearly. Once up to the entrance the light

Órmos Íou looking SW from the *chora*   *Nigel Patten*

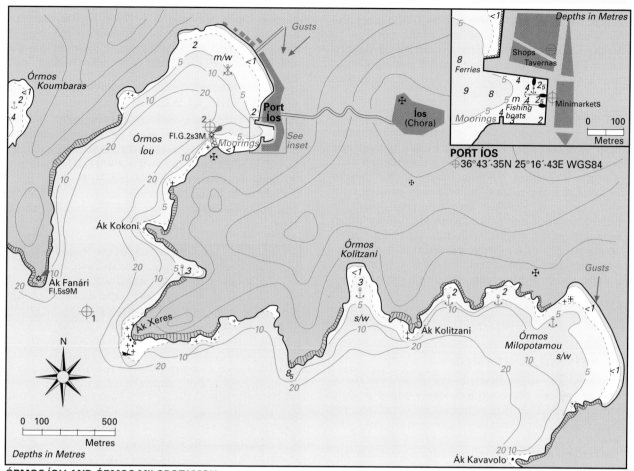

ÓRMOS ÍOU AND ÓRMOS MILOPOTAMOU
⊕₁ 36°42'·73N 25°15'·72E WGS84
⊕₂ 36°43'·36N 25°16'·21E WGS84

structure on Ák Fanári can be distinguished and a few buildings around the beach will be seen. The buildings around the harbour cannot be seen until you are into the bay.

By night Use the light on Ák Fanári Fl.5s9M and the light on the end of the rough stone breakwater Fl.G.2s3M.

Dangers
1. Care should be taken of the reef that runs S for about 100m from Ák Xeres.
2. With the *meltemi* there are strong gusts into the bay.

Mooring
Go stern or bows-to in the basin. The N quay is usually kept free during the day when the fast ferries are running. After 1800 the port police supervise yachts mooring along this quay. Use plenty of fenders and keep well pulled off the quay because of the surge from ferry wash. Even the slower ferries create substantial wash, with some arriving during the night. The bottom is mud – excellent holding.

Shelter All-round shelter out of the gusts from the *meltemi*. Ferries entering the harbour do so at speed and create a big surge in the basin. Yachts should keep pulled well-off or the surge will smash you onto the quay.

Authorities Port police and customs.

Note It is now prohibited to anchor in Órmos Íou as it obstructs the ferry turning area. All yachts must use the yacht harbour.

Facilities
Water A mini-tanker can deliver good drinking water.
Fuel A mini-tanker can deliver to the basin.

Ios harbour looking N

289

Provisions Most provisions can be found near the harbour. Ice from the NE corner of the harbour.
Eating out Tavernas and bars around the harbour.
Other PO. OTE. Bank. Greek gas. Camping Gaz in the *chora*. Hire motorbikes. Bus to the *chora*. Ferries to Piraeus, Thíra and Iraklion.

General

By night the waterfront throbs to the sound of music from bars and discos as young bodies weave their way from bar to bar to disco. Íos is the centre for the young backpackers sleeping rough on the nearby beaches. By day nudism rules (a sign painted on a cliff proclaims: 'Clothes are prohibited') and the nearby beaches are packed with the young of all nationalities complying with this sign. The *chora* above is a maze of streets packed with bars, boutiques and backpackers, although to be fair it is a more convivial place outside of high season.

ÓRMOS KOUMBARAS

The bay immediately N of Port Íos. Anchor in 3–4m. Indifferent shelter from the *meltemi*.

ÓRMOS MILOPOTAMOU

The large bay immediately S of Port Íos. On the N side of the bay there are four coves where a yacht can anchor. The two easternmost coves are the better sheltered. Anchor where convenient. The bottom is sand – good holding. Good shelter from the *meltemi* although there are strong gusts into the bay and some swell may enter with a prolonged blow. Open to the W and S. There are a number of hotels and tavernas on the beach. Much frequented by nudists.

ÓRMOS MANGANARI

A large bay on the S coast of Íos. In the NE corner of the bay there is a rocky islet. Anchor near the head of the bay in 3–8m or in the W or E of the bay. The bottom is sand, excellent holding. You can tuck into the cove on the W with a long line ashore to the

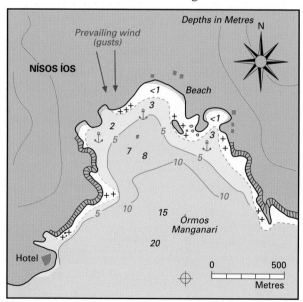

ÓRMOS MANGANARI
⊕36°39'·05N 25°22'·23E WGS84

N side. Open only to the S. Good shelter from the *meltemi* although there are gusts into the bay. A small hotel and tavernas ashore. A *caïque* brings the nature-lovers (topless and bottomless) daily from Íos.

ÓRMOS TRIS KLISES

A bay on the S coast about 1½ miles NE of Manganari. Anchor in either of the two coves in 3–5m. The bottom is rocky and not reliable holding. Good shelter from the *meltemi* although there are strong gusts into the bay. No facilities.

Care must be taken of a reef on the W side of the bay and of a shallow patch near the head of the E cove.

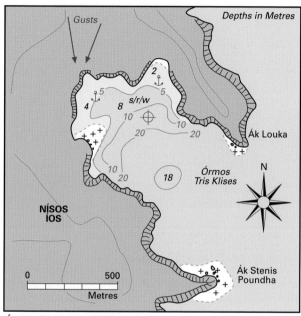

ÓRMOS TRIS KLISES
⊕36°40'·0N 25°23'·3E

Nísos Thíra
(Thera, Psira, Santorini)

Like Mílos, Thíra is a giant volcano. The principal island is Thíra, shaped like a new moon encircling the rim of the crater now filled with water. To the NW Thirasia forms another part of the rim and in the middle a black mass of cinder and lava (Kamméni and Néa Kamméni) is the volcanic plug. Thíra is steep-to on the west coast: variegated pumice cliffs in pastel shades of red, brown, grey, green and slate blue drop sheer into the sea from 150–300m and keep going down for another 300m. The east coast is low-lying, sloping evenly up to a hilly ridge running along the island. The summit of Thíra, Mt Áyios Ilías, is a conical peak in the SE of the island with a white monastery and a cluster of communication towers on top which are conspicuous from seaward. The white domed houses of the capital, Thíra (Fira), extend along the cliff top on the west coast about 213m (700ft) above the tiny harbour and present a remarkable (and much photographed) sight from seaward.

Legend has it that Thíra originated from a lump of earth presented to Jason and the Argonauts by Triton (a local African god) which was later dropped into the sea where Thíra (or *Kalliste* – the most beautiful – as it was called then) is now. The island was an important Minoan settlement until it blew itself to pieces in c.1440–1450 BC and destroyed the Minoan civilization as well (see 'Thíra and the Atlantis Legend' below). It was later subject to Athens and the Egyptian Ptolemys made it into a naval base. In the Middle Ages it was part of the duchy of Naxos. In the early 20th century it was a place of exile for political prisoners.

Thíra is unlike anywhere else in the world. The volcanic crater is some six miles long by four miles wide and viewing it from Thíra town, the mind cannot comprehend the sort of massive explosion that moved so much solid material to scoop out this deep bay. It may give you pause for thought to remember that the volcano is still active and that your yacht is moored in the crater.

The strange landscape breeds strange tales. Vampires are said to exist on the island and the inhabitants report that ghostly apparitions haunt the countryside at night. The volcanic soil is especially fertile and like the land around Mt Etna and Vesuvius the soil produces fine grapes for wine. Of the bottled wines Atlantis white or red and Nikteri white are good. Local wine can also be obtained from the barrel.

Thíra is unique and consequently it is one of the places in the Aegean that must be visited. In the summer as many as four cruise ships may be anchored in the bay beneath Thíra town disembarking thousands of sightseers. Yachtsmen are lucky in so far as they can visit Thíra town and then retire to the peace of another anchorage around the crater.

NISÍS THIRASIA

The westernmost island. The only anchorage is in Órmos Áyios Nikólaou (36°25'·3N 25°21'·2E). Anchor off the small hamlet at the foot of the cliffs. The short pier has 3m depths at its extremity but it is used by *caïque*-ferries from Thíra and Finikia. Good shelter from the *meltemi* although there is invariably some swell in the bay. Open to the S and E. Tavernas ashore. A zig-zag track leads up the cliffs to the village above where some provisions can be obtained.

NISÍS NÉA KAMMÉNI

The once hot lump of ash and cinders in the middle of the crater. There are a number of very small inlets around the island where a yacht can anchor. The anchor must have a trip line as the bottom consists of very large rocks which easily snag an anchor.

The best anchorage on Néa Kamméni is in a cove on the SE corner. There is a light structure on the S side of the entrance (Fl.3s5M). Unfortunately most of the quayed area here is used by the local tripper boats and there is little room for even small yachts. Squeeze in where you can. Care must be taken of a foul area off the W side of the cove where a sunken coaster lies on the bottom. There is a small chapel ashore. Open only to the E.

A yacht can also anchor immediately N of the entrance to the cove with a long line ashore. There is reasonable shelter from the *meltemi* here. Several coves N of this anchorage can also be used with care.

Caution Néa Kamméni is infested with very big and bold rats who will not hesitate to come aboard.

NÍSOS THÍRA

⊕**46** 0·5M W of Ák Epanomeria (Ammoúdhi Point/Thíra)
36°28'·1N 25°21'·6E
⊕**47** 0·5M W of Ák Akrotíri (Thíra) 36°21'·5N 25°20'·9E
⊕**48** 1M S of Ák Exomiti (Thíra) 36°19'·0N 25°26'·6E

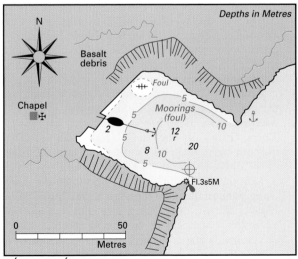

NÉA KAMMÉNI (SOUTHEAST COVE)
⊕36°24'·1N 25°24'·3E

Thíra and the Atlantis legend

Plato first recorded the Atlantis legend that has baffled historians to the present. His description of an ancient island civilization which vanished as the result of a great natural catastrophe has been variously fixed in the Antilles, America, an island somewhere on the continental shelf off the Mediterranean, Malta – and most often in Plato's imagination. In the last forty years the location of Atlantis has moved to Greece and many eminent authorities now believe that Thíra was in fact the fabled island.

We know that Thíra was populated before 2000 BC and that in the period before the catastrophic eruption an advanced and inventive Minoan civilization existed on Thíra and Crete. Although the excavations at Akrotíri on Thíra are interesting, the range of technological and artistic achievements of the Minoans is best seen at Iraklion and the Palace of Knossos. This civilization ended abruptly around 1400 BC and for some time it was hypothesized that a Mycenaean invasion had simply swept it away. Yet Thíra erupted at about the same time and the hypothesis of Professor Marinatos and others is that this mega-explosion not only destroyed Thíra but also caused a *tsunami* or seismic sea wave which destroyed the Cretan-based Minoans.

Thíra is the largest known active caldera in the Mediterranean and one of the largest in the world. It is about five times the size of Krakatoa near Java and the eruption of Thíra is estimated have been about three times greater than that of Krakatoa in 1883. Here is a description of that recent eruption:

'In the course of two days, 26-27 August 1883, 23 sq. km of Krakatoa disappeared as a result of a series of violent explosions. The biggest explosion at 10 a.m. on the 27th, was heard from Alice Springs in Australia to Martinique, and from Ceylon to Northern Malaya. Atmospheric shock waves from it travelled three and a half times round the globe. The blast caused serious damage to houses up to 160 km away. Tidal waves were associated with the explosions and that associated with the biggest explosion was reliably reported as 17m high at Vlakke Hoek lighthouse 88 km away from Krakatoa. The waves destroyed nearly 300 towns and villages on the surrounding coasts of Java and Sumatra, and a large proportion of the coast population, amounting to over 36,000 people, was drowned.'

J. V. Luce *The End of Atlantis*

From this it may be inferred that the earlier Thíra explosion could effectively destroy life on Crete only 60 miles away. The blast would destroy buildings and tidal waves perhaps 60–100m high moving at 160 km per hour would swamp nearby islands. Crete would have been covered in a layer of acidic ash between 10–75cm thick (10cm effectively destroys the soil for 2 years or more). And so in the end we come back to Plato's words: 'But afterwards there occurred violent earthquakes and floods; and in a single day and night of misfortune the island of Atlantis disappeared in the depths of the sea.'

The excavation of Akrotíri on the south of Thíra has revealed a prosperous city with three-storey mansions and wall paintings of quite exquisite beauty. However the excavations have added to the puzzle of Thíra as not a single inhabitant has been found buried in the ash and pumice. Excavations on Crete and other islands in the vicinity reveal previous eruptions and it is likely that Thíra was abandoned before the final catastrophic eruption that engulfed Akrotíri.

Since the great eruption of about 1400 BC the volcano of Thíra has remained active. In 236 BC it erupted again and separated Thirasia from the NW end of Thíra. In 196 BC Old Kameni (Hiera) appeared. In AD 1570 the south coast of Thíra collapsed into the sea. Three years later Small (Mikra) Kamméni appeared and in 1711–12 Néa Kamméni appeared. In 1866 a violent eruption began and lasted two years. At the end of 1868 an islet, Afotessa, appeared and then disappeared again. In 1925–26 another eruption joined Small Kamméni to Néa Kamméni. In July 1956 a massive earthquake caused much damage destroying many of the buildings at Finikia and Thíra. The epicentre of this earthquake was off the north coast of Amorgós and it produced tsunamis up to 17m high.

Thíra

BA 1541

The principal island. There are a number of anchorages around the island:

1. **Finikia (Epanomeria)** Lies on the N end of Thíra under Ák Epanomeria. There is a short pier with 6m depths at the extremity, but it is usually crowded with fishing boats and *caïque*-ferries. Anchor to the W of the mole in 10–20m. The bottom is rocky and the anchor should have a trip line. Some shelter from the *meltemi* although there is always some ground swell here. Completely open to the S.

   Tavernas on the waterfront. A track leads up the cliff to the village of Finikia above.

2. **Skála Thíra** The harbour for the capital of Thíra (Fira) on the steep slopes above. The harbour here, really just a quay cut into the base of the cliff, is very open and you should not leave a yacht unattended. Go stern or bows-to the quay using your anchor or a long line to the buoy. (See *Note*). If you are using the buoy there is invariably considerable confusion when a yacht on the inside wants to leave. All the yachts on one side or the other must drop their lines or pass them around the yacht leaving, an exercise which

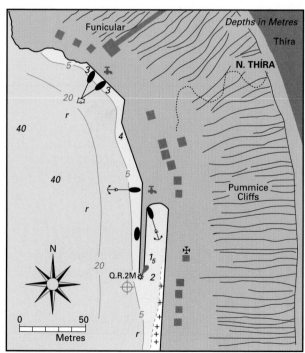

SKALA THÍRA
⊕36°25′·1N 25°25′·7E

Skála Thíra looking E   *Peter Kleinoth/MareTeam*

leaves ample scope for confusion. Getting out from the spider's web of lines is further complicated by the wash from tripper boats, ferries, and boats carrying passengers to and fro from the cruise ships anchored off. It is recommended you do not leave a yacht unattended on the quay.

Berths on the quay have a lee from the *meltemi* although there is a slop onto the quay. However the wash from other craft passing nearby, especially ferries and cruise ships, is significantly worse than any slop generated by the wind. The small harbour is mostly for local boats. There may be room in the NW corner of the harbour for a few yachts to go stern or bows-to. Alternatively yachts may be able to go alongside the outside of the mole. Make sure you have plenty of fenders out if alongside. The coastguard station in the main square in Thira appreciates a visit. There are plans to make the harbour more yacht-friendly.

Thíra looking down to the caldera from the *chora*   *Nigel Patten*

Water on the outer quay. There are several taverna/cafés by the harbour. A donkey can be hired for the climb up to the town above or you can take the recently installed funicular. At Thíra town there is good shopping for provisions and excellent restaurants and bars. The view from the *chora* is simply stupendous.

Note The buoy is not always in place and not always in the best condition. Winter storms or more likely galvanic corrosion in the sulphurous waters corrodes the mooring chain and it can take some time before the authorities replace it. If it is not in place there are few alternatives. You can drop an anchor and go stern or bows-to, but it shelves very steeply off the quay to 20 plus metres. In addition the bottom is foul with large boulders and a trip-line on the anchor is essential. If you take a long line to the buoy it is at your own risk. Americans should take note that a libel action against the port authorities is doomed to failure in the Byzantine intricacies of the Greek legal system.

3. **Athinios** A small harbour 4 miles ENE of Ák Akrotíri used for loading pumice from nearby quarries. It is usually crowded with coasters loading or waiting to be loaded. The village of Megálo Khorion stands atop the cliff behind. If you are going to berth here care must be taken of a submerged mole and debris immediately E of the short pier. There are mostly 6m depths off the quay. Go and reconnoitre by dinghy before attempting to berth. Shelter is not the greatest here as the prevailing wind pushes a swell straight onto the quay.

4. **Ák Akrotíri** On the S side of Ák Akrotíri there are a number of anchorages sheltered from the *meltemi*.

Directly under the cape there is a deserted bay used by a few local fishing boats on permanent moorings. Anchor in 4–6m on a boulder-strewn bottom – use a trip line. A light breeze blows around the W point of the bay and holds you into the ground swell making for a comfortable night's sleep.

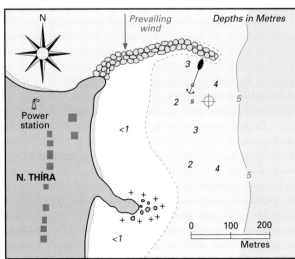

MONOLITHOS
⊕36°24'·8N 25°29'·3E

293

Approximately 1½ miles to the E there is a bight with a few houses and a taverna on the shore. Anchor in 4–5m. A further 1½ miles to the ESE there is another bight used by local fishing boats. The bottom off the S coast is coarse sand – good holding. These latter anchorages get some ground swell which causes yachts here to roll awfully.

5. *Monolithos* A small harbour approximately halfway along the E coast. A rough breakwater extends for 150m in an easterly direction with 2–3m depths inside the outer end. The western half of the harbour is shallow. Go bows-to with a long line ashore to the breakwater near its extremity. With the *meltemi* some swell works its way into the harbour. Ashore there is a taverna and showers.

VLIKADHA

Approach

Care is needed in the approach because of the old breakwaters now underwater and the associated rocks and reefs in the vicinity. From approximately ¾M off the coast head on a course of 45° for the chimneys on the shore. Approximately 400 metres off the harbour head for the end of the outer breakwater.

Conspicuous The chimneys and hotel immediately E of the harbour are easily identified. Closer in the outer breakwater and boats in the harbour will be seen.

By night The entrance is not lit at present and an approach by night would be dangerous because of the reefs in the approaches.

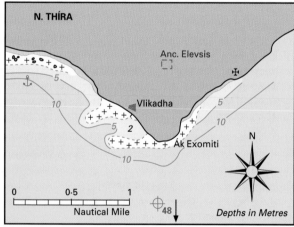

VLIKADHA APPROACHES

⊕48 1M S of Ák Exomiti (Thíra) 36°19'·0N 25°26'·6E

Dangers

1. Care is needed of the reefs which border both the E and W approaches to the harbour. At the time of writing the dangers are marked in a haphazard fashion with a red flag marking the end of the reef that must be left to starboard.

2. Unless you get exactly the right line into the harbour, depths are variable with some shallow patches. You should have someone up front conning you in.

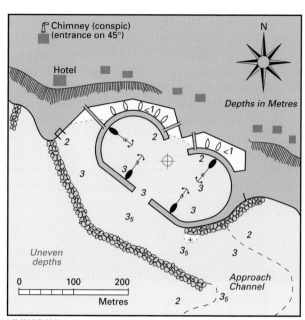

VLIKADHA
⊕36°20'·2N 25°26'·0E

3. In the entrance to the marina there is an underwater rock just off the inner breakwater and you should keep close to the end of the outer breakwater.

Note I have had reports of silting reducing depths in the approach channel to 2m. Recent reports from other yachts indicate depths are much as charted. Care is needed in the approach channel and yachts over 2m draught should go easy in the channel and maybe send someone ahead in the dinghy to reconnoitre.

Mooring

Go stern or bows-to where possible. Out of season some yachts go alongside.

Shelter Good all-round shelter.

Facilities

Services Water by mini-tanker. Water and electricity points to be installed.
Fuel By mini-tanker. Fuel jetty to be established on the E pier.
Eating out Taverna ashore.
Other Bus to *chora*. A taxi can be arranged from the hotel.

General

Vlikadha affords the best shelter on Thíra and for that it is worth making for. The entrance is tricky, although once you have piloted your way in it does not present the same adrenalin rush as the first time. You can get to *chora* from here and at least take your time over a visit without worrying about your boat down on the exposed quay at Skála.

NISÍDHES KHRISTIANA

Khristiana light 36°13'·3N 25°13'·7E

A group of jagged rocks lying about 9 miles SW of Ák Akrotíri on Thíra. There are no anchorages and they are uninhabited.

Nísos Anáfi

(Anaphe)

The southeasternmost of the Cyclades. A barren burnt lump of an island with a small *chora* and an exposed anchorage on the south coast. Legend has it that Apollo raised the island from the sea to provide refuge for Jason and the Argonauts during a storm – a myth probably connected to the Thíra eruption. A few backpackers are attracted to the island's long sandy beaches.

Skala Anáfi   *Nigel Patten*

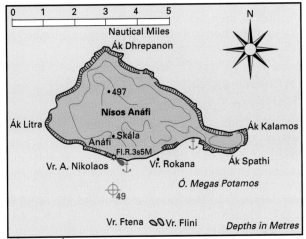

NÍSOS ANÁFI

⊕49 1M S of Ák Petradhia (Skála Anáfi) 36°19'·7N 25°46'·2E

SKÁLA ANÁFI

A bight on the S coast. The *chora* on the hill and the hamlet around the landing place are conspicuous. There is a light at Skála: Fl.R.3s5M. The eastern end of the island is a high precipitous peak separated by flat land from the rest of the island and looks like a separate island from the distance. A white chapel on the summit of the peak is conspicuous. Care must be taken of the low-lying Voi Rokana, a rock lying 1¼ miles E of the hamlet and approximately ¼ of a mile offshore.

Immediately W of the hamlet a broken-down breakwater running S provides some shelter from westerlies. Anchor in 3–6m and with the *meltemi* try to tuck yourself under the breakwater with a long line to it. There is a small pier, but it is always crowded with *caïques*. The bottom is sand – good holding. Although I have experienced a swell working its way around the island into here, others

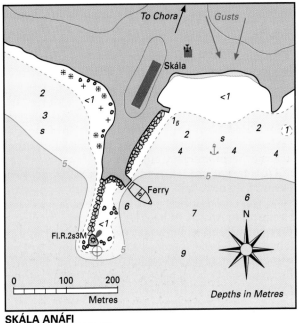

SKÁLA ANÁFI
⊕36°20'·6N 25°46'·2E

recommend the shelter at Anáfi and have had a comfortable time despite the *meltemi* screaming outside. Open to the SW–S–E. Limited provisions and tavernas in the hamlet. The Seashore (Poppy) taverna has been recommended.

About 3 miles to the E an open bay with a long sandy beach can be used in calm weather.

The eastern end of Anáfi looking NW. Note the conspicuous chapel perched on the summit

VI. Evia and the Northern Sporades

This chapter covers the island of Evia lying parallel to mainland Greece, the mainland coast itself from Ák Sounion to the Tríkeri peninsula, (Locris, Boeotia, Attica) and the northern Sporades. The inner route up the narrow gulf between Evia and the mainland is the more often travelled, there being sheltered waters and many safe harbours and anchorages. Along the east coast of Evia there are few safe anchorages sheltered from the prevailing wind. Nonetheless in the days of sail, *caïques* bound for the north would take the open water route making for Skiros and then slanting NW to Thessaloniki. The return trip was generally down the inner route.

In classical and Venetian times Evia and Skiros were important intermediate ports along the northern Aegean trade route between Athens and what is now northern Turkey. The trip from west to east was a gruelling slog (with a lot of rowing) against the prevailing winds.

The agricultural and mineral wealth of Evia ensured its own early development into a powerful state with a large fleet of its own, but it was later subdued by Athens. When the Venetians occupied it they considered it important enough to rank it as a kingdom and the standard of Negroponte (as Evia was called under the Venetians) was one of the three flown in St Mark's Square in Venice. Today, despite its proximity to Athens, Evia remains for the most part a wild and unspoiled island.

In ancient times an enemy of Athens wishing to invade the city-state would follow a fairly standard route from the north down through Evia and the adjacent mainland to southern Greece. The Pass of Thermopylae and the Plain of Marathon are probably the two best-known classical battle sites. The land force would be landed or supported from the sea and consequently this stretch of sea resounded to sea battles of which the Athenian harassment of Xerxes' fleet in the Tríkeri Channel is possibly best known. Not only the Persian invaders under Xerxes, but also the Macedonians, the Romans (under Glabrio and Cato), and the Turks, used this passage to get to southern and western Greece. In 1941 the British force (with the Australians and New Zealanders), retreating from the Germans in Macedonia, came down through here and were evacuated from beaches in Evia and the Saronic Gulf.

Kólpos Petalíon and the southern part of Evia are regularly cruised by Athens-based yachts, but further N there are fewer yachts to be seen except around the northern Sporades where a number of charter companies are based.

Weather patterns in Evia and the Northern Sporades

The prevailing wind in the summer is the *meltemi* blowing from the NE. As in the Cyclades the *meltemi* begins fitfully in June, blows strongest in July and August, and dies at the end of October. In July and August it blows at Force 4–6 and may reach Force 7 on occasion. In the spring and autumn the wind is again predominantly from the N (NE–NW) but there are regular winds from the S as well.

There are a number of local variations to the overall weather pattern. In the Tríkeri and Orei Channels (Stenón Tríkeri and Stenón Oréon) the wind is funnelled into the channel so that it blows from the E–ENE. In the gulf of Volos (Pagasitikós Kólpos) the prevailing wind is from the SE–SW. It can get up to a fresh breeze at times. A NW wind sometimes blows down from the head of the gulf in the spring and autumn.

In the winter, gales are more often than not from the NE and can be exceptionally harsh. In early December 1980 a gale from the NE reached Force 10 and snow covered most parts of Evia down to sea level. In the mountains, up to a metre of snow fell and transport, telecommunications and electricity facilities were knocked out for three days. Again in the winter of 2001–2 heavy snowfalls were recorded at sea level in this area. Snow on the decks is not what most people associate with Greece.

As in the Cyclades care must be taken of gusts off high land when the *meltemi* is blowing. Places noted for these squalls are the Evia coast in Kólpos Petalíon, the Evia coast N of Khalkís, and the E coast of Skiros.

In the summer the temperatures are high averaging 25°–26°C. Thessaly has the reputation of being the hottest place in Europe and certainly Volos is very hot in the summer (average temperature 27°C). In the spring and autumn there may be rain showers and thunderstorms. The latter may be accompanied by squalls, but they are normally short-lived affairs, usually over in an hour or so. The winters are harsher than those in more southern climes with colder temperatures and substantial snowfalls.

Quick reference guide

	Shelter	Mooring	Fuel	Water	Provisioning	Tavernas	Plan
Evia and adjacent mainland coast							
Gaïdhouromandra (Olympic Marina)	A	A	A	A	C	C	•
Lavrion	B	A	A	A	B	B	••
Órmos Thoriko	B	C	O	O	O	O	••
Tourkolimani	C	C	O	O	O	O	
Porto Rafti	B	AC	B	B	B	B	•
Órmos Vravronas	C	C	O	O	O	C	
Loutsa	A	A	O	A	C	C	
Rafina	C	A	B	B	B	B	•
Néa Mákri	C	A	B	B	B	C	
Órmos Marathonas	O	C	O	O	O	O	
Áy Apóstoliou	B	A	O	B	C	C	
Órmos Oropos	O	C	B	B	B	C	
Órmos Angistri	C	C	O	B	C	C	
Órmos Kastrí	B	C	O	O	O	O	•
Karistos	A	A	B	A	A	A	•
Nisídhes Petaloi	C	C	O	O	O	O	•
Néa Marmari	C	AC	B	A	B	B	•
Órmos Vlikho	B	C	O	O	O	O	
Órmos Animvoriou	B	C	O	O	O	O	•
Néa Stíra	C	C	O	B	C	C	
Nísos Stíra	B	C	O	O	O	O	•
Órmos Tigani	C	C	O	O	O	O	•
Almiropotamos	B	C	O	B	C	C	•
Voufalo	A	C	O	O	O	C	•
Aliverion	A	A	O	A	B	B	•
Amarinthos	O	BC	B	B	B	B	
Erétria	B	BC	B	B	A	B	•
Khalkís	B	ABC	A	A	A	A	•
Northern Evia Channel							
Órmos Skorponeriou	B	C	O	B	O	O	
Lárimna	C	C	B	A	B	C	•
Kólpos Atalántis	B	C	O	O	C	C	•
Skála Atalantis	B	AB	O	A	C	C	•
Áyios Konstandinos	O	AB	O	B	B	B	
Ayios Serafiou	B	B	O	O	O	O	
Néa Artaki	B	BC	B	B	A	B	•
Órmos Politika	A	AB	O	B	O	O	
Limni	A	AB	B	B	B	C	•
Loutra Adhipsou	A	BC	B	B	A	B	•
Órmos Yiali	C	C	O	O	O	O	
Áy Yeoryios	C	A	B	A	C	B	
N. Likhades	C	C	O	O	O	O	•
Stilidhos	B	AB	B	B	A	C	•
Karavomilos	C	C	O	B	C	C	
Rahes	C	C	O	B	C	B	
Akladhi	AC	BC	B	B	C	B	•
Órmos Vathikelon	A	C	O	O	O	O	•
Órmos Glifa	C	C	B	A	B	B	
Aryronísos	C	C	O	B	O	O	
Pirgos	B	AB	B	B	C	B	•
Orei	B	A	B	A	B	B	•
Gulf of Volos							
Órmos Ptelou	B	C	O	B	C	B	•
Órmos Nies	B	C	O	O	O	C	
Áy Kiriakí	C	C	O	B	C	C	•
Nisís Palaio Tríkeri	C	AC	O	O	C	C	•
Órmos Pithos	B	C	O	O	O	O	
Órmos Tríkeri	C	C	O	O	O	O	

	Shelter	Mooring	Fuel	Water	Provisioning	Tavernas	Plan
Órmos Vathoudhi	A	AC	B	B	C	C	•
Petraki	B	C	O	O	O	C	
Amalioupolis	C	AC	B	B	B	B	•
Fearless Cove	B	C	O	O	O	O	•
Néa Ankhialos	B	B	B	B	C	B	
Áy Yeóryios	B	AC	O	B	C	C	
Volos	A	AB	A	A	A	A	•
Órmos Agria	C	C	O	B	C	C	
Kato Gatsia	C	C	O	O	C	C	
Órmos Andriami	C	C	O	O	O	O	
Platania	B	BC	B	B	B	B	•
Pefki	B	A	O	A	B	B	•
Pondikonisi	C	C	O	O	O	O	
Kati Giorgyios	B	AC	O	O	C	C	
Skíathos							
Órmos Katavathra	C	C	O	O	O	C	
Koukounaries	A	AC	O	B	O	C	•
Órmos Platania	C	C	O	B	O	C	•
Skíathos	B	AC	B	A	A	A	•
Skópelos							
Loutráki	B	AC	B	A	C	B	•
Néa Klima	B	AB	O	O	O	O	
Órmos Panormou	B	C	O	O	C	C	•
Limonari	C	C	O	O	O	C	
Órmos Agnóndas	B	AC	O	B	O	C	•
Órmos Stafilos	C	C	O	O	O	C	•
Limín Skopelou	B	A	B	A	A	A	•
Alonissos							
Órmos Mourtia	C	C	O	O	O	C	•
Patitíri	B	A	B	A	B	B	•
Órmos Rousoumi	B	C	O	O	O	C	•
Votsi	B	C	O	B	O	C	•
Órmos Milia	C	C	O	O	O	C	•
Órmos Tzorti	B	C	O	O	O	C	•
Steni Vala	B	AC	O	B	C	C	•
Kalamakia	C	A	O	O	O	C	
Órmos Firaki	O	C	O	O	O	O	
Peristeri							
Órmos Peristera	B	C	O	O	O	O	•
Órmos Xero	B	C	O	O	O	O	•
Órmos Vasiliko	A	C	O	O	O	O	•
Pelagos							
Órmos Kira Panayía	C	C	O	O	O	O	•
Planitís	A	C	O	O	O	O	•
Skantzoura							
Órmos Prasso	C	C	O	O	O	O	•
Órmos Skantzoura	B	C	O	O	O	O	•
Skíros							
Áy Fokas	C	C	O	O	O	O	
Órmos Pevki	B	C	O	O	O	C	•
Linaria Cove	B	C	O	O	O	C	•
Limín Linaria	B	A	B	A	B	C	•
Órmos Akladhi	B	C	O	O	O	O	
Órmos Tristomou	O	C	O	O	O	O	
Órmos Renes	C	C	O	O	O	O	
Órmos Glifadha	B	C	O	O	O	O	
East Coast of Evia							
Órmos Petriés	B	AC	O	B	C	C	•
Kími	B	A	A	A	C	C	•
Áy Vasilikos anchorage	B	C	O	B	C	C	
Órmos Loutro	B	C	O	B	C	C	•

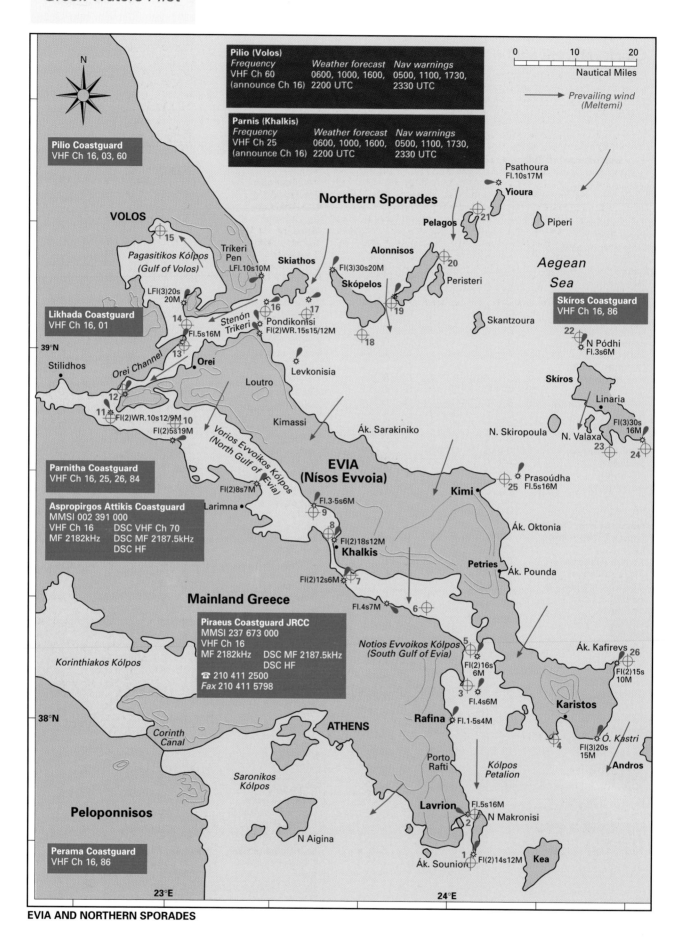

Pilio (Volos)
Frequency	Weather forecast	Nav warnings
VHF Ch 60	0600, 1000, 1600,	0500, 1100, 1730,
(announce Ch 16)	2200 UTC	2330 UTC

Parnis (Khalkis)
Frequency	Weather forecast	Nav warnings
VHF Ch 25	0600, 1000, 1600,	0500, 1100, 1730,
(announce Ch 16)	2200 UTC	2330 UTC

0   10   20
Nautical Miles

Prevailing wind
(Meltemi)

N

Pilio Coastguard
VHF Ch 16, 03, 60

VOLOS

Northern Sporades

Psathoura
Fl.10s17M

Yioura

Pelagos   21   Piperi

15

Pagasitikos Kólpos
(Gulf of Volos)

Tríkeri
Pen
LFl.10s10M

Skiathos

Alonnisos

20

Aegean
Sea

Fl(3)30s20M

Skópelos   Peristeri

Skíros Coastguard
VHF Ch 16, 86

LFl(3)20s
20M

16   17

Likhada Coastguard
VHF Ch 16, 01

14

Stenón
Trikeri

Pondikonisi
Fl(2)WR.15s15/12M

19

Skantzoura

22   N Pódhi
Fl.3s6M

39°N   Fl.5s16M

13   18

Stilidhos

Orei Channel   Orei

Loutro

Levkonisia

Skíros

12

11   10
Fl(2)WR.10s12/9M
Fl(2)5s19M

Kimassi   Ák. Sarakiniko

Linaria

N. Skiropoula   N. Valaxa
23

Fl(3)30s
16M

24

Parnitha Coastguard
VHF Ch 16, 25, 26, 84

Vorios Evvoikos Kólpos
(North Gulf of Evia)

**EVIA
(Nísos Evvoia)**

Prasoúdha
Fl.5s16M

Kimi   25

Aspropirgos Attikis Coastguard
MMSI 002 391 000
VHF Ch 16   DSC VHF Ch 70
MF 2182kHz   DSC MF 2187.5kHz
               DSC HF

Fl(2)8s7M
Larimna

Fl.3·5s6M

9

Ák. Oktonia

8
Fl(2)18s12M

Khalkis

Petries   Ák. Pounda

Mainland Greece

Fl(2)12s6M   7

Piraeus Coastguard JRCC
MMSI 237 673 000
VHF Ch 16
MF 2182kHz   DSC MF 2187.5kHz
               DSC HF
☎ 210 411 2500
Fax 210 411 5798

Fl.4s7M   6

Notios Evvoikos Kólpos
(South Gulf of Evia)

5

Ák. Kafirevs   26

Korinthiakos Kólpos

Fl(2)16s
6M

Fl(2)15s
10M

3
Fl.4s6M

Karistos

38°N

Rafina   Fl.1·5s4M

ATHENS

Corinth
Canal

Porto
Rafti

Kólpos
Petalion

Ó. Kastri

Fl(3)20s
15M

4

Andros

Saronikos
Kólpos

Lavrion   Fl.5s16M

2   N Makronisi

Peloponnisos

N Aigina

Perama Coastguard
VHF Ch 16, 86

Ák. Sounion   1   Fl(2)14s12M   Kea

23°E   24°E

EVIA AND NORTHERN SPORADES

Routes

Routes going N via Evia are basically up or down the outside of the island or the inside channel. The prevailing wind in the summer is the *meltemi* blowing from the NE and outside of the *meltemi* season most winds are still from the northerly quadrant. Yachts going N will usually take the inside channel which although still windy, offers more flat water and importantly more safe harbours and anchorages. Yachts coming S will often take the outside route and roar down to the Cyclades and Stenón Kafirevs with the wind behind. Some also take the inside channel and still have the wind behind.

Yachts heading N should, if they have time, leave in the spring or early summer before the *meltemi* begins or is not as strong as in mid to late summer. Often you will have days of calm and even some southerlies in the spring and early summer making going N a relaxed affair. If any depressions threaten there are more than enough safe harbours to take refuge in until the depression passes.

Yachts heading S in the summer or autumn will usually find that they have more than enough wind for a quick passage. There are several harbours along the E coast of Evia that can be used, although care is needed along what is in effect a lee shore most of the time. The seas can build up substantially, and as you get towards Stenón Kafirevs you will find some wicked steep cross-seas. In gales from any direction Stenón Kafirevs is a place to steer clear of – even big ships seek shelter in northerly gales rather than tackling the strait.

Data

PORTS OF ENTRY
Lavrion
Khalkis
Stilidhos
Volos
Skiathos

PROHIBITED AREAS
1. Navigation prohibited in Ormos Marathona during firing practice. Warnings are listed on Navtex.
2. Anchoring is prohibited in the northern part of Órmos Áyios Marina.
3. Landing is prohibited in the vicinity of Órmos Áyios Marina and on the nearby islands of Stíra, Verdhouyi and Kavaliani.
4. Landing is prohibited on Nísos Yiouri in the Northern Sporades.

MAJOR LIGHTS
Ák Angálistros Fl(2)14s12M
Ák Vrisáki Fl.5s16M
Nisís Mandhíli (Doro Channel) Fl(3)20s15M
Ák Veláni Fl.1·5s4M
Vrakhinisis Dhípsa Fl.4s6M
Nisídhes Verdhouyi (Nisís Ligia)

Fl(2)16s6M
Órmos Oropoú (SE point) Fl.4s7M
Ák Avlís (Dhíavlos Avlidhos) Fl(2)12s6M
Ák Kakokefalí Fl(2)18s12M
Ák Mníma Fl.3·5s6M
Ák Stalamáta Fl(2)8s7M
Ák Arkítsa Fl(2)5s19M
Nisís Strongilí (S islet) Fl(2)WR.10s12/9M
Ák Vasilína Oc.WG.5s14/11M
Ifalos Panagitsa (Orei Reef) Fl(2)12s9M
Aryiorónisos (E end) Fl.5s16M
Ák Tríkeri (Kavoúlia) LFl(3)20s20M
Ak Seskoulo (Volos) Fl.1·5s7M
Pondikonisi Fl(2)WR.15s15/12M
Ifalos Levthéris Fl(2)8s9M
Ák Sépia LFl.10s10M
Nisís Répi (Skíathos) Fl(2)WR.10s12/8M
Ák Gouroúni (Skópelos) Fl(3)30s20M
Ák Télion (Alonissos) Fl(3)12s12M
Nisís Psathoúra Fl.10s17M
Ák Lithári (Skíros) Fl(3)30s16M
Nisís Arápis (Ák Kafirevs) Fl(2)15s10M
Nisís Prasoúdha (Kími) Fl.5s16M
Levkonísia (NE Evia) Fl(3)15s10M

USEFUL WAYPOINTS
⊕1 0·15M S of Ák Angálistros (Makronisí S end)
37°38'·56N 24°01'·31E WGS84
⊕2 0·5M E of Ák Vrisáki
37°44'·63N 24°05'·29E WGS84
⊕3 1·5M E of Ák Marathonas
38°07'·4N 24°05'·4E
⊕4 1M S of Nisís Paximádhi (Órmos Karistou)
37°56'·6N 24°23'·3E
⊕5 Mid-channel between Vrak Levkasia and Áy Marina
38°11'·67N 24°05'·03E WGS84
⊕6 2M N of Áy Apóstoliou
38°19'·8N 23°53'·9E
⊕7 Mid-channel Stenón Avlídhou-Boúrtzi (Ák Avlís)
38°24'·42N 23°38'·09E WGS84
⊕8 Entrance to Vorios Limani (Khalkís)
38°28'·61N 23°35'·81E WGS84
⊕9 1M S of Ák Mníma
38°33'·51N 23°31'·88E WGS84
⊕10 2·5M N of Ák Arkitsa
38°47'·08N 23°02'·18E WGS84
⊕11 Likhades Channel Fairway
38°49'·43N 22°49'·67E WGS84
⊕12 0·5M N of Ák Vasalína
38°52'·76N 22°51'·07E WGS84
⊕13 0·5M E of E end of Aryíronisos
39°00'·59N 23°05'·22E WGS84
⊕14 Mid–channel Stenón Volou (1·5M N of Ák Stavrós)
39°03'·91N 23°04'·13E WGS84
⊕15 Ák Seskoulo (approaches to Volos)
39°20'·62N 22°56'·60E WGS84
⊕16 Mid–channel E end of Stenón Tríkeri (2·5M N of Pondikonisi)
39°05'·57N 23°20'·36E WGS84
⊕17 1M S of N Tsoungria (Skíathos)
39°05'·84N 23°30'·09E WGS84
⊕18 0·5M S of Ák Velona (Skópelos)
39°03'·59N 23°43'·19E WGS84
⊕19 Stenón Alonissou (mid-channel between N. Mikró and Ák Telio)
39°08'·42N 23°49'·24E WGS84
⊕20 Mid–channel N. Alonnisos – Ák Aspro (N. Peristeri)
39°14'·58N 23°58'·23E WGS84
⊕21 0·5M NE of Ák Kira (N. Pelagos)
39°22'·52N 24°05'·24E WGS84
⊕22 2M N of Nisís Vorios Pódhi (Skíros N end)
39°03'·2N 24°28'·1E
⊕23 1M S of Ák Valáxa light
38°47'·0N 24°29'·5E
⊕24 2M S of Nisís Sarakino light (Skíros S end)
38°43'·5N 24°37'·6E
⊕25 1M E of Ák Kími
38°38'·9N 24°10'·7E
⊕26 1M E of Nisís Arápis/Ák Kafirevs
38°09'·6N 24°37'·1E

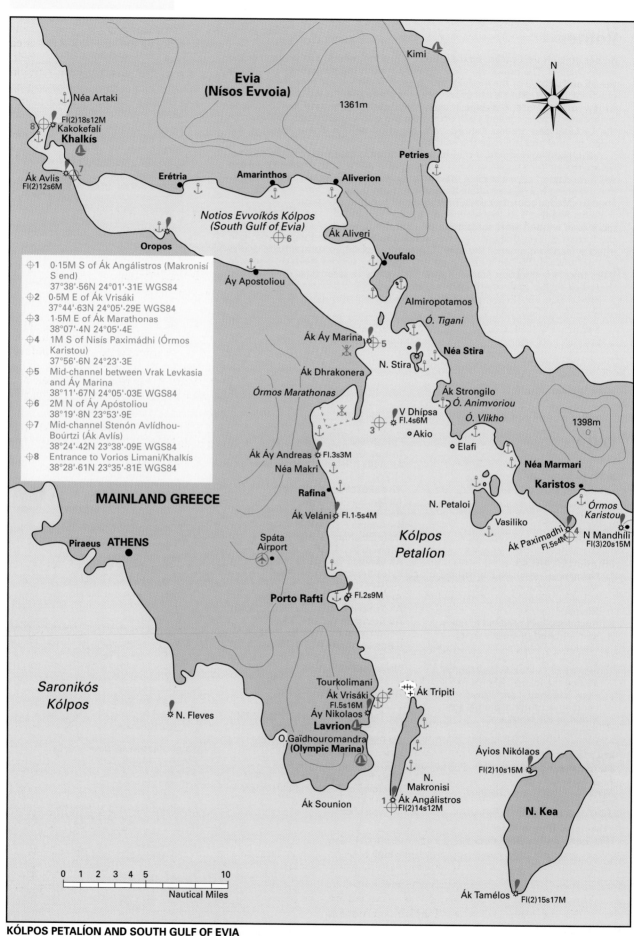

Evia
(Nísos Evvoia)

Kimi

1361m

Néa Artaki

Fl(2)18s12M
Kakokefalí
Khalkís

Petries

Ák Avlis
Fl(2)12s6M

Erétria

Amarinthos

Aliverion

Notios Evvoíkós Kólpos
(South Gulf of Evia)

Ák Aliveri

Oropos

Voufalo

Áy Apostoliou

Almiropotamos

Ó. Tigani

Ák Áy Marina

Néa Stira

N. Stira

Ák Dhrakonera

Órmos Marathonas

Ák Strongilo
Ó. Animvoriou

V Dhípsa
Fl.4s6M
Akio

Ó. Vlikho

1398m

Ák Áy Andreas ☼ Fl.3s3M

Elafi

Néa Marmari

Néa Makri

Karistos

Rafina

N. Petaloi

Órmos
Karistou

Ák Veláni ☼ Fl.1·5s4M

Vasiliko

Ák Paximadhi
Fl.5s4M

N Mandhíli
Fl(3)20s15M

**Kólpos
Petalíon**

MAINLAND GREECE

Spáta
Airport

Piraeus ATHENS

Porto Rafti ☼ Fl.2s9M

**Saronikós
Kólpos**

☼ N. Fleves

Tourkolimani
Ák Vrisáki
Fl.5s16M
Áy Nikolaos
Lavrion
O.Gaïdhouromandra
(Olympic Marina)

Ák Tripiti

Áyios Nikólaos
Fl(2)10s15M

N.
Makronisi

Ák Sounion

1 ☼ Ák Angálistros
Fl(2)14s12M

N. Kea

0 1 2 3 4 5   10
Nautical Miles

Ák Tamélos Fl(2)15s17M

KÓLPOS PETALÍON AND SOUTH GULF OF EVIA

West coast of Evia and adjacent mainland coast

This section covers the stretch of water hemmed in between the island of Evia and the adjacent mainland coast. The section is split into a further two sub-sections covering the sea area S of Khalkís (Kólpos Petalíon and Notios Evvoïkós Kólpos/the S Gulf of Evia) and N of Khalkís (Vórios Evvoïkós Kólpos/the N Gulf of Evia).

Evia (also Evoia, Euboea, or Euripos after the narrow channel at Khalkís) or Negroponte, the Venetian name, is the long mountainous island lying parallel in a NW–SE direction to the mainland coast. After Crete it is the largest Greek island. The irregular mountain range is geographically the continuation of the Pilion range running down the east side of the Gulf of Volos. Mt Dhirfis (Dhelfi), 45 miles NW of Ák Kafirevs, is the summit of the island at 1,874m (5,718ft). Ten miles further NW, Mt Pixaria is 1,445m (4,406ft) high, and at the southern end of the island Mt Okhi (*Okhi* = no, and here means the mountain defies all), is 1,398m (4,586ft) high. Between these considerable peaks the island is rugged and steep-to with little flat land except on the W coast. The peaks are covered in snow in the winter and often far into the spring. On the lower slopes the mountains are densely wooded in pine, plane, holm oak and olive trees. The coastal plains on the west are fertile and intensively cultivated in corn, vines, figs and market gardens. Lignite and magnesite are mined and marble quarried – Evian *cipollino* was prized above all others by the Romans.

The mainland coast opposite is also mountainous, although it is not in the league of the Evian mountains. Mt Knimis, standing inland from the cape of the same name in the N, is 946m (3,077ft) high, a peak opposite Khalkís with a conspicuous white patch near the summit rises to 1,030m (3,350ft), and Mt Pendelikon near Athens rises to 1,119m (3,638ft). For the most part the mainland mountains are barren or covered in maquis, but the coastal plain is wooded or cultivated. From a point opposite Khalkís the motorway north mostly follows the coastline.

In antiquity Evia was divided between seven city-states of which Khalkís and Eretria were the two most important. These two cities were rivals for the fertile Lelantine Plain lying between them with Khalkís finally winning by default when Eretria was razed by the invading Persians. After the Persian wars Evia came under the sway of Athens. It passed on to Rome and to Byzantium without too many hiccups.

When the Venetians took Evia they renamed the island, calling it Negroponte, meaning 'black bridge' – a corruption of the name of the bridge spanning the Euripos Channel. Under the Venetians it ranked as a kingdom. In 1470 the island was occupied by the Turks and remained under Turkish rule until it became part of modern Greece in 1830.

The proximity of the mainland coast to Athens (Rafina is only 18½ miles away) has raised this area to the dubious status of a summer commuter belt. Large villas line much of the coast between Lavrion and Khalkís and land development is beginning north of Khalkís. The opening of the new airport for Athens at Spáta near this coast will no doubt bring further development. Athenians have also started to go to Evia, but the poor roads and sheer size of the island ensure that large parts of it remain virtually untouched.

Coasts south of Khalkís

Mainland coast

OLYMPIC MARINA (Órmos Gaïdhouromandra)

Approach

From the S the marina and yard will not be seen until you are up to Ák Foniás. Once you have opened the bay the outer breakwater, yard buildings and the masts of yachts will be seen. From the N the buildings and harbour at Lavrion will be seen and closer in the breakwater and shoreside buildings at the Olympic yard.

By night Use the light on Ák Foniás Fl.2·5s6M. The marina entrance is lit Fl.R.3M.

VHF Ch 09 for Olympic Marine.

Mooring

Data 680 berths. Visitors' berths. Max LOA 30m+. Depths 2–10m.

Berth Where directed. Laid moorings.

Shelter Excellent all-round shelter.

Authorities Port police and customs. Harbourmaster and marina staff. Charge band 3.

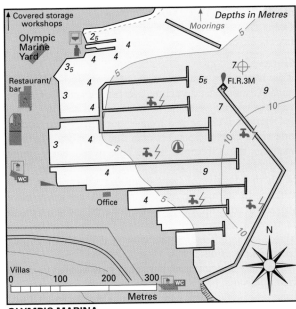

OLYMPIC MARINA
⊕37°41'·74N 24°03'·80E WGS84

Olympic Marina looking N

Facilities

Services Water and electricity at every berth. Shower and toilet block. Washing machines.

Fuel On the quay near the travel-hoist bay.

Repairs **Olympic Marine** 1,000 dry berths. 300 covered berths. 200/65/40-ton travel-hoists. Covered workshops. All mechanical and engineering repairs. GRP repairs including osmosis treatment and spray-painting facilities. Wood repairs. Electrical work. Liferaft certification. Sail repairs arranged. Chandlers.

Olympic Marine SA, GR 19500 Lavrion, Attica, Greece ☎ 22920 63700 *Fax* 22920 22569
Email olympicmarine@internet.gr
www.olmarine.com.

Provisions Minimarket planned in the marina. Better shopping in Lavrion (market on Thursdays).

Eating out A restaurant-cum-yacht club and a snack bar in the marina. Fotis, previously within the yard, has built a new restaurant outside just up the hill and those who have visited say he still cooks good food (☎ 60875). Otherwise tavernas in Lavrion.

Other Bank planned in the marina. Telephone and fax facilities. Hire cars and taxis. Bus to Athens.

General

The marina is now up and running and fairly full with Athens-based yachts, but there is still room for visiting yachts here.

Olympic Marine is a long-established yard and at one time Carter 33s, 37s and 39s were built here as well as the Olympic 45. There were even some ferrocement Endurance 45s built here in the '70s. With the demise of yacht-building Olympic Marine turned to laying up yachts and has an impressive infrastructure including large covered workshops. It is now a competent and well-run yard with just about all facilities for the care and repair of yachts ashore and afloat.

If it has a drawback it is that it is some distance from Athens and Piraeus where you may need to have specialist work carried out. The bus in and out can occupy the best part of a day by the time you have organised things in Athens, but with the much improved roads it is now fairly quick to get in and out by car, except, that is, until you arrive at the traffic snarl-ups in Athens itself.

LAVRION (Limín Lavriou)

BA 1571

Approach

Conspicuous The harbour lies immediately N of Gaïdhouromandra and from the S the buildings of the town are easily identified. From the N the two tall chimneys at Áy Nikólaos in the bay N of Lavrion (Órmos Thorikou) will be seen.

By night Use the lights on Ák Foniás Fl.2·5s6M and Ák Ergastíria Fl.1·5s4M. The entrance is lit Fl.G.3s5M/Fl.R.3s5M. The two chimneys at Áy Nikólaos are lit by fixed red lights with a good range.

Mooring

Go stern or bows-to the town quay or the L-shaped mole. A number of charter companies use Lavrion as a base and it can get crowded on turn-around days. Laid moorings tailed to the quay in places.

Shelter Good shelter. A bit of slop is pushed across the harbour onto the town quay, more uncomfortable than dangerous.

Authorities A port of entry: port police, customs and immigration.

Facilities

Services Water and electricity on the town quay. Water on the mole.

Fuel Near the quay on the W. A mini-tanker supplies yachts on the quay or go to the fuel quay at Olympic Marina nearby.

Repairs Most mechanical repairs. The extensive repair facilities of the Olympic Yard are nearby.

Provisions Good shopping for provisions nearby.

Eating out Tavernas in the town.

Other PO. OTE. Bank. Greek gas and Camping Gaz. Infrequent bus to Athens. Ferry to Kéa and Kíthnos.

Lavrion town quay looking across from the boatyard

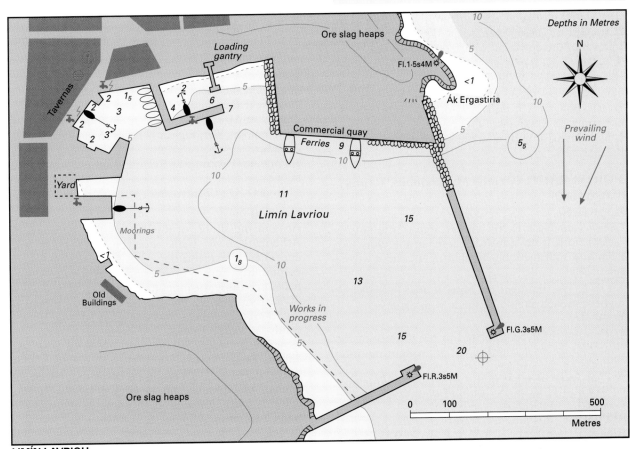

LIMÍN LAVRIOU
⊕37°42'·37N 24°04'·01E WGS84

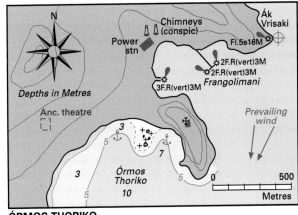

ÓRMOS THORIKO
⊕37°44'·7N 24°04'·9E

General

Lavrion was once an important port shipping cadmium and manganese and small amounts of lead from the reworking of the ancient mine tailings. The mines were probably worked as early as 1000 BC and in classical times large amounts of silver were extracted from the Lavrion mines whose wealth boosted Athens' commercial power.

Today Lavrion is a grubby 'has-been' port with piles of slag and ore littered around the coast. Yet it has its own charm, a sort of faded dignity and glimpses of old-world wealth in the villas around town. The waterfront has now been cleaned up and there are new cafés and bars along it. Most of those who spend some time here while working on a boat in the Olympic yard have a certain fondness for the place that is not readily apparent on a first visit.

ÓRMOS THORIKO

The large bay just over 1 mile N of Lavrion. Anchor in the NW of the bay taking care of the above water rocks off the shore. The bottom is sand and weed, good holding. Good shelter from the *meltemi* tucked under the N entrance point.

To the N of Órmos Thoriko is Frangolimani (Órmos Áyios Nikolaos), the site of a large power station and several other factories. Two very tall chimneys (red and white bands) are conspicuous from a considerable distance off. There is a substantial pier and quayed sections, but these are for supply ships only.

TOURKOLIMANI

Half a mile N of Ák Vrisáki this bay offers reasonable shelter from the *meltemi*. Anchor in the N cove. Open to the SE.

NÍSOS MAKRONISI (Nísos Eleni)

The long thin island lying parallel to the Attica coast between Ák Sounion and Nísos Kéa. It is a rugged hilly island rising to 274m (899ft) at the N end. The E coast of the island has numerous bays and coves along it that can be used according to the wind direction. Most of them are open to the *meltemi* blowing down from the NE although Órmos Angálistros at the S end and Órmos Yerolimonias about a third of the way up on the E side look as if

303

they would give some shelter from the *meltemi*. Care is needed of Ifalos Angálistros, the reef lying 0·15 miles S of the entrance to Órmos Angálistros.

Note When passing through Stenón Makronisou, the channel between Makronisi and the mainland coast, care must be taken of Ifalos Tripiti, a reef just awash, lying half a mile NW of Ák Tripiti, the N extremity of Makronisi. The remains of a wrecked coaster that formerly marked the reef have all but disappeared.

PORTO RAFTI (Órmos Markopoulo, Raptis, Mesoyaias)

Approach

Conspicuous Nisís Raftis with a large statue atop is conspicuous from seaward. Closer in the cluster of villas and apartment blocks skirting the shore will be seen.

By night Use the light on Nisís Raftis: Fl.2s9M. A night approach should be made with caution.

Dangers
1. Caution must be exercised in the vicinity of the anchorage on account of the permanent mooring floats on the surface.
2. Care must be taken of the remains of a mole now underwater on the N side of Limín Mesoyaias.

Mooring

Anchor in the NW corner in 4–10m. Care is needed of uneven depths in the NW part of the bay with some shallow patches. Proceed with care. Alternatively go stern or bows-to the quay in the cove on the N side of Ák Pounda if there is room. The bottom is mud or sand – good holding.

Shelter Good shelter from the *meltemi*. Although the bay is open to the E and SE these winds do not blow home and the islands in the entrance break up the swell. A number of yachts are wintered afloat here.

Authorities Port police.

Facilities

Water On the quay at Rafti.
Fuel Near the quay at Rafti.
Provisions Most provisions can be found at Rafti. A supermarket, although it is a fair distance from the harbour.
Eating out Tavernas at Rafti and others around the shore.
Other PO. OTE. Infrequent bus to Athens.

General

Around the shores of this fine natural harbour the Athenians have built their summer villas and apartments, transforming what was a simple fishing community into a prospering summer commuter belt. Incredibly the inhabitants have taken the worst of instant reinforced concrete non-architecture found around Athens and transplanted it here – the result is simply awful and were it not for the remarkable beauty of the bay, it would look like Athens itself.

The statue on Rafti Island probably dates from the Roman occupation and is known locally as 'the tailor' – whence the modern name of the harbour (*rafti* = tailor).

ÓRMOS VRAVRONAS
37°55'·8N 24°01'·4E

A large bay just over 2 miles N of Porto Rafti. Local boats are kept on permanent moorings and in calm weather a yacht can anchor here. It is partially sheltered from the NE by a small islet on the N side.

LOUTSA
37°58'·5N 24°00'·8E

Along the coast between Órmos Vravronas and Rafina, the coast is lined by villas and apartment blocks which stretch in an almost unbroken line along the coast. The effect is not attractive. At Loutsa there is a small private yacht harbour, the Artimedos Yacht Club, where small yachts may find a berth. Good shelter inside the harbour. Provisions and tavernas nearby.

RAFINA
Imray-Tetra G26

Approach

A ferry harbour 7 miles N of Porto Rafti. The cluster of buildings on a knoll above the harbour and the slopes behind is easily identified. Closer in the new mole and breakwater will be seen.

By night Use the light on Ák Veláni Fl.1·5s4M and the light on the outer mole Fl.G.3s3M and inner mole F.G.3M.

Note There is now so little safe berthing for yachts here that it is best to bypass the port if possible.

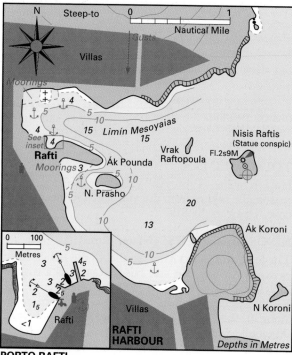

PORTO RAFTI
⊕37°53'·2N 24°02'·7E

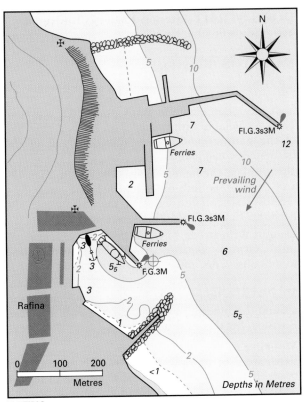

RAFINA
⊕38°01'·4N 24°00'·7E

Mooring

In calm weather try the basins on the S side or anchor off under the lee of the northernmost breakwater.

Shelter Poor in any moderate winds and untenable with strong N or S winds.

Authorities Port police and customs.

Facilities

Water on the quay. Fuel nearby. Provisions and tavernas in the town. PO. OTE. Ferries to Evia and the northern Cyclades. Bus to Athens.

General

The town is a pleasant enough place, but the uncomfortable harbour means that most yachtsmen's memories of it are less than favourable. Unless it is flat calm outside, the surge in the harbour is simply awful.

NÉA MAKRI

38°03'·5N 24°00'·0E

About 2 miles N of Rafina a dog-leg mole forms a small harbour offering shelter from the *meltemi*. The entrance is lit F.G/F.R. There are 1·5m depths in the entrance and 1–2m depths inside. With onshore winds a swell heaps up at the entrance and you should try elsewhere. The harbour is very small (approximately 50m x 50m in the outer basin) and only small yachts under 8 metres LOA should attempt to enter. NAOMA YC controls some of the berths.

Water and electricity on the quay. Tavernas along the beach.

ÓRMOS MARATHONAS

Ák Marathonas 38°07'·3N 24°03'·5E

In calm weather a yacht can anchor on the W side of the bay tucked as far up under Ák Marathonas as possible. Technically it is prohibited to anchor here, but either the prohibited area is not often enforced or you will be told when target practice is taking place, as a number of yachts have used the anchorage. (See Prohibited Anchorage notes that follow.) If the *meltemi* is blowing a considerable swell sets into the bay and it is unwise to anchor off this lee shore.

PROHIBITED ANCHORAGE AND LANDING

1. Anchoring is prohibited in the area enclosed by an imaginary line running 2¼ miles SW of Ák Marathonas and then 1½ miles NW (the N half of the bay). A floating target lies in this area.
2. Landing is prohibited between Ák Dhrakonera and a point 2 miles NW of Ák Áy Marina.
3. It is prohibited to enter the harbour enclosed by a mole under Ák Áy Marina.

These areas and the harbour at Áy Marina belong to the Greek army and are mostly used for recreational purposes.

ÁYIOS APOSTOLIOU

38°17'·6N 23°54'·0E

A small harbour on the mainland coast opposite Ák Aliveri. The harbour is very small and usually full of local craft so do not count on finding shelter here. There are 3m depths in the entrance and 2–3m depths on the outer dogleg of the mole. Care is needed of underwater ballasting off parts of the quay. Good shelter from the prevailing NE wind under the mole.

Water on the quay. Fuel nearby. Provisions and tavernas ashore.

ÓRMOS OROPOS
38°19'.0N 23°47'.7E

An open bay directly S of Erétria, it is the mainland ferry terminal for Erétria. Local craft are kept here in the summer on permanent moorings. Although open to the prevailing NE winds the anchorage can be used in light northerlies which are reported not to blow home. With any sort of fresh breeze it is best to seek shelter elsewhere. Anchor in 4–5m on mud keeping clear of the ferry quay. An extension to the central pier is planned to create a small enclosed harbour. Provisions and tavernas in Néa Palatea.

ÓRMOS ANGISTRI
38°20'.0N 23°44'.0E

This bay affords poor shelter from the prevailing winds but does have a boatyard that has been recommended. Evia Sea Centre can haul yachts up to 55ft on a hydraulic trailer. Hardstanding ashore. ☎ 22950 71963.

Evia coast south of Khalkís

ÓRMOS KASTRÍ

Lying 2 miles NE of Nisís Mandhíli on the SE coast of Evia, this bay affords good shelter to a yacht waiting for the wind and sea to moderate in the Doro (Kafirevs) Strait. Anchor at the head of the bay in 4–6m. There are strong gusts into the bay with the *meltemi* and it may be advisable to lay a second anchor for a sound nights sleep. The bottom is sand – good holding. Órmos Livádhi 1¼ miles NE of Kastrí also provides shelter from the *meltemi*. No facilities.

DORO STRAIT (Stenón Kafirevs/Kafireos)
See Andros in Chapter V.

KARISTOS (Karysto)
Approach
Conspicuous The town of Karistos at the foot of the high mountain range is easily seen from seaward. Nisís Áy Pelayia with a chapel on it lies a mile SW of the harbour and a fort immediately E of the harbour is conspicuous.

By night Use the lights on Nisís Paximádhi Fl.5s4M and Nisís Mandhíli Fl(3)20s15M and once into Órmos Karístou the lights at the entrance to the harbour: Fl.G.1·5s4M/2F.R(vert)3M.

Dangers With strong N winds there are violent gusts into Órmos Karístou off the surrounding mountains. Care must be taken if sailing into the bay.

Note The Admiralty *Pilot* states that light cloud around the summit of Oros Okhi, the peak inland of Karistos, heralds N winds.

Mooring
Berth stern or bows-to the town quay in the inner basin. It is often very crowded in here with fishing boats – if you can't find a berth go stern or bows-to the quay W of the ferry pier. The bottom is mud – good holding.

Shelter Good all-round shelter.

Authorities Port police and customs.

Anchorage Just to the E of the fort it is possible to anchor off the beach off the Hotel Apollon. Sheltered from the *meltemi* although there are strong gusts.

Facilities
Water On the town quay or in the square.

Fuel In the town. A mini-tanker can deliver to the quay.

Repairs Minor mechanical repairs.

Provisions Good shopping for provisions nearby in the town.

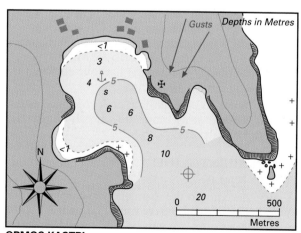

ORMOS KASTRI
⊕37°58'.4N 34°32'.7E

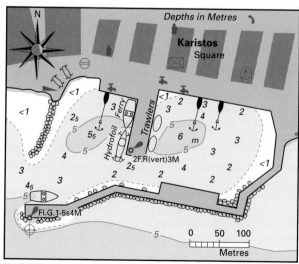

KARISTOS
⊕38°00'.7N 24°25'.0E

Eating out Good tavernas and bars around the waterfront.

Other PO. OTE. Bank. ATM. Greek gas and Camping Gaz. Infrequent bus to Khalkís. Ferry and hydrofoil to Rafina.

General

Karistos is a growing tourist resort situated on a narrow strip of land at the foot of a magnificent mountain range. In places the range drops sheer to the sea for 500m or more and if the seafarer is daring or foolhardy he can take a bus trip along the road cut into the mountainside. The rugged interior is well worth an excursion and there is good trekking in the hills behind.

Nisídhes Petaloi

This group of islands lies off the SW coast of Evia a short distance to the NW of Nisís Paximádhi. The two largest islands are Megálo Petali and Xero. There are numerous anchorages between them and it is possible to find shelter from just about all winds:

1. *Vasiliko* On the S side of Nisís Megálo Petali, this bay offers reasonable shelter from the *meltemi*. Anchor in 4–6m at the head of the bay. Sandy bottom. Open only to the S.

2. *Nisís Xero* A cove on the SW corner of the island off a large villa affords some shelter from the *meltemi*. Care needs to be taken in the approach of a reef off the SE corner of Nisís Tragos which is sometimes marked by a stake. There are now fish farms in here though it is still possible to get in. Between Nisís Xero and Nisís Mégalo Petali there are mostly 3m minimum depths, although it looks much less in places.

3. *Nisís Tragos* On the S side there is a large villa with a small harbour, but this is strictly private.

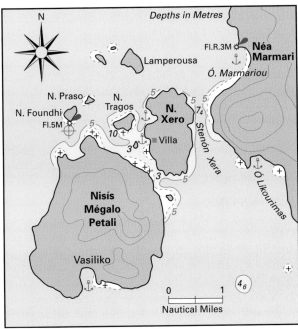

NISIDHES PETALOI
⊕38°01'·8N 24°14'·9E

Caution In Órmos Marmari between Evia and Nisídhes Petaloi there are strong gusts off the high land on Evia with the *meltemi*.

NÉA MARMARI

Approach

Órmos Marmariou is the bay opposite the northernmost of Nisídhes Petaloi. Néa Marmari is in the SE corner of the bay. The village is easily identified from seaward.

By night The end of the ferry pier is lit Fl.R.1·5s3M.

Dangers With the *meltemi* there are strong gusts down into the bay off the high land around it.

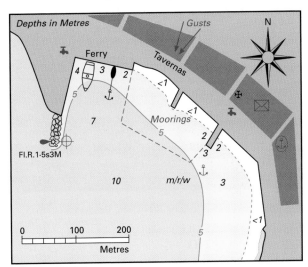

NÉA MARMARI
⊕38°03'·0N 24°19'·0E

Mooring

Go stern or bows-to the E end of the ferry quay. Alternatively anchor off clear of the area with permanent moorings. The bottom is mud and weed with some rocks.

Shelter Good shelter from the *meltemi* although there are fierce gusts into the bay. Open to the W when a swell is pushed onto the quay.

Authorities Port police.

Facilities

Water On the quay.

Fuel In the town. It may be possible to arrange a mini-tanker to deliver.

Provisions Good shopping for provisions nearby.

Eating out Tavernas on the waterfront.

Other PO. Bank. Ferry to Rafina.

General

Néa Marmari has changed from small fishing village to reinforced concrete tourist resort, though it still retains some charm and its situation under the steep-to mountains behind is spectacular. It is a handy stop on the way up the coast to stock up on provisions before the simpler places to come.

Néa Marmari on Evia looking WNW into Petalion Kólpos
Peter Kleinoth/MareTeam

ÓRMOS VLIKHO

38°05'·8N 24°14'·8E

In the NW corner of Órmos Marmariou you can also obtain shelter from the *meltemi*. Care is needed of the shoal patch off the E side of the entrance. Anchor off the beach in 3–6m on sand and weedy patches, good holding. Good shelter from the *meltemi* although there are gusts off the high land. Taverna ashore.

ÓRMOS ANIMVORIOU

38°07'·7N 24°12'·0E

The large bay under Ák Strongiló. On the N side of the bay some shelter from the *meltemi* can be found in several coves (Animvoriou = North wind bay). Care is needed of a reef running out from the point between the two N coves. Anchor in 4–5m on sand in the coves or off the long beach running around the NE side. Reasonable shelter from the *meltemi* although there are gusts and some swell tends to be pushed around Ák Strongiló.

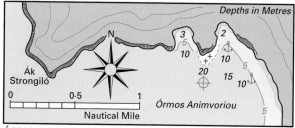

ÓRMOS ANIMVORIOU
⊕38°07'·7N 24°12'·0E

NÉA STÍRA

Three miles NE of Ák Strongiló lies the village of Néa Stíra. The natural camber of the coast provides some protection from the *meltemi* although there are strong gusts into the bay. There are 2–3m depths off the outer end of the pier and yachts can go alongside if there is room. The fishing harbour S of the pier has been partially dredged, with depths of mostly 2m in the S of the harbour. Depths are irregular further into the harbour and underwater ballast off the moles extends some distance. Immediately N of the harbour is a quay with greater depths, but like the fishing harbour it is usually full of local boats. The N pier is lit Fl.G.3s3M and the entrance to the fishing harbour is lit Fl.G.2s3M/Fl.R.2s3M but a night entrance into the harbour is not recommended. Alternatively anchor off in 4–5m. Mediocre shelter with gusts off the high land when the *meltemi* is blowing.

Provisions and tavernas ashore. Like Néa Marmari the fishing village has become something of a small resort.

NÍSOS STIRA

The island of Stira which sits in the entrance of Órmos Stira has a number of useful anchorages around it. In the approach from the NW care is needed of the reef running SE from the S end of Vrak Fonias.

1. **Nisís Petousi anchorage** On the NE side of Nisís Petousi there is a slight camber in the coast of the islet that affords some shelter from the prevailing wind. Anchor in 5–10m on sand.

NÍSOS STÍRA AND NÉA STÍRA
⊕₁ 38°11'·3N 24°10'·3E
⊕₂ 38°10'·8N 24°12'·4E

2. **Stíra E coast** About halfway up the E coast there is a bay which affords some shelter from the *meltemi*. Anchor in 5–10m tucked as far into the bay as depths allow.

3. **Marina Stíra** There are plans to build a marina on the W coast of Stira tucked under the islet of Nisís Áy Andreas. The plans are for a 400-berth marina with all facilities including travel-hoist and workshops ashore. There will be an associated hotel and apartment complex around the marina. To get to and from the marina and apartments there will be a ferry service from Áy Marina on the mainland coast opposite. Work has yet to begin on the marina and apartment complex which hopes to capitalise on the new airport at Spata. It remains to be seen whether the project gets off the ground.

4. **Stíra N coast** On the N coast there is a cove sheltered by an islet in the entrance which can be used in calm weather. Anchor in 4–6m on sand and weed.

ÓRMOS TIGANI

38°13'·6N 24°09'·5E

Under Ák Tigani ('the frying pan') some shelter from the *meltemi* can be found anchored off on the N side. Anchor in 5–10m. There are strong gusts with the *meltemi*.

ALMIROPOTAMOS (Almyro Potamo)

A long attractive bay with steep-to mountains above. There are strong gusts into the bay with the *meltemi*. The bottom is mostly sand and weed, good holding once you find a patch of sand. There are a number of anchorages:

1. At the entrance there is a cove on the W side though it is reported to be blocked by a fish farm.

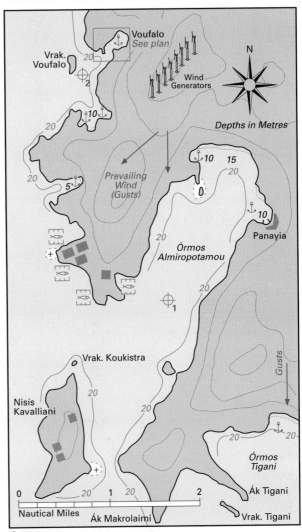

ÓRMOS TIGANI TO VOUFALO
⊕₁ 38°15'·0N 24°07'·8E
⊕₂ 38°17'·63N 24°06'·47E WGS84

2. In the cove NW of the islet at the head of the large bay. Anchor in 5–7m on mud and weed. Good shelter.

3. In the cove on the NE side. Several concrete piers and a ferry ramp have been constructed and it may be possible to berth stern or bows-to on one of the piers. Alternatively anchor off although it is quite deep in here and you will be anchoring in 10–12m. Good shelter.

Provisions and tavernas ashore. Ferry to Áy Marina. Irregular bus to Khalkis from the village above.

VOUFALO (Bouphalo)

An almost landlocked bay lying approximately 4 miles N of Nisís Kavaliani. The houses of the tiny hamlet in the inlet can be seen from the S. Wind generators on the hills surrounding Voufalo can been seen for some distance when approaching from any direction. Eight in a line on the ridge immediately E of the village are useful to pinpoint the inlet when approaching from the N.

A sand spit with trees along it extends from the E side and partially protects the anchorage. Anchor in

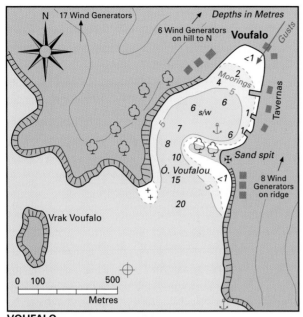

VOUFALO
⊕38°17'·63N 24°06'·47E WGS84

The anchorage at Voufalo looking SW   *Lu Michell*

5–6m behind the sand spit. Moorings at the head of the inlet restrict anchoring. A very small yacht can go bows-to the short pier (1m depths). The holding has been reported to be poor although others (including myself) have had no problems anchoring. Virtually all-round shelter tucked behind the sand spit.

Simple tavernas ashore.

Note Between Voufalo and Almiropotamos there are several bays which provide shelter from the *meltemi*. When coasting these can be investigated although fish farms occupy many on a more or less permanent basis. Most have a bottom of sand and weed and sufficient depths to anchor in. The surroundings here are wild and you are much removed from the resort areas around other parts of the coast. Simple tavernas ashore.

ALIVERION (Karastos)

BA 1571
Imray-Tetra G26

Approach

Conspicuous The two tall chimneys of Pirgos power station are visible from a considerable distance off. Closer in a small chimney and the harbour breakwaters are conspicuous.

By night Use the lights at the entrance to the harbour: Fl.G.4s7M/Fl.R.1·5s3M. The power station is lit up with bright lights at night.

Note
1. Works are in progress extending the W breakwater. The normal light Fl.R.1·5s3M is replaced with a buoy, Q.R.
2. In the bay SE of Aliverion is Milaki industrial harbour and cement factory. There are no facilities for yachts even if you did want to park next to a cement factory. The S pier is lit 2F.R(vert)5M.

Mooring

Go stern or bows-to behind the mole or on the town quay. A small cargo ship occasionally uses the long section of the town quay. There may be space towards the S end of the mole but care is needed of underwater ballast off the mole. The bottom is mud – excellent holding.

Shelter Good all-round shelter although strong S winds produce some surge and spray comes over the mole. Strong N winds do not blow home.

Authorities Port police.

Facilities

Water On the town quay and N side of harbour.
Fuel None available locally.
Provisions Limited provisions locally.
Eating out Several tavernas around the harbour with good local fare.
Other PO, OTE and bank in Aliverion town about 30 minutes away.

General

The harbour is properly called Karastos and the town a short distance away is Aliverion. It is a

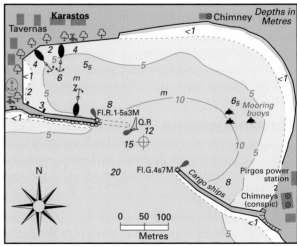

ALIVERION
⊕38°23·5N 24°02'·8E

captivating and friendly place that has mostly been bypassed by tourism. The giant power station of Pirgos on the opposite side of the bay is soon accepted as a part of the scenery and not the blot on the landscape it might first appear to be.

AMARINTHOS

38°23'·2N 23°53'·8E

A small resort and fishing village lying approximately 7 miles W of Aliverion. A yacht can anchor off here for provisions and a bite in settled weather, but although the *meltemi* does not blow strongly here, it is still a very exposed anchorage.

There is a small fishing harbour here with 3m depths in the entrance and 2–3m depths off the outer dogleg of the mole, but it is usually so crowded with fishing boats that it is all but impossible to find a berth. Water on the mole. Fuel in town. Provisions and tavernas ashore.

ERÉTRIA (Néa Psará)

BA 1571
Imray-Tetra G26

Approach

The bay lying approximately 5 miles W of Amarinthos. The approaches are surrounded by above and below-water rocks and a yacht should make the approach to the bay from the S. The light structure on the W side of the entrance (Fl.WR.1·5s5/3M red sector covers 061°-342°) is at the extremity of a sunken ancient mole running out from the coast.

Mooring

Anchor in the NE corner in 3–10m. There is a small *caïque* harbour on 'Dream' Island, but it is too small and mostly too shallow for even a small yacht. At the quay in the NW corner where the car ferries berth the depths are insufficient for a yacht. There may be space towards the S end of the mole but care is needed of underwater ballast off the mole. There is

some wash from ferries but it is more uncomfortable than dangerous. Good shelter from the *meltemi*. Open to the W and S.

Facilities

Port police and customs. Fuel in the town. Good shopping for provisions and good tavernas on the waterfront. Bus to Khalkís and ferry to Oropos.

General

Erétria is also called Néa Psará. In 1822 the Turks massacred the population of Khíos and nearby Psará after a rebellion and the survivors of Psará fled to Evia where they were given land at Erétria/Néa Psará. It is a growing tourist resort, hence the inevitable renaming of the island on the E side of the bay as 'Dream' Island.

NOTE

38°22'·31N 23°41'·91E WGS84

A dangerous wreck just underwater lies 3·5M SW of Ák Avlis in the position given above. It is marked by a spar buoy lit Fl(2)10s close N.

DHIAVLOS EVIRIPOU (Approaches to Khalkís)

BA 1554
Imray-Tetra G2, G26

S approach

Conspicuous Ák Avlis is the low–lying spit with a conspicuous lighthouse at the N end of Notios Evvoikos Kólpos. Once past Ák Avlis a shipyard in the SW corner and the cement works to the N are conspicuous. The channel through the middle of the bay is free from dangers, and Vrakis Passandasi beacon is easily identified. The huge cement factory complex on the W side of the entrance to the S harbour and the new road bridge (air height 36m) are conspicuous from a considerable distance off. There are always a number of ships anchored off the entrance to Órmos Mikró Vathi. The narrow buoyed entrance to the S harbour is easily negotiated.

By night Use the light on Ák Avlís Fl(2)12s6M and the light buoys: Q.G/Fl.G.2s. Further in use the light on Vrak Passándassi Fl.3s5M and in the approaches to the bridge the lights on the S side Fl.R.2s4M/2F.R.3M and the light buoys Q.G/Q.R.

Note
1. Overhead electric cables cross the strait 130m W of the new bridge with an air height of 37·3m.
2. Anchoring is prohibited in Dhíavlos Stenón.
3. The channel is often busy with commercial traffic and yachts should keep well clear of larger vessels in the vicinity.

N approach

Conspicuous The large modern buildings of Khalkís are visible from the distance. Ák Kakokefalí is conspicuous as a rocky promontory without buildings on it.

By night Use the light on Ák Kakokefalí Fl(2)18s12M, on the W bank Fl.G.2s3M, and the light buoys marking the channel: Q.G/Q.R.

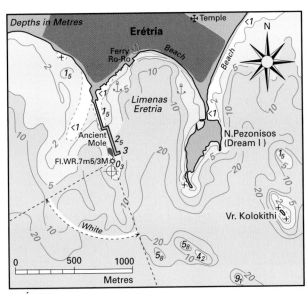

ERÉTRIA
⊕38°22'·9N 23°47·5E

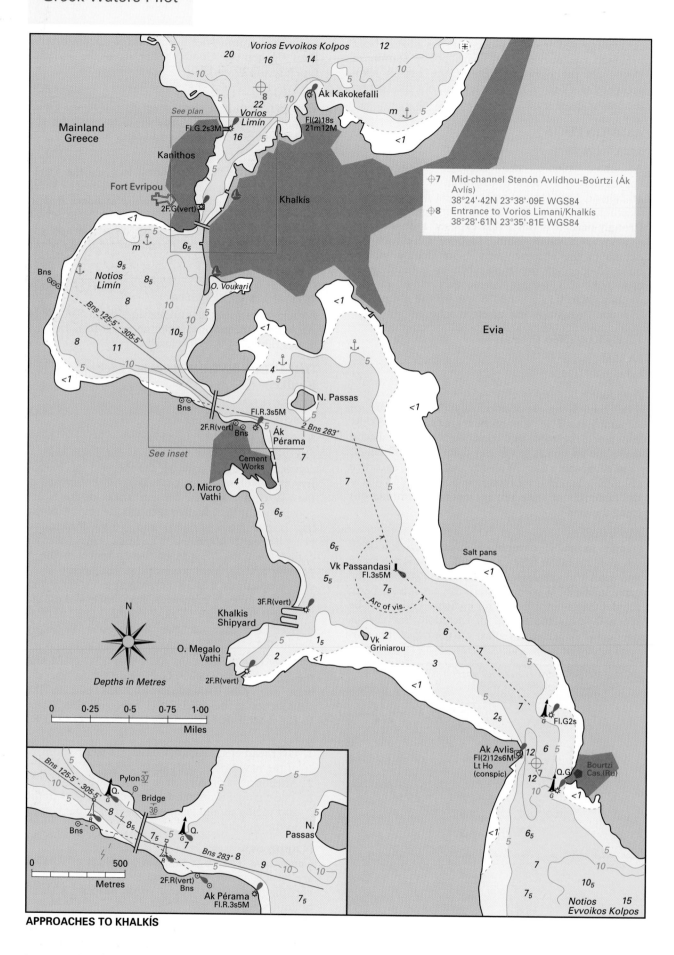

Vorios Evvoikos Kolpos

Mainland
Greece

Kanithos

Fort Evripou

Vorios Limín

Ák Kakokefalli

Fl.G.2s3M

Fl(2)18s
21m12M

2.F.G(vert)

Khalkís

⊕7 Mid-channel Stenón Avlídhou-Boúrtzi (Ák Avlís)
38°24'·42N 23°38'·09E WGS84
⊕8 Entrance to Vorios Limani/Khalkís
38°28'·61N 23°35'·81E WGS84

Evia

Notios Limín

Bns 125·5° - 305·5°

O. Voukari

N. Passas

Fl.R.3s5M

2.F.R(vert)

2 Bns 283°

Ák Pérama

See inset

Cement Works

O. Micro Vathi

Vk Passandasi
Fl.3s5M

Salt pans

Arc of vis.

N

Khalkis Shipyard

3.F.R(vert)

Vk Griniarou

O. Megalo Vathi

2.F.R(vert)

Depths in Metres

0   0·25   0·5   0·75   1·00
Miles

Ak Avlis
Fl(2)12s6M
Lt Ho
(conspic)

Fl.G2s

Q.G

Bourtzi Cas.(Ru)

Bns 125·5° - 305·5°

Pylon 37

Q.

Bridge 36

Q.

Bns 283° 8

N. Passas

Bns

2.F.R(vert)
Bns

0   500
Metres

Ak Pérama
Fl.R.3s5M

Notios Evvoikos Kolpos

APPROACHES TO KHALKÍS

KHALKÍS BRIDGE

The bridge spans the narrow gap between Evia and the mainland. The gap is 39·3m (129ft) wide and the bridge slides back into a recess under the road. The skipper of a yacht should go to the port police as soon as possible to find out what time the bridge is going to open and to pay the bridge fees.

The bridge invariably opens at night, usually after midnight, to minimise road traffic disruption. A current of 3–4 knots through the narrow gap is not unusual. Local fishermen in dinghies ride the tides in a wonderfully casual manner, but keep a lookout for them at night on the edges of the streams, as few of them carry lights. Radio contact with the bridge authorities can be patchy, especially if there is a lot of commercial traffic. Keep an eye on what other yachts are doing, as well as a listening watch on the radio. It is reported that the authorities have been known to leave the odd yacht out of the call. Traversing the gap under sail is prohibited.

VHF Ch 12.

Note The bridge is closed on Fridays. Yachts have been kept waiting for up to 30 hours, so it is wise to anticipate delays here.

Charge Around 20 Euros for an 11m yacht (2003). There is a 75% surcharge at weekends.

Signals These signals are displayed on the signal mast on the W side of the bridge platform.

By day	By night	Meaning
Three vertical black balls	Green, white, red vertical lights	Bridge closed
	White fixed light in the middle of the bridge	Bridge closed at night
Two black cones points together above a cone point down	Green, white, green vertical lights	Bridge open to S-bound vessels
Two black balls separated by a black cone point up	Red, white, red vertical lights	Bridge open to N-bound vessels.

A siren sounds and a flashing light warns boat traffic that the bridge is opening.

Tidal streams In the N harbour the spring range is about 0·8m (2·5ft) and the neap range about 0·2m (0·5ft). This must be borne in mind when mooring up or you may take the ground and miss the bridge. In the S harbour the spring and neap ranges are small. All depths given in the harbour plans are at mean low water springs. High water occurs in the N harbour approximately 1 hour 12 minutes after high water in the S harbour. The difference in time and range produces strong tidal streams which may reach 6–7 knots at springs. However, this is only in the very narrow section spanned by the bridge and a short distance N and S of the bridge the stream is considerably less.

Buoyage The direction of the buoyage system changes at Khalkis Bridge. S of the bridge the direction is for northbound traffic. N of the bridge the direction is for southbound traffic. This bizarre little system could cause confusion so it worth remembering when transiting from N–S or S–N.

KHALKIS

⊕8 Entrance to Vorios Limani/Khalkis
38°28'·61N 23°35'·81E WGS84

Mooring

S harbour The quay on the E side of Notios Limin is often full with commercial shipping. Khalkis Yacht Club in Ormos Voukari is reported to be very welcoming to visiting yachts, and will always try to find a berth. Yachts normally berth bows-to because ballasting extends a short distance out from the quay. Depths are variable with 1–2m off the quay. Water and electricity. Showers and toilets.

Anchorage Anchor under the fort in the N of the basin in 8–10m. The NW corner is sometimes buoyed off for water–skiing. The bottom is mud, excellent holding.

N harbour Go stern or bows-to or alongside the town quay where indicated on the E side of the harbour or stern or bows-to the short mole extending from the W side where a few local yachts are kept. Care is needed of rusting steel bars that protrude from the quay in places along the E quay. On this side a yacht is completely out of the current but on the W mole the weak current could make manoeuvring difficult. Large yachts should anchor off in the bay to the E of Ák Kakokefalí.

Facilities

Services Water and fuel on the quay in the N harbour (☎ 22609/22280 for fuel; ☎ 22213/29770 for water).

Repairs Some mechanical repairs. Yachts are hauled out in the boatyards in Voukari. Hardware shops.

Provisions Excellent shopping for all provisions. Ice

The road bridge S of Khalkís looking SE with the cement factory conspicuous　　　　　　*Lu Michell*

Khalkís bridge looking S　　　　　　*Lu Michell*

at the fish market.

Eating out Numerous good tavernas and restaurants nearby.

Other PO. OTE. Banks. ATMs. Greek gas and Camping Gaz. Hire cars, motorbikes and bicycles. Buses and trains to Athens.

General

Khalkís is the modern capital of Evia and the centre of communications for the island. The waterfront is a busy, pedestrianised area filled with bars of every persuasion. It's a lot more pleasant than its situation might suggest. Ancient Khalkís was similarly a prosperous city-state controlling the passage of commerce in the Evia channel.

The dangerous currents in the channel are mentioned by ancient sources: Livy, Cicero, Pliny

and Strabo commented on them and tradition has it that Aristotle flung himself into the channel because of his inability to explain the phenomenon. The channel was first spanned as early as 411BC. Under Justinian the fixed bridge was replaced by a movable wooden bridge. Under the Venetians the island took its name of Negroponte, the 'black bridge', from the bridge across to the mainland from Khalkís. In 1896 a Belgian company built an iron swing bridge that remained until 1962 when the existing bridge was built.

Coasts north of Khalkís
Mainland side of the channel

ÓRMOS SKORPONERIOU

38°31'·1N 23°22'·7E

The large bay under Ák Gatza with the islet of Gatza on the N side of the entrance. In the NW corner there is a cove which affords good shelter from the *meltemi*. Anchor in 7–10m on mud, good holding. In calm weather or with southerlies there is a useful anchorage on the W side of the headland on the S side of the bay. Anchor in 7–10m on mud, sand and weed. Camping ground ashore.

LÁRIMNA (Larmes)

The very tall chimney belching smoke at the cupronickel refinery is conspicuous from a considerable distance off. The chimney is painted in red and white bands and lit at night with red lights. Anchor off or go bows-to the short pier. The bottom is mud and shells – excellent holding. Fuel in town. Water near the pier. Most provisions available. Poor tavernas.

The village is grimy and blackened from the fumes of the refinery. These fumes deposit an unpleasant

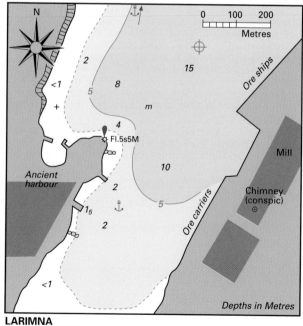

LARIMNA
⊕38°34'·8N 23°18'·9E

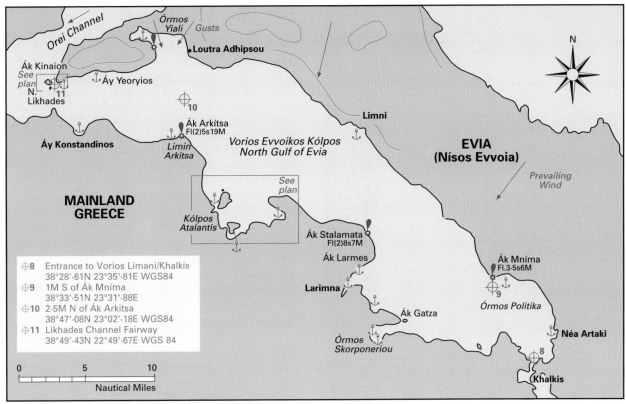

NORTH GULF OF EVIA (Vorios Evvoikos Kólpos)

oily grime over a yacht. The only reason for a visit here is to see the ancient harbour which is in good condition although parts of it have been wantonly destroyed in recent years.

UNNAMED BAY

38°35'·1N 23°18'·7E

About 2 miles SE of Ák Larmes there is a bay offering good shelter from the *meltemi*. The SW side of the bay is a low-lying islet connected to the land by a reef just below water. Some of the bay is now obstructed with fish farms, but there is still room to anchor in here. Anchor in 10m on sticky red clay, excellent holding.

KÓLPOS ATALÁNTIS (Atlandi, Atalante, Opuntius)

In this large bay on the W side of the gulf there are a number of anchorages affording shelter from the *meltemi*.

1. **Órmos Áy Ioánnis Theológos**
   38°39'·60N 23°11'·01E WGS84
   Anchor at the head of the bay. A short mole has been built out from the E end of the bay, but is usually full of local boats. Open to the W. Provisions and tavernas ashore.

2. **Órmos Amirou (Almyro)** In the S corner of Órmos Atalántis under the lee of Nisís Gáïdharos. In the middle of the entrance care must be taken of a below-water rock. There is now a fish farm and a mussel farm in the bay, but yachts can anchor to the W of them. All-round shelter can be found in this bay although there are strong gusts into it with W winds. The

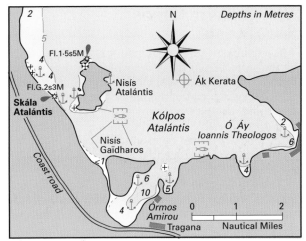

KÓLPOS ATALÁNTIS
⊕38°40'·58N 23°08'·20E WGS84

motorway N runs past the head of the bay.

3. **Nisís Atalántis** Anchor in a cove on the SW side of the island. There are now fish farms here. The island has a guardian on it who gets upset if you go ashore. A small church with a cupola is conspicuous next to the light structure on the islet.

4. **Skála Atalántis** (see harbour plan). A small fishing harbour opposite the cove on Nisís Atalántis. Moor stern or bows-to the outer end of the mole. Care must be taken entering the harbour as the entrance silts. Taverna and café at the root of the mole. Good shopping for provisions in Atalántis village on the low hill to the NNW of the harbour.

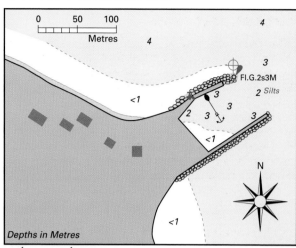

SKÁLA ATALÁNTIS
⊕38°40'·4N 23°04'·6E

LIMÍN ARKÍTSA

38°45'·1N 23°01'·9E

A small harbour on the W side of Ák Arkítsa. Ák Arkítsa is lit Fl(2)5s19M and off the harbour there is a light buoy Q.G. There are 2–3m depths in the entrance to the harbour and 1–2·5m depths inside. Good shelter inside the harbour. Ferry to Loutra Adhipsou.

ÁYIOS KONSTANDINOS

38°45'·5N 22°51'·6E

The mainland ferry terminal for Skíathos. Two jetties project from the shore which are used by the ferries. A 3F.G.3M is exhibited on the quay and a F.G.7M on the end of the mole. The roadstead and quays are completely open to the prevailing wind and it is untenable here if the *meltemi* is blowing. In calm weather it may be useful to provision up, but you should be prepared to move out if the wind picks up.

There is a small fishing harbour (50m by 15m!) but this is always crowded with fishing boats. Inside the fishing harbour there are 3–5m metre depths off the mole.

Ashore most provisions can be obtained and there are good tavernas.

AYIOS SERAFIOU

38°49'·8N 22°42'·2E

A new fishing harbour has been built off the sandy beach in front of a small village. The structure is in the shape of an unfinished 'P', with the entrance in the crook facing S. Depths of 2–3m reported in the entrance and inside.

Evia side of the channel

NÉA ARTAKI (Vatondas)
Approach
The harbour and anchorage lie approximately 3M NNE of Khalkis in a bight on the Evia coast. Apartments fringe the coast up from Khalkis, but the harbour is difficult to identify. To the N the soya silos are conspicuous. The breakwater and the low-lying spit of Ák Megali Manika will be seen when closer in, and the light structure and taverna on the headland are also conspicuous. Behind the harbour a church cupola shows up well.

By night The headland is lit Fl.1·5s5M and the entrance to the harbour 2F.R(vert)2M. Care is needed in a night approach because of the shoal water in the approaches.

Mooring
You may be able to go alongside the stub quay on the end of the breakwater but it is reported to be for the ferry. Anchor and take a long line to the W or S

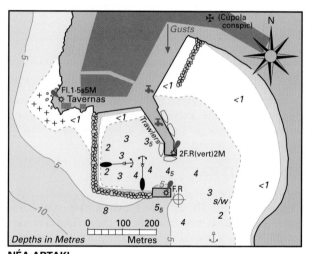

NÉA ARTAKI
⊕38°30'·64N 23°37'·93E WGS84

Néa Artaki looking NW   *Lu Michell*

breakwater. There is no quayed area on the W side so you need a long line and the dinghy to get ashore.

Shelter Reasonable shelter from the *meltemi* although there are gusts off the high land and some swell curves around the headland into the anchorage.

Note A concrete quay is planned along the S and W side of the harbour.

Facilities
Water on the quay. Provisions and tavernas ashore. PO.

ÓRMOS POLITIKA

38°34'·7N 23°32'·5E

The large bay under Ák Mníma. Ák Mníma is lit Fl.3·5s6M. The light structure, a white hexagonal hut, stands on a rock around 100m off the cape, and can be seen from some distance. You can anchor off the beach under the cape where there is reasonably good shelter from the *meltemi*. Anchor in 5–8m on sand and weed. There is a small pier here with 2–3m depths off the end.

Water tap ashore. Tavernas open in the summer. The village of Politika lies a few kilometres inland.

LIMNI

Approach
The buildings at Limni will be seen in a bight on the coast SE of Ák Yianitsa.

By night The stubby headland is lit on the end Fl.1·5s5M. The end of the mole is lit F.R(occas).

Mooring
Anchor off the village in 10–12m. It is everywhere fairly deep for anchoring. Alternatively you can try the harbour off the village. The entrance is a bit tricky as you need to make a sharp turn to port to enter. Go alongside or stern or bows-to the outer end of the mole if there is room.

Shelter Adequate shelter in settled weather at anchor although there are strong gusts off the high land with the *meltemi*. Good shelter in the harbour.

Facilities
Water near the harbour. Provisions and tavernas in town. PO.

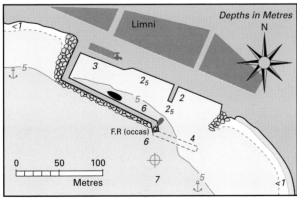

LIMNI
⊕38°46'·0N 23°19'·3E

LOUTRA ADHIPSOU

The ferry terminal on Evia for the ferries from Arkitsa. It is exposed off the ferry quay. The ferry quay is lit 3F.Y.3M. The fishing harbour here is usually crowded, but you may be able to find a berth inside. There are 4–5m depths in the entrance and mostly 2–4m depths inside. Go alongside or stern or bows-to where possible. Otherwise anchor off to the N outside the permanent moorings. The bottom is sand and weed, good holding once through the weed. Good shelter in the harbour.

Water on the quay. Provisions and tavernas ashore.

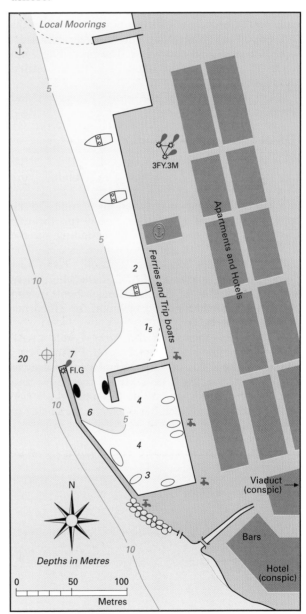

LOUTRA ADHIPSOU
⊕38°51'·44N 23°02'·38E WGS84

ÓRMOS YIALI

38°53'·0N 22°58'·0E

This large bay looks as if it should afford good shelter, but it is very deep for anchoring in most places. The W entrance is lit Fl.3s5M. There are a number of fish farms around the sides of the bay.

In the NW corner there is a bight where you can anchor off in 4–8m. Gusts with the *meltemi*. No facilities.

ÁY YEORYIOS

38°50'·3N 22°53'·0E

A village lying approximately 3½ miles E of the Likhades Islands. In front of the village there is a concrete quay and a mole which are mostly full with local boats. The ferries and local boats use the W side of the mole. Yachts can go stern or bows-to the E side where there are 3–4m depths reported at the end. Care needed of floating mooring lines. Depths of 1–2m off the village quay. Alternatively anchor off in 6–10m and sand and weed. The prevailing wind tends to blow off the land. Useful in settled conditions.

Water at the root of the mole. Provisions and tavernas ashore.

NISOI LIKHADES (Likada)

BA 1571

Lying close off Ák Lithada (Kinaion), the westernmost point of Evia, there is a narrow but easily navigable channel between the islands and the cape. A current of up to 2 knots may run through the channel in either direction depending on the wind direction. With the *meltemi* there is a S-going current, generally less than 2 knots. Keep just 50–80m off the sandy spit of Ák Lithada where there are good depths in the channel. Rocky shoals extend N into the channel for up to 500m off the SE corner of Nisis Monolia.

A yacht can anchor on the S or W side of Ák Lithada depending on wind direction. Fishing boats anchor on the S side of Nisís Monolia (open only to the E), but care must be taken of the above and below-water rocks surrounding this anchorage.

In the summer a beach bar opens on the N side of the island.

Northern Evia channels and the Gulf of Volos

(Maliakós Kólpos, Dhíavlos Oréon, Dhíavlos Tríkeri, Gulf of Volos or Pagasitikós Kólpos)

Mainland coast

MALIAKOS KÓLPOS

A shallow gulf bulging westwards from the W extremity of Evia. The coast is predominantly low-lying. The northbound motorway skirts the head of the gulf. The Pass of Thermopylae lies near the corner of the gulf.

STILIDHOS (Stilis, Stylis)

BA 1571

Situated on the N side of Maliakós Kólpos, Stilidhos is the port for the town of Lamia. It is surrounded by shoal water and a dredged channel leads into it. The channel is marked at the outer end by a pair of light buoys Q.G/Q.R and the beacon Fl.R.2s3M on Nisís Kaloyiros, a low sandy islet, and a beacon Fl.G.2s3M off the low shore on the other side. An orange inverted triangle on a light structure at the root of the mole DirLFl.Y.10s8M (300°-vis-330°) shows the channel.

Moor stern or bows-to or alongside the quay to the W of the central mole. The bottom is mud – good holding. Good shelter from the *meltemi*. Open to the S.

Fuel in the town. Small yachts can be craned onto the quay. Good shopping for provisions. Tavernas in the town. Buses to Athens and Volos.

The harbour is right on the edge of the main road northwards and is consequently not the quietest place around.

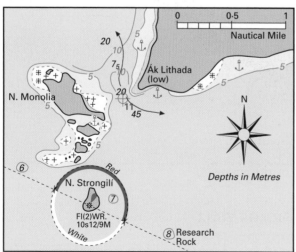

NISOI LIKHADES

⊕11 Likhades Channel Fairway 38°49'·43N 22°49'·67E WGS84

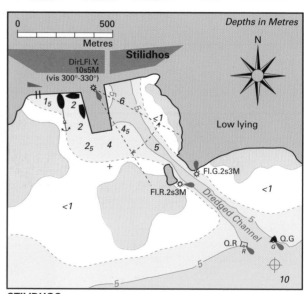

STILIDHOS
⊕38°53'·9N 22°37'·9E

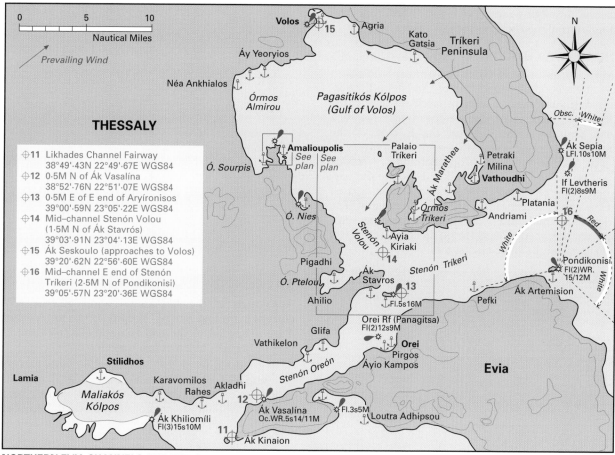

0   5   10
Nautical Miles

Prevailing Wind

N

THESSALY

⊕11 Likhades Channel Fairway
     38°49'·43N 22°49'·67E WGS84
⊕12 0·5M N of Ák Vasalína
     38°52'·76N 22°51'·07E WGS84
⊕13 0·5M E of E end of Aryíronisos
     39°00'·59N 23°05'·22E WGS84
⊕14 Mid–channel Stenón Volou
     (1·5M N of Ák Stavrós)
     39°03'·91N 23°04'·13E WGS84
⊕15 Ák Seskoulo (approaches to Volos)
     39°20'·62N 22°56'·60E WGS84
⊕16 Mid–channel E end of Stenón
     Tríkeri (2·5M N of Pondikonisi)
     39°05'·57N 23°20'·36E WGS84

Volos **15**   Agria
Kato Gatsia   Tríkeri Peninsula
Áy Yeoryios
Néa Ankhialos
Órmos Almirou   *Pagasitikós Kólpos (Gulf of Volos)*
Obsc.   White
Ák Sepia LFl.10s10M
Amalioupolis See plan   See plan   Palaio Trikeri   Petraki Milina   If Levtheris Fl(2)8s9M
Ó. Sourpis   Ák Marathea   **Vathoudhi**   Platania
Ó. Nies   *Órmos Tríkeri*   Andriami   **16**   Red
Pigadhi   *Stenón Volou*   Ayia Kiriaki   Stenón Tríkeri   White   White   Pondikonisi Fl(2)WR. 15/12M
Ó. Pteloú   Ák Stavros   **14**   Ák Artemision
Ahilio   **13** Fl.5s16M   Pefki
Glifa   Orei Rf (Panagitsa) Fl(2)12s9M
Vathikelon   **Orei** Pirgos   Áyio Kampos   **Evia**
Stilidhos   Karavomilos Rahes   Akladhi   *Stenón Oreón*
Lamia   *Maliakós Kólpos*   **12**   Ák Vasalína Oc.WR.5s14/11M   Fl.3s5M   Loutra Adhipsou
Ák Khiliomíli Fl(3)15s10M   **11**
Ák Kinaion

NORTHERN EVIA CHANNELS AND THE GULF OF VOLOS

KARAVOMILOS

38°53'·0N 22°42'·2E

Karavomilos is at the head of Órmos Ekinou about 4½ miles SE of Stilidhos and opposite Ák Khiliomíli. Local fishing boats are kept on moorings in the summer. Good holding in mud is reported on the E side of the bay near the military college. You may find space on the end of the mole to go stern or bows-to in 4–5m. Protection from the *meltemi* appears to be good. Provisions and tavernas ashore.

RAHES

38°52'·6N 22°46'·3E

Immediately E of Ák Dhrépanon is Rahes where local fishing boats and a few yachts are kept on moorings through the summer. A large cement factory and quayed area are conspicuous just E of Rahes. The shelter in the bight is better than it looks on the chart although a swell is reported to enter the bay with NE–E winds. Provisions and tavernas ashore.

AKLADHI

A small fishing harbour in the bay E of Ák Gounari. The end of the mole is lit F.G.3M. If there is room go alongside or stern or bows-to the mole. Good shelter from the prevailing E–ENE winds. Alternatively anchor off the village where the camber of the coast gives some shelter although a swell still runs into the bay.

Water on the foreshore. Provisions and tavernas in Akladhi.

Note Approximately 1M E of Akladhi is a quay for the Agroinvest factory. The quay is lit at either end 3F.G.3M/3F.R.3M.

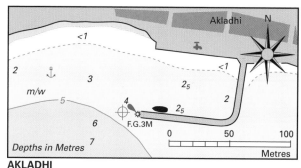

Akladhi   N
<1
2   <1
m/w   3   2₅
5   2
4   2₅
6   F.G.3M   2
Depths in Metres   7   0   50   100
Metres

AKLADHI
⊕38°53'·1N 22°48'·2E

Stenón Oréon
(Orei Channel)

This channel separates Evia from the Thessaly coast. The channel is very narrow – in places it is little more than a mile across and there can be currents of up to 2½ knots in places. The tidal range at springs is 0·8m (2·5ft) at Orei, the highest tidal range in the eastern Mediterranean. The coast is mostly mountainous and wooded although there is a narrow low-lying strip of land bordering the mountains along the Evia coast.

ÓRMOS VATHIKELON (Vathykelos)

Lying 1½ miles W of Glifa, this almost landlocked bay offers good all-round shelter. An islet off the W entrance point with a white church on it is easily identified. Care is needed of the dangerous rock lying approximately 20m off the E side of the entrance.

The bay is very deep for anchoring – mostly 10–20m around the NE side. The E side of the bay, where there are better depths for anchoring, is used to leave the car ferries from Glifa for the night. The bottom is mud and weed – good holding once through the weed. There are no facilities, just a few villas around the olive-clad slopes.

Aryronísos lighthouse on the E end of the island   *Lu Michell*

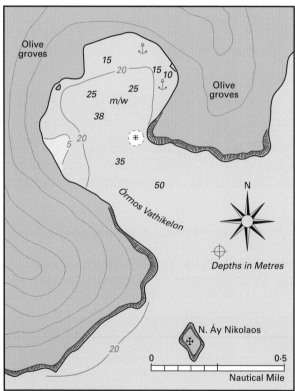

ÓRMOS VATHIKELON
⊕38°55'·8N 22°56'·7E

GLIFA (Glypha)

38°57'·0N 22°57'·8E

The ferry terminal for the car ferry running to Áyio Kampos under Ák Akrotiri on Evia. The short pier is used by the car ferry. With the *meltemi* some swell works its way into the bay. Anchor off the village or in the cove to the E. Passing ferries have been reported to push a dangerous swell into the bay. Part of the bay is sometimes buoyed off for swimming.

Fuel in the village and water on the quay. Most provisions available and several tavernas.

ARYRONÍSOS ANCHORAGES

Aryronisos is the flat island lying off the SW entrance to Pagasitikos Kólpos (Gulf of Volos). Care is needed of the reef running out from the N side of the islet to an above water rock.

1. A good lee from the prevailing E winds can be found under the SW side of the islet. Anchor in 8–15m on sand. The depths drop off quickly here so you will have to anchor fairly close in. The islet is private and while you can anchor, you cannot land.

2. On the mainland coast opposite you can anchor off the beach under a stubby headland in 5–8m on mud, sand and weed. There is a reasonable lee from the prevailing E wind although some swell enters. Camping ground ashore.

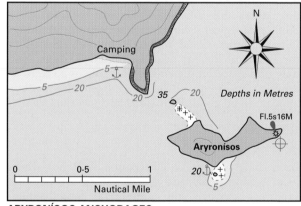

ARYRONÍSOS ANCHORAGES
⊕39°00'·5N 23°04'·6E

Evia side of Stenón Oréon

PIRGOS

A small fishing harbour off the resort of Pirgos. Apartment blocks around the beach and slopes near the harbour entrance are conspicuous. The end of the mole is lit Fl.G.3s3M. Small yachts can berth stern or bows-to on the end of the mole where possible. Reasonable shelter from the prevailing wind although some swell is pushed into the harbour making it uncomfortable at times.

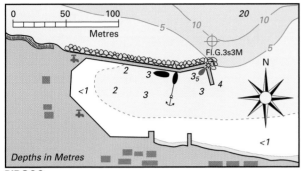

PIRGOS
⊕38°56'·37N 23°04'·13E WGS84

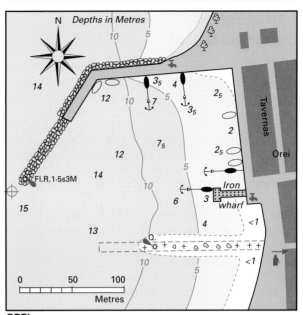

OREI
⊕38°56'·88N 23°05'·07E WGS84

Water on the quay. Provisions and tavernas ashore.

OREI (Oréon, Oreios)

Approach

Conspicuous This part of the coast is low-lying and wooded and it can be difficult to identify features. The metal tower with ⁑ topmark on Ifalos Oréon (Panagitsa) lying ½ a mile off the coast is easily identified – there are good depths in the fairway between the reef and the coast. Just N of the harbour a factory is conspicuous. Closer in the buildings of Orei and the mole and the light structure will be seen.

By night Use the light on Ifalos Oréon (Panagitsa) Fl(2)12s9M and at Orei Fl.R.1·5s3M. The end of the S mole is lit Q(occas).

Note The new W mole has been completed, but work appears to have halted on improvements to the S mole. Most of the blocks for the S mole are just underwater. The proposed final form of the S mole is shown on the plan.

Mooring

Go stern or bows-to on the N quay where convenient. Local boats use the E and W sides of the harbour. The old iron wharf has been re-opened to the public and yachts can go stern or bows–to on the end. Yachts on the N quay may be moved sometimes for a small coaster that uses the quay. There appears to be an old mooring chain running N–S in the harbour and a trip line is recommended. The bottom is sand and weed – good holding.

Shelter Good shelter from the prevailing winds. The *meltemi* does not blow home here. Strong E winds

are reported to cause a surge.

Authorities Port police and coastguard.

Note It should be remembered that the tidal range at Orei is 0·8m (2·5ft) at springs and allowance should be made for this. Some, like myself, lulled into a false sense of security in the virtually tideless Mediterranean, have found themselves stuck on the bottom here.

Facilities

Water At the root of the mole.
Fuel In town nearby.
Provisions Good shopping for provisions.
Eating out Pleasant tavernas on the waterfront.
Other PO. OTE. Irregular bus to Khalkís.

General

In ancient times Orei was an important maritime city. Above the harbour the remains of the Acropolis which guarded the harbour can be seen. In 1965 a Hellenistic marble bull was dredged from the sea by fishermen and placed in the town square. Today it remains a pleasant place with a modest summer tourist trade and the few yachts which venture into Stenón Oréou.

Orei harbour looking E   *Lu Michell*

321

Gulf of Volos
(Pagasitikós Kólpos)

This gulf opens up to the north from Stenón Vólou. The coast is mountainous except for the west coast which is low and marshy between Amalioupolis and Volos. The Tríkeri peninsula beginning at Mt Pilion (1,548m) is rugged and densely wooded. Mt Pilion is covered with snow in the winter and much of the spring – a ski lift operates in the winter. The gulf has a number of attractive anchorages and it is well worthwhile detouring from the northern channels to explore it.

Note The prevailing winds in the summer are from the NE or SE.

ÓRMOS PTELOU

The large bay on the W side of the entrance to Stenón Vólou entered between Ák Pigadhi and Ák Khondhros. The bay has now been much developed on the N side with clusters of villas around the slopes. There are several anchorages around the bay.

1. **Ahilio (Akhileion)** 39°00'·5N 22°57'·5E
   Although the anchorage off the village is exposed to the *meltemi*, it does not normally blow home. Tuck into the bight off the village as close as you can in 3–4m and there is reasonable shelter.

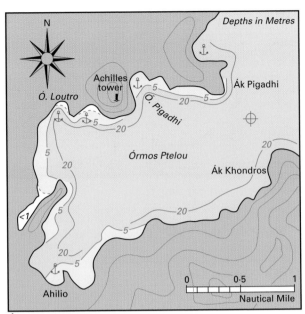

ÓRMOS PTELOU
⊕39°01'·8N 23°00'·0E

Ahilio in the SW of Órmos Ptelou

Good shelter with SE winds. The small fishing harbour is too shallow for yachts. Provisions and tavernas ashore.

2. **Ormiskos Loutró** 39°01'·8N 22°57'·6E
   The large bay in the NW corner bordered by low marshland. A ruined tower, called Achilles Tower, sits on the headland E of the bay. Anchor in the N where there is something of a lee from the *meltemi*. Open SE across the bay.

3. **Ormiskos Pigadhi** 39°02'·0N 22°58'·7E
   The bay immediately E of Loutró. Anchor in the cove on the E side of the bay in 6m. On the W side of the bay there is a small projecting quay to which you can go stern or bows-to with care. Good shelter from the *meltemi*. Open SE across the bay. The tower on the W side of the bay is locally called Achilles' Tower and Pigadhi is said to be the bay from which Achilles set sail for Troy.

4. Immediately N of Ák Pigadhi (Alkini) there is a cove with a settlement around it. There is a quayed area used by local fishing boats and there appears to be something of a lee from the *meltemi* here. Provisions and tavernas ashore.

STENÓN VOLOU (Volos Channel)

⊕13 0·5M E of E end of Aryíronisos 39°00'·59N 23°05'·22E WGS84
⊕14 Mid–channel Stenón Volou (1·5M N of Ák Stavrós) 39°03'·91N 23°04'·13E WGS84

ÓRMOS NIES

39°06'·8N 22°56'·0E

The bay running back S opposite the Tríkeri peninsula. On the E side near the entrance there is a cove affording reasonable shelter from the *meltemi*. Anchor in 4–6m on mud and weed. Alternatively anchor in the SE corner in 3–6m on mud, good holding. Good shelter although the *meltemi* tends to gust from the E–SE over the ridge into the anchorage. A camping ground in the SW corner and a number of villa developments along the W side of the bay.

Tríkeri Peninsula

ÁYIA KIRIAKÍ (Skála Tríkeri)

An open bay on the E side of the entrance to the Gulf of Volos. The village of Áyia Kiriakí on the hill above is conspicuous from seaward.

The bay is very deep. Anchor off the boatyard or in the SE corner of the bay, though the latter is crowded with fishing boats. Just to the E of the boatyard a new quay has been built. There are 2–3m depths off the quay but the bottom drops away quickly. Some 20m off the quay there are 20m depths and 25m off there are 30m depths. The bay is sheltered from the *meltemi*, but open to the W and S. The *meltemi* gusts down off the hills and creates a surge in the harbour. Perhaps the best place to be is anchored with a long line to the breakwater in the SE corner of the bay. There is another cove immediately W of the fishing hamlet where a yacht can anchor.

A large fleet of fishing boats is based at Áyia Kiriakí. Limited provisions and taverna/cafés ashore. The boatyard in the bay hauls out yachts. The village of Tríkeri (Áy Kiriakí) above the bay used to be dependent on the ferry from Volos until the road from Milina was built.

AK TRIKERI (Kavoulia)

⊕ 1M W of Ák Tríkeri 39°05'·80N 23°01'·64E WGS84

The cape on the E side of the entrance to the Gulf of Volos has a conspicuous square brick tower with a green light structure on top.

NISÍS PALAIO TRÍKERI (Palaeo Trikiri)

On the S side of this island there is the small village of Palaio Tríkeri which is conspicuous from the S. Go stern or bows–to on the quay on the W side, keeping clear of the ferry berth, or on the pontoon off the taverna in the NW corner. Depths 2–4m. Otherwise anchor off the village in 3–10m although there is limited space to swing. Good shelter from the *meltemi*. Taverna ashore. Drinking water from a public tap. Daily hydrofoil service to Volos.

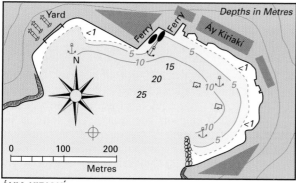

ÁYIA KIRIAKÍ
⊕39°05'·47N 23°04'·06E WGS84

Ayia Kiriaki looking NE into the bay   *Lu Michell*

The small harbour at Palaio Tríkeri looking N   *Lu Michell*

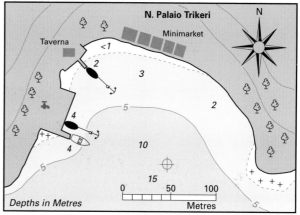

PALAIO TRIKERI
⊕39°09'·16N 23°04'·57E WGS84

ORMOS PITHOS

Mid–channel Ák Trakhili – N. Palaio Trikeri
39°09'·73N 23°06'·01E WGS84

A small bay E of Palaio Trikeri. Anchor with a long line ashore off the beach in the NE corner in 3–6m. Good holding and reasonable shelter in settled weather.

NISIS PITHU

There is a calm weather anchorage in beautiful surroundings off the S coast of the islet NW of Nisis Palaio Trikeri. Good shelter from the *meltemi*, but not really suitable for an overnight stop.

ÓRMOS TRÍKERI

Entrance 39°07'·8N 23°08'·0E

The deep bay running SW into the Tríkeri peninsula. In calm weather anchor off the small fishing village of Kotte (open to the NE–E). Spectacular scenery under the steep slopes above. Taverna ashore.

The bay in the SW corner now has a marble quarry at the head and is unsuitable for anchoring. There are several other anchorages suitable for lunch-stops on the W side of the bay.

ZASTENI ANCHORAGE (Avra)

39°07'·6N 23°09'·5E

¾ mile ESE of Ák Marathea there is an idyllic anchorage for a small yacht in a cove with a white house at the head. Open from N–W so really only suitable in calm weather. Anchor in 6–8m, mediocre holding on sand and weed.

ÓRMOS VATHOUDHI (Vathudi)

Situated in the SE corner of the Gulf of Volos (Pagasitikós Kólpos), this anchorage is protected by Nisís Alatas on the W and the Tríkeri peninsula on the E. The anchorage is normally entered from the N and there are good depths right into the bay. The

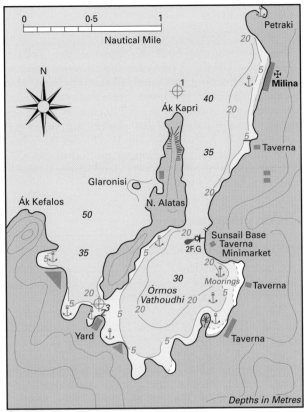

ÓRMOS VATHOUDHI AND APPROACHES
⊕₁ 39°10'·51N 23°12'·56E WGS84
⊕₂ 39°09'·03N 23°11'·78E WGS84

S entrance can be used in calm weather. Least depths of 3·2m in the fairway. There are a number of places to anchor:

1. Sunsail jetty in the NE side of the bay. Visiting yachts may be allowed to use the jetty, enquire first at the base. A charge is made. Laid moorings. Water on the quay. The jetty is lit 2F.G(vert)(occas). Taverna and minimarket ashore. More provisions and Camping Gaz from the supermarket in Milina. Fuel delivered by mini–tanker.

2. Anchor in 10–15m in the E side of the bay. The bottom is mud and sand – good holding. Good all-round shelter.

   A number of yachts are wintered afloat here and it can be difficult to find space to swing in the NE corner on account of the numerous permanently moored yachts there.

   Tavernas ashore. Provisions and tavernas at Milina, the village about 3 kilometres N.

3. Anchor in either of the two coves opposite the S end of Nisís Alatas. Care is needed to stay in the fairway of the channel to avoid the rocks and shoal water on either side of the channel before turning into the coves. There are 3·2m least depths in the fairway of the channel. There is a boatyard on the headland here that is used (exclusively) by the Sunsail base but may be of use in an emergency.

4. In the cove to the W of the S end of Nisís Alatas. Anchor in 3–5m on mud and weed, good holding.

Órmos Vathoudhi looking NNW over the anchorage to the Sunsail pier (left)
Lu Michell

PETRAKI

39°10'·8N 23°13'·0E

Half a mile N of Milina, Petrakia cove offers good shelter from the *meltemi*. Anchor in 5–10m on mud and weed, good holding. Open to the NW.

KHORTOS

39°11'·2N 23°12'·7E

In settled weather when the *meltemi* is not blowing hard you can anchor off the resort of Khortos. Anchor in 5–8m on mud. There is a jetty off the beach with 2–3m depths at the end. Provisions and tavernas ashore.

W side of the Gulf of Volos

AMALIOUPOLIS AND NEARBY ANCHORAGES (Órmos Mitzellas, Órmos Soupis)

On the W side of the entrance to the Gulf of Volos a steep-to headland juts out from the coast ending in Ák Periklis and Ák Almiros. The headland is indented with a number of bays and on the E side is the village of Amalioupolis at the head of Órmos Mitzellas.

Note Navigation is prohibited within a 5 mile radius of the military area at 39°13'·3N 22°48'·5E. However, in practice local yachts do not observe the prohibition and anchor at Amalioupolis and nearby anchorages.

1. *Amalioupolis*

   The village is conspicuous from seaward. Anchor off the town or go stern-to one of the two piers off the village (2·5m depths at the extremity). The bottom is sand – good holding. The small fishing harbour here is usually full of local boats. With

the *meltemi* some swell rolls into the anchorage. Good shelter from SE winds. Port police. Water near the pier. Good shopping for provisions. Tavernas and cafés.

2. Half a mile N of Amalioupolis there is an unnamed cove providing some shelter from the *meltemi*. Anchor near the head of the bay in 2–4m.

3. *Loutráki Amalioupolis (Fearless Cove)*
   39°10'·2N 22°52'·8E
   A sheltered cove in Órmos Sourpis on the W side of the headland. Anchor near the head of the cove in 3–6m. The bottom is mud, excellent holding. Good all-round shelter. Although the cove is open to the W for 1½ miles the wind does not blow home from that direction. A boatyard on the N side of the bay hauls yachts.

4. *Órmos Áy Ioánnis* Lies just to the S of Loutráki Amalioupolis. Anchor in 2–5m. Much of the bay is shallow towards the head. Good shelter from the *meltemi* and the SE.

Note On the W side of Órmos Sourpis there is a large factory complex with storage tanks, gantries and several long jetties.

NÉA ANKHIALOS (Néa Aghialos)

39°16'·53N 22°49'·29E WGS84

About 7 miles N of the factory complex in Órmos Sourpis and tucked into the W corner of the gulf is Néa Ankhialos. The entrance is difficult to make out until very close-to when a few boulders extending from the beach and a half submerged breakwater to port become visible. Here there is a small circular fishing harbour entered by a narrow channel. There is room for a couple of yachts alongside the outer end of the quay where there are 2–2·5m depths. Tucked under the end of the quay there is enough of a lee from the *meltemi* for it to be comfortable. The channel and basin are shallow with 1–<1m depths.

Provisions and tavernas nearby. The little harbour

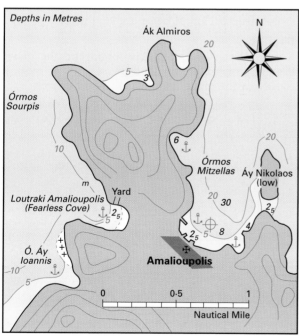

The small harbour at Néa Ankhialos looking out to the entrance is a pleasant enough stop despite the busy road along the shore. Just across the road from the harbour are the ruins of ancient Pyrasos.

ÁYIOS YEÓRYIOS

39°18'·00N 22°53'·93E WGS84

A bay lying under Ák Spilla. The inner part of the bay is mostly shallow, but you can tuck under the SW side as far as possible and find reasonable shelter from the *meltemi*.

There are also several other bays to the W that afford some shelter from the *meltemi*.

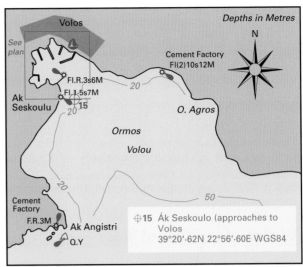

Áy Yeóryios looking SSW

VOLOS

BA 1571

Approach

Conspicuous The large city and a cement factory one mile to the E of the city are easily seen from the distance. The commercial docks, a large grey silo behind the docks and the church of Áyios Konstandinos (especially the clock tower) immediately behind the small yacht harbour are conspicuous. The harbour is generally full of cargo ships.

By night Use the light on Ák Seskoulo Fl.1·5s7M and at the cement factory Fl(2)10s12M. The NE end of the detached breakwater is lit Fl.R.3s. The end of the breakwater is lit Fl.G.3s4M, as is the extremity of the commercial pier F.G/F.R.

Note The detached breakwater sits very low in the water and can be difficult to pick out from the distance, but the light structure on the NE end of the detached breakwater stands out well.

Mooring

Most berths on the town quay are occupied by local boats. There is sometimes space to go stern or bows–to near the hydrofoil quay by the harbourmaster's office. There are laid moorings tailed to small buoys, although these have been reported as suspect so it may be best to use your own anchor. The bottom is mud and good holding although in parts of the harbour the bottom is very soft mud through which most anchors just plough furrows.

ORMOS VOLOU

The pontoon off the breakwater is often the only place for a visiting yacht but this area is used by local youths as a place to 'hang out'. Many of them are harmless, but theft and damage to yachts has been reported and drug abuse is apparent. Not a pleasant place to be, especially at weekends.

Shelter Regardless of the wind outside the gulf, the prevailing afternoon breeze sets from the SE–SW and can get up to a fresh breeze. Good shelter although there is a fetch across the bay with SW winds.

Authorities A port of entry: port police, customs and immigration. Charge band 2.

Note
1. Plans to turn the fishing harbour into a marina are raised periodically, although little has been done to move the project forward.
2. To the E of Volos harbour a small yacht harbour (near Áy Konstandinos church) has been constructed. Local boats are kept here.

Facilities

Services Water and electricity points on the quay. Water points on the breakwater.
Fuel Near the quay. A mini-tanker can deliver.

Volos looking N from Ák Seskoulo with the detached breakwater in the foreground

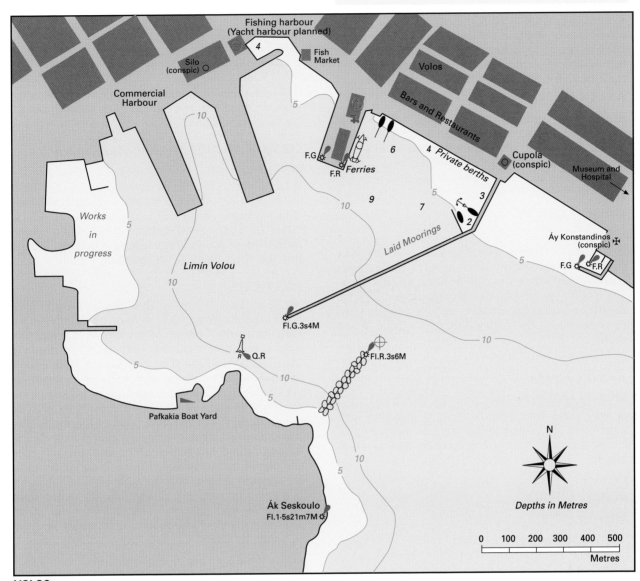

VOLOS
⊕39°20′·96N 22°56′·81E WGS84

Repairs Most mechanical repairs. General light engineering including stainless steel welding and machining work can be carried out. General electrical work. Yachts are hauled out in Pafkakia S of the commercial harbour (see separate entry). Good chandlers. Excellent hardware and tool shops.
Provisions Excellent shopping for all provisions. Good SPAR supermarket in the W of the town. Wine from the barrel. Ice from the fish market.
Eating out The tavernas and bars fronting the quay are fairly flashy and of varying quality. Towards the fishing harbour and further along to the SE are more convivial tavernas and there are a number of good *ouzeries* with good *mezedes*.
Other PO. OTE. Hospital. Banks. ATMs. Hire cars, motorbikes and bicycles. Buses and trains to Thessaloniki and Athens. Ferries to the northern Sporades. Internal flights to Athens. International flights due to start in 2004.

Note Volos is a good base from which to visit the spectacular monasteries at Meteori – buses and trains run regularly.

General
Volos is one of the most important commercial harbours in Greece, handling most of the Thessalian exports: cereals, silk, cotton, olive oil, sugar and soap. Until the disastrous earthquakes of 1954 and 1955 Volos rivalled Piraeus in commercial power. After the earthquakes, which flattened a large part of the city, it was rapidly rebuilt and once again it is prospering.

The present harbour was built in 1912, but Volos has always been an important maritime town. Jason and the Argonauts set sail from Volos (then Iolkos) – a fact commemorated by a bronze model of the *Argo* in a square by the harbour. The local wine is also called, appropriately enough, Argo.

The museum (towards the SE end of the city) contains an excellent collection of artefacts from Iolkos and Pagasai-Demetrias (across the bay S of Volos). Its collection of painted *stelai* is one of the best in the world and I recommend a visit. The faded paintings on the *stelai* show touching scenes from everyday life in ancient Greece – Protos, a muscular-looking man walking his dog, Metrophanes holding out his hands to his child, Hediste lying wan in bed – scenes far removed from the friezes of warriors and chariots and wounded lions we commonly think of as ancient funereal art.

PAFKAKIA BOATYARD

This family–run boatyard in the bay S of the main harbour is reported to be secure and efficient. Yachts, including catamarans, are hauled out on a trailer. Although facilities are limited it is a short walk to Volos and the owners are helpful.
☎ 24210 88612 (Gregory).

ÓRMOS AGROS

39°20'·4N 23°00'·7E

A large bay lying just over 3M ESE of Volos. The bay itself is fairly exposed but there is a small fishing harbour here where you may be able to find a berth. There are 2–3m depths in the entrance and 2–3·5m depths under the breakwater. Go alongside or stern or bows-to near the dogleg if there is a space. Good shelter.

Tavernas and cafés ashore.

KATO GATSIA

39°18'·5N 23°06'·0E

A very small fishing harbour. It is crowded with local boats. In calm weather you can anchor off in 3–5m on sand. Limited provisions and tavernas ashore.

Tríkeri Channel
(Stenón Tríkeri)

This channel separates Evia from the Tríkeri peninsula (Khersónisos Tríkeri). Although it is wider than Stenón Oreou, there can still be appreciable currents of up to 1½ knots, usually setting towards the SW. The coast is mountainous on both sides. The mountains of the Tríkeri peninsula drop sheer into the sea – they are scarred and scoured and mostly devoid of vegetation and habitation.

Off the mouth of the gulf, Athenian triremes had their first brush with the invading Persians under Xerxes. This was a delaying tactic by the Athenians rather than an attempt to hold the invaders. The tactic had an unforeseen success as soon afterwards a NE gale wrecked many of the Persian craft. Herodotus relates the story:

'The Persian fleet...made the Magnesian coast between Casthanea and Cape Sépias and on its arrival the leading ships made fast to the land, while the remainder, as there was not much room on the short stretch of beach, came to anchor and lay off-shore in lines, eight deep. In this position they remained during the night; but at dawn next day the weather, which was clear and calm, suddenly changed, and the fleet was caught in a heavy blow from the east – a 'Hellespontian' as the people there call it – which raised a confused sea like a pot on the boil. Those who realised in time that the blow was coming, and all who happened to be lying in a convenient position, managed to beach their vessels and to get them clear of

the water before they were damaged, and thus saved their own lives as well; but the ships which were caught well off-shore were all lost...'
Trans. Aubrey de Selincourt (quoted in Ernle Bradford *The Greek Islands*)

The modern yachtsman can only wonder why the Persian fleet did not choose the nearby natural harbour of Skíathos.

ÓRMOS ANDRIAMI (Khondhri Ammos)

39°07'·0N 23°13'·0E

A large bay on the N side of the channel. The huge quarry scar on Ák Sarakiniko is conspicuous in the S approaches. Anchor in a cove on the N side in 5–8m on mud, good holding. Reasonable shelter from the *meltemi* although some swell works around into the cove. Open S. No facilities.

PLATANIA

An open bay 2½ miles E of Andriami affording some shelter from the *meltemi*. The village of Platania at the bottom of a valley is conspicuous from seaward. A mole has been built out near the old short jetty at the E end of the bay. The end of the mole is lit Fl.G.3s3M. The mole much improves the shelter here if you can get on it or behind it. Go alongside or stern or bows-to if there is room. The hydrofoil berths at the outer end of the mole. The bay shelves gently to the shore with a mud and sand bottom so you can anchor off behind the mole near the permanent moorings if there is no space on it. Reasonable shelter from the *meltemi*.

Water tap near the bridge on the waterfront. Provisions and tavernas ashore. The bay is an attractive place with a wooded valley rising up from

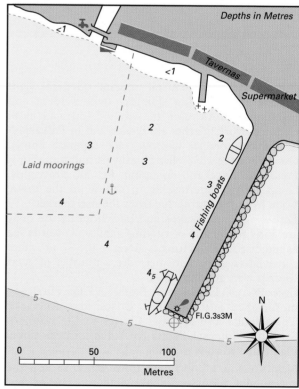

PLATANIA
⊕39°08'·4N 23°16'·5E

the bay with numerous plane trees dotted about – hence the name Platania.

PEFKI

A new fishing harbour on the N coast of Evia approximately 4 miles E of Ák Kefala. The mole head is lit: Fl.R.2s3M.

The harbour is full of fishing boats but it may be possible to find a berth. Alternatively anchor off clear of the permanent moorings. Good shelter from the *meltemi* under the mole.

Water tap ashore. Provisions and tavernas.

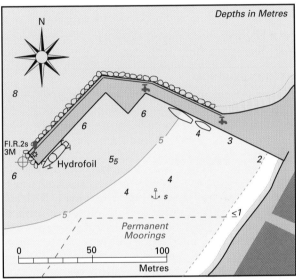

PEFKI
⊕39°00'·5N 23°12'·4E

Hydrofoil service. The area is a popular holiday destination for Greeks, with long sandy beaches along the adjacent coast.

PONDIKONISI

⊕16 Mid-channel E end of Stenón Tríkeri (2·5M N of Pondikonisi) 39°05'·57N 23°20'·36E WGS84

Lies on the S side of Stenón Tríkeri NE of Ák Artemision on Evia. A cove on the SW corner of the island gives good shelter from the *meltemi*. On the N side of the island is a landing leading up to the lighthouse.

Northern Sporades

The Sporades ('Sporades' means scattered or sown) are divided into two groups: the northern Sporades described here and the eastern Sporades lying along the coast of Asia Minor. The Dodecanese (the islands stretching from Kárpathos to Pátmos) are sometimes referred to as the Southern Sporades, but this is rare. The eastern Sporades (those islands north of Pátmos to Limnos) are less visited than the northern Sporades and consequently the name 'the Sporades' invariably refers to the northern group described here.

The main group of islands curves in a sickle shape from the southern corner of the Tríkeri peninsula northwards to the tiny sea-washed rock of Psathoúra. Forty miles north of here Mt Athos rises out of the sea at the bottom of the Khalkidhiki.

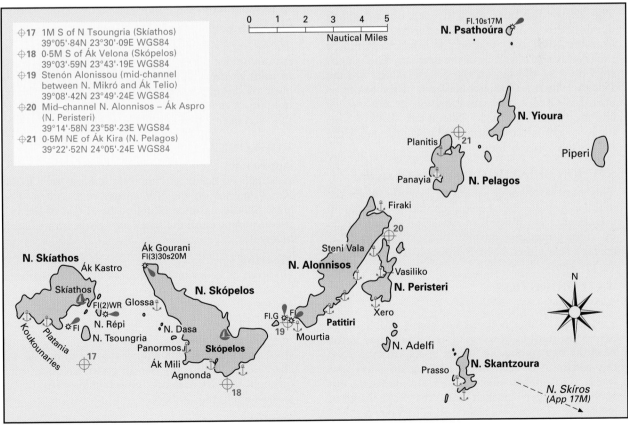

NORTHERN SPORADES

Skíros lies to the SE of the main group and although it belongs geographically and politically to these islands, it has tended to develop independently.

Lying out of the mainstream of history, the islands have few archaeological remains. Recently indications of Minoan occupation have been unearthed at Stafilos on Skópelos. The islands were subject-allies of Athens and later of Macedonia and Rome. Skíros has always been of more importance than the other islands, situated as it is on the trade route between Athens and Asia Minor.

During the Middle Ages the islands were easy prey for pirates. The inhabitants moved inland to fortified villages and not until the late 19th century did they begin to return to coastal villages. Consequently, most of the towns around the coast are of comparatively recent origin.

The popular architecture of the group is distinctive – the houses are washed in white, blue and pink and have gabled roofs with grey or red slates. Today the beautiful scenery and fine sandy beaches have been attracting growing numbers of tourists to the more accessible islands of the group.

Note The islands are not blessed with very much in the way of natural water supplies, nor when it is available is it always potable. The rapidly expanding tourism infrastructure ashore has cut supplies even further. Consequently water is in short supply and in harbours where it is available it is charged out at a high, not to say extortionate, rate.

Weather patterns in the northern Sporades

The *meltemi* does not blow as strongly down through the northern Sporades as it does further S. It blows from the NNE, but the direction is much altered by the islands and channels between them. The islands stop most of the sea on the S side except around Pelagos which gets the whole fetch of the sea from northern Greece. The combination of the *meltemi* and the flat seas on the lee side of the islands makes for some exhilarating sailing and not surprisingly the area is popular for flotilla holidays.

STENÓN SKÍATHOU (Skíathos Channel)

This narrow channel separates Skíathos from the mainland. Ifalos Levthéris (Lephtari Rock) lies in the channel 1¾ miles E of Ák Arápis. It is marked by a light structure (conspic): Fl(2)8s9M. A variable current sets either N or S through the channel at ½–1½ knots.

KATI GIORGYIOS

39°10'·6N 23°20'·7E

This small fishing harbour lies about 1M S of Ák Sepia. Go stern or bows–to on the small quay in the N of the bay among the fishing boats, or anchor off the beach in 3–6m. Good holding on sand and weed. Reasonable shelter from the *meltemi*, but some swell gets pushed into the bay. Limited provisions and taverna ashore. Bus to Volos.

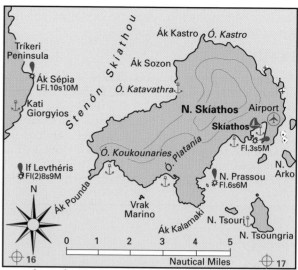

STENÓN SKÍATHOU

⊕16 Mid–channel E end of Stenón Tríkeri (2·5M N of Pondikonisi)
       39°05'·57N 23°20'·36E WGS84
⊕17 1M S of N Tsoungria (Skíathos)
       39°05'·84N 23°30'·09E WGS84

Nísos Skíathos

The nearest of the islands to the mainland coast. and referred to by some as 'The Greek Riviera'. With good ferry services and an airport it attracts more visitors than the other islands. From 1538 until 1830 the inhabitants moved to an almost inaccessible rocky spur on the northern end of the island. The Kástro, as it was called, was connected to the island by a drawbridge which could be raised in times of siege. Today most of the population lives in Skíathos town.

ORMOS KATAVATHRA

39°10'·97N 23°26'·51E

An anchorage on the NW side of Skíathos suitable in calm weather or a light *meltemi*. The approach is clear of dangers. Anchor in 4–6m on sand, good holding. A taverna on the beach, though it closes in the evenings.

KOUKOUNARIES

Approach
A small harbour in the NE corner of Órmos Koukounaries on the SW corner of Skíathos. The large Skíathos Palace Hotel at the E end of the bay is conspicuous and the small harbour is immediately below it.

Mooring
Go stern or bows-to either mole. The tiny harbour is usually crowded and you will probably have to anchor off.

Shelter Excellent shelter. A number of boats are wintered afloat here.

Anchorage Anchor off the beach clear of the ski channel in 4–6m on sand, good holding once through the hard sand. Good shelter from the *meltemi* anchored off here.

Facilities
Several tavernas nearby.

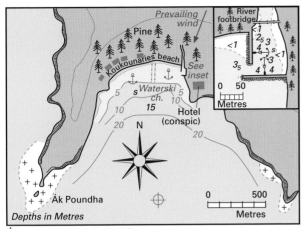

ÓRMOS KOUKOUNARIES
⊕39°08'·3N 23°24'·2E

General

Koukounaries is often said to be the best beach in the Aegean. It is a fine beach with the pines providing a wonderful aspect, but is not the best beach in the region in my opinion (see Khalkidhiki section).

ÓRMOS PLATANIA

A large bay to the E of Koukounaries with several hotels on the beach. Anchor off the beach in 4–8m on sand, good holding. Good shelter although there are strong gusts off the land with the *meltemi*.

Tavernas ashore.

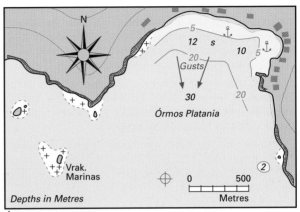

ÓRMOS PLATANIA
⊕39°07'·8N 23°26'·2E

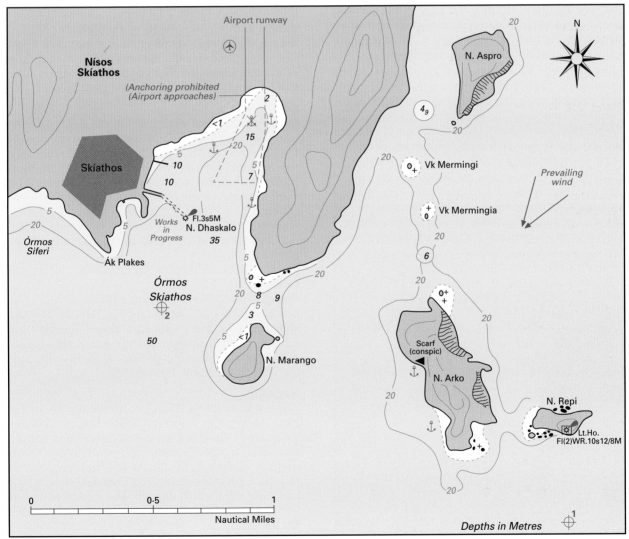

APPROACHES TO SKÍATHOS
⊕1 39°08'·29N 23°31'·70E WGS84
⊕2 39°09'·24N 23°29'·56E WGS84

SKÍATHOS

BA 1571
Imray-Tetra G25

Approach

Conspicuous The cluster of islands surrounding Skíathos harbour is easily identified. The lighthouse on Nisís Répi is conspicuous from the S and E. The buildings of Skíathos around the harbour, particularly a large building on the headland forming the E side of the old harbour and a church with a conspicuous clock tower on high ground to the N of the old harbour, are conspicuous.

Note Work is in progress extending the outer breakwater towards Nisís Dhaskalo (2003). Yachts should leave Nisís Dhaskalo to port in the approaches to Skíathos harbour.

By night Use the lights on Nisís Prassou Fl.6s6M, Nisís Répi Fl(2)WR.10s12/8M (red sector covers 261°-313°), and Dhaskalonísi in the immediate approaches Fl.3s5M.

VHF Ch 77 (Skíathos Marina)

Mooring

A triad of charter companies now controls the new pontoon and most of the town quay. You must call ahead for a berth. Charter operators protect their berths aggressively against anyone attempting to enter a vacant berth without authorisation.

Berth Go stern or bows–to on the pontoon or the town quay. Some laid moorings tailed to the quay. It is possible to anchor off the town to the N of the pontoon, but care is needed of the numerous moorings. The old harbour on the S side is reserved for excursion boats though there may be a few berths here for small yachts.

Shelter Good shelter from the *meltemi* in the new E harbour, but the wind does blow beam on, making manoeuvring into a berth a bit tricky at times. When the extension to the outer breakwater is complete shelter from southerlies should be much improved.

Skíathos harbour looking W with Skíathos town top middle. Photo taken before the extensions to the breakwater.

Peter Kleinoth/MareTeam

Authorities A port of entry: port police, customs and immigration. Charge band 2/3.

Anchorage It is also possible to anchor at the head of the bay and a number of yachts are wintered afloat here. Keep well clear of the area where anchoring is prohibited under the flight path of the airport. The bottom is mud, sand and weed – good holding.

Facilities

Services Water and electricity on the pontoon. The water is reported not potable. Around 50 metres from the pontoon just behind the bus stop there is a tap with good spring water. Some of the tavernas refill their mineral water bottles here! Showers.

Fuel Can be delivered to the harbour by mini-tanker.

Repairs Some mechanical repairs. Yachts are hauled out at the yard at the head of the bay. Chandlers. Hardware shops.

Provisions Good shopping for all provisions. Ice can be ordered.

Eating out Good tavernas in the town.

Other PO. OTE. Banks. ATMs. Greek gas and Camping Gaz. Hire cars, motorbikes and bicycles. Ferries and hydrofoils to Volos, Áyios Konstandinos and Skópelos. European charter flights. Internal flights to Athens and Thessaloniki.

General

The small town of Skíathos has grown in recent years to become a sort of junior league Míkonos with discos, bars and good restaurants livening up the night. In the summer the town is packed with tourists attracted to the sandy beaches, yet it remains a pleasant easy-going town and most of the locals are still friendly enough. But a quiet place it is not and those seeking less noise and fewer people are advised to head east.

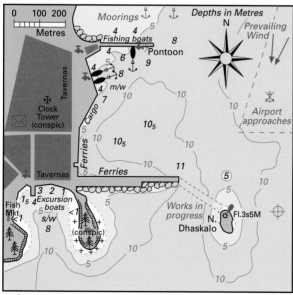

SKÍATHOS
⊕39°09′·7N 23°29′·8E

Nísos Skópelos

Skópelos (ancient Peparethos), like Skíathos, is densely wooded in pine over its slopes. It is also very fertile – vines, olives, almonds, pears, citrus fruit and plums, for which the island is famous, are grown. It is more intensively cultivated than Skíathos and the inhabitants (perhaps because they are farmers and not seafarers risking their lives at sea) are said to be more conservative.

The capital is Skópelos (*chora*-Skopélou) on the east side of the island. The island has long been considered a remote place – dissident Byzantines were exiled here far from the pleasures of Constantinople. In 1538 Barbarossa slaughtered the entire population of the island so presumably all the present inhabitants are immigrants who arrived in the 16th century. The island still has a remote feel to it in places and in the winter you can feel positively isolated on it. Today the islanders are an industrious and prosperous lot who seem quite happy to see tourists coming to their island, yet make few concessions to them outside Skópelos and Glóssa.

LOUTRÁKI (Glóssa)

Approach

Conspicuous From the S Ák Armenopetra, a sand-coloured knoll with off-lying rocks, is conspicuous. The village on the hill above the harbour is easily seen from a considerable distance off. A large brown church in the middle of the village is conspicuous. Closer in the small settlement behind the harbour will be seen.

By night The entrance is lit: Fl.G.3s3M/Fl.R.3s3M.

Dangers Hydrofoils enter and leave the harbour at speed and large ferries manoeuvre with considerable skill in the limited space. Keep well clear when they are in the harbour.

Mooring

Go stern or bows-to the pontoon in the NE corner. Space is limited on the pontoon in high season, but usually there is space to squeeze in. When using the inside berths on the N side of the pontoon, depths for laying your anchor come up quickly to <2m, limiting scope. The bottom is soft mud, sand and weed, good holding. Otherwise anchor fore and aft, or anchor and take a long line ashore to the wall, on the SE side of the pontoon. Alternatively anchor free in the S of the harbour clear of the ferry turning area.

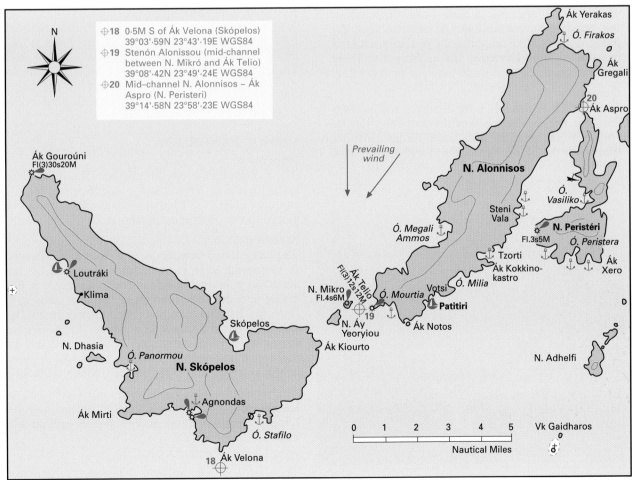

NISOI SKÓPELOS AND ALONNISOS

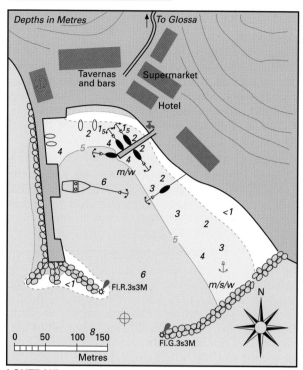

Depths in Metres

To Glossa

Tavernas and bars

Supermarket

Hotel

m/w

6

Fl.R.3s3M

m/s/w

N

0   50   100   8 150

Metres

Fl.G.3s3M

LOUTRÁKI
⊕ 39°09′·79N 23°36′·87E WGS84

Shelter Good shelter from the *meltemi*. Strong southerlies may be bothersome.

Facilities
There is a tap and hose at the root of the pontoon, but water is limited and should only be used for filling tanks. Good shopping for provisions. Good tavernas on the waterfront. Bus to Skópelos. Ferry to Skíathos.

General
Loutráki has grown into a modest tourist resort and the once sleepy village is now invaded every day by visitors from Skíathos who come for its splendid beaches to the SE of the harbour. Newly paved tree-

The yacht pontoon in Loutráki   *Lu Michell*

lined paths lead around the harbour to the waterside cafés in the village. Up the hill the village of Glossa is still worth the climb, if only to visit the restaurant Agnanti, with views and food to die for. Beware the perils of the goat-track on the way back down. A torch or a taxi is advisable.

NÉA KLIMA
39°08′·23N 23°38′·57E WGS84

A small harbour with a narrow entrance channel into a basin. The entrance is lit Fl.G.3s3M/Fl.R.3s3M. Care is needed in the channel and inside the harbour as depths are irregular. Depths in the channel are mostly 2–3m and in the basin 1·5–3m. The harbour is crowded with local boats and there is little chance of finding a berth.

ÓRMOS PANORMOU
Approach
The bay lies half a mile SE of Nisís Dhasia which is easily identified. From the S it is difficult to see the bay until close to. The apartment complex on the N side with red roofs is conspicuous.

Mooring
The large bay is very deep even close to the beach. A swimming area is sometimes cordoned off by small buoys in the NE side of the bay. Anchor in the E side outside the buoyed area. The inlet running S from the bay has better shelter. Anchor in the W side in 4–8m and take a line ashore. There can be strong gusts from the N and NW into the bay so make sure your anchor is well in. The bay is popular in the summer and often packed with yachts and other craft.

Facilities
Limited provisions and many tavernas around the beach.

General
The secluded inlet on the S features in Michael Carroll's *Gates of the Wind*. Anyone who has read

Loutráki on Skópelos looking S   *Lu Michell*

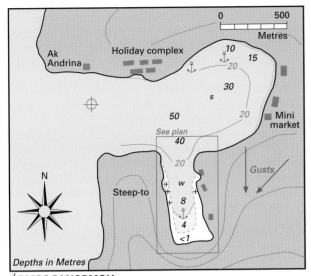

ÓRMOS PANORMOU
⊕39°06'·61N 23°39'·29E WGS84

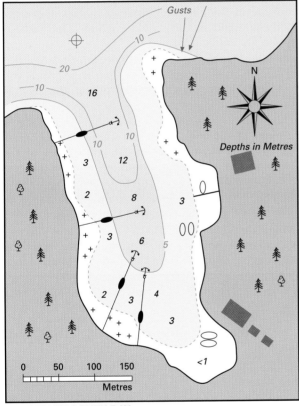

PANORMOU SOUTH BAY
⊕39°06'·61N 23°39'·52E WGS84

this book will immediately recognise his house on the E side of the inlet. Those who have not read it should obtain a copy (it is published in paperback by a Greek publisher and available locally) for the descriptions of the islands and particularly of Skópelos and Panormos just before the outside world learnt of these enchanted places.

Looking S from Agnóndas towards Ák Amarandos calm
weather anchorage   *Lu Michell*

Taverna/bars ashore. The pine-clad inlet is a
popular spot with Skopelites in the summer.

AK AMARANDOS

On the N side of Ak Amarandos yachts can anchor
with a long line ashore. This is a delightful little spot
and in calm weather suitable as an overnight
anchorage.

ÓRMOS STAFILOS (Staphylos)

An open bay on the S coast W of a craggy headland
joined by a low isthmus to Skópelos. Care needs to
be taken of the reef immediately S of an islet on the
W side of the bay although it is not in the obvious
approach to the bay.

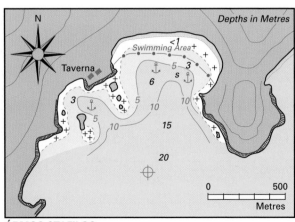

ÓRMOS STAFILOS
⊕39°04'·84N 23°44'·77E WGS84

The large bay offers good protection from the
meltemi although a swell often curves around into
the bay. Anchor outside the swimming area in
6–10m off the beach in the NE corner. Open to the
S.

A few summer villas have been built around the
slopes and the beach is popular in the summer.
Taverna and beach bar ashore.

The bay is named after a Minoan prince
(Staphylos), and recently archaeologists discovered
evidence of a Cretan settlement, including a gold-
plated sword handle and a gold diadem. This makes
Stafilos the most northerly Minoan settlement so far
unearthed.

LIMÍN SKOPÉLOU (SKÓPELOS)

BA 1571

Approach

Conspicuous From the E the town of Skópelos will
not be seen until you enter Órmos Skopélou. Once
you are in the bay the cluster of houses above the
harbour stand out in dazzling white. The harbour
moles are easily identified.

By night Use the light on Nisís Mikró Fl.4s6M and
the lights at the entrance Fl.G.2s6M and Fl.R (on
the light buoy off the works or on the new E
breakwater).

Dangers With strong NE winds (including a
prolonged *meltemi*) a steep and dangerous sea builds
up over the shoal water in the approaches to the
harbour. In these conditions it is difficult and
sometimes dangerous to enter or leave the harbour.
In this weather the ferry goes to Agnonda on the W
coast of Skópelos.

Mooring

Go stern or bows-to the N quay. A large mooring
chain lying 30m out from the quay and parallel to it

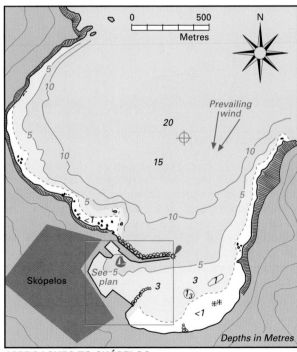

APPROACHES TO SKÓPELOS
⊕39°07'·71N 23°44'·13E WGS84

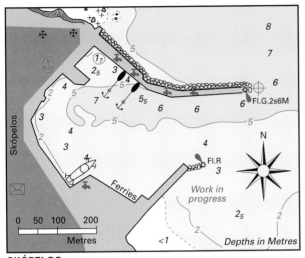

SKÓPELOS
⊕39°07′·40N 23°44′·11E WGS84

has been reported. Care is needed not to snag it with your anchor. The bottom is mud – excellent holding. Some laid moorings.

Shelter With a strong *meltemi* it can get very uncomfortable in the harbour. Ease off the warps and keep the yacht some distance off the quay. The wash from the numerous ferries and hydrofoils using the harbour is also bothersome. Otherwise shelter is good, with the best berths tucked into the NW corner.

Authorities Port police and customs.

Facilities
Water On the quay.
Fuel Can be delivered by mini-tanker. ☎ 34049.
Repairs Limited mechanical repairs. Hardware shops.
Provisions Good shopping for all provisions. Ice available.
Eating out Good tavernas on the waterfront and in the town.
Other PO. OTE. Bank. ATMs. Hire motorbikes and bicycles. Bus to Glóssa. Ferries and hydrofoils to Patitíri and Volos.

Limín Skopélou looking W   *Lu Michell*

General
The houses and churches (there are said to be 120) of the town are piled one upon another around a rock amphitheatre above the harbour. The houses are jammed together along narrow curving alleys that restrict access to pedestrians, donkeys and the occasional suicidal motorcyclist. An altogether delightful and relaxing place that has altered little (apart from acquiring some more tavernas and bars) despite the growing numbers of tourists discovering it.

Nísos Alonnisos
(Khelidromi)

In ancient times called Ilkos, this hilly wooded island relies on the donkey and the *caïque* as much as on motor vehicles. The old capital of Alonnisos, on a hill in the south of the island, was largely deserted after a severe earthquake in 1965. The islanders moved to Patitíri and Votsi, but eventually returned and most of the houses in the hill village have been restored. At Órmos Tzorti evidence of Neolithic and other ancient habitation has been discovered. Whether this was also the site of ancient Halonessos, a city that ancient commentators say disappeared into the sea during a catastrophic earthquake, is uncertain, as some believe Psathoúra, the northernmost island, to be the site.

ÓRMOS MOURTIA (Mourtias)
An open bay on the SW of Alonnisos offering some shelter from the *meltemi*. Open to the S and prone to swell entering. Anchor in 4–6m around the bay taking care to avoid the prohibited area where there are underwater cables. Taverna ashore.

The village of Alonnisos on the hill above is 30 minutes' steep climb up an unpaved road. In unsettled weather Patitíri is a safer harbour to leave a yacht in if you want to visit the hill village.

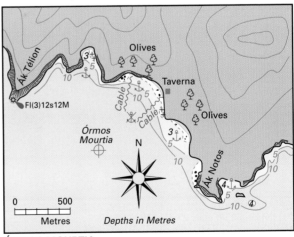

ÓRMOS MOURTIA
⊕39°08′·07N 23°50′·36E WGS84

337

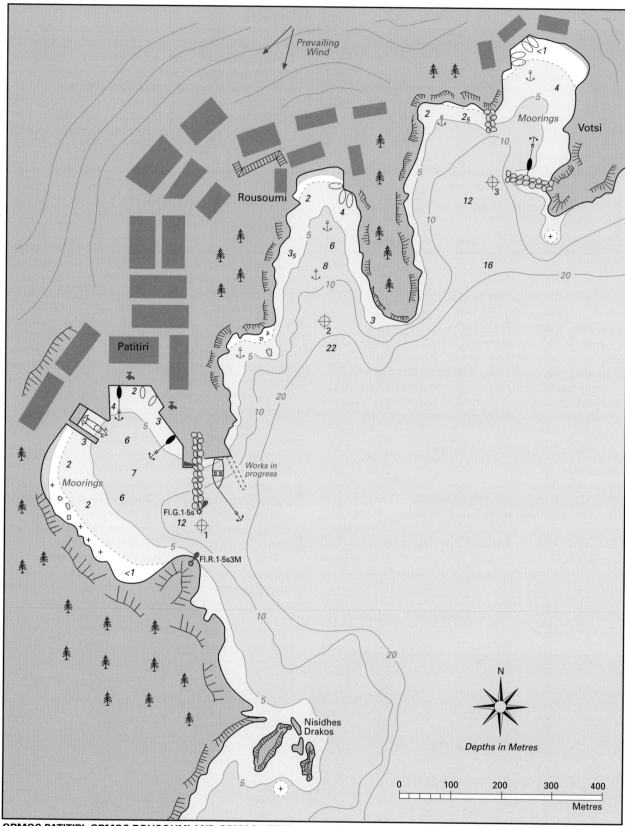

ORMOS PATITIRI, ORMOS ROUSOUMI AND ORMOS VOTSI
⊕₁ Patitíri 39°08′·55N 23°52′·11E WGS84
⊕₂ Rousoumi 39°08′·78N 23°52′·21E WGS84
⊕₃ Votsi 39°08′·86N 23°52′·44E WGS84

PATITÍRI

Approach
Conspicuous The old village of Alonnisos on the hill behind is visible from seaward. The village and harbour of Patitíri are not easily seen from the N or S until you are close to.

By night The entrance is lit: Fl.R.1·5s3M/ Fl.G.1·5s3M.

Dangers Care is needed of ferries entering and leaving the narrow entrance to the harbour.

Note Works in progress outside the E breakwater building a quay out eastwards. It would appear that another breakwater will be built parallel to the existing breakwater.

Mooring
Go stern or bows-to the NE quay. The bottom is sand and weed – good holding. There is little room to anchor in the harbour. Most of the S side is covered with permanent moorings.

Shelter Good shelter from the *meltemi*, although some swell tends to creep around into the harbour making it a bit rolly at times. Partially open to the E and SE.

Authorities Port police.

Facilities
Water Tap on the quay or a mini-tanker will deliver.
Fuel 200 metres away on the road to old Alonnisos. A mini-tanker can deliver to the quay.
Provisions Good shopping for provisions. Ice available.
Eating out Tavernas and bars on the waterfront.
Other PO. ATM. Ferries and hydrofoils to Skíathos and Volos.

General
As has recently happened on the other islands in the group, the capital of the island has moved from the hill village down to the harbour. Patitíri is a lovely spot surrounded by the cliffs on the S and pine-clad slopes behind, so inevitably it has attracted a growing number of tourists, but remains a pleasant spot still.

Patitíri on Alonnísos looking W. The hydrofoil quay has since been altered and work is in progress on the E side
Peter Kleinoth/MareTeam

ÓRMOS ROUSOUMI

A small and tranquil cove between Patitiri and Votsi. Good shelter from the *meltemi*. Anchor off the beach in 6–10m on sand and weed, good holding. The small quay in the NE corner is full of local boats. Tavernas ashore. A short walk over the hill into Patitiri.

Órmos Rousoumi looking SSW with the entrance to Patitiri in the background
Lu Michell

VOTSI

A cove immediately N of Rousoumi which a number of fishing boats use in preference to Patitíri. A short breakwater extends from the E side of the cove and a 'snoot' of a breakwater on the W. Room is very limited but it may be possible to anchor in 2·5–4m in the NE corner with a line ashore taking care of the numerous permanent moorings. Alternatively try the inside of the E breakwater. One or two yachts may find room to go bows-to the quay on the W side amongst the local fishing boats. Good shelter from the *meltemi* and open only to the S. The bottom shelves gradually towards the beach at the head of the bay.

Tavernas ashore.

Órmos Votsi looking N into the bay
Lu Michell

ÓRMOS MILIA

A large open bay on the SE side of Alonnisos. Reasonable shelter from the *meltemi* in the NE cove, otherwise open to E–SW and prone to some swell. Anchor and take a long line ashore in the NE corner, or anchor free in the other coves in settled weather. Beach bars open in the summer.

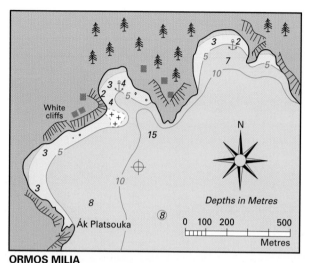

ORMOS MILIA
⊕39°09'·16N 23°53'·42E WGS84

ÁK KOKKINOKASTRO

Kokkinokastro is the red cliffy cape 2½ miles N of Patitíri (*kokkino* means 'red'). Kokkinokastro is thought to be the site of ancient Ilkos (about the fifth century BC).

ÓRMOS TZORTI

The bay immediately N of Ák Kokkinokastro. Care is needed of the above and below-water rocks extending out from Kokkinokastro. Anchor in 4–8m off the beach on sand and weed, good holding once the anchor is in. Good shelter from the *meltemi*.

A number of villas have been built around the bay. The beach is popular in the summer, but is usually deserted at night.

Immediately NE of Tzorti is another bay, Órmos

Leptos Yialos, which also gives reasonable shelter from the *meltemi* and is busy in summer. Anchor in 4–6m off the beach.

STENI VALA

A small cove on Alonnisos opposite the S end of Nísos Peristeri. Sheltered from the *meltemi* and only open SW. Depths immediately off the quay on the N side are reduced to only 1–1·5m by underwater ballast. Go bows–to to avoid rudder damage. Larger yachts may need to keep a short distance off the quay. It is reported that a large mooring chain runs the length of the bay so drop your anchor far enough out to avoid it. Several tavernas ashore. Showers available in some tavernas. Minimarket. The spot is popular with charter yachts.

Alternatively a yacht can anchor in a cove lined with pine trees and bamboo immediately S of the 'taverna' cove. Care is needed of the islet on the port side of the entrance. Good shelter.

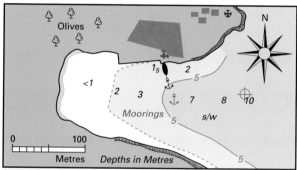

STENI VALA
⊕39°11'·48N 23°55'·75E WGS84

LIMIN KALAMAKIA

39°12'·08N 23°55'·85E WGS84

A small fishing harbour just under 1M N of Steni Vala. Light structures on the end of the breakwaters, but the entrance is not lit. Very narrow for manoeuvring inside, and in any case usually crowded with small local boats. Depths <1–3m. Indifferent shelter from the prevailing winds.

Steni Vala looking NW along the yacht quay   *Lu Michell*

ÓRMOS TZORTI
⊕39°10'·06N 23°54'·59E WGS84

ÓRMOS FIRAKI (Port Eiraka)

39°16'·2N 23°57'·0E

A bay on the N end of the island. The bay is very exposed and is untenable with the *meltemi*, but in calm weather makes a good lunch stop. At the head of the bay there is a small quay used by the tripper boats with 2–2·5m depths reported off it.

ÓRMOS MEGALI AMMOS (Kato Yioura)

39°10'·87N 23°52'·63E WGS84

A large bay on the W side of Alonnisos opposite Tzorti on the E side. In the NE corner there is a cove affording shelter from the *meltemi*. Anchor off the small beach in 5–8 metres. The bottom is sand and weed, good holding. Open WNW–SW.

No facilities and just a few villas ashore amongst the pines.

Nísos Peristeri

(Xero)

The island lying roughly parallel to and just to the E of Alonnisos.

ÓRMOS PERISTÉRA AND XERO

Two bays on the S end of Nísos Peristéra.

Órmos Peristéra Anchor off the beach at the head of the bay in 3–6m on mud and weed, good holding. Good shelter from the *meltemi*. A number of houses have now been built around the slopes.

Órmos Xero The bay immediately E of Órmos Peristéra. Anchor in 5–10m at the head of the bay. Adequate shelter from the *meltemi*.

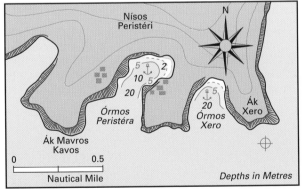

ORMOS PERISTÉRA AND XERO
⊕39°09'·7N 23°59'·0E

ÓRMOS VASILIKO

The bay at the N end of the large bay on the W coast. Care must be taken of the reef on the W side of the entrance. Anchor in 4–8m in the bay. Nearly all-round shelter. At the time of writing the bay is partially occupied by trawlers and a decommissioned ferry, but there is still room for yachts to anchor. Recent visitors have remarked that the bay and beaches nearby are knee-deep in rubbish, principally plastic and old tyres.

Several coves N of Vasiliko are attractive lunch stops.

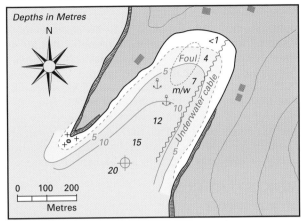

VASILIKO
⊕39°11'·86N 23°58'·41E WGS84

Órmos Vasiliko on Peristéri   *Nigel Patten*

ÓRMOS KLIMA

39°11'·4N 23°58'·7E

The large bay on the W side of Nísos Peristéri. In calm weather it is a spectacular spot to visit with a gorge running down to the head of the bay. The *meltemi* pushes a swell into the bay and although tenable in a light *meltemi*, if the wind pipes up it is not a good spot to be.

NOTE
The 3 fathom patch shown on the old Admiralty charts Nos. 1085 and 1087 extending across the northern passage between Alonnisos and Peristeri is in fact a smallish patch off the end of Peristeri. There are considerable depths in the fairway.

Nísos Pelagos

(Nísos Kira Panayía)

Lies 4 miles to the NE of Alonnisos. It is deserted except for large herds of goats, a herd of cows, some horses, a big black bull and a guardian. A number of sunken Byzantine ships have been discovered off the coast and in 1970 a quantity of pottery was recovered.

Note Pelagos Island is now a nature reserve. Along with Yioura and Piperi which are also nature reserves, this is one of the few remaining habitats of the Mediterranean Monk seal (*Monarchus monarchus*). Other habitats are around Cephalonia in the Ionian and the Atlantic coast of Morocco. At one time there was talk of banning yachts from the island, but this does not seem to have happened and yachts continue to visit the island. Yachtsmen should take care not to disturb wildlife around the island or they may find they are banned from here.

MONASTERY COVE

39°19'·3N 24°05'·6E

A small cove on the E side of the island where a yacht can moor in settled weather to visit the monastery. On BA 1062 it is the bay immediately S of the bay showing 8 and 2 fathoms. On Imray-Tetra G25 it is marked as Monastery Bay. The monastery itself is on a small headland at the S end of the bay. Anchor in 5m and take a line ashore. The cove is protected only from W winds and should be visited in calm weather only.

Steps are cut in the rock to climb to the monastery several hundred feet above. About a 40-minute walk. It is a lonely and haunted place inhabited by one old monk and caretaker keeping a last vigil here. Visitors should take care not to desecrate the spot whether believers or not.

KIRA PANAYIA (Áyios Petros)

A large bay on the SW corner of Pelagos. Nisís Pelérissa and the high plateau on the SE side of the bay are easily distinguished. There is deep water N and S of Nisís Pelérissa.

Good shelter from the *meltemi* can be found in Órmos Paigniou, although with northerlies there are vicious gusts into the bay. Anchor in the cove on the NW side or behind the islet in the middle of the bay and take a line ashore. The bottom is sand – good holding.

A yacht can also anchor in the coves on the SE side in 2–4m. The bottom is sand and thick weed – poor holding.

ÓRMOS PLANITIS (Planidhi)

A large landlocked bay on the N side of Nísos Pelagos. Nisís Sfika lies close to the W side of the narrow entrance which is difficult to see until you are close in. With strong N winds a considerable sea piles up at the entrance to Planitís and it is a frightening experience being pushed by the wind and sea towards the entrance which is only 82m (270ft) wide. Conversely with strong N winds it can

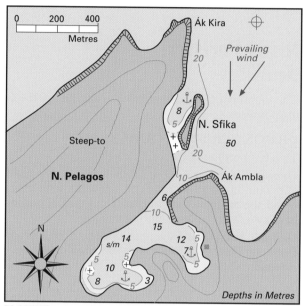

PLANITIS
⊕39°22'·02N 24°05'·14E WGS84

Planitís on Pelagos looking NE with Nísos Yioura at the very top of the photo   *Peter Kleinoth/MareTeam*

KIRA PANAYIA
⊕39°18'·8N 24°02'·3E

be difficult to leave the bay. There is a least depth of 6m over the bar at the entrance. Inside the bay the water is always smooth.

Anchor in either of the two forks of the bay. A favourite place is in 3–6m in the NE corner of the southernmost part of the bay. Excellent all-round shelter. The bottom is clay and mud with some weed – good holding. It is deserted apart from a large herd of goats, fishermen and yachts in the summer.

In calm weather you can anchor in between Nisís Sfika and the coast in delightful surroundings. The southern part of the passage is encumbered by a reef although local boats sometimes use it. It is not advised for yachts.

NISÍS YIOURA

A precipitous jagged island with no sheltered anchorages. A herd of the European wild goat, the now rare ibex, lives on the island and every year an armada of *caïques* sets out to cull the herd under the supervision of an official. Michael Carroll gives a lively description of the cullers and the culling in his *Gates of the Wind*.

NISÍS PIPERI

The Pepperpot. There are no anchorages around it.

NISÍS PSATHOÚRA

N. Psathoúra light (Fl.10s17M) 39°30'·3N 24°10'·9E

The northernmost of the northern Sporades, it is very low (12m/39ft), but the lighthouse (40m/131ft) is conspicuous. An extensive submerged city, possibly ancient Halonnesos, is reported to lie off the N end of the island.

Currents Around Psathoúra Island and also to the N of it the current sets strongly towards the SW. On passage between Porto Koufó and Pelagos in November, I estimated the current to be about 1½ knots to the SW. Quite possibly it is stronger at other times of the year. With strong winds from the N and S the seas in the vicinity of Psathoúra can be exceptionally disturbed and steep.

NÍSOS SKANTZOURA

Lies about 15 miles E of the S end of Skópelos. A number of small islands and shoals lie off the coast. A yacht can anchor in a number of places:

1. *Órmos Prasso* (opposite Nisís Prasso) which is made up of two small coves. Anchor in 4–6m sand.
2. *Nisís Prasso S side* On the S side of the islet there is a cove which you can tuck into. Anchor in 4–6m on sand and weed and take a long line to the shore. A large grapnel anchor with mooring lines attached to it is reported to lie on the S side about 25 metres off the coast. It is sometimes marked by a float.
3. *Órmos Skantzoura* A deep narrow bay on the S side of Skantzoura. Anchor in 3–5m and take a long line ashore.

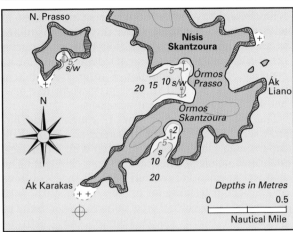

NÍSIS SKANTZOURA ANCHORAGES
⊕39°03'·0N 24°05'·9E

The bays here afford adequate if not always comfortable shelter from the *meltemi*. A swell usually works its way into the bays after the wind dies and the waves are not 'blown' past the anchorages. Open to the W–SW. The bottom is sand and weed. Excellent underwater fishing in the vicinity of the island.

Caution Nísos Skantzoura and the islets surrounding it are comparatively low-lying and are unlit. Care must be taken in the vicinity of the islands, especially at night.

Skíros
(Skyros)

The most easterly and the largest of the northern Sporades. It is nearly divided into two by a narrow isthmus in the middle. The summit of the island lies in the rugged southern half where Mt Kokhilas rises to 792m (2,600ft). The lower slopes of the high ground are wooded in pine and maquis. The northern half of the island is fertile and cultivated in parts.

The capital, Skiro or Khorio, is more like a Cycladic village than the villages on Skíathos or Skópelos. The white cubist houses with flat roofs are built on a steep slope with a Venetian castle on the summit. In the village there is an unusual amount of carved wood – doors, shutters, chairs and stools. Skíros embroidery is also much in evidence. Some of the best island folk art is contained in the Faltaitz Museum near the castle – one of the best of its kind in Greece.

Ancient Skíros was ruled by King Lykomedes. It was he who treacherously killed Theseus, king of Athens, by hurling him over a cliff into the sea. His body was recovered and forty years later taken to Athens for a burial befitting his rank. Later Achilles was sent here by his mother to keep him away from the Trojan Wars in which it had been prophesied he would die. The wily Odysseus, en route to the wars, discovered his identity and lured him away to his prophesied death.

The island has always been important because of its position on the trade route across the northern Aegean. The Athenians colonised it and the Venetians held it for some considerable time. The Venetian castle overlooking Khorio has ancient masonry incorporated in its construction and was the likely site of the ancient acropolis.

The island has its fair share of tourism and has been adopted by those of an alternative bent. You can do yoga workshops, be treated with alternative medicines of all persuasions, or just chill out. The islanders seem quite relaxed with all this and have always been a friendly lot on this windy outpost of the Sporades. A herd of wild ponies, descendants of the ancient breed called Pikermic and akin to Shetland ponies, roam the island. Despite the rough seas and strong winds around the island it is well worth a visit as the scenery is grand and wild.

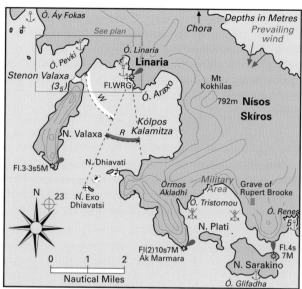

SKIROS – SOUTHWEST COAST

⊕23 1M S of Ák Valáxa light 38°47'·0N 24°29'·5E

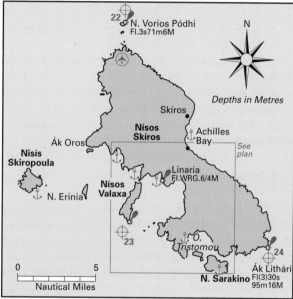

NÍSOS SKÍROS

⊕22 2M N of Nisís Vorios Pódhi (Skíros N end)
38°03'·2N 24°28'·1E
⊕23 1M S of Ák Valáxa light
38°47'·0N 24°29'·5E
⊕24 2M S of Nisís Sarakino light (Skíros S end)
38°43'·5N 24°37'·6E

ANCHORAGES

On this island battered by both wind and sea (its ancient name was Anemosa meaning 'windy'), the anchorages are mostly on the SW coast. From the N these are:

Órmos Áy Fokas Offers good shelter from the *meltemi* in attractive wooded surroundings. Anchor and take a long line to the shore to hold the bows into the slight swell that enters when the wind dies down in the evening. The bay is used by a few holiday-makers who come for the surroundings rather than the pebble beach. A taverna opens in the summer.

Órmos Pevki A large bay due N of the passage between Skíros and Nisís Valáxa. Good shelter from the *meltemi* and plenty of room to swing to anchor.

There is a quay and slipway for small craft on the S side of the bay. The long beach is popular in the summer and a couple of tavernas open for the season.

Stenón Valaxa There are depths of 2–5m in this passage. Keep to the centre of the passage or closer to the Skíros side. Usually you will encounter least depths of no less than 3·5–4m. It is scary but the ferry between Linaria and Kimi often uses this passage.

Ormiskos Linaria Lies further to the N from the ferry port of Linaria. Anchor in 3–6m on the W side of the bay. Good shelter from the *meltemi*. The bottom is mud – good holding. Taverna on the beach.

LIMÍN LINARIA

BA 1571
Imray-Tetra G18

Approach

Once past Nisís Valáxa some of the buildings around the harbour will be seen. The harbour proper will not be seen until you are right up to it when approaching from the S.

By night Use the light on the S end of Nisís Valáxa (Ák Valáxa) Fl.3·3s5M and the light on the end of the mole at Linaria Fl.WRG.2·5s6-4M (353°-R-021°-W-120°-G-300°).

Dangers With the *meltemi* there are strong gusts off the high land and confused seas in the approaches to the harbour.

Mooring

Go alongside where shown. The ferry and the lifeboat take up much of the limited quay space. Alternatively go stern or bows-to the quay on the SE side. Care is needed as ballasting extends a short distance underwater in places.

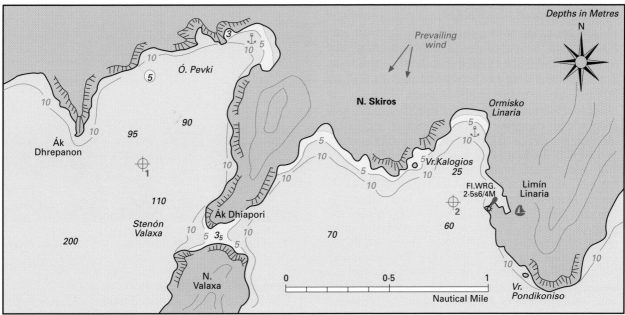

ORMOS PEVKI TO LIMIN LINARIA
⊕1 38°50'·75N 24°29'·8E
⊕2 38°50'·75N 24°29'·8E

LINARIA
⊕38°50'·6N 24°32'·2E

Linaria on Skíros looking WNW   *Peter Kleinoth/Mare Team*

Shelter Good shelter from the *meltemi*. Open to the NW–W.

Authorities Port police.

Facilities
Water On the quay.
Fuel On the quay.
Provisions Good shopping for provisions in Linaria. Better shopping in the *chora*.
Eating out Several tavernas nearby and others in the *chora*.
Other PO and OTE in the *chora*. Irregular bus to the *chora*. Ferries to Kimi and Volos and a hydrofoil to Skíathos.

General
Linaria is the place most yachts make for on Skíros and the small amount of quay space can be cluttered in the high season. It is more of a staging post for passengers on the ferry to get to the *chora* than a village as such, but is a pleasant enough place and really the only place from which to visit the *chora*.

Anchorages S of Linaria

Órmos Akladhi 38°46'·8N 24°34'·1E
Lying on the W side of Órmos Tristomou, this bay offers good shelter from the *meltemi*. Anchor in 3–5m near the head of the bay and take a long line ashore. The bottom is sand and weed.

Órmos Tristomou (Trebuki, Tris Boukes) If you want to visit the grave of Rupert Brooke anchor off the river mouth on the E side of Órmos Tristomou in 4–8m. The E side of the bay is now a military area and you should report to the shore station for permission to go ashore and visit Rupert Brooke's grave. The naval guards ashore have been helpful to visiting yachties once they have understood the purpose of the visit. However, there have also been recent reports that the bay is now strictly patrolled and although you can pass between Tristomou and Nisis Sarakino to reach Órmos Renes, you can no longer anchor in Tristomou. The bottom is sand and weed. To get to the grave follow the river bed for about 20 minutes and the grave will be found in an olive grove on the W side. I am not much of a fan of Rupert Brooke's poetry, more a fan of the man, but there are few of us who do not know the last lines of *The Old Vicarage*:

> 'And after, ere the night is born,
> Do hares come out about the corn?
> Oh, is the water sweet and cool,
> Gentle and brown above the pool?
> And laughs the immortal river still
> Under the mill, under the mill?
> Say, is there Beauty yet to find?
> And Certainty? and Quiet kind?
> Deep meadows yet, for to forget
> The lies, and truths, and pain?...oh! yet
> Stands the Church clock at ten to three?
> And is there honey still for tea?'

Órmos Renes Anchor in a cove in the NW or NE corner. There are mostly 5–8m depths to anchor in. The bottom is sand and weed. Good shelter from the *meltemi* although there are fierce gusts down into the bay.

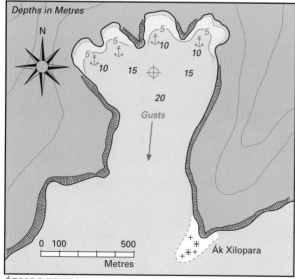

ÓRMOS RENES
⊕38°46'·4N 24°38'·0E

Órmos Akladhi on the SW coast of Skíros *Nigel Patten*

Ormiskos Glifadha 38°45'·0N 24°36'·8E
Lies on the S side of Nisís Sarakino. Anchor at the head of the creek in 4–6m. The bottom is sand and weed. Good shelter from the *meltemi*. Open only to the S.

Caution With a strong *meltemi* blowing there are violent gusts down onto the SW coast off the high mountains. These are especially fierce in Órmos Tristomou. Caution must be exercised on the lee side of the island on account both of the gusts and of the considerable seas raised by the *meltemi*.

ACHILLES BAY 'MARINA'

38°52'·3N 24°34'·5E

On the exposed E coast of Skíros a large new 'marina' has been built in Achilles Bay. This is on the N side of the low isthmus connecting the N and S parts of Skíros. The port is practically finished, complete with several dredging barges left half sunk inside the harbour. The entrance is lit Fl.G.3s3M/Fl.R.3s3M.

The entrance is fringed with rocks and reefs and with the entire NE Aegean as fetch for the *meltemi* there are horrendous seas at the entrance when any northerlies are blowing. I have not included a plan of the 'marina' here as not only is it dangerous to enter with any northerlies blowing, but it also has a heavy surge with moderate to strong northerlies making it pretty much untenable. Why it was built in this exposed position is a bit of a mystery as it offers no good shelter with the prevailing winds.

SKIROPOULA

The island lying approximately 8M W of Linaria on Skíros. On the SE of the island there is a bay affording some shelter from the *meltemi* (38°50'·0N 24°22'·0E). Care is needed in the approaches of the rocks and reefs running out from the SE side of the island and the approach to the anchorage should be made on a NE course. Anchor in either of the two coves at the head of the bay in 4–5m on sand. With the *meltemi* there are gusts into the anchorage.

East coast of Evia

For the most part this coast is rugged and precipitous with little shelter for yachts. The prevailing NE winds push considerable seas across the northern Aegean until they crash onto this coast. The coast is only sparsely populated and the scenery spectacular and wild. The only harbour of any size is Kimi approximately halfway along the coast, but there are a number of other anchorages offering some shelter from the prevailing winds.

ÓRMOS PETRIÉS (Áy Apostoli)

Lies 23½ miles NW of Ák Kafirevs tucked into the corner under Ák Pounda.

Approach

The entrance is difficult to identify from the N or S. Closer in the light structure at the entrance to the bay will be seen and once into the bay the village and breakwater are easily located. With the *meltemi* there is some swell at the entrance, but once into the bay the water is flat.

By night Use the light at the entrance to the bay Fl.5s4M and the lights at the entrance to the harbour: Fl.G.2s3M/Fl.R.2s3M.

Caution In the middle of the entrance to the harbour lies a sunken wreck of a small coaster about 35m long. The bow of the wreck faces N and the anchor winch here is just under 2m underwater. Otherwise it is covered with at least 3m. In calm weather it can be seen underwater. It is prudent to enter either close N or S of the entrance.

Recent reports say that the wreck is no longer here, but I would advise caution in the general vicinity.

Mooring

Anchor in 4–5m in the bay or go stern-to the

Petries looking WSW   *Hans van Rijn*

breakwater with a long line ashore. The bottom is sand and weed and not the best holding everywhere. There are numerous laid moorings and anchors on the bottom so a trip-line is advised. Good shelter from the *meltemi*.

Facilities

Several tavernas and mini-markets in the village. Public water tap.

General

The setting in the large bay is spectacular, but the village is a sorry collection of reinforced concrete houses mostly thrown up in the last few years. Nonetheless it is well worth a visit and the harbour is conveniently placed to break a voyage on the outside of Evia.

KÍMI (Kímis, Kymi, Paralia)

BA 1571
Imray-Tetra G26

Approach

Conspicuous From the S and E the village of Kími above the harbour is visible from seaward. From the north Nisís Prasoúdha and the lighthouse on it are easily identified and closer in a communication tower and dish on the ridge above the harbour are conspicuous. The harbour breakwater and entrance are easily identified.

By night Use the lights on Nisís Prasoúdha Fl.5s16M and at the harbour entrance Fl.R.3s3M/Fl.G.3s6M and Fl.R.1·5s3M/Fl.G.1·5s2M.

Dangers With the *meltemi* blowing a heavy sea rolls onto the Evia coast. There is invariably a confused swell around Ák Kími and at the entrance to the harbour.

Mooring

Go stern or bows-to the N mole or the N end of the W quay taking care to avoid the shallow patch. The harbour is often crowded with fishing boats and it can be difficult to find a berth. Care is needed of permanent moorings fouling the bottom. The

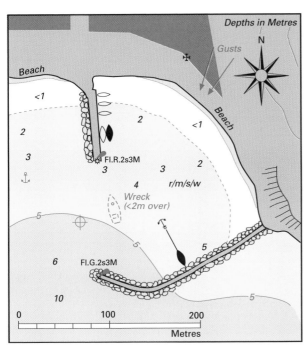

PETRIES
⊕38°24′·6N 24°11′·8E

Map labels: Depths in Metres · Beach · Gusts · N · Beach · Fl.R.2s3M · Wreck (<2m over) · r/m/s/w · Fl.G.2s3M · 0 100 200 Metres

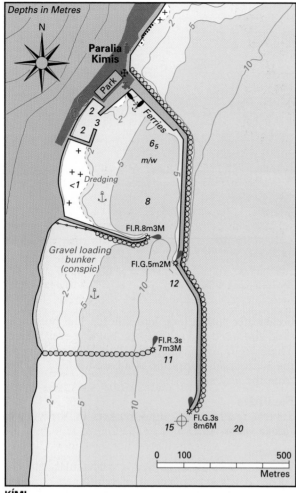

KÍMI
⊕38°37′·1N 24°08′·2E

bottom is mud – excellent holding.

Shelter Good shelter from the *meltemi*.

Authorities Port police and customs.

Facilities
Water On the quay or in the town.
Fuel Near the quay.
Provisions Some provisions available. Better shopping in Kími 30 minutes' walk up the hill. Ice available.
Eating out Several tavernas near the harbour.
Other Bus to Khalkís. Ferry to Skíros.

General
The grubby harbour and the hamlet around it (properly Paralia Kímis, Kími being the village on the hill above) are unprepossessing, but the setting is magnificent; the high mountains severed by deep gorges are densely wooded and drop down to long sandy beaches battered by the angry seas that crash onto this coast. It is a pleasant if steep walk up to Kími along the wooded road and the view from the village across the sea to Skíros is spectacular.

ÁK ÁY VASILIOS ANCHORAGES
38°52′·8N 23°26′·3E
Under Ák Áy Vasilios there are several coves which afford reasonable shelter from the *meltemi*. The best shelter is in the cove directly under the cape itself. Anchor in 4–5m on sand and weed, good holding once in. Alternatively anchor in the adjacent SW cove or off the beach fronting the small resort. The latter two anchorages are more exposed than the cove directly under the cape.

Some provisions and tavernas ashore.

ÓRMOS LOUTRO
Lies 9 miles SE of Ák Artemision. A reef runs from the NE side of the entrance in a SE direction for approximately 150m. Enter the bay from the S. Anchor in 3–4m in the bay. Sheltered from the *meltemi*. Open to the E and S. Some provisions and tavernas ashore.

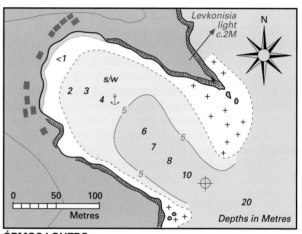

ÓRMOS LOUTRO
⊕38°56′·0N 23°25′·6E

VII. Northern Greece

This section covers the sea area from Thermaïkos Kólpos eastwards to Alexandroupolis in the northeast corner of Greece. It is a sea seldom cruised by yachtsmen, yet it offers some of the grandest scenery and without doubt the finest sandy beaches in Greece. Describe northern Greece to a yachtsman who has cruised solely in southern Greece, in the Saronic, Cyclades, Crete or the Dodecanese, and he will be inclined to think you are describing a country geographically removed from the Mediterranean.

The climate is Balkan rather than Mediterranean, with extreme differences between the summer and winter. The winters are harsh and cold with a high average rainfall and occasionally snow even at sea-level – no place for a yacht to spend the winter. The summers are hot and often described as languid. The terrain is mountainous and densely wooded. Pine, chestnut, plane, oak and poplar are common down to the water's edge. The coastal plains, deposited by the large rivers flowing through the region, are fertile and cultivated in maize, tobacco, rice, beans, sugar-beet, sunflowers and of course the vine. The fauna is prolific and said to include the jackal, wild cat, boar, roe deer and, in the remote areas, wolves. By the lakes and marshes bird life abounds: vultures, sea eagles, storks, herons, cormorants, pelicans, waders and ducks can be seen in large numbers. Flatfish, mussels and scallops are found in the shallows off the large rivers.

Just as the climate is Balkan rather than Mediterranean, so the peoples of this area are partly of Balkan origin. In ancient times the mountain-dwelling folk were regarded as wild and barbaric by the civilization centred around Athens. Around the coast the Greeks intermarried with the indigenous population and have always been regarded with suspicion by Greeks from the south. The objection by Greece to the adoption of the name Macedonia by the (now) FYRO Macedonia is ironic in that most of Greece used the term as an insult for those who came from northern Greece. Worried that northern Greece might join the FYRO Macedonia, politicians and others fell over backwards to adopt Macedonia as intrinsically Greek in culture and history when for years they had kept things Macedonian on the fringes.

The region reached its zenith when Alexander the Great toppled the Athenians and made Macedonia the centre of his empire. Not that things changed very much as the young Alexander was a great admirer of the Greeks and their civilization. After his death the power slipped away in the internecine struggles which went on for nearly two centuries. The usual succession of invaders followed the collapse of power, taking a harsher toll than in other regions since this was the first part of Greece they encountered after a long and hungry march over the mountains. The Goths, Huns, Ostrogoths, Bulgars, Slavs and Saracens laid waste to the region. By 1444 the Turks had secured the region and it remained under Turkish rule until 1913. At the beginning of the Second World War a combined Greek, English, Australian and New Zealand force was smashed by the German army and what had been an attempt to hold the German invasion turned into a frantic retreat to the southern beaches. The allied troops were evacuated from beaches on Evia and in the Saronic.

Until recently these northern provinces were little known to outsiders and indeed even Greeks from the southern regions viewed northerners with some suspicion. Today, tourism has opened up the area, especially around Kavala and on Thásos. Yet much of the coast has a solitude and beauty outside high season and most yachtsmen who visit northern Greece come back enchanted by the place.

Weather patterns

Because there is no outstanding weather pattern for the whole region the weather patterns are described in each section.

Routes

Like other parts of the Aegean, the *meltemi* is the prevailing wind in the summer blowing from the NE–E, but because it is not as consistent nor as strong as further S, it is not such a big component in determining routes in northern Greece. The matter is further complicated because a southerly sea breeze usually blows when the *meltemi* is not developed. This means that getting to northern Greece before the *meltemi* is established further S is the real problem and most people aiming to cruise around northern Greece will try to get up here in the late spring or early summer.

Once in the area yachts really can cruise only along a W–E axis from Thessaloniki to Samothrace. Going S after cruising here is comparatively easy whether you are headed back down to the Saronic or down through the eastern Sporades as you will have the *meltemi* behind you. It is worth remembering that the weather closes down quicker here and winter arrives earlier than further S with depressions winging through in the autumn and temperatures dropping at night to mid-European lows.

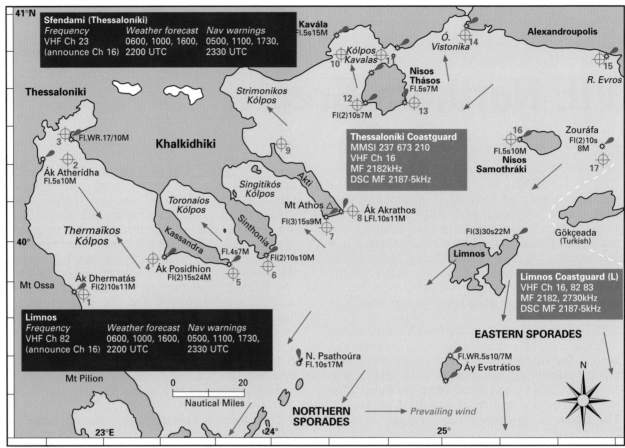

Data

PORTS OF ENTRY
Thessaloniki
Dhafni
Kavála
Alexandroupolis

PROHIBITED AREAS
Off the mouth of the Evros river near the Greek/Turkey
border. (Yet the local fishing boats frequent the area and
sometimes anchor off here whilst fishing.)

MAJOR LIGHTS
Ák Sépia LFl.10s10M
Ák Dhermatás Fl(2)10s11M
Ák Atherídha Fl.5s10M
Thessaloniki (Nisís Kavoúra. Axios) Fl(2)WRG.12s10-8M
Thessaloniki (Yacht Club) Dirlso.WRG.10s19M
Thessaloniki Airport Aero Al.WG.6s13M
Ák Mikró Émvolon Fl(3)G.15s5M
Ák Megálo Émvolon Fl.WR.10s17/10M
Ák Epanomí Fl(3)18s6M
Ák Posidhion (Kassandra) Fl(2)15s24M
Ák Psevdhókavos Fl(2)10s10M
Ák Pínnes Fl(3)15s9M
Ák Ákrathos LFl.10s11M
Nisídhes Stiliária N islet Fl.2·5s6M
Nisís Kavkanás Fl(3)18s7M
Ák Kará Ormán Fl.5s15M
Ák Ammódhis Fl(2)10s7M
Ák Keramotís Fl.WR.4s6/4M
Ák Fanári Fl.8s6M
Alexandroupolis Fl(3)15s24M
Ák Prínos (Thásos) Fl.5s7M
Ák Atspas (Thásos) Fl(2)10s7M
Ák Boumbouras (Thásos) Fl.3s7M
Ák Akrotíri (Samothráki) Fl.5s10M
Nisís Zouráfa (Samothráki) Fl(2)10s8M

USEFUL WAYPOINTS
⊕1 1M E of Ák Dhermatás
    39°47'·9N 22°52'·5E
⊕2 5M W of Ák Epanomí (N end of Thermaikos Kólpos)
    40°22'·5N 22°46'·5E
⊕3 1·5M W of Ák Megálo Émvolon (Fairway entrance to
    Kólpos Thessalonikos)
    40°30'·2N 22°47'·0E
⊕4 1M W of Ák Posidhion (Kassandra)
    39°57'·7N 23°20'·3E
⊕5 1M S of Ák Palioúri
    39°54'·2N 23°45'·0E
⊕6 0·5M S of Ák Psevdhókavos
    39°56'·32N 23°59'·45E WGS84
⊕7 1·5M S of Ák Pínnes
    40°05'·34N 24°18'·16E WGS84
⊕8 0·4M E of Ák Ákrathos
    40°08'·48N 24°24'·52E WGS84
⊕9 1M E of N. Stiliaria – N. Islet
    (Kólpos Ierissou)
    40°27'·4N 24°02'·1E
⊕10 2M E of Ák Vrasidhas (Kólpos Kavalas)
    40°49'·4N 24°23'·1E
⊕11 1M N of Ák Pakhis (Stenón Thasou)
    40°49'·15N 24°39'·12E WGS84
⊕12 0·3M W of Ák Atspas (SW Thásos)
    40°38'·35N 24°30'·25E WGS84
⊕13 1M E of Ák Boumbaras (SE Thásos)
    40°36'·5N 24°47'·9E
⊕14 1M S of Ák Fanári (O. Vistonikos)
    40°56'·5N 25°07'·5E
⊕15 1M S of Alexandroupolis (S mole)
    40°49'·1N 25°53'·9E
⊕16 1M W of Ák Akrotiri (Kamariotissa–Samothráki)
    40°28'·6N 25°25'·3E
⊕17 1M S of Nisís Zouráfa
    40°27'·4N 25°49'·7E

Quick reference guide

	Shelter	Mooring	Fuel	Water	Provisioning	Tavernas	Plan
Ó. Damoukhari	C	C	O	O	O	O	
Áy Íoannis	B	AB	O	B	C	C	•
Khorefto	B	AB	O	O	C	C	
Agrilia	B	B	O	O	O	C	
Ayios Kampos	B	AB	O	B	C	C	
Stómion	B	AB	B	A	B	B	•
Platamonas	B	AB	B	A	B	B	•
Litokhorou	B	AB	B	B	O	C	
Áy Katerini	A	AB	A	A	C	B	
Kitrous	B	C	O	O	O	O	
Ó. Methóni	C	C	O	B	C	C	
N. C. Thessaloníki	A	A	B	A	B	B	
Mikró Émvolon	A	A	B	A	B	B	•
Thessaloniki Marina (Aretsou)	A	A	B	A	A	A	•
Nea Epivates	C	AB	O	O	C	C	
Angelokhori	B	A	B	A	B	C	•
Néa Mikhaniona	B	AB	B	A	C	C	•
Ák Epanomí	O	C	O	O	O	O	
Néa Kallikrátia	B	AB	B	A	B	B	•
Néa Moudhania	A	AB	B	A	A	A	•
Potidhaias (Portas)	C	C	B	B	B	B	•
Porto Sani	A	A	B	A	C	C	
Néa Skioni	B	AB	B	A	C	B	•
Paliourion	O	C	O	B	O	C	
Port Marina	A	AC	O	B	O	C	
Kallithea	O	C	O	O	C	C	
Néa Fokaia	C	C	B	B	B	B	
Yerakini	C	C	O	O	C	C	
Nikitas	B	AB	O	B	C	C	
Néa Marmarás	B	A	B	A	A	A	•
Porto Carras	A	A	B	A	C	B	•
L. Toronis	B	C	O	O	O	C	
Porto Koufó	A	ABC	B	A	B	B	•
Órmos Kalamitsi	C	C	O	O	C	C	
Órmos Sikias	B	AC	O	B	C	C	•
Órmos Sarti	C	A	B	B	C	C	•
Akladhi	B	A	B	A	O	C	•
Nisís Dhiaporos	A	C	C	B	C	C	•
Panayía	B	AC	B	A	B	B	•

	Shelter	Mooring	Fuel	Water	Provisioning	Tavernas	Plan
Pirgadhíkia	C	C	B	B	C	C	
Ammouliani	B	AC	B	B	C	C	•
Ammouliani caïque harbour	B	AC	B	B	C	C	•
Ouranopolis	O	C	B	B	B	B	
Tripiti	C	AC	O	B	C	C	
Dhafni	C	AC	O	B	B	B	
Órmos Platí	B	C	O	O	O	O	•
Néa Rodha	B	AC	B	B	C	C	
Ierissós	B	AC	B	B	B	C	•
Stratonion	C	C	B	B	C	C	
Ó. Olimbiadhos	C	C	B	B	B	C	
N Kavkanás	C	C	O	O	O	O	
Stavrós	B	AC	B	A	B	B	•
Amphipoleos	C	C	O	O	O	O	
Órmos Elevtherón	A	ABC	B	B	B	B	•
Néa Iraklitsa	B	AB	B	A	B	B	•
Kavála	B	A	B	A	A	A	•
Keramotís	B	AB	B	A	B	B	•
Thásos							
Thásos Néa Limaní	A	AB	B	A	A	A	•
Port Thasos	A	A	B	B	A	A	•
Skala Rachoniou	O	A	O	B	C	C	
O. Prinos	C	AC	O	B	B	B	
Skála Sotiros	B	AB	O	B	C	C	•
Kallirakhis	B	A	B	A	B	C	•
Skala Marion	B	AC	O	B	C	C	•
Limenária	B	AC	B	B	A	B	•
Aliki	B	C	O	B	C	C	•
O. Potamias	C	C	O	O	O	O	
Mainland coast							
Port Lágos	A	AB	B	A	B	C	•
Fanarion	A	AB	B	B	C	C	•
Áy Kharalambos	A	AB	O	B	O	C	
Mákri	A	AB	O	B	O	C	
Alexandroupolis	A	AB	B	A	A	B	•
Samothráki							
Kamariótissa	A	AB	B	A	B	B	•
Therma	C	A	B	B	C	C	

Thermaïkos Kólpos and Thessaloníki

Thermaïkos Kólpos, the Gulf of Thermai, is enclosed by the northern Sporades in the south, by the high mountain range beginning at the Pilion range and extending north to towering Mt Olympus on the west, and by the relatively low-lying Kassandra Peninsula on the east. The gulf terminates in the small Kólpos Thessaloníkis in the north.

The dominating feature of the gulf is without doubt the massive mountain range on the west side stretching from Thessaly to Macedonia. In the south Mt Pilion at 1,545m (5,079ft) is the highest of the Pilion range. Thirty miles further north the first peak of the Olympus range, Mt Ossa (Kissavos), climbs to 1,978m (6,489ft). To the northwest of Mt Ossa the towering peaks of the Olympus Range proper begin: Mt Kato Olimbos (Low Olympus) at

1,587m (5,205ft) stands to the south of Pano Olimbos (High Olympus), the massif being topped by Mítikas (the needle) at 2,911m (9,550ft) and Stefani (the Throne of Zeus) at 2,909m (9,545ft). Surrounding the highest peak are nine other peaks standing over 2,680m (8,800ft). The range is the highest in Greece and peaks are covered in snow from autumn through to late spring.

Although there are other mountain ranges in Greece, also called Olympus, this is the one famous for its association with the gods. Here Zeus ruled and the gods dined, played, drank and argued in what the mortals down below believed was the ultimate in the good life. The first recorded ascent of Mítikas by mortals was as late as 1910 and the range was not properly mapped until 1921. Today the ascent is described as arduous rather than difficult and in fact the major part can be made by four-wheel drive and donkeys.

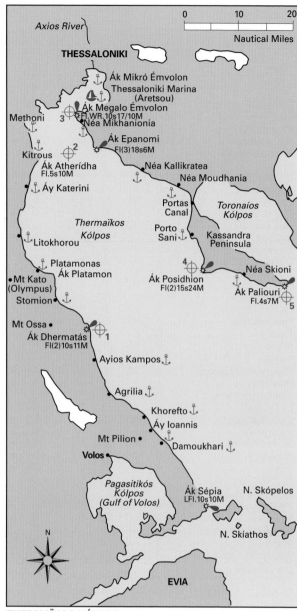

THERMAÏKOS KÓLPOS

⊕1   1M E of Ák Dhermatás 39°47'·9N 22°52'·5E
⊕2   5M W of Ák Epanomi (N end of Thermaïkos Kolpos)
      40°22'·5N 22°46'·5E
⊕3   1·5M W of Ák Megálo Émvolon (Fairway entrance to Kólpos
      Thessalonikos) 40°30'·2N 22°47'·0E
⊕4   1M W of Ák Posidhion (Kassandra) 39°57'·7N 23°20'·3E
⊕5   1M S of Ák Palioúri 39°54'·2N 23°45'·0E

Weather patterns in Thermaïkos Kólpos

In the summer months the *meltemi* blows in the gulf from the NE, but not with any consistency. In the S of the gulf it is more regular, normally blowing Force 3–5 although it may blow Force 6–7 on occasions, raising a short steep sea. Although the *meltemi* is not a regular occurrence in the N of the gulf, when it does blow it can be with considerable strength and it has on occasions reached Force 8.

The regular wind in the N half of the gulf, and in the S if the *meltemi* is not blowing, is from the

W–SW. This sea breeze gets up about mid-morning, blows Force 2–4, and dies down at night. A light northerly may blow at night.

In the spring and autumn the wind is predominantly from the N although S winds may also occur. In the winter, spring and the autumn a NW wind, locally called the *vardaris* and similar to the *mistral* that blows down the Rhône, may blow down the Axios river at Force 6–8 and can last from a day to a week.

Current

In March and April a strong current is reported to set out of the gulf, owing to the melting of snow in the mountains increasing the flow of fresh water into the sea.

ORMOS DAMOUKHARI

39°24'·4N 23°10'·8E

A small bay some 15M N of Ák Sepia. A rough stone breakwater provides shelter from the *meltemi*. Care needed in the approaches of off-lying rocky shoals to the N and S of the entrance. Approach on a WSW course into the bay. Anchor in 2–5m, taking care of rocks and a submerged platform towards the head of the bay.

ÁYIOS ÍOANNIS

A small harbour set into a bight on the coast. A dogleg mole shelters the harbour with the entrance on the S side. The entrance is lit Fl.G.3s3M. There are 3–4m depths in the entrance and 3–5m depths on the outer end of the quay along the mole. The harbour is very small and usually full of local boats, so do not rely on finding a berth here.

Provisions and tavernas ashore.

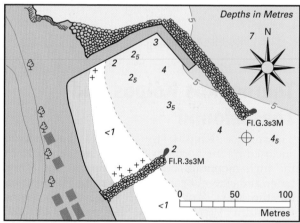

AYIOS IOANNIS
⊕39°25'·3N 23°09'·7E

KHOREFTO (Zagora)

39°26'·9N 23°08'·1E

A small fishing harbour 2M N of Áy Ioannis lying at the end of the long beach to the N. The dogleg mole provides some shelter from the *meltemi*, although with strong winds waves break over the mole. Depths of 5–6m in the entrance and 2–5m off the outer end of the quay along the mole. Poor holding on hard sand and rock.

Tavernas along the beach.

AGRILIA (Kamari)

39°34'·8N 22°55'·1E

A small harbour with two breakwaters extending out from the steep-to coast. The N longer breakwater is approximately 100m long. There are reported to be 5–6m depths in the entrance and 2–3m depths along the quay on the N breakwater. Go alongside where possible. The inner part of the harbour off the coast is shallow and rocky. Adequate protection although strong NE–E winds cause a surge.

Taverna ashore.

AYIOS KAMPOS

39°41'·1N 22°53'·5E

Midway between Agrilia and Ák Dhermatas is the two–harbour port of Ayios Kampos. The small harbour on the N side of the headland has excellent shelter but is mostly shallow and in any case full of local boats. The S harbour has greater depths, 4m in the entrance and 2–5m along the inside of the breakwater. Care is needed of rocks around the end of the breakwater and on the N and W side of the harbour. Water near the quay in the N harbour.

Some provisions and tavernas ashore.

STÓMION

A small harbour lying approximately 7M NW of Ák Dhermatás. The outer breakwater is easily identified. The entrance is lit Fl.G.2s3M/Fl.R.2s3M. There is also a light a little further NW at Stómion Fl.3s5M.

Go alongside or stern or bows-to under the breakwater. Good shelter. The harbour is a busy fishing port but small yachts can usually find a berth.

Water nearby. Provisions and tavernas ashore.

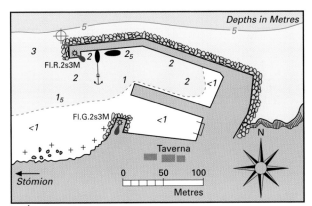

STÓMION
⊕39°51'·1N 22°44'·1E

PLATAMONAS

A small harbour off the town of Platamonas. The castle to the NW is conspicuous and closer in the buildings on the town are easily identified. The entrance is lit Fl.R.3s3M/Fl.G.3s3M. Go alongside

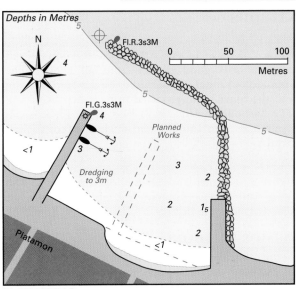

PLATAMONAS
⊕39°59'·6N 22°37'·6E

or stern or bows-to the outer end of the W mole. It is reported that the harbour is being dredged, and there are plans to complete the S quay and to add a concrete pier running parallel to the W mole. Good shelter.

Water nearby. Provisions and tavernas ashore.

LITOKHOROU

40°09'·4N 22°33'·1E

A small fishing harbour with a narrow and tricky entrance. Shoal water extends from the W side of the entrance and with fresh to strong onshore winds the entrance could be dangerous. The entrance is lit Fl.R.3s3M/Fl.G.3s3M. The shoals on the W side of the entrance may occasionally have a small buoy marking them. Stay close to the outer breakwater in the entrance before turning into the mole which forms one side of the retaining wall for the canalised creek that runs into the sea at the entrance. The entrance silts and is dredged periodically.

Go stern or bows-to the mole or anchor and take a long line to the breakwater. Most berths are occupied by small local craft. Good shelter.

Fuel on the main coast road running past the harbour. Taverna and café nearby.

ÁYIOS KATERINI

40°15'·7N 22°35'·9E

A small fishing harbour. Care is needed in the entrance of the shoal water off the outer end of the N breakwater. The entrance is lit Fl.R.3s3M/Fl.G.3s3M. Anchor and take a line to the E breakwater. Reasonable shelter although northerlies look as though they would blow straight in. The inner basin is very small and full of local boats. The basin silts and is dredged periodically. The basin silts and is dredged periodically.

Water on the quay. Fuel on the quay. Provisions and tavernas ashore.

KITROUS

40°22'·8N 22°38'·0E

Lying 1¾ NW of Ák Atherídha, this small-craft basin affords good shelter from all winds. The approach channel is reported to be dredged to 1·8m and the inner basin reported to have depths of 5m. The harbour entrance is lit Fl.R.3s3M/Fl.G.3s3M. Approach from the NE and anchor in convenient depths.

NOTE

Between Kitrous and Ormos Methoni large fish farms run in a continuous line up the coast. The seaward sides are lit Fl.Y.

ÓRMOS METHONI

Lying 6½ miles NW of Ák Atherídha is the open bay of Methóni which is used by fishing boats. Anchor in the SW corner. Care is needed as shallows run a considerable distance out from the coast. Tavernas ashore.

Thessaloníki

(Salonika)

BA 2070

The large built-up city is visible from a considerable distance off. Large cargo ships anchored in the bay and the commercial docks are conspicuous. A yacht should head for the yacht marina at Aretsou on the S side of Ák Mikró Émvolon.

NAUTICAL CLUB OF THESSALONÍKI

40°35'·4N 22°56'·5E

Note The club should be contacted in advance for a berth.

A private club harbour on the N side of Ák Mikró Émvolon. Care is needed in the approaches because of shoal water and rocks off the coast. Make the approach from the NW and then through the narrow entrance channel between the end of the breakwater and a beacon. There are 1–2·5m depths inside. Berth where directed.

The yacht club has a wonderful and quite exclusive clubhouse and restaurant overlooking the bay. There is also a small yard here where some yacht repairs can be arranged.

Nautical Club of Thessaloníki ☎ 2310 414 521.

MIKRÓ ÉMVOLON YACHT HARBOUR

Approach

Directly under Ák Mikró Émvolon is a yacht harbour (formerly a fishing harbour) that appears to offer good shelter. The harbour is difficult to spot from the distance as the outer breakwater is covered in grass and blends in with the slopes behind. A small white chapel on the end of the inner breakwater will be seen when closer in.

By night The end of the outer breakwater is lit F.R.

Mooring

Note The harbour is private and it is best to enquire for a berth in advance.

Berth Where directed. Catwalks run out from around the outer breakwater. Two pontoons extend out from the shore. Some laid moorings.

Shelter Excellent shelter.

Authorities Harbourmaster ☎ 2310 414 493/454 111.

Facilities

Services Water and electricity at or near most berths.
Fuel Can be delivered by mini-tanker.
Repairs Some yacht repairs can be arranged.
Provisions Good shopping in Aretsou suburb above.
Eating out Tavernas ashore and above in Aretsou.

THESSALONIKI
⊕40°35'·2N 22°55'·2E

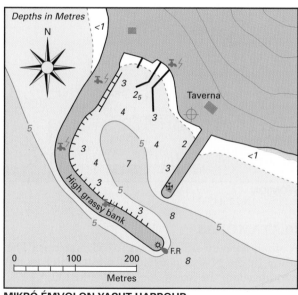

MIKRÓ ÉMVOLON YACHT HARBOUR
⊕40°34'·86N 22°56'·29E WGS84

Yacht harbour under Ák Mikró Émvolon and just W of Aretsou marina

General

You get the feeling that this harbour has an ancient pedigree somewhere under those grassy banks, but there seems little consensus on what it is amongst the locals, apart from: 'it is very old'.

THESSALONÍKI MARINA (Aretsou)

Approach

A church on the hill and a radio mast behind the marina are conspicuous. Closer in, the outer

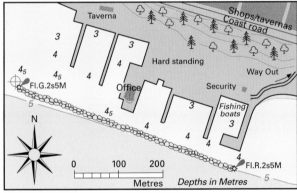

THESSALONIKI MARINA (ARETSOU)
⊕40°34′·6N 22°56′·5E

breakwater and the yachts in the marina can be easily seen.

By night Use the lights on Ák Megálo Émvolon Fl.WR.10s17/10M (red sector covers 335°-025°), Ák Mikró Émvolon Fl(3)G.15s5M and at the entrance to the marina Fl.G.2s5M/Fl.R.2s5M. The radio mast behind the marina is lit with F.R lights.

VHF Ch 09 for marina office.

Dangers With the *meltemi* blowing there are strong gusts into Órmos Thessaloníkis.

Mooring

Data 300 berths. Visitors' berths. Max LOA 30m. Depths 3–5m.

A marina attendant will direct you to a berth or go alongside the central jetty off the office to be allocated one. Moorings are laid and you pick up one of the small plastic buoys floating on the surface.

Shelter Excellent all-round shelter although W–SW winds cause an uncomfortable slop at some berths. Yachts are wintered afloat in the marina.

Authorities Port police and marina staff at the marina. Charge band 2.

Facilities

Services Water and electricity on the quay. Showers and toilets.

Fuel On the quay.

Repairs A crane can be arranged to haul yachts out onto the hard by the marina. Most mechanical repairs. Electrical repairs. Chandlers near marina entrance. More chandlers and hardware shops in the city.

Provisions Most provisions can be found in the vicinity of the marina. Better shopping in the nearby suburbs. Ice can be ordered.

Eating out Taverna in the marina and others up on the main road above.

Other PO and OTE in the city. Banks. ATMs. Greek gas and Camping Gaz. A gas filling station on the outskirts of the city. Hire cars and motorbikes. A regular bus runs every 15 minutes from just above the marina into the city. Buses to Kavala and Athens. Ferries to Limnos, Lésvos and Khíos.

Thessaloníki Marina looking SE towards the W entrance

Internal flights. Flights to some European countries.

General

Thessaloníki, or Salonika as it is still known to many, is the second largest city in Greece. Although it has an ancient pedigree, the modern office buildings and apartment blocks radiating from the centre effectively shroud this past. I must confess to an instant dislike of Thessaloníki – it is a noisy industrial city where the industry has covered the waters of the bay in a black oily scum and poisoned the fish. As in Athens it is wise in any fish restaurant to enquire as to whether the fish is local. If it is don't touch it.

The marina is sited outside the badly polluted bay in the green and wooded suburb of Aretsou. In the city the Archaeological Museum houses important finds from Neolithic to Byzantine times from all over northern Greece.

Note It is likely the marina will be privatised in the near future (as in other parts of Greece) and that things will change here.

NEA EPIVATES

40°30'·5N 22°54'·4E

A T–shaped mole off the S shore of Thessalonikos Kolpos is full of local boats. The only place you may find to berth is on the N side of the 'T' with shelter only from S winds. Berth where convenient in 2–1·5m.

Market and taverna ashore.

ANGELOKHORI

A busy fishing harbour just 600m S of Ák Megálo Émvolon. Care needed in the shallow waters of Vr. Vespanianos around the cape. Make the approach on a NNE course, keeping a close eye on the depth sounder. Depths in the entrance 4m, and inside mostly 2–3m. Berth where possible, taking care not to obstruct a fishing boat berth. Good all-round shelter. Water on the quay.

Tavernas ashore. Provisions in the village 20 minutes' walk away.

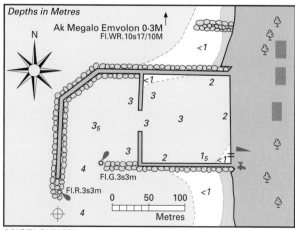

ANGELOKHORI
⊕40°29'·8N 22°48'·9E

NÉA MIKHANIÓNA (Kerasia)

Approach

A fishing harbour in the large bay under Ák Megálo Émvolon.

By night The entrance is lit F.G.3M/F.R.3M.

Mooring

Go stern or bows-to the quay in the S corner. Alternatively you may have to find a berth alongside a fishing boat.

Shelter Reasonable shelter although northerlies would probably cause some slop.

Facilities

Water on the quay. Fuel on the outskirts of the village. Provisions and tavernas.

Note A short distance S of the harbour is a yard which hauls yachts.

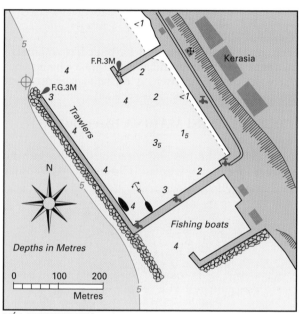

NÉA MIKHANIONA
⊕40°28'·3N 22°50'·8E

ÁKRA EPANOMÍ

Ák Epanomí light 40°22'·5N 22°53'·5E

The termination of a low-lying neck of land approximately 8½ miles SE of Ák Megálo Émvolon. The cape is marked by a light structure Fl(3)18s6M and a light buoy Fl.G at the outer end of the shoals extending from the cape. Anchor on either side of the cape according to the wind direction. Open to the W. On the N side of the cape is a small fishing harbour. The entrance is reported to have depths of 2m, but it is subject to silting and is dredged infrequently. There are also many fish farms on both sides of Ák Epanomi and care is needed in the vicinity, particularly at night.

NÉA KALLIKRÁTIA

Approach

The small resort town of Néa Kallikrátia lies approximately 10M SE of Ák Epanomí. The harbour sits under a cliff close NW of the village.

Néa Kallikrátia looking S

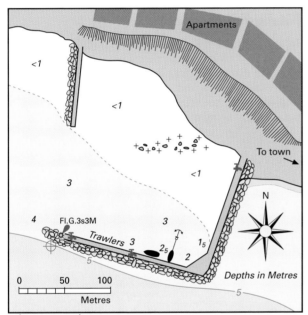

NÉA KALLIKRÁTIA
⊕40°18′·55N 23°03′·49E WGS84

The apartment blocks on top of the cliff are conspicuous.

By night The end of the mole is lit Fl.G.3s3M.

Dangers Although the immediate approaches are free of dangers, the inner half of the harbour is shallow and also has the remains of an old mole underwater. Care needed.

Mooring
The harbour is usually full of fishing boats. Try in the SE corner or see if you can go alongside a fishing boat.

Shelter Reasonable shelter although strong westerlies could make it uncomfortable and possibly untenable.

Facilities
Water on the quay. Fuel on the road running out of town. Provisions and tavernas in the village.

General
Néa Kallikrátia is predominantly a Greek resort which for some reason has also attracted the Russians looking for some sun. It is something of a pour-and-fill sort of place, but the fishing harbour is tucked away from the beach and the bodies.

NÉA MOUDHANIA
Approach
A village lying approximately 3M NW of the Portas Canal. Red cliffs along the coast to the S are conspicuous. The buildings of the town are easily identified and the harbour is situated in front of it. A church and cupola are conspicuous in the town. There is often a cargo ship or two unloading here which helps to identify where the harbour is.

By night The outer entrance is lit Fl.R.3s5M/Fl.G.3s3M and the entrance to the inner basin Fl.R.3s3M/Fl.G.3s3M. Although the characteristics are the same for the entrance and inner basin, a little care in the approach should sort out what is where.

Mooring
The quay in the outer port is for commercial ships. Proceed into the basin and try to find a berth in the NW corner or on the E mole.

Shelter Good all-round shelter.

Authorities Port police and customs.

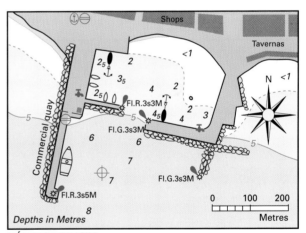

NÉA MOUDHANIA
⊕40°14′·20N 23°16′·63E WGS84

Néa Moudhania looking SW into the inner basin

357

Facilities

Water on the quay. Good shopping for provisions in town. Tavernas and cafés including a good internet café near the waterfront. PO. OTE. Banks. ATM. Bus to Thessaloníki.

General

Néa Moudhania is more of a working town than a resort and all the more pleasing for that. It serves as a hub for the Kassandra Peninsula and the agricultural interior. The waterfront is a busy place, busy with commerce rather than tourism, and in the harbour you are pretty well in the middle of town.

Khalkidhiki

(Halkidiki, Chalcidice)

The Khalkidhiki peninsula (Khalkidhiki Khersónisos) is the most prominent geographical feature of Macedonia. It is like a hand reaching down into the northern Aegean with three small peninsulas forming the fingers: Kassandra, Sinthonia, and Akti or Mt Athos. On the west side the Khalkidhiki is low-lying, with the highest point on the Kassandra peninsula rising to a miserly 353m (1,158ft). The rest of the Khalkidhiki is mountainous, with Mt Athos rising sheer from the sea to 2,033m (6,670ft) at the southern end of the Akti peninsula. The countryside is densely wooded – mostly with pine, but also with olive, hazel, oak and poplar. In many places the pine and poplar

grow down to the water's edge and shade what are, in my opinion, the finest sandy beaches in Greece.

The Khalkidhiki received its name from the colonies established there from Khalkís in Evia around 800 BC. The most important city to emerge from the colonisation was Olynthos, situated at the head of Toronaíos Kólpos (also called Kólpos Kassandras and the Gulf of Sinthonia). It reached its zenith in the fifth and fourth centuries BC. In 480BC Xerxes gathered his troops and ships here for the assault on Thessaly and Attica. Prior to this he had a canal cut across the narrow neck of land connecting the Akti peninsula to the rest of the Khalkidhiki to avoid the terrible storms encountered around Mt Athos. A few earth scars are all that remain of the canal-cut today.

Weather patterns around the Khalkidhiki

In the summer the *meltemi* blows with considerably less force than it does further south. Normally it will blow from the NE–E at Force 2–4, but often it does not blow for days and even weeks on end. In spring and early summer there will often be SE winds but these rarely blow more than Force 3–4.

⊕3 1·5M W of Ák Megálo Émvolon(Fairway entrance to Kólpos Thessalonikos) 40°30'·2N 22°47'·0E
⊕4 1M W of Ák Posidhion (Kassandra) 39°57'·7N 23°20'·3E
⊕5 1M S of Ák Palioúri 39°54'·2N 23°45'·0E
⊕6 0·5M S of Ák Psevdhókavos 39°56'·32N 23°59'·45E WGS84
⊕7 1·5M S of Ák Pínnes 40°05'·34N 24°18'·16E WGS84
⊕8 0·4M E of Ák Ákrathos 40°08'·48N 24°24'·52E WGS84
⊕9 1M E of N. Stiliaria – N. Islet (Kólpos Ierissou) 40°27'·4N 24°02'·1E

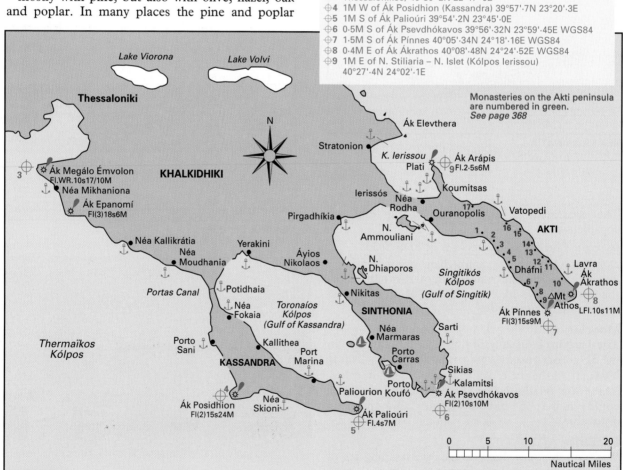

KHALKIDHIKI

The Akti Peninsula
(Khersónisos Akti, Áyios Oros)

This rugged peninsula has for over 10 centuries existed as a world unto itself. Divorced from the modern world, the holy community has no roads or electricity and few telephones. The medieval monasteries occupy spectacular sites on rocky bluffs and precipitous cliffsides and have been likened to Tibetan monasteries such as the Potala of Lhasa. Time is still reckoned by the Julian calendar (13 days behind the Roman calendar) and the day is ruled by the Byzantine clock with hours of variable length.

Females are not allowed to set foot in the monasteries and a yacht with women on board is not allowed to approach closer than 1M from the shores of the peninsula. In former times the rule was stricter, formulated by Constantine Monomachus in 1060: access was denied to 'every woman, every female animal, every child, and smooth-faced person'. Although officially the rule is still in force, female animals can now be found in the community and visitors do not have to be bearded.

Pressure is mounting within the European Parliament and other Western bodies for a lifting of the ban on women visitors. The only woman to have set foot on Mount Athos is Oriana Fallaci, the Italian author and journalist, who smuggled herself onto the peninsula.

The monasteries are divided into coenobite and idiorrhythmic communities. Coenobite monasteries are communal and the members are clothed alike and live from a common pool of resources. In the idiorrhythmic monasteries the members live apart and provide the clothes and food from their own resources. As well as 20 monasteries there are hermits (*Anchorites*) who live by themselves in what often seem to be inaccessible cells (particularly on the southern slopes of Mt Athos), the hermitage of two or three hermits (*Sarabaites*) and vagabond monks (*Gyrovakes*).

Although the peninsula is geographically and politically a part of Greece, it has administrative autonomy which includes financial and judicial authority. Monks of any race are accepted (apart from Greeks, the community includes Russians, Bulgarians, Serbs and Romanians) and on entering the holy community they become Greek subjects.

Without doubt the best way to see the Akti peninsula is from the sea. The medieval monasteries clinging to the cliffs at the edge of the wild interior (jackals are reported to be common) belong to a world that was bypassed by our modern age a long time ago. To visit the interior it is easiest to go on a conducted tour, although a more sedate visit to a single monastery captures more of the spirit of the place and is more convenient for a yacht on this desolate shore.

Permits are issued by the Grafio Proskyniton Ayiou Orous, the Pilgrims Office for Mount Athos, on the First Floor, Konstandinou Karamanli 14, Thessaloníki. ☎ 2310 833 733 *Fax* 2310 861 811. You must take your passport although you can fax for a permit if you fax the relevant pages of your passport to them. Given the small number of permits (10 per day in 2000) issued to heterodox foreigners, you are unlikely to get a permit around the time of the application and will probably just have to wait for a date to come up. Once you have your permit go to the Grafio Proskyniton (Pilgrims Bureau) at Ouranopolis for the Dhiamonitirion (a fee, typically 30 Euros, is charged) which entitles you to stay for four days on the Akti Peninsula. Many of the monasteries are often booked in advance so do not depend on staying in your chosen monastery, especially in high season. It is important to remember at all times that you are a guest here and for Greek Orthodox believers, this is the Holy Mountain.

A permit is not necessary to sail around the peninsula, but of course you cannot land. Ierissos is the safest place to leave a yacht if taking the local ferry to the community.

With strong winds from any direction, caution must be exercised in the vicinity of the Akti peninsula where there will be strong gusts off the high mountains. Around Mt Athos particular care must be taken as the gusts can be violent and the seas disturbed around Ák Pínnes and Ák Akrathos, although Xerxes was being over-cautious digging a canal to get his ships safely into Singitikos Kólpos.

PORTAS CANAL (Dhiórix Neas Potidhaias)

This shallow canal cuts the Kassandra peninsula off from the mainland. It is over ½ mile long and has a minimum width of 36m. A bridge spans the canal with a vertical clearance of 16m. The canal is dredged to 2·5m minimum depth, but is subject to silting particularly at the W entrance and at the edges. The W entrance is lit: Fl.R.2s3M/Fl.G.2s3M. The E entrance is lit: Fl.G.2s3M/Fl.R.2s3M.

At the W end there is a short quay usually occupied by local fishing boats and a small basin too shallow for most craft. At the E end there is a small basin in the N side of the canal where a small yacht might find a berth. It is shallow around the edges. The village of Portas or Potidhaia is on the S side of the canal. You can anchor off the E end of the canal where there are convenient depths and, at least in the morning, it is usually calm. Fuel station nearby. Provisions and tavernas.

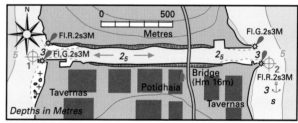

PORTAS CANAL
⊕1 40°11'·77N 23°19'·30E WGS84
⊕2 40°11'·81N 23°20'·08E WGS84

Portas Canal looking W from the bridge

PORTO SANI

40°05'·5N 23°18'·4E

At the Hotel Porto Sani on the W side of the Kassandra Peninsula, a small basin has been excavated with a dredged channel to it. The channel is reported to have 1·5m depths and the basin 1–1·5m depths. Good shelter inside. With any sort of onshore wind it would be unwise to enter and even small yachts are advised to reconnoitre beforehand.

Water on the docks. Provisions and tavernas ashore.

NÉA SKIONI

A fishing harbour lying approximately halfway between Ák Posidhion and Ák Palioúri on the SW coast of the Kassandra Peninsula. The approach is clear of dangers. Go stern or bows-to the stubby pier running out from the mole wherever there is a berth. The harbour is usually full of fishing boats and you may have to negotiate a berth alongside a fishing boat. Reasonable shelter although westerlies and southerlies would make it uncomfortable and possibly untenable at some berths.

Water on the quay. Fuel nearby in town. Provisions and tavernas ashore.

Néa Skioni is a modest resort with the fishing fleet to back it up when the tourists go home. The setting is wonderful although you can't help feeling that you walk into a different, less fishy, world when you leave the end of the harbour mole to go into town.

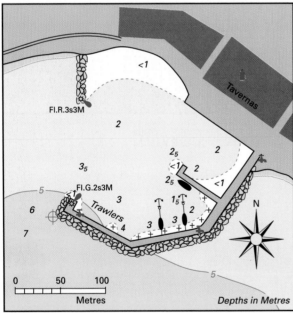

NÉA SKIONI
⊕39°56'·79N 23°31'·62E WGS84

Toronaiós Kólpos

(Gulf of Kassandra)

PALIOURION (Kannavitsa Bay)

N corner 39°57'·85N 23°40'·50E WGS84

An open anchorage NW of Ák Palioúri. Anchor in the N corner off the camping ground where there is a beach bar off the hotel. There is a pier in the S corner with 2·5m depths reported off the end. You should be ready to move out with any sort of onshore breeze. The large hotel on the beach has an abandoned look to it. Open to all sectors E. Anchor at the head of the bay off a pier which is reported to have 2·5m depths at its extremity. Fuel in the town and some provisions available.

PORT MARINA

A lagoon with a narrow and treacherous approach channel. The channel has 1·5–1·8m depths although the channel and the depths change with winter storms. There are rocks extending seawards either side of the channel. The best thing to do here is take a dinghy to reconnoitre the channel. In any sort of onshore breeze the channel should not be attempted. Once into the lagoon there are 1·5–3m

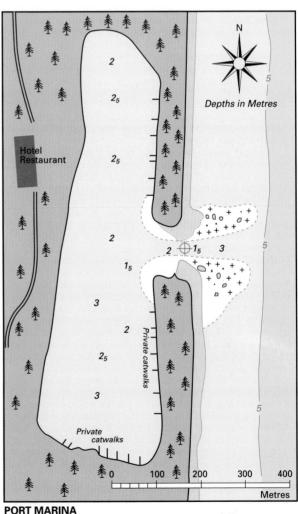

PORT MARINA
⊕39°59'·02N 23°39'·96E WGS84

depths between the entrance channel and the catwalks around the eastern side. Anchor and take a long line ashore or see if you can use one of the catwalks around the lagoon. A number of yachts are kept here permanently. All-round shelter.

Hotel, taverna and bar on the main road behind the lagoon. The large lagoon is wonderful, with sandy beaches along the coastal flat and mature pines all around. There are usually only a few local tourists and they all depart at night. I assume the place is called Port Marina because it will eventually become so.

KALLITHEA

A small resort. You can anchor off in calm weather. PO. Bank. Provisions and tavernas.

NÉA FOKAIA

40°08'·1N 23°24'·2E

A small resort about 8 miles SE of Portas Canal. A square stone tower on the bluff above the bight is conspicuous. Local fishing boats are kept on moorings in the bight on the N side of the bluff with the tower. There is a short jetty off the village. Provisions and tavernas ashore.

The setting is attractive although it is a pity about some of the new non-architecture ashore.

YERAKINI

40°16'·1N 23°26'·6E

Open anchorage at the head of Toronaios Kólpos off the beach resort of Skala Yerakinis. Anchor in 4–8m off the beach. The small jetty at the head of the bay is not really suitable for mooring. Care

needed of a small rocky patch some 450m S of the jetty, with 1–1·5m depths over. Otherwise the bottom is sand and weed, good holding. Reasonable shelter from the prevailing wind.

Taverna and provisions ashore.

NIKITAS

40°13'·1N 23°39'·9E

A small resort under steep slopes on the E side of the gulf. There is a small fishing harbour here with 2–4m depths reported under the mole, but it is usually crowded with local boats. See if you can get a berth in the harbour or anchor off.

Provisions and tavernas ashore.

NÉA MARMARÁS

Approach

The harbour lies under the S side of Ák Néa Marmarás. The buildings of the town 3 miles NE of Nisís Kelifos (Khelona Island) are easily identified. A church on the waterfront is conspicuous.

By night The entrance is lit: by a Fl.R.1·5s3M and a Q.R on the end of the wave-breaker pontoon.

Dangers The wave-breaker pontoon is very low in the water and difficult to distinguish until close to.

Mooring

Go stern or bows-to where directed or on a convenient berth on one of the pontoons. There are laid moorings tailed to a buoy to pick up. It is very tight for manoeuvring around and between the pontoons and you will need to take care to avoid the other yachts and moorings.

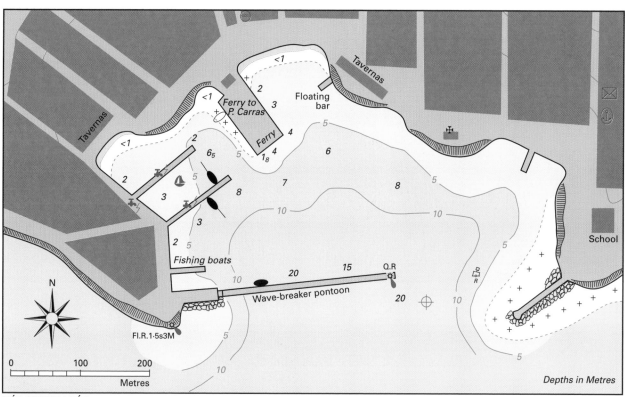

NÉA MARMARÁS
⊕40°05'·46N 23°47'·03E WGS84

Néa Marmaras looking SE from above the yacht pontoons

Shelter Good shelter although the sea breeze that often blows up the gulf can make it a bit rolly in here despite the wave-breaker pontoon. The breeze dies down at night so you get a good night's sleep. There is also some surge with W–NW winds.

Authorities Port police. Harbour attendant. Charge band 2.

Facilities
Services Water and electricity on the pontoons.
Fuel A mini-tanker can deliver to the quay.
Repairs Limited repairs only.

Provisions Good shopping for all provisions.
Eating out Good tavernas including good fish restaurants around the waterfront.
Other PO. OTE. Bank. ATM. Greek gas and Camping Gaz. Hire cars and motorbikes. Bus to Thessaloníki. Hydrofoil to the Northern Sporades.

General
There was probably a settlement here in ancient times pre-dating the Byzantine settlement that no doubt made use of the natural harbour. Greeks from Turkey were resettled here in 1922 in one of the exchanges of populations and the new village was christened Néa Marmarás. It has developed into a large resort town and the original village around the natural harbour now climbs up and over the steep-to hummock behind the harbour. It is a pleasing spot, the sort of place where you take an evening promenade along the waterfront to view the bar or restaurant for the night, nod politely to the locals and ponder whether you will or won't leave on the morrow.

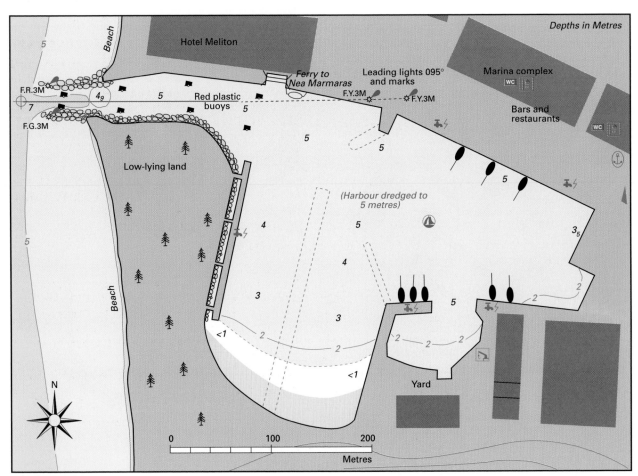

PORTO CARRAS
⊕40°04´·58N 23°47´·34E WGS84

PORTO CARRAS MARINA (Porto Karra)

Approach

Conspicuous From the N and W the two hyper-hotels and the buildings of the marina complex can be easily distinguished from the town of Néa Marmara. From the S only the town of Néa Marmara will be seen until you are into the bay.

By night The entrance is lit: F.R.3M/F.G.3M. There are leading lights through the entrance on 095°: front F.Y.3M and rear F.Y.3M.

VHF Ch 09 for marina office.

Dangers With strong NW–W–SW winds there is a disturbed swell at the entrance but it is quiet inside.

Note
1. The entrance channel is usually marked by 4 pairs of small red plastic buoys which are not lit.
2. Small ferryboats enter and leave the channel at speed, running to and from Nea Marmaras.

Mooring

Data 200 berths. Visitors' berths. Max LOA 45m. Depths 4–5m.

Go stern or bows-to where directed. There are laid moorings tailed to the quay or a buoy. Do not use your own anchor.

Shelter Good all-round shelter.

Authorities Harbourmaster and marina staff. Charge band 3.

Note
1. The harbour is mostly dredged to a least depth of 5m.
2. In the future it is planned to build a mini-breakwater on the N side and install pontoons where shown to increase the capacity of the marina.

Facilities

Services Water. Electricity (220V). Showers and toilets. Laundry service.

Fuel A mini-tanker can deliver.

Repairs It is planned to install a 50-ton travel-hoist. There will be hardstanding for around 35 yachts.

Porto Carras Marina looking SE　　*Photo Porto Carras*

Covered workshops. Some yacht repairs can be carried out including mechanical and engineering repairs.

Provisions Limited. Go to Néa Marmara.

Eating out Several restaurants and tavernas around the harbour.

Other PO. Exchange at the hotel. Bank in Néa Marmara. Medical centre. Golf course. Tennis. Horse riding centre. Telephone and fax service. Hire cars and bikes. Taxis. *Caïque* ferry to Néa Marmara.

Costas Livadiotis, Porto Carras, Sithonia 63081, Khalkidhiki, Greece
☎ 23750 71381 *Fax* 23750 72126
Email info@portocarras.com
www.portocarras.com

General

Porto Carras marina was developed along the lines of the Languedoc–Roussillon marinas in the S of France by the Greek shipping magnate John Carras – hence the name. As well as two hyper-hotels, the marina complex houses squash and tennis courts, a swimming pool, theatre, conference centre, casino, restaurants, bars and an array of boutiques and other shops.

When Porto Carras was built, a model farm was developed nearby and improved wine-making facilities were imported. The wines produced here with improved techniques are now excellent and the reds and whites bottled under the appellation Porto Carras Domaine are well worth sampling.

UNNAMED COVES S OF PORTO CARRAS

Less than a mile S of Porto Carras are two small coves with sandy beaches at the head. Open only to the W, they offer sufficient protection for an overnight stay in the summer. The more southerly of the two has a short quay where a small yacht can moor stern-to.

LIMÍN TORONIS

Limín Toronis is an inlet at the head of Órmos Toronis, the bay on the S side of Ák Papadhia. Good shelter from northerlies in the bay which is open only S.

PÓRTO KOUFÓ

Approach

Conspicuous From the distance the entrance to the landlocked bay is difficult to make out. A white hut on Ák Laimos (½ mile S of Ák Pagona) and Peristeronisi are conspicuous and closer in the red cliff to the W of the entrance and the houses on the E side of the bay can be seen.

By night Use the lights on Ák Pagona Fl.G.3s5M and Ák Spiliá Fl.R.3s4M. Care needed. The lights on Ák Pagona and Ák Spilia are not to be relied on.

Dangers With strong offshore winds there are severe gusts off the high land in the approaches to Porto Koufó.

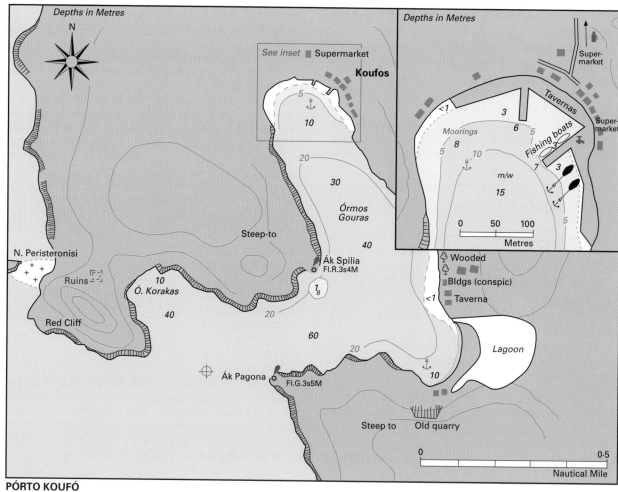

PÓRTO KOUFÓ
⊕39°57´·51N 23°54´·81E WGS 84

Mooring

A berth may be negotiated on either of the piers, or on the quay, but it can be smelly here in the summer. Anchor in 10–15m outside the permanent moorings in the N of the bay. In southerlies the S of the bay provides better shelter. The bottom is mud and weed – good holding once the anchor is through the weed.

Shelter Good shelter although there can be violent gusts with strong S winds.

Facilities

Water On the pier, though it is reported not to be potable.

Fuel On the road out to Néa Marmara. A mini-tanker can deliver.

Provisions Supermarket near the quay and another on the road out of town. Ice available.

Eating out Tavernas ashore, several with good fresh fish.

Pórto Koufó looking SSW towards the entrance   *Nigel Patten*

Porto Koufó looking NE along the quay   *Lu Michell*

Other Metered telephone. Greek gas and Camping Gaz. Bus to Néa Marmarás and Thessaloníki.

General

Porto Koufó must be one of the most magnificent natural harbours in the Mediterranean. Sheer red cliffs at the entrance open up to the large landlocked bay bordered by poplars and cultivated fields. What was a small fishing hamlet now caters for a few tourists in the summer. In the winter the harbour is a base for tunny fishing boats working around the Khalkidhiki.

Singitikós Kólpos

ÓRMOS KALAMITSI (Porto)

39°59'·0N 24°00'·0E

Two miles N of Ák Psevdhókavos is a bay with a number of above-water rocks in the entrance. In the southernmost cove a number of boats are kept on laid moorings in the summer. Anchor just clear of the moorings in 5–6m on sand. Some shelter from northerlies if you are tucked far enough up into the corner.

Limited provisions and tavernas ashore. A camping ground around the wonderful beach tucked in under the rocky coast.

ÓRMOS SIKIAS

Approach

Six miles N of Ák Psevdhókavos lies the large bay of Órmos Sikias. The rocks of Ifaloi Kepes (Kepes Reef) lying off the S entrance point can be identified and closer in the buildings at the head of the bay are conspicuous.

By night The S entrance point, Ák Ádholo, is lit Fl.1·5s4M, as is the end of the breakwater at Skála Sikias Fl.R.3s3M, but a night entrance is not really recommended.

Dangers

1. **Ifaloi Kepes** An above-water islet and reef borders the coast off the S entrance point for up to 700m off the coast.
2. **Ifalos Sikias** A reef with 2·8m over it lying about 600m SE of Ák Sikias, the N entrance point. There is also an islet with a reef extending SSE for 250m from it closer to the N coast and a reef off Ák Sikias itself.

Mooring

1. Anchor in either of the two coves on the N side of the bay. The bottom is sand and weed, mostly good holding. Reasonable shelter from northerlies but open to the E–SE.
2. Anchor at the head of the bay off the wonderful sandy beach around the head of the bay. Open NE–E.
3. **Skála Sikias** Anchor in the cove off the village in 3–5m or go bows-to the short mole if there is room. There are 3m depths at the extremity of the mole. Good shelter behind the mole from most winds.

Skála Sikias looking NE to the stubby mole

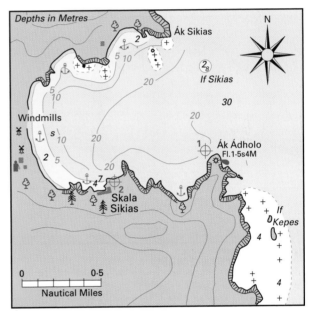

ÓRMOS SIKIAS
⊕₁ 40°02'·5N 24°00'·8E
⊕₂ 40°02'·07N 23°59'·75E WGS84

Shelter The bay suffers from an uncomfortable swell rolling in after NE winds except if you are tucked in behind the mole at Skála Sikias.

Facilities

Water and several tavernas at Skála Sikias. Other tavernas around the beach at the head of the bay. A mini-market and fuel on the main road back from the beach.

General

The beaches around the bay are composed of wonderful fine golden sand shaded by pine and poplar, the stuff tour operators' dreams are made of. Unfortunately much of the beach-front has been turned into a dusty camp site and caravan park. Skála Sikias remains a wonderful little cove away from the beach.

ÓRMOS SARTI

An open bay that affords some protection from N winds in the NW corner off the village. Care is needed of above water rocks and a reef just NW of the bay. Provisions and tavernas ashore. Fuel on the main road to the N.

AKLADHI

A cove immediately N of Sarti. There is a small fishing harbour here and small yachts may find room to go bows-to behind the mole. Care is needed of the underwater rocks off the end of the mole and on the coast side of the entrance. There are also rocks where the 1·5 sounding is shown. Go alongside or stern or bows-to wherever you can squeeze in. Good shelter tucked under the mole. The rocky patch inside the harbour is sometimes marked with a small can buoy.

Water on the mole. Taverna near the camping site on the coast.

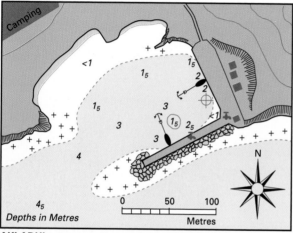

AKLADHI
⊕40°06′·18N 23°59′·04E WGS84

Akladhi N of Sarti

PORTO ZOGRAFU

A tiny inlet at the bottom of precipitous slopes between Ák Rigas and the Nisís Dhiaporos. It could be useful as a lunch stop in calm weather only. Taverna ashore and also, unfortunately, a caravan park.

NISÍS DHIAPOROS AND ADJACENT ANCHORAGES (Dhimítri Island)
Approach
S Passage This leads into Órmos Mesopanayia between Ák Xifaras and Ák Pláka, the SE extremity of Nisís Dhiaporos, on about 240°. A reef extends N from Ák Xifaras with Petronisi and Kalamonisia islets marking the extremity of the reef. The reef extends S and E from Ák Pláka with an above-water rock near the outer end. The S Passage lies between the last-mentioned rock and the Kalamonisia islets, all of which are clearly visible by day. There is 8m least depth in the fairway.

N Passage Leads into Órmos Dhimítri between Nisís Ambelitsi and Nisís Peristeri. A reef extends E and S from Peristeri with the SE edge of the reef marked by an above-water rock with a white chapel on it. A narrow rocky reef fringes Ák Zavos, the NW extremity of Nisís Dhiaporos, and the N Passage is between this reef and the reef surrounding Peristeri.

Caution On the accompanying plan it is impossible to show the reefs and above-water rocks in great detail. A yacht should proceed with caution and not attempt an approach by night. By day the reefs and above-water rocks are clearly visible and the approaches are in practice more straightforward than the accompanying notes might appear to indicate.

Mooring
There are numerous anchorages around Nisís Dhiaporos and the adjacent coast. The bottom is mostly mud or sand – good holding.

1. ***Órmos Mesopanayia*** Anchor on the N side under Nisís Dhiaporos in 5–6m on mud. Care needed of the reef which runs around the E side of the bay for some distance out. The S side of the bay is mostly shallow and a yacht should keep close to Nisís Dhiaporos when passing through Órmos Mesopanayia.
2. ***Órmos Koumaroudhes*** Anchor off the bight on Nisís Dhiaporos.
3. ***Órmos Kriftos*** The bay on the N side of Nisís Dhiaporos. Enter the bay on the E side of Nisís Ambelitsi. Anchor in 5–6m near the head of the bay or 8–10m in the bight on the E side about halfway down. All round shelter.
4. ***Órmos Dhimítri*** Anchor in the bight on the E side of the headland which encloses Órmos Kriftos in 5–6m. Alternatively anchor off the W side further down in 5–8m on mud. There is a fish farm here but still room to anchor. Care is needed of a detached reef here which will occasionally be marked.
5. ***Órmos Dhimitriaki*** Enter the bay between Nisís Kalogria and Ák Megas Toikhas. Anchor where convenient. Shelter is better than it looks in here with the normal summer settled weather.
6. ***Panayía*** Straightforward with good depths throughout. The best shelter is in the NE corner of the bay, but some care must be exercised as the bottom is foul with laid moorings. Anchor in 4–6m clear of the moorings. Good shelter.

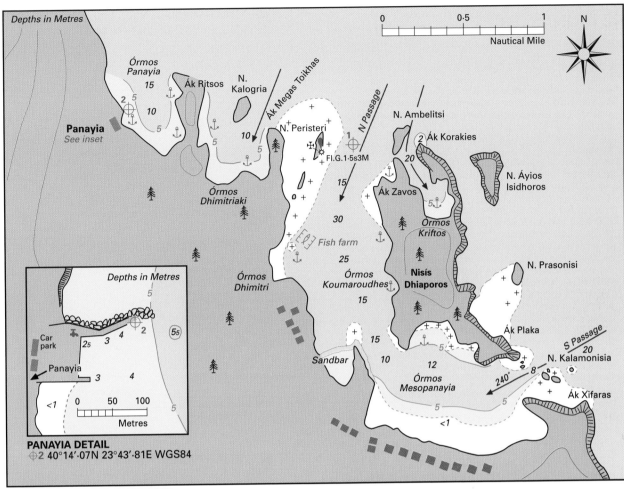

Depths in Metres

Órmos
Panayia
15
Ák Ritsos
N.
Kalogria
Ák Megas Toikhas
N. Passage
N. Ambelitsi
N. Peristeri
Fl.G.1·5s3M
2 Ák Korakies
20
N. Áyios
Isidhoros
Ák Zavos
5
Panayia
See inset
10
5
10
Órmos
Dhimitriaki
15
30
Órmos
Kriftos
25
Órmos
Dhimitri
25
Fish farm
Órmos
Koumaroudhes
15
**Nisís
Dhiaporos**
N. Prasonisi
Ák Plaka
S Passage
20
N. Kalamonisia
15
240°
8
Ák Xifaras
Sandbar
10
12
Órmos
Mesopanayia
5
5
<1

0   0·5   1
Nautical Mile
N

Depths in Metres
5
2
Car
park
2 5
3
4
2
55
Panayia
3
4
<1   0   50   100
Metres
5

PANAYIA DETAIL
⊕2 40°14'·07N 23°43'·81E WGS84

NISÍS DHIAPOROS ANCHORAGES
⊕1 40°13'·7N 23°46'·0E

On the W of the bay there is a pier used by a ferry that makes daily trips to the Akti peninsula. It can be used when the ferry is not in.

Facilities
Dhimítri Water from a camp site and a mini-market.

Panayía Water on the pier. Fuel in the village. Most provisions can be obtained – mini-market near the pier. Ice available. Several tavernas and cafés.

Panayía mole looking N

The village of Áyios Nikólaos about 2½km inland has additional facilities.

General
Behind the island the water is a little murky from the river draining into it, but everywhere else the water is clear, a wonderful turquoise over sand and rock. Numerous villas and a few small hotels have been built around the coastal flat at Mesopanayia, but apart from that the coast is little built up. Because

Anchorage in Órmos Dhimítriaki looking E to Nisís Kalogria

367

THE MONASTERIES

(see plan)

1. *Moní Konstamonitou.* Coenobite. Founded in the 11th century. Most of the buildings in the deep defile are of the 19th century. A yacht can anchor off in the bay in calm weather.
2. *Dhoheiariou (Dohiariou).* Idiorrhythmic. Founded in the 10th century. The central church, the Katholikon, is said to be one of the finest on Mt Athos.
3. *Xenofondos.* Coenobite. Founded in the 10th century by the monk Xenofon.
4. *Moní Ayíou Panteleimonos.* Coenobite. Founded in 1169, it once supported 1,500 Russian monks. It was badly damaged by fire in 1968 but it is still spectacular. There is a very small harbour nearby.
5. *Xiropotamou.* Idiorrhythmic. First mentioned in the 10th century, most of the buildings date from the 18th century.
6. *Simonopetra.* Coenobite. Founded in 1257 by St Simon, this is one of the most spectacular of the monasteries. The monastery is built on a rocky bluff connected to the cliff by a bridge. Heavy beams overhang the rock sides so that the parts of the monastery built on the beams literally hang in space above the sea and rocks below.
7. *Gregoriou.* Coenobite. Founded c. 1395.
8. *Dionysiou.* Coenobite. Founded in 1375, it stands on a spectacular precipitous rock.
9. *Ayíou Pavlou.* Coenobite. Founded in the 11th century, it occupies a spectacular site on a cliff overlooking a gorge below.
10. *Grand Lavra.* Idiorrhythmic. Situated under the massive height of Mt Athos, this is the largest of the monasteries. Apparently it alone has never suffered from the fires which have badly damaged the other monasteries.
11. *Karakallou.* Coenobite. Founded in the 15th century.
12. *Filotheou.* Idiorrhythmic First mentioned in the 12th century. The monks employ themselves woodcarving.
13. *Iviron.* Idiorrhythmic. Founded in 979. There is a pier here with 2m depths at its extremity. In calm weather it is possible to anchor off in 4–9m.
14. *Stavronikita.* Idiorrhythmic. Founded in 1542.
15. *Pantokrator.* Idiorrhythmic. Built in the 14th century on a sea-washed rock in a small cove. It appears to be possible to anchor off the monastery in calm weather.
16. *Vatopedi.* Idiorrhythmic. Founded in the 10th century, this is the most modern monastery with electricity, telephone and regular communication by ferry with Ierissós. Anchor off the monastery in 5–8m. Open to all sectors N.
17. *Esphigmenou.* Coenobite. First mentioned in 1034. The most northerly of the monasteries. A yacht can anchor off in calm weather.

Around the southern end of the Akti peninsula live scattered colonies of monks and hermits in almost inaccessible (or so it seems, looking up at them) huts clinging to the mountainside. The important colonies are one at St Anne's on the SW corner and a colony of painters and woodcarvers at Kerassia on the SE corner. A yacht can anchor close under Ák Dhiapori at Voulevtiria or at a small cove one mile ENE of Ák Pínnes in calm weather only. A yacht should not be left unattended and must be prepared to leave with the slightest hint of a change in the weather.

AKTI PENINSULA

Monastery on Athos   *Nigel Patten*

Panayia is used as the mainland port for the ferry to the Athos Peninsula and also by tripper boats, the little hamlet is overpowered by coaches waiting to drop off or pick up tour groups. Fortunately they all disappear off to Thessaloníki by the evening and the hamlet is once again a quiet little place. Around the various anchorages you are, thankfully, miles away from all this hubbub.

PIRGADHÍKIA

40°20'·2N 23°43'·2E

A small village at the head of the gulf in the NW corner. There is a small pier off the village with a light on the extremity (Q.R.3M). Fishing boats and a few small pleasure craft are kept on permanent moorings in the cove on the W side of the hummock the village is built on. Shelter is better than it looks although the anchorage should not be used in unsettled weather and in southerlies it is dangerous to remain here. Provisions and tavernas ashore. The little village is a gem of a place and well worth the effort to get up to.

NISÍS AMMOULIANI

Lying in the NE corner of Singitikós Kólpos, this island offers a number of good anchorages according to the wind direction. Off the NW extremity of the island lie the islets Nisídhes

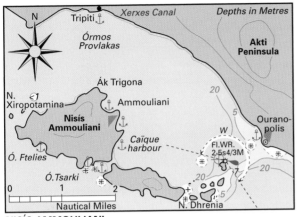

NISÍS AMMOULIANI
⊕40°19'·2N 23°57'·9E

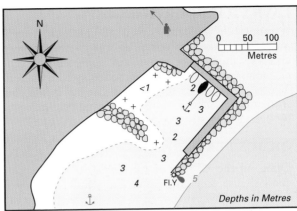

NISÍS AMMOULIANI - NEW CAIQUE HARBOUR

Xiropotamina and off the SE extremity the islets Nisídhes Dhrénia. In the channel between the easternmost of the Nisídhes Dhrénia and the Akti peninsula there are least depths of 4–7m in the fairway. Anchorages around the island are as follows:

1. *W side* On the W side of Nisís Ammouliani anchor in Órmos Ftelies (open to the W) or in Órmos Tsarki (open to the S). In both bays the holding is uncertain so make sure the anchor is well dug in and holding. Care is needed of the reefs on either side of Órmos Tsarki.

2. *Ammouliani village* On the NE corner of the island. A Fl.R.3s3M on the end of the mole. Go stern or bows-to the outer half of the mole. The central quay on the W is used by ferries. Alternatively anchor off N of the ferry quay in 3m. Provisions and tavernas ashore. Fuel from the supermarket near the root of the mole or on the outskirts of the village.

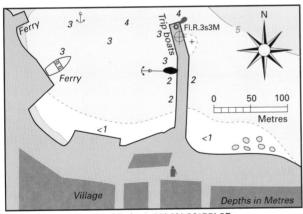

AMMOULIANI VILLAGE ⊕40°20'·2N 23°55'·3E

3. The bay immediately S of Ammouliani village. Anchor in 4–6m off the short mole. Indifferent shelter.

4. *Caïque harbour.* On the N of the large bay below Ammouliani village a small *caïque* harbour has been constructed. Small yachts may find a berth inside. There are 4m depths in the entrance and 2m depths off the quay. Alternatively anchor off to the SW of the harbour.

OURANOPOLIS

In fine weather a yacht can anchor off Ouranopolis in Órmos Provlakas. The square Prosforion Tower (24m high) is conspicuous on Ák Pirgos. Care must be taken of Ifalos Ouranoplis which is marked by a pole beacon with ⁑ topmark about 100m SW of the mole at Ouranopolis. The end of the jetty is lit Fl.G.3s3M and the beacon Fl(2)10s7M. The anchorage at Ouranopolis is not a secure one and in unsettled weather it is wise to return to one of the anchorages on Ammouliani Island.

Provisions and tavernas ashore. Fuel in the village. Ferries to Dhafni.

TRIPITI (Xerxes Canal S entrance)

40°21'·9N 23°55'·1E

A short jetty used by fishing boats immediately N of the site of Xerxes Canal. You may find a berth on the W side of the jetty. Depths 2–6m towards the end. A ferry to Ammouliani uses the end of the jetty. The head is lit Fl.R.2s3M.

Tavernas on the beach.

DHAFNI

The control port for the Akti peninsula.

Dháfni is situated about ½ mile N of Ák Kastanias in an open bay. There is limited shelter from N–NE winds from the natural camber of the coast but it is open from NW through W to S. The seabed rises abruptly making anchoring difficult. A short stone pier has 2m depths at its extremity and a yacht can go stern-to the pier. The bay is not safe in unsettled weather when the prevailing summer wind is funnelled in from the NW–W setting up an uncomfortable slop. A large mooring buoy in the bay is for ships.

CAUTION

Violent gusts blow off Mt Athos with strong winds from any direction. In calm weather it is interesting to stand inshore to see the monasteries. With strong winds the violent gusts and the considerable seas raised around the bottom of the Akti peninsula make it prudent for a yacht to keep some distance off.

LAVRA HARBOUR (Mandráki)

A minuscule harbour carved out of rock lying 2 miles N of Ák Ákrathos. The fort by the harbour and the monastery above are conspicuous. The entrance to the harbour is immediately S of the fort. There are reported to be 1·8m depths inside, but with any sort of swell running it would be dangerous for even a very small yacht to attempt to enter.

ÓRMOS PLATÍ

Lying on the W side of Ák Arápis, this bay offers good shelter from the prevailing winds. It is open only to the SW. Anchor in 5–8m depths in either of the two coves in Órmos Platí or in Órmos Frangou immediately N of Órmos Platí. The bottom is sand and weed – good holding.

Both bays are deserted although fishing boats from Ierissos and Koumitas occasionally shelter here.

The miniature harbour at Néa Rodha

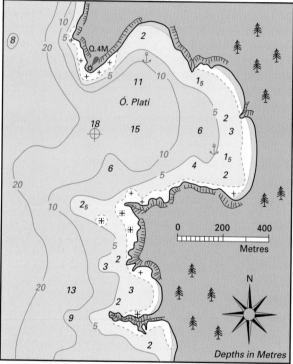

ORMOS PLATI
⊕40°26'·15N 23°59'·7E

NÉA RODHA

40°23'·0N 23°56'·0E

A village between Koumitsas and Ierissos. There is a short mole on the W side of the bay. A chapel on the bluff above the miniature harbour is conspicuous. A light is exhibited at the end of the mole: Fl.R.2s3M. A small yacht may be able to go bows-to the end of the mole where there are 2–3m depths although it is usually crowded with fishing boats. The inner half of the mole is shallow (less than a metre).

Provisions and tavernas in the village a dusty 20-minute walk away.

IERISSÓS

Approach

A small fishing harbour lying about ½ mile to the SE of Ierissós village. The large hotel behind it is conspicuous.

By night The entrance is lit Fl.R.3s3M/Fl.G.3s3M but a night entry is not advised.

Mooring

Go stern or bows-to with a long line to the breakwater in the outer half of the harbour or in the inner basin. Alternatively anchor inside the inner or outer parts of the harbour. The inner harbour is crowded with local fishing boats. Care must be taken of the very large mooring chains on the bottom and of the numerous mooring buoys and lines on the surface.

Shelter With strong N winds a swell rolls into the harbour – more uncomfortable than dangerous. The local fishing boats and a small ferry are moored here all year round.

Note This area is a part of the Akti peninsula and as such it is theoretically off-limits to yachts. Some yachts get away with anchoring here while others are told to leave. You take your chances and should be prepared to vacate the bay if asked to do so. The alternatives are limited, with Ierissós the closest and Stavros and even Thásos possibilities.

Caution The passage between Nisídhes Stiliária and Ák Arápis has less depth than that shown on the old BA 1679 and also appears more rock-bound than shown. Pass to seaward of the outermost of Nisídhes Stiliária.

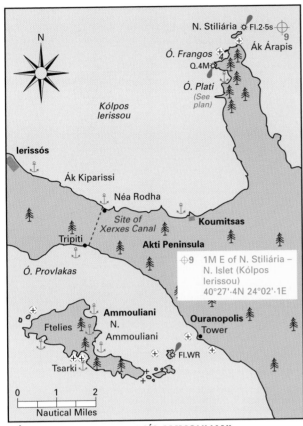

KÓLPOS IERISSOU AND NISÍS AMMOULIANI

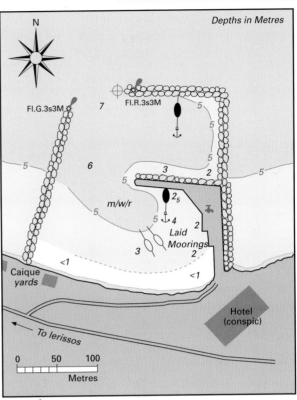

IERISSÓS
⊕40°23'·8N 23°53'·7E

Facilities
Tavernas at the harbour. Ierissós village is about one mile away from the harbour and here there is fuel and most provisions can be obtained. Also PO and OTE and several tavernas and cafés. A bus runs to Kavala. There are several yards building wooden fishing *caïques* along the beach from the harbour.

General
There are good beaches of coarse sand on either side of the harbour and the hinterland is pleasantly wooded with poplar, pine and olive trees. Ierissós has developed into a dusty ramshackle resort on the strength of the sandy beach nearby. The harbour is the nearest safe harbour to the site of Xerxes Canal 2 miles to the SE, although you are likely to be disappointed – there is little to see of the famous canal today.

STRATONION
40°30'·4N 23°50'·0E

Lies at the head of Órmos Stratonion in the NW corner of Kólpos Ierissou. Anchor off the village. To the N of the village there are two piers extending from the shore for loading ore from the nearby manganese mines. The bay is open to the E and S.

Provisions and tavernas ashore. Fuel in the village.

Between Stratonion and Ák Elevthera there are a number of coves offering good shelter from N winds, but open to the S. The cove nearest to Ák Elevthera offers the best shelter in beautiful surroundings. Open to the S and W.

The mainland coast
This section covers the mainland coast of Northern Greece from Strimonikos Kólpos to Alexandroupolis, including the nearby island of Thásos. The region is mountainous although not spectacularly so, and much of the high land is bordered by low-lying plains and marshes deposited by the four large rivers emptying into the sea along the coast: the Strimon, the Nestos, the Akmar and the Evros. The river Nestor is the boundary between Macedonia and Thrace and the river Evros is the border between Greece and Turkey. The countryside is for the most part densely wooded in pine and olive. The coastal plains are well-watered and fertile, producing large crops of grain and tobacco.

Ierissós looking NE

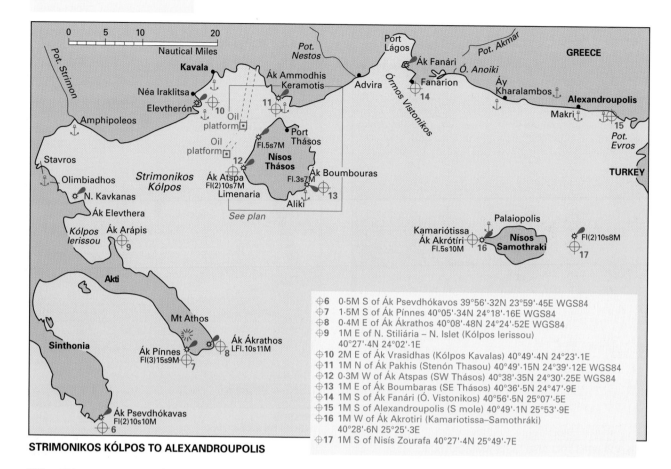

STRIMONIKOS KÓLPOS TO ALEXANDROUPOLIS

⊕6   0·5M S of Ák Psevdhókavos 39°56'·32N 23°59'·45E WGS84
⊕7   1·5M S of Ák Pínnes 40°05'·34N 24°18'·16E WGS84
⊕8   0·4M E of Ák Ákrathos 40°08'·48N 24°24'·52E WGS84
⊕9   1M E of N. Stiliária – N. Islet (Kólpos Ierissou) 40°27'·4N 24°02'·1E
⊕10   2M E of Ák Vrasidhas (Kólpos Kavalas) 40°49'·4N 24°23'·1E
⊕11   1M N of Ák Pakhis (Stenón Thasou) 40°49'·15N 24°39'·12E WGS84
⊕12   0·3M W of Ák Atspas (SW Thásos) 40°38'·35N 24°30'·25E WGS84
⊕13   1M E of Ák Boumbaras (SE Thásos) 40°36'·5N 24°47'·9E
⊕14   1M E of Ák Fanári (Ó. Vistonikos) 40°56'·5N 25°07'·5E
⊕15   1M S of Alexandroupolis (S mole) 40°49'·1N 25°53'·9E
⊕16   1M W of Ák Akrotiri (Kamariotissa–Samothráki) 40°28'·6N 25°25'·3E
⊕17   1M S of Nisís Zourafa 40°27'·4N 25°49'·7E

Weather patterns in Northern Greece

(These weather patterns also apply to Samothráki.)

In the summer months the *meltemi* blows only fitfully in this area. Normally the *meltemi* blows from the NE at Force 2–5, but on many days there will be little or no wind at all. If the *meltemi* does not blow a SW sea breeze will often set in about midday and blow at Force 2–4. In the winter, spring and autumn the wind is again from the NE or the S, but severe gales are most often from the NE.

In the comparatively shallow waters off this coast, particularly in Stenón Thasou, Órmos Vistonikos, Órmos Anoiko and the shallows off Alexandroupolis, a very short steep sea is kicked up with strong winds from the S. These seas can be aggravated by the W-going current setting along the coast which can vary from ½ to 1½ knots.

With S winds the sea level can increase by as much as 0·5m and conversely with N winds the sea level can decrease.

ÓRMOS OLIMBIADHOS

40°35'·6N 23°47'·4E

Lies 6½ miles to the NW of Ák Elevthera. Anchor off the village in 2–4m tucked as far under the stubby mole as possible. Adequate shelter although some swell usually penetrates. The outer end of the mole has 2–3m depths but is usually occupied by fishing boats. The mole is lit Fl.R.3s3M.

In the village there are provisions and tavernas. The setting on a coastal plain with mixed deciduous and pine all hemmed in by steep-to mountains is spectacular. The village is a sleepy little place that sees some tourism, but not a lot.

NISÍS KAVKANÁS

40°37'·0N 23°48'·5E

On the S side of the islet there is a bight that provides some shelter from the N and E. Care is needed of the reef off the W end of the islet. Anchor in 3–5m on sand and shingle.

The islet is lit on the SE corner Fl(3)18s7M.

STAVRÓS

A large bay in the SW corner of Strimonikos Kólpos. There is a short pier off the village and at the time of writing works were underway in the vicinity. As far as could be determined an additional mole was being built to form a small harbour enclosed by an

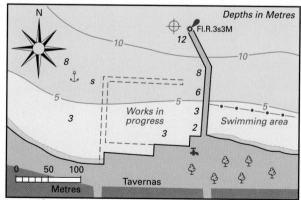

STAVRÓS
⊕40°40'·1N 23°42'·1E

L-shaped mole. A light is exhibited on the end of the pier (Fl.R.3s3M).

Fishing boats use the pier and are kept on permanent moorings off the village so shelter is probably better than it appears. Water on the quay. Fuel by mini-tanker.

The village has developed into a thriving resort with hotels, bars and cafés dotted around the shore. PO. Bank. Provisions and tavernas.

AMPHIPOLEOS

40°47'·0N 23°51'·5E

In the N corner of Strimonikos Kólpos at the mouth of the river Strimon there is a shallow basin which was formerly Amfipoleos harbour. However the entrance has silted to depths of less than 1m.

It is possible to anchor off the entrance to the basin in 3–4m, but there is little shelter to be gained here.

Caution At the mouth of the river Strimon the shoals are reported to extend further than indicated on the chart. A current of about 2 knots is also said to set to the S because of the considerable flow of fresh water from the river.

ELEVTHERÓN (Dhevtro)

BA 1687

Approach
This large bay lies 6 miles to the S of Kavála. A number of large hotels around the beach on the W side of the bay and a large silo at the root of the oil wharf are conspicuous.

By night Use the light on the N entrance point Fl.3s5M.

Mooring
In settled weather anchor off Néa Peramos or in the SW corner of the bay. In unsettled weather go stern or bows-to or alongside the N side of the large cargo pier in the NE corner of the bay. There are 7m depths along the outer end of the pier. The surroundings are not attractive but the shelter is nearly all-round. In strong S winds many of the fishing boats normally based in Kavála shelter here.

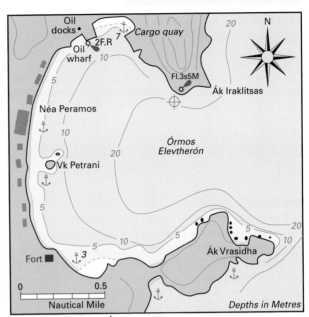

ÓRMOS ELEVTHERÓN
⊕40°50'·6N 24 19'·7E

Facilities
In Néa Peramos most provisions can be obtained and there are tavernas and cafés. Ferries to Thásos.

General
In settled weather the large bay has attractive anchorages on the S and W sides off long sandy beaches. The fort on the S side begs to be explored.

NÉA IRAKLITSA

A small fishing harbour in the SE corner of Kólpos Kavalas. The entrance is lit Fl.R.3s3M/Fl.G.3s3M. The end of the pier is lit F.R. Go alongside the end of the pier or go stern or bows-to the quay on the S. Good shelter.

Water on the quay. Fuel in the village. Provisions and tavernas ashore.

Elevtherón looking NE, across Órmos Elevtherón

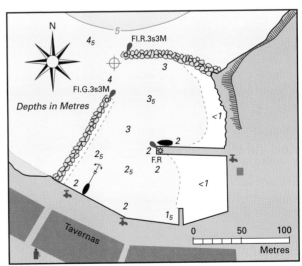

NÉA IRAKLITSA
⊕40°52'·1N 24°19'·1E

KAVÁLA

BA 1687

Approach

Conspicuous The large city on the rocky bluff and sprawled over the hills behind is conspicuous from the distance. Closer in, a fort and a church with a red cupola on the rocky bluff are conspicuous. The harbour moles are easily identified.

By night Use the light on Ák Kará Ormán Fl.5s15M and the lights at the entrance Fl.G.2s4M/ Fl.R.2s4M.

Mooring

Moor stern-to the N quay in the outer harbour if you can find room. The yacht club is strictly private with no facilities for visitors and, it is reported, few manners. The quay in the outer harbour is very high and you will have difficulty getting ashore unless you are near a ladder. The inner basin is usually crowded with fishing boats. You may be able to find a berth in the inner basin, but do enquire if it is OK to berth there – yachts which muscle into fishing boat berths should not be surprised to be unceremoniously evicted when boats return. The bottom is mud – excellent holding.

Shelter With strong S winds an uncomfortable surge develops and many of the fishing boats shelter at Elevtherón. However a number of yachts are moored all year round off the N mole and quay. Strong S winds are rare in the summer.

Authorities Port police, customs and immigration authorities.

Facilities

Water On the N quay and in the inner basin.

Fuel Can be delivered to the N quay and near the quay in the inner basin.

Repairs Most mechanical and general engineering repairs. Chandlers. Excellent hardware and tool shops.

Provisions Excellent shopping for all provisions. The best shopping area is immediately behind the fish market. Ice from the fish market.

Eating out Excellent tavernas including several fish

Kavála looking WNW from the root of the outer mole

tavernas near the fish market with delicacies such as sole, scallops and some of the best prawns in Greece.

Other PO. OTE. Banks. ATMs. Greek gas and Camping Gaz. A gas filling station some distance out of the city. Hire cars and motorbikes. Buses to Thessaloníki and Alexandroupolis. Ferries to Thásos. Internal flights to Athens.

General

Kavála is an important commercial port and first impressions of the city from a harbour churned up by ferries, tugs and workboats commuting to the oil rig are not likely to be favourable. Yet stay a day here and you begin to like this busy friendly city.

In the city an aqueduct (based on Roman design but built by the Turks in the 16th century) is prominent. On the rocky bluff the house of Mehmet Ali, a rich merchant of Kavála in the 18th century, who effectively ruled the city, has been preserved and is now a folklore museum. The archaeological museum near the harbour houses classical finds from the area.

KAVÁLA FISHING HARBOUR

40°56'·6N 24°25'·7E

On the E side of Ák Kará Ormán on the W side of Órmos Perigiali there is a fishing harbour where a small yacht may find a berth. Fuel nearby. A small boatyard close by hauls yachts. Provisions and tavernas ashore.

KAVÁLA WEST HARBOUR

40°55'·9N 24°23'·7E

On the W side of Órmos Kavála there is a dogleg breakwater extending NE for approximately 300m which protects a quayed area. This is a commercial port and not for yachts. The end of the breakwater is lit Fl(2)R.8s7M.

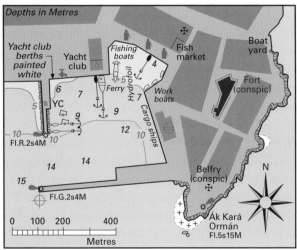

KAVÁLA
⊕40°55'·9N 24°24'·3E

KAVÁLA COMMERCIAL HARBOUR

40°57'·0N 24°28'·9E

Approximately 2 miles E of Kavála a large commercial harbour is under construction. Grandly titled the 'Phillip II of Macedonia' harbour, it is unlikely to offer much in the way of facilities for yachts. The entrance is lit Fl.R.4s3M/Fl.G.4s7M/3F.R.3M.

KERAMOTÍS

BA 1687

Approach

Keramotís is the principal ferry port connecting Thásos to the mainland. On the low-lying sand spit terminating in Ák Keramotís a few houses and the light structure will be seen before the sand spit itself. Once into the lagoon behind the sand spit, the village of Keramotís and the harbour are easily identified.

By night Use the lights on Ák Keramotís Fl.WR.4s6/4M and on the pier head Q.RG.2M.

Mooring

Go stern or bows-to or alongside the quay where shown. The wharf is usually crowded with coasters and fishing boats.

Shelter Is better than it looks. W winds cause a limited swell.

Authorities Port police and customs.

Facilities

Water on the quay. Fuel near the quay. Good shopping for provisions. PO. OTE. A number of tavernas and cafés. Buses to Alexandroupolis and Kavála. Car ferry to Thásos.

Note On the N side of the lagoon a number of mooring buoys (red and white vertical stripes) probably belong to the Greek navy. It would be prudent not to anchor in this area.

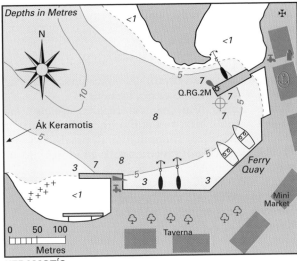

KERAMOTÍS
⊕40°51'·6N 24 42'·2E

OIL RIG PLATFORM

Lying 3½ miles NW of Ák Prínos on Thásos and 9½ miles SSE of Kavála is an oil rig platform which is conspicuous by day and night. Another platform was erected approximately 6·3 miles SSW of the original platform and approx. 4 miles from the coast of Thásos. Workboats regularly ply between the platform and Kavála. At night the platforms are lit by a battery of white lights (they could be mistaken for large ocean liners) and a Mo(U)15s10m.

ÁK AMMODHIS

A rock just under the water (0·9m) is reported to lie ½ mile SSW of Ák Ammódhis.

RIVER NESTOS

Shoaling is reported to extend as much as ½ mile further than indicated around the mouth of this river. I have noticed discoloured water as far as 1 mile off the coast, but a check on the depth showed no disparity with charted depths. Nonetheless it would be prudent to keep some distance off the river mouth. The land in the vicinity of the river mouth is very low-lying and it is often difficult to establish the limits of the coastal plain around it. A cluster of communication towers approximately ½ mile inland on the coastal plain (Pedhias Khrisoupoleos) is conspicuous.

STENÓN THASOU (Thásos Strait)

In the comparatively shallow water in the strait and in Órmos Vistonikos a short steep sea is quickly raised with strong winds. In Stenón Thasou a current sometimes sets to the E at a rate of ½–1½ knots.

Nísos Thásos

This round lump of marble separated from the mainland by a shallow sea strait enjoyed some power and prosperity in ancient times. Its position allowed it to be easily defended and it was and still is an enchanting and beautiful island.

The early colonists were the Parians who soon prospered from the Thasian gold mines. Despite being a well defended and powerful city-state, Thásos meekly submitted to the invading Persians. After Xerxes was defeated at Salamís the island had its ups and downs with Athens, but its merchants prospered on its mineral wealth (including Thasian marble which was renowned throughout the ancient world) and its famous black wine. In medieval times it suffered from pirate attacks until the Genoese Gattelusis and later the Turks occupied the island and restored order.

Today its prosperity is based on the natural beauty of the island: its sandy beaches, pine-clad hills, running streams (even in summer) and ancient monuments attract a growing number of tourists each year.

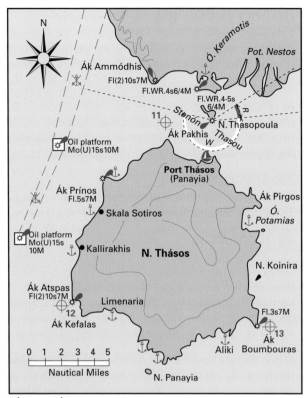

NÍSOS THÁSOS

⊕11 1M N of Ák Pakhis (Stenón Thasou)
    40°49'·15N 24°39'·12E WGS84
⊕12 0·3M W of Ák Atspas (SW Thásos)
    40°38'·35N 24°30'·25E WGS84
⊕13 1M E of Ák Boumbaras (SE Thásos)
    40°36'·5N 24°47'·9E

THÁSOS NÉA LIMANI

BA 1687

Approach

The harbour is situated immediately W of the old harbour on the NE side of the island. In the closer approaches the outer breakwater will be seen and the light structures at the entrance can be identified.

By night The entrance is lit: Fl.R.3s3M/ Fl.G.3s3M.

Thásos. The old harbour (foreground) and Nea Limani
(behind) looking W from the ancient theatre   *Lu Michell*

The entrance can be difficult to identify at night from the lights of ferries on either side of the harbour.

Mooring

Most yachts moor alongside either of the breakwaters. Despite hydrofoils coming and going (they berth on the E side of the harbour) the W breakwater is well sheltered from wind and wash.

Shelter Good all-round shelter.

Authorities Port police and customs.

Facilities

Water and electricity boxes are not connected yet.
   Also see Port Thásos.

PORT THÁSOS (Limín Panayía)

BA 1687

Approach

Conspicuous The buildings of the town in the natural amphitheatre at the foot of the hills can be seen from the distance, but the harbour moles are very low and difficult to see. The two white light structures on the extremities of the moles will be seen before the moles. A small orange buoy sometimes marks the end of the ancient breakwater to the NE of the harbour.

By night Use the light on the SE of Nisís Thasopoúla Fl.WR.4·5s6/4M and the lights at the entrance Fl.G.2s4M/Fl.R.2s4M.

Dangers Care should be taken of the remains of an ancient mole, mostly submerged, approximately 300m to the NE of the harbour. Approach the harbour from the N or NW.

Mooring

All but the N breakwater is usually full with local craft or trip boats. Most yachts should anchor and take a line ashore to avoid underwater rocks off the N breakwater. Smaller yachts can berth bows–to in places, but most will need to get ashore by dinghy. The bottom of the harbour was said to be originally constructed of marble, but I have found only mud and shingle – good holding.

Shelter Excellent all-round shelter.

Authorities Port police and customs (by the ferry quay).

Facilities

Water On the quay.
Fuel On the waterfront. A mini-tanker can be arranged to deliver to either harbour.
Repairs Limited mechanical repairs. *Caïques* are hauled out and built to the E of the old harbour.
Provisions Excellent shopping for all provisions.
Eating out Excellent tavernas with good fish on the waterfront.
Other PO. OTE. Bank. ATM. Greek gas and Camping Gaz. Hire cars and motorbikes. Buses around the perimeter of the island. Ferries to Keramotís and Kavála.

General

The town of Thásos is built on the same site as the ancient capital and wandering around the town you experience an architectural pot pourri of the old and the new. Most of the new town is within the 2½ miles of walls and towers that surrounded the ancient city. Thásos possessed two fine harbours. The surviving oval harbour was the ancient naval harbour. The ancient commercial harbour to the E is now mostly destroyed.

Close by this latter harbour is one of the most charming spots in the town – shaded by trees and close to the ruins of the *agora*, it is a short but steep walk up the hill behind to the ancient theatre and the *acropolis* that look out over Thásos. The theatre is undergoing a sympathetic 'make–over' to restore much of the stonework, and while the cranes and hammers do detract a little at the moment, the theatre retains its character. More than many of the other classic sites I have visited in Greece, Thásos conveys in both its substance and its atmosphere what an ancient Greek city was like. The museum houses most of the valuable finds from the site.

Harbours and anchorages around Thásos

(Going anti-clockwise around the island)

SKALA RACHONIOU

40°46'·95N 24°36'·83E WGS84

A small fishing harbour halfway between Ák Pakhis and Ák Prínos. The church in the village is conspicuous. The entrance is lit Fl.G.3s3M/Fl.R.3s3M. Limited quay space and depths <1–1·5m make it suitable only for very small yachts. The prevailing wind blows around the coast into the entrance of the harbour. Suitable in calm weather only.

Tavernas ashore.

ÓRMOS PRINOS

40°45'·59N 24°34'·56E WGS84

On the N side of Ák Prínos, this open bay affords some shelter from the prevailing NE winds by means of the natural camber of the bay. Off the

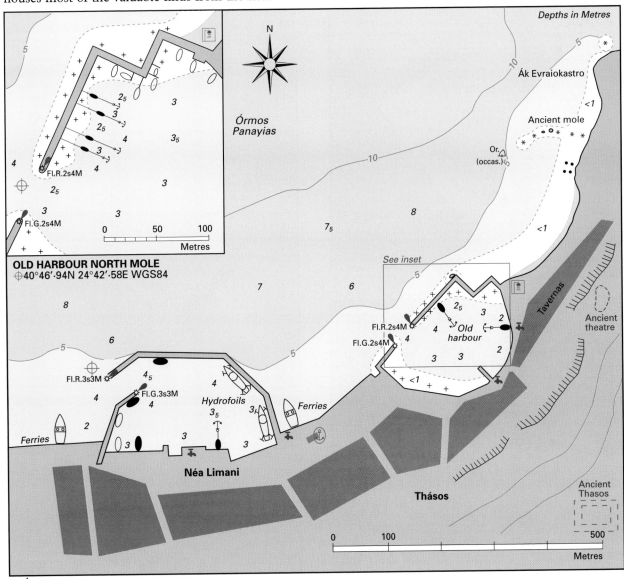

OLD HARBOUR NORTH MOLE
⊕40°46'·94N 24°42'·58E WGS84

Néa Limani

Thásos

THÁSOS
⊕40°46'·89N 24°42'·23E WGS84

village of Prínos there is a wharf and a short pier, but the latter is used by the car ferry to Kavála. Works are in progress developing the ferry quay and building a small harbour to the E. When finished there may be space for yachts to berth. Anchor in the bay. Some provisions available ashore and a number of good tavernas.

SKÁLA SOTIROS

A small fishing harbour approximately 2M S of Ák Prinos. A dogleg breakwater with the entrance N protects a small harbour. The entrance is lit Fl.G.3s3M/Fl.R.3s3M. Care needed of shallow water off the beach to the N of the harbour. Depths in the entrance 4m and depths in the harbour <1–3m. Permanent moorings in the W corner limit the available mooring space.

Some provisions and tavernas ashore.

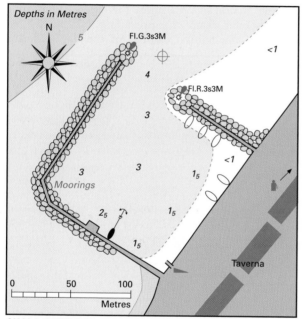

SKALA SOTIROS
⊕40°43′·76N 24°32′·82E WGS84

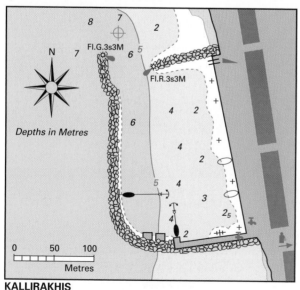

KALLIRAKHIS
⊕40°42′·68N 24°31′·86E WGS84

KALLIRAKHIS

A fishing harbour lying approximately 3·5M S of Ák Prinos. Depths are irregular off the E quay so, if possible, go stern or bows-to the outer part of S quay. Alternatively anchor and take a long line to the W breakwater. Good shelter.

Public tap on the quay. Fuel near the harbour. Provisions and tavernas along the beach.

SKALA MARION

A small fishing village built around two coves close N of Ák Atspas.

Approach

The light structure on Ák Atspas (Fl(2)10s7M) is conspicuous and closer in the village above the harbour will be seen. A statue of the Virgin Mary is conspicuous on the S side of the S cove. Around the headland to the N a breakwater has been built off the village. The end of the breakwater is lit Fl.G.3s3M.

Mooring

In the S cove a quay runs along the N side where the fishing boats moor. Limited space to berth among the fishing boats. The quay is high in places with

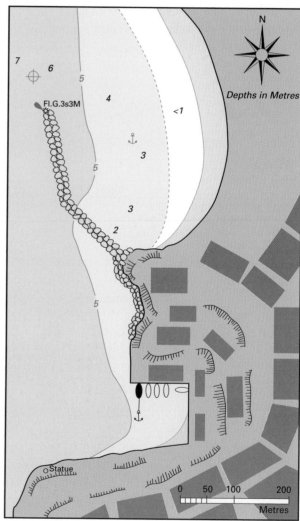

SKALA MARION
⊕40°38′·74N 24°30′·72E WGS84

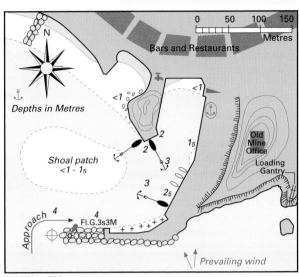

LIMENARIA
⊕40°37'·41N 24°34'·58E WGS84

Skála Marión S harbour. The breakwater of the N bay is visible left of picture *Lu Michell*

mooring rings set into the wall. Without further works the N harbour is open N but it does provide some shelter from prevailing winds and good shelter in southerlies. Anchor behind the breakwater in 2–6m off the beach. Water near the quay in the S cove.

Provisions and tavernas in the village.

ÓRMOS LIMENARIA

A busy fishing harbour and beach resort on the SW corner of Thasos.

Approach

Once into the bay the buildings around the beach to the W of the harbour will be seen. The old mine office perched on the top of the hill immediately E of the harbour is conspicuous. Care needed of a shoal patch in the centre of the W approaches off the beach. When entering the harbour keep close to the S breakwater (Fl.G.3s3M).

Mooring

Go stern or bows–to where there is room among the fishing boats on the S breakwater. Rocks reduce depths to <2m close to the quay in many places.

Limenaria looking SW. Note the shoal water in the entrance *Lu Michell*

Yachts also moor bows–to the quayed area on the knoll in the W side of the harbour. Again care is needed of underwater ballast off the quay. Old mooring chains are reported to lie on the bottom and a trip line is recommended. Better shelter than it looks from prevailing winds, but open W. Alternatively in settled weather anchor off the beach in 3–6m on sand and weed. Although shelter from northerlies is reasonable in the bay, there is usually some ground swell which can at times be uncomfortable.

Fuel and water on the waterfront. Good shopping for all provisions. Excellent tavernas and bars on the waterfront. Limenária was originally built to house workers from the nearby mines. In recent years it has developed into a large tourist resort.

PEFKARI (Rosongremou) and POTOS (Astris)

Along the coast to the SE of Limenária are Pefkari and Potos where a yacht can anchor off in settled weather. A small fishing harbour has been built off Potos, but it is little more than a rough breakwater. A swell rolls round into the bay from the S. There has been much development of beach-based tourism with lots of bars and restaurants around the bay.

ORMOS SOUROGKREMNOS (O. Áy Antonios)

40°35'·49N 24°37'·11E WGS84

An attractive settled weather anchorage on the S side of Ak Áy Antonios. Anchor off the beach in convenient depths. Beach bars ashore.

ORMOS ASTRIS

40°34'·71N 24°38'·32E WGS84

Large open bay between Ák Oxias and Ák Salonikos, with the off–lying island of N. Panayia to the S. Pretty lunch–stop anchorage with clear water and white sandy beaches.

Limited provisions and tavernas ashore.

ALIKI

On the SE corner of Thásos 2 miles to the W of Ák Babouras (Stravros) there are a number of small coves offering good shelter from N winds. Open only to the S, Aliki is the easternmost of the coves. Care is needed of the above and below-water rocks off the entrance. Anchor in 3–6m on sand and weed, good holding once the anchor is in. The prevailing wind tends to blow in over the head of the bay so it may be prudent to lay two anchors. In settled weather yachts anchor with a long line ashore to the S side to allow more space for others. On summer weekends parked cars line the roads for miles and it's hard to see the beach for the sunbathing bodies.

Some provisions and tavernas ashore.

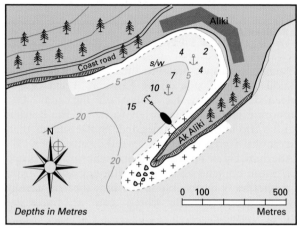

ALIKI
⊕40°36′·05N 24°44′·06E WGS84

ÓRMOS POTAMIAS

40°42′·56N 24°45′·78E WGS84

A large bay on the E coast of Thásos on the S side of Ák Pirgos. Anchor at the N end of the bay where there is reasonable shelter from NE winds. The bottom is sand and shelves gently to the shore. At the S end of the bay is a small fishing harbour open N, with a detached rough stone mole off the NW corner. Depths at the entrance and inside are subject to continuous silting, and unlikely to be much more than 1–1·5m. In settled weather anchor off to the E of the harbour with a long line ashore.

MAKRIAMMOS

On the NE corner of Thásos there is the open bay of Makriammos. In the N corner of the bay there is a short mole which provides some protection from NE winds. Moor bows-to near the extremity where there are 2m depths.

The Mainland coast

ADVIRA

40°55′·8N 24°58′·2E

A rockbound harbour with a buoyed channel into it. The entrance is lit Fl.G.3s3M/Fl.R.3s3M. It could be worth investigating but reconnoitre in the dinghy first.

PORT LÁGOS (Órmos Vistonikos)

BA 1636

Approach

Órmos Lágos lies in the NE corner of Órmos Vistonikos. It is a natural lagoon connected to the sea by a dredged channel. A hotel on Ák Fanári and a large factory and silo on the E side of the entrance to the harbour are conspicuous. The black conical buoy with a W cardinal topmark marking the outer edge of the shallows off Ák Fanári is difficult to see from seaward. Once inside Órmos Vistonikos, the buoys and beacons marking the dredged channel are easily identified and entry into the harbour is

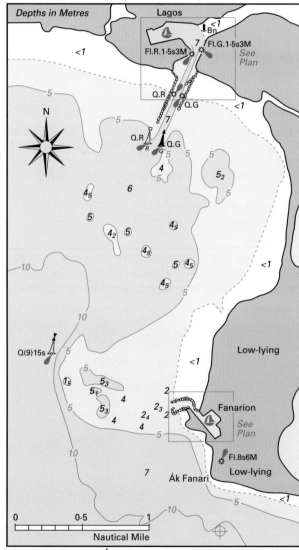

APPROACHES TO LÁGOS AND FANARION
⊕40°57′·0N 25°07′·8E

The basin at Lágos looking NE

straightforward. The channel and the harbour are kept dredged to 6m.

By night Use the light on Ák Fanári Fl.8s6M, the light buoy off the cape Q(9)15s, the light buoys marking the channel Q.R/Q.G and Fl.G.1·5s/ Fl.R.1·5s. There are leading lights: on 023°30′ F.Y.3M and F.Y.3M.

Mooring

Go alongside or stern or bows-to on the W quay.

Shelter Excellent all-round shelter.

Authorities Port police and customs.

Facilities

Water On the quay.

Fuel About 500m away.

Repairs Yachts are craned onto the hard in the SW corner.

Provisions Some provisions can be obtained. Ice available.

Eating out Tavernas.

Other Small Yacht Club.

General

Lágos is an important port for the shipment of grain from the hinterland. Although it is a commercial port, the approach to and setting of Port Lágos are

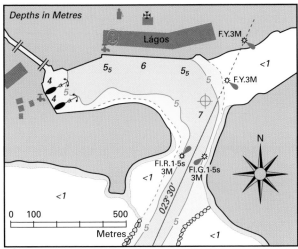

LÁGOS
⊕41°00′·4N 25°07′·6E

attractive. The surrounding marshes are a haven for all types of water birds rarely seen in other parts of Greece. The surrounding area is now a protected bird reserve and a walk through the lagoons is recommended. Just E of Lágos on the main road there is a delightful monastery built on an islet in the middle of one of the lagoons.

FANARION

A fishing harbour tucked into the W side of Ák Fanári. Care is needed in the approaches as the harbour is fringed by shoal water on the W side right out to the buoy (𝙄 topmark) marking the shallows in the approaches to Lágos. Make the approach from a WSW direction where the least depth should be 2·2m close off the entrance. The entrance is lit Fl.G.2s3M.

Care is needed in the harbour where there are irregular depths in the entrance channel of 1·8–2·5m depths. Go alongside or stern or bows-to the S quay. Good shelter.

Water near the quay. Fuel near the quay. Provisions and tavernas.

ÁYIOS KHARALAMBOS (Maronias)

40°52′·6N 25°30′·4E

One mile to the W of Ák Maronias at Áyios Kharalambos a rough stone L-shaped breakwater extends W and then N from the coast. There are reported to be 4–5m depths in the entrance and 2–3m depths off the quay on the E side. Good shelter.

Tavernas ashore.

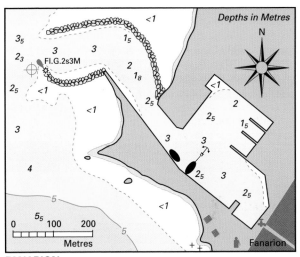

FANARION
⊕40°57′·9N 25°07′·5E

MAKRI

40°50′·8N 25°45′·1E

Seven miles to the W of Alexandroupolis lies a harbour serving the village of Mákri on the hill above. Go alongside or stern or bows–to inside the W breakwater with depths off the quay mostly 1·5–2·5m. Open S and E. In the NE corner is the original *caique* harbour. At the entrance there are less than 2m depths and it is rock-bound. Inside there would be excellent shelter. The entrance is lit F.G/F.R.3M. It deserves further exploration in settled weather.

ALEXANDROUPOLIS

BA 1636

Approach

Conspicuous The buildings of the large town are visible from the distance. The white lighthouse on the promenade and three red storage tanks behind the harbour are conspicuous. The outer mole of the harbour and the entrance are easily identified.

By night Use the main light Fl(3)15s24M and the lights at the entrance Fl.R.3s6M/Fl.G.3s3M.

Note Harbour works are in progress at the time of writing. Some of the lights listed may be in different positions and other lights may mark works being carried out. Care needed.

Dangers With strong S winds there is usually a lumpy sea over the shallow bank extending some miles off the coast in the approaches to the harbour.

Mooring

Go stern or bows-to or alongside the N quay near the entrance to the inner harbour or in the inner harbour itself. The bottom is sticky mud – excellent holding.

Shelter Good shelter, although strong S winds send in some swell – uncomfortable but not dangerous.

Authorities A port of entry: port police, customs and immigration authorities.

Facilities

Water On the quay in the inner harbour.
Fuel Near the quay.
Repairs Most mechanical and light engineering repairs. Excellent hardware shops.
Provisions Excellent shopping for all provisions. Ice from a fish shop near the waterfront.
Eating out Good tavernas in the town.

Other PO. OTE. Banks. ATM. Greek gas and Camping Gaz. Hire cars and motorbikes. Buses to Kavála and İstanbul. Train to Thessaloníki and İstanbul. Ferry to Samothráki. Internal flights to Athens.

General

Alexandroupolis, named after King Alexander (born 1893) and not Alexander the Great, is a modern bustling city and port. It is important as the major road and rail link with Turkey and also for the shipment of grain and tobacco from the hinterland. In the shallows 8 miles to the SE of the harbour where the Evros river flows into the sea, the local fishing boats net flatfish, mostly sole, and though most of it finds its way to Thessaloníki and Athens, some can be found in the tavernas at Alexandroupolis.

Samothráki
(Samothrace)

Until recently Samothráki has not had a secure harbour and for this reason has remained a solitary island shrouded in mystery. It is a forbidding-looking place, a gigantic lump of marble rising up to 1,600m (5,200ft) at the summit of Mt Fengari. On the west, Ák Akrotíri forms a shallow bay in which the harbour of Kamariótissa nesÿles.

The mysterious ancient inhabitants of the island, the Kabeiri (Cabeiri), were of pre-Greek origin, possibly of Phoenician or Phrygian stock, and worshipped the Great Earth Mother rather than the male gods which dominated classical times. The strength of the Kabeiri was such that Samothráki was regarded as a sacred island and a sanctuary for initiates of the cult, although this may have been a spin-off from the inaccessibility of the island.

They had a soft spot for seafarers, and initiation into their rites was deemed to be good luck and a

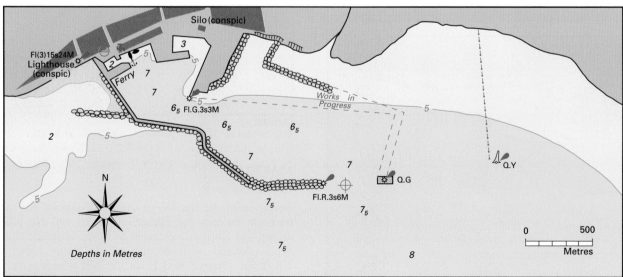

ALEXANDROUPOLIS
⊕40°50´.1N 25°53´.9E

safeguard against shipwreck. The power of the Kabeiri throughout the ancient world ensured Samothráki an independent existence throughout the Greek struggles until late into the Roman period.

The ruins of the ancient temple-city lie on a rocky ridge amongst wild olives and maquis. The American school of archaeologists have mainly been responsible for clearing the site and organising the small museum housing most of the finds that were not spirited away by early explorers. Of these the best known is the *Winged Victory of Samothrace* removed by the French in 1863 and now in the Louvre in Paris. The splendid site looking across to the mainland is well worth a visit. Above, in a craggy pocket, is the principal village (*chora*) of Samothráki.

KAMARIÓTISSA

Approach

Conspicuous From the N and W a tower on the NW corner of the island and the small village of Kamariótissa are conspicuous. From the S the low-lying sand spit terminating in Ák Akrotíri is not visible until you are very near it, but the light structure on the extremity is visible from some distance off. Four white wind generators are

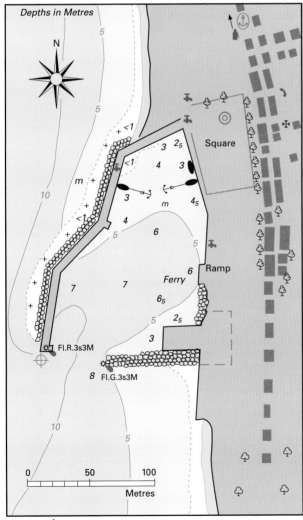

KAMARIÓTISSA
⊕40°28′·4N 25°28′·1E

conspicuous from the N and W. Closer in the cluster of buildings at Kamariótissa and the harbour mole are easily identified.

By night Use the light on Ák Akrotíri Fl.5s10M and the lights at the entrance: Fl.R.3s3M/Fl.G.3s3M.

Dangers By day or night caution must be exercised whilst navigating in the vicinity of the low-lying Ák Akrotíri when relative distances between the cape and the high mountains behind can be confused.

Mooring

Go stern or bows-to or alongside the mole or the quay wherever there is room. The bottom is sand and shingle – good holding. The harbour is usually crowded with fishing boats and it can be difficult to find a berth. You may have to go alongside a fishing boat and then move when it leaves.

Shelter Good all-round shelter although a strong SW wind might make the harbour uncomfortable.

Authorities Port police.

Facilities

Water At the root of the mole.
Fuel On the waterfront. A mini-tanker can deliver.
Provisions Most provisions can be obtained.
Eating out Good tavernas on the waterfront.
Other PO. OTE. ATM. Bus to the *chora*. Ferry to Alexandroupolis.

General

Kamariótissa is essentially a small fishing hamlet and the ferry port for Samothráki. The inhabitants are very friendly towards visiting yachtsmen as they rarely see a great number of yachts here. It is a safe place to leave a yacht when visiting the archaeological site on the N side of the island.

To get there take a taxi inland to Palaeopolis and then enquire at the hotel for admittance. It is a short walk to the site itself where there are remains of several of the initiation buildings including the Arsinion which was the largest circular building in ancient Greece. A small museum nearby houses finds from the site. While you are there it is worth going on to the *chora* which is not far away.

THERMA

40°30′·3N 25°36′·4E

A very small fishing harbour on the N coast of the island. An L–shaped mole gives some protection from the N–E winds, but with SW–NW winds it could be untenable. The mole head is lit Q.R. Depths of 2–4m along the mole are reported, but the entrance looks liable to silting and care is needed. Construction is not finished, and rusty iron bars are reported to protrude from the quayside. Tavernas ashore.

VIII. The Eastern Sporades

The eastern Sporades stretch down the coast of Asia Minor, linking northern Greece to the Dodecanese. Like the other islands in the Aegean, they are the peaks of mountains that once stood on the plain of the Aegean. Geographically Samothráki belongs to this group of islands, but politically it is administered from Alexandroupolis and its communications are with the north. Limnos, the most northerly of the group described here, hovers in its own limbo in the middle of the northern Aegean. Generally the islands are more fertile and greener than the Cyclades and the Dodecanese. Lésvos and Sámos in particular will surprise the visiting yachtsman with their well-watered, cultivated plains and extensive pine forests.

The history of the group of islands is patchy and difficult to summarise as a whole – the historical detail for each island can be found in the introduction to each one. Very early on Limnos was an important link between Europe and the islands to the south. It had a highly developed Bronze Age culture of a Minoan-Mycenaean type and metalworking probably filtered into the Cyclades and Crete from there. With the decline of Limnos, the Dorians and Ionians moved in. The Ionic Confederacy was centred around Khíos and Sámos and the adjacent mainland coast. The confederacy prospered and for some time rivalled Athens in its high life and appreciation of the arts. The chief cities of the group – Khíos, Ephesus, Smyrna and Miletus – endured as important centres long after the decline of the confederacy.

Lésvos existed outside the confederacy in a somewhat chaotic state until the beginning of the 6th century BC when Pittacus calmed the island and earned for himself a place as one of the Seven Sages of Greece. Soon afterwards, around 540 BC, Polykrates of Sámos achieved his meteoric rise to fame and fortune and control of the group revolved around this tyrannical genius and the Persians pushing up from Asia Minor.

The decisive Battle of Salamís ousted the Persians and ushered in the usual succession of invaders: the Romans, the Saracens, Byzantine rulers, the Venetians and the Genoese, and the Turks. Looking at the islands today (with the exception of Psará), it is hard to believe that they were often entirely abandoned by the native inhabitants as successive waves of invaders swept down on them and corsairs mopped up whatever was left. Indeed it is unlikely that the present populations of the islands are descended from the original inhabitants at all. The group became part of Greece in 1912 after the Balkan Wars.

Today the eastern Sporades are considered to be important military outposts and soldiers are stationed on all of the islands. Photographs of many of the harbours, much of the coastline and some of the interior are forbidden. A sign in Greek and English or of the pictorial type (a camera with a cross through it) will usually be found prohibiting photographs. It should be observed, or all your film may be confiscated and exposed!

With the exception of Sámos, the islands are to a large extent off the tourist track. Consequently many facilities are underdeveloped. Yacht equipment and servicing beyond the basic fisherman's needs is limited. In recent years a few more tourists have discovered the islands and there has been something of a revival in the main centres. You still won't find too many tavernas offering pseudo-sophisticated fare as in Corfu or Mikonos or Rhodes, but you will find a wider choice of places to eat and drink. However the friendliness of the locals more than makes up for these small deficiencies and prices on the whole are cheaper than elsewhere. The basics are there – good harbours, good centres for provisions and communications – but not the gloss. For many including myself that is a blessing.

Routes

The geography of the Eastern Sporades lying approximately north to south means that routes north in the summer are directly into the *meltemi* while routes south are off the wind.

With the *meltemi* blowing down the Turkish coast from the N–NNE some yachts use the coastal route up the Turkish coast, where the wind direction is modified by the coast and there is more possibility of getting some wind that is not directly on the nose. The wind is usually channelled into the gulfs along the Turkish coast and this can give some useful slants, enabling yachts to sail up the coast. Yachts heading N through the Eastern Sporades in the summer when the *meltemi* is blowing are in for a bash to windward and the going can be tough at times. If a yacht leaves in early summer or late autumn the northerlies are less frequent and less strong. You may even get a few southerlies to help you on your way.

Coming S down through the Eastern Sporades is a sleigh ride in the summer with the *meltemi* behind giving you good sailing all the way down and on through the Dodecanese. The wind direction will change somewhat as it is funnelled through the channels, but generally is aft of the beam.

If you are heading across to the Eastern Sporades from the Cyclades then it pays to stay high and head for somewhere like Andros or Tínos before setting off across to Lesvos, Khíos or Ikaria. Initially you will be close reaching, but the wind will free off the further you get across and it is a rollicking if wet ride with the *meltemi* across to the Eastern Sporades.

Data

PORTS OF ENTRY
Mirina (Limnos)
Mitilíni (Lésvos)
Limín Khíos
Pithagorion (Sámos)
Vathi (Sámos)

PROHIBITED AREAS
Khíos It is prohibited to enter or anchor in the N cove at Laghana.

Photographs of many of the harbours and parts of the coastline of Limnos, Lésvos, Khíos and Sámos are prohibited.

MAJOR LIGHTS
Limnos
Ák Pláka Fl(3)30s22M
Ák Moúrtzeflos Fl(2)14s13M
Ák Kástron Fl.6s11M
Vrak Kómbi (Ák Lena) Q(2)6s10M
Ák Kávos (Sagradha) Fl.3s5M

Áy Evstrátios
Ák Tripití Fl(2)10s8M
Nisís Áy Apóstoloi Fl.WR.5s10/7M

Lésvos
Ák Kórakas Fl.WR.5s11/8M
Ák Mólivos LFl.WG.10s12/8M
Nisís Sígri (Megalonisi)
Fl(2)15s21M
Nisís Kelloni Fl.3s6M
Ák Agriliós Fl(2)12s9M
Mitilíni Fl(3)14s6M
Nisídha Panayía Fl.10s7M

Psará
Ák Áyios Yeóryios Fl.10s25M

Khíos
Ák Anapómera (Vr Gertis)
Fl(3)12s11M
Vrak Stróvilo Fl.5s10M
Nisídha Venétiko Fl(2)15s12M
Limin Khiou Fl.G.3s12M
Ormiskos Mestá Fl.3s7M
Nisís Pasas Fl(2)20s11M
Nisís Prasonisia Fl(2)WR.10s6/4M

Ikaría
Ák Páppas Fl.20s25M
Ák Armenistís Fl(3)12s11M
Vrak Evdhilos (Kofinás) Fl.7·5s11M
Ák Dhrépanon Fl(3)24s12M

Sámos
Ák Kótsikas Fl(2)7·2s7M
Ák Gátos Fl(3)14s7M
Ák Áyios Dhoménikos Fl.3·6s5M
Ák Pangózi (Karlóvasi) Fl.5s11M

Foúrnoi
Ák Trakhíli Fl(2)15s7M
Ák Saíta (Malaki) Fl(2)12s8M

Quick reference guide

	Shelter	Mooring	Fuel	Water	Provisioning	Tavernas	Plan
Limnos							
Mirina	A	AC	B	A	A	B	•
Órmos Platí	B	C	O	O	O	C	•
Órmos Thanos	B	C	O	O	O	C	•
Órmos Áy Pavlou	C	C	O	O	O	O	•
Órmos Kondiá	B	C	O	O	O	C	•
Órmos Moúdhrou	A	AC	B	A	B	C	•
Órmos Plakas	C	A	O	O	O	O	
Órmos Hefaistia	C	C	O	O	O	O	
Órmos Kotsinas	C	C	O	O	O	O	
Órmos Moúrtzeflos	B	C	O	O	O	O	
Prasa	B	A	O	B	C	C	
Áyios Evstrátios	B	AB	O	A	C	C	•
Lésvos							
Mitilíni	A	A	B	A	A	A	•
Panayioudha	B	A	O	B	C	B	•
Pamfilla	C	C	O	B	O	C	
Skála Thermis	B	B	B	B	C	B	•
Skála Mistegna	B	AC	O	B	O	C	•
Skala Neo Kidonies	B	AB	O	B	B	B	
Órmos Mákris Yialos	O	C	O	O	O	O	
Tsonia	B	C	O	O	C	C	
Skála Sikaminéas	C	A	O	B	C	C	•
Mithimna	A	A	B	A	A	A	•
Pétra	B	AC	B	B	C	C	•
Ghavadholos	B	AB	O	B	C	C	•
Sígri	B	ABC	B	A	B	B	•
Erresos	B	AC	O	B	B	B	•
Kólpos Kalloni	C	C	O	B	C	C	•
Skála Polikhnitos	BC	A	B	B	C	B	•
Plomárion	A	A	B	A	A	B	•
Órmos Mersinia	B	C	O	O	O	C	•
Kólpos Yéras	BC	C	O	O	C	C	•
Perama	B	AB	B	A	C	C	
Psará	B	A	O	B	C	C	•
Oinoussa							
Mandráki	A	AC	O	A	C	C	•
Nisís Pasas	B	C	O	O	O	O	•

	Shelter	Mooring	Fuel	Water	Provisioning	Tavernas	Plan
Khíos							
Limín Khíou	B	AB	B	A	A	B	•
Khíos Marina	A	B	B	O	C	C	•
Vrondados	B	A	O	O	C	C	•
Daskaloptera	B	A	O	O	C	C	
O. Pantoukios	B	AC	O	B	C	C	
Órmos Kolokithias	C	C	O	B	C	C	•
Kardhamila (Marmaro)	B	A	B	A	B	B	•
Limnia (Volissos)	B	AB	B	B	C	C	•
O. Elinta	O	C	O	O	O	C	
Lithi	B	AB	O	B	C	C	•
Áy Eirini	C	C	O	O	O	C	
Ó. Mestá	C	AC	O	B	C	C	•
Áy Lorrias	B	C	O	O	O	C	
Ó. Kamari	B	C	O	B	C	C	•
Voukaria	C	A	O	A	C	C	
Komi	B	A	O	A	C	C	•
Kataraktis	B	AB	O	B	C	C	
Áy Ermioni	A	A	B	A	C	C	•
Ikaría							
Evdhilos	C	A	O	B	B	C	•
Áyios Kirikos	B	AC	B	A	A	B	•
Órmos Loutró	C	C	O	B	O	C	
Sámos							
Karlóvasi	B	AB	B	A	B	B	•
Áy Konstantinos	B	A	O	O	C	C	
Kokkari	C	C	O	B	O	C	
Vathi	C	AB	B	A	A	A	•
Órmos Mourtia	C	C	O	O	O	O	
Órmos Posidonion	B	C	O	O	O	O	
Pithagorion	A	AC	B	A	A	A	•
Pithagorion Marina	A	B	B	O	B	B	•
Ireon	B	C	O	O	C	C	
Samioupoula	O	C	O	O	O	C	
Marathakambos	B	AC	B	B	C	C	•
Órmos Limnionas	C	C	O	O	O	C	
Foúrnoi							
Órmos Fornoi	B	A	B	B	C	B	•
Foúrnoi anchorages	B	C	O	O	O	O	•

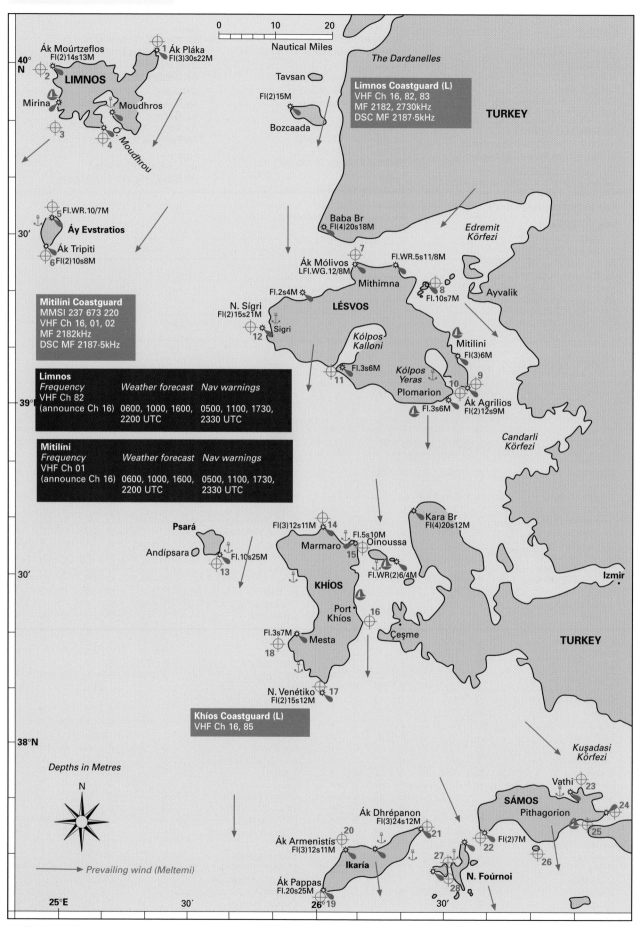

0   10   20
Nautical Miles

Ák Moúrtzeflos
Fl(2)14s13M
40°
N
2
LIMNOS
Mirina
Moudhros
Ó. Moudhrou
3
4

1 Ák Pláka
Fl(3)30s22M

The Dardanelles

Tavsan

Fl(2)15M

Bozcaada

Limnos Coastguard (L)
VHF Ch 16, 82, 83
MF 2182, 2730kHz
DSC MF 2187·5kHz

TURKEY

5 Fl.WR.10/7M
Áy Evstratios
Ák Tripiti
6 Fl(2)10s8M
30'

Baba Br
Fl(4)20s18M
7
Edremit Körfezi

Ák Mólivos
LFl.WG.12/8M
Mithimna

Fl.WR.5s11/8M
8
Fl.10s7M
Ayvalik

Fl.2s4M

N. Sígri
Fl(2)15s21M
12 Sigri

LÉSVOS

Kólpos Kalloni

Fl.3s6M
11

Kólpos Yeras
Plomarion
Fl.3s6M

Mitilini
Fl(3)6M
10
9
Ák Agrilios
Fl(2)12s9M

Candarli Körfezi

Mitilíni Coastguard
MMSI 237 673 220
VHF Ch 16, 01, 02
MF 2182kHz
DSC MF 2187·5kHz

39°

Limnos		
Frequency	*Weather forecast*	*Nav warnings*
VHF Ch 82		
(announce Ch 16)	0600, 1000, 1600, 2200 UTC	0500, 1100, 1730, 2330 UTC

Mitilíni		
Frequency	*Weather forecast*	*Nav warnings*
VHF Ch 01		
(announce Ch 16)	0600, 1000, 1600, 2200 UTC	0500, 1100, 1730, 2330 UTC

Psará
Andípsara
Fl.10s25M
13

Fl(3)12s11M 14
Marmaro
15
Fl.5s10M
Oinoussa

Kara Br
Fl(4)20s12M

Fl.WR(2)6/4M

KHÍOS

Izmir

30'

Port Khíos
16
Çeşme

Fl.3s7M
Mesta
18

TURKEY

N. Venétiko 17
Fl(2)15s12M

Khíos Coastguard (L)
VHF Ch 16, 85

38°N

Kuşadasi Körfezi

Depths in Metres

N

Prevailing wind (Meltemi)

Vathi 23
SÁMOS
Pithagorion
24

Ák Dhrépanon
Fl(3)24s12M
20
21
Ák Armenistís
Fl(3)12s11M
Ikaría
22 Fl(2)7M
25
27
26

Ák Pappas
Fl.20s25M
26° 19
N. Foúrnoi
28

25°E   30'   **26°**   30'

USEFUL WAYPOINTS

⊕1 1M N of Ák Pláka (Limnos)
    40°03'·1N 25°26'·8E

⊕2 1M W of Ák Moúrtzeflos (Limnos)
    39°59'·19N 25°00'·63E WGS84

⊕3 0·5M S of N. Tigani (Limnos)
    39°49'·24N 25°02'·65E WGS84

⊕4 0.5M S of N. Kastri
    (Ák Kómbi - Limnos)
    39°46'·88E 25°14'·17E WGS84

⊕5 1M N of Ák Áy Apóstoliou (Áy Evstrátios)
    39°26'·9N 24°59'·2E

⊕6 1M S of Ák Tripití (Áy Evstrátios)
    39°26'·9N 24°59'·2E

⊕7 0·25M N of Ák Mólivos (Lésvos)
    39°23'·05N 26°11'·05E WGS84

⊕8 0·25M E of N. Tomaria (Lésvos)
    39°18'·87N 26°27'·24E WGS84

⊕9 0.25M E of Ák Agriliós (Lésvos)
    39°00'·58N 26°36'·85E WGS84

⊕10 Entrance to Kólpos Yéras (Lésvos)
    (0·3M E of Ák Kavourolimni)
    39°00'·15N 26°33'·17E WGS84

⊕11 1M W of Vr Kalloni (Lésvos)
    39°04'·7N 26°03'·4E

⊕12 1M W of Vrak Sedhousa (Sígri/Lésvos)
    39°11'·9N 25°47'·8E

⊕13 2M S of Ák Áy Yeóryios (Psará)
    38°30'3N 25°36'·6E

⊕14 1M N of Vrak Gertis (Khíos)
    38°37'·4N 26°01'·6E

⊕15 Mid-channel N end of Stenón Oinoussa (Khíos)
    38°32'·73N 26°10'·32E WGS84

⊕16 0·3M E of Ák Eleni (Khíos)
    38°19'·76N 26°10'·15E WGS84

⊕17 0·5M N of Nisídha Venétiko
    38°08'·1N 26°00'·9E

⊕18 1M W of Ák Mestá (Khíos)
    38°14'·6N 25°50'·7E

⊕19 1M S of Ák Páppas (Ikaría)
    37°29'·8N 25°58'·8E

⊕20 1M N of Ák Armenistís (Ikaría)
    37°39'·2N 26°05'·0E

⊕21 1M E of Ák Dhrépanon (Ikaría)
    37°41'·5N 26°23'·1E

⊕22 1M S of Ák Áy Dhoménikos (Sámos)
    37°39'·7N 26°35'·5E

⊕23 1M N of Makronisi (Sámos)
    37°49'·12N 26°59'·90E WGS84

⊕24 0·5M E of Ák Gátos (Sámos)
    37°43'·53N 27°04'·67E WGS84

⊕25 Stenón Samou W end
    (Mid channel Bayrak Adasi N side)
    37°41'·86N 27°00'·80E WGS84

⊕26 1M S of Samioupoula
    37°36'·3N 26°48'·4E

⊕27 Mid-channel N end of Póros Fournon
    37°36'·0N 26°27'·8E

⊕28 Mid-channel S end of Póros Fournon
    37°33'·7N 26°27'·5E

Weather patterns in the eastern Sporades

The prevailing wind in the summer is the *meltemi*. It blows fitfully at first in June, getting up to full strength in July, August and September and dies in October. In July and August it blows strongly, about Force 4–6, and may reach Force 7 on occasions. In the more southerly islands of the group it blows from the N–NNW but in Limnos it blows from the NE. Around much of the group the *meltemi* is funnelled by the land including the adjacent Turkish coast so in places it can be blowing from the N, W or E. In the spring and autumn there are often S winds, but they rarely exceed Force 4–5.

In the winter strong winds may be from the SE or the NE. In the more northerly islands strong winds are most often from the NE and strong S winds can be expected to become strong NE winds which may blow for several days. In the winter exceptionally severe storms can strike the group and Force 10 and 11 gales have been recorded.

In common with the other islands in the Aegean there are gusts off the high land on the lee side of an island. With the *meltemi* these gusts are especially severe off Sámos and Ikaría and parts of Lésvos. With prolonged strong winds from the N the seas surrounding Limnos can become especially confused and it is prudent to wait a day after the wind has died to let the sea subside.

Limnos
(Lemnos)

Although it geographically belongs to the eastern Sporades, Limnos, situated as it is in the middle of the northern Aegean, is isolated from the other islands of the group. Few tourists go there and ships no longer call on the way to the Dardanelles – even the soldiers stationed there act as if the strategic significance of the island has been somehow overrated by the top brass and really they should be somewhere else. In ancient times none of this was true, when Limnos was an important island with one of the most advanced Bronze Age civilizations in Greece.

There were two main reasons for its importance. Lying halfway across the wind-tossed Aegean, it was the logical stepping stone between Europe and Asia Minor. It is likely that Troy was founded from Limnos and there was contact with Lésvos and northern Greece. As a stepping stone, Limnos possessed an abundance of well-sheltered natural harbours including the great Bay of Moudhros. Today, although the island is only partially wooded and cultivated on the east coast, it is easy to see how once, when the soft contours (there are no very high peaks) were covered in green woods, this was one of the finest islands in the northern Aegean.

The name Limnos is possibly derived from a cult of the Minoan mother-goddess, but the principal gods of the island were Hephaestus and the Kabeiri based on Samothráki. Hephaestus is supposed to have berated Zeus one day about his treatment of Hera whereupon he was thrown out of Olympus and

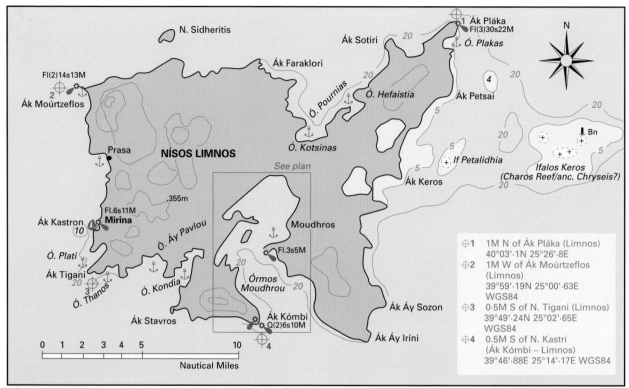

NÍSOS LIMNOS

fell onto Limnos – breaking both legs. Not until he had fashioned special leg-braces of gold could he walk. The myth probably derives from the volcanic nature of the island and also the tradition of metalworking that existed from early times when these skills spread from the north down to the Greek archipelago.

In classical times the island acquired ill repute from the so-called 'Limnian deeds'. The women of the island refused to serve Aphrodite who was making poor old Hephaestus miserable with her numerous affairs with other gods and mortals. Aphrodite responded by afflicting the unfortunate women with evil smells (Ernle Bradford suggests 'body odour and halitosis' in the euphemistic jargon of advertising) causing their husbands to ignore them. The incensed women of Limnos went on the rampage and murdered all males on the island. Jason and the Argonauts on their adventures discovered the island full of frustrated women and not surprisingly dallied two years repopulating it.

The site of the principal Bronze Age city is at Hephaestia on the east of the island. The Italians have excavated the site and also conducted underwater exploration of Charos Reef (Ifalos Keros) lying 7 miles off the east coast. The discovery of marble blocks gives some substance to the identification of the reef with ancient Chryseis. It is thought this was the site of the ancient city which, as Herodotus recorded, was engulfed by the sea after an earthquake.

Limnos achieved some prominence again when Moudhros Bay was the base for the Gallipoli campaign. Almost as if the failure of that campaign affected the island, ever since its importance has declined and even the tourist boom has only just touched the island. A local asked me when I was there: 'We have fine beaches, clear water, good harbours, friendly people, but no tourists – why?' I couldn't really tell him that I liked Limnos as it is, in its splendid isolation.

MIRINA (Myrinas, Merini, Kástro)

BA 1636

Approach

Conspicuous The castle on the rocky bluff on the N side of the entrance and a white church on a rocky bluff at the root of the outer breakwater are conspicuous. The buildings of the town can be seen from the N and W, but not from the S until you are into the bay. The S breakwater is easily identified.

By night Use the light on the castle Fl.6s11M and the lights at the entrance Q.R.3M/Q.G.3M. The inner basin is lit: F.R.2M.

Mooring

Go stern or bows-to the N quay. The bottom is mud, good holding.

Note A small ferry also uses the quay and stays overnight. Port police will inform you if you obstruct the berth.

Shelter Good shelter from the prevailing NE winds. Strong W-NW winds send a surge into the harbour, more uncomfortable than dangerous. Make sure your anchor has plenty of scope and you are pulled a little way off the quay. Southerlies may also cause a surge.

Authorities A port of entry: port police, customs and immigration. The most convenient port for clearing out to the Dardanelles.

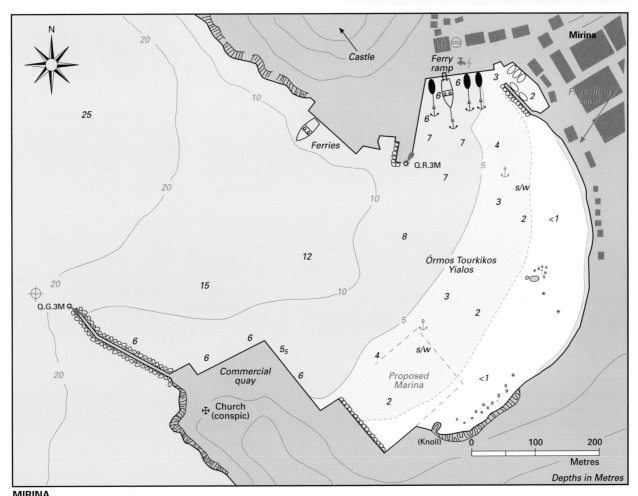

MIRINA
⊕ 39°52´·29N 25°02´·98E WGS84

Castle

Ferry ramp

Mirina

Prevailing wind

N

25

20

10

Ferries

Q.R.3M

7

7

7

6

6

6

6

3

2

4

5

s/w

3

8

12

Órmos Tourkikos Yialos

3

2

<1

*

*

15

10

20

Q.G.3M

6

6

6

5 5

6

5

s/w

3

2

4

Commercial quay

Church (conspic)

Proposed Marina

<1

*

2

2

(Knoll)

0   100   200

Metres

Depths in Metres

Mirina on Limnos looking S   *Lu Michell*

Note The inner harbour is invariably crowded with fishing boats. Under normal conditions the outer harbour affords good shelter so there is little to be gained by going into the inner harbour.

Anchorage It is possible to anchor off just inside the 5m line where convenient. The *meltemi* gusts down into the bay but the holding is good on sand and weed.

Note Works on the commercial quay appear to be complete. There are plans to build a marina in the S corner of the bay. Work has not yet begun.

Facilities

Services Water and electricity on the quay.
Fuel Can be delivered by mini-tanker.
Repairs Some mechanical repairs and light engineering work. Good hardware and tool shops.
Provisions Good shopping for all provisions. Ice available nearby.
Eating out Several good tavernas near the inner harbour and on the beach.
Other PO. OTE. Banks. ATMs. Greek gas. Buses to the principal villages. Ferries to Lésvos, Piraeus and Kavála. Internal flights to Thessaloníki and Athens.

General

Built near the site of the ancient capital, Mirina has only recently readopted its ancient name. Formerly it was called Kástro after the Genoese castle dominating the town. The castle is open both to visitors and to the herds of deer and goats that graze around it. The attitude to photography seems to be more relaxed, but caution is advised.

Few yachts visit Mirina and those which do use it primarily as the most convenient port for clearing for the Dardanelles. Yet it is a friendly place and a convenient base for visiting other anchorages around the island.

ÓRMOS PLATÍ

Lies N of Ák Tigani and provides good shelter from N winds. Open to the SW. Care should be taken of the reef extending SE from the N side of the entrance and a reef on the SE side of the bay. Anchor in 4–8m on sand. Tavernas on the beach.

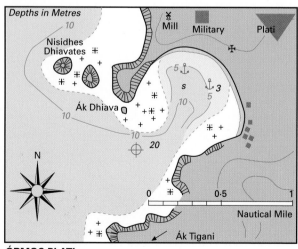

ÓRMOS PLATI
⊕39°51′·1N 25°03′·3E

ÓRMOS THANOS

The double-headed bay lying just E of Ák Tigani. Care is needed of the reef and shoal water extending for half a mile SSW of Ák Tigani. Ifalos Tigani, a rock which occasionally dries, lies approximately 0·2 of a mile SSW of Nisís Tigani. There is reported to be a passage between Ifalos Tigani and Nisís Tigani with 7m depths, but this is not recommended. A yacht should keep well off the cape before making the approach to the bay. There are several places a yacht can anchor.

1. *Órmos Stiri* Immediately under Ák Tigani there is a cove where a yacht can anchor with a long line to the shore. Anchor in 4–8m.
2. On the W side of the knobbly islet in Órmos Thanos. A yacht can anchor in 4–8m on sand. The head of this cove is rock-bound.
3. On the E side of the bay and the islet. This is the best anchorage. Anchor off the beach in 4–8m on sand. Good shelter from the *meltemi*. Taverna ashore.

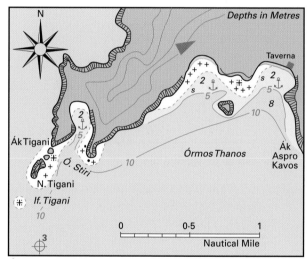

ÓRMOS THANOS

⊕3   0·5M S of N. Tigani (Limnos) 39°49′·24N 25°02′·65E WGS84

ÓRMOS ÁY PAVLOU

The large bay lying E of Órmos Thanos. Care is needed of the reef and above-water rock in the middle of the bay. It is easily identified in calm weather. There are a number of places a yacht can anchor around the large bay.

1. In the SW corner. The head and sides of the cove are obstructed by reefs and shoal water. Anchor in 4–5m in the middle of the cove. Mediocre shelter from the *meltemi*.
2. In the NW corner. The N side of the cove is obstructed by reefs and shoal water. Anchor in the SW of the cove in 4–5m on sand and weed. Mediocre shelter from the *meltemi*.

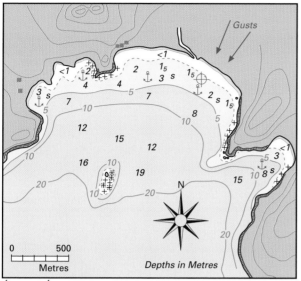

ÓRMOS ÁY PAVLOU
⊕39°50'·7N 25°07'·6E

3. At the head of the bay off the long beach. Anchor in 4–6m on sand and shingle. Reasonable shelter from the *meltemi*.

4. In the cove on the E side. Anchor in 3–6m on sand. Good shelter from the *meltemi*.

ÓRMOS KONDÍA

The large bay E of Órmos Áy Pavlou and N of Ák Stavrós. There are several places a yacht can anchor around the large bay.

1. On the W side of the bay there are several coves where a yacht can anchor. Mostly 3–8m on sand. Reasonable shelter can be found from the *meltemi*.

2. **Dhiapori** At the NE head of the bay is Dhiapori. Anchor in 4–7m off the hamlet on mud. Good shelter from the *meltemi*.

Tavernas ashore.

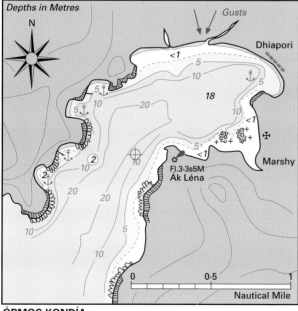

ÓRMOS KONDÍA
⊕39 50'·8N 25 09'·4E

ÓRMOS MOÚDHROU (Moudra)

BA 1636

Approach

Conspicuous The entrance to the large bay is easily identified. Nisís Kómbi and the light tower on it are conspicuous. Transit the channel between N. Pondokonisia and Ák Áspro Kávos on a bearing of 205°. Some of the channel markers are difficult to identify against the barren land behind. The twin cupolas of the cathedral are easier to pick up than the channel buoys in the approach to Moudhros. Care needed of four large mooring buoys to the N off the town. The end of the cargo quay has a broad RoRo ramp running into the water. The small harbour has light structures on the end of the breakwaters but no lights.

By night Use the lights on Nisís Kómbi Q(2)6s10M and Ák Áspro Kávos Fl.3s5M, the light buoys marking the channel Q.G/Q.R, and the lightbuoys at Moudhros (Q.G and Q.R, but not to be relied upon).

Dangers

1. Care must be taken of the reef extending for half a mile SW from Ák Velanidhia, the E entrance point.

2. Once up to Ák Áspro Kávos care is needed of the extensive reefs and shoal water bordering the coast and islets in the bay. The plan can only

MOUDHROS – HARBOUR AND ANCHORAGES
⊕₁ 39°47'·13N 25°14'·17E WGS84
⊕₂ 39°51'·01N 25°13'·70E WGS84

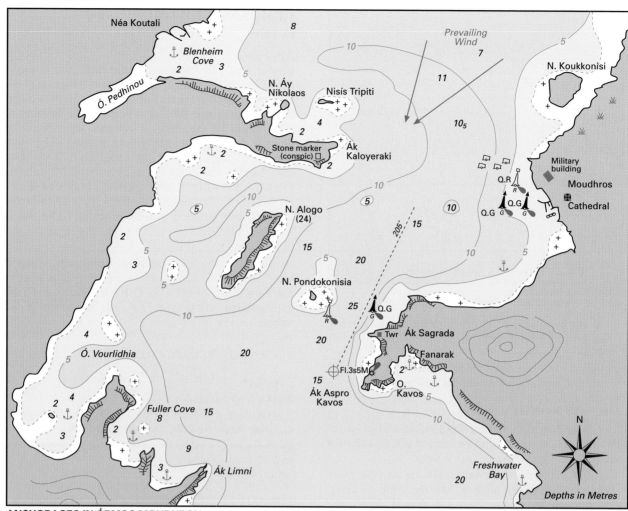

ANCHORAGES IN ÓRMOS MOUDHROU
⊕39°51'·01N 25°13'·70E WGS84

show these approximately and it is recommended you use BA 1636 if you intend to explore the bay in detail.

Mooring

Once into the bay there is a choice of anchorages or a yacht can proceed to the town of Moudhros on the E side of the bay.

Moudhros At Moudhros there are 3–4m depths off the outer half of the pier. Go alongside or stern or

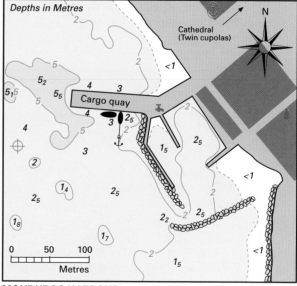

MOUDHROS HARBOUR
⊕39°52'·31N 25°15'·69E WGS84

bows-to as far towards the root of the pier as possible to leave room for local coasters to berth. The S side is recommended as giving better shelter from the *meltemi*. A small harbour with the entrance on the S side is mostly shallow, but with care a small

Ák Kómbi and Nisís Kastri on the W side of the entrance to Órmos Moúdhrou looking NW   *Lu Michell*

Freshwater Bay in Órmos Moudhrou   *Nigel Patten*

yacht can use it.

Shelter Good shelter from the *meltemi*.

Authorities Port police at Moudhros.

Anchorages There are numerous anchorages around the large bay:

1. **Blenheim Cove (Ó. Pedhinou)** Open NE–E.
2. N of Nisís Alogo under the headland ending in Ák Kaloyeraki.
3. **Órmos Vourlidhia** Open NE. Care is needed of the shoal in the bay. 3–4m depths on the E and SE of the shoal reported.
4. **Fuller Cove** Open NE.
5. **Tarrant Cove** Open NE.
6. **Órmos Kávos** 39°51'·11N 25°14'·54E WGS84
   Under Ák Áspro Kávos. The bottom is uneven with sand, rocks and weed. Anchor on a sandy patch in 4–5m. Open S. The beach is popular with Moudhriots in summer.
7. **Freshwater Cove** Good shelter from N winds reported here.

Facilities
(At Moudhros village)
Water On the quay.
Fuel In the town.
Provisions Most provisions can be obtained in the village.
Eating out Several tavernas.
Other PO. OTE. Bus to Mirina. The airport is near the head of the bay.

General
Órmos Moúdhrou is one of the finest fleet anchorages in the northern Aegean and it was from here the ill-fated Gallipoli campaign was launched. North of Moudhros village lies Australian pier and the remains of Egyptian pier. I find it difficult to conjure up what it must have been like when the bay was packed full of battleships, cruisers, destroyers and transport ships when looking at the forgotten and deserted bay today.

In the plan of Moudhros Bay I have identified Yam, Yrroc, Eb and Denmad Hills which when read

from right to left, as H. M. Denham points out, tells us what the British surveyors thought of their captain who was alleged to have worked them too hard and stopped their leave. Photographs are prohibited of some sites around the bay.

NOTE
SW-going currents along the S coast of Limnos cause a confused sea with wind over current.

East and north coast

On the E coast there are several large bays that can be used in calm weather. Care must be taken of Ifalos Petalidhia and Ifalos Keros (Charos Reef) lying off the E coast.

ÓRMOS PLAKAS
40°01'·2N 25°27'·0E

On the SE side of Ák Pláka there is a large bay with a short breakwater at the N end. There are 2–4m depths on the outer end of the quay where a yacht can go bows-to with care. Alternatively anchor in 3–5m in the lee of the breakwater.

ÓRMOS HEFAISTIA (Ekato Kefales)
39°58'·3N 25°20'·3E

The large bay of Órmos Pournias lies on the N coast between Ák Sotini and Ák Faraklon. On the E side of this bay is Órmos Hefaistia where some shelter can be found from the *meltemi*. Anchor in 5–8m on mud or sand.

ÓRMOS KOTSINAS
39°57'·0N 25°17'·5E

The bay on the SW side of Órmos Pournias. Some shelter from the *meltemi* tucked under the N side of the bay. Anchor in 5–8m. Military post ashore. Taverna on the S side of the bay.

ÓRMOS MOÚRTZEFLOS
39°58'·9N 25°02'·8E

On the S side of Ák Moúrtzeflos there is a small cove under the sand bar that affords good shelter from the *meltemi*. Open S. Anchor in 5–7m on sand and shingle.

PRASA
39°55'·6N 25°03'·8E

A tiny harbour 4M S of Moúrtzeflos, under Ák Kaloyeros. Good shelter under the N mole but the harbour is liable to silt and in any case is usually full of local boats.

Nísos Áyios Evstrátios

ÁYIOS EVSTRÁTIOS

Approach

Conspicuous The harbour lies 1½ miles SSW of Ák Kalamáki, beneath a small hill with a conspicuous whitewashed cemetery on the top.

By night The end of the mole is lit: Fl.R.2s3M.

Mooring

There are 3m depths along most of the length of the new quay and yachts can berth alongside or stern or bows-to. A sandy bottom with scattered rocks gives fair holding although there is some weed causing difficulty in places.

Shelter Shelter is much improved with the extension of the mole. Good shelter from the *meltemi*. Strong southerlies may still be a bit of a problem here.

Facilities

Water On the quay although a long hose is needed.
Provisions Most provisions can be found in the village.

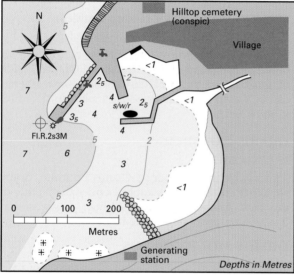

ÁYIOS EVSTRÁTIOS
⊕39°32'·4N 24°59'·2E

Áyios Evstrátios looking NW (extension to the mole not shown)
Nigel Patten

Eating out Taverna.
Other PO. Metered telephone at the taverna. Infrequent ferries in summer to Evia and Limnos.

General

Since the 1968 earthquake which destroyed many of the buildings the population has dwindled to about 300, almost all of whom live in the one fishing village.

The harbour is a useful stopover between the northern Sporades and Lésvos. The rest of the island is rocky and barren, but there are some pleasant beaches and caves under the cliffs. Until recently political offenders were deported to the island.

Nísos Lésvos
(Lesbos, Mitilíni, Mytilene)

One of the largest islands in the Aegean after Crete and Evia and the largest of the eastern Sporades, Lésvos is the jewel of the group. It is grander, greener and more fertile than any of the other islands. A prosperity founded on agriculture and local industry provides an economic balance rarely seen in the Greek islands and tourism simply provides the icing on the cake.

The island is roughly oval in shape with two deep landlocked gulfs on the southern side. It is mountainous throughout, rising from Mt Ordhimos (512m, 1,680ft) in the west to the twin peaks of Mt Olympus in the southeast and Mt Lebetimnos in the northeast (by coincidence they are both 958m or 3,176ft). In the west the island is mostly barren and rocky, but the interior and the east are forested with olives, chestnuts, oak, pine and poplar, though sadly forest fires raze large areas on a regular basis. The flat land is cultivated with market gardens and fields of tobacco. The olives of Lésvos have long been celebrated and today the plump olives and Lésvos olive oil are among the best in Greece.

Just as the spacious and wooded island is pleasing to the eye, so the ancient associations are memorable ones of the gentle arts of music and philosophy. Greatest of all is the poetess Sappho who was born on Lésvos about 612 BC, although it is uncertain exactly where she was born – perhaps Eressos or Mitilíni. Allegations that Sappho was a lover of her own sex gave the word Lesbian to the world, although this is based on just a few lines of her poetry (to Atthis – 'I was in love with you once Atthis, long ago . . .') and appears to have been contrived to cast a slur on her character and poetry after the 7th century AD. Today allegations of homosexuality matter less and we are only just beginning to uncover fragments of her poetry. For nearly 1,000 years Sappho was regarded almost as a goddess, Plato called her the tenth muse and later only Catullus and Horace came close to her flowing and sensual poetry. These lines are from a translation by Catullus:

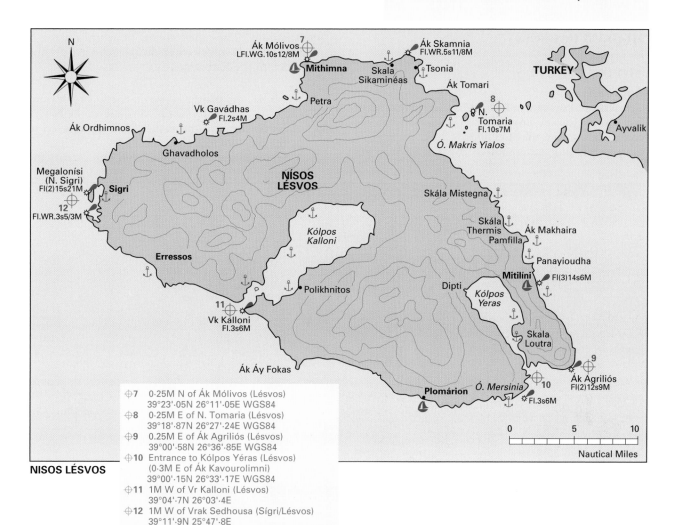

NISOS LÉSVOS

⊕7 0·25M N of Ák Mólivos (Lésvos)
39°23'·05N 26°11'·05E WGS84
⊕8 0·25M E of N. Tomaria (Lésvos)
39°18'·87N 26°27'·24E WGS84
⊕9 0·25M E of Ák Agriliós (Lésvos)
39°00'·58N 26°36'·85E WGS84
⊕10 Entrance to Kólpos Yéras (Lésvos)
(0·3M E of Ák Kavourolimni)
39°00'·15N 26°33'·17E WGS84
⊕11 1M W of Vr Kalloni (Lésvos)
39°04'·7N 26°03'·4E
⊕12 1M W of Vrak Sedhousa (Sígri/Lésvos)
39°11'·9N 25°47'·8E

'Godlike the man who
sits at her side, who
watches and catches
that laughter
which (softly) tears me
to tatters: nothing is
left of me, each time
I see her,
. . .tongue numbed; arms, legs
melting, on fire; drum
drumming in ears; head–
lights gone black.'

Sappho is said to have died in true poetic style, jumping off the cliffs on the southwest corner of Levkas when rejected by her lover Phaon – though in fact there is no real evidence that she ever visited Levkas. Still, it's an appropriately tragic story.

Sappho did not emerge from a cultural vacuum. The names associated with Lésvos are a rollcall of gentle artists and wise sages: Terpander the father of Greek music; Arion the dolphin-loving poet; Alcaeus, a contemporary of Sappho; Pitticus, who united the cities of the island and whose wise rule won him a place among the Seven Sages of Greece; Epicurus, whose benign humanitarian philosophy was forgotten after Christianity and only later rediscovered; Aristotle, who resided for some time here; and Aesop who wrote many of his fables on Lésvos. Indeed it is difficult to find anybody who was nasty living on Lésvos in ancient times, though I'm sure they were lurking in the background.

The geographical position of Lésvos and its sheltered natural harbours meant that from ancient times the island was an important trade link between Asia and Greece. Mitilíni is still reminiscent of the Levant and the old trading days, but the division between Greece and Turkey severed communications and destroyed the island's role as a commercial intermediary. After prosperity in ancient Greek and Roman times the island suffered from Saracen invasions and Byzantine expulsions of the invaders and, not surprisingly, the local inhabitants moved away from the sea to the hills. Not until the 14th century, when Lésvos was given to that remarkable Genoese adventurer Francesco Gattelusio, did the island again enjoy some measure of calm and prosperity. For a century the island was once more a trading centre. In 1462 the Turks occupied Lésvos and it effectively remained under Turkish occupation until 1912.

The heritage of the island is largely literary and cultural and its archaeological remains are few and undistinguished. It was Sappho who said that poets attain immortality and long after hewn stones have gone, her poetry and her loves will be remembered.

MITILINI (Mytilene)

BA 1675

Imray-Tetra G27

Approach

Conspicuous Two red and white-banded chimneys of the power station immediately N of Mitilini are conspicuous from all directions. Closer in, a large circular building and a monument in front of it are conspicuous. The squat round structure on the S end of the E breakwater helps to identify the entrance to the harbour.

Note

1. Work is in progress on a new breakwater enclosing Vórios Limineas Mitilinis on the N side of Ák Kástro and the castle. This is expected to be the new commercial port.

2. A detached breakwater has been built across the

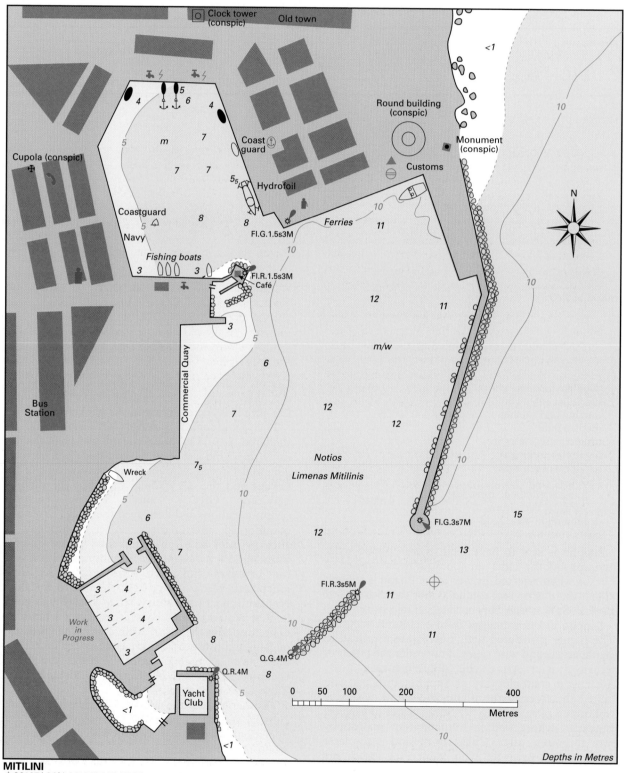

MITILINI

⊕39°05′·86N 26°33′·83E WGS84

Mitilíni (Lesvos) looking SSE *Lu Michell*

entrance to Mitilíni harbour. Entrance is between the E end of the detached breakwater and the old E harbour breakwater. The ends of the detached breakwater are marked by a green buoy at the W end and a red buoy at the E end.

3. A new yacht marina is under construction immediately N of the yacht club in the S of the harbour. The outer piers, slip and travel-hoist bay are complete and the inside has been dredged to 3–4m. Works continue but it is not yet open to yachts.

By night Use the lights on Ák Kástro (the castle headland) Fl(3)14s6M, on the outer breakwater Fl.G.3s7M, and at the entrance to the inner basin Fl.G.1·5s3M/Fl.R.1·5s3M. The Fl.G at the entrance to the inner basin is weak and cannot be confused with the Fl.G on the outer breakwater. The detached breakwater is lit Q.G and Fl.R.3s5M, and the yacht club pier Q.R.4M.

Mooring

Proceed into the inner harbour and moor alongside or stern or bows-to on the N or E side. The bottom is soft mud and some plough-type anchors will drag through it. The harbour can be smelly at times from sewage emptying into it.

Shelter Good all-round shelter, although the harbour can be uncomfortable with strong S winds. Moor in the SW corner of the inner harbour during these winds.

Authorities A port of entry: port police, customs and immigration authorities.

Facilities

Services Water and electricity on the N quay from the 'water man'.
Fuel Near the quay. A mini-tanker can deliver.
Repairs General mechanical repairs and light engineering work. A yard on the N side of the castle can haul yachts. Good hardware and tool shops. Limited chandlery.
Provisions Excellent shopping for all provisions.
Eating out Good tavernas including some fish tavernas on the S quay. The fishermen's café by the

miniature fishing harbour on the W side of the entrance to the inner harbour is a pleasant spot to while away an hour or so at sundown.
Other PO. OTE. Banks. ATMs. Greek gas and Camping Gaz. Hire cars and motorbikes. Buses to the principal towns and villages. Ferries to Piraeus and Ayvalik in Turkey. Internal flights and some European flights in the summer.

General

Mitilíni is the commercial heart of the island. Coasters, trading *caïques* and large fishing craft clutter the harbour. The town hums with local industry. In the old town the narrow winding streets are lined with market stalls and local craft shops – the atmosphere is redolent of an Oriental bazaar. The whole combines into a likeable Levantine mixture and the city, at first noisy and grubby, in the end charms the visitor.

On the waterfront and scattered around the outskirts of Mitilíni are some grand old baronial houses dating from the prosperous mercantile era of the harbour. The archaeological museum houses finds from the classical period and some wonderful mosaics from a Roman villa showing figures from Menander's comedies.

Panayioudha *caïque* harbour. The tower and warehouse buildings are conspicuous *Lu Michell*

PANAYIOUDHA

The small harbour of Panayioudha lies close NW of Ák Asfali, the prominent cape 1¾ miles N of Mitilíni. The old warehouses at the root of the N breakwater and the cupola of the church are conspicuous. The breakwater also shows up well. The entrance is lit F.G/F.R, though the lights should not be relied on. There is little room for yachts, but with care a small yacht can go bows-to the W quay. Care is needed of the shoal water extending from the N quay across to the end of the N breakwater. Good shelter from the *meltemi*.

Provisions and tavernas ashore.

Skála Thermís. Extreme caution is needed in the shallow and rocky approaches
Lu Michell

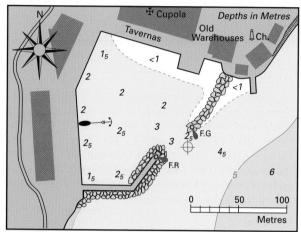

PANAYIOUDHA
⊕ 39°08'·61N 26°31'·84E WGS84

PAMFILLA

39°09'·7N 26°32'·4E

Lying close under Ák Makhaira there is an attractive bay sheltered from the *meltemi*. Anchor at the head of the bay N of the islet in 4–6m. Taverna ashore.

SKÁLA THERMÍS

Approach

The entire bay of Órmos Thermís is shallow and rocky. Nisís Thermís in the NE entrance to the bay is surrounded by reefs that extend for some distance to the S and W. Great care is needed in the approaches to Skála Thermís.

Conspicuous A windmill just to the N of Skála Thermís is conspicuous. To the S the old thermal spa buildings will be seen.

Dangers
1. An ancient breakwater just 80m E of the harbour entrance extends out N nearly 150m from the beach. It is very difficult to identify although it lies <1m under the surface.
2. There is a considerable area of rocky shoal water that extends out N and E from the breakwater.

The approach should be made on a SW course with great care. Only attempt in calm weather with someone on the bow conning you in.

The entrance is lit F.G/F.R, though the lights should not be relied on.

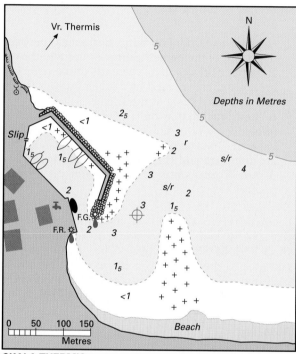

SKALA THERMIS
⊕ 39°10'·87N 26°30'·08E WGS84

Mooring

Go stern or bows-to or alongside the quay on the W side near the entrance. There is shoal water off the breakwater quay. Good shelter.

Water near the quay. Fuel nearby. Taverna.

General

Ancient Thermís is inland. The hot mineral springs still exist and a hotel has been built nearby. The springs were famous in the ancient world and a temple to Artemis and a complex of baths were excavated by the British School of Archaeology in the early 1930s.

SKÁLA MISTEGNA

Lying 7 miles NW of Mitilíni, this is the small harbour for the village of Mistegna on the hill above. The harbour is open to the SE–E. Moor bows-to the outer end of the mole taking care of the ballasting

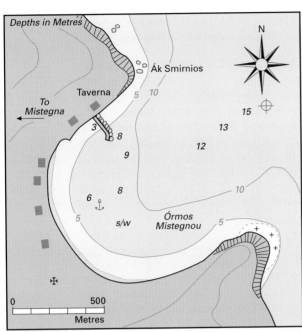

SKÁLA MISTEGNA
⊕39°12′·96N 26°28′·97E WGS84

Skála Mistegna harbour   *Lu Michell*

which extends underwater. The mole is usually crowded with local fishing boats so you will probably have to anchor in the more exposed S half of the bay. The bottom is mostly sand and weed with some rock patches. With strong winds from any sector this is not the best place to be.

Tavernas ashore and most supplies can be obtained in the village above.

SKALA NEO KIDONIES

39°14′·1N 26°27′·2E

A small harbour 2M NW of Mistegna. Care is needed of extensive reefs and shoal water off the cape to the N, and an isolated reef with 0.5m over in the S approaches. The entrance is lit Fl.R.3s3M/Fl.G.3s3M but a night approach is not recommended. Berth stern or bows-to on the N mole where there is room, in depths of 2–2·5m.

Good shelter inside the harbour, but entering or leaving with a *meltemi* blowing would be dangerous. Tavernas ashore.

ÓRMOS MAKRIS YIALOS

Nisídha Panayia light 39°18′·9N 26°26′·8E

In the large bay of Makris Yialos SW of Ák Tomari there are a number of coves on the N side providing some shelter from the *meltemi*.

Caution Órmos Makris Yialos and Nisídhes Tomaria in the bay are fringed by above and below-water rocks. Caution must be exercised in this area. Approximately one mile S of Ák Tomari a reef extends for some 400m in a NE direction from the shore. In the S part of Órmos Makris Yialos there is an islet known as Praselogos or Erimonisi which is fringed by underwater rocks. Special care must be taken of these as they are not well marked on earlier charts.

TSONIA

A small beach-side fishing village and low-key resort in the N side of Órmos Neos Limín on the NE corner of Lésvos. Nisís Monopetra is a low-lying island in the NE entrance to the bay, and care is needed of the rocks and reefs off the S end. Anchor off the village in 7–10m on sand, reasonable holding. Good shelter from the *meltemi* although there are strong gusts.

This is a wonderful spot with enough shelter from the *meltemi* to overnight here although a bit of swell creeps around into the bay – a bit uncomfortable rather than dangerous. Ashore there are a couple of simple tavernas with wonderful views over the bay.

SKÁLA SIKAMINEAS

A very pretty fishing village 1·5M SW of Ák Skamnia (Korakas). The church perched on the rock at the W end of the miniature harbour is conspicuous. Depths in the outer harbour are mostly 2–3m and less in the inner harbour. Small mooring blocks on the bottom reduce depths to less than 2m in places. A Fl.G.3s3M is exhibited at the end of the mole. Moor bows-to the extremity of the mole. Good shelter with N winds but in strong NE

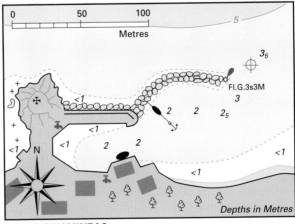

SKALA SIKAMINEAS
⊕39°22′·48N 26°18′·28E WGS84

Skála Sikamineas looking W from the entrance. The chapel perched on the rock is conspicuous *Lu Michell*

winds the harbour could be dangerous. The inner basin is crowded with local boats but you may find a space alongside or bows-to on the S quay.

A taverna and limited provisions available in the fishing hamlet.

The hamlet is an utter charmer and even with the harbour extension (when I first visited here in 1980 there was only what is now the inner basin) it is sad there is little room for yachts. In calm weather do try to visit. The chapel at the harbour is dedicated to the Panayia Gorgona – Our Lady of the Mermaid. The novelist Stratis Mirivilis was born here. I

confess to finding his novels difficult going (though that may be down to a bad translation).

MITHIMNA (Methymna, Mólivos)
Approach
Conspicuous The castle on the hill above the town is conspicuous from some distance off. Closer in, the town and the huddle of buildings around the small harbour at the foot of the hill can be seen.

By night Care needed. Use the light on Ák Mólivos LFl.WG.10s12/8M (green sector covers 219°-239° only). A Fl.R.3s3M is exhibited at the end of the mole.

Dangers
1. Above and below-water rocks fringe Ák Mólivos and the harbour mole for some distance off. The harbour should be entered from the SE.
2. The entrance to the inner basin is very narrow (about 10m wide but free of obstructions) and small yachts only will be able to enter the harbour which is crowded with fishing boats.

Mooring
Go stern or bows-to or alongside the outer mole where convenient. The bottom is mud, sand and weed, good holding. In the inner basin there is little room amongst the fishing boats. The bottom in the inner basin is thin mud over rock, bad holding.

Shelter Good shelter in the outer part of the harbour and excellent shelter in the inner basin.

Authorities Port police and customs.

Anchorage In calm weather a yacht can anchor in the

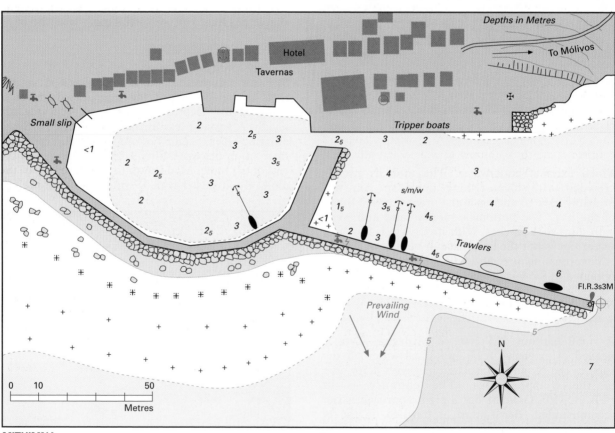

MITHIMNA
⊕39°22′·02N 26°10′·12E WGS84

Mithimna looking SW across the harbour *Lu Michell*

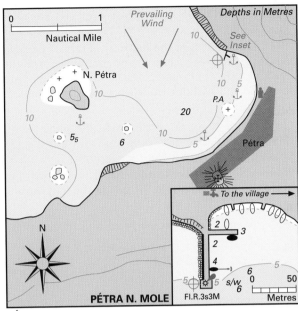

PÉTRA
⊕39°20′·21N 26°10′·70E WGS84

bay, but a swell sets in with the *meltemi* and the holding is uncertain.

Facilities
Services Water and electricity on the quay.
Provisions Good shopping for all provisions in the town. Ice on the quay.
Eating out Good tavernas in the town and around the harbour.
Other PO. OTE. Bank. ATM. Hire cars and bikes. Bus to Mitilíni.

General
Arion, the lyric poet (625 BC), who was saved from drowning by a music-loving dolphin, was born here. Presumably his spirit survives as the town has developed into something of an artists' resort as well as a tourist resort.

The town is a maze of cobbled streets and passages winding in and out of medieval fortifications, and a historical preservation order will hopefully keep it that way. The stone and timber houses, many with small timber balconies, look over the cliffs to the bay beneath. A growing number of tourists come to Mithimna as not only is the town pleasant and near to good bathing beaches, but the locals are welcoming – the clink of glasses will often be heard late into the night.

PÉTRA (Kavaki)
A small village off a sandy beach under Ák Kavaki. There is a small harbour N of Pétra village on the S side of Ák Kavaki. Anchor off the village in 5–10m on sand and weed. Poor shelter from the *meltemi* here. Under the mole on the N side of the bay there is reasonable shelter from the *meltemi*. A Fl.R.3s3M is exhibited on the end of the mole. Go stern or bows-to the outer end of the mole. Small fishing boats crowd the shore and occasionally a small coaster uses the end of the mole. Fuel delivered by mini-tanker.

The village of Pétra is a sleepy place with some modest tourism in the summer. Some provisions can be obtained and there are tavernas. The bay and

the village are a delight, being wooded and well-watered. In the village the church of Panayía Glykofiloussa built on a rocky bluff near the beach stands out from seaward.

Caution Care is needed of the reef in the bay off the village. A stick sometimes marks the reef but is not to be relied upon. In calm weather it is possible to anchor under the islet to the W – care is needed in the vicinity of the islet of the above and below-water rocks around it.

The pier at Pétra looking SE towards the village *Lu Michell*

GHAVADHOLOS (Gavatha)

Approach

The islet to the E of the harbour (Vrakhos Megálo Gavatha) and the church and bell-tower on the headland are conspicuous. Once around the island the mole and harbour entrance are easily identified.

Mooring

Go stern or bows-to or alongside the mole where there is room. The bottom is mud and weed, good holding. Good shelter from the *meltemi*.

Dangers You will have to turn sharply to starboard to avoid the shallows on the W side of the harbour.

Facilities

Water near the quay. Some provisions in the village and a taverna.

General

The little village is a friendly place where the locals eke out a living fishing or cultivating the fertile land around the head of the bay. There are reported to be hot springs here, but although I got whiffs of sulphuretted hydrogen from the shore by the village, I couldn't find them.

LIMÍN SIGRIOU (Sígri)

BA 1675

Imray-Tetra G27

Approach

From the N the narrow N channel between Megalonísi (Nísos Sígri) and Lésvos can be used by day. There are least depths of 4·5m in the fairway of the N channel. The reef extending NE from Megalonísi is marked by breakers. In the S channel between Vrak Sedhousa and Lésvos there are considerable depths.

Conspicuous From the S, Vrak Sedhousa, the lighthouse on Megalonísi and Sígri village are conspicuous.

By night Use the light on Megalonísi Fl(2)15s21M and the light on Ák Saratsina Fl.WR.3s5/3M (red sector covers 122°-160° and 219°-270°). Care is needed in a night approach from the S. The N

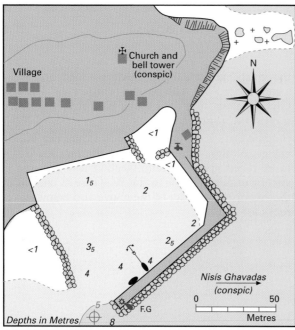

GHAVADHOLOS
⊕39°17'·0N 25°58'·55E

Ghavadholos looking SE from the hamlet

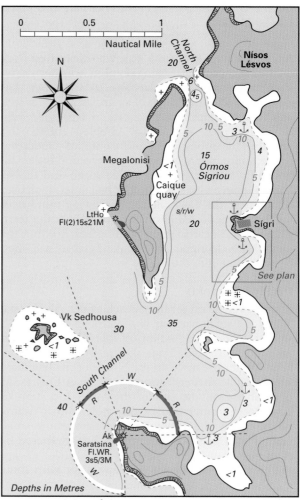

APPROACHES TO SÍGRI
⊕39°11'·4N 25°50'·0E

The fishing harbour at Sígri looking W towards Megalonisi
Lu Michell

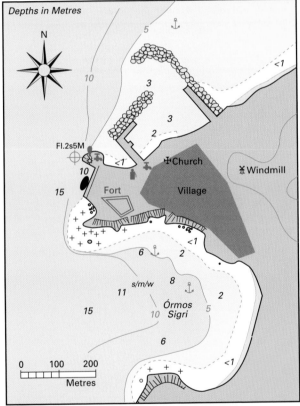

PORT SIGRI
⊕39°12'·71N 25°50'·94E WGS84

channel should not be attempted at night under any circumstances. The NW corner of the quay is lit Fl.2s5M.

Dangers Care is needed in the N channel when a heavy sea is running and breakers heap up over the shoal water in the vicinity and the channel itself.

Mooring
Anchor in the cove on the S side of Sígri village or go alongside the quay tucked as far as possible into the NE corner. Mooring is prohibited on the quay at certain times due to military restrictions. The bottom is sand, weed and rock and is poor holding in patches.

Shelter It can get a little bumpy on the quay, but not dangerous unless the wind turns to the W or S in which case anchor N of the promontory.

Note The fishing harbour on the N side of Sígri has been enlarged but there is little room for yachts.

Facilities
Water On the W quay and near the *caïque* harbour.
Fuel Near the quay.
Provisions Most provisions in the village.
Eating out Several tavernas and cafés.
Other PO. Bus to Mitilini.

General
A few tourists visit this fishing village for the nearby sandy beaches, but for the most part life carries on much as it has always done. It is one of those places that seems to attract outsiders looking for somewhere away from it all and that it is, perched on the remote western coast of Lesvos.

Sígri is noted in most guide books for its petrified forest on the W coast, but most visitors are not impressed by the sight. For the yachtsman the petrified remains near the lighthouse on Megalonísi (Nisís Sígri) are more accessible.

ERRESOS (Skála Erresos)
A small fishing harbour approximately midway between Sígri and Kólpos Kalloni. Care is needed in the approaches of an off-lying rock inside Vrak Niraki and the storm-damaged breakwater, both of which are just awash. A yacht should leave Niraki to

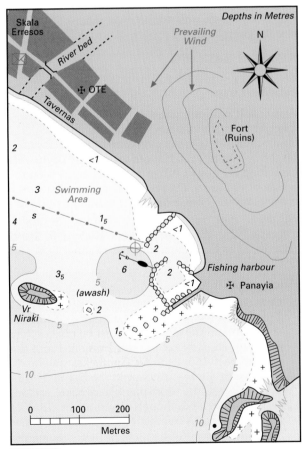

ERRESOS
⊕39°07'·83N 25°56'·07E WGS84

The fishing harbour at Erresos. The off-lying rocks are easily seen left of picture *Lu Michell*

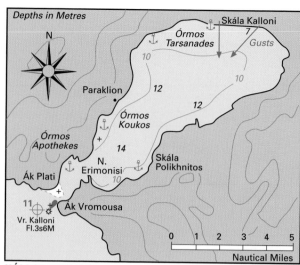

KÓLPOS KALLONI

⊕11 1M W of Vr. Kalloni (Lésvos) 39°04'·7N 26°03'·4E

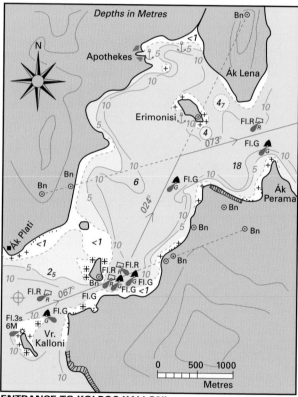

ENTRANCE TO KOLPOS KALLONI
⊕39°04'·9N 26°04'·6E

starboard in the approaches to the harbour.

In calm weather a yacht can anchor off the beach in 4–6m outside the buoys. Alternatively in settled weather anchor and take a long line to the mole, although it is not the most comfortable place to be. Small yachts may find a berth inside the small basin with local boats. Adequate shelter from the prevailing winds on the breakwater. Open S and W.

The village ashore is a small and amicable resort. Erresos has something of a reputation as a gay women's resort, but retains popularity with straights as well. PO. OTE. Exchange office. Provisions and tavernas. Taxis.

It is a pleasant walk to the main village of Erresos about 2km inland.

KÓLPOS KALLONI

BA 1675
Imray-Tetra G27

Approach and entrance

The narrow mountainous entrance to this large landlocked gulf is easily negotiated by day. Proceed on the N side of Vrak Kalloni taking care of the reef extending 0·15 miles NE of it. The channel is on the S side of the shoal and reef obstructing most of the channel on the N side. It is well marked by buoys.

By night Not recommended despite the lights available. Use the light on Vrak Kalloni Fl.3s6M and the light buoys marking the channel Q.R and Q.G.

Anchorages in the gulf

1. *Órmos Apothekes* 39°06'·62N 26°05'·75E WGS84
   This bay on the N side of the entrance affords the best shelter in the gulf. Care must be taken of the reefs and shoal water around Erimonisi and the isolated reef 250m off Ák Apothekes on the W entrance to the bay. Anchor in the bay in 5–10m or go bows-to the short pier where there are 3m depths off the end, though care must be taken of rock ballasting. A number of fishermen and their families inhabit the hamlet. At the root of the breakwater a taverna serves good simple fare, with fresh fish often on the menu.

2. *Órmos Koukos* A bay approximately 2½ miles N of the entrance to the gulf. Anchor in 8–10m. Some shelter from the *meltemi*.

3. *Paraklion* A bight just above Koukos. Anchor in 4–6m off a small breakwater. Poor shelter from the *meltemi*.

4. *Órmos Tarsanades* A bight in the NW corner of the gulf. Poor shelter from the *meltemi*.

5. *Skála Kalloni* 39°12'·35N 26°12'·54E WGS84
   An L-shaped mole protects a small harbour at the head of the gulf. There are 1·5–2m depths along the outer end of the mole. Go alongside if

Órmos Apothekes looking SE

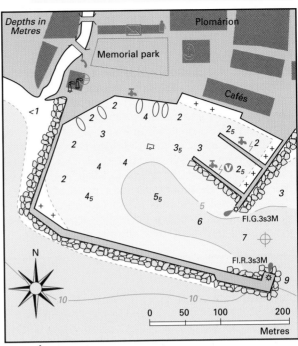

PLOMÁRION
⊕38°58'·39N 26°22'·26E WGS84

possible. Further inside it gets shallow. Alternatively anchor off the beach. Strong gusts with the *meltemi*. Provisions and tavernas ashore. PO.

6. **Skála Polikhnitos** A small harbour just E of the entrance to the gulf. Go bows-to (there is some underwater ballasting) the outer mole. Good protection from the *meltemi* although there are gusts.

Water on the quay and fuel nearby. Some provisions and tavernas ashore.

Note With the *meltemi* there are fierce gusts into Kólpos Kalloni and a considerable sea can be raised despite the limited fetch.

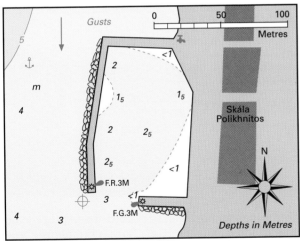

SKÁLA POLIKHNITOS
⊕39°06'·1N 26°10'·1E

PLOMÁRION (Plomari)

Approach
Conspicuous The town is conspicuous from some distance off. A cathedral with belfry behind the harbour and two chimneys near the root of the W breakwater are conspicuous. The harbour moles and light structures are easily identified.

By night Use the lights at the entrance: Fl.G.3s3M/Fl.R.3s3M.

Plomárion looking SW   *Lu Michell*

Mooring
Visiting yachts are allocated space inside the outer pier. Go stern or bows-to where convenient. Laid moorings at most berths.

Shelter Good all-round shelter, although there is still some surge with a strong *meltemi*.

Authorities Port police and customs.

Facilities
Services Water and electricity along the pier and the pontoon.
Fuel In the town and can be delivered by mini-tanker.
Repairs Some mechanical repairs possible. General hardware shops.
Provisions Excellent shopping for provisions.
Eating out Good tavernas on the waterfront and in the town.

405

Other PO. OTE. Bank. ATM. Hire cars and bikes. Bus to Mitilíni.

General

Plomárion was established in the 19th century (as Bilmar) when the islanders moved down to the shores after piracy had been suppressed. Narrow cobbled streets and passages wind in and out of the stone and timber houses built in a Turkish style with wooden balconies. Behind the town the countryside is covered in olive groves and thick chestnut and pine forest so that the town, sandwiched between the sea and the mountains, is a wonderful place. Plomárion is also famous for its ouzo, marketed as *Barbajanis Ouzo*, which is praised by connoisseurs of the aniseed-flavoured brew all over the Aegean.

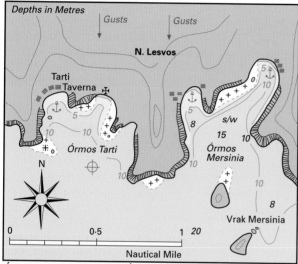

ÓRMOS MERSINIA AND ÓRMOS TARTI
⊕38°58′.3N 26°29′.8E

ÓRMOS MERSINIA AND ÓRMOS TARTI

A large bay lying 3 miles SW of the entrance to Kólpos Yéras behind Ák Petras. It is a double-headed bay. Anchor at the head of the W cove in 4–10m. The bottom is sand and weed – bad holding. It is difficult getting the anchor through the thick weed on the bottom. Good shelter from the *meltemi*, although there are gusts so make sure the anchor is properly dug in. Alternatively anchor in the E cove in 5–10m.

The bay sits under heavily wooded slopes and is a delightful place.

There is also a good anchorage in Órmos Tarti immediately W. Taverna at Órmos Tarti.

KÓLPOS YÉRAS

BA 1675
Imray-Tetra G27

Approach and entrance

This second landlocked gulf lies about 25 miles E of Kólpos Kalloni. The approach is straightforward by day but should not be attempted at night. Keeping well clear of Ák Kavourolimni which has a reef running N of it, pass between the cape and Vrak Kalóyeros, a reef marked by a stone beacon. Leave

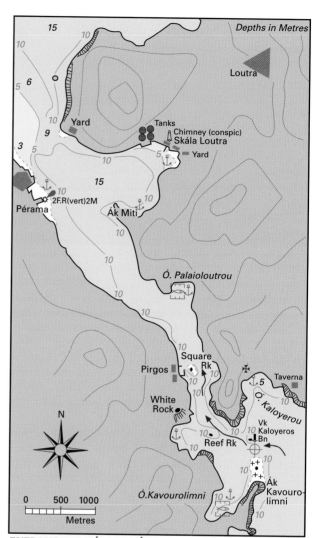

ENTRANCE TO KÓLPOS YÉRAS
⊕39°00′.51N 26°32′.72E WGS84

The stone beacon marking Vrak Kaloyeros in the entrance to Kólpos Yéras   *Lu Michell*

the beacon about 150m to starboard and proceed up the channel leaving Reef Rock (Vromonisi) and Square Rock (Áy Vasilios) to port.

Anchorages in Kólpos Yéras

1. *Órmos Kavourolimni* The bay tucked under the W entrance point to the gulf. There is a fish farm in here but still room to anchor. Also just N of Kavourolimni on the W side there is an attractive bay immediately W of Reef Rock.

2. *Órmos Kaloyerou* The bay tucked under the E entrance point looks to offer good shelter from the *meltemi*.

3. *Pirgos* A small fishing harbour on the W side of the channel adjacent to Square Rock. There may

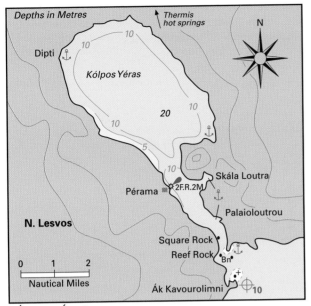

Depths in Metres

KÓLPOS YÉRAS

⊕10 Entrance to Kólpos Yéras (Lésvos) (0·3M E of Ák
Kavourolimni
39°00'·15N 26°33'·17E WGS84

be space to go alongside or stern or bows-to on
the N quay. Depths 2–4m. Good shelter. The
entrance is lit Fl.G.3s3M/Fl.R.3s3M.
4. ***Órmos Palaioloutrou*** In the cove in the
entrance channel S of Loutra. There is now a fish
farm here, but there is still room to anchor.
5. ***Pérama*** 39°02'·59N 26°30'·58E WGS84 On the W
side of the entrance channel. In calm weather a
yacht can go alongside or stern or bows-to where
convenient. Depths 3–5m off the quay. Water on
the quay. Fuel by mini-tanker. Large
coastguard/military presence. Port police.
6. ***Skála Loutra*** 39°02'·69N 26°31'·80E WGS84
The bay on the E side of the entrance channel.
There is a small fishing harbour at the head of the
bay. A chimney on the N side of the village is
conspicuous by day and is illuminated at night.

Skála Loutra in Kólpos Yéras on Lésvos looking NW
Peter Kleinoth/MareTeam

Four large fuel tanks by a new pier NW of the
village will also be seen. Anchor off the village in
settled weather or anchor and take a long line to
the breakwater. Depths of 2–4m off the
breakwater. A pair of pelicans has adopted the
harbour.
Water ashore. Several café/tavernas. There is a
caique yard at the S end of the village and another
on the NW corner of the bay.
The bay immediately E of Ák Miti provides
good shelter from S and W winds. Anchor in
6–12m on mud, good holding.
7. ***Kólpos Yéras SE corner*** In settled weather
there is a delightful cove in the SE corner of the
gulf.
8. ***Dipti*** (Dipti, Nipti) In the NW corner of the gulf.
There are 5m depths off the extremity of the mole
and a taverna ashore.

Note With the *meltemi* blowing there are gusts into
the gulf although they are not as fierce as those
blowing into Kólpos Kalloni.

Nísos Khíos and adjacent islands

Nísos Psará

Psará is a small barren island lying 10 miles west of
the north of Khíos. Together with Spétsai and
Hydra, Psará was one of the first islands to revolt
against the Turks. Its ships harried Turkish shipping
along the coast, scoring some notable successes. On
a number of occasions the Turks mounted
expeditions to squash the small island community,
but were unable to land because of bad weather
until June 1824. In that year Hosref Pasha landed a
large force and massacred the population. A few
survivors established Néa Psará (Erétria) on Evia.
The island has never recovered.

PSARÁ

BA 1058
Imray-Tetra G28

Approach
Conspicuous The small village on the low ridge of Ák
Trifilli is easily seen from the distance. Two large
churches in the village are conspicuous from the E
and S. Wind turbines to the NE are conspicous from
N and S. The mole will not be seen until close to. A
green conical buoy is reported to be in place
approximately 150m due E of the N entrance point.
By night Use the light on Ák Áy Yeóryios Fl.10s25M
and the light at the entrance Fl.R.1·5s3M. The
green buoy is lit Fl.G but should not be relied upon.
The inner mole is lit: F.R.3M. The harbour lights
are not always to be relied on.
Dangers When approaching from the W care should
be taken of the reefs fringing Nisís Andípsara and
Katonisi. These islands and rocks are not lit at night
making a night approach from the W difficult.

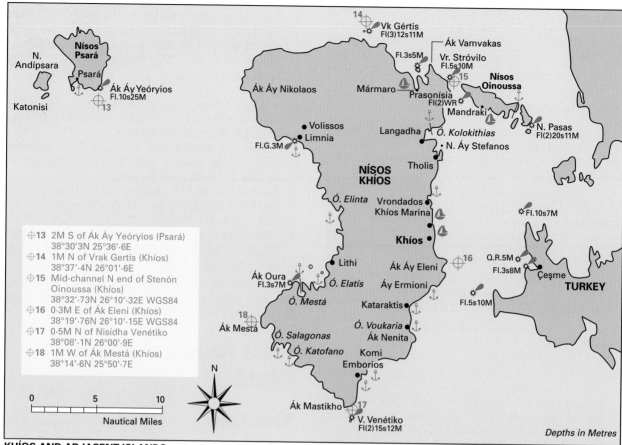

13 2M S of Ák Áy Yeóryios (Psará)
38°30'3N 25°36'·6E

14 1M N of Vrak Gertis (Khíos)
38°37'·4N 26°01'·6E

15 Mid-channel N end of Stenón
Oinoussa (Khíos)
38°32'·73N 26°10'·32E WGS84

16 0·3M E of Ák Eleni (Khíos)
38°19'·76N 26°10'·15E WGS84

17 0·5M N of Nisídha Venétiko
38°08'·1N 26°00'·9E

18 1M W of Ák Mestá (Khíos)
38°14'·6N 25°50'·7E

KHÍOS AND ADJACENT ISLANDS

Mooring

Go stern or bows-to where convenient. The bottom is mud and weed with some rocks – good holding.

Shelter Good all-round shelter although strong NE winds may make it uncomfortable.

Authorities Port police.

Facilities

Water Limited supplies on the island.

Provisions Limited provisions available but the villagers are dependent on the ferry from Khíos for many things.

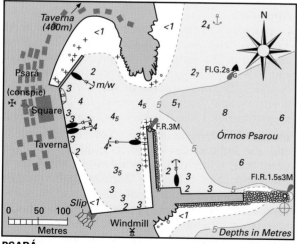

PSARÁ
⊕38°32'·4N 25°34'·1E

Psará harbour looking W   *Peter Kleinoth/MareTeam*

Eating out Several tavernas.
Other PO. Local ferry to Khíos.

General

There is little left of what was a prosperous town: a few crumbling houses and warehouses, windmills on the ridges and the large natural harbour. In recent years some of the houses have been restored and a little life is creeping back into the village.

Inland amongst the scorched rock of the island (there is little good earth for cultivation) is a Mycenaean necropolis, though it has not been systematically excavated to date. Homer mentioned the island, (he called it Psyrie), but said nothing about it, and apart from the brief age when it possessed a fine merchant fleet and lost it all against the Turks, to most people including Greeks the name Psará means little or nothing to this day.

Nísos Oinoussa

This barren island lies just over a mile to the east of the north of Khíos. At one time it supported a prosperous seafaring community, but today the population is much diminished.

MANDRÁKI (Oinoussa)

Approach

Conspicuous From the S the village is conspicuous from the distance. From the N Vrak Prasonísia and the light structure on it are easily identified. Closer in the church and light structure on Nisís Mandráki (Áy Pantelimonios) are easily seen and rounding Nisís Mandráki the harbour mole will be seen.

By night Use the light on Prasonísia Fl(2)WR.10s6/4M (red sector 301°-323°), on Nísis Mandráki Fl.2s4M, and the lights at the entrance Q.G.3M/Q.R.3M. The pier inside is lit: F.G.3M.

Caution The island of Oinoussa is fringed by reefs. Care should be taken of the reef lying approximately 0·7M SE of Prasonísia – it usually has breaking water over it. There are 10m depths in the fairway between this reef and Nísos Oinoussa. The three islets protecting Mandráki harbour are joined to one another by shallow rock-bound bars and there is no entrance between them.

Mooring

Go stern or bows-to where convenient or anchor off. The bottom is mud and weed – good holding.

Note Works in progress in the harbour. The N quay has been widened and straightened from the pier in the W to the miniature harbour at the E end. Work continues widening the commercial quay in the SE

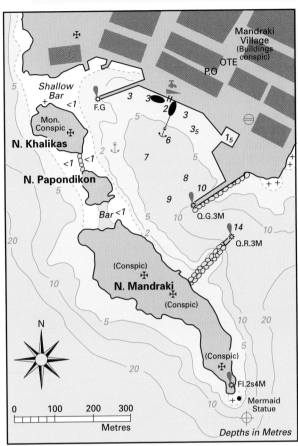

MANDRAKI (Oinoussa)
⊕ 38°30′·41N 26°13′·22E WGS84

corner of the harbour. Water and electricity boxes along the quay.

Shelter Good all-round shelter: a yacht can always find somewhere secure to moor in the harbour, even with strong SE winds which do not blow home.

Authorities Port police and customs.

Facilities

Water A tap near the quay.
Provisions Some provisions can be obtained but the villagers are largely dependent on the local ferry from Khíos.
Eating out A few tavernas – fresh fish is sometimes available.
Other PO. OTE. Bank. Local ferry to Khíos.

General

The smartening up of the waterfront in Mandráki seems to indicate something of a renaissance for the island. The large and elegant houses in the village, once neglected by globetrotting magnates, now have a fresh coat of paint. Luxury motor-yachts are a regular occurrence in the harbour. This apparently insignificant little island has produced the richest ship-owning families of Greece including the richest of them all, Costa Lemos. Contrary to popular belief the biggest Greek shipping magnate is not Niarchos or the late Onassis, but this private man whose name means nothing to most people. Apparently Greek ship owners control some 70 million tons of shipping, the same tonnage as all the other EU countries put together.

Mandraki harbour on Oinoussa looking NW. The new quay is just visible right of picture *Lu Michell*

409

NISÍS PASAS (Pashá) AND CHANNEL

BA 1625

Note The bay on the NW end of Nisís Pasas is now a military area and yachts are prohibited from entering the bay and immediate area.

Nisís Pasas lies off the E end of Nísos Oinoussa separated by a narrow channel with 3·5m least depth in the fairway. The W coast of Nisís Pasas is indented with several bays and coves which offer good shelter from the *meltemi*. Órmos Kambi on the E coast of Nísos Oinoussa also offers good shelter. The bottom is mostly sand with some weed – reported to be indifferent holding.

Recently a number of fish farms have sprung up in several of the bays and coves restricting the amount of space available around the island, though there is still room enough to find shelter here.

Caution The coasts of Oinoussa, Nisís Pasas and the islets in this area are fringed by reefs. By day these are readily picked out but care must be taken as the sketch plan can only show these reefs crudely.

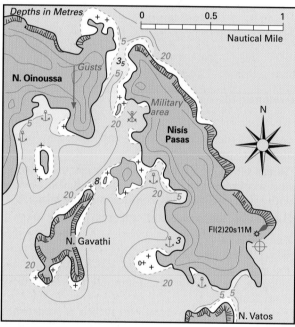

NISÍS PASAS
⊕38°30′·1N 26°17′·7E (Pasas light)

Nísos Khíos

(Chios, Hios)

Many islands claim to be the birthplace of Homer, but Khíos seems to be the most likely. Homer called the island 'craggy' and the epithet is deserved. Much of Khíos, especially the high mountain ridge running from Mt Profitis Ilías (1,297m, 4,255ft) in the north and terminating in low-lying Ák Mastikho in the south, is a lunar landscape of parched and pitted rock. Only on the northwest coast where thick pine forest covers the lower slopes and on the fertile plains in the south does the island bear any resemblance to ancient descriptions praising its fertility. In fact both the geography and history of Khíos are like a pattern that has been broken so many times that the original concept has been forgotten. Fertile plains rise up to barren rock, a severe plateau descends to a wooded valley, and the valley ends in a rocky bay scarred and broken by the sea.

The ancient history of Khíos was illustrious enough, but it has been somewhat overwhelmed by the tragedy of contemporary history. The name of the island was possibly derived from a word of Phoenician origin meaning 'mastic'. Along with Sámos and Smyrna (Izmir), Khíos became part of the Ionic Confederacy and enjoyed a considerable measure of affluence in which the arts prospered. Homer, that 'blind old man of rocky Khíos', Thales of Miletus, and later the tragic poet Ion were of the era. The Romans sacked it and thereafter the island sank into obscurity, being invaded by the Saracens and later becoming a pirate stronghold. With the Gattelusio family in control of Lésvos, the Genoese Giustianni family established control of Khíos in the early 14th century and it again became prosperous.

The Turks took it in 1566 and occupied the island until 1912. The Greek war of independence began in 1821 and in 1822 the Khians joined the revolt. The Turks took a terrible revenge that reverberated around the world. The towns on Khíos were razed, 25,000 Khians were massacred and 47,000 enslaved (in Néa Moni there is a bizarre chamber full of the bones of a few of those massacred). Delacroix commemorated the event in his famous picture and Victor Hugo was inspired to write his *The Child of Khíos*. The Greek Admiral Kanaris achieved a small revenge in the same year when he destroyed the Turkish flagship and its commander, but the real effect of the massacre was to awaken the world to the Greek struggle.

Those Khians who managed to escape were scattered all over Europe. Many later became prosperous merchants and ship owners (the Rallis brothers of London were from Khíos). Khíos had barely recovered when the great earthquake of 1881 shattered the island and killed 3,500. Yet the island has recovered and modern Khíos bustles and chatters still with the sounds of the Levant.

If there is one pattern to Khíos it is the cultivation of the mastic tree (*Pistacia lentiscus*) for its resin. Polunin and Huxley in their *Flowers of the Mediterranean* have this to say about the shrub:

'A resin is obtained from the punctured stems which is the mastic used in medicine and varnish-making; it is cultivated in the island of Chios for this purpose. Mastic has been used since classical times as a chewing-gum for preserving the gums and sweetening the breath. The Arabs produce an oil from the berries which is edible and used for illumination; it makes a popular sweet meat called masticha, and a liqueur known as 'mastiche'. Probably the balm of Genesis and the mastic tree of Susannah.'

Khíos harbour looking W. Yachts berth on the pier centre left
Peter Kleinoth/MareTeam

I might add that Sultans' ladies also believed it to be an aphrodisiac, ensuring its cultivation under Turkish occupation and today it is used mainly to make *mastika*, which is a potent liqueur, and in that strange concoction, the 'Submarine'. The latter is a spoonful of sickly sweet mastic jam in a glass of water, and just how you properly consume this treat without getting it all over yourself and the table I have yet to discover.

LIMÍN KHÍOU (Khíos, Hios)

BA 1625

Imray-Tetra G28

Approach

Conspicuous The tall buildings of the city are visible from some distance off. Four old windmills to the N of the harbour are conspicuous. A communications tower festooned with dishes is conspicuous to the S of the city. The harbour moles and harbour entrance are readily identified.

By night Use the lights at the entrance: Fl.G.3s12M/ Fl.R.3s12M. The N mole exhibits a F.R.17m, 209m from the head. The jetty off the S breakwater has a 2F.R(vert)3M on the end. The harbour lights are difficult to see against the lights of the city.

Dangers With the *meltemi* there is a disproportionately lumpy sea in the Khíos Channel and the approaches to Khíos harbour with the prevailing northerlies blowing against the north-going current. This can make the passage up the channel from the S an uncomfortable and prolonged affair.

Mooring

It is difficult to find a berth on either the mole or the new pontoon in the SE corner of the harbour. Yachts can berth stern or bows-to along the S quay, although the quay is quite high here and mooring rings are scarce. The quay to the N of the mole on the S side of the entrance has been squared off with depths off around 3m. Yachts sometimes moor alongside here but it is not recommended. High-speed ferries and coastguard boats enter and leave

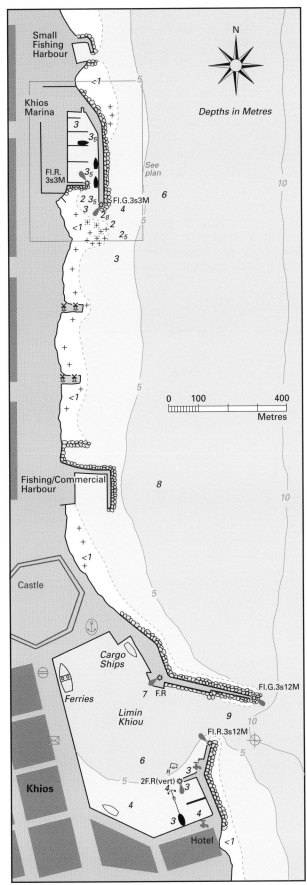

APPROACHES TO KHIOS
⊕38°22´·12N 26°08´·72E WGS84

the harbour at speed, sending a dangerous wash against the quay. Several yachts, mine included, have been badly damaged by this wash.

Shelter Good shelter from the *meltemi* tucked under the mole in the SE corner. Elsewhere in the harbour a slop is set up by the *meltemi* blowing across the large harbour (nearly half a mile long).

Authorities A port of entry: port police, customs and immigration authorities.

Note Sewers emptying into the harbour make it smelly in the summer.

Facilities

Water On the stub jetty in the SE corner.

Fuel In the town. A mini-tanker can deliver to the quay.

Repairs Most mechanical repairs. Light engineering work possible. Excellent hardware and tool shops.

Provisions Excellent shopping for provisions. A sort of permanent market will be found in the area behind the W quay. Ice available.

Eating out Tavernas in the town.

Other PO. OTE. Banks. ATMs. Greek gas and Camping Gaz. Hospital. Hire cars and motorbikes. Buses to the major villages. Ferries to Piraeus and Volos. Local ferries to Sámos, Oinoussa, Psará and Çeşme in Turkey. Internal flights.

General

Khíos is a noisy bustling harbour with an atmosphere closer to the Levant than to the islands to the W. Two-stroke three-wheelers buzz about, local ferries charge in and out, cranes creak unloading coasters – the only noise which penetrates the hubbub is the toot of the inter-island ferry.

The city largely dates from the 1881 earthquake which devastated the island and although a few of the old buildings survive they are overshadowed by the newer buildings. Even being generous, the city cannot be described as architecturally distinguished.

The town makes few concessions to tourism although an optimistically large hotel has been built near the SE corner of the harbour. A small museum in a converted mosque houses a few ancient finds. The dull white lumps of mastic are for sale everywhere.

KHÍOS MARINA

Approach

The marina has been built approximately 1M N of Khíos harbour. Four windmills to the S of the marina are conspicuous.

By night The entrance is lit Fl.G.3s3M/Fl.R.3s3M.

Dangers A reef and shoal water obstruct the direct entrance to the marina. The approach must be made on a course of due W towards the head of the breakwater, keeping very close to the breakwater and then turning sharply to starboard into the entrance. Least depths of 2·8m will be found off the breakwater increasing quickly to 3–4m inside it.

Note At present work has been abandoned on the marina and it is pretty much a building site.

Mooring

Data 275 berths. Visitors' berths. Max LOA 30m. Depths 2–3m.

Local fishing boats and trawlers have installed themselves in a lot of the berths but there is still room to go alongside in places. Makeshift moorings for fishing boats make it hazardous to go stern or bows-to, as your anchor may foul a block or chain on the bottom.

Shelter Good all-round shelter.

Authorities Harbourmaster to be appointed.

Facilities

All services including water, electricity and a toilet and shower block to be installed. It is planned to install a travel-hoist and workshops. Fuel can be delivered by mini-tanker. Limited provisions nearby. It is around 2km to Khíos town itself.

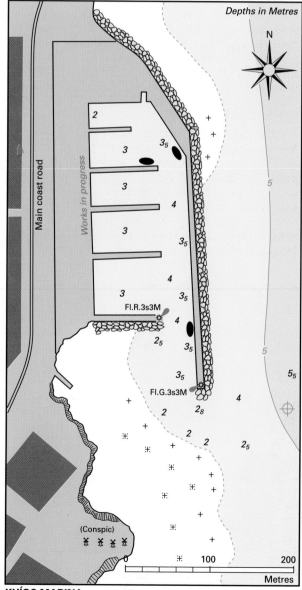

KHÍOS MARINA
⊕38°23'·19N 26°08'·69E WGS84

Khíos marina looking E. Approach from the E keeping close to the end of the breakwater *Lu Michell*

Vrondados fishing harbour *Lu Michell*

General

The superstructure is complete, the shelter is good, but work has come to a grinding halt. The surrounding wasteland is dusty and bare, save for the colour of the fishing boats that migrated here from the main harbour. Khíos 'marina' offers better shelter and safer mooring than Limín Khíou, though when or if it will ever be completed is not known.

VRONDADOS

A miniature fishing harbour lying 1 mile N of Khíos Marina. It offers some shelter for a small yacht, but is normally very crowded and you will have problems finding a berth. Care must be taken entering and berthing as the bottom is uneven and there is very little room for manoeuvring.

Water near the quay. Cafés and tavernas. The area now has mushrooming hotels and not inconsiderable numbers of tourists.

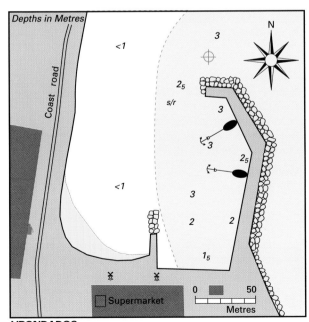

VRONDADOS
⊕38°24′·08N 26°08′·16E WGS84

DASKALOPETRA

38°25′·20N 26°08′·09E WGS84

A busy fishing harbour in very pretty surroundings about 1 mile N of Vrondados. Depths mostly 2–4m around the outer end of the mole, less towards the shore. Ballast off the quay in places. Yachts are unlikely to find a berth among the local boats.

ÁYIOS ÍOANNIS THOLOS

This narrow inlet lies immediately W of Ák Pakhis. At the head of the inlet there is a large yard which hauls out very big *caïques* and yachts. The owner states he can haul vessels out up to 1,000 tons – this figure should be taken with the proverbial grain of salt, but 200–300-ton *caïques* and a 25-ton displacement motorboat have been hauled. Apart from the yard the inlet is deserted.

ORMOS PANTOUKIOS

The bay adjacent to Órmos Tholos. A quay runs around the head of the bay with depths of 1–2·5m alongside, but the bottom falls away quickly to 20m making mooring stern-to difficult. Suitable in calm weather only.

ÓRMOS KOLOKITHIÁS

This large bay lies just N of Nisís Áyios Stefanos with the hamlet of Langadha in the SW corner. The bay in the SW corner is very deep for anchoring with 20–25m depths a short distance off the quay on the N side. On the S side there are 10–20m depths where a yacht can anchor and take a line ashore. Provisions and tavernas in the village.

Note The cove in the NW corner is a naval establishment and it is prohibited to enter it or navigate in the vicinity.

ÓRMOS PARAPANTA

The long inlet on the E side of Nisís Margaríti. Anchor near the head of the bay in 5–10m on sand. The *meltemi* pushes a swell down into here, but with light northerlies or any other wind the bay is tenable.

413

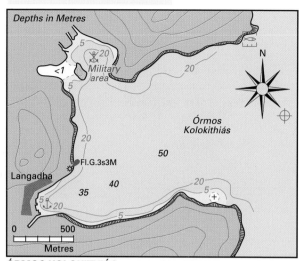

ÓRMOS KOLOKITHIÁS
⊕38°28'·89N 26°09'·55E WGS84

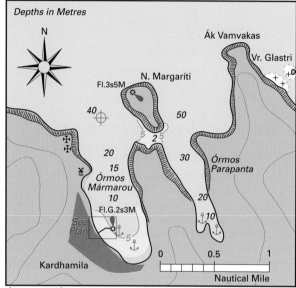

ÓRMOS MÁRMAROU AND ÓRMOS PARAPANTA
⊕38°33'·49N 26°06'·57E WGS84

KARDHAMILA (Mármaro)

Approach

Conspicuous The village cannot be seen until you are into the bay. A windmill on a rocky spur and the village and a cemetery above it are easily identified once you are in the entrance.

By night Use the lights on Nisís Margaríti at the entrance to the bay Fl.3s5M and on the end of the mole Fl.G.2s3M.

Dangers Depths of 2m or less have been reported between Nisís Margaríti and the coast although 10m depths are shown on the chart. The prudent course is to stay outside Margaríti.

Mooring

Go stern or bows-to the inside of the mole. The bottom is mud and weed, patchy holding.

Shelter Good shelter from the *meltemi*. When southerlies gust into the bay it may be better to anchor off in the SE corner of the bay.

Authorities Port police and customs.

Approach to Kardhamila on Khíos looking S. Note conspicuous windmill on rocky spur

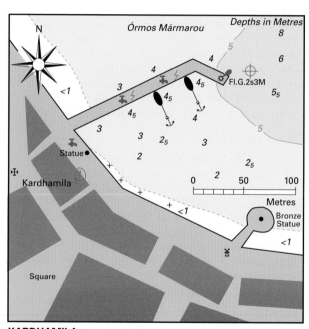

KARDHAMILA
⊕38°32'·70N 26°06'·61E WGS84

Facilities

Services Water and electricity (occas.) on the quay
Fuel Delivered by mini-tanker.
Provisions Most provisions can be found.
Eating out Tavernas on the waterfront.
Other PO. OTE. Bank. Buses to Khíos.

General

The village of Kardhamila is a delightful spot at the foot of a rough gorge cutting down through the mountains. A stream keeps everything watered and green through the summer in contrast to the parched and almost lunar mountains above the village. Around the shores are a number of large villas and houses which, I was told by a local, belong to the rich widows of Khiot captains. 'Now if I was single', he ventured, 'would I like an introduction?'

LIMNIA (Volissos)

The most northerly harbour on the W coast of Khíos, 7M SE of Ák Áy Nikolaos.

Approach

Conspicuous The village of Volissos and the castle above are visible from some distance off. Closer in the light structure on the SE side of the entrance can be seen.

By night Not recommended. The entrance is lit Fl.G.3s3M/Fl.R.3s3M. The inner mole is lit Fl.R.1·5s3M.

Dangers

1. Care should be taken of the above and below-water rocks fringing the coast in the approaches to the harbour.
2. Approximately 200m ESE of the end of the W breakwater lies a reef with 2m over. The approach should be made on a course due N towards the end of the W breakwater.

Note When rounding the NW coast of Khíos care should be taken of strong gusts from the *meltemi* accelerating off the mountains.

Mooring

Go stern or bows-to the quay in the NW corner. The bottom is sand and weed, good holding.

Shelter Good all-round shelter although SW winds make it a bit uncomfortable.

Facilities

Water From the taverna.
Fuel In Volissos village up the hill.
Provisions Most provisions can be obtained in Volissos about 1½ miles up the hill.
Eating out Tavernas by the harbour and several others in Volissos.
Other Bus to Khíos from Volissos village. Ferry to Psará.

General

The harbour is a quiet little place occupied only by a few fishermen and the odd tourist or two. The village above is crumbling and ruinous but engaging. There is a little tourism here but nothing overwhelming, and the village and harbour are well worth a detour up the W coast of Khíos.

ORMOS ELINTA

38°23'·0N 25°59'·1E

Between Limnia and Lithi are three capes all with conspicuous towers. Órmos Elinta is a calm weather anchorage under the second cape of Ák Pari. It is an isolated deep-sided bay with a sandy beach at the head.

LITHI

A small fishing harbour built on the W coast of Khíos above Mestá. Care is needed in the approach when the *meltemi* is blowing as heavy seas are set onto the W coast of Khíos. Go stern or bows-to the N mole. Good shelter from the *meltemi* despite its location.

Tavernas ashore. Sandy beach at the head of the bay.

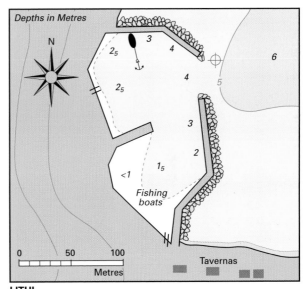

ÁYIOS EIRINI (Irini)

38°17'.72N 25°57'·97E WGS84

A short mole off the beach in the SE corner of Órmos Elatis. It is usually crowded with local boats, but in calm weather a yacht can anchor off the beach. Taverna ashore.

Alternatively anchor in the bay on the S side of Nisís Áy Sostis (the islet off the SW corner of Nisís Áy Stefanos), off the church. Reasonable shelter from the *meltemi* in idyllic surroundings.

MESTÁ (Limenas)

A long inlet on the W coast below Lithi. A light Fl.3s7M is exhibited on Ák Ourá on the W side of

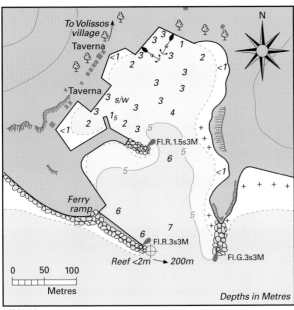

LIMNIA
⊕38°28'·07N 25°55'·07E WGS84

Órmos Mestá looking SW   *Lu Michell*

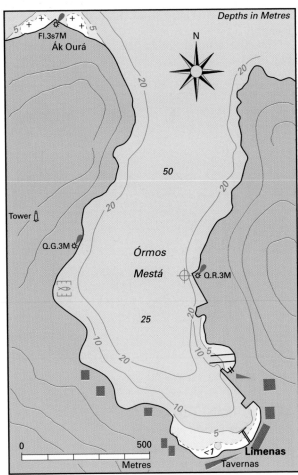

MESTÁ
⊕38°17´·60N 25°55´·71E WGS84

the entrance to the bay and further in the entrance to the inner part of the bay is lit Q.G.3M and Q.R.3M on the N quay end. The inner lights should not be relied on.

On the SE side of the inlet near the head there are several long quays with good depths off them. Recently two pontoons have been laid out from the

shore but may not always be in place. Berth stern or bows-to or alongside where convenient. Shelter from the *meltemi* is reported to be better than it looks in here. Good shelter from southerlies, but there may be a surge with strong westerlies.

Water from a tap near the root of the pier. Limited provisions and several tavernas ashore. The medieval village of Mestá 2M inland is worth a visit.

Southwest Khíos

ÁY LORRIAS, SALAGONA AND KATOFANO

On the S side of the SW corner of Khíos under Ák Venétiko there are several bays affording good shelter from the *meltemi*. They are all open to the S and in the event of southerlies a yacht should make for Órmos Mestá or proceed up the Khíos Channel to Khíos.

Anchor where shown in any of the bays on the plan. The bottom is mostly sand with some weed and is good holding.

Camping ground in Katofano. Small development at Salagona. Apart from a few olive groves and dwellings ashore nothing else disturbs this peaceful and quite enchanting corner of the island.

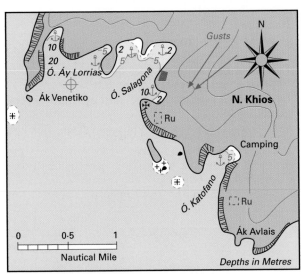

ÁY LORRIAS, SALAGONA & KATOFANO
⊕38°13´·0N 25°54´·0E

Southeast Khíos

ÓRMOS KAMARI (Emborios)

Lying 3 miles NNE of Ák Mastikho this small cove provides good shelter from the *meltemi*. The entrance is impressive between steep cliffs on either side. A ruined monastery on a hilltop immediately N is conspicuous. It is open to the SE. Anchor where convenient or anchor and take a long line ashore to the N side. The bottom is sand – good holding.

Tavernas and hotels ashore.

Órmos Kamari looking E out of the bay   *Lu Michell*

VOUKARIA

38°14'·56N 26°06'·41E WGS84

A small and shallow harbour. Depths vary from <1–2·5m but are subject to silting. It is dredged periodically. Water and electricity on the quay.

KATARAKTIS

38°15'·99N 26°06'·25E WGS84

A very crowded little harbour. Depths <1–4m. Sadly it is unlikely you will find a berth in this sleepy little gem of a place. Provisions and tavernas ashore.

ÁY ERMIONI

A fishing harbour on the S side of Ák Katomeri.

Approach

Care needed of rocks and shoal water some 100–150m E of the entrance to the harbour.

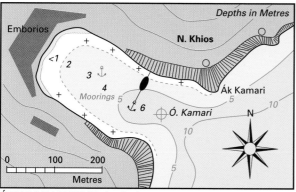

ÓRMOS KAMARI (Emborios)
⊕38°11'·25N 26°01'·84E WGS84

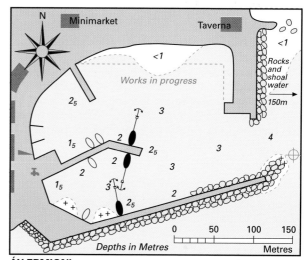

ÁY ERMIONI
⊕38°18'·03N 26°09'·07E WGS84

KOMI

A small fishing harbour, crowded with local boats, barely 1M N of Emborios. Depths 1·5–3m. Go bows-to where possible, taking care of shallower water immediately off the quay. Water and electricity on the quay. Pretty waterfront tavernas in this popular small resort.

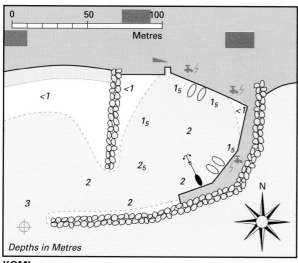

KOMI
⊕38°12'·07N 26°02'·90E WGS84

Áy Ermioni looking SW before work began on the N side of the harbour   *Peter Kleinoth/MareTeam*

Mooring

Berth on the S breakwater or central pier where possible, taking care of underwater ballast close to the quay in places. Depths <1–3m.

Note Works are in progress improving the N quay.

Facilities

Water tap at the root of the mole. Bars, restaurants and minimarkets close by.

Uninspiring modern concrete architecture ashore.

Nísos Ikaría
(Nicaria)

Ikaría is a huge precipitous slab of rock wedged into the sea to the west of Sámos. The island has green wooded and cultivated valleys in the north, but the high slopes and the south coast are mostly barren. The name probably derived from the Phoenician word *ikor* referring to an abundance of fish, and there are still considerable fleets working the waters here and around the nearby Nisídhes Foúrnoi.

The alternative and mythological origin of the name is derived from the legend of Daedalus and Icarus who contrived to escape from Crete by fabricating wings from feathers and wax. Icarus flew too high and the sun melted the wax so that he fell into the sea near Ikaría.

EVDHILOS

BA 1526

Approach

Conspicuous Vrakhonisís Kofinás with the light structure on it is conspicuous. From the E the village and the harbour mole are easily seen.

By night Use the light on Vrak Kofinás Fl.7·5s11M and the light on the end of the mole Fl.G.2s3M.

Mooring

Go stern or bows-to the mole or the pier in the S or anchor off. Much of the quay and parts of the mole

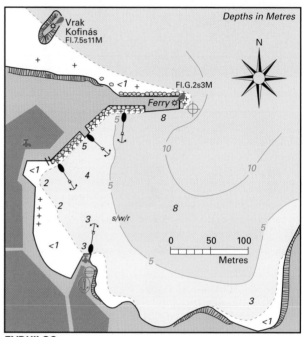

EVDHILOS
⊕37°38'·1N 26°11'·0E

⊕**19** 1M S of Ák Páppas (Ikaría) 37°29'·8N 25°58'·8E
⊕**20** 1M N of Ák Armenistís (Ikaría) 37°39'·2N 26°05'·0E
⊕**21** 1M E of Ák Dhrépanon (Ikaría) 37°41'·5N 26°23'·1E
⊕**22** 1M S of Ák Áy Dhoménikos (Sámos) 37°39'·7N 26°35'·5E
⊕**23** 1M N of Makronisi (Sámos) 37°49'·12N 26°59'·90E WGS84
⊕**24** 0·5M E of Ák Gátos (Sámos) 37°43'·53N 27°04'·67E WGS84
⊕**25** Stenón Samou W end (Mid channel Bayrak Adasi N side) 37°41'·86N 27°00'·80E WGS84
⊕**26** 1M S of Samíoupoula 37°36'·3N 26°48'·4E
⊕**27** Mid-channel N end of Póros Fournon 37°36'·0N 26°27'·8E
⊕**28** Mid-channel S end of Póros Fournon 37°33'·7N 26°27'·5E

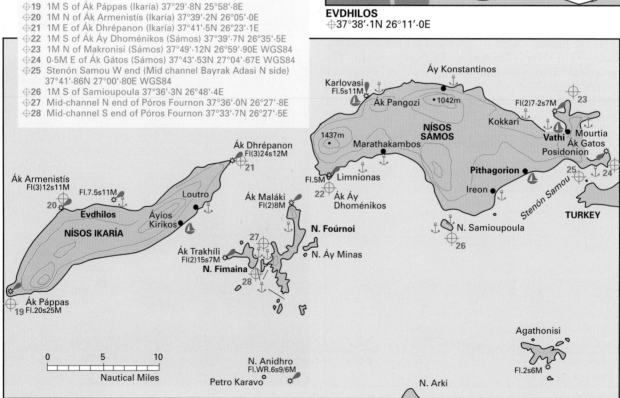

IKARIA AND SAMOS

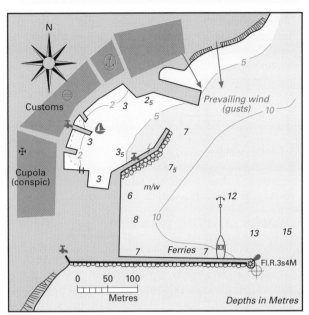

ÁYIOS KIRIKOS
⊕37°36'·8N 26°17'·9E

Evdhilos on Ikaría looking NW from the S side of the bay
Neville Bulpitt

have underwater ballasting extending out from them so it is best to go bows-to. The mole quay is also quite high and there are few places to secure warps to.

Shelter With a strong *meltemi* some swell creeps around the end of the mole. With strong NE winds the harbour is untenable.

Authorities Port police and customs.

Facilities
Water A tap near the quay.
Provisions Some provisions in the village.
Eating out Several tavernas and a number of cafés.
Other PO. Bus to Áyios Kirikos. Ferries to Sámos and Piraeus.

General
The tiny village sandwiched between a rocky bluff and high mountains is attractive and friendly. Ikaría doesn't get a lot of tourism compared to nearby Sámos although the new ferry service is changing that. Good fishing along the precipitous coast that drops sheer into the sea in the vicinity.

CAUTION
Along the S coast of Ikaría severe gusts sweep down off the high mountains.

ÁYIOS KIRIKOS (Agios Kirykos)

BA 1526
Imray-Tetra G32

Approach
The capital and ferry port of Ikaría lies on the SE side of the island.

Conspicuous The town and the harbour mole are easily identified from the distance.

By night Use the light on the end of the mole: Fl.R.3s4M.

Dangers With N winds there are severe gusts into the harbour and off the high land in the approaches – some caution is advised with the *meltemi*.

Mooring
Go alongside or stern or bows-to one of the piers inside the new inner breakwater. Care is needed towards the root of the piers where it shallows.

Shelter Adequate shelter from the *meltemi*. With moderate S winds the harbour should now be tenable with the construction of the new inner breakwater, but with gales from the S it may become untenable.

Authorities Port police and customs.

Facilities
Water On the pier.
Fuel In the town (about ¼ of a mile). A mini-tanker will deliver.
Provisions Good shopping for provisions.
Eating out Good tavernas.
Other PO. OTE. Bank. ATM. Hire motorbikes. Ferry to Piraeus.

General
The town is an attractive straggle of buildings up the steep slopes from the harbour and the locals are friendly. The only problem in this part of the world

Áy Kirikos looking SW
Nigel Patten

419

is the *meltemi* which howls down off the slopes and makes getting around the island a nightmare at times. Personally I think Icarus had his feathers blown off around here by the *meltemi* and didn't get anywhere near the sun.

Note It is reported a marina is to be built approximately 6 miles W of Áy Kirikos. No details are available.

KARKINAGRI

A small harbour situated W of Áy Kirikos has been reported. It has a difficult entrance and is crowded with local boats. No details are available.

ÓRMOS LOUTRÓ (Thermia)

37°37'·3N 26°18'·2E

Just over half a mile NE of Áy Kirikos is the bay of Loutró which affords reasonable shelter from the *meltemi*. Anchor in the bay, or small yachts can go on the quay off the old hydropathic institute. The former name of the place was Thermia, describing the hot springs now utilised by the hydropathic institute.

Loutró (Thermia) on Ikaría looking NE   *Nigel Patten*

ÁKRA DHREPANON

37°41'·3N 26°21'·8E

Immediately S of the cape there is an open bay partially protected from the *meltemi* which in calm weather could be used for visiting the ancient ruins of Drakanon. The ancient circular tower is conspicuous from seaward.

Nísos Sámos

While Lésvos is the jewel of the eastern Sporades, Sámos is the rough-cut diamond. The high mountain ridge running the length of the island is an extension of Mt Mykale in Turkey – from the southeast corner of the island it is a single sea mile across to Cape Mykale, making Sámos the closest of the Greek islands to Turkey. In the west the range rises sheer from the sea to Mt Kertetevs (1,437m, nearly 5,000ft) and runs east to the Ambelos range (1,041m, 3,730ft). Deep gullies score the mountainsides and peaks and bluffs assume shapes which even the restrained language of the Admiralty *Pilot* describes as 'fantastic'. Thick pine forest covers most of the lower slopes and villages perch precariously on small plateaus. There is a grandeur and grace to Sámos unequalled elsewhere.

In ancient times Sámos was lavishly praised: it was known as Parthenoarroussa for its beauty: Dryoussa for its oaks, Anthemis for its flowers, and Hydrele for its abundant springs. The name Sámos is probably derived from a Phoenician word meaning 'high'. As part of the Ionic Confederacy it prospered, but it was under the ambitious Polykrates that the island rose to the height of its prosperity in the 6th century BC.

Polykrates was equal parts tyrant and aesthete – a sort of latter-day Odysseus. He rose swiftly to power, conquering nearby islands and assembling a large fleet and army. To Sámos he invited poets and artists and under his patronage three of the greatest engineering feats in the ancient Greek world were achieved: the harbour at Pithagorion, the underground conduit and tunnel behind Pithagorion, and the temple to Hera near Ireon. The temple is now just ruins, but the remains of the harbour and the tunnel are still there. Polykrates was finally lured to the mainland coast and crucified by the Persians.

Sámos then passed from Sparta to Athens and thence to the Romans. Anthony sacked it before the Battle of Actium. Aided by Cleopatra, he gave a mammoth feast on the island to which all the civilized world was invited and which went on for months. This was his way of starting a war and the only question men had was what the victory feast would be like. As we know there was no victory feast, only defeat and hopeless suicide.

After the Roman occupation the island fell into obscurity and was the lair of pirates, apart from a brief period of Byzantine rule. The inhabitants fled to Khíos and Lésvos leaving the island open for the Turks to occupy in 1566. It became part of Greece in 1912.

You might expect an island ravaged and pillaged by corsairs for so long to be run down and poor in spirit. Not a bit of it. Sámos leaves you with the feeling of a happy island populated by friendly people. The scenery is superb from the extensive pine forests on the mountain slopes (Samian pine is considered to be the best for *caïque* building) to the cultivated plains. Sadly, forest fires have destroyed much of the pine forest on the S coast. Apart from the sweet white Sámos muscat wine, the excellent *Saimaina* dry white is available in Vathi, Karlóvasi and Pithagorion. A sweet red *moschata* is also produced.

KARLÓVASI

BA 1526

Imray-Tetra G32

Approach

Conspicuous From the distance the buildings of the town are easily identified. A church with a blue cupola on a precipitous rock bluff and two large churches with blue cupolas in the town are conspicuous. The harbour is to the W of the town and the harbour moles are easily identified.

By night Use the light on Ák Pangózi Fl.5s11M and the lights at the entrance Fl.G.4·5s5M/ Fl.R.4·5s4M. The main lights may not be in operation during harbour works.

Note

1. Work is in progress extending the outer breakwater. The light on the extremity is moved as work progresses but may not mark the end of underwater obstructions off the breakwater. Care needed in the immediate approaches.

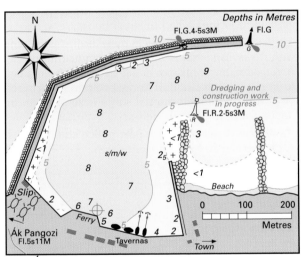

KARLÓVASI
⊕37°47'·68N 26°40'·83E WGS84

Karlóvasi looking E. Work is in progress on the east side of the harbour   *Lu Michell*

2. The end of the mole on the S side of the harbour has been destroyed. Dredging and construction work is in progress. Care needed when entering the harbour.

Dangers With the *meltemi* there can be a confused sea off the coast around the harbour and at the entrance.

Mooring

Go stern or bows-to or alongside where there is room on the S quay. The bottom is sand, mud and weed, good holding.

Shelter Good shelter, but with the *meltemi* some swell creeps around the end of the outer mole – uncomfortable but not dangerous. With strong S winds there are gusts off the high mountains behind.

Authorities Port police and customs.

Note Photographs of the coast to the W are prohibited.

Facilities

Water On the quay.

Fuel In the town about 2 miles away. A mini-tanker may be able to deliver.

Repairs Limited mechanical repairs. The yard in the SW corner of the harbour hauls out yachts.

Provisions Some provisions at the harbour. Good shopping for provisions in Karlóvasi village.

Eating out Tavernas on the waterfront.

Other PO and OTE in Karlóvasi village. Bus to Vathi.

General

The harbour is a sleepy little spot that seems to have seen more prosperous times. In recent years a little tourism has arrived to brighten up the harbour front. Inland, Karlóvasi proper is a straggling market village serving the agricultural needs of the hinterland. The centre is most attractive – all stone houses and cobbled streets.

AY KONSTANTINOS

37°48'·49N 26°49'·05E WGS84

A small crowded fishing harbour approximately halfway between Karlóvasi and Vathi along the N coast. Go stern or bows-to near the end of the mole if there is room, otherwise you may be able to moor alongside a fishing boat. Depths 1·5–4m. Reasonable shelter from the *meltemi*.

Tavernas and some provisions ashore.

AVLAKIA

37°47'·9N 26°51'·8E

Attractive calm weather anchorage under Ák Avlakia. Anchor off the beach in 6–10m. Suitable for a lunch stop only.

LIMONAKIA (Kokkari)

37°46'·7N 26°53'·8E

On the W side of Ák Kokkari a mole about 100m long has been built off the village of Limenakia. Depths of 2–5m have been reported along the mole, and there is good shelter from northerlies. Passing ferries are reported to send a dangerous swell into the bay.

Some provisions and tavernas ashore.

KOKKARI

Power station quay 37°46'·41N 26°54'·03E WGS84

The bay on the E side of Ák Kokkari. Care is needed of the reef off the end of the cape. In calm weather or light westerlies anchor off the village in 7–10m on sand and weed. Hotels and tavernas ashore.

Note Approximately halfway between Kokkari and Vathi a new power station has been built, complete with its own quay. The two red and white chimneys are conspicuous on the E side of the headland. Mooring and anchoring is prohibited.

VATHI (Sámos)

Approach

The capital and principal ferry port of Sámos lies in a large bay on the NE corner of the island.

Conspicuous The buildings of the town straggling around the bay and up the slopes behind are easily identified.

By night Use the light on Ák Kótsikas Fl(2)7·2s7M and the light on the end of the mole Fl.R.3s4M. The small yacht harbour is lit F.R.3M/F.G.3M.

Dangers Órmos Vathi is completely open to the N–NW and consequently the *meltemi* sends a heavy confused swell into the bay. There are also strong gusts off the high land in the vicinity.

Note
1. Work is in progress on the W side of the bay expanding the new commercial port.
2. Works are reported in the SE corner of the bay, reclaiming land and extending the quay.

Mooring

Go stern or bows-to or alongside the quay where shown, keeping clear of the ferry quay. If alongside it may pay to lay an anchor and use a bridle to keep the yacht pulled off the quay.

Vathí (Sámos) looking N. Yachts berth along the quay or in the small yacht harbour
Lu Michell

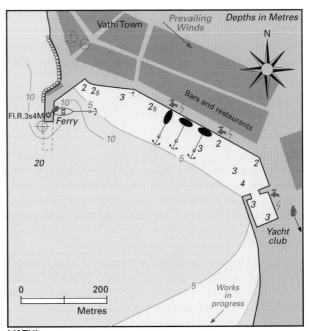

VATHI
⊕37°45'·34N 26°58'·21E WGS84

In the SE corner a small yacht harbour has been built and you may be able to find a berth in here. There are mostly 3m depths inside. Berth stern or bows-to in a vacant spot or where directed. There are laid moorings tailed to small buoys.

Shelter Shelter on the town quay is just adequate with the *meltemi* and is certainly very uncomfortable. A considerable surge can be set up and you will need to keep pulled well off. The yacht basin is sheltered from the *meltemi* although a surge is set up – more uncomfortable than dangerous.

Authorities A port of entry: port police and customs. A charge is made in the yacht basin.

Facilities

Services Water and electricity on the quay and in the yacht basin.

Fuel On the waterfront to the E. A mini-tanker can deliver to the quay.

Provisions Good shopping for all provisions nearby.

Eating out Good tavernas nearby.

Other PO. OTE. Banks. ATMs. Greek gas and Camping Gaz. Hire cars and motorbikes. Buses to the principal villages. Ferry to Piraeus, Kavála, Khíos and Kuşadasi in Turkey.

General

The bustling port town of Vathi is huddled around the waterfront, where everything seems to jump to the tune of the ships and ferries that call here. It is worth visiting the old island capital of Sámos in the hills over-looking the bay, if only to test your navigation skills in the labyrinthine passages winding through the town.

ORMOS ASPROKHORTI

37°47'·2N 26°58'·4E

The bay to the E of Ák Kotsikas is open to the prevailing wind, but tucked into the SE corner is a tiny cove that offers some shelter from the prevailing winds and good shelter from southerlies.

ÓRMOS MOURTIA

37°45'·5N 27°02'·3E

The large bay on the E end of Sámos. A monastery on the slopes is easily identified. Anchor in the cove at the head of the bay in 5m on a sandy bottom. Some shelter from the *meltemi* although a swell normally enters. Open to the S and E.

ÓRMOS POSIDONION

37°42'·5N 27°03'·4E

A small bay lying on the S side of Ák Gátos, the SE tip of Sámos. The light structure on the cape (Fl(3)14s7M) is easily identified from the N. Anchor in 5–10m on a sandy bottom. Good shelter from the *meltemi* although there are strong gusts down into the bay and channel. Ashore there are a few houses and several tavernas in attractive surroundings.

About 2 miles to the W at Psili Amos there is an anchorage behind an islet. Good shelter from the *meltemi*. A small development and a few tavernas ashore.

Stenón Samou
(Sámos Strait)

BA 1526
Imray-Tetra G32

The narrow strait between the E end of Sámos and mainland Turkey. (The Turks call the strait Dilek Boğazi.) At its narrowest the strait is less than a mile across. In the strait there is the small rocky islet of Bayrak Adasi (Turkish) with a light structure on it (Fl.5s8M). A yacht can pass either N or S of the islet. On the N side there is a rocky shoal with a least depth of 9m in the fairway. On the S side there are greater depths.

The narrow strait channels the fairly weak N-going current into a strong current with overfalls. The current sets to the E and may attain a rate of 3–4 knots in the narrow section of the strait although it is normally less at around 1–2 knots. The overfalls are usually worse on the N side than the S side. The overfalls combined with strong gusts off the high land of Sámos with the *meltemi* can make the passage very uncomfortable at times and care is needed.

PITHAGORION (Pythagoreon, Tigani)

BA 1526
Imray-Tetra G32

Approach

Conspicuous A line of 9 wind generators on the ridge E of Pithagorion are conspicuous and the buildings of the town are visible from some distance off. A large red-roofed hotel to the W of the town and Metamorfosis, a fortified stone monastery on the waterfront, are conspicuous. Closer in, the outer mole is easily identified.

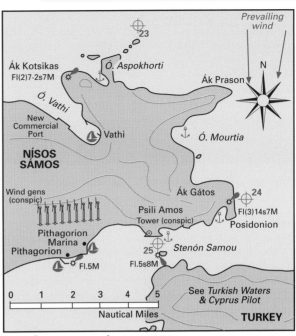

STENÓN SAMOU (SÁMOS STRAIT)

⊕23 1M N of Makronisi (Sámos) 37°49'·12N 26°59'·90E WGS84E
⊕24 0·5M E of Ák Gátos (Sámos) 37°43'·53N 27°04'·67E WGS84
⊕25 Stenón Samou W end (Mid channel Bayrak Adasi N side) 37°41'·86N 27°00'·80E WGS84

By night Use the light on Ák Foniás Fl.4s5M and the lights at the entrance Fl.R.2s3M/Fl.G.2s2M. From the W the lights at the entrance cannot be seen until close in. Care is needed of the beacon at the entrance to the inner harbour which is unlit.

Dangers With the *meltemi* there are strong gusts off the high land in the approaches to the harbour.

Note Once inside the outer mole the beacon marking the limit of the shallows on the S side of the entrance to the inner basin is easily identified.

Mooring

Go stern or bows-to the W quay. The bottom is mud – excellent holding.

Authorities A port of entry: port police, customs, and immigration. A small charge is sometimes made.

Facilities

Services Water and electricity on the quay. The connection charge is expensive.

Fuel About 3km out of town. A mini-tanker can deliver to the quay.

Repairs Some mechanical repairs. Hardware shops and limited chandlery.

Provisions Good shopping for provisions nearby. Fruit and vegetable van.

Eating out Tavernas on the waterfront and in town. I seem to have bad luck in Pithagorion with some pretty awful food served up in some of the waterfront tavernas. Choose carefully.

Other PO. OTE. Bank. ATMs. Various yacht agents in the town can arrange services. Greek gas and Camping Gaz collection and delivery by van. Hire cars, motorbikes and bicycles. Regular bus to Vathi. Ferries to Pátmos and Kuşadasi in Turkey. Internal flights to Athens.

Approach to Pithagorion looking N. Note wind generators

General

Set at the foot of pine-covered hills and looking over to the Turkish mountains, the town of Pithagorion is a busy tourist resort, and justifiably so. It is a thoroughly agreeable place, set in magnificent surroundings with high wooded mountains behind and just big enough to have good facilities yet small enough to be intimate.

The town was named Pithagorion comparatively recently, in 1955, in honour of Pythagoras who was born on Sámos. Formerly it was called Tigani meaning 'frying pan' – a name which is self explanatory once you have seen the shape of the harbour. Pithagorion is situated on the site of the ancient city of Sámos which rose to prominence under Polykrates the tyrant. During Polykrates' swift rise to power, what Herodotus described as three of the greatest engineering feats in the Greek world were achieved.

The first was the mole which protected the harbour and which survives in part today as part of the quay and the root of the outer mole.

The second was the temple of Hera built near Ireon. In its day bigger and better than any other, today only a single column remains standing amongst the ruins. A small museum in Pithagorion houses some of the finds from the temple site.

The third was the tunnel hewn through the mountain to bring water to the city and also probably as an escape route. It still exists today although the middle section has collapsed. The original was a mile long and 2·4m (8ft) square and for its day an extraordinary engineering feat. The entrance is immediately behind Pithagorion and a part of the tunnel can be explored by those who don't suffer from claustrophobia, though considerable care is needed. It is open six times a week on three days – enquire at the tourist office.

PITHAGORION MARINA

Imray-Tetra G32

Approach

The new marina lies immediately E of Pithagorion harbour on the E side of Ák Foniás. From the S the entrance to the 'marina' is in line with the easternmost wind turbine on the hill above. For the moment work goes slowly on the marina and it is pretty much a building site. A few yachts use it but most prefer to berth in Pithagorion itself.

By night Use the light on Ák Foniás Fl.4s5M and the lights at the entrance Fl.G.2s3M/Fl.R.2s3M.

VHF Ch 09 will be used.

Note All the main quays are complete. The six pontoons planned for the W of the basin are not yet in place.

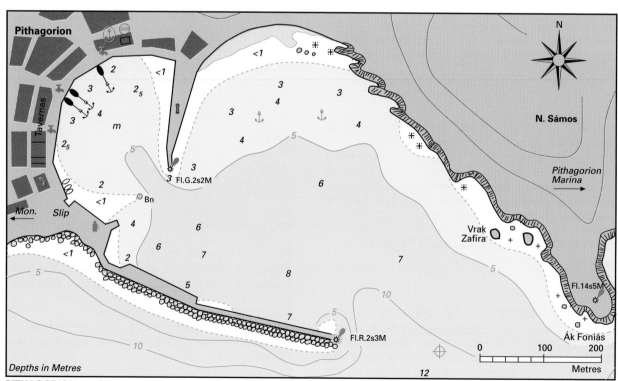

PITHAGORION
⊕37°41′·19N 26°57′·06E WGS84

Pithagorion on Sámos looking SW across the harbour   *Lu Michell*

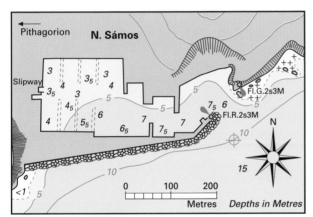

PITHAGORION MARINA
⊕37°41′·36N 26°57′·53E WGS84

Mooring

Data 250 berths. Visitors' berths. Max LOA 20m. Depths 3–7·5m. Laid moorings to be installed. Some local boats use the harbour, but there is plenty of room to go alongside where convenient.

Shelter Good all-round shelter.

Authorities Harbourmaster to be appointed.

Facilities

All services to be installed including water, electricity, toilets and showers. It is planned to install a travel-hoist and workshops. No shops or tavernas. It is a 20 minute walk into Pithagorion.

IREON

37°39′·59N 26°52′·94E WGS84

At the W end of the large bay running around to Pithagorion is the village and small fishing harbour at Ireon. A short breakwater provides some shelter. Anchor off in 3–4m. The *meltemi* does not gust into this corner as strongly as elsewhere along this coast.

Provisions and tavernas ashore.

The Temple of Hera is about 1km from the harbour.

NISÍS SAMIOUPOULA (Samopoula)

⊕26 1M S of Samioupoula 37°36′·3N 26°48′·4E

A *caïque* from Pithagorion runs tourists out to the island in the summer and anchors in a cove on the E side of the island. Ashore there is a small hamlet with a taverna.

MARATHAKAMBOS

A fishing harbour on the SW of Sámos. 11 wind turbines are conspicuous on the hill behind the harbour. An outer breakwater runs E from a natural bight with a short inner breakwater extending S from the coast. There are 3–4m depths in the entrance and outer part of the harbour. Anchor in the outer part or go bows-to the short pier running out from the shore. There are 2m depths at the extremity of the pier. With the *meltemi* there are strong gusts off the land so ensure your anchor is holding well.

Provisions and tavernas ashore. The surroundings are spectacular with precipitous cliffs and hills rising abruptly from the shore. Sadly much of the pine has been burnt in recent forest fires.

Note This is a military area although now opened up for a little tourism. Photographs are prohibited.

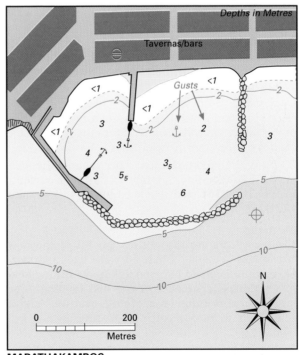

MARATHAKAMBOS
⊕37°42′·52N 26°42′·12E WGS84

425

Marathokambos harbour looking ESE   *Lu Michell*

ÓRMOS LIMNIONAS

37°41'·2N 26°37'·6E

Lying close SW of Ák Khondhros Kávos, this bay offers shelter from N winds, but is subject to fierce gusts off the mountains above. It is open to the S.

Taverna opens in the summer.

CAUTION

On the W and S sides of Sámos severe gusts sweep down off the high mountains with the *meltemi*. Unless a yacht is proceeding to Limnionas or Marathakambos it is a good policy to keep at least 2–3 miles off the S coast.

Nisídhes Foúrnoi

(Phournoi)

FOURNOI (Órmos Korseon, Kampos)

BA 1625

Approach

The steep-to high islands (of Foúrnoi and Fimaina) are visible from many miles away (Nisís Foúrnoi is 515m, 1,686ft high at its northern point).

Conspicuous From the N the village of Foúrnoi (Korseon) and 2 windmills on the ridge to the SW of the village are conspicuous. From the S the village cannot be seen but the windmills are conspicuous.

By night Not recommended. There is only the light on Ák Svistokáminos (S side of Órmos Korseon): Fl.WR.3·5s4/3M (red sector covers 034°-138° and 172°-243°).

Mooring

Visiting yachts are directed to the SE of the new jetty on the NE quay. There are some laid moorings. Go stern or bows-to or better still find a fishing boat to go alongside because of the bad holding. The bottom here is a thin layer of mud over rock and it is difficult to find a patch where the anchor will hold.

Shelter Shelter is good but there is some surge in the harbour with a strong *meltemi*.

NISIDHES FOÚRNOI

⊕27 Mid-channel N end of Póros Fournon 37°36'·0N 26°27'·8E
⊕28 Mid-channel S end of Póros Fournon 37°33'·7N 26°27'·5E

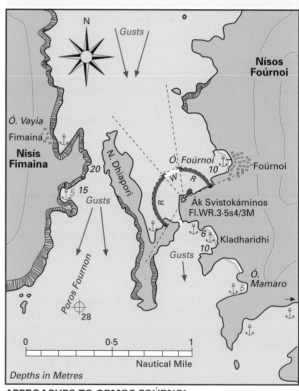

APPROACHES TO ORMOS FOÚRNOI

⊕28 Mid-channel S end of Póros Fournon 37°33'·7N 26°27'·5E

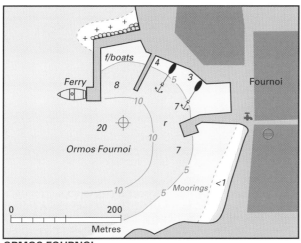

ORMOS FOURNOI
⊕37°34'·5N 26°28'·8E

Anchorage on the bottom of Nísos Foúrnoi · · · · · · · *Nigel Patten*

Note The SE of the harbour is full of permanent moorings off the beach.

Authorities Port police and customs.

Facilities
Water Tap near the quay.
Fuel Small quantities may be available.
Provisions Some provisions can be obtained but the villagers are largely dependent on the ferry from Samos for supplies.
Eating out Several tavernas – fresh fish is often available.
Other PO. Ferry to Sámos.

General
Foúrnoi (Korseon, Kambos) is the only major village on the island and the population and facilities are concentrated here. A large fishing fleet is based here and the locals are generally friendly to visiting yachts. The coves S of the village are mostly deserted and the surrounding jagged coastline offers good fishing.

ANCHORAGES AROUND THE ISLANDS
1. *Fimaina (Órmos Vayia)* The bay on Nisís Fimaina opposite Órmos Korseon. Poor shelter from the *meltemi*. Taverna ashore.
2. *Nisís Dhiapori* The bay on the E side immediately SW of Ák Svistokáminos.
3. *Cliff Bay* The cove on Nisís Fimaina on the W side of the narrow channel between Fimaina and Dhiapori. Some shelter from the *meltemi*.
4. *Kladharidhi* Anchor in the bay sheltered on the W by Nisís Dhiaporoi. Posts are set into the rocks along the N shore to take long lines. Three mooring buoys in the N of the bay are reported to have been used by visiting yachts. A new mole in the centre of the bay is reported to have depths of 3m off. You are beam on to the prevailing wind here. Tavernas ashore in summer.
5. *Órmos Mármaro* Anchor at the N end of the bay with a long line ashore. Depths are considerable. Good protection from the *meltemi*.
6. *Quarry Bay* In the large bay immediately S of Mármaro there is reported to be good shelter

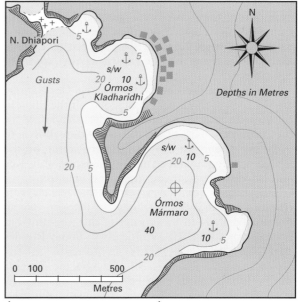

ÓRMOS KLADHARIDHI AND MÁRMARO
⊕37°33'·3N 26°28'·7E

from the *meltemi*. Anchor at the head of the bay in 5–8m, good holding once the anchor is in. Ashore there is an ancient marble quarry with unfinished columns and other bits and pieces lying around.
7. At the S end of Nisís Foúrnoi there is a large bay immediately W of Ák Agridhio that looks as though it would offer good shelter from the *meltemi*. There is also another inlet NW of it.
8. *Órmos Khrisomilia* On the N end of Foúrnoi on the W side there is the large bay of Khrisomilia. A yacht can anchor off here in calm weather though depths are considerable. To the E there is the small cove of Vali which is said to afford some shelter from the *meltemi*, though again depths are considerable.

CAUTION
With the *meltemi* there are severe gusts off the high land of the islands and in the strait between Fimaina and Foúrnoi (Póros Fournon) considerable confused seas are pushed down. Care is needed when navigating in the vicinity of the islands which in the *meltemi* season are very windy places indeed.

427

IX. The Dodecanese

The Dodecanese, the Twelve Islands, lie in a crescent chain down the Asiatic Turkish coast curving west towards Crete. The name 'Dodecanese' is of comparatively recent origin. It came into use in 1908 when twelve islands of this group excluding Lipso, Kós and Rhodes, but including an outsider, Ikaría, protested about their deprivation of the special privileges and tax exemptions they had been granted in the 16th century by the Turks. Since then the name has come to include Lipso, Kós and Rhodes, but to exclude Ikaría. The group is also known as the Southern Sporades.

Like most of the Greek Islands, the Dodecanese are the tops of mountains that stood on the plain of the Aegean long since flooded. The islands are for the most part bare of vegetation, although not to such an extent as the Cyclades. Several of the islands with abundant natural springs, notably Kós and Rhodes, are relatively green and wooded.

The history of the Dodecanese has largely revolved around the fortunes of Rhodes, which dominated trade in this corner of the Aegean from ancient times until the 19th century. Today Rhodes dominates the new trade in tourists in the Dodecanese. In the early Middle Ages the Knights of St John, based in their fortress in Rhodes, stamped the area with their military signatures. Most of the military architecture is not the ubiquitous Venetian and Genoese architecture so prevalent in other parts of Greece, but that of the Knights. The occupation of the Knights nonetheless ensured the Venetians access to the trade in this part of the world. After the Knights finally capitulated to the Turks in 1522, the Dodecanese were to remain under Turkish rule until 1912.

Despite such a long period of unbroken occupation the islands have remained intrinsically Greek, and there is as little here to remind you of the long years under Turkish rule as elsewhere in Greece. After the Italo-Turkish war (1911–12) the islands were awarded to Italy although they were to be passed on in due course to Greece. This promise was later conveniently forgotten and the Dodecanese remained under the Italians until the Second World War. Finally in 1947 they officially became part of Greece. For those not familiar with modern Greek history it comes as quite a shock to learn that these islands have been a part of Greece for such a short time, when visually and culturally they appear to be as much a part of Greece as any of the other islands.

Routes

In the summer routes through the Dodecanese are basically off the wind or bashing into the wind. The *meltemi* blows from the N–NW around Pátmos, curving down through the islands to blow from the W around Rhodes. The problem here is really how to get N and W in the summer. There are not too many options. The *meltemi* does have something of a thermal component which means the wind is augmented in the afternoon by a sea breeze blowing onto Asia Minor. With any luck if you leave early in the morning there will be less wind than in the afternoon. We are really talking of relative amounts of wind here and at times the *meltemi* can blow all through the night with as much force as in the day.

If you are heading W through the Cyclades the usual plan is to head as far N as possible in the Dodecanese and then dive off through the Cyclades where the *meltemi* will blow from the N in the middle and the NE towards the westerly Cyclades. An alternative is to head W and SW around the bottom Cyclades to Serifos and then up to the Saronic. The *meltemi* tends not to be as strong around the southern edges of the Cyclades and towards the Peloponnese.

In the spring and autumn you will likely pick up southerlies and if you are planning to go N to the eastern Sporades or Northern Greece then spring and early summer is the time to do it before the *meltemi* is well established. Then you can come back S with the *meltemi* aft of the beam.

Weather patterns in the Dodecanese

In the summer the prevailing wind is the *meltemi* blowing from the NW–W. It starts fitfully in June, blows strongly in July through to September and again fitfully in October. In the summer months it regularly blows Force 4–6 and may on occasion reach Force 7. It does not blow every day, but may blow without a break for 5–10 days.

In the spring and autumn the wind frequently blows from the SE, about Force 2–4, although it may be stronger on occasion. In the winter the wind is predominantly from the SE although gales may come from the N or S.

When the *meltemi* is blowing at full strength in July and August the gusts off the lee side of an island can be considerably stronger than the wind strength in the open sea. Gusts are particularly strong off Pátmos, Kalimnos, Kós, Nísiros, Tílos, Kárpathos and Astipálaia. In the comparatively open stretch of sea between Astipálaia and Kárpathos a large and disturbed sea is set up when the *meltemi* blows for days on end.

In the summer months it is very hot in the Dodecanese, although the *meltemi* provides some relief. Temperatures may reach 35°C although the average temperature is less. In the winter the climate is mild.

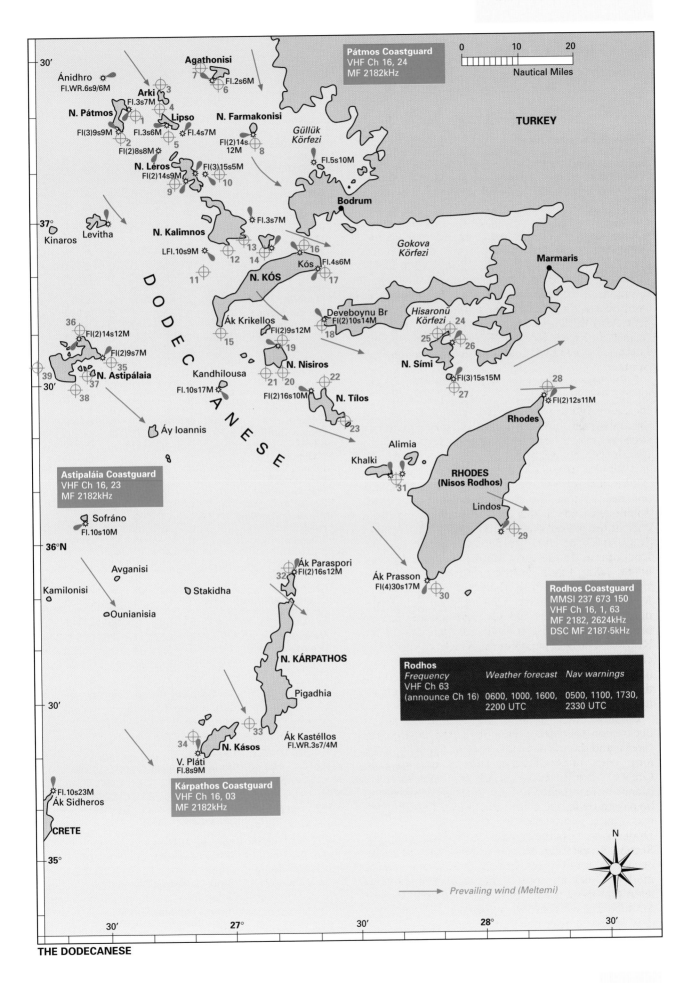

THE DODECANESE

Quick reference guide

	Shelter	Mooring	Fuel	Water	Provisioning	Tavernas	Plan
Pátmos and adjacent islands							
Skála Pátmos	B	AC	B	B	B	A	•
Anchorages near							
Skála Pátmos	BC	C	O	O	O	C	•
Ormos Stavros	C	C	O	O	O	C	
Nísos Arki							
Port Augusta	A	AC	O	B	C	C	•
Port Stretto	B	C	O	O	O	O	
N. Marathos	B	C	O	O	O	C	•
Lipso							
Órmos Lipso	B	AC	B	A	B	B	•
Lera Lipso	B	C	O	O	O	C	•
Agathonisi							
Áy Yeóryiou	B	AC	B	B	C	C	•
East Bay	B	C	O	O	O	O	•
Nisís Farmakonisi							
O Tholou	C	C	O	O	O	O	•
Léros							
Port Lakkí	B	A	B	A	B	B	
Partheni	A	C	B	B	C	C	•
N. Arkhangelos	C	C	O	O	O	O	•
Órmos Plakoudi	C	C	O	O	O	O	•
Órmos Alindas	C	AC	B	A	B	B	•
Pandeli	B	AC	B	B	C	B	•
Xerokambos	B	AC	O	B	C	C	•
Kalimnos							
Limín Kalímnos	A	A	B	A	A	A	•
Órmos Akti	C	C	O	O	O	C	
Vathi	B	A	O	B	C	C	•
Órmos Palionisou	O	C	O	O	O	O	
Emborios	B	C	O	B	C	C	•
Mirties	C	C	O	B	C	C	
Telendhos	O	C	O	B	C	C	
Órmos Linarias	O	C	O	C	C	C	
Vlikadia	B	C	O	B	C	C	
Psérimos	C	AC	O	O	C	B	•
N. Platí	C	C	O	O	O	O	
Kós							
Limín Kós	B	A	B	A	A	A	•
Kós Marina	A	A	A	A	B	B	•
Kardamena	B	AC	O	B	C	B	•
Órmos Kamáres	B	AC	O	A	C	C	•
Limnionas	BC	AC	O	O	C	C	
Mastikhari	B	AB	O	A	C	B	
Nisís Yialí	C	C	O	O	O	O	
Nísiros							
Mandráki	C	AB	B	A	B	B	•
Palon	B	A	O	A	C	B	•

	Shelter	Mooring	Fuel	Water	Provisioning	Tavernas	Plan
Nísos Tílos							
Livádhi	A	AB	B	A	B	C	•
Áy Andonis	C	C	O	B	O	C	
Sími							
Sími	B	A	B	A	A	A	•
Pethi	B	AC	O	B	C	C	•
Áy Marina	B	C	O	O	O	C	
E coast anchorages	C	C	O	O	O	C	
Nisís Seskli	C	C	O	O	O	O	
Panormittis	A	C	O	O	C	C	•
Áy Emilianos	C	AC	O	O	O	O	•
O. Emborios	O	C	O	O	O	O	
Rhodes							
Mandráki	A	A	A	A	A	A	•
Rhodes Marina	A	AB	B	B	A	A	•
Ák Ladhiko	B	C	O	O	O	C	
Faliraki	C	C	O	O	B	A	
Lindos	B	C	O	B	C	A	•
Áy Apostoli	C	C	O	O	O	O	
Órmos Lardhos	O	C	O	O	O	C	
Istros/Vigli	O	C	O	O	O	O	
Ák Prasso	B	C	O	O	C	B	
Órmos Langonia	O	C	B	B	B	C	
Fanai	B	A	O	B	O	C	
Órmos Trianda	O	C	O	O	O	O	
Khálki	B	AC	O	A	C	C	•
Potamós	B	C	O	O	O	C	
Alimia	B	C	O	O	O	O	•
Kárpathos							
Port Karpathos	C	AB	B	A	B	B	•
Órmos Amorfos	C	C	O	O	O	O	
Órmos Mákri Yialo	C	C	O	O	O	O	
Finiki	C	A	O	B	C	C	•
Trístoma	B	C	O	O	O	O	•
Dhiafani	C	AC	O	O	C	C	
Kásos							
Limín Kasou	C	A	B	B	C	C	•
Limín Fri	A	AB	B	B	B	B	•
Órmos Khelatronas	C	C	O	O	O	O	
Astipálaia							
Skála	B	ABC	B	A	B	B	•
Maltezana	B	BC	O	B	C	C	•
Órmos Agrilithi	B	C	O	O	O	O	•
Vathi	A	C	O	O	C	C	•
Panormos	B	C	O	O	O	C	•
Órmos Livádhi	C	C	O	O	O	O	•
N. Áy Ioánnis	B	C	O	O	O	O	

Data

PORTS OF ENTRY
Kós
Sími
Rhodes (Rodhos)

PROHIBITED AREAS
Léros It is prohibited to navigate and land on the S side of Órmos Lakkí in the vicinity of the naval buildings.

MAJOR LIGHTS
Nisís Ànidhro Fl.WR.6s9/6M

Pátmos
Ák Yeranós Fl.3s7M
Ák Ilías Fl(3)9s9M

Lipso
Ák Gátos Fl.3s6M
Nisís Kalapódhia Fl.4s7M
Vrak Saráki Fl(2)8s8M
Nisís Gáïdharos Fl.2s6M
Nisís Farmakonisi (S summit) Fl(2)14s12M

Léros
Órmos Alíndas Fl.3s5M
Vrak Áy Kiriakí Fl(3)15s5M
Órmos Lakkí (Ák Lakkí) Fl(2)14s9M
Nisís Gláros Fl.2s4M

Kalimnos
Nisís Kalólimnos Fl.3s7M
Limín Kalímnou Fl.R.2s4M
Vrak Safonídhi LFl.10s9M

Psérimos
Ák Rousa Fl(2)WR.10s12/9M
Vrak Nekrothikes Fl.WR.5s6/4M

Kós
Ák Ammóglossa Fl.R.4s9M
Ák Loúros Fl(3)WR.15s6/4M
Ák Foúka Fl.4s6M
Nisís Yialí Áy Andónios Fl.2s5M
Nísiros Ák Palos Fl(2)9s12M
Nisís Kandheliousa Fl.10s17M

Tílos
Vrak Gáïdharos Fl(2)16s10M

Sími
Nisís Marmarás Fl.3s6M
Nisís Khondrós Fl.3s5M
Ák Koutsoúmba Fl.3s5M

Vrak Kouloundrós (Troumbeta Rock) Fl(3)15s15M
Nisís Khálki (Skála) Fl.WR.6s8/6M

Rhodes
Nisís Tragusa Fl(2)WR.14s8/6M
Kámiros Skála Fl.3s8M
Ák Milon (Zonari) Fl.WR.4s6/4M
Rhodes Harbour (Áy Nikólaos) Fl(2)12s11M
Vrak Paximádha Fl.WR.4s9/6M
Ák Prasson Fl(4)30s17M

Kárpathos
Ák Kastéllos Fl.WR.3s7/4M
Nisídha Dhespotiko Fl.5s6M
Ák Paraspóri (Saria) Fl(2)16s12M
Nisís Stakidha Fl.3s8M
Ounianísia Fl(2)16s7M
Nisís Megálo Sofráno Fl.10s10M
Vrak Strongilí Fl(2)WR.10s7/5M

Kásos
Vrak Platí Fl.8s9M

Astipálaia
Ák Floúdha Fl(2)14s12M
Ák Exópetra Fl(2)9s7M

USEFUL WAYPOINTS

⊕1 0·5M SE of Ák Yeranós (Pátmos)
37°20'·01N 26°37'·31E WGS84
⊕2 1M S of Ák Ilias (Pátmos)
37°15'·2N 26°34'·3E
⊕3 0·5M N of Ák Koumaro (Arki)
37°25'·30N 26°43'·13E WGS84
⊕4 0.25M S of N. Grilousa (Arki)
37°21'·12N 26°42'·39E WGS84
⊕5 Mid-channel Frangonisi – Makronisi (Lipso)
37°15'·64N 26°43'·95E WGS84
⊕6 0·25M S of Ák Stifí (Agathonisi)
37°26'·35N 26°57'·65E WGS84

⊕7 0·4M W of Ák Nera (Agathonisi)
37°28'·53N 26°54'·96E WGS84
⊕8 1M S of Ák Petronkopis (Farmakonisi)
37°15'·5N 27°05'·3E
⊕9 1M W of Ák Lakki (Léros)
37°06'·8N 26°48'·2E
⊕10 1M E of Vrak Áy Kiriakí (Léros)
37°08'·8N 26°54'·4E
⊕11 3M S of Vrak Safonídhi (Kalimnos-Kós Channel)
36°50'·27N 26°54'·49E WGS84
⊕12 0·5M S of Áy Yeóryios (Kalimnos)
36°54'·97N 26°59'·21E WGS84
⊕13 0·75M S of Ák Khali (Kalimnos)
36°55'·95N 27°02'·97E WGS84
⊕14 0·25M S of Vrak Krevvatio (Psérimos)
36°54'·82N 27°09'·39E WGS84
⊕15 0·5M S of Ák Krikellos (Kós)
36°39'·80N 26°58'·43E WGS84
⊕16 0·75M N of Ák Ammóglossa (Kós)
36°55'·70N 27°16'·42E WGS84
⊕17 0·25M E of Ák Áy Fokas (Kós)
36°51'·67N 27°21'·69E WGS84
⊕18 0·75M W of Deveboynu Bükü (Knidos/Turkey)
36°41'·45N 27°20'·90E WGS84
⊕19 0·5M N of Ák Katsouni (Nísiros)
36°37'·70N 27°11'·36E WGS84
⊕20 0·5M S of Ák Loutros (Nísiros)
36°32'·92N 27°11'·66E WGS84
⊕21 1M S of Ák Levkhos (Nísiros)
36°32'·72N 27°08'·28E WGS84
⊕22 0·5M N of Ák Angistrou (Tílos)
36°29'·58N 27°21'·10E WGS84
⊕23 Mid-channel between Tílos and Andítilos
36°22'·6N 27°26'·9E

⊕24 1M N of Ák Makria (Sími)
36°41'·1N 27°51'·5E
⊕25 W entrance of Nímos Passage (Sími)
36°38'·72N 27°49'·76E WGS84
⊕26 0·25M N of Ák Koutsoumba (Sími)
36°38'·17N 27°52'·35E WGS84
⊕27 1M S of Vrak Kouloundros (Sími)
36°30'·0N 27°52'·2E
⊕28 1M N of Ák Milon (Rhodes)
36°28'·45N 28°13'·25E WGS84
⊕29 0·4M E of Ák Lindos (Rhodes)
36°03'·20N 28°05'·78E WGS84
⊕30 1M S of Ák Prasso (Rhodes)
35°51'·53N 27°45'·24E WGS84
⊕31 1M S of Vrak Nisáki (Khálki)
36°12'·0N 27°38'·0E
⊕32 1M N of Ák Paraspóri (Kárpathos)
35°55'·3N 27°13'·7E
⊕33 1M S of If Kárpathos
35°25'·92N 27°03'·10E WGS84
⊕34 100m N of If Kasou (Kásos)
35°25'·01N 26°51'·73E WGS84
⊕35 0·3M S of Ák Exópetra (Astipálaia)
36°34'·44N 26°28'·55E WGS84
⊕36 1M N of Ák Floúdha (Astipálaia)
36°39'·6N 26°22'·8E
⊕37 0·2M S of Nisís Ligno (Astipálaia)
36°33'·32N 26°23'·97E WGS84
⊕38 0·2M S of Ák Khilos (Astipálaia)
36°30'·16N 26°21'·94E WGS84
⊕39 1M S of Nisís Ofidhousa (Astipálaia)
36°30'·63N 26°08'·77E WGS84

Nísos Pátmos

The northernmost of the Dodecanese. The island is composed of three barren volcanic lumps joined to one another by narrow isthmuses. The natural harbour of Skála lies on the central isthmus and above it is the focal point of the island – the *chora* of Pátmos crowned by the monastery of St John the Divine. The *chora*, like that of Astipálaia, belongs more to the Cyclades than to the Dodecanese. The glaring white squat houses and courtyards contrast vividly with the grey stone monastery above.

Pátmos belongs to the Christian age rather than to antiquity. St John the Divine was banished to Pátmos by the Emperor Domitian. Here he dictated the wild poetry of the Apocalypse, found in the book of Revelations, to his disciple Prochorus. Halfway up the road between Skála and the *chora* is the Church of the Apocalypse and the Cave of St Anne where St John transmitted the fiery words of God to his disciple – at least so legend says, as we have no real proof that St John did actually write the Apocalypse whilst on Pátmos.

For centuries the island was the home of Saracen pirates until 1088 when St Christodoulos was granted permission to establish a monastery in honour of St John. The continued presence of the pirates dictated the fortified walls surrounding the monastery. The monastery prospered and its library became one of the largest in Greece outside Mt Athos. Many of the manuscripts have since been dispersed (many of them to England), but the valuable *Codex Porphyrius* written on purple vellum in silver and gold, and some excellent Byzantine illuminations, remain. The Treasury has a number of valuable icons and stoles. Special arrangements have to be made to see items not on display.

Pátmos is the spiritual centre of the Greek Orthodox Church after Mt Athos. Near the Church of the Apocalypse stands the new theological college attended by students from all over Greece. At Easter celebrations are carried out with considerable pomp and later much gusto.

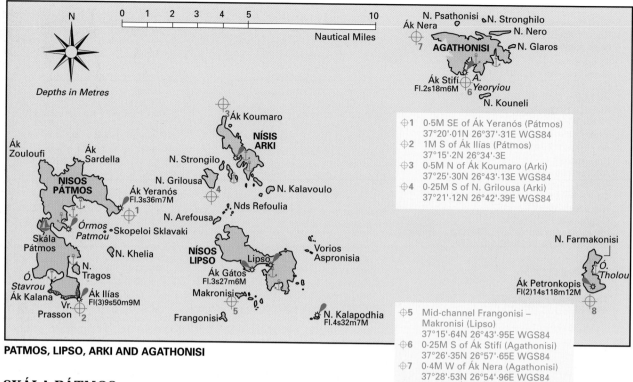

PATMOS, LIPSO, ARKI AND AGATHONISI

Worldwide positions list:

⊕1 0·5M SE of Ák Yeranós (Pátmos)
37°20'·01N 26°37'·31E WGS84
⊕2 1M S of Ák Ilías (Pátmos)
37°15'·2N 26°34'·3E
⊕3 0·5M N of Ák Koumaro (Arki)
37°25'·30N 26°43'·13E WGS84
⊕4 0·25M S of N. Grilousa (Arki)
37°21'·12N 26°42'·39E WGS84

⊕5 Mid-channel Frangonisi –
Makronisi (Lipso)
37°15'·64N 26°43'·95E WGS84
⊕6 0·25M S of Ák Stifí (Agathonisi)
37°26'·35N 26°57'·65E WGS84
⊕7 0·4M W of Ák Nera (Agathonisi)
37°28'·53N 26°54'·96E WGS84
⊕8 1M S of Ák Petronkopis
(Farmakonisi)
37°15'·5N 27°05'·3E

SKÁLA PÁTMOS

BA 1531

Imray-Tetra G32

Approach

Conspicuous In the approaches to Skála Pátmos there are a number of rocks and islets which are easily identified by day. Pátmos *chora* and the fortress-like monastery on the crown of the hill S of Skála Pátmos are conspicuous from some distance off. Skála Pátmos lies almost in the middle of the island at the lowest point. The white houses of Skála Pátmos are easy to see as you enter the bay.

By night Use the light on Ák Ilías Fl(3)9s9M, Vrak Kavouronísia (Tragos Rock) Fl(2)WR.12s5/3M (red sector covers 087°-232° over the reef N of the islet), Ák Áspri Fl.WR.2s5/3M (red sector covers 272°-320° over Ifalos Khelia, Nisís Khelia and Skopeloi Sklavaki), and the light at Skála Pátmos Fl.R.1·5s3M. The E cardinal buoy to the N of the ferry quay is lit Q(3)7s.

Dangers

1. Care should be taken of the numerous reefs associated with the rocks and islets in the

Approach to Pátmos looking W. The houses of the *chora* and the fortress-like monastery are easily identified

ÓRMOS PATMOU
⊕1 37°19'·80N 26°36'·52E WGS84
⊕2 37°18'·81N 26°36'·44E WGS84

approaches. Skopeloi Tragos lies 0·1 mile N of Vrak Kavouronísia (Tragos Rock). Ifalos Khelia lies 0·6 miles S of Nisís Khelia. Ifalos Sklavaki lies 0·2 miles SW of the more westerly of the two Sklavaki islets.

Note Ifalos Khelia is at the limit of the red sector of Ák Aspri light.

2. With the *meltemi*, strong gusts blow into the bay off the surrounding high land.

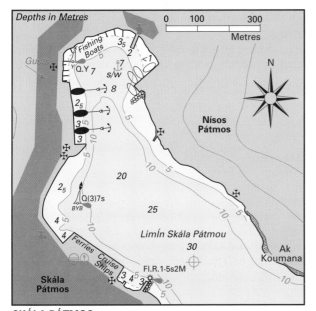

SKÁLA PÁTMOS
⊕37°19'.37N 26°32'.95E WGS84

Mooring

Go stern or bows-to the quay in the NW corner of the bay. Stern-to is better as the *meltemi* gusts down across the quay from the NW. The bottom is sand, mud and weed, good holding.

Shelter Shelter from the *meltemi* is better than it looks on the plan. The bay is open SE and with moderate SE winds it is uncomfortable – with strong SE winds probably untenable.

Authorities Port police and customs.

Anchorage Yachts can anchor near the head of the bay in 6–10m. Good shelter from the *meltemi*.

Facilities

Water Delivered by mini-tanker.
Fuel Can be obtained from a station at the head of the bay. There is a jetty near the fuel station with 2–3m depths at its extremity. A mini-tanker will deliver to the quay at Skála Pátmos.
Repairs A slip at the head of the bay hauls out local *caïques*. Some mechanical repairs can be carried out at Skála Pátmos. Good general hardware shops.
Provisions Good shopping for provisions at Skála.
Eating out Good tavernas on the waterfront.
Other PO. OTE. Bank. ATM. Greek gas and Camping Gaz. Hire motorbikes and bicycles. Bus to the monastery. Daily ferry to Piraeus and Rhodes and local ferry to Kós and Sámos.

General

Skála Pátmos has largely grown up to meet the needs of cruise ships and the daily ferry and hydrofoils bringing people to see the monastery of St John. Most of the buildings around the harbour date from the Italian occupation and unlike many of the towns that grow up around a busy ferry port, Skála is a pleasant town in itself. Remember when visiting the monastery to dress appropriately – bikinis and even shorts are inappropriate.

Skála Pátmos looking NNW across to Órmos Mérikha on the other side of Pátmos Island   *Peter Kleinoth/MareTeam*

OTHER ANCHORAGES NEAR SKÁLA PÁTMOS

BA 1531
Imray-Tetra G32

These anchorages near to Skála are all protected from the *meltemi* although subject to gusts off the high land.

1. ***Órmos Meloyi*** The first bay to the NE of Skála Pátmos. Anchor at the head of the bay in 5–7m. The bottom is sand and weed. Open to the SE. Taverna ashore.
2. ***Órmos Livádhi*** Immediately N of Órmos Meloyi. An islet, Nisís Panayía, in the entrance to the bay is easily recognised. Anchor at the head of the bay in 4–6m. With the *meltemi* there are gusts into the bay. Open SE.
3. ***Órmos Kambos*** Immediately NE of Livádhi. Anchor where convenient. Holding as for Meloyi, but open to the S as well as the SE. There are a number of villas around the bay, a taverna, and a shop where basic provisions can be obtained.
4. ***Órmos Grikou*** Lies 2 miles to the SE of Skála. Anchor in 8–10m off the hamlet at the head of the bay. A jetty on the N side is reported to have 2m depths alongside. The bottom is thick weed – difficult to get through so make sure your anchor is well dug in. Open to the SE although Nisís Tragos provides some protection from this direction. Taverna ashore. Bus to Skála in the summer.

ÓRMOS STAVRÓS

37°17'·4N 26°33'·3E

On the W coast of Pátmos almost opposite Órmos Griko. The bay is quite deep. Anchor in 5–10m in the N part of the bay or in 5–10m in the N end of the E part of the bay. The bottom is sand and weed, reasonable holding. Reasonable shelter from the *meltemi* although some swell may work around into the bay – more uncomfortable than dangerous.

Nísos Arki

A much indented island lying six miles ENE of Ák Yeranós on Pátmos. About halfway along the W coast lie Port Augusta and Port Stretto, protected by a number of small off-lying islands.

PORT AUGUSTA
Approach

The dogleg inlet on the W side of Arki. The islets in the approach are easily recognised. The light structure is conspicuous. A light (Fl.3s5M) is exhibited on the N side of the entrance but a night entrance is not advised. Care is needed of the reef running out for approximately 15m from the N entrance point.

Mooring

The inlet is very narrow once around the dogleg. In the middle of the inlet there are 4–5m depths shelving gradually to the sides. Go stern or bows-to the quay at the head of the inlet where there are mostly 2–4m depths. Alternatively anchor in the entrance and take a long line ashore to the E side. The bottom is mud and weed with a few rocks, good holding. Good all-round shelter in attractive surroundings.

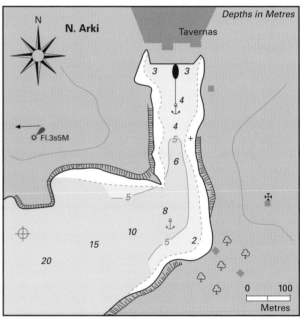

PORT AUGUSTA
⊕37°22'·59N 26°43'·88E WGS84

ARKI AND LIPSO

⊕3 0·5M N of Ák Koumaro (Arki)
   37°25'·30N 26°43'·13E WGS84
⊕4 0·25M S of N. Grilousa (Arki)
   37°21'·12N 26°42'·39E WGS84
⊕5 Mid-channel Frangonisi – Makronisi (Lipso)
   37°15'·64N 26°43'·95E WGS84

Port Augusta looking NE inside the inlet

Facilities

Two tavernas on the waterfront.

PORT STRETTO

37°22'·5N 26°44'·4E

Two inlets lying immediately S of Port Augusta. Anchor in 4–5m in the W inlet and in 10–12m in the E inlet. The head of the W inlet is shallow. The bottom is sand and weed – good holding. Good shelter from the *meltemi* but open S.

Nisís Marathos

The island lying in the approaches to Port Augusta and Port Stretto. Between the S tip of Nisís Marathos and the small islet of Spalato immediately E there is a dangerous reef with less than 2m over it. The reef is normally visible as a greenish patch. Between the reef and Marathos there is a passage with 5–8m depths and between the reef and Spalato depths of 5-7m. You should have someone up front to con the way through. Enter the anchorage from the E rather than between Marathos and Spalato.

In the cove on the SE side of Maratho two tavernas open in the summer. There are laid moorings which can be picked up. Good shelter from the *meltemi* but open S. The tavernas use VHF Ch 12 and are helpful to yachties.

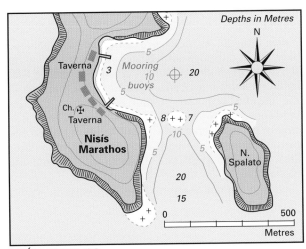

NISÍS MARATHOS
⊕37°21'·99N 26°43'·70E WGS84

Nísos Lipso

(Lipsa)

The island lying two miles S of Arki. It supports a small population in the village of Lipso (Sokora) on the S side of the island. There is a harbour here in a dogleg bay, and there are a number of small bays under the SW tip of the island.

ÓRMOS LIPSO (Sokora)

A 1531

Approach

Conspicuous Nisídhes Khalava, the islets off the SW corner of Lipso, are easily identified from the distance. Closer in, a white church on the S side of

the entrance and the light structure on the N side of the entrance will not be seen until the bay opens up and the houses of Lipso become visible.

By night Use the light on Ák Gátos Fl.3s6M and on the quay in the bay F.R.3M/2F.R(vert)6M.

Caution With the *meltemi* there are fierce gusts into the bay.

Mooring

Go stern or bows-to inside the new pier extension or alongside the pontoon in the NW corner. The inner harbour has been dredged to 3-5m. The bottom is sand, mud and weed – bad holding.

Note Harbour works continue in the SE corner of the harbour where the water-boat moors off the chapel on the corner.

Shelter Good shelter from the *meltemi* although there are strong gusts. In the event of strong southerlies anchor in 4–5m at the southern end of the bay.

Authorities Customs and port police.

Anchorage Beaches on the N side of the bay provide useful anchorages. The small bay off the chapel is the best place to be with good shelter from the *meltemi*.

Facilities

Services Water and electricity boxes on the pier but not connected yet. Water can be delivered by mini-tanker. Water on the pontoon in the NW corner and electricity connection can be arranged

Fuel On the SE side of the harbour.

Provisions Most provisions can be obtained in the village.

Eating out Numerous good tavernas on the waterfront, some with good fresh fish.

Other PO. Exchange. Ferry to Pátmos. Hydrofoils to Kós/Pátmos.

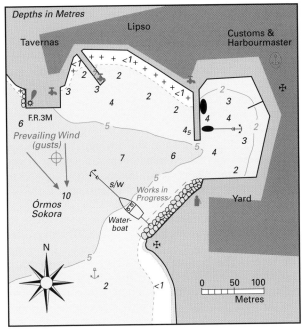

LIPSO
⊕37°17'·67N 26°45'·86E WGS84

Lipso harbour looking SW with Nisídhes Khalava at the top of the picture (new works not shown)   *Peter Kleinoth/MareTeam*

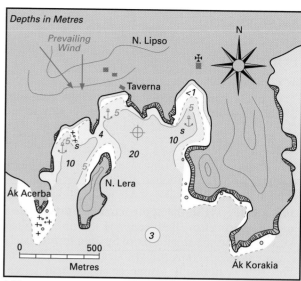

LERA LIPSO
⊕37°16′·5N 26°46′·5E

Lipso harbour looking W over the new pier extension towards the entrance to Órmos Sokora   *Lu Michell*

General

The small village is attractive in a higgledy-piggledy sort of way. Increasing numbers of tourists in recent years have reduced the reliance on agriculture and fishing on the island. Lipso produces some quaffable white wines.

LERA LIPSO

On the S side of Lipso in the bay situated between Ák Acerba and Ák Korakia there are several coves affording good shelter from the *meltemi*.

Care must be taken of a reef extending S from Ák Acerba. Proceed around either side of the islet (Lera) in the bay and anchor where convenient in any of the coves around the N side. Off the taverna there are stakes on the shore to which a long line can be taken. The bottom is sand and weed and good holding. Good shelter from the *meltemi* but completely open to the S. There is a small taverna on the beach in the centre cove but otherwise there are no facilities.

Nísos Agathonisi
(Gaïdharos)

The much-indented island lying 10 miles NE of Arki and 8 miles W of the Turkish coast. It is easily identified from the distance. I am not sure whether the island is technically part of the Dodecanese or the eastern Sporades, but include it here for convenience.

Note On the E side of Agathonisi the passage between Agathonisi and Nisís Gláros is shown on BA and Greek charts as having least depths of 8m. In fact a sand bar obstructs most of the passage in the middle and you should not attempt to pass between Agathonisi and Nisís Gláros. There is a deeper passage reported close to Agathonisi, but the prudent course is to go to seawards of Nisís Gláros and spare yourself the trouble of finding the channel.

On the S coast there are two deep bays.

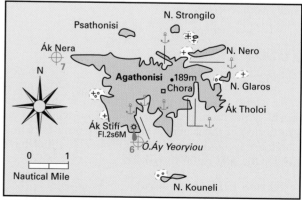

NISOS AGATHONISI
⊕6 0·25M S of Ák Stifi (Agathonisi)
     37°26′·35N 26°57′·65E WGS84
⊕7 0·4M W of Ák Nera (Agathonisi)
     37°28′·53N 26°54′·96E WGS84

ÁY YEORYIOU

Approach

This is the triple-headed bay near the SW end of the island. The entrance is lit on the W side (Ák Stifi) Fl.2s6M.

Mooring

At the head of the bay there is a quay where you can go stern or bows-to the N corner. Alternatively anchor near the head of the bay or in either the W or E coves. It is fairly deep for anchoring and you will generally be dropping anchor in 7–12m. The bottom is mud and weed, generally good holding.

Shelter Good shelter from the *meltemi*. Open S.

Facilities

Fuel station near the quay. Some provisions and tavernas. Ferry to Pithagorion.

General

Ashore there is the fishing village and the *chora* is a short distance inland. This has always been a fishing port and often the boats will stray across into Turkish waters to poach the richer fishing grounds there.

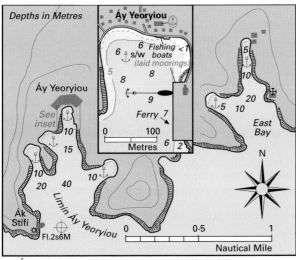

LIMÍN AY YEORYIOU AND EAST ANCHORAGE
⊕37°26'·65N 26°57'·91E WGS84

Áy Yeoryiou on Agathonisi looking SE   *Lu Michell*

The hamlet is a delightful spot. You can swim right off the boat and then wander ashore for a drink or a meal. The locals are friendly and there is only a little tourism here. Mark it up as one of those special places.

AGATHONISI EAST BAY

37°27'·3N 26°59'·7E

Approximately 1½M E of Áy Yeoryiou is another deep indented bay. Anchor in either the W cove or at the head of the bay in 4–7m on sand and weed. Good shelter from the *meltemi*.

Nisís Farmakonisi

(Pharmako Island)

Note In recent years there has been a military presence on the island and yachts have been prohibited from anchoring in the bay on the E side. I include the details of the island here as the restrictions may be relaxed, as they have been in previous years.

This small island lies 14 miles E of Lipso just off the Turkish coast. On the E side of the island there is a small cove in Órmos Tholou offering some shelter from the *meltemi*, but completely open to the S and E. The cove can be recognised by four arches near the shore, the remains of a Roman villa.

Ashore there are a few ruins dating from the Romans and a small Byzantine church. It is here that Julius Caesar was captured by pirates and held to ransom for 38 days. H M Denham relates that he kept in good spirits and exercised and jested with his captors. Once released after the ransom was paid, he gathered an expedition together and in turn captured the pirates who were sentenced to death by crucifixion.

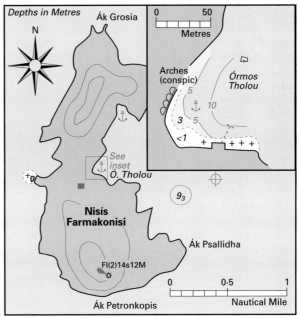

FARMAKONISI
⊕37°17'·7N 27°06'·5E

Nísos Léros

Léros lies close north of Kalimnos and the two islands were referred to as one in antiquity – the Kalydnian Isles of Lero-Kalimno.

Léros is less harsh than its sister island Kalimnos. The hills are rounded and the countryside around Órmos Lakkí and Platanos is wooded and green. Platanos itself is a jumble of hibiscus, jasmine, bougainvillea and oleander. It is a thoroughly likeable island capital with friendly inhabitants and a fine view over Órmos Alindas and Pandeli.

The island was associated in antiquity with the cult of Artemis. The worship of the mother-goddess when most of the civilized world had switched to the worship of the father-god left the islanders out of kilter with the rest of the islands and Leros had something of a reputation as a 'strange' island. During the carnival (in February or March) satirical verses are composed which the children recite at parties given in the houses of newly-weds. Stuart Rossiter in the *Blue Guide to Greece* considers these customs to derive from ceremonies associated with Dionysus of Eleusis. Whatever the mythopoeic origins everyone has a good time.

PORT LAKKÍ (Porto Lago)

BA 1531

Approach

Conspicuous From the W the entrance to Órmos Lakki is difficult to identify. Seven wind turbines on the hill to the N of Órmos Gournes are conspicuous. The group of rocks NW of the entrance and the light structures on either side of the entrance can be seen only when closer in. At the entrance to the bay the fort and 4 windmills at Alinda will be seen, but they are obscured by a hill as you proceed further into the bay. The buildings of Lakkí and the mole are conspicuous once inside the bay.

By night Use the lights on either side of the entrance to Órmos Lakkí (Ák Lakkí Fl(2)14s9M and Ák Angistro Fl.2·5s5M) and the light on the end of the mole at Lakkí Fl.R.3s4M.

VHF Ch 11 for the marina at Lakkí and Ch 10 for Evros boatyard.

Dangers

1. With the *meltemi* there are strong gusts off the high land in the approaches and in the bay. There is also a confused sea at the entrance to the bay.
2. With strong southerlies there are gusts and a confused sea in the entrance to the bay and a considerable swell penetrates right into the bay itself.

Note

1. It is prohibited to approach within 200m of the naval establishment on the S side of Órmos Lakkí. The buildings of the naval establishment are clearly visible once inside the bay.
2. There are fish farms inside the N and S entrance points although the locations may vary as they are moved around.

Mooring

Data c.30 berths. Visitors' berths. Max LOA 24m. Depths 3–5m.

Berths Go stern or bows-to in the marina where directed. There are laid moorings to pick up. You can also berth at Evros Boatyard where there are laid moorings off the quay and moorings in the bay.

Shelter Good shelter from the *meltemi* although there are gusts into the harbour. With S winds a surge develops in the bay and harbour.

Port Lakkí on Léros looking W across the boatyard to the yacht harbour
Peter Kleinoth/MareTeam

NISOS LEROS

⊕9 1M W of Ák Lakki (Léros) 37°06'·8N 26°48'·2E
⊕10 1M E of Vrak Áy Kiriakí (Léros) 37°08'·8N 26°54'·4E

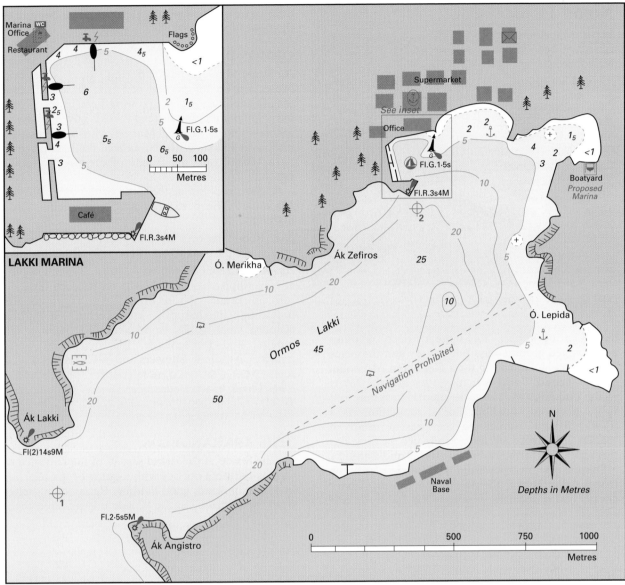

LAKKI MARINA

ORMOS LAKKI
⊕₁ 37°06′·72N 26°49′·78E WGS84
⊕₂ 37°07′·52N 26°50′·95E WGS84

Authorities Marina staff. Port police and customs. Charge band 2.

Agmar Marine SA (Lakki Marina)
Leros Island, 85400 Dodecanese, Greece
☎ 22470 25240/24812 *Fax* 22470 28200
Email yacht_services@agmar.gr

Facilities

Services Water and electricity at every berth. WC and showers. Laundry facilities.
Fuel A mini-tanker can be arranged at the marina.
Repairs
Agmar Marine The company which runs Lakki Marina also has a boatyard. For details see entry for Partheni.
Evros Boatyard At the head of Lakkí Bay. 50-ton travel-hoist. Mechanical and some engineering repairs. Showers and toilets.
Note A marina is planned in association with the boatyard. At the time of writing there are 10 berths with laid moorings off the shore. Until the proposed protective mole is built all berths are exposed to the W–SW.

Evros Marine SA (Leros Marina)
Leros Island, PO Box 30, 85401, Greece
Evros Boatyard ☎ 22470 24733 *Fax* 22470 23947
Email lerosmar@hol.gr
Provisions Good shopping for most provisions nearby. Supermarket (free delivery) two blocks back from Lakki Marina.
Eating out Taverna at the marina. Tavernas nearby. Good restaurant in town next to the PO.
Other PO. OTE. Banks. ATMs. Hire motorbikes and bicycles. Bus to Platanos, the island's capital near Órmos Alindas. Taxis. Ferries to Piraeus and Rhodes.

General

The large buildings surrounding Órmos Lakkí all date from the Italian occupation when the bay was

Lakki marina looking NE towards the town   *Lu Michell*

the Italian naval base. The large art deco buildings are arranged around wide boulevards and the place has the feel of a mock-up for a film about Mussolini or any Second World War movie set in Italy. Many of the buildings were used as mental hospitals and Leros acquired something of a reputation as a 'Devil's Island', something the present influx of tourists that arrive by ferry rarely see as they flee through Lakkí to the resorts at Alinda and Pandeli.

Despite the overpowering architecture and the recent scandals over the mental institutions, I have always had a sneaking fondness for Lakki. It is a little out of kilter just like Leros used to be, and is the better for it.

ÓRMOS PARTHENI

A large dogleg bay offering good all-round protection on the N side of Léros. It would seem that the military who once were here in force may have down-sized and instead there is now a boatyard ashore run by Agmar Marine who also run the marina at Lakkí. With the *meltemi* the best place to be is tucked into the E side of the bay. Tavernas ashore.

Anchor in 3–8m at the head of the bay off Ayias Matronas. The bottom is mud and weed – good holding.

Note Recent reports are that anchoring is restricted off Ayias Matronas to allow room for fishing boats.

Agmar Marine 70-ton travel-hoist. 3–3·5m depths at travel-hoist bay. 350 berths on hardstanding. 3-ton jib crane. 2-ton crane. All yacht repairs including mechanical, engineering (including stainless steel work), wood and GRP repairs, sail repairs, and gardiennage. Electricity and water points. Chandlers. Showers and WC. Canteen.

Agmar Marine SA (Partheni Boatyard)
Léros Island, 85400 Dodecanese, Greece.
☎ 22470 26009/26010 *Fax* 22470 22120
Email yacht_services@agmar.gr

NISÍS ARKHANGELOS

On the S side of the island just W of the entrance to Órmos Partheni is a bay with a sandy beach. Anchor in 4–5 m on sand, good holding. Reasonable shelter from the *meltemi*. On the W side it is reported there

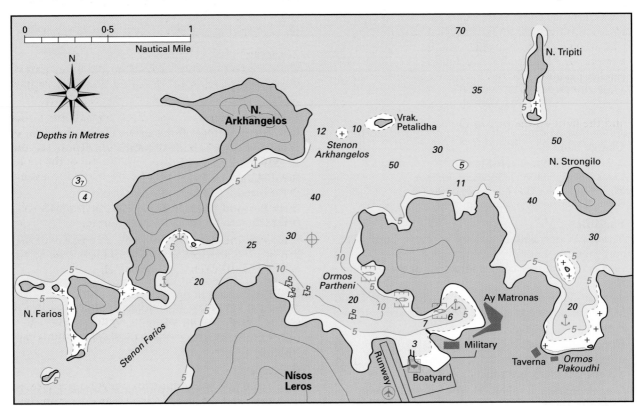

ORMOS PARTHENI AND APPROACHES
⊕37°12'·0N 26°47'·5E

Áy Matronas in Órmos Partheni looking SE *Lu Michell*

are stakes ashore to take a long line to. Good fishing around the nearby rocks.

ÓRMOS PLAKOUDI

On the NE coast of Léros, Órmos Plakoudi offers good shelter in all except NE–E winds. In the middle of the entrance to the bay the group of above-water rocks can be left to either side (5m depths and over on both sides). Anchor off the small fishing hamlet in 4–7m. The SW corner is usually the best place to be. Taverna opens in summer.

It is around 1½km over to Áy Matronas on the other side of the headland.

ÓRMOS ALINDAS

Approach

This deep bay situated on the E coast of Léros is the alternative ferry port in strong W–SW winds.

Conspicuous The Venetian castle on the rocky summit of Ák Kastello and four windmills on the saddle of a hill above the town are conspicuous from some distance off.

By night Use the light W of Ák Kastello Fl.3s5M and the light on the pier in the bay F.R.3M.

Dangers With the *meltemi* there are strong gusts into the bay.

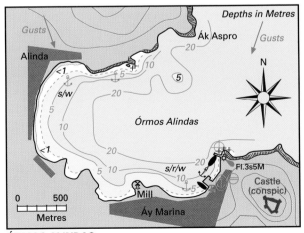

ÓRMOS ALINDAS
⊕37°09′·62N 26°51′·23E WGS84

Mooring

When northerlies are not blowing go stern or bows-to the short mole off Ák Kástro or stern or bows-to the central pier. Alternatively anchor off on the W side of the pier. The bottom is hard sand and rock – bad holding. When the *meltemi* is blowing strongly the best place to be is in the NW corner of the bay. Anchor in 3–8m.

Shelter The *meltemi* gusts into the bay from W–NW setting up an uncomfortable choppy sea. With a strong *meltemi* the anchorage off Áy Marina is untenable. Anchor in the NW corner or go to Pandeli.

Facilities

Water Near the quay at Áy Marina.
Fuel In the town. A mini-tanker can deliver to the quay.
Provisions Most provisions can be found nearby.
Eating out Tavernas and bars on the waterfront.
Other PO. OTE. Bank. ATMs.

General

The village of Áyia Marina is the village near the water while on the saddle of the hill above the bay, about fifteen minutes' walk away, is Lero or Platanos, the main town of the island. Both Áyia Marina and Lero are thoroughly pleasant places with an abundance of bougainvillea and clematis adorning the houses, giving the place an Italianate air.

PANDELI (Panali)

Approach

On the S side of Ák Kastello and Ák Pandelis lies a large bay and in the NW corner is Pandeli with a small harbour off the beach.

By night The end of the mole is lit Fl.G.3s3M.

Mooring

Go alongside or stern or bows-to the outer part of the mole or anchor off the beach in 4–8m depths. The bottom is sand and weed – good holding.

Note It is reported that port regulations forbid yachts from using the harbour from the end of August to the end of May during the fishing season. In summer yachts may berth on the end of the mole, but may still have to vacate the berth for fishing boats.

Shelter Good shelter from the *meltemi*. Strong southerlies could make it uncomfortable.

Anchorage Immediately SW there is a small cove that can be used although shelter from the *meltemi* is not as good as the anchorage at Pandeli.

Facilities

Water on the quay. Diesel can be delivered to the quay. Provisions ashore and better shopping in Platanos up the hill. Tavernas and cafés. Showers in some of the cafés.

General

The setting is wonderful with a few houses around the beach and the local fishing boats drawn up close to the beach. Oleander, bougainvillea and tamarisk

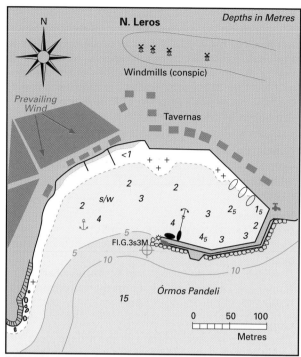

PANDELI
⊕37°09'·00N 26°51'·80E WGS84

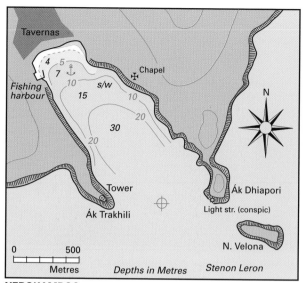

XEROKAMBOS
⊕37°05'·94N 26°52'·86E WGS84

STENÓN LEROU

⊕ Channel fairway (N. Mikro Glaronisia and N. Velona)
37°05'·63N 26°53'·26E WGS84

The channel between N. Mikro Glaronisia and N. Megálo Glaronisia is shallow and rock bound and should not be used. The main channel between N. Mikro Glaronisia and N. Velona is free of dangers in the fairway.

Nísos Kalimnos

The sister island of Léros, lying immediately S of it and separated by Stenón Lerou. This great craggy lump of rock is for the most part steep-to and bare of vegetation. Kalimnos imparts a feeling of prehistoric permanence – long after the human race has disappeared, you feel that Kalimnos will remain much as it is today. It is not so much the height of

Pandeli harbour looking SE   *Lu Michell*

grow profusely in the village, with fishing nets strung up to dry along the beach. Platanos is about a fifteen minute walk up the hill.

ÓRMOS XEROKAMBOS

On the S side of Léros this large bay offers good shelter from the *meltemi*, being open only to the S. Anchor off or pick up a laid mooring off one of the tavernas. There is a miniature fishing harbour in the SW corner. There may be room to berth bows-to near the end of the breakwater. Depths around 2–3m. Care needed of underwater ballast close in.

Tavernas ashore. A number of houses and villas have been built around the slopes above the bay.

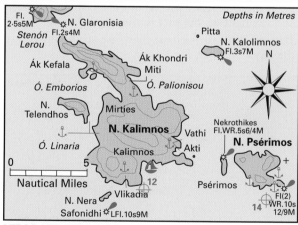

LEROS AND KALIMNOS

⊕12   0·5M S of Ák Áy Yeóryios (Kalimnos)
       36°54'·97N 26°59'·21E WGS84
⊕13   0·75M S of Ák Khali (Kalimnos)
       36°55'·95N 27°02'·97E WGS84
⊕14   0·25M S of Vrak Krevvatio (Psérimos)
       36°54'·82N 27°09'·39E WGS84

the mountain range (Mt Profitis Ilías or Parasivia is a scant 679m, 2240ft) but the sheer bulk of it which is impressive from seaward.

In ancient and medieval times the island followed the fortunes of Kós. The Italian occupation in 1912 was actively opposed by the Kalimniots who painted the Greek national colours everywhere to annoy their masters. During the Second World War many of the islanders, faced with starvation when their livelihood of sponge-fishing was denied them, emigrated all over the world. You will meet many American and Australian Greeks in the capital who have returned home to live here.

The grubby sprawling capital of Pothia (Port Kalimnos) is the centre of sponge-fishing in Greece. In ancient times the sponge was used much as we use artificial sponges today – for washing and cleaning up the after-dinner mess. It also had other uses:

'The servants in the 'Odyssey' swabbed tables with it, while it was in great demand with artisans, who used it to apply paint, and with soldiers who had no drinking vessels to hand. In the Middle Ages, burned sponge was reputed to cure various illnesses. Together with olive oil it has been used from time immemorial as a contraceptive pessary by the oldest professionals – who oblivious of the fact that they figure in the pages of Athenaeos, still

flourish in Pláka today – using roughly the same sort of slang, in which the word 'sponge' finds many a picturesque use.'

Lawrence Durrell *The Greek Islands*

Artificial sponges have replaced many of the uses of this little animal and most of the natural sponges being washed out in Kalimnos harbour are sold to tourists.

LIMÍN KALIMNOS (Kalymnos, Pothia)

BA 1531

Imray-Tetra G34

Approach

Conspicuous From the E the buildings of Kalimnos town around the bay and a number of white oil storage tanks to the E of the town are conspicuous. From the W the town will not be seen until you are up to the entrance of the bay. Closer in, the monastery on the hill above the town, the silver cupola of the cathedral on the waterfront and the outer mole are easily identified.

By night Use the lights at the entrance: Fl.R.2s4M/ Fl.G.2s3M. The harbour lights are difficult to make out against the loom of the town lights. The church on the top of the ridge and a large cross lower down the slopes are floodlit at night.

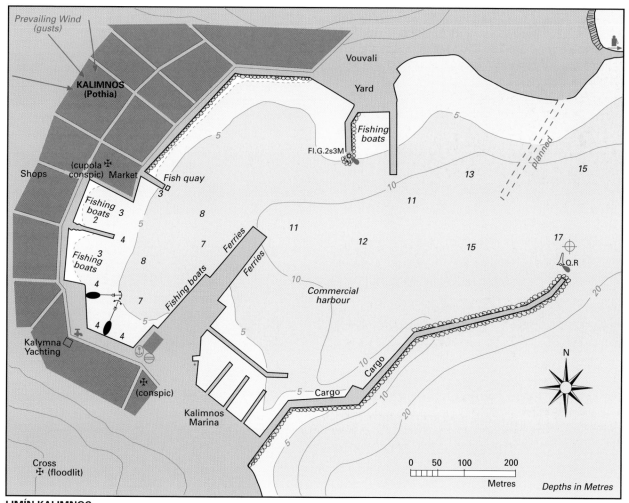

LIMÍN KALIMNOS
⊕36°56′·84N 26°59′·69E WGS84

Note At the time of writing the Fl.R had been removed and the buoy marking the end of the works was lit Q.R. The Fl.R will be repositioned at the end of the extended breakwater.

Dangers
1. With the *meltemi* blowing there are strong gusts off the high land down into the approaches and in Órmos Kalímnou itself.
2. At the time of writing the breakwater extension was still largely underwater. Its extremity is marked by a smallish red buoy (Q.R). Works are expected to be completed on the breakwater in the near future.

Mooring

Note Work on the basic structure of Kalimnos Marina was completed in 2002, but it is not yet fully operational.

Data 80 berths. Visitors' berths. Max LOA c.20m. Depths 2–5m.

There are to be laid moorings tailed to the pontoons.

Shelter Good shelter.

Authorities Harbourmaster. Port police and customs on the main ferry pier. A charge will be made in the marina.

Note If the marina is not operational then go stern or bows-to the S quay on the W side of the ferry pier. It is very crowded here and it can be difficult to find a berth. The bottom is mud and weed and not everywhere good holding. Good shelter although the *meltemi* gusts down onto the quay so make sure your anchor is well in.

Facilities

Services (Kalimnos Marina) Water and electricity to be installed. A shower and toilet block to be built. Water and electricity on the town quay.

Fuel At the fuel quay on the N side of the bay outside the harbour.

Repairs Most mechanical repairs can be carried out. Some light engineering work. Kalymna Yachting on the yacht quay can provide a haul-out service using a crane and slings for yachts up to 10 tons. They also arrange repairs and gardiennage. A boatyard to the E of the town hauls out large *caïques* and a few yachts. Good hardware and tool-shops. Basic chandlery can be obtained from a number of shops near the fish quay.

Kalymna Yachting, PO Box 47, 85200 Kalimnos
☎ 22430 24083/24084/23043 *Fax* 22430 29125
Email kalymna@europlanet.com

Provisions Good shopping for all provisions. Ice available.

Eating out Tavernas on the waterfront and in the town. Noisy bars on the waterfront.

Other PO. OTE. Banks. ATMs. Greek gas and Camping Gaz. There is a gas filling factory just outside the town. Hire cars, motorbikes and bicycles. Intermittent bus service to the other villages on the island. Daily ferries to Piraeus and Rhodes.

General

Kalimnos is the home of the Kalimniot sponge-divers – the sponge-boats, most of the *trehandiri* type and about 10–12m in length, are built in the boatyard immediately E of the town. Originally the sponge-divers fished in shallow waters, jumping overboard with a heavy stone slab and scooping the sponges off the bottom into a net. Nowadays a

Limín Kalimnos looking N from the coast. Note the works on the outer breakwater

compressor is used and deeper waters off Africa and Cyprus are fished. An interesting book worth getting on the harrowing lives of the sponge fishermen has just been published by a resident Kalimniot: *Bitter Sea* by Faith Warn (available locally).

The town of Kalimnos is attractive from the distance. Many of the houses are washed in various shades of blue – a practice continued from the days of the Italian occupation when the blue houses reminded their Italian masters of the Greek colours. On closer inspection the town is rather dusty and grubby, with the hustle and bustle of tripper boats and fishing boats loading and unloading their cargoes, and trucks, cars, vans, motorbikes, three-wheeler mini-trucks and vans buzzing along the waterfront. Sponges are, of course, for sale everywhere.

ÓRMOS AKTI (Ati, Katsouni)

36°57'·7N 27°02'·8E

Immediately NW of Ák Kahli, the SE extremity of Kalimnos, lies Órmos Akti. Much of the bay is now obstructed by fish farms, though there is still room to anchor. With a strong *meltemi* a swell enters the bay and there are gusts off the surrounding hills. Care is needed of an underwater rock near the head of the bay which is sometimes marked by a white buoy. Anchor in 10m on the S side of the submerged rock. Tavernas ashore.

VATHI

One mile N of Órmos Akti lies the deep fjord of Vathi. From the E the deep slit in the hills can be seen from the distance. Go bows-to the pier or the quay after the pier, leaving the quay for the tripper boats clear. Care is needed as there is underwater ballasting extending out in places. It may also be possible to anchor fore and aft further in although it is reported there are now numerous local moorings here. The bottom is sand and weed – good holding.

Note It is reported that the bay is to be dredged and pontoons installed on the N side.

Good shelter from the *meltemi* although there are strong gusts off the surrounding hills.

Dangers It is reported that a new high speed ferry passing outside the bay sends in a considerable

Kalimnos. Vathi looking W from near the entrance to the inlet
Nigel Patten

wash. Substantial damage has been caused to yachts thrown against the quay. Keep pulled off the quay and make sure your anchor is well in.

In the small hamlet at the shallow head of the inlet, limited provisions can be obtained and there are several tavernas. Water on the quay. A 'yacht club' near the quay.

The valley inland from Vathi is extremely attractive – orange and lemon groves and lush market gardens contrast with the steep red rock hills in this, one of the few lush parts of Kalimnos.

ÓRMOS PALIONISOU (Baia Isolavecchia)

37°01'·92N 26°59'·63E WGS84

A bay on the S side of Ák Poundha. Although this bay appears suitable, the holding (rock covered by a thin layer of sand and weed) is bad. There is a short jetty at the head of the bay to which you can take a long line. The bay is surrounded by spectacular pitted cliffs, with just a flash of green grass and a few houses at the head. A primitive taverna occasionally opens in the summer.

EMBORIOS (Emporios, Vorio Bay)

A bay lying on the SE side of Ák Kefala. The islet of Kalavros lying in the entrance is difficult to identify against the land behind. Closer in, the hamlet at the head of the bay will be seen. Pick up one of the laid moorings in the bay. If you are anchoring here the holding is poor and it is useful to take a long line ashore if possible. The bottom of mud and sand has thick weed over it. A jetty in the N of the bay has 4m off the end but is usually occupied by fishing boats. Good shelter from the *meltemi* although there are strong gusts into the bay.

Minimarket and tavernas ashore. The bay is an attractive spot and usefully located on the W coast of Kalimnos. If you are picking up one of the moorings in the bay then you should really go and eat at the taverna inscribed on the mooring buoy.

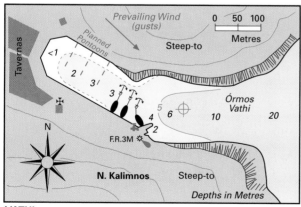

VATHI
⊕*36°58'·5N 27°02'·2E*

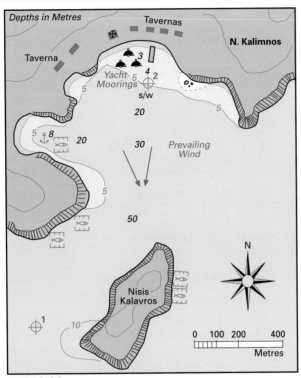

EMBORIOS
⊕1 37°01´·91N 26°55´·43E WGS84
⊕2 37°02´·71N 26°55´·70E WGS84

MIRTIES

36°59´·7N 26°55´·8E

A small village on the Kalimnos side of Stenón Telendhou. There is a small harbour here used by local *caïques* and tripper boats running to Nísos Telendhos. Although there are 2–3m depths off the outer part of the mole, most of the harbour from around the middle is shallow. As the harbour is very small anyway, this leaves little room for manoeuvring. In calm weather you can anchor off the village, but it is too exposed if there is any wind about.

Note It has been reported that Kalimnos port police are preventing yachts from anchoring in the bay.

Provisions and tavernas ashore.

NISÍS TELENDHOS

36°59´·87N 26°55´·47E WGS84

In calm weather anchor in 6–10m off the small hamlet on the E coast. Just adequate shelter from the *meltemi* with very strong gusts off the high land. Shallow draught boats may be able to get onto the quay but reconnoitre first.

The craggy lump of Telendhos conveys a prehistoric permanence – 'always has been there and always will be' – and indeed has been inhabited since prehistoric times as well as by the Greeks, Romans and later in the Middle Ages. The island was joined to Kalimnos up until the 15th century when an earthquake rearranged the topography and submerged the land-bridge.

ÓRMOS LINARIAS

Is virtually untenable except in calm weather. It is open to all sectors westward and subject to strong gusts off the hills in southerly winds.

ÓRMOS VLIKADIA (Vlikhadhia)

36°55´·5N 26°58´·0E

On the S coast of Kalimnos, one mile W of Ák Áyios Yeóryios, Vlikhadia is open only to the S. It provides good shelter from the *meltemi* although there are gusts off the surrounding hills. Anchor in 5–6m keeping clear of the swimming area at the head of the bay. The bottom is mostly rock so anchoring is difficult. Make sure your anchor is well in if going ashore.

Summer villas and tavernas ashore.

Nísos Psérimos

ÓRMOS PSÉRIMOU

Situated on the SW side of Nísos Psérimou, the entrance to Órmos Pserimou is difficult to see except from the SW. Once at the entrance the houses of the hamlet and the rough stone mole are easily seen. In the summer the tripper boats take up all the sheltered quay space and there is little chance of finding a slot. After the tripper boats have returned to Kós in the evening you will be able to go on the quay until they return around mid-morning. The bottom is sand and weed with some rocky ledges – good holding on the sand. With a *meltemi* blowing a swell enters the bay but if a yacht can manage to tuck itself into the NW corner behind the mole it is not unduly uncomfortable.

Tavernas on the beach. The hamlet of gleaming whitewashed houses is a holiday place for the locals from Kós and Kalimnos and when the tripper boats arrive the beach is packed solid with sunbathers.

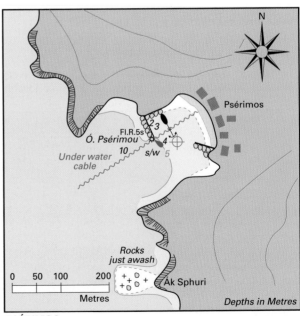

PSÉRIMOS
⊕36°55´·8N 27°07´·8E

Órmos Psérimou on the W coast of Psérimos looking W
Peter Kleinoth/MareTeam

Caution Care must be taken to avoid the reef just N of Ák Sphuri off the island. The outer rocks are awash and easily spotted.

NISÍS PLATÍ

36°57'·2N 27°05'·7E (Vrak Nekrothikes light)

The long thin islet lying N to S off the W coast of Pserimos. In settled weather tripper boats anchor off the bight about in the middle of the islet and also at the NE end. Here there is some protection from the *meltemi* which has mostly been funnelled to blow from the WNW. Anchor in 3–5m on sand.

Nísos Kós

(Stanko, Istankoy)

Kós lies tucked into the Gulf of Kós (the ancient Ceramic Gulf, Turkish Gökova Körfezi) between the Myndus peninsula to the north and the Dorian promontory to the south. The fingers of Turkey reach out to touch the island, enclosing the ancient triangle of trading power that vied with Rhodes to dominate the southwestern Aegean. Kós was probably not an important partner in the power

hexapolis, and not until the city of Kós was founded in 366 BC on the present site of the modern capital did it prosper and become an important maritime power. Today the harbour is probably much as it was when Kós was a powerful city.

The island has always been much praised for its fertility. A mountain ridge runs its length (the summit attains a height of 845m (2788ft) near the NE end) and on the eastern side it is precipitous and barren. It is the western side which is well-watered and fertile. Sandy beaches fringe the cultivated plain which produces fine vegetables, melons and grapes. The Kós variety of lettuce was introduced to England from here. Perhaps the mulberry trees on which the silkworm feeds also covered these slopes in antiquity. Kós was once famous for its silk and in particular the *Coae vestes*, the diaphanous flowing silk dresses prized by Roman women – sadly no longer made or worn.

Ancient Kós had many famous citizens but above them all stands Hippocrates, the great physician of antiquity and the father of modern medicine. We know little of the old healing methods but we do know that for the Hippocratic school the site of the sanatorium was as important as the methods. (The tranquillity of Epidavros, of mysteries earlier than Hippocrates, is proof enough.) The Aesculapion (Ascelepion) is just outside Kós town and should not be missed. The three terraces lie in a peaceful setting near to medicinal springs on a limestone hill overlooking the Gulf of Kós. The Italians rebuilt much of the Aesculapion to the original plan without destroying the calm of the place. It is the appropriate place to remember the Hippocratic Oath:

'I shall look upon him who shall have taught me this art even as one of my parents. I will share my substance with him and relieve his need should he be in want. His children shall be as my own kin, and I will teach them the art, if they so wish, without fee or covenant...The regimen I adopt shall be for the benefit of my patients according to my ability and judgement, and not for their hurt or for any wrong. I will give no deadly drug to any, though it be asked of me, nor will I counsel such, and especially I will not aid a woman to procure abortion. Whatsoever house I enter, there I will go for the benefit of the sick refraining from all wrong doing or corruption, and especially from any act of seduction, of male or female, of bond or free. Whatever things I may hear concerning the life of men during my attendance of the sick, or even apart from them, which should be kept secret, I will keep my own counsel upon, deeming such things as sacred secrets.'

Ák Ammóglossa on the NE corner of Kós looking E. The shoal water off the end is deceptive and care is needed

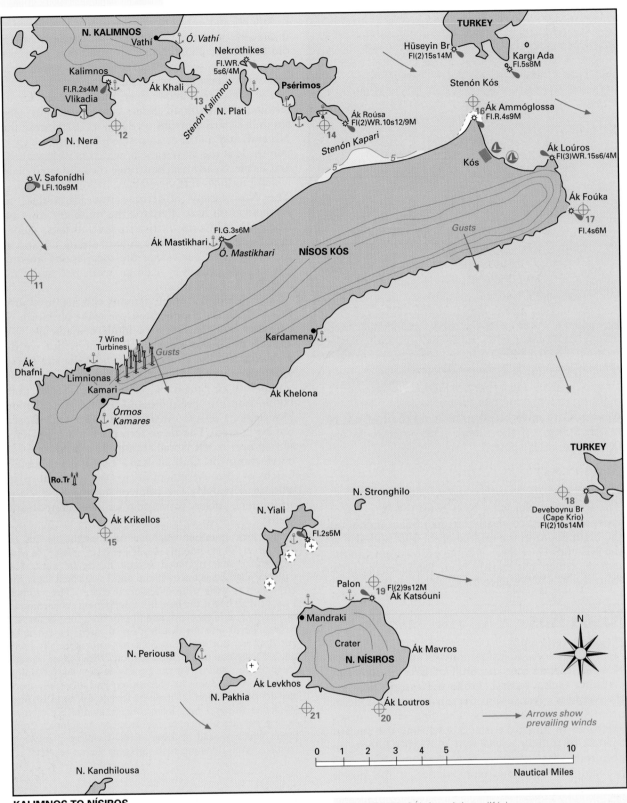

KALIMNOS TO NÍSIROS

⊕11 3M S of Vrak Safonídhi (Kalimnos-Kós Channel)
36°50'·27N 26°54'·49E WGS84
⊕12 0·5M S of Áy Yeóryios (Kalimnos)
36°54'·97N 26°59'·21E WGS84
⊕13 0·75M S of Ák Khali (Kalimnos)
36°55'·95N 27°02'·97E WGS84
⊕14 0·25M S of Vrak Krevvatio (Pserimos)
36°54'·82N 27°09'·39E WGS84
⊕15 0·5M S of Ák Krikellos (Kós)
36°39'·80N 26°58'·43E WGS84

⊕16 0·75M N of Ák Ammóglossa (Kós)
36°55'·70N 27°16'·42E WGS84
⊕17 0·25M E of Ák Áy Fokas (Kós)
36°51'·67N 27°21'·69E WGS84
⊕18 0·75M W of Deveboynu Buku (Knidos/Turkey)
36°41'·45N 27°20'·90E WGS84
⊕19 0·5M N of Ák Katsouni (Nísiros)
36°37'·70N 27°11'·36E WGS84
⊕20 0·5M S of Ák Loutros (Nísiros)
36°32'·92N 27°11'·66E WGS84
⊕21 1M S of Ák Levkhos (Nísiros)
36°32'·72N 27°08'·28E WGS84

Recently more tourists have been discovering Kós and several large hotels have been built around the sandy beaches. In many ways it resembles Rhodes – the green slopes, large hotels, the bustling harbour under the castle of the Knights – and like Rhodes it wants to have an ever larger slice of the tourist pie whatever the cost.

KÓS (Ko, Stanko)

BA 1531

Imray-Tetra G35

Approach

Conspicuous From the E the fort on the S side of the entrance, the palace, a chimney near the entrance and a minaret in the town are conspicuous. From the N and W a large brown hotel on the spit ending in Ák Ammóglossa is conspicuous from some distance off. Rounding the point the entrance to the harbour is easily seen.

By night Use the lights on Ák Ammóglossa Fl.R.4s9M, Ák Foúka Fl.4s6M, and Ák Loúros Fl(3)WR.15s6/4M. The entrance to the old harbour is lit Fl.G.3s3M/Fl.R.3s3M.

Dangers The shoals extending from Ák Ammóglossa should be given a good offing. With a strong *meltemi* blowing there are often confused seas off Ammóglossa, but once around it the sea is comparatively flat.

Mooring

Go stern or bows-to the quay on the E side. The bottom is mud – excellent holding.

Note The harbour is very crowded in the summer and it can be difficult to find a berth. Unless you specifically want to be here it is better to go to the marina.

Shelter With a strong *meltemi* there is often an uncomfortable surge in the harbour although shelter on the E side is good. With gales from the N–NE the harbour is close to untenable.

Authorities A port of entry: port police, customs, health and immigration authorities.

Anchorage Large yachts can anchor off the beach S of the entrance in settled weather. Care is needed to keep clear of the approaches to the hydrofoil quay.

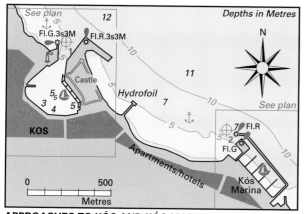

APPROACHES TO KÓS AND KÓS MARINA
⊕₁ 36°53′·88N 27°17′·34E WGS84
⊕₂ 36°53′·84N 27°17′·97E WGS84

Facilities

Water On the quay. The water man usually does the rounds twice a day.

Fuel In the town. A mini-tanker can deliver to the quay.

Repairs Some mechanical repairs. Hardware shops and some chandlery available.

Provisions Excellent shopping for provisions and a good market just up from the harbour. Ice from a factory on the outskirts of town.

Eating out Good tavernas in the town.

Other PO. OTE. Banks. ATMs. Greek gas and Camping Gaz. Hire cars, motorbikes and bicycles. Intermittent bus service to the other villages on the islands. Daily ferries to Piraeus and Rhodes and to Bodrum in Turkey. European and internal flights to Kós airport.

General

Kós is a likable mixture of medieval Frankish and Turkish architecture with a few contributions of Italian monumental. Oleander, bougainvillea, jasmine and hibiscus grow in profusion and classical remains from the era of Greek prosperity are used in novel ways – a sarcophagus forms the basin for a fountain, fragments of ancient marble prop up the branch of a tree, part of a marble column forms the base for a flower box, huge hewn blocks of stone line the path in a park. The fort and the adjacent park, shaded by old spreading plane trees (one of which is reputed to be that which Hippocrates taught under,

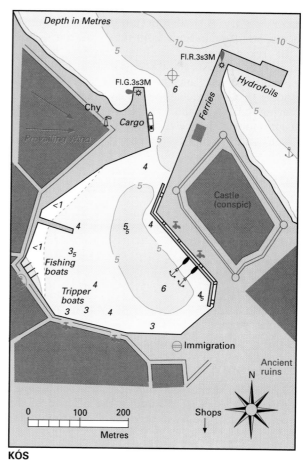

KÓS
⊕36°53′·88N 27°17′·34E WGS84

Kós harbour looking SSW in from the entrance
Peter Kleinoth/MareTeam

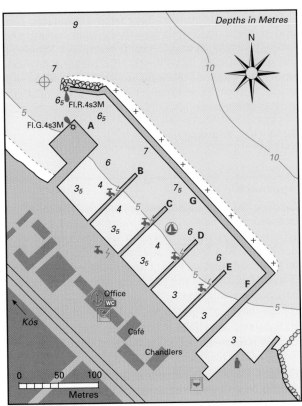

KÓS MARINA
⊕36°53'·84N 27°17'·97E WGS84

although it is only 400–500 years old – a nice tradition anyway) and cooled by the *meltemi*, is quite one of the most pleasant places to be on a hot summer's day. A small museum in the town houses Greek and Roman finds from the excavations.

In recent years Kós has attracted growing numbers of tourists and it seems as if the city of Kós is set to revive ancient rivalries and challenge Rhodes for the valuable annual cargo of bodies craving sun and sand. The town has changed to accommodate this new trade and though I think it retains much of its character, you may, like some others, think it has become 'all fast food and discos'.

KOS MARINA

Approach
The marina lies approximately ¾M SE of the old harbour at Kós town. The approach and entrance are straightforward.

By night The entrance is lit Fl.G.4s3M/Fl.R.4s3M. VHF Ch 77. (Callsign *Kós Marina*).

Mooring
Data 250 berths. Visitors' berths. Max LOA c.25m. Depths 3–6m.

Berths Berth where directed. A RIB will often come out to escort you to a berth. Laid moorings tailed to the quay.

Shelter Good shelter although northerlies including a strong *meltemi* cause a surge at the SE end of the marina. If possible try to berth on the first two piers in from the entrance.

Authorities Marina staff. A port of entry. Port police on site. Passport control in the main ferry terminal

in the old harbour. Charge band 2.

Kos Marina ☎ 22420 57500 *Fax* 22420 20877
Email info@kosmarina.gr
www.kosmarina.gr

Facilities
Services Water and electricity at all berths. Shower and toilet block. Laundry services.
Fuel Fuel quay near the travel-hoist bay.
Repairs 100-ton travel-hoist. Chandlers. Repair facilities.
Provisions Minimarket in the marina. Better shopping on the outskirts of Kos.
Eating out Café in the marina. Tavernas and restaurants nearby on the waterfront.
Other An ATM, boutiques and a restaurant and bar to be established within the marina.

Kos Marina looking NW towards the entrance

General

The marina has been up and running for a few years now and sets a standard for other Greek marinas to emulate. Most people vote it one of the best marinas in Greece. The boatyard is open and gaining a reputation for competent work. It is a bit out of the way compared with the old harbour at Kos, but then for some that will be a blessing.

NOTE

Off the SE coast of Kós fierce gusts blow down off the surrounding hills when a strong *meltemi* is blowing. The worst spots seem to be off the three prominent capes, Krikellos, Khelona, and Foúka. Around Cape Krio on mainland Turkey there are also fierce gusts and disturbed seas.

KARDAMENA

Approach

The small harbour lies almost exactly halfway along the SE coast of Kós. The long sprawl of hotels and bars and tavernas along the coast is easily identified. Care needs to be taken of two swimming platforms lying off the harbour (lit: F.R).

Caution With the *meltemi* there are fierce gusts off the high land of Kós and care is needed.

Mooring

Go stern or bows-to off the pier running out from the beach, or alongside on the breakwater, checking first to see you are not taking a local's berth. The bottom is sand and weed, good holding.

Shelter Good shelter from the *meltemi* which gusts off the land.

Facilities

Water At the root of the pier.

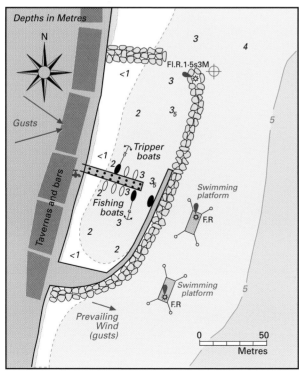

KARDAMENA
⊕36°47′·0N 27°08′·9E

Fuel About 200m away in the village.
Provisions Good shopping for provisions.
Eating out Numerous tavernas and bars nearby.
Other PO. OTE. Exchange. Hire cars and motorbikes. Internal and international flights from the airport about 5 km away.

General

Once a small fishing village, Kardamena is now a sprawl of a resort, catering for package holidaymakers who want little to do with things Greek and frequent any establishment that remotely resembles the 'local' at home. The resort is only 5 kilometres from the airport so getting the hordes to and from Kardamena is simplified. The prize of the resort is the wonderful long sandy beach often described as the best in the Dodecanese. At night the resort fairly pulsates to the sound of over-amplified music of all descriptions, so don't bank on getting a lot of sleep.

ÓRMOS KAMARES (Kamara, Palaeokastro)

Situated on the S end of Kós, this bay and the small harbour offer good shelter from the *meltemi*. A large white hotel on the N side of the bay is conspicuous from some distance off and the small harbour is on the W side of the bay. Anchor in the bay in 4–6m or go stern or bows-to or alongside the outer end of the mole. There is also room in the small fishing harbour for a few yachts. The bottom is sand and weed – good holding. With the *meltemi* blowing the gusts into the bay are not strong or prolonged.

Water at the root of the mole. Also a taverna at the root of the mole and a disco further round the beach.

Kamáres is no longer a tranquil spot, being plagued with waterbikes and water-ski boats which not only make an irritating noise, but appear to be driven largely by irritating people.

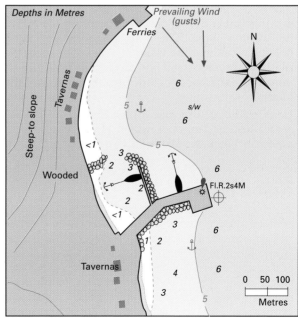

KAMARES
⊕36°44′·2N 26°58′·3E

451

LIMNIONAS

36°46'·5N 26°57'·8E

A small fishing harbour on the NW corner of Kós. Care needed of uneven depths under the mole. Go stern or bows-to where there is room, although it is usually full of local boats. Good shelter from the *meltemi* if you can tuck in behind the mole. Taverna ashore.

MASTIKHARI

36°51'·2N 27°04'·6E

A harbour about halfway along the NW coast of Kós. An L-shaped breakwater provides good protection from the *meltemi*. The entrance is lit (Fl.G.3s6M) though the light is not to be relied upon. The harbour is used by local ferries and tripper boats.

The harbour appears to have silted since it was built and care is needed over depths. Go stern or bows-to the N quay close to the 'square' quay in the corner. The bottom is soft mud and dead weed, poor holding. The SW quay has mostly less than 1m depths off it.

Provisions and tavernas ashore. Ferry to Kalimnos.

Nisís Yialí

(Yalí)

BA 1531

⊕ 0·25M E of Yiali/1·75M W of Strongili
36°40'·79N 27°08'·61E WGS84

Three miles NW of Nísiros an open bay on the S coast of Nisís Yialí offers some lee from the *meltemi*. The island is scarred by extensive quarries and in the bay a large loading chute extends into the sea. From the S and E the quarry scars are conspicuous. The sea is usually discoloured by dust from the quarry. A yacht seeking shelter here should anchor in 5–6m under the saddle of the island to the NE of the loading chute. The bottom is sand and good holding. Care must be taken of a reef 350m S of the islet (Áy Antonios) off the E end of Yialí and of numerous large mooring buoys in the vicinity of the quarry.

Caution About half a mile off the SW tip of Yialí lies a reef just under water which is not easily seen, especially when the *meltemi* is blowing.

Nísos Nísiros

Almost square, Nísiros is an extinct volcanic crater poking out of the sea SW of Deveboynu Burun (Cape Krio) in Turkey. The rich soil on the slopes of the cone is terraced and cultivated with olives and citrus trees. Until recently the hot sulphurous springs were renowned for their medicinal properties, but the hydropathic institute looks abandoned today. If the weather allows, it is a thoroughly pleasant excursion to the crater (2½ miles across) where there is a spectacular view of the surrounding sea and islands. If Mandráki harbour is untenable, which it usually is with a strong *meltemi*, tuck into Palon where there is better shelter.

LIMÍN MANDRAKI

Approach
The buildings around the harbour and the harbour mole on the NW corner of the island are easily identified from the N. The harbour actually lies a short distance E of Mandráki village.

By night A Q.G.3M is exhibited on the end of the mole.

Mooring
Go alongside or stern-to the mole or the quay. With a strong *meltemi* a swell creeps around the end of the mole making the harbour uncomfortable and possibly dangerous. With a strong N–NE wind the harbour is untenable. Port police.

Note Care is needed of the ferry calling here, which does not normally anchor but holds itself off with its propeller against lines ashore, causing a lot of wash for yachts berthed nearby.

Facilities
Good shopping in the nearby village. Good tavernas. PO. OTE. Daily ferry to Kós.

General
The village on the terraced slopes is most attractive and in calm weather the harbour is well worth a visit. A bus runs from Mandráki (there is one at 1000 hours) to the crater and it is an excursion which shouldn't be missed.

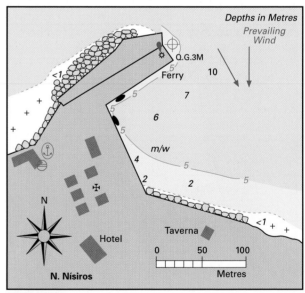

MANDRAKI
⊕36°36'·9N 27°08'·5E

PALON (Palos)

Approach
This small harbour lies 2 miles to the E of Mandráki harbour.

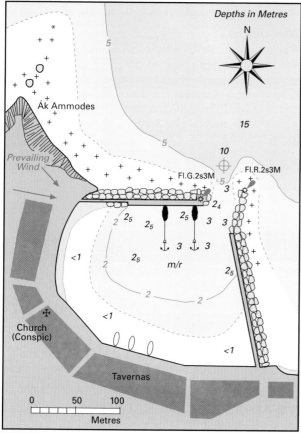

PALON
⊕36°37'·24N 27°10'·30E WGS84

Conspicuous From the E the buildings of the abandoned hydropathic institute, a cluster of large stone buildings with red roofs immediately E of Palon, are conspicuous. From the W the harbour will not be seen until you are around the rocky headland sheltering it, but a gantry and a cluster of buildings on the coast immediately W of the headland will be seen. Closer in a church in the village and the harbour breakwaters are easily identified.

By night The entrance is lit: Fl.G.2s3M/Fl.R.2s3M.

Nísiros. Palon harbour looking E from the ridge above

Dangers
1. Care needs to be taken of the reef running N for about 100m from Ák Ammodes. The final approaches to the harbour should be made on a course due S towards the entrance.
2. With the *meltemi* there are fierce gusts and a wicked short sea off the N side of Nísiros.
3. The entrance is narrow with a least depth over rocks of 2·4m. Care is needed with any swell being pushed down into the entrance when depths could be reduced.

Mooring
Go stern or bows-to the N mole. The bottom is mud, sand, and rocks, good holding.

Shelter Reasonable shelter from the *meltemi* although there may be a surge with a prolonged blow which can it uncomfortable. Keep pulled well off.

Facilities
Water on the quay from the water man (number on the quay). A minimarket and several tavernas in the village. Good fish sometimes available. Irregular bus to Mandráki.

General
The little harbour and the village are wonderful. You can swim in the harbour. The hinterland is green and wooded. The tavernas sit on the edge of the harbour and you can spend most of the day in one sipping cold beer and watching the locals watching you. Around Palon there is good if steep walking, or you can wander along the coast to the old hydropathic institute.

NISÍS PERIOUSA
Approximately 4½ miles WSW of Mandráki is Nisís Periousa. Local fishing boats sometimes shelter in the bay on the E coast where there is some shelter from the *meltemi*.

Nísos Tílos

Situated between Nísiros and Khálki, this long thin island has always existed on the fringes of its more popular cousins, though in recent years it has attracted more tourists to its shores. It was known in medieval times as Episcopi, a name that probably referred to its watchtowers from which it could signal to Rhodes of an approaching enemy. The Italians revived the name, calling it Piscopi. Today, as in many of the small islands off the main tourist track, many of the young leave for the big cities of Rhodes or Athens. There is some tourism in Livádhi, but otherwise Tílos remains off the beaten track.

ÓRMOS LIVADHIOU (Livadhia)
BA 1532

On the E coast of Tílos lies the large bay of Livádhia with a harbour and ferry quay.

Approach
Once the bay is opened the village of Livádhi will be seen.

453

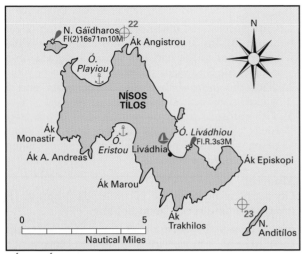

NÍSOS TÍLOS

⊕22 0·5M N of Ák Angistrou (Tílos)
36°29'·58N 27°21'·10E WGS84
⊕23 Mid-channel between Tílos and Andítílos
36°22'·6N 27°26'·9E

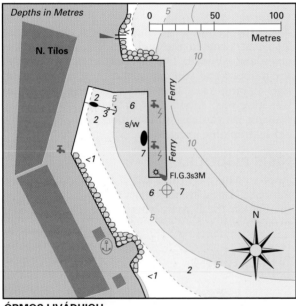

ÓRMOS LIVÁDHIOU
⊕36°25'·02N 27°23'·18E WGS84

Tílos. Livadhiou harbour looking S   *Lu Michell*

By night The end of the new mole is lit Fl.G.3s.

Mooring

Yachts moor stern or bows-to or alongside on the new mole, keeping clear of the trip boat berth in the corner. Alternatively go bows-to on the town quay. Care is needed here as depths come up to <1m close to the quay. Ferries and larger yachts use the outside of the new mole. The bottom is sand and weed, good holding.

Shelter With a strong *meltemi* blowing there are gusts off the surrounding hills and a swell works its way into the bay, but tucked inside the new mole there is good shelter.

Authorities Port police.

Facilities

Water and electricity boxes on the new mole. Most provisions can be obtained and there are a lot of tavernas for such a small place.

General

Although increasing numbers of tourists have boosted the number of tavernas in town, the locals seem indifferent to all the activity. Even the arrival of another ferry causes little more than a ripple around the small square.

LIVÁDHIA FISHING HARBOUR

36°25'·0N 27°24'·2E

In the SE corner of the bay there is a very small fishing harbour which has 2m depths in the entrance and off the N breakwater. A small yacht may be able to squeeze in here with care. The entrance is lit: Fl.R.3s3M.

ÁYIOS ANDONIS

36°27'·6N 27°20'·0E

A small fishing harbour in the SE corner of Órmos Playiou on the N end of the island. A dogleg mole extends for about 120m from the coast with another shorter mole inside it. There are reported to be 3–4m depths at the entrance and 2–3m depths inside. It is very small and yachts over 8–9m should not even poke a nose inside.

Tavernas ashore.

ÓRMOS ERISTOU 36°25'·6N 27°21'·0E

A large bay on the S side of Tílos that provides some shelter from the *meltemi* although a swell usually works its way around into here. Anchor in 3–5m off the beach. Gusts into the bay with the *meltemi*.

You can walk up to the *chora* N of the anchorage.

Nísos Sími

Sími lies in the entrance to the Gulf of Doris (Turkish – Hisarönu Körfezi) looking like a giant Rorschach ink blob. From seaward it is a barren precipitous island, but inland there are patches of pine forest. The indentations in the coastline

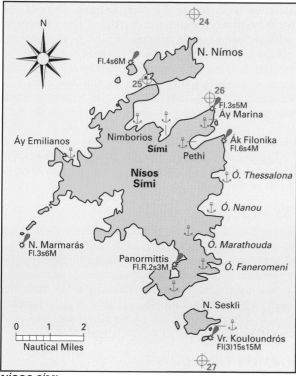

NÍSOS SÍMI

⊕24   1M N of Ák Makria (Sími) 36°41'·1N 27°51'·5E
⊕25   W entrance of Nímos Passage (Sími)
      36°38'·72N 27°49'·76E WGS84
⊕26   0·25M N of Ák Koutsoumba (Sími)
      36°38'·17N 27°52'·35E WGS84
⊕27   1M S of Vrak Kouloundrós (Sími)
      36°30'·0N 27°52'·2E

provide numerous anchorages and in fact the principal harbour is an entirely natural feature.

Sími was once famous for shipbuilding and sponge-diving. Simiot shipwrights built many of the fast galleys for the Knights of St John and later for their Turkish masters. Even today Simiot *caïques* seem to be better cared for than in many of the other islands. Simiot divers were once known as the best in the Aegean, although Kalimniot divers would contest that claim. Today few Simiots risk the dangers of sponge-fishing and Kalimnos is the undisputed centre.

SÍMI (Limín Simis, Symi, Syme)

BA 1532
Imray-Tetra G35

Approach

Conspicuous From the N the houses of Sími on the ridge above the town are conspicuous. From the S and E the harbour will not be seen until you are right into the bay. From the S it is easy to confuse the entrance to Pethi, the large bay immediately SE, with that of Sími. Entering Órmos Simis the houses of Sími town are immediately conspicuous. A clock tower and a white church on the N quay are also conspicuous.

By night Use the light on Ák Koutsoúmba Fl.3s5M and the light on the quay Fl.G.3s3M.

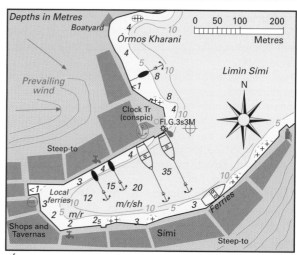

SÍMI
⊕36°37'·09N 27°50'·40E WGS84

Mooring

Go stern or bows-to the quay on the N side of the harbour taking care to leave the part of the quay allotted to the ferries clear. A harbour attendant will usually whistle or wave you into a berth. Most of the western quay is reserved for local trip boats and the local ferry. The depths in the harbour drop off rapidly and you should be prepared to let go your anchor in 12–20m. The bottom is mud and rock – poor holding in places.

Shelter Good shelter from the *meltemi*. With strong S winds there is a considerable surge in the harbour which can become dangerous with prolonged southerlies. The ferries (five or more in the summer) create a considerable wash when they arrive about mid-morning.

Authorities A port of entry. Port police and customs. Charge band 2.

Anchorage In settled weather it is possible to anchor in Órmos Kharani and take a long line ashore. Reasonable shelter from the *meltemi* with the only problem being the wash from ferries as they charge into Port Sími. Keep pulled well off.

Sími harbour looking W from the ridge above the town

Nigel Patten

455

Facilities

Services Water on the quay. The harbour attendant will open it up for you. Electricity can be connected on request.

Fuel The harbour attendant can arrange for fuel to be delivered.

Repairs Limited mechanical repairs. A boatyard hauls out large *caïques* and the occasional yacht in the cove N of the harbour.

Provisions Good shopping for provisions.

Eating out Excellent tavernas in some delightful locations in the town.

Other PO. OTE. Banks. ATM. Greek gas and Camping Gaz. Hire motorbikes. Daily ferries to Rhodes.

General

Discovering Sími is like discovering an exotic plant in the desert. The muted blue, amber, cream and rose-hued houses have been built one upon the other up the steep sides of the inlet like a child's building block version of a town. On the S side of the harbour a staircase leads up the hill to the houses on the top and though this heart-thumping climb takes it out of you in the summer, it is worth the effort both for the views from the top and for the fine old houses built on rocky projections and inclines on the way. The people of Sími remain detached from the daily onslaught of tourists from Rhodes and you can almost hear the sigh when the ferry departs.

PETHI (Pedhi)

Over the hill to the SE of Sími lies the deep inlet of Pethi. The S entrance is lit: Ák Filonika Fl.6s4M. Care needs to be taken of an above-water rock in the middle of the entrance – it is easily seen by day.

Anchor in 6–10m N of the pier or in front of the hotel on the S side of the pier. The water-tanker that used to use the end of the pier is no longer in evidence. There may be room for a few yachts to go

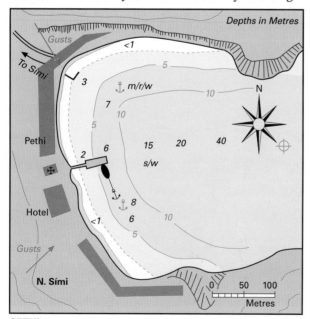

PETHI
⊕36°36'·95N 27°51'·70E WGS84

stern or bows-to on the pier, keeping clear of the local boats and water-taxi berths. The bottom is sand and weed, poor holding in places. The holding off the hotel on the S side of the pier is reported to be better though I haven't found it to be any better than the holding elsewhere in the bay (read 'I dragged' for that). Shelter from the *meltemi* is good but there are strong gusts into the bay so make sure your anchor is properly dug in or lay a second anchor to be on the safe side.

Tavernas on the waterfront. It is a long hike over the steep ridge to Sími town or take the bus from in front of the hotel.

ÁY MARINA

Immediately N of the entrance to Pethi there is an attractive anchorage behind the islet of Áy Marina. A reef connects the islet to the coast on the N so the approach must be made from the S. Anchor in 4–5m on a sandy bottom. There is a lee from the *meltemi* here remarkable for its calm. A good bathing beach ashore under an elaborate stone wall and beautiful clear water. Taverna ashore.

ÓRMOS THESSALONA

36°35'·83N 27°52'·78E WGS84

Lies just over half a mile S of Ák Filonika. Magnificent precipitous cliffs drop straight into the sea at the head of the bay. Anchor where depths are convenient although much of the bay is too deep. Some protection from the *meltemi* although a swell will sometimes roll in depending on the strength of the *meltemi*.

ÓRMOS NANOU

36°34'·97N 27°52'·56E WGS84

A large bay just S of Thessalona. A good lunch stop with wild steep-to scenery and clear water. Pine trees run down the steep-sided valley to the shore. A café bar opens in the summer.

ÓRMOS MARATHOUDA

36°33'·89N 27°52'·30E WGS84

Three miles S of Pethi lies Órmos Marathouda open only to the E. Anchor in 4–8m at the head of the bay. Subject to gusts off the hills. Over the saddle at the head of the bay lies a small hamlet.

ÓRMOS FANEROMENI

36°33'·0N 27°52'·5E

One mile S of Marathouda lies the deep inlet of Órmos Faneromeni open only to the E. Anchor at the head of the bay. Also subject to gusts off the hills.

NISÍS SESKLI ANCHORAGE

36°31'·0N 27°52'·2E (Vrak Kouloundrós light)

Nisís Seskli lies off the S end of Sími separated by a deep channel (Stenón Seskli). On the SE side of Nisís Seskli lies Órmos Skomisa, immediately N of Vrakhonisís Kouloundrós (Troumbeta). A small islet, Artikonisi, partially protects the cove from the

W–SW. The cove should be approached from the E. Anchor in the middle of the cove in 5–6m sand and rock, doubtful holding. On the W side there is a small quay you can take a line to. Good shelter from the *meltemi* in attractive deserted surroundings.

PANORMITTIS

BA 1532

Approach

An enclosed bay on the SW corner of Sími. A white windmill on the E side of the entrance and the large white buildings of the monastery are conspicuous.

By night Use the light on Nisís Marmarás Fl.3s6M and the light on the NE side of the entrance Fl.R.2s3M. Care is needed of yachts at anchor which may not be carrying anchor lights.

Dangers With the *meltemi* there can be gusts and confused seas off the entrance.

Mooring

Anchor in 3–6m in the NE side of the bay. There is sometimes room on the pier in the S corner although most of the space is taken up by local ferries and tripper boats and by the water tanker which calls here. The bottom is sand and weed with some rocks – good holding once the anchor has cut through the weed.

Shelter Good all-round shelter.

Facilities

Limited provisions and tavernas ashore. Bread available at the monastery.

General

The bay is attractive in a sparse sort of way and the monastery on the SE side complements it, being a sparse sort of place itself. When the ferries and tripper boats arrive the bay is transformed into a noisy crowded place for a few hours, but outside that it is a peaceful spot.

Looking into the entrance of Panormittis on the SW corner of Sími *Lu Michell*

ÁY EMILIANOS

36°36'·4N 27°46'·5E

On the W coast of Sími some shelter from the *meltemi* can be found under a short headland on the E side of Ák Kefala. From the N the monastery of Áy Emilianos on the headland and another monastery on the slopes inland are easily identified. Anchor in 8–10m on the S side of the headland. There is only the monastery ashore.

NISÍS NÍMOS

(Nemos)

Nisís Nímos, immediately N of Nísos Sími, is separated from the latter by a narrow channel (Stenón Nimou). There is a least depth of 4m in the fairway of the channel and although it looks daunting the first time through, it is a convenient short cut that avoids circumnavigating Nímos. With a strong *meltemi* blowing into the channel the depth at the trough of any swell may reduce the depth a little, something less than half a metre at most. Just look straight ahead and not at the variegated sea bottom passing under the keel.

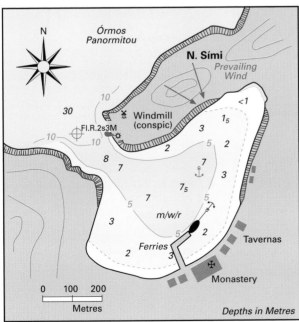

PANORMITTIS
⊕36°33'·12N 27°50'·53E WGS84

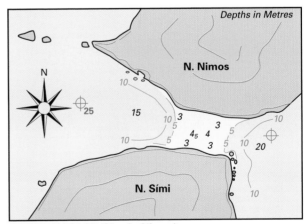

NIMOS PASSAGE (Stenón Nimou)
⊕36°38'·66N 27°50'·30E WGS84

⊕25 W entrance of Nímos Passage (Sími)
36°38'·72N 27°49'·76E WGS84

ORMOS EMBORIOS

36°37'·6N 27°49'·4E

On the W side of Órmos Sími is an open bay suitable for lunch stops in light to moderate winds. Depths are mostly very deep even close in to the shore. Anchoring off the beach is popular with the tripper boats. On the S side of the bay off the hamlet there is a 7–10m patch where you can anchor on mud and weed. Tavernas ashore in the hamlet and on the beach.

Rhodes
(Nísos Rodhos)

The largest island of the Dodecanese, Rhodes lies at the southern end of the chain of islands stretching down the west coast of Asiatic Turkey. Its name is of uncertain origin but possibly comes from the Greek word for the rock-rose which grows all over the island. In antiquity it had many names: Stadia, referring to its ellipsoid shape; Ophioussa, from the many snakes on the island; Poeissia, referring to its fertility; Olyessa, because it is earthquake prone; and Makaria, calling it simply the blessed isle.

As the ancient name, Stadia, states, the island is roughly ellipsoid or diamond-shaped. A mountain range runs from N to S with the highest peak, Mt Ataviros (1,215m, 4009ft), situated in the middle of the west coast. Unlike many of the other islands of the group, Rhodes is fertile not only in the valleys and on the plains but also on the high hills. Pine, olive, orange and lemon, fig and pear trees grow well. Maquis and wild flowers (including the rock-rose) grow in the countryside, while hibiscus, bougainvillea and jasmine run riot over village houses. Butterflies seem to be everywhere – so much so that Rhodes has been called the butterfly island. In addition to butterflies, the fauna is said to include deer, foxes, hares, badgers, partridges, vultures, jackdaws, jays and the Rhodes dragon – a lizard growing as long as 50cm (14in) – though you are unlikely to find any of these around the crowded north end of the island.

This garden island with its dry hot summers and mild winters (the climate resembles that of Sicily) has been popular throughout history: smiled upon by the sun-god Helios; extravagantly praised by Strabo; beloved by Tiberius who deserted Capri for a time, bringing his entire retinue with him; the Knights of St John were reluctant to leave their castle even when surrounded by hostile neighbours; and the Italians, who occupied Rhodes in 1912 intent on creating another Capri. Today Rhodes is without doubt the most popular tourist island in Greece. Hotels stretch along the east and west coasts from Rhodes city where sun and sandy beaches create an irresistible lure for sun-starved northerners.

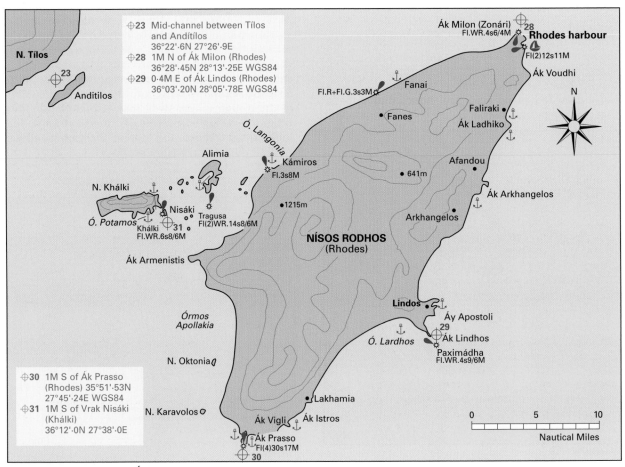

RODHOS, ALIMIA AND KHÁLKI

The significant history of Rhodes is neatly compacted into two periods: the story-book times of ancient Greece and the violent period of the Knights of St John. Moreover, such has been the influence of Rhodes on the surrounding islands that its history can to a large extent be read as the history of most of the Dodecanese.

The island has always been important as a trading centre between Asia and Africa and Greece and Italy. Homer mentions three cities on Rhodes: Lindos, with its natural harbour on the east; Ialysos, in the northwest; and Kamiros, about 20 miles down the west coast from Ák Milon (Zonari). Rhodes, along with Kós, Knidos and Halicarnassus, monopolised trade in this southwest corner of the Aegean.

In 408 BC the three cities mentioned by Homer decided to pool their resources and found the city of Rhodes on its present site. Hippodamus of Miletus designed the new city and built a series of harbours on the eastern side of the low-lying peninsula on which the city was built. The new city and its splendid harbour complex swiftly eclipsed the other three cities to become the most important city and trading centre in the southwestern Aegean. The Rhodians built up their own fleet of merchant vessels to become a major sea power. And they managed all this without upsetting the major warring powers around them – in effect a little Switzerland growing ever more prosperous.

The Rhodians managed successfully to evade being caught up in the international politics of the time until the death of Alexander the Great, when the Mediterranean was plunged into chaos. Rhodes refused to help Antigonus invade Egypt (which was, after all, its major trading partner). Demetrius Polioketes, a would-be Alexander, enters the history books at this point. To teach the Rhodians a sharp lesson he assembled a large force and also the gargantuan siege machine for which he is famous – the Helepolis. The contraption was estimated to be nine storeys high, weighed perhaps 125 tons and rolled up to the city walls on giant oak wheels. It sprouted huge catapults, drawbridges which could be dropped down to release troops, a nest on top for archers, and was shielded against enemy arrows.

Around Rhodes today, piled in heaps or lying about the castle walls, you can see the heavy stone balls believed to be the missiles Demetrius flung at the city. He did a lot of damage, but at the end of a year he had still not beaten the stubborn Rhodians. He signed a treaty with them and ordered all his siege machinery to be sold and the money donated to the Rhodians for a statue to commemorate the great siege. Thus the statue of the sun-god Helios was born. Chares began the statue in 302 BC and twelve years later the Colossus of Rhodes was complete. Perhaps it did stand astride Mandráki harbour, as commentators say, and perhaps not. Wherever the precise site of the 35 metre high statue was, it became a landmark for all ships nearing the island until it was toppled by the earthquake of 227 BC.

Rhodes endured as an important economic and sea power until 43 BC when Cassius sacked the city and destroyed it. Rhodian marine law was universally admired, parts were absorbed into the Venetian sea code and its spirit is with us today. For centuries the city attracted artisans and artists. In Roman times Caesar, Brutus, Anthony, Cicero and Tiberius all studied in Rhodes. Pliny counted over 2,000 statues when he was there and yet today a mere handful remain, so complete was Cassius' sacking of the city.

Until 1309 Rhodes drifted with the mainstream of history: ruled by Byzantium; sacked by the Saracens; ruled by the Venetians and later by the Genoese who in 1306 gave shelter to the Knights of St John. In 1309 the refugees became the masters of Rhodes. They built the huge fortified castle that dominates the town today and acquired a fleet of fast galleys which harried Turkish merchant vessels up and down the coast. They expanded from Rhodes to Khálki and Alimia, Sími and Tílos, Kós and Kalimnos, and the adjacent coast of Asia Minor. In all of these places the castles or the remains of castles built by the Knights can be seen today.

The huge fortifications of Rhodes withstood two great sieges – in 1444 from Egypt and in 1480 from the Turks. In 1522 Suleiman I assembled a force reckoned to number over 100,000 men against 650 Knights and 1,200 supporters. The defence of the Knights against such a force is one of history's great battles. They held out for five months before the Grand Master, Villiers de l'Isle Adam, capitulated on honorable terms. It is said that Suleiman, watching the Grand Master leave, remarked, 'It is not without some regret that I oblige this old Christian to leave his home.'

Rhodes remained under Ottoman rule until the Italians occupied it in 1912. Intent on recreating the glory of Rhodes, they set about restoring and tidying up the castle and the town. They have been much criticized for their restoration work, but I do not think it is overdone, and most of it gives a good feeling of what medieval fortifications were like. For the student of military warfare, Rhodes has probably the best preserved medieval fortifications in Greece. During the Second World War the island was occupied by the Germans and in 1947 it became Greek along with the rest of the Dodecanese.

RHODES HARBOUR – MANDRÁKI

BA 1532
Imray-Tetra G3, G35

Approach

Conspicuous From the W and N the city of Rhodes on a low-lying spit of land can be identified from a long way off. Large hotels line the beach on the W. From the S and E a chimney S of the town and the E mole of Rhodes Marina and Limín Akandia are conspicuous. The large ferries in Limín Emborikós also show up well. Mandráki basin, where a yacht should make for, is easily identified by the small fort with the lighthouse (Áyios Nikólaos), a cupola, the

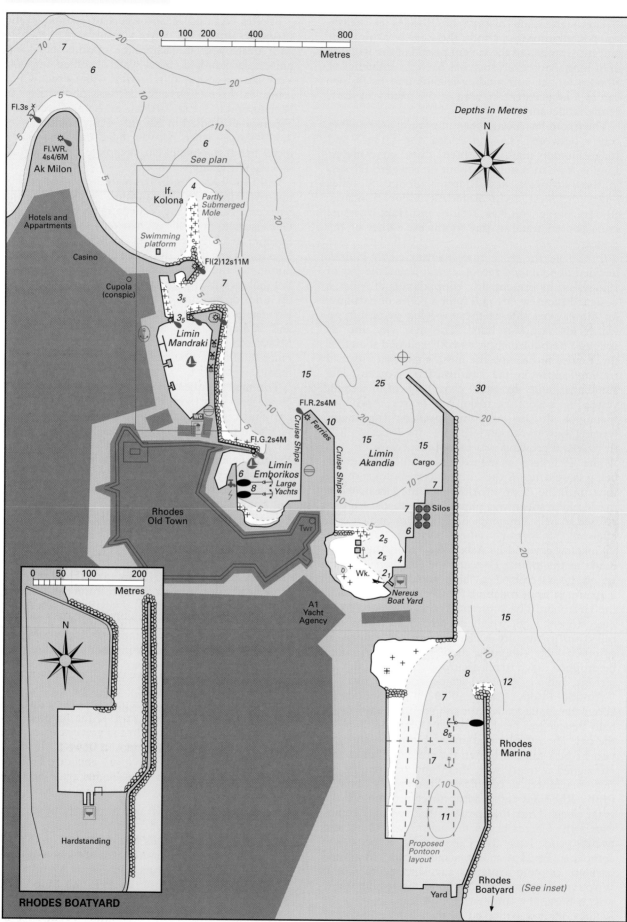

Depths in Metres

N

RHODES BOATYARD

APPROACHES TO RHODES
⊕36°27´·04N 28°14´·12E WGS84

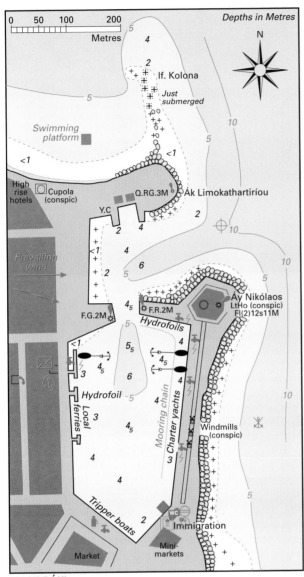

MANDRÁKI
⊕36°27'·12N 28°13'·67E WGS84

Mandráki looking into the entrance with Áy Nikólaos on the left of picture   *Lu Michell*

belfry, the market and the three windmills on the mole forming the E side of Mandráki. On either side of the entrance to Mandráki there is a tower with a bronze deer on top.

By night Use the light on Ák Milon Fl.WR.4s6/4M (red sector covers Ifalos Kolóna over 286°-314°), Áy Nikólaos Fl(2)12s11M, the W breakwater head Fl.G.2s4M, Limín Emborikós Fl.R.2s4M, and the lights at the entrance to Mandráki Q.RG.3M, F.R and F.G.2M. Some of the lights are difficult to identify against the loom of the city lights. Approaching from the W the light at Rhodes airport (AlFl.WG) some 10 miles S of the city is easily picked up.

Dangers
1. Keep well off Ák Milon (Zonári) and the shoal water running N from it and the reef (Ifalos Kolóna) extending N from the outer mole protecting the entrance to Mandráki.
2. Care should be taken when strong southerlies and easterlies are blowing as there is a disturbed

swell at the entrance to Mandráki, although once inside the basin there are no problems.

Mooring
Mandráki
The harbour is hopelessly crowded in the summer, with charter operators zealously guarding their berths. Mandráki is now designated as a marina, although apparently vacant berths do not necessarily translate to the automatic allocation of a berth. Yachts can also go on the pontoon inside the entrance on the W side of the harbour if there is room. There are a few laid moorings both here and in the 'marina', but crossed anchors and frayed tempers are more the order of the day in Mandráki. Try to arrive mid-week rather than at the weekend when charter companies are doing change-overs.

Limín Emborikós
Large yachts moor on the quay on the W side of Limín Emborikós. Call A1 Yacht Agency for a berth. If there are vacant berths smaller yachts may be permitted to berth here, although it can be uncomfortable with a surge from the *meltemi* and wash from numerous cruise ships being manoeuvred into and out of berths on the other side of the harbour.

Rhodes Marina
Work is due to recommence on Rhodes Marina. A new consortium (including A1 Yachting) has been formed to take over the completion and running of the marina. The southern end of the harbour has become something of a hydrofoil graveyard and will take some clearing up. Go stern or bows-to the quay on the E side or if there is room anchor off in the centre. No doubt when work begins again and the place is cleaned up then yachts will not be permitted until the marina proper is open. The planned layout of the pontoons is shown in the plan.

Projected Data c.300 berths. All services including water and electricity, shower and toilet blocks, fuel quay and yacht services

Shelter Good all-round shelter in Mandraki. Numerous boats winter afloat here.

Note Fouled anchors are a common occurrence in Mandraki simply because there are so many yachts.

A large mooring chain lying approximately 30m out from the quay is also easily fouled.

Authorities Marina/yacht charter staff. A port of entry: port police, customs and immigration authorities. Customs and immigration are at the root of the E mole in Mandráki and the port police are on the W side. Charge band 2.

Facilities

Services Water and electricity on the quay. You buy pre-paid cards in the office for water and electricity. Showers and toilets.

Fuel A mini-tanker delivers to the quay.

Repairs **Nereus Boatyard** 60-ton travel-hoist. The channel to the hoist basin is normally dredged to 2–2·5m. Go first to the boatyard where the leading marks for the channel will be described. Reservations are advisable if you want to leave your boat here for the winter. All mechanical repairs. Most engine spares can be obtained within a few days from Piraeus. Wood and GRP repairs. Light engineering work including stainless steel work carried out. Electrical and some electronic repairs. Sail repairs. Life raft service. Good hardware and tool shops. Several chandlers.

Nereus Boatyard, Odos Australis 19, Rodhos, Dodecanese, Greece ☎/*Fax* 0241 22717.

A1 Yacht Trade Consortium SA is a long-established company (formerly Yacht Agency Rhodes) who have a well-stocked chandlery, including many imported items and a good stock of books and charts. They can arrange berths in Mandráki or Emborikós and charge a handling fee for doing so. Large yachts will need to book ahead to get a berth. They are also brokers and charter agents. The staff are knowledgeable and helpful and can usually obtain most bits of gear. Mail can be sent to them and will be held for collection.

A1 Yacht Trade Consortium SA,
PO Box 393, Byronos 1 & Kanada St,
85 100 Rhodes, Greece
☎ 22410 22927 *Fax* 22410 23393
Email rhodes@a1yachting.com
VHF Ch 73 (call sign *A1 Yachting*)

The office is on the waterfront between Nereus boatyard and the commercial port.

Provisions Good shopping in the new town around the harbour and in the white octagonal market. Ice available.

Eating out Good tavernas – ask around for recommendations. Le Bistrot, Araliki and Sea Star, all in the old town, have been recommended.

Other PO. OTE. Banks. ATMs. Greek gas and Camping Gaz. Turkish baths in the old town. Hire cars, motorbikes and bicycles. Bus service to the important villages. Organised excursions to Lindos, the Valley of the Butterflies, Kamiros etc. Daily ferries to Piraeus via Crete or the northern Cyclades. Daily ferries to Marmaris in Turkey in the summer. European and internal flights.

Mandráki harbour looking SSW   *Peter Kleinoth/MareTeam*

General

Rhodes city – you either love it or hate it. After the sleepy peace of many of the other islands in this area, Rhodes town fairly hums and bustles as only the most important tourist town in Greece can. But it is not overpowering, and once you are accustomed to the fact that you are back in a busy city the place does grow on you.

Rhodes city consists of two distinct parts: the old city surrounded by the walls built by the Knights and the new town largely built by the Italians during their occupation of the island. Much of the old city was restored by the Italians and although they have been criticized for producing 'Hollywood' castles and towers, with the passing of time the reconstruction has weathered and blended into the original medieval stonework. In the new town the buildings lining the waterfront were also largely built by the Italians in a monumental style to designs by Florestano di Fausto. The other notable buildings mostly date from the Turkish occupation.

Mandráki was probably the harbour used by the Knights to keep their swift galleys in, although some believe the basin now called Emborikós was the galley harbour and Mandráki was occupied only by small boatbuilders. The word Mandráki is the diminutive of *mandra* meaning 'a sheep fold' and is used in many other places to describe a small enclosed harbour.

Here in ancient times the Colossus of Rhodes may have stood – the bronze statue of Helios the sun-god, one of the seven wonders of the world (despite the postcards which show him looking more like a ridiculous jolly green giant). Although the popular opinion is that the statue did not stand astride the harbour entrance, I agree with Ernle Bradford that there is no reason why this should not have been so:

'My opinion is that, as is so often the case, the ancient story is true; the statue of the Sun God literally be-straddled the narrow entrance to the galley harbour. It is a small boat harbour, and one must bear in mind that the ships of the ancients were, by modern standards, only small boats. Most of them, no doubt, lowered their masts when entering harbour under oars – just as the galleys often did in the time of the knights. In any case, a statue with a total height of 105 feet would have given plenty of clearance between its legs even if their masts were raised.'

Ernle Bradford *The Greek Islands*

The statue was destroyed by an earthquake in 227 BC and 80 years later sold as scrap.

Beyond the old and new city stand the blank reinforced concrete hotels and suburbs of the holiday town relieved only by the abundance of oleander, bougainvillea and hibiscus. On Ák Zonari stands the Hydrobiological Institute, housing an interesting collection of preserved and live marine animals caught in local waters.

RHODES BOATYARD

A separate project S of Rhodes Marina for a huge yard with protected basin. 550 and 200-ton travel-hoists. Slipway. 100,000sq.m of hardstanding. This is a government project which will be put out to private tender when complete. No completion date is available.

NOTE

When on passage between Rhodes and Lindos there are fierce gusts off the high land when the *meltemi* is blowing strongly. If you are heading to Rhodes from Lindos it is best to leave very early in the morning when the *meltemi* sometimes dies off for a while.

Between Rhodes city and Lindos there are several bays and coves that can be used in settled weather.

ÁK LADHIKO ANCHORAGE

36°19'·3N 28°12'·8E

A small bay under Ák Ladhiko. Care is needed of shoal water in the entrance (2m) and off the E entrance. The best policy is to stay closer to the W entrance point. Anchor in 4–5m on sand and rock, reasonable holding once you find a good sandy patch. Good shelter from the *meltemi*.

Tavernas ashore.

FALIRAKI

36°20'·8N 28°13'·3E

A small fishing harbour and notorious tourist resort lying to the N of Órmos Ladhiko. The entrance is rock bound from some distance out and should only be attempted in calm weather with someone in the bow to con you in. An approach on a course of 225° to the N side of the harbour is recommended.

LINDOS (Limín, Lindhou)

BA 1532

Approach

The castle and the town are conspicuous. By night there are no lights although on a clear night entry is possible with care.

Mooring

Anchor outside the buoyed area near the pier or in the N bay. The bottom is sand with some rock – good holding although a trip line is recommended in the N bay where there are some large boulders. The

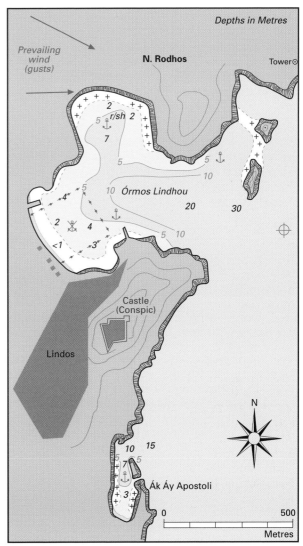

LINDOS
⊕36°05'·73N 28°05'·82E WGS84

bay is open to the E and southerlies send in a swell. With the *meltemi* there are fierce gusts down into the bay so make sure your anchor is well in before leaving a yacht unattended.

Facilities

Water Limited from local sources.
Provisions Most provisions can be found.
Eating out Numerous excellent if somewhat expensive tavernas.
Other PO. OTE. Banks. ATM. Hire cars, motorbikes and bicycles. Buses to Rhodes.

General

Early in the morning or late in the afternoon, Lindos, with its small winding streets between medieval houses and the toy castle perched on a rock summit as if about to topple into the bay, is uniquely beautiful. In the heat of the day coaches and ferries transport hundreds of tourists from Rhodes – the narrow streets are packed tight, the beach resembles something from Cannes or Nice and the bay buzzes with speedboats towing inflatable rafts, but by dusk they have all departed.

Lindos, commanding the superb natural harbour,

Lindos on the E coast of Rhodes Island looking SSW
Peter Kleinoth/MareTeam

was the principal city of the island before the foundation of Rhodes in about 408 BC. The acropolis within the medieval castle affords an all-round view over land and sea – before 1000 hours or after 1600 hours there are few people about. In the village the old houses with black and white pebble mosaic courtyards and staircases are a legacy from the prosperous Middle Ages.

ÁY APOSTOLI

Situated immediately S of Órmos Lindou. It is possible to anchor here – take a line ashore as there is limited swinging room. The enclosed inlet appears to offer good shelter, but any swell rebounds around the bay making it uncomfortable.

ÓRMOS LARDHOS

36°04'·0N 28°01'·5E

To the S of Lindos under the rocky Ák Lindhos lies the wide bay of Lardhos. In settled weather anchor off the small hamlet at the E end of the bay. There is a friendly taverna ashore. The gusts off the hills here are often less bothersome than in Lindos.

ÁK ISTROS

35°55'·8N 27°51'·9E

The cape 6 miles NE of Ák Prasso which is the southernmost tip of Rhodes. There is an anchorage off a small hamlet on the SW side of the cape. In the N side of the bay is a pier providing reasonable shelter from the *meltemi*. A new breakwater has been reported to be under construction S of Ák Istros.

Note There is a wreck dangerous to navigation 0·5M S of the cape.

ÁK VIGLI

Lies 1 mile SW of Ák Istros. It can be easily distinguished by a tower on the extremity of the cape. There is an anchorage on the N side of the cape in 3–6m giving some shelter from the *meltemi*.

ÁK PRASSO

35°52'·8N 27°45'·1E (Ák Prasso light)

The southernmost tip of Rhodes. It is connected to Rhodes by a low neck of land and from the distance looks like an island. The cape and the lighthouse on it are conspicuous from some distance off. On the N side of the cape there is good shelter from S winds in 2–4m depths. On the S side of the cape there is good shelter from the *meltemi* in a small cove in 2–4m depths. The bottom in both anchorages is sand and good holding.

Wind and kite-surfing are popular around the windy cape (which will give you a bit of a clue about what sort of winds to expect). The natural sand-bar which connected the islet to Rhodes has been partially washed away in recent winter storms, leaving a narrow channel which is not navigable by yachts.

NOTE

When on passage along the E coast of Rhodes, the Khina Rocks lying 4 miles SE off Ák Vigli, are low-lying and difficult to pick out.

ÓRMOS LANGONIA (Kámiros Skála)

36°16'·4N 27°49'·5E

On the W coast of Rhodes one mile to the E of Ák Kopriá lies Langonia. It offers only limited shelter from the W and some shelter from the S. A light is exhibited here Fl.3s8M. There is a quay where the *caïque* ferry from Khálki berths. Fuel and water ashore.

FANAI (Mais)

36°22'·0N 27°58'·6E

A small harbour on the NE coast of Rhodes approximately midway between Ák Milon and Kamiros. The entrance is lit Fl.G.3s3M/Fl.R.3s3M. Care is needed in the entrance as silting is occurring and there is a bar at the entrance which may build up over time. Although depths are 1·5–2m inside the harbour, there may be less over the bar. Reconnoitre by dinghy first. Go stern or bows-to wherever you can find a berth. Good shelter from the *meltemi*. NE winds may cause a problem.

Tavernas ashore. The village of Fanai (Fanes) is a short distance inland.

ÓRMOS TRIANDA

36°25'·8N 28°11'·0E

Situated on the NE tip of Rhodes, this open bay offers shelter from the S and SE only. It is untenable with the *meltemi*. Anchor in 4–8m off the beach which is lined with large hotels. The bottom is sand and good holding.

Nísoi Khálki and Alimia

Lying off the W coast of Rhodes, these two islands have always been dependent on their large neighbour. Khálki has a small dwindling population – nearly all of it living around the harbour. Alimia is deserted.

Nísos Khalki

KHALKI (Halkia, Skála, Emborios)

Approach

Conspicuous The three windmills on top of the ridge behind the village are conspicuous from a long way off. The harbour proper will not be seen until you are into the bay.

By night A night approach is not recommended because of the numerous unlit rocks and reefs in the approaches. Use the light on Nisáki Fl.WR.6s.8/6M (232°-R-244° and 280°-R-297°) and on the N entrance Fl.3s6M.

Dangers Care must be taken of the numerous above- and below-water rocks in the approaches and the strait between Khálki and Alimia. Xera rock although above water is difficult to see and the reef immediately due W of Nisáki is only just awash and difficult to spot. Most of the other rocks and islets can be identified by day even off a comparatively small scale chart, though care is needed.

Mooring

In summer a pontoon is placed to the N of the ferry quay. Go stern or bows-to where directed or where there is room. Otherwise go stern or bows-to or alongside the ferry quay. If you are on the ferry berth when the ferry is due the port police will ask you to move off for the 30 minutes or so which it stays. Recent reports say the pontoon is not always in place. The bottom is sand and rock – uncertain holding in places.

Shelter Good shelter from the *meltemi* although there are gusts into the bay. With strong S winds a considerable swell enters the harbour.

Authorities Port police.

Anchorage Anchor off clear of the ferry turning area and the laid moorings for local craft. The best place to be is tucked into the N side of the bay.

Facilities

Water On the pontoon. Limited supplies locally.
Provisions Most provisions can be found although the island is dependent on the ferry for most things.
Eating out Several convivial tavernas. Fresh fish sometimes available.
Other PO. OTE. Ferry to Skála Kamiros on Rhodes.

General

Although many of the houses are in ruins the village on the slopes around the bay is attractive. In many ways it reminds me of Sími town on a smaller and poorer scale. The fort on the precipitous rock behind the village (cone-shaped and 670m high), like the fort on Alimia, was a watchtower for

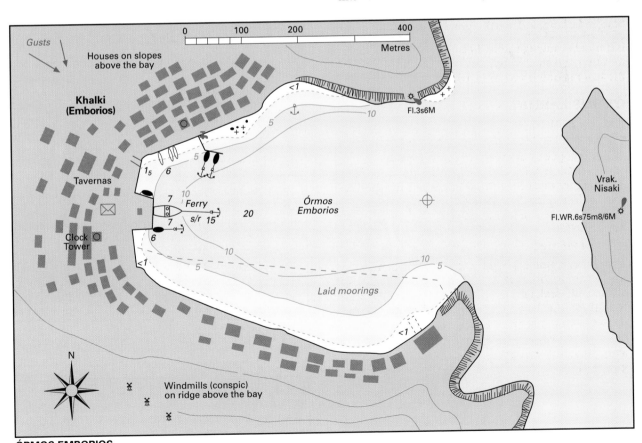

ÓRMOS EMBORIOS
⊕36°13'·3N 27°37'·5E

465

Rhodes. Inside is the small church of Áy Nikólaos.

ÓRMOS POTAMOS

36°13'·1N 27°36'·3E

The bay on the S of Khálki immediately W of Khálki harbour. Good shelter from the *meltemi*. Care is needed of a reef and shoal patch before you get to the NW corner and of shoal water fringing the head of the bay. Anchor at the head of the bay in 4–6m closer to the E side than to the W. The bottom is sand and rocks, reasonable holding.

Taverna ashore. It is a short walk over the headland into Khalki.

Nisís Alimia

ÓRMOS ALIMIA

Approach

The large bay on the S of Nisís Alimia. From the N and S the ruined fort above the bay is conspicuous. A few white houses and a small church are conspicuous once you are at the entrance to the bay.

By night Not recommended. There are no lights and the unlit rocks and reefs in the approaches make it dangerous.

Dangers Care must be taken of the numerous above- and below-water rocks in the approaches and the strait between Khálki and Alimia. See notes for Khálki.

Mooring

Anchor in either of the two bays. The S bay is mostly quite deep compared to the N bay. The bottom is sand and weed – good holding.

Shelter The S bay offers good shelter from the *meltemi* although there are gusts. The N bay may get some swell pushed in by a strong *meltemi* although there is some shelter tucked in behind the spit the church is built on.

Facilities

None.

General

Nobody lives on Alimia, although a few fishermen from Khálki have houses there. The fort above the E bay is a long hot walk up the rocky hill – from the summit there is a commanding view over Khálki and Rhodes. In the S bay there are a number of deserted buildings left over from the Second World War. In one of these nostalgic German soldiers drew a series of cartoons depicting what life was like back home and what life might have been like on some distant tropical island if there had been no war.

Nísoi Kárpathos and Kásos

These two sea-swept islands are the most southerly of the Dodecanese. Lying between Crete and Rhodes in a stretch of angry sea, the islands seem to have been bypassed by history. Today only a few tourists visit them and, of the islanders themselves, it is said that more Karpathiots live in Athens than in Kárpathos.

Kásos is ellipsoid in shape and steep-to on all sides. Very little vegetation is to be seen on the island even around the major village of Fri. In 1824 the Egyptians ravaged the island and from all appearances Kásos never recovered. (The Kasiots remember it as the Holocaust.) When I entered

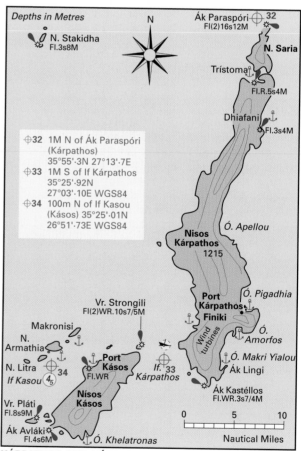

KÁRPATHOS AND KÁSOS

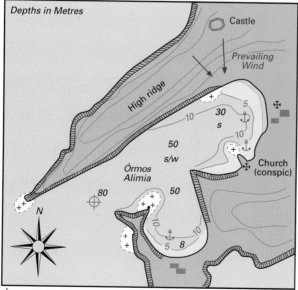

ÓRMOS ALIMIA
⊕36°15'·8N 27°41'·5E

Órmos Khelatronas for the first time there appeared to be people lining the cliffs surrounding the bay – on closer inspection these were scarecrows. Yet nothing is grown in the vicinity of the bay and my imagination ran wild speculating that these scarecrows were a device, perhaps an old custom, designed to let any invading Egyptians know the Kasiots were ready and waiting this time.

Kárpathos (also known by its medieval name of Scarpanto) is also mountainous and steep-to, but by comparison with Kásos is a green and fertile island. A mountain ridge runs from NE to SW with Mt Kalolimni (Lastra) at 1,200m (3960ft) the highest in the centre of the island. The W coast is mostly barren except in the valleys, but the E coast is covered in pine. On the S coast there are fertile valleys and plains planted in olives, citrus and fruit trees. Most of the population lives in the southern part of the island and there are many small and attractive villages in this region. It is well worth making an excursion inland from Pigadhia if the weather permits you to leave your yacht there safely.

CAUTION

During the *meltemi* season strong gusts blow off the S and E sides of Kásos and Kárpathos. Against this there is often a current of 1 knot or so running northwards up the east coast of Kárpathos past Ák Patella. Large and disturbed seas will be encountered in Stenón Kasou (Kásos Strait) between Kásos and Crete and especially in Stenón Karpathou (Kárpathos Strait) near the southern tip of Rhodes. In the latter sea area the bottom comes up quickly from 600–700m to 100–200m causing a wicked cross-sea.

PORT KÁRPATHOS (Pigadhia)

BA 1532

Approach

Conspicuous From the S the large cross on the N side of Ák Patella is conspicuous. The rocky outcrops of Nisídha Despotika and Garonisos are easily identified but the lower lying Nisidha Afoti is difficult to make out. A cupola immediately N of the outer breakwater is conspicuous and closer in the buildings of the town will be seen.

By night Use the light on Nisídha Dhespotika Fl.5s6M and the light on the end of the mole Fl.R.4s8M. A fixed red light is also exhibited on a television repeater just W of the town.

Dangers With the *meltemi* there are fierce gusts in the approaches.

Mooring

Go stern or bows-to the new mole in the SW corner. Care needed as some yachts have springs running across the quay. It may be possible for small yachts to squeeze in under the mole – care is needed of the depths under the mole and it would be best to reconnoitre first.

Shelter There is always some surge with the *meltemi* which gusts across the mole. In the morning there are sometimes gusts from the N–NE and there is a

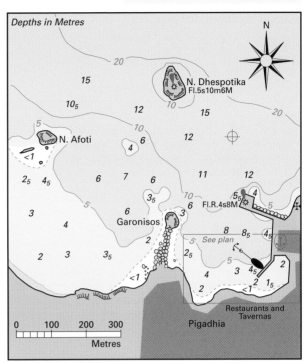

APPROACHES TO PORT KARPATHOS (Pigadhia)
⊕35°30′·72N 27°12′·88E WGS84

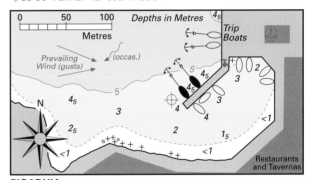

PIGADHIA
⊕35°30′·54N 27°12′·84E WGS84

Port Kárpathos (Pighadia) looking SW   *Nigel Patten*

467

surge with strong S winds.

Authorities Port police and customs.

Facilities

Water On the mole.

Fuel Can be delivered by mini-tanker.

Provisions Good shopping for provisions in the village.

Eating out Good tavernas in the town.

Other PO. OTE. Bank. ATM. Greek gas. Hire motorbikes. Ferry to Piraeus and Rhodes.

General

The small town of Pigadhia more than makes up for the uncomfortable harbour – fringed by green trees and gardens, it is both attractive and friendly. In recent years the place has acquired a modest tourist trade, though not an overpowering one. It is the best place to use as a base for exploring the island. Don't panic if you hear sirens going in the town – it's probably the parrot that lives on the balcony above Café Karpathos running through his impressive repertoire.

ÓRMOS AMORFOS (Amorphi Bay)

35°27'·7N 27°12'·0E

The large bay under Ák Volokas. Anchor in the NW cove. Care is needed of the reef off low-lying Ák Skopi in the S of the bay and of rocks and shoal water fringing the shore. The bottom is sand with some rocks, good holding. This bay has been reported to be less subject to gusts off the hills than Mákri Yialo to the S. Open to the S and SE.

Hotel and tavernas ashore.

ÓRMOS MAKRI YIALO (Makris Yialos)

35°26'·40N 27°10'·93E WGS84

A deserted bay lying near the S end of the island close northward of Ák Lingi. The wreck on the reef off Ák Lingi is conspicuous from some distance. Anchor in 4–8m near the head of the bay. The bottom is sand – good holding. The bay offers good shelter from the *meltemi* although the bay is subject to strong gusts. Open to the E.

FINIKI (Foiniki)

Approach

The small harbour lies on the N side of the bay close N of Ák Palaiokastro. The houses around the bay will be seen closer in.

By night The end of the breakwater is lit: Fl.R.3s3M.

Dangers Care must be taken of a reef reported lying approximately 60m SE from the extremity of the breakwater. Keep close to the end of the rough stone breakwater.

Mooring

Go stern or bows-to the quay where there are 2–4m depths off. The N and E sides of the bay are shallow.

Shelter Adequate shelter from the *meltemi* but open to the S. With southerly winds dangerous gusts are reported to blow off the high land and a swell enters the harbour.

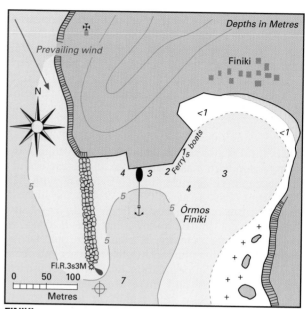

FINIKI
⊕35°29'·4N 27°06'·9E

Facilities

Ashore in the small fishing hamlet there is a café/taverna and little else.

TRISTOMA

This long sheltered inlet on the NW corner of Kárpathos appears on the chart to offer the best shelter on the island. However, with a strong *meltemi* heavy seas pile up at the entrance and there are fierce gusts off the hills. With strong southerlies there are also gusts off the surrounding hills. Entry is by the southernmost passage. Anchor at the head of the inlet or in the cove on the NE side. There is a short quay in the corner with depths off it around 1·8–2m.

The village of Tristoma is now reported to be deserted with most buildings destroyed.

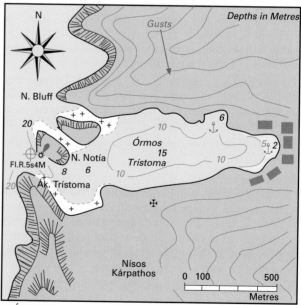

TRÍSTOMA
⊕35°49'·3N 27°12'·3E

DHIAFANI

35°45'·5N 27°13'·0E

A small harbour has been built to the N of the light on the cape. Care is needed of reefs with 3m over in the E approaches. Three windmills behind the harbour are conspicuous. The main light is on Ák Dhiafani Fl.3s4M and the end of the breakwater is lit Fl.R.3s3M. There is another light 2F.R(vert)3M on the pier to the N of the entrance but a night approach is not recommended. The dogleg mole is open to the N–NW and though the *meltemi* gusts down into here it is more uncomfortable than dangerous. Go stern or bows-to or alongside on the quay if there is room. Otherwise anchor off the village where convenient. The bottom is rocky with sand and shingle, not everywhere good holding and a trip line is recommended.

NISÍS SARIA (Saros)

Lies immediately N of Kárpathos separated only by a narrow channel. The channel has been reported to have 2·8m minimum depths and to be easily navigated in calm weather. (I have not navigated the channel and cannot confirm these depths.) With strong winds gusts blow out of the channel and short steep waves are generated.

IFALOS KÁRPATHOS (Kárpathos Rock)

⊕**33** 1M S of If Karpathos 35°25'·92N 27°03'·10E WGS84

A reef in the channel between Kásos and Kárpathos near the SW end of Kárpathos. The reef has less than 2m depths over it but is easily identified now by the wrecked coaster atop.

Nísos Kásos

ÓRMOS FRI

A new harbour has been built W of the small harbour at Limin Kasou, close E of the miniature harbour at Fri.

LIMÍN KASOU (Port Kásos, Emborió, Ophris, Ofris, Fri)

Approach

This small fishing harbour lies 0·5M E of the new harbour of Limin Fri.

Conspicuous From the W the town of Fri to the W of the harbour and a pink-roofed church fronted by palms near the harbour are conspicuous. From the E a white church on the headland to the E of the harbour and the mole are also conspicuous.

By night The end of the mole is lit: Fl.G.1·5s3M.

Dangers With the *meltemi* there are gusts and a confused sea in the approaches to the harbour.

Mooring

Go stern or bows-to the mole. The bottom is rock and sand.

Shelter Reasonable shelter from the *meltemi* although there is a surge in the harbour with a prolonged blow. Open to the NE. With strong winds from the S there are gusts off the high hills behind. With southerlies the fishermen either move elsewhere or anchor on the S side of the harbour with a line ashore.

Facilities

Water on the quay. Most provisions in Fri. Taverna at the harbour.

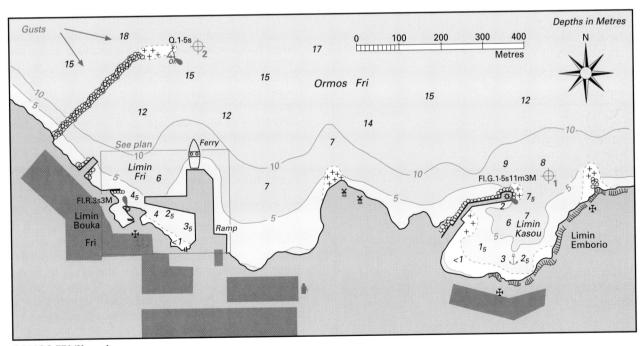

ORMOS FRI (Kasos)
⊕1 35°25'·14N 26°56'·03E WGS84
⊕2 35°25'·32N 26°55'·47E WGS84

LIMIN FRI

Approach

The new harbour lies 0·5M W of the fishing harbour of Limin Kasou.

Conspicuous From the W the outer breakwater and the blue cupola behind the harbour will be seen. The entrance to the new inner harbour is narrow and should not be confused with the entrance to the miniature harbour (Limin Bouka) immediately to the W.

By night The light on Ák Áy Yeóryios Fl.WR.3s5/3M covers Nisidhes Kasonisia and If Kasou in the W approaches (083°-175°) and Vrak Kalothonas in the E approaches (241°-251°). The end of the outer breakwater is lit by a buoy Q.1·5s. The entrance is not lit, but the entrance to the miniature harbour is lit Fl.R.3s3M.

Mooring

Go alongside where convenient in the inner harbour. The outer quay is used by ferries.

Shelter Good shelter from the *meltemi*. Strong southerlies could make it uncomfortable. Fri is a welcome secure harbour in this windy corner of the Aegean.

Authorities Port police and customs.

Facilities

Services Water on the quay. Electricity not yet connected.

Fuel The service station on the outskirts of the village may deliver by mini-tanker.

Provisions Some provisions in the village. It is much dependent on the ferry delivering supplies.

Eating out Several tavernas in the village. Good fresh fish sometimes available.

Other PO. ATM. Greek gas. Tripper ferry to Karpathos. Ferries to Crete and Piraeus.

General

The village of Fri sits excluded in this windy corner of the Aegean, a bit of a wallflower in its dowdy old-fashioned way. That is its charm. The village, all whites and blues with the church in the middle,

The new harbour at Fri looking NE over the miniature fishing harbour
Lu Michell

Limín Kasou looking N

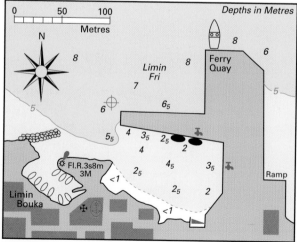

LIMIN FRI
⊕35°25'·09N 26°55'·37E WGS84

straggles around the new harbour and the miniature *caïque* harbour squeezed into a rocky hole in the low cliffs and looks out over the stormy waters of the Kasou channel. In bad weather the ferry cannot come here and the island is cut off apart from the small turbo-prop plane that flies across from Karpathos to the short airstrip W of the village. It is an enchanting place, a bit of island life caught in a time warp, and if you visit here stay for a while, although the odds are that the weather may keep you bottled up here anyway.

KASONISIA (Kaso Islets)

Shelter from the *meltemi* can be obtained in a number of small coves on the S side of these islands – sponge-boats fishing the area often use the low-lying Makronisi or Armathia (the largest of the group) where some shelter from N winds can be obtained. The bottom is sand and reported to be good holding. Good fishing around the islands.

IFALOS KASOU (Kásos Rock)

⊕34 100m N of If Kasou (Kásos)
35°25'·01N 26°51'·73E WGS84

Lies in the channel between Kásos and Kasonisia. It is no real danger to most sailing yachts since the least depth over it is 4·5m. A transit of Ák Áy Yeóryios and Nisís Kolofonos clears it.

ÓRMOS KHELATRONAS

35°20'·0N 26°52'·5E

At the S end of Kásos this deserted bay offers good shelter from the *meltemi*. Anchor in 4–8m at the head of the bay. The bottom is sand with not a patch of weed in sight – excellent holding. The *meltemi* gusts down off the hills and a swell invariably works its way around into the bay making it a little rolly, but you are safe enough. Idyllic and sometimes spooky surroundings.

Nísos Astipálaia
(Astypalaea, Stampalia)

Lying like an almost forgotten part of the Dodecanese, 35 miles west of Nísiros, Astipálaia (also called Stampalia in the Middle Ages and again during the Italian occupation) consists of two mountain ranges joined by a long slender isthmus. When approaching from the north or south it appears to be two islands. The coastline is much indented and offers a number of safe anchorages. Until the Romans and later the English suppressed piracy in the Aegean, the island was a natural lair for pirates, with good shelter and a strategic position to pounce on merchant shipping.

In antiquity the island was famed for its seafood and its fertility. Pliny praised its mussels and the surrounding seabed was supposed to have the best sponges in the Aegean. Today little of this is evident – the land is mostly barren or scrubby, the mussels nonexistent, and the sponge-divers go to the African coast. However, crayfish often appear on taverna menus. In the Middle Ages the Venetian family Quirini ruled the island. In 1912 it was the first of the Dodecanese to be occupied by the Italians. These last occupants built little and the character of the island is more like that of the Cyclades than that of the Dodecanese.

CAUTION

From Ák Exópetra (Poulari) across the S coast of Astipálaia to Ák Khilos there are strong gusts off the land when the *meltemi* is blowing.

SKÁLA ASTIPÁLAIA (Periyialo)
Approach

Conspicuous The castle with two white churches inside is conspicuous from some distance off. The white houses of the *chora* and a line of 4 windmills

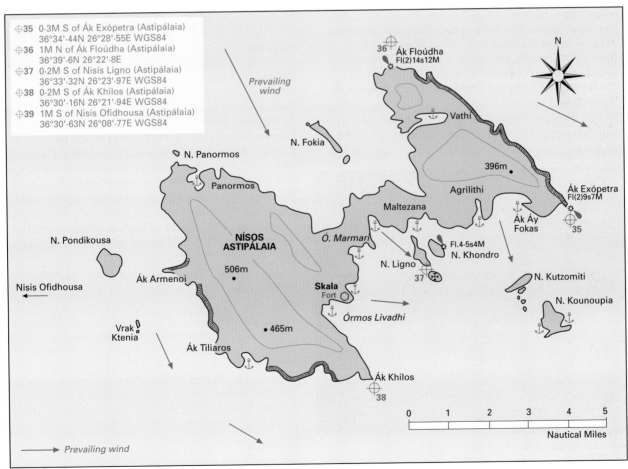

⊕35 0·3M S of Ák Exópetra (Astipálaia)
36°34'·44N 26°28'·55E WGS84
⊕36 1M N of Ák Floúdha (Astipálaia)
36°39'·6N 26°22'·8E
⊕37 0·2M S of Nisís Ligno (Astipálaia)
36°33'·32N 26°23'·97E WGS84
⊕38 0·2M S of Ák Khilos (Astipálaia)
36°30'·16N 26°21'·94E WGS84
⊕39 1M S of Nisís Ofidhousa (Astipálaia)
36°30'·63N 26°08'·77E WGS84

ASTIPÁLAIA (Astypalaea, Stampalaia)

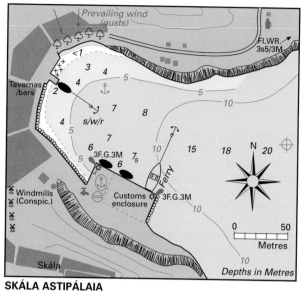

SKÁLA ASTIPÁLAIA
⊕36°32'·83N 26°21'·53E WGS84

on the hills are also conspicuous. Entering the bay, the houses along the waterfront and the quay are easily seen.

By night Use the light on the N side of the bay Fl.WR.3s5/3M (red sector covers 261°-293°) and the two lights on the quay: 3F.G.3M and 3F.G.3M in inverted triangle configurations.

Dangers With the *meltemi* there can be strong gusts off the high land in the approaches.

Mooring

Moor alongside the ferry quay, although you may have to move off for a short time when the ferry is due. Alternatively anchor in the bay. With care a couple of yachts can go bows-to the short pier off the town. The bottom is sand and weed, reasonable holding.

Shelter With the *meltemi* there are gusts into the bay which can make a berth on the quay uncomfortable. The bay is completely open to the SE and in the

Skála Astipálaia looking NW across the quay and the chora on the hill on the S side of the entrance *Peter Kleinoth/MareTeam*

472

event of such a wind the local fishermen go to Maltezana.

Authorities Port police and customs.

Facilities

Water Near the quay.
Fuel On the N side of the bay. A mini-tanker can deliver to the quay.
Provisions Most provisions can be obtained in the village, but the island is largely dependent on the ferry for supplies and there may be a shortage of some items (particularly fruit and vegetables).
Eating out Good tavernas around the waterfront, several with superb views over the bay.
Other PO. OTE. Bank. ATM. Hire motorbikes. Ferry to Piraeus and Rhodes.

General

The harbour and the *chora* above, which virtually form one town straggling from the bay to the summit, are most attractive from seaward although a little dilapidated on closer inspection. The castle dominating the *chora* (variously named Astipálaia or Stampalia or Kastello after the castle) was built in the 13th century by John Quirini. Legend has it that the castle was successfully defended on one occasion by the defenders throwing beehives onto the attackers. From the castle there is a magnificent view across to Maltezana to the NE and Órmos Livádhi to the SW.

ÓRMOS MALTEZANA (Analipsis)

BA 1541

Imray-Tetra G34

Approach

This bay is situated on the middle of the S coast where the island is almost divided into two by the isthmus. The normal entrance is on either side of Nisís Khondró.

Conspicuous Nisís Áy Kiriakí, the low islet just S of Ligno, has a conspicuous white chapel in the middle. Nisís Khondró and Nisís Ligno are easily identified from the distance and closer in the mole and the hamlet behind it are easily seen.

By night Not recommended. Use the light on Nisís Khondró Fl.4·5s4M and the light on the extremity of the mole Fl.G.2s4M. The fuel barges and buoys are marked by a F but this is not to be relied upon (not working 2000).

Dangers With the *meltemi* there are gusts in the approaches.

Note

1. It is possible to enter and leave Órmos Maltezana by the passage between the islet connected by a reef to Nisís Ligno and the islet N of it. There are 5·5m least depths in the fairway. The passage is easily negotiated by day though the clarity of the water makes it look shallower than it really is.
2. Care is needed of the fuel barges moored in the middle of the bay.

Mooring

Anchor in the bay or go alongside the pier if there is room. Do not take berths belonging to local fishing

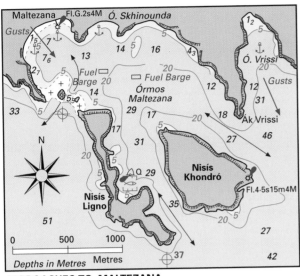

APPROACHES TO MALTEZANA
⊕ 36°34'·48N 26°23'·15E WGS84

⊕37 0·2M S of Nisís Ligno (Astipálaia)
    36°33'32N 26°23'·97E WGS84

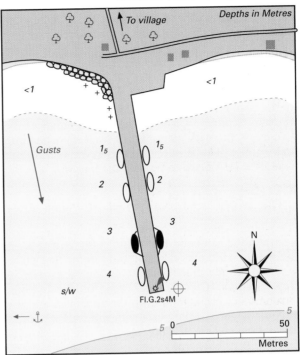

MALTEZANA
⊕36°34'·6N 26°23'·3E

Maltezana looking towards the pier from the anchorage

boats on the pier. The bottom is sand and weed, good holding although it can be a bit of a struggle to get the anchor in first time.

Shelter Good shelter from the *meltemi* with few gusts. Although partially open to the SE the wind does not blow home and little swell enters the bay.

Facilities
Some provisions in the hamlet. Several tavernas and cafés ashore.

General
The bay is attractive with an anomalous (for Astipálaia) green foreshore under the barren burnt slopes behind and clear water in the bay. The good lee from the *meltemi* also comes as a blessed relief. On the slopes NW of the hamlet there is an airstrip.

ÓRMOS AGRILITHI
A deserted inlet lying approximately 1 mile NE of Nisís Khondró. Good shelter from the *meltemi* although there are gusts off the slopes. Anchor where convenient and take a long line ashore. The

bottom is sand – good holding. The deserted bay is a wonderful wild spot which, with the *meltemi* howling outside, can feel like your own private paradise.

Note The 4·5m shoal patch (Ifalos Baraka) lying approximately half a mile SE of the E entrance point to Agrilithi is visible in calm weather but is difficult to spot with the *meltemi* kicking up a chop.

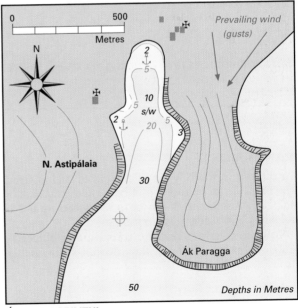

ÓRMOS AGRILITHI
⊕36°35'·0N 26°25'·4E

ÓRMOS VLIKADHA
The large bay tucked under Ák Áy Fokas. It is very deep for anchoring around the bay and really the only place is tucked into the E part of the bay. Here

there are gusts off the land from the N when the *meltemi* is blowing so it is not a safe place to be.

NISÍS KOUNOUPIA

36°32'·0N 26°28'·2E

The southernmost islet off Ák Áy Fokas. The S end of the island has two inlets with a sand bar between. In calm weather a yacht can anchor in either of the two inlets, but with the *meltemi* a swell is pushed into the W inlet. The E inlet offers more protection but is not the best place to be with the *meltemi*.

VATHI

BA 1666

This landlocked inlet on the NE tip of the island offers good all-round shelter. The entrance is somewhat difficult to pick out from the cliffs. Anchor off the small hamlet in the W corner in 3–5m depths. There is thick weed on the bottom, but find a clear patch to drop the anchor in and the holding is good. Mild gusts with the *meltemi*. A few large trawlers are usually moored off the fishing hamlet. A café/taverna.

There are also suitable depths for anchoring in at the E end of the inlet.

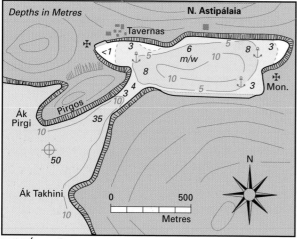

VATHÍ
⊕36°36'·5N 26°23'·0E

PANORMOS

In the bay at the NW tip of Astipálaia shelter from the *meltemi* can be found in a cove on the W side of the bay. Anchor in 4–5m on a sandy bottom. No facilities but peaceful surroundings.

In calm weather there are several other places to anchor nearby, although they do not offer shelter from the *meltemi*.

ÓRMOS LIVÁDHI

36°32'·3N 26°21'·0E

On the S side of the *chora* (Skála Astipálaia) is the large bay of Livádhi with a pleasant anchorage at the head off the beach. Anchor in 5–10m tucked up into the NW corner. The bottom is sand and the gusts from the *meltemi* are not too bad here.

Tavernas ashore.

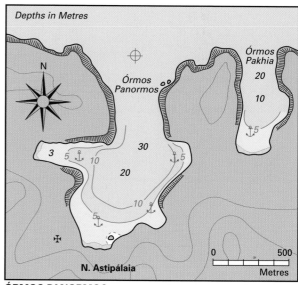

ÓRMOS PANORMOS
⊕36°35'·8N 26°17'·0E

Nisís Áy Íoannis (Nisís Sirina)

36°17'·0N 26°44'·5E (Nisís Plakhida light)

A high domed island lying approximately 19 miles SE of Astipálaia. Nisídhes Adelfia, a group of high jagged islands approximately 4 miles NW of Sirina, are conspicuous and the bold outline of Áy Íoannis is easily identified. A light is exhibited on Nisís Plakidha (Fl.WR.3s9/6M), the largest island of Nisídhes Trianísia to the SE of Áy Íoannis, but navigating in the vicinity of these islands and rocks at night should be avoided.

On the S of Áy Íoannis there is a large bay which local fishermen use. It is reported that most of the bay is quite deep with a rock-strewn bottom, but in the NE corner there is a patch of sand suitable for anchoring in. The fishermen have a permanent mooring here and don't seem to mind visitors using it when they leave at night to fish around Nisídhes Trianísia. Good shelter from the *meltemi*. The bay is only open S.

Ashore there is little except two chapels and a herd of goats.

X. Crete
(Kriti)

Crete is the largest and most important island in the Aegean. Lying across the mouth of the southern Aegean, it both commands the southern approaches to Greece and forms the link between the Peloponnisos and Asia Minor through Kásos, Kárpathos, and Rhodes. While it is politically and geographically a part of Greece, its inhabitants have always thought of themselves as being Cretans first and Greeks second.

Crete is dominated by the high mountain backbone which runs throughout its length. Approaching from seaward the peaks of the mountains, snow-capped in the winter and well into the spring, can be seen from a considerable distance off. On the western end of the island the Levka Ori (White Mountains) are a mountain range reaching 2,469m (8,100ft); in the middle of the island the Idhi Ori (Ida) are three conspicuous peaks with the highest peak (Oros Psiloriti or Mt Ida) reaching 2,456m (8,060ft); and at the eastern end the Oros Dhikti (Lasithi Mountains) attain 2,133m (7,000ft).

For the most part the island is rocky and barren except for the plains on the north coast which are cultivated and the high Lasithi Plateau, a fertile bowl in the mountains. On the south coast the land drops away abruptly to the sea except around Ierapetra. The favourable climate enables a wide variety of fruit and vegetables to be grown: olives, grapes, carob beans, bananas, peaches, oranges (said to be the best in Greece), melons, tomatoes (early season tomatoes for Greece are grown at Ierapetra), and a wide variety of other fruits and vegetables. The flora of Crete is varied, with some 140 indigenous species including many varieties of the orchid family.

The history of Crete, both ancient and modern, has often been turbulent. It was inhabited in Neolithic times and again during the Cycladic period, but to most people Crete is known as the centre of the Minoan civilization which ruled over the eastern Mediterranean from 2000–1450 BC (middle and late Minoan). Perhaps one of the more gentle civilizations to exist, it gave us the beautifully decorated pottery which can be seen in the museum at Iraklion and the graceful palaces that Sir Arthur Evans lovingly excavated and recreated. The palace of Knossos is the best known, but the palaces at Phaistos on the south coast and Kato Zakros on the east coast, though there is less to see, are worth visiting for both the superb sites and the peace away from the crowds at Knossos. The Minoan civilization disappeared almost overnight around 1450 BC, probably as a result of the eruption on Thíra when it is thought tidal waves, earthquakes and ash obliterated the palaces, the fleet, and the land.

By about 800 BC the Dorians had established themselves on Crete and in the classical period small city-states were scattered around the island. There was an orderly progression through the Roman occupation into the Byzantine period. Many beautiful frescoes still exist from the Byzantine era in churches on Crete and a Cretan school of fresco painting flourished – so much so that Cretan artists were in demand all over Greece. Towards the end of the Byzantine period the Saracens occupied Crete and remained for over a century. The island was retaken for Byzantium by the Emperor Nikephoros who employed the bizarre device of catapulting the heads of captured prisoners into the stronghold of Iraklion (then Kandak or Kandia), so demoralizing the defenders that they eventually capitulated.

After the Fourth Crusade the island was ruled by the Genoese until the 13th century when it was sold to Venice. The Venetians occupied the island until 1669 and most of the castles and forts still standing date from this era. The harbours on the northern coast were of vital importance in the Venetian trade route from the Peloponnisos to Asia Minor and they fought long and hard to stop the Turks taking Crete. The Turks won through in 1669 and were to hold Crete until 1898. For the Cretans it was a time of much hardship and poverty and there were many insurrections, bloodily put down by the Turks. The spirit and the independence of the Cretans in their battle against the Turks is immortalised in the prose of Nikos Kazantzakis. Crete became a part of Greece in 1913.

The Cretans, battered by the misfortune of history, but never beaten, have today recovered some degree of prosperity through tourism. However much you despise the reinforced concrete dormitories lining the beaches, you cannot at the same time deny the rise in living standards they have brought with them. Crete is a booming tourist island and the yachtsman is lucky enough to be able to explore its more remote parts and so sample something of the island that is denied to most. The Cretan has a certain reserve that can be mistaken for hostility, but once this has been overcome visitors will find they are welcome and will be treated as privileged guests.

Data

PORTS OF ENTRY
Khania
Soúdha
Rethimno
Iraklion
Áyios Nikólaos
Sitia
Kali Limenes

PROHIBITED AREAS
1. Navigation is prohibited in an area extending 500m N, NE and E of Ák Maléka.
2. Navigation and anchorage are prohibited in Órmos Soudhas except for the channel running up the middle of the bay (not marked) and at Limín Soudhas. It is prohibited to enter at night.
3. It is prohibited to anchor in an area extending ¾ mile E and SE of Ák Soúdha.
4. Navigation and anchorage are prohibited in the areas shown around Ák Sidheros.

MAJOR LIGHTS
Nisís Gramvoúsa (NW point) Fl.WR.10s17/13M
Ák Maléka Fl(2)12s10M
Ák Dhrépanon Fl(3)30s20M
Nisís Soúdha Fl.G.4·8s6M
Rethimon Fl.G.3s12M
Ák Khondrós Kávos Fl.WR.6s12/8M
Ák Stavrós Fl(2)14s11M
Iraklíon (N mole head) LFl.G.6s9M
Iraklíon (Pier head) LFl.R.6s9M
Nisís Dhía (N point) LFl.12s9M
Nisís Dhía (Ák Stavrós) Fl.6s12M
Ák Áy Ioánnis Fl(2)12·8s11M
Órmos Áy Nikólaos (Mikrónisos) Fl.3s26m4M
Ák Vamvakiá Fl(3)18s10M

Nisís Paximádha Fl.WR.6s12/8M
Ák Sidheros Fl.10s23M
Nisídhes Kaválloi Fl(3)12s6M
Koufonísi Fl(2)16s10M
Gaïdhouronísi Fl(2)12s10M
Ák Theófilos Fl(2)12s10M
Megalonísi Fl(3)24s11M
Ák Lítinos Fl.6s12M
Gavdhopoúla (NW point) Fl.8s12M
Nísos Gávdhos (S point) Fl(2)16s12M
Nisís Loutró LFl.10s6M
Nisís Skhistó Fl.8s8M
Nisís Elafónisos Fl(3)24s12M

Weather patterns in Crete

In the summer the prevailing wind is the *meltemi* blowing from the NW–WNW. In common with the rest of the Aegean it blows strongest in July and August. It does not usually blow more than Force 5–6 off the northern coast and is more often Force 3–4. In the spring and autumn the wind is predominantly from the S, about Force 2–4.

The southern coast is notorious for the squalls that blow off the high mountains with the prevailing summer winds. The Admiralty Pilot tersely warns that: 'Strong squalls blow down from the mountains during northerly winds. These squalls often begin suddenly, and they may be violent close inshore.'

Iraklion/Knossos		
Frequency	Weather forecast	Nav warnings
VHF Ch 83		
(announce Ch 16)	0600, 1000, 1600, 2200 UTC	0500, 1100, 1730, 2330 UTC

Sítia		
Frequency	Weather forecast	Nav warnings
VHF Ch 85		
(announce Ch 16)	0600, 1000, 1600, 2200 UTC	0500, 1100, 1730, 2330 UTC

Moistakos		
Frequency	Weather forecast	Nav warnings
VHF Ch 04		
(announce Ch 16)	0600, 1000, 1600, 2200 UTC	0500, 1100, 1730, 2330 UTC

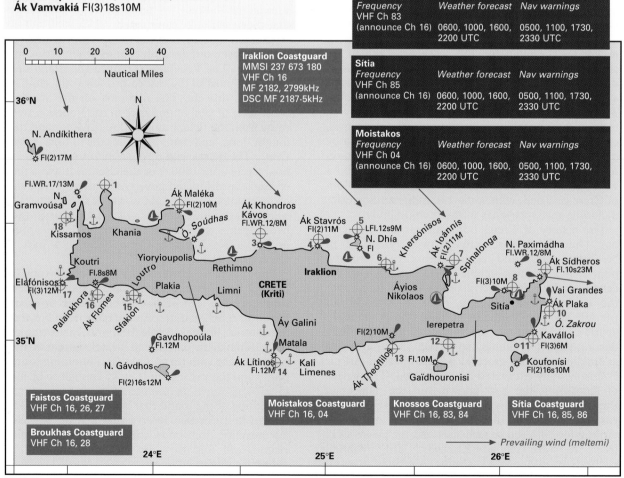

CRETE

USEFUL WAYPOINTS

⊕**1** 1M N of Ák Spáthi
35°42'·8N 23°44'·0E

⊕**2** 1M N of Ák Maléka
35°36'·21N 24°10'·50E WGS84

⊕**3** 0·25M N of Ák Khondros Kàvos
35°25'·94N 24°42'·01E WGS84

⊕**4** 0·5M N of Ák Stavrós
35°26'·49N 24°58'·36E WGS84

⊕**5** 1M N of Ák Marmara (N. Dhía)
35°29'·0N 25°13'·0E

⊕**6** 1M N of Ák Khersónisos
35°21'·40N 25°23'·40E WGS84

⊕**7** 0·5M N of Ák Áy Ioánnis
35°21'·02N 25°46'·36E WGS84

⊕**8** 0·5M N of Ák Vamvakia
35°13'·95N 26°06'·98E WGS84

⊕**9** 1M N of Ák Sidhero
35°20'·02N 26°18'·73E WGS84

⊕**10** 1M E of Ak Plaka
35°11'·9N 26°20'·2E

⊕**11** 1M S of Nisís Kaválloi
35°00'·7N 26°13'·7E

⊕**12** 1M S of Ák Iereptra
34°59'·3N 25°44'·3E

⊕**13** 1M S of Ák Theofilos
34°58'·0N 25°30'·3E

⊕**14** 1M S of Ák Lítinos
34°54'·4N 24°44'·0E

⊕**15** 1M S of Ák Mouros
35°10'·6N 24°04'·6E

⊕**16** 1M S of Nisís Skhistó
35°12'·3N 23°40'·3E

⊕**17** 1¼M W of Nisís Elafónisos
35°16'·2N 23°30'·0E

⊕**18** 1M E of Pondikonisi
35°35'·2N 23°30'·0E

In the summer months Crete is very hot: the average temperatures often get to 35°–36°C in July and August and can reach 40° at times. In the winter the mountains are covered in snow down to the lower slopes, but the coastal plains have a mild winter climate and the coastal towns are agreeable places to winter afloat.

Routes

Routes in the summer are fairly straightforward. Along the northern coast you can proceed quietly along from W to E with the prevailing wind, or with a little more effort proceed from E to W. Although the *meltemi* tends to come from a westerly direction, there are usually enough days when the wind is light or there is a morning calm to make reasonable progress from E to W.

On the S coast the ferocity of the gusts off the mountains mean that it can be difficult whichever way you go. The wind also tends to blow around either end of Crete so you will have a bit of a bash getting out from either end.

In the winter, southerlies set large seas onto the S coast and the preferred route has to be along the N coast.

Quick reference guide

	Shelter	Mooring	Fuel	Water	Provisioning	Tavernas	Plan
North Coast							
Kissamos	B	ABC	O	B	O	C	•
Khania	A	A	B	A	A	A	•
Soúdha	A	BC	B	B	B	B	•
Ormos Milati	B	C	O	O	C	C	
Yioryioupolis	B	BC	B	B	B	B	
Rethimno	B	A	B	A	A	A	•
Pánormos	B	A	O	B	C	C	•
Órmos Balí	B	C	O	O	O	C	
Palaiokastro	B	AB	B	B	O	O	•
Iraklion	A	AB	B	A	A	A	•
Khersónisos	B	AC	B	B	B	A	•
Sissi	A	AB	O	B	C	C	•
Milatos	B	AB	B	B	C	C	•
Spinalonga	A	C	B	B	B	B	
Áy Nikólaos Marina	A	A	B	A	A	A	•
Pahia Ammos	C	A	O	B	B	B	
Sitía	B	A	B	A	A	A	•
Ák Sidheros	B	C	O	O	O	O	•
South Coast							
Nisís Gramvoúsa	B	C	O	B	O	O	•
Koutris	O	C	O	O	O	O	
Palaiokhora	B	ABC	B	B	B	B	•
Loutró	B	C	O	B	C	C	•
Sfakion	OA	C	B	B	B	B	•
Plákia	O	C	B	B	B	B	
Limni	O	C	O	O	O	O	
Áy Galini	B	A	B	A	B	B	•
Pirgos	B	AB	B	A	C	C	•
Matala	C	C	B	B	B	B	
Kali Limenes	B	C	B	B	C	C	•
Ierepetra	B	AB	B	A	B	B	•
Órmos Zakros	C	C	O	O	O	C	
Órmos Grandes	C	C	O	O	C	C	
Órmos Kouremenos	B	ABC	B	B	C	C	•
Vai	B	C	O	O	C	C	

Northern coast of Crete

KISSAMOS (Kavonisi, Kastelli)

Approach

The harbour lies in the SW corner of Kólpos Kissamos to the E of a rocky spur. The town of Kastelli and the harbour mole are easily identified.

By night The entrance is lit: Fl.G.2s3M/Fl.R.2s3M.

Note If there is a blow from the N you can get stuck in here for a while. The bay is around 14 miles deep before you can get out to turn the corner.

Dangers Care is needed of the shoal water extending NNE from the headland the harbour is built under. There is 4m shoal patch approximately 600m N of the headland and a 2m shoal patch approximately 400m N of the headland.

Mooring

Berth alongside or anchor off inside the mole.

Shelter Good shelter from the W and NW although there is often some surge inside. Open to the E and SE.

Authorities Port police.

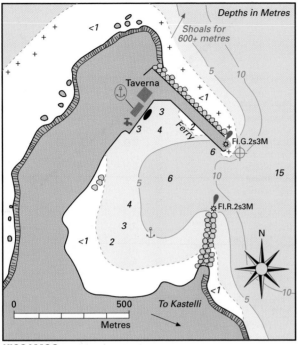

KISSAMOS
⊕35°31'·0N 23°38'·4E

Facilities

Water standpipe. A taverna/café and a telephone at the harbour. Bus to Kastelli. In Kastelli fuel and provisions can be obtained.

General

Kissamos is the harbour for Kastelli town about one mile to the E. The harbour is used by a few fishing boats and coasters and the ferry.

KHANIA (Khania, Hania)

BA 1707
Imray-Tetra G37
35°31'·35N 24°01'·09E WGS84

Approach

Conspicuous The town is visible from some distance off. Closer in a white mosque on the waterfront, the lighthouse on the E side of the entrance, and a number of chimneys in the town are conspicuous.

By night Use the light on the E side of the entrance Fl.R.2·5s7M and the lights on either side of the entrance to the inner harbour: F.G.3M/F.R.3M. The E end of the detached breakwater is lit Fl.G.4s5M, but should not be relied upon as it is not always in place.

Dangers The approach is difficult with strong onshore winds. A dangerous sea heaps up on the shoal water at the entrance and care is needed in the immediate approaches. The new detached breakwater improves matters, but it is still difficult with onshore winds.

Note The new detached breakwater has subsided somewhat and is now only 1m above water.

Mooring

The E basin marina is mostly full of local yachts and it is unlikely you will find a berth here. Visiting yachts usually go stern-to immediately inside the inner harbour on the S quay. Laid moorings at most berths.

Shelter Good all-round shelter, although strong northerlies cause a surge in the harbour and spray comes over the outer mole. A number of yachts have wintered afloat here, but in bad northerly gales

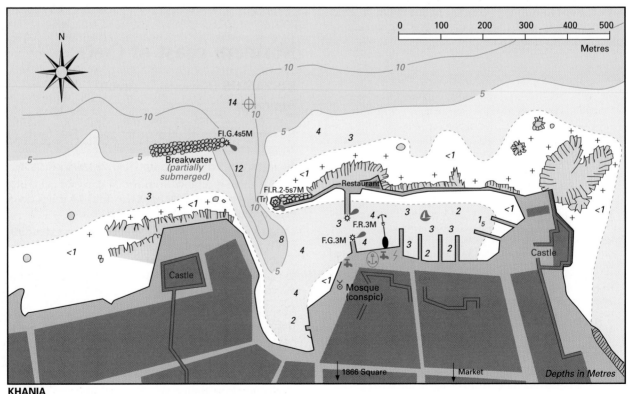

KHANIA
⊕35°31'·35N 24°01'·09E WGS84

Khania yacht quay looking E   *Lu Michell*

additional lines are needed.

Authorities Port of entry: port police, customs, and immigration. Harbourmaster. Charge band 2.

Facilities

Services Water and electricity at or near every berth. WC and shower block.

Fuel In the town. A mini-tanker can deliver to the quay.

Repairs Mechanical repairs. Some light engineering work. Good hardware and tool shops. Chandlers at Skrydlof 26 near 1866 Square.

Provisions Excellent shopping for all provisions. Ice available.

Eating out Good tavernas near the waterfront and in the town.

Other PO. OTE. Banks. ATMs. Greek gas and Camping Gaz in 1866 Square. Hire cars, motorbikes and bicycles. Buses to Iraklion. Ferries from Soúdha. Internal flights to Athens.

General

Khania was for centuries the capital of Crete and was only recently demoted in favour of Iraklion. The Venetian city around the harbour is a fascinating place – cobbled streets, imposing Venetian houses, mosques and minarets, and the market. The lighthouse on the mole is of Venetian-Turkish origin. None of this has been tarted up and turned into a toy town – the city exists with modern additions and crumbling edges and a bustling, busy life to it. In recent years it has become popular with tourists, but the harbour provides a sanctuary from the hurly-burly if you need it.

Everyone who has wintered here has recommended it, even though the harbour can be uncomfortable at times. The town has a buzz to it that is there even when the tourists have departed and, unlike many other tourist spots, doesn't die in the winter.

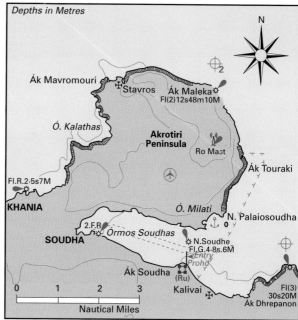

AKROTIRI PENINSULA

⊕ 0·5M N of Ak Dhrepanon 35°29'·03N 24°14'·46E

⊕2 1M N of Ák Maleka 35°36'·21N 24°10'·50E WGS84

ÓRMOS SOÚDHAS

BA 1706
Imray-Tetra G37

Approach

Conspicuous The high plateau of Akrotíri peninsula is easily recognised from the distance. Atop the peninsula are a number of high towers with military scanners. Nisís Soúdhas, with a fort and naval buildings, is conspicuous. The narrow entrance to the channel free for navigation is marked by two light buoys (Fl.R/Fl.G) which are difficult to pick out. On either side of the light buoys and extending to the shore are large black mooring buoys holding the anti-submarine net. The channel free for navigation which runs down the middle of the bay is unmarked. A large flour mill near the harbour is conspicuous. Proceed to the harbour taking care to avoid the restricted area around the naval dockyard.

Soudha fishing harbour and yacht pier looking S into Soudha Bay   *Lu Michell*

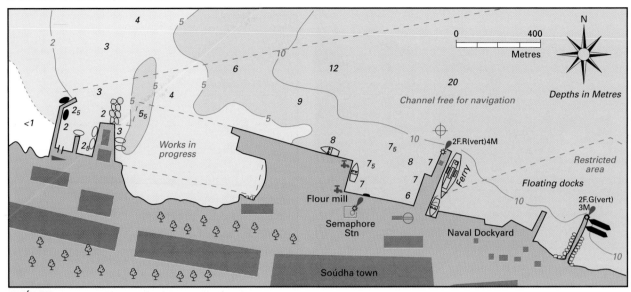

SOÚDHA
⊕35°29'·5N 24°04'·7E

By night It is prohibited to enter Órmos Soúdhas at night.

Caution Órmos Soúdhas is the NATO southern base and care must be taken to avoid the prohibited area to the N and E of the Akrotíri peninsula (extending out approximately 0·75 to 1 mile from the coast) and the prohibited area N and S of the channel free for navigation in Órmos Soúdhas (the channel runs 283° true from the buoys at the entrance and is 0·2 mile wide). In practice I am not sure there are anti-submarine nets across the entrance any more, but it would be silly to exclude the possibility.

Mooring

Go alongside on the end of the mole in the fishing harbour. Care needed of works in progress in the immediate approaches.

Shelter Good shelter – so much so that the wind in Órmos Soúdhas is generally no indication of conditions outside.

Authorities Port police, customs.

Facilities
Water On the quay.
Fuel In the town. A fuel tanker can be arranged.
Provisions Good shopping for provisions. Ice available.
Eating out Tavernas ashore.
Other PO. OTE. Bank. ATM. Greek gas. Ferry to Piraeus – this is the ferry port for Khania. Regular bus service (every ten minutes) to Khania.

⊕3 0·25M N of Ák Khondros Kàvos
    35°25'·94N 24°42'·01E WGS84
⊕4 0·5M N of Ák Stavrós
    35°26'·49N 24°58'·36E WGS84
⊕5 1M N of Ák Marmara (N. Dhía)
    35°29'·0N 25°13'·0E
⊕6 1M N of Ák Khersónisos
    35°21'·40N 25°23'·40E WGS84
⊕7 0·5M N of Ák Áy Ioánnis
    35°21'·02N 25°46'·36E WGS84

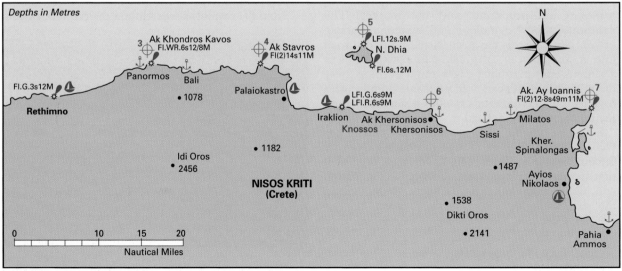

RETHIMNO TO AY NIKOLAOS

General

Soúdha is a naval base so it does not have any of the trappings of a tourist resort. For many this is a blessing and the simple homespun pleasures of Soúdha are a relief from the touts outside tavernas in some of the large Cretan resorts. Khania is nearby if you need an injection of pace into your life.

ORMOS MILATI

35°30'·19N 24°10'·31E WGS84

This bay on the SE corner of the Akrotiri peninsular appears to lie within the prohibited zone, but during the summer the beach is crowded and the bay is busy with small local craft.

A breakwater around the beach is packed with small local boats. Anchor off the beach on hard sand and rock or off the islet (Nisis Palaiosoudha) in settled weather. Holding is poor and generally better off the beach. The small quay on the outside of the breakwater looks tempting but is open to considerable wash from ferries passing to and from Soúdha. Tavernas and bars ashore.

YIORYIOUPOLIS (Georgioupolis)

BA 1707

Imray-Tetra G37

A small harbour at the mouth of the Almiros river in the SW corner of Órmos Almirou. From seaward the church on the small island connected by a causeway to the land and a hotel on the beach are conspicuous. Care must be taken in the approach because of the shoal water and underwater rocks in the bay. The approach has depths of 1·5–2·5m, but it would be wise to reconnoitre in the dinghy before entering. Moor alongside. Good shelter except from strong N–NE winds.

Water in the town. Most provisions can be obtained and there are several tavernas in the village. Buses to Khania and Iraklion. An attractive friendly little place well worth visiting.

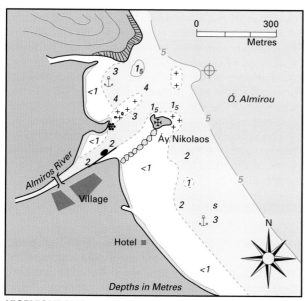

YIORYIOUPOLIS
⊕35°22'·1N 24°16'·0E

RETHIMNO (Rethymno)

BA 1707

Imray-Tetra G37

Approach

Conspicuous From the W the fort on the headland and the buildings of the town are conspicuous. From the E a white church on a hill to the E of the town and two minarets in the town stand out clearly. Closer in the breakwater is easily identified.

By night Use the lights at the entrance: Fl.G.3s12M/Fl.R.4s6M. The mole sheltering the inner harbour is lit on the extremity: F.G.3M.

Dangers There is often a rolling swell at the entrance.

Note The development of the E quay into a marina continues steadily. The S and E quays have been completed and the concrete slabs for the pontoons are stacked along the S quay. Service boxes have been installed but are not all connected. The basin has been dredged and the S quay is full of small local boats. Laid moorings are reported to be ready to put in.

Mooring

At present nobody seems to be in charge of mooring, and yachts go stern or bows-to where convenient clear of fishing boat berths. Alternatively you may find a berth in the old Venetian harbour, tucked in amongst *caïques*, pirate ships and parascending speedboats. Space is very tight inside the harbour so it is best to enquire first before entering.

Data c.250 berths (planned). Visitors' berths. Max LOA c.17m. Depths 2·5–4m.

Shelter Good all-round shelter. Excellent shelter in the Venetian harbour.

Authorities Port police and customs in the Venetian harbour.

Facilities

Services Water on the quay. Water and electricity at all marina berths when completed.
Fuel Can be delivered by tanker.
Repairs Some mechanical repairs. Hardware shops.
Provisions Good shopping for all provisions. Ice available.
Eating out Excellent tavernas including several good fish restaurants around the Venetian harbour.
Other PO. OTE. Banks. ATMs. Greek gas and Camping Gaz. Hire cars, motorbikes and bicycles. Buses to Khania and Iraklion.

General

The basic marina infrastructure provides good shelter for yachts in Rethimno. Unfortunately, though, the huge unrestricted expanse of concrete along the E breakwater is used as a car and motorbike drag strip by the local youths, often running late into the night.

The old Venetian town and harbour is one of the most attractive spots on Crete. The town also shows signs of the Turkish occupation with wooden

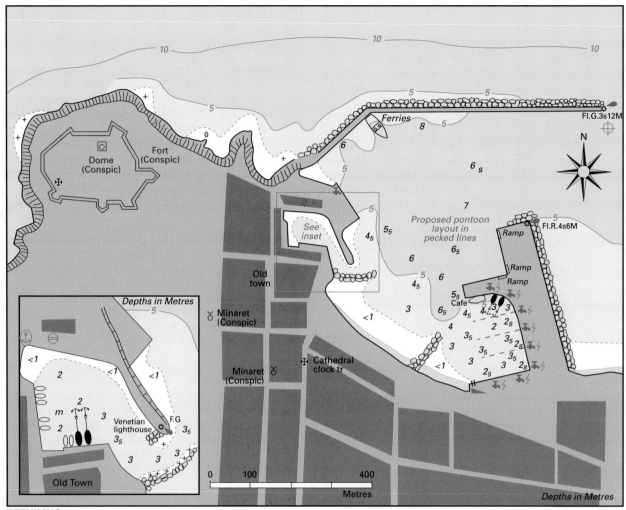

RETHIMNO
⊕35°22'·39N 24°29'·22E WGS84

Rethimno 'Marina' looking N   *Lu Michell*

balconies on some of the houses and two well-preserved minarets. In the last week of July the Cretan wine festival is held here.

AK LIANOS KAVOS

35°25'·38N 24°39'·02E WGS84

The huge hotel complex on the cape is conspicuous from some distance. A new watersports harbour has been built in association with the hotel, but is not really suitable even for small yachts.

PÁNORMOS

35°25'·3N 24°41'·6E

A small harbour approximately 2M E of Ák Lianos Kávos. From the W the light structure on Ák Khondros Kavos is small but easily identified. The buildings of the town and a huge hotel complex lie immediately E. The entrance is lit Fl.G.3s3M/Fl.R.3s3M. Go stern or bows-to or alongside the outer end of the mole. Reasonable shelter although the harbour is open to N–NE and would likely be uncomfortable and probably untenable with strong winds from this direction.

Water ashore. Some provisions and tavernas.

The village around the harbour has some tourism, but remains a sympathetic little place compared to some of the mass tourism running along other parts of this coast.

ÓRMOS BALI

35°24'·81N 24°47'·08E WGS84

A large bay approximately 16 miles E of Rethimon. Care is needed of the rocks extending out from the W entrance to the bay. Anchor in 4–8 metres tucked as far into the W side of the bay as practical. There is good shelter here in settled conditions from the prevailing W–NW wind although some swell rolls

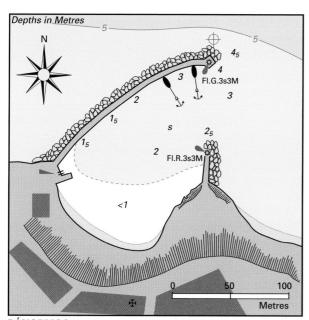

PÁNORMOS
⊕35°25'·21N 24°41'·54E WGS84

Órmos Bali looking WNW into the bay. You can see the small harbour on the W side   *Lu Michell*

around into the bay. The bay and the small harbour are dangerous in strong NE winds. The bottom is sand and weed, good holding.

In a cove on the W side a mole provides good shelter and you may be able to find a berth stern-to tucked under the end. The end of the mole is lit Fl.G.3s3M. There are 3–5 metres along most of the outer part of the mole, but the little harbour is cluttered with permanent moorings and local boats, so don't rely on finding a berth here. The inner part of the harbour is shallow. Coastguard ashore. Some provisions and tavernas and bars around the harbour.

The bay is all turquoise and green water over sand and is a handy stop along the coast. The hamlet of Bali is a pleasant place with a bit of upmarket tourism and a convivial spot for a run ashore.

PALAIOKASTRO

A new harbour has been constructed close N of the oil terminal W of Iraklion.

Approach

The jetties extending out for 200m from the oil terminal are conspicuous, as are the tankers moored close by. From the N the ruins of the Venetian castle which lends its name to the village will be seen. Closer in the breakwaters are easy to identify.

By night The entrance to the N basin is lit Fl.R/Fl.G and the entrance to the S basin is also lit. The jetties off the oil terminal are lit 2F.R.3M and 3F.R.3M.

Mooring

The S harbour is mostly shallow and yachts should head for the N entrance into the larger basin.

Most berths are occupied by small local craft, with very little room for yachts. The inside of the breakwater is used by fishing boats, mostly alongside, where it may be possible to squeeze in or to go alongside a fishing boat. Alternatively go stern or bows-to on one of the jetties. Care is needed of underwater concrete blocks which reduce depths in places, particularly off the end of the two piers and in places along the quay.

Facilities

No facilities at the harbour.

Knossos

Situated a short distance outside Iraklion (about a 2½ mile walk, or buses leave regularly from the town centre) are the remains of Knossos. In common with other well-known archaeological sites in Greece, Knossos is crowded in the summer and the bustling noisy tour parties detract somewhat from the architectural merits of the place. Nonetheless it is well worth a visit and in the early morning or late afternoon when most of the tourists have left, something of the atmosphere of Knossos can be felt.

Knossos was not the only Minoan palace in Crete, but it is considered to be the archetype of such palaces and reconstruction by Sir Arthur Evans makes it easier for the layman to visualize what Minoan architecture was like compared to, say, Phaistos or Zakros. The existing palace, lovingly excavated by Sir Arthur Evans from 1900 and later by the British School in Athens, was built around 1700BC. The heart of Knossos was the central court where business was conducted and the locals idled away the day discussing matters great and small. Around the central court were placed the archives, the storerooms, devotional areas and some living quarters – forming a whole unit that was light and airy and architecturally pleasing. The palace was not only a pleasant place to live in, but also boasted amenities such as running water and a proper drainage system. Some criticism has been levelled at Sir Arthur Evans' reconstruction of Knossos, but without his work there would be little for the layman to see.

The eruption of Thíra probably destroyed Knossos and the other Minoan palaces in Crete, indeed it effectively destroyed the Minoan civilization, and reduced to rubble a structure that outstripped much of the nearby contemporary architecture.

Palaiokastro looking S over the harbour towards Iraklion

Lu Michell

IRAKLION (Herakleion, Candia)

BA 1707

Imray-Tetra G38

Approach

Conspicuous From the NW the town and the long N mole (over a mile long) are easily distinguished. The fort at the entrance to the inner harbour and the ferries in the outer harbour are conspicuous. From the E a large brown building at the airport to the E of the city and the white oil storage tanks in the SE corner of the harbour are also conspicuous. The gantries of cranes in the harbour are also conspicuous.

By night Use the lights at the entrance LFl.G.6s9M/ LFl.R.6s9M and at the entrance to the inner harbour F.G.2M/F.R.2M. The commercial pier is lit Fl.R.1·5s3M. There is also a light at the airport to the E of the harbour: Aero Al.WG.4s15M.

Dangers

1. With the *meltemi* there can be a confused swell at the entrance, but inside it is quiet.

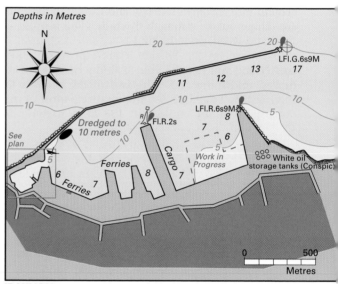

IRAKLION
⊕35°21′·0N 25°09′·2E

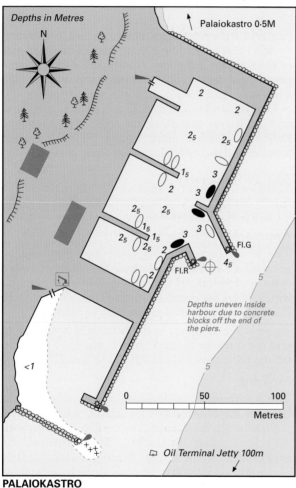

PALAIOKASTRO
⊕35°21′·27N 25°02′·61E WGS84

Iraklion. The inner old Venetian harbour looking E

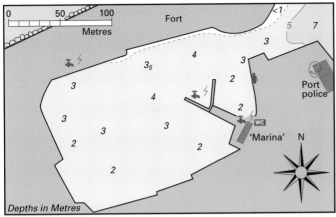

VENETIAN INNER HARBOUR, IRAKLION

2. Care is needed of the numerous ferries coming and going from the harbour.

Mooring

Proceed to the inner Venetian harbour and berth stern or bows-to at the so-called marina on the E or on the quay on the N where there are sufficient depths. Two pontoons have been installed off the 'marina'. Good holding in mud. The inner harbour is often full and it can be difficult to find a place to berth. The outer harbour has high quays, few mooring bollards, and poor shelter. In NW winds yachts can find reasonable shelter just outside the Venetian harbour E of the wreck. It is difficult to get ashore on the high quay and it is easier to take the dinghy into the Venetian harbour.

Shelter Excellent shelter in the inner harbour although there is an uncomfortable surge with strong NE winds. The occasional boat winters here.

Authorities A port of entry: port police, customs and immigration.

Facilities

Services Water and electricity on the quay.
Fuel On the quay at the entrance to the inner basin.
Repairs Some mechanical repairs. Light engineering work possible. Small yachts can be hauled out in the 'marina'. Large *caïques* are hauled out at the slip in the SE corner of the harbour. Hardware shops.
Provisions Excellent shopping for provisions. Ice available. Fish is often for sale on the SW corner of the inner harbour.
Eating out Excellent tavernas including several good fish tavernas. Some good tavernas around the market in the centre of town.
Other PO. OTE. Banks. ATMs. Greek gas and Camping Gaz. There is a factory to the W of the city where gas bottles can be filled. Launderette nearby. Hire cars, motorbikes and bicycles. Buses to most parts of the island. Daily ferry service to Piraeus; less regularly to Rhodes. European and internal flights.

General

Iraklion is the fifth largest city in Greece and appears to be a city composed almost entirely of travel agents and car-hire agencies:

'On the first day, one knows beyond contradiction that Iraklion is one of the least pleasant cities of the Mediterranean and nothing to do with that splendid imagined Crete of mountains and mountaineers, ancient palaces and tiny churches rich in paintings.'

Hopkins *Crete: Its past and people*

Adam Hopkins goes on to say that for some people . . .'It becomes possible to like Iraklion . . .only people born there actually love it' (*ibid*), but for yachtsmen there is little attractive to find about the city in the short time they are likely to be there. The attraction lies outside the city at Knossos and later in the museum at Iraklion, where you can mull over the Minoan world that was.

NISÍS DHÍA (Standia)

⊕5 1M N of Ák Marmara (N. Dhía) 35°29'·0N 25°13'·0E

A barren rocky island lying 6 miles NNE of Iraklion. On the S coast Órmos Mesarios offers some shelter from northerly winds.

GOUVES MARINA

35°20'·2N 25°17'·8E

Along the coast between Iraklion and Khersónisos a small harbour has been built in association with a hotel complex. No details are available yet but it is unlikely to be suitable for visiting yachts.

KHERSÓNISOS (Limín Khersonisou)

Imray-Tetra G38

Approach

Conspicuous From the W a white church and a mill on Ák Khersónisos are conspicuous. Rounding the cape the headland behind which the harbour lies and a number of large white hotels to the E of the harbour are conspicuous.

By night The end of the mole is lit Fl.G.2s5M but a night approach would be dangerous given the numerous underwater rocks and shoals in the

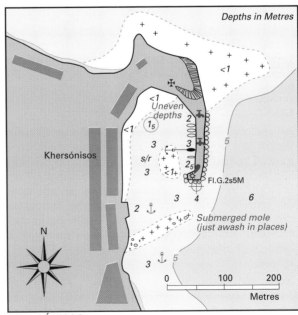

KHERSÓNISOS
⊕35°19'·3N 25°23'·6E

485

approach and in the harbour.

Dangers
1. There are numerous reefs fringing the coast and harbour. Care should be taken of the reef off Ák Khersónisos, the reef around the square rock between the cape and the harbour, and the reef that projects N and E of the headland and the harbour.
2. On entering the harbour, care must be taken to avoid the submerged mole which has only a few rocks just above water, and to avoid the shoal patch immediately W of the head of the built-up mole (see plan).

Mooring

Go bows-to the built-up mole or anchor off. Care must be taken in the harbour where the depths are uneven – reconnoitre first in a dinghy. The bottom is sand and rock, poor holding.

Note The harbour is reported to be so crowded with local boats that it is difficult to find a berth.

Shelter Good shelter from the *meltemi* and open only to the SE.

Anchorage It is possible to anchor off in the bay immediately S of Ák Khersónisos, although there is usually some swell in here.

Facilities

Water In the town, though care is needed as it is not all potable. Enquire first.
Fuel In the town.
Provisions Good shopping for provisions in the town.
Eating out A wide choice of tavernas of all types.
Other PO. OTE. Bank. ATMs. Hire cars, motorbikes and bicycles.

General

Khersónisos is built on the ancient town of Chersonesos, though there is little left to see amid the concrete wilderness that has engulfed the site and spread out all along the coast. The resort has become something of a by-word for the sort of tasteless development akin to that in Benidorm where those who come on holiday are looking only for the proverbial sun, sand and sex. If you can find your way through the British thronging the streets there is a Venetian mosaic fountain in one of the hotels.

SISSI

An enclosed harbour on the mouth of a small river. Works are in progress extending the protective mole. The entrance looks liable to silting and depths are likely to change. Reconnoitre in a dinghy first. With the prevailing onshore wind seas can pile up at the entrance and entry should not be attempted except in calm weather. The small basin has excellent shelter among the *caïques* but care is needed of moorings and floating lines. Tavernas ashore.

Note 1M E of Sissi the Kalimera Kriti Hotel complex has a short breakwater protecting the beach, and should not be confused with Sissi harbour entrance.

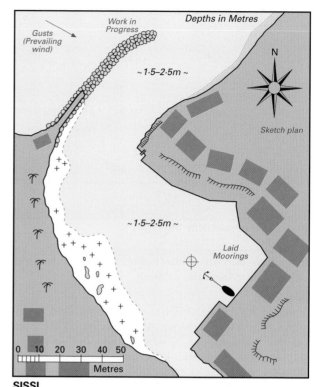

SISSI
⊕35°18′·48N 25°31′·17E WGS84

MILATOS

A small harbour approximately 2M E of Sissi. The entrance is lit Fl.G.3s3M/Fl.R.3s3M. In the immediate approaches and in the entrance depths are uneven with some large boulders scattered around the seabed. With the prevailing wind waves pile up at the entrance making the final approach tricky and possibly dangerous in all but the morning calm. Go stern or bows-to or alongside off the outer end of the mole. The bottom is sand and rock. Good shelter although there is a surge with the prevailing wind. With strong onshore winds it may become untenable in here.

Water on the quay. Some provisions and tavernas ashore.

Milatos is not a bad place for a visit to the Minoan

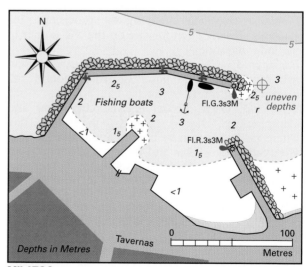

MILATOS
⊕35°19′·22N 25°33′·75E WGS84

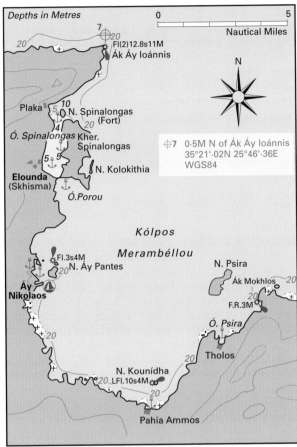

KÓLPOS MERAMBÉLLOU

Palace at Malia. The palace has not been reconstructed as at Knossos, but there is enough of the ground-plan intact to make it interesting and it has the advantage of being less crowded than Knossos. Also near Milatos is a cave that was used by Cretans to shelter from the Turks in 1823. In the end they were starved out and taken into slavery or slaughtered.

SPINALONGA LAGOON

37°17'·85N 25°44'·3E

Approach

Conspicuous From the W and E Nisís Spinalongas with a Venetian fort on top is conspicuous.

Entrance There are 3–4m depths over the sand bar between Nisís Spinalongas and the W shore of Crete. In the lagoon the depths vary between 3–6m.

Dangers There are usually strong gusts off the high land between Ák Áyios Ioánnis and Nisís Spinalongas with the *meltemi*. Once in the lagoon the gusts are less hard and not so frequent.

Mooring

Anchor where convenient in the lagoon. A reasonable lee can be found under Nisís Spinalongas. There is some shelter with few gusts at Skhisma. Here there is a short pier with 1·5–2·5m depths off it, though it is invariably crowded with tripper boats.

Facilities

At Skhisma: Most provisions can be obtained.

Excellent tavernas including several good fish tavernas. PO. OTE. Hire cars, motorbikes and bicycles.

General

It is fascinating to sail in the enclosed lagoon watching the sea bottom slip past a few metres under the keel. At one time the flat waters of the lagoon were a seaplane base.

Do not miss Nisís Spinalongas. Beneath the Venetian fort which is a small deserted settlement which was once a leper colony. The settlement and the fort surrounded by the shallow waters of the lagoon are most picturesque. Nisís Spinalongas makes a good lunch-stop before going on to Áyios Nikólaos.

ÁYIOS NIKÓLAOS (Limín Ayíou Nikoláou)

BA 1707

Imray-Tetra G38

Approach

Conspicuous From the N and E, Nisís Áy Pantes with a white church on its summit is conspicuous. The buildings of the town including many large hotels along the foreshore are also conspicuous. Yachts should head for the yacht marina on the S side of the town and not for the main harbour.

By night Use the light on Nisís Mikrónisos Fl.3s4M and the light on the extremity of the mole Fl.R.2s7M. The entrance to the marina is lit Fl.G.3s3M/Fl.R.3s3M. The protective moles along the beach are lit Fl.Or on each end.

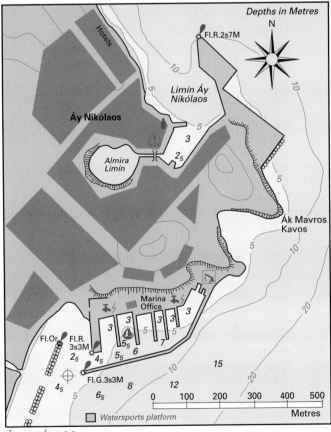

ÁY NIKÓLAOS
⊕35°11'·10N 25°42'·99E WGS84

Áy Nikólaos Marina looking SW to the entrance   *Lu Michell*

VHF Ch 12 for Áyios Nikólaos Marina.

Note Depths at the entrance to the marina are subject to silting. There are usually 4·5m least depths, but if you have any doubts call up the marina who will assist entry or buoy the deepwater channel for deep draught yachts.

Mooring

Data 250 berths. Visitors berths. Max LOA c.25m. Depths 3–6m. Depths in entrance 4·5m.

Berth Where directed. Laid moorings tailed to a buoy and to the quay.

Shelter Good all-round shelter. Yachts are left afloat through the winter and in fact it is claimed that winds in winter are more benign than in summer.

Authorities Port police and customs in the old harbour. Marina staff. Charge band 2.

Ay Nikolaos Marina, 72100 Ay Nikolaos, Crete
☎ 28410 82384 *Fax* 28410 82386
Email oanak@agn.forthnet.gr or depaman@otenet.gr
www.forthnet.gr/internetcity/yachting/marina

Facilities

Services Water and electricity at or near every berth. WC and shower cubicles.

Fuel Can be delivered by mini-tanker to the marina. A travel-hoist is to be installed. 50-berth hardstanding area.

Repairs Minor mechanical repairs. Hardware shops.

Provisions Good shopping nearby for provisions. Ice available.

Eating out Numerous tavernas nearby.

Other PO. OTE. Banks. ATMs. Greek gas and Camping Gaz. Hire cars, motorbikes and bicycles. Buses to Iraklion and Sitía.

General

Áyios Nikólaos may once have been a small fishing village – now it is a booming tourist resort festooned with large hotels. Some people like the place, but personally I find the heart and soul of the town have been sold off to the tour operators. In the old town itself there are some convivial spots, especially around the inner lake (Almira Limin) and it pays to stick around here rather than stray into the package

holiday zones. The lake is said to be bottomless (though it is apparently 67 metres deep) and is an old volcanic crater.

In the marina you are at least some distance away from the din of thousands of holiday-makers who are concentrated on the W side of Áy Nikólaos. A number of yachts have wintered here and rightly recommend the place.

PAHIA AMMOS (Pakhias Ammou)

35°06'·76N 25°48'·23E WGS84
BA 1707
Imray-Tetra G38

A small harbour in the SW corner of Kólpos Merambellou. Care must be taken of the reefs around the two small islets 100m and 400m NNW of the harbour. Approach from the NE. There are 2–3m depths at the extremity of the mole, though silting appears to be taking place so go slowly. Sometimes a small coaster is moored stern-to the extremity of the mole and a warp is taken right across to the pier on the opposite side of the harbour effectively stopping any yacht entering. With the normal NW wind a swell works its way around the mole making the harbour uncomfortable. Open to the NE–E.

Some provisions can be obtained and there are several tavernas and cafés in the small village ashore.

SITÍA

BA 1707
Imray-Tetra G38

Approach

Conspicuous From the W the white light structure on Ák Vamvakiá is conspicuous. The buildings of Sitía and the outer (N) mole are conspicuous once the cape has been rounded. From the E the buildings of the town and the fort on the hill are conspicuous.

By night Use the light on Ák Vamvakiá Fl(3)18s10M, the light on the N mole Fl.G.2s5M and the lights at the entrance F.G.3M/F.R.3M.

Mooring

Go stern or bows-to the S mole. Yacht berths are marked between lines painted on the quay wall. The bottom is sand and weed with some rock and care is needed of numerous small craft moorings and floating lines.

Shelter With the *meltemi* there is a gentle surge of no consequence in the harbour. Open to the NE.

Authorities Port police and customs.

Facilities

Services Water and electricity on the quay.

Fuel In the town. Delivery by mini-tanker may be arranged.

Repairs Limited mechanical repairs. Hardware shops.

Provisions Good shopping for provisions. Ice available.

Eating out Good tavernas including several fish restaurants, some in wonderful locations at the edge of the harbour.

Sitía looking NE over the old harbour to the ferry mole
Lu Michell

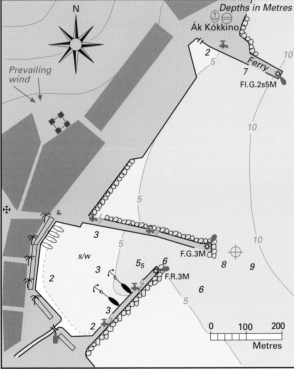

SITÍA
⊕35°12'·46N 26°06'·70E WGS84

Other PO. OTE. Bank. ATMs. Greek gas and Camping Gaz. Hire cars, motorbikes and bicycles. Buses to Áyios Nikólaos, Iraklion and Ierapetra.

General

Approaching from the sea, Sitía appears as a huddle of houses and some pretty awful apartment blocks on a bare rocky hillside. Once in the inner harbour the tree-lined esplanade fronting the harbour comes as an unexpected surprise. Here you can sit in a friendly taverna over a good meal and watch dusk fall over the bay. Further inland is a green fertile plain mainly planted with vines. Sitía was formerly called La Sitía from whence the name of the province – Lasithi.

ÁK SIDHEROS

Approach

The lighthouse on the cape is easily identified. Approach the cape with caution because of the above and below-water rocks fringing it. A night approach would be dangerous because of these rocks and reefs.

Dangers
1. ***Ifalos Spitfaiar*** (*Spitfire*) A detached reef lying 3 miles W of Ák Sídheros. It is difficult to see with any swell running.
2. ***Vrákhoi Pinakl* (*Pinnacle*)** above and below-water rocks lying close off the coast just over a mile W of Ák Sídheros. The above-water rocks are easily identified.
3. ***Nisís Sidhero*** The islet half a mile W of Ák Sídheros. Approximately 200m N of the islet there is an isolated reef, Vk Sídheros.
4. ***Skopeloi Sídheros*** The above and below-water rocks NNE of Ák Sidheros. The above-water rocks are easily identified.
5. ***Vrákhoi Navayion*** A reef just awash SE of Ák Sídheros.
6. Off the E side of Ák Sídheros a reef fringes the coast. It is just awash in places.

Mooring

By day anchor in any of the bays and coves shown on the plan. In the small cove immediately S of Ák Sídheros it is necessary to anchor fore and aft or take a long line ashore. The bottom is mostly sand, rock and weed.

Note It is prohibited to use the anchorages on the W side of Ák Sídheros which are designated as a military zone.

Facilities
None.

General
There are no inhabitants here, bar the lighthouse

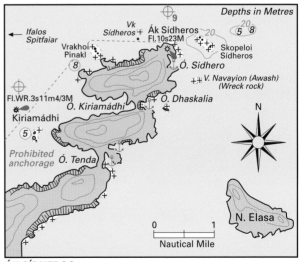

ÁK SÍDHEROS

⊕9 1M N of Ak Sidhero 35°20'·02N 26°18'·73E WGS84

⊕ 0·65M N of Kiriamadhi 35°18'·69N 26°15'·77E WGS84

keeper and a few fishermen. The scenery is on a grand scale and the isolation, the utter quiet, the razor-back reefs surrounding the coast, can instill a sense of dread as the sun goes down.

Southern coast of Crete
(Includes W and E coasts from W to E)

NISÍS GRAMVOÚSA (Grambusa)

Imray-Tetra G37

On the SE side of this island there is a bay sheltered from northerly winds (NW–NE). Anchor in the bay on the S side of Nisís Gramvoúsa in 3–6m. In southerlies anchor under the isthmus formed by Khersónisos Tigani. On Gramvoúsa there is a quay with reasonable depths where a yacht can go bows-to with care.

Water from a well by the chapel. No facilities. At one time the island was a notorious pirate stronghold until an Anglo-French expedition flushed the pirates out in 1828.

ÓRMOS KOUTRIS

35°29'·6N 23°34'·0E

The large bay under Ák Koutri. Shelter from N through to SE. Open NW to SW. Care is needed of the islet and reef running SSW for nearly 1M from the N entrance point. Anchor at the N end in 3–5m on sand.

No facilities.

Ashore at the N end is the ancient city and

The quay and anchorage on the S side of Nisís Gramvoúsa looking SSE   *Nigel Patten*

harbour of Phalasarna. The ancient harbour, hewn from the rock, now lies some 6m above the present sea level. The elevated harbour is dramatic evidence of the geological subsidence of Crete with the E and N 'tipping' downwards into the sea and elevating the S and W.

AKTI

35°28'·8N 23°34'·1E

A small and mostly shallow harbour tucked into the S corner of Órmos Koutris. The approaches are rock-bound and it is best to reconnoitre first by dinghy. The mole is lit Fl.G.3s3M.

CAUTION

All along the S coast there are severe gusts off the high mountains with westerly and northerly winds. Care must be taken under these conditions as the squalls can be of exceptional violence. If a yacht is making a longish passage along the coast it is worthwhile standing off about 5 miles, as suggested by the Admiralty *Pilot*.

PALAIOKHORA (Palaeohora)

BA 1707

Imray-Tetra G37

An anchorage lying near the SW tip of Crete. A prominent headland with a fort on it is easily recognised. Go alongside or stern or bows-to in the new harbour on the E side of the rocky headland. Alternatively anchor on either side of the headland according to the wind direction.

Note When entering the harbour do so from the E and keep close to the S mole in the entrance to avoid the underwater rocks off the end of the stubby N mole. Work is in progress on the harbour at an intermittent rate so keep an eye open for any changes to the harbour plan.

Water on the quay. Fuel in town, but a mini-tanker can deliver to the harbour. Good shopping for all provisions. Good tavernas. Bus to Khania.

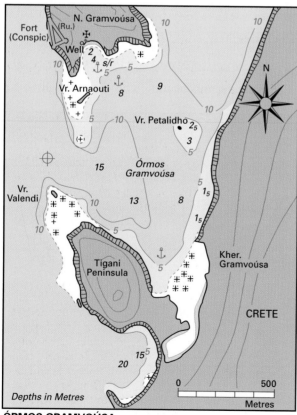

ÓRMOS GRAMVOÚSA
⊕35°35'·9N 23°34'·7E

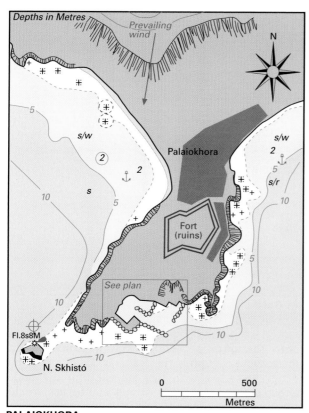

PALAIOKHORA
⊕35°13'·3N 23°40'·3E (N. Skhistó light)

Loutró looking SW *Nigel Patten*

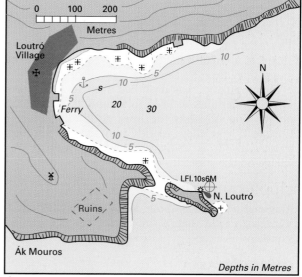

ÓRMOS LOUTRÓ
⊕35°11'·8N 24°05'·0E

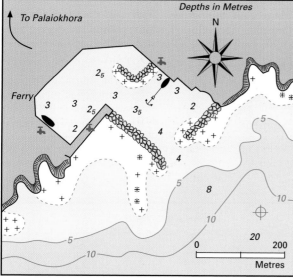

PALAIOKHORA HARBOUR
⊕35°13'·6N 23°40'·7E

SOUGIA (Souyia)

35°14'·75N 23°48'·5E

There is a miniature harbour here about 500m W of the village. A small yacht could go on the outside of the W quay.

ÓRMOS FOINIKIAS AND ÓRMOS LOUTRÓ

On either side of Ák Mouros shelter can be found depending on the wind direction. On the W side there is Órmos Foinikias sheltered from NE–E. On the E side there is Órmos Loutró offering better shelter from N–W–SW. In Órmos Loutró anchor in 4–10m off the village. The bottom is sand, good holding. Both bays are open to the S.

A few tavernas and limited provisions available ashore. Loutró is the ancient Phoenix described by St Luke in Acts (27:12) and was much used in those days by Alexandrian shipping.

SFAKION

Imray-Tetra G37

In calm weather anchor off the village taking care of the above and below-water rocks in the vicinity. Just SE of the village a new yacht harbour is under construction. The outer breakwater is complete but there are no quayed areas at present. With care a yacht may be able to find a spot inside with a long line to the shore or the breakwater. It is reported there is a shoal patch in the entrance so it would be best to reconnoitre by dinghy first. The once small village has become a booming tourist resort in recent years. Good tavernas and good shopping for all provisions. Daily buses to Khania.

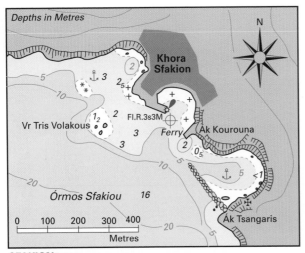

SFAKION
⊕35°11′·9N 24°08′·3E

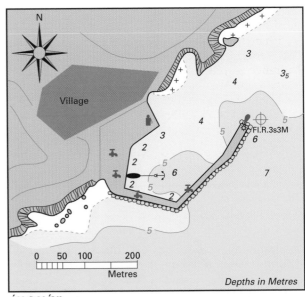

ÁY GALÍNI
⊕35°05′·8N 24°41′·5E

NÍSOS GAVDHOS

(anc. Claudia)

34°48′·3N 24°07′·3E (Ák Tripití/SE end of Gavdhos)

The island lying about 20 miles S of Ák Mouros. There is a small quay inside the NW tip that the *caïque* ferry from Palaiokhora uses. Two tavernas.

The population has dwindled over the years from some 350 families in 1945 to around 70 individuals today. The island is the most southerly point of Europe if you allow islands into the geographical framework. It is about a 40-minute walk to the village on the summit.

FRANGOKASTELLI

An open anchorage about 6 miles E of Sfakion. A Venetian castle (hence the name 'Frank's castle') stands on the cape.

ÓRMOS PLAKIA

35°10′·3N 24°23′·8E

Lies 8 miles E of Kakomouri headland. Suitable only in settled weather. Anchor in 3–6m off the beach. There are severe gusts into the anchorage. There is a short mole here but it is rockbound and of no use to yachts.

LIMNI

A cove at the foot of a ravine 5 miles E of Plakia. During the Second World War it was used to evacuate British, Australian and New Zealand troops from Crete to Egypt.

ÁY GALINI (Erimoupolis)

BA 1707

Imray-Tetra G37

Approach

From seaward the village and the mole are conspicuous. The end of the mole is lit: Fl.R.3s3M.

Mooring

Go stern or bows-to or alongside the quay. The bottom is sand – good holding. Reasonable shelter from the prevailing summer winds, but gusts blow onto the quay so fender well if alongside. In moderate southerlies the harbour should now be better protected with the extension to the mole although it is still likely strong southerlies would cause problems.

Port police and customs.

Facilities

Water on the quay. Fuel on the quay. Good shopping for all provisions. Good tavernas. PO. OTE. Buses to Iraklion and Rethimon.

General

At one time an important port for shipping produce from the hinterland, its importance declined when lorries began taking the produce to Iraklion for shipment. Recently it has become a popular tourist spot and hotels have been built around the shore.

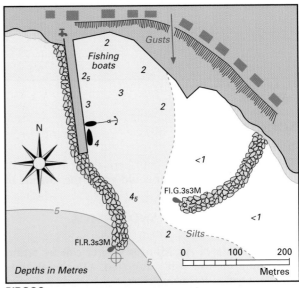

PIRGOS
⊕35°04′·8N 24°44′·2E

PIRGOS

A fishing harbour lying nearly 3M ESE of Áy Galini. The entrance is lit Fl.R.3s3M/Fl.G.3s3M. The entrance is prone to silting and you should keep close to the W breakwater at the entrance. Go stern or bows-to or alongside on the end of the quayed section of the W breakwater. Good shelter from northerlies. Strong southerlies would probably cause a problem in here.

Water at the root of the breakwater. Fuel ashore. Tavernas.

MATALA

34°59'·7N 24°44'·8E

BA 1707

A horseshoe-shaped bay on the W side of Ák Lítinos. Suitable only in calm weather as the prevailing wind causes a swell to roll in. Good shopping for provisions and good tavernas ashore. Daily buses to Iraklion.

Matala is mentioned in the Odyssey as the place where Menelaus' ships were wrecked when returning from Troy. It was known to be an important Roman port and was used at least up until Byzantine times.

KALI LIMENES (Kalon Limenon)

BA 1707

Imray-Tetra G38

Approach

A small bay on the E side of Ák Lítinos. A church on the S side of the bay and the oil storage tanks on Nisís Áy Pavlos are conspicuous. There is a light on Megalonísi: Fl(3)24s11M.

Mooring

Anchor in the bay in 3–6m. Good shelter from the N and W, but open to the E and S. It is also possible to anchor under Nisís Trafos to the E where some shelter from easterlies can be found. Port police and

Kali Limenes looking NE   *Nigel Patten*

customs.

Facilities

Limited provisions and tavernas in the village.

General

Nisís Áy Pavlos is a bunkering station and the 'T' piers on the island are used by large ships. Kali Limenes (Fair Haven or Good Harbour) was visited by St Paul in AD 59 when he was en route from Myra to Rome in a Roman corn ship. Bad weather had forced the ship to go south of Crete and it being late in the year, they considered wintering in Kali Limenes. Eventually a decision was made to leave and the ship was later wrecked in Malta.

GAÏDHOURONISI (Donkey Island)

During strong southerlies a yacht can find a useful lee under the northern shores of the island. A *caïque* ferry from Ierepetra runs tourists to the island in the summer. A taverna on the island.

IEREPETRA

BA 1707

Imray-Tetra G38

Approach

Conspicuous The town at the foot of a plain is conspicuous from the distance. Closer in, a chimney in the town and the fort and a clock tower behind the harbour are conspicuous.

By night The entrance is lit Fl.R.3s4M, but a night approach is hazardous because of the reefs and shoal water in the immediate approach.

Dangers

1. Care must be taken of the reef lying close off the entrance. It is sometimes marked by two buoys, but these cannot be relied on to be in place. The entrance to the harbour is best made between the reef and the end of the breakwater. Keep close to the end of the breakwater, though not too close because of above and below water rocks off it. An approach leaving the reef to port is possible, but the extent of the reef is difficult to determine.

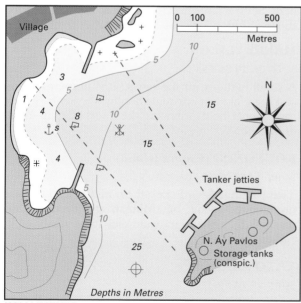

KALI LIMENES

⊕34°55'·7N 24°48'·3E

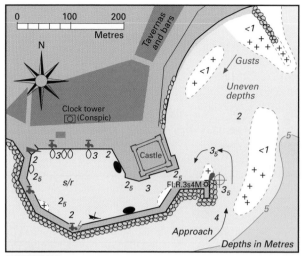

IEREPETRA
⊕35°00'·21N 25°44'·33E WGS84

KATO ZAKROS TO ÓRMOS ERIMOUPOLIS

⊕10 1M E of Ak Plaka 35°11'·9N 26°20'·2E

Care is needed as the violent winter storms in this area seem to rearrange the sea bottom.
2. With strong southerlies there is a confused swell off the entrance which makes the entry through the narrow entrance difficult.

Mooring

Go alongside the quay under the W side of the castle, or along the S breakwater, wherever there is room. Care is needed of ballasting underwater and where some silting has taken place, especially near the entrance.

Shelter With the *meltemi* there are strong gusts into the harbour and although they are off the land, a bit of a surge is set up. In southerly gales waves break over the breakwater and there is a considerable surge in the harbour which may make it dangerous.

Authorities Port police and customs.

Note For a number of years there have been plans to extend the outer mole, but it seems likely that for the present further work will be confined to repairing storm damage to the existing harbour.

Facilities

Water On the quay.
Fuel In the town. A mini-tanker can deliver to the quay.
Repairs Some mechanical repairs. Hardware shops.
Provisions Good shopping for all provisions.
Eating out Good tavernas on the waterfront.
Other PO. OTE. Banks. ATM. Greek gas and Camping Gaz. Hire cars and motorbikes. Bus to Iraklion and Sitía. Ferry to Gáïdharos.

General

Ierepetra (pronounced 'Erepetra') was an important town in Minoan and again in Roman times although few architectural remains are to be found today. Its importance now lies in its mild summer and winter climate: the nearby market gardens grow early produce for the European market and recently an increasing number of tourists have been attracted here. Several large hotels have been built around the shores of the bay to cater for the latter trade.

MAKRI YIALOS

35°02'·2N 25°58'·5E

A small harbour off the resort. It is prone to silting and there are not adequate depths for yachts. In any case tripper boats servicing the resort take up much of the space.

KOUFONISI (Kuphu Island)

34°56'·0N 26°08'·6E (Koufonisi light)

These islands lie off the SE tip of Crete. They are uninhabited today, but Minoan and Roman ruins on the largest island indicate they were inhabited in earlier times.

KATO ZAKROS

35°05'·8N 26°16'·2E

A large sandy bay at the foot of a dramatic gorge. In settled weather anchor in the N of the bay. Care must be taken of a reef running out from the middle of the bay and of other rocks around the shore. Tavernas on the shore.

At the foot of the gorge on an exquisite site are the ruins of a Minoan summer palace.

ÓRMOS GRANDES

⊕ 0·5M N of Ak Plaka 35°12'·43N 26°19'·16E WGS84

The large bay on the N side of Ák Pláka. The best anchorage is at Kouremenos in the N of the bay where there is good shelter from the prevailing winds. At Kouremenos there is a short mole providing additional protection. It is usually crowded with fishing boats but a yacht may find a berth alongside the outer end where there are 2–3m depths. Water on the quay. Tavernas around the bay.

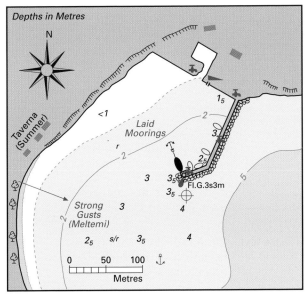

KOUREMENOS
⊕35°12'·88N 26°16'·21E WGS84

VAI

Two miles to the N of Kouremenos is Vai, where a yacht can anchor off. The sandy beach is easily identified by the extensive groves of palm trees along the foreshore. A yacht reported being anchored off Vai for two weeks in June and experiencing only the normal summer winds blowing off the land.

A hotel and tavernas ashore. *Vai* is probably an old word for palms and the place is named on modern Greek charts as Finikodassos (palm grove).

Appendix

I. USEFUL ADDRESSES

National Tourism Organisation of Greece (NTOG) offices

Australia – New Zealand
Greek National Tourism Organization
51, Pitt St, Sydney, NSW 2000 PO Box R203, Royal Exchange NSW 2000 Australia
☎ 00 61 2 92411663/4/5, 92521441 *Fax* 92352174

Austria
Griechische Zentrale Für Fremdenverkehr
A-10105 Wien, Opernring 8
☎ 00 43 1 5125317 or 170
Fax 5139189

Belgium
Office National Héllenique du Tourisme
172 Avenue Louise, Louizalaan, B-1050 Bruxelles
☎ 00 32 2 6475770, 6475944 *Fax* 6475142

Canada
Toronto
Greek National Tourism Organisation
1300 Bay Street Main Level, Toronto, Ontario, Canada M5R 3K8
☎ 00 1 416 9682220
Fax 9686533
Montreal
Greek National Tourism Organisation
1170 Place du Frère André, 3rd Floor, Montreal, Quebec, Canada H3B 3L6
☎ 00 1 514 8711535
Fax 8711498

Denmark (information office)
Det Graeske Turistbureau
Vester Farimagsgade 6, 1606-København
☎ 00 45 33 325332, 325368
Fax 157376

Finland (information office)
Kreikan Valtion Matkailutoimisto
Iso Roobertinkatu 10 A3, 00120 Helsinki 12
☎ 00 35 89 607113, 607552
Fax 601313

France
Office National Héllenique du Tourisme
3 Avenue de l' Opera, Paris 75001
☎ 00 33 1 42 60 65 75
Fax 42 60 10 28

Germany
Frankfurt
Griechische Zentrale Für Fremdenverkehr
Neue Mainzerstr. 22, 60311 Frankfurt-Main
☎ 00 49 69 236561/2/3
Fax 236576
München
Griechische Zentrale Für Fremdenverkehr Pacellistr. 5 W 80333 München
☎ 00 49 89 222035/6
Fax 297058
Hamburg
Griechische Zentrale Für Fremdenverkehr Abteistr. 33, 20149 Hamburg
☎ 00 49 40 454498
Berlin
Griechische Zentrale Für Fremdenverkehr
Wittenbergplatz 3a, 10789 Berlin
☎ 00 49 30 2176262/3
Fax 00 49 30 2177965

Israel
Greek National Tourism Organisation
5 Shalom Aleichem St, PO Box 2620, Tel Aviv 61262
☎ 00 97 23 517 0501, 517 0351
Fax 00 97 23/517 0487

Italy
Rome
Ente Nazionale Ellenico Per Il Turismo
Via L. Bissolati 78-80, Roma 00187
☎ 00 39 06 4744249, 4744301 *Fax* 4883905
Milan
Ente Nazionale Ellenico Per Il Turismo
Piazza Diaz 1, (Angolo Via Rastrelli) 20123 Milano
☎ 00 39 02 860470/860477
Fax 72022589

Netherlands
Griekse Nationale Organizatie Voor Toerisme
Kerkstraat 61, 1017GC Amsterdam
☎ 00 31 20 6254212/3/4
Fax 6207031

Norway
Den Grekse Stats Turistbyrå
Ovre Slottsgate 15B, 0157 Oslo 1
☎ 00 47 2 426501/2

Spain
Oficina Nacional Hellenica de Turismo
C/Alberto Aguilera 17-1, Madrid 28015
☎ 00 34 91 5484889/90
Fax 5428138

Sweden
Grekiska Statens Turistbyrå
Birger Jarlsgatan 30, Box 5298 Stockholm
☎ 00 46 86796480, 6796580 *Fax* 6118802

United Kingdom and Ireland
Greek National Tourism Organisation
4 Conduit Street, London W1R ODJ
☎ 00 44 20 7734/5997
Fax 7287 1369
www.tourist-offices.org.uk

United States of America
New York
Greek National Tourism Organisation
Olympic Tower, 645 Fifth Ave, New York, NY 10022
☎ 00 1 212 4215777
Fax 8266940
Chicago
Greek National Tourism Organisation
168 North Michigan Avenue/Suite 600, Chicago, Illinois 60601
☎ 00 1 312 782108
Fax 7821091
Los Angeles
Greek National Tourism Organisation
611 West Sixth Street/Suite 2198, Los Angeles, California 92668
☎ 00 1 213 6266696/9
Fax 4899744

Consular offices in Greece
☎ prefix 00 30

United Kingdom
Embassy
1 Ploutarchou Street, 106 75 Athens, Greece
☎ 1 727 2600 *Fax* 727 2722 (Consular Section)
www.british-embassy.gr
Email britania@hol.gr
Consulates
Corfu 2 Alexandras Avenue, 491 00 Corfu
☎ 661 30 055
Fax 661 37 995
Crete 16 Papa-Alexandrou St, 71202 Heraklion
☎ 81 224 012
Fax 81 243 935
Kos 8 Annetas Laoumtzi St, 85300 Kos
☎ 242 215 49
Fax 242 259 48
Patras 2 Votsi Street, 262 21 Patras
☎ 61 277 329
Fax 61 225 344
Thessaloniki 8 Venizelou Street, Eleftheria Square, PO Box 10322, 541 10 Salonika
☎ 31 278 006 269 984
Rhodes 11 Amerikis St, 85100 Rhodes
☎ 241 272 47
Fax 241 226 15

United States of America
Embassy
91 Vasilissis Sophias Boulevard, Athens, Greece
☎ 1 721 2951
www.usisathens.gr
Email consul@ibm.net
Consulate
43 Tsimiski, 76th Floor, 54623, Thessaloniki, Greece
☎ 31 242 905

Germany
Odos Karoli Kai, Dimitriou 3, Athens
☎ 1 724 801

Canada
Embassy
4 Ioannou Gennadiou Street, Athens, Greece 115 21
☎ 1 727 3400/725 4011
Fax 727 3480
Consulate
c/o Bank of Nova Scotia 17, Tsimiski Street, 546 24 Thessaloniki, Greece
☎ 31 256 350 *Fax* 256 351

II. USEFUL BOOKS AND CHARTS

Admiralty publications
Mediterranean Pilot Volume III (NP 47)
Covers the Ionian Sea.
Mediterranean Pilot Volume IV (NP 48)
Covers the Aegean Sea.
List of Lights Volume E (NP 78)
Mediterranean, Black and Red Seas.

Yachtsman's pilots
Imray Mediterranean Almanac editor Rod
Heikell (Imray). A biennial publication
with light lists, radio, harbour plans
and other associated information.
Mediterranean Cruising Handbook Rod
Heikell (Imray). Companion volume to
Mediterranean Almanac.
The RYA Book of Mediterranean Cruising
Rod Heikell (Adlard Coles Nautical).
*The Ionian Islands to the Anatolian Coast: a
sea-guide* H M Denham (John
Murray).
*The Aegean: a sea-guide to its coasts and
islands* H M Denham (John Murray).
Classic yachtsman's guides, although
no longer revised and kept up-to-date.
Contain much interesting information,
particularly on naval history.
West Aegean Rod Heikell (Imray). Covers
the Saronic Gulf, eastern Peloponnisos
and Western Cyclades in detail.
Ionian Rod Heikell (Imray). Covers the
Ionian, in detail.
East Aegean Rod Heikell (Imray). Covers
the Dodecanese and adjacent Turkish
coast, in detail.
Häfen und Ankerplätze in Griechenland
Gerd Radspieler. Covers the Ionian,
Saronic Gulf and Eastern Peloponnisos
only. In German.
Guide Pratique de Grèce et Turquie Jacques
Angles (Editions du Pen Duick).
Covers the Dodecanese. In French.
Turkish Waters and Cyprus Pilot Rod
Heikell (Imray).

Other guides
Yacht Charter Handbook Rod Heikell
(Imray).
The Blue Guide to Greece Edited by Stuart
Rossiter. (A and C Black). The usual
excellent quality of this series.
The Greek Islands Lawrence Durrell
(Faber). Lots of glossy photographs
and Durrell's own inimitable
description of the islands.
The Greek Islands Ernle Bradford (Collins
Companion Guide). An excellent
background guide from an author who
has sailed his own yacht around
Greece.
Dumont Guide to the Greek Islands Edited
by Evi Melas and translated by Russell
Stockman. Stewart (Tabori & Chang,
NY; or Webb & Bower, UK). Good
guide with glossy photos.
The Rough Guide to Greece Ellingham,
Jansz and Fisher (Routledge and
Kegan Paul). Down-to-earth guide.
The Mediterranean Greenpeace.
Berlitz Guides to:
Athens/Corfu/Crete/Greek Islands/
Peloponnese/Rhodes/Salonica and
Northern Greece. Good, compact and
necessarily brief, guides.
The Peloponnese E. Karpodini-Dimitriadi
(Ekdotike Athenon).

*Prospero's Cell: a guide to the landscape and
manners of the island of Corcyra*
Lawrence Durrell (Penguin). On
Corfu.
*Reflections on a Marine Venus: a companion
to the landscape of Rhodes* Lawrence
Durrell (Penguin). On Rhodes.
Bitter Lemons Lawrence Durrell (Faber).
On Cyprus.
Crete: Its Past, Present and People Adam
Hopkins (Faber). Excellent general
introduction to Crete.
Crete John Freely (Weidenfeld &
Nicolson). Good guide.
Pausanias Guide to Greece Volumes I & II
Translated by Peter Levi (Penguin).
Pausanias was a doctor who spent
twenty years travelling around Greece
in the reign of Hadrian recording
details of Greek cities, customs and
beliefs. Interesting and useful to this
day.
Herodotus The Histories (*Historiai*).
Greek Society Antony Andrewes (Pelican).
The World of Odysseus M. I. Finley
(Penguin). Life in Homeric times.
The Penguin Atlas of Ancient History Colin
McEvedy.
*Fortresses and Castles of Greece Volumes I &
II and Fortresses and Castles of Greek
Islands* Alexander Paradissis.
Translated by S. A. Paradissis
(Efstathiadis Brothers). The most
detailed descriptive work on all Greek
forts and castles. Published and readily
available in Greece.
The Venetian Empire Jan Morris (Penguin).
Very readable account of the Venetian
maritime empire that touched so many
Greek islands and coastal harbours,
leaving its forts and castles everywhere.
Recommended.
The Greek Adventure David Howarth
(Collins). Excellent and very readable
account of the Greek War of
Independence.
The End of Atlantis J. V. Luce (Paladin).
Good account of the Thíra eruptions.

General
The Colossus of Maroussi Henry Miller
(Penguin). A 'must' to read even if you
are not going to Greece.
Zorba the Greek Nikos Kazantzakis
(Faber).
Freedom and Death Nikos Kazantzakis.
Cavafy: a critical biography Robert Liddell
(Duckworth). The biography of the
forgotten poet of Alexandria.
The Alexandrian Quartet Lawrence Durrell.
The Poems of Catullus Translated by Peter
Whigham (University of California
Press).
Mani: travels in the Southern Peloponnese
and *Roumeli: travels in Northern Greece*
Patrick Leigh Fermor (Penguin).
Contain much interesting and esoteric
information on Greece and the Greeks
in general as well as on the areas
covered.
Eleni Nicholas Gage (Fontana). Easy read
on the Civil War in Greece.
Hellas – A Portrait of Greece Nicholas Gage
(Collins Harvill). Contains some
interesting information not found in
other 'portraits'.
A Literary Companion to Travel in Greece

Edited by Richard Stoneman
(Penguin).
Sappho to Shelley. Greek Literature: An
Anthology. Edited by Michael Grant
(Penguin).
*The Jason Voyage: the quest for the Golden
Fleece* and *The Ulysses Voyage: sea
search for the Odyssey* Tim Severin
(Arrow Books: Jason and Hutchinson:
Ulysses). The conventional and
unconventional interpretations of two
ancient voyages after retracing the
routes in a replica galley.
Gates of the Wind Michael Carroll (John
Murray) Interesting account of the
Northern Sporades.
Bitter Sea Faith Warn (Guardian Angel
Press).

Flora
Flowers of Greece and the Aegean Anthony
Huxley and William Taylor (Chatto &
Windus).
Flowers of the Mediterranean Anthony
Huxley and Oleg Polunin (Chatto &
Windus).
Both the above have excellent colour
photographs and line drawings for
identification.
Herbs of Greece Alta Niebuhr.
Trees and Bushes of Britain and Europe Oleg
Polunin (Paladin). Excellent guide
with colour photographs for
identification.
Trees and Shrubs of Greece George Sfikas.

Marine life
*Hamlyn Guide to the Seashore and Flora
and Fauna of the Mediterranean* A C
Campbell. Comprehensive guide to
Mediterranean marine life.
The Yachtsman's Naturalist M Drummond
and P Rodhouse (Angus & Robertson).
About Britain and northern Europe,
but many species are common to the
Mediterranean.
British Whales, Dolphins and Porpoises F C
Fraser. As above.
Mediterranean Wildlife. The Rough Guide.
Peter Raine (Harrap-Columbus).
Patchy guide that includes a chapter
on Greece.
Fishes of Greece Published by the
Efstathidis Group and available in
Greece. A poor guide.
Dangerous Marine Animals B W Halstead,
P S Auerbach and D R Campbell
(Wolfe Medical). The standard
reference work.

Food
Greek Cooking Robin Howe.
Food of Greece Vilma Chantiles.
The Best of Greek Cooking Chrissa
Paradissis.
Food in History Reay Tannahill (Paladin).
Contains some interesting details on
Greek food as part of a general history.

British Admiralty charts

No	Chart	Scale
180	Aegean sea	1,100,000
186	Vlorë to Bar and Brindisi to Vieste	300,000
188	Entrance to the Adriatic Sea, including Nísos Kérkira	300,000
189	Nísos Sapiéntza to Nísos Paxoí	300,000
203	Nísos Zakínthos to Nísos Paxoí	150,000
206	Nísos Kérkira and approaches	150,000
	Vórion Stenón Kérkiras	25,000
236	Nísos Ródhos to Taşlik Burnu,	300,000
	Finike	12,500
1030	Southwest entrance channels to the Aegean Sea	150,000
1031	Ákra Yérakas to Nísos Kéa	150,000
1037	Nisís Falconera to Nísos Íos	150,000
1038	Stenó Sífnou to Stenó Kafiréa	150,000
	Stenó Dhísvaton	40,000
1040	Nísos Íos to Vrakhonisída Kandhelioússa	150,000
1041	Nísos Náxos to Vrákhoi Kalóyeroi	150,000
1055	Rhodes Channel and Gökova Körfezi	150,000
1058	Nísos Khíos and Izmir Körfezi	150,000
1062	Nísoi Voríoi Sporádhes	150,000
1085	Stenó Kafiréa to Thessaloníki	300,000
1086	Strimonikös Kölpos to Edremit Körfezi	300,000
1087	Stenó Kafiréa to Edremit Körfezi	300,000
1091	Nísos Kríti	300,000
1092	Western approaches to the Aegean Sea	300,000
1093	Stenó Andikithíron to Edremit Körfezi	3000,000
1095	Stenó Kafiréa to Rhodes Channel	300,000
1099	Eastern approaches to the Aegean Sea	300,000
1439	Sicilia to Nísos Kriti	1,100,000
1440	Adriatic sea	1,100,000
1513	Kólpos Elevsínas	25,000
1526	Sámos Strait with harbours in the islands of Sámos, Ikaría and Foúrnoi	
	Marathokámbos	5,000
	Áyios Kírikos, Évidhilos, Liménas Karlóvasi and Pithagoríon	7,500
	Sámos	10,000
	Póros Fóurnon and Órmos KovSeón	25,000
	Sámos Strait	50,000
1531	Harbours in Northern Dhodhekánisos	
	Nísos Pátmos, Approaches to Skála	30,000
	Nísos Pátmos, Skála	7,500
	Nisídha Lipsoí, Lipsoí	30,000
	Nísos Kálimnos, Órmos Kalímnou	7,500
	N Yialí and N Nísiros, Órmos Yialí	50,000
	Nísos Kós, Órmos Kos	10,000
	Nísos Léros, Órmos Lakkí	10,000
1532	Harbours in Southern Dhodhekánisos	
	Nísos Tílos, Órmos Livádhia	10,000
	Nísos Ródhos, Ródhos	7,500
	Nísos Sími, Sími	10,000
	Nísos Sími, Panormítis	5,000
	Nísos Ródhos, Órmos Líndhou	10,000
	Nísos Kárpathos, Órmos Pigádhia	10,000
	Nísos Kásos, Órmos Frí and Limín Emborió	5,000
1538	Plans in the northern Kikládhes	
	Órmos Ày Nikólau	10,000
	Órmos Livádhi	10,000
	Órmos Mérikha	10,000
	Órmos Fáros	10,000
	Limín Tínou	10,000
	Órmos Kamáres	10,000
	Órmos Foínika	15,000
	Limín Sírou and approaches	15,000
	Órmos Kástro	20,000
	Órmos Gávrio	25,000
	Míkonos and approaches	25,000
1539	Plans in the Central Kikládhes	
	Órmos Mílou	30,000
	Stenái Kimólou with Órmos Voúdhia	25,000
	Stenó Andípárou with Órmos Paroikías	25,000
	Órmos Naoúsis	25,000
	Órmos Náxou	15,000

No	Chart	Scale
	Paroikía	5,000
1541	Plans in the Southern Kikládhes and Nísos Astipálaia	
	Órmos Athiniós	5,000
	Órmos Thíras	5,000
	Ormískos Skála	7,500
	Órmos Katápola	10,000
	Órmos Karavostási	10,000
	Órmos Manganári	10,000
	Órmos Análipsis	15,000
	Órmos Fou	15,000
	Órmos Vathi	15,000
	Nísos Thíra	60,000
1554	Nótios Evvoïkós Kólpos	110,000
	Approaches to Porthmós Evrípou	27,500
	Porthmós Evrípou	7,500
	Dhíavlos Stenó	10,000
1556	Vórias Evvoïkós Kólpos and approaches to Vólos	110,000
1571	Plans in the western Aegean sea	
	Liménas Linariás	5,000
	Stenó Valáxa	7,500
	Lávrion	7,500
	Skíathos	7,500
	Órmos Alivéri	10,000
	Stilís	12,500
	Kímis	12,500
	Skópelos	15,000
	Erétria	20,000
	Vólos and approaches	20,000
	Nisídhes Likhádhes	25,000
	Kólpos Kalamítsas	30,000
	Approaches to Liménas Skiáthou	30,000
1596	Piraiévs	12,500
1598	Póros Megáron Áyios Theódhoroi and Elevsís	
	Elevsís	7,500
	Ayois Theódhoroi (oil terminal)	10,000
	Póros Megáron	12,500
1599	Órmos Falírou and Liménas Pórou	
	Órmos Falírou	12,500
	Liménas Pórou and approaches	15,000
1600	Korinthiakós Kólpos	100,000
	Dhióriga Korínthou	25,000
1625	Khíos Strait and Ildir Körfezi	50,000
	Khíos	10,000
	Çeşme	15,000
1636	Plans in the northern Aegean Sea	
	Nísos Límnos	150,000
	Órmos Moúdhrou	25,000
	Lágos and approaches	25,000
	Alexandroúpoli	20,000
	Míruna	12,500
1657	Saronikós Kólpos	100,000
1675	Plans in the eastern Aegean Sea	
	Mitilíni	7,500
	Órmos Sígri	20,000
	Entrance to Kólpos Kallonís	20,000
	Entrance to Kólpos Yéras	25,000
	Approaches to Ayvalik	50,000
1676	Prokólpos Pátron to entrance of Korinthiakós Kólpos	100,000
1683	Plans on the south and east coasts of Pelopónnisos	
	Limín Monemvasías	5,000
	Návplion: Spétsai	7,500
	Koróni; Yíthion	10,000
	Órmos Methónis	15,000
	Kólpos Monemvasías Stenó Spetsó	25,000
1687	Port and anchorages in northern Greece	
	Kólpos Kaválas and approaches	75,000
	Keramotí	20,000
	Néa Kaváli	20,000
	Órmos Elevtherón	20,000
	Stratónion	12,500
	Kavála	12,500
	Thásos	6,000

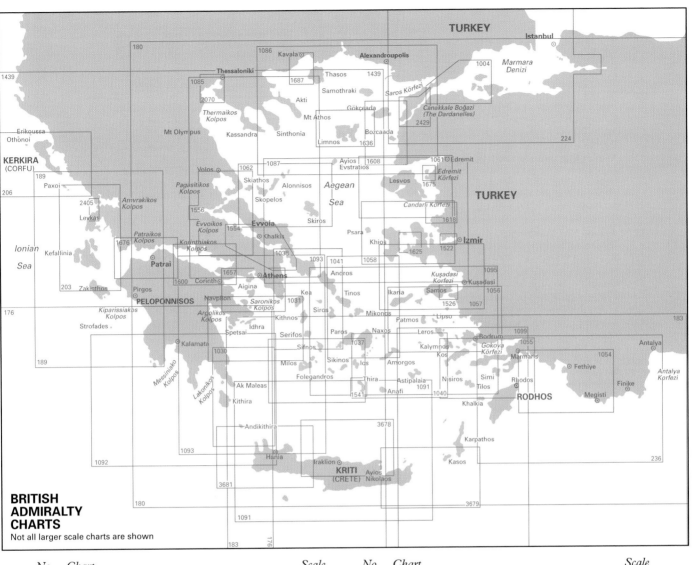

**BRITISH
ADMIRALTY
CHARTS**
Not all larger scale charts are shown

No	Chart	Scale
1706	Órmos Soúdhas and approaches	25,000
	Limín Soúdhas	7,500
1707	Greece, harbours and anchorages in Nísos Kríti	
	Ormoi Palaiokhóras; Órmos Kaloí Liménas	12,500
	Iereptra; Áyios Nikólaos; Iráklion	10,000
	Réthimon; Órmos Mátala; Sitía	7,500
	Khaniá; Áy Galíni	5,000

Imray-Tetra charts

G1 Mainland Greece and the Peloponnísos Passage Chart
Plans Approaches to Piraeus and Ormos Falírou — 1:729,000

**G11 North Ionian Islands
Nísos Kérkira to Nísos Levkas**
Plans Ormos Gouvion (N. Kérkira), Vorion Steno Kérkiras, Límin Kérkiras (N. Kérkira), Limin Alipa (N. Kérkira), Ormos Lakka (N. Paxoi), Limin Paxon (N Paxoi)
Insets Amvrakikos Kólpos, Nísos Othonoi — 1:182,400

**G12 South Ionian Islands
Nísos Levkas to Nísos Zákinthos**
Plans Kólpos Aetou (N. Ithaca), Dhioriga Levkadhos (Levkas Canal), Ormos Argostoliou (N. Kefallinia), Ormos Zákinthou (N. Zákinthos) — 1:188,200

G121 The Inland Sea
Plans Ormos Ayias Eufimas (N. Kefallina), Ormos Frikou (N. Ithaca), Ormos Fiskardho (N. Kefallina), Ormos Vasilikas (N. Levkas), Dhioriga Levkadhos (Levkas Canal) — 1:93,400

G13 Gulfs of Patras and Corinth
Plans Mesolongiou, Ormos Loutrákiou, Kiaton, Patrai, Ormos Andíkiron, Ormos Aiyiou, Krissaios Kólpos, Dhiorix Korinthou (Corinth Canal) — 1:218,800

G14 Saronic and Argolic Gulfs
Plans Marina Alimos, Ormos Falírou, Límin Porou (N. Póros), Steno Spétson (N. Spetsai), Límin Aiginis (N. Aigina) — 1:189,000

**G141 Saronikos Kolpos
Corinth Canal to Akra Sounio and Nisos Poros** — 1:109,000

**G15 Southern Peloponnísos
Ormos Navarinou to Nisos Kithíra and Akra Tourkovigla**
Plans Kalamata, Ormos Navarínou, Yíthion, Monemvasía (Yefira), Methóni, Koróni — 1:189,700

G16 Western Peloponnisos. Killini to Kalamata
Plans Killini, Kiparissia, Steno Methonis, Pilos, Katakolon — 1:189,000

G2 Aegean Sea (North Part) Passage Chart
Plans Canakkale Boğazi (The Dardanelles) — 1:720,500

G25 Northern Sporades and North Evvoia
Plans Linaria (N. Skiros), Ormos Skiathou (N. Skiathos), Ormos Skopelou (N. Skopelos) 1:183,800

No	Chart	Scale

G26 Nisos Evvoia
Plans Approaches to Khalkis, Linaria
(N. Skiros), Kimis (N. Evvoia), Eretria
(N. Evvoia), Limenas Aliveriou (N. Evvoia),
Rafina   1:184,600

G27 Nísos Lésvos and the Coast of Turkey
Plans Dikili (Turkey), Kólpos Yéras – N. Lésvos
(Greece), Kólpos Koloni – N. Lésvos (Greece),
Sígri – N. Lésvos (Greece), Mitilíni – N. Lésvos
(Greece), Ayvalík (Turkey)   1:185,300

G28 Nísos Khíos and the Coast of Turkey
Plans Limin Khíou – N. Khíos (Greece),
Ceşme Körfezi (Turkey), Siğacik Limani
(Turkey), Izmir (Turkey), Limin Psarou –
N. Psará (Greece), Foça Limani (Turkey),
Ormos Mandráki – N. Oinoússa (Greece)   1:187,500

G3 Aegean Sea (South Part) Passage Chart
Plan Límin Rodhou (N. Rodhos)   1:758,800

G31 Northern Cyclades
Plans Mikonos Marina (N. Mikonos),
Ormos Gávriou (N. Andros), Límin A.
Nikolaou (Nísos Kea), Limin Sirou (N. Siros),
Ormos Naousis (N Paros)   1:189,700

G32 Southern Sporades and Coast of Turkey
Plans Kuşadasi Liman (Turkey),
Límin Karlóvasi (N. Samos), Límin A. Kirikou
(N. Ikaria), Steno Samou (N. Samos),
Límin Pithagóriou (N. Samos), Ormos
Patmou (N. Patmos)   1:189,700

G33 Southern Cyclades (Sheet 1 – West)
Plans Steno Kimolou (N. Kimolos), Ormos
Livadhiou (N. Serifos), Steno Andíparou (N. Paros),
Ormos Naxou (N. Naxos)   1:190,000

No	Chart	Scale

G34 Southern Cyclades (Sheet 2 – East)
Plans Ormos Kalímnou (N. Kalimnos),
Ormos Analipsis
(N. Astipálaia)   1:190,000

G35 Dodecanese and Coast of Turkey
Plans Bodrum (Turkey), Rodhos – N. Rodhos
(Greece), Kós Marina – N. Kós (Greece),
Marmaris (Turkey), Limin Simi –
N. Simi (Greece)   1:190,000

G36 South Coast of Turkey. Marmaris to Geyikova Adasi
Plans Marmaris (Turkey), N. Rodhos
(Greece), Meyisti (Greece), Approaches to
Meyisti and Kaş (Greece/Turkey), Fethiye
(Turkey), Göçek (Turkey)   1:193,000

G37 Nisos Kriti (West)
Plans O. Gramvousa, Hania, Rethimno,
A. Galinis, Soudha, Palaiokhora, O. Sfakion   1:193,000

G38 Nisos Kriti (East)
Plans Iraklion, Sitia, A. Nikolaos, Ierapetra,
Kaloi Limenes, Khersonisos   1:193,000

G39 Nisos Karpathos to Nisos Rodhos
Plans Ormos Tristoma, Ormos Fri and
Limin Emborio, Ormos Pigadhia,
Ormos Lindhou   1:194,000

G40 Kaş to Antalya
Plans Kekova Demiryeri (Turkey), Kemer
Marina (Turkey), Finike (Turkey), Uçağiz
Limani (Turkey), Antalya (Turkey), Setur
Antalya Marina (Turkey), Approaches to
Kaş and Megisti (Turkey/Greece)   1:193,000

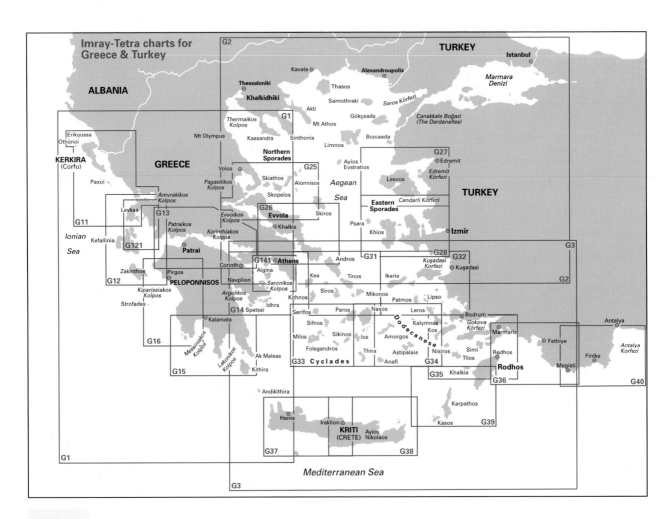

Index

Abbreviations used in index: L. =
Limín, Limeniskos; N. = Nisís,
Nisidhes, Nísos, Nisoi; Ó. =
Órmos, Órmiskos